KW 60

DATE DUE

Demco, Inc. 38-293

WITHDRAWN

D1492340

Property and Conveyancing Library

THE LAW OF EASEMENTS

AUSTRALIA
Law Book Co.
Sydney

CANADA and USA
Carswell
Toronto

HONG KONG
Sweet & Maxwell Asia

NEW ZEALAND
Brookers
Wellington

SINGAPORE and MALAYSIA
Sweet & Maxwell Asia
Singapore and Kuala Lumpur

PROPERTY AND CONVEYANCING LIBRARY

GALE
ON
EASEMENTS

EIGHTEENTH EDITION

BY

JONATHAN GAUNT Q.C.

AND

THE HONOURABLE MR JUSTICE MORGAN
One of Her Majesty's Justices of the High Court

LONDON
SWEET & MAXWELL
2008

First edition	(1839)	By Charles James Gale and Thomas Denman Whatley
Second edition	(1849)	By Charles James Gale
Third edition	(1862)	By W.H. Willes
Fourth edition	(1868)	By David Gibbons
Fifth edition	(1876)	By David Gibbons
Sixth edition	(1888)	By George Cave
Seventh edition	(1899)	By George Cave
Eighth edition	(1908)	By Raymond Roope Reeve
Ninth edition	(1916)	By T.H. Carson
Tenth edition	(1925)	By W.J. Byrne
Eleventh edition	(1932)	By F. Graham Glover
Twelfth edition	(1950)	By D.H. McMullen
Thirteenth edition	(1959)	By Michael Bowles
Second Impression	(1962)	
Fourteenth edition	(1972)	By Spencer G. Maurice
Second Impression	(1975)	
Fifteenth edition	(1986)	By Spencer G. Maurice
Sixteenth edition	(1997)	By Jonathan Gaunt and Paul Morgan
Second Impression	(1999)	
Third Impression	(2001)	
Seventeenth edition	(2002)	By Jonathan Gaunt and Paul Morgan
Eighteenth edition	(2008)	By Jonathan Gaunt and Paul Morgan

Published in 2008 by
Sweet & Maxwell Limited of 100 Avenue Road,
http://www.sweetandmaxwell.co.uk
Typeset by LBJ Typesetting of Kingsclere.
Printed and bound in Great Britain by
CPI William Clowes, Beccles, NR34 7TL.
No natural forests were destroyed to make this product;
only farmed timber was used and re-planted.

British Library Cataloguing in Publication Data

A CIP catalogue record for this book
is available from the British Library

ISBN 978-1-847032-22-5

PREFACE

It is a fact that in the long history of this work, first published in 1839, no previous editor has survived to produce a third edition. We therefore embarked on our task with some trepidation but are happy to report that between publication of the 17th and 18th editions nothing worse has befallen either of us than the appointment of one of the team to the Chancery Bench.

One consequence of our now having had three goes is that we estimate that between us we can claim to be the authors of over half the book. In this edition, it has been possible, armed with the Land Registration Rules 2003, to give a more comprehensive treatment in Chapter 5 to registered land and the important topic of overriding interests. We have also added to Chapter 14 a completely new section (paras 14–112 *et seq*.) of nearly thirty paragraphs on the subject of damages and, in particular, damages in lieu of injunction, which we hope practitioners will find of assistance.

Moreover, there have been some important developments in the law of easements since the last edition. First, there have been three interventions by the House of Lords. In *Bakewell v Brandwood* [2004] 2 A.C. 219, the House at last sorted out the mess caused by *Hanning v Top Deck Travel* (1994) 68 P. & C.R. 14, which had caused much anxiety to persons who found they were being held to ransom to obtain access to their homes across common land. In *R. (Beresford) v Sunderland City Council* [2004] 1 A.C. 889, the House gave valuable guidance on the meaning of "as of right" and the difference between user which is "*precario*"—and thus does not give rise to prescriptive rights—and user which is merely acquiesced in, which does. In *Moncrieff v Jamieson* [2007] 1 W.L.R. 2620, the House confirmed that a right to park can exist as an easement.

The Court of Appeal have also been at work. *McAdams Homes v Robinson* [2004] 3 E.G.L.R. 93 contains an analysis of the scope of rights acquired impliedly or by prescription and what therefore constitutes excessive use. Recently, in *RHJ Limited v F.T. Patten (Holdings) Limited* [2008] 2 W.L.R. 1096, they considered the effect of clauses designed to preserve the right to build. In addition to those we have included about forty other appellate decisions.

There has also been an upsurge of interest in rights of light, the remedies for their infringement and the measure of damages. In *Midtown v City of London Real Property Co* [2005] 1 E.G.L.R. 65, the Court refused an injunction which would have prevented the building of a large block of offices which interfered with the light to the offices on the opposite side of the street. In *Regan v Paul Properties Limited* [2007] Ch. 135, however, the Court of Appeal reaffirmed the principle that a party whose property right is infringed is prima facie entitled to an injunction and in *Tamares Limited v Fairpoint Properties Limited* [2007] 1 W.L.R. 2167, the Court awarded damages in lieu of injunction on a profits related basis. These last two decisions have so altered the balance of negotiation for developers that we would not be surprised to see some correction in future cases and also wonder whether one may expect greater use of the powers to over-ride easements contained in section 237 of the Town and Country Planning Act 1990 and some resulting case law on that subject.

In the preface to the supplement to the 17th edition, published in 2005, we made a plea to the judiciary to include maps or plans in their judgments in easement cases. This has gone largely unheeded, so perhaps we may be forgiven a wry smile upon finding Arden L.J. making the very same point—but in relation to counsels' skeleton arguments—in *Hunte v E. Bottomley & Sons Limited* [2007] EWCA Civ 1168 (cited at para.14–140, below). What's sauce for the goose . . .

Finally, in the preface to our last edition we looked forward to the day when the Law Commission would direct their shovels to the Augean stable that is the law of easements. That day dawned just before we delivered our copy to the publishers with the publication of Law Commission Consultation Paper No. 186. The Commission kindly invited our assistance prior to the production of their Paper and generously acknowledge at several points in the Paper the help they derived from this work. They also quote verbatim the criticisms of the law of easements we made in the preface to the previous edition. We have incorporated some discussion of the Commission's proposals in the present edition but time did not permit us to give them the consideration they deserve. It would be most gratifying if, by the publication of the next edition of this work, there was some new legislation to incorporate.

We have endeavoured to state the law as at August 1st 2008.

Jonathan Gaunt QC   The Hon Mr Justice Morgan
Falcon Chambers   Royal Courts of Justice

August 2008

PREFACE TO THE FIRST EDITION

The want of a treatise upon those important rights known in the Law of England by the name of "Easements" has, it is believed, been sensibly felt by the Profession.

The length of time which has elapsed without any attempt having been made to supply this want affords a sufficient reason for the appearance of the present Essay. The difficulties which arise from the abstruseness and refinements incident to the subject, have been increased by the comparatively small number of decided cases affording matter for defining and systematising this branch of the law. Upon some points, indeed, there is no authority at all in the English law; of the decisions some depend upon the circumstances of the particular case, and some are irreconcilable with each other.

Watercourses are the only class of easements with regard to which the law has been settled with any degree of precision.

A desire to remedy an admitted defect led to the passing of the Prescription Act—a statute, which has not only failed in effecting its particular object, but has introduced greater doubt and confusion than existed before its enactment. In fact, had it not been held, that the statute did not repeal the common law, many rights which have been enjoyed immemorially would have been put an end to by circumstances which never could have been intended to have that effect.

As in many other branches of the Law of England, the earlier authorities upon the law of easements appear to be based upon the civil law, modified, in some degree, probably, by a recognition of customs which existed among our Norman ancestors. The most remarkable instance of an adoption by the English law from this source is the doctrine known in the French law by the title of "Destination due père de famille."

In the majority of cases, both ancient and modern, probably from a consideration of this being the origin of the law, recourse has been had for assistance to the civil law. It has, therefore, been considered that the utility of the work would be increased by the introduction of many of the provisions of that refined and elaborate system with respect to Praedial Servitudes, and the doctrine of Prescription; as well as some of the observations of Pardessus—an eminent French writer on Servitudes.

With the same view the authority of decisions in the American courts has been called in aid upon the subject of watercourses—questions which the value of water as a moving power, and the frequent absence of ancient appropriation, have often given rise to in the United States. In those judgments the law is considered with much care and research, and the rights of the parties settled with precision. The result of the authorities is stated by Chancellor Kent, in his well-known Commentaries, with his usual ability.

Upon many points, particularly upon the construction of the Prescription Act, the observations contained in the following pages are, in some degree, unsupported by direct authority. It has, however, been thought better to endeavour to open the law upon the doubts which presented themselves than to pass them over in silence.

Temple,
July 1839.

TABLE OF CONTENTS

PART I

CHARACTERISTICS OF AN EASEMENT

1. Characteristics of an Easement

2. Equitable Rights to Easements

PART II

THE ACQUISITION OF EASEMENTS

3. Creation of Easements by Known Transactions

4. Establishment of Easements by Prescription

PART III

PARTICULAR EASEMENTS AND PARTICULAR NATURAL RIGHTS OF A SIMILAR CHARACTER

PART IV

EXTINGUISHMENT OF EASEMENTS

12. Extinguishment of Easements

PART V

DISTURBANCE OF EASEMENTS

13. What Amounts to a Disturbance

14. Remedies for Disturbance

APPENDICES

STATUTES, RULES AND ORDERS

TABLE OF CASES

TABLE OF STATUTES

References in bold type indicate where the text of the section appears

TABLE OF STATUTORY INSTRUMENTS

References in bold type indicate where the text of the section appears

TABLE OF PRACTICE DIRECTIONS

TABLE OF CIVIL PROCEDURE RULES

PART I

CHARACTERISTICS OF AN EASEMENT

CHAPTER 1

CHARACTERISTICS OF AN EASEMENT

1.—INTRODUCTION

What is an easement?

An easement[1] is a right over the land of another, which has certain limiting charac-   **1–01**
teristics. First, it is a right which is appurtenant to other land of the proprietor of the
right, which it must accommodate, and cannot exist on its own (in legal terminology,
"in gross"). Secondly, it is a proprietary, not a personal, right and will therefore
bind successors to the servient land and enure for the benefit of successors to the
dominant land. Thirdly, a right to take something from the land of another (such as
game, fish, turf or timber) is not an easement but a "profit" (and can exist in gross).
An easement is said to be a right "without profit". Fourthly, it is not such a right as
entitles the proprietor to the exclusive use of the servient tenement; the owner of the
servient tenement retains absolute dominion over his land and all the rights of an
owner and can use it as he likes, subject to such limitations as are imposed upon it

---

[1] The word comes from the old French "*aisement*", meaning "convenience" or "accommodation".
The modern French word is servitude, which is also the word used in Scottish law. "Easement" was
an expression recognised in legal parlance at least by 1695 because it is fully discussed in *Peers v
Lucy* (1695) 4 Mod. 362; see Holdsworth, *A History of English Law*, 1925, Vol. 7, p. 322.

by the easement. Fifthly, there are some advantages (for example a right to a view or privacy or protection from the weather or of television reception) which cannot exist as easements (although they may be protected in other ways, as by restrictive covenants or the law of nuisance).

An easement therefore, being a proprietary right, is an interest in or over the land of another and is one of the incorporeal rights recognised by English law, but it is not an estate in land. It is an interest which is capable of being conveyed or created at law provided that it is an interest equivalent to either of the estates that can exist at law, namely an estate in fee simple absolute in possession or a term of years absolute.[2]

Easements may be divided into three categories:

(1) positive easements: the right to do something or make use of some installation on your neighbour's land, such as a right of way or a right to instal and use a drain;

(2) negative easements: a right to receive something from your neighbour's land without your neighbour obstructing or interfering with it, such as light, air, support or water;

(3) a right to do something on your own land which would otherwise amount to a private nuisance, for example acts which give rise to noise, smoke, smells or pollution.[3]

Easements and profits à prendre

1–02 An easement relates only to user of land, that is, it merely confers a right to utilise the servient tenement in a particular manner, or to prevent the commission of some act on that tenement, whereas a *profit à prendre in solo alieno* confers a right to take from the servient tenement some part of the soil of that tenement or minerals under it or some of its natural produce or the animals *ferae naturae* existing upon it.[4] For example, the right to depasture cattle,[5] or to graze sheep[6] is a profit, and so is the right to take sea-washed coal from the foreshore.[7] The subject-matter of a profit must be something which is capable of ownership.[8]

[2] Law of Property Act 1925, s.1(2)(a).

[3] For examples, see para.1–73, below. Category 3 may be regarded as positive easements in that the nuisance affects the neighbour's land but they represent a distinct category in that the act in question is committed on the dominant tenement.

[4] *Alfred F. Beckett Ltd v Lyons* [1967] Ch. 449 at 482, per Winn L.J., approving the statement in *Halsbury's Laws of England* (3rd ed., Vol. 12, p. 522), para. 1129; and see *Duke of Sutherland v Heathcote* [1892] 1 Ch. 475 at 484, and paras 1–141 – 1–145, below.

[5] *Bailey v Appleyard* (1838) 8 A. & E. 161.

[6] *White v Taylor (No. 2)* [1969] 1 Ch. 150 at 177.

[7] *Alfred F. Beckett Ltd v Lyons* [1967] Ch. 449 at 474, per Harman L.J.; at 482, per Winn L.J. In the expression *profit à prendre in solo alieno* the words *in solo alieno* are not equivalent to *ex solo alieno*: per Winn L.J. at 480.

[8] *Alfred F. Beckett Ltd v Lyons* [1967] Ch. 449 at 481, 482, per Winn L.J. The nature of *profits à prendre* (including the right to kill and carry away game and fish) is discussed in *Wickham v Hawker* (1840) 7 M. & W. 63; *Ewart v Graham* (1859) 7 H.L.C. 344; *Fitzhardinge v Purcell* [1908] 2 Ch. 163; *White v Williams* [1922] 1 K.B. 727; *Peech v Best* [1931] 1 K.B. 1; *Mason v Clarke* [1955] A.C. 778.

Hence the right to take water (except water appropriated or confined in some receptacle) is not a profit, for water (unless so confined) is not capable of being owned,[9] but the right is or may be an easement.[10]

While the nature of a profit is thus essentially different from that of an easement, the rules and principles governing the acquisition, extinguishment and disturbance of profits are generally applicable to the acquisition, extinguishment and disturbance of easements. For this reason, although this work is not one on the law of profits,[11] reference will be made to the classification of profits[12] and the subject of profits will be referred to whenever to do so appears to be helpful in expounding the law of easements.

A possessory right cannot be an easement

The grantee of the exclusive use of land has an estate in the land and not an easement. So Lopes L.J. in *Reilly v Booth* said[13]:   **1–03**

> "The exclusive or unrestricted use of a piece of land, I take it, beyond all question passes the property or ownership in that land, and there is no easement known to law which gives exclusive and unrestricted use of a piece of land."

It can on occasions be difficult to tell on which side of the line which divides exclusive use and an easement parking and storage rights fall.[14]

A right to build in airspace has been held to be a grant of the fee simple in the air space and not an easement.[15]

The status, for rating and similar purposes, of railway tunnels, gas mains, and the like, belonging to statutory undertakers, has been considered in a number of cases in which no question arose as to the rights of the undertakers vis-à-vis the owners of the surrounding soil, but the distinction between easement and ownership was

---

[9] *Alfred F. Beckett Ltd v Lyons* [1967] Ch. 449 at 481, per Winn L.J.

[10] *Race v Ward* (1855) 4 E. & B. 702; *Manning v Wasdale* (1836) 5 A. & E. 758; *Paine & Co v St Neots Gas and Coke Co* [1939] 3 All E.R. 812 at 823; *Simeon, Re* [1937] Ch. 525. In *Mitchell v Potter* [2005] EWCA Civ 88, *The Times*, January 24, 2005, the county court judge had held that the right to take water from a reservoir was a profit but the Court of Appeal held that it was not necessary to determine whether the right was a profit or an easement.

[11] As will be seen (paras 1–141 — 1–145, below), a profit may be a "sole" or "several" profit, or a profit "in common" or right of common. For a detailed discussion of the law of profits and commons, see, e.g. *Halsbury's Laws of England* (4th ed., 2003 Reissue, Vol. 6), title *Commons*, *Halsbury's Laws of England* (4th ed., Reissue, Vol. 16(2)), title *Easements and Profits A Prendre*, Gadsden, *The Law of Commons* (1988), and Ubhi and Denyer-Green, *Law of Commons and of Town and Village Greens*. For older works see Hall, *Law of Profits à Prendre and Rights of Common*; Williams *on Commons*; Woolrych *on Commons*; Harris and Ryan, *An Outline of the Law Relating to Common Land*.

[12] See in particular section 9 of this chapter, paras 1–141 — 1–145, below.

[13] (1890) 44 Ch. D. 12 at 26. See also *Capel v Buszard* (1829) 6 Bing. 150 at 159; *Clifford v Hoare* (1874) L.R. 9 C.P. 362 at 371.

[14] See paras 9–96 to 9–110, below.

[15] *Bursill Enterprises Pty Ltd v Berger Bros Trading Co Pty Ltd* (1971) 124 C.L.R. 73 (High Court of Australia); *Tileska v Bevelon* (1989) 4 B.P.R. 97306 (Supreme Court of New South Wales–Equity Division, Waddell C.J.).

referred to. Such cases appear to be *sui generis*, and it is difficult, for instance, to find a dominant tenement.[16] Usually no easement is created.[17] In *South Eastern Railway v Associated Portland Cement Manufacturers (1900) Limited*[18] the reservation, in a conveyance to a railway company, of the right for the conveying party, his heirs and assigns, to make a tunnel under the land conveyed (the proposed railway) was treated by Swinfen Eady J. as a reservation of an easement, but by the Court of Appeal as an assignable personal contract. The owner of an exclusive right to use a tunnel is, in fact, almost certainly, the owner of the tunnel itself.[19]

This chapter

1–04   The remainder of this chapter is divided into the following parts:

Part 2.—Essential characteristics of an easement
Part 3.—Examples of easements
Part 4.—Rights analogous to easements
Part 5.—Incidents of easements
Part 6.—Statutory rights
Part 7.—Licences
Part 8.—Extent and mode of enjoyment
Part 9.—Classification of profits
Part 10.—Law reform

2.—ESSENTIAL CHARACTERISTICS OF AN EASEMENT

Essential characteristics

1–05   The essential characteristics of an easement appear from *Ellenborough Park, Re*.[20] In that case the question arose whether the owners of certain houses in Ellenborough Park, an open space, comparable with the garden of a London "square", in Weston-super-Mare, had any right to participate in a compensation rental and dilapidations payment received by the owners of the park under the Compensation (Defence) Act 1939. Such a right could only exist if the houseowners had some interest in the park;

---

[16] *Metropolitan Railway v Fowler* [1892] 1 Q.B. 165; [1893] A.C. 416; *Holywell Union and Halkyn Parish v Halkyn Drainage Co* [1895] A.C. 117; *R. v Chelsea Waterworks Co* (1833) 5 B. & Ald. 156; *Southport Corp v Ormskirk Union Assessment Committee* [1894] 1 Q.B. 196; *Ystradyfodwg and Pontypridd Main Sewerage Board v Bensted* [1907] 1 K.B. 490 at 497; *Taff Vale Ry v Cardiff Ry* [1917] 1 Ch. 299 at 317.
[17] *Newcastle-under-Lyme Corp v Wolstanton Ltd* [1947] Ch. 427 at 456, 457. This case was considered in detail by the High Court of Australia in *Commissioner of Main Roads v The North Shore Gas Company Ltd* (1967) 120 C.L.R. 118: see, in particular, per Windeyer J. at pp. 132–133. It seems clear, however, that a particular house or piece of land can have an easement to maintain and use a drain on other land: see paras 1–22 and 1–54, below.
[18] [1910] 1 Ch. 12.
[19] *Bevan v London Portland Cement Co* (1892) 67 L.T. 615; *Pearson's Will, Re* (1900) 83 L.T. 626; and see (1916) 32 L.Q.R. 70.
[20] [1956] Ch. 131.

their only possible interest was an easement, and the question thus became one of easement or no easement. The facts were shortly as follows: Ellenborough Park was a rectangular piece of land[21] surrounded by a road, on three sides of which (the fourth faced the sea) were rows of houses. In or about 1864 the sites of the houses, and also of other houses further away, formed part of a building estate which was sold in plots. The conveyance of one of these plots, which was accepted as typical, contained a grant of the plot, together with the dwelling-house in course of erection thereon, and together with easements over the roads and drains in the estate:

> "And also the full enjoyment . . . at all times hereafter in common with the other persons to whom such easements may be granted of the pleasure ground . . . [Ellenborough Park] . . . but subject to the payment of a fair and just proportion of the costs charges and expenses of keeping in good order and condition the said pleasure ground."[22]

There was a detailed covenant by the purchaser to complete the house in accordance   **1–06**
with specifications and plans, similar in every respect externally and in a uniform manner with a particular house already built, and a covenant by him against alteration of the external elevation or structure, and against user for commercial purposes. The vendors covenanted with the purchaser, and his successors in title and all other persons to whom the right of enjoyment of the park might be granted, to keep the park as an ornamental pleasure ground, and not at any time to "erect or permit to be erected any dwelling-house and other building (except any grotto bower summerhouse . . . or other ornamental erection) within or on any part of the" park, but that the same should at all times remain as an ornamental garden or pleasure ground. A similar right of user was granted in respect of some nine or ten other plots, not actually fronting the park but separated from the road round it only by houses so fronting.

The right to use the park was held by the Court of Appeal,[23] affirming Danckwerts   **1–07**
J., to be an easement, and for the purposes of the decision it was agreed between counsel, and accepted by the Court, that the following four characteristics[24] are essential to an easement:

1. There must be a dominant and a servient tenement.[25]
2. An easement must accommodate the dominant tenement.[26]
3. Dominant and servient owners must be different persons.[27]
4. A right over land cannot amount to an easement unless it is capable of forming the subject-matter of a grant.[28]

---

[21] More exactly, it was two pieces of land, intersected by a main road.
[22] It may be observed that the grant of a similar right was provided for in an agreement, made in 1843, for a lease of a house in a similar crescent in Brighton: *Lawrence v South County Freeholds Ltd* [1939] Ch. 656 at 660.
[23] The judgment of the Court was delivered by Sir Raymond Evershed, M.R.
[24] As formulated in *Cheshire's Modern Real Property* (13th ed.), pp. 490 *et seq.*
[25] See paras 1–08 *et seq.*, below.
[26] See paras 1–23 *et seq.*, below.
[27] See paras 1–31 *et seq.*, below.
[28] See paras 1–36 *et seq.*, below.

These four characteristics to some extent overlap, but it will be convenient to consider each of them separately.

(1) *There must be a dominant and a servient tenement*

1–08   In other words, an easement requires that some diminution of the natural rights incident to the ownership of an estate in one piece of land be reflected in a corresponding artificial right superimposed on the natural rights incident to another piece of land. Lord Cairns L.J. in *Rangeley v Midland Railway Company*[29] said:

> "There can be no easement properly so called unless there be both a servient and a dominant tenement. . . . There can be no such thing according to our law, or according to the civil law, as what I may term an easement in gross. An easement must be connected with a dominant tenement."

Again, Lord Coleridge C.J. in *Hawkins v Rutter*[30] said:

> "No doubt the term 'easement' has, somewhat loosely and inaccurately perhaps,[31] but still with sufficient accuracy for some purposes, been said to define the case of a public right of way, in which case there exists no dominant and servient tenement; but in strictness, and according to the proper use of legal language, the term 'easement' does imply a dominant tenement in respect of which the easement is claimed, and a servient tenement upon which the right claimed is exercised."

Again, Winn L.J. in *Alfred F. Beckett Ltd v Lyons*[32] said:

> "I think it is an essential element of any easement that it is annexed to land, and that no person can possess an easement otherwise than in respect of and

---

[29] (1868) 3 Ch. App. 306 at 310, 311. The question here was whether a railway company could divert a public footpath without acquiring and paying for the new site, and the passage quoted was dealing with an argument that this would not be permanently used, within s.84 of the Lands Clauses Consolidation Act 1845, and that the company would have a mere easement, the ownership of the site remaining as before. As Lord Cairns L.J. pointed out (at 311) "a public road or highway is not an easement, it is a dedication to the public of the occupation of the surface of the land for the purpose of passing and repassing, the public generally taking upon themselves (through the parochial authorities or otherwise) the obligation of repairing it". In Sturley, "Easements in Gross" (1980) 96 L.Q.R. 556, it is suggested that the rule against easements in gross exists on the weakest of authority for reasons which are no longer compelling; see also Gardner (1982) 98 L.Q.R. 305.

[30] [1892] 1 Q.B. 668 at 671, deciding that the right of a member of the public to ground his barge on the bed of a navigable river was not an "easement" for the purpose of the County Courts Act 1888, s.60.

[31] For instance, in *Dovaston v Payne* (1795) 2 H.Bl. 527, the soil of a highway was said to be subject to an easement for the benefit of the public, but a public right of way cannot be an easement, for there is no dominant tenement. In *Taff Vale Ry v Cardiff Ry* [1971] 1 Ch. 299 at 317, Scrutton L.J. pointed out that "Parliament and parliamentary draftsmen have used the term 'easement' in relation to various rights which no lawyer would ordinarily describe as 'easements'."

[32] [1967] Ch. 449 at 483.

in amplification of his enjoyment of some estate or interest in a piece of land: compare Rangeley v. Midland Railway Company."[33]

More recently, Peter Gibson L.J. in *London & Blenheim Ltd v Ladbroke Retail Parks*[34] said: "It is trite law that there can be no easement in gross: see Rangeley v. Midland Railway Company."

It follows that an easement, being annexed to the dominant tenement, cannot   **1–09**
be separated from it by being assigned to a stranger.[35] This does not mean, however, that the use of the dominant tenement is confined to the dominant owner personally. In the first place, a lease or tenancy of dominant land operates as a lease or tenancy of the land plus the easement, and anyone for the time being entitled to an interest in the land which, vis-à-vis the owner, gives him the right to possession is entitled, vis-à-vis whoever is in possession of the servient land, to use the easement.[36] If the tenant is entitled to the protection of Part II of the Landlord and Tenant Act 1954 and, thereby, to a continuation and renewal of the tenancy, that protection extends to a right of way included in the lease.[37] Secondly, the grant of an easement normally operates as a grant of the right to such user as the enjoyment of the dominant land reasonably requires, and this includes user by strangers.[38] In *Proud v Hollis*[39] it was said that the landlord of land to which a right of way is annexed may use the way to view waste, or to demand rent, or to remove an obstruction. Perhaps the true view is that user by a landlord for any purpose connected with the dominant tenement could be justified as had under the licence, express or implied, of the tenant.

Identification of the dominant tenement

The dominant tenement must exist and must be identified before there can be a   **1–10**
grant, or a contract for the grant, of an easement sufficient to create an interest in land binding successors in title to the servient land. Thus it was said[40]:

> "A right intended as an easement and attached to a servient tenement before the dominant tenement is identified would ... be an incident of a novel kind."

---

[33] (1868) 3 Ch. App. 306.
[34] [1994] 1 W.L.R. 31 at 36H.
[35] *cf. Ackroyd v Smith* (1850) 10 C.B. 164 at 188.
[36] *Skull v Glenister* (1864) 16 C.B. (n.s.) 81 (parol letting from year to year), *cf.* Law of Property Act 1925, s.187(1). On the other hand it seems that, in the absence of clear words enabling him to do so, the owner of a dominant tenement could not authorise the public to use a right of way annexed thereto: see *Johnstone v Holdway* [1963] 1 Q.B. 601 at 613.
[37] *Nevill Long & Co (Boards) v Firmenich & Co* (1982) 44 P. & C.R. 12 (applying *Whitley v Stumbles* [1930] A.C. 544, HL, and *Dodson Bull Carpet Co Ltd v City of London Corp* [1975] 1 W.L.R. 781).
[38] See paras 9–71 to 9–74, below.
[39] (1822) 2 B. & C. 8.
[40] *London & Blenheim Ltd v Ladbroke Ltd* [1994] 1 W.L.R. 31 at 37H; followed in *Voice v Bell* (1993) 68 P. & C.R. 441; these cases are discussed at paras 2–32 to 2–34, below.

A dominant tenement can usually be identified without much difficulty. Although it is obviously good conveyancing practice in a deed granting an easement to specify the dominant tenement clearly, failure so to do is not necessarily fatal to the grant, for extrinsic evidence, including evidence of the manner in which a purchaser intends to use land in the future, is admissible to identify the dominant tenement when its identity does not appear clearly from the deed. This rule is illustrated by two modern cases.[41]

1–11   In *Johnstone v Holdway*[42] a vendor held certain land, including a quarry, in trust for a company. The vendor as trustee and the company as beneficial owner conveyed part of the land to a purchaser, who was the defendant's predecessor in title. The quarry was not included in the land conveyed, but was adjacent to it on its north-western boundary. There was a public highway on the south-eastern boundary of the land conveyed, and the conveyance contained a reservation and exception in favour of the company and its successors in title of a right of way for use "at all times and for all purposes (including quarrying)" over the land conveyed from a point on its north-western boundary to a point on its south-eastern boundary. The reservation did not specify the dominant tenement for the benefit of which the right of way was given, but it was intended to be the quarry. The plaintiffs became the owners of the quarry as the company's successors in title, and they claimed a declaration that they had a right of way over the defendant's land from the highway to the quarry. For the defendant it was submitted that it was not permissible to identify the dominant tenement by inferences from facts and circumstances which must have been known to the parties at the time of the conveyance.

1–12   Delivering the judgment of the Court of Appeal, Upjohn L.J. referred to *Thorpe v Brumfitt*.[43] In that case, in the course of a rearrangement of boundaries a triangular piece of land, containing five-and-a-half square yards and intended to be thrown into the yard of an inn to which a right of way had previously been enjoyed, was conveyed with a right of way at all times and for all purposes over a passage described as being "between" the highway and the north side of the piece of land conveyed. In an action for obstruction, it appears to have been argued, in reliance on *Ackroyd v Smith*,[44] that the right was in gross. Rejecting this, Mellish L.J. said that the words "between", etc., might fairly be construed as making the right appurtenant to the five-and-a-half square yards. James L.J. went further, and said that the right to and from the five-and-a-half square yards must be construed reasonably, in the circumstances, as meaning a right of way between

---

[41] See also *Laurie v Winch* (1952) 4 D.L.R. 449; *Gamble v Birch Island Estates* (1971) 13 D.L.R. (3d) 657; *Harada v Registrar of Titles* [1981] V.R. 743. An example of the admission of extrinsic evidence to identify the dominant tenement is provided in *Hamble Parish Council v Haggard* [1992] 1 W.L.R. 122. The rule for easements is less strict than the rule as to the annexation of the benefit of a restrictive covenant, in which case the land intended to be benefited by the covenant must be sufficiently defined in the conveyance so as to be readily ascertainable (for which latter purpose extrinsic evidence is admissible): *Crest Nicholson Ltd v McAllister* [2004] 1 W.L.R. 2409 at [31]–[34].

[42] [1963] 1 Q.B. 601.

[43] (1873) 8 Ch. App. 650.

[44] (1850) 10 C.B. 164; see para.1–16, below.

the highway and the yard, of which the five-and-a-half square yards were to form part, and that the right would therefore pass as appurtenant to the inn.

Upjohn L.J. said[45] that it was quite plain that James L.J. took the view that you must look at the whole of the relevant facts which must have been known to the grantor and the grantee at the time of the grant and take into consideration the whole object of the transaction. Upjohn L.J. referred[46] to *Callard v Beeney*[47] in which a vendor conveyed a farm to a purchaser together with a right of way over a field No. 171 belonging to the vendor "for the purpose of access to and from the point marked 'X' on the said plan to the field numbered 169", and the Divisional Court held as a matter of construction that the dominant tenement was the whole of the 70 acres or so of land conveyed by the deed and that the right of way was appurtenant to those lands and not limited to use for purposes connected with field No. 169 only. Upjohn L.J. pointed out that Wright J. in his judgment in *Callard v Beeney*[48] dealt with the matter purely as a matter of construction and cited the observations of Lord Wensleydale in *Lord Waterpark v Fennell*[49] that:

"The construction of a deed is always for the court; but, in order to apply its provisions, evidence is in every case admissible of all material facts existing at the time of the execution of the deed, so as to place the court in the situation of the grantor."

In the light of those authorities Upjohn L.J. said[50]:

"In our judgment, it is a question of the construction of the deed creating a right of way as to what is the dominant tenement for the benefit of which the right of way is granted and to which the right of way is appurtenant. In construing the deed the court is entitled to have evidence of all material facts at the time of the execution of the deed, so as to place the court in the situation of the parties."

It seemed to the Court of Appeal perfectly plain that in the case before it the dominant tenement was the land and quarry.

Easement may be appurtenant to land other than that conveyed

The Shannon Limited v Venner Limited,[51] in which the Court of Appeal applied **1–13** *Thorpe v Brumfitt*[52] and *Johnstone v Holdway*,[53] not only is authority on the admissibility of extrinsic evidence but also shows that the easement granted may,

---

[45] [1963] 1 Q.B. 601 at 611.
[46] [1963] 1 Q.B. 601 at 611.
[47] [1930] 1 K.B. 353.
[48] [1930] 1 K.B. 353 at 360.
[49] (1859) 7 H.L.C. 650 at 684.
[50] [1963] 1 Q.B. 601 at 612.
[51] [1965] Ch. 682.
[52] (1873) 8 Ch. App. 650.
[53] [1963] 1 Q.B. 601.

when the dominant tenement is not specified in the deed of grant, be appurtenant to other land besides that conveyed by the deed.

In 1927 the plaintiff company bought certain land in Surrey on which it built a factory so constructed that it could be extended. In 1930 adjoining land, described as land "to the north of land recently sold by the vendor to the company", was conveyed to it by the same vendor "together with a right of way for all purposes for the company and their successors in title their tenants and servants and all persons authorised by the company in common with the vendor and all others authorised by him over and along the private estate drive of the vendor as" identified on a plan. There was no physical division between the land conveyed and the land acquired by the company in 1927. The company claimed a declaration that the right of way was appurtenant to the adjacent land which it had previously acquired. Pennycuick J. admitted evidence that at the time of its purchase the company intended to use the further land in connection with its factory, and that that intention was communicated to the vendor before the execution of the conveyance, but, founding his conclusion on the reference to the company and its successors in title and the inclusion of the grant of the right of way between the parcels and the *habendum*, held that the words of the conveyance were clear and that the right of way was not appurtenant to the land previously acquired by the company.

1–14   The Court of Appeal allowed an appeal from Pennycuick J.'s decision, holding that proper conveyancing practice required not merely a reference to "successors in title" but an identification of the owner or occupier of identified dominant land for the benefit of which an easement was created; that the identification of the dominant tenement was not clear or sufficient in the conveyance, which did not in terms identify the dominant tenement at all; and that extrinsic evidence was therefore admissible concerning the circumstances in which the conveyance was executed.

Danckwerts L.J., delivering the judgment of the Court of Appeal, said[54]:

> "It is one thing to allow a party to say: 'By the words in the deed, I meant this meaning' (which is not admissible), and quite another thing to advance evidence that, in acquiring a particular piece of land, the purchaser had certain plans for the use of that land which may explain the form which the document took. The evidence was rightly admitted as throwing light upon the circumstances in which the document came to be executed.
>
> It is sufficient to refer to the words of Upjohn L.J., giving the judgment of the court, in Johnstone v. Holdway."[55]

Having cited the words from the judgment in *Johnstone v Holdway* quoted above, Danckwerts L.J. continued[56]:

> "That is the situation in the present case, and we are entitled to have the benefit of the evidence of the surrounding circumstances. A document intended

[54] [1965] Ch. 691.
[55] [1963] 1 Q.B. 601 at 612; see para.1–12, above.
[56] [1965] Ch. 691 at 692.

to have legal effect is not executed in a vacuum. It is drafted and executed to deal with the situation in which the parties find themselves. Of course, if the words used in the deed are perfectly clear, they must be given their meaning, and extrinsic evidence is not admissible, because that would be contradicting the terms of the deed.

. . . Of course the deed must be looked at, and then, if the meaning is not plain, the court is entitled to consider the surrounding circumstances so as to see whether light as to the construction is to be gained from these."

It had been submitted for the defendant company that, in the absence of a statement identifying the dominant tenement, there must be a presumption, and possibly an inference, that the land actually conveyed by the deed must be the dominant tenement, and reliance was placed upon *Callard v Beeney*,[57] as support for the proposition to that effect on p. 8 of the 13th edition of this work. The Court of Appeal thought[58] that that might be so in the absence of evidence causing an inference that some other land was the dominant tenement for the benefit of which the easement was created, but held that it could not be an irrebuttable presumption. *Callard v Beeney* was a case where the contest was between the whole of the land conveyed and a single field forming part of it. It did not seem to be the same point as that which the Court had to consider in the case then before it.

The description of a right of way may limit the dominant tenement to some part only of the land conveyed. In *Henning v Burnet*[59] a conveyance of a house and a field beyond it contained a grant of a right of way over a road which was described as "leading" to the house; in fact it passed alongside it and then turned in so as to divide the house from the field. It was held that the way was to the house only, and was not annexed to the field also. In *British Railways Board v Glass*,[60] on the other hand, a conveyance of land acquired for the construction of a railway line contained an exception in favour of the grantor and his heirs and assigns of "a right of crossing the said railway to the extent of twelve feet in width on the level thereof with all manner of cattle to and from one part of the said close of land hereinbefore described and called Cowshed or Cowleaze . . . to the other part of the said close severed by the said . . . railway" and it was held that the reference to the field called Cowshed as containing the two ends of the crossing place was merely used so as to identify the position of the crossing; that is to say, the description of a part of the dominant land was not restrictive of the dominant tenement but merely intended to show where the right of way would be exercised.

In *Ackroyd v Smith*,[61] where a close and other lands were conveyed, together with the right for the grantee, his heirs and assigns, owners and occupiers for the time being of the said close and other lands, of passing and repassing, with or without horses, cattle, carts, and carriages, for all purposes, in, over, along and

1–15

1–16

---

[57] [1930] 1 K.B. 353.
[58] [1965] Ch. 691 at 692, 693.
[59] (1852) 8 Exch. 187.
[60] [1965] Ch. 538.
[61] (1850) 10 C.B. 164.

through a certain road described as running between a certain turnpike road and a certain lane called Legram's Lane, or through some other road in the same direction to be formed by the grantee, the court expressed the opinion that the grant, on its true construction, was not only for the purposes of the land conveyed but also for purposes unconnected with it, and was therefore a grant of a right in gross, not appurtenant to the land conveyed and not capable of passing by a subsequent conveyance of it with its appurtenances. It seems reasonable to suppose, however, that a right granted in the same quite common form would now be treated as annexed to the land conveyed.

In *Todrick v Western National Omnibus Co*[62] Romer L.J. said:

> "I doubt, however, whether at the present day any judge would hold that the right granted in that case was as a matter of construction a grant of a right of way for all purposes whether connected or unconnected with the land in question."

The topography of *Ackroyd v Smith* is obscure, but it seems[63] that the land to which it was sought to make the way appurtenant was not at the end of the road. So far as can be gathered,[64] this road either led into or passed the end of an accommodation road, part of the "lands" granted and leading to other of these lands.

An incorporeal hereditament can be a dominant tenement

1–17 The dominant tenement usually consists of corporeal property. It was, however, held by Buckley J. in *Hanbury v Jenkins*[65] that a right of way can be appurtenant to a right of fishing. He adopted note 7 to Hargrave and Butler's edition of Co. Litt. 121b, that the true test of appurtenancy was the propriety of relation between the principal and the adjunct, which might be found out by considering whether they so agreed in nature and quality as to be capable of union without incongruity.

In *Att-Gen v Copeland*,[66] a highway authority claimed an easement of discharging water on the defendant's land by means of a pipe running from a highway. The action was dismissed by Lord Alverstone C.J. on the ground that the public right of passage over the road was not such a right as was capable of having the easement claimed attached to it, and that therefore the claim to the easement failed for want of a dominant tenement. This decision was reversed by the Court of Appeal, on the ground that the pipe in question was a "drain" within the meaning of section 67[67] of the Highway Act 1835; Lord Collins M.R. adding[68] "that a legal origin was

---

[62] [1934] Ch. 561 at 583; and *cf. Thorpe v Brumfitt* (1873) 8 Ch. App. 650 at 658; *Gaw v Córas Iompair éireann* [1953] I.R. 232.
[63] See *Thorpe v Brumfitt* (1873) 8 Ch. App. 650 at 657; *Todrick v Western National Omnibus Co* [1934] Ch. 561 at 590, 591.
[64] See (1850) 10 C.B. 164 at 176.
[65] [1901] 2 Ch. 422.
[66] [1901] 2 K.B. 101. On appeal [1902] 1 K.B. 690.
[67] Now repealed.
[68] [1902] 1 K.B. 690 at 693.

possible and ought to be presumed", for the right claimed, and the Lords Justices apparently concurring. This case is therefore inconclusive on the question whether a dominant tenement can consist of an incorporeal hereditament.

Applying the test in *Hanbury v Jenkins*, it is submitted that if the owner of a right **1-18** to take certain minerals[69] under close A obtained from the owner of an adjacent close, B, a grant of a way over the close B, or a right to discharge water over it, for him, his heirs and assigns, as appurtenant to the right of mining, an easement would undoubtedly be created and would be appurtenant to the incorporeal right already vested in the grantee. It is clear that if the grantee, in the case above supposed, was already the owner, not merely of the incorporeal hereditament, but of the substratum itself containing the minerals, and obtained such a grant from the owner of B, he would thus become entitled to an easement appurtenant to his soil; and what reason is there for holding that such would not also be the result in the case first put? If the question were raised in the form above suggested, the difficulty could not be evaded by holding that the first incorporeal right is enlarged by the grant of the second, and that both together form one entire right, as they would do if they had originally been conferred by the same grantor in one grant.[70]

Salvin's Indenture, Re[71] indicates that a dominant tenement may consist of both **1-19** corporeal and incorporeal hereditaments. The defendants were the water authority for an important area in the county of Durham. The plaintiff's predecessors in the title had some years before purported to grant to the defendants' predecessors in title (who were at that time the water authority for the area in question) "the free and uninterrupted right easement liberty leave licence power and authority" in consideration of a small yearly rentcharge "to make and maintain and from time to time lay . . . enlarge alter . . . cleanse drain and repair all or any mains and pipes necessary or proper for the conveyance or transit of water for the purposes of the water authority. The plaintiff took out an originating summons for the construction of this grant, and on his behalf it was contended unsuccessfully that it had not operated as the grant of an easement, but only as the grant of a licence, on the ground that the defendants' system of pipes was not a dominant tenement to which the right of conveying water could have been annexed. Dealing with this argument, Farwell J. said[72]:

---

[69] The right to take minerals out of the soil of another is an incorporeal right; the right to a stratum of minerals is a corporeal right: *Doe d. Hanley v Wood* (1819) 2 B. & Ald. 724; *Wilkinson v Proud* (1843) 11 M. & W. 33; *Hamilton v Graham* (1871) L.R. 2 Sc. & Div. 166.

[70] The instance given above, with substantially the conclusions stated, was originally from the hand of Mr W.H. Willes, the editor of the 3rd edition (1862).

[71] [1938] 2 All E.R. 498. Farwell J.'s decision is criticised in an article, Brett, "The Dominant Estate", in 14 Conv. (n.s.) 264, 267 *et seq. Salvin's Indenture, Re* was followed in *Gas & Fuel Corp of Victoria v Barba* [1976] V.R. 755 (grant of easement for gas pipe-line) and distinguished in *Harada v Registrar of Titles* [1981] V.R. 743 (right to lay electrical wires and to erect poles and towers not a proprietary right). See also *Paul v Canadian Pacific Ltd* (1989) 53 D.L.R. (4d) 487 (easement to lay railway line, where dominant tenement was the land owned by the railway company) and *Shelf Holdings Ltd v Husky Oil Operations Ltd* (1989) 56 D.L.R. (4d) 193 (easement to lay oil pipe-line). For a dissenting voice, see Windeyer J. in *Commissioner of Main Roads v North Shore Gas Co Ltd* (1967) 120 C.L.R. 118 at 133.

[72] [1938] 2 All E.R. 498 at 506.

"In my judgment, that is not sound. The undertaking in this case, which is now vested in the defendants, consists of corporeal hereditaments and incorporeal hereditaments, the corporeal hereditaments being the lands which the company acquired for the purpose of its object—that is to say, lands for the erection of reservoirs and other similar purposes—and the incorporeal hereditaments being the rights which it acquired in land of others, to lay pipes and for other purposes. The undertaking, in my judgment, being composed of corporeal and incorporeal hereditaments, is capable of being the dominant tenement in respect of such a grant as this."[73]

Right of burial

1–20   The exclusive right of burial may be granted in perpetuity, under a faculty if the vault is in a church or churchyard[74] and, if it is elsewhere, by statute.[75] The validity of a non-statutory perpetual grant of this kind appears to be undoubted,[76] but the nature of the right created is questionable, and it is submitted that no easement is created,[77] for there is no dominant tenement. A true easement, of burying in the chancel of a church any person dying in a certain house, was recognised in *Waring v Griffiths*.[78]

Servient tenement

1–21   If no servient tenement is ascertainable there is, of course, no easement. In *Woodman v Pwllbach Colliery Co Ltd*,[79] where a lessee claimed, unsuccessfully, that his lease contained an implied grant of the right to cause a nuisance by allowing coal dust to dissipate itself over adjoining land of the lessor (to which no reference was made in the lease), the Court of Appeal,[80] who refused to infer any such grant, intimated that the right, if granted, could not be an easement, for no servient tenement was ascertainable. Lord Cozens Hardy M.R. said[81]:

"... if it is an easement it is elementary to say that you must have a dominant and a servient tenement. You cannot have a dominant tenement without

---

[73] But see *Stockport Waterworks Co v Potter* (1864) 3 H. & C. 300 at 327.

[74] *De Romana v Roberts* [1906] P. 332.

[75] Cemetery Clauses Act 1847, s.40; the Local Authorities' Cemeteries Order 1977 (S.I. 1977/204), art.10 and Sch.2 (made under the Local Government Act 1972, s.214(3)); and see *Hoskins-Abrahall v Paignton U.D.C.* [1929] 1 Ch. 375; *Reed v Madon* [1989] Ch. 408.

[76] See, e.g. *De Romana v Roberts*, above; *Kellett v St. John's, Burscough* (1916) 32 T.L.R. 571 and *cf.* the Burial Act 1853, s.4.

[77] This was conceded in *London Cemetery Co v Cundey* [1953] 1 W.L.R. 786, but on the ground that there was no servient tenement. See *Kellett v St. John's Burscough*, above, at 572. This was the conclusion in the Australian case of *Beard v Baulkham, Hills Shire Council* [1986] 7 N.S.W.L.R. 273, and see (1965) 39 A.L.J. 50, where the authorities are reviewed. The nature of an exclusive right of burial was considered in *Reed v Madon* [1989] 1 Ch. 408 at 419–420, *West Norwood Cemetry, In re* [1994] Fam. 210 at 218 and *West Norwood Cemetry, In re* [2005] 1 W.L.R. 2176 at [28]–[30].

[78] (1758) 1 Burr.440.

[79] (1914) 111 L.T. 169; affd. [1915] A.C. 634.

[80] And see, per Lord Summer [1915] A.C. 634 at 648, 649.

[81] (1914) 111 L.T. 169 at 172.

some definition of what is the tenement which goes by the name of the servient tenement. There is no reference whatever to be found in this deed which enables one to answer that question. ... It may have been [the lessor's] whole property for all I know. ... You cannot have a servient tenement without an area. You must have lines defining some area."

Swinfen Eady L.J. said[82]: "It is necessary for an easement that there should be a servient tenement that can be defined and pointed out."

Difficulty in identifying the servient tenement, though not any doubt as to its **1–22** existence, may arise where, for instance, a house is granted with the right to receive water, or discharge drainage, through a pipe in adjoining property retained by the grantor. In such a case the servient tenement may be thought to consist of the adjoining property or some part of it, or of the pipe itself, if this is not part and parcel of the dominant land,[83] or of the adjoining property and the pipe.[84]

For most practical purposes the question is of little importance, for it is clear that such a right is an easement,[85] and that, whatever the servient tenement may be, the pipe is entitled to protection from interference,[86] including, presumably, interference by withdrawal of support.[87] Furthermore, in cases of doubt the deed will be construed against the grantor.[88] In other similar cases the identity of the servient tenement may bear on the question whether the so-called easement is not repugnant to the proprietary rights of the servient owner.[89]

(2) *An easement must accommodate the dominant tenement*

This and the first condition mean, in effect, that no right over land can be an ease-   **1–23** ment unless it in fact[90] accommodates other land (the dominant tenement). It is

---

[82] (1914) 111 L.T. 169 at 174.

[83] If a pipe is laid in the land of another, then, in the absence of express agreement, the application of the maxim *quicquid plantatur solo, solo cedit* depends upon the circumstances and the language of the grant: *Simmons v Midford* [1969] 2 Ch. 415, where *Lancaster v Eve* (1859) 5 C.B. (n.s.) 717, *Wake v Hall* (1883) 8 App. Cas. 195 and *Armstrong v Sheppard & Short Ltd* [1959] 2 Q.B. 384 at 401, per Lord Evershed M.R. are considered, but part of the reasoning in *Simmons v Midford* was disapproved in *Melluish v B.M.I. (No. 3) Ltd* [1996] A.C. 454; see also *Goodhart v Hyett* (1883) 25 Ch. D. 182 at 186; *Newcastle-under-Lyme Corp v Wolstanton Ltd* [1947] Ch. 427 at 439.

[84] *Paine & Co v St Neots Gas & Coke Co* [1939] 3 All E.R. 812 at 823.

[85] "The right to the free passage of water through my neighbour's land and for that purpose to maintain a pipe or other channel therein is one of the commonest forms of easement" (Warrington L.J., *Schwann v Cotton* [1916] 2 Ch. 459 at 474); and see *Nuttall v Bracewell* (1866) L.R. 2 Exch. 1 at 10.

[86] *Schwann v Cotton*, above.

[87] The pipe has, however, no right to participate in any right of support which the soil enclosing it may itself have; *Newcastle-under-Lyme Corp v Wolstanton Ltd* [1947] Ch. 427.

[88] *Dunn v Blackdown Properties Ltd* [1961] Ch. 433 at 442; but where on the conveyance of the servient tenement an easement is reserved, the reservation will be construed against the grantee and in favour of the grantor of the servient tenement; see para.3–13, below.

[89] See paras 1–54 *et seq.*, below.

[90] "An incident of this nature cannot, even by express words in a deed, be connected with the estate by the mere acts of the parties"; per Byles J. in *Bailey v Stephens* (1862) 12 C.B. (n.s.) 91 at 115, pointing out that a grant to the owner of land in Kent of a right of way over land in Northumberland would not create an easement.

no objection that other land, or other people, could equally be accommodated by the same right,[91] or that the grant of the right has the effect of conferring some benefit on other land also.[92]

As Lord Evershed M.R. said delivering the judgment of the Court of Appeal in *Ellenborough Park, Re*[93] what is required is that the right "accommodates and serves the dominant tenement, and is reasonably necessary for the better enjoyment of that tenement, for if it has no necessary connection therewith, although it confers an advantage upon the owner and renders his ownership of the land more valuable, it is not an easement at all, but a mere contractual right personal to and only enforceable between the two contracting parties."

1–24   In applying this to the grant of "the full enjoyment" of Ellenborough Park, the Court of Appeal decided that the right did "accommodate and serve" each of the houses with which it was granted, in that the use of the park was an extension of the normal use of the house. The Court recognised that mere increase in value is not decisive, and that some rights, granted with a house, may fail to qualify as easements because they are not connected or are too remotely connected, with the normal enjoyment of the house, the question whether or not a connection exists being primarily one of fact, and depending largely on the nature of the alleged dominant tenement and the nature of the right granted. The test in the present case was whether the park constituted, in a real and intelligible sense, the garden (albeit the communal garden) of the houses to which its enjoyment was annexed.

1–25   The Court of Appeal found a close analogy in

> "the case of a man selling the freehold of part of his house and granting to the purchaser, his heirs and assigns, the right, appurtenant to such part, to use the garden in common with the vendor and his assigns. In such a case, the test of connection, or accommodation, would be amply satisfied; for just as the use of a garden undoubtedly enhances, and is connected with, the normal enjoyment of the house to which it belongs, so also would the right granted, in the case supposed, be closely connected with the use and enjoyment of the part of the premises sold. Such, we think, is in substance the position in the present case. The park became a communal garden for the benefit and enjoyment of those whose houses adjoined it or were in its close proximity. Its flower beds, lawns and walks were calculated to afford all the amenities which it is the purpose of the garden of a house to provide; and, apart from the fact that these amenities extended to a number of householders, instead of being

---

[91] *Ellenborough Park, Re* [1956] Ch. 131 at 172, explaining a dictum of Willes J. in *Bailey v Stephens*, above; followed in *Riley v Pentilla* [1974] V.R. 547 (liberty to use an area of land "for the purpose of recreation or a garden or a park").

[92] *Simpson v Godmanchester Corp* [1897] A.C. 696 at 702, 703. "It is, no doubt, one of the essential characteristics of an easement that its exercise shall be for the use and benefit of the dominant estate. But there is no law to the effect that an easement, which is serviceable and beneficial to that estate, shall cease to exist whenever, from the very nature of the right, its exercise by the dominant estate confers, or tends to confer, some benefit upon other lands or tenements" (Lord Watson at 703).

[93] [1956] Ch. 131 at 170; quoting and adopting *Cheshire's Modern Real Property*, (7th ed.), p. 457. See para.1–07, above.

confined to one (which on this aspect of the case is immaterial), we can see no difference in principle between Ellenborough Park and a garden in the ordinary signification of that word. It is the collective garden of the neighbouring houses, to whose use it was dedicated by the owners of the estate, and as such amply satisfied, in our judgment, the requirement of connection with the dominant tenements to which it is appurtenant."[94]

In *Hill v Tupper*[95] the plaintiff, to whom a canal company had granted a lease of   **1–26** land adjoining the canal, together with "the sole and exclusive right or liberty to put or use boats on a certain canal, and to let the same . . . for the purposes of pleasure", sued the defendant, who also had premises on the canal, for damages for letting out pleasure boats and so infringing the plaintiff's alleged right. The action failed, on the ground that the "exclusive right" granted had no connection with the use and enjoyment of the plaintiff's land, and was unknown to the law.[96] The grant operated as a licence or covenant on the part of the canal company, and was binding as between the canal company and the plaintiff, but gave him no right of action in his own name against the defendant for any infringement of the supposed exclusive right. Of this case it was said in *Ellenborough Park, Re*[97] that

> "what the plaintiff was trying to do was to set up, under the guise of an easement, a monopoly which had no normal connexion with the ordinary use of his land, but which was merely an independent business enterprise. So far from the right claimed sub-serving or accommodating the land, the land was but a convenient incident to the exercise of the right."[98]

The mere fact that an easement is acquired for the purposes of a business carried   **1–27** on on the dominant tenement does not disqualify it under this head.[99]

In *Simpson v Godmanchester Corporation*[100] the corporation established, by prescription, alternatively under a lost grant, an easement to open lock gates in times of flood. It was admitted that there was some municipal land which was thereby protected from floodwater.

In *Clos Farming Estates v Easton*,[101] the question was whether a right to enter   **1–28** the servient land, to carry out viticulture work and to harvest the grapes and sell them was capable of existing as an easement. The New South Wales Court of Appeal held that one reason why it was not so capable was that the right claimed

---

[94] [1956] 1 Ch. 131 at 174, 175. *Cf. Robins v Evans* (1863) 2 H. & C. 410.
[95] (1863) 2 H. & C. 121.
[96] *cf. Att-Gen v Horner* [1913] 2 Ch. 140 at 180, 196, 197.
[97] [1956] Ch. 131 at 175.
[98] Interference with the right to put boats on the canal would, however, have been actionable; see per Bramwell B. in *Nuttall v Bracewell* (1866) L.R. 2 Exch. 1 at 11, 12.
[99] *Moody v Steggles* (1879) 12 Ch. D. 261 (right to fix a signboard on adjoining property); *Henry Ltd v M'Glade* [1926] N.I. 144 (stationary sandwich-man); *Copeland v Greenhalf* [1952] Ch. 488 (claim to keep things for business purposes on neighbouring land).
[100] [1897] A.C. 696.
[101] [2002] NSWCA 389.

did not accommodate the allegedly dominant tenement. Santow J.A. asked "What does 'accommodation' mean in this context?". His answer was[102]:

> "First, it requires there to be a natural connection between the dominant and servient tenements. The right must be reasonably necessary for the enjoyment of the dominant tenement and not merely confer advantage on the owner of that tenement, as would a mere contractual right ... [The trial judge] concluded that whether the right granted accommodated and served the dominant tenement depended on whether the right granted was connected with the normal enjoyment of the dominant tenement. That is a question of fact, dependant on the nature of the dominant tenement and the right granted. It was not enough that the land be a convenient incident to the right. Rather the nexus must exist in a real and intelligible sense. Additionally, [the trial judge] recognised that the facilitation of the business or the commercial use in which the dominant land is involved may, in limited circumstances, be nonetheless sufficient to create the requisite nexus, provided the criteria for an easement is satisfied. ... It was submitted that the requirement that the easements sufficiently accommodate the dominant tenement is in effect a requirement that the easement make property better and more convenient. This may be achieved, it was argued, merely by benefiting some trade carried out on the property. ... In sum, the appellant contended that, as lot 86 was used for the purposes of carrying out farming and harvesting works, and the servient Clos Farms were used for viticultural purposes, this clearly established the necessary nexus between the dominant and servient lots. ... The respondents acknowledged that a right benefiting a trade carried out on the dominant tenement may in appropriate circumstances be a valid easement. But this is provided that the conduct of the trade is a necessary incident to the normal enjoyment of the land, not merely an independent business exercise. ... The supposed dominant tenement was not relevantly benefited by the rights [in question] because it was merely a convenience and matter of efficiency that lot 86 be used for the purposes of farm management ... There was no feature of lot 86 that rendered it the natural or only place from which to carry out harvesting and associated works. ... There was no evidence which indicated that farm management, as distinct from storage, was actually carried on on that lot. The supposed connection was not a real one. I would agree."

1–29 In *Clapman v Edwards*[103] a 99-year lease of a petrol station of the defendant included "the right to use the flank walls of [certain adjoining premises of the lessor] for advertising purposes". The defendant granted to a bill-posting company the right, for a year, to post bills, etc., on these premises, whereupon the plaintiff, who derived title to both properties under the lessor, sought to restrain the defendant from permitting any other person to use the flank walls for advertising, his contention being that the right granted was an easement appurtenant to the petrol station and therefore could not be assigned separately from the station; alternatively, that any advertisements must be confined to advertisements relating to the business of the station. Bennett J. held that there was nothing in the words quoted to confine the permitted advertisements to advertisements connected with the petrol station, and that the right of advertising, not being connected with the station or any other land, was not an easement but a licence.

If land to which a right purports to be annexed is in fact accommodated by the use of the right, the right qualifies as an easement whether the dominant and servient tenements are contiguous or not.[104] A right of way, not ending anywhere on the land to which it is annexed, will be a valid easement if the owner of the land owns, or otherwise has the right to pass over, the intervening land.[105]   **1–30**

(3) *Dominant and servient owners must be different persons*

The meaning is that the owner and occupier of land cannot subject it to an easement in favour of other land also owned and occupied by himself.[106] It is obvious that if A owns and occupies a piece of land (or several pieces of land) any use made by him of part in connection with another part is referable to his rights of ownership,[107] and does not involve any diminution of, or accretion to, natural rights. "In order to obtain an easement over land you must not be the possessor of it, for you cannot have the land itself and also an easement over it."[108] "You cannot have an easement over your own land."[109] "Of course, strictly speaking, the owner of two tenements can have no easement over one of them in respect of the other. When the owner of Whiteacre and Blackacre passes over the former to Blackacre, he is not exercising a right of way in respect of Blackacre; he is merely making use of his own land to get from one part of it to another."[110]   **1–31**

---

[104] *Todrick v Western National Omnibus Co* [1934] Ch. 561; *cf. Moody v Steggles* (1879) 12 Ch. D. 261 at 267.

[105] *Todrick v Western National Omnibus Co*, above; *Pugh v Savage* [1970] 2 Q.B. 373, where there was a right of way to and from field C over field A, passing over an intervening field B with the consent of the tenant of field B: the right subsisted after the owner of field C became the owner of field B; *Robinson Webster (Holdings) Limited v Agombar* [2002] 1 P. & C.R. 243.

[106] *B. & W. Investments Ltd v Western Scottish Friendly Society* (1969) 20 N.I.L.Q. 325. This proposition is thought not to be affected by s.72(3) of the Law of Property Act 1925, which provides that a person may convey land (which is defined to include, unless the context otherwise requires, an easement) to himself. The question might conceivably arise if the owner-occupier of land purported to grant to himself an easement over part of it, and then disposed of that part. In such a case, however, an easement might well be held to have been granted *de novo*, by implication, under the disposition.

[107] It is pointed out in *Bolton v Bolton* (1879) 11 Ch. D. 968 at 970, 971, that the user of part in connection with another part is referable to the ownership of the part used, and not necessarily to the ownership of the other part, and therefore that the right could not pass, under a conveyance of the other part, as "appurtenant" to it. See also *Sovmots Investments Ltd v Secretary of State for the Environment* [1979] A.C. 144 at 169, per Lord Wilberforce.

[108] *Ladyman v Grave* (1871) 6 Ch. App. 763 at 767, per Lord Hatherley L.C.

[109] *Metropolitan Ry v Fowler* [1892] 1 Q.B. 165 at 171, per Lord Esher M.R.

[110] *Roe v Siddons* (1888) 22 Q.B.D. 224 at 236, per Fry L.J.

Accommodations enjoyed by an owner or occupier of land over part of it are usually described as "quasi-easements", and may become actual easements if the part accommodated is disposed of separately.[111]

1–32   An owner of two pieces of land can, of course, grant, expressly or impliedly, an easement over one to a tenant of the other. Such grants constantly arise by implication.[112] A tenant cannot, however, obtain an easement over other land of his landlord, either under section 2 of the Prescription Act 1832[113] or by prescription at common law,[114] or under the doctrine of lost modern grant.[115] This is because a tenant can only prescribe in right of his landlord,[116] and because an easement cannot be obtained by prescription for a limited time only.[117] A tenant can, however, under section 3 of the Prescription Act, prescribe against his landlord for an easement of light.[118]

1–33   It appears from *Deny v Sanders*[119] that, by the custom of the manor, a copyhold tenant could prescribe for an easement against another copyhold tenant, or against the lord. Such a right would[120] survive enfranchisement under the Copyhold Act 1894 (see s.23), and if so, would, it seems, survive enfranchisement under the Law of Property Act 1922 (see Sch.12, para.(5))[121]; but it would not, unless expressly reserved, survive a common law enfranchisement of the servient tenement. In *White v Taylor (No. 2)*[122] (where the right claimed was a *profit à prendre*) Buckley J. held that enjoyment of grazing facilities by tenants of the lord of the manor holding under leases or tenancy agreements could not establish a reputation of rights appurtenant to the lands comprised in their holdings.

---

[111] See paras 3–53 *et seq.*, below.

[112] See, e.g. *Beddington v Atlee* (1887) 35 Ch. D. 317 at 322. An easement granted expressly or impliedly to a tenant determines with the expiration or determination of the tenancy (at 322–324; the tenancy ended by reason of a forfeiture); and see *M.R.A. Engineering Ltd v Trimster Co Ltd* (1988) 56 P. & C.R. 1 at 4, where the tenancy ended by surrender. A different conclusion was reached where the lessee of the dominant tenement, with the benefit of an easement for the term of his lease, acquired the freehold reversion on his lease and the lease merged in the freehold; it was held that the person who was the lessee and who was now the freehold owner of the dominant tenement retained the benefit of the original easement for a period equivalent to the original term of the lease: *Wall v Collins* [2007] Ch. 390. The two other authorities referred to in this footnote were not cited. In any event, it was held in *Wall v Collins* that the lessee who acquired the freehold acquired the same easement (in fee) under s.62 of the Law of Property Act 1925 (as to the operation of s.62 see paras 3–126 *et seq.*). This second conclusion appears sound whereas the first conclusion is more doubtful. See also an article in [2007] Conveyancer 464.

[113] *Kilgour v Gaddes* [1904] 1 K.B. 457; *Gayford v Moffat* (1868) 4 Ch. App. 133 at 135.

[114] *Large v Pitt* (1797) Peake, Add. Cas. 152.

[115] *Simmons v Dobson* [1991] 1 W.L.R. 720, applying *Wheaton v Maple & Co* [1893] 3 Ch. 48 and dicta in *Kilgour v Gaddes* [1904] 1 K.B. 457, *Deny v Sanders* [1919] 1 K.B. 223 and *Cory v Davies* [1923] 2 Ch. 95; but see the exceptional case of *Bosomworth v Faber* (1995) 69 P. & C.R. 288, which concerned a 2,000-year term which could be enlarged into a fee simple under Law of Property Act 1925, s.153.

[116] *Gayford v Moffatt*, above.

[117] *Wheaton v Maple & Co* [1893] 3 Ch. 48 at 63; *Kilgour v Gaddes* [1904] 1 K.B. 457 at 460, 466, 467.

[118] *Morgan v Fear* [1907] A.C. 425; see para.4–25, below.

[119] [1919] 1 K.B. 223.

[120] [1919] 1 K.B. 223 at 239, 243, per Scrutton L.J.

[121] *Quaere*, however, whether the "other easements" referred to in para.(5) are not confined to mining easements.

[122] [1969] 1 Ch. 160 at 185.

The question whether land owned by a person as trustee can have or be   **1–34**
subject to an easement over or in favour of other land owned by the same person
beneficially was touched on in *Ecclesiastical Commissioners for England v
Kino*,[123] but does not appear to have arisen for decision. In that case, where the
owners of a church, until recently owned by the rector, sought an interim injunction to restrain a threatened obstruction of light to the church by the then owners
of adjoining land, until recently part of the glebe and also owned by the rector,
it was objected that the unity of possession prevented the acquisition of a right
to light. The Court of Appeal doubted this; at least they thought the point not
so clearly sound as to justify the refusal of an interim injunction, and Brett L.J.
said that his present inclination of opinion was that the rector, as beneficial owner
of the glebe, might make it a servient tenement to the church of which he was
only trustee.

It seems that A and B as co-owners of the servient tenement can grant an easement   **1–35**
to A, the sole owner of the dominant tenement,[124] and that A and B as co-owners
of the servient tenement can grant an easement to A and C as co-owners of the
dominant tenement.[125]

(4) *To amount to an easement a right must be capable of forming the subject-matter of a grant*

Positive rights

It is thought that the right to do any definite positive thing can be the subject-   **1–36**
matter of a grant, and that such a right, if the other three conditions mentioned
above are satisfied, will rank as an easement; but that the negative rights, or rights
of immunity, capable of being the subject-matter of a grant (as distinct from a
restrictive covenant) are strictly limited. On the other hand, a right which depends
upon the exigencies of the other owner's use of his land at any time, and therefore his consent, cannot be the subject of a legal grant.[126]

It is difficult to imagine any right to do some positive act on servient land that
could not, by the use of intelligible words, be the subject of a grant. If a right of way
over A's land can be granted, why should the right to do any other positive act on A's
land not be capable of being granted? Although the right to do, on dominant land, a
positive act infringing the natural rights of the servient land (for instance to create a
nuisance) is seldom, if ever, granted expressly, but is more usually acquired (if at all)
by prescription, which presumes a grant, or under the doctrine against derogation

---

[123] (1880) 14 Ch. D. 213.
[124] *McDonald v McDougall* (1897) 30 N.S.R. 298 at 300 (Henry J.) and on appeal at 311 and 312.
[125] *Lonegren and Reuben, Re* (1987) 37 D.L.R. (4d) 491 (Lander J.).
[126] *Green v Ashco Horticulturalist Ltd* [1966] 1 W.L.R. 889; *Lay v Wyncoll* (1966) 198 E.G. 887,
    explained in *Goldsmith v Burrow Construction Ltd, The Times*, July 31, 1987, CA, and referred to
    in *Mills v Silver* [1991] Ch. 271 at 282.

from grant, there is no reason to suppose that any particular right to do a positive act on dominant land is incapable of being granted.[127]

1–37 "No particular words are necessary to a grant",[128] and words of covenant or agreement may operate as a grant. Thus an agreement between A, owner of land, and B, owner of mines beneath it, that the owners of the mines should not be liable for (in effect) damage to the surface, was construed as a grant of the right to let down the surface,[129] and an agreement between A and B that A and his successors in title should have the control of a stream on B's land, and that such stream should be allowed to flow in a free and uninterrupted course into A's land, was held to be an easement of the watercourse.[130] In *Russell v Watts*,[131] Lord Blackburn said that a covenant may, if it is necessary to carry out the intention, operate as a grant.

Negative rights

1–38 Negative rights, or rights of immunity, stand on a different footing. Such rights are naturally acquired by means of covenants; and a grant to the owners of Whiteacre that it shall not be lawful for the owners of Blackacre to do on Blackacre some particular thing that might otherwise be lawfully done is a doubtful conception. Even in regard to the right to light, which undoubtedly is an easement, and, like all other easements, must originate (at common law[132]) in a grant, express, implied or presumed, it has been repeatedly said that this cannot be the subject of a grant; and indeed the judicial utterances to that effect are almost as numerous as those which support the contrary view. Thus, in *Moore v Rawson*,[133] Littledale J. said:

> "... although ... a right of way, being a privilege of something positive to be done or used in the soil of another man's land, may be the subject of legal grant, yet light and air, not being to be used in the soil of the land of another, are not the subject of actual grant; but the right to insist upon the non-obstruction and non-interruption of them more properly arises by a covenant which the law would imply not to interrupt the free use of the light and air."

1–39 In *Rowbotham v Wilson*,[134] Cresswell J. said that "rights, such as the right to light and air, are not the subject-matter of a grant". In *Scott v Pape*,[135] Bowen L.J. said that before the Prescription Act the right to light depended "on the implication,

---

[127] *Pwllbach Colliery Co Ltd v Woodman* [1915] A.C. 634 at 649, Lord Summer said that a right for A to spread coal dust, emanating from his land, anywhere on adjoining land can be the subject of a grant, but he also expressed the opinion that it is too indeterminate to be an easement proper.
[128] *Rowbotham v Wilson* (1860) 8 H.L.C. 348 at 362, per Lord Wensleydale.
[129] *Rowbotham v Wilson* (1860) 8 H.L.C. 348.
[130] *Northam v Hurley* (1853) 1 E. & B. 665.
[131] (1885) 10 App. Cas. 590 at 611.
[132] No presumption of grant is required for the purposes of s.3 of the Prescription Act 1832; see para. 4–25, below.
[133] (1824) 3 B. & C. 332 at 340.
[134] (1857) 8 E. & B. 123 at 143.
[135] (1886) 31 Ch. D. 554 at 571.

derived from user, of some supposed covenant by the owner of the servient tenement". In *Birmingham, Dudley and District Banking Co v Ross*,[136] Lindley L.J.
said that "the grant of an easement of this kind [light] is, properly speaking, an
implied covenant by the grantor not to use his own land so as to injure the rights
of [the dominant owners]"; and in *Hall v Lichfield Brewery Co*[137] Fry J., in awarding damages for obstruction of the access, long enjoyed, of air through windows
of a slaughterhouse, expressed the opinion that the right so recognised could not
be claimed by grant, and therefore (prescription being the implication of a grant)
could not be the subject of prescription, but must rest on implied covenant.

On the other hand, in *Dalton v Angus*,[138] Lord Selborne, after stating his opin-   **1–40**
ion that a right of support can be gained by prescription, proceeded:

> "Some of the learned Judges" [i.e. those who were summoned to give their
> opinion] "appear to think otherwise, and to doubt whether it could be the sub-
> ject of grant. For that doubt I am unable to perceive any sufficient foundation.
> Littledale J., in Moore v Rawson,[139] spoke of the right to light as being prop-
> erly the subject, not of grant, but of covenant. If he had said (which he did not),
> that a right to light could not be granted, in the sense of the word 'grant' neces-
> sary for prescription, I should have doubted the correctness of the opinion,
> notwithstanding the great learning of that eminent Judge. . . . the light which
> enters a building by particular apertures does and must pass over the adjoining
> land in a course which, though not visibly defined, is really certain and, in that
> sense, definite. Why should it be impossible for the owner of the adjoining land
> to grant a right of unobstructed passage over it for that light in that course?"

There are many other judicial references to a "grant" of light,[140] and it is thought that,   **1–41**
provided that the channel is sufficiently defined, the right to an uninterrupted flow or
passage of light, water, or anything else can be granted as a negative easement. Even
so, no right, except the right of support,[141] of immunity against the doing on servient
land of some otherwise lawful act (not involving interference with the flow of something), appears to have been accepted as an easement, and it is thought that the class
of negative easements is now closed. In *Phipps v Pears*[142] Lord Denning M.R.
said[143] that a negative easement must be looked at with caution, because the law has
been very chary of creating any new negative easements. The question is important,
for although, by taking a restrictive covenant, a man can acquire for his land immunity

---

[136] (1888) 38 Ch. D. 295 at 312. See also per Bowen L.J. at 313.
[137] (1880) 49 L.J. Ch. 665. See also the opinion of the same judge in *Dalton v Angus* (1881) 6 App.
Cas. 740 at 771, 773, 776.
[138] (1881) 6 App. Cas. 740 at 794; see also at 823, per Lord Blackburn.
[139] (1824) 3 B. & C. 332 at 340.
[140] See, e.g. *Jones v Tapling* (1862) 12 C.B. (n.s.) 826 at 864; *Booth v Alcock* (1873) 8 Ch. App. 663
at 665, 666; *Leech v Schweder* (1874) 9 Ch. App. 463 at 474; *Phillips v Low* [1892] 1 Ch. 47 at 50.
[141] It is a question whether the right of support is purely negative. Regarded as the right to exert thrust
on the supporting land or buildings, it is positive: *Dalton v Angus* (1881) 6 App. Cas. 740 at 793.
[142] [1965] 1 Q.B. 76. See para.1–45, below.
[143] [1965] 1 Q.B. 76 at 82, 83.

from almost anything,[144] a restrictive covenant is not enforceable against a purchaser for value without notice, whereas an easement is valid against all comers.[145]

In *Hunter v Canary Wharf Limited*[146] people living in the London Docklands area claimed damages for interference with the reception of television broadcasts said to be caused by the erection of the Canary Wharf tower, some 800 feet high. They sued in nuisance and did not claim an easement of television but Lord Hoffmann said that he did not think such an easement could exist.[147] His reasoning was as follows: the general principle is that one may build what one likes on one's own land; if the effect is to interfere with the light, air or view of one's neighbour, that is his misfortune; that right can only be restrained by covenant or the acquisition (by grant or prescription) of an easement. It is settled that easements of light or air may be acquired but only for the benefit of particular windows or defined apertures. Such defined rights of air, light and support are strictly a matter between immediate neighbours. The building entitled to support, the windows entitled to light and the apertures entitled to air will be plain and obvious. The restrictions on the freedom of the person erecting the building will be limited and precise. By contrast, to allow the acquisition by prescription of a right to a view would impose a burden on a very large and indefinite area.[148] Likewise the effect of a right not to have television reception interfered with would not be limited to immediate neighbours and would impose a large burden on anyone wishing to erect a tall building. This tends to support the suggestion in the previous paragraph that the class of negative easements is now closed.

Significance of the fourth characteristic

1–42   In *Ellenborough Park, Re*[149] the Court, after remarking[150] that the exact significance of this fourth and last characteristic[151] is, at first, perhaps, not entirely clear, said that, for the purposes of that case, the cognate questions involved under it were: (a) whether the rights purported to be given were expressed in terms of too wide and vague a character (or[152] whether the right conferred was too wide and vague); (b) whether, if and so far as effective, such rights would amount to rights of joint occupation or would substantially deprive the park owners of proprietorship or legal possession; (c) whether, if and so far as effective, such rights constituted mere rights of recreation, possessing no quality of utility or benefit, and on such grounds could not qualify as easements. It is convenient to consider (a) and (c) together, and then (b).

---

[144] *National Trust v Midlands Electricity Board* [1952] Ch. 380, a covenant, intended to preserve the view from certain land of the Trust, that "no act or thing shall be done or placed or permitted to remain upon [certain land of the covenators] which shall injure prejudice affect or destroy the natural aspect and condition of the land" was held void for uncertainty.

[145] A right in the nature of an easement and enforceable against successors in title without notice may arise, under the doctrine forbidding derogation from grant, from an express grant for a particular purpose. See paras 3–32 *et seq.*, below.

[146] [1997] A.C. 655.

[147] [1997] A.C. 655, at 709H.

[148] See per Lord Blackburn in *Dalton v Angus* (1881) 6 App. Cas. 740 at 824.

[149] [1956] Ch. 131; see para.1–06, above.

[150] [1956] Ch. 131 at 164.

[151] See para.1–07, above.

[152] [1956] Ch. 131 at 175.

Easements that are not recognised

As to (a) and (c), there appears to be no reported case in which an express grant   **1–43**
of a supposed easement has been held to create no easement because the wording
of the grant is too vague, but under this head can be considered the cases in which
a prescriptive right to the unobstructed general flow of air from an allegedly
servient tenement over an allegedly dominant tenement has been rejected. In
Webb v Bird,[153] it was decided that the owner of a windmill could not become
entitled, either under section 2 of the Prescription Act, or by presumed grant, to
the general flow of air from adjoining land; the reason being that the right
claimed was, in the nature of things, incapable of being interrupted. This was followed in *Bryant v Lefever*,[154] and *Harris v De Pinna*,[155] where a building erected
on adjoining land affected the draught of the plaintiff's chimneys, and in *Chastey
v Ackland*,[156] where the erection of a building on adjoining land prevented the
dissipation of foul air coming from the plaintiff's premises.

It appears to be undoubted that an express grant of a general right to receive air
from adjoining premises would not create an easement.[157] It has been repeatedly said
that a grant will not be presumed when the grantor could not have reasonably prevented the enjoyment of the subject of the grant,[158] and it may be true to say that a
grant of the right to receive what the grantee must inevitably receive in any case is
a grant of nothing; but the general passage of air can be at least partially obstructed,
as appears from the cases just cited, and probably the true reason for refusing to
recognise an easement of the general flow of air is that the subject-matter is too
vague, and that it would be inconvenient to do so.[159]

For the same or similar reasons the law does not recognise an easement of   **1–44**
prospect,[160] or privacy.[161] That there is no natural right to either is clear,[162] and it is
thought that the cases in footnotes 160 and 161 sufficiently establish that no such

---

[153] (1861) 10 C.B. (n.s.) 268; (1862) 13 C.B. (n.s.) 841.
[154] (1879) 4 C.P.D. 172.
[155] (1886) 33 Ch. D. 238.
[156] [1895] 2 Ch. 389; compromised on appeal [1897] A.C. 155.
[157] "The principle . . . I conceive to be that, until defined and confined, there is in those cases [water],
as in light and air in its natural state, no subject-matter capable of being the subject of a lawful
grant": *Dalton v Angus* (1881) 6 App. Cas. 740 at at 759, per Field J.
[158] See, e.g. per Wightman J., *Chasemore v Richards* (1859) 7 H.L.C. 349 at 370; per Fry J., *Dalton
v Angus* (1881) 6 App. Cas. 740 at 776; per Lopes L.J., *Chastey v Ackland* [1895] 2 Ch. 389
at 397.
[159] See per Lindley L.J., *Harris v De Pinna* (1886) 33 Ch. D. 238 at 262; but *cf.* the view of Lord
Denning M.R. in *Phipps v Pears* [1965] 1 Q.B. 76 at 83; see para.1–45, below.
[160] *Aldred's Case* (1610) 9 Co.Rep. 57(b); *Dalton v Angus* (1881) 6 App. Cas. 740 at 824; *Harris v
De Pinna* (1886) 33 Ch. D. 238 at 262; *Browne v Flower* [1911] 1 Ch. 219 at 225; *Campbell v
Paddington Corp* [1911] 1 K.B. 869 at 875, 876; and see *Leech v Schweder* (1874) 9 Ch. App. 463
at 475, where "attach . . . to the land" clearly means "attach as an easement"; applied by analogy
to preclude an action in nuisance for interference with television reception in *Hunter v Canary
Wharf Ltd* [1997] A.C. 655.
[161] *Chandler v Thompson* (1811) 3 Camp. 80; *Dalton v Angus* (1881) 6 App. Cas. 740 at 764; *Browne
v Flower* [1911] 1 Ch. 219 at 225.
[162] *Tapling v Jones* (1865) 11 H.L.C. 290 at 305; *Fishmongers' Co v East India Co* (1752) 1 Dick.
163; *Potts v Smith* (1868) L.R. 6 Eq. 311 at 318; *Campbell v Paddington Corp* [1911] 1 K.B. 869
at 878, 879; *Hurdman v North Eastern Ry Co* (1878) 3 C.P.D. 168 at 174.

right can be acquired as an easement. It seems also that, except by agreement, there can be no separate right to have maintained unobstructed the view of premises by for example prospective customers.[163]

1–45   In *Phipps v Pears*[164] the Court of Appeal held that there was no right to be protected from the weather and Lord Denning M.R. (with whom Pearson and Salmon L.JJ. agreed), having referred to cases dealing with prospect and air coming through an undefined channel, said[165]:

> "The reason underlying these instances is that if such an easement were to be permitted, it would unduly restrict your neighbour in his enjoyment of his own land. It would hamper legitimate development: see Dalton v. Angus, per Lord Blackburn.[166] Likewise here, if we were to stop a man pulling down his house, we would put a brake on desirable improvement. Every man is entitled to pull down his house if he likes.[167] If it exposes your house to the weather, that is your misfortune. It is no wrong on his part. Likewise every man is entitled to cut down his trees if he likes, even if it leaves you without shelter from the wind or shade from the sun; see the decision of the Master of the Rolls in Ireland in Cockrane v. Vemer.[168] There is no such easement known to the law as an easement to be protected from the weather."

The practical effect of this decision, however, and the statement that, if a man pulls down his house and exposes yours to the weather, it is no wrong on his part, has been largely negatived by the decision of the Court of Appeal in *Rees v Skerret*[169] to the effect that the person who does those acts owes a duty to his neighbour to take reasonable steps to provide adequate protection from the weather to his neighbour's exposed wall.

1–46   In *Dennis v Ministry of Defence*,[170] the Ministry of Defence asserted a prescriptive right to commit a nuisance, namely the noise caused by low flying jets from RAF Wittering. It was held that, though a prescriptive right to commit a nuisance can be acquired, it must be (a) capable of forming the subject-matter of a grant and (b) as of right. The test for certainty suggested by Counsel was "Could a

---

[163] *Smith v Owen* (1866) 35 L.J.Ch. 317; *Butt v Imperial Gas Co* (1866) 2 Ch. App. 158. For the policy behind this rule see *Hunter v Canary Wharf Ltd* [1997] A.C. 655 and para.1–41, above.

[164] [1965] 1 Q.B. 76. This decision is criticised in (1964) 80 L.Q.R. 318. It was applied by Sir Douglas Frank Q.C. in *Marchant v Capital & Counties Property Co Ltd* (1982) 263 E.G. 661 (reversed on other grounds [1983] 2 E.G.L.R. 156, CA) and in *Giltrap v Busley* (1970) 21 N.I.L.Q. 342, and cf. *Bradburn v Lindsay* [1983] 2 All E.R. 408; see para.10–27, below. *Sedgewick Forbes Bland Payne Group Ltd v Regional Properties Ltd* [1981] 1 E.G.L.R. 33 (it was left undecided whether *Phipps v Pears* applied to a roof of an office block).

[165] [1965] 1 Q.B. 76 at 83.

[166] (1881) 6 App. Cas. 740, at 824.

[167] This is not, of course, entirely accurate because he may be prevented from doing so by statute.

[168] (1895) 29 I.L.T. 571.

[169] [2001] 1 W.L.R. 1541, applying *Leakey v National Trust* [1980] Q.B. 485. See also the Party Wall etc. Act 1996, s.2(2)(n): right of building owner to expose party-wall subject to providing adequate weathering.

[170] [2003] 2 E.G.L.R. 121; see in particular at paras [50]–[54].

conveyancer draft it?". The amount of noise authorised by the alleged right had not been defined or established and the claim failed.

It has been held that, if A sends water, for his own purposes, from one part of his land to another, a right in an adjoining owner to take from the latter part such water as happens to be there from time to time (the amount, if any, depending on the will of A) cannot arise by implication.[171]   **1–47**

Jus spatiandi

In *Ellenborough Park, Re*[172] it was further argued that the grant of a right to full enjoyment of the park was too wide and vague, was a right of mere recreation and amusement and not of utility and benefit, and was a *jus spatiandi*, and, on each of those grounds, failed to rank as an easement. The court decided, however, that the right, on its proper interpretation, was a right well defined and commonly understood; and that, assuming that a mere right of recreation and amusement is incapable of ranking as an easement,[173] this was not such a right, but was a beneficial attribute of the houses in respect of which it was granted.   **1–48**

In regard to *jus spatiandi*, the argument was based on certain dicta of Farwell J. in *International Tea Stores Co v Hobbs*[174] and *Att-Gen v Antrobus*.[175] In the first case the learned judge expressed the opinion that if a house or lodge at the vendor's park gates were conveyed with the rights conferred by section 6 of the Conveyancing Act 1881,[176] the purchaser would not acquire a right to use the garden and park, because such a right "being a mere jus spatiandi, is unknown to the law".[177] This was obiter dictum. In the second case, the learned judge declined to presume a lost grant or lost statute creating a public right to visit Stonehenge, because the public as such cannot prescribe, "nor is jus spatiandi known to our law as a possible subject-matter of grant or prescription".[178]

The court in *Ellenborough Park, Re* doubted whether the right which it was there considering could be said to constitute a mere *jus spatiandi*, for the essence and main purpose of *jus spatiandi* is wandering at large, whereas a private garden is an ordinary attribute of the residence to which it is attached, and the right of wandering in it is only one method of enjoying it. On the assumption, however, that the right there in question did constitute a *jus spatiandi*, or that it was analogous thereto, the court put to itself the question "Whether the right which is in question in these proceedings is, for that reason, incapable of ranking in law as an   **1–49**

---

[171] *Burrows v Lang* [1901] 2 Ch. 502. The case is otherwise if the right to the water is expressly granted: *Beauchamp v Frome R.D.C.* [1937] 4 All E.R. 348 at 357. In *Mitchell v Potter* [2005] EWCA Civ 88, *The Times*, January 24, 2005, the express grant of a right to water was construed as giving the grantee the right to take such water as was reasonably required and not just such water as remained from time to time after the servient owner had abstracted water.

[172] [1956] 1 Ch. 131 at 136.

[173] See paras 1–52 *et seq*.

[174] [1903] 2 Ch. 165.

[175] [1905] 2 Ch. 188.

[176] See now the Law of Property Act 1925, s.62.

[177] [1903] 2 Ch. 165 at 172.

[178] [1905] 2 Ch. 188 at 198.

easement". After considering the judgments of Farwell J., and pointing out that he cited no authority for his proposition that *jus spatiandi* is unknown to the law and incapable of being granted, and after considering *Duncan v Louch*,[179] the court concluded that (a) while the decision in *Att-Gen v Antrobus* was unquestionably right, for no public right of wandering at will over an undefined open space can be granted or prescribed for, the dictum in *International Tea Stores Co v Hobbs* could not be accepted as an exhaustive statement of the law, and, in reference at least to such a case as was being considered in *Ellenborough Park, Re* could not be regarded as authoritative; (b) the reasoning of the decision in *Duncan v Louch*, and the circumstances of the case, no less than the language used, involved "acceptance as an easement of a right such as that with which, according to our interpretation of the effect of the relevant deeds, we are here concerned".

1-50   It was also pointed out that *Keith v Twentieth Century Club*[180] had, in the peculiar circumstances of that case which need not here be stated, no authoritative force. The court was careful to confine its decision to the case before it, and it did not, at any rate in terms, address itself to the abstract question whether a *jus spatiandi* is capable of ranking as an easement; but the decision at least establishes that there is no authority against this view, and it seems safe to assume that, while in some cases a *jus spatiandi* might possibly fail as an easement because it does not accommodate the supposedly dominant tenement, such a right will not fail merely on the ground of vagueness. It is possible, however, that a *jus spatiandi* alleged to have been acquired by mere user might be more difficult to establish than a right acquired by express grant capable of being read and construed. Mere user, moreover, might well be assumed to have been had by permission, and not as of right.[181]

1-51   In *Duncan v Louch*,[182] the plaintiff declared for a right of passing and repassing into a certain close called Terrace Walk, and of walking there, and of passing and repassing into and upon a certain erection at the other end called the Water Gate. He proved a grant to a predecessor of "the free liberty, use, benefit and privilege of the Terrace Walk". An objection that a right so granted was not a right of way, but a right to use the walk for pleasure only, and was therefore improperly stated in the declaration, was overruled, on the ground that the right claimed, namely, a right of way from one end of the walk to the other, was less than, but included in, the right proved, namely, a right of passage backwards and forwards over every part of the walk. Such a right was evidently regarded as a valid easement.

Recreation and amusement

1-52   The proposition[183] that a right of mere recreation and amusement cannot rank as an easement was founded, in argument in *Ellenborough Park, Re*[184] on a passage

---

[179] (1845) 6 Q.B. 904; see above.
[180] (1904) 73 L.J. Ch. 545.
[181] cf. *Bourke v Davis* (1890) 44 Ch. D. 110 at 121. The *jus spatiandi* is considered in an article, Peel, "What is an Easement?" in 28 Conv. (n.s.) 450, 460 *et seq.*
[182] (1845) 6 Q.B. 904.
[183] See para.1–48, above.
[184] [1956] Ch. 131.

in Theobald's *The Law of Land* (2nd ed.), p. 263, where two cases are referred to. One, *Solomon v Vintners' Co*,[185] which relates to support, contains, on this point, nothing more than two interlocutory and inconclusive observations[186] which seem, if anything, to negative the proposition, and in *Ellenborough Park, Re* were regarded as unimportant. In the other, *Mounsey v Ismay*,[187] it was decided that a customary public right to hold horse races was not an "easement" within section 2 of the Prescription Act. Martin B., delivering the judgment of the court, considered, without deciding, whether an easement in gross was within the statute,[188] and proceeded,[189]

> "But, however this may be, we are of opinion that to bring the right within the term 'easement' in the second section it must be one analogous to that of a right of way which precedes it and a right of watercourse which follows it, and must be a right of utility and benefit, and not one of mere recreation and amusement."

Of this, the Court of Appeal in *Ellenborough Park, Re* said[190]:

> "The words which we have quoted were used in reference to a claim for a right to conduct horse races and, in our judgment, the formula adopted by Theobald should be used in the light of that circumstance. In any case, if the proposition be well-founded, we do not think that the right to use a garden of the character with which we are concerned in this case can be called one of mere recreation and amusement, as those words were used by Martin B. . . . We think, therefore, that the statement of Baron Martin must at least be confined to exclusion of rights to indulge in such recreations as were in question in the case before him, horse racing or perhaps playing games, and has no application to the facts of the present case."

The decision in *Mounsey v Ismay* was that the Prescription Act does not apply to   **1–53** customary rights acquired by the inhabitants of a district. The last sentence of the judgment[191]: "What we think [the Prescription Act] contemplated were incorporeal rights incident to and annexed to property for its more beneficial and profitable enjoyment, and not customs for mere pleasure", might be taken to indicate that a right of mere pleasure cannot accommodate land, but the case is some way from being an authority on this point, or for the general proposition asserted by

---

[185] (1859) 5 H. & N. 585.
[186] "Pollock C.B.—If I build a wall at the extremity of my land, and my neighbour plays racquets against it for twenty years, is it contended that he would acquire a right to have it kept up? Bramwell B.—Probably a right not to have it pulled down, if he had used it for that purpose as of right" (at 593).
[187] (1865) 3 H. & C. 486.
[188] It is now clear that there cannot be an easement in gross. See para.1–08, above.
[189] (1865) 3 H. & C. 486 at 498.
[190] [1956] Ch. 131 at 179.
[191] (1865) 3 H. & C. 486 at 499.

Theobald. In practice, rights of playing games on another's land are usually enjoyed by permission; express grants of such rights, or circumstances in which the user "as of right" required by the Prescription Act could be alleged with any prospect of success, must be rare.[192]

Right amounting to joint or exclusive occupation

1–54 As to (b)[193]: an easement, as already mentioned, involves a diminution of natural rights of ownership, and a grant under which the proprietary rights of the so-called servient owner are either usurped or held jointly with another cannot create an easement. For instance, "no man can be considered to have a right of property, worth holding, in a soil over which the whole world has the privilege to walk and disport itself at pleasure".[194] The line is difficult to draw, and each new case would probably be decided on its own facts in the light of common sense.[195] This point is further discussed in paragraph 1–58 below.

1–55 It may happen that what appears to be the subject of an easement is in fact part and parcel of the dominant tenement. Thus in *Francis v Hayward*[196] a fascia on one (A) of two houses, A and B, in common ownership, had at all material times been used to advertise the business of the tenant for the time being of B. B was let in 1855 for 21 years, and in 1874 A was let to the defendant. At the expiration of the lease of B, and during the lease of A, B was let to the plaintiff, who claimed a right to use the fascia. It was argued that the defendant's lease was granted subject, at most, to a reservation of an easement for the term of the then existing, and since expired, lease of B, and that no grant could be implied in the plaintiff's existing lease, in derogation of the pre-existing lease to the defendant, which contained no express reservation. The court was inclined to think that A was let subject to, and B was let with, a right to use the fascia, but the decision was that the fascia was part of B and included in the demise to the plaintiff.

1–56 It is obvious that the identity of the servient tenement is, at least in theory, a relevant consideration. If Blackacre has a right to receive water through a pipe laid under A's field, the right is clearly not repugnant to A's proprietary rights in the field, and if the servient tenement is considered to be the field, there is no difficulty on principle in establishing an easement.[197] A, however, could sell the greater part of the field entirely free from the easement; the servient tenement must, it is thought, consist at most of the space occupied by the pipe and so much

---

[192] In *City Developments Pty Ltd v Registrar-General (NT)* (2000) 156 F.L.R. 1, it was held that a grant in favour of houses in a development of a right to use a foreshore and a lake "for private recreational purposes" was neither too vague nor too exclusive to be an easement.

[193] See para.1–42, above.

[194] *Lord St Leonards, Dyce v Lady James Hay* (1852) 1 Macq. 305 at 309, negativing an alleged public *jus spatiandi* over private property; and see *Metropolitan Ry v Fowler* [1893] A.C. 416 at 426, per Lord Watson.

[195] The line was described as "ill defined" in *Hair v Gillman* [2000] 3 E.G.L.R. 74 at 75G.

[196] (1882) 20 Ch. D. 773; (1882) 22 Ch. D. 177, considered in *William Hill (Southern) Ltd v Cabras Ltd* (1987) 54 P. & C.R. 42 and see para.11–40, below.

[197] This analysis of the identity of the servient tenement was rejected in *Moncrieff v Jamieson* [2007] 1 W.L.R. 2620 per Lord Scott at [57].

of the soil on each or one side as is necessary for access for repair. Of the servient tenement so constituted A is very nearly (and certainly of the space occupied by the pipe) deprived of possession; yet the validity of an easement of this kind is undoubted.[198] On the other hand, a right to make and use on another's land an embankment for the purpose of a railway or tramway cannot, it seems, be an easement, for the proprietary rights of the landowner in the embankment and its site are entirely excluded.[199]

If the right to possession of the supposedly servient tenement is vested in two   **1–57** persons jointly, one of them does not have an easement as against the other. Joint entitlement to a right is different from a case where one party is entitled to the land but the other party has a limited right over that land. If A grants or lets to B part of a house together with the right to use, in common with A or others, a particular room of which A retains control, then, while in a sense B "shares" with A, A does not share with B,[200] and in such a case there is no difficulty in establishing an easement.

The question of whether the right granted or claimed by prescription is too   **1–58** extensive to be an easement has been considered in a large number of decided cases. Unfortunately, the law is not clear and precise as to the boundary between a right which can be an easement and a right which is too invasive of the rights of the owner of the land to be an easement. Reference will be made to the relevant cases but, first, it is appropriate to refer to the most recent discussion of the topic in the House of Lords in *Moncrieff v Jamieson*.[201] That case discussed whether a right to park could be an easement. It was held that it could be. The House of Lords discussed the so-called "ouster" principle, i.e. that the right granted or claimed would not be an easement if the owner was ousted from his enjoyment of the land affected.[202] Lord Scott said[203]:

> "Every servitude or easement will bar some ordinary use of the servient land. For example, a right of way prevents all manner of ordinary uses of the land over which the road passes. The servient owner cannot plough up the road. He cannot grow cabbages on it or use it for basketball practice. A viaduct carrying water across the servient land to the dominant land will prevent the same things. Every servitude prevents any use of the servient land, whether ordinary or otherwise, that would interfere with the reasonable exercise of the servitude. There will always be some such use that is prevented.
>
>   . . .

---

[198] See para.1–22, fn.85, above; and see *Chelsea Waterworks Co v Bowley* (1851) 17 K.B. 358.
[199] *Taff Vale Ry v Cardiff Ry* [1917] 1 Ch. 299 at 316, 317.
[200] *Rogers v Hyde* [1951] 2 K.B. 923 at 931, 932; *Baker v Turner* [1950] A.C. 401 at 415, 416, 422, 432, 433, 437, 438 (both cases on the Rent Acts).
[201] [2007] 1 W.L.R. 2620. This was an appeal from Scotland. It should not be assumed that Scottish law and English law are identical on this subject (see per Lord Neuberger at [136]) but the speeches contained a valuable discussion of the English cases. The case is discussed in an article at [2008] S.L.T. 1.
[202] See the article at [2007] Conveyancer 223.
[203] At [54], [57] and [59].

The servient land in relation to a servitude or easement is surely the land over which the servitude or easement is enjoyed, not the totality of the surrounding land of which the servient owner happens to be the owner. If there is an easement of way over a 100-yard roadway on a 1,000-acre estate, or an easement to use for storage a small shed on the estate access to which is gained via the 100-yard roadway, it would be fairly meaningless in relation to either easement to speak of the whole estate as the servient land. Would the right of way and the storage right fail to qualify as easements if the whole estate bar the actual land over which the roadway ran and on which the shed stood, with or without a narrow surrounding strip, were sold? How could it be open to the servient owner to destroy easements by such a stratagem? In my opinion such a stratagem would fail. It would fail because the servient land was never the whole estate but was the land over which the roadway ran and on which the shed stood. Provided the servient land was land of which the servient owner was in possession, the rights of way and of storage would continue, in my opinion, to qualify as easements.

. . .

I do not see why a landowner should not grant rights of a servitudal character over his land to any extent that he wishes. The claim in *Batchelor v Marlow* for an easement to park cars was a prescriptive claim based on over 20 years of that use of the strip of land. There is no difference between the characteristics of an easement that can be acquired by grant and the characteristics of an easement that can be acquired by prescription. If an easement can be created by grant it can be acquired by prescription and I can think of no reason why, if an area of land can accommodate nine cars, the owner of the land should not grant an easement to park nine cars on the land. The servient owner would remain the owner of the land and in possession and control of it. The dominant owner would have the right to station up to nine cars there and, of course, to have access to his nine cars. How could it be said that the law would recognise an easement allowing the dominant owner to park five cars or six or seven or eight but not nine? I would, for my part, reject the test that asks whether the servient owner is left with any reasonable use of his land, and substitute for it a test which asks whether the servient owner retains possession and, subject to the reasonable exercise of the right in question, control of the servient land."

1–59   In *Moncrieff v Jamieson* Lord Neuberger said[204]:

"At least as at present advised, I am not satisfied that a right is prevented from being a servitude or an easement simply because the right granted would involve the servient owner being effectively excluded from the property.

. . .

---

[204] At [140], [143] – [144].

Accordingly, I see considerable force in the views expressed by Lord Scott in paragraphs 57 and 59 of his opinion, to the effect that a right can be an easement notwithstanding that the dominant owner effectively enjoys exclusive occupation, on the basis that the essential requirement is that the servient owner retains possession and control. . . . However, unless it is necessary to decide the point to dispose of this appeal, I consider that it would be dangerous to try and identify [the] degree of ouster [that] is required to disqualify a right from constituting a servitude or easement, given the very limited argument your Lordships have received on the topic.

. . .

I am also concerned that, if we were unconditionally to suggest that exclusion of the servient owner from occupation, as opposed to possession, would not of itself be enough to prevent a right from being an easement, it might lead to unexpected consequences or difficulties which have not been explored in argument in this case. Thus, if the right to park a vehicle in a one-vehicle space can be an easement, it may be hard to justify an effectively exclusive right to store any material not being an easement, which could be said to lead to the logical conclusion that an occupational licence should constitute an interest in land."

Reference will now be made to the cases before *Moncrieff v Jamieson*,[205] many of which were discussed by the House of Lords in that case.[206] In *Heywood v Mallalieu*[207] an alleged right to use the kitchen of a house for washing and drying clothes was assumed, in proceedings for specific performance of an agreement for sale of the house, to be an easement. In *Miller v Emcer Products, Ltd*[208] a grant to the lessee of an office of the right to use a lavatory in common with the landlords and others was held to create easement. Romer L.J. said[209]: **1–60**

"In my judgment the right had all the requisite characteristics of an easement. There is no doubt as to what were intended to be the dominant and servient tenements respectively, and the right was appurtenant to the former and calculated to enhance its beneficial use and enjoyment. It is true that during the times when the dominant owner exercised the right the owner of the servient tenement would be excluded, but this in greater or less degree is a common feature of many easements (for example, rights of way) and does not amount to such an ouster of the servient owner's right as was held by Upjohn J. to be incompatible with a legal easement in Copeland v. Greenhalf."[210]

---

[205] [2007] 1 W.L.R. 2620.
[206] At [140], [143]–[144].
[207] (1883) 25 Ch. D. 357.
[208] [1956] Ch. 304.
[209] [1956] Ch. 316.
[210] [1952] Ch. 488; see para.1–62, below.

1–61   In *Att-Gen of Southern Nigeria v John Holt and Company (Liverpool) Ltd*[211] the
Judicial Committee expressed the opinion that a right to store goods on the land
of another could be created as an easement. "There is nothing in the purposes for
which the easement is claimed inconsistent in principle with a right of easement
as such."[212]

In *Smith v Gates*[213] a prescriptive right to keep chicken coops on a common was
established. In *Philpot v Bath*[214] the grant of an easement was inferred from an act
which might, if an intention to dispossess had been established, have operated to
dispossess the servient owner and give the dominant owner a statutory title to the
servient tenement. The defendant, who had recently erected certain works on the
foreshore on which his premises abutted, and was defending an action for an order
on him to remove the works, sought to establish a statutory title on the ground that
his predecessors had dispossessed the owner of the foreshore by bringing on to it
a number of large boulders. It was held that these boulders had been installed for
the purpose not of dispossessing the owner but of protecting the defendant's premises from the sea, and that the defendant had not acquired a statutory title, but had
acquired an easement. An order made against him to remove the works was
expressed to be without prejudice to his right to an easement over the foreshore for
the purpose of protecting his premises from encroachment by the sea by means of
rocks, stones or piles placed on the foreshore.

In *Thomas W. Ward Ltd v Alexander Bruce (Grays) Ltd*[215] on the other hand,
the Court of Appeal held that, even though there may be a prescriptive right to
break up vessels in a dock, that does not include the right to maintain the silt over
the area in question. Such a right cannot be the subject-matter of a legal easement,
because it involves the almost complete exclusion of the alleged servient owner.

1–62   In *Copeland v Greenhalf*[216] the defendant claimed a prescriptive right to
deposit and repair vehicles on a strip of land varying in width from 15 feet to 35
feet, and leading from a village street to an orchard. Upjohn J. found[217] that

> "The practice established [by the evidence] is this, that for 50 years past the
> defendant and his predecessor, his father, have been in the habit of storing

---

[211] [1915] A.C. 599.

[212] [1915] A.C. 617. In this case the land over which the easement was claimed (by prescription) was
held to belong to the Crown, subject to a perpetual right in the company, under an implied licence,
to use it for its business purposes. There could be no easement properly so called, because during
the period of user the company had thought itself to be, as in effect it was, the owner of the land.
A claim to an easement by prescription which fails because the right claimed is too wide may succeed as a claim to title by adverse possession, and a claim to title which fails may succeed as a
claim to an easement: see an article, Goodman, "Adverse Possession or Prescription? Problems of
Conflict," 32 Conv. (n.s.) 270. For cases which considered both adverse possession and prescription, see *Pavledes v Ryesbridge Properties* (1989) 58 P. & C.R. 459; *Central Midlands Estates Ltd
v Leicester Dyers* [2003] 2 P. & C.R. D2; and contrast *Burns v Anthony* (1997) 74 P. & C.R. D41.

[213] [1952] C.P.L. 814.

[214] [1905] W.N. 114.

[215] [1959] 2 Lloyd's Rep. 472.

[216] [1952] Ch. 488.

[217] [1952] Ch. 488, at 491.

on the south-east side of the strip vehicles awaiting repair to their wood-work, and that they have been stored on any part of the south-east side of the strip provided that an adequate means of access to Barebones orchard is left, such adequate means being a width of something like 10 feet. Subject to that, the defendant and his predecessors have for the last 50 years used the south-east side of the strip for depositing vehicles awaiting repair, for put-ting vehicles there which have been repaired and were awaiting collection, and for repairing them there themselves. The nature of the vehicles placed on the strip has, of course, changed with changing conditions of life. Lorries and other vehicles of that sort are now placed there and repaired, or while awaiting repair. I am fully satisfied that that is what the defendant and his father have done for 50 years."

On these facts the learned judge decided that no easement had been acquired. He said[218]:   **1–63**

"I think that the right claimed goes wholly outside any normal idea of an easement, that is, the right of the owner or the occupier of a dominant tene-ment over a servient tenement. This claim (to which no closely related authority has been referred to me) really amounts to a claim to a joint user of the land by the defendant. Practically, the defendant is claiming the whole beneficial user of the strip of land on the south-east side of the track there; he can leave as many or as few lorries there as he likes for as long as he likes; he may enter on it by himself, his servants and agents to do repair work thereon. In my judgment, that is not a claim that can be established as an easement. It is virtually a claim to possession of the servient tenement, if necessary to the exclusion of the owner; or, at any rate, to a joint user, and no authority has been cited to me which would justify the conclusion that a right of this wide and undefined nature can be the proper subject-matter of an easement. It seems to me that to succeed, this claim must amount to a suc-cessful claim of possession by reason of long adverse possession. I say noth-ing, of course, as to the creation of such rights by deed or covenant; I am dealing solely with a right arising by prescription."

Such questions must be questions of degree. A prescriptive claim based on user,   **1–64**
where a grant has to be invented or imagined by the court, may well have more difficulty in qualifying as an easement than a right actually granted and capable of being scrutinised; and it is not inconceivable that the right asserted by the defendant in Copeland's case might be acquired, as a valid easement, under a judiciously-worded express grant. Moreover, in *Wright v Macadam*[219] (which was not cited in *Copeland v Greenhalf*[220]), the plaintiff established a right, under

---

[218] [1952] Ch. 488, at 498.
[219] [1949] 2 K.B. 744; see para.3–137, below.
[220] [1952] Ch. 488.

section 62 of the Law of Property Act 1925, to use a coal-shed on the defendant's land, although the practical effect was to exclude the defendant from the coal-shed.

1–65   *Copeland v Greenhalf* was distinguished by Ungoed-Thomas J. in *Ward v Kirkland*.[221] The plaintiff in that case owned a cottage, the northern wall of which was built on his boundary and abutted on to the defendant's farmyard. The plaintiff claimed a right to go on to the defendant's land to do maintenance work on the side of his cottage. It appeared that there had been no case in which such a right had been accepted as an easement, and it was objected that such a right constituting an easement would amount to an exclusion of the servient owner from possession of his land. Ungoed-Thomas J. pointed out that the facts of the case were very different from those of *Copeland v Greenhalf*.[222] Dealing with the argument that such a right as that claimed would in effect exclude the defendant from the use of part of the farmyard next to the cottage or interfere substantially with such use, his Lordship pointed out that similar considerations arose even in cases of rights of way, because the owner of the servient tenement cannot exercise his property rights in such a manner as to defeat the easement which exists over the way, and had no difficulty in coming to the conclusion that such a right as the plaintiff claimed was not a right which would be defeated upon the ground that it would amount to the possession or joint possession of part of the defendant's property, that is to say, that part over which the plaintiff would be exercising his right to maintain his wall.

1–66   In *Grigsby v Melville*[223] the defendant claimed an easement of storage in the cellar of a property adjoining his own. While not deciding the case on this point, Brightman J. thought it clear that the defendant's claim would give, to all intents and purposes, an exclusive right of user over the whole of the cellar, and he would have followed *Copeland v Greenhalf*[224] had it been necessary to do so. It had been suggested that *Copeland v Greenhalf*[225] was inconsistent with *Wright v Macadam*[226] but Brightman J. said that he was not convinced that there was any real inconsistency between the two cases, adding that, as to the extent of the claim, the precise facts in *Wright v Macadam*[227] were not wholly clear from the report, and it was a little difficult to know whether the plaintiff in that case had exclusive use of the coal-shed or of any defined portion of it. To some extent a problem of this sort might be one of degree. In *Hanina v Morland*[228] it was held that the use of a flat roof by the tenant of an upper floor maisonette as an extension of her home, the landlord only claiming to have retained control for purposes of repair, amounted to exclusive occupation and so could not, if permissory, ripen into an easement under section 62 of the

---

[221] [1967] Ch. 194 at 222, 223.
[222] [1952] Ch. 488.
[223] [1972] 1 W.L.R. 1355. In Smythe, "Storage: Prescription or Limitation?" (1974) 118 S.J. 305, it is suggested that such a right of storage as was here in question might be acquired by limitation.
[224] [1952] Ch. 488.
[225] [1952] Ch. 488.
[226] [1949] 2 K.B. 744.
[227] [1949] 2 K.B. 744.
[228] (2000) 97 (47) L.S.Gaz. 41, CA.

Law of Property Act 1925. Likewise in *Clos Farming Estates Pty Ltd v Easton*,[229] it was held that a right to cultivate a vineyard was incapable of forming the subject-matter of a grant because it neutralised the servient owners' rights and left them powerless to control or influence what was to happen to their agricultural land.

In *Newman v Jones*[230] Megarry J. said that in view of *Wright v Macadam* he felt **1-67** no hesitation holding that a right for a landowner to park a car anywhere in a defined area near the dominant tenement is capable of existing as an easement and in *London & Blenheim Estates v Ladbroke Retail Parks Limited*[231] H.H. Judge Paul Baker Q.C. said that he regarded the right to park claimed as valid easement, although

> "If the right granted in relation to the area over which it is to be exercisable is such that it would leave the servient owner without any reasonable use of his land, whether for parking or anything else, it could not be an easement though it might be some larger or different grant."

In *Batchelor v Marlow*, the deputy judge[232] held that an easement to park cars on **1-68** a strip of land during business hours on weekdays could be acquired by prescription because the right claimed, being limited in point of time, did not amount to such exclusion of the owner as to preclude it subsisting as an easement. His decision was reversed by the Court of Appeal[233] who held that the right claimed was incapable of being an easement because the owner would not have had any reasonable use of the land for parking or other purposes; the curtailment of his right to use the land for intermittent periods would make his ownership illusory. This decision must now be regarded as suspect after *Moncrieff v Jamieson*.[234]

It appears therefore that it is possible for the claimant's user to be too comprehensive to enable him to acquire an easement by prescription, while being insufficiently exclusive to enable him to acquire title by adverse possession.[235] In *Clos Farming v Easton*,[236] Bryson J. said that it appears from Lord Evershed M.R.'s observations in *Ellenborough Park, Re* that an intervention less extreme than an exclusive and unrestricted use of a piece of land can invalidate a supposed easement.

---

[229] [2002] NSWCA 389; although the servient owner owned the vines, he did not have the ability to do anything to or with them and was merely left with the ability to picnic and take walks among them.

[230] Unreported but cited at length in *Handel v St Stephens Close Ltd* [1994] 1 E.G.L.R. 70 at 72A.

[231] [1992] 1 W.L.R. 1278 at 1288C. The point seems to have been assumed to be correct for the purpose of the appeal at [1994] 1 W.L.R. 31. For a full discussion of the right to park, see paras 9–96 to 9–110, below.

[232] [2001] 1 E.G.L.R. 119.

[233] (2001) 82 P. & C.R. 459, and see *Central Midland Estates Ltd v Leicester Dyers* (2003) 2 P. & C.R. D2. As to parking rights, see further para.9–96, below.

[234] See per Lord Scott at [59]–[60] and per Lord Neuberger at [143].

[235] See *Simpson v Fergus* (2000) 79 P. & C.R. 398, where the marking out and regular use of four parking bays in a road over which others had rights of way was held not to amount to "possession" so as to entitle the claimant to sue in trespass.

[236] (2001) 10 B.P.R. 97,897 at [45]. Bryson J. refers to [1956] 1 Ch. 131 at 168 but he appears to have in mind the question formulated at 164 "whether such rights . . . would substantially deprive the park owners of proprietorship or legal possession". Bryson J.'s decision was upheld on appeal at [2002] NSWCA 389.

In *Evanel Pty Limited v Nelson*[237] there was an express grant of a right of footway qualified by a proviso containing a covenant by the grantor not to use the
land the subject of the right otherwise than on June 30 in each year. In fact the
land in question was used as part of the garden of the dominant tenement and was
inaccessible from the rest of the grantor's land. It was held that this right, though
not correctly characterised as a right of way, was capable of forming the subject-
matter of a grant. In *Wilcox v Richardson* Handley J. suggested that the fact that
the use of a parking space by the dominant owner amounts in practice to exclusive possession is no objection to the right being an easement "because the
servient owner's other rights are not affected". It is difficult to see how either of
these cases can be reconciled with *Batchelor v Marlow*.[238]

1–69   The Court of Appeal in *Jackson v Mulvaney*[239] applied the decision in
Ellenborough Park, Re in a case which well illustrates the principles discussed in this
section. In that case, cottages were built around a small yard, intended originally to
accommodate outside lavatories and coal sheds and the means of access to those facilities. With the coming of improved sanitary arrangements and central heating, these
facilities became redundant and the yards in time were converted to gardens tended
on a co-operative basis by the surrounding householders. Without warning, the owner
of the yard/garden grubbed up a flowerbed and a grassed passage in order to lay a
gravel surface with a view to creating an access to neighbouring land. One of the
householders sued claiming a right to cultivate the garden. The Court at first instance
declared that she was entitled to reinstate and maintain her flowerbed and awarded
her damages. The owners of the yard appealed contending (a) that the right claimed
was too extensive to be capable of being the subject-matter of a grant of an easement,
and (b) that such an easement could not in any event be acquired by prescription.

The Court of Appeal analysed the situation as follows:

(1) the right to enjoy the land as a communal garden was a right that was
capable of subsisting as an easement provided that there was the necessary connection between the dominant and the servient tenement;

---

[237] (1995) 7 B.P.R. 97,559 (Supreme Court of New South Wales).
[238] *Wilcox v Richardson* (1997) 8 B.P.R. 97,652 at 15,500. The leading English cases were considered
in *Mercantile General Life Reassurance Co v Permanent Trustee Australia Ltd* (1988) 4 B.P.R.
97,229, Supreme Court of New South Wales—Equity Division, where it was held that the English
authorities showed that it was possible to grant expressly, as an easement, a right to use a portion
of the servient tenement to the exclusion of the servient owner, or to use the whole of the servient
tenement in common with the servient owner, or with another deriving title under him, or in common with the servient owner and with another deriving title under him. It was also stated that the
cases in which the existence of an easement involving the exclusive use of part of the servient tenement or the use, in common with the servient owner, of the whole or substantially the whole, of
the servient tenement has been denied appear to be cases involving a claim to a prescriptive easement (as in *Copeland v Greenhalf*) or an implied easement (as in *Grigsby v Melville*) in which
cases the relevant claim, in reality, amounts to a claim to the title to the land by reason of long
adverse possession. This distinction between the possibility of there being a right which could be
an easement if it was expressly granted but not an easement if it were claimed pursuant to an
implied grant or by reason of prescription does not appear to be sound.
[239] [2003] 1 W.L.R. 360.
[240] [2004] 1 P. & C.R. 242.

(2) the fact that the owners of the dominant tenements had in fact maintained the garden did not as a matter of law mean that the servient owner
had been excluded from using it;

(3) the dominant owners had simply been carrying out that which they were
entitled to do, namely such works as were necessary to enable them to
enjoy the right to use the garden as such;

(4) the servient owners retained the right to enter the garden area and do
whatever they wished on it provided that such acts did not destroy or
detract from the character of the area as a garden which could be
enjoyed by the dominant owners;

(5) the servient owner was entitled to remodel the garden but only upon
giving reasonable notice, putting forward reasonable proposals (which
maintained the character of the area as a garden) and for good reasons;

(6) as to whether such an easement can be acquired by prescription, while in the
absence of an express grant the Court has the more difficult task of assessing the evidence as to alleged use in order to determine whether the claimed
right has been established, nevertheless if it is clear from that evidence
that use has been made of the land for the requisite period which is capable
of amounting to an easement, the Court should not be deflected from
declaring the existence of an easement which can be sensibly formulated.

The Court, however, held that the right created by the proved use only restricted the
use which the servient owner could make of the land to the extent necessary to
ensure that the garden could still be enjoyed by the dominant owners as a communal garden; the declaration by the trial judge that the claimant was entitled to restore
the flowerbed in its original position was wrong, albeit that the act of removing the
flowerbed without notice had been unlawful. Whether any particular proposal by the
servient owners to create a driveway through the garden would substantially interfere with the dominant owner's rights was a question of fact. The Court therefore
substituted for the declaration made by the trial judge a declaration that the claimant
was entitled to a right to use the land in question as a communal garden for recreational and amenity purposes. The Court stated that this would inevitably require the
servient owners, if they wish to carry out any works on the land in question, (a) to
do so in a way which would substantially maintain its character of the communal
garden and (b) to demonstrate that any proposed work would maintain that character; in practice this was likely to require prior consultation and preferably agreement
if not to amount to a significant interference with the respondent's rights.

Mulvaney extends the decision in *Ellenborough Park, Re* to a case where (a)
there was no express grant; (b) there was no obligation by the servient owner to
maintain the area as a garden or any obligation by the dominant owners to pay for
the cost of maintenance; and (c) the dominant owners were claiming not merely
a right to enjoy but a right to cultivate as ancillary to the right to enjoy as a garden. These rights, while undoubtedly extensive, were nevertheless not exclusive,
because the servient owner was still entitled to do things on the land which would
not detract from its character as a garden, such as forming a gravelled driveway.

1–70   In *P&S Platt v Crouch*,[241] where a claim was made to rights to moor boats, erect signs and fish along a section of riverbank, it was held that such rights would not deprive the owners of any reasonable user of the land and so were capable of being an easement.

1–71   The most recent illustration of the application of the principle, as to when a right is too extensive to be an easement, is of course the decision of the House of Lords in *Moncrieff v Jamieson*[242] itself. Reference has been made above to the general principles which are considered in that case. The House of Lords proceeded to apply those principles to the claimed right to park. The detailed facts of that case and the state of the law as to the easement of parking are considered at paragraphs 9–96 to 9–110 below and that discussion will not be repeated here.

Class of possible easements not closed

1–72   Such, then, are the essential characteristics of an easement. Notwithstanding certain nineteenth-century dicta to the effect that rights of a novel kind cannot be annexed to land,[243] it is clear that any right having these characteristics will rank as an easement, and that, while the category of negative easements is, in the nature of things, limited, so that a negative easement must be looked at with caution,[244] and it is unlikely that any new negative easements will be recognised, the class of possible easements is not closed.[245]

3.—EXAMPLES OF EASEMENTS

1–73   The following among other rights have been recognised by the courts, in many cases inferentially or by tacit assumption, as easements:

Positive easements

1–74   Rights of way.[246]

Right to place over neighbouring land clothes on lines.[247]

---

[241] [2004] 1 P. & C.R. 18.

[242] [2007] 1 W.L.R. 2620.

[243] *Keppell v Bailey* (1834) 2 My. & K. 517 at 535; *Ackroyd v Smith* (1850) 10 C.B. 164 at 188; *Hill v Tupper* (1863) 2 H. & C. 121 at 127; *Nuttall v Bracewell* (1866) L.R. 2 Exch. 1 at 10. "A tendency in the past to freeze the categories of easements has been overtaken by the defrosting operation in Re Ellenborough Park": *Dowty Boulton Paul Ltd v Wolverhampton Corp (No. 2)* [1976] Ch. 13 at 23, per Russell L.J. It has more recently been said that the law is reluctant "to recognise new forms of burdens on property conferring more than contractual rights": *London & Blenheim Ltd v Ladbroke Ltd* [1994] 1 W.L.R. 31 at 37 G–H.

[244] *Phipps v Pears* [1965] 1 Q.B. 76 at 82, 83, per Lord Denning M.R.

[245] *Ward v Kirkland* [1967] Ch. 194 at 222; and see *Ellenborough Park, Re* [1956] Ch. 131; *Simpson v Godmanchester Corp* [1896] 1 Ch. 214 at 219; *Dyce v Lady James Hay* (1852) 1 Macq. 305 at 309.

[246] *Drewett v Towler* (1832) 3 B. & Ald. 735.

[247] *Drewett v Towler* (1832) 3 B. & Ald. 735.

Right to move a timber traveller through and over neighbouring land,[248] or to cause bowsprits of vessels in dock to project over adjoining land.[249]

Right in working mines,[250] or quarries,[251] to make spoil banks on the surface.

Right to mix muck on a neighbour's land.[252]

Right to deposit on a neighbour's land house refuse, or trade goods.[253]

Right to place a signpost,[254] or chicken-coops,[255] on a common.

Right to nail fruit trees on a neighbour's wall.[256]

Right to use a fascia on a neighbour's house.[257]

Right to fix a signboard on a neighbour's house.[258]

Right to use the chimney of a neighbour's house for the passage of smoke.[259]

Right to use the kitchen of a neighbour's house for washing.[260]

Right to use a lavatory.[261]

Right to use a coal-shed.[262]

Right of landing nets on another's land.[263]

All necessary rights to enable the grantee to obtain water from the land of the grantor.[264]

Right to place a pile in the bed of a river.[265]

Right to place stones on the foreshore for protection of adjoining land.[266]

Right to go on the land of another to clear a mill-stream and repair its banks[267]; or to open locks in time of flood.[268]

Right for the occupier of a messuage to water cattle at a pond and take water for domestic purposes.[269]

---

[248] *Harris v De Pinna* (1886) 33 Ch. D. 251.

[249] *Suffield v Brown* (1864) 4 De G.J. & Sm. 185.

[250] *Rogers v Taylor* (1857) 1 H. & N. 706; see *Marshall v Borrowdale Plumbago Mines* (1892) 8 T.L.R. 275.

[251] *Middleton v Clarence* (1877) Ir.R. 11 C.L. 499.

[252] *Pye v Mumford* (1848) 11 Q.B. 666.

[253] *Foster v Richmond* (1910) 9 L.G.R. 65; *Att-Gen for S. Nigeria v Holt* [1915] A.C. 599 at 617.

[254] *Hoare v Metropolitan Board of Works* (1874) L.R. 9 Q.B. 296.

[255] *Smith v Gates* [1952] C.P.L. 814.

[256] *Hawkins v Wallis* (1763) 2 Wils. 173.

[257] *Francis v Hayward* (1882) 22 Ch. D. 177 at 182, per Bowen L.J.

[258] *Moody v Steggles* (1879) 12 Ch. D. 261; *William Hill (Southern) Ltd v Cabras Ltd* (1986) 54 P. & C.R. 42, CA.

[259] *Hervey v Smith* (1855) 1 K. & J. 389; 22 Beav. 299; see *Jones v Pritchard* [1908] 1 Ch. 630.

[260] *Heywood v Mallalieu* (1883) 25 Ch. D. 357.

[261] *Miller v Emcer Products Ltd* [1956] Ch. 304; see also *West Pennine Water Board v Jon Migael (North West)* (1975) 73 L.G.R. 420, CA.

[262] *Wright v Macadam* [1949] 2 K.B. 744.

[263] *Gray v Bond* (1821) 2 Brod. & Bing. 667.

[264] *Simeon, Re* [1937] Ch. 525 at 537.

[265] *Lancaster v Eve* (1859) 5 C.B. (n.s.) 717.

[266] *Philpot v Bath* [1905] W.N. 114.

[267] *Beeston v Weate* (1856) 5 E. & B. 986; *Peter v Daniel* (1848) 5 C.B. 568; *Roberts v Fellowes* (1906) 94 L.T. 279.

[268] *Simpson v Godmanchester Corp* [1897] A.C. 696.

[269] *Manning v Wasdale* (1836) 5 A. & E. 758.

Right to go on a neighbour's land and draw water from a spring there,[270] or from a pump.[271]

Right to discharge rainwater by a spout or projecting eaves.[272]

Right to discharge polluted water into another's watercourse.[273]

Right to send water across a neighbour's land by an artificial watercourse.[274]

Right to use or affect the water of a natural stream in manner not justified by a natural right, e.g. by damming it.[275]

Right to place a fender in a mill-stream to prevent waste of water.[276]

Right to commit a private nuisance by creating noise[277]; or by polluting water[278]; or by polluting air by smoke or smell.[279]

Right to a pew in a church.[280]

Right to construct and maintain a ventilation duct.[281]

Right to enter on adjoining land to repair an outside wall.[282]

Right to use the area alongside a wharf for the loading and unloading of vessels, and possibly for breaking up vessels.[283]

Right to use an airfield.[284]

Right to park a car anywhere in a defined area near to the dominant tenement.[285]

[270] *Race v Ward* (1855) 4 E. & B. 702.
[271] *Polden v Bastard* (1865) L.R. 1 Q.B. 156 (but in that case the right was not proved).
[272] *Harvey v Walters* (1872) L.R. 8 C.P. 162.
[273] *Wright v Williams* (1836) 1 M. & W. 77.
[274] *Beeston v Weate* (1856) 5 E. & B. 986; *Abingdon Corp v James* [1940] Ch. 287.
[275] *Beeston v Weate* (1856) 5 E. & B. 986.
[276] *Wood v Hewett* (1846) 8 Q.B. 913.
[277] *Elliotson v Feetham* (1835) 2 Bing.N.C. 134; *Ball v Ray* (1873) 8 Ch. App. 467 at 471; *The State Electricity Commission of Victoria & Joshua's Contract, Re* [1940] V.L.R. 121.
[278] *Baxendale v McMurray* (1867) Ch. App. 790.
[279] *Crump v Lambert* (1867) L.R. 3 Eq. 409 at 413.
[280] "There may be annexed to a house, as appurtenant to it, by means of a faculty, the exclusive right to use a pew": *Phillips v Halliday* [1891] A.C. 228 at 233; and see *St Mary's, Banbury, Re* [1986] Fam. 24; *St Mary of Charity, Faversham, Re* [1986] Fam. 143 at 155. A lost faculty will be presumed in appropriate circumstances, but for this purpose evidence is required of acts of user, e.g. repair, which are more consistent with a right under a faculty than with occupation by permission of or arrangement with the church authorities: *Crisp v Martin* (1876) 2 P.D. 15; *Halliday v Phillips* (1889) 23 Q.B.D. 48; *Stileman-Gibbard v Wilkinson* [1897] 1 Q.B. 749. It seems that as a matter of law a right of way over consecrated ground cannot be conferred by a faculty and so an easement of way, as opposed to a licence of indefinite duration, cannot arise under the doctrine of lost modern grant: *St Martin Le Grand, York, Re* [1990] Fam. 63.
[281] *Wong v Beaumont Property Trust Ltd* [1965] 1 Q.B. 173; followed in *Auerbach v Beck* [1985] 6 N.S.W.L.R. 424; on appeal at 454 and in *Wilcox v Richardson* (1997) 8 B.P.R. 97,652.
[282] *Ward v Kirkland* [1967] Ch. 194; followed in *Auerbach v Beck* [1985] 6 N.S.W.L.R. 424; on appeal at 454; but there is no right to have a structure protected from the weather (which would be a negative easement): *Phipps v Pears* [1965] 1 Q.B. 76; *Marchant v Capital & Counties Property Co Ltd* (1982) 263 E.G. 661 (reversed on other grounds [1983] 2 E.G.L.R. 156, CA). See para.1–45, above.
[283] *Thomas W. Ward Ltd v Alexander Bruce (Grays) Ltd* [1959] 2 Lloyd's Rep. 472, CA; but there is no right to maintain silt; see para.1–90, below.
[284] *Dowty Boulton Paul Ltd v Wolverhampton Corp (No. 2)* [1976] Ch. 13.
[285] per Sir Robert Megarry V.-C. in *Newman v Jones* (unreported) but cited at [1994] 1 E.G.L.R. 70 at 72A; *Handel v St Stephens Close Ltd* (*ibid.*); *Bye v Marshall* [1993] C.L.Y. 208; *Sweet & Maxwell v Michael-Michaels (Advertising)* [1965] C.L.Y. 2192; *London & Blenheim Estates Ltd v Ladbroke Retail Parks Ltd* [1992] 1 W.L.R. 1278 at 1288B (assumed to be correct for the purpose of appeal at [1994] 1 W.L.R. 31).

Right to fillet fish in a filleting bay for sale from a takeaway fish and chip shop.[286]

Right to construct and maintain underground rock-anchors for securing the wall of a road cutting.[287]

Negative easements

Right to receive light for a building.[288]   **1–75**
Right to receive air by a defined channel.[289]
Right of support of buildings from land[290]; or from buildings.[291]
Right to receive a flow of water in an artificial stream.[292]

In *Elliott v Burn*[293] where surface owners had granted to mineral owners the right to let down the surface on terms of paying a tonnage rent and compensation for any damage, it was held by the House of Lords, negativing a claim for income tax on the tonnage rents as profits arising from an easement ("hereditament") under the Income Tax Act 1918, Sch.A, No.I, r.7,[294] that what was granted was not an easement at all, but (it seems)[295] merely a release from the liability of being sued on letting down the surfaces, for damages for a nuisance, or for an injunction.

Qualified easements

A qualified easement may exist; as, for instance, the right of a landowner to dam   **1–76**
up a stream running through the servient land, and divert it into an artificial cut through the servient land to the dominant land, subject to the right of the servient owner to use the water in the cut for irrigation, when required,[296] or a right to enclose part of a river into a fishing-weir, subject to the right of a mill-owner on the opposite side to open the weir when water is scarce.[297]

Easements in common

Section 187(2) of the Law of Property Act 1925 provides that nothing in the Act   **1–77**
affects the right of a person to hold or exercise an easement, right or privilege

---

[286] *Wilcox v Richardson* (1997) 8 B.P.R. 97,652.
[287] *Pennant Hills Golf Club Ltd v Roads and Traffic Authority of New South Wales* (1999) 9 B.P.R. 97,761.
[288] See Ch.7, below.
[289] *Bass v Gregory* (1890) 25 Q.B.D. 481.
[290] *Dalton v Angus* (1881) 6 App. Cas. 740.
[291] *Lemaitre v Davis* (1881) 19 Ch. D. 281; *Waddington v Naylor* (1889) 60 L.T. 480.
[292] *Nuttall v Bracewell* (1866) L.R. 2 Exch. 1 at 10; *Schwann v Cotton* [1916] 2 Ch. 459; *Keewatin Power Co v Lake of the Woods Milling Co* [1930] A.C. 640.
[293] [1935] A.C. 84.
[294] See now the Income and Corporation Taxes Act 1988, ss.119 and 120, *Earl Fitzwilliam's Collieries Co v Phillips* [1943] A.C. 570.
[295] See *IRC v New Sharlston Collieries Co* [1937] 1 K.B. 583 at 605.
[296] *Beeston v Weate* (1856) 5 E. & B. 986.
[297] *Rolle v Whyte* (1868) L.R. 3 Q.B. 286.

over or in relation to land for a legal estate in common with any other person, or the power of creating or conveying such an easement, right or privilege. The meaning appears to be that several pieces of land in different ownership can have an easement, for example a right of way, over the same site.

4.—Rights Analogous to Easements

Fencing easements

1–78   As has been seen,[298] a true easement is either a right to do something or a right to prevent something. A right to have something done is not an easement, nor is it an incident of an easement, and an obligation to do something on one's own land can only arise, speaking generally, by statute or contract.[299] Moreover, the burden of a contractual obligation of that kind does not run with the land.[300] Anomalously, however, the courts have recognised an obligation on the owners and occupiers of a piece of land to maintain a fence thereon for the benefit of the owners and occupiers of adjoining land.[301] Although not a true easement,[302] this right is commonly referred to as a fencing easement. The obligation has been established by proof of long usage under which the quasi-servient owner or occupier has consistently repaired the fence when told to do so by the quasi-dominant owner or occupier,[303] and therefore inferentially in performance of a binding obligation, and when land has been enclosed from a common and the person taking it has maintained a fence against the rest of the common, an obligation to do so for the benefit of the commoners and their successors has been inferred.[304] The right is of such a nature that it can pass under section 62 of the Law of Property Act 1925.

1–79   The right has been considered in three modern cases, *Jones v Price*,[305] *Crow v Wood*[306] and *Egerton v Harding*.[307] In *Jones v Price* the plaintiff claimed damages

---

[298] See para.1–01, above.

[299] *cf. Hilton v Ankesson* (1872) 27 L.T. 519. The obligation to fence a railway imposed by the Railway Clauses Consolidation Act 1845, s.68 may continue after the railway has been abandoned: *R. Walker & Sons v British Railways Board* [1984] 1 W.L.R. 805.

[300] *Rhone v Stephens* [1994] 2 W.L.R. 429; approving *Austerberry v Oldham Corp* (1885) 29 Ch. D. 750, which had overruled *Cooke v Chilean* (1876) 3 Ch. D. 694; see also *Haywood v Brunswick Building Society* (1881) 8 Q.B.D. 403; *E. & G.C. Ltd v Bate* (1935) 79 L.Journal 203. In *Jones v Price* [1965] 2 Q.B. 618 at 639, Diplock L.J. said that the assumption in *Boyle v Tamlyn* (1827) 6 B. & C. 329 that the obligation could be created by covenant could not survive *Austerberry v Oldham Corporation* (1885) 29 Ch. D. 750 and was not in any event easy to reconcile with *Spencer's Case* (1583) 5 Co.Rep. 16a.

[301] *Lawrence v Jenkins* (1873) L.R. 8 Q.B. 274, where earlier cases are referred to. The obligation is on the occupier, not on the owner if not in occupation: *Cheetham v Hampson* (1791) 4 Term Rep. 318.

[302] In old editions of this book it was referred to as a spurious easement; see, e.g. the 4th edition (1868) at p. 460, quoted in *Lawrence v Jenkins* (1873) L.R. 8 Q.B. 274 at 279. In *Jones v Price* [1965] 2 Q.B. 618 at 633, Willmer L.J. referred to it as a quasi-easement.

[303] *Star v Rookesby* (1710) 1 Salk. 335; *Hilton v Ankesson*, above; *Jones v Price*, above; *Egerton v Harding* [1975] Q.B. 62.

[304] *Barber v Whiteley* (1865) 34 L.J.Q.B. 212; approved in *Sutcliffe v Holmes* [1947] K.B. 147. Such cases are in a special category: *Jones v Price* [1965] 2 Q.B. 618 at 647, per Winn L.J.

[305] [1965] 2 Q.B. 618.

[306] [1971] 1 Q.B. 77.

[307] [1975] Q.B. 62.

for cattle trespass and the defendant by way of defence alleged an obligation on the part of the plaintiff to maintain a hedge which the Court of Appeal found was a boundary fence.[308] The Court of Appeal found that the right to require the owner of adjoining land to keep the boundary fence in repair was a right which could arise by prescription and was commonly established by proof of immemorial user or by the doctrine of a lost grant,[309] but that there was no evidence to establish against the plaintiff a prescriptive right to have the hedge kept in repair, either by such usage or by a lost grant. Diplock L.J. said[310] of the right, "It is tempting to think that its real origin lies in local custom, but this explanation was rejected in 1670 in Polus v. Henstock."[311]

Crow v Wood[312] was another case in which the plaintiff claimed damages for **1–80** cattle trespass. A large sheep moor with several adjoining farms remained for many years in common occupation. The farms were let to individual farmers who had the right to stray a certain number of sheep on the moor and who agreed to keep their fences and walls in good repair. In 1951 one of the farms was sold together with the right to stray 40 sheep on the moor. That right was let in 1962 to the defendant, who put 40 sheep on the moor. In 1956 and 1966 respectively two other adjacent farms were sold to the plaintiff together with rights of stray which she did not exercise. From 1966 the plaintiff ceased to keep up the walls and fences on her farm against sheep from the moor and in consequence sheep, and in particular the defendant's sheep, often got into her farm. The plaintiff sought damages and an injunction, and the defendant claimed that the plaintiff was under a duty by implied grant at common law and/or by section 62 of the Law of Property Act 1925 to keep up her fences and walls for the benefit of holders of grazing rights on the moor; and that his sheep had only entered her land because of her failure to do so.

The plaintiff succeeded in the Malton County Court, but the Court of Appeal **1–81** allowed the defendant's appeal, holding that the right to have one's neighbours keep up fences was a right in the nature of an easement which was capable of being granted by law so as to run with the land and be binding on successors. It was of such a nature that it could pass under section 62 of the Law of Property Act 1925. The county court judge had held that there was a custom of the moor by which each of the farmers adjoining the moor was bound to keep up the fences and walls of his own farm, but Lord Denning M.R. said that this was not sufficient of itself to put an obligation on the plaintiff to fence her land, adding[313]: "It appears from the old books that a right to have fences kept up does not arise by custom", a statement which his Lordship supported by reference to *Bolus v Hinstorke*[314] another name, in another report, for *Polus v Henstock*.[315] Lord

---

[308] By s.5(6) of the Animals Act 1971, the existence of a duty on the part of a landowner to fence provides a defence to an action by such a person for trespass by livestock.
[309] As in *Barber v Whiteley* (1865) 34 L.J.Q.B. 212; approved in *Sutcliffe v Holmes* [1947] K.B. 147.
[310] [1965] 2 Q.B. 618 at 639.
[311] (1670) 1 Vent. 97.
[312] [1971] 1 Q.B. 77.
[313] [1971] 1 Q.B. 77 at 83.
[314] (1670) 2 Keb. 686.
[315] (1670) 1 Vent. 97.

Denning also said,[316] *obiter*, that there was in every conveyance to a farmer who bought his farm from a common owner, and who had a right to put sheep on the moor and to have his neighbours repair fences, implied an obligation, ancillary to that right, to keep up his own fences.

1–82   The nature of the obligation to fence, and the circumstances in which it can arise, appear, it is thought definitively, in the judgment of the Court of Appeal (delivered by Scarman L.J.) in *Egerton v Harding*.[317] The plaintiff's cottage and the defendants' farm adjoined common land over which they both enjoyed grazing rights. The plaintiff did not exercise her rights but the defendants had grazed cattle on the common since 1968. In 1971 cattle belonging to the defendants strayed into the plaintiff's garden, and she sued for damages for cattle trespass. The defendants counterclaimed alleging failure to fence. The judge of the Aldershot and Farnham County Court found that a custom to fence against the common land had been proved and that owners of land adjoining the common were under a liability to fence against cattle lawfully on the common; but he found that there was no evidence of enclosure, grant, or presumption of lost modern grant. He dismissed the plaintiff's claim and awarded the defendants nominal damages on their counterclaim. The plaintiff appealed against the finding that a duty to fence could arise by custom and that a valid custom to fence had been proved.

1–83   The Court of Appeal found that a duty to fence against another's land could originate in prescription or lost modern grant (in which case the right has the nature of an easement) or in custom, these two possible origins being totally distinct from one another. Scarman L.J. explained them as follows[318]: "Custom, being local law, displaces within its locality the common law; an easement is a matter of private right and obligation recognised and enforceable by the general law." In order to succeed on the ground of obligation it is necessary to adduce evidence directly implicating the occupiers of the allegedly servient tenement of prescriptive right or of lost modern grant. Fencing as a matter of obligation is essential. The Court of Appeal disapproved a dictum of Edmund Davies L.J. in *Crow v Wood*[319] to the effect that it was enough to show that land was accustomed to be fenced and that it was immaterial that a party had voluntarily fenced his premises simply for, it might be, his own protection. On the facts of *Egerton v Harding*[320] the Court of Appeal found that there was no evidence of any enclosure of the plaintiff's cottage, and no evidence directly implicating its occupiers of prescriptive right or of lost modern grant, although it was very likely that there had been an enclosure, which would provide a legal origin of the practice of fencing; since where the lord of a manor allowed a freeholder or a copyholder to enclose a piece of common land, thereby effectually destroying common rights over the land enclosed, he almost invariably required that the land be fenced against the common.

[316] [1971] 1 Q.B. 77 at 85.
[317] [1975] Q.B. 62.
[318] [1975] Q.B. 62 at 68.
[319] [1971] 1 Q.B. 77 at 86, 87.
[320] [1975] Q.B. 62.

The Court of Appeal held, however, that there was evidence on which the **1–84** county court judge could properly find the existence of immemorial usage, and rejected the passages in the judgments of Diplock L.J. in *Jones v Price*[321] and Lord Denning M.R. in *Crow v Wood*[322] quoted above, which the Court of Appeal found to be historically unsound, and to be founded on a misunderstanding of *Polus v Henstock*,[323] which, as Scarman L.J. pointed out,[324] "is authority to the effect that an easement or a right akin to an easement, which is limited to a particular boundary, could not arise by custom: but it does not go so far as to decide that within a manor there could be no manorial custom to fence against the waste (i.e. the common)." Having considered the authorities, Scarman L.J. said[325] that the old law appeared to have been as follows:

"A duty to fence against another's land could arise by grant or custom. As between freeholders it was a duty enforceable by the writ de curia claudenda[326]: if it was a duty for the benefit of a manorial waste in which copyholders had an interest recognised by their lord, it arose by custom upon which copyholders could rely because, by reason of the 'imbecility' of their estate, they could not prescribe. In short, the duty was recognised as one that could arise; whether its juridical basis was grant or custom depended upon the character of the landholding and the circumstances prevailing in the vill or manor."

In the present case the county court judge was not to be faulted for having found **1–85** that the duty to fence came from custom proved by immemorial usage: but the Court of Appeal found that, once there was established an immemorial usage of fencing against the common as a matter of obligation, that was enough to prove the duty to fence, provided always that it could be shown that such a duty could have arisen from a lawful origin. In the present case the history of the common and the origin of the usage under which the owners of land adjoining regarded themselves as obliged to fence the common might never be known, but it was known that the usage could have derived from one of several lawful origins.[327]

---

[321] [1965] 2 Q.B. 618 at 639.

[322] [1971] 1 Q.B. 77 at 83.

[323] (1670) 1 Vent. 97; reported as *Bolus v Hinstorke* (1670) 2 Keb. 686. In that case (as Scarman L.J. pointed out in *Egerton v Harding* at 71) the court relied on Co. Litt. (1823), Vol.1, p. 113b (Scarman L.J.'s citation), where the distinction between prescription and custom is explained: the former is personal, "being made in the name of a certain person and of his ancestors, or those whose estate he hath"; while the latter is local and applicable to all within the manor. See also *Godfrey v Godfrey*, Y.B. 10 Edw. IV 18; *Barber v Whiteley* (1865) 34 L.J.Q.B. 212.

[324] [1975] Q.B. 62 at 70.

[325] [1975] Q.B. 62 at 71.

[326] *Pomfret v Ricroft* (1669) 1 Saund. 321 at 322a, there is a note as follows: "The ancient remedy was by the writ de curia claudenda, which lay for the tenant of the freehold against another tenant of land adjoining to compel him to make a fence or wall, which he ought, by prescription, to make between his land and the plaintiff's."

[327] Scarman L.J. pointed out in *Egerton v Harding*, above, at 72, an analogous situation was considered in *London and North-Western Ry v Fobbing Levels Sewers Commissioners* (1897) 75 L.T. 629, where the plaintiff's liability to repair a sea wall was in issue.

Ways in gross

1–86   Although this is no longer considered to be good law, there is no doubt that in former times a grant of a perpetual right of way in gross was considered to be valid, in the sense that it created a heritable and presumably assignable right which the owners for the time being of the quasi-servient tenement were bound to recognise. For instance, in *Senhouse v Christian*,[328] which was an action of trespass, the defendant pleaded that in 1722 H. Senhouse (the plaintiff's father) granted by deed to John Christian (the defendant's grandfather), his heirs and assigns, a way over a certain slip of land; that John Christian by virtue of this deed became seised of the said way in gross; that the same on his death descended to Evan Christian, as his son and heir, and on the death of Evan, to one John Christian, as the brother and heir to Evan; and from the last-mentioned John Christian, upon his death, to the present defendant Christian, as his son and heir, who justified, under that deed, the acts complained of. The question argued and decided was whether the defendant's acts were within the terms of the grant; no suggestion was made that he had no right, and it was evidently assumed without question that he and the plaintiff had the same rights and obligations as the original grantor and grantee; in other words, that the right granted had descended to the defendant and bound the plaintiff.

1–87   A right of this kind is clearly not an easement, for there is no dominant tenement. The 15th edition of this work had asked why it should not be possible now, as it was before, to grant, for an interest equivalent to an estate in fee simple, an assignable and transmissible right binding the land over which it is exercised, and comparable with a *profit à prendre* in gross. It was suggested in early editions of this work[329] that *Ackroyd v Smith*[330] was no authority against this possibility on the basis that all that was decided there was that a right of way for purposes not connected with the land to which it was supposed to be appurtenant did not pass to successive owners of the land. As late as 1911 the late Mr Charles Sweet wrote[331]: "It is possible to create a perpetual way in gross by grant, if the deed is clearly expressed and proper words of limitation are used."[332] More recently, however, it has been said that the law is reluctant "to recognise new forms of burden on property conferring more than contractual rights" and it was held that a right to park cars (which could otherwise be an easement) was a contractual right only, and not a property right binding a successor of the grantor, because there was no dominant tenement in existence before the transfer of the allegedly servient land to the successor of the grantor.[333]

---

[328] (1787) 1 T.R. 560.
[329] See, e.g. the 3rd ed., by Mr W.H. Willes, p. 13.
[330] (1850) 10 C.B. 164.
[331] *Challis' Real Property* (3rd ed.), p. 55; and see his article in (1908) 24 L.Q.R. 259.
[332] See also *Lord Hastings v North Eastern Ry* [1898] 2 Ch. 674; and *cf.* para.1–20, above, as to rights of burial.
[333] *London & Blenheim Ltd v Ladbroke Ltd* [1994] 1 W.L.R. 31 at 36 (followed in *Voice v Bell* (1993) 68 P. & C.R. 441), relying on *Ackroyd v Smith* (1850) 10 C.B. 164 at 188.

Special immunities under the doctrine as to non-derogation from grant

The same situation as if an easement had been created, although none has been,   **1–88**
can arise from the doctrine that no one can derogate from, that is to say, impede
the purpose of, his grant.[334] The immunity obtained may be of a special kind not
recognised as an easement. On the other hand, it may have all the qualities of a
recognised easement. Furthermore, the rule in *Wheeldon v Burrows*,[335] under
which a positive right may be acquired, is a branch of the general rule against
derogation from grant. Accordingly, the acquisition of rights by reference to the
doctrine will be considered[336] on the basis that those rights are easements,
although strictly they are not.

5. — INCIDENTS OF EASEMENTS

Easements and title by adverse possession under the Limitation Act 1980

A person who acquires a statutory title to land does not thereby acquire a way of   **1–89**
necessity to it over adjoining land of the dispossessed person.[337] The reason is
that while the title of the former owner is extinguished, the Limitation Act 1980
does not operate as a statutory conveyance; and hence it must follow that no new
easement of any kind can arise in such a case, for there is no disposition by the
common owner[338] under which an easement can arise by implication.

The question whether a person who acquires a statutory title to land becomes
entitled to an easement[339] which is already annexed to it does not appear to have
arisen for decision.

Such a person is bound by an easement[340] already affecting the land which he
acquires.[341] In *Williams v Usherwood*[342] it was held that where the true owner
makes use of the land in the possession of the squatter but where the use by the
true owner is not sufficient to prevent the squatter from being in possession and
acquiring a statutory title, the title so acquired will be subject to rights in favour
of the true owner to enable him to continue such use.

---

[334] For the statement of the principle by Parker J. in *Browne v Flower* [1911] 1 Ch. 219 at 226, see
para.3–32, below.
[335] (1879) 12 Ch. D. 31 at 49, per Thesiger L.J.
[336] See paras 3–32 *et seq.*, below.
[337] *Wilkes v Greenway* (1890) 6 T.L.R. 449. This decision is discussed in *Jourdan on Adverse
Possession* (2003), chapter 23 where it is suggested (at para.23–25) that the reasoning is inconsistent with *Williams v Usherwood* (1983) 45 P. & C.R. 235.
[338] See para.3–17, below.
[339] Or a restrictive covenant. This question is discussed in *Jourdan on Adverse Possession* (2003) at
para.23–15 where it is suggested that an easement appurtenant to the land would benefit the squatter in possession both during and after the period of limitation.
[340] Or a restrictive covenant.
[341] *Nisbet and Potts' Contract, Re* [1905] 1 Ch. 391 at 400; [1906] 1 Ch. 386 at 401.
[342] (1983) 45 P. & C.R. 235.

Ancillary easements

1–90 The grant of an easement is also the grant of such ancillary rights as are reasonably necessary to its exercise or enjoyment.[343] Where the use of a thing is granted, everything is granted by which the grantee may have and enjoy such use.[344] The ancillary right arises because it is necessary for the enjoyment of the right expressly granted.[345]

In *Central Electricity Generating Board v Jennaway*,[346] in which the plaintiff had under statutory powers a wayleave to place electric lines above the ground over the defendant's land, Lloyd-Jacob J. held that the wayleave carried with it the right to place on the defendant's land towers to support the lines. In *White v Taylor (No. 2)*[347] Buckley J. held that the plaintiffs, who had a profit of grazing sheep on the defendant's down, were entitled, as an ancillary right under an implied grant, to water their sheep on the down by means of suitably located troughs supplied by carted water. In *Besley v John*,[348] it was held that a right to graze sheep on a common did not carry with it the right to bring additional feed onto the common but did permit the grantee to come onto the common to attend to the welfare of the sheep; this latter right could be exercised by using a vehicle, given the large area of the common; the right was to be exercised reasonably and with the minimum interference with the rights of the owner of the common. The grant of an easement over land for parking lot purposes does not carry with it, as a necessary incident, the right to erect a sign advertising the parking lot.[349]

In *Moncrieff v Jamieson*[350] there was an express grant of a "right of access". It was conceded by the servient owner that there was a right of access with or without vehicles and that the grant carried with it an ancillary right to turn a vehicle on the way, to stop a vehicle on the way for the purpose of loading and unloading and to leave a vehicle on the way for the duration of short visits to the dominant tenement, e.g. by tradesmen. The House of Lords also decided a disputed

---

[343] Parker J., *Jones v Pritchard* [1908] 1 Ch. 630 at 638; and see *Bulstrode v Lambert* [1953] 1 W.L.R. 1064. *Cf. Thomas W. Ward Ltd v Alexander Bruce (Grays) Ltd* [1959] 2 Lloyd's Rep. 472, CA: a prescriptive right to break up vessels and scuttle them on a bed of silt does not carry right to maintain the silt so as to prevent the servient owner from dredging. See also *V.T. Engineering Ltd v Richard Barland & Co Ltd* (1968) 19 P. & C.R. 890: a grant of a right of way over a road for all purposes includes a right to halt vehicles on the way while being loaded or unloaded, but does not entitle the grantee to station loading equipment on the way. *Duke of Westminster v Guild* [1985] 1 Q.B. 688, CA; a grant in a lease of a right of drainage entitled the tenant to go upon his landlord's adjacent land to repair the drain.

[344] *Pomfret v Ricroft* (1669) 1 Wms.Saund. 321, 323. And see *Liford's Case* (1614) 11 Co. Rep. 46b, 52a; *Senhouse v Christian* (1787) 1 Term Rep. 560; *Gerrard v Cooke* (1806) 2 Bos. & Pul.N.R. 109; *Dand v Kingscote* (1840) 6 M. & W. 174; Shep. Touch. 100.

[345] Lord Parker, *Pwllbach Colliery Co Ltd v Woodman* [1915] A.C. 634 at 646, and see 643. The principle is expressed in the maxim "*Lex est cuicunque aliquis quid concedit concedere videtur et id sine quo res esse non potuit.*"

[346] [1959] 1 W.L.R. 937.

[347] [1969] 1 Ch. 160.

[348] [2003] EWCA Civ 1737.

[349] *Lean Asper Amusements Ltd v Northmain Carwash* (1966) 56 D.L.R. (2d) 173.

[350] [2007] 1 W.L.R. 2620.

question as to whether the dominant owner had a right to park a number of vehicles on the way. It was held that in the unusual circumstances of that case,[351] there was such a right to park either as a right ancillary to the grant of the right of access or as a grant implied into the transaction which involved the severance of the dominant land from the servient land and the grant of a right of access over the servient land.

Right to repair

The question of ancillary easements commonly arises in connection with repairs. **1–91**
Thus the grantee of an easement for a watercourse through his neighbour's land may, when reasonably necessary, enter his neighbour's land for the purpose of repairing, and may repair, such watercourse.[352] "If a man gives me a licence to lay pipes of lead in his land to convey water to my cistern, I may afterwards enter and dig the land to mend the pipes, though the soil belongs to another and not to me."[353] The owner of a building entitled to support from an adjoining building is entitled to enter and take the necessary steps to ensure that the support continues by effecting repairs, and so forth, to the part of the building which gives the support.[354] The grantee of a right of way is entitled to repair the way; he is entitled to enter the servient owner's land for this purpose but only to do necessary work in a reasonable manner.[355]

Repair for this purpose can include making alterations to and improving the subject of the easement,[356] alteration to meet altered conditions[357]; also replacement.[358] A person can alter the surface of the servient land to accommodate the right granted, as by building a made road or spreading gravel on it, so long as there is not undue interference with the rights of the owner of the servient land. So where the right of way is steeply inclined or goes over a cliff, the dominant owner may be entitled to construct steps or a staircase.[359] The extent of the ancillary right has to be determined in the light of the particular circumstances of the grant; it is not limited to the minimum standard to make the grant effective.[360] Nor is it limited to the width of the track existing at the date of grant.[361]

---

[351] See paras 9–100–9–103.
[352] Parker J., *Jones v Pritchard* [1908] 1 Ch. 630 at 638; and see para.1–90, above.
[353] *Pomfret v Ricroft* (1669) 1 Wms.Saund. 321 at 323, and see para.1–90, above. *Duke of Westminster v Guild* [1985] 1 Q.B. 688, CA (drainpipes).
[354] *Bond v Nottingham Corp* [1940] Ch. 429 at 439.
[355] See the summary of the law in *Carter v Cole* [2006] EWCA Civ 398; see paras 9–86–9–92, below.
[356] *Newcomen v Coulson* (1877) 5 Ch. D. 133 at 144 (way); *cf. Hodgson v Field* (1806) 7 East 613; *Lawrence v Griffiths* (1987) 47 S.A.S.R. 455 (grantee entitled to carry out substantial earthworks to constrain carriageway). But a way can only be improved to the extent reasonably necessary for the enjoyment of the easement granted: *Butler v Muddle* (1995) 6 B.P.R. 97,532.
[357] *Finlinson v Porter* (1875) L.R. 10 Q.B. 188.
[358] *Hoare v Metropolitan Board of Works* (1874) L.R. 9 Q.B. 296; *Stokes v Mixconcrete (Holdings) Ltd* (1978) 38 P. & C.R. 488.
[359] *Hanny v Lewis* (1998) 9 B.P.R. 97,702; *Hemmes Hermitage Pty Limited v Abdurahman* (1991) 22 N.S.W.L.R. 343.
[360] *Nationwide Building Society v James Beauchamp* [2001] 3 E.G.L.R. 6.
[361] *Wimpey Homes Holdings Limited v Collins* 1999 S.L.T. (Sh Ct) 16.

In this respect, express grants differ from prescriptive rights: if a right of way is granted for all purposes the dominant owner may improve it to make it available for a purpose not in contemplation at the time of the grant, but a prescriptive right is limited by the nature of the use from which it has arisen and the servient tenement cannot be improved so as to increase the burden upon it.[362] The servient owner can maintain and repair the way if he chooses. The common law "has contemplated with equanimity the prospect that both the servient owner and the dominant owner have the right of repair".[363]

1–92   The dominant owner, having a right to enter and repair, is entitled to prevent anything being done which substantially interferes with the exercise of that right. Thus in *Goodhart v Hyett*[364] the owner of a pipe easement in another's land, and in *Abingdon Corporation v James*[365] a local authority with a statutory duty to maintain a pipe, laid and owned by it, obtained in the one case an injunction restraining the erection of a proposed building, and in the other a mandatory order for the removal of an existing building, over the line of the pipe. The limit up to which interference remains not actionable, that is whether the exercise of the right must be made practically impossible,[366] or merely substantially more difficult, has not been precisely determined.[367] In *Goodhart v Hyett*[368] North J. said: "the question is not whether [repair] can be done as a matter of engineering skill, but whether practically the plaintiffs will have the same opportunity of enjoying the right as before", but the proposed building in that case would clearly have made access for repair underneath it practically impossible.

In *Prospect County Council v Cross*[369] an electricity authority sought an injunction to prevent interference with an easement for power lines. The interference in question was the erecting of swimming pools and other obstructions underneath the power lines which prevented engineers obtaining access to repair the lines. It was held that this was an actionable interference.

Perlman v Rayden[370] concerned an express grant of a right of access onto the servient tenement to repair the dominant tenement. The servient owner intended to build on the servient tenement in a way which would reduce the area available to the dominant owner in the exercise of the right. It was held that the servient owner had to leave enough land available to the dominant owner as was needed to exercise the right in a convenient and efficient way with space for the storage and preparation of materials and a convenient, rather than a minimal area, in which contractors could actually carry out the intended works of repair.

---

[362] *Mills v Silver* [1991] Ch. 271 at 286H–287C; and see *Alvis v Harrison* (1990) 62 P. & C.R. 10 at 15, HL (a Scottish case).
[363] *Carter v Cole* [2006] EWCA Civ 398.
[364] (1883) 25 Ch. D. 182.
[365] [1940] Ch. 287, followed in *Rickmansworth Water Co v J. W. Ward & Son Ltd* [1990] E.G.C.S. 91, where a mandatory injunction requiring the removal of a building was also granted.
[366] cf. *Mayor of Birkenhead v London and North Western Ry* (1885) 15 Q.B.D. 572 at 580.
[367] *Abingdon Corp v James* [1940] Ch. 287.
[368] (1883) 25 Ch. D. 187. And see *Metropolitan Water Board v L.N.E. Ry* (1924) 131 L.T. 123.
[369] (1990) 21 N.S.W.L.R. 601.
[370] [2004] EWHC 2192 (Ch) at [55]–[61].

Obligation to repair—dominant owner

Generally speaking, a dominant owner is not bound to keep the subject of his **1–93** easement in repair. In *Taylor v Whitehead*[371] where the owner of a right of way unsuccessfully asserted a right to deviate on the way becoming flooded, Lord Mansfield said[372] that by common law he who has the use of a thing ought to repair it; but this means that the servient owner is not bound to repair,[373] and if the dominant owner wants the way repaired he must repair it himself.[374]

Nevertheless, a dominant owner, though not compellable to repair, may be practically obliged to do so in order to avoid committing a trespass or nuisance. In *Ingram v Morecraft*[375] Sir John Romilly M.R. said *obiter*: "If I grant a man a right to lay pipes over my land, it follows that he must keep them watertight, for otherwise the escape of water is a trespass." This situation[376] was explained by Parker J.[377] as follows:

> ". . . there is undoubtedly a class of cases in which the nature of the easement is such that the owner of the dominant tenement not only has the right to repair the subject of the easement, but may be liable to the owner of the servient tenement for damages due to any want of repair. Thus, if the easement be to take water in pipes across another man's land and pipes are laid by the owner of the dominant tenement and fall into disrepair, so that water escapes on to the servient tenement, the owner of the dominant tenement will be liable for damage done by such water. Strictly speaking, I do not think that even in this case the dominant owner can be said to be under any duty to repair. I think the true position is that he cannot, under the circumstances mentioned, plead the easement as justifying what would otherwise be a trespass, because the easement is not, in fact, being fairly or properly exercised."

The fact that the pipe also serves the servient tenement, and that it is open to the servient owner to repair, does not, it seems, make any difference.[378]

---

[371] (1781) 2 Doug. K.B. 745.

[372] (1781) 2 Doug. K.B. 745, at 749.

[373] *Jones v Pritchard* [1908] 1 Ch. 630 at 638, per Parker J. *Duke of Westminster v Guild* [1985] Q.B. 688 at 700F.

[374] *Duncan v Louch* (1845) 6 Q.B. 904 at 909, 910, per Coleridge J; *Carter v Cole* [2006] EWCA Civ 398.

[375] (1863) 33 Beav. 49 at 51, 52. This was directed to the point that it is for the grantee of a right of way, and not the grantor, to do what is necessary to make the right available. The defendant had granted to the plaintiff the right to use a way, not yet made up and crossed at one point by a fence. The plaintiff having knocked down the fence in order to pass, and the defendant having put it up again, an injunction restraining this alleged obstruction was refused. The Master of the Rolls was not satisfied that the defendant was not entitled to have the fence, provided it did not prevent the use of the way. The real question, he said, was, to make a gate in the fence, and his impression was that it was for the plaintiff to do this, but the question who was to be at the expense of £1 for a gate was not, he thought, a fit subject for a Chancery suit.

[376] See also *Abingdon Corp v James* [1940] Ch. 287 at 295 and *Duke of Westminster v Guild* [1985] 1 Q.B. 688 at 703A.

[377] *Jones v Pritchard* [1908] 1 Ch. 638.

[378] *Buckley (R.H.) & Sons Ltd v Buckley (N.) & Sons* [1898] 2 Q.B. 608.

1–94   If the dominant owner does repairs to the subject-matter of the easement, there will generally be no right to a contribution from the servient owner to the costs incurred, in the absence of an express agreement to that effect.[379] The same rule applies where the servient owner does repairs to the subject-matter of the easement. It is a common practice to grant a right of way to a purchaser "the purchaser and his successors in title contributing" some proportion of the cost of keeping the way in repair. There is a curious dearth of authority as to the effect of such a provision. It seems reasonable to suppose that the dominant owner for the time being could be restrained from using the way while the stipulated obligation remained unperformed; but whether the right determines on default once occurring, or is merely suspended until the default is made good, is not established.[380] Depending upon the precise way in which the provision is expressed, it may create an obligation by way of covenant,[381] and, as such, it could be enforced against the original grantee of the easement by the servient owner for the time being,[382] but not (if the easement were perpetual) against a successor of the original grantee. A successor in title of the original grantee could, however, it seems, be held liable to make the prescribed contribution under the principle *qui sentit commodum sentire debet et onus*, i.e he who takes the benefit must also take the burden.[383]

There are however, limits to this principle. As Lord Templeman said in *Rhone v Stephens*[384]:

> "Conditions can be attached to the exercise of a power in express terms or by implication. . . . It does not follow that any condition can be rendered enforceable by attaching to it a right nor does it follow that every burden imposed by a conveyance may be enforced by depriving the covenantor's successor in title of every benefit which he enjoyed thereunder. The condition must be relevant to the exercise of the right."

So the mere fact that the grant of an easement is expressed to be "subject to" another provision does not mean that the right to enjoy the easement is conditional on compliance, in particular where the obligation in question is personal.[385]

---

[379] *Konstantinidis v Townsend* [2003] EWCA Civ 537; *Carter v Cole* [2006] EWCA Civ 398 at [8] proposition no. (6).

[380] See *Duncan v Louch* (1845) 6 Q.B. 904, *per curiam*.

[381] See the discussion in *Westacott v Hahn* [1918] 1 K.B. 495 and *Brookes v Drysdale* (1877) 3 C.P.D. 52. In *IDC Group Ltd v Clark* [1992] 1 E.G.L.R. 187, it was suggested that with the principle of "he who takes the benefit must also take the burden", the way in which the obligation is enforced was not by action but by withholding the benefit until the burden was discharged: see at p. 190F. This topic was not considered by the Court of Appeal on an appeal in that case: (1992) 65 P. & C.R. 179.

[382] *cf. Smith and Snipes Hall Farm Ltd v River Douglas Catchment Board* [1949] 2 K.B. 500.

[383] *cf. Aspden v Seddon* (1876) 1 Ex D. 496; *Westhoughton U.D.C. v Wigan Coal & Iron Co* [1919] 1 Ch. 159 at 171, establishing that any person having a right to let down the surface subject to making compensation for damage must, if he exercises the right, pay the compensation; *Halsall v Brizell* [1957] Ch. 169; "wholeheartedly" approved by the House of Lords in *Rhone v Stephens* [1994] 2 A.C. 310. The subject of "benefit and burden" is considered in great detail in *Tito v Waddell (No. 2)* [1977] Ch. 106 at pp. 289–311. See also *Four Oaks Estate Ltd v Hadley* (1986) 83 L.S.Gaz. 2326 and *Parkinson v Reid* (1966) 56 D.L.R. (2d) 315 at 319–320.

[384] [1994] 2 A.C. 310 at 322F.

[385] *Allied London Industrial Properties Ltd v Castleguard Properties Ltd* (1997) 74 P. & C.R. D43, CA.

It is now settled that there are two requirements for the enforceability of a positive covenant against a successor in title to the covenantor under this doctrine: first, the condition of discharging the burden must be relevant to the exercise of the rights that enable the benefit to be obtained; secondly, the successor must have the opportunity to choose whether to take or renounce the benefit and thereby escape the burden. So a successor does not have to contribute to the cost of a facility which he is either not entitled to or chooses not to enjoy.[386]

If such a provision were contained in a grant of an easement for a term of years, its benefit and burden would run, no doubt, in accordance with the rules applicable to covenants in leases. In such cases the grantor is considered to have the reversion to the easement which he created *de novo* himself.[387]

In *Carter v Cole*[388] the grant of the right of way was expressed to be conditional upon the grantee contributing 80 per cent of the cost of maintenance and upkeep of the way to the grantor within 28 days of being requested to do so. The condition did not apply in the case of a reasonable dispute as to costs or the need for, or the quality of, maintenance. It was held that if the grantee did not pay within 28 days of being requested to do so, then subject to the reasonable dispute provision, the grantee could not use the way. It was further held that the grantor was not entitled to demand a contribution based upon an estimate of the costs to be incurred on the works but was only entitled to be paid when a sum due in respect of the works had become payable by the grantor.

Obligation to repair–servient owner

Apart from statute[389] or any special local custom or express contract, the owner of a   **1–95** servient tenement is not ordinarily bound to execute any repairs necessary to ensure the enjoyment of the easement by the owner of the dominant tenement.[390] The grantor of a way over a bridge is not by common law liable, nor does he impliedly

---

[386] *Thamesmead Town Limited v Allotey* [1998] 3 E.G.L.R. 97, applying *Rhone v Stephens* [1994] 2 A.C. 310.

[387] *Martyn v Williams* (1857) 1 H. & N. 817, where, a right (*profit à prendre*) to get china clay in certain land having been granted to the defendant for a term of years, a successor in title to the land successfully enforced a covenant by the defendant to deliver up works in repair. And see *Grant v Edmondson* [1931] 1 Ch. 1 at 33. A converse case (assignee of the right held liable) is *Norval v Pascoe* (1864) 34 L.J. Ch. 82. *Martyn v Williams* (1857) 1 H. & N. 817 was applied in *Nevill Long & Co (Boards) Ltd v Firmenich & Co* (1984) 47 P. & C.R. 59 which was followed in *Cardwell v Walker* [2004] 2 P. & C.R. 122, discussed at para.1–98, below.

[388] [2006] EWCA Civ 398.

[389] *cf.* the Railways Clauses Consolidation Act 1845. See *British Railways Board v Glass* [1965] Ch. 538; *Greenhalgh v British Railways Board* [1974] 1 W.L.R. 781; *Sampson Associates Ltd v British Railways Board* [1983] 1 All E.R. 257; *Walton & Son v British Railways Board* [1984] 2 All E.R. 249.

[390] "An easement requires no more than sufferance on the part of the occupier of the servient tenement": *Jones v Price* [1965] 2 Q.B. 618 at 631, per Willmer L.J. *Duke of Westminster v Guild* [1985] 1 Q.B. 688 at 700F.

contract, to keep the bridge in repair for the convenience of the grantee.[391] If the servient owner does carry out repairs, then he is generally not entitled to a contribution from the dominant owner to the costs incurred, in the absence of an agreement to that effect. If, however, there is disturbance of the easement on the part of the servient owner, he may incur an obligation to repair. In *Saint v Jenner*[392] the defendants, in order to slow down traffic using a metalled lane running across their land over which the plaintiffs had a right of way, caused to be constructed a series of ramps. These did not at first amount to a disturbance, but later the surface of the lane deteriorated and pot-holes, which appeared at the ends of the ramps, caused a substantial interference. The defendants gave undertakings to repair and maintain the lane's surface, but the question arose whether, if a successor in title of the servient tenement failed to maintain the lane's surface and did not remove the ramps, he would be liable to the owners of the dominant tenement for disturbance of the easement. The Court of Appeal, applying *Sedleigh-Denfield v O'Callaghan*,[393] found that he would be so liable, as he would be adopting a nuisance. In effect, therefore, if he retained the ramps, he would be bound to repair. Moreover, an owner of a house which allows it to fall into disrepair so that damage is occasioned to an adjoining house enjoying a right of support, may be liable to the adjoining owner.[394]

1–96   A lessor who lets part of a building with a right to use a staircase, or other common part, retained by himself is under an obligation to the tenant to take reasonable care to keep the staircase in a reasonably safe condition.[395] Whether this obligation rests on implied contract or arises at common law is not entirely clear,[396] but it is thought that the duty, however arising, is owed to the tenant as tenant of the demised premises rather than as a dominant owner.[397]

---

[391] Parker J., *Jones v Pritchard* [1908] 1 Ch. 630 at 637; and see *Taylor v Whitehead* (1781) 2 Doug. K.B. 745, 749; *Colebeck v Girdlers Co* (1876) 1 Q.B.D. 234, 243; *Bond v Nottingham Corp* [1940] Ch. 429 at 438; *Urich v Local Health Authorities for St Andrew-St David* (1964) 7 W.L.R. 482; *Kelfy v Dea* (1965) 100 I.L.T.R. 1; *Parkinson v Reid* (1966) 56 D.L.R. (2d) 315, 319; *Stokes v Mixconcrete (Holdings) Ltd* (1978) 38 P. & C.R. 488; *Carter v Cole* [2006] EWCA Civ 398. It was said by Mr Serjeant Williams in the note to *Pomfret v Ricroft* (1669) 1 Wms. Saunders, 6th ed., 321, 322a, that "the grantor of a right of way may be bound either by express stipulation or prescription to repair it", and he cites *Rider v Smith* (1790) 3 Term Rep. 766 in which, on demurrer in an action against the owner of a close for not keeping in repair a footway running across it, the Court held that a declaration alleging that by reason of his possession the defendant ought to repair was good, and that the special matter of the objection might be given in evidence, thus recognising, at all events, the possibility of such an obligation being established. However, this possibility appears to be ruled out by the later decisions.

[392] [1973] Ch. 275, CA; applied by analogy in *Cardwell v Walker* [2004] 2 P. & C.R. 122.

[393] [1940] A.C. 880, HL.

[394] *Bradburn v Lindsay* [1983] 2 All E.R. 408 (in negligence or nuisance); *Holbeck Hall Hotel Ltd v Scarborough Borough Council* [2000] Q.B. 836 and *Rees v Skerrett* [2001] 1 W.L.R. 1541. These cases are discussed in detail at paras 10–35 to 10–38, below.

[395] *Dunster v Hollis* [1918] 2 K.B. 795; *Liverpool City Council v Irwin* [1977] A.C. 239 (stairs, lifts and rubbish chutes).

[396] *Cockburn v Smith* [1924] 2 K.B. 119 and *Hargroves, Aronson & Co v Hartopp* [1905] 1 K.B. 472, distinguished in *Duke of Westminster v Guild* [1985] 1 Q.B. 688 at 702, where a distinction is drawn between cases where there is an escape from the landlord's premises and where the tenant's right is merely obstructed.

[397] As to the statutory liability under the Occupier's Liability Act 1957 and the Occupiers' Liability Act 1984, see paras 1–99 *et seq.*, below.

It seems clear on principle[398] that if a servient owner covenants to keep in repair **1–97** the subject of a perpetual easement, the covenant, being a positive covenant, cannot be enforced against a successor in title. The devolution of the benefit of such a covenant was considered in *Gaw v Coras Iompair Eireann*.[399] There a railway company, more than a hundred years ago, in making the Dublin-Wicklow line along the seashore, had acquired a strip of land from A, who owned a house on the top of a cliff and land, including the strip, extending down the cliff to the sea, and had granted to A a right of way over this strip, which it covenanted to keep in repair. The plaintiff, on whom the house, land and right of way had devolved without any express assignment of the benefit of the covenant, successfully enforced this against the defendant, who had succeeded by statute to the obligations of the original railway company, and was thus practically in the position of an original covenantor. Dixon J. decided two things: first that the covenant did not touch and concern the house and land so as to run with them,[400] but ran, if at all, with the easement; and, secondly, that there is no clear authority that the benefit of a covenant cannot run with an incorporeal hereditament in the same manner as a corporeal one; furthermore, that the old case of *Holmes v Buckley*,[401] properly understood, is some authority that it can; and that the covenant touched and concerned, and therefore its benefit ran with, the right of way. The learned judge made a careful and informative review of the authorities, and concluded that *Milnes v Branch*[402] did not decide that the benefit of a covenant to pay a rentcharge does not run with the rentcharge, and did not prevent him from deciding that the benefit of a covenant to repair the subject of an easement can run with the easement.

Unfortunately the case of *Grant v Edmondson*,[403] in which the English Court of Appeal followed *Milnes v Branch*,[404] and decided the very point that Dixon J. thought was not decided there, was not cited, and this omission deprives the conclusion of Dixon J. of most of its authority. There has been much learned discussion[405] as to whether an easement, incapable as it is, or was, of descending independently of the land to which it is appurtenant, can properly be described, as a rentcharge can, as an incorporeal hereditament; and even if it can, a decision

---

[398] *Austerberry v Oldham Corp* (1885) 29 Ch. D. 750 approved in *Rhone v Stephens* [1994] 2 W.L.R. 429; *E. & G.C. Ltd v Bate* (1935) 79 L. Journal 203; and see *Morris v Cartwright* (1963) 107 S.J. 553; *Parkinson v Reid* (1966) 56 D.L.R. (2d) 315.

[399] [1953] I.R. 232.

[400] Depending upon the facts of the case, it may be possible to argue in another case that the benefit of the covenant does touch and concern and therefore run with the dominant tenement.

[401] (1691) Prec. in Chanc. 39; doubted in *Austerberry v Oldham Corp* (1885) 29 Ch. D. 750. In this case a covenant, by a grantor of a watercourse, to clean it was enforced by an assignee of the watercourse against an assignee of the land through which it ran. The explanation, so far as the benefit of the covenant is concerned, may be that the watercourse served adjoining land of the covenantee, and the benefit of the covenant ran with that land (per Cotton L.J. at 777), but "the case is too loosely reported to be a guide on the point" (per Lindley L.J., at 782).

[402] (1816) 5 M. & S. 411.

[403] [1931] 1 Ch. 1.

[404] (1816) 5 M. & S. 411.

[405] See, e.g. *Challis' Real Property* (3rd ed.), p. 55; *Brotherton's Estate, Re* (1907) 77 L.J. Ch. 58.

on a covenant to pay a rentcharge, or to build for the better security of a rentcharge, does not necessarily apply to a covenant to repair the subject of an easement,[406] but, however that may be, the decision in *Gaw's* case[407] cannot be regarded as authoritative, and *Holmes v Buckley*,[408] which appears to be the only other reported case on the same point, is of doubtful authority also. *Gaw's* case was cited with apparent approval by Lord Oliver in *Swift Investments v Combined English Stores Group* where he said: "Certainly it appears that some incorporeal hereditaments (for instance an easement) rank as 'land' for this purpose: see *Gaw v Coras Iompair Eireann*.[409] Further, the proposition that the rules about the benefit of a covenant touching and concerning land are satisfied where the benefit of the covenant touches and concerns an easement is supported by the reasoning in *Cardwell v Walker*.[410]

1–98   The burden and benefit of a covenant entered into by the grantor of an easement for a term of years devolves, no doubt, in accordance with the rules applicable as between landlord and tenant.[411] In *Cardwell v Walker*, a landowner granted a lease of a residential property and granted the lessee an easement entitling the lessee to take a supply of electricity across adjoining land owned by the lessor. By a subsequent arrangement, the lessor and the lessee agreed that the supply of electricity should be through a meter operated by tokens and the lessor agreed to make such tokens available to the lessee. Subsequently still the lessor sold the reversion on the lease of the residential property to one purchaser and the ownership of the adjoining land to another purchaser, the defendant. The defendant discontinued the supply of tokens and argued that as a successor in title he was not bound by his predecessor's obligation to supply tokens. The defendant was held, on various grounds, to be liable to provide tokens to the lessee. One of the grounds was that the defendant was bound by the obligation if there was privity of estate between himself and the lessee and if the obligation to supply tokens touched and concerned the easement under which the lessee was entitled to take a supply of electricity. It was held that the defendant had a reversion on the lease as the easement granted to the lessee bound the defendant's land.[412] Further, the easement was "land" for the purposes of the principle that the benefit of the covenant had to touch and concern "land". Further, on the facts the benefit of the covenant did touch and concern the easement. The result was that the defendant was bound by the obligation to provide tokens.

---

[406] As pointed out by Romer L.J. in *Grant v Edmondson* [1931] 1 Ch. 1 at 28, 29, it is impossible to reason on these questions by analogy. "Apart from decisive authority one way or another, it seems to me that it is impossible to answer the question whether a covenant to pay runs with a rentcharge one way or the other. The question 'Why should it?' cannot be answered by reference to principles with any greater conviction than can the question 'Why should it not?' "

[407] [1953] I.R. 232.

[408] (1691) Prec. in Chanc. 39.

[409] [1989] A.C. 632 at 640. Consider also s.78 of the Law of Property Act 1925 which refers to "a covenant relating to any land of the covenantee" and s.205(1) which defines "land" so as to include an easement, and see *Cardwell v Walker* [2004] 2 P. & C.R. 122 at [45].

[410] [2004] 2 P. & C.R. 122 at [45]; see at para.1–98, below.

[411] See above.

[412] Applying *Nevill Long & Co (Boards) Ltd v Firmenich & Co* (1984) 47 P. & C.R. 59.

Occupier's liability

In the absence of contract the owner of the servient tenement had no duty at common law towards persons coming on to it to keep it safe. The position under the Occupiers' Liability Act 1957 was considered in *Greenhalgh v British Railways Board*.[413] In that case, Lord Denning M.R. (with whom Davies and Widgery L.JJ. agreed) said that a person using a public or a private right of way was not a "visitor" to whom the occupier of the servient tenement owed the "common duty of care" under section 2(1) of the Occupiers' Liability Act 1957 because at common law such a person was never regarded as an invitee or licensee or treated as such. The case was concerned with a public right of way so that, strictly speaking, Lord Denning's reference to a private right of way was *obiter*, but in *Holden v White*,[414] in which the plaintiff sought against the servient owner damages for injuries sustained when he trod on a defective manhole cover in a private right of way, the Court of Appeal (reversing the decision of Stocker J.) applied *Greenhalgh v British Railways Board*[415] and held that the owner of land over which there was a right of way owed no duty at common law to those using the right of way, and that the Occupiers' Liability Act 1957 did not extend the common law duties of an occupier, so that the servient owner's liability was restricted to her visitors: the plaintiff was not her visitor, so his claim failed.

Oliver L.J. (with whom Ormrod L.J. and Wood J. agreed) said[416]:

> "It was well established that, in the absence of contract, the servient owner had no duty at all to the dominant owner himself to keep the way in repair, and it is difficult to see any logical reason why he should have been burdened with a duty to the licensees or invitees of the dominant owner. The owner of the servient tenement is simply a person who takes his land subject to an incumbrance which he can do nothing to avoid. No doubt he owes the ordinary duty of an occupier to persons whom, either expressly or impliedly, he invites onto his land or to whom he can be said to have granted permissive entry. But it is entirely unreal to regard him as having in any sense issued any invitation or permission to persons who enter the land in exercise of the dominant owner's rights. That would, I think, be so even in the case of the original grantor, but it is a fortiori the case where, as here, the owner of the servient tenement acquired the land already burdened with the easement, for at no time does he have any choice about whether to admit the invitees or licensees of the dominant owner nor does he have any control over the activities of such persons so long as they do no more than exercise the right conferred on their invitor or licensor by virtue of his estate in the land."

1–99

---

[413] [1969] 2 Q.B. 286 at 293. The Court of Appeal applied the dictum of Willis J. in *Gautret v Egerton* (1867) L.R. 2 C.P. 371 at 373.

[414] [1982] Q.B. 679. Followed in *Clutterham v Anglian Water Authority, The Times*, August 14, 1986 (which left open whether the servient owner was liable for positive misfeasance which left the way dangerous).

[415] [1969] 2 Q.B. 286.

[416] [1982] Q.B. 683.

1–100   These authorities were approved and applied by the House of Lords in *McGeown v Northern Ireland Housing Executive*[417] (in the context of a public right of way). Lord Keith said[418]:

> "These authorities . . . are sufficient to show that the rule in Gautret v. Egerton is deeply entrenched in the law. Further, the rule is in my opinion undoubtedly a sound and reasonable one. Rights of way pass over many different types of terrain, and it would place an impossible burden upon landowners if they not only had to submit to the passage over them of any one who might choose to exercise them but also were under a duty to maintain them in a safe condition. Persons using rights of way do so not with the permission of the owner of the solum but in the exercise of a right. There is no room for the view that such persons might have been licensees or invitees of the landowner under the old law or that they are his visitors under the English and Northern Irish Acts of 1957. There may indeed be a question whether the owner of the solum is occupier of the right of way for the purposes of these Acts. Doubts about that were expressed in Holden v. White but it is unnecessary for present purposes to decide it."

1–101   There are two important qualifications which emerge from that decision and which ought to be stressed. First, the mere granting of a right of way to the dominant owner does not of itself exculpate the grantor from liability to a person using the way. That person may well be an implied licensee or invitee of the grantor. As Lord Browne-Wilkinson pointed out[419]:

> "A landowner who for purposes which benefit him licenses or invites people to use a means of access comes under a duty of care to them. The lowest level of such case is that illustrated by the present case and by the Fairman and Jacobs cases. The owner of tenanted premises lays out access routes to the flats or shops which he lets: the users of such access are his licensees. The next level is illustrated by Brackley v. Midland Railway. The occupier of the land (i.e. the footbridge) encourages his own customers to use the way as part of the facilities provided for his customers. Until the way becomes a public right of way, customers using it are his invitees. The highest level is illustrated by the modern shopping centre or shopping mall. The owner lays out the ground floor (and frequently upper floors) as a large open space, furnished with amenities (benches, fountains, flowerbeds, etc.) specifically designed to attract people to the centre where they will shop. The more people attracted, the greater the profitability of the development and the higher the rent payable by tenants of the shops. Such open spaces are the means whereby the public gain access to the shops. In my judgment, people using such areas would be his invitees."

---

[417] [1995] 1 A.C. 233.
[418] [1995] 1 A.C. 233, at 243E.
[419] [1995] 1 A.C. 233, at 247C.

Secondly, the House of Lords left open the question whether the owner of the **1–102** solum is an "occupier" of the right of way for the purposes of the Occupiers' Liability Acts, a point which had been discussed in *Holden v White*. This question is critical because section 1 of the Occupiers' Liability Act 1984 provides that the occupier of land owes the common duty of care "to persons other than his visitors" in certain circumstances. These are that:

(a) he is aware of the danger or has reasonable grounds to believe that it exists;
(b) he knows or has reasonable grounds to believe that the other person is in the vicinity of the danger; and
(c) the risk is one against which, in all the circumstances of the case, he may reasonably be expected to offer the other some protection.

Where these conditions are satisfied, therefore, it will not be enough to rely on the principle that the user of the way is not a "visitor", but it becomes necessary to inquire whether the servient owner is an "occupier".

Whether a person is an "occupier" for the purposes of the Acts is to be deter- **1–103** mined in accordance with the common law.[420] The test as explained by Lord Denning in *Wheat v Lacon*[421] is as follows:

". . . wherever a person has a sufficient degree of control over premises that he ought to realise that any failure on his part to use care may result in injury to a person coming lawfully there, then he is an occupier . . . If a person has any degree of control over the state of premises it is enough."

In *Holden v White*[422] the servient owner conceded that she was the "occupier" for **1–104** the purposes of the Occupiers' Liability Act 1957, but Wood J. said[423] that he was far from satisfied that for the purposes of section 1 of that Act the servient owner was the occupier vis-à-vis the plaintiff, and Oliver and Ormrod L.JJ. seem to have had doubts on this point. Oliver L.J. said[424] that it seemed that Stocker J. had treated ownership as equivalent to occupation, and added that whether that was strictly correct need not be further considered because of the concession which had been made. Ormrod L.J. said[425] that whether the easement owner was to be regarded as the "occupier" was a point which might have to be decided in a later case.

Oliver L.J. referred to the fact that Stocker J. was clearly influenced by the thought that, if there was no duty owed by the servient owner, there was no duty owed by anybody, and said[426]:

---

[420] Occupiers' Liability Act 1984, s.1.
[421] [1966] A.C. 552 at 578C and at 579A.
[422] [1982] Q.B. 679.
[423] [1982] Q.B. 679, at 687.
[424] [1982] Q.B. 679, at 683.
[425] [1982] Q.B. 679, at 687.
[426] [1982] Q.B. 679, at 686.

"It is unnecessary for the purposes of the present appeal to decide the point, but I am not, speaking entirely for myself, convinced that this assumption is right. There is no statutory definition of an 'occupier' and in Wheat v. E. Lacon & Co. Ltd[427] Lord Denning M.R. favoured a definition which would include having any degree of control over the state of the premises. In the instant case, for example, the manhole cover set in the path prima facie would appear to have been put there for the benefit of, and presumably maintained by the [dominant owners] and, without expressing any concluded view on the point, it may well be that those owners, whose visitor the plaintiff was, had a sufficient degree of control to render them occupiers for the purposes of the Act of 1957."

1-105   It was suggested in the 15th edition of this work that *Holden v White* at least suggests that there is very great doubt whether a servient owner, having regard to his lack of control over the exercise of rights over the servient tenement, can be the occupier thereof vis-à-vis the person exercising those rights and the view was therefore expressed that he was not, as such servient owner, an "occupier of premises" within section 1 of the Occupiers' Liability Act 1984 and not, therefore, affected by the extension of an occupiers' liability imposed by that Act. The present editors do not agree that the owner of the solum can never be liable qua servient owner.[428] It is submitted that whether he is to be regarded as an "occupier" must depend in each case on what degree of control he has over the state of the premises and, in particular, of the feature causing the damage or injury. His degree of control over the exercise of rights over the servient tenement and his relationship to persons exercising those rights, though material to the question whether they are his visitors, would not appear to be material to the question whether he is an "occupier". If, as Oliver L.J. suggests in the passage cited above, the dominant owner may have a sufficient degree of control to make him an "occupier",[429] the same may be equally true of the servient owner. In practice, it may well be that, where the feature causing the damage was installed for the benefit of/maintained by the dominant owner, the conditions for liability under the 1984 Act would be unlikely to be met in the case of the servient owner.

"Rent" for easements

1-106   Rent, properly so called, cannot be reserved on the grant of an easement.[430] The enforceability of a covenant by a dominant owner to make some payment for the

---

[427] [1966] A.C. 552 at 579.

[428] In this we would appear to be in agreement with the editors of Clerk & Lindsell, *The Law of Torts* (19th ed.), para.12–79. This passage in the text of *Gale* was approved by Toulson J. in *Vodden v Gayton* [2001] P.I.Q.R. P52 at [62].

[429] For an example of a person who undertook the repair of the feature in question being held liable as an "occupier", though not the owner, see *Collier v Anglian Water Authority, The Times*, March 26, 1983 (water authority maintaining promenade along top of sea wall).

[430] Co.Litt. 47a; *Capel v Buszard* (1829) 6 Bing. 150 (affirming (1828) 8 B. & C. 141), where a distress on barges lying on land between high- and low-water in the Thames, of which land the plaintiffs were found by special verdict to have "the exclusive use" (which was treated for the present purpose as an easement and not as a demise of the land itself) was held bad.

use of the easement against a successor in title of the covenantor must depend on the same considerations as a covenant by him to repair.[431] In *Lord Hastings v North Eastern Railway*[432] the owner of land demised to a railway company a wayleave or right to make and use a railway over the land, reserving to himself, his heirs and assigns, a periodical payment calculated on the tonnage of coal, etc., carried to a certain port over any part of the railways comprised in the company's special Act. The right to recover the payments was held to have devolved on a successor in title to the land, as the owner of the reversion to the right, but this right cannot have been an easement, for there was no dominant tenement. In *Rance v Elvin*[433] Nicholls J. held that a water supply paid for by the servient owner, but towards the costs of which the dominant owner was prepared to contribute, was incapable of being an easement and thereby passing on conveyance. This was because, save in the anomalous case of an easement of fencing,[434] a right in the nature of an easement can only impose negative obligations on the servient owner. In the Court of Appeal, however, his decision was reversed and Browne-Wilkinson L.J. distinguished a right to a supply of water and a right to the passage of water. In this instance there was an easement of passage for water in the pipe. There was no obligation to supply water to the pipes but if water was so supplied there would be a remedy in quasi-contract for reimbursement of expenditure incurred on supplying water impliedly on request. The same analysis was applied to a right to the passage of electricity and said to apply to all utilities in *Duffy v Lamb*.[435]

Easements and the rule against perpetuities

The rule against perpetuities in relation to the creation of easements was examined by Cross J. in *Dunn v Blackdown Properties Ltd*.[436] In that case two plots of land were, by two conveyances dated respectively December 17, 1926, and January 11, 1938, conveyed to the plaintiff's predecessors in title, together with the right for the grantees, their heirs and assigns to use the sewers and drains "now passing or hereafter to pass" under a private road on which the plots abutted and belonging to the defendant's predecessors in title. At some date after January 11, 1938, the defendant's predecessors in title constructed a surface water sewer along the road and a soil sewer which passed from their land lying north of the road, ran under the road for some distance, and turned on to other land belonging to them. The two plots together with the foregoing right were conveyed to the plaintiff on September 20, 1945. The plaintiff claimed a declaration that she was entitled to the right to use the sewers and drains then passing or thereafter to pass under the road in connection with the two plots, and Cross J. held that, since no

1–107

---

[431] See paras 1–93 *et seq.*, above.
[432] [1898] 2 Ch. 674; affirmed [1899] 1 Ch. 656; [1900] A.C. 260.
[433] (1985) 50 P. & C.R. 9, CA.
[434] See paras 1–78 *et seq.*, above.
[435] (1997) 75 P. & C.R. 364.
[436] [1961] Ch. 433. This decision is discussed in an article by Battersby, "Easements and the Rule against Perpetuities," in 25 Conv. (n.s.) 415.

sewers or drains were in existence at the date of the conveyance to the plaintiff's predecessors in title, the grant of the right to use the sewers and drains "hereafter to pass" was a grant of an easement to arise at an uncertain date in the future not limited to take effect within the perpetuity period and was, therefore, void.

1–108   Cross J. said[437] that, subject to the operation of section 162 of the Law of Property Act 1925 (which contains restrictions on the rule), there was no doubt that the rule applied to grants of easements. It followed that, where the grant was not immediate but was of an easement to arise in the future, it would be void unless it were limited to take effect only within the perpetuity period. It seems clear, however, that the "wait and see" rule introduced by section 3 of the Perpetuities and Accumulations Act 1964 might save a grant made on or after the date of commencement of that Act (July 16, 1964: see s.15(5)) and not expressly confined within the perpetuity period.[438]

1–109   Cross J. continued by saying that it was not always easy to decide whether the grant in question was of an immediate right or of a right to arise in the future. He illustrated the difficulty by comparing *South Eastern Railway Co v Associated Portland Cement Manufacturers (1900) Ltd*[439] with *Sharpe v Durrant*.[440]

In *S.E. Railway Co v Associated Portland Cement Manufacturers (1900) Ltd*[441] an agreement under hand between the plaintiff's agent and A, a landowner, and made in contemplation of the acquisition by the plaintiff of a strip of land for a railway, provided that A, his heirs and assigns, should have the right to make a tunnel under the proposed railway, and this was followed by a grant of the strip which reserved a like right. An action by the plaintiff to restrain the assignees of the lessees of the devisee of the grantor from doing so was dismissed by Swinfen Eady J. who, treating the right reserved as an easement, held that this was an immediate right, and that there was no question as to the validity of a grant *in futuro*. An appeal was dismissed on the ground that the agreement was a personal contract which the defendant company, which held under a lease containing an assignment of the benefit of the agreement, was entitled to enforce.

The Court of Appeal did not express any view on the question whether the reservation was of an immediate or a future easement.

1–110   In *Sharpe v Durrant*[442] a conveyance of a strip of land for a tramway contained a reservation to the vendors of the right of passing over the tramway by crossings to be made by the purchaser, who covenanted to make crossings as, and at any two places that, the vendors should require. One crossing-place was selected, but it was held by Warrington J. that the reservation was void for remoteness, for until the selection was made there was no easement. His Lordship also held that the personal covenant to make crossings, involving as it did an obligation not to interfere with the passage across, was, although "a personal agreement not creating any

[437] [1961] Ch. 438.
[438] See *Adam v Shrewsbury* [2006] 1 P. & C.R. 474, in particular at [43].
[439] [1910] 1 Ch. 12.
[440] (1911) 55 S.J. 423; [1911] W.N. 158, CA.
[441] [1910] 1 Ch. 12.
[442] (1911) 55 S.J. 423; [1911] W.N. 158, CA.

interest in land", a negative covenant which the defendants could enforce against the plaintiff who had acquired the tramway, with notice, after the selection of the crossing-place; consequently there was a declaration that the defendants were entitled to a right of way over the crossings. An appeal was dismissed, but the appeal is not reported, and it is possible, of course, that the Court of Appeal differed from the opinion of Warrington J. as to the validity of the reservation.

Cross J. in *Dunn v Blackdown Properties Ltd* said[443]:   **1–111**

> "I do not find the views expressed by Swinfen Eady J. and Warrington J. as to the effect from the point of view of perpetuity of a right given to the grantee to select the site of an easement at all easy to reconcile. I do not think, however, that I am compelled to choose between them in this case. If there had been a sewer under [the defendant's road] at the dates of the grants to her predecessors in title the plaintiff could have claimed, on authority of the Associated Portland Cement case,[444] that the owners of [her land] had from the first a right exercisable at any time to make connections with and use that sewer or any sewer substituted for it, but, as there was no sewer under the road, the plaintiff must rely on the words 'or hereafter to pass'. It is not for the owners of the [plaintiff's land] to decide whether or not a sewer will or will not pass under the road in future. That is for the owner of the road to decide, and I do not see how this part of the right granted can be treated as anything but the grant of an easement to arise at an uncertain date in the future.
>
> Counsel for the plaintiff submitted that in the Associated Portland Cement case[445] the right to construct the tunnel only arose if the railway company decided to build the railway and that Swinfen Eady J. must have thought that this fact did not make the reservation bad for perpetuity. I do not so read the facts or the judgment. It is to my mind reasonably clear that the reservation in question was of an immediate right to build a tunnel exercisable as from the date of the conveyance to the railway company, whether or not a railway was built."

It was also argued for the plaintiff in *Dunn v Blackdown Properties Ltd*,[446] that,   **1–112** assuming that the grants would have been void at common law, they were saved by section 162 of the Law of Property Act 1925. That section provides:

> "(1) For removing doubts, it is hereby declared that the rule of law relating to perpetuities does not apply and shall be deemed never to have applied . . .
>
>> (d) to any grant, exception or reservation of any right of entry on, or user of, the surface of land or of any easements, rights, or privileges over or under land for the purpose of—

[443] [1961] Ch. 433 at 440.
[444] [1910] 1 Ch. 12.
[445] [1910] 1 Ch. 12.
[446] [1961] 1 Ch. 433.

> (i)   winning, working, inspecting, measuring, converting, manufac-
>   turing, carrying away, and disposing of mines and minerals;
> (ii) inspecting, grubbing up, felling and carrying away timber and
>   other trees, and the tops and lops thereof;
> (iii) executing repairs, alterations, or additions to any adjoining
>   land, or the buildings and erections thereon;
> (iv) constructing, laying down, altering, repairing, renewing, cleans-
>   ing and maintaining sewers, watercourses, cesspools, gutters,
>   drains, water-pipes, gas-pipes, electric wires or cables or other
>   like works.
>
> (2) This section applies to instruments coming into operation before or
>   after the commencement of this Act."

This argument also failed because Cross J. held[447] that on its true construction section 162(1)(d)(iv) was only intended to make it clear that if a basic right of sewage was not itself void for perpetuity an ancillary right to construct works to make the basic right effective was not to be treated as void for perpetuity because it might be exercised outside the perpetuity period.

1–113   Three further cases which illustrate the operation of the rule in regard to easements are *Smith v Colbourne*,[448] *Ardley v Guardians of the Poor of St Pancras*[449] and *Adam v Shrewsbury*.[450]

In *Smith v Colbourne*, where a purchaser objected to title on the ground that a former owner, A, had agreed with a neighbour, B, that the light to a certain window in the property was enjoyed by the revocable licence of B and his successors, and that, if the licence were revoked, A or his successors would block up the window, and, if they did not, B or his successors might do so, the Court of Appeal intimated that if the conditional right last mentioned was an easement, which they thought it was not, it was void for remoteness, the reason being, no doubt, that it would not arise until A or his successors had failed to block up after revocation of the licence, neither of which events would necessarily occur in due time, or at all.

1–114   In *Ardley v Guardians of the Poor of St Pancras*[451] an underlease of land reserved to the underlessor and his heirs a right of way over the east side of the land to the other land comprised in the lease, during such time as they should hold such other land, and, if they disposed of it, then there was reserved to the underlessor, his heirs and assigns, a right of ingress and egress over the same east part for the purpose of building or repairing on a different piece of land belonging to the underlessor in fee. The defendants, who were assignees of that other land, claimed to be entitled to the right first reserved, and contended that a right of way granted or reserved until alienation of the dominant tenement is absolute, the

---

[447] [1961] Ch. 433 at 441, 442.
[448] [1914] 2 Ch. 533; and see *Newham v Lawson* (1971) 22 P. & C.R. 852.
[449] (1870) 39 L.J. Ch. 871.
[450] [2006] 1 P. & C.R. 474, in particular at [43].
[451] (1870) 39 L.J. Ch. 871.

attempted limitation being void as a restraint on alienation. Lord Romilly M.R., after rejecting this contention and holding that the first right had ceased, added that the second right (not belonging to the defendants) still continued; that is *semble*, had begun on the cesser of the first. His Lordship said[452]:

> "I do not think there is anything illegal in a man reserving to himself and his heirs a right of way for a limited purpose, and when that purpose is accomplished to say that the right of way shall cease, reserving to himself after that a different and distinct right of way for another and separate purpose.
>
> I am of opinion, therefore, that when the houses [on the other land] were built, the right of way into [that land] ceased. The right of ingress and egress still continues for the purpose of repairing and rebuilding any of the houses [on the underlessor's own land]. That, however, is not what the defendants claim, and I am of opinion they have no right of way over the eastern portion of the [land underleased]."

The validity of the reservation of the second right was not questioned in argument, nor was it material. This case may perhaps support the view that the grant of a right for certain purpose until a certain event, and then for a different purpose, is valid if the dominant tenement is the same throughout, for such a grant might well be regarded as an immediate grant of a single but variable right.

In *Adam v Shrewsbury* one analysis of the facts was that there was an implied   **1–115**
grant of a right of way over a road as and when it was constructed. The grantor was not under an obligation to build the road and had not done so. It was held that the parties had to "wait and see" for a 21-year perpetuity period whether the road had been constructed but if at the end of that period a road had not been constructed, then the grant failed for perpetuity.

No easement on easement

A servient owner as such has no right to have an easement continued. This is par-   **1–116**
ticularly illustrated by drainage easements. If A, in order to drain his land or mines, sends water through the land of B, B can either prevent this, or, if the water is useful to him, accept the water. If A, by grant or prescription, acquires a right to send the water, B has no rights at all; he must accept the water but he cannot demand it; and a right to demand it, or to prevent A from turning it off, cannot be acquired by prescription.

So Lord Abinger C.B. in *Arkwright v Cell* said[453]:

---

[452] (1870) 39 L.J. Ch. 871, at 874.
[453] (1839) 5 M. & W. 203, 232. The effect of the final sentence ("though . . .") is not entirely clear. It was adopted by Lord Cozens-Hardy M.R., in *Schwann v Cotton* [1916] 2 Ch. 459 (see para.3–55, below), and applied to a case where water flowed through a pipe not for the purpose of draining the property in which it arose, but for supplying other property: see also per Warrington L.J. at 475. See also *Chamber Colliery Co v Hopwood* (1886) 32 Ch. D. 549 at 558; *Wood v Waud* (1849) 3 Exch. 748 at 777; *Greatrex v Hayward* (1853) 8 Exch. 291; *Burrows v Lang* [1901] 2 Ch. 502 at 509; *Bartlett v Tottenham* [1932] 1 Ch. 114 at 129; *Deed (John S.) & Sons Ltd v British Electricity Authority* (1950) 66 T.L.R. (Pt 2) 567.

"Several instances were put in the course of the argument of cases analogous to the present, in which it could not be contended, for a moment, that any right was acquired. A steam-engine is used by the owner of a mine to drain it, and the water pumped up flows in a channel to the estate of the adjoining landowner, and there is used for agricultural purposes for twenty years. Is it possible, from the fact of such a user, to presume the grant by the owner of the steam-engine of the right to the water in perpetuity, so as to burden himself and the assigns of his mine, with the obligation to keep a steam-engine for ever, for the benefit of the landowner? Or, if the water from the spout of the eaves of a row of houses were to flow into an adjoining yard, and be there used by its occupiers for twenty years for domestic purposes, could it be successfully contended that the owners of the houses had contracted an obligation, not to alter their construction so as to impair the flow of water? Clearly not. In all, the nature of the case distinctly shews that no right is acquired as against the owner of the property from which the course of water takes its origin: though, as between the first and any subsequent appropriator of the watercourse itself, such a right may be acquired."

So also Erle C.J. in *Gaved v Martyn* said[454]:

"If there is uninterrupted user of the land of the neighbour for receiving the flow as of right for twenty years, such user is evidence that the land from which the water is sent into the neighbour's land has become the dominant tenement, having a right to the easement of so sending the water, and that the neighbour's land has become subject to the easement of receiving that water. But such user of the easement of sending on the water of an artificial stream is of itself alone no evidence that the land from which the water is sent has become subject to the servitude of being bound to send on the water to the land of the neighbour below. The enjoyment of the easement is of itself no evidence that the party enjoying it has become subject to the servitude of being bound to exercise the easement for the benefit of the neighbour. A right of way is no evidence that the party entitled thereto is under a duty to walk; nor a right of eaves-dropping on the neighbour's land, that the party is bound to send on his rain-water to that land. In like manner, we consider that a party by the mere exercise of a right to make an artificial drain into his neighbour's land either from mine or surface, does not raise any presumption that he is subject to any duty to continue his artificial drain, by twenty years' user, although there might be additional circumstances by which that presumption would be raised or the right proved."

1–117   The proposition is, however, subject to the qualification that "if it be proved that the stream was originally intended to have a permanent flow, or if the party by whom or on whose behalf the artificial stream was caused to flow is shown to

[454] (1865) 19 C.B. (n.s.) 732 at 758.

have abandoned permanently without intention to resume the works by which the flow was caused, and given up all right to and control over the stream, such stream may become subject to the laws relating to natural streams".[455]

In *Mason v Shrewsbury and Hereford Railway Co*[456] a canal company acting **1–118** under statutory powers had diverted to its canal, over a period of about 60 years, most of the water in a natural stream, from a point above the land of the plaintiff, who was a riparian owner. The defendant company, having acquired power to buy the canal and discontinue it, restored the water to its natural course, which by then had become silted up and incapable of holding the water, which thus flooded the plaintiff's land. The plaintiff unsuccessfully claimed damages for causing the flood, and for disturbance of an alleged easement to have the water diverted. Cockburn C.J. said[457]:

> "I am far from saying that the grant of an easement might not be accompanied by stipulations on the part of the grantor; as, for instance, that the easement should not be discontinued without his consent, or that on its discontinuance certain things should be done. I am far from saying that such a stipulation would not give a right of action. My observations are intended to apply to a case in which nothing appears beyond the existence of an easement. In such a case, it appears to me beyond doubt that the servient owner acquires no right to the continuance of the easement and the incidental advantages arising to him from it, if the dominant owner thinks proper to abandon it."

6. — STATUTORY RIGHTS

Generally

Rights which have all the characteristics of an easement can be created by **1–119** statute.[458] However, in addition to the cases where statutes create easements properly so called, there is a great variety of statutory provisions which bring into existence rights over the land of another which rights are not easements properly so called, usually on the ground that there is no dominant tenement.[459] Although these statutory rights are not easements and although they exhibit many characteristics

---

[455] *Gaved v Martyn* (1865) 19 C.B. (n.s.) 759, per Erle C.J.
[456] (1871) L.R. 6 Q.B. 578.
[457] (1871) L.R. 6 Q.B. 578, 588.
[458] See paras 3–02—3–03, below.
[459] But see *Salvin's Indenture, Re* [1938] 2 All E.R. 498 where it was held in the case of an express grant to a water authority of a right to lay mains and pipes that the dominant tenement was the land of the water authority acquired in order to perform its functions and also the incorporeal rights acquired to lay mains and pipes in the land of third parties; see, further, the Australian and Canadian cases cited at para.1–19, above, dealing with installations in connection with electricity, gas and oil and a railway line; compare the gas pipes in *Commission of Main Roads v North Shore Gas Co Ltd* (1967) 120 C.L.R. 118. The topic of statutory "easements" is discussed in (1956) 20 Conv. 208 (J.F. Garner).

different from easements, and from each other, depending on the precise terms of the statutes which create them, it is appropriate to make brief reference to some of the more important rights of this kind. These are:

(1) rights in relation to electricity;
(2) rights in relation to gas;
(3) rights in relation to water;
(4) rights in relation to pipelines;
(5) rights in relation to telecommunications;
(6) rights in relation to mining.

1. Rights in relation to electricity

1–120 The relevant statute is the Electricity Act 1989. Under section 6 of that Act,[460] the Secretary of State may grant licences authorising the licence-holder to generate, transmit and supply electricity to any person in the licence-holder's authorised area. Under section 10, the licence-holder has a number of specified powers which include the acquisition of what are called "wayleaves".[461] The right to acquire a wayleave arises where, for any purpose connected with the carrying on of the activities which he is authorised by his licence to carry on, it is necessary or expedient for a licence-holder to instal and keep installed an electric line on, under or over any land and the owner or occupier of the land has failed to give the wayleave after he has been formally asked to do so or has only been prepared to give the wayleave subject to conditions which are unacceptable to the licence-holder. In this provision, "land" has the meaning given to it by the Interpretation Act 1978 where "land" is defined to include buildings and other structures, land covered with water, and any estate, interest, easement, servitude or right in or over land.[462] In those circumstances, the Secretary of State may grant the wayleave to the licence-holder, subject to such terms and conditions as the Secretary of State thinks fit. The Secretary of State may not entertain such an application where the land is covered by a dwelling and the line is to be installed on or over the land.[463]

1–121 Before granting the wayleave, the Secretary of State must give the occupier and, if different, the owner of the land an opportunity of putting their case to a person appointed by the Secretary of State. The procedure for the hearing is governed by the Electricity (Compulsory Wayleaves) (Hearings Procedure)

---

[460] As substituted by the Utilities Act 2000, s.30.
[461] Under the Electricity Act 1989, Sch.4, para.6.
[462] *British Waterways Board v London Power Networks* [2003] 1 All E.R. 187 where the land in question was a service tunnel under a water-filled cutting.
[463] "Dwelling" is defined so as to include a garden: Electricity Act 1989, Sch.4, para.6(8); *ibid.*, para.6(4) does not preclude the Secretary of State from entertaining an application for a wayleave when the line already existed and he is applying to keep the installation rather than to make a new one. There is an intelligible difference between the situation of a person confronted with a proposal for a new line which he does not want and that of a landowner who has come with open eyes to land over which a line already runs: *R. v Secretary of State for Trade & Industry Ex p. Wolf* (2000) 79 P. & C.R. 299.

Rules 1967.[464] The rights conferred by such a wayleave do not give the licence-holder an interest in land but simply a right of occupation.[465] Where a wayleave is granted to a licence-holder, the occupier of the land and, if different, the owner of the land may recover from the licence-holder compensation in respect of the grant.[466] Where in the exercise of any right conferred by a wayleave, any damage is caused to land or movables, any person having an interest in the land or movables may recover compensation in respect of such damage and where, in consequence of the exercise of such a right, a person is disturbed in his enjoyment of any land or movables, he may recover compensation in respect of such disturbance.[467] Compensation may be recovered as a lump sum or by periodical payments or partly in one way and partly in the other.[468] Where the wayleave has been granted by agreement it is a question of construction of the agreement as to whether the agreement exclusively governs the right to compensation and, if so, what compensation the agreement provides for.[469] The basis for determining compensation has been considered in a number of cases.[470]

2. Rights in relation to gas

The relevant statute is the Gas Act 1986. Under section 7 of that Act,[471] the Gas and Electricity Markets Authority may authorise a person to be a gas transporter. The 1986 Act does not confer on a gas transporter a general right to acquire a wayleave. Such a transporter may place pipes, conduits, service pipes, cables, sewers and other works and pressure governors, ventilators and other apparatus in or under any street[472] but this provision does not empower the transporter to lay down

1–122

---

[464] As construed in accordance with the Electricity Act 1989 (Consequential Modifications of Subordinate Legislation) Order 1990.

[465] *Newcastle-under-Lyme Corp v Wolstanton Ltd* [1947] Ch. 427 at 456–457; there is a special statutory provision which deems there to be an interest in land for the purposes of the Mines (Working Facilities and Supports) Act 1966. In *Central Electricity Generating Board v Jennaway* [1959] 1 W.L.R. 937 (discussed at para.1–90, above) the right was treated as sufficiently analogous to an easement so that the rules as to incidental rights attached to an easement applied also to such a right; however, this case ought to be reconsidered in relation to the Electricity Act 1989 in view of the decision in *Sovmots Investments Ltd v Secretary of State for the Environment* [1979] A.C. 144 to the effect that the ambit of expropriatory orders should not be open to debate and that if ancillary rights are to be conferred, they must be expressly mentioned. The decision in *Newcastle-under-Lyme Corp v Wolstanton Ltd* was followed in *Commission for Main Roads v North Shore Gas Co Ltd* (1967) 120 C.L.R. 118 (itself followed in *Harada v Registrar of Titles* [1981] V.R. 743) and distinguished in *Gas & Fuel Corp v Barba* [1976] V.R. 755.

[466] Electricity Act 1989, Sch.6, para.7(1).

[467] Electricity Act 1989, Sch.6, para.7(2).

[468] Electricity Act 1989, Sch.6, para.7(3).

[469] *Christian Salvesen (Properties) Ltd v Central Electricity Generating Board* (1984) 48 P. & C.R. 465; *Mayclose Ltd v Central Electricity Generating Board* [1987] 2 E.G.L.R. 18; *Allen v South Eastern Electricity Board* [1988] 1 E.G.L.R. 171.

[470] *Tunis Investments Ltd v Central Electricity Generating Board* [1981] 1 E.G.L.R. 186; *George v South Western Electricity Board* [1982] 2 E.G.L.R. 214; *Clouds Estate Trustees v Southern Electricity Board* [1983] 2 E.G.L.R. 186; *Naylor v Southern Electricity Board* [1996] 1 E.G.L.R. 195; *Welford v EDF Energy Networks (LPN) Ltd* [2007] 2 E.G.L.R. 470.

[471] Substituted by Gas Act 1995, s.5 and amended by Utilities Act 2000 and Energy Act 2004.

[472] Gas Act 1986, s.9(3), Sch.4, para.1(1).

or place any pipe or other works into, through, or against any building, or in any land not dedicated to public use.[473] Accordingly, if a gas transporter wishes to acquire rights to lay pipes and other works, it must use its powers of compulsory acquisition.[474] These powers extend to acquiring rights over land by creating new rights as well as acquiring existing ones.[475] Such new rights can be easements if there is a dominant tenement.[476] In relation to the compulsory powers of the gas transporter, the Acquisition of Land Act 1981 applies and the Compulsory Purchase Act 1965 applies with modifications, which include a substitute section 7 of the 1965 Act laying down a different measure of compensation.[477]

3. Rights in relation to water

1–123   The relevant statutes are the Water Resources Act 1991 and the Water Industry Act 1991. These statutes contain almost identical provisions dealing with the power of the National Rivers Authority or a relevant undertaker to lay pipes in private land. The Water Resources Act 1991 continued the existence of the National Rivers Authority[478] but with effect from April 1, 1996 its functions were transferred to the Environment Agency.[479] Under the Water Resources Act 1991, the Agency has power to lay a relevant pipe (whether above or below the surface) in private land and to keep that pipe there.[480] The power is exercisable after giving reasonable notice of the proposed exercise of the power to the owner and to the occupier of the land where the power is to be exercised.[481] Subject to any provision to the contrary contained in an agreement between the Agency and the person in whom an interest in the pipe is or is to be vested, every such pipe vests in the Agency.[482] The Water Resources Act 1991 provides for the payment of compensation.[483] The Water Industry Act 1991 empowers the Secretary of State to appoint a company as a water undertaker or sewerage undertaker.[484] A relevant undertaker has powers to lay a relevant pipe (whether above or below the surface) in private land and to keep that pipe there; the statutory provisions are almost

---

[473] Gas Act 1986, Sch.4, para.3(1). There is a limited exception in Sch.4, para.3(2) in the case of a street which has been laid out but not dedicated to public use.

[474] Conferred by Gas Act 1986, s.9(3), Sch.3.

[475] Gas Act 1986, Sch.3, para.1(2).

[476] For the nature of the rights acquired by a local authority who laid gas pipes under statutory powers, see *Newcastle-under-Lyme Corp v Wolstanton Ltd* [1947] Ch. 427 and the cases cited in fn.465, above. In that case, the rights were not easements but amounted to an exclusive right of occupation of the space in the soil taken up by the pipes together with an implied right of support for the pipes themselves.

[477] Gas Act 1986, Sch.3, paras 4–13. For compensation cases dealing specifically with gas pipelines, see *Blandrent Investment Development Ltd v British Gas Corporation* [1979] 2 E.G.L.R. 18; *Whelan v British Gas* [1993] 2 E.G.L.R. 243; *Jackson v British Gas* [1996] 36 R.V.R. 239.

[478] Water Resources Act 1991, s.1.

[479] Environment Act 1995, s.2(1).

[480] Water Resources Act 1991, s.160(1).

[481] Water Resources Act 1991, s.160(2).

[482] Water Resources Act 1991, s.175.

[483] Water Resources Act 1991, Sch.21, para.2; see para.3 as to the assessment of that compensation.

[484] Water Industry Act 1991, s.6.

identical to those which apply to the Environment Agency.[485] The basis for determining compensation has been considered in a number of cases.[486]

4. Rights in relation to pipe-lines

The relevant statute is the Pipe-lines Act 1962.[487] The Secretary of State may make an order known as a "compulsory rights order" which authorises a person to place a pipe-line, or a length of pipe-line in the land described in the order and may grant a number of ancillary rights, subject to the conditions set out in the order.[488] The 1962 Act contains provisions as to how an application for such an order is to be made and as to the consideration of objections.[489] The compulsory rights order enures for the benefit of the owner of the pipe-line, after the line is placed in the land.[490] The 1962 Act provides for the payment of compensation.[491]

1–124

5. Rights in relation to telecommunications

The relevant statutes are the Telecommunications Act 1984 and the Communications Act 2003. Schedule 2 to the 1984 Act introduced what was described as "the telecommunications code" and this code is now known as "the electronic communications code". The code replaces the provisions of 12 separate Acts which made up the Telegraph Acts 1862 to 1916. Under section 106 of the 2003 Act, the rights under the code can be made available to a person to whom it is applied by a direction given by OFCOM and to certain government departments where the department is providing or proposing to provide an electronic communications network. Paragraphs 2 and 3 of the code provide that the agreement of the occupier of land is required for the operator to be able to have and to exercise certain rights. However, paragraph 5 of the code creates a procedure which allows an operator to give notice to the relevant persons in relation to an area of land that the operator requires those persons to agree to confer specified rights on the operator. If those persons do not agree to confer the required rights, then the operator may apply to the court for an order conferring those rights. The relevant court is the county

1–125

---

[485] The relevant provisions of the Water Industry Act 1991 are ss.159 (the power), 179 (vesting of works) and Sch.12, paras 2 and 3 (compensation). Although a water undertaker is given an express power to discharge water into a water course as ancillary to its pipe laying power by s.165, there is no express or implied power for a sewage authority to discharge into a water course or onto land of another without consent of the owner: *British Waterways Board v Severn Trent Water Limited* [2002] Ch. 25.

[486] See *St John's College, Oxford v Thames Water Authority* [1990] 1 E.G.L.R. 228; *Collins v Thames Water Utilities Ltd* [1994] 2 E.G.L.R. 209; *King v West Dorset Water Board* (1962) 14 P. & C.R. 166; *Felthouse v Cannock Rural District Council* (1973) 227 E.G. 1173; *Bestley v North West Water Limited* [1998] 1 E.G.L.R. 187; *Wickham Growers Ltd v Southern Water Plc* (1996) 73 P. & C.R. 301.

[487] The Pipe-lines Act 1962 does not apply to all pipe-lines: ss.58 to 64 of the 1962 Act specify a number of cases to which the 1962 Act does not apply.

[488] Pipe-lines Act 1962, s.12 as amended by the Deregulation (Pipe-Lines) Order 1999, SI 1999/742.

[489] Pipe-lines Act 1962, s.12(3), Sch.2.

[490] Pipe-lines Act 1962, s.12(4).

[491] Pipe-lines Act 1962, s.14.

court.[492] The code lays down certain matters of which the court must be satisfied before it confers the rights requested by the operator.[493] The court may confer the right on terms and subject to conditions specified in its order.[494] These terms and conditions must include:

(1) such terms with respect to the payment of consideration in respect of the giving of the agreement, or the exercise of the rights to which the order relates, as it appears to the court would have been fair and reasonable if the agreement had been given willingly and subject to the other provisions of the order; and

(2) such terms as appear to the court appropriate for ensuring that that person and persons from time to time bound by the rights conferred are adequately compensated (whether by the payment of such consideration or otherwise) for any loss or damage sustained by them in consequence of the exercise of those rights.[495]

1–126   In *Mercury Communications Ltd v London and India Dock Investments Ltd*[496] the amount of the consideration under (1) above was considered in detail.[497] It was held that the determination of the amount of such consideration necessarily involved an element of subjective judgment, rather than a finding of fact as to "market value" or the like. It followed that what was fair and reasonable was not necessarily the same as what would have been the result had the agreement been entered into willingly. The market value was an obvious starting point. However, circumstances could arise in which the court could properly conclude that the likely market value was not a result which was fair and reasonable. Compulsory purchase principles, and in particular the principle that one left out of account the scheme of development which prompted the compulsory acquisition,[498] did not apply. Similarly, it was not appropriate to have regard to the commercial benefits which would accrue to the operator as a result of the order conferring the rights. That might, however, be appropriate where there was a single capital payment to be made and the amount of the benefit could be easily quantified. What was fair

---

[492] Para.1(1) of the code. For transitional provisions relating to consents given and agreements made before 1984, see para.28 of the code and *British Telecommunications Plc v Humber Bridge Board* [2000] N.P.C. 144.

[493] Para.5(3) of the code.

[494] Para.5(4), (5) of the code.

[495] Para.7 of the code.

[496] (1993) 69 P. & C.R. 135. In *Cabletel Surrey and Hampshire Ltd v Brookwood Cemetry* [2002] EWCA Civ 720 the Court of Appeal was invited by both parties to the appeal to proceed on the basis of the decision in *Mercury Communications* and the Court of Appeal did so, summarising and applying those principles. The issue on the appeal was whether the county court judge was right to prefer one expert witness to another.

[497] The court did not apply the approach laid down in *B.P. Petroleum Developments Ltd v Ryder* [1987] 2 E.G.L.R. 233 in relation to s.8 of the Mines (Working Facilities and Support) Act 1966; see para.1–127, below.

[498] *Pointe Gourde Quarrying and Transport Co Ltd v Sub-Intendent of Crown Lands* [1947] A.C. 565.

and reasonable in that case was ultimately determined by reference to comparable transactions, bearing in mind the respective bargaining positions of the parties.[499]

6. Rights in relation to mining

In relation to minerals other than coal, the relevant statute is the Mines (Working **1–127** Facilities and Support) Act 1966. This Act empowers the court[500] to confer a wide range of working facilities set out in section 1,[501] together with ancillary rights as defined in section 2.[502] Where rights are granted under the 1966 Act, the court may determine the amount and the nature of compensation or consideration to be paid or given and the persons to whom it is to be paid or given, either at the time when it determines whether the right should be granted or at any subsequent time.[503] The compensation or consideration in respect of any right is assessed by the court on the basis of what would be fair and reasonable between a willing grantor and a willing grantee, having regard to the conditions subject to which the right is or is to be granted.[504] The basis for assessing compensation has been considered in a number of cases.[505] The authorities were reviewed in *B.P. Petroleum Developments Ltd v Ryder*[506] where it was held that compulsory purchase principles applied. In relation to coal, licensed operators under the Coal Industry Act 1994 are given a statutory right to withdraw support from land.[507] The Coal Mining Subsidence Act 1991 makes provision for remedial action and compensation in relation to subsidence damage.

The Mining Code

The rights and liabilities of statutory undertakers or their privatised successors **1–128** with regards to mines and minerals may be governed by the Mining Code which, as enacted, applies to railway companies, but has often been incorporated into deeds by which other undertakers have acquired lands or rights over land. The Mining Code is contained in the Railway Clauses Consolidation Act 1845,

---

[499] The circumstances in which compensation for depreciation was payable under para.4 of the code were considered in *Finsbury Business Centre Ltd v Mercury Communications Ltd* [1994] R.V.R. 108.

[500] The court is the Chancery Division of the High Court: see CPR 8PD 15.3.

[501] As substituted by the Mines (Working Facilities and Support) Act 1974 and amended by the Coal Industry Act 1994, s.67 and Schs 9 and 11.

[502] The powers under the 1966 Act were considered in *B.P. Petroleum Developments Ltd v Ryder* [1987] 2 E.G.L.R. 233, which was the first case under the Act dealing with the exploitation of petroleum.

[503] Mines (Working Facilities and Support) Act 1966, s.8(1).

[504] Mines (Working Facilities and Support) Act 1966, s.8(2).

[505] *Markham Main Colliery Ltd, Re* (1925) 134 L.T. 253; *Denaby and Cadeby Main Collieries, Re, Colliery Guardian*, p. 2180, November 30, 1928; *Consett Iron Co Ltd v Clavering* [1935] 2 K.B. 42; *Consett Iron Co Ltd's Application, Re* [1938] 1 All E.R. 439; *Naylor Benzon Mining Co Ltd, Re* [1950] Ch. 567; *Associated Portland Cement Manufacturers Ltd's Application, Re* [1966] 1 Ch. 308; *B.P. Petroleum Developments Ltd v Ryder* [1987] 2 E.G.L.R. 232.

[506] [1987] 2 E.G.L.R. 233; distinguished in *Mercury Communications Ltd v London and India Dock Investments Ltd* (1993) 69 P. & C.R. 135 in relation to Sch.2 to the Telecommunications Act 1984, see para.1–126, above and not followed in *Bocardo SA v Star Energy UK Ltd* [2008] EWHC 1756 (Ch.).

[507] Coal Industry Act 1994, ss.38 to 41.

sections 77–85 as amended by the substitution of sections 78–85E by Part II of the Mines (Working Facilities and Support) Act 1923.

The point of the Mining Code was to enable railway companies to acquire the surface without acquiring or having to pay for the underlying minerals (if any) and to oblige them to pay compensation only if and when minerals, the extraction of which was likely to cause damage to the undertaking, came to be worked. Where it applies, it supplants the surface owner's ordinary common law rights, namely:

(a) the right of support from subjacent and adjacent land inherent in the ownership of the surface; and

(b) any easements of support for buildings or works which might otherwise have been acquired by prescription as a result of 20 years' enjoyment.

The operation of the Code was explained by Lord Cranworth in *Great Western Railway Co v Bennett*[508] thus:

"It was obviously the intention of the legislature . . . to create a new code as to the relation between mine owners and railway companies, where lands were compulsorily taken for the purpose of making a railway. The object of the statute evidently was to get rid of all the ordinary law on the subject, and to compel the owner to sell the surface, and if any mines were so near the surface that they must be taken for the purposes of the railway, to compel him to sell them, but not to compel him to sell anything more. The land was to be dealt with just as if there were no mines to be considered; nothing but the surface. That being so, justice obviously requires that when the mine owner thinks it beneficial to him to work his mines, and proceeds to do so, he should be just in the same position as if he had never sold any part of the surface at all. If he had not compulsorily parted with the surface, he might have worked his mines, sinking his shaft from the very surface unto the very bottom of the mine. The object of the statute was that, for the purpose of the railway, the company was to take (and it was a very beneficial provision for the company), that and that only, which is necessary for the purpose of the railway; and that all the rest should be left to be dealt with whenever the time for working the mine should arrive."

The Code provides that, if the mineral owner wishes to extract the minerals in the vicinity of the works of the undertaker within the area of protection, he must serve a notice of approach.[509] The undertaker may then serve a counter-notice specifying what minerals are to be left unworked.[510] If a counter-notice is served,

---

[508] [1867] L.R. 2 H.L. 27 at page 40.

[509] Railway Clauses Consolidation Act 1845, s.78(1), as substituted by the Mines (Working Facilities and Support) Act 1923, s.15; for definition of "the area of protection", see *ibid.*, s.78(5).

[510] Railway Clauses Consolidation Act 1845, s.78(2).

the mineral owner must stop but is entitled to be paid compensation "for the loss caused by the specified minerals being left unworked".[511] This extends to all losses which are not too remote provided that the mineral owner has acted reasonably.[512] If no counter-notice is served, the mineral owner may proceed with his extraction as long as he does so in a proper manner and according to the usual manner of working such minerals in the district.[513] In the absence of agreement the amount of compensation is to be determined by arbitration.[514]

The mine owner is also entitled to compensation for:

(a) any increase in the cost of working his other minerals caused by the giving of a late counter-notice;[515]

(b) losses caused by the continuous working of the mine being interrupted; and

(c) any loss caused by the mine having to be worked in such a way as not to injure the protected works of the undertaker.[516]

There is also provision for the mine owner to have rights of access through the specified minerals[517] and requiring him to contribute to the expenses incurred by the undertaker in making good any damage to its works caused by authorised working within the area of protection.[518]

7.—LICENCES

A licence in relation to land is a permission which makes it lawful for the licensee **1–129** to do what would otherwise be a trespass.[519] A licence properly so called, without more, does not create an estate or interest in land.[520] Such a licence does not bind a successor in title of the licensor. Licences in relation to land can be granted in a great range of circumstances and take many forms. A licence may be express or implied. A licence may be conferred gratuitously. Such a licence is often called "a bare licence" and can be revoked at any time on reasonable notice without rendering the licensor liable in damages.[521] In such a case, the licensee will not be a

---

[511] Railway Clauses Consolidation Act 1845, s.78(4).

[512] The right to compensation therefore extends to the loss of the profits which could have been earned from the void which would have been available for landfill purposes following extraction and are not limited merely to the value of the minerals left unworked: *National Grid Gas Plc v Lafarge Aggregates Limited* [2006] EWHC 2559 (Ch.). See also *London & North Eastern Ry Co v BA Collieries* [1945] A.C. 143, applying *Bwllfa and Merthyr Dare Steam Colliery v Pontypridd Waterworks Co* [1903] A.C. 436.

[513] Railway Clauses Consolidation Act 1845, s.79(1).

[514] Railway Clauses Consolidation Act 1845, s.78A(1).

[515] Railway Clauses Consolidation Act 1845, s.78A(2).

[516] Railway Clauses Consolidation Act 1845, s.81.

[517] Railway Clauses Consolidation Act 1845, s.80.

[518] Railway Clauses Consolidation Act 1845, s.79A.

[519] *Thomas v Sorrell* (1673) Vaugh. 330 at 351.

[520] *Ashburn Anstalt v Arnold* [1989] Ch. 1.

[521] *Aldin v Latimer Clark, Muirhead & Co* [1894] 2 Ch. 437; *Armstrong v Shephard & Short Ltd* [1959] 2 Q.B. 384.

trespasser until he has had reasonable notice to leave the land or to stop doing that which had been permitted by the licence.[522] A licence may be granted as part of a contractual arrangement. The relationship of the parties is then governed by the law of contract as to the interpretation of its express terms and as to the implication of terms and as to the termination of the contract. There may be a licence coupled with a grant, for example, the grant of a *profit à prendre*. Such a licence will last for the time that the profit endures. If the licensor acts contrary to the terms of a contractual licence or a licence coupled with a grant, the court has available to it its usual remedies for breach of contract, including the remedies of injunctions and damages.[523] Whether or not the benefit of the licence is transmissible depends upon the nature of the licence. The benefit of a personal licence will not be assignable. The benefit of a bare licence will generally not be assignable, or at any rate, the question may be largely academic if it is capable of being revoked at any time. The benefit of a contractual licence which is not a personal licence will be assignable. A licence coupled with a grant will generally be assigned upon an assignment of the right granted. The burden of a contractual licence does not pass to a successor in title of the licensor. This is because the licence does not create an interest in land. If the licensor transfers the land in question to a successor who is not bound by the licence at a time when the licensor was not entitled to determine the licence, the licensor will be in breach of contract. If the successor in title knowingly induced the breach of contract by the licensor, he may be liable in tort in accordance with general principles. A licence coupled with a grant will bind a successor in title of the grantor if the right granted binds such successor. There are many cases where the courts have held that the licensee had not only the rights of a licensee but had greater rights acquired in accordance with the principles relating to proprietary estoppel or constructive trusts.[524] The principal cases which involved equitable rights akin to easements are considered in the next chapter.

1–130   In *Armstrong v Sheppard & Short Ltd*,[525] the Court of Appeal held that if A gives authority to B for the doing of an act on his land, and the act is done and completed, then whatever be the description of the authority, it is generally too late for A to complain and, accordingly, the plaintiff could not complain of a sewer which the defendant had constructed on the plaintiff's land after the plaintiff had informed the defendant orally that he did not object to the construction of it. On the other hand, the Court of Appeal held that an oral licence to discharge water through another's land, to be irrevocable during the licensor's tenure of the land, must have the necessary qualities of a contract binding on the parties, and

[522] *Canadian Pacific Railway v The King* [1931] A.C. 414; *Australian Blue Metal v Hughes* [1963] A.C. 74.

[523] *Winter Garden Theatre (London) Ltd v Millennium Productions Ltd* [1948] A.C. 173; *Verrall v Great Yarmouth Borough Council* [1981] Q.B. 202.

[524] The better known cases include *Errington v Errington* [1952] 1 K.B. 290; *Binions v Evans* [1972] Ch. 359; *D.H.N. Food Distributors v L.B. Tower Hamlets* [1976] 1 W.L.R. 852 and *Sharpe, Re* [1980] 1 W.L.R. 219.

[525] [1959] 2 Q.B. 384. This decision is discussed in an article by Cullity, "The Executed Licence", 29 Conv. (n.s.) 19.

be supported by consideration, and that, there being no consideration for the licence granted by the plaintiff to the defendant, the plaintiff was entitled to revoke the licence and had, on the facts, done so.

In *IDC Group Limited v Clark*[526] it was held that a deed which purported to **1–131** "grant licence and consent" to the use of a fire escape route did not create an easement and so did not bind successors in title to the grantor (even though they were included in the definition of the grantor); a licence properly so called is permission to do something on or over land which creates no interest in it and the word must be taken to have been used by a conveyancer in that sense.[527]

8.—EXTENT AND MODE OF ENJOYMENT

As every easement is a restriction upon the rights of property of the owner of the **1–132** servient tenement, no alteration can be made in the mode of enjoyment by the owner of the dominant tenement, the effect of which will be to increase such restriction beyond its legitimate limit.[528] In the case of an express grant of the easement the limit depends on the words used.[529] Supposing no express grant to exist, the right must be limited and defined by the user proved.[530]

The extent of an easement acquired by user was considered in detail by the **1–133** Court of Appeal in the important case of *McAdams Homes Limited v Robinson*.[531] This case concerned a right acquired by an implied grant rather than a fictitious grant (i.e. by prescription) but it was said that, at least in the great majority of cases, there should be little difference in the principles applicable to the two types of case.[532] The case concerned a right of drainage rather than a right of way but the leading right of way cases in this area were considered in detail and were relied upon for the purpose of stating general principles which apply both to rights of way and other easements. The first judgment in *McAdams Homes* was given by Neuberger L.J. He held that the cases established the following propositions:

---

[526] (1992) 65 P. & C.R. 179.

[527] This approach is markedly different from that adopted by the courts when deciding whether an arrangement constitutes a licence or a tenancy, when the label counts for very little: see *Addiscombe Garden Estates Limited v Crabbe* [1958] 1 Q.B. 513; *Street v Mountford* [1985] A.C. 809. The Court of Appeal explained the difference on the basis that "those cases depend mainly on exclusive possession given to the licensee, a state of affairs which cannot arise where all that is given is a right to pass and repass over another's land".

[528] e.g. as to light: *Ankerson v Connelly* [1906] 2 Ch. 554; [1907] 1 Ch. 678; *News of the World v Allen Fairhead & Sons* [1931] 2 Ch. 402.

[529] See, e.g. in the case of an express grant of a watercourse, the judgment of Jessel M.R. in *Taylor v St Helens Corp* (1877) 6 Ch. D. 271; and in the case of grants of rights of way, Ch.9, below.

[530] *Miner's Safe Co v G.N. & City Ry* [1907] 1 Ch. 229; *Att-Gen v G.N. Ry* [1909] 1 Ch. 775; *British Railways Board v Glass* [1965] Ch. 538; *Thomas W. Ward Ltd v Alexander Bruce (Grays) Ltd* [1959] 2 Lloyd's Rep. 472; *Woodhouse & Co Ltd v Kirkland (Derby) Ltd* [1970] 1 W.L.R. 1185; see further, paras 9–03 *et seq.*, below.

[531] [2005] 1 P. & C.R. 520.

[532] See at [22] and [79].

(1) where the dominant land is used for a particular purpose at the time an easement is created, an increase, even if substantial, in the intensity of that use, resulting in a concomitant increase in the use of the easement, cannot of itself be objected to by the servient owner[533];

(2) excessive use of an easement by the dominant land will render the dominant owner liable in nuisance; in most cases where the extent, and even the nature, of the grant is in dispute the question of excessive user will be unhelpful because one can only determine whether the use is excessive once one has decided the extent of the grant[534];

(3) where there is a change in the use of, or the erection of new buildings on, the dominant land, without having any effect on the nature or extent of the use of the easement, the change, however radical, will not affect the right of the dominant owner to use the easement[535];

(4) a number of cases bear on the converse question, namely, the effect of a change in the use of the dominant tenement which results, or may result, in an alteration in the manner or extent of the use of the easement[536];

(5) the issue as to the extent of an easement acquired by implied grant or by prescription should be determined by answering two questions;

(6) the first question was: whether the development of the dominant land represented a "radical change in the character" or a "change in the identity" of the dominant land as opposed to a mere change or intensification in the use of the dominant land;

(7) the second question was: whether the use of the dominant land as redeveloped would result in a substantial increase or alteration in the burden on the servient land;

(8) it is only if the redevelopment of the dominant land resulted in a radical change in its character and would lead to a substantial increase in the burden that the dominant owner's right to enjoy the easement would be suspended or lost;

(9) where both requirements are satisfied, the dominant owner's right to enjoy the easement will be ended, or at least suspended, so long as the radical change of character and substantial increase in burden are maintained;

---

[533] This proposition was supported by *British Railways Board v Glass* [1965] Ch. 538 and *Cargill v Gotts* [1981] 1 W.L.R. 441.

[534] The Lord Justice quoted with approval para.6–90 of the 17th edition of this work and *British Railways Board v Glass* [1965] Ch. 538.

[535] This proposition was supported by *Luttrel's Case* (1601) 4 Co. Rep. 86a, *Watts v Kelson* (1870) 6 Ch. App. 166, *Atwood v Bovis Homes Limited* [2001] Ch. 379 and *Harvey v Walters* (1873) L.R. 8 C.P. 162.

[536] These cases included *Williams v James* (1867) L.R. 2 C.P. 577, *Wood v Saunders* (1875) 10 Ch. App. 582, *Wimbledon and Putney Commons Conservators v Dixon* (1875) 1 Ch. D. 362, *Milner's Safe Company Limited v Great Northern & City Railway Company* [1907] 1 Ch. 208, *RPC Holdings Limited v Rogers* [1953] 1 All E.R. 1029, *British Railways Board v Glass* [1965] Ch. 538, *Giles v County Building Constructors (Hertford) Limited* (1971) 22 P. & C.R. 978 and *Ray v Fairway Motors (Barnstaple) Limited* (1968) 20 P. & C.R. 261.

(10) although not all the cases were entirely consistent and clear, the above approach was principled, consistent and coherent;

(11) it was a potentially unsatisfactory feature of the principles that both questions might be said to involve an exercise which may have a rather uncertain outcome; the questions had to be expressed in a generalised way and each case would very much turn on its own facts, with regard to the particular easement, the position on the ground at the date of the grant, the surrounding circumstances at the date of grant, and the nature and effect of the redevelopment that has subsequently taken place; (this comment was made in the context of a case which involved an implied grant and the comment needs adaptation in a case where one is concerned with an easement acquired by prescription).

Neuberger L.J. then applied these principles to the facts of the case; the facts of this case are discussed at para.6–94 below.

Nourse L.J. gave the second judgment in *McAdams v Robinson*. He made the following observations about the authorities: **1–134**

(1) in general, authorities on prescriptive easements apply equally to implied easements and vice versa;

(2) in general, authorities on rights of way apply equally to rights of drainage;

(3) the authorities on rights of way from *Williams v James*[537] onwards establish that the right impliedly granted or prescriptively acquired is a right for all purposes according to the ordinary and reasonable use to which the dominant tenement might be applied at the time of the implied or supposed grant;

(4) the authorities on rights of way subsequent to *Williams v James* fall into two broad categories; first, those where there has been a change in the character of the dominant tenement leading to a substantial increase in the burden of the easement, in which cases use of the right has been restrained; secondly, those in which there has been no such change but a considerable increase in the use of the right in which cases the use has been allowed to continue;

(5) in the first category of case are *Wimbledon and Putney Commons Conservators v Dixon*[538] and *RPC Holdings Limited v Rogers*[539]; in the second category of case are *British Railways Board v Glass*,[540] *Giles v County Building Constructors (Hertford) Limited*[541] and *Cargill v Gotts*.[542]

Peter Gibson L.J. gave a short judgment in *McAdams v Robinson* which concentrated on the fact that the right arose pursuant to an implied grant. The grant of   **1–135**

---

[537] (1867) L.R. 2 C.P. 577.
[538] (1875) 1 Ch. D. 362.
[539] [1953] 1 All E.R. 1029.
[540] [1965] Ch. 538.
[541] (1971) 22 P. & C.R. 978.
[542] [1981] 1 W.L.R. 441.

the easement was to correspond to the facility which the grantor himself found necessary to use at the time of the implied grant. To determine whether the subsequent user is excessive, comparison must be made with what was the user at the time of the implied grant. The question was one of fact and degree.

1–136   In the case of the easement of light, the dominant owner may obtain an increase of light by altering his mode of framing and glazing.[543] On the other hand, a dominant tenement, having ancient windows overlooking the servient tenement, may not be so altered,[544] unless the alteration is one which might reasonably have been expected,[545] so as to make the unobstructed access of light to the ancient windows more necessary to the enjoyment of the dominant tenement than they were before the alteration, and thereby to render actionable an obstruction which would not, before the alteration, have been an illegal interference with the light.[546]

1–137   In the case of water rights, a mill-owner who has the right of diverting water cannot alter his sluice so as to divert more water.[547] Nor can a riparian owner who has acquired a prescriptive right to pollute water increase the pollution to the prejudice of others.[548] Nor can a riparian owner increase the burden of the lower riparian owner by making structures which increase the flow of water.[549] But where the burden is not increased, trifling variations can be made in the user of the easement. Thus, where a right existed to supply cattle-sheds by a watercourse, the dominant owner could erect cottages in the place of the cattle-sheds.[550]

On the construction of grants, it has been held that a grantee of a watercourse could not enlarge the channel.[551] A grant of the running of water, etc., from land did not authorise the discharge of a sewage effluent,[552] or of the refuse of tan pits.[553]

1–138   In *Wood v Saunders*[554] the plaintiff, being entitled by express grant to a mansion with the free passage of water and soil to a cesspool on the defendant's land, enlarged the mansion so as to increase the amount of soil. The defendant having stopped the drains leading to the cesspool, the case came before Hall V.-C., who restrained the defendant from preventing the free use and passage of water and soil in and to the cesspool, but added that his order was only to protect the plaintiff in the

---

[543] *Turner v Spooner* (1861) 1 Dr. & Sm. 467.

[544] i.e. the dominant owner may make the alteration but this does not produce the result that there is an actionable interference with his light when there was none before the alteration.

[545] *Carr-Saunders v Dick McNeill Associates Ltd* [1986] 1 W.L.R. 922 at 928–929, applying *Moore v Hall* (1878) 3 Q.B.D. 178 at 182 and *Colls v Home and Colonial Stores Ltd* [1904] A.C. 179.

[546] *Ankerson v Connelly*, above; *News of the World v Allen Fairhead & Sons* [1931] 2 Ch. 402; *Smith v Evangelization Society Trust* [1933] Ch. 515. See *Bailey (W.H.) & Sons Ltd v Holborn and Frascati Ltd* [1914] 1 Ch. 598.

[547] *Bealey v Shaw* (1805) 6 East 208.

[548] *Crossley & Sons Ltd v Lightowler* (1867) 2 Ch. App. 478; *McIntyre Bros v M'Gavin* [1893] A.C. 268.

[549] *Frechette v Compagnie Manufacturière de St Hyacinthe* (1883) 9 App. Cas. 170.

[550] *Watts v Kelson* (1870) 6 Ch. App. 166. See also *Saunders v Newman* (1818) 1 B. & Ald. 258; *Greenslade v Halliday* (1830) 6 Bing. 379.

[551] *Taylor v St Helens Corp* (1877) 6 Ch. D. 264.

[552] *Phillimore v Watford R.D.C.* [1913] 2 Ch. 434.

[553] *Chadwick v Marsden* (1867) L.R. 2 Exch. 285.

[554] (1875) 10 Ch. App. 582. This case was considered in detail in *McAdams v Robinson* [2005] 1 P. & C.R. 520 at [45]–[47]. See also *Metropolitan Board of Works v L. & N.W. Ry* (1881) 17 Ch. D. 246; *New Windsor (Mayor) v Stovell* (1884) 27 Ch. D. 665.

reasonable use of such cesspool to the extent to which the same was used prior to the date of the grant. On appeal the decree was varied, the plaintiff submitting to be restrained from allowing the drainage from the additional buildings erected by him to go into the cesspool, and the defendant being restrained from preventing the free passage of water and soil into the cesspool. The court apparently treated the drainage from the additional buildings as severable from the drainage from the original building; and thus the case became a question of "excess" rather than of construction.

In *Graham v Philcox*[555] the plaintiffs occupied the first floor of a coach house   **1–139** which had been converted into residential premises and the first floor of which enjoyed a right of way over land adjoining the building. Later the plaintiffs acquired the ground floor of the coach house and occupied the whole of it as one residence. The alteration of the dominant tenement by its enlargement did not affect the existence of the right of way because there was no evidence that the plaintiffs' use of it was or would be excessive.

The pulling down of a house for the purpose of repair does not, by the law of   **1–140** England, even when construed most strictly, cause the loss of any easement attached to it, if it be accompanied by an intention, acted upon within a reasonable time, of rebuilding it.[556] This intention will be presumed.[557] The reason is that it is incidental to all houses to be repaired and at some time to be rebuilt, and the right when acquired is acquired for the tenement with such incidents. If this were not so, no prescriptive right could be acquired in respect of a messuage or any other artificial structure.[558]

A mere alteration in the mode of enjoyment, as the change of a mill from a fulling to a grist mill, or the like,[559] whereby no injury is caused to the servient tenement, or a trifling alteration in the course of a watercourse,[560] does not destroy the right. On the other hand in *Clarke v Somersetshire Drainage Commissioners*[561] it was held that an easement to pollute a stream with the refuse of a fellmongery and with the waste dyes used in making coloured rags had been lost by the place in which those businesses had been carried on being utilised as a leather-board factory, because the resulting pollution was of a different kind, although less objectionable.

9.—Classification of Profits

Profits and rights of common

The nature of a *profit à prendre* and the essential differences between an easement   **1–141** and a profit have already been noticed.[562] The classification of profits will now be briefly considered.

---

[555] [1984] Q.B. 747.
[556] *Luttrel's Case* (1602) 4 Rep. 86.
[557] *Smith v Baxter* [1900] 2 Ch. 138.
[558] See further, paras 12–26 *et seq.*, below.
[559] *Luttrel's Case* (1602) 4 Rep. 86; *Baxendale v McMurray* (1867) 2 Ch. App. 790.
[560] *Hall v Swift* (1838) 4 Bing.N.C. 381.
[561] (1888) 57 L.J.M.C. 96.
[562] See para.1–02, above.

A *profit à prendre* may be enjoyed to the exclusion of all other persons, in which case it is termed a "sole" or "several" profit. On the other hand, a profit may be enjoyed in common with one or more persons, including the owner of the servient land, when it is called a profit "in common" or right of common.[563] Every right of common is, therefore, a *profit à prendre*, but not every *profit à prendre* is a right of common.

Historically, rights of common came first, being based upon the former system of landholding which gave rise to the communal enjoyment of certain types of *profits à prendre*, for example, rights of pasture. The enjoyment of profits in severalty was a later development and indeed most modern instances of profits are also of rights of common.[564]

1–142   Lord Lindley, delivering the judgment of the Court of Appeal in *Duke of Sutherland v Heathcote*, gave the following exposition[565]:

> "A profit à prendre is a right to take something off another person's land; such a right does not prevent the owner from taking the same sort of thing from off his own land; the first right may limit, but does not exclude, the second. An exclusive right to all the profit of a particular kind can, no doubt, be granted; but such a right cannot be inferred from language which is not clear and explicit."

On the other hand, a grant of a several (that is exclusive) right of fishing may be made without the use of the word "several".[566] Similarly, in the case of the reservation of right of fishing, a mere reservation, without more, in the absence of factors pointing the other way, will give rise to an exclusive right.[567]

Appurtenant or in gross

1–143   As with an easement, a *profit à prendre* may be appurtenant to a dominant tenement. Unlike an easement, however, a profit may also exist in gross, that is, it

---

[563] For the distinction between a profit in common and a profit sole or several profit, see Halsbury's *Laws of England* (4ᵗʰ Ed, Vol. 16(2) Reissue), title Easements and Profits a Prendre, para. 258, Ubhi and Denyer-Green, *The Law of Commons and of Town and Village Greens*, paras 4.9.1–4.9.5 and Harris and Ryan, *An Outline of the Law Relating to Common Land*, pp. 34, 35. The general principles referred to in the present work relate to all profits, whether in common or in severalty.

[564] All rights of common should now be registered: Commons Registration Act 1965. This Act will be repealed and replaced by the Commons Act 2006 (the relevant provisions of which are not yet in force). For the effects of the 1965 Act, see Halsbury's *Laws of England* (4ᵗʰ Ed, Vol. 6, 2003 Reissue), title Commons and Harris and Ryan, *An Outline of the Law Relating to Common Land*. For the 1965 Act and the 2006 Act, see Ubhi and Denyer-Green, *The Law of Commons and of Town and Village Greens*.

[565] [1892] 1 Ch. 475 at 484, 485.

[566] *Malcomson v O'Dea* (1863) 10 H.L.C. 593; *Neill v Duke of Devonshire* (1882) 8 App. Cas. 135; *Hanbury v Jenkins* [1901] 2 Ch. 401 at 414; *Duke of Beaufort v John Aird & Co* (1904) 20 T.L.R. 602 at 603.

[567] *Lady Dunsany v Bedworth* (1979) 38 P. & C.R. 546.

may be unconnected with the ownership of any dominant tenement.[568] A profit which is appurtenant to land will run with the dominant tenement into the hands of successive owners thereof and will be carried by the general words of section 62 of the Law of Property Act 1925.[569] A profit which is appurtenant cannot be unlimited in its extent; it must have either a definite limit (or "stint") or be limited by reference to the needs of the dominant tenement.[570] Thus, the common of pasture appurtenant must be limited to a definite number of cattle or to cattle *levant* and *couchant*, that is, the number that the dominant tenement is capable of supporting in winter.[571] Where, therefore, an exclusive right of grazing over a moor had been granted by a conveyance of an adjoining farm, but on a later conveyance of the farm no reference was made to the right, an action for a declaration that the right had become annexed in perpetuity to the fee simple of the farm failed, as an appurtenant right of grazing without limit (though such a right might exist in gross) was unknown to the law.[572] Generally, a profit appurtenant cannot be severed or enjoyed apart from its dominant tenement, although where the right has a definite limit, not by reference to the needs of the dominant tenement, before the coming into force of section 9 of the Commons Act 2006, it could be severed, at least in the case of the common of pasture.[573] On and after June 28, 2005 the position in relation to a right of common, which is registered in a register of common land or town or village greens as attached to any land, is governed by section 9 of the Commons Act 2006 which restricts the circumstances in which such a right may be severed from the dominant land to the cases provided in Schedule 1 to that Act or any case authorised by any other Act.[574]

A profit in gross is not limited by the needs of any dominant tenement and can **1–144** exist without a definite limit. There may be a right in gross to take the proceeds of another man's land without stint.[575] A profit in gross is an interest in land and can be dealt with and will devolve in the same way as other interests in land.[576]

---

[568] *Lord Chesterfield v Harris* [1908] 2 Ch. 397 at 421, per Buckley L.J. And see *Shuttleworth v Le Fleming* (1865) 19 C.B. (n.s.) 687; *Johnson v Barnes* (1873) L.R. 8 C.P. 527; *Webber v Lee* (1882) 9 Q.B.D. 315, CA.

[569] *White v Williams* [1922] 1 K.B. 727; *Anderson v Bostock* [1976] Ch. 312; *Broxhead Common, Whitehill, Hampshire, Re* (1977) 33 P. & C.R. 451.

[570] *Bailey v Stephens* (1862) 12 C.B. (n.s.) 91; *Lord Chesterfield v Harris* [1908] 2 Ch. 397, CA (affirmed sub nom. *Harris v Earl of Chesterfield* [1911] A.C. 623).

[571] *Lord Chesterfield v Harris* [1908] 2 Ch. 397, CA, at 421, per Buckley L.J.

[572] *Anderson v Bostock* [1976] Ch. 312, applying *Lord Chesterfield v Harris* [1911] A.C. 623.

[573] *Daniel v Hanslip* (1672) 2 Lev. 67; *Bunn v Channen* (1813) 5 Taunt. 244; and see discussion on this point in *White v Taylor (No. 2)* [1969] 1 Ch. 160 at 189, 190, per Buckley J. and authorities therein cited. This probably applies to all profits where the limit is fixed, e.g. rights to take a fixed amount of turves, wood or fish. *Bettison v Langton* [2002] 1 A.C. 27 (right to pasture 10 cows and 30 sheep on Tawna Down in Cornwall).

[574] For the transfer of a right of common which is registered in such a register but where it is not shown as attached to any land, see Commons Act 2006, s.12 (not yet in force).

[575] *Lord Chesterfield v Harris* [1908] 2 Ch. 397, CA, at 421, per Buckley L.J.; *Staffordshire and Worcestershire Canal Navigation v Bradley* [1912] 1 Ch. 91. In *Lovett v Fairclough* (1990) 61 P. & C.R. 385, a claim to have acquired by prescription a profit in gross of piscary failed on the facts.

[576] *Staffordshire and Worcestershire Canal Navigation v Bradley* [1912] 1 Ch. 91, where the right to take fish could have been the subject of a lease; and see *Webber v Lee* (1882) 9 Q.B.D. 315.

1–145   There may also exist a profit appendant, that is, annexed to land by operation
of law. This type of right arose when the lord of the manor subinfeudated arable
land. The feoffee would take a right to pasture on the manorial waste animals necessary to plough and manure the land granted to him. The Statute of *Quia
Emptores* 1289–90[577] ended subinfeudation, so that a profit appendant must have
come into existence before the statute. The right was limited to animals *levant*
and *couchant*.[578]

A profit may also exist in the form of a common *pur cause de vicinage*, which
is restricted to rights of pasture. The right arises where there is inter-commoning
between two contiguous pieces of common land.[579]

10.—LAW REFORM

1–146   In March 2008, the Law Commission published a Consultation Paper entitled
Easements, Covenants and Profits a Prendre.[580] The Consultation Paper invites
the views of consultees as to the Law Commission's list of provisional proposals
and specific consultation questions. Of relevance to this chapter are the following
provisional proposals or specific questions:

(1) The Law Commission's provisional view is that the current requirement
that an easement be attached to a dominant estate in the land serves an
important purpose and should be retained. It does not believe that easements in gross should be recognised as interests in land.

(2) The Law Commission considers that the basic requirements that an easement accommodate and serve the land and that it has some nexus with
the dominant land serve an important purpose and should be retained.

(3) The Law Commission provisionally proposes that in order to comprise
an easement:

(a) the right must be clearly defined, or be capable of clear definition,
and it must be limited in its scope such that it does not involve the
unrestricted use of the servient land; and

(b) the right must not be a lease or tenancy, but the fact that the dominant owner obtains exclusive possession of the servient land should
not, without more, preclude the right from being an easement.

(4) The Law Commission provisionally proposes that where the benefit and
burden of an easement is registered, there should be no requirement for
the owners to be different persons, provided that the dominant and
servient estates in land are registered with separate title numbers.

---

[577] 18 Edw. 1, c. 1.
[578] *Robertson v Hartopp* (1889) 43 Ch. D. 484 at 516, 517.
[579] *Tyrringham's Case* (1584) 4 Co.Rep. 37.
[580] Law Com. Consultation Paper No. 186.

CHAPTER 2

EQUITABLE RIGHTS TO EASEMENTS

Legal easements and equitable rights

A legal easement is one which is created for an interest equivalent to a fee **2–01** simple absolute in possession or a term of years absolute.[1] It may be created by statute,[2] or by grant by deed *inter vivos*,[3] or by will,[4] in which last case the legal title is perfected by an assent, which, unless made by a corporation, need not be under seal.[5]

Inasmuch as an easement attaches to the dominant tenement in respect of which it is granted, it is obvious that an easement already in existence as a legal easement cannot be disposed of separately, and that there can be no question of creating

---

[1] Law of Property Act 1925, s.1(2).

[2] See para.3–02, below.

[3] See paras 3–04 *et seq.*, below. If the servient tenement is registered under the Land Registration Act 2002, the express grant or reservation of an easement will only create a legal, as distinct from an equitable, easement, when the easement is duly registered.

[4] See para.3–15, below.

[5] Law of Property Act 1925, s.52(1), (2)(a); *Hewlins v Shippam* (1826) 5 B. & C. 221. Possibly a parol lease of land plus an easement, taking effect in possession for a term not exceeding three years, and at the best rent reasonably obtainable, would create a legal easement: Law of Property Act 1925, ss.52(2)(d), 54(2). Note that in *Sweet v Sommer* [2004] EWHC 1504 (Ch) and [2005] EWCA Civ 227 it was conceded that an easement *reserved* by an assent which was under hand but not under seal took effect in equity only.

an interest in an existing easement apart from the land to which it belongs.[6] If an easement over Whiteacre is granted by deed to A, owner of Blackacre, in fee simple, and C afterwards becomes entitled in equity to Blackacre (as for instance by paying his purchase-money under an agreement for sale, but not taking a conveyance), then C, it is thought, could exercise the easement to which Whiteacre has already been subjected, although his interest in Blackacre and the easement is only equitable. But it would be impossible for A to create an equitable interest in the easement as a separate thing; no one could claim a right to the easement otherwise than by virtue of an interest in Blackacre.

2–02   Questions seldom arise as to the rights of a person entitled to an equitable interest in an existing legal easement. There are however cases where the only right to an easement is an equitable one. The principal cases where this occurs are cases of equitable easements:

(1) which are the subject of express grant in relation to a servient tenement which is registered under the Land Registration Act 2002 but where the grant is not completed by due registration;
(2) which arise as a result of the operation of the principles relating to proprietary estoppel; and
(3) equitable easements which arise pursuant to contracts to create legal easements.[7]

The effect of non-registration under the Land Registration Act 2002

2–03   The express grant or reservation of an easement (other than one which is capable of being registered under the Commons Registration Act 1965) is a disposition which is required to be completed by registration.[8] This reference to an express grant does not include a grant of an easement as a result of the operation of section 62 of the Law of Property Act 1925.[9] It follows from the use of the word "express" that an implied grant or reservation of an easement is not a disposition that requires to be completed by registration. If a disposition of a registered estate requires to be completed by registration, it does not operate at law until the relevant registration

---

[6] The position is to be contrasted with that relating to profits. The common law rule was that grazing rights appurtenant to land, if limited to a fixed number of animals, could be severed from the land to which they were attached, thereby converting them from rights appurtenant to rights in gross and this rule was not affected by the Commons Registration Act 1965 (see *Bettison v Langton* [2002] A.C. 27) but is now subject to Commons Act 2006, s.9 in relation to those rights of common which are registered as attached to any land: compare Commons Act 2006, s.12 in relation to rights of common not so registered.

[7] The position was well described by the New Brunswick Court of Appeal in *Salisbury (Village) v Collier* (1998) 169 D.L.R. (4d) 560 where it was said that if an owner agrees to grant an easement for valuable consideration, equity considers that the easement has been granted and that it is binding on parties taking with notice; the same result follows even if there was no consideration given by the dominant owner as long as he incurred expenditure or did work pursuant to the agreement. For further discussion of the subject, see Crane, "Estoppel Interests in Land" 31 Conv. 332; Poole, "Equities in the Making" 32 Conv. 90; and Jackson, "Equitable Easements" 33 Conv. 135.

[8] Land Registration Act 2002, s.27(2)(d).

[9] Land Registration Act 2002, s.27(7).

requirements are met.[10] The relevant registration requirements in relation to the express grant or reservation of an easement are set out in Schedule 2 to the 2002 Act.[11] These are that a notice in respect of the interest created must be entered in the register and, if the interest is created for the benefit of a registered estate, the proprietor of the registered estate must be entered in the register as its proprietor. The practical steps which must be taken to effect registration are explained in the Land Registry Practice Guide 62. It should be noted that an easement granted or reserved by a lease is a registered disposition. The Land Registry Practice Guide 62 explains the steps that should be taken to effect registration where the lease is a registered lease and where the lease is not a registered lease. The treatment of easements under the Land Registration Act 2002 is considered in detail in Chapter 5.

Proprietary estoppel

An equitable easement or an equitable right in the nature of an equitable easement can arise as a result of the operation of the principles of equity relating to proprietary estoppel. A full discussion of the equitable principles is beyond the scope of a work on easements.[12] Proprietary estoppel is a means by which property rights may be affected or created. It is also sometimes referred to as "estoppel by acquiescence". The reference to proprietary estoppel is a reference to the equitable jurisdiction of the court to interfere in cases where the assertion of legal rights is unconscionable. Although this jurisdiction is of long standing, it has been significantly developed in recent times. Because the principles are equitable and apply in cases of unconscionability, they are intended to remain flexible. This flexibility restricts the ability to describe them other than in broad terms. The essential elements of proprietary estoppel can be summarised as follows:

2–04

(1) an equity arises where the owner of land induces or encourages or allows another to believe that he has or will enjoy some right or benefit over the owner's property; in reliance upon this belief, the other acts to his detriment to the knowledge of the owner; and the owner then seeks to take unconscionable advantage of the other by denying him the right or benefit which he thought he had or expected to receive;

(2) the equity gives the other person the right to seek relief; the claim is an equitable one and is subject to the normal principles governing equitable remedies;

(3) the court has a wide discretion as to the manner in which it will give effect to the equity, having regard to all the circumstances of the case and to the expectations and conduct of both parties;

(4) the relief which is available to the court may be negative, that is, in the form of restraining the owner from asserting his legal rights, but it may

---

[10] Land Registration Act 2002, s.27(1).
[11] Land Registration Act 2002, s.27(4), Sch.2, para.7.
[12] A summary of the relevant principles is to be found in Megarry & Wade, *The Law of Real Property* (6th ed., 2000), Ch.13, pp. 727–751; a shorter summary is in *Snell's Equity* (30th ed.), pp. 637–643.

be positive, by ordering the owner to grant or convey to the other some estate, right or interest in or over his land, or to pay the other compensation, or both, or to act in some other way;

(5) it is in a case where the operation of these principles gives rise to an order that the owner grant the other a right in the nature of an equitable easement, that the case may be regarded as one where an equitable easement has been created by the operation of the principles of proprietary estoppel.[13]

2–05   In *Crabb v Arun District Council*[14] Scarman L.J. said that the law was correctly stated in Lord Kingsdown's dissenting speech in *Ramsden v Dyson*.[15] Lord Kingsdown said:

> "The rule of law applicable to the case appears to me to be this: If a man, under a verbal agreement with a landlord for a certain interest in land, or, what amounts to the same thing, under an expectation, created or encouraged by the landlord, that he shall have a certain interest, takes possession of such land, with the consent of the landlord, and upon the faith of such promise or expectation, with the knowledge of the landlord, and without objection by him, lays out money upon the land, a Court of equity will compel the landlord to give effect to such promise or expectation."

As Scarman L.J. said,[16] that statement of the law was put into the language of landlord and tenant because it was a landlord and tenant situation with which Lord Kingsdown was concerned, but it has been accepted as being of general application.

2–06   The requirements of such an estoppel were set out in more detail in *Willmott v Barber* by Fry J., referring to "five probanda".[17] These *probanda* have been recited and applied in some cases but not regarded as essential in others. The courts have now consistently indicated that they prefer a broad approach based on determining whether the behaviour of the person alleged to be estopped is unconscionable. Thus in *Taylors Fashions Ltd v Liverpool Victoria Trustees Co Ltd*,[18] Oliver J. said:

> "The more recent cases indicate that the application of the Ramsden v. Dyson principle–whether you call it proprietary estoppel, estoppel by acquiescence

---

[13] Amongst the leading cases on proprietary estoppel (not involving rights akin to easements) are *Dillwyn v Llewelyn* (1862) De G.F. & J. 517; *Ramsden v Dyson* (1866) L.R. 1 H.L. 129; *Willmot v Barber* (1880) 15 Ch. D. 96; *Plimmer v Mayor of Wellington* (1884) 9 App. Cas. 699; *Inwards v Baker* [1965] 2 Q.B. 29; *Taylors Fashions Ltd v Liverpool Victoria Trustees Ltd* [1982] Q.B. 133n.; and *Gillett v Holt* [2001] Ch. 210. In *Cobbe v Yeoman's Row Management Ltd* [2006] 1 W.L.R. 2964, the Court of Appeal considered in detail the approach to be adopted as to the relief to be granted where a claim based on a proprietary estoppel succeeded. The principal cases on proprietary estoppel involving rights akin to easements are *Ward v Kirkland* [1967] Ch. 194; *E.R. Ives Investments Ltd v High* [1967] 2 Q.B. 379; *Crabb v Arun D.C.* [1976] Ch. 179, and *Bexley LBC v Maison Maurice Ltd* [2007] 1 E.G.L.R. 19.
[14] [1976] Ch. 179 at 193, 194.
[15] (1866) L.R. 1 H.L. 139 at 170.
[16] *Crabb v Arun D.C.* [1976] Ch. 179.
[17] (1880) 15 Ch. D. 96 at 105–106.
[18] [1982] Q.B. 133n.

or estoppel by encouragement is really immaterial–requires a very much broader approach which is directed rather at ascertaining whether, in particular individual circumstances, it would be unconscionable for a party to be permitted to deny that which, knowingly, or unknowingly, he has allowed or encouraged another to assume to his detriment than to inquiring whether the circumstances can be fitted within the confines of some preconceived formula serving as a universal yardstick for every form of unconscionable behaviour."[19]

Illustrations

Rochdale Canal Co v King provides an early example of the application of the   **2–07** equitable principles. The company, which had obtained a decision at law that the defendant, the owner of a mill adjoining the company's canal, was not entitled to use the water for generating steam, applied first for an interim injunction,[20] and then for a perpetual injunction,[21] restraining the defendant from doing so. Both were refused. Lord Cranworth said[22]:

"The defendants by their answer swear that, to their belief, when the mill was originally built by James King [their father] in 1830, express notice was given by him to the canal company of his intention to make a communication with the canal in order to draw from it water, not only for the purpose of condensing steam [which was allowed], but also for the purpose of raising it, and for other purposes; that the servants and agents of the company superintended the laying down of the pipes, and were aware of the uses to which they were to be applied, and made no objection, although they were cognisant of the great expense incurred. Now, unquestionably, if this be true, the plaintiffs can have no relief in this court . . . I entirely assent to the argument . . . that mere acquiescence (if by acquiescence is to be understood only the abstaining from legal proceedings) is unimportant. Where one party invades the rights of another, that other does not, in general, deprive himself of the right of seeking redress merely because he remains passive . . . But the evidence of long-continued use of the water for all purposes, by the adjacent mill-owners, may be very important, as tending to satisfy this court that when the mill of the defendants was erected the plaintiffs must have known that King, who was building it, was laying out his money in the expectation that he would have the same privilege of using the water as was enjoyed by all his neighbours."

---

[19] At 151. See also *Crabb v Arun D.C.* [1976] Ch. 179 at 194, per Scarman L.J.; *Shaw v Applegate* [1977] 1 W.L.R. 970; *Amalgamated Investment and Property Co Ltd v Texas Commerce International Bank Ltd* [1982] Q.B. 84 at 103, per Robert Goff J.; *Habib Bank Ltd v Habib Bank AC Zurich* [1981] 1 W.L.R. 1265 at 1285, per Oliver L.J.; *John v George* [1996] 1 E.G.L.R. 7; *Gillett v Holt* [2001] Ch. 210.
[20] (1851) 2 Sim. (n.s.) 78.
[21] (1853) 16 Beav. 630.
[22] (1851) 2 Sim. (n.s.) 88.

On the later motion Sir John Romilly M.R. said[23]:

> "I am of opinion that, so far as concerns this mill, which was constructed in
> 1829, I must, on this evidence, come to the conclusion that the company have
> encouraged James King in so constructing his mill as to derive, from the canal,
> water for the purposes of steam, and that they cannot now, after the lapse of
> eighteen years, dispute his right to do so . . .[24]: I think that the Plaintiffs had
> then distinct notice that James King intended to employ the water of the canal
> for the purpose of steam, in addition to the condensation thereof, and having
> sent their engineer to inspect the laying down of the pipes for this purpose
> from the canal, I am of opinion that they must be held to have assented to the
> use of the water for such purposes relating to the generation or employment
> of steam, as the construction of his mill would manifestly and plainly have
> disclosed to anyone conversant in such matters."

In a judgment delivered two days later in another case,[25] Sir John Romilly referred
to "the principle . . . that he who stands by and encourages an act, cannot afterwards
complain of it".

2–08   In *Catching v Bassett*[26] the plaintiffs had pulled down a building, which had
windows with an easement of light over the defendants' adjoining property, and
built another, which, by arrangement made between them and the defendants for
the benefit of the defendants, was no higher than a line of light drawn from the top
of a wall at the back to the top of a party-wall, belonging to the plaintiffs and the
defendants, in front. The defendants, having given notice under the Metropolitan
Building Act 1855[27] of intention to raise the party-wall, and so to deprive the new
building of light, were restrained from doing so.

In *Williams v Earl of Jersey*[28] the plaintiffs sought to restrain the defendant
from proceeding with an action at law for alleged nuisance caused by copper
works on the plaintiffs' land. The bill alleged that the defendant was well aware
of the works being erected and the purpose for which they were intended, and of
the deleterious effect on vegetation produced by the manufacture of copper, but
nevertheless he acquiesced in and encouraged their erection and the expenditure
of money thereon. A demurrer was overruled.

The defendant in *Davies v Sear*[29] took from A an assignment of a lease, granted
to A, of a house under which was an arch, marked "gateway" on the plan, and
leading to a mews. At this time the mews was not fully enclosed, but A was under
contract to build round it so as to leave no other means of access than under the
arch, and this the plaintiff, A's successor in title to the mews and surrounding

---

[23] (1853) 16 Beav. 641.
[24] The defendants were his successors in title.
[25] *Duke of Beaufort v Patrick* (1853) 17 Beav. 60, 74 (not a case of easement).
[26] (1862) 32 Beav. 101.
[27] Now repealed.
[28] (1841) Cr. & Ph. 91.
[29] (1869) L.R. 7 Eq. 427.

land, did. The defendant, after the mews had been completely enclosed, was restrained from depriving it of all means of access by blocking up the arch, on the ground[30] that the physical appearance of the arch put him on inquiry as to how the land surrounding the mews was intended to be developed.

In *Ward v Kirkland*[31] the plaintiff's predecessor in title had in 1928 purchased a **2–09** cottage which was part of the glebe. The cottage was built on the northern boundary of the land conveyed and abutted onto a yard of a farm which was also part of the glebe. In 1942 the defendant's husband became tenant of the farm. In 1954 the cottage was conveyed to the plaintiff. In 1955 the plaintiff wished to instal a bathroom and water closets in the cottage and he asked for, and was given, permission by the defendant to lay drains. He then advised the rector of his plans and asked permission from him to lay drains through the farmyard and to connect them to the septic tank on his own premises. The rector gave permission for the bath water to be so drained without imposing any limit on the time during which the drains might remain. Nothing was said about effluent from the water closets. The plaintiff did the work, laying drains for the effluent and bath water and constructing his septic tank so as to take both and also surface water, which since before 1928 had come through the defendant's land on to his. In 1958 the defendant purchased the freehold of the farm. The defendant alleged that the drains laid under the farmyard constituted a trespass and she purported to terminate any licence which might have been given to the plaintiff and demanded that they should be removed.

Ungoed-Thomas J. found that the drains in the farmyard had been laid at the plaintiff's expense in reliance on the permission given by the fee simple owner without any stipulation as to period, and, in those circumstances, the plaintiff had an equitable right to keep the drains in position permanently for the purpose of draining off the bath water, and he was accordingly entitled to an injunction restraining the defendant from interfering with that right. Furthermore, Ungoed-Thomas J. held that although the plaintiff's equity related only to the drainage of bath water, the defendant's claim for an injunction to restrain the drainage of effluent failed, because she had herself given consent to the installation of the drains and had stood by while they were put in, not objecting until much later; and that, although the plaintiff had trespassed in using the drains in excess of the permission granted, that was an insubstantial and trivial trespass entitling the defendant to nominal damages only.

Ward v Kirkland[32] was applied in *E.R. Ives Investment Limited v High*.[33] The **2–10** defendant, who was a builder, in 1949 bought the site of a bombed house and started to build a new house on it. At about the same time one Westgate bought an adjoining double site and started to build on it a block of flats. Westgate encroached on the defendant's site, putting the foundations of the flats about a foot over the boundary into the defendant's land some feet below ground level. The defendant objected to this trespass but at a meeting between the parties it was orally agreed

---

[30] It was also held that a way of necessity arose. See paras 3–115 *et seq.*, below.
[31] [1967] Ch. 194.
[32] [1967] Ch. 194.
[33] [1967] 2 Q.B. 379.

between them that Westgate was to be allowed to keep the foundations of the flats on the defendant's land and that the defendant was to have a right of way from the back of his house across the yard of Westgate's flats so as to get access to a side road. There were letters evidencing the agreement, which was acted upon by both sides. In 1950 Westgate sold his site to a Flight Lieutenant and Mrs Wright, who knew of the agreement. Soon afterwards both the defendant's house and the block of flats were finished. The defendant used the way across the yard and, in 1959, relying on the right of way, he built a garage which was so constructed that it could only be used by means of the yard. The Wrights raised no objection to the building of the garage or to the defendant's use of the yard for access to it. Moreover, in 1960, the Wrights got the defendant to resurface the yard and he paid one-fifth of the cost of so doing. In 1962 the Wrights put up the flats for sale by auction, the particulars of sale referring to the defendant's right of way over the yard. The plaintiff company bought this property at the auction and the conveyance to the company from the Wrights stated that the property was conveyed subject to the right of way. The right of way was never registered as a land charge and the plaintiff claimed that it was void against it under section 13 of the Land Charges Act 1925.[34] The plaintiff brought an action for damages and trespass and an injunction restraining the defendant from trespassing on the yard.

The judge of the Norwich County Court dismissed the claim and an appeal by the plaintiff to the Court of Appeal failed. Lord Denning M.R. and Danckwerts L.J.[35] held that the defendant had in equity a good right of way across the yard arising in two ways, first by reason of the mutual benefit and burden under the agreement made between Westgate and the defendant in 1949, and secondly, by reason of the acquiescence of the plaintiff's predecessors in the rights thereby acquired. Winn L.J.[36] put the defendant's rights slightly differently, saying that a very clear equity and also an estoppel arose against the plaintiff preventing it from denying the defendant's use of the right of way.

2–11   In *Crabb v Arun District Council*,[37] the plaintiff owned a piece of land from which access to the public highway was obtained at point A over a road belonging to the defendant. The plaintiff wished to sell his land in two parts and agreed with the defendant's representative a second access at point B. The defendant fenced the boundary between its road and the plaintiff's land, with gates at points A and B. The plaintiff sold the piece of land with access at point A without reserving any right in favour of the other piece, thus leaving it land-locked, unless there

---

[34] Repealed. See now the Land Charges Act 1972, s.4(6), as amended by the Finance Act 1975, s.52(1) and Sch.12.

[35] Danckwerts L.J. referred (at 399) with approval to *Snell's Equity* (26th ed., 1966), pp. 629–633, where the equitable ground in question was discussed under the name of "proprietary estoppel" and the comment is made (at p. 633) that "the doctrine thus displays equity at its most flexible". Both Lord Denning M.R. and Danckwerts L.J. applied *Hopgood v Brown* [1955] 1 W.L.R. 213 and *Halsall v Brizett* [1957] Ch. 169.

[36] Winn L.J. referred (at 405) to *Halsall v Brizett* [1957] Ch. 169 at 182, per Upjohn J.

[37] [1976] Ch. 179. *Cf. McBean v Howey* [1958] N.Z.L.R. 25; *Dewhirst v Edwards* [1983] 1 N.S.W.L.R. 34 (where the claim failed on the facts); and *Hill v AWJ Moore & Co Pty Ltd* (1990) 5 B.P.R. 97,358 (where the claim succeeded).

was access at point B on to the defendant's road. The defendant removed the gate at point B and fenced the gap.

In the Court of Appeal Scarman L.J. said[38] that if the plaintiff had any right, it was an equity arising out of the conduct and relationship of the parties, and that it was well settled law that the court, having analysed and assessed the conduct and relationship of the parties, had to answer three questions: "First, is there an equity established? Secondly, what is the extent of the equity, if one is established? And, thirdly, what is the relief appropriate to satisfy the equity?"

The Court of Appeal held that the defendant was estopped from denying to the plaintiff the access at point B. The defendant knew through its representative that the plaintiff intended to sell his land in two parts. It led him to believe that he would be granted an access at point B and, by erecting the gates and failing to disabuse the plaintiff of his belief, had encouraged him to act to his detriment in selling part of his land without reservation over it of any right of way, thereby giving rise to an equity in his favour. In those circumstances Scarman L.J.[39] analysed the minimum equity to do justice to the plaintiff as a right either to an easement or to a licence upon terms to be agreed. In fact the court held that the plaintiff should have an easement.

In subsequent proceedings,[40] in which the plaintiff applied for damages for loss which he had suffered by the sterilisation of his land over some five to six years, the Court of Appeal dismissed his claim. Damages could have been awarded under the Chancery Amendment Act 1858 (Lord Cairns' Act),[41] but, since no question of damages had been raised at the hearing, it was now too late to inquire into that matter. The right to damages as an equitable remedy was discretionary. **2–12**

It is to be observed that, while estoppel has in the past often been referred to as being a shield and not a sword, in such a case as *Crabb v Arun District Council*,[42] in which new rights and interests are created by estoppel in or over land, those rights can give rise to a cause of action. There are also earlier cases in which a man has executed works, etc., on the understanding that he is to have an easement on terms, but no terms have been agreed. In such cases interference with the intended right has been restrained, the terms being settled by the court.[43]

In *Valentine v Allen*[44] various parties involved in a scheme of development orally agreed on a layout which would allow all of them access to the properties **2–13**

---

[38] [1976] Ch. 179 at 192, 193.
[39] [1976] Ch. 179 at 198.
[40] *Crabb v Arun District Council (No. 2)* (1976) 121 S.J. 86.
[41] Repealed by the Supreme Court Act 1981, s.152(4), Sch.7: see now *ibid.*, s.50. See further, para.14–86, below.
[42] [1976] Ch. 179 at 187, per Lord Denning M.R.
[43] *Powell v Thomas* (1848) 6 Hare 300; *Duke of Devonshire v Eglin* (1851) 14 Beav. 530; *Laird v Birkenhead Ry Co* (1859) John. 500; *cf. Covering's Case*, referred to by Lord Loughborough, 5 Ves. 690; 6 Hare 304n.; L.R. 10 Eq. 147. In *East India Co v Vincent* (1740) 2 Atk. 83, where the defendant agreed, in return for a promise by the company to employ him, that certain proposed new windows in the company's building should have a right of light (both agreements being oral), and on the faith of this the windows were put in but the company did not employ as agreed, whereupon the defendant built a wall obstructing the light, Lord Hardwicke ordered the defendant to pull down the wall, and the company to perform its agreement.
[44] [2003] EWCA Civ 915.

in which they were interested. Their underlying assumption was that earlier deeds of grant enabled the development to be carried out in accordance with that layout. The parties embarked on the development on the basis of that common assumption so that they (and their successors in title) would not be allowed to assert rights inconsistent with that assumption in circumstances where it would be unfair or unjust to do so.

2–14   In *Sweet v Sommer*[45] Mr Lovering owned both Old Forge Yard and Forge Meadow. In April 1988, he transferred Old Forge Yard to himself and his wife. The transfer did not expressly reserve any right to way to Forge Meadow which he initially retained. The trial judge held that a way of necessity was to be implied but he went on to consider arguments as to proprietary estoppel on the basis that there was no implied way of necessity. The Court of Appeal did not find it necessary to consider the argument as to a way of necessity and decided the case on the basis of the claim to a proprietary estoppel. In October 1988, Mr Lovering transferred Forge Meadow to the predecessor of the claimants. The transfer of October 1988 purported to grant a right of way over Old Forge Yard to the predecessor of the claimants. The case proceeded on the basis that this grant was not effective because it was made by Mr Lovering alone and not by Mr and Mrs Lovering who, in October 1988, were the joint owners of Old Forge Yard. However, Mrs Lovering knew of the terms of the grant in the October 1988 transfer. Later, Forge Meadow was transferred to the claimants and Old Forge Yard was transferred to the defendant. The defendant contended that there had not been an effective grant of a right of way over Old Forge Yard in favour of Forge Meadow. It was held that if Mrs Lovering had sought to challenge the grant in the October 1988 transfer she would have been estopped from doing so. She knew of the grant, she (and Mr Lovering) both believed the grant was effective, the purchaser believed the grant was effective, and the purchaser incurred expense in reliance on that belief to the knowledge of Mr and Mrs Lovering. Any estoppel which would have bound Mrs Lovering in equity was also binding on the defendant as successor in title to Old Forge Yard as the equity was an overriding interest under rule 258 of the Land Registration Rules 1925.[46]

2–15   In *Bexley London Borough Council v Maison Maurice Ltd*[47] the defendant had a right of access to an existing highway. The Council as highway authority wished to build a relief road which would cut across this access. Its plan was carried into effect and the relief road, called Albion Way, was built. The Council retained title to a strip of land between the defendant's land and Albion Way. The defendant agreed terms with the Council which included the reservation of a right of way across the strip of land to Albion Way. Later, the defendant wished to create an alternative access to Albion Way. The proposed new access would be safer to use. The defendant obtained planning permission from the Council for the new access. One of the conditions attached to the planning permission was that the existing access was to be stopped up and extinguished. The defendant instructed the works

---

[45] [2004] EWHC 1504 (Ch) and [2005] EWCA Civ 227.
[46] This point is discussed at para.2–43, below.
[47] [2007] 1 E.G.L.R. 19.

department of the Council to construct a crossover to form the new access. The previous access was physically stopped up. Between 1996 and 1998, the defendant used the new access without objection from the Council. In 1998, the Council asked the defendant for payment equating to 50 per cent of the value of the land in return for the grant of a right of access for the new crossover. It was held that the defendant had the benefit of a proprietary estoppel which prevented the Council denying that the defendant had a permanent access across the new crossover. A reasonable person in the position of the defendant would have believed that it had simply exchanged one means of access for another without there being a requirement that the land for the new access had to be bought from the Council. The defendant did so believe. That belief had been encouraged by the Council. The detriment suffered by the defendant was not confined to the expenditure on creating the new access but included giving up the old access in circumstances where it might not get planning permission (which would be needed) to re-open the old access. The conduct of the Council was unconscionable. In fashioning a remedy, the court adopts a flexible approach. One possible starting point is to fulfil the relevant expectations which had been encouraged by the Council. This may not be appropriate where the expectations are uncertain, or extravagant, or out of all proportion to the detriment suffered. In this case, the fulfillment of the defendant's expectations was not extravagant or disproportionate to the detriment suffered.

Limits on proprietary estoppel

While proprietary estoppel will come to the assistance of a party who has clearly **2–16** been encouraged to rely upon the acquiescence of another, it is not possible to acquire on the basis of acquiescence a right to do something, or to produce a result, not reasonably capable of being supposed to have been contemplated by the acquiescing party.

In *Bankart v Houghton*[48] Sir John Romilly M.R. thought it "impossible to be reasonably contended that, because a man has acquiesced in the erection of certain works which have produced little or no injury, he is not afterwards to have any remedy, if, by the increase of the works, at a subsequent period, he sustains a serious injury".

In *Bankart v Tennant*,[49] where a tenant under an agreement for a lease had started a copper factory and for a time, without objection by the lessor, had used surplus water from the lessor's canal, no agreement for the use of this was imputed to the lessor, for the canal water was not essential to the factory.[50]

Negotiations for the grant of property rights, such as an easement, are often car- **2–17** ried on subject to the express stipulation that they are "subject to contract". This is a well understood phrase which is intended to convey to the negotiating parties the message that neither side will be legally bound until a contract is concluded and up to that point either party is free to withdraw from the negotiations. Thus, in a "subject to contract" case, it may not be possible for a party claiming a proprietary

[48] (1860) 27 Beav. 425.
[49] (1870) L.R. 10 Eq. 141.
[50] *cf. Pwllbach Colliery Co v Woodman* [1915] A.C. 634.

estoppel to demonstrate that it had a belief that it had acquired rights, or an expectation that it would be granted rights (unless of course a contract were to be made). Further, in such a case, it would not generally be considered unconscionable for a party to withdraw from negotiations and assert that the other party had not acquired any rights in the absence of a concluded contract, given that the withdrawing party had expressly reserved the right to withdraw.[51] It is possible but unlikely that in some circumstances a party to negotiations which began as "subject to contract" would be able to satisfy the court that the parties had subsequently agreed to convert the negotiations into a contract or that some form of estoppel had arisen to prevent both parties from refusing to proceed with the transaction envisaged, for example, by making a representation or inducing a belief to the effect that he would not withdraw from the negotiations notwithstanding the "subject to contract" label.[52] However, a "subject to contract" case needs to be distinguished from a case where there is no contract but yet there is the necessary expectation that rights will be granted and the circumstances are such that the other party would be acting unconscionably if he were to defeat those expectations. The all-important difference seems to rely heavily on the express use of the words "subject to contract" amounting to an express reservation of a right to withdraw from negotiations and therefore a right to defeat whatever expectations might otherwise have arisen.[53]

2–18   In *Armstrong v Sheppard & Short Limited*[54] the plaintiff owned a small strip of land at the rear of his premises on which the defendant company had entered and constructed a sewer for the discharge of sewage and effluent. The plaintiff claimed damages for trespass and an injunction to restrain the discharge of effluent through the sewer. The judge of the Willesden County Court found as a fact that the plaintiff had orally informed the defendant that he did not object to the construction of the sewer; but he also found that the plaintiff, when he so informed the defendant, was not aware that he was the owner of the strip of land or that he had a right to object to the construction of the sewer. In those circumstances the Court of Appeal held that the plaintiff was not debarred from asserting his legal right against one who was shown to have infringed it on the ground of acquiescence, unless it was clear that at the time when he acquiesced he was aware of his proprietary right and, accordingly, that there was no equity which barred the plaintiff from asserting his legal title, though in the circumstances he should not be granted an injunction.

---

[51] *Attorney General of Hong Kong v Humphreys Estate (Queen's Garden) Ltd* [1987] A.C. 114. And see *Derby & Co Ltd v ITC Pension Trust Ltd* [1977] 2 All E.R. 890 and *London & Regional Investments Ltd v TBI Plc* [2002] EWCA Civ 355 at [41]–[44].

[52] *Attorney General of Hong Kong v Humphreys Estate (Queen's Garden) Ltd* [1987] A.C. 114 at 127H–128B; *Cobbe v Yeoman's Row Management Ltd* [2006] 1 W.L.R. 2964 at [57].

[53] *Cobbe v Yeoman's Row Management Ltd* [2005] W.T.L.R. 625 at [118]–[122] (Etherton J.) and [2006] 1 W.L.R. 2964 at [53]–[57] (Court of Appeal). In *Kilcarne Holdings Ltd v Targetfollow (Birmingham) Ltd* [2005] 2 P. & C.R. 105 it was said at [229] that in this respect equity follows the law; the point was not considered on appeal at [2006] 1 P. & C.R. D55.

[54] [1959] 2 Q.B. 384. The Court of Appeal applied *Ramsden v Dyson* (1865) L.R. 1 H.L. 129 and *Willmott v Barber* (1880) 15 Ch. D. 96; see also *Ward v Kirkland* [1967] Ch. 194, 235–241.

Further, there will be no estoppel if the party enforcing his legal right is not act-   **2–19**
ing unconscionably. In *Lovett v Fairclough*[55] the defendant unsuccessfully claimed
to have acquired by prescription a profit in gross in piscary in common and without
stint. In the alternative, the defendant claimed to be entitled to such a profit pursuant
to a proprietary estoppel; it was held on the detailed facts that it was not unconscionable or inequitable for the plaintiffs to assert their legal rights to prevent the
defendant from fishing.

There is no reported case in which a man, merely because he has encouraged
the erection of a building by his neighbour, has had imputed to him an agreement
that the light to the windows of the building shall not be obstructed. As a general
rule it is clear that the right to build on land is one of the natural rights of ownership, and that one who builds on the edge of his land takes his chance of his
neighbour doing the same, to his prejudice.[56]

Actual agreement

It appears that an agreement which complies with the relevant statutory formalities,   **2–20**
made for valuable consideration for the grant of an easement, or to the effect that
some easement shall be exercisable, creates in equity a valid easement which can be
exercised against the servient party and his successors in title, not being a purchaser
for value without notice[57]; and that the same result may follow as a result of an estoppel[58] from an agreement not made for valuable consideration but involving expenditure or work actually incurred or done by the dominant party, as, for instance, an
agreement, oral or under hand only, made between A and B and acted on by B, that
B shall have the right to lay and maintain a pipe in A's land for the use of B's land.[59]

The statutory formalities

Before September 27, 1989, an agreement for the grant of an easement was not   **2–21**
enforceable by action unless it complied with section 40 of the Law of Property
Act 1925,[60] which provided that no action could be brought on an agreement
for the sale or other disposition of an interest in land, unless the agreement or

---

[55] (1990) 61 P. & C.R. 385. More generally, as to the need to keep the right claimed in proportion to
the detriment suffered, see *Cobbe v Yeoman's Row Management Ltd* [2006] 1 W.L.R. 2964;
Sledmore v Dalby (1996) 72 P. & C.R. 196; and *National Westminster Bank Plc v Somer
International (UK) Ltd* [2001] EWCA Civ 970; [2002] 1 All E.R. 198. In *Evans v Cynon Valley
B.C.*, unreported, CA, January 16, 1992, a claim to a right of way on the basis of an equitable estop-
pel failed because the defendant borough council was not acting unconscionably.

[56] *Tapling v Jones* (1865) 11 H.L.C. 290, 305; *Allen v Seckham* (1879) 11 Ch. D. 790 at 792, 797;
Truscott v Merchant Tailors' Co (1856) 11 Exch. 855 at 864, 865; *Hunter v Canary Wharf Ltd*
[1997] A.C. 655.

[57] See para.2–36, below. *Thatcher v Douglas* [1996] N.L.J. 282; *Smith v Curry* (1918) 42 D.L.R. 225;
Leon Asper Amusements Ltd v Northmain Carwash (1966) 56 D.L.R. (2d) 173.

[58] *cf.* the cases referred to at paras 2–04 *et seq.*, above; *James Jones & Sons Ltd v Earl of Tankerville*
[1909] 2 Ch. 440 at 443.

[59] In *E.R. Ives Investment v High* [1967] 2 Q.B. 379, see para.2–10, above, the Court of Appeal found
that there was a concluded agreement which the parties contemplated would be put into force, but
this was not the ratio decidendi in that case.

[60] Replacing Statute of Frauds 1677, s.4.

some memorandum or note thereof was in writing and signed by the party to be charged or by some other person thereunto by him lawfully authorised. However, if the person seeking to enforce the agreement could show part performance by him of the agreement, he did not have to establish a memorandum or note in writing.[61]

2–22   On and after September 27, 1989, the position is governed by section 2 of the Law of Property (Miscellaneous Provisions) Act 1989. This provides that a contract for the sale or other disposition of an interest in land can only be made in writing and only by incorporating all the terms which the parties have expressly agreed in one document or, where contracts are exchanged, in each.[62] An easement is within the definition of "interest in land".[63] The grant of an easement is a "disposition".[64] The terms may be incorporated in a document either by being set out in it or by reference to some other document.[65] The documents incorporating the terms or, where contracts are exchanged, one of the documents incorporating them (but not necessarily the same one), must be signed by or on behalf of each party to the contract.[66] Where a contract for the sale or other disposition of an interest in land satisfies the conditions of this section by reason only of the rectification of one or more documents in pursuance of an order of a court, the contract comes into being, or is deemed to have come into being, at such time as may be specified in the court's order.[67] Section 2 applies only to contracts which are executory and not to contracts which have been executed, e.g. by the grant of the interest in land.[68]

2–23   These provisions make major changes in the law. The contract must be in writing and it is not sufficient to have a note or memorandum which evidences the contract. All the agreed terms must be set out in the single document or in each part of the exchanged documents. Thus it is no longer possible, as it was under section 40 of the Law of Property Act 1925, to construct a contract, and a note or memorandum of it, out of an exchange of letters. "Exchange of contracts" requires there to be a formal exchange of signed parts of the contract involving a formal delivery by each party of its part into the actual or constructive possession of the other with the intention that the parties will become actually bound when exchange occurs, but not before.[69]

2–24   The document must set out all the terms of the contract. Thus one must ask: did the terms upon which the parties agreed to dispose of the relevant interest include

---

[61] For a detailed treatment of section 40 and of the law relating to part performance, see Megarry & Wade, *The Law of Real Property* (6th ed., 2000), 12.015–12.017.

[62] 1989 Act, s.2(1).

[63] 1989 Act, s.2(6).

[64] 1989 Act, s.2(6) incorporating the definition in s.205(1)(ii) of the Law of Property Act 1925.

[65] 1989 Act, s.2(2).

[66] 1989 Act, s.2(3).

[67] 1989 Act, s.2(4). For an example of this, see *Wright v Robert Leonard Developments* [1994] E.G.C.S. 69. For a case where the written document omitted terms which had been expressly agreed but where the omission could not be cured by rectification, see *Oun v Ahmad* [2008] EWHC 545 (Ch).

[68] *Tootal Clothing v Guinea Properties Ltd* (1992) 64 P. & C.R. 452, explained and distinguished in *Kilcarne Holdings Ltd v Targetfollow (Birmingham) Ltd* [2005] 2 P. & C.R. 105 at [198] (this point was not discussed on appeal at [2006] 1 P. & C.R. D55).

[69] *Commission for the New Towns v Cooper* [1995] Ch. 259.

a term that has not been incorporated in the document which they have signed?[70] It had been said that the provisions do not apply to a contract which is merely collateral to the contract for the disposition of an interest in land,[71] but this approach has been questioned.[72] Any alterations that are made to a concluded written contract must themselves comply with section 2; this cannot be achieved by an exchange of letters and the parties will have to exchange identical signed copies of the variation or they will both have to sign one document which makes the change. If the parties do not comply with section 2 in relation to such alterations, then the alterations will be a nullity and the original contract will remain enforceable because no binding agreement has superseded it.[73] It may no longer be possible to adduce extrinsic evidence to identify the land.[74]

The contract must be signed[75] by each party to it and not merely by the party **2–25** against whom the contract is sought to be enforced. A letter and a plan referred to in the letter will not normally constitute a single document. The document relied on as a single document must be self-evidently a single document. But it is possible for a contract to be created by the signing by both parties of one document which refers to a further document in which some or all of the contract terms are set out. The purpose of the reference must be to incorporate in the primary document the terms set out in the further document. Thus a letter and an accompanying plan did not create a contract where the plan, but not the letter, had been signed by both parties.[76]

The doctrine of part performance has been abolished.[77] Section 2 of the 1989 Act **2–26** does not affect the creation or operation of resulting, implied or constructive trusts.[78] Thus, in a case where the parties made an oral agreement under which one party was to carry out building works on a house and was then to be granted a lease of the house and where that party performed his side of the agreement, the circumstances were such that he was entitled to an interest in the house, applying the principles of proprietary estoppel, and the same facts could be relied upon to establish a constructive trust which had effect notwithstanding section 2 of the 1989 Act.[79]

---

[70] *Grossman v Hooper* [2001] EWCA Civ 615, [2001] 2 E.G.L.R. 82 at [20]; *Kilcarne Holdings Ltd v Targetfollow (Birmingham) Ltd* [2005] 2 P. & C.R. 105 at [198] (this point was not discussed on appeal at [2006] 1 P. & C.R. D55); *Dolphin Quays Development Ltd v Mills* [2007] 1 P. & C.R. 12.

[71] *Record v Bell* [1991] 1 W.L.R. 853; *Tootal Clothing Ltd v Guinea Properties Management Ltd* (1992) 64 P. & C.R. 452; *Lotteryking v AMEC Properties* [1995] 2 E.G.L.R. 15.

[72] *Grossman v Hooper* [2001] EWCA Civ 615, [2001] 2 E.G.L.R. 82 at [20], [34]–[37].

[73] *McCausland v Duncan Lawrie Ltd* [1997] 1 W.L.R. 38.

[74] *Rudra v Abbey National Plc* (1998) 76 P. & C.R. 537 at 541, 542; extrinsic evidence was admitted in *Freeguard v Rogers* [1999] 1 W.L.R. 375 but the effect of s.2 of the 1989 Act on the admissibility of the evidence was not argued.

[75] "Signed" is to be given its ordinary meaning: *Firstpost Homes v Johnson* [1995] 4 All E.R. 355; thus a letter drafted by one party and addressed to that party with the intention that it be signed by the other party was not without more "signed" by the addressee.

[76] *Firstpost Homes v Johnson* [1995] 4 All E.R. 355.

[77] Law of Property Act 1925, s.40(2), which preserved the doctrine of part performance is repealed by the 1989 Act, s.2(8); *Yaxley v Gotts* [2000] Ch. 162 at 172F, but see *Singh v Beggs* (1995) 71 P. & C.R. 120.

[78] Law of Property (Miscellaneous Provisions) Act 1989, s.2(5).

[79] *Yaxley v Gotts* [2000] Ch. 162.

Illustrations

2–27   In *McManus v Cooke*,[80] the plaintiff and defendant, being owners of adjoining houses, had entered into an oral agreement, under which a party-wall was to be pulled down and rebuilt at their joint expense, and each party was to be at liberty to make a lean-to skylight resting on the new party-wall and running up to the sill of the first-floor window of his own building. The defendant having shaped his skylight so as to show above the wall and obstruct some of the light coming to the plaintiff's skylight, Kay J. granted an injunction, holding that the agreement was for an easement of light, and that if the Statute of Frauds[81] applied, as in his opinion it did, the plaintiff, having provided the defendant with the benefit intended for him, was entitled to the benefit intended for himself. The order, after reciting that the alleged agreement as to pulling down and rebuilding the party-wall, and the position of the skylights on each side of it, had been proved, restrained the defendant from permitting his skylight to remain, and from placing any other skylight which would obstruct the light to the plaintiff's skylight more than the skylight which the defendant agreed to erect would have done, the plaintiff giving a corresponding undertaking as to his skylight; and it directed, if necessary, the execution of a proper deed to secure these easements to both parties.

2–28   In *May v Belleville*[82] a right of way reserved to the plaintiff, pursuant to a sale agreement, in a conveyance by him not executed by the purchaser and so not operating as a legal grant of the way,[83] was enforced against a successor in title of the purchaser taking with notice of the agreement.

In *White v Grand Hotel, Eastbourne*,[84] where it was proved that P and F, predecessors in title of the parties, had made and acted on a verbal arrangement under which F was to set back into his land a boundary wall between his land and a passage belonging to P, so widening the passage, and in return was to be allowed to open a gateway in the new wall and have a right of way over the passage, the rights of the parties in regard to the passage were determined exactly as they would have been if the right had been actually granted.

2–29   In *Cory v Davies*[85] three adjoining pieces of land, west, middle and east, fronting on a road, had been demised in 1857 separately to three related persons called Cory, each of whom covenanted with the lessor to develop in accordance with plans and specifications said in the lease to have been agreed. A terrace of seven houses, standing back from the road, was built, two (W1 and W2) on the west plot, three on the middle plot, and two (E1 and E2) on the east plot. A wall was built along the side of the road, with a gate at each end, opposite W1 and E2. Inside was a roadway, suitable for vehicles but without turning space, the result being that a vehicle going to any of the houses had to use both gates and the whole of the roadway.

---

[80] (1887) 35 Ch. D. 681.
[81] The predecessor of the Law of Property Act 1925, s.40.
[82] [1905] 2 Ch. 605.
[83] But see now the Law of Property Act 1925, s.65, and para.3–12, below.
[84] (1912) 106 L.T. 785; [1913] 1 Ch. 113; 82 L.J. Ch. 57, CA; 110 L.T. 209, HL.
[85] [1923] 2 Ch. 95.

The defendant, who had taken an assignment of E2, the piece of roadway in front of it and the east gateway, refused to allow vehicles to pass his house, and unsuccessfully defended an action by the assignees of the leasehold interest in the other six houses. Judgment was given on alternative grounds, one of which was that the circumstances justified the inference that the three original lessees, before building the houses and making the roadway and gates, had mutually agreed that each should grant the others the easements required for vehicular access, that the Statute of Frauds[86] was no defence, for each intended grantee had performed his part by making, or contributing to the expense of, his portion of the terrace, roadway and gates, and that each of the three plots thus acquired in equity the requisite easement over the others. The defendant took (as it was held) with notice of the easement acquired by the other two plots, and was thus bound by them.

An argument that the assignee of E1, which had been leased together with E2, had no rights against E2, because the assignment of E2 contained no express reservation in favour of E1, was rejected on the ground that, as the assignment of E2 carried inferentially a right over the portion of roadway belonging to E1, it could be considered to reserve by implication a similar right over the roadway belonging to E2; alternatively, an actual verbal agreement to that effect could be assumed to have been made. The same conclusion was reached on the alternative ground that, in the circumstances, there ought to be implied in each of the three leases a grant of the right to use the roadway and gates not included in the demise, and a reservation to the lessor and his lessees, owners and occupiers of the other plots, of the right to use the roadway and gates, so far as constructed on the demised plot.

In *Celsteel Ltd v Alton House Holdings Ltd*[87] a specifically enforceable contract   **2–30**
to grant a lease of a garage together with a right of way to the garage was held to create an equitable easement over the route of the way.

In *Thatcher v Douglas*,[88] the plaintiff, T, agreed with the adjoining landowner,   **2–31**
Mr Williams, to share the use of a slipway leading down to tidal mud-flats. Part of the slipway intruded onto T's land. Thereafter, W sold his property and it eventually came into the ownership of the defendant, D. T continued to use the slipway until his use was objected to by D. The court held that in many cases where there was an informal agreement between friendly neighbours, the natural inference was that the agreement was intended to be personal to them. However, in this case as a result of certain evidence given and, in particular, in view of the fact that the quid pro quo for the user of the slipway was the permission to continue the trespass on T's land and that trespass was likely to continue indefinitely, the right to use the slipway was also to continue indefinitely and enure for the benefit of T's successors in title and be binding on W's successors in title. It was also held that as W's land was registered land, the agreement for the easement was an overriding interest under section 70(1)(a) of the Land Registration Act 1925.[89]

---

[86] The predecessor of the Law of Property Act 1925, s.40.
[87] [1985] 1 W.L.R. 204 at 219H.
[88] [1996] N.L.J. 282.
[89] See para.5–10, below.

Dominant tenement must be identified

2–32   It has been seen that a contract to grant an easement at once or upon a future con-
tingency gives rise to an immediate interest in land potentially binding on and
enuring for the benefit of the parties' successors in title. Moreover, an option to
acquire an easement also qualifies as an interest in land.[90] However, a contract
to create what is intended to be an easement for the benefit of land which is to
be identified in the future does not create a proprietary interest and will not,
therefore, be binding on successors in title of the grantor,[91] at least if they acquire
the servient land before the dominant tenement is identified.[92] The law requires
that there should be a dominant tenement before there can be a grant, or a contract for the grant, of an easement sufficient to create an interest in land binding
successors in title to the servient land. The reasons for this have been said to be,
first, the policy against encumbering land with burdens of uncertain extent and,
secondly, the reluctance of the law to recognise new forms of burden on property
conferring more than contractual rights.[93]

2–33   So in *London & Blenheim Estates Limited v Ladbroke Retail Parks Limited* the
Court of Appeal held that the grant of a right to nominate additional land as the
dominant tenement so as to enjoy the right to use a car park did not create an
interest in land which bound successors in title to the servient tenement. It was
accepted by counsel and assumed by the Court without decision that, if the notice
nominating the additional land had been served before the grantor had disposed
of the servient tenement, an interest in land would have arisen but the Court
expressed some doubt whether an interest in land can arise on the occurrence of
an event after the grant of the relevant rights.[94]

Similarly in *Voice v Bell*,[95] it was held that a clause which provided that if the
transferor were to acquire property at the rear of the land transferred, the trans-
ferees and their successors should not object to him demolishing a wall so as to
provide access for motor vehicles to the property in question was enforceable
only as a matter of contract and did not bind a successor to the servient tenement.

2–34   Although it is of the essence of an easement that there must be both a dominant and servient tenement, the fact that the affected part of the servient land
remains to be identified in the future does not prevent the creation of a proprietary
interest, provided that the rule against perpetuities is not infringed.[96]

---

[90] *Gas & Fuel Corporation of Victoria v Barba* [1976] V.R. 755.
[91] *London & Blenheim Estates Limited v Ladbroke Retail Parks Limited* [1994] 1 W.L.R. 31.
[92] *Voice v Bell* (1993) 68 P. & C.R. 441.
[93] [1994] 1 W.L.R. 31 at 37G–H.
[94] [1994] 1 W.L.R. 31, at 38D–E.
[95] Above.
[96] See paras 1–107 *et seq.*, above. In *London & Blenheim Estates Limited v Ladbroke Retail Parks
Limited* (above) the right granted was to park on any part of the retained land set aside as a car
park when the transferor's development had been completed. A similar conclusion was reached in
relation to the effect of an option to call for an area of land (to be identified subsequent to the
agreement) within an identified larger area: the option created an equitable interest binding the
whole of the larger area, until the smaller area was identified: *Sainsbury's Supermarkets Ltd v
Olympia Homes Ltd* [2006] 1 P. & C.R. 289 at [56]–[66].

An agreement to grant a profit

The same principle is applied in the case of a *profit à prendre* which, to exist as a legal interest, must be granted by deed.[97] An enforceable contract will give the grantee an equitable right to a profit.[98] In the case of an agreement made before September 27, 1989, if not supported by part performance, there must be a sufficient memorandum in writing to satisfy section 40 of the Law of Property Act 1925[99]; if there is evidence in writing, or if the grant is supported by acts of part performance, the grantee may sue for interference with the right.[100] In the case of an agreement made on or after September 27, 1989, the parties must comply with section 2 of the Law of Property (Miscellaneous Provisions) Act 1989.[101]

2–35

The position of third parties

An easement to which an equitable right has arisen in any of the ways mentioned in this chapter, enures, it is thought, like a legal easement, for the benefit of the dominant tenement.[102] The general rule of the law of equity, and subject to statutory requirements as to registration (considered in detail below) is that the equitable right is binding on a purchaser with notice of it or upon a donee irrespective of whether he has notice of it.[103] If the equity is to be regarded as a mere equity,[104] then even a purchaser of an equitable interest without notice of the equity will take free of it.[105] Thus, in *Prinsep v Belgravian Estate Ltd*,[106] a house built under a building agreement eventually followed by a lease was held not to have an easement of light against adjoining property which had been sold by the lessor, after the agreement but before the lease, to a purchaser without notice of the agreement.

2–36

In *Hervey v Smith*,[107] where the outside wall of a new house contained two flues reserved for the use of an adjoining house which was afterwards built and connected with them, the adjoining owner making a payment under the London Building Act and so becoming entitled in equity to an easement, a subsequent purchaser for value of the first house, who blocked up the flues and claimed to

---

[97] Law of Property Act 1925, s.52(1); see *Mason v Clarke* [1955] A.C. 778 at 798, per Lord Morton of Henryton. This was also the case at common law: *Wood v Leadbitter* (1845) 13 M. & W. 838 at 842, 843. Moreover, to create a legal interest, the grant must be for an interest equivalent to an estate in fee simple absolute in possession or a term of years absolute: Law of Property Act 1925, ss.1(2)(a), 205(1)(ix), (x).

[98] *White v Taylor (No. 2)* [1969] 1 Ch. 160 at 181; see also *Mills v Stokman* (1967) 41 A.L.J.R. 16 (contract to sell slate).

[99] *Webber v Lee* (1882) 9 Q.B.D. 315.

[100] *Frogley v Earl of Lovelace* (1859) John. 333; *Mason v Clarke* [1955] A.C. 778.

[101] See para.2–22, above.

[102] *E.R. Ives Investment v High* [1967] 2 Q.B. 379; and see *Inwards v Baker* [1965] 2 Q.B. 29 at 37, per Lord Denning M.R.; also *Hopgood v Brown* [1955] 1 W.L.R. 213; *Armstrong v Sheppard & Short Ltd* [1959] 2 Q.B. 384; *Ward v Kirkland* [1967] Ch. 194.

[103] *Voyce v Voyce* (1991) 62 P. & C.R. 290 at 294, 296.

[104] For the meaning of "mere equity", see para.5–29, below, and Megarry & Wade, *The Law of Real Property* (6th ed., 2000), para.5–012.

[105] *Westminster Bank Ltd v Lee* [1956] Ch. 7 at 18, 19; *National Provincial Bank Ltd v Ainsworth* [1965] A.C. 1175 at 1238.

[106] [1896] W.N. 39.

[107] (1855) 1 K. & J. 389; subsequent proceedings, 22 Beav. 299.

have taken without notice, was held to be put on inquiry by the mere existence of the flues. Page Wood V.-C. said[108] that the question of notice concerning the right to an easement of this kind is like those cases in which notice of possession by a tenant is notice of the terms of his holding.

The general equitable rules are subject to the rules as to registration of land charges (in the case of unregistered land) and the scheme of land registration.

Unregistered land: the Land Charges Act 1972

2–37   In the case of unregistered land, an equitable easement which had arisen as a result of the operation of the principles of proprietary estoppel was considered in *E.R. Ives Investment Ltd v High*.[109] The plaintiff's case that as such an equitable easement had not been registered as a land charge under Class C(iv) as an estate contract or under Class D(iii) as an equitable easement, it was void against the plaintiff under section 13(2) of the Land Charges Act 1925.[110] It was said, in particular, that the right was an "equitable easement" within Class D(iii). This class is defined as "Any easement right or privilege over or affecting land created or arising after the commencement of this Act, and being merely an equitable interest". Lord Denning M.R. pointed out[111] that those words were almost identical with those used in subsection (3)(iii) of section 2 of the Law of Property Act 1925, which is concerned with equitable interests which cannot be overreached. He said that the words should be given the same meaning and must be read in conjunction with sections 1(2)(a), (3) and 4(1) of the Law of Property Act.

It then appeared that an "equitable easement" was a proprietary interest in land such as would before 1926 have been recognised as capable of being conveyed or created at law, but which since 1926 only took effect as an equitable interest. An instance of such a proprietary interest was a *profit à prendre* for life. It did not include a right, liberty or privilege arising in equity by reason of "mutual benefit and burden", or arising out of "acquiescence", or by reason of a contractual licence, because before 1926 these were not proprietary interests such as were capable of being conveyed or created at law; they only subsisted in equity. Accordingly they did not need to be registered as land charges, so as to bind successors, but took effect in equity without registration.[112]

Danckwerts L.J. also held[113] that the charge in question was not a registrable charge; accordingly section 199 of the Law of Property Act 1925, which provides that a purchaser shall not be prejudicially affected by notice of any instrument

[108] (1855) 1 K. & J. 389 at 394.
[109] [1967] 2 Q.B. 379.
[110] Repealed. See now the Land Charges Act 1972, s.4(6), as amended by the Finance Act 1975, s.52(1) and Sch.12.
[111] [1967] 2 Q.B. 379 at 395. See also *Poster v Slough Estates Ltd* [1969] 1 Ch. 495 at 506, 507, per Cross J. (right to re-enter premises after termination of a lease and to remove fixtures not an "equitable easement" for the purposes of the Land Charges Act 1925).
[112] In so holding, Lord Denning M.R. adopted the views expressed by Mr C.V. Davidge in an article, "Equitable Easements" in 59 L.Q.R. 259 and of Professor H.W.R. Wade in [1956] Cambridge Law Journal 225, 226.
[113] [1967] 2 Q.B. 400.

or matter capable of registration under the provisions of the Land Charges Act 1925[114] which is void or not enforceable against him under that Act, had no application. The decision of the Court of Appeal was referred to with approval by Lord Wilberforce in *Shiloh Spinners Ltd v Harding*[115] where the House of Lords held that a right of re-entry was equitable and did not fall within either Class C(iv) or Class D(iii).

Where there is a specifically enforceable contract to grant a legal easement over   **2–38**
unregistered land the purchaser has an equitable right to a legal grant. This right would seem to fall outside the Land Charges Act 1972, s.2(5)(iii), Class D(iii); it is not an "equitable easement" because there is no easement presently exercisable. In any event having regard to *E.R. Ives Investments Ltd v High*,[116] it could not be registered under Class D(iii) because it is an interest which even before 1926 would not have taken effect at law. Such an agreement would not seem to be an estate contract which is defined as "a contract by an estate owner or by a person entitled at the date of the contract to have a legal estate conveyed to him to convey or create a legal estate, including a contract conferring either expressly or by statutory implication a valid option to purchase, a right of pre-emption or any other like right".[117] An easement is not an estate[118] and so a contract to grant an easement is not a contract to convey or create an estate.[119]

Registered land

In relation to registered land, prior to October 13, 2003 matters were governed by   **2–39**
the Land Registration Act 1925 and the rules made thereunder and since that date matters are governed by the Land Registration Act 2002 and the rules made thereunder. In view of the fact that it will still be necessary for some time to come to analyse the effect of transactions which took place before October 13, 2003, the scheme under the 1925 Act will be described. The general treatment of easements under the Land Registration Act 1925 and under the Land Registration Act 2002 is considered in detail in Chapter 5.

Registered land: the Land Registration Act 1925

In relation to the 1925 Act, the nature of a contract to grant an easement over   **2–40**
registered land was considered in *Celsteel Ltd v Alton House Holdings Ltd*.[120] The

---

[114] Repealed. See now the Land Charges Act 1972.
[115] [1973] A.C. 691 at 721.
[116] [1967] 2 Q.B. 379, para.2–10, above.
[117] Land Charges Act 1972, s.4(6) as amended by the Finance Act 1975, s.52(1) and Sch.12.
[118] See s.1 of the Law of Property Act 1925.
[119] This point was dealt with somewhat oddly in *E.R. Ives Investments Ltd v High* [1967] 2 Q.B. 379; counsel for the appellant submitted that a contract to grant an easement was an estate contract (see at 384G); counsel for the respondent seemed to agree (see at 389D); Lord Denning M.R. said in terms that there was no contract to convey a legal estate (see at 395C) and Winn L.J. appeared to accept the appellant's submission that in so far as the matter rested upon the contract to grant an easement, that contract was void for non-registration as a land charge (see at 403F).
[120] [1985] 1 W.L.R. 204 (revd. in part, but not on this point, [1986] 1 W.L.R. 512). For comment, see [1986] Conv. 31 (M.P. Thomson); [1999] Conv. 11 (Greed) and (1999) 115 L.Q.R. 89 (D.G. Barnsley).

third plaintiff agreed to take a lease of a garage together with vehicular rights of way from the public highway, and he had for over four years been in actual occupation of the garage and had been exercising his easement of way, but the intended lease had not yet been granted, nor were his rights protected by any notice, caution or other entry against the registered title to the servient land. The question arose whether this was an overriding interest. Section 70(1)(a) of the Land Registration Act 1925 protects as overriding interests:

"Rights of common, drainage rights, customary rights (until extinguished), public rights, profits à prendre, rights of sheepwalk, rights of way, watercourses, rights of water, and other easements not being equitable easements required to be protected by notice on the register."

Rule 258 of the Land Registration Rules 1925[121] provides:

"Rights, privileges, and appurtenances appertaining or reputed to appertain to land or demised, occupied, or enjoyed therewith or reputed or known as part or parcel of or appurtenant thereto, which adversely affect registered land, are overriding interests within section 70 of the [Land Registration] Act, and shall not be deemed incumbrances for the purposes of the Act."

2–41   Scott J. said[122] that the meaning and scope of the provision "equitable easements required to be protected by notice on the register" was somewhat obscure, but having considered *E.R. Ives Investment Ltd v High*[123] and *Poster v Slough Estates Ltd*[124] and the limited meaning given by Lord Denning M.R.[125] to the expression "equitable easements" in the former case, declined to give that expression a similarly limited meaning in section 70(1)(a):

"because in general the clear intention of the Land Registration Act 1925 is that equitable interests should be protected either by entry on the register or as overriding interests and, if equitable easements in general are not within the exception in paragraph (a), it would follow that they would rank as overriding interests and be binding upon registered proprietors of servient land even though such proprietors did not have and could not by any reasonable means have obtained any knowledge of them. That result could not possibly be supported. In my view, therefore, the dicta in the two cases are not applicable to the construction of 'equitable easements' in paragraph (a) of section 70(1)."

[121] SR & O 1925/1093. The rules were made under s.144 of the Land Registration Act 1925. Having regard to the wide power to make rules conferred by sub-para.(xxi) of subs.(1) of s.144, Scott J. rejected ([1985] 1 W.L.R. 221) an argument that r.258 was ultra vires.
[122] [1985] 1 W.L.R. 219 at 220.
[123] [1967] 2 Q.B. 379.
[124] [1969] 1 Ch. 495.
[125] [1967] 2 Q.B. 379 at 395.

His Lordship went on to find that the words "required to be protected" in section **2–42**
70(1)(a) should be read in the sense "need to be protected". The exception was
intended to cover all equitable easements other than such as by reason of some
other statutory provision or applicable principle of law could obtain protection
otherwise than by notice on the register; for example, equitable easements which
qualified for protection under paragraph (g) of section 70(1) as part of the rights
of a person in actual occupation. Prima facie, therefore, the right to an easement
of way of the third plaintiff in *Celsteel Ltd v Alton House Holdings Ltd*[126] needed
the protection of an entry on the register (which, as has been seen, it did not
have). Scott J. found, however, that the right was a right enjoyed with land for
the purposes of rule 258 of the Land Registration Rules 1925 and therefore
ranked as an overriding interest, not needing to be protected by an entry on the
register, and binding against the lessee of the land over which the right of way
was exercised. The decision was approved by the Court of Appeal in *Thatcher v
Douglas*.[127]

Celsteel Ltd v Alton House Holdings Ltd[128] was applied in *Sweet v Sommer.*[129]   **2–43**
It was held that the equity, taking the form of an equitable easement, arising from
a proprietary estoppel, was an overriding interest within rule 258 of the Land
Registration Rules 1925 as it was being openly exercised at the relevant time.
Sweet v Sommer also raised a further point in relation to rule 258. In respect of
another plot of land, the Northern Field, a right of way had been purportedly
reserved over Old Forge Yard. However, the reservation was in an assent which
was under hand and not under seal and it was conceded that the reservation took
effect in equity only. Initially, the right of way was registered against the registered title to the servient tenement. However, the Land Registry were later
persuaded to remove the entry because the reservation was not effective at law
but only in equity. The owner of the Northern Field, relying on rule 258, contended that the equitable right of way was an overriding interest binding Old
Forge Yard. This contention was upheld. Even though the right of way was not
much used at the relevant time, it was known or reputed as appertaining to the
Northern Field and that sufficed. The servient owner also alleged that the equitable right of way could not be an overriding interest because it had initially been
registered against the servient tenement. Section 3(xvi) of the 1925 Act defined
overriding interests as rights *not* entered on the register. It was held that if it had
been wrongly registered and the entry had been removed, then there was no
barrier to the right being an overriding interest.

It is suggested that (in relation to the scheme under the Land Registration Act   **2–44**
1925) it will always be wise to protect a contract to grant a right (whether or
not an equitable easement) over registered land so as to ensure that subsequent

---

[126] [1985] 1 W.L.R. 204 (revd. in part, but not on this point, [1986] 1 W.L.R. 512).
[127] [1996] New L.J. 282; the facts of that case are set out at para.2–31, above.
[128] [1985] 1 W.L.R. 204.
[129] [2004] EWHC 1504 (Ch) and [2005] EWCA Civ 227. The facts of *Sweet v Sommer* are set out at
para.2–14 above.

proprietors of the servient land are bound.[130] An equitable easement may be protected by notice,[131] or by caution.[132] A caution will also be accepted to protect an equitable right in land which does not amount to an equitable easement but, by reason of an express agreement or an estoppel, becomes binding on successive owners who acquire the land with notice of it.[133] Such a right may, instead, be noted on the register because it is within the words "any other right, interest, or claim which it may be deemed expedient to protect by notice instead of by caution" within the meaning of section 49(1)(f) of the Land Registration Act 1925.[134]

2–45   In *Holaw (470) Ltd v Stockton Estates Ltd*,[135] the claimant contended that it was entitled to rectification of a transfer of land so as to include the reservation of a right of way over the land transferred. It was held that the reservation of such a right had been intended but had been omitted from the transfer. The claim to rectification was brought against the defendant in circumstances where it was necessary for the claimant to show that the right to rectification of the transfer was an overriding interest within section 70(1)(g) of the Land Registration Act 1925. That paragraph refers to the "rights of every person in actual occupation of the land". It was held that although a right to rectification of a transfer can be a right within section 70(1)(g),[136] the claimant and its predecessors were not in actual occupation of the servient tenement even though the way was being used. The judge said[137]: "I do not consider that use, even intensive use, of a right of way can involve the user being in occupation of the way". The claim to rectification therefore failed.

2–46   In *Allen v Jones*,[138] the owners of adjoining properties made a homemade agreement to vary a right of way; the claimant permitted his neighbour to lay gravel on part in return for giving up part. There was no deed and an entry in respect of the unvaried right of way remained on the register. The neighbour sold his property to the defendant without telling him of the agreement to give up part of the way or of the claimant's proposals to fence the part given up. The claimant's case was that the easement had been extinguished by agreement at law or in equity and that the agreement took effect in equity against a successor with notice; alternatively, the purchaser was bound by reason of the doctrine of benefit and burden or of estoppel. It was held that there was no release at law because of the absence of a deed; nor in equity as against the purchasers, since they had

---

[130] See the Land Registration Act 1925, ss.20(1)(a), 23(1)(b), as amended by the Finance Act 1975, s.52(1) and Sch.12. An easement granted by a registered proprietor which is to be appurtenant to registered land must be registered before it becomes a legal easement: *ibid.*, ss.19(2), 22(2). Until registration it will take effect in equity only and should be protected accordingly.

[131] Land Registration Act 1925, s.49(1)(c); and see Ruoff & Roper, *Registered Conveyancing* (London: Sweet & Maxwell), paras 6.06, 35.27.

[132] Land Registration Act 1925, s.54(1).

[133] Ruoff & Roper, *Registered Conveyancing*, para.36.11.

[134] *Registered Conveyancing*, para.35.33, where it is observed that in *Poster v Slough Estates Ltd* [1969] 1 Ch. 495 (see fn.97, para.2–35, above) Cross J. did not consider this provision when he expressed some criticism of the registered system.

[135] (2000) 81 P. & C.R. 404.

[136] See *Blacklocks v J.B. Developments (Godalming) Ltd* [1982] Ch. 983 and *Nurdin & Peacock Plc v D.B. Ramsden & Co Ltd* [1999] 1 E.G.L.R. 119.

[137] (2000) 81 P. & C.R. 404 at 423.

[138] [2004] EWHC 1119.

no notice; while an estoppel might have operated against the vendor, it did not operate against the purchaser because the equity was not entered on the register and was not an overriding interest.[139]

Registered land: the Land Registration Act 2002

The treatment of easements generally under the Land Registration Act 2002 is considered in Chapter 5. It is useful to consider at this point the way in which the 2002 Act deals with the specific case of an equitable easement. If the easement is clearly equitable, the Land Registry will not enter the benefit of it in the register for the dominant land either on first registration or subsequently. This is because the 2002 Act makes provision only for the registration of *legal* interests.[140] Hence, only the benefit of appurtenant *legal* easements can be entered in the register on first registration[141] and only the benefit of *legal* easements can be entered when the dominant land is already registered.[142] However, on first registration of an estate, that estate vests in the registered proprietor "together with all interests subsisting for the benefit of the estate" and this can extend to equitable easements.[143]   **2–47**

If the servient land is registered, an application should be made to enter an agreed or unilateral notice in respect of the equitable easement. Where an equitable easement is granted in a transfer of registered land, the Land Registry will automatically enter notice of the easement in the register for the servient land providing that the title number is entered in panel 2 of Form AP1. On first registration of the servient land, the Land Registry will enter a notice in the register in respect of an equitable easement.

As to the possibility of an equitable easement being an overriding interest, an equitable easement cannot be an overriding interest on first registration of the servient tenement and will not be an overriding interest on a registered disposition of the registered servient tenement unless it was an overriding interest before October 13, 2003. Reference should also be made to the more detailed treatment in Chapter 5 of easements under the 2002 Act.

The treatment of equitable easements under the Land Registration Act 2002 will be very different from the position under the 1925 Act. Indeed the position as disclosed by the decision in *Celsteel Ltd v Alton House Holdings Ltd*[144] was considered by the Law Commission to be unsatisfactory.[145] Under the 2002 Act, an equitable easement cannot have overriding status (unless it already had that status on October 13, 2003). It can only be protected by entry of a notice on the   **2–48**

---

[139] In *Valentine v Allen* [2003] EWCA Civ 915, for the facts of which see para.2–13 above, Hale L.J. suggested that there might be difficulties in regarding an oral agreement to grant a right of way as constituting an overriding interest but the Court held that the parties had proceeded on a common assumption and that the claimant was therefore estopped.

[140] Land Registration Act 2002, s.2.

[141] Land Registration Rules 2003, rule 33(1).

[142] Land Registration Act 2002, Sch.2, para.7 and Land Registration Rules 2003, rules 73 and 74.

[143] Land Registration Act 2002, s.11(3).

[144] [1985] 1 W.L.R. 204.

[145] See the Law Commission's consultative document, (1998) Law Com. No. 254 at paras 5.1–5.24 and its final report, (2001) Law Com. No. 271 at para.8.67.

register.[146] The 2002 Act also makes express provision as to equities arising by reason of estoppel and mere equities.[147] Section 116 declares, for the avoidance of doubt, that in relation to registered land, an equity by estoppel and a mere equity have effect from the time the equity arises as an interest capable of binding successors in title; this provision makes clear that the status of an equity by estoppel and a mere equity is that of an interest in land, a proprietary interest. Such an interest can be protected by a notice on the register. The provision is subject to the rules in the 2002 Act as to the effect of dispositions on priority.

Under the 2002 Act, an equitable easement (which was not already an overriding interest on October 13, 2003) can never override a registered disposition. So mere agreements to grant an easement as in *Celsteel*[148] and *Thatcher v Douglas*,[149] however apparent on the ground, will not be binding on a successor, nor will easements coming into existence as a result of an estoppel arising from the conduct of a predecessor. It remains to be seen whether there may still be some scope for the operation of the doctrine of benefit and burden in a case where the successor wishes to continue to enjoy the benefit of a transaction entered into by his predecessor; if he takes free of the equity, he can hardly continue to enjoy the benefit. The right analysis may be that he adopts or becomes bound himself by the estoppel, as in *Valentine v Allen*,[150] by showing that he intends to proceed on an existing common assumption: see para.2–13 above.

[146] The position in relation to the 2002 Act is discussed in more detail at paras 5–12 *et seq.*, below.
[147] See para.5–29, below.
[148] [1985] 1 W.L.R. 204; see para.2–40, above.
[149] [1996] New L.J. 282; see para.2–31, above.
[150] [2003] All E.R. (D)79.

PART II

THE ACQUISITION OF EASEMENTS

CHAPTER 3

CREATION OF EASEMENTS BY KNOWN TRANSACTIONS

An easement may be created by or under a particular statute, or *inter partes* by a **3–01** grant *inter vivos* or a testamentary disposition. It may be granted expressly by the terms of a conveyance and it may be expressly reserved over land granted. It may be created by the general words contained in a conveyance or imported into the conveyance by section 62 of the Law of Property Act 1925. It may arise by implication, founded on presumed intention, under a grant or an agreement for a grant of land, as where land is disposed of for a particular purpose, or the ownership of land becomes divided and continuous and apparent easements pass in accordance with the rule in *Wheeldon v Burrows*.[1] Only exceptionally can an easement be reserved by implication. The express grant or reservation of an easement is a conveyancing matter which, given a competent grantor and a competent grantee, should present no difficulty. If the servient tenement is registered under the Land Registration Act 2002, the express grant or reservation of the easement must be completed by registration in order for it to be a legal, as distinct from an equitable, easement. The creation of easements by implication and by general words is considered below.[2] An easement may also be established under the doctrine of prescription or lost modern grant, which are considered in the next chapter.[3]

---

[1] (1879) 12 Ch. D. 31 at 49.
[2] See paras 3–17 *et seq.*, 3–126 *et seq.*, below.
[3] *cf.* those cases where special immunities arise under the doctrine of non-derogation from grant, paras 3–32 *et seq.*, below, and those cases where rights to easements arise in equity, Ch.2, above.

1.—CREATION BY OR UNDER STATUTE

3–02   There are, or have been, very many public and private Acts, under which, or by the exercise or performance of powers or obligations contained in them, easements or rights analogous thereto can arise.[4] The following are some examples.

(1) Private Inclosure Acts, and awards made under the Inclosure Acts 1801 and 1845, whereby land subject to rights of common was parcelled out in severalty, nearly always created rights of way and other easements.[5]

(2) The owner of land severed by a railway acquires the right to pass over level crossings and other accommodation works made under section 68 of the Railway Clauses Consolidation Act 1845.[6]

(3) Government departments and other public bodies have various powers to acquire and grant easements. Thus, section 17(4) of the New Towns Act 1981[7] empowered a development corporation to create easements over land which it acquires. Examples of statutes which permit a public body to acquire an easement include National Parks and Access to the Countryside Act 1949, ss.103(6), 114(1) (as amended), Highways Act 1980, s.250 (as amended) and Local Government (Miscellaneous Provisions) Act 1976, s.13 (as amended).[8] Where the statute is intended to confer a right to acquire and to grant an easement, it is normally to be expected that the statute will make express provision as to the existence of the power and the circumstances in which it may be exercised. The Local Government (Miscellaneous Provisions) Act 1976, s.13 reversed the decision of the House of Lords in *Sovmots Investments Ltd v Secretary of State for the Environment*.[9] In that case, the London Borough of Camden unsuccessfully sought to acquire for the benefit of maisonettes (which were the subject of a compulsory purchase order) certain ancillary rights (including a right of support from the building below and a right of passage for water and other services) which were not part of the order and were in any case not (with only some possible exceptions) in existence when the order was made. The House of Lords held that a power to acquire land compulsorily did not of itself authorise compulsion of an owner of land not being acquired to grant over that land new rights in the nature of easements. The definition of "land" in subsection (1) of section 189 of the Housing Act 1957[10] as including "any right over land" was confined to existing rights; nor were

---

[4] For a discussion of this subject, see Garner, "Statutory Easements", 20 Conv. 208.

[5] See, e.g. *Newcomen v Coulson* (1877) 5 Ch. D. 133; *Finch v G.W. Railway* (1880) 5 Ex. D. 254; *Gotobed v Pridmore* (1971) E.G. 759; *Benn v Hardinge* (1992) 66 P. & C.R. 246.

[6] The servient owner may have a statutory duty to repair: see paras 1–95 *et seq.*, above. See further for the operation of this section, paras 9–53–9–54, below.

[7] Before its amendment by the New Towns and Urban Development Corporation Act 1985, s.4(1), Sch.3.

[8] The 1976 Act, s.13 is amended by the Acquisition of Land Act 1981, s.34(3), Sch.6.

[9] [1979] A.C. 144, reversing the decision of the Court of Appeal [1977] Q.B. 411, which had reversed the decision of Forbes J. "Expropriation cannot take place by implication or through intention: it is authorised or not authorised": per Lord Wilberforce [1979] A.C. 171.

[10] Repealed by the Housing (Consequential Provisions) Act 1985, s.3(1) and Sch.1.

the rights claimed included by reason of the definition in that subsection of "house" as including "appurtenances belonging thereto or usually enjoyed therewith". The decision of the House of Lords has, however, been reversed for the future by section 13 of the Local Government (Miscellaneous Provisions) Act 1976, which permits the acquisition by means of a compulsory purchase order of rights which are not in existence when the order is made.[11] Further, it may be possible to hold that the empowering statute has by implication granted the right to acquire an easement. Thus, the simultaneous provision of a power to construct works and of a right to compensation in respect of consequent damage raises the implication that the empowering statute gives a right of support to the works after construction.[12] A statutory power to acquire an easement may impliedly include necessary ancillary rights.[13]

(4) There are various statutes which allow a lessee or a group of lessees to acquire the freehold of the leased property or of the block of flats which have been leased or to acquire a long lease of the same. These statutes make provision for the grant and reservation of appropriate easements.[14] The position under the Leasehold Reform Act 1967 was considered in detail in *Kent v Kavanagh*.[15] In general, the way in which the 1967 Act is intended to operate is that both the rights which benefited and which bound the lessee should be carried through into his new status as freeholder. That case was complicated because the facts concerned two enfranchisements of adjoining properties with reciprocal easements. It was held that where properties, A and B, are separately leased with reciprocal rights over the other property and the lessees of A and B both acquire their respective freeholds under the 1967 Act, then the former lessees (as owners of the freehold) continue to enjoy the same rights over each other's property as they did while they each were tenants of their property. If they were entitled to reciprocal easements under the former leases, those easements are (in effect) enfranchised. The easements subsist for the benefit of (and as a burden on) the respective freehold interests. It is immaterial which of the two plots was the first to be enfranchised.[16]

(5) The Landlord and Tenant Act 1954, Part II, provides for security of tenure for business tenants who occupy all or a part of their demised premises for the purposes of a business carried on by them. One form of the security

---

[11] See also Housing (Consequential Provisions) Act 1985, s.28, Sch.3. *Sovmots Investments Ltd v Secretary of State for the Environment* [1979] A.C. 144 remains of considerable importance because of the consideration given by the House of Lords to *Wheeldon v Burrows* (1879) 12 Ch. D. 31 and s.62 of the Law of Property Act 1925, and their Lordships' approval of *Bolton v Bolton* (1879) 11 Ch. D. 968 and *Long v Gowlett* [1923] 2 Ch. 177: see paras 3–129 and 3–130, below.

[12] *Corporation of Dudley, Re* (1881) L.R. 8 Q.B.D. 86, 93, per Brett L.J.; *London and North Western Ry Co v Evans* [1893] 1 Ch. 16, 31, per A.L. Smith L.J.

[13] *Central Electricity Generation Board v Jennaway* [1959] 1 W.L.R. 937; see para.1–90, above.

[14] See Leasehold Reform Act 1967, ss.8, 10; Housing Act 1985, Sch.6; and Leasehold Reform, Housing and Urban Development Act 1993, s.57, Schs 7 and 9.

[15] [2007] Ch. 1.

[16] [2007] Ch. 1, at [58].

which is provided is that in certain circumstances a tenant is entitled to be granted a new tenancy of the demised premises or part of them.[17] Where there is an order for the grant of a new tenancy, the new tenancy will include rights enjoyed by the tenant in connection with the premises included in the new tenancy, except as otherwise agreed between the parties or determined by the court.[18] The rights there referred to can include easements. The power to include such rights does not permit the tenant to acquire greater rights than those subsisting under the current tenancy.[19] Where the only subject-matter of a tenancy is an easement, an issue may arise as to whether the tenant is "occupying" the thing demised i.e. the easement for the purposes of a business so as to be protected by the 1954 Act. It has been held that one does not "occupy" a right of way[20] but that one can "occupy" a right which is a right to use parking spaces.[21]

(6) The Access to Neighbouring Land Act 1992 empowers the court to make an access order permitting access onto land for the purpose of carrying out certain works to adjoining or adjacent land.[22]

(7) Section 68 of Countryside and Rights of Way Act 2000 and Regulations made under that section provided for the creation of a vehicular right of way at a time when it was considered that certain vehicular rights of way could not be acquired by prescription.[23] Section 68 of the 2000 Act has now ceased to have effect by reason of the Commons Act 2006, section 51 (in force in England with effect from October 1, 2006[24] and in Wales with effect from September 6, 2007[25]).

3–03   *Profits à prendre* may also be created by statute. When land was allotted to commoners under the Inclosure Acts, shooting rights were frequently reserved to the lord of the manor.

2.—CREATION INTER PARTES

Competent grantors

3–04   An individual owner of land can subject it to an easement for any estate or interest for which he could alienate it,[26] and a corporation whose power to alienate its

---

[17] Landlord and Tenant Act 1954, ss.23, 29.

[18] Landlord and Tenant Act 1954, s.32(3).

[19] *J Murphy & Sons Ltd v Railtrack Plc* [2002] 2 E.G.L.R. 48.

[20] *Land Reclamation Co v Basildon DC* [1979] 1 W.L.R. 767; *Nevill Long & Co (Boards) Ltd v Firmenich Ltd* [1983] 2 E.G.L.R. 76.

[21] *Pointon York Group Plc v Poulton* [2007] 3 E.G.L.R. 37.

[22] The 1992 Act is considered in detail at paras 11–41 to 11–69.

[23] Section 68 of the Countryside and Rights of Way Act 2000 and the Regulations made thereunder are considered at para.4–126, below.

[24] Commons Act 2006 (Commencement No. 1, Transitional Provisions and Savings) (England) Order 2006 (SI 2006/2504), art.2(d).

[25] Commons Act 2006 (Commencement No. 1, Transitional Provisions and Savings) (Wales) Order 2007 (SI 2007/2386,W197), art.3(j).

[26] There is no legal objection to the creation of an easement in reversion to take effect upon the determination of a tenancy: *Wolland v Marshalsea*, unreported, November 10, 1994, CA.

land is restricted can grant an easement which is not inconsistent with the purposes for which it holds the land.[27]

The statutory power of sale of a mortgagee includes power, if the mortgage was executed after 1911,[28] and does not provide to the contrary, to sell part of the mortgaged property with a grant or reservation of a right of way or other easement over either the part retained or the part sold.[29]   **3–05**

Similarly, on any sale or other disposition or dealing under the powers conferred by the Settled Land Act 1925 (which are exercisable by trustees for sale and personal representatives[30]), an easement, right or privilege of any kind may be reserved or granted over or in relation to the settled land or any part thereof or other land, including the part disposed of, and, in the case of an exchange, the land taken in exchange.[31] A person exercising Settled Land Act powers can also (apparently) sell[32] or lease[33] an easement over his land as an independent transaction, that is to a person already the owner of the dominant tenement. In the case of a lease in such circumstances, the "best rent" required by section 42(1)(ii) is presumably recoverable by the estate owner for the time being.[34] The requirement of a proviso for re-entry (s.42(1)(iii)), does not apply.[35] Such a person may also subject his land to an easement in exchange for the grant of an easement over other land,[36] or, with or without consideration, including the release of an easement over his land,[37] release other land from an easement accommodating his land.[38]   **3–06**

The incumbent of a benefice, or, during a vacancy, the bishop of the diocese in which the benefice is situated, has power to take an easement for the benefit of any land which forms part of the property of the benefice and to grant an easement over such land, but the exercise of such powers requires the consent of the Church Commissioners, the diocesan dilapidations board and, where the power is   **3–07**

---

[27] *Gonty and Manchester, Sheffield and Lincolnshire Ry* [1896] 2 Q.B. 439; *cf. Stourcliffe Estates Co Ltd v Bournemouth Corp* [1910] 2 Ch. 12; and see *British Transport Commission v Westmorland C.C.* [1958] A.C. 126. In *Housden v Conservators of Wimbledon and Putney Commons* [2007] 1 W.L.R. 2543, it was held (at first instance) that a statutory prohibition on the owner of land "disposing" of any part of the land prevented the owner being a competent grantor of an easement over the land but this interpretation of the statute was rejected on appeal: [2008] 1 W.L.R. 1172. It has been held in Australia that, provided that he did not interfere with his co-owner's rights in, and enjoyment of, the land, a tenant in common or joint tenant could incumber the land so as to bind both the co-owners and their successors in title: *Medley v Roberts* [1977] V.R. 282. It is, however, thought that an incumbrance in the nature of an easement would usually interfere with such rights and enjoyment.

[28] In *Born v Turner* [1900] 2 Ch. 211, where the mortgage was executed before 1912, and the mortgagee sold part of the mortgaged property, a right of light over the retained part was held to pass by implication. Whether the mortgagee could have expressly granted a right which would not arise by implication was not decided.

[29] Law of Property Act 1925, s.101.

[30] Law of Property Act 1925, s.28; Administration of Estates Act 1925, s.39.

[31] Settled Land Act 1925, s.49(1)(a).

[32] Settled Land Act 1925, ss.38, 39.

[33] Settled Land Act 1925, ss.41, 42.

[34] *Lord Hastings v North Eastern Ry* [1898] 2 Ch. 674; see para.1–136, above.

[35] *Sitwell v Earl of Londesborough* [1905] 1 Ch. 460 at 465.

[36] Settled Land Act 1925, s.38(1)(iii).

[37] Settled Land Act 1925, s.61(2)(e).

[38] Settled Land Act 1925, s.59(2).

exercised by the incumbent, the bishop.[39] The grant or taking of an easement in such a case may be made or done either without monetary consideration or in consideration of the payment of a capital sum, any capital sum payable in respect of the grant of an easement being payable to the commissioners to be applied for the purposes for which the proceeds of sale of the land over which the easement is granted would be applicable.[40]

3–08   The absence of consent, either express or through acquiescence, where such consent is required, will prevent the acquisition of an easement by prescription. The plaintiffs in *Oakley v Boston*[41] owned a strip of land which had until 1952 been glebe. In 1973 they brought an action against the adjoining owner to restrain him from trespassing over the strip. By virtue of section 20 of the Ecclesiastical Leases Act 1842 and section 1 of the Ecclesiastical Leases Act 1858 the consent of the Church Commissioners (as the successors of the Ecclesiastical Commissioners) was required for the grant of a valid easement over the strip. Because there was no direct evidence of consent having been given, or of the commissioners having knowledge of acquiescence on the part of the incumbent to the use of the strip, the Court of Appeal rejected the defendant's claim that he had acquired an easement by the doctrine of lost modern grant. (On the facts there had, since 1962, been insufficient use to support a claim under section 2 of the Prescription Act 1832: but in this respect too the absence of consent or acquiescence would have been fatal to the defendant's case.) It is clear from the judgment of Goulding J. that it will generally be difficult to show acquiescence on the part of a person in a fiduciary position. His Lordship said[42]:

> "There are also considerable difficulties in applying a doctrine of acquiescence to persons in a fiduciary position who have an active duty to others to fulfil before they can exercise their powers. The commissioners in the present case in particular were not entitled to let anything go by default: it was their duty only to alienate if satisfied of the permanent benefit of the transaction."

Persons entitled to rights of common have no power, prima facie, to grant an easement over the common.[43]

3–09   Clearly a person entitled to land cannot subject it to an easement more extensive than his own interest.[44] If, however, a person expressly grants an easement over land to which he has no title, and then acquires the fee, the land will be bound

---

[39] Church Property (Miscellaneous Provisions) Measure 1960, s.9(1); as amended by the Patronage (Benefices) Measure 1986, s.34(2), Sch.5. See *Hamble Parish Council v Haggard* [1992] 1 W.L.R. 122 (no consents required because churchyard not property of benefice). As to the power of the bishop to delegate: Church of England (Miscellaneous Provisions) Measure 1983, s.8.

[40] Church of England (Miscellaneous Provisions) Measure 1983, s.9(2), (3).

[41] [1976] Q.B. 270, followed in *St Clement's, Leigh-on-Sea, Re* [1988] 1 W.L.R. 720.

[42] [1976] Q.B. 270 at 285.

[43] *Paine & Co v St Neots Gas & Coke Co* [1938] 4 All E.R. 592; [1939] 3 All E.R. 812.

[44] *Beddington v Atlee* (1887) 35 Ch. D. 317 at 327; and *cf. Daniel v Anderson* (1861) 31 L.J. Ch. 610.

by estoppel.[45] On the other hand, no grant will be implied, or arise from general words, in excess of the interest of the grantor at the time of the grant. In *Booth v Alcock*[46] where the defendant, being lessee of land and owner of a house adjoining it, granted to the plaintiff a lease of the house with its appurtenances, including "lights", and then acquired the reversion in fee of the land, it was held that the plaintiff acquired a right to light for the residue of the term of the lease of the land, and that the defendant's acquisition of the reversion made no difference. "General words in a grant must be restricted to that which the grantor had then power to grant, and will not extend to anything which he might subsequently acquire."[47]

In *Quicke v Chapman*,[48] where the defendant, having entered into a building agreement under which he was to build houses on a number of plots, and was to have a lease of each house on completion and in the meantime a licence to enter only, took and assigned to the plaintiff a lease of a completed house before completing and acquiring a lease of the adjoining house, the plaintiff was held not entitled to restrain interference with the light of his house by the adjoining house when completed. The implication of a grant of right to light was negatived by the consideration that the defendant, when he assigned the lease to the plaintiff, had no interest in the adjoining land which would have enabled him to grant the right expressly.

Similarly, no easement will arise by implication, or under general words in a conveyance, if the vendor, before agreeing to sell the supposedly dominant tenement (A), has agreed to sell the supposedly servient tenement (B), without reserving the alleged easement. The reason is that the vendor, on agreeing to sell B, becomes a trustee of B for his purchaser, and a subsequent contract by him to sell A cannot be assumed to include a contract to create an incumbrance on B.[49] Hence it appears to follow that if the owner of two properties, A and B, agrees to sell B, and then agrees to sell A, with an express grant of an easement over B, the grant of the easement will be ineffectual unless the grantee is a purchaser for money or money's worth without notice of the contract to sell B. As the purchaser of A is presumably a purchaser of "an interest in" B, within section 4(6) of the Land Charges Act 1972, it seems to follow that if the contract to sell B has not been registered as a land charge Class C(iv) under section 2(4)(iv) of that Act, the contract will be void under section 4(6) against the purchaser of A, and by virtue of section 199(1) of the Law of Property Act 1925 he will not be prejudicially affected by notice of it.

3–10

[45] *Rowbotham v Wilson* (1857) 8 El. & Bl. 123 at 145; (1860) 8 H.L.C. 348 at 364. *Quaere* as to the position if the grantor, having some interest in the land, expressly grants an easement in excess of the interest, and afterwards acquires the excess interest. See *Booth v Alcock* (1873) 8 Ch. App. 663; *Universal Permanent Building Society v Cooke* [1952] Ch. 95 at 102; Co.Litt. 47b; 2 Wms.Saund. (1871) 829, 830.

[46] (1873) 8 Ch. App. 663.

[47] per Mellish L.J. (1873) 8 Ch. App. 667.

[48] [1903] 1 Ch. 659.

[49] *Beddington v Atlee* (1887) 35 Ch. D. 317; and see *Davies v Thomas* [1899] W.N. 244, where the purchaser of property having an apparent pipe easement over adjoining property belonging to the vendor, but then mortgaged, failed to establish the easement against a subsequent purchaser from the mortgagee.

Competent grantees

3–11   It seems that no easement can be effectually granted in excess of the interest, if any, of the grantee in the dominant tenement.[50] However, if, on the grant of a perpetual easement to one who is only tenant for years of the dominant tenement, it appears to have been contemplated that the grantee will acquire the fee, and he does so, the grant may take effect according to its tenor.[51]

A grant to an equitable owner may be construed as a grant of a legal easement. In *Johnstone v Holdway*[52] a vendor held land, including a quarry, in trust for a company and on a sale of part of the land, not including the quarry, the conveyance contained an exception and reservation in favour of the company and its successors in title of a right of way for the benefit of the quarry over the land sold. The exception and reservation operated by way of regrant by the purchaser to the vendor and the question arose whether, as a matter of construction, the purchaser granted to the company a legal easement or an equitable easement. The Court of Appeal held that it would be unreasonable to suppose that the parties intended that the purchaser should grant an equitable easement to the company, retaining a bare legal right in himself to be held upon trust for the company. The company was the beneficial owner of the quarry and the party interested to preserve its right to go to the quarry; the vendor was not interested. The Court accordingly held that the exception and reservation operated as a grant at law and not only in equity.

An authorised mode of application of capital money is the purchase in fee simple, or for a term of 60 years or more, of any easement convenient to be held with the settled land for mining or other purposes.[53]

Grant inter vivos

3–12   As already mentioned,[54] the general rule is that a legal easement cannot be created *inter vivos* otherwise than by deed. An easement so otherwise granted or agreed to be granted takes effect, if at all, in equity. Further, if the servient tenement is registered under the Land Registration Act 2002, the express grant or reservation of an easement will only create a legal, as distinct from an equitable, easement when the easement is duly registered.[55] Whether an equitable easement will bind a purchaser for value of the servient tenement depends on whether the matter is governed by the law as to unregistered conveyancing or by the Land Registration Act 1925 or the Land Registration Act 2002.[56]

---

[50] *Smeteborn v Holt* (1347) Y.B. 21 Edw. 3, fo. 2, pl. 5.

[51] *Rymer v McIlroy* [1897] 1 Ch. 528, where the grant also operated as a covenant; the circumstances were unusual. This case was considered in *Wall v Collins* [2007] Ch. 390 at [34]–[38] where it was concluded that the result depended upon the construction of that particular arrangement. *Wall v Collins* itself concerned the effect of a merger of a lease in a freehold upon an easement enjoyed by the lessee; and see para.1–32, above.

[52] [1963] 1 Q.B. 601 at 612, 613; see also paras 1–11 and 1–12, above.

[53] Settled Land Act 1925, s.73(1)(xii).

[54] See para.2–01, above.

[55] See para.5–22, below.

[56] See paras 2–36 *et seq.*, above.

It is not necessary to use the word "grant"[57] or, since 1925 at any rate, to use words of limitation.[58] The words used to effect an express grant of an easement will be construed in accordance with ordinary principles as to the construction of legal documents. Many of the cases of express grant which are considered in later chapters, and in particular Chapter 9 dealing with rights of way, illustrate the operation of the general principles as to the interpretation of legal documents in the context of easements.

Before 1926 an easement purporting to be reserved by the grantor was in truth granted by the grantee,[59] and for this reason an easement reserved to the vendor in a conveyance not executed by the purchaser took effect in equity only.[60] Section 65 of the Law of Property Act 1925 provides,[61] however, that after 1925, (1) a reservation of a legal estate operates at law without any execution of the conveyance by the grantee of the legal estate out of which the reservation is made, or any regrant by him, and operates to create the legal estate reserved, and to vest the same in possession in the person (whether being the grantor or not) for whose benefit the reservation is made, and (2) a conveyance of a legal estate expressed to be made subject to another legal estate not in existence immediately before the date of the conveyance is to operate as a reservation, unless a contrary intention appears.[62] In spite of the absence of execution by the grantee, the reservation operates by way of regrant by him. For the purposes of the rule that in the event of doubt upon the construction of a grant it should be construed against the *proferens*, the grantee is still to be regarded as the *proferens*, so that the reservation will be construed against him and in favour of the grantor of the servient tenement.[63]

If a vendor wishes to reserve an easement over the land conveyed in favour of the land which he retains he should do so in specific terms.[64] It may, however, be possible to construe a reservation from general words which refer to current user   **3–13**

---

[57] Law of Property Act 1925, s.5(2).

[58] Law of Property Act 1925, s.60. The necessity for the use of words of limitation before 1926 was considered in three articles in (1908) 24 L.Q.R. 199, 259, 264.

[59] "It is neither parcel of the thing granted, nor is it issuing out of the thing granted, the former being essential to an exception, and the latter to a reservation": Lord Tyndal C.J., *Durham and Sunderland Ry v Walker* (1842) 2 Q.B. 940 at 967. In the years 1882–1925 a conveyance to the use that the vendor or some other person might have, for an estate not exceeding in duration the estate conveyed in the land, an easement over the land conveyed, operated to vest the easement in that person for that estate: Conveyancing Act 1881, s.62(1).

[60] *May v Belleville* [1905] 2 Ch. 605.

[61] See also *Mason v Clarke* [1954] 1 Q.B. 460 at 466, per Denning L.J.; [1955] A.C. 778 at 786, per Viscount Simonds (a case of a *profit à prendre*).

[62] See *Wiles v Banks* (1985) 50 P. & C.R. 80. Having regard to s.56(2) of the Law of Property Act 1925, it is immaterial that the grantee is not named in the conveyance.

[63] *St Edmundsbury and Ipswich Diocesan Board of Finance v Clark (No. 2)* [1975] 1 W.L.R. 468 at 478–480, CA, following *Johnstone v Holdway* [1963] 1 Q.B. 601 at 612, CA, disapproving *Cordell v Second Clanfield Properties Ltd* [1969] 2 Ch. 9. See also *Bulstrode v Lambert* [1953] 1 W.L.R. 1064 at 1068, per Upjohn J., *Mason v Clarke* [1954] 1 Q.B. 460 at 467, per Denning L.J., [1955] A.C. 778 at 786, per Lord Simonds (a case of a *profit à prendre*).

[64] As to the effect of a reservation of a right of fishing, see *Lady Dunsany v Bedworth* (1979) 38 P. & C.R. 546 and para.1–142, above.

of the land conveyed for the benefit of the land retained.[65] In *Pitt v Buxton*[66] this question was considered by the Court of Appeal. In 1946 one of the plaintiff's predecessors in title purchased certain fields, which adjoined a public road, and through which passed a roadway. There was no specific mention of the roadway in the conveyance which was expressed to be "subject to all rights of way . . . (including all quasi-easements and methods of user hitherto used or enjoyed by the vendor in connection with his adjoining or neighbouring property) if any . . . existing over or affecting [the property conveyed] . . . and to all occupation and other roads". The property conveyed adjoined a small enclosure which itself adjoined a lake, both the properties of the vendor. In 1953 another of the plaintiff's predecessors in title purchased the small enclosure from the owner of the lake, the conveyance again being made subject to "quasi-easements", "methods of user" and "occupation ways" affecting the property conveyed. The defendant, who was the present owner of the lake, claimed a right of way on foot or by vehicle, for himself, his tenants and licensees for the purpose of passing from the public road to the lake to fish. The question on appeal was whether the general words in the 1946 and 1953 conveyances operated as grants of rights of way over the roadway and the enclosure for access to the lake for fishing. Russell L.J. said[67]:

> "I do not see, in principle, that it is not possible to constitute an express regrant by the use of general words referring to current de facto accommodation of the latter by the former. Whether there is a grant must be a question of the intention of the parties to be gathered from the language of the instrument in the circumstances in which that language was used. If land is conveyed subject to 'rights' of way hitherto enjoyed, it may well be that mere accommodations or quasi-easements are not by such language elevated to the status of an easement: see, for example, *Russell v. Harford*,[68] but see also *May v. Belleville*.[69] If, however, express reference is made to all quasi-easements and methods of user hitherto enjoyed, it seems to me that the proper conclusion is that a grant by the purchaser is intended, the nature and extent of the easement being determined (if at all) by the facts of user which obtained, though it must be for the vendor (or his successors) to establish with some precision what were the facts and, consequently, what was the right said to be created."

There was some evidence that at the time of the two conveyances persons were permitted to use the roadway and the small enclosure, on foot and with vehicles, to reach the lake from the public road for the purpose of fishing. The evidence,

---

[65] Here the surrounding circumstances are giving meaning to expressions in the conveyance. This should not be confused with implied reservation, as to which see paras 3–85 *et seq.*, below.

[66] (1970) 21 P. & C.R. 127.

[67] (1970) 21 P. & C.R. 127, at 133. Sachs L.J. assumed, without deciding, that general words may give rise to a reservation: *ibid.*, at 135, 136. Phillimore L.J. did not add to the judgments.

[68] (1866) L.R. 2 Eq. 507.

[69] [1905] 2 Ch. 605.

however, was exiguous and it could not be said that there was such a regular and established method of user of or quasi-easement over the roadway in favour of the lake for fishing purposes as would support the view that an easement was created by the language of the 1946 conveyance. There was even less evidence in support of the necessary extent of user at the time of the 1953 conveyance.

In *Pallister v Clark*[70] one (No.2) of a pair of semi-detached cottages was sold and   **3–14** the conveyance provided: "It is hereby agreed and declared between the parties hereto . . . as between the property and land hereby conveyed and such adjoining land and premises of the vendors all rights of light air way water drainage support and other easements and quasi-easements shall continue to be enjoyed as hitherto." By a later conveyance the other cottage (No.1) was conveyed subject to, and with the benefit of, that agreement and declaration. The Court of Appeal, affirming the judgment of the judge of the Darlington County Court and applying the passage in the judgment of Russell L.J. in *Pitt v Buxton*[71] quoted above, held that the words of the agreement and declaration were capable of constituting a regrant of the rights mentioned for the benefit of cottage No.1.

Grant by will

Easements may be created by will where the testator owns and makes separate   **3–15** dispositions of the dominant and servient tenements. Until the personal representative gives a written assent,[72] the easement takes effect in equity only.[73] There is apparently nothing to prevent a testator from subjecting, by his will, land owned by him to a new easement in favour of land not owned by him.

Indorsement of memorandum

Section 200 of the Law of Property Act 1925 provides that (1) where land (other   **3–16** than registered land) having a common title with other land is disposed of to a purchaser (other than a lessee or mortgagee) who does not hold or obtain possession of the documents forming the common title, such purchaser, notwithstanding any provision to the contrary, may require that a memorandum giving notice of any provision contained in the disposition to him restrictive of the user of, or giving rights over, any other land comprised in the common title, shall, where practicable, be written or indorsed on, or, where impracticable, be permanently annexed to some one document selected by the purchaser but retained in the possession or power of the person who makes the disposition, and being or forming part of the common title; but (2) the title of a person who omits to do so is not to be prejudiced.

---

[70] (1975) 30 P. & C.R. 84.
[71] (1970) 21 P. & C.R. 127 at 133.
[72] Administration of Estates Act 1925, s.36. Where the easement arises by implication, it should be expressly included in the assent relating to the dominant tenement, and the assent relating to the servient tenement should be expressed to be subject to it.
[73] Law of Property (Amendment) Act 1924, s.9, Sch.9, para.3.

3.—CREATION BY IMPLICATION

(1) *Categories of implication*

3–17   An easement may arise by implication under a grant, including a lease and a testamentary gift,[74] of land if an intention to grant it can properly be inferred. This intention may be inferred:

1. Where the grant contains particular words of description. Alternatively, in such a case, the easement may be created by estoppel.[75]
2. Where the circumstances indicate that it was contemplated that the land granted would be used in some particular manner. The easement may be implied by the necessity of the case.[76]
3. Under the doctrine of non-derogation from grant, by virtue of which, as already noticed,[77] there may be acquired not only easements but also immunities of a special kind not recognised as easements.
4. Under the rule in *Wheeldon v Burrows*,[78] which is a branch of the general rule against derogation from grant, but which is commonly considered under a separate head.[79]
5. Where without a means of access or other right, the land granted or retained would be rendered completely inaccessible or unusable.[80]

3–18   The occasion on which an easement most commonly arises without being granted or reserved in express terms is when the owner, or lessee,[81] of land sells or lets[82]

---

[74] Where an easement created by will arises by implication, it should be expressly included in the assent relating to the dominant tenement, and the assent relating to the servient tenement should be expressed to be subject to it.

[75] See *Mellor v Walmesley* [1905] 2 Ch. 164 at 175, 176.

[76] In *Sovmots Investments Ltd v Secretary of State for the Environment* [1977] Q.B. 411 at 440, 441, Forbes J. adopted as correctly stating the law two passages in Megarry and Wade, *The Law of Real Property* (4th ed.), p. 839. First, "A purchaser of land is ordinarily entitled by the contract to existing easements or profits which are appendant or appurtenant to the land sold. As regards quasi-easements, he is entitled to such rights as may fairly be implied into the contract." Secondly, "It therefore seems that there is no general rule that a contract entitles the purchaser to all the rights which an unrestricted conveyance would pass to him. He is rather entitled only to existing easements, and such quasi-easements as are necessary or intended." Forbes J. said that what might be "intended" or "fairly implied into the contract" might be determined from the surrounding circumstances "including, and most important, the way in which both parties knew the premises were to be used."

[77] See para.1–88, above.

[78] (1879) 12 Ch. D. 31.

[79] See, e.g. *Ward v Kirkland* [1967] Ch. 194. This case is considered further at paras 3–35 and 3–54, below.

[80] Although it is possible to have an implied reservation of an easement of necessity as well as an implied grant of a way of necessity, the law adopts a more strict approach with a claim to an implied reservation: see *Adealon International Ltd v Merton LBC* [2007] 1 W.L.R. 1898.

[81] For the present purpose it makes no difference whether the disposing party is owner in fee, or lessee or tenant (see *Key v Neath R.D.C.* (1905) 93 L.T. 507, affirmed (1907) 95 L.T. 771); but an easement created or a disposition by a lessee will not, of course, bind the reversion, nor will it do so if the reversion is afterwards acquired by the lessee: see *Booth v Alcock* (1873) 8 Ch. App. 663, above, para.3–09.

[82] The case of a voluntary conveyance of part does not seem to have come before the courts.

part of it and retains the rest; or disposes of both parts to different persons at the same time. An easement impliedly agreed to be granted or reserved in such a case takes effect as an equitable easement pending the execution of the conveyance or lease, and thereafter, whether expressly granted or not, takes effect as a legal easement.[83]

At this point it should be observed that an easement arising or acquired by implication may at the same time arise under general words, either set out in the conveyance[84] or, as is more probable today, imported into it by section 62 of the Law of Property Act 1925.[85] The two classes of obligations, the one implied from the surrounding circumstances and the fact of the grant, and the other found as a matter of construction from the words of the grant, are quite distinct from one another, as appears from the judgment of Bowen L.J. in the Court of Appeal in *Bayley v Great Western Railway Company*.[86]

In many cases in which the question arises it is sufficient, for practical purposes, to see whether the right in question is included in the general words, for if it is, it will have arisen and can be enforced. Nevertheless, it is thought that the first question in such cases is whether the right would have arisen apart from the general words, for if it would, it will have passed under the conveyance or other disposition whether it is included in the general words or not, unless the disposition shows a contrary intention; and if it would not, then, although it may be included in the general words, these may, where the pre-conditions for rectification are satisfied, be liable to rectification on the ground of mutual mistake. Moreover, the question may arise between contract and conveyance, as when it is sought to modify the general words in a proposed conveyance so as to exclude the grant of an easement which the contract does not import; or to include in the conveyance an express grant of an easement which the contract does import. Furthermore, where the owner of the land disposed of and the land retained is also the occupier of both, no right can arise under general words which is not imported by the contract.

3–19

An easement may also arise if an intention to reserve it can properly be inferred, but the general rule is that a grantor who intends to reserve a right over the tenement granted must do so expressly, so that it is only in exceptional cases that an easement can be reserved by implication.[87]

---

[83] Inasmuch as the rights of the purchaser or lessee arise from the contract, he is, it is thought, clearly entitled to have an express grant, in his conveyance or lease, of the easement which would otherwise be implied. See *Williams on Vendor and Purchaser* (4th ed.), pp. 659, 660.

[84] For an example of general words in a conveyance, see *William Hill (Southern) Ltd v Cabras Ltd* (1986) 54 P. & C.R. 42, where a right to exhibit signs on the landlord's premises passed under a demise of the premises "together with the appurtenances thereto", even though the grant of any easements "except ones as are specifically granted by this lease" was expressly negatived.

[85] In *Ward v Kirkland* [1967] Ch. 194 the plaintiff claimed an easement by implication of law, by the application of the doctrine of derogation from grant, by general words under s.62 of the Law of Property Act 1925 and by prescription. General words are considered at paras 3–126 *et seq.*, below.

[86] (1883) 26 Ch. D. 434 at 452. See Elliott, "Non-Derogation from Grant" (1964) 80 L.Q.R. 224 for an interesting discussion of the distinction.

[87] *Wheeldon v Burrows* (1879) 12 Ch. D. 31 at 49 per Thesiger L.J.; see paras 3–85 *et seq.*, below.

(2) *From description in parcels*

3–20   Of the cases in which an intention to grant an easement was inferred from the language of the conveyance or lease, the earliest seems to be *Roberts v Karr*.[88] Pratt had released to Compigné a piece of land of varying width, described as abutting east on a new road on Pratt's own land. It abutted in the widest part on the road; but in the narrower part a strip of the grantor's land intervened between the road and the premises granted. Pratt alleged that he had intended to reserve the strip, but it was held that, even admitting such an intention, he and those claiming under him were precluded by the description in Compigné's release from preventing Compigné or his assigns from coming out into the road over the strip of land. "Is it not", asked Lord Mansfield C.J.,[89] "a sufficient answer to say, you have told me in your lease, 'this land abuts on the road': you cannot now be allowed to say that the land on which it abuts is not the road."

3–21   In *Harding v Wilson*[90] a lease of premises to one Bolton described them as abutting on "an intended way of thirty feet wide", the soil on that side of the premises demised being the property of one Sloane, the lessor. The defendant, as tenant of the adjoining land under a subsequent demise from Sloane, afterwards built to within 27 feet of the land demised to Bolton. The plaintiff, an underlessee from Bolton, having brought his action claiming a right of way over the whole 30 feet, it was admitted that he was entitled (independently, as it seems, of the description) to a convenient way, his premises not being otherwise accessible from the high road; but it was held that he was not entitled to more. "Adverting", said Lord Abbott C.J.,[91] "to the lease from Sloane to Bolton, the former does not grant a way thirty feet wide, but only describes the land demised as bounded by an intended way of that width. There is merely an expression and declaration of intention." The argument was somewhat complicated by the fact that the plaintiff's underlease did not specify any particular width; but this was held to be immaterial. This case does not seem to have received very much consideration.

3–22   In *Espley v Wilkes*[92] the defendant's lease described the premises demised as "bounded on the east and north by newly-made streets", and the new streets were shown on the plan indorsed. The lessee covenanted to kerb the causeways adjoining the land demised. The way to the east was never made or marked out, and the site was subsequently leased by the same landlord to the plaintiff. It was held that the effect of the defendant's lease was to give him a private right of way over both streets; for the lessor was by his own description estopped from denying that there were streets which were in fact ways. Lord Kelly C.B. relied on *Harding v Wilson*[93] as an authority for the defendant, apparently treating that decision, so far as it affirmed the plaintiff's right to a convenient way, as proceeding on estoppel.

---

[88] (1809) 1 Taunt. 495.
[89] (1809) 1 Taunt. 495, at 503.
[90] (1823) 2 B. & C. 96.
[91] (1823) 2 B. & C. 96, at 96.
[92] (1872) L.R. 7 Exch. 298.
[93] (1823) 2 B. & C. 96.

It is, however, difficult to understand why, if the lessor in that case was estopped from denying that the plaintiff was entitled to some way, he was not equally estopped from denying that the way should be thirty feet wide. It is conceived that the "convenient way" in *Harding v Wilson* was a way of necessity.[94]

In *Mellor v Walmesley*,[95] where land conveyed was described with full dimen-   **3–23** sions and reference to a plan and also, inconsistently with these, as "bounded on the west by the 'seashore'" (which was construed as "foreshore", i.e. the land between ordinary high- and low-water marks), it was held by Vaughan Williams and Stirling L.JJ. that if, as they thought, the western boundary was in fact, on the proper construction of the conveyance, east of the foreshore, the defendants as successors in title of the grantor were estopped as against the plaintiffs, as successors in title of the grantees, from denying that the intervening land west of this boundary was part of the "seashore"; and that the plaintiffs were entitled to unrestricted access over the intervening land to the sea.

In *Rudd v Bowles*[96] leases of four new houses with back gardens, bounded at   **3–24** the rear by land of the lessor, were granted by reference to a plan, on which a strip, part of the lessor's land at the back and running along the boundaries of the gardens, but not mentioned in the body of the lease, was shown coloured. Except through the houses themselves there was no other means of access to the gardens, and each garden had a gate opening into the strip. In the circumstances it was held that each lease contained an implied grant of a right of way over the strip, the grounds being that, reading the leases in the light of the surrounding circumstances, an intention to grant such a right must necessarily be inferred, and that the colouring on the plan was intended to denote a way or passage, either made or intended to be made, along the backs of the gardens.

It is sometimes a question whether, in parcels, such words as "as the same was   **3–25** late in the occupation of X" are merely additional words of identification, or import that the property is to be held with or subject to the rights that affected it when occupied by X. It seems that such words will generally be regarded as words of identification.[97]

(3) *From the particular use intended*

The contemplated user may appear from the circumstances of the grantee, as in   **3–26** *Hall v Lund*.[98] The owner of two mills had leased one to the defendant. In the lease he was described as a bleacher, and the premises leased as lately occupied by Pullan. Pullan had formerly carried on the business of a bleacher in this mill,

---

[94] *Harding v Wilson* and *Espley v Wilkes* were referred to by Cave and A.L. Smith JJ. in *Roe v Siddons* (1888) 22 Q.B.D. 224, but the decision ultimately turned on another point. See also *Cooke v Ingram* (1893) 68 L.T. 671.

[95] [1905] 2 Ch. 164.

[96] [1912] 2 Ch. 60.

[97] *Martyr v Lawrence* (1864) 2 De G.J. & S. 261 (not in fact a case concerned with an easement); *Polden v Bastard* (1865) L.R. 1 Q.B. 156.

[98] (1863) 1 H. & C. 676.

and had drained his refuse into a watercourse which supplied the other mill. The lessor having afterwards sold the mills to the plaintiff, it was held that there had been an implied grant to the defendant of the right to use the watercourse as Pullan had used it,[99] for the purposes of the bleaching business, notwithstanding that such user caused a nuisance.

Again, the contemplated user may appear from the condition of the relevant property, as in *Jones v Pritchard*,[100] a case concerned with a party wall. There was an implied reservation as well as an implied grant.[101]

3–27   In *Lyttleton Times Co Ltd v Warners Ltd*,[102] which was an action by a lessee of part of a building to restrain the commission by the lessor of a nuisance by noise on the rest, it appeared that, when the lease was negotiated, both parties had agreed to a rebuilding of the premises on the terms that the lessee company was to rent from the lessor the upper floors as additional bedrooms for its adjoining hotel, and the lessor was to use the ground floor as a printing works, both parties believing, wrongly as it turned out, that this would not cause any nuisance. There was no evidence that the printing works were carried on improperly, and the action failed because the lessor company was doing nothing more than what had been contemplated, and so must be taken to have impliedly reserved the right to do what it was doing. "If it be true that neither has done or asks to do anything which was not contemplated by both, neither can have any right against the other."[103] This case is authority for the proposition that a nuisance may be legalised by grant.[104]

3–28   In *Pwllbach Colliery Co v Woodman*[105] Lord Parker said: "The law will readily imply the grant or reservation of such easements as may be necessary to give effect to the common intention of the parties to a grant of real property, with reference to the manner or purposes in and for which the land granted or some land retained by the grantor is to be used."[106] Lord Parker referred to *Jones v Pritchard*[107] and *Lyttelton Times Co Ltd v Warners Ltd*. He added:

---

[99] The grant would not, *semble*, have extended to a nuisance caused by some different method of working afterward adopted; see *Pwllbach Colliery Co v Woodman* [1915] A.C. 634 at 648.

[100] [1908] 1 Ch. 630.

[101] See para.3–92, below.

[102] [1907] A.C. 476, considered in *Southwark LBC v Mills* [2001] 1 A.C. 1.

[103] [1907] A.C. 481, per Lord Loreburn L.C.

[104] In *The State Electricity Commission of Victoria & Joshua's Contract, Re* [1940] V.L.R. 121, the Commission acquired land for the purpose of erecting an electrical substation; it was held that there was an implied grant of an easement to transmit noise across the retained land of the vendors.

[105] [1915] A.C. 634 at 646. Cited in *Sovmots Investments Ltd v Secretary of State for the Environment* [1979] A.C. 144 at 175, per Lord Edmund-Davies and applied in *Davies v Bramwell* [2007] EWCA Civ 821.

[106] In *Vanderpant v Mayfair Hotel Co* [1930] 1 Ch. 138, which was an action for nuisance by noise from, inter alia, the kitchen of a large hotel, the defendant attempted, unsuccessfully on the facts, to apply this principle to a case where, before the hotel was built, the plaintiff had secured, by agreement, immunity from the obstruction of light to this house by any future building other than the hotel, and certain other rights, all of which it was alleged were granted on the understanding that the part of the hotel opposite should be used as a kitchen. See also *Horton v Tidd* (1965) 196 E.G. 697; the grant of a lease to a cricket club did not carry an implied right to hit cricket balls into adjoining premises.

[107] [1908] 1 Ch. 630.

"... it is essential for this purpose that the parties should intend that the subject of the grant or the land retained by the grantor should be used in some definite and particular manner. It is not enough that the subject of the grant or the land retained should be intended to be used in a manner which may or may not involve this definite and particular use."

In that case it was held that a lease which recognised that the lessee would, or might, carry on mining operations did not grant by implication the right to create a nuisance by dissipating coal dust over the lessor's land by the use of screening plant installed for the purposes of mining operations begun after the date of the lease. There was no evidence that the trade could not be carried on otherwise.

In *Keewatin Power Co v Lake of the Woods Milling Co*[108] a grant by the Crown **3–29** of land which included a mill and artificial channels from a lake was held to include, by implication from the circumstances, the right to use, for the purposes of the mill, all the water that the channels, at the time of the grant, could bring.

In *White v Taylor (No. 2)*[109] in which the plaintiffs claimed a *profit à prendre* of grazing sheep, Buckley J. also referred to Lord Parker's dictum in *Pwllbach Colliery Co v Woodman*[110] and said that the court should be no less ready to give effect to the common intention of the parties in resolving a latent ambiguity in the language than in perfecting the transaction by implying what they had omitted to say. Buckley J. held, applying Lord Parker's dictum and also *Jones v Pritchard*,[111] that the plaintiffs, who had established their right to depasture sheep, were entitled, as an ancillary right under an implied grant, to water the sheep so depastured by means of troughs supplied by carted water and to do anything else necessary for the proper care and maintenance of the sheep.

In *Stafford v Lee*[112] a conveyance of an area of woodland contained no express **3–30** grant of a right of way over a private roadway which provided the only practical means of access. It was common ground that a right of way was to be implied but the question was whether it was limited to the purposes necessary for the use of the land as woodland or extended to the activities involved in building and using a house on the land. The Court of Appeal inferred from the plan annexed to the conveyance that the parties intended that the plot should be used for the construction of a dwelling and that a right of way for the purpose of building and using a dwelling was therefore to be implied. Nourse L.J. emphasised that there are two hurdles which the person claiming such an easement must surmount: (1) he must establish on the balance of probabilities a common intention that the land is to be put to some definite and particular use; (2) he must show that the easements he claims are necessary to give effect to it.[113]

---

[108] [1930] A.C. 640.
[109] [1969] 1 Ch. 160 at 183, 184.
[110] [1915] A.C. 634 at 646.
[111] [1908] 1 Ch. 630.
[112] (1992) 65 P. & C.R. 172.
[113] (1992) 65 P. & C.R. 172, at 175; these principles were applied in *Mobil Oil Co Limited v Birmingham City Council* [2002] 2 P. & C.R. 168.

3–31   In *Green v Lord Somerleyton*[114] the reservation of an easement of drainage was implied into a conveyance which had been expressed to be made "subject to and with the benefit of" a deed of covenant as to draining marshes of the same date and between the same parties, which deed imposed a duty on the dominant owner to maintain a pump for draining the marshes and a duty on the servient owner to keep dykes on the servient land cleansed and open.

(4) *Special immunities under the doctrine of non-derogation from grant*

3–32   Reference has already briefly been made, in considering in Chapter 1 the characteristics of an easement, to the doctrine of non-derogation from grant from which can arise the same situation as if an easement had been granted, although none has been.[115] The doctrine is most conveniently considered by reference to the judgment of Parker J. in *Browne v Flower*.[116] His Lordship said[117]:

> "The plaintiffs next relied on the maxim that no one can be allowed to derogate from his own grant. This maxim is generally quoted as explaining certain implications which may arise from the fact that, or the circumstances under which, an owner of land grants or demises part of it, retaining the remainder in his own hands. The real difficulty is in each case to ascertain how far such implications extend. It is well settled that such a grant or demise will (unless there be something in the terms of the grant or demise or in the circumstances of the particular case rebutting the implication) impliedly confer on the grantee or lessee, as appurtenant to the land granted or demised to him, easements over the land retained corresponding to the continuous or apparent quasi-easements enjoyed at the time of the grant or demise by the property granted or demised over the property retained."

Parker J. was here referring to the rule in *Wheeldon v Burrows*[118] and he proceeded to give examples of the manner in which the easements might arise by reference to the rule and to point out that the terms of the grant or demise or the special circumstances of the case might, on the other hand, rebut the implication. His Lordship then continued[119]:

> "But the implications usually explained by the maxim that no one can derogate from his own grant do not stop short with easements. Under certain circumstances there will be implied on the part of the grantor or lessor

---

[114] [2004] 1 P. & C.R. 520.
[115] See para.1–88, above.
[116] [1911] 1 Ch. 219.
[117] [1911] 1 Ch. 219 at 224, 225 (applied in *Lyme Valley Squash Club Ltd v Newcastle-under-Lyme B.C.* [1985] 2 All E.R. 405).
[118] (1879) 12 Ch. D. 31. See paras 3–53 *et seq.*, below.
[119] [1911] 1 Ch. 225, 226. See also *Popplewell v Hodkinson* (1869) L.R. 4 Ex. 248, para.10–03, below; *Robinson v Kilvert* (1889) 41 Ch. D. 88.

obligations which restrict the user of the land retained by him further than can be explained by the implication of any easement known to the law. Thus, if the grant or demise be made for a particular purpose, the grantor or lessor comes under an obligation not to use the land retained by him in such a way as to render the land granted or demised unfit or materially less fit for the particular purpose for which the grant or demise was made."

His Lordship went on to refer to examples as follows[120]:

"In Aldin v. Latimer Clark, Muirhead & Co.[121] land having been demised for the purpose of carrying on the business of a timber merchant, the lessor came under an obligation not to build on land retained by him so as to interrupt the access of air to sheds on the demised property used for drying timber, although the law does not recognise any easement of air unless it comes through or to some defined passage or aperture. Similarly in the case of Grosvenor Hotel Co. v. Hamilton[122] the lessee was held entitled to prevent the lessor from using property retained by him in such a way as to cause on the demised property vibrations which did not amount to a legal nuisance, though there is no such easement known to the law as an easement of freedom from vibration any more than there is an easement of freedom from noise. Once again, though possibly there may not be known to the law any easement of light for special purposes, still the lease of a building to be used for a special purpose requiring an extraordinary amount of light might well be held to preclude the grantor from diminishing the light passing to the grantee's windows, even in cases where the diminution would not be such as to create a nuisance within the meaning of the recent decisions: see Herz v. Union Bank of London.[123] In none of these cases would any easement be created, but the obligation implied on the part of the lessor or grantor would be analogous to that which arises from a restrictive covenant. It is to be observed that in the several cases to which I have referred the lessor had done or proposed to do something which rendered or would render the demised premises unfit or materially less fit to be used for the particular purpose for which the demise was made."[124]

In *Harmer v Jumbil (Nigeria) Tin Areas Ltd*,[125] in which Younger L.J.[126] **3–33** described the rule against derogation from grant as "a principle which merely

---

[120] [1911] 1 Ch. 226.
[121] [1894] 2 Ch. 437.
[122] [1894] 2 Q.B. 836.
[123] (1854) 2 Giff. 686.
[124] See also *Frederick Betts Ltd v Pickfords Ltd* [1906] 2 Ch. 87.
[125] [1921] 1 Ch. 200.
[126] [1921] 1 Ch. 200 at 225. See also *Sovmots Investments Ltd v Secretary of State for the Environment* [1979] A.C. 144 at 175, per Lord Edmund-Davies. Indeed, the principle is not restricted to cases involving real property: see *British Leyland v Armstrong Patents* [1986] A.C. 577 (right of owner of car to have access to a free market in spare parts); *Johnston & Sons Ltd v Holland* [1988] 1 E.G.L.R. 264 at 267K.

embodies in a legal maxim a rule of common honesty", it was established that the application of the rule is not confined to physical interference with the land granted. Land was leased with the express purpose that it should be used for the purposes of an explosives magazine, and further land was held under a tenancy agreement which permitted the erection thereon of a shed for packing explosives. Subsequently adjoining land was leased to the defendant company by a lessor who was the successor in title of both the grantor of the lease of the site of the explosives magazine and the grantor of the tenancy of the land on which the shed was sited. The defendant proposed to erect buildings which would have occasioned the withdrawal of the plaintiff's licence for the magazine and packing shed under the Explosives Act 1875.

The Court of Appeal held that in the circumstances in which the lease was granted there must be implied on the part of the lessor an obligation not to do anything which would violate the conditions under which the licence was held, so as to cause a forfeiture of it; that the acts of the defendant would, if done by the lessor, have been in derogation of his grant; and that inasmuch as the defendant was for this purpose in the same position as the lessor, the acts of the defendant must be regarded as being done by him. This case is not only authority for the proposition that a successor in title of the grantor may be restrained from acting in derogation of the grant; it is also one of the few cases[127] in which a right of immunity acquired under the doctrine of non-derogation has been successfully asserted by a successor in title of the grantee. It is thought, however, that, at least so long as the original purpose of the grant is adhered to,[128] the right, even if it is of a kind not recognised as an easement, attaches to the premises granted in the same way as an easement.

3–34   The statement by Parker J. in *Browne v Flower*[129] that the obligation implied on the part of the lessor or grantor would be analogous to that which arises from a restrictive covenant requires qualification, for unlike the obligation which arises under a restrictive covenant, the obligation implied on the part of the lessor or grantor binds successors without notice. This appears from *Cable v Bryant*.[130] A stable and an adjoining yard were in common ownership, the yard being subject to a lease. The freeholder let the stable, in which were two windows or ventilators, to the plaintiff. A few months later the freeholder conveyed the yard to the defendant, the lessee joining to surrender the lease. The defendant then erected a hoarding in the yard close to the stable, so blocking the windows or ventilators; and the plaintiff obtained an injunction. The immunity, so recognised, of interference with air and light appears to have had the characteristics of an easement, but

---

[127] *Johnston & Sons Ltd v Holland* [1988] 1 E.G.L.R. 264 is another such case.
[128] If the premises were used for some different purpose, the right might well be considered to have been abandoned.
[129] [1911] 1 Ch. 219 at 226.
[130] [1908] 1 Ch. 259; followed in *Johnston & Sons Ltd v Holland* [1988] 1 E.G.L.R. 264. In *Molton Builders Ltd v Westminster LBC* (1975) 30 P. & C.R. 182 at 186, Lord Denning M.R. approved a passage in Megarry & Wade, *The Law of Real Property*, now contained in the 6ᵗʰ ed. at para.14–208, to the effect that the principle binds the grantor and persons claiming under him and the right to enforce it passes to those claiming under the grantee.

it was argued that as the yard was let when the plaintiff took his lease, no implication of the grant of an easement could arise, because the easement could not
have taken effect in possession. Neville J. expressed no opinion as to this, and
decided the case on the principle of non-derogation from grant; that is, on the
ground that the lessor, having let the stable, was under an obligation not to interfere with its reasonable use for the purposes of a stable for which it was granted.
He held that the rule against derogation from grant did not depend on implied
covenant but was a rule of law and that the obligation to which it gave rise
affected a successor in title, with or without notice.

In *Ward v Kirkland*,[131] in which the plaintiff claimed a right to go onto the   **3–35**
defendant's property for the purpose of doing certain works to the advantage
of the plaintiff's property, Ungoed-Thomas J. said[132] that the question of derogation from grant generally arose in cases where the grantor did something on
his own property which defeated the enjoyment of the property granted as it
existed and was contemplated at the time of the grant. His Lordship said that
clearly there was a distinction between the two categories of case, but it seemed
to him that the underlying principle of the doctrine applied to both categories.
It was (he said) with hesitation and with an appreciation of the difficulties that
he came to that conclusion, and he preferred, in upholding the plaintiff's claim,
to rely upon the operation of the general words under section 62 of the Law
of Property Act 1925; so that his views on the operation of the doctrine were
obiter dictum.

In *Woodhouse & Co Ltd v Kirkland (Derby) Ltd*,[133] however, Plowman J. held,   **3–36**
distinguishing *Cable v Bryant*,[134] that, although a purely negative right over the
servient or quasi-servient tenement might be acquired under the doctrine forbidding derogation from grant in a manner which was indistinguishable from an
implied grant, this was not true of a positive right, such as a right of way. The
plaintiff company's premises enjoyed a right of way over a passageway belonging to the defendant company which gave access from the plaintiff's yard to the
public highway. In 1965 the plaintiff acquired from the defendant company a
small strip of land near the entrance to the passageway from the yard in order to
improve the access from the yard. The plaintiff, having acquired the strip of land,
increased the width of the gateway leading into its yard. The plaintiff alleged that
the defendant was aware of the plaintiff's intention to increase the width of the
gateway and must be taken to have increased the width of the right of way by
opening it out at the end where the plaintiff's gates were situated. The defendant
erected posts so as to bar entry to the yard except over the original width of the
passageway. Plowman J. held that the 1965 conveyance did not operate as an
implied grant of an extended right of way, though he did find that the erection of

---

[131] [1967] Ch. 194.
[132] [1967] Ch. 194 at 227.
[133] [1970] 1 W.L.R. 1185. Rather surprisingly, *Ward v Kirkland* [1967] Ch. 194 was not cited in argument.
[134] [1908] 1 Ch. 259.

the posts amounted to a derogation from grant in that they rendered the land conveyed in 1965 materially less fit for the purpose for which the grant was made, namely, to improve the access to the yard.

3–37   The authorities were reviewed in the important case of *Johnston & Sons Ltd v Holland*.[135] The defendant, Miss Holland, had a long lease of a property, the flank wall of which was used as an advertisement hoarding which could be viewed from the highway across an intervening open site, used as a car park. The defendant's predecessor in title had granted a sub-lease of the property but had reserved the use of the exterior of the flank wall of the premises for the purpose of affixing posters or advertisements thereto and the right to grant licences therefor. At the time of the grant of the sub-lease, the open site adjoining the flank wall was owned by a third party. Subsequently, the plaintiff company acquired the term of the sub-lease and the freehold of the open site (and, indeed, the freehold of the premises subject to the long lease). The plaintiff erected a hoarding on the open site so that the advertisements on the flank wall were obscured. The defendant sued for damages asserting a breach of the plaintiff's obligation not to derogate from the grant consisting of the reservation out of the sub-lease, a reservation in favour of the defendant's predecessor in title from the sub-lease to the plaintiff's predecessor in title. The plaintiff contended that because the hoarding was on the open site and because the original sub-lessee had no right or interest in the open site when the reservation was taken, the obligation not to derogate from that reservation did not extend to anything done on the open site. Nicholls L.J., giving the only judgment in the Court of Appeal said[136]:

> "We have not been referred to any case in which it has been decided, or even suggested, that the non-derogation from grant principle can apply in respect of activities of the grantor on neighbouring land subsequently acquired by him. Despite this, a rigid inflexible limitation excluding such activities by a grantor from the scope of the principle in all circumstances is capable of producing such unattractive results that, given the rationale underlying the principle, I am emboldened to consider whether, indeed, there is any such overriding limitation."

Having reviewed the authorities, he concluded that the broad principle to be applied was as follows:

> ". . . if one man agrees to confer a particular benefit on another, he must not do anything which substantially deprives the other of the enjoyment of that benefit; because that would be to take away with one hand what is given with the other."[137]

---

[135] [1988] 1 E.G.L.R. 264.
[136] [1988] 1 E.G.L.R. 264 at 267J.
[137] [1988] 1 E.G.L.R. 264, at 267M citing *Molton Builders Ltd v City of Westminster* (1975) 30 P. & C.R. 182 at 186, per Lord Denning M.R.

Nicholls L.J. continued[138]:

"In a case such as the present, that exercise involves identifying what obligations, if any, on the part of the grantor can fairly be regarded as necessarily implicit, having regard to the particular purpose of the transaction when considered in the light of the circumstances subsisting at the time the transaction was entered into. It is at this point that I find myself unable to see why that exercise should be subject to the overriding limitation contended for by [counsel for the plaintiff] in the present case . . .", and

"Of course in considering what is necessarily implicit in a transaction in a case where the grantor owns no other land, very great weight indeed must be given to that factor. It will be a very exceptional case for it to be necessarily implicit in a lease that the activities of a lessor who owns no adjoining land, and has no plans to buy any adjoining land, are to be restricted on the adjoining land should he ever become owner or tenant of that land. Whether it is so implicit or not will depend on all the circumstances, including the purpose of the grant and the nature of the activities sought to be restrained. But if the facts in a given case point clearly to such a restriction being implicit, I can see no reason in principle why the law should treat that case differently from one where the lessor already owns the adjoining land at the time of the lease."

Accordingly, the plaintiff was held liable as successor in title[139] to the original sub-lessee for derogating from the reservation in the sub-lease by erecting hoardings so as to obscure the defendant's advertisements on the flank wall.

The immunities acquired by virtue of the doctrine depend upon the common **3–38** intention, to be gathered either from the express words of the grant or the circumstances in which the grant was made.[140] Prima facie the obligation involved in the grant for use for a particular business is confined to the ordinary purposes of that business, and does not extend to special branches of it which require extraordinary protection.[141] Furthermore, no act can be complained of, under the doctrine, which does not make the land granted unfit for the particular purpose for which it was granted or, at least, where the purpose can only be achieved at greater expense or with less convenience.[142] In *Browne v Flower*,[143] for example, where

---

[138] [1988] 1 E.G.L.R. 264 at 267M.

[139] Following *Cable v Bryant* [1908] 1 Ch. 259, and see para.3–34, above.

[140] *Birmingham, Dudley and District Banking Co v Ross* (1888) 38 Ch. D. 295; *Myers v Catterson* (1889) 43 Ch. D. 470; *Corbett v Jonas* [1892] 3 Ch. 137; *Lyttelton Times Co v Warners Ltd* [1907] A.C. 476, 481; *Johnston & Sons Ltd v Holland* [1988] 1 E.G.L.R. 264.

[141] *Aldin v Latimer Clark Muirhead & Co* [1894] 2 Ch. 437 at 444; *Robinson v Kilvert* (1889) 41 Ch. D. 88.

[142] *O'Cedar Ltd v Slough Trading Co Ltd* [1927] 2 K.B. 123 at 127, per Branson J., cited with approval by Lord Templeman in *British Leyland v Armstrong Patents* [1986] A.C. 577.

[143] [1911] 1 Ch. 219; see para.3–32, above. See also *O'Cedar Ltd v Slough Trading Co* [1927] 2 K.B. 123 (use of adjoining land in a manner calculated to raise the fire insurance premium for the demised building held not to be a derogation); *Port v Griffith* [1938] 1 All E.R. 295 (similar decision as to a lease of adjoining premises for a business which the plaintiff was bound to carry on under her lease); *Kelly v Battershell* [1949] 2 All E.R. 830 (similar decision as to the incorporation of the rest of a house, in which the plaintiff had a flat, into a hotel on adjoining premises).

the plaintiff was tenant of a residential flat, and the landlords and those representing them had erected a staircase leading from the outside to the flat above, so affecting the plaintiff's privacy, the plaintiff's action failed because, although there had been interference with her amenities, the land was still no less capable of being used as a flat than it had been before.

Modern examples

3–39   It is easy to state the obligation that a grantor must abstain from doing anything which will render the premises unfit or materially less fit to be used for the purpose for which the grant was made, but less easy to apply it. What sort of acts will the courts regard as rendering premises unfit? What is meant by "materially less fit"? How do you define the purpose of the grant? Some further examples may help to answer these questions.

3–40   It is important to look at what both parties contemplated the other would do with his land. So where upper floors were let as hotel bedrooms, the lessee being fully aware that the ground floor would be used as a printing press, it was held that the use of the ground floor as a printing press was not a derogation from grant.[144] It is not a derogation to do what you were always expected to do, even if it has unforeseen consequences.

3–41   A landlord let premises adjacent to the demised premises to a woodworker, as a result of which the insurance premium on the former premises was increased. It was held that merely to render it substantially more expensive to conduct the business for which the premises had been demised was not a breach.[145] It did not go to the "fitness" of the premises.

3–42   A landlord let a shop for 21 years for use for the sale of wool and general trimmings. Six years later he let the adjoining shop for the sale of tailoring and dressmaking trimmings and cloths. It was held that there was no implied obligation not to let premises to a competitor.[146]

3–43   A tenant took a pre-let of a shop in a proposed shopping centre which the lessor agreed to construct "approximately as shown on the layout in the plans submitted" by his architect. Subsequently the landlord adapted its plans and built a unit twice the size of the tenant's which it proposed to let to Woolworths, a direct competitor. It was held that there was no derogation from grant.[147]

3–44   A farmer sold off some cottages next to his farmyard. Shortly afterwards he began to use the yard for keeping pigs and stacking manure. The court refused to imply an obligation inhibiting the use of the yard for "any customary and normal agricultural purpose".[148]

---

[144] *Lyttleton Times Co Ltd v Warners Ltd* [1907] A.C. 476.
[145] *O'Cedar Ltd v Slough Trading Company Ltd* [1927] 2 K.B. 123.
[146] *Port v Griffiths* [1938] 1 All E.R. 295, applied in *Romulus Trading v Comet Properties* [1996] 2 E.G.L.R. 70, but explained and distinguished in *Oceanic Village Ltd v Shiryama Shokusan Co Ltd* [2001] L. & T.R. 478 which shows that there may be special circumstances in which letting to a competitor who intends to sell the same products may amount to derogation from grant.
[147] *Clarks-Gambol of Canada Ltd v Grant Park Plaza Ltd* [1967] 64 D.L.R. (2d) 570.
[148] *Milner v Spencer* [1976] 2 E.G.L.R. 111.

A landlord owned a row of shops with a service road at the rear. He let the shops on leases which contained tenants' covenants not to allow their vehicles to obstruct the service road. The landlord failed to enforce the covenants with the result that the lessee of the end shop could not effect deliveries. The landlord was held liable in nuisance and for derogation from grant for failing to enforce the covenant.[149]   **3–45**

A landlord granted a 23-year lease of three commercial units with a right to use the forecourt and exclusive right to park vehicles on part of the forecourt for loading and unloading. He then let two other units to other tenants who continually parked their vehicles on the forecourt in breach of the terms of their leases. The landlord consented to or connived at this behaviour and this was held to amount to a derogation from grant.[150]   **3–46**

A tenant had a shop in a shopping mall which sold puzzles and executive toys. Subsequently her landlord let an adjoining unit to a pawnbroker. The pawnbroker only let in one customer at a time and the waiting customers deterred the customers of the shop. The court held that the purpose of the letting was as a shop in a mall; it was implicit that other tenants would be subject to similar forms of lease which prohibited the tenants from committing nuisances and conferred on the landlord a rule making power for the management of the mall; while the letting to the pawnbroker was not derogation, the landlord's failure to take steps to control the pawnbroker's clientele and the manner in which the pawnbroker conducted his business was a derogation from grant.[151]   **3–47**

A council which owned a 184-acre site designated for outdoor recreation let part of it as an equestrian centre together with the right to use bridle paths over the retained land. The tenant complained that the council had committed or suffered on the retained land a variety of activities which had damaged its business, interfered with its use of the bridle paths and caused occasional injury to its horses, including noisy parties, authorised and unauthorised football games obstructing the bridle paths, the flying of model aircraft and the holding of motor rallies near the bridle paths, use of the bridle paths by anglers driving to a lake and use by trespassers for kite flying. It was held: (a) that no action lay for uses contemplated by the parties at the time of the lease, unless the activity in question was carried out in an unreasonable way; and (b) that a failure to control trespassers could be a breach. Damages were awarded in respect of some of the activities complained of.[152]   **3–48**

A landlord let a shop in a new shopping centre in the Kings Road, Chelsea to a retailer of ladieswear. The original concept had been to have "exclusive designer labels and select fashion retailers" on that floor of the scheme but these aspirations were never entirely realised and the scheme attracted few well-known brand names. The landlord sought ways to enhance the number of customers and hit on the idea of converting the atrium and the lower ground floor into a glass-sided unit to be let   **3–49**

[149] *Hilton v James Smith and Sons (Norwood) Ltd* [1979] 2 E.G.L.R. 44.
[150] *Nynehead Developments Ltd v R.H. Fibreboard Containers Ltd* [1999] 1 E.G.L.R. 7.
[151] *Chartered Trust v Davies* [1997] 2 E.G.L.R. 83.
[152] *Yankwood Ltd v Havering L.B.C.* [1998] E.G.C.S. 75.

to a well-known record company, thus equipping the centre with an anchor trader. A year after the new unit opened, the tenant closed asserting that the landlord was in repudiatory breach of its obligation not to derogate from grant by reason of having altered the centre physically, changed the tenant mix by letting large units to non-fashion retailers and permitted the new retailers to display prominent signage. The judge held that he was "far from persuaded" that the landlord was under any "necessarily implicit" obligation to maintain the original tenant mix; that to do something which it was not foreseeable would damage the tenant's business was no derogation from grant; that he was "inclined to think" that the circumstances of the grant did impose an obligation on the landlord not so to alter or use the common parts of the centre in such manner as to cause it to lose its character as a retail shopping mall; that the landlord could not do or permit something which it was reasonably foreseeable would render a particular shop materially less fit for the commercial purpose for which it had been let; that on the facts the creation of the new unit had not caused the centre to lose its character as a retail shopping mall; that the signage might have contributed to the adverse effect on the tenant's trade but was not a breach because that could not have been reasonably expected.[153] It appears from this decision that the obligation not to derogate from grant is not absolute but is an obligation not to do something which it is reasonably foreseeable will damage the grantee.

3–50   A tenant took a lease of a kiosk situated within the exit from Goodge Street Underground Station. The judge held on the facts that it had been contemplated by the parties at the date of grant that the exit would be part of the station operation during the hours when the station was open. In fact, the exit was only operational during the morning rush hour and the tenant's trade from the kiosk was accordingly affected. It was held that the closure of the exit at other times amounted to derogation from grant.[154]

3–51   The cases referred to above contain four examples of the landlord being held liable for failing to prevent others interfering with express easements granted by him to his tenants. In *Hilton*, he was liable for failing to prevent his tenants obstructing a service road. In *Nynehead*, he was held liable for conniving with his other tenants' illicit parking. In *Chartered Trust*, he was held liable for not regulating the way one tenant ran his business so that his customers put off customers to another tenant's shop. In *Yankwood*, he was held liable for letting licensees and trespassers frighten horses on the bridle paths. A landlord may, therefore, be liable not only where he himself directly interferes with the enjoyment of an easement which he has granted[155] but also where he fails to exercise powers which he has reserved to control others.

Summary of principles relating to non-derogation from grant

3–52   The above cases concerning the principle of non-derogation from grant establish the following propositions:

---

[153] *Petra v Jeffrey Rogers* (2001) 81 P. & C.R. 21.
[154] *Platt v London Underground Ltd* [2001] 2 E.G.L.R. 121.
[155] See Chapter 13, below.

1. the principle is that if a grant or demise be made for a particular purpose, the grantor or lessor is under an obligation not to do anything which will render the premises granted or demised unfit or materially less fit for the particular purpose for which the grant or demise was made;
2. this doctrine goes beyond the law of easements in that it can confer rights which cannot exist as easements and does not depend on the existence at the date of grant of any defined servient tenement[156];
3. it also goes beyond the law of restrictive covenants in that the obligations which it creates can be enforced against successors without notice, can impose restrictions on what the grantor can do with land which it did not own at the date of grant but acquired later and can impose positive obligations on successors in title;
4. the derogation doctrine does not apply:

    (i)   to acts known to be intended at the date of the lease, even if they have unforeseen consequences;
    (ii) to situations which existed at the date of the lease[157];
    (iii) to acts which affect the amenity rather than the fitness of the land;
    (iv) to acts which merely increase the cost of running the premises or affect the profitability of the trade without impinging on the ability of the premises to be used for the contemplated purposes;
    (v)   to acts which in fact cause damage to the tenant's trade but in a manner that could not reasonably have been foreseen.

5. the doctrine can apply:

    (i)   to acts which render premises legally unfit, not merely physically unfit;
    (ii) to omissions to enforce obligations against other tenants (thus imposing positive duties);
    (iii) to acts which render the exercise of the tenants' rights over the landlord's retained land less convenient, though not impossible.[158]

(5) *The rule in Wheeldon v Burrows*

The rule in *Wheeldon v Burrows*[159] is limited to continuous and apparent easements **3–53** impliedly granted when the owner of a piece of land grants away part of it. As

---

[156] Indeed it has been applied in contexts that have nothing to do with real property, such as patent law: *British Leyland v Armstrong Patents* [1986] A.C. 577.

[157] *Southwark L.B.C. v Mills* [2001] 1 A.C. 1.

[158] See further para.13–02, below.

[159] (1879) 12 Ch. D. 31. The terms of a contract may be such as to oust any implication of any right under the rule: *Squarey v Harris-Smith* (1981) 42 P. &. C.R. 118 (not cited in *Lyme Valley Squash Club v Newcastle-under-Lyme B.C.* [1985] 2 All E.R. 405); so may the terms of the conveyance: see, per Peter Gibson L.J. in *Wheeler v J.J. Saunders Ltd* [1996] Ch. 19 at 32 (as to the relevance of a fencing covenant); *Wheeler v J.J. Saunders* was considered and applied in a further case involving a fencing covenant: see *Hillman v Rogers* [1997] EWCA Civ 3069; further, the terms of the conveyance may limit the extent of the implication: *Nickerson v Barraclough* [1981] Ch. 426.

appears from the judgment of Thesiger L.J. in that case, this common law rule for determining what easements are implied in favour of the grantee against the grantor is really a branch of the general rule against derogation from grant. The facts of the case are less important than the rule but may be shortly stated. A workshop and an adjacent piece of land belonging to the same owner were put up for sale by auction. The workshop was not then sold, but the piece of land was, and it was soon after-wards conveyed to the purchaser. A month after this the vendor agreed to sell the workshop to another person, and in due course conveyed it to him. The workshop had windows overlooking and receiving their light from the piece of land first sold, and Lord Bacon V.-C. and the Court of Appeal held that, as the vendor had not when he conveyed the piece of land reserved the right of access of light to the win-dows, no such right passed to the purchaser of the workshop, and that the purchaser of the piece of land could build so as to obstruct the windows of the workshop. The case itself was thus concerned with an alleged implied reservation, but Thesiger L.J.'s judgment (which was the judgment of the court) stated the rules governing implied grant as well as implied reservation. His Lordship said[160]:

> "We have had a considerable number of cases cited to us, and out of them I think that two propositions may be stated as what I may call the general rules governing cases of this kind. The first of these rules is, that on the grant by the owner of a tenement of part of that tenement as it is then used and enjoyed, there will pass to the grantee all those continuous and apparent easements (by which, of course, I mean quasi-easements), or, in other words, all those easements which are necessary to the reasonable enjoyment of the property granted, and which have been and are at the time of the grant used by the owners of the entirety for the benefit of the part granted. The second proposition is that, if the grantor intends to reserve any right over the tene-ment granted, it is his duty to reserve it expressly in the grant. Those are the general rules governing cases of this kind, but the second of those rules is subject to certain exceptions. One of those exceptions is the well-known exception which attaches to cases of what are called ways of necessity; and I do not dispute for a moment that there may be, and probably are, certain other exceptions, to which I shall refer before I close my observations upon this case.[161] Both of the general rules which I have mentioned are founded upon a maxim which is as well established by authority as it is consonant to reason and common sense, viz. that a grantor shall not derogate from his grant."

Thesiger L.J. proceeded to review the leading cases on the subject,[162] including those dealing with ways of necessity, and then continued[163]:

---

[160] (1879) 12 Ch. D. 49.

[161] Where the title to the ownership of the surface of land has been lost by reason of adverse posses-sion, the former owner may still have a right to go upon the land to repair overhanging projections such as eaves: *Williams v Usherwood* (1983) 45 P. & C.R. 235.

[162] See in particular *Suffield v Brown* (1864) 4 De G.J. & S. 185 and the speech of Lord Westbury at 194, from which Thesiger L.J. in the passage cited above freely quoted.

[163] (1879) 12 Ch. D. 58 at 59.

"These cases . . . support the propositions that in the case of a grant you may imply a grant of such continuous and apparent easements or such easements as are necessary to the reasonable enjoyment of the property conveyed, and have in fact been enjoyed during the unity of ownership, but that, with the exception which I have referred to of easements of necessity, you cannot imply a similar reservation in favour of the grantor of land."[164]

In *Ward v Kirkland*[165] in which the plaintiff, as stated above,[166] claimed the right **3–54** to go on to the defendant's property for the purpose of doing certain works for the advantage of the plaintiff's cottage, Ungoed-Thomas J. referred to the passage in *Wheeldon v Burrows*[167] last quoted and said that, reading that passage on its own, on first impression, it would appear that the "easements which are necessary to the reasonable enjoyment of the property conveyed" might be a separate class from "continuous and apparent easements."[168] His Lordship said that it had been recognised that there was some difficulty in those descriptions, and that it had been suggested that perhaps the "easements necessary to the reasonable enjoyment of the property conveyed" might refer to negative easements, whereas the case with which his Lordship was dealing was concerned with positive easements. However that might be, there is no reported case in which positive easements not "continuous and apparent" have been held to come within the doctrine of *Wheeldon v Burrows*.[169] Ungoed-Thomas J. took the words "continuous and apparent" to be directed to there being on the servient tenement a feature which would be seen on inspection and which was neither transitory nor intermittent; for example, drains and paths, as contrasted with the bowsprits of ships overhanging a piece of land. On the facts of the case before him, his Lordship held that there was no continuous and apparent easement within the requirements of *Wheeldon v Burrows*, and so the easement claimed was not created by implication of law.

Wheeldon v Burrows[170] was considered by the House of Lords in *Sovmots* **3–55** *Investments Ltd v Secretary of State for the Environment*.[171] The speeches of Lord Wilberforce and Lord Edmund-Davies are particularly important. Lord

---

[164] See also *Bayley v Great Western Ry* (1884) 26 Ch. D. 434 and 452, per Bowen L.J.; *Brown v Alabaster* (1888) 37 Ch. D. 490; *Birmingham, Dudley and District Banking Co v Ross* (1888) 38 Ch. D. 295 at 308, per Cotton L.J.; *Nicholls v Nicholls* (1899) 81 L.T. 811; *Browne v Flower* [1911] 1 Ch. 219 at 225, when Parker J. tacitly converted "continuous and apparent" into "continuous or apparent".

[165] [1967] Ch. 194 at 224–226.

[166] See para.3–35, above.

[167] (1879) 12 Ch. D. 31 at 58–59.

[168] To the contrary effect is Peter Gibson L.J. in *Wheeler v J.J. Saunders Ltd* [1996] Ch. 19 at 31 referring to the earlier passage from Thesiger L.J. at (1879) 12 Ch. D. 31 at 49; and see *Auerbach v Beck* [1985] 6 N.S.W.L.R. 424 at 443 (Powell J.); on appeal [1985] 6 N.S.W.L.R. 454.

[169] (1879) 12 Ch. D. 31. In *St Clement's, Leigh-on-Sea, Re* [1988] 1 W.L.R. 720, a concrete path which had previously existed had been removed by the date of the sale; no longer being apparent, a right of way over the path did not pass under the sale.

[170] (1879) 12 Ch. D. 31.

[171] [1979] A.C. 144.

Wilberforce emphasised[172] that there will pass by virtue of the rule only those easements necessary to the reasonable enjoyment of the property granted which have been used and are, at the time of the grant, used by the entirety of the property for the benefit of the part granted. His Lordship referred[173] to the rule as "a rule of intention, based on the proposition that a man may not derogate from his grant. He cannot grant or agree to grant land and at the same time deny to his grantee what is at the time of the grant obviously necessary for its reasonable enjoyment". Lord Edmund-Davies also treated[174] the line of cases to which *Wheeldon v Burrows*[175] belongs as exemplifying the rule against derogation from grant, but his Lordship, having quoted[176] the propositions stated by Thesiger L.J.,[177] pointed out that their basis was, as Lord Parker of Waddington had said and stressed in *Pwllbach Colliery Co Ltd v Woodman*[178] that "The law will readily imply the grant or reservation of such easements as may be necessary to give effect to the common intention of the parties to a grant of real property . . ." Lord Edmund-Davies did not suggest that any distinction was to be made between the acquisition of positive and negative easements.

3–56   It is, however, suggested that a negative easement acquired on the disposition of part of a tenement is more correctly attributed to the operation of the rule that no one can be allowed to derogate from his grant than to an implied grant.[179] In other words, while the owner of a house served by a drive and overlooking a field can fairly be said, on selling the house without the drive, to have intended to grant with the house a right of way over the drive, it seems more natural, if he sells the house and retains the field, to ascribe to him the intention, not actually to grant with the house a right to light, but to charge the field with the uninterrupted passage of light to the house. The result, however, appears to be the same on either view. The manner in which different types of positive and negative easements are acquired on a disposition of part will now be considered.

3–57   In *Moncrieff v Jamieson*[180] it was stated that the principle in *Wheeldon v Burrows*[181] was an example of the general and well established principle which applies to contracts, whether relating to grants of land or other arrangements, to the effect that the law will imply a term into a contract where, in the light of the terms of the contract and the facts known to the parties at the time of the contract, such a term would have been regarded as reasonably necessary or obvious to the parties.

---

[172] [1979] A.C. 144 at 168.
[173] [1979] A.C. 144 at 168.
[174] [1979] A.C. 144 at 175.
[175] (1879) 12 Ch. D. 31.
[176] [1979] A.C. 144 at 175.
[177] (1879) 12 Ch. D. 31 at 49.
[178] [1915] A.C. 624 at 646.
[179] See paras 3–32 *et seq.*, above. Although the principle of derogation from grant applies to both positive and negative easements, generally it is applied to negative easements: *Ward v Kirkland* [1967] Ch. 194 at 226, 221, per Ungoed-Thomas J.
[180] [2007] 1 W.L.R. 2620 at [112] per Lord Neuberger.
[181] (1879) 21 Ch. D. 31.

Positive easements: (a) Rights of way

Borman v Griffith[182] provides a clear formulation of the principles under consid-   **3–58**
eration and shows that the rule in *Wheeldon v Burrows*[183] remains of importance
in spite of the statutory importation of general words by section 6 of the
Conveyancing Act 1881, and its successor, section 62 of the Law of Property Act
1925, if only because the general words will not always be imported. In *Borman
v Griffith*[184] A had been the owner of a private park, in which a drive ran from the
main road past the front door of a house (formerly a gardener's lodge) called The
Gardens, and on to another house called The Hall. In 1923 A agreed under hand
to demise to the plaintiff for seven years The Gardens with the adjoining paddock, orchard and gardens, but not the drive. At this time the plaintiff was making, and he afterwards completed, an unmetalled way leading from the main road
to the paddock at the rear; but there was no road across the paddock, and the
plaintiff used the drive, which was the natural way of approaching The Gardens,
until it was obstructed by the defendant, who had taken a lease of The Hall and
the rest of the park, including the drive, in 1926. Maugham J., giving judgment
for the plaintiff, decided, first, that no general words were to be imported into the
agreement, for an agreement for a lease exceeding a term of three years is not, for
the purposes of section 62 of the Law of Property Act 1925, a "conveyance" as
defined in section 205(1)(ii)[185]; and he proceeded[186]:

> "In my opinion, however, the position of the court in granting specific per-
> formance of a contract such as this is the same, in effect, so far as regards
> rights of way, as if there had been, before the coming into force of the
> Conveyancing Act 1881,[187] a conveyance of this property with no mention
> of rights of way: in other words, the doctrine that a grantor may not derogate
> from his own grant would apply in the circumstances of this case. The plain-
> tiff being entitled to specific performance, the court would decide that he
> must be given all such rights of way as, according to the doctrine of the court
> in regard to implied grants, would pass upon a conveyance or demise. In my
> view, the principles laid down in such cases as Wheeldon v. Burrows,[188]
> Brown v. Alabaster,[189] and Nicholls v. Nicholls,[190] are applicable. Without
> going through all the cases in detail, I may state the principle as follows—
> namely, that *where, as in the present case, two properties belonging to a
> single owner and about to be granted are separated by a common road, or*

---

[182] [1930] 1 Ch. 493. This case was applied in *Horn v Hiscock* (1972) 223 E.G. 1437 (tenancy agreement under hand).
[183] (1879) 12 Ch. D. 31.
[184] [1930] 1 Ch. 493.
[185] See para.3–126, below.
[186] [1930] 1 Ch. 493 at 498, 499. The italics are the editors'.
[187] i.e. s.6, repealed and reproduced, as to conveyances made after 1881, by s.62 of the Law of
Property Act 1925.
[188] (1879) 12 Ch. D. 31.
[189] (1888) 37 Ch. D. 490.
[190] (1899) 81 L.T. 811.

where a plainly visible road exists over the one for the apparent use of the other, and that road is necessary for the reasonable enjoyment of the property, a right to use the road will pass with the quasi-dominant tenement, unless by the terms of the contract that right is excluded[191]: and in my opinion, if the present position were that the plaintiff were claiming against the lessor specific performance of the agreement of October 10, 1923, he would be entitled to be given a right of way for all reasonable purposes along the drive, including the part that passes the farm on the way to the orchard.

It is true that the easement, or, rather, quasi-easement, is not continuous. But the authorities are sufficient to show that a grantor of property, in circumstances where an obvious, i.e. visible and made road is necessary for the reasonable enjoyment of the property by the grantee, must be taken prima facie to have intended to grant a right to use it."

3–59   In *Goldberg v Edwards*[192] the formula italicised above was accepted by the Court of Appeal, subject to the possible addition[193] of the words "and convenient" after "reasonable". In that case, where an annexe to a house was let separately from the house and access to the annexe was either through the house or (much less conveniently) along a passage outside, it was held on the facts that access through the house was not necessary for the reasonable or convenient enjoyment of the annexe. Evershed M.R. said[194]:

"In my judgment it does not follow that a way through the front door of another's premises and through the ground floor and passages is even prima facie necessary for the reasonable or convenient enjoyment of the premises behind. It would take strong evidence to show that it was so, for the right to pass through another's premises, particularly when they are business premises, is, I think, a considerable burden upon the servient tenement in any case."

3–60   In *Brown v Alabaster*[195] the lessee of two plots of land, A and B, had built on B two houses, Westbourne and Cottisbrook, each with a garden to which the only means of access, except through the houses themselves or a narrow passage with two steps down into the garden, was through a gate at the back and thence along an enclosed way, part of A, to a street. It was held that an assignment of the lease of the two houses included a right of way over the way on A. Kay J. said[196]:

"... it seems to me that the law is this–that a particular formed way to an entrance to premises like these, 'Westbourne' and 'Cottisbrooke', which leads to gates in a wall part of these demised premises, and without which

---

[191] As in *Squarey v Harris-Smith* (1981) 42 P. & C.R. 118.
[192] [1950] Ch. 247.
[193] Taken from a passage in previous editions of this book.
[194] [1950] Ch. 247 at 254.
[195] (1888) 37 Ch. D. 490.
[196] (1888) 37 Ch. D. 507.

those gates would be perfectly useless, may pass . . . by implied grant without any large general words, or indeed without any general words at all . . .
That it was intended, looking at all the facts, that the persons to whom
'Westbourne' and 'Cottisbrook' were conveyed should have the use of those
two gates and of this back-way, is, to my mind, beyond all doubt. Then,
although I agree that it is not for all purposes a way of necessity, do I want
an express grant? It seems to me to be clear on the authorities that an express
grant is not wanted in such a case as this."

In *Nicholls v Nicholls*[197] an agreement for the partition of two houses behind which   **3–61**
was a formed road was held to include an agreement to grant to each house a right
of way over the road. Stirling J. said that although in general a way not being a way
of necessity does not pass by implication, still it was established by many cases that
a formed road over one tenement to and for the apparent use of the other does.

If the land disposed of can be reached by two formed ways over the land
retained, and has no other means of access, the purchaser is entitled to a way of
necessity over one of them, to be selected by the grantor[198] but if there is another
satisfactory means of access, then the right claimed will not be necessary for the
reasonable enjoyment of the property and will not be implied.[199]

In *Millman v Ellis*[200] the conveyance granted to the purchaser a right of way   **3–62**
over part of a layby which gave access from the dominant tenement to a highway.
It was held that the purchaser was also entitled to a right of way over the remainder of the layby under the rule in *Wheeldon v Burrows*. The use of all of the layby
for the purpose of gaining access to the highway was continuous and apparent
and the implication of such a right was not excluded by the more limited express
grant. A right of way over all of the layby was necessary for the reasonable and
convenient enjoyment of the dominant tenement because the use of the part of the
layby which was the subject of the express grant, without also using the remainder of the layby, for the purpose of gaining access to the highway, although such
access was possible, was dangerous.

Maugham J., in *Borman v Griffith*,[201] referred to a "road", but the implication   **3–63**
can equally apply to a passage or path if the use of this appears to be necessary
for the reasonable or convenient enjoyment of the property. In *Hansford v
Jago*,[202] where a right of way was held to have passed, by implication, over an
enclosed strip of land, not made up but constituting, as in *Brown v Alabaster*,[203]
practically the only means of access to the backyards of the cottages in respect of
which the right was claimed, Russell J. said[204]:

---

[197] (1899) 81 L.T. 811.
[198] *Bolton v Bolton* (1879) 11 Ch. D. 968; and see *Hughes and Ashley's Contract, Re* [1900] 2 Ch.
595.
[199] *Wheeler v J.J. Saunders Ltd* [1996] Ch. 19.
[200] (1995) 71 P. & C.R. 158.
[201] [1930] 1 Ch. 493; see para.3–58, above.
[202] [1921] 1 Ch. 322.
[203] (1888) 37 Ch. D. 490; see para.3–60, above.
[204] [1921] 1 Ch. 322 at 342.

"What is required in the case of a quasi-easement is the quality of being apparent. That quality may be arrived at in different ways, and, no doubt, the easiest case is that of a made-up road; it is most important, if not essential, that the road should be made up when it is sought to establish the apparency of a quasi-easement of way over an enclosed piece of land. But when every other possible indication is present as here, and they all point to a defined and enclosed strip having been set aside to provide an access to the rear of certain houses, I certainly decline to hold, unless compelled to do so by authority, that the absence of a made-up road prevented the establishment of an implied grant. . . . It is often very important that there should be a made-up road, especially where the right is claimed over unenclosed land, but, where there are other indicia to show that a strip of land was intended to be used as a way, it is not necessary that there should be a made-up road to establish the right."[205]

3–64   It appears moreover from *Donnelly v Adams*[206] that if the termini of the alleged way raise the obvious inference that a way between them was intended to be included, the way itself need not be marked out at all. In that case, where a lease had been granted of a house with a back garden and a garden wall, in which was a door opening on a piece of waste ground which was retained by the lessor and had on its further side a wall in which were two gates opening on public passages, the Irish Court of Appeal inferred, from the circumstances and evidence, an intention to grant a right of way for the purpose of carrying coal across the waste land between the garden door to one of the passages, by such route and through such of the two gates as the lessor should from time to time appoint.[207]

3–65   In *Walmsley and Shaw's Contract, Re*[208] where a plot of land was sold under a contract not referring, either expressly or generally, to rights of way, Eve J. held that the vendor was entitled to exclude from the conveyance the statutory general words and to substitute "together with all . . . easements rights and appurtenances . . . appertaining or appurtenant thereto"; so (presumably), in effect, excluding all rights not already appurtenant, including a right of way, which the purchaser claimed, over a farm cart-track, not made up and not in any sense constructed as a means of access to the property sold. This case, *Bolton v Bolton*[209] and *Peck and London School Board, Re*[210] which the learned judge followed, may appear to be

---

205 See also *Rudd v Bowles* [1912] 2 Ch. 60, referred to at para.3–24, above, where the further side of the strip was not fenced off from the remaining land of the lessor. *Hansford v Jago* was applied in *Robinson Webster (Holdings) Ltd v Agombar* [2002] 1 P. & C.R. 243 at [76] but it was held on the detailed facts that no right of way was intended.

206 [1905] 1 I.R. 154, which would have been applied in *Donaldson v Smith* [2007] 1 P. & C.R. D4 at [24] but for the fact that there were no clear termini for the way claimed. Compare *Wheeler v J.J. Saunders Ltd* [1996] Ch. 19.

207 Whether *Polden v Bastard* (1865) L.R. 1 Q.B. 156, where it was decided that a devise of a house did not include the right to go from it (whether by a formed or visible path does not appear) across the garden of an adjoining house of the testatrix to fetch water from a pump there, would be decided in the same way now, *quaere*.

208 [1917] 1 Ch. 93.

209 (1879) 11 Ch. D. 968.

210 [1893] 2 Ch. 315.

authorities for the proposition that a contract to sell a piece of land "with its appurtenances" is a contract to sell the land with such easements, if any, as are already appurtenant to it (and which would pass automatically) and nothing else, but it is thought that they are not. Eve J. said that he thought that the contract was, as in the other cases just referred to, a contract for the sale of the premises with such rights of way only as were legally appendant or appurtenant to them; and this part of the judgment, taken by itself, appears to suggest that a contract for sale, at any rate a contract to sell "with appurtenances", negatives any implication of intention to grant *de novo* a right not already appurtenant; but, if that is what is meant, the learned judge would not have gone on to point out, as he did, that when a property with a particular mode of access apparently and actually constructed as a means of access to it is contracted to be sold, there is a strong presumption that the means of access is included in the sale, but that the farm track there in question was not so constructed.

In *Moncrieff v Jamieson*[211] it was held that there could be implied into a trans-   **3–66** action, which involved the severance of the dominant tenement from the servient tenement and the express grant of a right of access to the dominant tenement across the servient tenement, a right to park vehicles on the servient tenement. It was held that such a right was reasonably necessary for the convenient enjoyment of the rights expressly conveyed or granted by the transaction.

Positive easements: (b) Drainage

Where the property disposed of is drained through a pipe or the like in the prop-   **3–67** erty retained, the right to continue to drain will pass by implication.[212] The same, no doubt, applies to eavesdrop.[213]

Positive easements: (c) Right to withdraw support

The grant of minerals separately from the surface does not, under the general law,   **3–68** include by implication the right to withdraw support from the surface.[214]

Negative easements: (a) Water supply

It appears to be undoubted that where water is conveyed to the property granted   **3–69** through a pipe or the like in the land retained, the right to the continued flow of water through the pipe will pass by implication. In *Watts v Kelson*[215] the owner of two pieces of land having made on one a tank, fed by a natural stream, from which two pipes carried water to cattle sheds on the other, sold first the land with the cattle sheds to the plaintiff, and then the land with the tank to a predecessor

---

[211] [2007] 1 W.L.R. 2620; see in particular per Lord Neuberger at [112] – [113] and [118] – [127].
[212] *Pyer v Carter* (1857) 1 H. & N. 916; *Ewart v Cochrane* (1861) 4 Macq. 117; 10 W.R. 3.
[213] See *Pyer v Carter*, above.
[214] *Butterknowle Colliery Co v Bishop Auckland Industrial Co-operative Society* [1906] A.C. 305. The rights of operators licensed under the Coal Industry Act 1994 to withdraw support from land are governed by s.38 of that Act.
[215] (1870) 6 Ch. App. 166.

in title of the defendant. The plaintiff was held entitled to the same flow of water through the pipes as was enjoyed at the time of the sale to him, and this notwithstanding that at the time of the action the sheds had been replaced by a house and the water was used for domestic purposes. In this case the land first sold appears to have had the exclusive right to the water in the tank, and in such a case the use to which the water is put from time to time is plainly immaterial.[216]

3–70   In *Schwann v Cotton*[217] at the death of a testator there were three adjoining properties, Nugent's, Malta and Braxton. An underground pipe conveyed water from a well in Nugent's, through Braxton, which belonged to the testator, to Malta, which also belonged to him. The testator having left a will giving Malta and Braxton respectively to the predecessors in title of the plaintiff and the defendant, it was held that Malta had acquired, by implication, against Braxton the right to the uninterrupted flow of such water as came through the pipe. The possibility that the owner of Nugent's, who was not a party, might have the right to stop the water at the well made no difference.

3–71   In *Nicholas v Chamberlain*[218]:

> "It was held by all the Court upon demurrer, that if one erect a house and build a conduit thereto in another part of his land, and convey water by pipes to the house, and afterwards sell the house with the appurtenances, excepting the land, or sell the land to another, reserving to himself the house,[219] the conduit and pipes pass with the house; because it is necessary, et quasi appendant thereto; and he shall have liberty by law to dig in the land for amending the pipes, or making them new, as the case may require."

3–72   In *Wheeldon v Burrows*[220] James L.J. suggested that what was thought by the court to pass was not merely the right to the passage of water, but the conduit itself as a corporeal part of the house[221]; and thus it may be that on a conveyance of a house, cisterns, sewers, gutters, drains, etc., serving the property conveyed exclusively may pass as part and parcel of that property under the general words imported by section 62(2) of the Law of Property Act 1925. In *Schwann v Cotton*[222] it was thought unnecessary to consider whether the property in the pipe itself, so far as it passed through Malta, vested in the devisee of Braxton.

---

[216] *cf. Holker v Porritt* (1875) L.R. 10 Exch. 59, 62. As to the effect of a grant of the right "as now enjoyed in common with others having the same right" to receive spring water through a pipe, see *Beauchamp v Frome R.D.C.* [1938] 1 All E.R. 595, distinguished in *Mitchell v Potter* [2005] EWCA Civ 88, *The Times*, January 24, 2005, where the express grant of a right to water was construed as giving the grantee the right to take such water as was reasonably required and not just such water as remained from time to time after the servient owner had abstracted water.

[217] [1916] 2 Ch. 459. See also *Westwood v Heywood* [1921] 2 Ch. 130.

[218] (1606) Cro.Jac. 121, 122 (Court of King's Bench).

[219] See para.3–90, below.

[220] (1879) 12 Ch. D. 31.

[221] *cf. Truckell v Stock* [1957] 1 W.L.R. 161, where the footings and eaves of a house, extending beyond the boundary shown on the plan, were held to have been included in the conveyance of the house. And see para.1–22, above.

[222] [1916] 2 Ch. 459; and see para.1–22, above.

No right will be implied, however, where the water is sent onto the land **3–73** granted for the purpose of draining the land retained, and not for the purpose of supplying the land granted[223]; and where the owner of land made a conduit conducting the water to a mill-pond on his land, and sold land abutting on the pond, no right passed by implication, or under the statutory general words, to have the flow to the pond continued, or to take water from the pond for the purpose of watering cattle if there should be any water to take.[224]

Negative easements: (b) Support

Where one of two buildings in common ownership and supporting each other is **3–74** disposed of and the other retained, or both are disposed of at the same time, each acquires, by implied grant or reservation,[225] a right of continued support against the other.[226] It seems that a right of support arises also where a building is disposed of separately from vacant land adjoining.[227] Furthermore, where the owner of land sells or leases part of it to someone who is known to be acquiring it for building purposes, the building when erected acquires, prima facie, by implication a right of support against the adjoining land, or the subjacent minerals if these are owned and reserved by the grantor.[228] This implication may, however, as always, be negatived by the circumstances. It seems that if, at the time of a contract for the grant of land, it is known to the purchaser that the grantor, or a purchaser from him, intends to build in a certain way on adjoining land of the grantor, the grantor or his purchaser is entitled to build as intended, and in so doing to let down the surface of the land granted, whether built on or not[229]; and that if the grantee has notice of a general intention to build on the retained land, the land granted is liable to such deprivation of support as reasonable building on the land retained entails.[230]

Negative easements: (c) Light

It is settled that, on a disposition of a building deriving light from adjoining **3–75** land[231] of the disposing party, the building acquires prima facie, by implication,

---

[223] *Bartlett v Tottenham* [1932] 1 Ch. 114.

[224] *Burrows v Lang* [1901] 2 Ch. 502.

[225] As to implied reservation on the disposition of part, see para.3–85, below.

[226] *Richards v Rose* (1853) 9 Exch. 218; *Dalton v Angus* (1881) 6 App. Cas. 740 at 792, 793; *Scouton & Co (Builders) Ltd v Gifyott & Scott Ltd* (1971) 221 E.G. 1499. No implication was made from a reversionary lease taking effect in possession 24 years after its date: *Howarth v Armstrong* (1897) 77 L.T. 62.

[227] See *Shubrook v Tufnell* (1882) 46 L.T. 886, and the cases in the next note.

[228] *Caledonian Ry v Sprot* (1856) 2 Macq. 449; *Rigby v Bennett* (1882) 21 Ch. D. 559; *Siddons v Short* (1877) 2 C.P.D. 572.

[229] *Murchie v Black* (1865) 19 C.B. (n.s.) 190.

[230] *Rigby v Bennett* (1882) 21 Ch. D. 559, per Cotton L.J. In this case the plaintiff agreed to take, and afterwards took, a lease requiring him to build to the satisfaction of the lessor. After the agreement by the plaintiff, the defendant entered into a similar agreement relating to adjoining land. The defendant then started to excavate for his building, and in so doing let down the house built by the plaintiff. The plaintiff had notice that some building was to be erected on the defendant's land, but there was no evidence that it was not possible to build on it without affecting the plaintiff's house. The defendant was held liable.

[231] The land need not be immediately adjoining: *Birmingham, Dudley and District Banking Co v Ross* (1888) 38 Ch. D. 295 at 300, 312, 314.

a right to light over the adjoining land. Thus in *Swansborough v Coventry*[232] Tindall C.J. said:

> "It is well established by the decided cases, that where the same person possesses a house, having the actual use and enjoyment of certain lights, and also possesses the adjoining land, and sells the house to another person, although the lights be new, he cannot, nor can anyone who claims under him, build upon the adjoining land so as to obstruct or interrupt the enjoyment of those lights."

So again, in *Leech v Schweder*[233] Mellish L.J. said:

> "It is perfectly established that if a man owns a house, and owns property of any other kind adjoining that house, and then either conveys the house in fee simple or demises it for a term of years to another person, a right to light unobstructed by anything to be erected on any land which at the time belonged to the grantor passes to the grantee."

This principle applies where at the time of the disposition, or, if this is preceded by an agreement, the agreement for it, the grantor knows that the land is being acquired for building purposes. In such a case the right attaches to the buildings when built.[234]

3–76   Where the building and the land are included in a mortgage, the implication arises on a mortgagee's authorised disposition of the building[235]; and also, it is submitted, on a similar disposition by the mortgagor, for example a lease granted under statutory powers, or otherwise binding on the mortgagee. It seems that a disposition, not binding on a mortgagee of a quasi-servient building, would carry a right to light against the mortgagor and his successors,[236] but not against the mortgagee and his successors.[237]

3–77   The implication, however, based as it is on intention, may be negatived or modified by the circumstances. It will not be made so as to deprive the grantor of the right to do anything which at the date of the grant (or, it is submitted,[238] at the date of the contract for it if there was one, and if on the facts the choice of date

---

[232] (1832) 9 Bing. 305 at 309.
[233] (1874) 9 Ch. App. 463 at 472. See also *Palmer v Fletcher* (1663) 1 Lev. 122; *Rosewell v Prior* (1701) 6 Mod.Rep. 116; *Bayley v Great Western Ry* (1884) 26 Ch. D. 434; *Myers v Catterson* (1890) 43 Ch. D. 470; *Phillips v Low* [1892] 1 Ch. 47; *Broomfield v Williams* [1897] 1 Ch. 602; *Born v Turner* [1900] 2 Ch. 211; *Pollard v Gare* [1901] 1 Ch. 834; *Frederick Betts Ltd v Pickfords Ltd* [1906] 2 Ch. 87.
[234] *Miles v Tobin* (1868) 17 L.T. 432; *Robinson v Grave* (1873) 21 W.R. 569; *Bailey v Icke* (1891) 64 L.T. 789; *Pollard v Gare* [1901] 1 Ch. 834; *Frederick Betts Ltd v Pickfords Ltd* [1906] 2 Ch. 87.
[235] *Born v Turner* [1900] 2 Ch. 211.
[236] *Beddington v Atlee* (1887) 35 Ch. D. 317 at 322; see para.3–101, below and *cf. Poulton v Moore* [1915] 1 K.B. 400 (release by mortgagor).
[237] *Davies v Thomas* [1899] W.N. 244.
[238] See *Broomfield v Williams* [1897] 1 Ch. 602 at 616; and para.3–101, below.

is material) it was in the contemplation of both parties that he should do. A leading case on this topic is *Birmingham, Dudley and District Banking Co v Ross*.[239] There the plaintiffs were assignees of a lease granted by the Birmingham Corporation to one Daniell, and the defendant was a lessee from the Corporation of neighbouring land. Both properties were included in an area which was subject to an improvement scheme made some years previously by the Corporation under statutory powers, and this scheme included a new main street called Corporation Street. In 1880 the Corporation agreed to grant to Daniell, on the completion of certain buildings which he thereby agreed to build, a lease of a piece of land fronting on the proposed site of Corporation Street on the west, and on another proposed new street or passage, to be called Warwick Passage, on the south. The Corporation undertook to make these new streets. In 1883, Daniell's buildings being completed, he was granted a lease. In 1886 the Corporation agreed to grant to the defendant a lease, for building purposes, of a piece of land bounded on the north by Warwick Passage and also fronting on Corporation Street. At this time there was a low building on the defendant's land, and this he proceeded (evidently in pursuance of his agreement) to demolish and replace by a larger one which materially affected the light coming to the plaintiffs' building. It appeared from the evidence that it was well known to Daniell, when his lease was granted, that the land afterwards agreed to be leased to the defendant belonged to the Corporation, was included in the improvement scheme, was a valuable site, and would sooner or later be built on. It also appeared that the plaintiffs' buildings were lower than the average of those fronting Corporation Street, while the height of the defendant's building, having regard to the importance of Corporation Street, was not unreasonable.

In these circumstances the Court of Appeal, affirming Kekewich J., decided   **3–78** that no right to light had passed by implication[240] to Daniell. Cotton L.J. said[241]:

> "When the question is as to an implied obligation we must have regard to all the circumstances which existed at the time when the conveyance was executed which brought the parties into that relation from which the implied obligation results; I quite agree that we ought not to have regard to any agreement during the negotiations entered into between the plaintiffs and the corporation; except in this way; if we find that any particular space in fact was left open at the time when the lease was granted, and that that open space was contracted to be left open during the negotiation which took place, and is not referred to in the lease, we must have regard to the fact of that open space being left, and we must have regard to the fact that by agreement between the parties the lessor had bound himself not to build that space; and also we must, in my opinion, in determining what obligation results from the position in which the parties have put themselves, have regard to all the

[239] (1888) 38 Ch. D. 295.
[240] Or under the statutory general words: see paras 3–126 *et seq.*, below.
[241] (1888) 38 Ch. D. 295 at 308, 309.

other facts which existed at the time when the conveyance was made, or when the lease was granted, and which were known to both parties."

3–79   Lindley L.J. said[242] that the only implied grant that he could infer from the terms of the deed and the surrounding circumstances was of a right to such an amount of light as would come over the corporation land to Daniell's house after the Corporation had built what they liked on the other side of the 20-foot street, Warwick Passage; and Bowen L.J. said[243]:

> " . . . coming to the amount of enjoyment of light that is supposed by the law to accompany in an ordinary case the lease or the grant of a house which is erected with window-lights, where the grantor of the house is also the owner of premises either adjoining or neighbouring, then this presumption arises, that the grantor intends the grantee to enjoy so much light unobstructed as must under the circumstances have been assumed by both parties to be reasonably necessary for the fair and comfortable use of the premises which are the subject of the grant. That seems to me to be the real definition and measure of the ordinary implication that arises . . . [The obligation] must be measured by all the surrounding circumstances. The presumption that arises in favour of the ordinary measure can be rebutted by showing that the circumstances are not ordinary circumstances, or, to speak more accurately, it is not a case of rebutting a presumption, it is a question of the proper inference to be drawn from a consideration of all the facts. I do not think any hard and fast line can be laid down beyond which you are not to admit evidence to rebut the presumption, or rather—as I should prefer to say—to measure the implication itself. Here we have some salient facts which seem to me to prove to demonstration that the plaintiffs are not entitled to the right which they claim . . . All the parties here knew and intended that there should be buildings on the opposite side of Warwick Passage; and that the parties, when they negotiated for this grant, left the height of these buildings undefined. If Daniell had desired to protect himself further than by the width of the passage, in my opinion, he ought to have done so expressly . . . I will not say what would be the case if the light had been absolutely destroyed."

3–80   The same principle was applied by Joyce J. in *Godwin v Schweppes Ltd*.[244] In that case, at the time of the conveyance by A to B of the building, now owned by the plaintiffs, in respect of which the implied right was claimed, the adjoining land over which the right was claimed was the subject of an agreement for the grant by A to B of a building lease, in pursuance of which B had made plans for the erection, and had laid the foundations, of a building which would leave a well or area, shown on

---

[242] (1888) 38 Ch. D. 295, at 311, 312.
[243] (1888) 38 Ch. D. 295, at 313–316.
[244] [1902] 1 Ch. 926. A somewhat similar case is *Quicke v Chapman* [1903] 1 Ch. 659; see para.3–09, above.

the plan to the conveyance, between it and the plaintiffs' building. These plans were afterwards abandoned, and the defendants, successors in title to A of the adjoining land, built on it a building which obstructed the plaintiffs' lights to a lesser extent than the building originally intended would have done, and did not impinge on the site of the proposed area. It was held that, in the circumstances, B did not acquire against A any right to have his lights unobstructed by any future building on the adjoining ground, not being a building within the contemplated area.

The onus of negativing the implication that prima facie arises is on the grantor.[245] It will not necessarily be negatived or limited by the fact that the grantee knows of a general intention on the part of the grantor to build somewhere on the land retained. In *Broomfield v Williams*,[246] where in the conveyance to the plaintiff the adjoining land was described as "building land", it was held that the implication was not negatived, but having regard to the circumstances it was conceded by the plaintiff, and would probably have been held, that he would not be entitled to complain of obstruction by a building erected (as the building in fact erected was not) more than four feet nine inches away from his boundary. Lindley and Rigby L.JJ. decided the case on the ground that a right to light passed under the general words imported by section 6 of the Conveyancing Act 1881 and that the reference to "building land" did not show an intention to exclude them.   **3–81**

In *Pollard v Gare*,[247] the purchaser's knowledge that the adjoining land was part of a building estate marked out on a plan in lots, with a building line, did not affect the implication. The vendor remained entitled to build, but there was no inference that he was to be entitled to build so as to obstruct the plaintiff's light. But in *Swansborough v Coventry*[248] where a house conveyed "with all lights and easements to the same belonging" was described as bounded by "a piece of freehold building ground" and on this ground had stood a low building, recently demolished, the vendor and his successors were held entitled to build to the extent of the former building, but no further.   **3–82**

In *Myers v Catterson*,[249] where the plaintiff had acquired his land from a railway company with knowledge that the adjoining land would be required for the purposes of the railway, it was held that the company entered into an implied obligation not to interfere with the plaintiff's lights by anything not necessarily required for those purposes. The plaintiff's house enjoyed light through arches in the railway viaduct, and accordingly the defendant, who had taken a lease of the arches from the company, was restrained from blocking them up.   **3–83**

Negative easements: (d) Other negative rights

It has already been pointed out that, where land is granted for a special purpose, the operation of the rule against derogation from grant prevents the grantor, or his   **3–84**

---

[245] *Broomfield v Williams* [1897] 1 Ch. 602 at 610, 613.
[246] [1897] 1 Ch. 602.
[247] [1901] 1 Ch. 834.
[248] (1832) 9 Bing. 305.
[249] (1890) 43 Ch. D. 470.

successors, with or without notice, from anything that interferes with that purpose.[250] Where a building is granted without any intention known to the grantor to use it for any special purpose, the parties will be supposed to have intended that it shall remain capable of use and enjoyment for ordinary purposes, and on this ground the grantor and his successors will be restrained from interfering with the access of air through existing apertures in the building.[251] Whether in such a case the grantee could acquire immunity against interference, not actionable as between strangers, of any kind not discussed in this section seems doubtful, for the reason that it is difficult to envisage any other immunity that could be required, and it is thought that the class of negative easements is confined to those here mentioned.[252]

Implied reservation on the disposition of part

3–85   After some fluctuation in the earlier authorities, it is now settled[253] that prima facie, on a disposition of part of the land of the disposing party, no reservation of any easement in favour of the part retained will be implied.

If, therefore, the grantor intends to reserve any right over the tenement granted, it is his duty to reserve it expressly in the grant,[254] and quasi-easements enjoyed by one piece of land over another in common ownership and not reserved on the severance will be lost.[255] In *Suffield v Brown*[256] Lord Westbury said:

> "When the owner of two tenements sells and conveys one for an absolute interest therein,[257] he puts an end, by contract, to the relation which he had himself created between the tenement sold and the adjoining tenement; and discharges the tenement so sold from any burthen imposed upon it during his joint occupation; and the condition of such tenement is thenceforth determined by the contract of alienation and not by the previous user of the vendor during such joint ownership."

In *Crossley & Sons Ltd v Lightowler*[258] Lord Chelmsford said:

---

[250] See paras 3–32 *et seq.*, above.

[251] *Cable v Bryant* [1908] 1 Ch. 259; para.3–34, above.

[252] See paras 1–41 and 1–72, above. It has been held that a right to a view, protection from the weather and uninterrupted television reception cannot exist as easements.

[253] *Wheeldon v Burrows* (1879) 12 Ch. D. 31; *Webb's Lease, Re* [1951] Ch. 808. The latter case was applied in *Kwiatkowski v Cox* (1969) 213 E.G. 34. A claim resting on an implied reservation of a right of access to inspect and maintain a flank wall and (in particular) to cleanse guttering and to paint a down-pipe failed.

[254] *Wheeldon v Burrows* (1879) 12 Ch. D. 31 at 49, per Thesiger L.J.

[255] *Wheeldon v Burrows*, above; *Ray v Hazeldine* [1904] 2 Ch. 17 (light); *Liddiard v Waldron* [1934] 1 K.B. 435; *Aldridge v Wright* [1929] 2 K.B. 117; *Taws v Knowles* [1891] 2 Q.B. 564 (right of way); see, generally, (1964) 80 L.Q.R. 244 (D.W. Elliot).

[256] (1864) 4 De G.J. & S. 185, 195. Thesiger L.J. in *Wheeldon v Burrows* (1879) 12 Ch. D. 31 freely quoted from Lord Westbury's speech.

[257] The same principle applies when a term of years is granted (*Webb's Lease, Re,* above), or assigned (*Aldridge v Wright* [1929] 2 K.B. 117), and on a mortgage of the property at least if the mortgagee takes possession (*Taws v Knowles* [1891] 2 Q.B. 564).

[258] (1867) 2 Ch. App. 478 at 486.

"It appears to me to be an immaterial circumstance that the easement should be apparent and continuous, for non constat that the grantor does not intend to relinquish it unless he shows the contrary by expressly reserving it."

The exceptions to the prima facie rule have never been exhaustively stated. One **3–86** is where the property retained is landlocked, and a case for a way of necessity arises.[259] Again, if one of two houses supporting each other is granted, and thus obtains by implication a right of continued support against the house retained,[260] the one retained acquires by implied reservation a similar right against the house granted.[261] "Rights will be impliedly reserved which are in their nature reciprocal to rights which the grant must be taken to have conferred upon the grantee."[262] In *Kent v Kavanagh*[263] a common freeholder granted a lease of a house followed by a lease of an adjoining house to two lessees. The houses were separated by a pathway which was three feet wide. Each lease demised one-half of the width of the pathway. It must have been appreciated that the pathway could not be used by either lessee without passing over the other half which was included in the other lease. It must have been the intention of the parties to those leases that that was how the pathway was to be used. In those circumstances, the necessary grant and reservation of reciprocal rights of way were implied.[264]

It was said, however, by Jenkins L.J. in *Webb's Lease, Re*[265] that these two **3–87** exceptions do not exhaust the list, which is incapable of exhaustive statement, as the circumstances of any particular case may be such as to raise the necessary inference that the common intention of the parties must have been to reserve some easement to the grantor, or such as to preclude the grantee from denying the right consistently with good faith; in such circumstances the court would imply the appropriate reservation.

The scope for implication is, nonetheless, more restricted in the case of a reservation than that of a grant. The reason is that in the case of implied reservation, the implied term will to some extent run counter to the express term of the instrument in question, whereas in the case of an implied grant, the implied term will be designed to enable what is expressly granted to be the better enjoyed by the grantee.[266]

---

[259] See paras 3–115 *et seq.*, below.
[260] See para.3–74, above.
[261] *Richards v Rose* (1853) 9 Exch. 218; *Wheeldon v Burrows* (1879) 12 Ch. D. 31 at 59; *Russell v Watts* (1884) 25 Ch. D. 559 at 573; *Aldridge v Wright* [1929] 2 K.B. 129 at 134.
[262] Evershed M.R., *Webb's Lease, Re* [1951] Ch. 808 at 816, 817. *Cf. Hopgood v Brown* [1955] 1 W.L.R. 213; *Cory v Davies* [1923] 2 Ch. 95.
[263] [2007] Ch. 1.
[264] [2007] Ch. 1, at [63] – [65].
[265] [1951] Ch. 808. The approach in *Webb* was held by the Court of Appeal to remain the law in *Peckham v Ellison* (1999) 77 P. & C.R. 276 and accordingly applied in *Holaw (470) Ltd v Stockton Estates Ltd* (2001) 81 P. & C.R. 404 at 428–431.
[266] *Chaffe v Kingsley* (1999) 77 P. & C.R. 404 at 417 per Jonathan Parker J.

The "appropriate reservation" referred to by Jenkins L.J. must be that which the parties intended to be reserved. A common intention to reserve a right of some kind, but which is unspecific as to the precise nature and extent of the right, is not enough.[267] Nor is it enough to show that, had the parties foreseen the eventuality which in fact occurred, they would have wished to make provision for it, unless it can also be shown either that there was only one contractual solution or that one of several possible solutions would without doubt have been preferred.[268] Indeed, the Court of Appeal have recently emphasised that the correct test in law is that stated by Jenkins L.J. in *Webb's Lease, Re*,[269] namely whether the circumstances raise a necessary inference of an intention common to both parties that the right in question should be reserved; before such an inference can be drawn, the party claiming the reservation must show that the facts are not reasonably consistent with any other explanation; it is not enough that they are simply consistent with such an explanation.[270]

The express reservation of other rights shows that the parties turned their minds to what rights ought to be reserved and militates against the implication of further rights.[271]

3–88   In *Pyer v Carter*,[272] at the time of the sale of one (A) of two adjoining houses (A and B), water from the eaves of A fell on B, and then flowed down a spout into a drain which ran under B, and thence under A, to the common sewer. B was drained through this drain. A and B having been successively sold, the owner of B obtained a verdict in an action against the owner of A for stopping the drain where it entered A. The Court of Exchequer, making no distinction between implied grant and implied reservation, decided that the owner of B was, by implied grant,[273] entitled to have the use of the drain for the purpose of conveying the water from his house, as it was used at the time of the defendant's purchase. It seemed in accordance with reason that, on a sale of one of two or more adjoining houses, that house should be entitled to the benefit of all the drains from it, and be subject to all the drains then necessarily used for the enjoyment of the adjoining house, and that without express reservation or grant. This decision, so far as it implies that there is no difference between implied reservation and implied grant, was dissented from by Lord Westbury in *Suffield v Brown*[274] and is contrary to modern principle; but it can perhaps be supported on the ground that the drain in respect of which the right was sought was used by both properties in common.

---

[267] *Chaffe v Kingsley* (1999) 77 P. & C.R. 404, at 417.
[268] *Philips v British Sky Broadcasting* [1995] E.M.L.R. 472.
[269] [1951] Ch. 808 at 829.
[270] *Peckham v Ellison* (1999) 77 P. & C.R. 276.
[271] *Chaffe v Kingsley* (above) at 418; see also *Frogmore Developments Ltd v Shiryama Shokusan Ltd* [2001] E.G.L.R. 121 at 125H.
[272] (1857) 1 H. & N. 916.
[273] i.e. implied reservation.
[274] (1864) 4 De G.J. & S. 185.

In *Wheeldon v Burrows*[275] Thesiger L.J. said that he could see nothing unrea- **3–89** sonable in supposing that in such a case as *Pyer v Carter*[276] where the defendant under his grant was to take the easement, which had been enjoyed during the unity of ownership, of pouring his water on the grantor's land, he should also be held to take it subject to the mutual and reciprocal easement by which that very same water was carried into the drain on that land and then back through the land of the person from whose land the water came. It is curious that the Lord Justice made no reference to the water coming from the plaintiff's land, but that no doubt is implicit.

In *Wheeldon v Burrows*[277] Thesiger L.J. mentioned that easements of necessity **3–90** are excepted from the general rule; but it is questionable whether any easement, other than access and support, can be "of necessity".[278] In *Union Lighterage Co v London Graving Dock Co*[279] Stirling L.J. expressed the opinion that an ease- ment of necessity, in this context, is one without which the property retained can- not be used at all, and not one merely necessary to the reasonable enjoyment of the property. This dictum and principle was applied by the Court of Appeal in *M.R.A. Engineering Ltd v Trimster Company Ltd*,[280] where the Court declined to imply a reservation of a vehicular way of necessity over the land sold because the land retained enjoyed access by foot via a public footpath.

The status of *Nicholas v Chamberlain*[281] so far as it decided that the reserva- **3–91** tion of the right to use a conduit supplying water to a house will be implied on a sale of the land in which the conduit is, without the house, and of *Simpson v Weber*,[282] where it was held that, on the sale of one of two houses, a right was impliedly reserved to maintain on the wall of the house sold a creeper growing on the property retained and extending up that wall, and also certain plugs in the same wall which supported a gate-post belonging to the property retained, is doubtful. It does not appear that a right to light has ever been regarded as an ease- ment of necessity.

In *Jones v Pritchard*,[283] where a house had been built with fireplaces and flues **3–92** in the outside wall, some connected with and used by the house, and others useless for it but capable of being used by an adjoining house if built, and the

---

[275] (1879) 12 Ch. D. 31 at 59.
[276] (1857) 1 H. & N. 916.
[277] (1879) 12 Ch. D. 31 at 50, 59.
[278] In *Pryce v McGuiness* [1966] Qd.R. 591, a claim to a way of necessity succeeded but a claim to allegedly necessary easements of electrical wires and for sewerage and drainage failed.
[279] [1902] 2 Ch. 557.
[280] (1987) 56 P. & C.R. 1. See also *Manjang v Drammeh* (1990) 61 P. & C.R. 194 where there was no implied reservation of a way of necessity because there was available access over water to the land.
[281] (1606) Cro.Jac. 121, p. 113, above; and see comments of Vaughan Williams L.J. in *Union Lighterage Co v London Graving Dock Co* [1902] 2 Ch. 565 at 566.
[282] (1925) 133 L.T. 46.
[283] [1908] 1 Ch. 630. See also *Lyttleton Times Co Ltd v Warners Ltd* [1907] A.C. 476. Both these cases were referred to by Lord Parker when, in *Pwllbach Colliery Co v Woodman* [1915] A.C. 634 at 646, he said that the law will readily imply the grant or reservation of such easements as may be necessary to give effect to the common intention of the parties; see para.3–28, above.

plaintiff, owner of the house, granted to the adjoining owner, who intended to build and afterwards built a house connecting with the fireplaces and flues designed for it, the outside moiety of the wall, including a moiety of the flues, it was held by Parker J. that there must be implied a reservation to the grantor and a grant to the grantee of such easements as would be necessary to enable each to use the flues connected with the fireplaces on his side of the wall.[284]

3–93   The case must be rare in which a grantee can be shown positively, or, for instance, by necessary inference from the effect on the property granted or some physical characteristic of the property retained, to have recognised and acquiesced in an intention on the part of the grantor to use his retained property, or part of it, in some definite manner detracting from the natural rights incident to the ownership of the property granted. Clearly it is not enough that the grantee knows that the grantor retains adjoining land and would probably wish to use it in the same way as before.

3–94   The subject was considered in *Webb's Lease, Re*.[285] There the plaintiff, the owner of a building, painted on one of the outside walls an advertisement of a business carried on by him on the ground floor, and granted to a company a licence, which was exercised, to use another outside wall as an advertising site. He then, first in 1939 and afterwards in 1949, let the first and second floors to the defendant, and, disputes having arisen after a long period of acquiescence by the defendant, he issued an originating summons asking whether, in the circumstances, he was entitled, without the defendant's consent, to continue to use the two outside walls, comprised in the lease, for advertising. The Court of Appeal answered this question in the negative, on the ground that the circumstances did not justify a departure from the general rule.

3–95   The burden which faces a grantor who seeks to show an implied reservation is readily apparent from the judgment of Jenkins L.J. who said[286]:

> "That question must be approached with the following principles in mind: (i) If the landlord intended to reserve any such rights over the demised premises it was his duty to reserve them expressly in the lease of August 11, 1949 (Wheeldon v. Burrows[287]); (ii) The landlord having failed in this duty, the onus was upon him to establish the facts to prove, and prove clearly, that his case was an exception to the rule (Aldridge v. Wright[288]); (iii) The mere fact that the tenant knew at the date of the lease of August 11, 1949, that the

---

[284] The point in the case was that, as a result of a defect in the plaintiff's half of one of the flues used by the adjoining house, smoke from that house found its way into the plaintiff's house and damaged his decorations and furniture. It was held that the adjoining owner, not having been guilty of negligence, or want of reasonable care and precaution, was not liable. The subject of reservations in leases is considered in Samuels, "Reservations and Exceptions of Easements and Similar Rights by Landlords" 27 Conv. (n.s.) 187.

[285] [1951] Ch. 808.

[286] [1951] Ch. 808 at 828–830.

[287] (1879) 12 Ch. D. 31.

[288] [1929] 2 K.B. 117; see para.3–105, below.

landlord was using the outer walls of the demised premises for the display of the advertisements in question did not suffice to absolve the landlord from his duty of expressly reserving any rights in respect of them he intended to claim, or to take the case out of the general rule; see Suffield v. Brown[289]; Crossley & Sons Ltd v. Lightowler.[290]

Applying these principles to the present case, I ask myself whether the landlord has on the meagre facts proved discharged the onus which lies on him of proving it an exception to the general rule. He can, so far as I can see, derive no assistance from the passage quoted above from Lord Parker's speech in the Pwllbach Colliery case.[291] It might, I suppose, be said to have been in the contemplation of the parties that the landlord would continue to use the ground floor of the premises for the purposes of his business as a butcher and provision merchant, but it cannot in my view be contended that the maintenance during the term of the lease of his advertisement over the door was a necessary incident of the user so contemplated. This applies a fortiori to the 'Brymay' advertisement, the display of which on the outer wall of the demised premises by the . . . licensees of the landlord was, so far as I can see, not related in any way to the use or occupation of the ground floor for the existing or any other purpose. . . .

The mere fact that the tenant knew of the presence of the advertisements at the date when the lease of August 11, 1949, was granted being, as stated above, beside the point, nothing is left beyond the bare circumstance that the advertisements were not only present at the date of the grant but had been continuously present without objection by the tenant since the commencement of the original tenancy in 1939. Does this circumstance suffice to raise a necessary inference of an intention common to both parties at the date of the lease that the landlord should have reserved to him the right to maintain these advertisements throughout the twenty-one years' term thereby granted? I cannot see that it does. The most that can be said is that the facts are consistent with such a common intention. But that will not do. The landlord must surely show at least that the facts are not reasonably consistent with any other explanation. Here he manifestly fails. . . .

In short, I can hold nothing more established by the facts proved than permissive user of the outer walls by the landlord for the display of the advertisements during the original tenancy and thereafter from the granting of the lease until the tenant's objection in January, 1950; with nothing approaching grounds for inferring, as a matter of necessary inference, an intention common to both parties that such permissive user should be converted by the lease into a reservation to the landlord of equivalent rights throughout the twenty-one years' term thereby granted."

[289] (1864) 4 De G.J. & S. 185.
[290] (1867) 2 Ch. App. 478.
[291] [1915] A.C. 634 at 646; i.e. the passage quoted at para.3–28, above.

3–96   In regard to *Simpson v Weber*,[292] Evershed M.R. said[293] that he would not criti-
cise the decision in it, and Jenkins L.J.[294] expressed the opinion that the physical
circumstances might perhaps have sufficed to support an implication of an intention common to the parties that the easements in question should be reserved; but
both expressed disapproval of the grounds on which the decision was apparently
arrived at, namely, that in a case where an easement might reasonably have been
reserved if the parties had thought of it, it will be taken to have been impliedly
reserved unless there is evidence of an intention not to do so.

3–97   The principles in *Webb's Lease, Re* were applied in *Peckham v Ellison*.[295] Two
adjoining residential properties, No. 15 and 16, were owned freehold by the local
authority and let to two separate tenants. There was a means of access over a piece
of land which lay alongside No. 15 for the occupier of No. 16 to go from the front
of No. 16 to the rear of No. 16. In 1982, the tenants of No. 15 acquired the freehold of
No. 15 under the right to buy provisions of the Housing Act 1980. There was no
express reservation of a right of way over the piece of land at the side of No. 15 for
the benefit of No. 16. In 1989, the tenants of No. 16 acquired the freehold of No. 16
under the right to buy provisions of the Housing Act 1985. The issue was whether
there had been impliedly reserved from the 1982 transfer of No. 15 a right of way
for the benefit of No. 16 over the land to the side of No. 15. The Court of Appeal
considered the detailed evidence as to the intentions of the parties. It was held that
the facts were not reasonably consistent with any explanation other than there was a
common intention on the part of the parties to the 1982 transfer that the claimed right
of way was to be reserved. The facts of the case were described as exceptional.

3–98   The principles in *Webb's Lease, Re* were again applied in *Chaffe v Kingsley*[296]
where no reservation was implied. The only appropriate reservation was one
which the parties intended to be reserved. It was not enough to show only a non-
specific intention to reserve a right of some unspecified kind. The facts fell short
of establishing any intention to reserve a right in perpetuity and indeed it was not
right to imply even a reservation which was limited in time. The relevant conveyances contained express reservations of rights which showed that the parties
had turned their minds to what rights should be reserved and the express rights
did not extend to the rights being claimed.

3–99   In *Holaw (470) Ltd v Stockton Estates Ltd*,[297] the court considered the principles in, and the facts of, both *Webb's Lease, Re* and *Peckham v Ellison* and held
that no reservation was to be implied on the facts before it.

Easements acquired on simultaneous dispositions

3–100   Where separate parts of land held by the same person are disposed of at the same
time, each part acquires by implication the same easements over any other part as

---

[292] (1925) 133 L.T. 46.
[293] [1951] Ch. 808, at 820.
[294] [1951] Ch. 808, at 827.
[295] (1998) 79 P. & C.R. 276.
[296] (1999) 79 P. & C.R. 404.
[297] (2001) 81 P. & C.R. 404.

it would if that other part had been retained, and the other part becomes subject to the easement so acquired. In *Russell v Watts* Fry L.J. said[298]:

> "As the same vendor is selling to two persons at the same time, each purchaser is entitled, in favour of the house he buys, to the benefit of the maxim that no man shall derogate from his own grant but, at the same time, he has the burden of the same maxim in favour of his neighbour's house; and the result is, that all the quasi-easements which existed between the two lots in the hands of the one owner, the vendor, are perpetuated by way of implied grant, in the hands of the respective purchasers."

It was said by the Deputy Judge in *Donaldson v Smith*[299]:

> "The concept of simultaneity must be in my judgment understood and interpreted in context, not least because these rules are ultimately guides to the ascertainment of the transferor's presumed intentions. It is therefore not in my view the degree of chronological proximity as such which is of importance as the pointer which it may give as to the interconnection of the two dispositions by the owner to separate transferees of the two parts of his land. Ultimately the question is whether they are to be regarded as in effect part and parcel of a single transaction."

This rule applies not only where the dispositions are for value,[300] but also where they are testamentary,[301] or voluntary conveyances *inter vivos*.[302] Where the dispositions are testamentary, it makes no difference that one is specific and the other residuary, or that one disposition is expressed to be free from incumbrances.[303]

Where dispositions are preceded by contracts, the rights of the parties depend on the circumstances in which, including the dates on which, the contracts were made, **3–101**

---

[298] (1884) 25 Ch. D. 559 at 584. The majority decision in this case was reversed ((1885) 10 App. Cas. 590) on consideration of the very special documents and circumstances. In the passage quoted it is assumed (and see *Allen v Taylor* (1880) 16 Ch. D. 355 at 358) that each purchaser or grantee knows that the other land is being disposed of. If either does not, then it would seem that, as between the purchasers, the rule applies; and each acquires by implication the appropriate easements over the part taken by the other; but *quaere* whether, as between the ignorant purchaser and the owner, a reservation of the right acquired by the other purchaser can be implied, and whether the owner could not be made liable on covenants for title. The case does not seem to have arisen.

[299] [2007] 1 P. & C.R. D4 at [16]. In that case, having regard to the somewhat unusual circumstances, it was held that two appointments by trustees, which were separated by four and a half months, were sufficiently "simultaneous".

[300] As in *Swansborough v Coventry* (1832) 9 Bing. 305, para.3–82, above (light) and *Nicholls v Nicholls* (1899) 81 L.T. 811; *Hansford v Jago* [1921] 1 Ch. 322; *Cory v Davies* [1923] 2 Ch. 95 (rights of way).

[301] *Allen v Taylor* (1880) 16 Ch. D. 355; *Phillips v Low* [1892] 1 Ch. 47 (light); *Milner's Safe Co Ltd v Great Northern and City Railway* [1907] 1 Ch. 208 (right of way); *Schwann v Cotton* [1916] 2 Ch. 459 (water supply).

[302] *Phillips v Low* [1892] 1 Ch. 47, 51. The case of a common owner making a voluntary conveyance of part only, retaining the rest, does not appear to have come back before the court.

[303] *Phillips v Low*, above.

and not on the dates of the conveyances. Any doubt which was previously thought to exist as to the accuracy of this proposition appears to have been removed by the judgment of Buckley J. in *White v Taylor (No.2)*[304] (a case concerned with *profits à prendre*) where his Lordship followed *Beddington v Atlee*,[305] in which an unsuccessful claim to light was made in the following circumstances. In 1881, A, the owner of the equity of redemption in a house and adjoining land, leased the house for 21 years, thereby, as it was held, conferring on the lessee by implication (although A had not the legal estate), a right to light for the term of the lease. Afterwards, on January 19, 1882, he agreed to sell the house, subject to the lease, to a nominee of the plaintiff, and this contract was completed in February, 1882, by a conveyance of the house by A and his mortgagees to the plaintiff, subject to the lease. In May, 1882, A conveyed the adjoining land on sale to the defendant. In September the plaintiff determined the lease under a proviso for re-entry, and in 1885 he commenced these proceedings to restrain the defendant from obstructing the light to the house by building on the adjoining land. If these had been the only material facts, A would have been considered to have granted to the plaintiff, with the house, a right to light against the adjoining land retained by A, and the defendant, who took his conveyance after the plaintiff took his, would have taken subject to the plaintiff's right. In fact, however, the conveyance to the defendant was made in pursuance of a contract made on January 4, 1882, before the contract with the plaintiff; and it was held that inasmuch as A was not in a position to grant an easement over the adjoining land which he had agreed to sell, the plaintiff was not entitled, either by implied grant or under the statutory general words, to the right which he claimed. As the plaintiff's contract and conveyance were both later in date than the contract with the defendant, the date of the plaintiff's conveyance might, equally with the date of his contract, have been regarded as the date when the plaintiff's rights crystallised; but it is implicit in the judgment that the question depended on the relative dates of the contracts, and that, if the plaintiff's contract had preceded the defendant's, and the course of events had been contract with plaintiff, contract with defendant, conveyance to defendant, conveyance to plaintiff, the result would have been different. It was further held that the right to light impliedly granted by the lease of the house, which was for 21 years from August 1881, did not survive the actual determination of the lease.

3–102   In *White v Taylor (No.2)*[306] lots carrying grants of sheep rights were sold at auction. All the contracts were entered into on the same day and the purchasers thereupon became entitled in equity to the rights as appurtenances to the land which they bought. Buckley J. held that each purchaser must be taken to have known that the vendor was at the same time selling the other lots to the other purchasers

---

[304] [1969] 1 Ch. 160.
[305] (1887) 35 Ch. D. 317. See also *Birmingham, Dudley and District Banking Co v Ross* (1888) 38 Ch. D. 295; *Quicke v Chapman* [1903] 1 Ch. 659; *Broomfield v Williams* [1897] 1 Ch. 602, per Rigby L.J. at 616 (the dates of the contracts do not appear); the reference to "the contract" in *Rigby v Bennett* (1882) 21 Ch. D. 559 at 567 *ad fin*; and per Lord Westbury in *Suffield v Brown* (1864) 4 De G.J. & S. 185 at 195, para.3–88, above.
[306] [1969] 1 Ch. 160 at 181–183.

upon the terms of the conditions of sale. As in *Beddington v Atlee*,[307] the state of affairs upon which the language employed in the conveyances operated was governed by the contracts for sale.

In regard to assents by personal representatives, no question can arise, for an **3–103** assent relates back to the death, unless a contrary intention appears.[308] It is suggested that, where different parts of an estate devolve separately, the easements with and subject to which each part is to be held ought to be specified in the assents.

The principle set out in para.3–100 above as to simultaneous dispositions is **3–104** often applied to other transactions by conditions of sale[309] which provide that a vendor of part of his land is entitled to have expressly reserved out of the conveyance such rights as would be implied in favour of a purchaser of the retained land if the vendor had conveyed the land to be sold and the land to be retained by simultaneous conveyances to different purchasers. Without that condition the vendor would not be entitled to any implied easements (other than easements of necessity or those required to carry out the common intention of the parties) and section 62 of the Law of Property Act 1925 would not operate in favour of the retained land. The effect of such a condition is to "level the playing field" between vendor and purchaser as to the grant and reservation of easements. Nonetheless, the creation of rights under the rule in *Wheeldon v Burrows* depends on the presumed intention of the parties and section 62 also yields to any expression of contrary intention. So where the context in which an option to repurchase land was granted showed that it was the intention of the parties merely to restore the *status quo ante* if a development project did not proceed, the vendor was not entitled to the reservation as easements of the "rights" his retained property had previously enjoyed over the land reconveyed but over which he had not acquired easements by prescription at the date of the original sale.[310]

Easements acquired on grant of a lease

Questions of difficulty often arise where properties, originally in common own- **3–105** ership, are let, or one of them is. If an owner (or lessee) of land grants a lease of part of it, his lessee will acquire by implication, for the term of the lease, any easement over the part retained which would be acquired by a grantee in fee simple.[311] During the term of the lease, any later lease or grant of the part retained must take effect subject to the right so acquired; and in that sense the right, if not expressly reserved in the later lease or grant, will be impliedly reserved. In *Aldridge v Wright*[312] Greer L.J. stated (referring to *Thomas v Owen*[313]) that:

---

[307] (1887) 35 Ch. D. 317.
[308] Administration of Estates Act 1925, s.36(2).
[309] See Standard Conditions of Sale (4th ed.) condition 3.4 and Standard Commercial Property Conditions of Sale (2nd ed.) condition 3.3.
[310] *Selby District Council v Samuel Smith Old Brewery (Tadcaster)* (2000) 80 P. & C.R. 466.
[311] *Borman v Griffith* [1930] 1 Ch. 493 (agreement for a lease); *Horn v Hiscock* (1972) 223 E.G. 1437 (tenancy agreement under hand); see para.3–58, above.
[312] [1929] 2 K.B. 117 at 130, 131; see also *Liddiard v Waldron* [1934] 1 K.B. 435 at 447, per Greer L.J.
[313] (1887) 20 Q.B.D. 225.

"If the owner of two adjoining properties, A and B, grants to the tenant of A a tenancy from year to year with a right of way during his tenancy over B, and subsequently leases B, the lease of B is subject to a reservation of the right of way which has ex hypothesi been granted to the tenant of A if it is shown that the lessee of B was aware of a long continued exercise of the right by the tenant of A";

but it is submitted that the reference to notice on the part of the subsequent lessee does not imply that an easement granted by implication is only binding on a successor in title of the grantor with notice. If the previous disposition created a legal estate or interest, and the easement is thus a legal easement, the easement must, so it is submitted, bind all persons interested in the servient tenement, with or without notice. The reference to notice on the part of the subsequent lessee perhaps imports that, admitting that this lessee takes subject to the right already acquired by the other, a reservation will be implied, if the subsequent lessee has notice, as between him and the landlord, so as to absolve the landlord from liability on covenants for title.

3–106   In *Thomas v Owen*, the plaintiff, lessee of a farm, established against the defendant, lessee under the same landlord of an adjoining farm, a right of way over a lane through the defendant's land. This lane was in a cutting, with steep banks on each side; it had no communication with the defendant's land, and its only visible purpose was to give access from and to the high road to and from the plaintiff's farm. In 1873, when each party was a yearly tenant of his farm, the landlord granted a lease of the defendant's farm, including the site of the lane, to the defendant; and in 1878 he granted a lease of the plaintiff's farm to the plaintiff. The grounds of the decision of the Court of Appeal in favour of the plaintiff have never been considered clear; but the decision was summarised by Lawrence L.J. in *Liddiard v Waldron*[314] as follows:

"The Court of Appeal came to the conclusion, paying special regard to the fact that the lane was of no use to the defendant as a road and that it had been used and repaired exclusively by the plaintiff for many years, that a grant of a right of way over the lane was included in his yearly tenancy and that a reservation of the right ought to be implied in the 1873 lease because at the date of [that] lease . . . it had already been granted to the plaintiff, the tenant of the quasi-dominant tenement."

3–107   If the court in *Thomas v Owen*[315] had merely implied a reservation from the defendant's lease of the right then incident to the plaintiff's yearly tenancy, that reservation, it might be supposed, would have been co-terminous with the tenancy; but the court went further, and held that the lease granted in 1878 to the plaintiff included the right of way; and thus they must have regarded the reservation from

[314] [1934] 1 K.B. 435 at 444.
[315] (1887) 20 Q.B.D. 225.

the defendant's lease as a reservation for the whole of its term. *Thomas v Owen* was followed in *Westwood v Heywood*[316] where the plaintiff established, as incident to the land (D) conveyed to him, a right to the flow of water through a pipe from a source on adjoining land (S) belonging at the time of the conveyance to his vendor, and at the time of the action to a successor in title of the vendor. If S had been unlet at the time of the plaintiff's purchase, the right would clearly have passed by implication[317]; but S had been let, to the defendant, without reservation. If that had been all, the conveyance of D could not have conferred any right against the tenant of S; but D was also let, and this letting was earlier than the letting of S and was still on foot at the time of the conveyance. Astbury J. held that the letting of D carried the water right, that the letting of S was subject to an implied reservation of the right so granted to the tenant of D, and that at the date of the plaintiff's conveyance there was nothing to prevent the vendor from granting the water right in fee simple. It was in fact unnecessary to decide this question, because after the date of the plaintiff's conveyance, and before the action, the defendant acquired the fee simple of S, and in these circumstances it was held that, even if the defendant, as tenant of S, was not bound by the right, the conveyance of it to the plaintiff, made while the defendant was tenant, carried the right against the reversion of S subsequently acquired by the defendant.

It may, perhaps, be suggested that *Thomas v Owen* should be regarded as an isolated case so far as it decides, if it does, that an owner who grants first a lease of dominant land of his, and then a longer lease, without any express reservation, of the servient land, is able to make another disposition of the dominant land which will bind the servient land during the subsistence of the servient lease and after the determination of the dominant lease; and that it is more in accordance with principle to suppose that if a lease of the dominant land is followed by a lease or conveyance of the servient land not containing any reservation, the servient land will not be bound after the determination of the dominant lease. That was decided in *Warner v McBryde*.[318]   **3–108**

In *Flanigan and McGarvey and Thompson's Contract, Re*[319] the owner of land   **3–109** who, having let the dominant part on a quarterly tenancy protected by the Rent Acts, agreed to sell the servient part, was held entitled to have the conveyance so worded as to convey the property subject, during the existing tenancy of the dominant part and any tenancy that might supersede it, to such right of way as was incident to the tenancy; and not to reserve in perpetuity in the conveyance the right of way enjoyed by the tenant. Black J. expressed the opinion that that result would have followed if the conveyance had been executed without any express reservation.

---

[316] [1921] 2 Ch. 130.
[317] *Watts v Kelson* (1870) 6 Ch. App. 166; see para.3–69, above.
[318] (1887) 36 L.T. 360. See also *Beddington v Atlee* (1887) 35 Ch. D. 317, para.3–101, above.
[319] [1945] N.I. 32. Black J. said (at 43): "I have read and re-read Thomas v. Owen, and I think all the subsequent reported cases in which Thomas v. Owen has been referred to, in an earnest endeavour to see if I could formulate the precise principle in a logical framework of exceptions to the principle of Wheeldon v. Burrows. I cannot profess to have succeeded."

3–110   In *Coutts v Gorham*,[320] where the owner of two houses, D and S, leased S, and then leased D, which had windows overlooking S, to the plaintiff, and then granted a new lease of S to the defendant, it was held that the lease of D to the plaintiff carried the right to light against S, except during the original lease of S, and that, the lease of S to the defendant having been granted out of a reversion which was subject to the right already granted by the lease of D, the defendant was not entitled to obstruct D's light.

3–111   If the owner of two properties, D and S, grants a lease of D with a right to light over S, and then conveys D subject to the lease, S being all the time in hand, the conveyance of the reversion to D will carry the right to light on ordinary principles,[321] the result being, it seems, that the right is annexed to the estate or interest of both the lessee and the reversioner.[322]

If S is leased without any reservation of an easement in favour of D, and D is then granted, the grantee of D cannot, of course, have any easement over S during the lease of S. Any negative right over S which would pass by implication on the grant of D if S were on hand will, it seems, be acquired by D on the expiration of the lease of S, under the doctrine forbidding derogation from grant[323]; but it is questionable whether a positive right, such as a right of way, will be so acquired; at any rate, there seems to be no decision that it will.[324]

3–112   Where two lessees or tenants of property, formerly owned by the same person but since conveyed separately, are in dispute as to an alleged easement for the benefit of one of them, and it is not shown that the easement has been granted by one tenant to another, the proper approach would seem to be to investigate the history of the tenancies, and see whether they or either of them were granted by the common owner, and if so, which was granted first; and, if neither was granted by the common owner, to see whether the claiming lessee's landlord became entitled, under his conveyance from the common owner, to the easement claimed.

3–113   In *Aldridge v Wright*,[325] which was an action to restrain trespass, the defendant, who was lessee of a house, No. 28, sought to establish against the plaintiff, who was lessee of the house next door, No. 30, a right of way over that house's garden. The two houses had been the subject of separate contemporaneous leases granted to the same person, whose successor to both houses had first assigned the lease of No. 30 to A, without reserving any rights, and afterwards assigned the lease of No. 28 to B. The plaintiff and defendant became tenants of No. 30 and No. 28 respectively, and afterwards acquired the leasehold reversions. It was held that, as

---

[320] (1829) Moo. & M. 396. A similar case is *Davies v Marshall (No.1)* (1861) 1 Dr. & Sm. 557; see also *Westwood v Heywood* [1921] 2 Ch. 130; also *Cable v Bryant* [1908] 1 Ch. 259, para.3–34, above, where an owner having (i) leased the servient part of his land, (ii) conveyed the dominant part to the plaintiff and then (iii) conveyed the servient part to the defendant, the lessee joining to surrender the term, the plaintiff was held to have acquired a right to air against the defendant.

[321] In particular, the application of section 62 of the Law of Property Act 1925, as to which, see *Kent v Kavanagh* [2007] Ch. 1 and *Wall v Collins* [2007] Ch. 390.

[322] *Barnes v Loach* (1879) 4 Q.B.D. 494.

[323] *Cable v Bryant* [1908] 1 Ch. 259.

[324] *cf.* the argument, as to which the court expressed no opinion, in *Cable v Bryant*, above.

[325] [1929] 2 K.B. 117.

the lease of the allegedly servient tenement, No. 30, had been assigned first, no right was impliedly reserved to the assignor, and that the defendant, deriving title under him, had no easement.

A similar case is *Liddiard v Waldron*[326] where the plaintiff, owner of a house, **3–114** No. 22, claimed against the defendant, owner of the next house, No. 21, a right of way over a path behind and belonging to No. 21. No. 21 had been conveyed by the common owner first, without reservation, and it was held that no easement passed on the later conveyance of No. 22. It appeared that, at the time of the conveyance of No. 21, the right claimed was being used by the weekly tenant of No. 22; and hence it was argued, in reliance on *Thomas v Owen*[327] (and this argument succeeded in the Divisional Court[328]), that the common owner, having granted a right to the tenant of No. 22, must be taken to have reserved that right in perpetuity in the subsequent conveyance of No. 21. The Court of Appeal reversed the Divisional Court on the ground that there was no evidence that the user by the weekly tenant of No. 22 was of right, and that the case depended on *Wheeldon v Burrows*.[329] The tenancy of No. 22 appears to have determined before the conveyance of No. 22, and it is submitted that, even if the right had been annexed to that tenancy, the result would have been the same.

(6) *Easements of necessity*

A way of necessity, strictly so called,[330] may arise where, on a disposition by a **3–115** common owner[331] of part of his land, either the part disposed of or the part retained is left without any legally enforceable means of access.[332] In such a case the part so left inaccessible may be entitled, as of necessity, to a way over the other part. The principle no doubt applies where both parts are disposed of simultaneously, either by grant *inter vivos*,[333] or by will.[334]

> "If I have a field enclosed by my land on all sides, and I alien this close to another, he shall have a way to this close over my land, as incident to the

---

[326] [1934] 1 K.B. 435.

[327] (1887) 20 Q.B.D. 225; para.3–106, above.

[328] [1933] 2 K.B. 319.

[329] (1879) 12 Ch. D. 31.

[330] As opposed to a way necessary (a) for the enjoyment of some right expressly granted by the conveyance (as where the grant of a right to draw water from a spring will imply a right of way to the spring), or (b) in order to give effect to the common intention of the parties: *Nickerson v Barraclough* [1980] Ch. 325 at 332, per Sir Robert Megarry V.-C.; and see para.1–90, above (ancillary easements), and paras 3–26–3–30, above (common intention).

[331] Including a trustee; *Howton v Frearson* (1798) 8 Term Rep. 50.

[332] See *Manjang v Drammeh* (1990) 61 P. & C.R. 194 at 197 for a concise statement of the essentials for the implication of such an easement by Lord Oliver (approved by the Court of Appeal in *Adealon International Ltd v Merton LBC* [2007] 1 W.L.R. 1898). For a comparative study of legal solutions on access to landlocked land, see Bradbrook (1982) 10 Syd.L.R. 39.

[333] See para.3–106, above.

[334] See para.3–106, above; *Pearson v Spencer* (1861) 1 B. & S. 571; *Pheysey v Vicary* (1847) 16 M. & W. 484.

grant; for otherwise he cannot have any benefit from the grant. And the grantor shall assign the way where he can best spare it."[335]

"Where a man having a close surrounded with his own land, grants the close to another in fee, for life or for years, the grantee shall have a way to the close over the grantor's land, as incident to the grant, for without it he cannot derive any benefit from the grant. So it is where he grants the land, and reserves the close to himself."[336]

Although the principles which apply have been stated so that they apply to claims to implied reservations as well as to implied grants, it is now clear that the law is more strict in relation to a claim to an implied reservation.[337]

3–116   In *Nickerson v Barraclough*[338] the Court of Appeal held that the doctrine of way of necessity is founded upon an implication from the circumstances and rejected the suggestion[339] that public policy was a possible foundation of the doctrine. Accordingly, the suggested implication could be negatived by the express terms of the transaction. Brightman L.J. pointed out[340] that it is well established that a way of necessity is never found to exist except in connection with a grant of land, so that land acquired by escheat[341] or by adverse possession[342] gets no way of necessity, and he saw no reason why, if a way of necessity were based upon public policy, land acquired by escheat or by adverse possession should be excluded. In *Hillman v Rogers*[343] the existence of an express fencing covenant which would have negatived the implication of an easement on the basis of the principles in *Wheeldon v Burrows*[344] would not have negatived an implication of an easement of necessity.

3–117   Although earlier cases had tended to treat the relevant principles as equally applicable to claims as to implied reservation and to claims as to implied grant, it is now clear that a distinction can be drawn and that the principles are to be more strictly applied in the case of a claim to an implied reservation of an easement of necessity. In this context, as elsewhere, the presumption of non-derogation of grant works in favour of the grantee but against the grantor. The difference can be seen to have particular application in a case where there is at the time of the

---

[335] Rolle's Abridgment, tit. Graunt, pl. 17.

[336] 1 Wms.Saund. (1871 ed.) 570; adopted in *Pinnington v Gotland* (1853) 9 Exch. 1 at 12; discussed in *Adealon International Ltd v Merton LBC* [2007] 1 W.L.R. 1898.

[337] *Adealon International Ltd v Merton LBC* [2007] 1 W.L.R. 1898.

[338] [1981] Ch. 426; see at 440, per Brightman L.J., at 446, per Eveleigh L.J., and at 447, per Buckley L.J. The Court of Appeal reversed on this point the judgment of Sir Robert Megarry V.-C. [1980] Ch. 325. The Court of Appeal and the Appeal Committee of the House of Lords refused leave to appeal. See also *Antigua v Boxwill* (1969) 15 W.I.R. 56, Guyana CA; *North Sydney Printing Pty Ltd v Sabemo Investment Corp Pty Ltd* [1971] 2 N.S.W.L.R. 150 (discussed in *Adealon International Ltd v Merton LBC* [2007] 1 W.L.R. 1898).

[339] In *Packer v Wellstead* (1658) 2 Sid. 39, 111, and *Dutton v Taylor* (1701) 2 Lut. 1487; and see the 14th ed. of this book at p. 117.

[340] [1981] Ch. 440.

[341] *Proctor v Hodgson* (1855) 10 Exch. 824.

[342] *Wilkes v Greenway* (1890) 6 T.L.R. 449. See para.1–89, above.

[343] [1997] EWCA Civ 3069.

[344] (1879) 12 Ch. D. 31.

transaction a possibility of (albeit no pre-existing legal entitlement to) an alternative right or advantage over the land of third parties. The grantee's normal expectation is that the relevant necessary right, if not otherwise available, will be allowed as an incident of the grant, and thus that it will be provided by the grantor over land within his control. Where the roles are reversed, the grantor has no equivalent expectation. On the contrary, the presumption is that any rights he requires over the land transferred will have been expressly reserved in the grant, and the burden lies on the grantor to establish an exception. To that issue, the existence of other realistic possibilities of an alternative right or advantage, even if not legally enforceable at the time of the grant, is clearly relevant.[345]

Where a way of necessity arises, whether in favour of the grantee of the enclosed land,[346] or of the grantor retaining the enclosed land,[347] its line is to be chosen by the grantor[348]; but it is for the person entitled to it to make it up.[349] It has been said that the line, once established, cannot be altered by the servient owner.[350] **3–118**

It has been seen[351] that if a house or land with a drive or other obvious means of approach is granted without the drive or any right over it, a right over the drive will arise by implication. No case of necessity arises, because a right over a defined way is impliedly granted, and in this sense it is true to say[352] that a way of necessity is not a defined way. Whether, if the drive is granted and the (otherwise inaccessible) house retained, the grantor obtains a right over the drive, by implication, because it is a necessary means of access to the house,[353] or a right over some way, to be chosen by him, as of necessity, does not seem clear[354]; but the question can seldom be a live one, for if in such a case a true way of necessity arises, the grantor will presumably choose the existing way.[355]

Clearly no way of necessity arises if, at the time of the grant, the claiming party owned other land which gave access.[356] Where there is no legal entitlement to a right as an alternative to the claimed necessary right, then a realistic possibility of an alternative right or advantage may be relevant, but a distinction is to be **3–119**

---

[345] *Adealon International Ltd v Merton LBC* [2007] 1 W.L.R. 1898.

[346] *Clark v Cogge* (1607) Cro.Jac. 170; *Brown v Alabaster* (1888) 37 Ch. D. 490 at 500; *Barry v Hasseldine* [1952] Ch. 835 at 838.

[347] *Packer v Wellstead*, above.

[348] *Bolton v Bolton* (1879) 11 Ch. D. 968. Only one way is allowed, and it must be a convenient way; *ibid.*, and see *Pinnington v Galland* (1853) 9 Exch. 1 at 12.

[349] *Osborn v Wise* (1837) 7 Car. & P. 761 at 764; *cf.* para.1–91, above.

[350] *Pearson v Spencer* (1861) 1 B. & S. 571 at 584, per Blackburn J.; affirmed 3 B. & S. 761. In this case a right over an existing defined way appears to have passed by implication under the will. *Cf. Deacon v S.E. Ry* (1889) 61 L.T. 377. In *Wynne v Pope* (1960) 3 S.A. 37, however, it was held by the Supreme Court of South Africa that an easement of necessity can be altered by the owner of the servient tenement if he can afford to the owner of the dominant tenement another route as convenient as the original route. See also Garner, "Ways of Necessity" 24 Conv. (n.s.) 205.

[351] See para.3–58, above.

[352] See *Brown v Alabaster* (1888) 37 Ch. D. 490; para.3–60, above.

[353] See *Pinnington v Galland* (1853) 9 Exch. 1 at 12.

[354] See *Pearson v Spencer* (1861) 1 B. & S. 571 at 584, 585; *Holmes v Goring* (1824) 2 Bing. 76, 84.

[355] In *Nickerson v Barraclough* [1981] Ch. 426 at 445, 446, Eveleigh L.J., finding an implied provision for access, said that it was for the grantor to choose the actual route.

[356] See, e.g. *Midland Ry v Miles* (1886) 33 Ch. D. 632 at 644.

drawn between a case of a claim to an implied grant and a claim to an implied reservation.[357] In a case of a claim to an implied grant of a right of way, merely permissive user of other land as a means of access was disregarded.[358] In a case of a claim to an implied reservation of a right of way, the court looked broadly at all the relevant facts and held that there was insufficient in the facts to rebut the presumption that the grantor did not intend to derogate from its grant by claiming an implied reservation of a right of way.[359] Where a building, under which was an archway leading to a mews retained by the lessor, was demised to a lessee who had notice that the lessor intended to develop his retained land in such a way as to leave it inaccessible except through the archway, the lessee was restrained from blocking this up, on the ground, among others, that a way through the archway was reserved as a way of necessity.[360]

It is not essential that the inaccessibility of the land granted (or retained) be due to the fact that it is surrounded by land of the grantor (or grantee) and no other person[361]; but speaking generally it does appear to be essential that the land is absolutely inaccessible or useless.[362] If, however, a particular part of the property cannot, without the right claimed, be used for its designed purpose, then it is probably true to say that a right of access for that purpose will arise as of necessity. For instance, in *Hansford v Jago*,[363] where earth closets belonging to the cottages sold could not be emptied without either infringing a local byelaw or passing over the strip of land over which the right of way was claimed, Russell J. would probably have decided, if it had been necessary, that a way of necessity for this purpose had been made out. On the other hand the use of an adjoining passage for carrying coals or other things which can, though not conveniently, be carried through a house is not necessary in this sense.[364] Moreover, in *Titchmarsh v Royston Water Co*[365] where land, otherwise inaccessible, adjoined a highway lying in a cutting 20 feet below, it was held that no way of necessity arose over other adjoining land. In *Manjang v Drammeh* the Privy Council held that an available access by water, albeit less convenient than access across terra firma, is

---

[357] See para.3–117, above.
[358] *Barry v Hasseldine* [1952] Ch. 835 approved by the Court of Appeal in *Adealon International Ltd v Merton LBC* [2007] 1 W.L.R. 1898 in preference to the *obiter* comments in *Titchmarsh v Royston Water Co* (1899) 81 L.T. 673. *Barry v Hasseldine* was followed at first instance in *Sweet v Sommer* [2004] EWHC 1504 (Ch) at [23], a case involving an implied reservation, but this was before the decision in *Adealon*. *Barry v Hasseldine* was distinguished by Robert Walker L.J. in *Hillman v Rogers* [1997] EWCA Civ 3069, where access was available over an agricultural holding tenanted by the family partnership.
[359] *Adealon International Ltd v Merton LBC* [2007] 1 W.L.R. 1898.
[360] *Davies v Sear* (1869) L.R. 7 Eq. 427.
[361] *Barry v Hasseldine* [1952] Ch. 835.
[362] *Union Lighterage Co v London Graving Dock Co* [1902] 2 Ch. 557 at 573, applied in *M.R.A. Engineering v Trimster Co Ltd* (1987) 56 P. & C.R. 1; *Nickerson v Barraclough* [1980] Ch. 325 at 332, per Sir Robert Megarry V.-C. (The Court of Appeal did not disagree on this point.)
[363] [1921] 1 Ch. 322; para.3–63, above, para.3–127, below.
[364] *Aldridge v Wright* [1929] 2 K.B. 117; *cf. Liddiard v Waldron* [1934] 1 K.B. 435.
[365] (1899) 81 L.T. 673. This decision was considered in *Adealon International Ltd v Merton LBC* [2007] 1 W.L.R 1898 as being based on a finding that the claimed right was not truly necessary.

sufficient to negative any implication of a way of necessity.[366] In *Sweet v Sommer*, it was suggested that the claimed right of way was not necessary because the dominant owner could demolish a structure on his own land and thereby gain access from the dominant tenement to a highway. It was held at first instance that where access to the retained land is only available either over the land transferred or by destruction of a physical barrier the continued existence of which was obviously contemplated by the parties, it was consistent with doctrine and not contradicted by authority to say that a way over the property transferred was impliedly reserved as a matter of necessity; it was also stated that whether a particular way is necessary, and whether vehicular use of that way was necessary, was a question of fact to be determined by a consideration of all the surrounding circumstances.[367] The Court of Appeal dismissed an appeal but did so on the basis of a proprietary estoppel and did not express any views on the claim to an easement of necessity.[368]

It seems that a way acquired as of necessity, whether by the grantee or the grantor, is such a way as is necessary for the use of the servient land as it is at the time of the grant, or for such use as is then contemplated by both parties. In *Gayford v Moffatt*,[369] where a lease had been granted of a counting-house and vaults, to which the only means of access was over a courtyard held by the lessor, and the lessor afterwards began to build on part of the courtyard, it was held that the lessee became entitled to a way of necessity over the courtyard,

3–120

> "and that way must be a way suitable to the business to be carried on on the premises demised, namely, the business of a wine and spirit merchant. That is the position in which the tenant stood after the lease was granted, and is the position in which he now stands. The question is therefore reduced to this, whether there remained, after the building was erected, such a way as the plaintiff would have been entitled to the day after the lease was granted."[370]

It was decided that enough room was left for the plaintiff to bring pipes of wine in wagons to the vault entrance in the courtyard, and the bill was dismissed.

In *Serff v Acton Local Board*[371] land acquired by the defendant Board under compulsory powers for the purpose of sewage works was conveyed to it by the

---

[366] (1990) 61 P. & C.R. 194, applying *Menzies v Breadalbane* (1901) 4 F. 59; *Fitchett v Mellow* (1898) 29 O.R. 6 and *Harding v Herr* (1965) 47 D.L.R. (2d) 13. Under New Zealand's Law of Property Act 1952, section 129B, the Court can make an order granting access through the land of a neighbour if land is "landlocked". Land is "landlocked" if there is no reasonable access to it. In *Kingfish Lodge (1993) Limited v Archer* [2000] 3 N.Z.L.R. 364 a 12-hectare site at the coast which had been developed as a tourist lodge which was accessible only by sea was held not to be "landlocked" in this sense.

[367] [2004] EWHC 1504 (Ch), see at [24] and [30].

[368] [2005] EWCA Civ 227.

[369] (1868) 4 Ch. App. 133.

[370] (1868) 4 Ch. App. 136, per Lord Cairns; and see *Nickerson v Barraclough* [1980] Ch. 325 at 329, per Sir Robert Megarry V.-C.

[371] (1886) 31 Ch. D. 679.

plaintiff, to whom that and adjoining land had been conveyed by a conveyance containing full recitals of the proposed works. The Board was held entitled, as of necessity, to the use of a way over the plaintiff's retained land for all purposes for which it could be required for sewage works.

3–121   In *Corporation of London v Riggs*[372] the defendant had conveyed to the Corporation the outer part of a piece of agricultural land in Epping Forest, retaining a part which was entirely surrounded by the land conveyed. There was no defined means of access to the part retained, which was used solely for agricultural purposes. The defendant having started to build a public tea-room on the part retained, the Corporation brought this action, alleging that he had unlawfully drawn timber and other building materials across the land conveyed, and that he threatened to continue to do so and to attract and cause the public to cross the land conveyed, both in carriages and on foot; and it claimed a declaration that the defendant was entitled to no more than a way of necessity over the land conveyed, sufficient for its use for agricultural purposes only; that, if necessary, the position and other particulars of that way might be set out and defined; and an injunction in accordance with the declaration. The defendant demurred to the statement of claim, except so far as it claimed to have the way set out, and he alleged that, except as aforesaid, the claim was bad in law on the ground that he was entitled to a way for all purposes, and not for agricultural purposes only. Lord Jessel M.R., after observing that the point did not appear to be covered by authority, overruled the demurrer, on the ground that a way of necessity must be limited by the necessity at the time of the grant. He said[373]:

> "The object of implying the re-grant, as stated by the older judges, was that if you did not give the owner of the reserved close some right of way or other, he could neither use nor occupy the reserved close, nor derive any benefit from it. But what is the extent of the benefit he is to have? Is he entitled to say, I have reserved to myself more than that which enables me to enjoy it as it is at the time of the grant? And if that is the true rule, that he is not to have more than necessity requires, as distinguished from what convenience may require, it appears to me that the right of way must be limited to that which is necessary at the time of the grant; that is, he is supposed to take a re-grant to himself of such a right of way as will enable him to enjoy the reserved thing as it is. . . . If you imply more, you reserve to him not only that which enables him to enjoy the thing he has reserved as it is, but that which enables him to enjoy it in the same way and to the same extent as if he reserved a general right of way for all purposes: that is—as in the case I

---

[372] (1880) 13 Ch. D. 798, considered in *Dwyer Nolan Developments Ltd v Kingscroft Developments Ltd* [1998] 1 E.H.C. 125; [1999] 1 I.L.R.M. 141 (High Court of Ireland) where it is pointed out that English and Irish jurisprudence differ on this point; see Peter Bland, *The Law of Easements and Profits à Prendre*, 1997 ed. at p. 225. In *Adealon International Ltd v Merton LBC* [2007] 1 W.L.R. 1898 at [12], *Corporation of London v Riggs* was described as a "classic case" of an easement of necessity.

[373] (1880) 13 Ch. D. 798 at 806, 807.

have before me–a man who reserves two acres of arable land in the middle of a large piece of land is to be entitled to cover the reserved land with houses, and call on his grantee to allow him to make a wide metalled road up to it. I do not think that is a fair meaning of a way of necessity: I think it must be limited by the necessity at the time of the grant."

The Master of the Rolls added that, where the grant is of the enclosed piece, it might be that the grantee obtains a larger way of necessity than the grantor does under the implied regrant; but he did not think so.

In *Chappell v Mason*[374] the lessee of a house, A, took a lease from a different landlord of the top part of the adjoining house, B, not including the stairs from the street. By permission of the landlords the party wall was opened, on the top floor, so as to give communication between the two premises, and the lessee afterwards took a lease of the top part of B for a further term. While B was so leased the landlord of A took possession (the lease of A having evidently come to an end by effluxion of time or otherwise), and blocked up the opening, so leaving the demised part of B inaccessible except by the stairs. It was held nevertheless that the lessee had no right to use the stairs. **3–122**

There is no conceptual objection to an inchoate way of necessity which matures into a full right of way when the necessity eventuates.[375] In *Holmes v Goring*[376] the Court of Common Pleas considered that a way of necessity does not survive the necessity under which it arose, and that, if the person entitled to it acquires adjoining land which gives access to the dominant tenement, the right will cease. The case is not clear, however, and it may be that, at the time of the grant of the allegedly servient tenement, the necessity for a way over it had already ceased.[377] The case has now been followed at first instance.[378] It has been stated that there is no reason why the intention to be presumed should not be limited to an intention to reserve the easement for so long as may be necessary. As the implied reservation of a way of necessity involves an implied derogation from grant, it should be limited to the minimum in time, as in every other respect. If more is desired by the transferor, he can always reserve an easement expressly. **3–123**

Easements of necessity most often arise in connection with access. In *Wong v Beaumont Property Trust Limited*,[379] however, the plaintiff successfully claimed a right to construct a ventilation duct on the defendant's land. The tenant under a lease covenanted to keep the demised premises open as a popular restaurant, to **3–124**

---

[374] (1894) 10 T.L.R. 404.
[375] *Hillman v Rogers* [1997] EWCA Civ 3069 per Ward L.J. (Robert Walker and Butler-Sloss L.JJ.'s views, in agreement with Ward L.J., were *obiter*); *Donaldson v Smith* [2007] 1 P. & C.R. D4 at [34].
[376] (1894) 2 Bing. 76.
[377] See per Fry J., *Barkshire v Grubb* (1881) Ch. D. 616 at 620. The facts in *Holmes v Goring* were unusual and complicated, and the leading judgment is difficult to analyse. The decision was doubted by Parke B. and Alderson B. in *Proctor v Hodgson* (1855) 10 Exch. 824, 828. The point is referred to, inconclusively, in *Huckvale v Aegean Hotels Ltd* (1989) 58 P. & C.R. 163, and, also inconclusively, in *B.O.J. Properties Ltd v Allen's Mobile Home Park Ltd* (1979) 108 D.L.R. (3d) 305.
[378] *Donaldson v Smith* [2007] 1 P. & C.R. D4 at [34].
[379] [1965] 1 Q.B. 173.

control and eliminate all smells and odours caused by such use of the premises and to comply with the health regulations so that they should not become or cause an annoyance or nuisance to the landlord or to the tenants and occupiers of adjacent buildings belonging to the landlord. At the time of the execution of the lease the covenants as to ventilation could not be complied with unless a ventilation system was installed with a duct fixed to the outside back wall of the landlord's building. That fact was not then appreciated by the parties to the lease, so that this case is also authority for the proposition that an easement of necessity may impliedly be granted even though the parties do not realise that necessity at the time of the grant. The judge of the Exeter County Court granted the plaintiff, who had bought the remainder of the lease, a declaration that he was entitled to enter the landlord's premises for the purpose of constructing, maintaining and repairing a ventilation system for use in connection with the restaurant.

3–125   The Court of Appeal, dismissing the landlord's appeal and applying the dictum of Lord Parker in *Pwllbach Colliery Company v Woodman*,[380] held that since at the time of the grant of the lease and thereafter a ventilation system with an air duct on the wall of the landlord's premises was necessary in order that the business of a popular restaurant could legally be carried on in the demised premises in accordance with the terms of the lease, the plaintiff had established an easement of necessity and was entitled to the declaration. Lord Denning M.R. said[381]:

> "There is one point in which this case goes further than the earlier cases which have been cited. It is this. It was not realised by the parties, at the time of the lease, that this duct would be necessary. But it was in fact necessary from the very beginning. That seems to me sufficient to bring the principle into play. In order to use this place as a restaurant, there must be implied an easement, by the necessity of the case, to carry a duct up this wall."

Pearson L.J. said[382] that the choice was either to say that the provisions of the lease could not be carried out and must remain inoperative, or to imply an easement of necessity into the lease. The court should read the lease in such a way that *res magis valeat quam pereat*, and therefore the right course was to imply an easement of necessity.

Salmon L.J. said[383] that it seemed to be plain on the authorities that if a lease were granted which imposed a particular use on the tenant and it was impossible for the tenant so to use the premises legally unless an easement were granted, the law did imply such an easement as of necessity.

---

[380] [1915] A.C. 634 at 646. In *Nickerson v Barraclough* [1980] Ch. 325 at 332, Sir Robert Megarry V.-C. pointed out that although Lord Denning M.R. in *Wong v Beaumont Property Trust Ltd* [1965] 1 Q.B. 173 was referring to easements of necessity in the strict sense, he cited in support only Lord Parker's speech, which was concerned with an easement necessary in order to give effect to the common intention of the parties: see para.3–115, above.

[381] [1965] 1 Q.B. 173 at 181.

[382] [1965] 1 Q.B. 173 at 183.

[383] [1965] 1 Q.B. 173 at 189.

4. — CREATION BY GENERAL WORDS

Law of Property Act 1925, s.62

Prior to the coming into force, on January 1, 1882, of section 6 of the Conveyancing **3–126** Act 1881, it was common to set out in a conveyance "general words", operating as a species of express grant, by virtue of which easements could be claimed as being established for the benefit of the land granted. The court was not, however, inclined to establish the easement claimed unless it had previously existed and afterwards became extinguished through unity of ownership, and then only if the subsequent conveyance by the common owner contained some such general words as "together with all ways (etc.) used or enjoyed therewith".[384]

Statute has, as a matter of conveyancing, eliminated the necessity of setting out the general words by deeming them to be set out.[385] By section 62 of the Law of Property Act 1925 (which re-enacts section 6 of the Conveyancing Act 1881) it is provided that:

"(1) A conveyance of land shall be deemed to include and shall by virtue of this Act operate to convey, with the land, all buildings, erections, fixtures, commons, hedges, ditches, fences, ways, waters, watercourses, liberties, privileges, easements, rights, and advantages whatsoever, appertaining or reputed to appertain to the land, or any part thereof, or, at the time of conveyance, demised, occupied, or enjoyed with, or reputed or known as part or parcel of or appurtenant to the land or any part thereof.

(2) A conveyance of land, having houses or other buildings thereon, shall be deemed to include and shall by virtue of this Act operate to convey, with the land, houses, or other buildings, all outhouses, erections, fixtures, cellars, areas, courts, courtyards, cisterns, sewers, gutters, drains, ways, passages, lights, watercourses, liberties, privileges, easements, rights and advantages whatsoever, appertaining or reputed to appertain to the land, houses, or other buildings conveyed, or any of them, or any part thereof, or, at the time of conveyance, demised, occupied, or enjoyed with, or reputed or known as part or parcel of or appurtenant to, the land, houses, or other buildings conveyed, or any of them, or any part thereof.

(3) A conveyance of a manor shall be deemed to include and shall by virtue of this Act operate to convey, with the manor, all pastures, feedings, wastes, warrens, commons, mines, minerals, quarries, furzes, trees, woods, underwoods, coppices, and the ground and soil thereof, fishings, fisheries, fowlings, courts leet, courts baron, and other courts, view of frankpledge and all that to view of frankpledge doth belong, mills, mulctures, customs, tolls, duties, reliefs, heriots, fines, sums of money, amerciaments, waifs, estrays, chief-rents, quit-rents, rentscharge, rents seek, rents of assize, fee farm rents,

---

[384] See, e.g. *Langley v Hammand* (1868) L.R. 3 Exch. 161 at 168.
[385] *Peck and the School Board for London, Re* [1893] 2 Ch. 315 at 318.

services, royalties, jurisdictions, franchises, liberties, privileges, easements, profits, advantages, rights, emoluments, and hereditaments whatsoever, to the manor appertaining or reputed to appertain, or, at the time of conveyance, demised, occupied, or enjoyed with the same, or reputed or known as part, parcel, or member thereof . . . .

(4) This section applies only if and as far as a contrary intention is not expressed in the conveyance, and has effect subject to the terms of the conveyance and to the provisions therein contained.[386]

(5) This section shall not be construed as giving to any person a better title to any property, right, or thing in this section mentioned than the title which the conveyance gives to him to the land or manor expressed to be conveyed, or as conveying to him any property, right, or thing in this section mentioned, further or otherwise than as the same could have been conveyed to him by the conveying parties.

(6) This section applies to conveyances made after the 31st day of December, 1881."

"Conveyance" includes (s.205(1)(ii)) a mortgage, charge, lease, assent, vesting declaration, vesting instrument, disclaimer, release, and every other assurance of property or an interest therein by any instrument, except a will. It includes a tenancy agreement for a term not exceeding three years,[387] but not an agreement for a lease exceeding three years,[388] nor a mere oral tenancy.[389]

"Land" includes (s.205(1)(ix)) land of any tenure, and mines and minerals, whether or not held apart from the surface, and buildings or parts of buildings (whether the division is horizontal, vertical or made in any other way), and other corporeal hereditaments.

Appertaining or reputed to appertain to

3–127   The modern tendency, as has been seen,[390] is to rest the right to an easement on the supposed intention of the parties to the contract, or, if there was no contract, on the intention of the testator or grantor, irrespectively of the presence or absence of general words in the conveyance. Often an easement which arises by implication is created also by the operation of the statutory general words. It is uncommon, on the other hand, for an easement to arise solely under the general words and not also by implication. It is thought that the only rights, not being rights arising by implication, which pass under the statutory words in a

---

[386] The effect of a contract may be to exclude the general words from the conveyance: *Squarey v Harris-Smith* (1981) 42 P. & C.R. 118; not cited in *Lyme Valley Squash Club Ltd v Newcastle-under-Lyme B.C.* [1985] 2 All E.R. 405.

[387] *Wright v Macadam* [1949] 2 K.B. 744.

[388] *Borman v Griffith* [1930] 1 Ch. 493; see para.3–58, above. See also *Horn v Hiscock* (1972) 223 E.G. 1437.

[389] *Rye v Rye* [1962] A.C. 496.

[390] See para.3–17, above.

conveyance³⁹¹ are rights, advantages, etc., enjoyed at the time of the conveyance³⁹²
by an occupier of the land conveyed³⁹³ over other land of the grantor, and rights
"reputed to appertain" to the land conveyed.³⁹⁴ Section 62 cannot, of course, create new rights when there has been no actual enjoyment of the facility claimed by
the owner or occupier of the dominant tenement over the servient tenement.³⁹⁵ It
has been held that an inchoate right, in the course of being acquired by prescription but where the full period for prescription has not elapsed, can be passed on
to the lessee pursuant to a lease which is a conveyance within section 62.³⁹⁶ This
means that the person to whom the property is leased can add the period of user
before the lease to a period of user after the lease to make up the relevant period
for prescription.

The words "appertaining or reputed to appertain to" refer, in their strict mean-   **3–128**
ing,³⁹⁷ to easements already existing and annexed to the estate granted and not to
future rights. In that sense they are superfluous,³⁹⁸ and it does not seem that an
easement could ever arise under the statutory words "appertaining . . . to". On the
other hand "appurtenances" easily admits a secondary meaning, such as "usually
occupied",³⁹⁹ and in a conveyance will carry a right of way used by a tenant over
adjoining land of the vendor.⁴⁰⁰ Such a right would also pass as a right "enjoyed
with" the property.⁴⁰¹ In *White v Taylor (No. 2)*⁴⁰² the tenants of the vendor, the
common owner of a number of properties which were offered for sale by auction,
had sheep grazing rights over one of the properties. These rights could not be

---

³⁹¹ As defined by s.205(1)(ii) of the Law of Property Act 1925.

³⁹² *Nickerson v Barraclough* [1981] Ch. 426. (S.62 is not concerned with future rights.) Where a common owner sells his land in lots at one sale, the conveyances are for this purpose regarded, irrespective of their actual dates, as contemporaneous; see *Lewis v Meredith* [1913] 1 Ch. 571.

³⁹³ Including a purchaser who takes possession between contract and conveyance; *Goldberg v
Edwards* [1950] Ch. 247.

³⁹⁴ In *Beddington v Atlee* (1887) 35 Ch. D. 317 (see para.3–76, above); *Birmingham, Dudley and
District Banking Co v Ross* (1888) 38 Ch. D. 295 (see para.3–63, above); *Godwin v Schweppes
Ltd* [1902] 1 Ch. 926 (see para.3–64, above) and *Quicke v Chapman* [1903] 1 Ch. 659 (see paras
3–09 and 3–64, above), which have all been considered above in connection with claims to light
by implication, and in all of which the claim by implication failed, a claim under the statutory
general words also failed. See also *Salaman v Glover* (1875) L.R. 20 Eq. 444.

³⁹⁵ *Payne v Inwood* (1996) 74 P. & C.R. 42 at 47.

³⁹⁶ *Midtown Ltd v City of London Real Property Co Ltd* [2005] 1 E.G.L.R. 65 at [23].

³⁹⁷ *Bolton v Bolton* (1879) 11 Ch. D. 968 at 970; *Thomas v Owen* (1887) 20 Q.B.D. 225 at 231;
Nickerson v Barraclough [1981] Ch. 426.

³⁹⁸ *Beddington v Atlee* (1887) 35 Ch. D. 317 at 326. Strictly, it is not necessary to rely on section 62
in relation to existing easements which are appurtenant to the land conveyed as these pass automatically with the land and without express mention: see *Godwin v Schweppes Ltd* [1902] 1 Ch.
926 at 932 and *Snell and Prideaux Ltd v Duttons Mirrors Ltd* [1995] 1 E.G.L.R. 259 at 264L–M.

³⁹⁹ *Thomas v Owen* (1887) 20 Q.B.D. 225 at 231–232.

⁴⁰⁰ *Hansford v Jago* [1921] 1 Ch. 322 at 329–331, following on this point *Thomas v Owen*, above. No
question was raised as to the power of the vendor to grant the right as against the adjoining property. Both were sold at one auction, and at that time were occupied by tenants who (apparently)
became the purchasers.

⁴⁰¹ The words "enjoyed with" refer to incorporeal hereditaments and not to physical property: *C.N.T
v JJ Gallagher Ltd* [2003] 2 P. & C.R. 24 at [64]. Similarly, in accordance with the ordinary meaning of the word "appurtenant", land should not be regarded as appurtenant to other land.

⁴⁰² [1969] 1 Ch. 160 at 186–189.

appurtenant to the other properties and the purchasers had notice of this fact. Buckley J. accordingly held that the rights were not "reputed or known as part or parcel of or appurtenant to the land or any part thereof", and in so holding distinguished *White v Williams*,[403] where a reference to particulars of sale operated to grant a sheepwalk by reason of admissions in the particulars. Although, as that case shows, a right of grazing can pass under section 62, such a right must be a valid right. That means that it must be limited to the needs of the dominant tenement. An exclusive right of grazing without limit is unknown to the law.[404]

The need for some diversity of ownership or occupation

3–129   A relatively clear case where section 62 operates to grant an easement to a transferee of the dominant tenement is where the dominant tenement is occupied by a tenant to whom the freehold is then transferred. If such a tenant had rights over the servient tenement pursuant to the terms of his tenancy, then those rights are *demised with* the dominant tenement (for the purposes of that phrase in section 62) and after the transfer of the freehold to the tenant, the tenant continues to enjoy the rights previously enjoyed but now in the capacity of freeholder, rather than tenant.[405] If such a tenant did not have rights over the servient tenement pursuant to the terms of his tenancy, but such advantages were actually enjoyed with the dominant tenement, then again on the tenant acquiring the freehold of the dominant tenement, the former advantages will be upgraded into rights pursuant to section 62 and enjoyed by the transferee of the freehold in the capacity of freeholder.[406] In these cases, there is clear diversity of occupation of the dominant and the servient tenements and no particular difficulty under section 62 arises. However, the position is more controversial where there is no diversity of occupation. In *Titchmarsh v Royston Water Co Ltd*[407] and *Long v Gowlett*[408] there are suggestions that the operation of section 62 is limited, where there is unity of occupation, to continuous and apparent quasi-easements. In *Sovmots Investments Ltd v Secretary of State for the Environment*[409] there are dicta of Lord Wilberforce[410] and Lord Edmund-Davies[411] which give approval to *Long v Gowlett*[412] and to the proposition that there is no room for the operation of section 62 unless there has been some diversity of ownership or occupation of the quasi-dominant and quasi-servient tenements prior to the conveyance. These dicta, which ordinarily would have great weight, lose some of their force because when *Sovmots Investments Ltd v Secretary of State for the Environment* reached

---

[403] [1922] 1 K.B. 727.
[404] *Anderson v Bostock* [1976] Ch. 312; see para.1–143, above.
[405] See *Kent v Kavanagh* [2007] Ch. 1, in particular at [73].
[406] See *Wall v Collins* [2007] 3 W.L.R. 459 at [46].
[407] (1899) 81 L.T. 673.
[408] [1923] 2 Ch. 177 at 202–204.
[409] [1979] A.C. 144.
[410] [1979] A.C. 144 at 169.
[411] [1979] A.C. 144 at 176.
[412] [1923] 2 Ch. 177.

the House of Lords[413] it was not argued that section 62 was relevant in the particular circumstances of the case, and the views expressed by Lord Wilberforce and Lord Edmund-Davies[414] cannot easily be reconciled with the other cases which (because of the circumstances) their Lordships did not consider in detail.[415]

It is clear that where there is unity of occupation it is not possible to claim that **3–130** a right is "appurtenant" to the grantee's land, and it is a question of fact whether it is "enjoyed with" it. If it is so enjoyed (and in both *Titchmarsh v Royston Water Co Ltd*[416] and *Long v Gowlett*[417] it was found that the right claimed was not enjoyed with the land conveyed), there seems to be no reason why the right should not pass, although it is not a continuous and apparent easement.[418] So in *Wardle v Brocklehurst*[419] Williams J. in the Court of Exchequer Chamber said:

".. . Inasmuch as the unity of ownership extinguishes the easement, the right of way cannot pass as simply appurtenant to the land to which it was formerly attached, though it continues to exist in point of user. But, though it does not exist as a right, it will pass by a conveyance of the land, if proper words be used to pass it, as, if all ways 'used and enjoyed' with the land are conveyed."

Moreover, *Broomfield v Williams*,[420] a decision of the Court of Appeal, contra- **3–131** dicts the contention that, where there is unity of occupation, section 62 is limited to continuous and apparent quasi-easements. Sargant J. in *Long v Gowlett*[421] sought to explain *Broomfield v Williams* as involving a right to light which he said[422] was "extremely similar to a continuous and apparent easement", but there

---

[413] [1979] A.C. 144. The House of Lords reversed the decision of the Court of Appeal [1977] Q.B. 411, which had reversed the judgment of Forbes J.

[414] Lord Fraser of Tullybelton, Lord Russell of Killowen (who delivered a dissenting speech) and Lord Keith of Kinkel merely referred to the fact that the reliance placed on s.62 had not been pursued in their Lordships' House.

[415] *Sovmots Investments Ltd v Secretary of State for the Environment* [1979] A.C. 144 is discussed in detail in a series of articles in The Conveyancer, Harpum, "Easements and Centre Point: Old problems resolved in a new setting," (1977) 41 Conv. 415; Smith, "Centre Point: faulty towers with shaky foundations", (1978) 42 Conv. 449; and Harpum, "Long v. Gowlett: a strong fortress", also (1979) 43 Conv. 113. See also Jackson, "Easements and General Words", (1966) 30 Conv. 340 and *The Law of Easements and Profits* (1978) by the same author, pp. 101, 102. *Cf.* Megarry and Wade, *The Law of Real Property*, (6th ed.), para.18–114, where the dicta of Lord Wilberforce and Lord Edmund-Davies are accepted as stating the law. The views of Lord Wilberforce were quoted with apparent approval in *Kent v Kavanagh* [2007] Ch. 1, in particular at [46].

[416] (1899) 81 L.T. 673.

[417] [1923] 2 Ch. 177.

[418] This accords with the views expressed by the learned editors of Megarry and Wade, *The Law of Real Property* (6th ed.), para.18–114, and Foa's *Law of Landlord and Tenant* (8th ed.), pp. 75, 76. A right of support passed under s.62 when title to two adjoining buildings was severed in *Scouton & Co (Builders) Ltd v Gilyott & Scott Ltd* (1971) 221 E.G. 1499.

[419] (1860) 1 E. & E. 1058 at 1065, 1066.

[420] [1897] 1 Ch. 602; see para.3–81, above. See also *Lyme Valley Squash Club Ltd v Newcastle-under-Lyme Borough Council* [1985] 2 All E.R. 405.

[421] [1923] 2 Ch. 177.

[422] [1923] 2 Ch. 177 at 202.

is nothing in the judgments in *Broomfield v Williams*[423] to suggest that the statutory words should be confined in the way suggested by Sargant J.

3–132   There is a difference between the case where, for example, the common owner of Blackacre and Whiteacre exercises acts of ownership over Blackacre which are not attributable to his ownership of Whiteacre, as in *Long v Gowlett*,[424] and the case where, for example, such a common owner walks regularly across Blackacre to reach Whiteacre so that the way across Blackacre is enjoyed with Whiteacre.[425] In *Ward v Kirkland*[426] Ungoed-Thomas J. considered *Long v Gowlett*[427] and explained it as turning on the "distinction . . . between enjoyment exclusively for the purposes of the alleged dominant tenement or enjoyment of an advantage which might be attributable to the possession and ownership of the alleged servient tenement". Ungoed-Thomas J. rejected the view that a right to pass under section 62 must be continuous and apparent, but he did not accept that every de facto advantage would pass. He accepted as correct the objection of Sargant J. in *Long v Gowlett*[428] to the creation under section 62 of rights involving user which was both intermittent and non-apparent. In *Ward v Kirkland*[429] the right claimed was to enter the farmyard included in the alleged servient tenement to carry out repairs to the cottage on the alleged dominant tenement. The right claimed was apparent, because it was obvious that the only possible and practicable way of maintaining the wall was by using the farmyard to obtain access to it.

3–133   In *Payne v Inwood*[430] the Court of Appeal considered the effect of *Long v Gowlett, Broomfield v Williams, Wardall v Brocklehurst* and the dicta in the *Sovmots* case. Roch L.J., considering *Broomfield*, stated that a right to light is in a special category in that it is continuous (during daylight hours) and does not involve the dominant owner going upon the servient tenement but merely the servient owner abstaining from interfering with the access of light to the windows of the building on the dominant tenement; the light appertains to the house sold and at the time of the conveyance is enjoyed by the house being conveyed, independently of who is the owner and occupier of the house. He concluded that *Broomfield* was to be confined to cases dealing with such advantages as light to buildings and was an exception to the general rule. Section 62 does not apply unless there has been, before the severance of ownership, a de facto enjoyment of the right, however precarious, by the occupier of that part of the land "altogether apart from" the ownership or occupation of the other part.

---

[423] See fn.420.

[424] [1923] 2 Ch. 177. See Jackson, "Easements and General Words", (1966) 30 Conv. 340, 344, 345.

[425] See *Kay v Oxley* (1875) L.R. 10 Q.B. 360; *Peck and the School Board for London, Re* [1893] 2 Ch. 315.

[426] [1967] Ch. 194 at 228.

[427] [1923] 2 Ch. 177.

[428] [1923] 2 Ch. 177.

[429] [1967] Ch. 194.

[430] (1996) 74 P. & C.R. 42 at 48–51, a case in which there had not in fact been any enjoyment of the way claimed by the vendor; followed in *Robinson (Webster) Holdings Ltd v Agombar* [2002] 1 P. & C.R. 243.

More recently, section 62 has been applied in a case where there might have been, but was not, attention given to whether the section applied when there was no diversity of occupation. In *P&S Platt Ltd v Crouch*[431] the defendant transferred to the claimant land comprising a hotel. Prior to the transfer the hotel had been run on the basis that hotel guests would be able to use river moorings adjacent to the hotel and other facilities. The transfer did not expressly mention the use of the moorings and other facilities. The transfer did not exclude the operation of section 62. The principal argument addressed to the Court of Appeal in relation to section 62 was to the effect that the background circumstances showed that the parties did not intend that the transferee should be granted rights to use the moorings and the other facilities. This argument was rejected on the facts. That being so, the Court held that the rights in question did appertain to and were reputed to appertain to and were enjoyed with the hotel, being part of the hotel business and advertised as such and enjoyed by the hotel guests. The rights were said to be continuous and apparent so that it did not matter that prior to the sale of the hotel there was no prior diversity of occupation of the dominant and servient tenements.[432] None of the cases referred to above in relation to the suggested need for diversity of occupation are referred to in the judgments.

3–134

Permissive enjoyment

It is settled that general words in a conveyance to a sitting tenant will operate to grant to him, as an easement, any right or advantage which is exercised by him, as tenant, over other land of the grantor, and is capable of being granted as an easement, including "rights" exercised by permission and not of right.[433] In such cases the general words appear to operate automatically and independently of intention. The conversion, under general words, of permissive user into a legal right was first illustrated in *International Tea Stores Co v Hobbs*,[434] where Farwell J. held that the statutory general words in a conveyance to a tenant operated to grant, as an easement, a right of access to and from adjoining land retained by the vendor, which the tenant at the time of the conveyance was exercising by permission of the vendor. The access was in fact "enjoyed with" the property conveyed, and the statutory general words therefore operated. His Lordship (considering section 6(2) of the Conveyancing Act 1881) said[435]:

3–135

"The real truth is that you do not consider the question of title to use, but the question of fact of user; you have to inquire whether the way has in fact been used, not under what title it has been used, although you must of course take into consideration all the circumstances of the case."

---

[431] [2004] 1 P. & C.R. 242.
[432] [2004] 1 P. & C.R. 242, at [42].
[433] *Miller v T.G. Dobson & Co Ltd* (1971) 220 E.G. 1595; *Hair v Gillman* [2000] 3 E.G.L.R. 74.
[434] [1903] 2 Ch. 165.
[435] [1903] 2 Ch. 165 at 172.

3–136 So, too, in *Lewis v Meredith*[436] Neville J. said[437] with reference to an artificial watercourse which had long been enjoyed by the tenants of the plaintiff's predecessor in title:

> "Easement or right in the strict sense there could not be, for the common ownership precluded the acquisition of any right or easement by the occupiers, but International Tea Stores Co. v. Hobbs[438] shows that 'a right' permissive at the date of the grant may become a legal right upon the grant by force of the general words in section 6 of the Conveyancing Act 1881. From this point of view the circumstances under which the quasi right was enjoyed became immaterial so long as it was actually enjoyed and was of a nature which could be granted, that is to say, a right known to the law."

3–137 Both these cases were cited with approval by the Court of Appeal in *Wright v Macadam*,[439] where, at the time of the grant by the defendant to the plaintiffs of a tenancy for one year of a flat in the defendant's house, one of the plaintiffs was statutory tenant of the flat and used a shed in the garden, by permission of the defendant, for the purpose of storing coal. It was held by the Court of Appeal that, the tenancy agreement being a "conveyance" as defined[440] for the purposes of section 62, and the right to use the shed for storing coal for the purposes of the flat being a right or easement recognised by the law and capable of being granted expressly, and being a right de facto exercised at the time of the tenancy agreement, and the case not being one in which it could be said to have been in the contemplation of the parties that the enjoyment of the right (that is, *semble*, the existence of the shed) should be purely temporary, the general words imported into the tenancy agreement operated to grant, as part of the tenancy, the right to use the shed for the purpose of storing coal, together with the necessary means of access to it.

3–138 The previous paragraph was said in *Hair v Gillman*[441] to identify the distinction between a right that is temporary, in the sense that it is merely precarious so that it can be withdrawn at any time, and a right that is temporary in the sense that the parties know that it will only be capable of being enjoyed for a limited period because of the nature of the property over which it is to be enjoyed. The right to use the coal shed would have been "temporary" in the sense meant by Jenkins L.J. in *Wright v McAdam* if it had been known to both parties that the landlord intended within a limited period to demolish the shed. The fact that a permission could have been withdrawn at any time does not make it "temporary" in this sense and thus prevent it being a privilege or right enjoyed with land such as to attract the operation of section 62.

---

[436] [1913] 1 Ch. 571.
[437] [1913] 1 Ch. 571 at 579.
[438] [1903] 2 Ch. 165.
[439] [1949] 2 K.B. 744.
[440] By s.205(1)(ii) of the Law of Property Act 1925. See para.3–126, above.
[441] [2000] 3 E.G.L.R. 74 at 76F. *Wright v Macadam* and *Hair v Gillman* were considered in *P&S Platt Ltd v Crouch* [2004] 1 P. & C.R. 242 at [36]–[37].

In *Ward v Kirkland*[442] Ungoed-Thomas J. said that the plaintiff's claim to a   **3–139**
right to enter the defendant's farmyard to maintain the wall of the plaintiff's cottage would not be defeated by reason of permission to do so being given on each
occasion of user while the farmyard and the cottage were in common ownership;
hence the right was by the operation of section 62 transformed into an easement
on the cottage being conveyed to the plaintiff.

The principle applies equally where the right is exercised by a tenant or some   **3–140**
other person who is not the grantee under the conveyance. In such a case, if the
right is incident to the tenancy, the general words in the conveyance will, provided that the grantor has power to do so,[443] annex the right to the estate or interest granted as well, as in *Graham v Philcox*,[444] where the Court of Appeal applied
International Tea Stores Co v Hobbs,[445] *Lewis v Meredith*,[446] and *Wright v
Macadam*.[447] M, the freehold owner of a property comprising a large dwelling-
house with a garden and coach house, let the first floor of the coach house to B
for five years together with a right of way over the entrance drive to the property
and through the garden. B assigned his interest in the lease to D, who became a
statutory tenant. Later M let the ground floor of the coach house to W, with a similar right of way but over the other side of the garden. The dwelling-house was
converted into two semi-detached houses, 6A and 6B, the former being adjacent
to the right of way granted to B. M having died, his executors conveyed to W the
land on which the coach house stood. M's executors then conveyed 6A to the
defendants subject to the right of the tenant of the first floor of the coach house
to use the way originally granted to B. Finally, W's successors in title conveyed
the coach house to the plaintiffs, who, after D had given up his statutory tenancy
of the first floor, occupied the whole coach house as one residence. The defendants refused to allow the plaintiffs to continue to use the right of way which had
been enjoyed by B and D.

The Court of Appeal held that the duration of that easement was not co-terminous   **3–141**
with the lease to B or the statutory tenancy, and that by virtue of section 62(2) the
conveyance of the coach house to W operated to carry also the right of way then
enjoyed with the first floor. Moreover, the Court of Appeal held, distinguishing
Harris v Flower,[448] that, as there was no evidence that the plaintiffs' actual or anticipated use of the way would be excessive, the alteration of the dominant tenement
by the enlargement of the dwelling comprising the first floor flat to take in the
ground floor as well did not affect the existence of the right of way.

---

[442] [1967] Ch. 194 at 230; see para.2–09, above. In fact Ungoed-Thomas J. held that the user had been
enjoyed by the separate occupier of the cottage without his having obtained his neighbour's
permission.
[443] *M.R.A. Engineering Ltd v Trimster Company Ltd* (1987) 56 P. & C.R. 1, where the grantor had previously conveyed away the land over which a right of way had been enjoyed by a tenant without
reserving any right over it; and see para.3–152, below.
[444] [1984] Q.B. 747; and see *Barnes v Loach* (1879) 4 Q.B.D. 494; *White v Williams* [1922] 1 K.B. 727.
[445] [1903] 1 Ch. 165.
[446] [1913] 1 Ch. 571.
[447] [1949] 2 K.B. 744.
[448] (1904) 91 L.T. 816. See para.12–105, below.

Privileges and advantages

3–142   It seems that general words will carry a privilege or advantage not amounting to an easement. In *Goldberg v Edwards*[449] the first defendant, in pursuance of an oral agreement made in January, granted to the plaintiffs, in July 1947, a lease of the annexe to a house for two years from January 1947. The plaintiffs had taken possession in January, and at the date of the lease they were using the house, by permission of the defendant landlord, as a means of access to the annexe, but this permission was personal to them, in the sense that it did not extend to servants and the like, or (apparently) assignees.

The Court of Appeal, following *Wright v Macadam*,[450] held that the rights so enjoyed at the date of the lease passed under the statutory general words, and, further, that the relevant date for this purpose, that is "the time of the conveyance", was the date (July) when the lease was granted, and not the date (in January) from which the term granted was calculated. Lord Evershed M.R. said that he guarded himself from saying that rights which were purely personal, in the strict sense of that word, would necessarily in every case be covered by section 62, and he based himself on the view that the right there given, though limited to the lessees, was given to them *qua* lessees, and as such it was covered by the principle of *Wright v Macadam*,[451] and by section 62. If it is right to suppose that the privilege was not to be exercisable by assignees, it is difficult to see how it could have been annexed to the tenancy as an easement, and questionable whether it would bind an assign of the reversion. Nevertheless the right, whatever it was, was held to pass under the general words.

3–143   In *Crow v Wood*[452] the Court of Appeal held that a right to have one's neighbour keep up fences, though not an easement strictly so called, because it involved the servient owner in the expenditure of money, was a right which was capable of being granted by law, because it was in the nature of an easement. Accordingly, it was of such a nature that it could pass under section 62 when, as in that case, it was "enjoyed with" the dominant tenement.

3–144   In *Regis Property Co Ltd v Redman*,[453] on the other hand, the Court of Appeal held that an obligation to supply constant hot water or central heating, which involved the performance of services and was essentially a matter of personal contract, was not a right, easement or privilege capable of being granted by lease or conveyance so as to pass under section 62.

3–145   In *Green v Ashco Horticulturist Ltd*[454] permission was given to the plaintiff to use a way intermittently, subject to the exigencies of the owner's business and the requirements of the owner's tenants, and Cross J. held that the right over the way which the plaintiff claimed could not have been the subject of a legal grant;

---

[449] [1950] Ch. 247; para.3–59, above.
[450] [1949] 2 K.B. 744.
[451] [1949] 2 K.B. 744.
[452] [1971] 1 Q.B. 77; see paras 1–78–1–85, above.
[453] [1956] 2 Q.B. 612.
[454] [1966] 1 W.L.R. 889; see para.1–36, above.

accordingly, section 62 could not operate. In *White v Taylor (No. 2)*[455] Buckley J. said that to prove that grazing rights for sheep were at the time of the conveyance "enjoyed with" the land sold, it had to be shown that a particular number of sheep was being depastured on the land retained.

In *Burrows v Lang*[456] Farwell J. held that a right to take from a mill pond such **3–146** water as its owner, being competent to cut off the supply, might allow to be there was a right unknown to the law, incapable of passing under general words. So, too, in *Phipps v Pears*[457] the Court of Appeal held that there was no such easement known to the law as an easement to be protected from the weather.

A facility of parking cars on waste land, enjoyed by the public at large, includ- **3–147** ing a neighbouring tenant of the owner of the land, without protest by the owner, was held not to pass under the statutory general words in a conveyance to the tenant of the reversion to his property. The user, being open to anyone, in the sense that the owner had never stopped anyone from trespassing by parking his car, was considered not to be enjoyed with the tenant's particular property. The same result was reached on the alternative ground that, before the conveyance, the owner had told the tenant that such user would no longer be allowed.[458] But a right to park cars can exist as an easement[459] and can be created under section 62.[460]

Reputed rights

Rights which are reputed to appertain to property conveyed will pass under the **3–148** statutory general words.[461] The necessary degree of "reputation", and the persons among whom it must be had, do not seem to have been defined. In *Clark v Barnes*[462] a right of way over a barely visible track had been annexed to plot A, but became extinguished (subject to the rights of a tenant of plot A) on the plaintiff, the owner of the site, acquiring also plot A. At the time of the conveyance of plot A to the defendant the track was still used by the tenant, and it was held, on the evidence, to pass[463] as a right "reputed to be enjoyed with" plot A under the conveyance; but the words quoted do not appear in section 62,[464] and it seems more probable[465] that the right was considered to be "[occupied or] enjoyed with" the plot.

Similarly in *Peck and the School Board for London, Re*[466] a way over waste **3–149** land, which "had been", and perhaps was being, used for convenience by tenants

---

[455] [1969] 1 Ch. 160 at 185, 186; see para.3–29, above.
[456] [1901] 2 Ch. 502.
[457] [1965] 1 Q.B. 76; see para.1–45, above.
[458] *Le Strange v Pettefar* (1939) 161 L.T. 300.
[459] See para.1–67, above and paras 9–96 to 9–110, below.
[460] *Sweet & Maxwell v Michael-Michael (Advertising) Ltd* [1965] C.L.Y. 2192; *Newman v Jones*, unreported, March 22, 1982, Megarry J.; *Handel v St Stephens Close Ltd* [1994] 1 E.G.L.R. 70; *Hair v Gillman* (2000) 80 P. & C.R. 108.
[461] See subss.(1) and (2) of s.62, para.3–126, above.
[462] [1929] 2 Ch. 368.
[463] According to the report in [1929] 2 Ch. 380.
[464] See para.3–126, above.
[465] See the argument at [1929] 2 Ch. 378.
[466] [1893] 2 Ch. 315.

of property agreed to be sold, would have passed under the conveyance, if the statutory general words had been left to operate, as a right either "reputed to appertain to" or "enjoyed with" the property. It may be that the farm track in *Walmsley and Shaw's Contract, Re*[467] which had formerly been used permissively by occupiers of the property agreed to be sold, would have passed under the conveyance as a reputed right, had the wording of the conveyance not excluded it.

3–150   In *White v Taylor (No. 2)*[468] Buckley J. held that the enjoyment of grazing facilities by former copyholders could not establish a reputation of rights appurtenant to their lands, and thus the grazing facilities could not be said to be "appertaining or reputed to appertain to the land or any part thereof" within section 6 of the Act of 1881. In *Green v Ashco Horticulturist Ltd*,[469] Cross J. said that, in considering whether the user was such that section 62 would operate, one ought to look at a reasonable period of time before the grant in question in order to see whether there was anything over that period which could be called a pattern of regular user in any particular way or ways.

3–151   This approach was applied by the Court of Appeal in *Pretoria Warehousing Co Ltd v Shelton*[470] where a shopping centre had been laid out with all the shops having access to a central concourse but, shortly before the grant of two subsequent leases, the landlords had formed two new units in part of the area over which the shop tenants had previously enjoyed rights. It was held that free use of the central concourse had been reputed to appertain to all the shop units and that that reputation had not been lost by the date of grant of the later leases. As Megarry J. said in *Costagliola v English*,[471] reputations do not die in a day. In that case at the date of the relevant conveyance, much of the use of a right of way had ceased 11 months before, but it had gone on long enough before that to become established as a normal means of access to the dominant tenement and it was held that an established means of access which ceases to be actively enjoyed to any great extent for less than a year does not thereby cease to be a quasi-easement. But section 62 does not "resurrect mere memories of past rights".[472]

Competent grantor

3–152   Section 62 will not, of course, operate so as to confer on the transferee any right which the transferor has no power to grant.[473] In *M.R.A. Engineering Limited v Trimster Company Limited*[474] the plaintiffs had sold a plot of land to the defendants and at the same time granted to them an option to purchase certain land at the rear of the plot conveyed, which land was let to a tenant with the benefit of a right of way across the plot conveyed. When, subsequently, the defendants exercised the

---

[467] [1917] 1 Ch. 93; see para.3–65, above.
[468] [1969] 1 Ch. 160, 185; see para.3–29, above.
[469] [1966] 1 W.L.R. 889 at 898; see para.1–36, above.
[470] [1993] E.G.C.S. 120; [1993] N.P.C. 98.
[471] (1969) 210 E.G. 1425.
[472] *Penn v Wilkins* (1974) 236 E.G. 203 (Megarry V.-C.).
[473] See paras 3–05–3–10, above, and s.62(5).
[474] (1987) 56 P. & C.R. 1.

option (the tenancy having been surrendered), the question arose whether the option land was to be valued on the basis that it enjoyed a right of way over the land previously sold off. No such right had been reserved at the time of the sale. The plaintiffs argued that a conveyance of the option land would carry with it the right of way which had been enjoyed by the tenant by reason of section 62 but it was held that the section can only apply where the owner of the land over which the right of way is impliedly granted has a sufficient estate to support making such a grant.[475] Nourse L.J. said[476]:

> "It is essential to the application of section 62 to quasi-easements, as it was to the application of the rule in Wheeldon v Burrows before it, that the conveyancing party should be the owner of the quasi-servient tenement at the time that he conveys away the quasi-dominant tenement. It is his ability to make the right the subject of an express grant which, by the application of the doctrine of non-derogation from grant, prevents him from denying that it has passed under an implied grant. If he does not have that ability, no implication is to be made against him."

In *St Clement's, Leigh-on-Sea, Re*[477] it was held that because the incumbent of a churchyard could not, without appropriate authority, expressly grant an easement over the churchyard, no such rights would pass by reason of section 62 as a result of a conveyance made without that authority. **3–153**

Contrary intention

Section 62 applies only if and as far as a contrary intention is not expressed in the conveyance, and it has effect subject to the terms of the conveyance and to the provisions therein contained.[478] The few cases on the subject show that, in order to negative the creation, under the statutory general words, of an easement which, apart from the section, would arise by implication, clear words are required. In *Gregg v Richards*[479] Sargant L.J. said: **3–154**

> "It is to be noticed that it is by way of express grant that [the section] operates and not by way of implied grant, and that it is for the grantor who seeks to show that that express grant is limited to prove affirmatively that there is some limitation of that express grant."

The use of the words "with the appurtenances" is not in itself an indication of a contrary intention.[480]

---

[475] (1987) 56 P. & C.R. 1, at 5, per Dillon L.J.
[476] (1987) 56 P. & C.R. 1, at 7.
[477] [1988] 1 W.L.R. 720.
[478] Subs.(4), para.3–126, above.
[479] [1926] Ch. 521 at 535; considered in *Handel v St Stephens Close Ltd* [1994] 1 E.G.L.R. 70; applied in *Stafford v Pearson-Smith* (1962) 182 E.G. 539.
[480] *Hansford v Jago* [1921] 1 Ch. 322.

3–155   In *Gregg v Richards*[481] the plaintiff had purchased a house and land. The conveyance contained an express grant to the plaintiff of the right to use a way described as coloured green on the plan indorsed on the deed. The part coloured green was a foot-way four feet wide, part of a wider way running along the farther side and back of the adjoining premises to the back premises of the plaintiff's house. At the time of the conveyance a right of access for vehicles to the plaintiff's back premises over the whole way was enjoyed with her house. The *habendum* in the conveyance was "to hold the same with the benefit of all such easements and privileges in the nature of easements as are now subsisting in respect of the property hereby conveyed". The plaintiff claimed that the right to use the whole width of the way for the purpose of access of vehicles to her back premises passed to her under the statutory general words. It was held by the Court of Appeal, reversing the decision of Russell J., that the maxim *expressio unius exclusio alterius* did not apply, and that no contrary intention, within subsection (4) of section 62, had been expressed. Warrington L.J. attached importance to the wording of the *habendum*, but Lord Pollock M.R. and Sargant L.J. did not base their judgments on this narrow ground, and Sargant L.J. expressed the opinion[482] that even if there had been a more limited grant of way and nothing else, that would not of itself have been sufficient to exclude the larger right of way which was given by the Act.[483]

3–156   Similarly, in *Pretoria Warehousing Co Ltd v Shelton*[484] the Court of Appeal held that an express right of uncertain meaning granted by a lease did not operate to exclude the general right conferred by section 62.

In *Snell and Prideaux Ltd v Dutton Mirrors Ltd*[485] Hoffmann L.J. pointed out that it is in no way inconsistent for there to be a grant of a limited right so as to restrict the ambit of the covenant for title and at the same time an implied grant under section 62 or the common law of a wider right in so far as the grantor is able to grant it.

3–157   It has been seen[486] that easements may arise by implication, apart from the general words imported by the section. If the section is in some respect negatived by words in the conveyance, the question whether the words prevent the easement so negatived from arising by implication must, it is thought, depend on the circumstances. Words in a conveyance to the effect that the section is not to apply, or that a particular easement is not included, or reserving to the grantor the right to build on adjoining land as he pleases[487] would, no doubt, prevent any easement, or the easement excluded, from arising at all; but that result does not necessarily follow. In *Broomfield v Williams*[488] Lindley L.J., after deciding that the description in a conveyance of adjoining land as "building land" did not show

---

[481] [1926] Ch. 521.
[482] [1926] Ch. 535.
[483] And see *Hapgood v J.H. Martin & Son Ltd* (1934) 152 L.T. 72, where Horridge J. treated *Gregg v Richards* as having been decided on the broader ground.
[484] [1993] E.G.C.S. 120; [1993] N.P.C. 98.
[485] [1995] 1 E.G.L.R. 259 at 264M.
[486] See paras 3–17 *et seq.*, above.
[487] See, e.g. Key and Elphinstone's *Conveyancing Precedents* (15th ed.), Vol. 1, p. 1033 and the cases collected at para.4–28, below.
[488] [1897] 1 Ch. 606 at 610; see para.3–81, above.

an intention to exclude the section so far as it related to light, added that, even if it did, he would still hold that the grantee had a prima facie unrestricted right to light. In *Hansford v Jago*[489] Russell J., after deciding that section 62 was not excluded by the use of the word "appurtenances" in the conveyance, proceeded to hold that, if he were wrong in that, a right of way still passed, on the sale, by implication. In *Green v Ashco Horticulturist Ltd*,[490] Cross J. held that a clause in a lease which reserved to the lessor unlimited power to deal with the land and premises adjoining that demised, including power to build without regard to the diminution of light or air enjoyed by the lessee which might result, was not applicable to rights of way. In *Hillman v Rogers*,[491] a fencing covenant negatived the implication of a right of way on the basis of the principles in *Wheeldon v Burrows* and was a sufficient contrary intention for the purposes of section 62(4) but would not have been a sufficient contrary intention to defeat the implication of a way of necessity.

It is not unusual to find an express provision in a conveyance which states that   **3–158**
no easements other than those expressly granted are to be "implied". Such a provision would, no doubt, prevent the implication of an easement but would it evince a contrary intention to the operation of section 62? Strictly, the operation of section 62 does not involve the "implication" of an easement. The true analysis as shown by *Gregg v Richards*[492] is that the easement is created by reason of the statute applying to the circumstances of the case. On this analysis, an express term that no easements are to be "implied" would not suffice to prevent the operation of section 62. But yet, it is not unusual to describe the operation of section 62, somewhat loosely perhaps, as resulting in the grant of an easement being implied, presumably implied by statute. If it is desired to exclude the operation of section 62, the safer course is to state in terms that section 62 is not to apply to the conveyance in question rather than to rely on the less clear statement that no easements are to be "implied".

It has been said in one textbook that even in a case where there is no contrary   **3–159**
intention expressed in the conveyance:

> " . . . the section is also subject to any contrary intention which might be implied from circumstances existing at the time of the grant."[493]

The textbook then goes on to illustrate this proposition by reference to the cases which show that section 62 does not apply to a case where the right which is claimed under section 62 is based upon previous enjoyment of something which was temporary in the sense that it was only capable of being enjoyed for a limited period because of the nature of the property over which it was enjoyed. Those cases have been considered in paras 3–135 to 3–141, above. The passage in the

---

[489] [1921] 1 Ch. 322; see para.3–63, above.
[490] [1966] 1 W.L.R. 889, see para.1–36, above.
[491] [1997] EWCA Civ 3069.
[492] [1926] Ch. 521.
[493] Megarry & Wade, *Law of Real Property*, 6th ed., para.18–115.

textbook has been cited with apparent approval by the Court of Appeal in *P&S Platt Ltd v Crouch*[494] but it would seem that this was on the basis that certain rights which are temporary in this sense do not come within section 62. In *C.N.T. v JJ Gallagher Ltd*[495] it was said, relying on the word "expressed" in section 62(4), that section 62 applied unless there was an express rebuttal of its application. The passage in the textbook should not be read as meaning that the operation of section 62 can be ousted by an alleged contrary intention to be derived from the background circumstances of the case.

Rectification

3–160   In many cases the creation of an easement by the statutory general words is contrary to the intention of the grantor. If such creation is the result of a mistake common to both parties, the conveyance can be rectified on ordinary principles[496]; but the question is what amounts, for this purpose, to a mutual mistake. Clearly, if the court is satisfied that both parties positively did not intend the conveyance to include the easement, and that the omission to modify or exclude the statutory general words was, in this sense, due to their mutual mistake, a case for rectification arises. The purchaser in such a case may, however, have had no definite ideas about the included easement, or he may not have been aware of its potential existence, and it is not entirely clear whether proof of mere lack of intention to include, as distinct from a positive intention not to include, is sufficient.[497]

3–161   Again, the contract on its proper construction may not have included the right in fact created by the general words. In such a case it would seem reasonable to suppose that the conveyance ought to be rectified as a matter of course, but the rectification would be based, not on actual intention, but on imputed intention. In *Clark v Barnes*[498] where the conveyance to the defendant was rectified, Luxmoore J. said:

> " . . .the contract itself does not include any provision which will entitle the defendant to claim to have such a right of way as he claims, granted to him. The question then is, is the plaintiff entitled to have words inserted in the deed of conveyance, to limit the operation of the Law of Property Act 1925, s.62; and to prevent the grant of such a right of way by implication? It is plain that if this point had been raised before the conveyance had been executed and the court had been asked to determine what the form of the conveyance would be, such a limitation would undoubtedly have been inserted, and on this ground the plaintiff is entitled to have the conveyance rectified";

---

[494] [2004] 1 P. & C.R. 242 at [37].
[495] [2003] 2 P. & C.R. 24 at [60].
[496] Reference should be made to the standard works dealing with the equity of rectification for the general principles applicable.
[497] The language of Morton J. in *Wallington v Townsend* [1939] 2 All E.R. 235 at 237, may be thought to imply that it is. In that case a strip of land was in dispute.
[498] [1929] 2 Ch. 368 at 380, 381. *Cf. Stait v Fenner* [1912] 2 Ch. 504.

but the learned judge went on to find as a fact that the right of way to which the action related had been the subject of a conversation between the parties, and that it was understood and agreed between them that there should be no such right.

In *Slack v Hancock*[499] where the plaintiff, owner of land over which the occu-   **3–162**
pier of adjoining land exercised certain rights, agreed to sell the first land to the defendant–who did not know of these rights–subject to all rights exercised over it by occupiers of the adjoining land, but omitted to reserve any rights in the conveyance, a claim to have the conveyance rectified on the ground of mutual mistake was not established.

The equity of a party to a grant to have this rectified is not enforceable against   **3–163**
a purchaser for value from the other party without notice.[500]

5.—LAW REFORM

In March 2008, the Law Commission published a Consultation Paper entitled   **3–164**
"Easements, Covenants and Profits a Prendre".[501] The Consultation Paper invites the views of consultees as to the Law Commission's list of provisional proposals and specific consultation questions. Of relevance to this chapter are the following provisional proposals or specific questions:

(1) The Law Commission provisionally proposes that an easement which is expressly reserved in the terms of a conveyance should not be interpreted in cases of ambiguity in favour of the person making the reservation.

(2) It invites the views of consultees as to whether it should be possible for parties to create short-form easements by reference to a prescribed form of words. Where the prescribed form of words is used, a fuller description of the substance of the easement would be implied into the instrument creating the right.

(3) It invites the views of consultees as to which easements should be so dealt with and the extent to which parties should be free to vary the terms of short-form easements.

(4) It provisionally proposes that in determining whether an easement should be implied, it should not be material whether the easement would take effect by grant or by reservation. In either case, the person alleging that there is an easement should be required to establish it.

(5) It provisionally proposes that section 62 of the Law of Property Act 1925 should no longer operate to transform precarious benefits, enjoyed

---

[499] (1912) 107 L.T. 14.

[500] *Smith v Jones* [1954] 1 W.L.R. 1089; unless the effect of the rectification accords with what the purchaser believed he was acquiring: *Newman v Jones*, unreported, March 22, 1982, Megarry J.; and, for the position in relation to rectification of a registered title, consider *Blacklocks v J.B. Developments Ltd* [1982] Ch. 183 and *Holaw (470) Ltd v Stockton Estates* (2001) 81 P. & C.R. 29 (right to rectify capable of being an overriding interest).

[501] Law Com. Consultation Paper No. 186.

with the owner's licence or consent, into legal easements on a conveyance of the dominant estate.

(6) It invites the views of consultees as to whether it should be provided that the doctrine of non-derogation from grant should not give rise to the implied acquisition of an easement.

(7) It invites consultees' views on the following:

   (a) Whether they consider that the current rules whereby easements may be acquired by implied grant or reservation are in need of reform.

   (b) Whether they consider that it would be appropriate to replace the current rules (i) with an approach based upon ascertaining the actual intentions of the parties; or (ii) with an approach based upon a set of presumptions which would arise from the circumstances.

   (c) Whether they consider that it would be appropriate to replace the current rules with a single rule based on what is necessary for the reasonable use of the land.

(8) It invites consultees' views as to whether it would be desirable to put the rules of implication into statutory form.

CHAPTER 4

ESTABLISHMENT OF EASEMENTS
BY PRESCRIPTION

1.—INTRODUCTION

Definition of prescription

Prescription may be defined as: a title acquired by use or enjoyment had during **4–01**
the time and in the manner fixed by law. "Prescriptio est titulus ex usu et tempore
substantiam capiens ab authoritate legis."[1]

Modes of acquiring title

The mode of acquiring title to an easement by prescription requires a considera- **4–02**
tion of:

    (1) The length of time during which the enjoyment must continue, whether
        (i) for the purpose of prescription at common law, or (ii) under the

---

[1] Co. Litt. 133b.

doctrine of lost grant, or (iii) by reference to the Prescription Act 1832.[2]

(2) The persons against and by whom the enjoyment must be had.

(3) The qualities of that enjoyment.

Prescription and human rights

4–03   It is suggested that the existence of a law of prescription is not inconsistent with the property rights of the servient owner, over whose land a right is acquired by prescription. The point has not arisen directly for decision but the above conclusion is supported by the decision of the House of Lords in *Oxfordshire CC v Oxford CC*.[3] That case concerned a town or village green where the claim was that rights to use the green for recreation had been acquired by 20 years' user for the purposes of the Commons Registration Act 1965. At the time of the decision, the European Court of Human Rights had held that English law as to the acquisition of title by adverse possession infringed a landowner's Convention rights, in particular his right under Article 1 of the First Protocol not to be deprived of his possessions, at any rate in a case where the landowner's title was registered under the Land Registration Act 1925.[4] Lord Hoffmann distinguished this decision on two grounds.[5] The first was that acquisition of title extinguished the landowner's rights whereas acquisition of a right to use the land as a town or village green did not. That reasoning would also apply to the acquisition of an easement by prescription. His second ground was that the 1965 Act operated to preserve open spaces in the public interest rather than for the benefit of one private individual. That reasoning would not apply to the acquisition of an easement. However, Lord Scott seemed to regard it as being in the public interest to "prevent the disturbance of long-established *de facto* enjoyment"[6] and that reasoning could apply to acquisition of an easement by prescription. Further, since that decision the Grand Chamber of the European Court of Human Rights has reversed the earlier decision as to acquisition of title by adverse possession.[7]

Exclusion of prescription by force of statute

4–04   It has been expressly enacted that no right of way as against the relevant railway authority can be acquired by prescription over any road, footpath, thoroughfare or place, which is the property of that authority and which forms an access or

---

[2] In *Tehidy Minerals Ltd v Norman* [1971] 2 Q.B. 528 at 543, the Court of Appeal expressed the view that the coexistence of three separate methods of prescribing is anomalous and undesirable, for it results in much unnecessary complication and confusion.

[3] [2006] 2 A.C. 674.

[4] *Pye (Oxford) Ltd v United Kingdom* [2005] 3 E.G.L.R. 1; the decision was by a chamber of the former Fourth Section of the Court.

[5] [2006] 2 A.C. 674 at [58]–[59].

[6] [2006] 2 A.C. 674 at [86].

[7] [2007] ECHR 44302/02.

approach to any station, goods yard, wharf, garage or depot or any dock or harbour premises of that authority.[8]

2.—THE LENGTH OF TIME DURING WHICH THE ENJOYMENT MUST CONTINUE

(1) *Prescription at common law*

Time of legal memory

It has been said that any legal system must have rules of prescription which prevent   **4–05**
the disturbance of long-established de facto enjoyment.[9] However, English law had two different rules; one was a rule of limitation which related to the time at which a possessory claim was barred by the lapse of time; the other is what English law calls prescription where one presumes an initial grant conferring a legal origin for the subsequent user. In order to understand the common law of prescription it is necessary to describe briefly the history of English law as to limitation. The matter was described in *R. v Oxfordshire County Council Ex p. Sunningwell P.C.* as follows[10]:

> "[The common law] did not treat long enjoyment as being a method of acquiring title. Instead, it approached the question from the other end by treating the lapse of time as either barring the remedy of the former owner or giving rise to a presumption that he had done some act which conferred a lawful title upon the person in de facto possession or enjoyment. Thus the medieval real actions for the recovery of seisen were subject to limitation by reference to various past events. In the time of Bracton the writ of right was limited by reference to the accession of Henry I (1100). The Statute of Merton 1235 . . . brought this date up to the accession of Henry II (1154) and the Statute of Westminster 1275 . . . extended it to the accession of Richard I in 1189. The judges used this date by analogy to fix the period of prescription for immemorial custom and the enjoyment of incorporeal

---

[8] British Transport Commission Act 1949, s.57. By Railways Act (Consequential Modifications) (No. 2) Order 1999 (SI 1999/1998) the relevant authority is any successor of the British Railways Board.

[9] *R. v Oxfordshire C.C. Ex p. Sunningwell P.C.* [2000] 1 A.C. 335 per Lord Hoffmann at 349D. In its 14th report, *The Acquisition of Easements and Profits by Prescription*, Cmnd. 3100 (1966), the Law Reform Committee recommended that it should cease to be possible to acquire easements and profits by prescription. In the alternative, it proposed a new system for the acquisition of easements by prescription which would have eliminated many of the unsatisfactory features of the present law. The recommendations were not implemented. In its consultative document on Land Registration, (1998) Law Com. No. 254, the Law Commission proposed that it should cease to be possible to acquire easements or profits by prescription at common law or by presumed lost grant; the only method of prescription should be in accordance with the Prescription Act 1832. However, in its later report, (2001) Law Com. No. 271, the Law Commission made no recommendation in relation to prescription. The reasons for this were given at *ibid.*, paras 1.19, 5.37 and 5.38. They included the fact that the Law Commission was undertaking a comprehensive review of easements and land obligations, which review would include the subject of prescription.

[10] *R. v Oxfordshire C.C. Ex p. Sunningwell P.C.* [2000] 1 A.C. 335 per Lord Hoffmann at 349G–350B.

hereditaments such as rights of way and other easements. In such cases, however, the period was being used for a different purpose. It was not to bar the remedy but to presume that enjoyment was pursuant to a right having a lawful origin. In the case of easements, this meant a presumption that there had been a grant before 1189 by the freehold owner."

By the Limitation of Prescription Act 1540[11] it was, however, provided that there should be a progressive period of limitation of 60 years for a writ of right and of 50 years for a possessory action; and by the Limitation Act 1623 the limitation period for the recovery of land was diminished to 20 years. It would have been logical if in the case of incorporeal rights the analogy to writs of right which existed until 1540 had been maintained, and the length of enjoyment for which a prescriptive right might be inferred had been reduced to 20 years; but the analogy was abandoned and in the case of easements and *profits à prendre* 1189 has remained for prescription at common law the extent of legal memory.[12]

Presumption from long enjoyment

4–06   The extreme difficulty of giving proof of enjoyment for so long a period was less-ened by its being held that evidence of enjoyment for so long as anyone could remember raised a presumption that such enjoyment had existed for the period of legal memory.[13] In *Angus v Dalton*[14] Lush J. said: "Theoretically an ancient house at this period was a house which had existed from the time of Richard I. Practically, it was a house which had been erected before the time of living mem-ory, and the origin of which could not be proved." The evidence in such a case need not cover any particular continuous period.[15]

Where, on the other hand, the actual origin of the enjoyment was shown to have been of more recent date than the time of legal memory, the right was held to be defeated. Thus, in *Bury v Pope*,[16]

---

[11] Despite its name the Act was concerned only with limitation, not prescription in the sense which that word has today.

[12] The history of the rule was considered by Cockburn C.J. in *Bryant v Foot* (1867) L.R. 2 Q.B. 161 at 179–182. See also Blackstone's *Commentaries* (4th ed., adapted by Robert Malcolm Kerr, 1876), Bk.II, Ch.17; Megarry and Wade's *The Law of Real Property* (6th ed., 2000), pp. 1124, 1125.

[13] *Jenkins v Harvey* (1835) 1 Cr. M. & R. 877 at 894.

[14] (1877) 3 Q.B.D. 85 at 89. In *Aynsley v Glover* (1875) 10 Ch. App. 283, where the court presumed a pre-1189 grant of light to cottages (date of building not proved) on evidence of enjoyment for so long as living memory went, and *R.C.P. Holdings Ltd v Rogers* [1953] 1 All E.R. 1029 (right of way), a claim under the Prescription Act 1832 would have failed, in the former case, because of unity of possession during the statutory period, and in the latter case, because no user could have been proved in the years immediately before the commencement of the action. "When the existence of a way is spoken to over a period extending as far back as living memory goes, and there is noth-ing to show that there must have been a time when it did not exist, a case of prescription at com-mon law is made out" (per Harman J. [1953] 1 All E.R. 1029 at 1031). See, also, *R. v Oxfordshire C.C. Ex p. Sunningwell P.C.* [2000] 1 A.C. 335 at 350B–D.

[15] *R.P.C. Holdings Ltd v Rogers* [1953] 1 All E.R. 1029 at 1031, 1032.

[16] (1586) Cro.Eliz. 118. And see *Norfolk (Duke) v Arbuthnot* (1880) 5 C.P.D. 390 at 392, 393; *Wheaton v Maple & Co* [1893] 3 Ch. 48 at 62, 67, 69; *Bowring Services Ltd v Scottish Widows Fund and Life Assurance Society* [1995] 1 E.G.L.R. 158 at 160.

"It was agreed by all the justices, that if two men be owners of two parcels of land adjoining, and one of them doth build a house upon his land, and makes windows and lights looking into the other's lands, and this house and the lights have continued by the space of thirty or forty years, yet the other may upon his own land and soil lawfully erect an house or other thing against the said lights and windows, and the other can have no action; for it was his folly to build his house so near to the other's land: and it was adjudged accordingly."

Effect of unity of possession

Unity of possession without unity of ownership may not prevent the establish-   **4–07**
ment of a claim to prescription at common law. "If a man have common by prescription, unity of possession of as high and perdurable estate is an interruption
of the right."[17] It is in the last-mentioned sense that "unity of possession" is used
by Lord Mansfield in *Morris v Edgington*,[18] where he speaks of a right of way or
common extinguished by "unity of possession", that is, unity of ownership. The
dictum of Martin B. in *Winship v Hudspeth*,[19] that a claim by immemorial prescription at the common law would be defeated by proof of unity of possession
at any time, must not be taken as applying to mere unity of possession without
unity of ownership, which did not exist in that case.

(2) *Lost grant*

Presumption of modern lost grant

Although the courts refused in form to shorten the time of legal memory by   **4–08**
analogy to the later Statutes of Limitation, they obviated the inconvenience which
must have arisen from allowing long enjoyment to be defeated by showing that it
had not had a uniform existence during the whole period required by introducing
a new kind of title by presumption of a grant made and lost in modern times.[20]
On this ground, although it appeared that a right of way which existed formerly had been extinguished by unity of possession,[21] or even by an Act of
Parliament,[22] it was held that a new title might be obtained by an enjoyment for

---

[17] Co. Litt. 114b.

[18] (1810) 3 Taunt. 24 at 30.

[19] (1854) 10 Exch. 5 at 8.

[20] The earliest reported decision to this effect is that of *Lewis v Price* in 1761 (2 Wms. Saund. (1871 ed.) p. 504) per Lord Blackburn in *Dalton v Angus* (1881) 6 App. Cas. 812.

[21] *Keymer v Summers*, cited in *Read v Brookman* (1789) 3 T.R. 151, 157.

[22] *Campbell v Wilson* (1803) 3 East 294; see also *Hull v Homer* (1774) 1 Cowp. 102; *Eldridge v Knott* (1774), *ibid.* at 214; *Holcroft v Heel* (1799) 1 Bos. & P. 400; *Dartmouth v Roberts* (1812) 16 East 334; *Doe d. Fenwick v Reed* (1821) 5 B. & Ald. 232; *Livett v Wilson* (1825) 3 Bing. 115; *Codling v Johnson* (1829) 9 B. & C. 933. As to the rule that a man cannot prescribe against a public Act of Parliament, see para.4–123, below.

20 years. In a later case, where windows were shown to have existed for 20 years, proof that they did not exist 22 years before the obstruction was insufficient to defeat an action.[23]

This was in reality prescription shortened by analogy to the period of limitation fixed by the Limitation Act 1623, and introduced into the law under a new name; for "the law allows prescription only in supply of the loss of a grant, and therefore every prescription presupposes a grant to have existed".[24] The expedient "is ancillary to the doctrine of prescription at common law, and applicable in cases where something prevents the operation of the common law prescription from time immemorial, and is therefore only applicable when the right claimed is such as, if immemorial, might have been the subject of prescription".[25]

4–09   The gist of the principle upon which a modern lost grant is presumed is that the state of affairs is otherwise unexplained. "When the court finds an open and uninterrupted enjoyment of property for a long period unexplained, omnia praesumuntur rite esse acta, and the court will, if reasonably possible, find a lawful origin for the right in question."[26]

In *Tehidy Minerals Ltd v Norman*[27] the Court of Appeal, observing that "in the case of an easement it has long been recognised as the law that twenty years' enjoyment is or may be sufficient to give rise to a presumption of a lost grant", proceeded on that basis in considering a claim on the part of the defendants that they had acquired rights of common of grazing. The defendants could not show that they had enjoyed the rights claimed for more than 30 years before action brought, and so could not make out a case under section 1 of the Prescription Act 1832,[28] but some were on the facts able to show prescription at common law and under the doctrine of lost grant.

Objections to doctrine of lost grant

4–10   The introduction of this doctrine was attended with considerable opposition, and it was contended[29] that to sustain a claim founded upon such a lost grant the jury must actually believe in its existence, or, at all events, they must find it as a fact, though they did not believe it. Doubts and difficulties arose from the vague and uncertain language frequently made use of by judges in leaving questions to the jury—enjoyment being sometimes treated as affording a conclusive presumption, whilst at others such user was only considered to be "cogent evidence" of

---

[23] *Penwarden v Ching* (1829) Moo. & Mal. 400. In *Phillips v Halliday* [1891] A.C. 228 a faculty for a pew was presumed after long possession.

[24] 2 Bl.Com. 265, citing *Potter v North* (1669) 1 Vent. 387; see *Gardner v Hodgson's Kingston Brewery Co* [1903] A.C. 229.

[25] *Dalton v Angus* (1881) 6 App. Cas. 740 at 816, per Lord Blackburn.

[26] *Att-Gen v Simpson* [1901] 2 Ch. 671 at 698, per Farwell J.

[27] [1971] 2 Q.B. 528 at 546.

[28] See para.4–21, below, and see *Oakley v Boston* [1976] Q.B. 270; *Ward (Helston) Ltd v Kerrier D.C.* [1984] R.V.R. 18 (Lands Tribunal).

[29] By Sir W. D. Evans, 2 Evans' Pothier 136.

prescription,[30] the presumption of which judges were in the habit of recommending juries to adopt. The history of the development of the doctrine of modern lost grant was described in *Bryant v Foot* as follows[31]:

> "Juries were first told that from user, during living memory, or even during 20 years, they might presume a lost grant or deed; next they were recommended to make such presumption; and lastly, as the final consummation of judicial legislation, it was held that a jury should be told, not only that they might, but also that they were bound to presume the existence of such a lost grant, although neither judge nor jury, nor any one else, had the shadow of a belief that any such instrument had ever really existed."

The doctrine was fully considered in *Dalton v Angus*,[32] first in the Queen's Bench Division and then on appeal in the Court of Appeal and in the House of Lords. Before considering that case in detail, it is useful to set out a modern statement of its effect.

In *Tehidy Minerals Ltd v Norman*[33] Buckley L.J., delivering the judgment of the Court of Appeal, stated the effect of *Angus v Dalton*[34] as follows[35]:   **4–11**

> "In our judgment Angus v. Dalton decides that, where there has been upwards of twenty years' uninterrupted enjoyment of an easement, such enjoyment having the necessary qualities to fulfil the requirements of prescription, then unless, for some reason such as incapacity on the part of the person or persons who might at some time before the commencement of the twenty-year period have made a grant, the existence of such a grant is impossible, the law will adopt a legal fiction that such a grant was made, in spite of any direct evidence that no such grant was in fact made.
>
> If this legal fiction is not to be displaced by direct evidence that no grant was made, it would be strange if it could be displaced by circumstantial evidence leading to the same conclusion, and in our judgment it must follow that circumstantial evidence tending to negative the existence of a grant (other than evidence establishing impossibility) should not be permitted to displace the fiction. Precisely the same reasoning must, we think, apply to a presumed lost grant of a profit à prendre as to an easement."

---

[30] *R. v Joliffe* (1823) 2 B. & C. 54. See *Best on Presumptions* (1844), p. 103; and per Bowen J. in *Dalton v Angus* (1881) 6 App. Cas. 740 at 781: "The twenty years' rule . . . in truth . . . was nothing but a canon of evidence."

[31] (1867) L.R. 2 Q.B. 161 at 181, per Cockburn C.J.

[32] (1877) 3 Q.B.D. 85; (1878) 4 Q.B.D. 162; (1881) 6 App. Cas. 740.

[33] [1971] 2 Q.B. 528.

[34] (1877) 3 Q.B.D. 85; (1878) 4 Q.B.D. 162; (1881) 6 App. Cas. 740.

[35] [1971] 2 Q.B. 528 at 552. Buckley L.J. went on to say that in *White v Taylor (No. 2)* [1969] 1 Ch. 160 (in which *Angus v Dalton* (1877) 3 Q.B.D. 85; (1878) 4 Q.B.D. 162; (1881) 6 App. Cas. 740 was not cited to him) he was wrong when he refused to presume a grant: see [1969] 1 Ch. 160 at 195. Part of the passage quoted from *Tehidy Minerals Ltd v Norman* [1971] 2 Q.B. 528 was cited with approval by Lord Scott of Foscote in *Bakewell Management Ltd v Brandwood* [2004] 2 A.C. 519 at [29].

Dalton v Angus[36]

4–12   In the Queen's Bench Division[37] all the judges appear to have been of opinion
that the presumption was capable of being rebutted by some means or other[38]; but
they differed upon the question of what evidence or admission was sufficient for
the purpose.

The plaintiffs had proved enjoyment of the support claimed for their factory
since its erection 27 years before the accident which gave rise to the action, and
claimed the right under the doctrine of lost grant; but it was either proved or
admitted at the trial that no grant had ever in fact been made. Notwithstanding
this admission, Lush J. at the trial directed a verdict for the plaintiffs; and, on the
motion for judgment, he adhered to his opinion

> "that the mere absence of assent, or even the express dissent of the adjoin-
> ing owner, would not prevent the right to light and support from being
> acquired by uninterrupted enjoyment, and that nothing short of an agree-
> ment, either express or to be implied from payment or other acknowledge-
> ment, that the adjoining owner shall not be prejudiced by abstaining from
> the exercise of his right, would suffice to rebut the presumption. In other
> words, that it would be presumed, after the lapse of 20 years, that the ease-
> ment had been enjoyed by virtue of some grant or agreement, unless it were
> proved that it had been enjoyed by sufferance."[39]

Cockburn C.J., on the contrary, held that when it was proved or admitted that
the assent of the defendant's predecessor was not asked for or obtained, by grant
or in any other way, to any support being derived from the soil, the presumption
was at an end.[40] He was also of the opinion that, the enjoyment of the support
claimed not being capable of being interrupted, no grant could be implied from
the failure to interrupt it. Mellor J. agreed on both points with Cockburn C.J., and
judgment was given for the defendants.

4–13   The Court of Appeal was also divided upon the question now under consideration. Brett L.J. considered that the question of grant or no grant was a pure
question of fact to be found by the jury, and that to exclude evidence tending
to show that there never was a grant would be to usurp the functions of the

---

[36] (1877) 3 Q.B.D. 85; (1878) 4 Q.B.D. 162; (1881) 6 App. Cas. 740. This case is now a leading
authority upon several branches of the law of easements, and notably upon the following points,
each of which is considered in its place: (1) the presumption of lost grant and the evidence admissible to rebut it; (2) the acquisition of negative easements under the Prescription Act 1832; (3)
secrecy of enjoyment; (4) the effect of an enjoyment which it is impossible or difficult to interrupt;
(5) the characteristics of the easement of support generally; and (6) the liability of an employer for
the acts of his contractor.

[37] (1877) 3 Q.B.D. 85.

[38] See especially the cases collected by Cockburn C.J. (1877) 3 Q.B.D. 85 at 106; and the observations of Brett L.J. (1878) 4 Q.B.D. 162 at 200.

[39] (1877) 3 Q.B.D. 85 at 93.

[40] (1877) 3 Q.B.D. 85 at 117, 120.

legislature[41]; quoting the observation of Lord Mansfield in *Hull v Horner*[42] that "length of time, used merely by way of evidence, may be left to the consideration of the jury to be credited or not, and to draw their inference one way or the other according to circumstances". Thesiger L.J., while holding that the presumption of lost grant might be negatived by showing "a legal incompetence as regards the owner of the servient tenement to grant an easement,[43] or a physical incapacity of being obstructed as regards the easement itself,[44] or an uncertainty and secrecy of enjoyment putting it out of the category of all known easements",[45] was of the opinion that the presumption could not be rebutted by mere proof that no grant had in fact been made.

> "The presumption of acquiescence", he said, "and the fiction of an agreement or grant deduced therefrom, in a case where enjoyment of an easement had been for a sufficient period uninterrupted, is in the nature of an estoppel by conduct which, while it is not conclusive so far as to prevent denial or explanation of the conduct, presents a bar to any simple denial of the fact, which is merely the legal inference drawn from the conduct."[46]

Cotton L.J. agreed with Thesiger L.J.[47] In the result, the court directed that the defendants should elect within 14 days whether they would take a new trial, which the court thought them entitled to upon the point of notice, and that, if they did not so elect, judgment should be entered for the plaintiff.

The defendants did not elect to take a new trial, but appealed to the House of Lords,[48] where the case was twice argued, and the questions were put to seven judges of the High Court. Of the judges, three[49] based their opinions upon grounds which rendered it unnecessary for them to consider in what manner the presumption of lost grant might be rebutted; three[50] in effect agreed with Thesiger and Cotton L.JJ. that the presumption could not be rebutted merely by showing that no grant had in fact been made; while the seventh[51] was of opinion that proof by the defendants that the right claimed had not been granted either by deed or by equitable agreement was sufficient to rebut the presumption. **4–14**

The opposite points of view of the four last-named judges on this question are fully expressed in the opinions of Lindley and Bowen JJ., respectively.

---

[41] (1878) 4 Q.B.D. 162 at 201. Compare the observations of the same judge in *Duke of Norfolk v Arbuthnot* (1880) 5 C.P.D. 393 and in *Earl De la Warr v Miles* (1881) 17 Ch. D. 590.

[42] (1774) Cowp. 102.

[43] See *Barker v Richardson* (1821) 4 B. & Ald. 579; and see para.4–62, below.

[44] See *Webb v Bird* (1863) 13 C.B. (n.s.) 841.

[45] See *Chasemore v Richards* (1859) 7 H.L.C. 349.

[46] (1878) 4 Q.B.D. 162 at 173.

[47] (1878) 4 Q.B.D. 162 at 186.

[48] (1881) 6 App. Cas. 740.

[49] Pollock B., and Field and Manisty JJ.

[50] Lindley, Lopes and Fry JJ., the last-named bowing to authority, but questioning the principle of the decided cases.

[51] Bowen J.

"The theory of implied grant", said Lindley J., "was invented as a means to an end. It afforded a technical common law reason for not disturbing a long-continued open enjoyment. But it appears to me contrary to the reason for the theory itself to allow such an enjoyment to be disturbed simply because it can be proved that no grant was ever in fact made. If any lawful origin for such an enjoyment can be suggested, the presumption in favour of its legality ought to be made."[52]

Bowen J., on the other hand, treated the rule as to presuming a grant or agreement from 20 years' enjoyment as nothing more than a canon of evidence, similar to the presumption of death arising from seven years' absence without news received, or to the presumption of the satisfaction of a bond after 20 years, and similarly liable to be displaced by counter-evidence.

"It seems a contradiction in terms to maintain that the rebuttable presumption of the existence of a grant would not at any time have been necessarily counteracted by actual proof that no such grant had ever been made . . . . But . . . it would not now be sufficient to disprove a legal origin, unless the possibility of an equitable origin were negatived as well."[53]

Lindley and Lopes JJ. agreed with Bowen J. that the question of notice should have been submitted to the jury; but, the defendants having rejected a new trial, this was now immaterial to the particular case.

4–15   The House,[54] after hearing the judges, unanimously affirmed the decision of the Court of Appeal, Lord Penzance alone questioning the principle, but following the previous decisions. Lord Blackburn appears to have proceeded on the grounds which influenced Pollock B. and Field and Manisty JJ., looking upon the right claimed as springing directly from the long enjoyment, without the interposition of a grant inferred or imputed; and he did not therefore consider the question here discussed. Lord Selborne, while expressing an opinion that the right claimed was conferred by the Prescription Act 1832,[55] thought that the same result could be reached by the doctrine of presumed grant, and expressed his concurrence with the majority of the Court of Appeal.[56] Lord Watson in effect agreed with Lord Selborne, and Lord Coleridge concurred generally.

Although the Lords do not expressly discuss the general question as to what evidence is admissible to rebut the presumption of lost grant, the effect of their judgment is to affirm the opinion of Thesiger and Cotton L.JJ. It follows that the presumption cannot be displaced by merely showing that no grant was in fact made; the long enjoyment either estops the servient owner from relying on such

[52] (1881) 6 App. Cas. 740 at 765.
[53] (1881) 6 App. Cas. 740 at 779–783.
[54] Lord Selborne L.C. and Lords Penzance, Blackburn, Watson and Coleridge.
[55] See paras 4–22 and 4–23, below.
[56] (1881) 6 App. Cas. 740 at 800.

evidence or overrides it when given,[57] and the court will make any possible presumption necessary to give that long enjoyment a legal origin.[58] It appears, however, to be still the law that an incapacity to grant the easement will rebut the presumption in question and negative the claim so far as it rests on the fiction of a lost grant.[59] It would not be reasonable to presume a grant when the evidence of user does not support in extent the right claimed.[60] It is clear that the claim may be resisted on any ground which would prevent the right from being acquired by prescription from time immemorial.[61]

Application of doctrine of lost grant

It should be noted here that in modern times the courts have had frequent recourse   **4–16** to this doctrine and have repeated and applied in various ways the words of Lord Herschell in *Phillips v Halliday*[62]:

> "Where there has been long-continued possession in assertion of a right, it is a well-settled principle of English law that the right should be presumed to have had a legal origin if such a legal origin was possible, and the courts will presume that those acts were done and those circumstances existed which were necessary to the creation of a valid title."

The doctrine of modern lost grant has been resorted to as an alternative not only to prescription at common law but also to prescription under the Prescription Act 1832.[63] The courts have presumed a lost grant of a right to ventilate a cellar through adjoining property[64]; a grant in the nature of an agreement substituting one way for another[65]; and as to paying a quit rent.[66] The court will presume not

---

[57] *cf. Goodman v Saltash Corp* (1882) 7 App. Cas. 633; *Bass v Gregory* (1890) 25 Q.B.D. 481; *Phillips v Halliday* [1891] A.C. 228.

[58] *Att-Gen v Simpson* [1901] 2 Ch. 671 at 698; *East Stonehouse U.D.C. v Willoughby Bros Ltd* [1902] 2 K.B. 318 at 332; *Dawson v M'Groggan* [1903] 1 I.R. 92 at 98.

[59] See the opinion of Thesiger L.J. in *Angus v Dalton* (1878) 4 Q.B.D. 162 at 173–175 and the cases there quoted: *Tyne Improvement Commissioners v Imrie* (1899) 81 L.T. 174; *Neaverson v Peterborough R.D.C.* [1902] 1 Ch. 557; *Hulley v Silversprings Bleaching and Dyeing Co* [1922] 2 Ch. 268; *Green v Matthews* (1930) 46 T.L.R. 206; *Bakewell Management Ltd v Brandwood* [2004] 2 A.C. 519.

[60] *Alfred F. Beckett v Lyons* [1967] Ch. 449.

[61] See, e.g. *Roberts & Lovell v James* (1903) 89 L.T. 282.

[62] [1891] A.C. 228 at 231. Those words were repeated, by Lord Halsbury in *Clippens Oil Co v Edinburgh District Water Trustees* [1904] A.C. 64; by Joyce J. in *Hulbert v Dale* [1909] 2 Ch. 570; by Buckley L.J. in *Att-Gen v Horner* [1913] 2 Ch. 177; by Lord Reading in *General Estates Co v Beaver* [1914] 3 K.B. 926; and by Lord Denning M.R. in *Davis v Whitby* [1974] Ch. 186. The doctrine of lost modern grant was again applied, by the House of Lords, in *Bakewell Management Ltd v Brandwood* [2004] 2 A.C. 519. As to pleading a lost grant, see para.14–54, below.

[63] *Simpson v Godmanchester Corp* [1897] A.C. 696. In *Tisdall v McArthur & Co (Steel and Metal) Ltd* [1951] I.R. 228, it was contended that a prescriptive right to light cannot arise under a presumption of modern lost grant, but this was not accepted. This was described as "the modern and better view" in *Marlborough v Wilks Head & Eve* per Lightman J., December 20, 1996, unreported.

[64] *Bass v Gregory* (1890) 25 Q.B.D. 481.

[65] *Hulbert v Dale* [1909] 2 Ch. 570.

[66] *Bomford v Neville* [1904] 1 I.R. 474; *Foley's Charity Trustees v Dudley* [1910] 1 K.B. 317.

only a grant from an individual but an award[67] or a faculty from the ordinary[68]; or a regulation of a port authority.[69] As regards the Crown, the courts have presumed a grant of a lost charter.[70] They have presumed a grant from the Crown to a corporation of the right to discharge sewage into a tidal river.[71] They have also presumed the grant of a manor,[72] or of a several fishery in tidal waters.[73] Lost grants by the Crown have also been presumed of a franchise ferry, whether from point to point[74] or from vill to vill.[75]

4–17   At the time of passing of the Prescription Act 1832, a "20 years' rule" had become established, whereby a presumption of lost grant was raised by user as of right for 20 years.[76] Since the Act this rule has become blurred. The doctrine must not be applied blindly or unrealistically.[77] The presumption of a legal grant should be applied only when no other explanation is forthcoming; when another explanation is equally possible, the court should not presume a legal origin.[78] A mistaken belief, however, does not amount to an alternative explanation within the meaning of that proposition, which contemplates such things as permission from time to time, neighbourly tolerance and the like.[79] A temporary permission or series of permissions is to be distinguished from a permanent, irrevocable permission attributable to a lost grant.[80] Nor does "toleration" of user amount to an alternative explanation; on the contrary, acquiescence by the servient owner is a necessary ingredient in the acquisition of rights by prescription and lost grant.[81]

4–18   In *Healey v Hawkins*[82] Goff J., on the basis that enjoyment for 20 years might not have continued right down to the time of action brought (so that the Prescription

---

[67] *East Stonehouse U.D.C. v Willoughby Brothers Ltd* [1902] 2 K.B. 332.

[68] *Phillips v Halliday* [1891] A.C. 228; *Stileman-Gibbard v Wilkinson* [1897] 1 Q.B. 749. It seems that a right of way over consecrated ground cannot be granted by faculty and so cannot arise by the application of the doctrine of lost grant: *St Martin le Grand, York, Re* [1990] Fam. 63.

[69] *Att-Gen v Wright* [1897] 2 Q.B. 318.

[70] *Goodtitle v Baldwin* (1809) 11 East 490; and see *Lord Rivers v Adams* (1878) 3 Ex.D. 365. As to a lost grant by the Crown of a market, see *Att-Gen v Horner* (1885) 11 App. Cas. 66; *Att-Gen v Horner (No. 2)* [1913] 2 Ch. 140.

[71] *Somersetshire Drainage Commissioners v Bridgwater Corp* (1904) 81 L.T. 729.

[72] *Merttens v Hill* [1901] 1 Ch. 851.

[73] *Goodman v Saltash Corp* (1882) 7 App. Cas. 633.

[74] *Dysart v Hammerton* [1914] 1 Ch. 822. See also the same case in the House of Lords [1916] A.C. 57 at 80.

[75] *General Estates Co v Beaver* [1914] 3 K.B. 918.

[76] See, e.g. *Campbell v Wilson* (1803) 3 East 294; *Bryant v Foot* (1867) L.R. 2 Q.B. 161 at 181; *Dalton v Angus* (1881) 6 App. Cas. 740 at 780–812.

[77] *Duke of Norfolk v Arbuthnot* (1880) 5 C.P.D. 390, 394; *Tilbury v Silva* (1890) 45 Ch. D. 98; *Att-Gen v Simpson* [1901] 2 Ch. 673 at 698; *Gardner v Hodgson's Kingston Brewery Co* [1903] A.C. 229 at 235.

[78] *Alfred F. Beckett Ltd v Lyons* [1967] Ch. 449 at 473–476, CA; *Odey v Barber* [2008] Ch. 175.

[79] *Bridle v Ruby* [1989] 1 Q.B. 169 at 177F. The reference to "tolerance" is to be understood in the way described in *Mills v Silver* [1991] Ch. 271.

[80] [1989] 1 Q.B. 169 at 178B.

[81] *Mills v Silver* [1991] Ch. 271 at 279G, 281G and 287H.

[82] [1968] 1 W.L.R. 1967 at 1976. Goff J. did not, however, accept as a principle of general application the suggestion in the 13th ed. of this work, at p. 126, that it would seem right to expect the doctrine to be applied where enjoyment for a period of 20 years has not continued right down to the time of action brought.

Act was not available), presumed on the facts before him a lost modern grant. If evidence is given of user as of right during living memory and there is nothing to rebut the consequent presumption of a pre-1189 grant,[83] no presumption of a modern grant is required.[84]

(3) *The Prescription Act 1832*

Purpose and effect

The long title to the Prescription Act 1832[85] is "An Act for shortening the Time   **4–19** of Prescription in certain cases". The preamble is as follows:

> "Whereas the expression 'time immemorial, or time whereof the memory of man runneth not to the contrary,' is now by the law of England in many cases considered to include and denote the whole period of time from the reign of King Richard the First, whereby the title to matters that have been long enjoyed is sometimes defeated by showing the commencement of such enjoyment, which is in many cases productive of inconvenience and injustice; for remedy thereof be it enacted . . ."

The real intention behind the Prescription Act 1832 is a matter of speculation. The preamble suggests an intention to prevent claims "at common law", that is based on immemorial user, from being defeated by evidence of commencement of user after 1189; but this object had been achieved by the doctrine of modern lost grant, above referred to; and it seems that the chief purpose was to found on a statutory presumption the grant which, under that doctrine, unbelieving juries were required to find, as a fact, to be the basis of long user.[86] The Act, however, contains provisions much more extensive than are necessary merely to attain this object.[87]

The Act has not superseded either of the pre-existing methods of claiming by   **4–20** prescription. An easement is still capable of being established by prescription at

---

[83] See para.4–05, above.

[84] *R.P.C. Holdings Ltd v Rogers* [1953] 1 All E.R. 1029 at 1031.

[85] Formerly known as Lord Tenterden's Act. Although, as in previous editions, individual sections are set out and considered in this chapter, the whole Act has been printed in the Appendix, below. The citations in the text are printed as amended.

[86] "The Act," said Parke B. (referring to the relief of the consciences of jurymen), "was intended to accomplish this object by shortening in effect the period of prescription, and making that possession a bar or title of itself which was so before only by the intervention of the jury" (*Bright v Walker* (1834) 1 C.M. & R. 211 at 218); and see per Cockburn C.J. in *Angus v Dalton* (1877) 3 Q.B.D. 85 at 105, 106; and per Lord Macnaghten in *Gardner v Hodgson's Kingston Brewery Co* [1903] A.C. 229 at 238. The Report of the Real Property Commissioners (1829) which preceded the 1832 Act is referred to in *Housden v Conservators of Wimbledon and Putney Commons* [2008] EWCA Civ 200 at [41].

[87] Mr Gale added "and it certainly is to be lamented that its provisions were not more carefully framed". The present editors respectfully agree.

common law, or under the doctrine of modern lost grant[88] and it is not unusual to plead all three methods alternatively.[89] The Act merely provides a statutory method of establishing an easement in some cases. It is not affected by anything in Part I of the Law of Property Act 1925.[90]

It should be noticed that in *Hyman v Van den Bergh*[91] Farwell L.J., basing himself on *Tapling v Jones*,[92] expressed (*obiter*) his personal opinion that (a) the doctrine of modern lost grant is no longer applicable to claims to light, and that (b) in regard to light, a defence based on agreement in writing (section 3 of the Act), or interruption (section 4) cannot be evaded by setting up a claim otherwise than under the Act. The first proposition was considered and not accepted by Kingsmill Moore J. in *Tisdall v McArthur & Co (Steel and Metal) Ltd*.[93] The second seems inconsistent with *Duke of Norfolk v Arbuthnot*,[94] where the Court of Appeal, after negativing, on the ground of interruption, a claim to light under the Act, proceeded to negative, on the facts, an alternative claim under the doctrine of modern lost grant, from which it may be inferred that the claim might, on other facts, have been established.

Claims to profits à prendre

4–21   Section 1 of the Prescription Act 1832 is as follows:

> "1. No claim which may be lawfully made at the common law, by custom, pre-scription, or grant, to any right of common or other profit or benefit to be taken and enjoyed from or upon any land of our sovereign lord the King, or any land being parcel of the Duchy of Lancaster, or of the Duchy of Cornwall, or of any ecclesiastical or lay person, or body corporate, except such matters and things as are herein specially provided for, and except tithes, rent, and services, shall, where such right, profit, or benefit shall have been actually taken and enjoyed by any person claiming right thereto without interruption for the full period of thirty years, be defeated or destroyed by showing only that such right, profit, or benefit, was first taken or enjoyed at any time prior to such period of thirty years, but nevertheless such claim may be defeated in any other way by which the same is now liable to be defeated; and when such right, profit, or benefit, shall have been so taken and enjoyed as aforesaid for the full period of sixty years, the right thereto shall be deemed absolute and indefeasible, unless it shall appear that the same was taken and enjoyed by some consent or agreement expressly made or given for that purpose by deed or writing."

[88] "The statute only applies where you want to stand upon thirty years' user; but here, where the title is one of 200 or 300 years, that statute is not needed, and the title can be rested on the original right before the passing of the statute" (per Lord Hatherley L.C. in *Warrick v Queen's College, Oxford* (1871) 6 Ch. App. 716 at 728); see also *Aynsley v Glover* (1875) 10 Ch. App. 283; *Gardner v Hodgson's Kingston Brewery Co* [1903] A.C. 229 at 238; *Housden v Conservators of Wimbledon and Putney Commons* [2008] 1 W.L.R. 1172 at [43].
[89] See *Tehidy Minerals Ltd v Norman* [1971] 2 Q.B. 528 and para.14–52, below.
[90] Law of Property Act 1925, s.12.
[91] [1908] 1 Ch. 167 at 176–178.
[92] (1865) 11 H.L.C. 290.
[93] [1951] I.R. 228. The Court of Appeal in Ireland expressed no opinion on the point.
[94] (1880) 5 C.P.D. 390.

This section concerns rights of the nature of *profits à prendre*, not easements, but its terms are similar to those of section 2 below which does concern easements. Its interpretation and effect on the acquisition of *profits à prendre* are therefore of relevance also to the law of easements.[95]

Rights of way, etc.

Section 2 of the Prescription Act 1832 is as follows: **4–22**

> "2. No claim which may be lawfully made at the common law, by custom, prescription or grant, to any way or other easement, or to any watercourse or the use of any water to be enjoyed or derived upon, over, or from any land or water of our said lord the King, or being parcel of the Duchy of Lancaster or of the Duchy of Cornwall, or being the property of any ecclesiastical or lay person, or body corporate, when such way or other matter as herein last before mentioned shall have been actually enjoyed by any person claiming right thereto without interruption for the full period of twenty years, shall be defeated or destroyed by showing only that such way or other matter was first enjoyed at any time prior to such period of twenty years, but neverthe-less such claim may be defeated in any other way by which the same is now liable to be defeated; and where such way or other matter as herein last before mentioned shall have been so enjoyed as aforesaid for the full period of forty years, the right thereto shall be deemed absolute and indefeasible, unless it shall appear that the same was enjoyed by some consent or agree-ment expressly given or made for that purpose by deed or writing."

This section applies to all positive easements[96] and is not, as suggested in *Webb v Bird*,[97] confined to rights of way and water.[98] A right to adulterate the water of a nat-ural stream has been held to be a watercourse[99] but not a claim to water occasionally escaping from a lock.[100] The section does not apply to easements of light,[101] which is separately dealt with by section 3, nor was it apparently regarded in *Dalton v Angus*[102] as applying to other purely negative easements. It was, however, evidently

---

[95] Profits annexed to a dominant tenement and also profits in gross may be claimed by prescription at common law and under the doctrine of modern lost grant in the same manner as easements. On the other hand, s.1 of the Prescription Act 1832 almost certainly does not apply to profits in gross, which appear to be excluded from its operation by s.5. In other respects, and apart from the differ-ent periods of enjoyment which are requisite, the Act applies the same rules to easements and to profits. It applies to profits *pur cause de vicinage*: see *Prichard v Powell* (1845) 10 Q.B. 589.

[96] *Dalton v Angus* (1881) 6 App. Cas. 740 at 798; *Bass v Gregory* (1890) 25 Q.B.D. 481; *Simpson v Godmanchester Corp* [1897] A.C. 696 at 709. It was suggested *obiter* in *Crisp v Martin* (1876) 2 P.D. 15 at 28 that the Act did not apply to the right to use a pew in the parish church.

[97] (1861) 10 C.B. (n.s.) 268 at 283.

[98] (1861) 10 C. B. (n.s.) 268 at 283.

[99] *Wright v Williams* (1836) 1 M. & W. 77; *Carlyon v Lovering* (1857) 1 H. & N. 784 at 797, 798.

[100] *Staffordshire & Worcestershire Canal Co v Birmingham Canal Co* (1866) L.R. 1 H.L. 254.

[101] *Perry v Eames* [1891] 1 Ch. 658; *Wheaton v Maple & Co* [1893] 3 Ch. 48. See s.3 below.

[102] (1881) 6 App. Cas. 740 at 798 *et seq*. As to the distinction between positive and negative easements, see para.1–01, above.

assumed in *Harris v De Pinna*[103] that the section would apply to a negative easement in the form of a right to the passage of air through a defined channel.

Apart from the temporal limits expressed, the section does not appear to alter the common law. User for either of the two periods of 20 and 40 years must be "as of right", that is, *nec vi, nec clam, nec precario*,[104] and the right enjoyed must have been enjoyed as an easement.[105] A claim based on user during either period (extended or not extended by section 7 or section 8[106]) can be defeated by proof of unity of possession of both tenements at any time during the period, for during such unity the user cannot be "as of right" in the sense intended, that is as an easement.[107] A claim based on enjoyment for the shorter period can be defeated in any way (except proof of commencement of enjoyment within the time of legal memory) in which a claim could be defeated before the Act. A claim based on user for the longer period is prima facie capable of being defeated only by proof of consent in writing. The question[108] whether the positive enactment that the right is to be deemed absolute makes it unnecessary to presume a grant, and so enables a right to be established, by 40 years' user of the kind required by the Act, against a servient owner who was incapable of granting it is considered later in this chapter.

Right of light

4–23   Section 3 of the Prescription Act 1832 is as follows:

> "3. When the access and use of light to and for any dwelling-house, workshop, or other building shall have been actually enjoyed therewith for the full period of twenty years without interruption, the right thereto shall be deemed absolute and indefeasible, any local usage or custom to the contrary notwithstanding, unless it shall appear that the same was enjoyed by some consent or agreement expressly made or given for that purpose by deed or writing."

This section is concerned exclusively with easements of light.[109] Unlike sections 1 and 2, it does not name or bind the Crown.[110] It must be read with section 4, so that no right can become absolute and indefeasible until called in question in some action or suit.[111] The words "other building" do not necessarily include any structure.[112]

---

[103] (1886) 33 Ch. D. 250.

[104] *Harbidge v Warwick* (1849) 3 Exch. 552; *Gaved v Martyn* (1865) 19 C.B. (n.s.) 732; *Chamber Colliery Co v Hopwood* (1886) 32 Ch. D. 549; *Gardner v Hodgson's Kingston Brewery Co* [1903] A.C. 229. As to enjoyment as of right and generally as to the qualities and character of the necessary enjoyment, see paras 4–77 *et seq.*, below.

[105] *Onley v Gardiner* (1838) 4 M. & W. 496.

[106] See paras 4–50–4–56, below.

[107] *Damper v Bassett* [1901] 2 Ch. 350; *Onley v Gardiner*, above.

[108] See paras 4–71–4–79, below.

[109] The special characteristics of easements of light are considered in Ch.7, below.

[110] *Perry v Eames* [1891] 1 Ch. 658; *Wheaton v Maple & Co* [1893] 3 Ch. 48.

[111] *Colls v Home and Colonial Stores* [1904] A.C. 179 at 189; *Hyman v Van den Bergh* [1908] 1 Ch. 167 at 172.

[112] See para.7–03, below.

They have been held to include a church,[113] an unconsecrated chapel,[114] a picture gallery, a greenhouse,[115] and an open-sided garage,[116] but not a structure for storing timber,[117] nor does it seem that they would apply to a trade fixture removable by a tenant at the end of his tenancy.[118] The quantum of light that can be claimed is not diminished by the user of a room for purposes requiring less than a normal amount of light, for instance as a scullery[119]; nor is the claim affected by the fact that the light is transmitted through the glass roof of an adjacent yard,[120] or that the light, if apparently capable of being admitted, has not been admitted continuously,[121] or that the dominant house has been unoccupied.[122]

It is not necessary that the claim to light should be exercised "as of right"[123] for, unlike section 2, section 3 does not contain the words "claiming right thereto". There must, however, be evidence on which "actual enjoyment" can be found as a fact[124] and the access of light must be enjoyed in the character of an easement, and therefore enjoyment while the dominant and servient tenements are in the same occupation is not sufficient.[125]   **4–24**

No alteration of a building, which would not involve the loss of a right to light when indefeasibly acquired, will, if made during the currency of the statutory period, prevent the acquisition of the light.[126]

The interruption of light is subject to the same general considerations as the interruption of other easements.[127] In particular it has been held that a fluctuating or temporary obstruction caused, for instance, by the stacking of empty packing

---

[113] *Ecclesiastical Commissioners v Kino* (1880) 14 Ch. D. 213; *Anderson v Francis* [1906] W.N. 160. A contrary view is suggested in *Duke of Norfolk v Arbuthnot* (1880) 5 C.P.D. 392, but that decision seems to turn rather on the unusual nature of the aperture, evidence of interruption, and the known history of the buildings concerned.

[114] *Att-Gen v Queen Anne Gardens and Mansions Co* (1889) 60 L.T. 759.

[115] *Clifford v Holt* [1899] 1 Ch. 698; *Allen v Greenwood* [1980] Ch. 119; see also para.7–18, below.

[116] *Smith & Co (Orpington) v Morris* (1962) 112 L.J. 702, County Ct.

[117] *Harris v De Pinna* (1886) 33 Ch. D. 238.

[118] *Maberley v Dowson* (1827) 5 L.J. (o.s.) K.B. 261.

[119] *Price v Hilditch* [1930] 1 Ch. 500.

[120] *Tisdall v McArthur & Co (Steel and Metal) Ltd* [1951] I.R. 228.

[121] *Cooper v Straker* (1888) 40 Ch. D. 21; *Collis v Laugher* [1894] 3 Ch. 659; *Smith v Baxter* [1900] 2 Ch. 138.

[122] *Courtauld v Legh* (1869) L.R. 4 Exch. 126.

[123] *Colls v Home and Colonial Stores* [1904] A.C. 179 at 205. This may be the explanation of *Voyce v Voyce* (1991) 62 P. & C.R. 290; the plaintiff was the legal owner of a farmhouse and cottage but the defendant was the equitable owner of the cottage and entitled to a conveyance of the cottage as a result of an equitable estoppel binding on the plaintiff; the Court of Appeal appear to have held that the plaintiff was entitled, by prescription, to a right of light over the land occupied by the defendant, for the benefit of the farmhouse, but there is no detailed reasoning on this point.

[124] *Smith v Baxter* [1900] 2 Ch. 138; *Tamares Ltd v Fairpoint Properties Ltd* [2007] 1 W.L.R. 2148 at [6]–[16].

[125] *Harbidge v Warwick* (1849) 3 Exch. 552, where unity of possession existed throughout the whole period relied on. The decision of Lord Hatherley (Page Wood V.-C.) in *Simper v Foley* (1862) 2 J. & H. 555, that s.3 is satisfied by enjoyment for 20 years, followed by a period of unity of possession, and his dictum in *Ladyman v Grave* (1871) 6 Ch. App. 763 at 768, that a right can be established under s.3 by enjoyment for two periods, together making 20 years but separated by a period of unity of possession, would not, it is thought, now be followed; see *Hyman v Van den Bergh* [1907] 2 Ch. 516 at 525–528; [1908] 1 Ch. 176.

[126] *Andrews v Waite* [1907] 2 Ch. 500.

[127] *Smith v Baxter* [1900] 2 Ch. 138. See paras 4–43–4–47, below.

cases which are removed from time to time is not of itself an interruption within the section[128] nor is the installation of a glass roof.[129] The conventional method of interrupting the access of light, in order to prevent the acquisition of an ease-ment, is by the erection of a screen or hoarding near the boundary of the prospec-tively servient property.[130]

4–25   It is settled that enjoyment as against an owner of the servient tenement who cannot dispose of the fee may be sufficient, for it is not necessary to presume an absolute grant. This result follows from the words of section 3, as to which Lord Westbury laid down in the House of Lords that the right to light now depends on positive enactment. "It is a matter juris positivi, and does not require, and there-fore ought not to be rested on, any presumption of grant."[131]

Where the servient tenement is in the occupation of a lessee for years, the right is under section 3 of the Act acquired as against all persons interested in the servient tenement, including owners in fee,[132] even if the owner of the servient tenement be also the owner of the dominant tenement.[133]

4–26   A claim will be defeated by written consent or agreement affecting the enjoy-ment during any part of the period of 20 years preceding action brought.[134] An agreement not in writing is ineffective to prevent the acquisition of the right,[135] but the signature of the servient owner is unnecessary, and an agreement signed by the dominant owner,[136] or his tenant[137] or any person in actual occupation,[138] is sufficient. If a lease or conveyance excepts the right to light in such a way as merely to negative the implication of a grant, the exception does not constitute an

---

[128] *Presland v Bingham* (1889) 41 Ch. D. 268. The temporary nature of such an obstruction shifts the onus on to the defendant: per Lindley L.J., *ibid.*, at 276.

[129] *Tisdall v McArthur & Co (Steel and Metal) Ltd* [1951] I.R. 228.

[130] Corporations holding their land for special purposes have usually the same rights in this respect as individuals: see *Banner v G.W.R.* (1883) 24 Ch. D. 1; *Myers v Catterson* (1889) 43 Ch. D. 470; *Foster v London, Chatham & Dover Ry* [1895] 1 Q.B. 711; *Paddington Corp v Att-Gen* [1906] A.C. 1.

[131] *Tapling v Jones* (1865) 11 H.L.C. 290 at 304. See *Jordeson v Sutton Co* [1898] 2 Ch. 614 at 618, 626, where the servient tenement belonged to a gas company, as to whom it was objected that they were under a statutory incapacity to grant a right of light, and North J. overruled the objection, holding that no presumption of grant was necessary. The fact that a presumption of grant is not required for the purposes of the Act does not import that a grant cannot be presumed independ-ently of it: *Tisdall v McArthur & Co (Steel and Metal) Ltd* [1951] I.R. 228, where *Tapling v Jones* is explained. See also *Healey v Hawkins* [1968] 1 W.L.R. 1967.

[132] *Simper v Foley* (1862) 2 J. & H. 555 at 564; *Ladyman v Grave* (1871) 6 Ch. App. 763 at 769.

[133] *Morgan v Fear* [1907] A.C. 429, affirming CA [1906] 2 Ch. 406. This decision seems to have been arrived at in deference to the following earlier authorities, viz.: *Frewen v Philipps* (1861) 11 C.B. (n.s.) 449; *Mitchell v Cantrill* (1887) 37 Ch. D. 56; *Robson v Edwards* [1893] 2 Ch. 146.

[134] *Hyman v Van den Bergh* [1908] 1 Ch. 167. In this case at first instance, [1907] 2 Ch. 516, Parker J. stated that the consent or agreement referred to in the 1832 Act was the same consent or agree-ment as would prior to the Act have been fatal to the acquisition of an easement by prescription at common law or by presumption of a grant: see at 530. Parker J.'s analysis was approved in the Court of Appeal: see [1908] 1 Ch. 167 at 172. This analysis would seem to suggest that the con-sent or agreement must be by or on behalf of the servient owner. However, a submission to this effect was rejected in *Paragon Finance Plc v City of London Real Property Co Ltd* [2002] L. & T.R. 139; [2002] 1 E.G.L.R. 97; an appeal to the Court of Appeal was compromised.

[135] *Mallam v Rose* [1915] 2 Ch. 222.

[136] *Bewley v Atkinson* (1879) 13 Ch. D. 283.

[137] *Hyman v Van den Bergh* [1908] 1 Ch. 167.

[138] [1908] 1 Ch. 167, at 179.

agreement within the section[139] but the case is otherwise, and an "agreement" is constituted, if the instrument contains words which positively authorise the grantor to build as he pleases.[140] Whether the particular provision comes within the exception in section 3 depends upon the true construction of the provision, applying the general rules as to the construction of legal documents. There is no special rule of construction in this context. It is not necessary for the provision to expressly refer to "light". It is not necessary for it expressly to say that the enjoyment of light is "permissive". What is needed is that the clause makes it clear that the enjoyment of light is not absolute and indefeasible.[141]

In *Mitchell v Cantrill*[142] a lease demised land and its appurtenances "except rights, if any, restricting the free use of any adjoining land or the conversion or appropriation at any time thereafter of such land for building or other purposes, obstructive or otherwise"; it was held that the quoted phrase was an exception from the grant but was not a consent or agreement within section 3 with the result that the lessee was able to rely upon 20 years' enjoyment of light and acquired a right of light by prescription. The same result was reached where a conveyance stated that the transfer was "not including any easements of implied easements of light and air".[143]   **4–27**

Conversely, in *Haynes v King*,[144] a lease contained a declaration   **4–28**

"notwithstanding anything herein contained, the lessors shall have power, without obtaining any consent from, or making any compensation to, the lessee, to deal as they may think fit with any of the premises adjoining or contiguous to the hereditaments hereby demised and to erect, or suffer to be erected, on such adjoining or contiguous premises, any buildings whatsoever, whether such buildings shall or shall not affect or diminish the light or air which may now, or at any time during the term hereby granted, be enjoyed by the lessee, or the tenants or occupiers of the hereditaments hereby demised";

it was held that this declaration was a consent or agreement within section 3 and prevented an easement of light being acquired by prescription. The same result was reached in *Foster v Lyons & Co Ltd*[145] ("reserving nevertheless to the lessor, and his lessees and tenants, full right to build to any height upon the land adjoining the land and premises hereby demised, notwithstanding such buildings may obstruct any light on the land hereby demised"), *Willoughby v Eckstein*[146]

---

[139] *Mitchell v Cantrill* (1887) 37 Ch. D. 56; *Hapgood v Martin* (1934) 51 T.L.R. 82.
[140] *Haynes v King* [1893] 3 Ch. 439; *Foster v Lyons & Co* [1927] 1 Ch. 219; *Willoughby v Eckstein* [1937] Ch. 167; *Blake and Lyons Ltd v Lewis Berger & Sons Ltd* [1951] 2 T.L.R. 605; *Marlborough (West End) Ltd v Wilks Head & Eve*, Lightman J., December 20, 1996 (unreported); *Paragon Finance Plc v City of London Real Property Co Ltd* [2002] L. & T.R. 139; [2002] 1 E.G.L.R. 97; *Midtown Ltd v City of London Real Property Co Ltd* [2005] 1 E.G.L.R. 65; *RHJ Ltd v F T Patten (Holdings) Ltd* [2008] 2 W.L.R. 1096.
[141] *RHJ Ltd v F T Patten (Holdings) Ltd* [2008] 2 W.L.R. 1096.
[142] (1887) 37 Ch. D. 56.
[143] *Hapgood v Martin & Son* (1934) 51 T.L.R. 82.
[144] [1893] 3 Ch. 439; the judgment also considered the meaning of "adjoining or contiguous".
[145] [1927] 1 Ch. 219; the judgment also considered the meaning of "adjoining".
[146] [1937] 1 Ch. 167.

("subject to the adjacent buildings or any of them being at any time or times rebuilt or altered according to plans both as to height elevation extent and otherwise as shall or may be approved of the ground landlord for the time being"), *Blake and Lyons Ltd v Lewis Berger & Sons Ltd*[147] ("subject to the adjacent buildings being at any time or times rebuilt or altered according to plans both as to height elevation extent or otherwise as shall or may be approved by the ground landlord for the time being") and *Marlborough v Wilks Head & Eve*[148] ("it is hereby agreed and declared that notwithstanding that the Building Owners have placed windows in that part of their new buildings which overlook the premises occupied by the adjoining owner no right or easement of light or air exists in respect thereof or has been or shall at any future time be acquired by the Building Owners or anyone deriving title through or under them and the adjoining owner and the freeholders and all persons deriving title through or under them or either of them shall have the right to intercept light and air coming to the said windows"). In *Paragon Finance Plc v City of London Real Property Co Ltd*[149] it was held in relation to a complicated clause dealing with future building on other land that the other land must be land belonging to the landlord rather than to a third party. In a further judgment in the same case,[150] it was held that the other land must be land belonging to the landlord at the date of the lease so that if the landlord subsequently acquired other land, the landlord would not have the benefit of the clause in relation to that land. In *Midtown Ltd v City of London Real Property Co Ltd*,[151] where the provision was unusually framed as a covenant, it was held that there was in substance an agreement for the purposes of section 3 of the Prescription Act 1832. In *RHJ Ltd v F T Patten (Holdings) Ltd*[152] one provision in the lease expressly excluded the grant of rights by implication and a second provision excepted and reserved to the lessor and others the right to build on certain other land; it was held that the second provision came within the exception in section 3.

4–29   The facts in *Ruscoe v Grounsell*[153] were a little unusual. The court had to consider whether a stone tablet set into the wall of a building in 1816 amounted to an agreement or consent within section 3. The tablet said that the stone was placed by the purchaser of the building to perpetuate the right of the vendor (the owner of the adjoining land) to build within nine inches of the first building. The court was prepared to assume that the stone amounted to an "agreement" and was "in writing". The question remained whether the stone was an express agreement relating to light and made for the relevant purpose. The court held that it was

---

[147] [1951] 2 T.L.R. 605; it was held that the land which had the benefit of the clause was not restricted to land which was the property of the ground landlord.

[148] Lightman J., December 20, 1996, unreported; it was also held that the clause meant that the enjoyment of light was precarious so that a right to light was not acquired under the doctrine of lost modern grant.

[149] [2002] L. & T.R. 139; [2002] 1 E.G.L.R. 97.

[150] [2002] 1 E.G.L.R. 97.

[151] [2005] 1 E.G.L.R. 65.

[152] [2008] 2 W.L.R. 1096.

[153] (1903) 89 L.T. 426; considered in *RHJ Ltd v F T Patten (Holdings) Ltd* [2008] 2 W.L.R. 1096.

unable to say what the purpose of the stone was and, accordingly, it did not suffice for the exception in section 3.

What is to happen where the dominant tenement or the servient tenement **4–30** change hands?

Section 3 of the 1832 Act refers to consent or agreement. It would seem that the consent is one given by someone having a relevant interest in the servient tenement to the person who is benefitting from the user of light. It would also seem that the relevant agreement would be between such persons.

What happens if the person with the interest in the servient tenement, who gave the consent or made the agreement, transfers his interest or his interest being a limited interest comes to an end? What is the position when the person with the interest in the dominant tenement, who has the benefit of the consent or the benefit of the agreement, transfers his interest or his interest being a limited interest comes to an end?

First, as regards the person with the interest in the dominant tenement who has **4–31** the benefit of the consent or agreement, it may be, depending upon the circumstances and the terms in which the consent or agreement is expressed, that the permission is personal to that person with the interest in the dominant tenement. In such a case, the consent or agreement would lapse when that person transfers his interest in the dominant tenement or that interest comes to an end. The question would then arise whether continued use by the successor or another relevant person with an interest in the dominant tenement is referable to the acquiescence of the servient owner in user as of right (and therefore time will run) or whether the continued use could support an inference that the original consent or agreement has been renewed (and therefore time will not run).

Secondly, as regards the person with the interest in the servient tenement who **4–32** granted the consent or who was a party to the agreement, the general rule is that a consent or agreement (which does not create an interest in land) will not bind the successor in title to the servient tenement[154] and a person with a prior interest in the servient tenement would also not be bound.

In a number of cases concerning the easement of light and section 3 of **4–33** the Prescription Act 1832, the court has referred to the dominant owner "denouncing" a permission given by the servient owner and holding that it was open to the dominant owner to act in that way so that continued user after the permission is "denounced" would be user as of right and not pursuant to the permission.[155]

In the case of a provision which reserves to the servient owner the right to build **4–34** on the servient land notwithstanding any interference with the light passing to the dominant tenement, the position may be capable of being analysed in a different way. In a number of the cases which concerned such provisions, the right reserved to the servient owner is described as a "right" in terms which suggest

---

[154] *Ashburn Anstalt v Arnold* [1989] Ch. 1.
[155] *Bewley v Atkinson* (1879) 13 Ch. D. 283; *Greenhalgh v Brindley* [1901] 2 Ch. 324; and *Smith v Colbourne* [1914] 2 Ch. 533.

that the right may be an interest in land.[156] Further, it is tentatively suggested that such a right could be an easement, namely, an easement to do something on one's own land which would otherwise be a nuisance to an adjoining owner. Speaking generally, a right to commit that which would otherwise be a nuisance can be an easement.[157] It is rather more easy to consider such a right as an easement where the right is to discharge something from one parcel of land onto adjoining land. However, there are decisions where the right in the nature of an easement has been to carry on an activity on one's own land, such as a noisy activity, which would otherwise be a nuisance to the adjoining land.[158] Although there are difficulties in acquiring such an easement by prescription,[159] those difficulties would not arise where the right in question had been expressly granted and the issue being discussed is as to the legal character of the right and whether the benefit and burden passes to successors of the original parties.

4–35 A consent or agreement for the purposes of section 3 of the 1832 Act does not infringe the law as to perpetuities.[160]

4–36 The application of a written agreement to given circumstances will ordinarily be a question of construction; thus a reference to a "window" has been held to include a skylight.[161]

4–37 The section effectively destroys local customs by which the right to light might be defeated.[162]

The Rights of Light Act 1959

4–38 The Rights of Light Act 1959[163] embodied the recommendations of a committee appointed in March 1957 and presided over by Mr Justice (later Lord Justice) Harman.[164] Recognising the problems of the user of sites left vacant by war damage in the 1939–1945 War, the Act temporarily extended the period of prescription for the acquisition of rights of light,[165] but this temporary provision is now spent.

The Committee also recognised that on the one hand it would be a mistake to suppose that planning legislation had deprived the right of light of its former practical importance, in the sense that permission was unlikely to be given for any building which would obstruct light to the point of nuisance, and on the other

---

[156] *Foster v Lyons & Co Ltd* [1927] 1 Ch. 219 at 228 per Eve J.; *Willoughby v Eckstein* [1937] 1 Ch. 167 at 174 and *Paragon Finance Plc v City of London Real Property Co Ltd* [2002] 1 E.G.L.R. 97 at 102.

[157] See paras 4–128–4–130.

[158] *Elliottson v Feetham* (1835) 132 E.R. 53; *Crump v Lambert* (1867) L.R. 3 Eq. 409 at 413; and *Sturges v Bridgman* (1879) 11 Ch. D. 852.

[159] *Pwllbach Colliery Co Ltd v Woodman* [1915] A.C. 634 at 646, 647 and 649.

[160] *Bewlay v Atkinson* (1879) 13 Ch. D. 283 at 289.

[161] *Boston v Isted* [1903] 1 Ch. 405.

[162] *Cooper v Hubbuck* (1862) 12 C.B. (n.s.) 456; *Truscott v Merchant Tailors' Co* (1856) 11 Exch. 855.

[163] Referred to in this chapter as "the Act of 1959". The text of the Act (as amended) and the relevant rules are printed in the Appendix, below. The operation of the Act of 1959 is described in *Bowring Services Ltd v Scottish Widows Fund & Life Assurance Society* [1995] 1 E.G.L.R. 158.

[164] The Report of the Committee on the Law Relating to Rights of Light (Cmnd. 473), published on May 12, 1958.

[165] Rights of Light Act 1959, s.1: repealed by the Statute Law (Repeals) Act 1974, s.1, Sch., Pt IV.

hand that the conventional erection of a screen to interrupt the flow of light was sometimes refused planning permission, so that there was a practical problem (not only in the case of war-damaged property) calling for a remedy in respect of prospectively servient property. Accordingly the Act of 1959 provides for the notional interruption of light as an alternative to actual interruption and so modifies section 3 of the Prescription Act 1832.[166]

The Act of 1959[167] enables the owner[168] of land over which light passes to a **4–39** dwelling-house, workshop or other building to apply to the local authority for the registration of a notice in the register of local land charges.[169] The application must identify the servient land and the dominant building and specify the position and dimensions of an opaque structure to which the notice is intended to be equivalent. The Lands Tribunal, before the application is made, must have certified[170] either that adequate notice has been given to all persons who appear to the Lands Tribunal to be likely to be affected by the registration of such a notice or that the case is one of exceptional urgency. (In this latter case the certificate must specify the length of time for the notice to be on the register.) When an application has been properly made a notice should then be registered by the local authority.

In principle, the decision of the Lands Tribunal to issue a certificate under the **4–40** Act of 1959 and the registration of a notice by the local authority are open to challenge by way of judicial review under Civil Procedure Rules, Pt 54, brought against the Lands Tribunal and possibly also the local authority. However, judicial review is a discretionary remedy and the court would need to consider the availability to the applicant of an alternative remedy, such as the issue of a writ for infringement of the right to light. However, it is not open to such a complainant to commence proceedings by writ challenging the issue of the certificate and the registration of the notice on grounds which could have been put forward on an application for judicial review under Civil Procedure Rules, Pt 54 and a writ issued in such circumstances will be struck out as an abuse of the process of the court.[171] It is not possible to appeal by way of case stated against the issue of a certificate by the Lands Tribunal.[172]

---

[166] See para.4–23, above.

[167] Rights of Light Act 1959, s.2.

[168] "Owner" includes a lessee where the lease has not less than seven years unexpired and a mortgagee in possession: s.7, as amended by the Local Land Charges Act 1975, s.17(2), Sch.1.

[169] The Local Land Charges Rules 1977 (SI 1977/985), made by the Lord Chancellor under the Local Land Charges Act 1975, s.14, regulate the registration of light obstruction notices in Pt 11 of the register of local land charges under s.2 of the Act: see in particular r.10. The rules, as amended from time to time, are in the Appendix, below.

[170] The Lands Tribunal Rules 1996 (SI 1996/1022), made by the Lord Chancellor under the Lands Tribunal Act 1949, s.3, and the Law of Property Act 1969, s.28(6), regulate applications to the Lands Tribunal for a certificate under s.2 of the Act of 1959. See in particular rr.21–24 (Pt VI). 938 definitive certificates and 211 temporary certificates were issued between 1959 and 1980: see (1978) 122 S.J. 515, 534; (1981) 259 E.G.L.R. 123 (W.A. Greene).

[171] *Bowring Services Ltd v Scottish Widows Fund & Life Assurance Society* [1995] 1 E.G.L.R. 158, applying *O'Reilly v Mackman* [1983] 2 A.C. 237.

[172] *Bowring Services Ltd v Scottish Widows Fund & Life Assurance Society* [1995] 1 E.G.L.R. 158.

4-41   A notice has effect until the expiry of one year beginning with the date of registration[173] or, where the certificate of the Lands Tribunal certifies the case to be one of exceptional urgency, at the end of the period specified in the certificate, whichever event occurs first. In either case the notice may cease to have effect on an earlier date if the registration is cancelled.[174]

Where a notice is registered, then, for the purposes of determining whether any person is entitled (by virtue of the Prescription Act 1832 or otherwise) to a right to the access of light to the dominant building across the servient land, the access of light of that building shall be treated as obstructed to the same extent as if an opaque structure of the specified dimensions had on the date of registration of the notice been erected by the applicant in the specified position, and had remained in that position only during the period for which the notice has effect.[175]

Any person who would have had a right of action in respect of the erection of such a structure as is specified in the application, as infringing a right to the access of light to the dominant building, has the like right of action in respect of the registration of the notice.[176] He may be granted such declaration as the court considers appropriate, and an order cancelling or varying the registration.[177] In order to avoid the problem of an interruption during the final year of the prescriptive period under section 3 of the Prescription Act 1832, it is provided in the Act of 1959 that the dominant owner may treat his enjoyment as having begun one year earlier than it did.[178]

4-42   For the purposes of section 4 of the Prescription Act 1832 (under which a period of enjoyment is not to be treated as interrupted except by a matter submitted to or acquiesced in for one year after notice thereof) persons interested in the dominant building are deemed to have notice of the registration and of the applicant, and until an action is brought in respect of the registration all such persons are deemed to acquiesce in the notional obstruction. If the action fails, the court may direct that such persons shall continue to be deemed to acquiesce in the notional obstruction as if the action had not been brought.[179]

The Act of 1959 applies in relation to land in which there is an interest belonging to the Queen in right of the Crown or of the Duchy of Lancaster, or belonging to the Duchy of Cornwall, or belonging to a government department, or held in trust for the Queen for the purposes of a government department[180]; but section

---

[173] Where a temporary notice is registered and within the time permitted by the temporary notice a certificate under s.2(3)(a) of the Act of 1959 is lodged, the period of 12 months referred in s.3(2)(b) runs from the date of registration of the temporary notice and not from some later date: *Bowring Services Ltd v Scottish Widows Fund & Life Assurance Society* [1995] 1 E.G.L.R. 158, where the plaintiff failed to establish a right of light under s.3 of the 1832 Act because it issued its writ more than 12 months after the date of registration of the temporary notice.

[174] Rights of Light Act 1959, s.3(2).

[175] Rights of Light Act 1959, s.3(1).

[176] Rights of Light Act 1959, s.3(3).

[177] Rights of Light Act 1959, s.3(5). See *Hawker v Tomalin* (1969) 20 P. & C.R. 550 (Harman J.) as to the desirable form of declaration and as to the exercise of the court's discretion under s.3(5).

[178] Rights of Light Act 1959, s.3(4).

[179] Rights of Light Act 1959, s.3(6).

[180] Rights of Light Act 1959, s.4(1), (3).

3 of the Prescription Act 1832 (as modified by the Act of 1959) is not to be construed as applying to any such land to which that section would not apply apart from the Act of 1959.[181] It appears, therefore, that the acquisition of a right of light for the benefit of any such land may be prevented by notional interruption, although it remains impossible to acquire a right of light under section 3 of the Prescription Act 1832 against the Crown.

Periods of enjoyment: interruption

Section 4 of the Prescription Act 1832 is as follows: **4–43**

> "4. Each of the respective periods of years hereinbefore mentioned shall be deemed and taken to be the period next before some suit or action[182] wherein the claim or matter to which such period may relate shall have been or shall be brought into question; and no act or other matter shall be deemed to be an interruption, within the meaning of this statute, unless the same shall have been or shall be submitted to or acquiesced in for one year after the party interrupted shall have had or shall have notice thereof, and of the person making or authorising the same to be made."

This section is qualified by the provisions as to disability in section 7.[183] The enjoyment which gives an easement under the Act is enjoyment ("as of right" under sections 1 and 2 but this is not necessary under section 3[184]) during a period, of the prescribed length, running back from the commencement of an action; and not during any period of the specified length, whenever occurring.[185] Consequently, unless or until the claim or matter is brought into question in some action, the right under the Act remains inchoate[186]; but the commencement of such an action fixes the period and enables the right to be established.[187]

The actual user is only sufficient to satisfy the statute if during the whole of the   **4–44** statutory period (whether acts of user be proved in each year or not) the user is enough at any rate to carry to the mind of a reasonable person who is in possession of the servient tenement the fact that a continuous right to enjoyment is being asserted and ought to be resisted if such right is not recognised and if resistance to it is intended.[188] Whether the actual user is thus sufficient is a question of

---

[181] Rights of Light Act 1959, s.4(2).

[182] Including an objection to the registration of a right of common: Commons Registration Act 1965, s.16(2).

[183] See paras 4–50 and 4–51, below.

[184] See para.4–24, above.

[185] *Wright v Williams* (1836) 1 M. & W. 77; *Jones v Price* (1836) 3 Bing.N.C. 52; *Richards v Fry* (1838) 7 A. & E. 698; *Flight v Thomas* (1841) 8 Cl. & Fin. 231; *Tilbury v Silva* (1890) 45 Ch. D. 98; *Colls v Home and Colonial Stores* [1904] A.C. 179 at 189.

[186] *Colls v Home and Colonial Stores* [1904] A.C. 179 at 189; *Hyman v Van den Bergh* [1907] 2 Ch. 516 at 524, 525; [1908] 1 Ch. 167 at 171, 175.

[187] *Cooper v Hubbuck* (1862) 12 C.B. (n.s.) 456; *Beytagh v Cassidy* (1868) 16 W.R. 403.

[188] *Hollins v Verney* (1884) 13 Q.B.D. 304 at 315; see also *Bower v John Etherington Ltd* (1965) 53 D.L.R. (2d) 338, Nova Scotia Supreme Court.

fact.[189] Suggestions that actual user in the first and last years of the period relied on[190] or in every year of such a period[191] must necessarily be proved have not been adopted or followed by the Court of Appeal.[192] In *Hollins v Verney*[193] Lindley L.J. said that:

> "a cessation of user which excludes an inference of actual enjoyment as of right for the full statutory period will be fatal at whatsoever portion of the period the cessation occurs; and, on the other hand, a cessation of user which does not exclude such inference, is not fatal, even although it occurs at the beginning, or the end of, the period."

A claim to an easement of parking failed on the facts in *Central Midlands Estates Ltd v Leicester Dyers Ltd*,[194] where the user was described as "of an occasional nature".

4–45   An "interruption" within the section may arise from any actual discontinuance of enjoyment by reason of an obstruction acquiesced in for one year. It may result from adverse[195] obstruction by the servient owner[196] or by a stranger[197]; but the commencement of proceedings by the servient owner is not an "interruption".[198] A statement by the servient owner that he would or might interrupt the user in the future is not an interruption; if the servient owner acquiesces in the user continuing in the meantime, then that period of acquiesence can be relied upon in support of a claim to prescription.[199] The movement of a passageway by agreement does not interrupt the running of time so as to prevent the acquisition of an easement after 20 years' user.[200]

Since an interruption is required by section 4 to be acquiesced in for one year, it follows that an enjoyment for a period exceeding 19 years which is then obstructed can be protected if proceedings are brought after 20 years have run and

---

[189] *Smith v Baxter* [1900] 2 Ch. 138. In *White v Taylor (No. 2)* [1969] 1 Ch. 160 non-user for two periods, each of five or six years, defeated a claim under the Act: see [1969] 1 Ch. 194. See also *Mills v Silver* [1991] Ch. 271 and *Williams v Sandy Lane (Chester) Ltd* [2007] 1 E.G.L.R. 10 at [33]–[34]. In *Estey v Withers* (1975) 48 D.L.R. (3d) 121, use of a wood in the summer months only to gain access to a summer house, the road being barricaded in the spring and autumn of the year, was sufficiently continuous.

[190] See *Bailey v Appleyard* (1838) 8 A. & E. 161; *Parker v Mitchell* (1840) 11 A. & E. 788; *Carr v Foster* (1842) 3 Q.B. 581.

[191] per Parke B. in *Lowe v Carpenter* (1851) 6 Exch. 825.

[192] *Earl De la Warr v Miles* (1881) 17 Ch. 535 at 600; *Hollins v Verney* (1884) 13 Q.B.D. 304 at 313, 314 (approving *Hall v Swift* (1838) 4 Bing.N.C. 381; *Lawson v Langley* (1836) 4 A. & E. 890).

[193] (1884) 13 Q.B.D. 314.

[194] [2003] 2 P. & C.R. DG1.

[195] The party's own obstruction of his light does not defeat him (*Smith v Baxter* [1900] 2 Ch. 138, 143).

[196] *Plasterers' Co v Parish Clerks' Co* (1851) 6 Exch. 630.

[197] *Davies v Williams* (1851) 16 Q.B.D. 558.

[198] *Reilly v Orange* [1955] 2 Q.B. 112.

[199] *Samuel v Fatih*, unreported, June 20, 2000, CA.

[200] *Davis v Whitby* [1974] Ch. 186, applying the dictum of Patteson J. in *Payne v Shedden* (1834) 1 M. & Rob. 383.

before the obstruction has lasted one year.[201] If, however, the proceedings are brought before the 20 years have run, the claimant's right is still inchoate and he has no protection by injunction or otherwise.[202]

An interruption from natural causes of the flow of a stream will not prevent prescription,[203] nor will a fluctuating interruption.[204] Repeated interruptions, each for less than a year, may be evidence of contentious user so as to show that the enjoyment is not "as of right" under section 2[205] or they may result in the acquisition of a qualified easement only.[206]   **4–46**

A person asserting an interruption must prove that some notice other than the mere existence of a physical obstruction was given to the person interrupted.[207] Acquiescence is then a question of fact.[208] It may be negatived by evidence of protests made in anticipation of the interruption even if not subsequently renewed during the year following its completion.[209]

In order to negative submission or acquiescence, it is not essential to bring an action or to remove the obstruction.[210] There is no acquiescence in an interruption when the owner of the dominant tenement refuses to exercise his right under a permission given by the owner of the servient tenement.[211] The onus is on the party claiming a right by prescription to prove (a) that at the time of action brought any existing interruption of a permanent character has lasted for less than one year, or (b) if it has lasted for more than one year, that he did not submit to or acquiesce in it.[212] In order to disprove "submission", a party must prove both unwillingness on his part to accept the interruption and some words or act by which his opposition is made clear to the person responsible for the interruption.[213] Discontent, not effectively communicated to the other party, is not enough.[214] If, therefore, the discontented party consults his solicitor, the solicitor should make an immediate protest; it may be fatal to delay while legal aid is sought, evidence collected and counsel instructed to settle proceedings.[215]   **4–47**

---

[201] *Flight v Thomas* (1841) 1 A. & E. 688; 8 Cl. & Fin. 231; see the explanation of this case by Lord Campbell in *Eaton v Swansea Waterworks Co* (1851) 17 Q.B. 267 at 272. Enjoyment continues, though interrupted, unless the interruption be acquiesced in for a year. See also *Bowring Services Ltd v Scottish Widows Fund & Life Assurance Society* [1995] 1 E.G.L.R. 158.

[202] *Bridewell Hospital (Governors) v Ward, Lock Bowden & Co* (1893) 62 L.J.Ch. 270; *Battersea v London City Sewers Commissioners* [1895] 2 Ch. 708.

[203] *Hall v Swift* (1838) 4 Bing.N.C. 381; see *Carr v Foster* (1842) 3 Q.B. 581.

[204] *Presland v Bingham* (1889) 41 Ch. D. 268.

[205] *Eaton v Swansea Waterworks Co* (1851) 17 Q.B. 267, applied in *Newnham v Willison* (1988) 56 P. & C.R. 8, followed in *Smith v Brudenell-Bruce* [2002] 2 P. & C.R. 51. See paras 4–86 and 4–87, below.

[206] *Rolle v Whyte* (1868) L.R. 3 Q.B. 286.

[207] *Glover v Coleman* (1874) L.R. 10 C.P. 108; *Seddon v Bank of Bolton* (1882) 19 Ch. D. 462.

[208] *Bennison v Cartwright* (1864) 5 B. & S. 1.

[209] *Davies v Du Paver* [1953] 1 Q.B. 184.

[210] *Glover v Coleman* (1874) L.R. 10 C.P. 108.

[211] *Ward v Kirkland* [1967] Ch. 194 at 231, 232; and see para.4–97, fn.371, below.

[212] *Dance v Triplow* (1991) 64 P. & C.R. 1, CA. See paras 14–44–14–53, below.

[213] (1991) 64 P. & C.R. 1, CA at 5, per Glidewell L.J.

[214] (1991) 64 P. & C.R. 1, CA at 14, per Balcombe L.J.

[215] As was the case in *Dance v Triplow*, above: see at 9.

What the claimant may allege

4–48   Section 5 of the Prescription Act 1832 is as follows:

> "5. In all actions upon the case and other pleadings, wherein the party claiming may now by law allege his right generally, without averring the existence of such right from time immemorial, such general allegation shall still be deemed sufficient, and if the same shall be denied, all and every the matters in this Act mentioned and provided, which shall be applicable to the case, shall be admissible in evidence to sustain or rebut such allegation; and in all pleadings to actions of trespass, and in all other pleadings wherein, before the passing of this Act it would have been necessary to allege the right to have existed from time immemorial, it shall be sufficient to allege the enjoyment thereof as of right by the occupiers of the tenement in respect whereof the same is claimed for and during such of the periods mentioned in this Act as may be applicable to the case, and without claiming in the name or right of the owner of the fee, as is now usually done; and if the other party shall intend to rely on any proviso, exception, incapacity, disability, contract, agreement, or other matter hereinbefore mentioned, or on any cause or matter of fact or of law not inconsistent with the simple fact of enjoyment, the same shall be specially alleged and set forth in answer to the allegation of the party claiming, and shall not be received in evidence on any general traverse or denial of such allegation."

This section relates to pleading.[216] The requirement that enjoyment must be alleged to have been "as of right" does not apply where an easement of light is being claimed.[217] The reference to "the tenement in respect whereof the same is claimed" shows that the Act does not apply to profits à prendre in gross.[218]

No presumption to be allowed

4–49   Section 6 of the Prescription Act 1832 is as follows:

> "6. In the several cases mentioned in and provided for by this Act, no presumption shall be allowed or made in favour or support of any claim, upon proof of the exercise or enjoyment of the right or matter claimed for any less period of time or number of years than for such period or number mentioned in this Act as may be applicable to the case and to the nature of the claim."

---

[216] See paras 14–44 *et seq.*, below.

[217] *Colls v Home and Colonial Stores* [1904] A.C. 179 at 205. See para.4–24, above.

[218] *Shuttleworth v Le Fleming* (1865) 19, C.B. (n.s.) 687; *Mercer v Denne* [1904] 2 Ch. 534 (affirmed [1905] 2 Ch. 538 at 586); *Ramsgate Corp v Debling* (1906) 22 T.L.R. 369; *Lovett v Fairclough* (1990) 61 P. & C.R. 385 at 396.

In *Hanmer v Chance*[219] Lord Westbury said:

"The meaning seems to be that no presumption or inference in support of the claim shall be derived from the bare fact of user or enjoyment for less than the prescribed number of years; but where there are other circumstances in addition, the statute does not take away from the fact of enjoyment for a shorter period its natural weight as evidence, so as to preclude a jury from taking it, along with other circumstances, into consideration as evidence of a grant."

Proviso for disabilities

Section 7 of the Prescription Act 1832 is as follows:

4-50

"7. Provided also, that the time during which any person otherwise capable of resisting any claim to any of the matters before mentioned shall have been or shall be an infant, idiot, non compos mentis, feme covert, or tenant for life, or during which any action or suit shall have been pending, and which shall have been diligently prosecuted, until abated by the death of any party or parties thereto, shall be excluded in the computation of the periods hereinbefore mentioned, except only in cases where the right or claim is hereby declared to be absolute and indefeasible."

In *Hulley v Silversprings Bleaching and Dyeing Co Ltd*[220] Eve J. observed that the intention of section 7 was "to preserve the rights-to the extent therein mentioned-of persons incapable of making the grant on the presumption of which the whole structure of statutory prescription is founded, or of suing to prevent an invasion of their rights and property". With the coming into force of the Married Women's Property Act 1882 on January 1, 1883,[221] coverture ceased to have any significance save in the case of property acquired before that date by a married woman whose marriage was still subsisting: there can be no property so affected now. Inasmuch as land belonging to a minor must now be vested in trustees for him,[222] and a tenant for life under a settlement holds the legal estate in fee simple on the trusts of the settlement, it would seem that by analogy the protection given by the section should no longer extend to minors and tenants for life; but the generally accepted view is that their rights are preserved by section 12 of the Law of Property Act 1925, which provides that nothing in Part I[223] thereof affects

---

[219] (1865) 4 De G.J. & S. 626 at 631; and see *Carr v Foster* (1842) 3 Q.B. 581; *Hollins v Verney* (1884) 13 Q.B.D. 304.

[220] [1922] 2 Ch. 268 at 279.

[221] See ss.1, 2, 25.

[222] Law of Property Act 1925, ss.1(6), 19.

[223] Pt I (now amended) consists of ss.1–39. The position of a tenant for life is created directly by the Settled Land Act 1925, but it could perhaps be considered to originate in s.1(6) (*cf.* also s.39) of the Law of Property Act 1925, *cf.* ss.12 and 31 of the Law of Property Act 1922 and *Turner's Will Trusts, Re* [1937] Ch. 15.

the operation of any statute or of the general law with reference to the acquisition of easements or rights over or in respect of land.[224]

No provision is made for absence beyond the seas, but in such a case, although the time of such absence could not be excluded under this section, it might be used to show ignorance on the part of the servient owner of the enjoyment, so as to bring the case within the rule as to knowledge of the servient owner.[225]

4–51   It is to be observed that it is only in computing the shorter periods specified in sections 1 and 2 (30 years under section 1, and 20 years under section 2) that the period of disability is to be excluded; it is not excluded in computing any period after which a right is declared to be absolute and indefeasible (60 years under section 1, and 40 years under section 2), so that there is no exclusion in the case of a claim to a right of light under section 3 (by which it is provided that the right shall be absolute and indefeasible after enjoyment for 20 years). Where it is applicable the effect of section 7 is to prolong the specified period, down to the time of action brought, of continuous enjoyment as of right and as an easement, by so long a time as the disability has lasted; in other words, enjoyment of the necessary character must be shown for a period of 20 (or, in the case of profit, 30) years, either wholly before the disability, if it is still subsisting, or partly before and partly after, if it has ended[226]; and also during the period of disability.[227]

Extension of the period of 40 years

4–52   Section 8 of the Prescription Act 1832 is as follows:

> "8. Provided always, that when any land or water upon, over or from which any such way or other convenient watercourse or use of water shall have been or shall be enjoyed or derived hath been or shall be held under or by virtue of any term of life, or any term of years exceeding three years from the granting thereof, the time of the enjoyment of any such way or other matter as herein last before mentioned, during the continuance of such term, shall be excluded in the computation of the said period of forty years, in case the claim shall within three years next after the end or sooner determination of such term be resisted by any person entitled to any reversion expectant on the determination thereof."

The full meaning and effect of this section have never been authoritatively decided. It is intended to protect the reversioner on a tenancy for life, or for more than three years, by conditionally excluding the period of the tenancy.

---

[224] This is the view of the authors of Megarry and Wade's *The Law of Real Property* (6th ed., 2000), p. 1133. It may still be possible to presume a lost grant by a tenant for life: consider the powers of a tenant for life to grant easements conferred by Settled Land Act 1925, s.38(i); but see *Roberts and Lovell v James* (1903) 89 L.T. 282.

[225] See paras 4–53 and 4–54, below, as to the effect of ignorance or notice of dissent on the part of a reversioner.

[226] *Clayton v Corby* (1842) 2 Q.B. 813.

[227] *Onley v Gardiner* (1838) 4 M. & W. 496; *Clayton v Corby*, above. The same considerations apply where the period of a lease is excluded under s.8.

Section 8 is expressly confined to "the said period of forty years", which is the longer period mentioned in section 2.[228] It clearly cannot therefore apply to profits, etc., under section 1, or to easements of light under section 3. Its application to the 20-year period under section 2 was considered in *Palk v Shinner*[229] where the Court of Queen's Bench held that it applies only to the period of 40 years, and therefore that the time during which the premises are under lease for a term exceeding three years is not to be excluded in the computation of the period of 20 years' enjoyment of a right of way. But the question whether the tenancy for years, though not excluded for the purposes of section 8, might not be made use of in another way to defeat the user, is a different matter.

4–53

In *Palk v Shinner*[230] a way had been used for 20 years, during the first 15 of which the servient tenement had been under lease; it did not appear whether the reversioner knew of the user during the lease, but at all events no resistance was made either during the 15 years or the remaining years for which the land was in possession of the reversioner. Erle J. told the jury that the fact of the land having been in lease for the 15 years would not defeat the user; and, upon a rule *nisi* for a new trial for misdirection, the question principally argued was whether section 8 of the statute applied to a 20 years' user, so that the tenancy should be excluded, and the court expressed a clear opinion that it did not. Moreover, Erle J. said[231] that if this case had arisen before the statute, "there would have been good evidence to go to the jury of a user as of right for twenty years, notwithstanding the existence of the tenancy".

It would seem that any objection in respect of the land having been in lease which might have been taken at the common law, for instance absence of knowledge on the part of the reversioner, may still be taken to a user for 20 years under section 2 of the statute, although the statutory process of excluding the time of the lease is not open except in the case of 40 years' user.

On the other hand, in the case of 40 years' user, unless the reversioner should resist the claim within three years from the termination of the tenancy, he could not set up the existence of the lease in any way. He could not set it up by way of exclusion from the computation by reason of the express condition, imposed by section 8, of resisting within the three years above mentioned. Nor could he set it up as at the common law by reason of the provisions of section 2, which, though they allow a 20-years' user to be defeated "in any other way" in which the same at the common law might be defeated, do not allow the 40-years' user to be so defeated, but only by showing that the enjoyment was had under a written agreement. So that but for section 8 the reversioner could make no use of the fact of the tenancy at all.

In short, there are two distinct ways in which advantage may be taken of the existence of a term of years:

4–54

(1) as showing, in connection with the other circumstances of the case, that there has not been enjoyment binding against the reversioner, such as

---

[228] See para.4–22, above.
[229] (1852) 18 Q.B. 568.
[230] *Staffordshire & Worcestershire Canal Co v Birmingham Canal Co* (1866) L.R. 1 H.L. 254.
[231] (1866) L.R. 1 H.L. 254 at 575.

enjoyment for 20 years, commencing during the tenancy and continuing through it, and unknown to him and his agents;[232]

(2) as entitling the reversioner to have the period of enjoyment of the term excluded from the period of computation, so as virtually to extend the period of enjoyment required to be proved.

The first way was open at the common law, and is left untouched by the statute in so far as the period of 20 years' user under section 2 is concerned, but is not left in the case of the 40 years' user. The second way is the creature of the statute, and, according to the case of *Palk v Shinner*[233] is only applicable to a case of 40 years' user. If, however, the person resisting the claims does not, by resisting it within three years from the end of the term, comply with the condition upon which alone he can under section 8 take advantage of the period of enjoyment, he is debarred from setting up the fact of the existence of the tenancy for years at all, except[234] in so far as it may assist him in showing his ignorance of the claimant's enjoyment or some defect in the character of that enjoyment.

4–55   Two questions arise from the wording of the section. In the first place, the section applies only to "a way or other convenient watercourse or use of water". "No doubt", said Parke B., in *Wright v Williams*,[235] "there is a mistake in the eighth section, probably a miscopying in the insertion of the word 'convenient' instead of 'easement' ". In *Laird v Briggs*[236] Fry J. adopted this construction *sub silentio*, but the Court of Appeal in the same case[237] expressly left the point open.

In the second place, the section refers to resistance by "any person entitled to any reversion expectant on the determination" of the term of life or term of years previously mentioned. This has been held not to apply to a person entitled in remainder expectant on a life estate.[238] It seems, however, questionable whether the section could now apply to any period of life tenancy, even if no other interest were created and a reversion remained in the settlor; for freehold life interests now take effect as equitable interests, and it is difficult to see how land could be said to be "held" under an equitable interest. Moreover it may be suggested that the expression "term of life" was intended to connote, as in *Bright v Walker*,[239] a lease for life or lives, now capable of taking effect only as a lease for 90 years determinable.[240]

4–56   After an enjoyment of 40 years, the extent of the exemption contained in section 8 appears to amount to this. The period during which the owner of the servient inheritance has not been *valens agere*, in consequence of the existence of

---

[232] As to which, see paras 4–66 and 4–113, 4–114, and 4–115, below.

[233] (1852) 18 Q.B. 568.

[234] See *Davies v Du Paver* [1953] 1 Q.B. 184 and paras 4–104 *et seq.*, below.

[235] (1836) 1 M. & W. 77. The suggestion does not appear by the report to have been made by the judge in this case; but it is found in counsel's argument, as reported in 1 Tyr. & G. 375 at 390.

[236] (1880) 16 Ch. D. 440.

[237] (1881) 19 Ch. D. 22.

[238] *Symons v Leaker* (1885) 15 Q.B.D. 629.

[239] (1834) 1 Cr.M. & R. 211.

[240] Law of Property Act 1925, s.149.

a lease for life or for more than three years, is altogether excluded in the computation of the 40 years, provided such owner contests the claim within three years after the lease expires. If the first 20 of the 40 years' enjoyment occurred at a time when the servient tenement was not held under lease, it seems that the owner of the servient inheritance (even though he brought his action within three years from the expiration of the lease) would be prevented by a 20 years' valid enjoyment from successfully challenging the claim to an easement. Again, if the servient tenement had been held without lease during the first 18 and the last 2 of the 40 years, it would seem that the owner of the servient inheritance would be equally prevented by a 20 years' valid enjoyment from successfully challenging the claim. The time of enjoyment during the leases is simply to be excluded, and there appears to be nothing to prevent the tacking together of the two periods of 18 and 2 years during which there has been a valid enjoyment. The case appears by the express enactment of the statute—that the time during which the property was so held on lease shall be excluded from the computation of the period of 40 years—to be exempted from the rule requiring 20 years' enjoyment next before action brought.[241]

Effect of Prescription Act 1832

The general effect of the Act is to confront the claimant with two difficulties   **4-57**
which do not exist at common law. First, the user must be proved for the period computed next before the commencement of the action in which the claim is contested. Secondly, there must be nothing in the facts inconsistent with the continuous enjoyment of the easement as such during the whole period. Thus, unity of possession at any time during the period is fatal under the Act,[242] however small the claimant's interest may be. This is not so at common law, though a claim resting on a presumed pre-1189 grant can be defeated by proof of such unity of both possession and ownership as would extinguish the right so presumed to have been granted.[243] On the other hand, the Act does not, except as to light, assist mere enjoyment per se. A claim based on enjoyment for one of the shorter periods specified in section 1 or section 2 is liable to be defeated on any ground which would defeat it at common law; and while a claim based on enjoyment for one of the longer periods is declared to be absolute unless it was had by written consent or agreement, the enjoyment must still have been "as of right".

Difficulties have arisen as to the relationship between sections 7 and 8. If a   **4-58**
servient tenement has been subject to a lease during which, under section 8, the 40-year period does not run, the question arises whether user for 20 years when there was no such lease can be defeated as in ordinary cases; for instance, by showing that the owner of the inheritance was during the whole or part of that

---

[241] The views here advanced (which are those of Mr Gale) are confirmed by *Clayton v Corby* (1842) 2 Q.B. 813, and *Pye v Mumford* (1848) 11 Q.B. 675 (upon the effect of excluding the periods of disability under s.7). See also the text to fnn.226 and 227, para.4–51, above.

[242] See *Onley v Gardiner* (1838) 4 M. & W. 496, and paras 4–22 and 4–24, above.

[243] See para.4–07, above.

time under disability. By section 7, the provision in favour of disabilities does not apply to the cases "where the right or claim is declared to be absolute and inde-feasible"; and it may be urged that the policy of the law is, after so long an enjoy-ment, to clothe such user with the legal right without allowing the general object to be defeated by too minute provisions. To this, however, it may be replied that if the period of the subsistence of the lease is to be excluded, the reversioner does not obtain complete protection unless he stands in the same position to all intents and purposes as he would do in the ordinary case of a user of 20 years, when the servient tenement was not under lease; and that the words of section 7 may be satisfied by supposing it to mean only that, in the computation of the period of 40 years, for the purpose of throwing upon the owner of the inheritance the onus of showing that he was under the particular disability of a reversioner, no time of general disability is to be deducted; but that the fact of his being a reversioner being once established, and the question, therefore, then being whether there has been a valid user of 20 years, that must be decided as if it stood completely abstracted from the time during which the servient tenement was in lease; or that, in other words, in computing the period of 40 years, disability under section 7 shall never be deducted—in computing that of 20 years, always, if properly set up in the pleading.[244]

In considering the general effect of the Act it should be noted that the claim to light under section 3 differs from claims to other easements in that the claim need not be as of right, cannot be defeated by pleas of disability or a lease under sections 7 and 8 respectively, and cannot be claimed as against the Crown.

3.—THE PERSONS AGAINST WHOM AND BY WHOM THE ENJOYMENT MUST BE HAD TO GIVE RISE TO A PRESCRIPTIVE TITLE

(1) *Against whom the enjoyment must be had*

Presumed grant by owner of servient tenement

4–59   As it is essential to the existence of an easement that one tenement should be made subject to the convenience of another, and as the right to the easement can exist only in respect of such tenement, the continued user by which the easement is to be acquired by prescription must be by a person in possession of the domi-nant tenement. Moreover, as such user is only evidence of a previous grant—and as the right claimed is in its nature not one of a temporary kind, but one which permanently affects the rights of property in the servient tenement—it follows that by the common law such grant can only have been legally made by a party capable of imposing such a permanent burden upon the property—that is, the owner of an estate of inheritance.[245] Further, in order that such user may confer

---

[244] The judgments in *Clayton v Corby* (1842) 2 Q.B. 813 and *Pye v Mumford* (1848) 11 Q.B. 675 (see fn.241 para.4–56, above) establish these propositions.
[245] *Daniel v North* (1809) 11 East 372.

an easement, the owner of the servient inheritance must have known that the easement was enjoyed, and also have been in a situation to interfere with and obstruct
its exercise, had he been so disposed. His abstaining from interference will then
be construed as an acquiescence.[246] *Contra non valentem agere non currit prae-
scriptio.*

There are thus two distinct points which need to be considered, namely (1) the
servient owner's interest in the servient tenement; and (2) such owner's knowledge of the user of the easement. In the present section it is proposed to consider
the first of these points; the second will be considered in section 4.

According to the common law, all prescription presupposes a grant,[247] and   **4–60**
(apart from the special case of light claimed under section 3 of the Act) the general rule is that, to establish a prescriptive title to an easement, the court must presume a grant of the easement by the absolute owner of the servient tenement to
the absolute owner of the dominant tenement.[248] Furthermore, for the purpose of
such a grant it must be shown that there was a competent grantor and a competent grantee.[249] An enjoyment of the easement as against an owner of the servient
tenement who could not dispose of the fee is normally not sufficient.

In connection with this question the provisions in sections 7 and 8 of the
Prescription Act 1832, in relation to persons under disability and to tenants for
life and for years, must, where the claim is made under the Act, be carefully borne
in mind. For instance, disability on the part of the servient owner might prevent
the presumption of a grant.

The general doctrine requires to be considered in some detail, bearing in mind
that the Prescription Act 1832 has not taken away any of the methods of claiming easements which previously existed.[250] In considering the present question it
is important to distinguish the method in which the particular easement is
claimed, and as to this it is to be remembered that there are three ways in which
prescriptive rights can arise: namely (1) at common law; (2) by presumption of a
lost grant; and (3) under the Act.

1. Claims based on prescription at common law

In the case of an easement claimed by prescription at common law there must   **4–61**
have been enjoyment as against an absolute owner of the servient tenement. It
was laid down by Lindley L.J. in *Wheaton v Maple & Co*[251] (a case where the
easement of light was in question) that a right claimed by prescription must be
claimed as appendant or appurtenant to land and not as annexed to it for a term

---

[246] *Gray v Bond* (1821) 2 Brod. & Bing. 667; *Liverpool Corp v Coghill* [1918] 1 Ch. 307.
[247] *Goodman v Saltash Corp* (1882) 7 App. Cas. 654 at 655; *Gardner v Hodgson's Kingston Brewery
Co* [1903] A.C. 229 at 239.
[248] *Wheaton v Maple & Co* [1893] 3 Ch. 63; *Kilgour v Gaddes* [1904] 1 K.B. 466; *Simmons v Dobson*
[1991] 1 W.L.R. 720.
[249] The need to have a competent grantor and a competent grantee has already been referred to in considering the creation of easements *inter partes*: see paras 3–05 *et seq.* and 3–11, above.
[250] See para.4–20, above.
[251] [1893] 3 Ch. 63 at 65.

of years; also that an easement for a limited time only cannot be gained by prescription at common law. Vaughan Williams J. in *Fear v Morgan*[252] seems to have been of the opinion that by prescription at common law a right to light can only be acquired between absolute owners. Again, it was said by Mathew L.J. in *Kilgour v Gaddes*[253] (referring to a right of way): "Such an easement can only be acquired by prescription at common law where the dominant and servient tenements respectively belong to different owners in fee." It follows that where the fee simple in both dominant and servient tenements belongs to the same owner no easement can be acquired by prescription at common law.[254]

This rule does not, however, apply to a case where the lessee had at the material time a unilateral right pursuant to section 153 of the Law of Property Act 1925 to enlarge his leasehold interest into the fee simple without anyone else's consent.[255]

2. Claims based on lost grant

4–62 Where the claim to an easement is based on the doctrine of lost grant, it would seem to follow from the language used by Lindley L.J. in *Wheaton v Maple & Co* that the same rule should apply, and that an enjoyment as against an owner of the servient tenement who cannot dispose of the fee is not sufficient.[256] In *Barker v Richardson*,[257] where the light of a presumably modern house had been enjoyed for more than 20 years over land which during part of that period had been glebe land, no easement was acquired, the ground of the decision being thus stated by Abbott C.J.[258]:

> "Admitting that twenty years' uninterrupted possession of an easement is generally sufficient to raise a presumption of a grant, in this case, the grant, if presumed, must have been made by a tenant for life, who had no power to bind his successor; the grant, therefore, would be invalid . . . ."

---

[252] [1906] 2 Ch. 415 at 416.
[253] [1904] 1 K.B. 467.
[254] "It is well settled that a lessee cannot acquire a right of way over the land of another lessee under the same lessor either by prescription at common law, or under the doctrine of a lost grant, or by prescription under the Prescription Act 1832": per P.O. Lawrence J. in *Cory v Davies* [1923] 2 Ch. 95 at 107, citing *Wheaton v Maple & Co* (above) and *Kilgour v Gaddes* (above). The point may not previously have been settled as a matter of decision in the case of lost grant, but it is now by *Simmons v Dobson* [1991] 1 W.L.R. 720.
[255] *Bosomworth v Faber* (1992) 69 P. & C.R. 288, where the Court of Appeal was prepared to presume a lost modern grant.
[256] [1893] 3 Ch. 69; applied to lost modern grant in *Simmons v Dobson* [1991] 1 W.L.R. 720; see para. 4–61, above.
[257] (1821) 4 B. & Ald. 579. Compare *Runcorn v Doe d. Cooper* (1826) 5 B. & C. 696 (a case of adverse possession under the old Statutes of Limitation). It should be noted that in *Barker v Richardson* the incapacity of the owner of the servient tenement to make an absolute grant covered only part of the period of enjoyment. So, again, in *Roberts & Lovell v James* (1903) 89 L.T. 287, an absolute grant could at one time during the enjoyment have been made by the owners of the servient tenement. In both cases, however, the court refused to presume a grant. As to a grant over glebe land today, see *Oakley v Boston* [1976] Q.B. 270 and para.3–08, above.
[258] (1821) 4 B. & Ald. 579 at 582.

In *Bradbury v Grinsell*[259] the rule is stated as follows: **4–63**

> "Though an uninterrupted possession for twenty years or upwards should be
> sufficient evidence to be left to a jury to presume a grant; yet the rule must
> ever be taken with this qualification, that the possession was with the acqui-
> escence of him who was seised of an estate of inheritance: for a tenant for
> life or years has no power to grant such right for a longer period than during
> the continuance of his particular estate. If such a tenant permits another to
> enjoy an easement on his estate for twenty years or upwards without inter-
> ruption, and then the particular estate determines, such user will not affect
> him who has the inheritance in reversion or remainder; but when it vests in
> possession the reversioner may dispute the right to the easement, and the
> length of possession will be no answer to his claim."

In *Roberts v James*[260] Romer L.J. said that it was clear law that where there was a   **4–64**
tenant for life in possession of land a lost grant of a right of way could not be implied
as against the reversioner merely from the user of the way during the lifetime of the
tenant for life, one ground being that the reversioner not being in possession would
have no power to prevent the user, and he ought not to have his reversion affected
because he could not prevent it. Stirling L.J. referred to *Bradbury v Grinsell*[261] and
said that the rule showed that the person who has the inheritance in remainder or
reversion might when it vested in possession assert his right to dispute the claim to
the easement. It was only by proving his acquiescence that the lost grant could be
assumed, and he added that in order to establish acquiescence one must show knowledge on the part of the person against whom the knowledge is asserted of the fact
that the easement was enjoyed, and that that was very clearly established by *Daniel
v North*,[262] in which the doctrine was applied to the obstruction of light and air coming over a servient tenement in the possession of a tenant for years.

 On the other hand, in *Bright v Walker*,[263] where a lessee holding the dominant   **4–65**
tenement claimed a right of way on the ground of user over a servient tenement also
held by a lessee, Parke B., referring to the old doctrine of lost grant, stated that user
for 20 years would before the Prescription Act have been evidence to support a
claim to a non-existing grant by the termor in the *locus in quo* to the termor under
whom the plaintiff claimed, although such a claim was by no means a matter of
ordinary occurrence, and in practice the usual course was to state grant by an owner
in fee to an owner in fee. Again, in referring to the doctrine of lost grant, it was said
by Channell J. in *East Stonehouse U.D.C. v Willoughby Brothers Ltd*[264] that in
recent times the doctrine had been applied more widely than formerly.

---

[259] 2 Wms. Saund. (1871 ed.) 509–512.
[260] (1903) 89 L.T. 287.
[261] 2 Wms. Saund. (1871 ed.) 509–512.
[262] *Daniel v North* (1809) 11 East 372. Compare *Cross v Lewis* (1824) 2 B. & C. 686.
[263] (1834) 1 Cr.M. & R. 211 at 221.
[264] [1902] 2 K.B. 318 at 332. In Ireland the law has developed differently: see *Hanna v Pollock* [1900]
    2 Ir.R. 664; *Macnaghten v Baird* [1903] 2 Ir.R. 731; and *Flynn v Harte* [1913] 2 Ir.R. 326, where
    the earlier decisions are reviewed by Dodd J.

"In particular it can be applied between termors when there is a difficulty in applying the statute owing to the freeholder not being bound."

4–66   In *Pugh v Savage*,[265] the Court of Appeal held that the fact that a tenancy of the servient tenement came into existence during the course of the period of user was not, in the absence of evidence that the servient owner had no knowledge of the user while the tenant was in possession, fatal to the presumption of a lost grant, although it was a matter to be considered. On the other hand, a distinction could properly be drawn between cases where the tenancy was in existence at the beginning of the period of user and cases where the tenancy came into existence in the course of the period of user, and in the former type of case it might well be unreasonable to imply a lost grant by the owner at the beginning of the user. He might not have been able to stop the user, even if he knew about it.

4–67   The case where the fee simple in both the dominant and the servient tenement belongs to the same owner may be a special one. The question of presuming a lost grant in such a case is governed by the rules that a lessee for years must prescribe in right of his lessor and not in right of himself; and that the lessor cannot have an easement over his own land. It is now settled that a tenant cannot acquire an easement by the doctrine of lost modern grant against another tenant holding under the same landlord.[266]

3. Claims under the Prescription Act 1832

4–68   Here it is necessary to make a distinction between the cases where a claim is made to an easement other than light and the case where a claim is made to light, because, as has already been seen,[267] it follows from the words of section 3 of the Act that in the case of light a presumption of an absolute grant is not required and a right can be acquired by enjoyment as against an owner of the servient tenement who cannot dispose of the fee. In the case of a claim based on section 2 of the Act it is relevant to the question of the servient owner's interest in the servient tenement whether the enjoyment has been only for the shorter period of 20 years or for the full period of 40 years.

4–69   (a) *Twenty years' enjoyment.* For a claim under section 2 based upon 20 years' enjoyment only to succeed it is necessary to show title against all persons having interests in the servient tenement. The principle is explained in *Bright v Walker*[268] where for more than 20 years the plaintiff, holding Blackacre under a lease for lives from a bishop, enjoyed without interruption a way over Whiteacre held by the defendant under a lease for lives from the same bishop. The plaintiff

---

[265] [1970] 2 Q.B. 373, considered further, para.4–113, below, in connection with claims under the Prescription Act 1832.

[266] *Simmons v Dobson* [1991] W.L.R. 720; but note the exceptional case of *Bosomworth v Faber* (1992) 69 P. & C.R. 288 and see para.4–61, above.

[267] See para.4–25, above.

[268] (1834) 1 Cr.M. & R. 211. This case is referred to in connection with lost modern grant at para.4–65, above.

claimed the right of way under the Prescription Act, but the claim failed. Parke B., delivering the judgment of the Court of Exchequer, said[269]:

> "The important question is, whether this enjoyment, as it cannot give a title against all persons having estates in the locus in quo, gives a title as against the lessee and the defendants claiming under him, or not at all? We have had considerable difficulty in coming to a conclusion on this point; but, upon the fullest consideration, we think that no title at all is gained by an user which does not give a valid title against all, and permanently affect the Fee. Before the statute, this possession would indeed have been evidence to support a plea or claim by a non-existing grant from the termor, in the locus in quo, to the termor under whom the plaintiff claims, though such a claim was by no means a matter of ordinary occurrence; and in practice the usual course was to state a grant by an owner in fee to an owner in fee. But, since the statute, such a qualified right, we think, is not given by an enjoyment for twenty years. For, in the first place, the statute is 'for shortening the time of prescription'; and if the periods mentioned in it are to be deemed new times of prescription, it must have been intended that the enjoyment for those periods should give a good title against all, for titles by immemorial prescription are absolute and valid against all. They are such as absolutely bind the fee in the land. And, in the next place, the statute nowhere contains any intimation that there may be different classes of rights, qualified and absolute–valid as to some persons, and invalid as to others. From hence we are led to conclude, that an enjoyment of twenty years, if it give not a good title against all, gives no good title at all; and as it is clear that this enjoyment, whilst the land was held by a tenant for life, cannot affect the reversion in the bishop now, and is therefore not good as against every one, it is not good as against any one, and, therefore, not against the defendant."

It is, of course, to be observed that in this case the fee simple in both the dominant and the servient tenement belonged to the same owner (the bishop). It was this fact, not the existence of a tenancy of the servient tenement, which was fatal to the existence of an easement.

(b) *Forty years' enjoyment.* It seems that an enjoyment which has continued for 40 years will confer a right to the easement unless the reversioner resists the claim within three years after the determination of the particular estate; as in the cases of conditional estates, a valid right is given as against all the world, until by the happening of the condition the estate is defeated.[270] This view is supported by *Wright v Williams*[271] (a case relating to water rights) in which Parke B. during the course of the argument said that it was the intention of the Prescription Act that   **4–70**

---

[269] (1834) 1 Cr.M. & R. 211 at 220, 221.
[270] This was the view of Mr Gale himself.
[271] (1836) Tyr. & G. 375 (see in particular at 392, 393, 400).

an enjoyment of 20 years should be of no avail against an idiot or other person labouring under incapacity, but that one of 40 years should confer an absolute title even as against parties under disabilities; also that a user for 40 years confers a prima facie title which is good, unless the reversioner pursues his remedy within the three years mentioned in section 8. In delivering the judgment of the Court of Exchequer, Lord Abinger held that, even where a tenancy for life existed, the enjoyment of an easement for 40 years gave an indefeasible title. It seems to follow that, in the opinion of the then judges of the Court of Exchequer, it was not necessary to presume an absolute grant where a claim under the Act to an easement was based on a 40 years' enjoyment.[272]

Where the fee simple in both the dominant and the servient tenement belongs to the same owner, it is clear that (except in the case of light) the tenant of one close cannot as such acquire under the Act a prescriptive easement over another close belonging to the same landlord either by 20 years' user[273] or by 40 years' user.[274]

Incompetent grantors

4–71 It will have been seen[275] that as a general rule the enjoyment of an easement as against an owner of the servient tenement who is unable to dispose of the fee is not sufficient to give rise to a prescriptive title, and that the ordinary cause of such an inability arises from a deficiency of estate, as where a servient owner is tenant for life or tenant for years. The inability to dispose of the fee may, however, arise from other causes, for instance by reason of the doctrine of ultra vires or where the owner of the servient tenement is restrained from alienation.

Thus, where the owner of the servient tenement is a company whose powers of disposition are limited, and a grant of the easement by such company would be ultra vires, it seems that no prescriptive title will arise either where an easement of any kind is claimed by prescription at common law or under the doctrine of lost grant, or where an easement other than light is claimed on the ground of a 20 years' enjoyment under section 2 of the Prescription Act. The prescriptive title will not arise, because the necessary grant cannot be presumed.[276] The relevant principle was considered in *Bakewell Management Ltd v Brandwood*.[277] It was argued by the servient owner that because the user relied upon had involved the commission of a criminal

---

[272] For further discussion, see paras 4–73 and 4–75, below.

[273] *Gayford v Moffatt* (1868) 4 Ch. App. 133; *Bailey v G.W. Ry* (1884) 26 Ch. D. 434 at 441; *Sturges v Bridgman* (1879) 11 Ch. D. 852 at 855.

[274] *Kilgour v Gaddes* [1904] 1 K.B. 457. As to the position in Ireland see the cases referred to in fn.264, para.4–65, above.

[275] See paras 4–59 and 4–60, above.

[276] *Rochdale Co v Radcliffe* (1852) 18 Q.B. 287 at 315; *Att-Gen v G.N. Ry* [1909] 1 Ch. 775 at 778. Compare *Neaverson v Peterborough R.D.C.* [1902] 1 Ch. 557; *Hulley v Silversprings Bleaching and Dyeing Co* [1922] 2 Ch. 268; *Green v Matthews* (1930) 46 T.L.R. 206; also *Mill v New Forest Commissioner* (1856) 18 C.B. 60, in which last case a *profit à prendre* was enjoyed as against the Crown for 30 years, and a claim made under s.1 of the Prescription Act was defeated on the ground that the Crown was by statute incapacitated from making a grant.

[277] [2004] 2 A.C. 519.

offence, such user could not be relied upon for the purposes of prescription. The land in that case was a common to which section 193 of the Law of Property Act 1925 applied. Section 193(4) made it an offence for a person to drive a motor vehicle over such a common "without lawful authority". The grant of an easement normally would be lawful authority. It was held that the relevant statutory provision did not in general make it ultra vires for the servient owner to grant an easement to drive a vehicle across the common and so the principle referred to in this paragraph would not generally prevent an easement being acquired by prescription in such a case.[278] Lord Scott of Foscote identified some circumstances where the owner of the servient tenement would not be able to authorise (by the grant of a purported easement) certain activities on the common, for example where the activities would be an unreasonable interference with the rights of the commoners (see section 30 of the Commons Act 1876) so as to constitute a nuisance. Further, the owner of the common could not grant the right to drive cars on the common to too many people if that would constitute a nuisance.[279]

If, however, a claim were made to the easement of light over land owned by a disabled company on the ground of 20 years' enjoyment under section 3 of the Prescription Act, it is clear that it would not be necessary to presume a grant, and a right to the easement might be established.[280]   **4–72**

There has for a long time been a difference of view as to what the legal position is in a case where an easement (other than light) is claimed under section 2 of the Prescription Act on the ground of a 40-years' enjoyment over land owned by a disabled company. The words which in section 2 are applied to 40 years' enjoyment of an easement other than light are similar, and possibly identical, to the words which in section 3 are applied to a 20-years' enjoyment of light. It has been argued that the result which in the latter case was held to follow as regards light should also in the former case follow as regards easements other than light—namely that it is not necessary to presume an absolute grant.[281] Further, the words of sections 7 and 8 of the Prescription Act 1832 appear to have a material bearing on the question. If where an easement is claimed under section 2 of the Act on the ground of a 40-years' enjoyment it is necessary to presume an absolute grant, this alone would, where the servient tenement is owned by a person under disability or a tenant for life or for years, prevent a prescriptive title from arising, and the special provisions as to exclusion which in fact are contained in sections 7 and 8 would seem inappropriate. The language used by the judges in *Wright v Williams*,[282] which was decided under section 8, and in which a question arose as to the effect of a 40-years' enjoyment of an easement other than light, the servient tenement being held by a tenant for life, seems to show that in their opinion it was not necessary in such a case to presume an absolute grant.   **4–73**

---

[278] See, in particular, per Lord Walker of Gestingthorpe at [50]–[56].
[279] per Lord Scott of Foscote at [24].
[280] *Tapling v Jones* (1865) 11 H.L.C. 304; *Jordeson v Sutton, Southcoates and Drypool Gas Co* [1898] 2 Ch. 614 at 618, 626.
[281] See the words of Lord Selborne in *Dalton v Angus* (1881) 6 App. Cas. 800.
[282] (1836) Tyr. & G. 375. See para.4–70, above.

4–74   On the other hand, in *Staffordshire and Worcestershire Canal Navigation (Proprietors) v Birmingham Canal Navigation (Proprietors)*,[283] where an easement was claimed on the ground of a 40-years' enjoyment, and it was objected that the servient tenement was owned by a company which had no power to make a grant, it was said in the House of Lords that, if the Prescription Act 1832 applied to the case, it would be necessary to show that the right claimed could have been granted, and it was said, further, that under the circumstances a grant would have been ultra vires and void. The question posed in paragraph 4–73 above has now been answered in *Housden v Conservators of Wimbledon and Putney Commons*.[284] At first instance in this case, it was held that it would have been ultra vires for the servient owner to have granted the easement claimed. The dominant owner relied upon 40 years' user for the purposes of section 2 of the 1832 Act. The judge held that he was bound by the decision in the *Staffordshire* case to hold that section 2 could not be relied upon to found prescription even where the user had continued for 40 years. He held that the opening words of section 2 which referred to a claim "which may be lawfully made at the common law", which words did not appear in section 3, meant that neither the 20-year nor the 40-year period referred to in section 2 gave rise to an easement by prescription in the case of a putative grantor who did not have power to grant the easement.[285] In the Court of Appeal, the actual decision was that the servient owner was not disabled from granting the easement claimed and so, strictly, the question of the effect of 40 years' user did not arise. The Court of Appeal however decided to deal with the issue. The judge's conclusion was upheld. It was held that the court was bound by the *Staffordshire* case and had to proceed on the basis that the House of Lords in that case had regarded the opening words of section 2 as a ground for distinguishing the operation of section 2 from the operation of section 3 in a case where the servient owner was unable to grant the easement claimed.[286]

4–75   In *Lemaitre v Davis*[287] a right of support was claimed under section 2 of the Prescription Act. The fee simple in the servient tenement belonged to the rector and churchwardens of a parish—an ecclesiastical corporation—who were restrained from alienation.[288] Hall V.-C. held that the fact that the servient tenement was held by such a corporation did not prevent a title to the easement being acquired under the Act. If the claim there was based upon an enjoyment for the shorter period of 20 years mentioned in section 2, the decision would seem to be wrong. It was pointed out in *Housden v Conservators of Wimbledon and Putney Commons*[289] that the *Staffordshire* decision was not cited in *Lemaitre v Davis*,

---

[283] (1866) L.R. 1 H.L. 254 (see at 260, 262, 268 and 278).
[284] [2007] 1 W.L.R. 2543 (first instance) and [2008] 1 W.L.R. 1172 (Court of Appeal).
[285] [2007] 1 W.L.R. 2543 at [77] and [81].
[286] [2008] 1 W.L.R. 1172 at [66] and [77].
[287] (1881) 19 Ch. D. 281 at 291.
[288] As to acquiring by prescription an easement over ecclesiastical property, see *Barker v Richardson* (1821) 4 B. & Ald. 579; *Ecclesiastical Commissioners v Kino* (1880) 14 Ch. D. 213; *Oakley v Boston* [1976] Q.B. 270; and see paras 3–08 and 4–62, fn.257, above.
[289] [2008] 1 W.L.R. 1172 at [67].

which cannot therefore be treated as a reliable authority as to the operation of section 2 in the case of a restraint on alienation and 40 years' user.

(2) *By whom the enjoyment must be had*

Competent grantee

According to the general rule requiring the presumption of an absolute grant **4–76** which is applicable in the establishment of a prescriptive title to an easement,[290] it is not only necessary to show that there was a competent grantor as regards the servient tenement, but it is also necessary to show that there was a competent grantee as regards the dominant tenement.[291] Thus it seems that a statutory company cannot by prescription acquire rights more extensive than are conferred upon it by the legislature; and accordingly a company which has been reconstituted as a railway company could not by prescription acquire water rights.[292] So, again, the "inhabitants" of a village cannot *eo nomine* acquire by prescription a right of way, "inhabitants" not being competent grantees.[293]

While a prescriptive easement must be claimed as appurtenant to the fee simple of the dominant tenement,[294] it is sufficient in pleading to claim it on the ground of an enjoyment as of right by the occupiers of such tenement.[295] Accordingly, the enjoyment of an easement by a tenant for life in possession of the dominant tenement will enure for the benefit of the fee simple and be a sufficient foundation for presuming an absolute grant.[296]

As regards the enjoyment of an easement by a tenant for years, the possession of the tenant is the possession of his landlord.[297] Thus where Blackacre, the dominant tenement, is demised by A to B, and B enjoys an easement over the adjoining Whiteacre, B's enjoyment enures for the benefit of A's fee. But where Whiteacre also belongs to A in fee, no easement is acquired by B's enjoyment.[298]

---

[290] See paras 4–59 and 4–60, above.

[291] Upon the question by whom the enjoyment must be had, Mr Gale wrote as follows:

"Although the user by which it is sought to acquire an easement must be that of the party in possession of the dominant tenement, yet any user under a claim of right in respect of such tenement will be in contemplation of law user by such possessor. Hence it appears that there is no disability of any kind to destroy the effect of such user."

The correctness of that proposition must today be considered doubtful.

[292] *National Guaranteed Manure Co v Donald* (1859) 4 H. & N. 8. See *Traill v McAllister* (1890) 25 L.R.Ir. 524, where it was held that a prescriptive title to an easement cannot result from acts of the dominant owner which are prohibited by statute.

[293] *Foxall v Venables* (1590) Cro.Eliz. 180.

[294] *Wheaton v Maple & Co* [1893] 3 Ch. 63; *Kilgour v Gaddes* [1904] 1 K.B. 466.

[295] Prescription Act 1832, s.5; see para.4–48, above.

[296] As to the rules laid down before the Prescription Act, see *Grimstead v Marlowe* (1792) 4 T.R. 717; *Att-Gen v Gauntlett* (1829) 3 Y. & J. 93; *Codling v Johnson* (1829) 9 B. & C. 933.

[297] *Gayford v Moffatt* (1868) 4 Ch. App. 133 at 135; *Pugh v Savage* [1970] 2 Q.B. 373 at 383, per Cross L.J. *Midtown Ltd v City of London Real Property Co Ltd* [2005] 1 E.G.L.R. 65 at [15].

[298] See paras 4–61, 4–67 and 4–70, above.

Where a permanent artificial stream in Cornwall had been used from time immemorial by tin-bounders (who merely were entitled by custom to work tin on the dominant tenement), such user was sufficient to give water rights by immemorial prescription to the owner in fee of the dominant tenement; the presumption being that the privilege was originally acquired by arrangement with such owner as well as with the tin-bounders.

4.—Qualities and Character of the Necessary Enjoyment

(1) *In general*

Enjoyment as of right

4–77 In order that the enjoyment, which is the quasi-possession of an easement, may confer a right to it by length of time, it must have had certain qualities and been of a certain character. In delivering the judgment of the Court of Exchequer in *Bright v Walker*,[299] in which a right of way was claimed under the Prescription Act 1832, and the qualities of an enjoyment necessary to clothe it with right by lapse of time were considered, Parke B. made the following general remarks[300]:

> "In order to establish a right of way, and to bring the case within this section,[301] it must be proved that the claimant has enjoyed it for the full period of twenty years, and that he has done so 'as of right', for that is the form in which by section 5 such a claim must be pleaded; and the like evidence would have been required before the statute to prove a claim by prescription or non-existing grant. Therefore, if the way shall appear to have been enjoyed by the claimant, not openly and in the manner that a person rightfully entitled would have used it, but by stealth, as a trespasser would have done—if he shall have occasionally asked the permission of the occupier of the land—no title would be acquired, because it was not enjoyed, 'as of right'. For the same reason it would not, if there had been unity of possession during all or part of the time: for then the claimant would not have enjoyed 'as of right' the easement, but the soil itself. So it must have been enjoyed without interruption. Again, such claim may be defeated in any other way by which the same is now liable to be defeated; that is, by the same means by which a similar claim, arising by custom, prescription, or grant, would now be defeasible; and, therefore, it may be answered by proof of a grant, or of a licence, written or parol, for a limited period, comprising the whole or part of the twenty years, or of the absence or ignorance of the parties interested in opposing the claim, and their agents, during the whole time that it was exercised."

[299] (1834) 1 Cr.M. & R. 211.
[300] (1834) 1 Cr.M. & R. 211 at 219.
[301] Prescription Act 1832, s.2. See para.4–22, above.

The authority of this case, and the doctrines laid down by the court in it, were fully recognised in *Monmouthshire Canal Co v Harford*[302] and *Tickle v Brown*.[303]

In *R. (Beresford) v Sunderland City Council*[304] it was said that "as of right" did   **4–78** not mean "of right" but was closer to "as if of right"; user can be "as of right" even though it is not adverse to the interests of the servient owner.[305] "As of right" requires one to look at the quality and character of the user and to ask whether the user is of a kind which would be enjoyed by a person having such a right. The user must be such as to convey the impression that such a right is asserted; it is not relevant to inquire into the subjective beliefs of the persons carrying on the user and, in particular, it is not necessary for such persons to show that they believed that they already possessed the right claimed.[306] If a person with the benefit of an express grant of a right of way uses the way in a manner which is outside the scope of the express right of way but he tells the servient owner that by his use he does not intend to acquire any prescriptive rights outside the scope of the express right of way, his user will not be of such a character as to bring home to the servient owner that a continuous right of enjoyment, wider than the express right of way, is being asserted.[307] A claim to an easement of parking failed on the facts in *Central Midlands Estates Ltd v Leicester Dyers Ltd*[308] where the user was described as "of an occasional nature".

Knowledge of user

The effect of the enjoyment being to raise the presumption of a consent on the   **4–79** part of the owner of the servient tenement, it is obvious that no such inference of consent can be drawn, unless it be shown that he was aware of the user, and, being so, made no attempt to interfere with its exercise.[309] Still less can such consent be implied, but rather the contrary, where he has contested the right to the user, or where, in consequence of such opposition, an interruption in the user has actually taken place. Even supposing those defects of the user not to exist, still the effect of the user would be destroyed if it were shown that it took place by the express permission of the owner of the servient tenement, for in such a case the user would not have been had with the intention of acquiring or exercising a right. The presumption, however, is that a party enjoying an easement acted under a claim of right until the contrary is shown.[310]

[302] (1834) 1 Cr.M. & R. 614.
[303] (1836) 4 A. & E. 369; and see *Winship v Hudspeth* (1854) 10 Ex. 5.
[304] [2004] 1 A.C. 889, Lord Walker of Gestingthorpe at [72].
[305] per Lord Walker of Gestingthorpe at [91]–[92].
[306] *R. v Oxfordshire C.C. Ex p. Sunningwell P.C.* [2001] 1 A.C. 335, a decision which concerns "as of right" in the Commons Registration Act 1965 but which also reviews the law as to easements.
[307] *Field Common Ltd v Elmbridge Borough Council* [2005] EWHC 2933 (Ch.) at [37]; the dominant owner's statement may also create an estoppel if the other ingredients of an estoppel are present: *ibid.* at [46].
[308] [2003] 2 P. & C.R. DG1.
[309] See paras 4–104 *et seq.*, below.
[310] *Campbell v Wilson* (1803) 3 East 294.

User nec vi, nec clam, nec precario

4–80   The civil law expressed the essential qualities of the user, by the clear and concise rule that it should be "nec vi, nec clam, nec precario".[311] The law of England, as cited by Coke,[312] from Bracton,[313] exactly agrees with the civil law:

> "Both to customes and prescriptions these two things are incidents inseparable, viz. possession or usage, and time. Possession must have three qualities: it must be long, continual and peaceable; 'longa, continua et pacifica': for it is said, 'transferuntur dominia, sine titulo, et traditione, per usucaptionem, scilicet per longam, continuam, et pacificam possessionem. Longa, i.e., per spatium temporis per legem definitum. . . . Continuam dico, ita quod non sit legitime interrupta. Pacificam dico, quia si contentiosa fuerit, idem erit quod prius, si contentio fuerit justa. Ut si verus dominus, statim cum intrusor vel disseissor ingressus fuerit seisinam, nitatur tales viribus repellere, et expellere, licet id quod inceperit perducere non possit ad effectum, dum tamen cum defecerit, diligens sit ad impetrandum et prosequendum. Longus usus nec per vim, nec clam, nec precario, etc."[314]

4–81   The words of Coke have been repeated by modern judges in stating the present rule. Thus it was said by Willes J.:

> "In the case of prescription, long enjoyment in order to establish a right must have been as of right, and therefore, neither by violence, nor by stealth nor by leave asked from time to time."[315]

> "An enjoyment as of right," said Lord Davey, "must be 'nec vi, nec clam, nec precario.' "[316]

Lord Davey's concise explanation will suffice for the present purpose; but reference may be made to the longer explanations given by Lord Denman in *Tickle v Brown*,[317] by Brett L.J. in *Earl De la Warr v Miles*,[318] and by Cozens-Hardy J. in *Gardner v Hodgson's Kingston Brewery Co*.[319]

---

[311] Cod. 3, 34, 1, *de serv.*; Dig. 8, 5, 10, *si serv. vind.*

[312] Co. Litt. 113b.

[313] Bracton, Lib. 2, f. 51b, 52a, Lib. 4, f. 222b.

[314] "Rights of ownership are transferred without title and livery through usucaption, that is to say, through long, continuous and peaceful possession. Long, that is, for the length of time prescribed by law ... Continuous, I say, in such a way that it is not lawfully interrupted. Peaceful, I say, because if it shall have been contentious, it will be the same as before, if the dispute shall have been just. As if the true lord, immediately after an intruder or disseisor shall have entered into seisin, attempts to repulse and expel such persons by force, even if he is not able to effect that which he began, yet when he has failed, is diligent in impetration and prosecution. Long use is neither by force, nor secretly, nor by permission, etc."

[315] *Mills v Colchester Corp* (1867) L.R. 2 C.P. 476 at 486.

[316] *Gardner v Hodgson's Kingston Brewery Co* [1903] A.C. 229 at 238. Lord Davey was repeating the words used by Erle J. in *Eaton v Swansea Waterworks Co* (1851) 17 Q.B. 275.

[317] (1836) 4 A. & E. 369.

[318] (1881) 17 Ch. D. 591.

[319] [1900] 1 Ch. 592 at 597.

Proof of enjoyment as of right

The words "as of right" occur in section 5 of the Prescription Act; and the mod-   **4–82**
ern rules as to the necessity of proving an enjoyment of this character appear to
be as follows: where light is claimed under section 3 of the Act, it is not necessary that the enjoyment should have been as of right,[320] but where an easement
other than light is claimed under section 2 of the Act, it is settled that the enjoyment on which the claim is based (whether for the period of 20 years or for that
of 40 years) must be shown to have been "as of right".[321] In the case of claims by
prescription at common law or under the doctrine of lost grant, whether to light
or to any other kind of easement, it is also necessary to show an enjoyment as of
right.[322] It is essential that the evidence is consistent only with user as of right. If
the evidence points to permission, the claim will not succeed. If the user is
equally consistent with user by permission and user as of right then the user is not
sufficient for prescription.[323] Thus, in referring to the doctrine of lost grant, it was
said by Fitzgibbon L.J.:

> "The whole doctrine of presumed grant rests upon the desire of the law to
> create a legal foundation for the long-continued enjoyment, as of right, of
> advantages which are prima facie inexplicable in the absence of legal title.
> In cases such as this, where the grant is admittedly a fiction, it is all the more
> incumbent on the judge to see, before the question is left to the jury, that the
> circumstances and character of the user import that it has been 'as of right.'
> It appears to me, in the present case, that the evidence is inconsistent with
> right, and that the user is consistent only with permission to enjoy what the
> supposed grantor did not want, if and so long as that user might be consis-
> tent with the rights of third parties, and also with the grantor's right to use
> his own property from time to time in a reasonable manner. Such a user
> could never have been 'as of right' in its inception; it could never acquire
> during its continuance any higher than a permissive character, and it there-
> fore never could be, or become, a foundation for the presumption of a
> grant."[324]

In *Alfred F. Beckett Ltd v Lyons*,[325] in which local inhabitants had collected and
carried away sea-washed coal from the foreshore without believing that what they
did was done as of right, the practice was not sufficient to support a claim as of
right such as to require the court to find a legal origin for it in the fiction of a lost
grant.

---

[320] *Colls v Home and Colonial Stores* [1904] A.C. 179 at 205.
[321] *Kilgour v Gaddes* [1904] 1 K.B. 462.
[322] See the above words of Willes J. in *Mills v Colchester Corp*, above.
[323] *Odey v Barber* [2008] Ch. 175 at [36].
[324] *Hanna v Pollock* [1900] 2 I.R. 664 at 671; see per Buckley L.J. in *Att-Gen v Horner* [1913] 2 Ch. 140 at 178.
[325] [1967] Ch. 449, explained and discussed in *Mills v Silver* [1991] Ch. 271 at 282F–284B.

(2) *Rules for acquisition of easements by prescription*

4–83   The following rules may be laid down as applying to the acquisition by prescription of easements generally; though not (except where otherwise stated) to the acquisition of the right to light under section 3 of the Prescription Act.

1. Nec vi

4–84   The enjoyment must not be by violence.

At common law any acts of interruption or opposition from which a jury might infer that the enjoyment was not rightful were sufficient to defeat the effect of the enjoyment, the question being whether, under all the facts of the case, such enjoyment had been under a concession of right. By section 4 of the Prescription Act, it is enacted that nothing shall be deemed to be an interruption, unless it shall be submitted to or acquiesced in for the space of a year after the party interrupted shall have had notice thereof, and of the person making or authorising the same. It is certainly by no means clear what the precise intention of the legislature was; but it appears hardly possible that it should have been intended to confer a right by user during the prescribed period, however "contentious" or "litigious" such user may have been.

4–85   In *Eaton v Swansea Waterworks Co*[326] the question was raised as to what would be the effect in law of a state of "perpetual warfare" between the dominant and servient owners, and it was held by the Court of Queen's Bench that interruptions acquiesced in for less than a year might show that the enjoyment never was of right. The inference drawn from this decision by Bowen J.[327] was that the user ought to be neither violent nor contentious. The neighbour, without actual interruption of the user, ought perhaps, on principle, to be enabled by continuous and unmistakable protests to destroy its peaceful character, and so to annul one of the conditions upon which the presumption of right is raised.

4–86   In *Newnham v Willison*[328] the principle that contentious user is not user "as of right" was applied in the following circumstances. The issue arose whether the plaintiff was entitled to the use of a "swept curve" at the junction of two tracks over which he enjoyed a right of way or only to a sharp-angled corner. The evidence established that there had been use of the swept curve without objection from 1960 to the spring of 1983. In the spring of 1983 the defendants erected a post and other obstacles. In July the plaintiff's predecessor objected by letter and removed the obstacles. In August the defendant erected a fence which made the turning into a sharp angle. The plaintiff ceased to use the track and commenced his proceedings in June 1984, more than a year after the erection of the post. The Court of Appeal held that once there is knowledge on the part of the person seeking to establish prescription that his user is

---

[326] (1851) 17 Q.B. 267.
[327] In *Dalton v Angus* (1881) 6 App. Cas. 740 at 786. See also *Lyell v Hornfield* [1914] 3 K.B. 916 followed in *Field Common Ltd v Elmbridge Borough Council* [2005] EWHC 2933 (Ch.).
[328] (1987) 56 P. & C.R. 8. The claim to the easement was based on s.2 of the Prescription Act 1832; it is not clear why the plaintiff did not rely on the doctrine of lost modern grant.

being objected to and that the use which he claims has become contentious and, if he then overcomes the objections, particularly if he does so physically as by removing an obstruction, then that is sufficient evidence to show that the user was no longer "as of right".[329] Accordingly, the Court held that the claim to prescription failed both because of section 4 of the Prescription Act 1832 (interruption for more than a year) and because there had not been a period of 20 years' user as of right immediately before action brought.[330]

It is at least open to question whether *Newnham v Willison* was correctly decided. The Court appears to have lost sight of the requirement of section 4 of the Prescription Act 1832 that to defeat a claim to a prescriptive right any interruption must have been submitted to or acquiesced in for one year.[331] The plaintiff, in that he removed the initial obstruction and protested by solicitor's letter, does not appear to have been either submitting to or acquiescing in the acts relied on as an interruption.[332] If a single incident of obstruction promptly removed by the claimant can defeat a claim, what is the point of the requirement in the section? The judgments in *Eaton v Swansea Water Works Co* are to the effect that interruptions acquiesced in for less than a year may be of importance "on the question whether there ever was a commencement of an enjoyment as of right"[333] and may show "that the enjoyment never was of right",[334] but do not suggest that such interruptions may be relied upon to defeat the claim on the ground that user as of right became "no longer as of right".[335] At any rate, the decision emphasises the importance of instituting proceedings promptly after any interruption in any case where the period necessary for prescription has already run.

Newnham v Willison[336] was followed in *Smith v Brudenell-Bruce*[337] where it   **4–87** was held that two letters written in forceful terms by the servient owner objecting to continued user of a way meant that such user thereafter was contentious and not as of right. However, because there had been 20 years' user as of right before the letters, the claim to prescription based on the doctrine of lost modern grant succeeded even though a claim under the 1832 Act failed.

In *Dennis v Ministry of Defence*[338] a claim to prescription failed on the ground   **4–88** that the user was "*vi*". The Ministry of Defence was the occupier of an airfield

---

[329] (1987) 56 P. & C.R. 8, at 19, per Kerr L.J.
[330] (1987) 56 P. & C.R. 8, at 20, per Eastham J., who appears to have regarded the mere sending of a letter as sufficient to constitute a "contentious" situation which (a) amounted to an interruption within s.4 and (b) prevented further use being "as of right".
[331] See paras 4–43 to 4–47, above.
[332] These would appear to have been sufficient acts to negative "submission" as explained in *Dance v Triplow* (1991) 64 P. & C.R. 1 at 5; see para.4–47, above.
[333] (1851) 17 Q.B. 267, at 273, per Lord Campbell C.J.
[334] (1851) 17 Q.B. 267, at 275, per Coleridge J.
[335] The expression used by Kerr L.J. at (1987) 56 P. & C.R. 19.
[336] (1987) 56 P. & C.R. 8.
[337] [2002] 2 P. & C.R. 51. It should be noted that lost modern grant was not relied on in *Newnham v Willison* even though it seems that the user of the swept curve had continued from 1960 to 1983: see (1987) 56 P. & C.R. 8 at 15. See also *Field Common Ltd v Elmbridge Borough Council* [2005] EWHC 2933 (Ch.) where protests by the servient owner and threats from the servient owner of an injunction meant that the user was contentious and therefore "*vi*".
[338] [2003] 2 E.G.L.R. 121 (and see the discussion at 127G–K).

near to the claimants' property. The RAF used the airfield as an operating and training base for jump-jet Harrier aircraft, which were very noisy. The claimants contended that the use of the airfield in this way constituted an actionable nuisance at common law, a contention which the court upheld. The Ministry argued that the user had continued for a sufficient length of time such that it had acquired a prescriptive right to continue the activity. The argument failed on two grounds. The first ground was that the right claimed could not form the subject-matter of a grant on account of the uncertainty in expression of the alleged right.[339] The second ground was that the claimants had complained and protested over the years, but the Ministry's attitude was that the flying had to continue. It was held that the claimants' protests coupled with the Ministry's insistence on continuing, which the claimants were powerless to stop, meant that the user was with force or "*vi*". The claimants were held not to have acquiesced in the user.

4–89   An act of partial interruption, instead of destroying the easement claimed, may qualify it, and be evidence of another easement. Thus, where a weir across a river was claimed by prescription, and a miller, whose mill was on its banks, had caused a fender to be shut down, the court held this not fatal to the claimant's right, thinking that there was nothing to prevent a second easement being acquired, as subordinate to that already existing, if the subject-matter admitted of it.[340]

2. Nec clam

4–90   The enjoyment must not be secret.

The user of an easement may be secret, either by reason of the mode in which a party enjoys it, or by reason of the nature of the easement itself.

Instances of the former kind are where the right is exercised by stealth, or in the night.[341] Instances of the latter kind occur where a man who secretly excavates his own land on which a house is standing subsequently and in consequence of the excavation claims an extraordinary degree of support for the house from the neighbouring soil,[342] or where extraordinary support is claimed in consequence of a peculiarity in the internal structure of the house,[343] not visible to the neighbour.

4–91   A consideration of this rule would, it appears, afford an answer in the affirmative to the question incidentally raised in *Dodd v Holme*[344]—whether, in order to

---

[339] See para.4–128, below.
[340] *Rolle v Whyte* (1868) L.R. 3 Q.B. 302.
[341] *Talis usus non valebit, cum sit clandestinus, et idem erit si nocturnus*: Bracton, Lib. 2, f. 52b. *Aut in absentia domini*: *ibid.*, Lib. 4, f. 221a. See *Dawson v Norfolk* (1815) 1 Price 246; *Liverpool Corp v Coghill* [1918] 1 Ch. 307.
[342] *Partridge v Scott* (1838) 3 M. & W. 229.
[343] *Angus v Dalton* (1878) 4 Q.B.D. 162; see per Thesiger L.J. at 181–183 and per Cotton L.J. at 187. The defendants elected not to take a new trial, so that the decision on this point of the Court of Appeal was not, strictly speaking, open to review by the House of Lords; but the point was referred to on the appeal: see the same case in (1881) 6 App. Cas. 740 at 751 (Pollock B.), 757 and 760 (Field J.), 766 and 767 (Lindley L.J.), 777 and 779 (Fry J.), 787 and 789 (Bowen J.), 801 (Lord Selborne), 807 (Lord Penzance), 827 and 828 (Lord Blackburn).
[344] (1834) 1 A. & E. 493.

acquire a right to support for a house by antiquity of possession, it must originally have been built with that degree of strength and coherence which may reasonably be expected to be found in a well-built house. For as there might be nothing in the external appearance of the house to give notice to the owner of the adjoining land that the weakness with which it was built caused it to require a greater degree of support from his soil than a well-built house would have required, and as *quoad* such additional support the enjoyment would have been secret, no presumption of a grant of it on his part could be implied. The same reasoning would also apply to the case of an ancient house, originally well built, becoming weaker from the want of proper repair. A man believing there were no minerals on his own land might be willing to subject it to the easement of support to a well-built house, which would diminish the value of his property only in the event of his wishing to mine in it, although he would refuse to restrict himself from digging a foundation for any building he might require; which would possibly be the case were he bound to afford the support necessary to sustain a rickety and ill-built edifice. There is also the case of a house originally requiring no more than an ordinary degree of support, but subsequently altered so as to require an unusual amount of lateral pressure to support it. But here, it seems that, if the alteration be openly and honestly made, the servient owner is fixed with notice that an additional burden of some kind is being imposed upon his tenement, and, if he makes no inquiry, will in time become subject to the obligation of increased support.[345] This reasoning also applies to the claim of an extraordinary degree of support from adjoining houses.[346]

Secrecy of enjoyment was one of the difficulties in establishing the easement **4–92** of support considered in the leading case of *Dalton v Angus*.[347] It was established by that decision that there must be some knowledge or means of knowledge on the part of the servient owner against whom the right is claimed.[348] In the simple case where a prescriptive easement of support is claimed by the owner of one of two adjoining houses against the owner of the other, it must be shown that the owner of the servient tenement knew or had the means of knowing that his house was affording support to the other.[349] Again, in *Union Lighterage Co v London Graving Dock Co*[350] where the sides of a wooden dock had for more than 20 years been supported by underground rods which were not themselves visible, but certain nuts which fastened them were visible, claim to support for the dock from the rods was defeated on the ground that the enjoyment had been "*clam*". It was held

---

[345] *Dalton v Angus* (1881) 6 App. Cas. 740; per Lord Selborne at 801.
[346] See per Bramwell B. in *Solomon v Vintners' Co* (1859) 4 H. & N. 585 at 601. In *Angus v Dalton*, Cockburn C.J. appears to have considered that the very possibility of acquiring any prescriptive right to support was excluded by the secrecy of the enjoyment (3 Q.B.D. 117), but this opinion was negatived by the Court of Appeal and the House of Lords. See *Lloyds Bank v Dalton* [1942] Ch. 466.
[347] (1881) 6 App. Cas. 740.
[348] *Union Lighterage Co v London Graving Dock Co* [1902] 2 Ch. 557.
[349] *Gately v Martin* [1900] 2 Ir.R. 269; *Wilsons Brewery Ltd v West Yorkshire M.B.C.* (1977) 34 P. & C.R. 224. See *Lemaitre v Davis* (1881) 19 Ch. D. 291.
[350] [1902] 2 Ch. 557.

by Romer and Stirling L.JJ. that, on the facts, knowledge of the rods ought not to be attributed to the servient owner; Vaughan Williams L.J. holding, on the other hand, that there was sufficient means of knowledge.[351]

4–93   In *Liverpool Corporation v Coghill*[352] it was held that the claimants' intermittent discharge, at night, of borax solution into the plaintiffs' sewers without their knowledge was a secret enjoyment which did not entitle them to an easement although practised for more than 20 years before proceedings were brought in May 1917. Moreover, time would not have commenced to run against the plaintiffs until there had been an invasion of a legal[353] right and, as the effluent was innocuous prior to the year 1908, the requisite period had not elapsed. In any case it was doubtful if the plaintiffs, in view of their statutory duties, could have made such a grant as the prescriptive right contended for implied.

In connection with the rule that enjoyment as of right must not be "*clam*", reference should be made to the cases quoted later[354] laying down that the user on which a claim to a prescriptive easement is based must be a user of which the servient owner has knowledge either actual or constructive.

3. Nec precario

4–94   The enjoyment must not be precarious.

What is precarious? "That which depends not on right, but on the will of another person."[355] "Si autem", says Bracton,[356] "(seisina) precaria fuerit et de gratia, quae tempestive revocari possit et intempestive, ex longo tempore non acquiritur jus."[357]

Enjoyment had under a licence or permission from the owner of the servient tenement confers no right to the easement. Each renewal of the licence rebuts the presumption which would otherwise arise, that such enjoyment was had under a claim of right to the easement.[358] Permission granted by a tenant who is in occupation of the servient tenement is sufficient to defeat a claim under the doctrine of lost grant or on the basis of section 2 of the Prescription Act.[359]

4–95   The law draws a distinction between acquiescence by the owner on the one hand and licence or permission from the owner on the other hand. In some circumstances, the distinction may not matter but in the law of prescription, the distinction is fundamental. This is because user which is acquiesced in by the owner

---

[351] This principle will tend to be an obstacle to the acquisition of a right of underground drainage or sewerage by prescription. Such a claim failed in *Barney v B.P. Truckstops Ltd* [1995] N.P.C. 5.

[352] [1918] 1 Ch. 307.

[353] See *Goldsmid v Tunbridge Wells Improvement Commissioners* (1866) 1 Ch. App. 349.

[354] See paras 4–104 *et seq.*, below.

[355] per Farwell J., *Burrows v Lang* [1901] 2 Ch. 502 at 510.

[356] Lib. 4, f. 221a.

[357] "If seisin shall have been from mere favour and from grace, which can be revoked in season and out of season, no right is acquired from a long period of time."

[358] *Monmouthshire Canal Co v Harford* (1834) 1 C.M. & R. 614; *Tone v Preston* (1883) 24 Ch D. 739; *Chamber Colliery Co v Hopwood* (1886) 32 Ch. D. 549.

[359] *Ward v Kirkland* [1967] Ch. 194 at 233, 234.

is "as of right"; acquiescence is the foundation of prescription. However, user which is with the licence or permission of the owner is not "as of right". Permission involves some positive act or acts on the part of the owner, whereas passive toleration is all that is required for acquiescence. The positive act or acts may take different forms. The grant of oral or written consent is the clearest and most obvious expression of permission. But there is no reason in principle why the grant of permission should be confined to such cases. Permission may also be inferred from the owner's acts. It may be that there will not be many cases where, in the absence of express oral or written permission, it will be possible to infer permission from an owner's positive acts. Most cases where nothing is said or written will properly be classified as cases of mere acquiescence. But there is no reason in principle why an implied permission may not defeat a claim to use "as of right". Such permission may only be inferred from overt and contemporaneous acts of the owner.[360]

The question of "*nec precario*" was considered by the House of Lords in *R.* **4–96** *(Beresford) v Sunderland City Council*.[361] That case did not involve a claim to an easement but concerned a claim to a town or village green within section 22 of the Commons Registration Act 1965, where the status of town or village green had been acquired by prescription. Lord Scott of Foscote suggested[362] that the principles as to prescription under the Prescription Act 1832 (dealing with easements) and under the Highways Act 1980 (dealing with dedication of a public highway) and under the Commons Registration Act 1965 were not necessarily identical and indeed to apply principles applicable to one type of right to another type of right without taking account of their differences could be "dangerous". However, the House of Lords considered cases on easements amongst other things and it is thought that it is possible to derive from the decision statements of principle of application as to prescription in the law of easements.

Lord Rodger of Earlsferry described the position in Roman law and referred to the law as described by Bracton. In Roman law, "*precarium*" was the name given to a gratuitous grant of enjoyment of land or goods which is revocable at will. The arrangement is informal and is based on the grantor's goodwill, whether more or less enthusiastic. But, however informal, the arrangement does involve a positive act of granting the use of the property, as opposed to mere acquiescence in its use. Bracton took over the noun *precarium* and its congeners from the vocabulary of Roman law and used them in a number of contexts, but always with reference to a gratuitous grant which is revocable at any time at the grantor's pleasure. In connection with easements, Bracton used *precarium* to mean the same as "*de gratia*" i.e. of grace. English law distinguishes between a temporary licence or permission for an activity (which is *precarium*) and acquiescence.[363]

---

[360] *R. (Beresford) v Sunderland City Council* [2002] Q.B. 874 (Court of Appeal) at [11]–[12].
[361] [2004] 1 A.C. 889.
[362] [2004] 1 A.C. 889, at [34].
[363] [2004] 1 A.C. 889, at [57]–[58]. Lord Rodger approved the meaning of "*precarium*" given in *Burrows v Lang* [1901] 2 Ch. 502 at 510 and in *Sturges v Bridgman* (1879) 11 Ch. D. 852 at 863.

Lord Scott of Foscote pointed out that whilst the normal position was that use which was the subject of a licence or permission was "*precario*" and not as of right, this was not invariably so. Lord Scott gave two examples of the exceptions. He referred to a case of proprietary estoppel where the owner of the servient land would be estopped by his statements from revoking a permission he had given. He suggested that user in those circumstances would not be "*precario*" and that after 20 years' enjoyment of the equity which arose from the proprietary estoppel, the beneficiary of the permission would be able to claim a legal easement under the Prescription Act 1832. Lord Scott's second example concerned an agreement to grant an easement which was not completed by a deed of grant even though the consideration for the grant was paid. He suggested that 20 years' user pursuant to the agreement would have entitled the purchaser of the easement to a legal easement by prescription as the user would not have been "*precario*"; the purchaser would have been "claiming right" to the easement. Lord Scott referred to the position of a purchaser in possession under an uncompleted contract of sale.[364]

One of the main points in the *Beresford* case was whether the relevant licence or permission had to be express or whether a licence or permission which was to be implied from all the circumstances could mean that the user was "*precario*". It was held that user pursuant to such an implied licence would indeed be "*precario*".[365] The House of Lords therefore agreed with the judge at first instance and the Court of Appeal on this question of principle. However, the House of Lords disagreed with the lower courts as to whether it was proper to imply a permission on the facts of that case. It was held that the essential distinction which was relevant was between a revocable licence or permission and acquiescence on the part of the servient owner. A revocable licence or permission would constitute "*precarium*" and would defeat prescription whereas acquiescence was of the essence of prescription. Encouragement of the user by the owner of the servient tenement did not necessarily signify an implied licence or permission and, accordingly, although the owner had encouraged the user in that case that amounted to a case of acquiescence and not a case of implied licence or permission.

An example of an implied licence or permission was a case where a charge was made for entering on the land.[366] It may also be possible to have a case where consent is given by non-verbal means.[367]

4–97   The name "*precarium*" suggests, and the Roman law Digests indicate, that in Roman law the paradigm case is of a grant in response to a request.[368] In *Odey v Barber* it was argued that "*precarium*" could *only* be shown where the permission had been asked for and that an unsolicited permission, even when acted upon, did

[364] [2004] 1 A.C. 889 at [37]–[38] and see *Bridges v Mees* [1957] Ch. 475 at 484–485.
[365] [2004] 1 A.C. 889 at [5], [43], [59], [75] and [83], subject possibly to the exceptional cases discussed by Lord Scott.
[366] [2004] 1 A.C. 889 at [74]–[75].
[367] [2004] 1 A.C. 889 at [75].
[368] [2004] 1 A.C. 889 at [57].

not suffice. That argument was rejected.[369] In that case, the permission had been acted upon. In such a case it is not difficult to say that the user is referable to the permission and therefore not "as of right". That decision did not involve any question as to what the result would be where the dominant owner repudiates the proffered permission and continues the user asserting that he does so as of right and not pursuant to the permission.[370] If the servient owner obstructs the user as of right and instead offers a permission to continue the user and that permission is not taken up, then the dominant owner does not acquiesce in the obstruction for the purposes of section 4 of the 1832 Act.[371]

Before the Prescription Act, any admission, whether verbal or otherwise, that **4–98** the enjoyment had been had by permission of the owner of the servient tenement was sufficient to prevent the acquisition of the right, however long such enjoyment might have continued. Since the Prescription Act, where an easement is claimed under the Act, the effect of permission for the enjoyment having been given by the owner of the servient tenement has been considered in many cases.

A claim to an easement (other than light) under section 2 of the Act on the ground of an enjoyment for 20 years is defeated by an oral consent given at the beginning of and extending throughout the user.[372] If user has continued for 40 years a claim will still be defeated by permission given during the period, or by user which continues on a common understanding that the user is and continues to be permissive,[373] but not by prior parol permission.[374] Once permission has been given, the user remains permissive and is not capable of ripening into a right (save where the permission is oral and the user has continued for 40 years) unless and until, having been given for a limited period only, it expires or, being general,

---

[369] [2008] Ch. 175, following, in particular, *Rafique v Trustees of the Walton Estate* (1992) 65 P. & C.R. 356 and the Australian decision of *O'Mara v Gascoigne* (1996) 9 B.P.R. 16,349, where it was held that an unsolicited permission was sufficient to prevent prescription: "acting on leave volunteered is as much acceptance of it as if it had been asked for in the first place": see at 16,355. The decision in *Rafique* had been criticised in (1994) Conv. 196 (Prof. H. Wallace) citing *Mills v Colchester Corp* (1867) L.R. 2 C.P. 476 at 486 and *Tickle v Brown* (1836) 4 A. & E. 369 at 382, which refer to permission being "asked for" rather than unilaterally given. The same article also discussed *B.P. Properties Ltd v Buckler* (1987) 55 P. & C.R. 337, where the unilateral grant of a licence to occupy prevented the person in possession of the land from being in adverse possession; in this case, however, it was suggested that the position might be different if the person in possession of the land had repudiated the grant of the unilateral permission; see at 346.

[370] Consider *Bewlay v Atkinson* (1879) 13 Ch. D. 283, *Greenhalgh v Brindley* [1901] 2 Ch. 324 and *Smith v Colbourne* [1914] 2 Ch. 533 where there are references to a permission otherwise available being "denounced".

[371] See *Ward v Kirkland* [1967] Ch. 194 at 231.

[372] *Healey v Hawkins* [1968] 1 W.L.R. 1967 (considering and explaining dicta of Lord Denman C.J. in *Tickle v Brown* (1836) 4 A. & E. 369 at 383, and Alderson B. in *Kinloch v Nevile* (1840) 6 M. & W. 795 at 806). See also *Reilly v Orange* [1955] 2 Q.B. 112 at 119.

[373] See *Jones v Price and Morgan* (1992) 64 P. & C.R. 404 at 407, per Parker L.J.

[374] *Gardner v Hodgson's Kingston Brewery Co* [1903] A.C. 229, affirming CA [1901] 2 Ch. 198; *Healey v Hawkins* [1968] 1 W.L.R. 1967; and see *Tickle v Brown* (1836) 4 A. & E. 369; *Beasley v Clarke* (1836) 2 Bing.N.C. 705; *Earl De la Warr v Miles* (1881) 17 Ch. D. 535 at 596. Written permission, in order to defeat a claim based on an enjoyment for 40 years, must be properly pleaded, a general traverse of enjoyment as of right being insufficient: *Tickle v Brown*, above, 369 at 383; see *Gardner v Hodgson's Kingston Brewery Co* [1900] 1 Ch. 594, per Cozens-Hardy J.; [1901] 2 Ch. 213, per Rigby L.J.; *Lowry v Crothers* (1872) I.R. 5 C.L. 98.

it is revoked, or there is a change of circumstances from which revocation may fairly be implied.[375]

If the enjoyment was originally by permission, it is a question of fact, depending upon the evidence, and the inferences to be drawn therefrom, whether it has so continued.[376] The fact that a gate, through which a right of way was claimed, had always been kept locked, the key having been kept by the proprietor of the servient tenement, but always having been asked for by the proprietor of the dominant tenement as a matter of right, when it was required, and never having been refused, did not prevent the acquisition, by prescription, of the easement.[377] But the fact that a gate across a way is installed and kept locked for substantial periods may well show that user was not as of right: the principle is that the party claiming to have acquired a right by prescription will fail if he can show no more than casual user permitted by a neighbour's tolerance and good nature.[378] There is, however, no general principle that if user has been "tolerated" by the servient owner, no prescriptive right can arise, for this would be inconsistent with the whole notion of acquisition of rights by prescription, in which acquiescence by the servient owner is a necessary element.[379]

4–99   In *Rose v Krieser*[380] the parties had originally entered into an agreement for the grant of mutual easements. Over the years the dominant owner had used an access way which was not the same as that granted or to be granted pursuant to the agreement. The trial judge held that the user had given rise to a right of way by prescription but he also held that the user "found its origin" in the original agreement. The servient owner contended that this meant that the user was permissive and could not be relied upon for the purposes of prescription. The argument was rejected. First, it was said that the reference in the Canadian equivalent of the Prescription Act 1832 to a consent or agreement only extended to a consent or agreement which prevented the user being "as of right"[381] and, further, the user relied upon related to land which was different from that which was the subject of the agreement. Accordingly, the finding of an easement by prescription was upheld.

---

[375] *Healey v Hawkins* [1968] 1 W.L.R. 1967, applying *Gaved v Martyn* (1865) 19 C.B. (n.s.) 732. In *Odey v Barber* [2008] Ch. 175 at [38]–[42], it was held that the relevant user was within the permission from the servient owner.

[376] *Gaved v Martyn* (1865) 19 C.B. (n.s.) 732; *Healey v Hawkins* [1968] 1 W.L.R. 1967. See "Prescription under the Statute" by P. St J. Lagan in 32 Conv. (n.s.) 40.

[377] *Roberts v Fellowes* (1906) 94 L.T. 279.

[378] *Goldsmith v Burrow Construction Limited*, *The Times*, July 31, 1987 (Court of Appeal (Civil) Transcript No. 750 of 1987) explaining and applying *Lay v Wyncoll* (1966) 198 E.G. 182 and *Green v Ashco Horticultural Limited* [1966] 1 W.L.R. 889.

[379] *Mills v Silver* [1991] Ch. 271 at 279G–280B, per Dillon L.J. and at 288A–G, per Parker L.J., explaining *Goldsmith v Burrow Construction* (above) and distinguishing and disapproving dicta in *Patel v W.H. Smith (Eziot) Limited* [1987] 1 W.L.R. 853, a decision which can only be upheld on the basis that the defendants had conceded in correspondence that they did not have the rights for which they were contending.

[380] [2002] 212 D.L.R. (4th) 123.

[381] Consider, also, Lord Scott's observations in *R. (Beresford) v Sunderland City Council* [2004] 1 A.C. 889 at [37]–[38], noted at para.4–96, above.

Where the easement of light is claimed under section 3 of the Act, it has been   **4–100**
laid down in the House of Lords that enjoyment as of right need not be alleged or
proved, and that the right is acquired by 20 years' enjoyment without interruption
and without written consent.[382] A written consent would negative the effect of the
enjoyment (see section 3), but not a verbal consent.[383]

The rule that an enjoyment which is by permission is not an enjoyment as of
right is illustrated by cases as to water rights. Thus, in *Wood v Waud*[384] it was said
that the nature of an artificial watercourse showed that though the water in fact
had flowed for 60 years, yet from the beginning it was only intended to flow so
long as the coal-owners did not think fit otherwise to drain their mines, and so
was precarious.[385] It was said also that the decision of the Court of Exchequer in
the last-mentioned case was in fact a decision that an enjoyment for more than a
statutable period is not an enjoyment as of right if during the period it is known
that it is only permitted as long as some particular purpose is served.[386]

It is for the party claiming the prescriptive right to prove that his user was "as
of right". If the evidence material to this assertion is rejected, the claim will fail
even if the court cannot make a positive finding that the user was permissive.[387]

If a permission has been given by the servient owner to the dominant owner,   **4–101**
what is the position as regards successors in title to the original parties to that permission?

First, as regards the benefit of the permission, it may be, depending upon the
circumstances and the terms in which the permission is expressed, that the permission is personal to the original dominant owner. In such a case, the permission
would lapse when the original dominant owner transfers the dominant tenement.
The question would then arise whether continued use by the successor is referable to the acquiescence of the servient owner in user as of right (and therefore
time will run) or whether the continued use could support an inference that the
original permission has been extended to the successor to the dominant tenement
(and therefore time will not run).

Secondly, as regards the burden of the permission, the general rule is that a permission does not create an interest in the land,[388] and therefore the permission
will not bind the successor in title to the servient tenement.

In a number of cases concerning the easement of light and section 3 of the
Prescription Act 1832, the court has referred to the dominant owner "denouncing" a permission given by the servient owner and holding that it was open to the

---

[382] *Colls v Home and Colonial Stores* [1904] A.C. 179 at 205.
[383] *London Corp v Pewterers' Co* (1842) 2 Moo. & R. 409; *Judge v Lowe* (1873) I.R. 7 C.L. 291; see
Plasterers' Co v Parish Clerks' Co (1851) 6 Exch. 630; *Mallam v Rose* [1915] 2 Ch. 222.
[384] (1849) 3 Exch. 748.
[385] See *Mason v Shrewsbury & Hereford Ry* (1871) L.R. 6 Q.B. 578 at 584; *Schwann v Cotton* [1916]
2 Ch. 459 at 475, where Warrington L.J. explains the judgment (at 3 Exch. 779) in *Wood v Waud*,
above.
[386] (1849) 3 Exch. 748, see *Staffordshire & Worcestershire Canal Co v Birmingham Canal Co* (1866)
L.R. 1 H.L. 254.
[387] *Jones v Price & Morgan* (1992) 64 P. & C.R. 404 at 408.
[388] *Ashburn Anstalt v Arnold* [1989] Ch. 1.

dominant owner to act in that way so that continued user after the permission is "denounced" would be user as of right and not pursuant to the permission.[389]

4. Enjoyment under a mistake

4–102   The fact that enjoyment takes place under a mistaken view of his rights entertained by the dominant owner does not prevent enjoyment being "as of right" so as to defeat prescription. So, in *Earl De la Warr v Miles*[390] a claim to take litter did not fail because of an erroneous belief that a certain decree conferred the right. In *Bridle v Ruby*[391] the acquisition of a prescriptive right over a driveway was not defeated because the driveway had been used in the mistaken belief that the right to use it derived from an earlier conveyance. In *Bosomworth v Faber*[392] the acquisition of a right to a supply of water by lost modern grant was not defeated by the fact that the supply had been enjoyed by virtue of a grant which was void on account of being perpetuitous. As Cotton L.J. put it in *Earl De la Warr v Miles*:

> "It is not necessary, . . . that the acts done should at the time have been attempted to have been justified in a way in which we think they can legally be justified, if the person doing them was claiming to do them as of right. What particular right the person doing the act alleged, unless there was permission from time to time given by the lord, in my opinion is not material under the statute."[393]

4–103   Previous editions of this work suggested the law was otherwise on the authority of *Chamber Colliery Co v Hopwood*.[394] There, Blackacre was demised to a tenant who during the lease made and enjoyed a watercourse on it for the benefit of an adjoining property of his own: both landlord and tenant believed that such enjoyment was authorised by the lease: assuming that it was not so authorised, the Court of Appeal held that there was no enjoyment as of right. The apparent discrepancy between this case and *Earl De la Warr v Miles* was initially explained[395] on the basis that in the latter case there was no consensual element, whereas in the former case the tenant's erroneous belief was acquiesced in by the landlord. In *Bridle v Ruby* the Court of Appeal has now drawn a more convincing distinction, namely that:

---

[389] *Bewley v Atkinson* (1879) 13 Ch. D. 283; *Greenhalgh v Brindley* [1901] 2 Ch. 324; and *Smith v Colbourne* [1914] 2 Ch. 533.
[390] (1881) 17 Ch. D. 535.
[391] [1989] 1 Q.B. 169.
[392] (1992) 69 P. & C.R. 288. See also *Capar v Wasylowski* (1983) 146 D.L.R. (3d) 193.
[393] (1881) 17 Ch. D. 535 at 597.
[394] (1886) 32 Ch. D. 549.
[395] In *Thomas W. Ward Limited v Alexander Bruce (Grays) Limited* [1959] 2 Lloyd's Rep. 472, where a grant for loading and unloading vessels was exceeded by breaking up vessels: there was no evidence that either party believed this to be within the grant and the dominant owner failed to show that his user was not "*precario*".

"In the Chamber Colliery case, both parties believed the enjoyment of the water course was under and for the period of the lease. There was a common belief therefore that nothing was being asserted or claimed and nothing acquiesced in greater than a right for a limited term."[396]

In general, the subjective belief of the person carrying on the user is irrelevant; what is relevant is the character of the user; is it user of the kind that would be carried on if the person carrying it on had the right claimed?[397] User in a mistaken belief that it is justified by a right of limited duration, which belief is acquiesced in, cannot be made the foundation of a grant of unlimited duration but to say that no user based on a mistaken belief could found a claim to prescription would be to say that the law will only presume a grant in favour of someone who is aware that he is a wrongdoer.[398]

Where, however, a right has been asserted and acquiesced in on a particular basis, the claimant cannot thereafter set up his claim on any other ground, but this does not mean that where a claimant asserts a right in the mere belief that such right has been conferred when it has not, this negatives any claim to prescription.[399]

5. Knowledge of servient owner

The enjoyment must be one of which the servient owner has either actual knowledge   **4–104**
or the means of knowledge.[400] This rule will be best illustrated in the first instance by the following statements of law made by judges in cases where easements were called in question.

In *Sturges v Bridgman*[401] Thesiger L.J., delivering the judgment of the Court of Appeal, said:

"The law governing the acquisition of easements by user stands thus: Consent or acquiescence of the owner of the servient tenement lies at the root of prescription, and of the fiction of a lost grant, and hence the acts or user, which go to the proof of either the one or the other, must be, in the language of the civil law, nec vi nec clam nec precario; for a man cannot, as a general rule, be said to consent to or acquiesce in the acquisition by his neighbour of an easement through an enjoyment of which he has no knowledge, actual or constructive,[402] or which he contests and endeavours to interrupt, or which he temporarily licenses. It is a mere extension of the same notion, or rather it is a principle into which by strict analysis it may be

---

[396] [1989] 1 Q.B. 169 at 176H, per Parker L.J.
[397] *R. v Oxfordshire C.C. Ex p. Sunningwell P.C.* [2000] 1 A.C. 335.
[398] *Bridle v Ruby* [1989] 1 Q.B. 169 at 177D.
[399] [1989] 1 Q. B. 169, at 177B, explaining *Att-Gen v Horner (No. 2)* [1913] 2 Ch. 140; *Campbell v Wilson* (1803) 3 East 294; and *Lord Rivers v Adams* (1878) 3 Ex.D. 361.
[400] *Diment v Foot (N.H.)* [1974] 1 W.L.R. 1427 at 1433, per Sir John Pennycuick V.-C.; *Williams v Sandy Lane (Chester) Ltd* [2007] 1 E.G.L.R. 10 at [33].
[401] (1879) 11 Ch. D. 852 at 863. See also per Stirling L.J., *Roberts v James* (1903) 89 L.T. 282 at 287.
[402] See *Liverpool Corp v Coghill* [1918] 1 Ch. 307 at 314.

resolved, to hold, that an enjoyment which a man cannot prevent raises no presumption of consent or acquiescence."[403]

4–105   Again, in delivering his opinion to the House of Lords in *Dalton v Angus*,[404] Fry J. said:

> "In my opinion, the whole law of prescription and the whole law which governs the presumption or inference of a grant or covenant rest upon acquiescence. The courts and the judges have had recourse to various expedients for quieting the possession of persons in the exercise of rights which have not been resisted by the persons against whom they are exercised, but in all cases it appears to me that acquiescence and nothing else is the principle upon which these expedients rest. It becomes then of the highest importance to consider of what ingredients acquiescence consists. In many cases, as, for instance, in the case of that acquiescence which creates a right of way, it will be found to involve, first, the doing of some act by one man upon the land of another; secondly, the absence of right to do that act in the person doing it; thirdly, the knowledge of the person affected by it that the act is done; fourthly, the power of the person affected by the act to prevent such act either by act on his part or by action in the courts; and lastly, the abstinence by him from any such interference for such a length of time as renders it reasonable for the courts to say that he shall not afterwards interfere to stop the act being done. In some other cases, as, for example, in the case of lights, some of these ingredients are wanting; but I cannot imagine any case of acquiescence in which there is not shown to be in the servient owner: 1, a knowledge of the acts done; 2, a power in him to stop the acts or to sue in respect of them; and 3, an abstinence on his part from the exercise of such power. That such is the nature of acquiescence and that such is the ground upon which presumptions or inferences of grant or covenant may be made appears to me to be plain, both from reason, from maxim, and from the cases."

Referring to the above opinions of Fry J., Lord Penzance, in his speech in the House of Lords in *Dalton v Angus*, stated that he was in "entire accord" with that judge; the opinion being also described by Lord Blackburn as "a very able one".[405] Lord Blackburn's own view seems to have been to base prescription not so much upon acquiescence as upon utility, *bono publico*.[406] But later decisions appear to have followed rather the lines laid down by Fry J. than those laid down by Lord Blackburn. In *Union Lighterage Co v London Graving Dock Co*[407]

---

[403] For a good example of a case where the owner of the servient tenement was held to have had either actual knowledge or constructive notice of the enjoyment of the easement claimed, see *Lloyds Bank v Dalton* [1942] Ch. 466; see para.4–106, below.

[404] (1881) 6 App. Cas. 740 at 773.

[405] (1881) 6 App. Cas. 740 at 803, 823.

[406] (1881) 6 App. Cas. 740 at 818, 826.

[407] [1902] 2 Ch. 557, affirming [1900] 2 Ch. 300, per Cozens-Hardy J.; see also *Diment v Foot (N.H.)* [1974] 1 W.L.R. 1427, para.4–114, below.

Vaughan Williams L.J. distinctly prefers the view of Fry J., stating, however, at the same time that actual knowledge is not essential to acquiescence, but that means of knowledge is sufficient.[408] Romer and Stirling L.JJ. also indicated that means of knowledge is sufficient.[409]

In *Lloyds Bank v Dalton*[410] Bennett J. found as a fact that the defendants, own- **4–106** ers of dye-works which had in fact supported the plaintiff's yard and outbuilding, either must have known or must be taken to have had a reasonable opportunity of knowing that the said yard and outbuilding had been supported by the dye-works. The decision is clear authority for the view that constructive as opposed to actual knowledge is enough to prevent the owner of the servient tenement from setting up the defence that the enjoyment of the easement claimed was "*clam*". In *Loder v Gaden*[411] where there was a right of way for agricultural purposes, it was held that a wider right of way had not been acquired by prescription when there was no hint that the dominant tenement was being used for a wider use than agricultural purposes.

The cases in which the importance of knowledge on the part of the servient **4–107** owner has been most frequently discussed are those where the servient tenement has during the enjoyment been in the possession of a tenant for life or years. It seems that in such cases the want of acquiescence of the owner of the inheritance of the neighbouring tenement may be inferred, either from the circumstance that he is not in possession, or from the nature of the enjoyment of the right being such as to be out of his view and knowledge, though he is in possession. With respect to the former question an important point arises, whether, if the knowledge in fact of the owner of the inheritance of the hostile enjoyment of an easement be shown, he is bound by it. Cases decided before the Prescription Act certainly lay down that if knowledge in fact of the reversioner be shown, he would be bound; but in *Daniel v North*[412] Le Blanc J. took a distinction between two divisions of ease-ments, expressing an opinion to the effect that an enjoyment of a negative ease-ment would not bind the reversioner, unless his knowledge were positively shown, though it would be otherwise in the case of an affirmative easement. If it be taken as law that a reversioner can be bound by his knowledge in fact of a user enjoyed during the time his land is in the possession of a tenant, as his acquies-cence in such cases is inferred from his offering no opposition, it would seem that he must, by law, have some valid mode of preventing the right from vesting by the continuance of the user. With respect to a negative easement, it is clear the user gives no right of action to any person; and even as to some positive

---

[408] [1902] 2 Ch. 557, at 568, 569. On the facts Vaughan Williams L.J. dissented from the other mem-bers of the Court of Appeal. A servient owner who had been in possession of the servient tenement throughout was presumed to have notice, actual or constructive, of the use to which the servient land was being openly and continuously subjected: *Bower v John Etherington Ltd* (1965) 53 D.L.R. (2d) 338, Nova Scotia Supreme Court.

[409] [1902] 2 Ch. 571 at 574.

[410] [1942] Ch. 466.

[411] (1999) 78 P. & C.R. 223.

[412] (1809) 11 East 372; and *semble* Parke J. in *Gray v Bond* (1821) 2 Brod. & Bing. 667 also took this distinction.

easements, such as a right of way, it is doubtful whether the reversioner could maintain an action[413]; and during the continuance of the tenancy he may be unable either to interrupt the enjoyment or to compel his tenant to do so. Unless, therefore, some positive act, as a notice, intimating his dissent, be sufficient to obviate the effect of the user giving a right, he would not be brought into the condition of a *valens agere*, without which the prescription ought not to run against him.[414]

4–108   Bracton,[415] treating of the qualities of a possession necessary to confer a right, appears to consider that such a notice, at all events if followed up by an action as soon as the party is in a condition to bring one, will amount to an interruption.

> "Continuam dico ita quod non sit interrupta; interrumpi enim poterit multis modis sine violentia adhibita, per denuntiationem et impetrationem diligentem, et diligentem prosecutionem, et per talem interruptionem, nunquam acquiret possidens ex tempore liberum tenementum."[416]

Moreover, in speaking of this precise case—of a particular estate existing in the servient tenement during the user of the easement—he[417] seems to be clearly of opinion that such a prohibition will be sufficient to preserve his right.

> "Si autem fuerit seisina clandestina, scilicet in absentia dominorum vel illis ignorantibus, et si scirent essent prohibituri, licet hoc fiat de consensu vel dissimulatione ballivorum, valere non debet."[418]

4–109   In *Daniel v North*,[419] which was an action before the Prescription Act for obstructing ancient lights, the premises on which the obstruction was erected had been occupied during 20 years by a tenant at will, and there was no evidence that the owner of those premises was aware of such enjoyment. Lord Ellenborough observed, on the argument for a new trial:

> "How can such a presumption be raised against the landlord, without showing that he knew of the fact, when he was not in possession, and received no immediate injury from it at the time?"

---

[413] As to the power of the reversioner to sue, see paras 14–17 *et seq.*, below.

[414] This passage (in the 14th ed. of this work) was approved by Sir John Pennycuick V.-C. in *Diment v Foot (N.H.)* [1974] 1 W.L.R. 1427 at 1435.

[415] Lib. 2, f. 51b.

[416] "Continuous, I say, in the sense that it is not interrupted; for it will be able to be interrupted in many ways without the use of violence, by means of denial and diligent impetration, and diligent prosecution, and, by reason of such interruption, the possessor will never acquire a free tenement from lapse of time."

[417] Lib. 4, f. 221.

[418] "If, moreover, seisin shall be clandestine, that is to say, in the absence of the lords or without their knowing, and had they known they would have forbidden it, although this be done with the consent or dissimulation of the bailiffs, it ought not to be valid."

[419] (1809) 11 East 372 at 374.

In delivering his judgment his Lordship said:

"The foundation of presuming a grant against any party is, that the exercise of the adverse right on which such presumption is founded was against a party capable of making the grant: and that cannot be presumed against him unless there were some probable means of his knowing what was done against him. And it cannot be laid down as a rule of law, that the enjoyment of the plaintiff's windows during the occupation of the opposite premises by [a tenant], though for twenty years, without the knowledge of the landlord, will bind the latter. And there is no evidence stated in the report from whence his knowledge should be presumed."[420]

The Prescription Act 1832 introduced two questions of difficulty upon the point **4–110** how far the reversioner is bound by an enjoyment had during the continuance of a particular estate. First, supposing the reversioner, being aware of the fact, from time to time gives a parol or written notice of his dissent to the enjoyment of the easement, any active interference on his part being prevented by the existence of the particular estate. Secondly, supposing the reversioner being in total ignorance of any such enjoyment having been had during the continuance of the particular estate, in consequence of such ignorance does not avail himself of the exception in his favour contained in the statute. Would a valid right to an easement be acquired in either of these cases?

In the case of light the answer to this question is in the affirmative.[421] In the case of other easements the answer would appear to depend upon whether the user is of 20 years or 40 years, and, if of 20 years, whether the reversioner is entitled expectant on a term of years, or on a life tenancy. If the user is of 20 years the reversioner expectant on a life tenancy would not be bound, by reason of the exclusion of the period of disability under section 7. As, however, section 7 does not exclude the period during which the servient tenement shall have been in lease for a term of years, and section 8 applies only to the period of 40 years, it would seem that, so far as the statute is concerned, the reversioner would be bound, if his reversion was expectant on a term of years. If the user is of 40 years, he would be bound, unless he resisted within three years from the expiration of the term, under section 8; or unless the circumstances were such (as, for example in *Kilgour v Gaddes*[422]) as not to admit of the user having been "as of right" against him.

---

[420] (1809) 11 East 372, at 374, 375. For the present rule where light is claimed under the statute, see paras 4–23 to 4–37, above.

[421] See the cases cited, at paras 4–25 to 4–26, above. In particular, see *Morgan v Fear* [1907] A.C. 425, where *Frewen v Phillips* (1861) 11 C.B. (n.s.) 449 was approved. In his judgment in *Frewen v Phillips*, Pollock C.B. used the following words: "It may be that, if a man opens a light towards his neighbour's land, the reversioner may have no means of preventing a right thereto from being acquired by a twenty years' enjoyment, unless he can prevail upon his tenant to raise an obstruction, or is able to procure from the other party an acknowledgment that the light is enjoyed only by consent."

[422] [1904] 1 K.B. 457, para.4–61, above, and see *Davies v Du Paver* [1953] 1 Q.B. 184, para.4–116, below.

4–111   At all events, if the user of any easement actually commenced before the property over which it is claimed passed into the possession of the lessee, the mere fact of such tenancy having continued during a period of 20 years will not, it seems, be sufficient to defeat the right acquired by the lapse of time, unless it be shown that the landlord, up to the time of granting the lease, was in ignorance that any such right was claimed.[423] Thus, in *Cross v Lewis*,[424] where a house was proved to have been built for 38 years, during the whole of which time there had been windows towards the adjoining premises, and these premises had belonged for a number of years to a family residing at a distance, none of whom was proved to have ever seen them, and they had been occupied by the same tenant during the last 20 years, the court held that, after such a long enjoyment, the windows must be considered ancient windows, and that the plaintiff was consequently entitled to recover for their obstruction. Bayley J. in his judgment said[425]:

> "The right is proved to have existed for thirty-eight years; the commencement of it is not shown. It is possible that the premises, both of the plaintiff and defendant, once belonged to the same person, and that he conferred on the plaintiff, or those under whom she claims, a right to have the windows free from obstruction. Daniel v. North[426] has been relied upon, to show that the tenancy rebutted the presumption of a grant; but this is a very different case; [the] tenancy was shown to have existed for twenty years, but the origin of the plaintiff's right was not traced."

Littledale J. added[427]:

> "It was proved that the windows had existed for thirty-eight years, and [the] tenancy for twenty. How the land was occupied for eighteen years before that time did not appear. I think that quite sufficient to found the presumption of a grant."[428]

4–112   As the claim of an easement is in derogation of the ordinary rights of property, it lies upon the party asserting such claims, in opposition to common right, in all cases to support his case by evidence.[429] In *Cross v Lewis*[430] the absence of any evidence as to the earlier state of the windows was indeed held to operate in favour of the plaintiff, the party claiming the easement; but the substantial proof, namely of the user for a period of 20 years, had already been given by the claimant; and this, unrebutted by any evidence to take the case out of the ordinary

---

[423] But see *Davies v Du Paver* [1953] 1 Q.B. 184, para.4–116, below.
[424] (1824) 2 B. & C. 686; and see *Morgan v Fear* [1907] A.C. 425.
[425] (1824) 2 B. & C. 686 at 689, 690.
[426] (1809) 11 East 372.
[427] (1824) 2 B. & C. 686 at 690.
[428] See *Palk v Shinner* (1852) 18 Q.B. 568, para.4–53, above.
[429] Applied in *Rhys Jones v Scott* [2006] EWHC 2908 (Q.B.) at [25]–[26]; see, also, *Field Common Ltd v Elmbridge Borough Council* [2005] EWHC 2933 (Ch.) at [33].
[430] (1824) 2 B. & C. 686.

rule, was of course sufficient to establish the easement. From the observations of the learned judge in that case, it would appear that, provided that the existence of the easement prior to the commencement of the tenancy is shown, and a sufficient length of enjoyment has taken place to afford evidence of a grant, the burden of proof will be thrown upon the owner of the land sought to be made liable to the easement; and unless he can show such previous user to have taken place without his knowledge, the right to the easement will be established.[431] Indeed, it seems from this case that proof of enjoyment for 20 years is in all cases prima facie evidence of a title which must be rebutted by the owner of the servient tenement; and where the servient tenement has been in the possession of a tenant for years, but an easement over it has been enjoyed for a long time, it has been laid down that the landlord may be presumed to have been aware of it.[432]

In *Pugh v Savage*[433] the plaintiff was the owner in fee simple of a farm, which **4–113** he had bought from R in 1950. The farm included field A, which was approached from the highway along a lane, part of which bordered the plaintiff's land. A footpath ran from the highway along the lane into field A, across field A into field B, and across field B into field C. Until 1966 field B was owned by an estate company, and field C formed an isolated part of another farm. In 1966 the estate company bought field C and let it, together with field B and a large field fronting on to the highway, to the defendant. When he took the tenancy the defendant was informed that he would be entitled to a private right of way on foot and with vehicles over field A and along the lane into the highway. When, however, the defendant purported to exercise that right, the plaintiff, while admitting that there was a public footpath, denied the existence of any private way for vehicles. In 1968 the plaintiff ploughed up field A and partially obstructed the lane with hedge-cuttings. The defendant therefore took his vehicles over other parts of the plaintiff's land to reach the highway. The plaintiff claimed an injunction and damages for trespass, and the defendant claimed a right of way across field A and along the lane and counterclaimed for damages. The defendant claimed that such a right of way had been enjoyed without interruption by him and his predecessors, the occupiers of field C, for over 30 years immediately prior to the commencement of the proceedings. At the hearing of the action it was agreed that shortly after 1940 R had let the field to his son on an oral tenancy which was surrendered when the plaintiff bought the farm in 1950.

The Court of Appeal, applying *Cross v Lewis*[434] and *Palk v Shinner*,[435] held that where a tenancy of a servient tenement came into existence during the course of the period of user, the grant of the tenancy would not, in the absence of evidence that the servient owner had no knowledge of the user while the tenant was in possession, be a fatal objection to the presumption of a grant or to a claim made under the Prescription Act, although it was a matter to be considered; and that

---

[431] See *Gray v Bond* (1821) 2 Brad. & B. 667.
[432] *Davies v Stephens* (1836) 7 C. & P. 570.
[433] [1970] 2 Q.B. 373; applied by Burgess V.-C. in *Davis v Whitby* [1973] 1 W.L.R. 629 at 630, 631.
[434] (1824) 2 B. & C. 686; see para.4–111, above.
[435] (1852) 18 Q.B. 568; 17 Jur. 372; see para.4–53, above.

where, as in the case before the Court, there had been long user of the way, the law should support it. On the other hand, the Court took the view that a distinction was to be drawn between cases where the tenancy was in existence at the beginning of the period of user and cases when the tenancy came into existence in the course of the period of user. In the former case it might well be unreasonable to imply a lost grant by the owner at the beginning of the user. He might not have been able to stop the user, even if he knew about it.[436]

4–114   The effect of the Court of Appeal's decision is, as Sir John Pennycuick V.-C. said in *Diment v Foot (N.H.)*[437] (which was also concerned with an alleged right of way), that, in a case where long user has been shown, there is a presumption that the owner of the land knew of it and the burden of proof is then on him: that is to say, instead of the dominant owner having to establish affirmatively that the servient owner did have knowledge, the latter must establish that he did not.[438] The question which arose in *Diment v Foot (N.H.)*[439] was whether that presumption extended to the servient owner's agent. The learned Vice-Chancellor rejected an argument that knowledge or imputed knowledge on the part of the agent must be treated as the knowledge of the servient owner as principal, and that the presumption could only be rebutted by showing that the agent did not in fact have knowledge or means of knowledge, saying that there could not be a presumption, merely by reason of the relationship of principal and agent, and without reference to the particular circumstances, that the agent had knowledge or means of knowledge of any particular act on the land. His Lordship said that that would be carrying the presumption altogether beyond anything which was said in *Pugh v Savage*.[440] Where there is an agent the role of establishing knowledge or means of knowledge must rest on the person claiming the right, who might discharge the burden by direct evidence or by inference, the inference depending upon the particular circumstances.

4–115   In *Williams v Sandy Lane (Chester) Ltd*,[441] the law was summarised as follows:

> ". . . it is possible to derive from the decision of this Court in *Pugh v Savage* the following principles applicable to cases where the servient land is, or has been, subject to a tenancy. First, in a case where the grant of the tenancy of the servient land predates the user by or on behalf of the owner of the dominant land, it is necessary to ask whether, notwithstanding the tenancy, the freehold owner of the servient land could take steps to prevent user during the tenancy. The answer to that question is likely to turn on the terms of the tenancy. Second, if (notwithstanding the tenancy) the owner of the servient land could take steps to prevent the user, then it is necessary to ask whether (and, if so, when) the freehold owner had knowledge (actual or imputed) of

---

[436] The claim to prescription failed for this reason in *Piromalli v Di Masi* [1980] W.A.R. 173.
[437] [1974] 1 W.L.R. 1427 at 1434, 1435.
[438] Not followed in *Axler v Chisholm* (1977) 79 D.L.R. 97.
[439] [1974] 1 W.L.R. 1427 at 1434, 1435.
[440] [1970] 2 Q.B. 373.
[441] [2007] 1 E.G.L.R. 10.

that user by the owner of the dominant land. The fact that the freehold owner of the servient land was out of possession when the user began and throughout the term of the tenancy may well lead to the conclusion that knowledge of that user should not be imputed. But if, on the facts, the owner of the servient land does have knowledge of the user and could (notwithstanding the tenancy) take steps to prevent that user, but does not do so, then (prima facie) acquiescence will be established. Third, in a case where user of the servient land by the owner of the dominant land began before the grant of the tenancy, it is necessary to ask whether the freehold owner of the servient land had knowledge (actual or imputed) at or before the date of the grant. If so, then it is likely to be immaterial whether the terms of the tenancy are such that the owner of the servient land could (or could not) take steps to prevent that user. That is because if (with knowledge of the user) the owner of the servient land grants a tenancy of that land on terms which put it out of his power to prevent that user, he can properly be said to have acquiesced in it. Fourth, if the owner of the servient land did not have knowledge of the user at the date of the grant, then the position is the same as it would be if the grant had pre-dated the user. It is necessary to ask whether (notwithstanding the tenancy) the freehold owner can take steps to prevent the user; and, if so, whether (and if so when) the owner had knowledge of the user."

In *Davies v Du Paver*[442] where a right of sheepwalk, based on user for 60 years, **4–116** was claimed by prescription at common law, alternatively under section 1 of the Act, over land which had been let during all these years except a few towards the end, it was held that the onus was on the plaintiff to show that the owner had some knowledge, or reasonable means of knowledge, of the user, and that in the absence of such evidence the claim failed, the plaintiff not showing user "as of right". Common local knowledge of the user was established, but, in the circumstances, this was considered not to extend to the owner.

6. Enjoyment must be capable of interruption

The enjoyment must be one which the servient owner could have prevented or **4–117** interrupted.

This rule is well illustrated by the case of *Sturges v Bridgman*.[443] There the question arose as regards two adjoining houses in London. One of these belonged to confectioners, who for more than 60 years before action had caused noise on their premises by the use of a pestle and mortar in their kitchen. The other house was purchased a few years before action by a doctor, who thereupon built a consulting room close to the kitchen. Shortly afterwards he brought an action against the confectioners to restrain them from causing the noise, which, on the evidence, the court held, amounted to a nuisance to the plaintiff's premises after

---

[442] [1953] 1 Q.B. 184.
[443] (1879) 11 Ch. D. 852.

the erection of his consulting room, but not before. The confectioners contended by way of defence that a right to cause the noise had been acquired by user, and that a grant should be presumed. The court, however, decided against the contention; holding that, before the erection of the consulting room, the noise could not have been legally prevented, either physically or by means of an action, and that accordingly there was no sufficient user from which a grant could be presumed. The same doctrine was applied where claims were made to the access of air to chimneys over an unlimited surface of the servient tenement[444] and to subterranean water percolating in unknown channels.[445] In neither of these cases could the servient owner have prevented the user.

4–118   In *Angus v Dalton*[446] Cockburn C.J. and Mellor J. gave judgment against a claim of lateral support for buildings, partly upon the ground that the enjoyment of such support cannot be resisted or prevented by the adjoining owner by any means short of an excavation which may be destructive of his own tenement,[447] but the majority of the Court of Appeal, while conceding that an enjoyment physically incapable of interruption would confer no right,[448] held that the decided cases precluded them from applying the principle to the easement in question,[449] and their decision was upheld by the House of Lords.

> "That power of resistance", said Lord Selborne,[450] "by interruption does and must in all such cases exist, otherwise no question like the present could arise. It is true that in some cases (of which the present is an example) a man acting with a reasonable regard to his own interest would never exercise it for the mere purpose of preventing his neighbour from enlarging or extending such a servitude. But, on the other hand, it would not be reasonably consistent with the policy of the law in favour of possessory titles, that they should depend, in each particular case, upon the greater or less facility or difficulty, convenience or inconvenience, of practically interrupting them. They can always be interrupted (and that without difficulty or inconvenience), when a man wishes, and finds it for his interest, to make such a use of his own land as will have that effect. So long as it does not suit his purpose and his interest to do this, the law which allows a servitude to be established or enlarged by long and open enjoyment, against one whose preponderating interest it has been to be passive during the whole time necessary for its acquisition, seems more reasonable, and more consistent with

---

[444] *Bryant v Lefever* (1879) 4 C.P.D. 173.

[445] *Chasemore v Richards* (1859) 7 H.L.C. 349.

[446] (1877) 3 Q.B.D. 85; (1878) 4 Q.B.D. 162; sub nom. *Dalton v Angus* (1881) 6 App. Cas. 740.

[447] (1877) 3 Q.B.D. 85 at 117, 125 *et seq.*

[448] (1878) 4 Q.B.D. 162 at 175.

[449] (1878) 4 Q.B.D. 162 at 176–181.

[450] (1881) 6 App. Cas. 740 at 796. Some of the judges even hinted that the enjoyment of lateral support was capable of being resisted by the simple method of bringing an action for trespass; and Lord Selborne appears to have concurred in this view, without making it the basis of his judgment. See per Lindley and Bowen JJ. at 763, 784, and the contrary opinion of Fry J. at 775; Lord Selborne's opinion on this point is reported at 793, and Lord Watson's at 831.

public convenience and natural equity, than one which would enable him, at any distance of time (whenever his views of his own interest may have undergone a change), to destroy the fruits of his neighbour's diligence, industry, and expenditure."

Lord Penzance concurred in the judgment, feeling himself bound by previous decisions; but his own opinion was that the enjoyment must, in order to confer a right, be capable of interruption "without extravagant and unreasonable loss or expense".[451]

With regard to a right to discharge a noxious effluent, time will not run against the servient owner during such time as the effluent remains harmless.[452]

The question as to what interruption will be sufficient to defeat a claim under the Act to an easement is considered in the cases referred to in connection with section 4.[453]

7. Enjoyment as an easement

The enjoyment must have been an enjoyment of the easement in the character of an easement, distinct from the enjoyment of the land itself.

4–119

This rule has been so laid down as regards a right of way,[454] and also as regards the right of light[455]; and bears upon the case of unity of possession.[456] For where there is unity of possession of the dominant and servient tenements there is no enjoyment of an easement as an easement. The case of unity may also be referred to the preceding rule about prevention of enjoyment. Thus, where the same person has been in legal occupation as tenant of the servient and dominant tenements[457] it is obvious that the user of the servient tenement by the common occupier could not be prevented by the owner of that tenement.[458] The operation of the unity is to destroy the effect of the previous user by breaking the continuity of enjoyment.

8. Enjoyment must be definite and continuous

The enjoyment must be definite and sufficiently continuous in its character. Thus: "Non-user which would not be sufficient to establish an abandonment of a right acquired may be enough to prevent the acquisition of that right under the [Prescription] Act."[459]

4–120

---

[451] (1881) 6 App. Cas. 740 at 805. The opinions of the judges on this point will be found reported at 749 (Pollock B.), 764 (Lindley J.), 774 (Fry J.), and 785 (Bowen J.).

[452] *Liverpool Corp v Coghill* [1918] 1 Ch. 307, para.4–93, above.

[453] See paras 4–43 *et seq.*, above.

[454] *Battishill v Reed* (1856) 18 C.B. 702.

[455] *Harbidge v Warwick* (1849) 3 Exch. 552.

[456] See para.4–57, above.

[457] *Harbidge v Warwick*, above. See as to rights of way, *Damper v Bassett* [1901] 2 Ch. 350; *Hulbert v Dale* [1909] 2 Ch. 570.

[458] See *Outram v Maude* (1881) 17 Ch. D. 391 at 405.

[459] *Smith v Baxter* [1900] 2 Ch. 138, per Stirling J. at 146; and see *Hulley v Silversprings Bleaching and Dyeing Co* [1922] 2 Ch. 268 at 281; *Hollins v Verney* (1884) 13 Q.B.D. 304, and other cases quoted under s.4 of the Prescription Act, paras 4–43 *et seq.*, above.

Continuity may be interrupted by the act of the servient owner or by that of the person claiming the prescriptive right. In the first case, section 4 of the Prescription Act 1832 will apply[460]; in the second case it is mainly a question of fact and degree whether the nature of a given enjoyment establishes an easement of an intermittent character or whether the enjoyment is so lacking in continuity as to be otiose. Thus it is not to be understood that the enjoyment of an easement must necessarily be incessant; although, in a great variety of cases, it would obviously be so, such as in the case of windows, or rights to water. In those easements which require the repeated acts of man for their enjoyment, as rights of way, it would appear to be sufficient if the user is of such a nature, and takes place at such intervals, as to afford an indication to the owner of the servient tenement that a right is claimed against him—an indication that would not be afforded by a mere accidental or occasional exercise.[461] On the other hand, the evidence may disclose a casual use, dependent for its continuance upon the tolerance and good nature of the servient owner, and not such as to put him on notice that a right is being asserted.[462]

4–121   The continuity of enjoyment may be broken either by the cessation to use, or by the enjoyment not being had in the proper manner.

> "An enjoyment of an easement for one week", said Parke B. in *Monmouthshire Canal Co v Harford*[463] "and a cessation to enjoy it during the next week, and so on alternately, would confer no right."[464]

So it is where the enjoyment has been had under permission asked from time to time, which, upon each occasion, amounts to an admission that the asker had then no right. Indeed, the very mode in which this enjoyment, under constantly renewed permission, operates in defeating the previous user is that it breaks the continuity of the enjoyment[465]; and it is expressly laid down by the Court of

---

[460] See para.4–43, above.

[461] *Per curiam* in *Bartlett v Downes* (1825) 3 B. & C. 621; and in *Hollins v Verney* (1884) 13 Q.B.D. 304, 315; as to light, see *Smith v Baxter* [1900] 2 Ch. 138; *Andrews v Waite* [1907] 2 Ch. 500; see also *Bower v John Etherington Ltd* (1965) 53 D.L.R. (2d) 338, Nova Scotia Supreme Court. The passage in the text (which appeared also in the 14th ed. of this work) was cited with approval by Goff L.J. in *Ironside, Crabb and Crabb v Cook, Cook and Barefoot* (1981) 41 P. & C.R. 326, CA.

[462] *Ironside, Crabb and Crabb v Cook, Cook and Barefoot* (1981) 41 P. & C.R. 326, CA, and *Goldsmith v Burrow Construction Ltd*, *The Times*, July 31, 1987, CA, where the fact that a gate was locked from time to time indicated that its use at other times was permissive, both explained and discussed in *Mills v Silver* [1991] Ch. 271, where the fact that a track was not passable by vehicles in wet weather (five months of the year) did not break the continuity of enjoyment so as to defeat the presumption of a lost grant.

[463] (1834) 1 C.M. & R. 631.

[464] This does not mean a cessation in the actual user, as, for instance, by reason of the claimant having no occasion to use the easement; otherwise a right to a way or other non-continuous easement could not be acquired. It means a cessation in the user as of right, as in the case cited in the text, where the asking of permission during the period, by admitting that the person asking had no right at that time, interrupted the continuity of the enjoyment as of right. See the question discussed in *Hollins v Verney* (1884) 13 Q.B.D. 304, para.4–44, above.

[465] *Monmouthshire Canal Co v Harford* (1834) 1 C.M. & R. 631, per Lord Lyndhurst.

King's Bench, in their judgment in the case of *Tickle v Brown*,[466] that the breaking of the continuity is inconsistent with the enjoyment during the periods of either 20 or 40 years, and that for that reason evidence of the breaking of such continuity is admissible on a traverse of the enjoyment.

In a claim to sheep rights under section 1 of the Prescription Act, the claimant   **4–122** need not establish that the right has been exercised continuously, for the right, of its nature, would only be used intermittently. On the other hand the user must still be shown to have been of such a character, degree and frequency as to indicate an assertion by the claimant of a continuous right and of a right of the measure of the right claimed.[467]

Where a riparian owner claimed a prescriptive right to pollute the stream, it was held that a progressive increase, during the period relied on, in the plant of the polluting mill and in the volume of water polluted was "destructive of that certainty and uniformity essential for the measurement and determination of the user by which the extent of the prescriptive right is to be ascertained".[468] On the other hand, easements to take water, whether express or prescriptive, are rarely if ever defined by reference to quantity as well as, or instead of, by reference to the purposes for which the water may be abstracted.[469] In *Green v Lord Somerleyton*[470] it was held that there was, on the facts of that case, sufficient certainty and continuity for an easement of drainage to have been acquired by prescription by way of a lost modern grant.

9. Compliance with statute or custom

All prescription is founded on the presumption of a grant. A grant cannot be pre-   **4–123** sumed where such a grant would have been in contravention of a statute.[471] Similarly, a grant cannot be presumed where such a grant would have been contrary to the common law.[472] In *Neaverson v Peterborough Rural Council*[473] after referring to the long user in question, it was said[474]:

> "The question is whether that ought to be treated as evidence of a lost grant, which might have had a legal origin. If such a grant could not have had a legal origin, then it is not competent for us to presume its existence."

---

[466] (1836) 4 A. & E. 369 at 383; *Beasley v Clarke* (1836) 2 Bing.N.C. 705; *Gardner v Hodgson's Kingston Brewery Co* [1903] A.C. 229. See paras 4–94 to 4–101, above.

[467] *White v Taylor (No. 2)* [1969] 1 Ch. 160 at 192–195.

[468] *Hulley v Silversprings Bleaching and Dyeing Co Ltd* [1922] 2 Ch. 268 at 281.

[469] *Cargill v Gotts* [1981] 1 W.L.R. 441 at 446, per Templeman L.J. (considering *Hulley v Silversprings Bleaching and Dyeing Co Ltd*, above).

[470] [2004] 1 P. & C.R. 520.

[471] Blackstone, *Commentaries on the Law of England*, Vol. 2, p. 265. The matter is described differently at Co. Litt. 115a where it is said that one may not prescribe against a statute and a distinction is drawn between affirmative and negative statutes.

[472] e.g., where the user amounts to a public nuisance; see para.4–130, below.

[473] [1902] 1 Ch. 557.

[474] [1902] 1 Ch. 557 at 563, per Collins M.R.; see also at 571, 578, 579.

This was followed in *Hulley v Silversprings Bleaching and Dyeing Co*[475] where it was said[476]:

> "A lost grant cannot be presumed where such a grant would have been in contravention of a statute and as title by prescription is founded on the presumption of a lost grant, if no grant could lawfully have been made no presumption of the kind can arise."

If the statutory prohibition was for the benefit of a particular individual or body, a waiver of the prohibition by that individual or body may be presumed, on appropriate evidence.[477] It has also been said that there are cases where by the doctrine of a lost grant or lost patent or by some similar presumption individuals have, notwithstanding the terms of a statute, acquired rights apparently in contradiction of it.[478] Whether the statute prohibits the grant contended for is a matter of interpretation of the relevant statute. Thus in *Campbell v Wilson*[479] it was held that the enjoyment of a way for 20 years was sufficient evidence from which to presume a grant or other lawful origin of a right of way; an earlier Inclosure Act had, prior to that enjoyment, extinguished a like right over the same land, so that the 20 years' enjoyment was attributable to the neglect of the owner of the servient tenement to avail himself of the provisions of the Act; however the Inclosure Act did not prohibit the presumed grant which was contended for and the decision is not at variance with the rule stated above. The object of the Act in *Campbell v Wilson* was simply to benefit the owners of allotted lands by exempting them from the burden of existing rights of way, but not to injure the allottees by restricting the power of each allottee to dispose of or burden his own land as he might think proper; and there was nothing in the statute prohibiting the creation of new rights. Where, on the other hand, the acts of user relied upon are contrary to some statutory provision, so that an actual grant of the right which is sought to be established by user would be void, and it cannot possibly be referred to any legal origin, the common law rule prevails, and no right is acquired.[480] The decisions in *Neaverson v Peterborough Rural Council* and *Hulley v Silversprings Bleaching and Dyeing Co* were approved by the House of Lords in *Bakewell Management Ltd v Brandwood*.[481]

4–124   The rule as stated above was at one time thought to go further and the above cases were interpreted as supporting a wider proposition. Thus in *Cargill v*

---

[475] [1922] 2 Ch. 268.
[476] [1922] 2 Ch. 268 at 282; and see *Green v Matthews* (1930) 46 T.L.R. 206.
[477] *Goldsmid v G.E. Ry* (1884) 9 App. Cas. 927; *George Legge & Son Ltd v Wenlock Corp* [1938] A.C. 204 at 222.
[478] *George Legge & Son Ltd v Wenlock Corp* [1938] A.C. 204 at 222.
[479] (1803) 3 East 294; see, also *Dynevor (Lord) v Richardson* [1995] Ch. 173.
[480] *Rochdale v Radcliffe* (1852) 18 Q.B. 287; *Race v Ward* (1857) 7 E. & B. 384; *National Guaranteed Manure Co v Donald* (1859) 4 H. & N. 8; *Staffordshire & Worcestershire Canal Co v Birmingham Canal Co* (1866) L.R. 1 H.L. 267 at 278; *Neaverson v Peterborough R.D.C.* [1902] 1 Ch. 557; *Hulley v Silversprings Bleaching and Dyeing Co* [1922] 2 Ch. 268; *Green v Matthews* (1930) 46 T.L.R. 206.
[481] [2004] 2 A.C. 519.

Gotts[482] where the user for part of the period was illegal under section 23(1) of the Water Resources Act 1963, it was held that such user could not be relied upon in support of a claim to prescription.

It was said that "the court will not recognise an easement established by illegal activity." However, in the same case, it was held that if an easement had been validly established, it was not extinguished by reason of the fact that it subsequently became necessary to obtain a licence, prescribed by statute, in order to exercise it lawfully. Even if the acts relied upon would have been lawful if authorised by the landowner, if they were prohibited by statute for the benefit of the public, they could not be relied upon to establish an easement by prescription. Again, in *Hanning v Top Deck Travel Group Limited*[483] the Court of Appeal held that vehicular use of the track across Horsell Common in breach of section 193(4) of the Law of Property Act 1925[484] could not give rise to prescriptive rights, despite the fact that such use could have been authorised by the freeholders. It is also relevant to note that section 34 of the Road Traffic Act 1988 makes it a criminal offence to drive a mechanically pro-pelled vehicle on to or upon any common land, moorland or land of any other description, not being land forming part of a road or on any road being a footpath, bridleway or restricted by-way.[485] This section and its predecessors had been relied upon to defeat claims to a public vehicular right of way.[486] In a case where the user relied on was in breach of planning control but where no enforcement notice had been served and so no criminal offence had been committed, it was held that the decision in *Hanning* did not prevent the user being relied on.[487]

The statement in *Cargill v Gotts*[488] (referred to at paragraph 4–124, above) was disapproved, and the decision in *Hanning v Top Deck Travel Group Ltd*[489] was overruled by the House of Lords in *Bakewell Management Ltd v Brandwood*,[490] which also involved section 193 of the Law of Property Act 1925. The House of Lords accepted that one could not acquire an easement by prescription, whether under the doctrine of lost modern grant or under the 1832 Act, where there was not a competent grantor at the relevant time. The law as to the need for a competent

4–125

---

[482] [1981] 1 W.L.R. 441.

[483] (1993) 68 P. & C.R. 14; followed in *Massey v Boulden* [2003] 1 W.L.R. 1792 (a case on section 34 of the Road Traffic Act 1988) and *Hayling v Harper* [2004] 1 P. & C.R. 563 (also on section 34 of the Road Traffic Act 1988 and its predecessors).

[484] "Any person who without lawful authority draws or drives upon land to which this section applies any carriage, cart, caravan, truck or other vehicle . . . shall be liable on summary conviction to a fine . . ."

[485] Substituted by the Countryside and Rights of Way Act 2000, s.67 and Sch.7; there is an exception for land within fifteen yards of a road for the purpose of parking the vehicle. Similar provisions were contained in Road Traffic Acts since the Road Traffic Act 1930. "Road" is defined in Road Traffic Act 1988, s.192(1); this definition has been considered in a large number of cases which are collected in the *Encyclopedia of Highway Law and Practice*, vol. 1, para.3–557 and see, in par-ticular, *Clarke v Kato* [1998] 1 W.L.R. 1647.

[486] *Robinson v Adair, The Times*, March 2, 1995; *R. v Hereford and Worcester Ex p. Pick* (1995) 51 P. & C.R. 231; *Stevens v Secretary of State for the Environment* (1998) 76 P. & C.R. 503.

[487] *Batchelor v Marlow* [2001] 1 E.G.L.R. 119; this part of the decision was not the subject of the appeal at (2001) 82 P. & C.R. 459.

[488] [1981] 1 W.L.R. 441.

[489] (1993) 68 P. & C.R. 14.

[490] [2004] 2 A.C. 519.

grantor applied not only where the alleged grant would have been ultra vires but also where the alleged grant was of an alleged right to do something contrary to the criminal law; no such right could be granted. However, the position under section 193 of the Law of Property Act 1925 was different from either of these cases. Even in a case where section 193 applied to the land in question (the suggested servient land) the owner of that land retained power to grant an easement[491] and the servient owner was not even a fiduciary in relation to the power to grant such an easement; he could grant the easement in return for a payment which he was entitled to keep. Thus such a grant would have been an effective grant and the cases as to the need for a competent grantor did not prevent an easement being acquired by prescription over land which was subject to section 193 of the Law of Property Act 1925. This reasoning depended on the reference to "without lawful authority" in section 193(4) and accordingly also applies to the similar argument based on section 34(1) of the Road Traffic Act 1988, where again the words "without lawful authority" are used. The House of Lords having analysed the earlier authorities in this way, the question became one of public policy. Should it be possible to acquire an easement by prescription when the user relied upon was criminal at the time it was carried on? The House of Lords pointed out that prescription usually involves tortious activity, i.e. trespass on the servient land.[492] Public policy did not prevent activity that was illegal in that sense from leading to the acquisition of property rights. Public policy did not operate to prevent prescription in a case which involved a criminal offence under section 193 of the Law of Property Act 1925 or section 34 of the Road Traffic Act 1988 because the user was criminal only because there had not actually been a grant of lawful authority. The user of land which was made criminal by section 193(4) of the 1925 Act, or by section 34(1) of the 1988 Act, had more in common with use of land that is illegal because it is tortious than with use of land that is illegal because it is criminal. Lord Walker of Gestingthorpe stated[493]:

"In my opinion, it is the landowner's unfettered power of dispensing from criminal liability, exercisable at his own discretion and if he thinks fit for his own private profit, which is the key to the disposal of this appeal. Since a dispensing power of that sort is very unusual, it is unlikely to apply to many other cases of criminal illegality."

4-126   Before the House of Lords decision in *Bakewell Management Ltd v Brandwood*[494] the law as laid down in *Hanning*[495] was modified by section 68 of the Countryside and Rights of Way Act 2000 and regulations made thereunder.

---

[491] Subject to a qualification spelt out by Lord Scott of Foscote in respect of a case where the suggested grant would create a public nuisance: see para.4–71, above.
[492] In *Williams v Sandy Lane (Chester) Ltd* [2007] 1 E.G.L.R. 10, there was also a breach of covenant, but that was irrelevant to the question of prescription.
[493] [2004] 2 A.C. 519 at [60].
[494] [2004] 2 A.C. 519.
[495] (1993) 68 P. & C.R. 14.

Section 68 applied to a way which the owner or occupier (from time to time) of any premises had used as a means of access for vehicles to the premises, if that use of the way: (i) was an offence under an enactment applying to the land crossed by the way, but (ii) would otherwise have been sufficient to create on or after May 5, 1993,[496] and to keep in existence, an easement giving a right of way for vehicles.[497] Where the section applied, regulations could provide for the creation on the application of the owner of the premises concerned and on compliance by him with prescribed requirements, of an easement subsisting at law for the benefit of the premises and giving a right of way for vehicles over that way.[498] The section permitted the regulations to provide for certain specified matters.[499] One of those matters was payment by the applicant for the easement.[500] The relevant regulations made under section 68 of the Countryside and Rights of Way Act 2000 were the Vehicular Access Across Common and Other Land (England) Regulations 2002[501] and the Vehicular Access Across Common and Other Land (Wales) Regulations 2004.[502]

Section 68 of the Countryside and Rights of Way Act 2000 has now been repealed[503] with effect from October 1, 2006 in England[504] and from September 6, 2007 in Wales.[505]

Custom

The existence of a custom which is inconsistent with the right claimed will prevent the user relied upon giving rise to a presumed grant of such a right.[506] However, where section 3 of the Prescription Act 1832 (dealing with prescription to a right to light) applies, the effect of the section is to override any local usage or custom to the contrary.   **4–127**

5.—PRESCRIPTIVE RIGHT TO CAUSE NUISANCE

It is settled that many acts done upon a man's own property which are in their nature injurious to the adjoining land, and consequently actionable as private nuisances,   **4–128**

---

[496] This is the date prescribed by the relevant regulations and was the date of the decision in *Hanning v Top Deck Travel Group Ltd* (1993) 68 P. & C.R. 14.
[497] Countryside and Rights of Way Act 2000, s.68(1). "Enactment" is defined to include an enactment in a local or private Act and a bye-law, regulation or other provision having effect under an enactment: see s.68(5).
[498] Countryside and Rights of Way Act 2000, s.68(2).
[499] Countryside and Rights of Way Act 2000, s.86(4).
[500] Countryside and Rights of Way Act 2000, s.68(4)(d).
[501] SI 2002/1711.
[502] SI 2004/248.
[503] By section 51 of the Commons Act 2006.
[504] See SI 2006/2504, art.2(d).
[505] See SI 2007/2386, art.3(j).
[506] *Wynstanley v Lee* (1818) 2 Swans. 333; *Perry v Eames* [1891] 1 Ch. 667; *Bowring Services Ltd v Scottish Widows Fund and Life Assurance Society* [1995] 1 E.G.L.R. 158, and see para.7–30, below.

are capable, at least in theory, of being legalised by prescription.[507] Thus, the right not to receive impure air is an incident of property, and for any interference with this right an action may be maintained; but by an easement acquired by his neighbour a man may, it appears, be compelled to receive the air from him in a corrupted state, as by the admixture of smoke or noisome smells. So, too, he may be compelled to submit to noises caused by the carrying on of certain trades. Again, with regard to flowing water, the right not to have impure water discharged on to a man's land is one of the ordinary rights of property, the infringement of which can only be justified by an easement previously acquired by the party so discharging it.

Thus, it is said in Viner's *Abridgment*[508] that an ancient brewhouse, though erected in Fleet Street or Cheapside, is not a nuisance. So, it seems that an ancient user may be a justification for the exercise of a noisy[509] or offensive trade, or for discharging water in an impure state upon the adjoining land,[510] or for discharging coal dust on a neighbour's wharf.[511] A claim to a prescriptive right to commit a nuisance failed in *Dennis v Ministry of Defence*.[512] The Ministry of Defence was the occupier of an airfield near to the claimants' property. The RAF used the airfield as an operating and training base for jump-jet Harrier aircraft, which were very noisy. The claimants contended that the use of the airfield in this way constituted an actionable nuisance at common law, a contention which the court upheld. The Ministry argued that the user had continued for a sufficient length of time such that it had acquired a prescriptive right to continue the activity. The argument failed on two grounds. The first ground was that the right claimed could not form the subject-matter of a grant on account of the uncertainty in expression of the alleged right. The Ministry were not able to identify the level of decibels to be referred to in the imaginary grant, nor to define the permitted flight circuit. It would not be right to assume a grant of an open-ended right to commit a noise nuisance. It would also not be right to take the maximum noise measurement which had been recorded because there was no evidence that that level had continued for 20 years. The second ground was that the claimants' protests coupled with the Ministry's insistence on continuing, which the claimants were powerless to stop, meant that the user was with force or "*vi*".[513] The claimants were held not to have acquiesced in the user.

From what period time runs

4–129   Until a nuisance arises, no one can complain, and no question of prescription can arise until a nuisance is first committed.[514] It follows that a right to carry on an

---

[507] A private nuisance may be legalised by implied grant: see *Lyttleton Times Co Ltd v Warners Ltd* [1907] A.C. 476 at 481; *cf. Pwllbach Colliery Co v Woodman* [1915] A.C. 634; and see paras 3–26–3–30, above.

[508] Nuisance, G.

[509] *Elliotson v Feetham* (1835) 2 Bing.N.C. 134; *Crump v Lambert* (1867) L.R. 3 Eq. 409 at 413.

[510] *Wright v Williams* (1836) 1 M. & W. 77; *Brown v Dunstable Corp* [1899] 2 Ch. 378.

[511] *Royal Mail Steam Packet Co v George and Branday* [1900] A.C. 480.

[512] [2003] 2 E.G.L.R. 121 (and see the discussion at 127G–K); followed in Ireland in *Lanigan v Barry* [2008] IEHC 29 (a case of noise nuisance).

[513] See para.4–88, above.

[514] *Halsey v Esso Petroleum Co Ltd* [1961] 1 W.L.R. 683 at 702.

offensive trade, or to pollute water with sewage, is not acquired merely by having carried on the trade or having polluted the water for 20 years; but it must be shown that the air over the plaintiff's land, or the water to which he is entitled, has been corrupted for that period,[515] and corrupted to the extent of the right claimed,[516] and so as to be actionable or preventible by the plaintiff or his predecessors.[517] The difficulties would usually be insuperable, and it does not seem that a contested claim to a prescriptive right to commit a nuisance by noise, smell or the like has ever, in fact, succeeded. The fact that the nuisance varied throughout the 20-year period was a difficulty in the way of presuming a grant in *Dennis v Ministry of Defence*.[518]

No prescription for a public nuisance

There can be no prescription to make a public nuisance, which is a prejudice to all people, because it cannot have a lawful beginning, by licence or otherwise, being against the common law.[519] Thus a prescription for the inhabitants of a town to lay logs in a highway was held void,[520] and so of a prescription to maintain in a navigable river a weir not erected before the time of Edward I[521]; similarly, a claim to a right to use a public footway for wheeled traffic after 40 years' user for that purpose was held bad on the ground that the user was in its inception, and had been all along, a public nuisance.[522]

4–130

On the same ground a prescription to discharge sewage into a river was held bad.[523] As regards the right to discharge sewage into a tidal river or the sea, there is no such common law right,[524] but it seems that an "easement" in gross of this nature might be acquired by the corporation of a town (on behalf of the inhabitants), the right being based on a lost grant from the Crown,[525] or possibly on prescription at common law.[526] The noise nuisance in *Dennis v Ministry of Defence*[527] was not alleged to be a public nuisance.

---

[515] *Flight v Thomas* (1839) 10 A. & E. 590; *Murgatroyd v Robinson* (1857) 7 E. & B. 391; *Goldsmid v Tunbridge Wells Improvement Commissioners* (1866) 1 Ch. App. 349; see also *Liverpool Corp v Coghill* [1918] 1 Ch. 307.

[516] *Crossley & Sons Ltd v Lightowler* (1867) 2 Ch. App. 478; *Heather v Pardon* (1878) 37 L.T. 393; *Hulley v Silversprings Bleaching and Dyeing Co* [1922] 2 Ch. 268; *cf. Lemmon v Webb* [1894] 3 Ch. 1; [1895] A.C. 1.

[517] *Sturges v Bridgman* (1879) 11 Ch. D. 852.

[518] [2003] 2 E.G.L.R. 121, discussed in para.4–128, above and followed in Ireland in *Lanigan v Barry* [2008] IEHC 29 (a case of noise nuisance).

[519] See *Butterworth v West Riding Rivers Board* [1909] A.C. 57; *Mott v Shoolbred* (1875) L.R. 20 Eq. 24. See also para.4–123, above.

[520] *Fowler v Sanders* (1618) Cro.Jac. 446; *Dewell v Sanders* (1618) Cro.Jac. 490; 2 Rolle Ab., 265; Vin.Ab., Prescription, F; Com.Dig. Prescription, F. 2.

[521] *Rolle v Whyte* (1868) L.R. 3 Q.B. 286; *Leconfield v Lonsdale* (1870) L.R. 5 C.P. 657.

[522] *Sheringham U.D.C. v Holsey* (1904) 91 L.T. 225.

[523] *Att-Gen v Barnsley Corp* [1874] W.N. 37.

[524] *Foster v Warblington U.C.* [1906] 1 K.B. 665; *Hobart v Southend-on-Sea Corp* (1906) 75 L.J.K.B. 304, compromised on appeal (1906) 22 T.L.R. 530.

[525] *Somersetshire Drainage Commissioners v Bridgwater Corp* (1899) 81 L.T. 732.

[526] *Foster v Warblington U.C.* [1906] 1 K.B. 665.

[527] [2003] 2 E.G.L.R. 121.

6. LAW REFORM

4–131   In March 2008, the Law Commission published a Consultation Paper entitled *Easements, Covenants and Profits a Prendre*.[528] The Consultation Paper invites the views of consultees as to the Law Commission's list of provisional proposals and specific consultation questions. Of relevance to this chapter are the following provisional proposals or specific questions:

(1) The Law Commission provisionally proposes that the current law of pre-scriptive acquisition of easements (that is, at common law, by lost mod-ern grant and under the Prescription Act 1832) be abolished with prospective effect.

(2) It invites the views of consultees as to:

    (a) whether prescriptive acquisition of easements should be abolished without replacement;

    (b) whether certain easements (such as negative easements) should no longer be capable of prescriptive acquisition, and, if so, which; and

    (c) whether existing principles (for example, proprietary estoppel) suf-ficiently serve the function of prescriptive acquisition.

(3) It provisionally proposes:

    (a) that it should be possible to claim an easement by prescription on proof of 20 years' continuous qualifying use;

    (b) that qualifying use shall continue to within 12 months of application being made to the Registrar for entry of a notice on the register of title;

    (c) that qualifying use shall be use without force, without stealth and without consent; and

    (d) that qualifying use shall not be use which is contrary to law, unless such use can be rendered lawful by the dispensation of the servient owner.

(4) It invites consultees' views as to whether prescriptive acquisition of easements should only be possible in relation to land the title to which is registered following service of an application on the servient owner.

(5) It invites consultees' views as to whether the registration of a prescrip-tive easement should be automatic or subject to the servient owner's veto.

(6) It invites the views of consultees as to whether the rule that easements may only be acquired by prescription by or against the absolute owners of the dominant and servient lands should be relaxed, and if so in what circumstances.

[528] Law Commission Consultation Paper No. 186.

(7) It invites the views of consultees as to whether adverse possessors should be treated any differently from others who claim an easement by prescription.

(8) It invites the views of consultees on the issue of the capacity of both servient and dominant owners.

(9) It invites the views of consultees on the appropriate approach to be adopted in relation to prescriptive claims over land the title to which is not registered.

CHAPTER 5

EASEMENTS AND REGISTERED LAND

1.—INTRODUCTION

This chapter discusses two separate schemes of land registration. The first part of **5–01**
the chapter describes the way in which easements were dealt with under the former scheme of land registration created by the Land Registration Act 1925 and
the rules made under that Act. The second part of the chapter describes the way
in which easements are now dealt with under the current scheme of land registration created by the Land Registration Act 2002 and the rules made under that Act.
The scheme under the Land Registration Act 1925 was considered and criticised
in a consultative document issued by the Law Commission.[1] This was followed
by a Law Commission Report which recommended a comprehensive reform of
the law of land registration and included detailed proposals in relation to easements in respect of registered land.[2] Those recommendations were implemented
by the Land Registration Act 2002. The principal provisions of the 2002 Act came
into effect on October 13, 2003.[3] It is desirable to consider the former scheme
under the 1925 Act in some detail because, even though it has been replaced by
the scheme created by the 2002 Act, it will often be necessary to analyse events
which have occurred in the past and which were governed by the 1925 Act at that
time. Further, the 2002 Act contains transitional provisions which refer back to
the scheme under the 1925 Act.[4]

---

[1] (1998) Law Com. No. 254; see, in relation to easements, at paras 5–1–5–24 and 10–79–
10–94.

[2] (2001) Law Com. No. 271; see, in relation to easements, at paras 4–24–4–26, 5–37–5–38,
8–23–8–25 and 8–65–8–73.

[3] The Commencement Order which is of principal relevance is the Land Registration Act 2002
(Commencement No. 4) Order 2003 (SI 2003/1725).

[4] Land Registration Act 2002, s.134 and Sch.12; Sch.12, paras 9 and 10 contain transitional
provisions as to easements.

2.—The Scheme under the Land Registration Act 1925

Effect of registration of the dominant land

5–02   Upon the registration of any freehold or leasehold interest in land with an absolute or good leasehold title, then subject to any entry to the contrary on the register, any easement which is appurtenant to that interest becomes appurtenant to the registered land in like manner as if it had been granted to the proprietor who is so registered.[5] The registration of a person as the proprietor of land, whether as first or subsequent proprietor, passes the benefit of easements without mention thereof on the register.[6]

Registration of an easement

5–03   The proprietor may, if he so wishes, apply (whether on first registration or at any other time) to have a specific entry on the register of any legal easement to which he may be entitled.[7] The Registrar must thereupon give such notice (if any) to the person in possession of the servient land as he may deem advisable.[8] If that land is registered, he must give notice to the proprietor and to every person appearing by the register to be interested, and he must, if he thinks fit, enter notice of it against such land.[9] If the Registrar is satisfied that there is a legal easement appurtenant to the land, he may enter it as part of the description of the land in the Property Register, and the effect of such entry is to confer an absolute, good leasehold, qualified or possessory title to the easement, according to the nature of the title to the land.[10] If the Registrar is not satisfied that the right is appurtenant he must enter it with such qualification as he deems advisable or he may merely enter notice of the fact that the proprietor claims it.[11]

The benefit of an easement must not be entered on the register except as appurtenant to a registered estate, and then only if it is a legal easement.[12]

Registered disposition of land

5–04   On any registered disposition of the land or of a charge thereon, the benefit of the easement which has been entered on the register accrues, on registration, to the grantee as part of the registered estate, but without prejudice to any express

---

[5] Land Registration Act 1925, s.72. See also *ibid.*, ss.5 and 9, which refer specifically to registration as first proprietor; ss.6 and 11 which refer to possessory title; and ss.7 and 12 which refer to qualified title.

[6] The Land Registration Rules 1925, SR & O 1925/1093, r.251. The Land Registration Act 1925, s.3(xxiv), defines "registered land" as including any easement appurtenant thereto. See *Evans' Contract, Re* [1970] 1 W.L.R. 583.

[7] Land Registration Rules 1925, r.252.

[8] Land Registration Rules 1925, r.25(1).

[9] Land Registration Rules 1925, r.253(2).

[10] Land Registration Rules 1925, r.254(1). This will be so even if there was, in fact, no title to the easement; see *Peachey v Lee* (1964) 192 E.G. 365.

[11] Land Registration Rules 1925, r.254(2).

[12] Land Registration Rules 1925, r.257. See Land Registration Act 1925, s.144(1)(xx).

exception or reservation.[13] Quite apart from easements entered on the register, a registered disposition will confer on the transferee or grantee all easements which are appurtenant to the registered land.[14] A person who has contracted to purchase registered land together with an easement appurtenant thereto cannot insist upon the vendor obtaining registration of the easement.[15]

Creation of easements by the proprietor

The proprietor of registered land may in the prescribed form expressly grant or reserve an easement or *profit à prendre* thereover.[16] The easement must be entered on the register against the registered servient tenement.[17] If the easement is to be appurtenant to registered land it will not take effect as a legal interest until registered as such,[18] but where the dominant land is unregistered it is neither necessary nor possible to have the easement positively registered.[19]

5–05

General words

The general words implied in conveyances by virtue of section 62 of the Law of Property Act 1925 apply, so far as applicable thereto, to dispositions of a registered estate.[20] Therefore, in a transfer of registered land there are implied those rights and advantages which are enjoyed over the land retained by the registered proprietor. When the new proprietor is registered these rights will mature into legal easements, as on a conveyance of unregistered land.[21] Unlike the case where there is an express grant of an easement by a registered proprietor, there is here no requirement[22] for express registration of the easement or entry against the registered servient tenement. The creation of easements in this manner applies upon registration of the transfer irrespective of whether the land retained is registered or unregistered. If the vendor wishes to exclude the general words of section 62 of the Law of Property Act 1925, he should do so in the transfer, and an entry may be made on the register excluding them.[23]

5–06

Implied grant

There is no clear provision which includes those rights which will pass by implication on a disposition of part of a tenement, in particular those quasi-easements

5–07

---

[13] Land Registration Rules 1925, r.256.

[14] Land Registration Rules 1925, ss.20, 23, 72. Land Registration Rules 1925, r.251.

[15] *Evans' Contract, Re* [1970] 1 W.L.R. 583.

[16] Land Registration Act 1925, ss.18(1), (2), 21(1).

[17] Land Registration Act 1925, ss.19(2), 22(2). There seems to be no discretion in the Registrar to enter notice of the interest. See *Burr v Copp* [1983] C.L.Y. 2057 (Bloomsbury and Marylebone County Court).

[18] Land Registration Act 1925, ss.19(2), 22(2). Until registration it will be an equitable easement.

[19] Land Registration Act 1925, ss.19(2), 22(2), 141(1)(xx). Land Registration Rules 1925, r.257.

[20] Land Registration Act 1925, ss.19(3), 22(3).

[21] Land Registration Act 1925, ss.20(1), 23(1); Land Registration Rules 1925, r.251.

[22] Registration of the easement may, if it is so desired, be obtained: Land Registration Rules 1925, rr.252–254.

[23] Land Registration Act 1925, ss.20(1), 23(1).

which are discussed in *Wheeldon v Burrows*.[24] In some cases, such rights will be covered by the general words of section 62 of the Law of Property Act 1925. More important is the apparent lack of any provision for easements of necessity to be implied in a disposition of registered land.[25]

Implied reservation

5–08   There appears to be no provision by which a reservation of an easement will be implied in a disposition of registered land in those circumstances where a reservation would be implied in unregistered conveyancing, for example easements of necessity and those arising from the common intention of the parties.[26]

Of course, in the case of both implied grants and implied reservations the contract will contain the implication, and the purchaser or the vendor, as the case may be, can insist upon a transfer containing words sufficient to carry out the intention in the contract.

Prescription and registered land

5–09   Easements adversely affecting registered land may be acquired in equity by prescription in the same manner and to the same extent as if the land were not registered.[27] It is provided that if the easement so acquired is capable of taking effect at law it shall take effect at law also[28] and, being an overriding interest, the Registrar may, if he thinks fit, enter notice of it on the register.[29]

If a legal easement has been acquired by prescription for the benefit of registered land, it may, if the Registrar thinks fit, be registered as part of the description of the land.[30]

Overriding interests

5–10   Registered land is subject to "overriding interests", that is, those interests which are enforceable against a proprietor of registered land even though they do not appear on the register. Overriding interests include the following: "Right of common, drainage rights, customary rights (until extinguished), public rights, profits à prendre, rights of sheepwalk, rights of way,[31] watercourses, rights of water, and other easements not being equitable easements required to be protected by notice

---

[24] (1879) 12 Ch. D. 31. Previous editions of *Ruoff and Roper on Registered Conveyancing* (dealing with the Land Registration Act 1925) suggested that such quasi-easements were adequately covered by the wording in the Land Registration Act 1925, s.20(1), and the Land Registration Rules 1925, r.251.

[25] Such easements would seem to be omitted from Land Registration Act 1925, ss.20(1) and 23(1), and from Land Registration Rules 1925, r.251, because they need not be appurtenant to the land nor would they necessarily pass under s.62 of Law of Property Act 1925 if the land were unregistered.

[26] There may be an express reservation: Land Registration Act 1925, ss.18(1)(d), (e), (2), 20(1)(c), (d).

[27] Land Registration Act 1925, s.75(5); Land Registration Rules 1925, r.250(1).

[28] Land Registration Rules 1925, r.250(2).

[29] Land Registration Rules 1925, r.250(2)(a); Land Registration Act 1925, s.70(3).

[30] Land Registration Rules 1925, r.250(2)(b).

[31] *Celsteel Ltd v Alton House Holdings Ltd* [1985] 1 W.L.R. 204 (reversed in part [1986] 1 W.L.R. 512).

on the register."[32] Legal easements[33] and *profits à prendre* will therefore bind registered land although not protected by entry on the register.[34] An easement which was created before the land became registered will bind the first and subsequent registered proprietors of the land; and an easement properly created in registered land will bind the grantor and subsequent proprietors.[35]

A purchaser of registered land, therefore, may frequently be bound by easements and *profits à prendre* of which he had no knowledge and which were not discoverable by searching the register. There are, however, certain provisions which envisage entry of these rights on the register.

Where at the time of first registration an easement or *profit à prendre* created by an instrument and appearing on the title adversely affects the land, the Registrar must enter a note thereof on the register.[36] The status of such an easement or *profit à prendre* as an overriding interest is not affected if a note is not made.[37]

In any event, where the existence of an overriding interest is proved to the satisfaction of the Registrar or admitted, he may enter notice of the same or of a claim thereto on the register, but no claim to an easement or *profit à prendre* is to be noted against the title to the servient land if the proprietor of such land (after the prescribed notice is given to him) shows sufficient cause to the contrary.[38]

In *Holaw (470) Ltd v Stockton Estates Ltd*[39] the claimant was able to show that a transfer of registered land had omitted the reservation of a right of way contrary to the intention of the parties and in circumstances where the transfer was liable to be rectified. The claim to rectification was asserted in circumstances where the claimant had to show that the right to rectification was an overriding interest within section 70(1)(g) of the Land Registration Act 1925 being within "the rights of every person in actual occupation of the land". Although a right to rectification of the transfer could be a right within section 70(1)(g)[40] and although there was actual use of the right of way at the relevant time, it was held that use, even intensive use, of a right of way did not amount to occupation of the servient tenement and the claim failed.[41]

---

[32] Land Registration Act 1925, s.70(1)(a). For the meaning of "other easements not being equitable easements required to be protected by notice on the register" and the effect of Land Registration Rules 1925, r.258, see *Celsteel Ltd v Alton House Holdings Ltd* (above) and discussion at paras 2–40 to 2–43, above.

[33] As to the question of whether equitable easements are overriding interests, see paras 2–40 to 2–42, above. *Profits à prendre* seem to be overriding interests, whether legal or equitable.

[34] Land Registration Rules, r.258.

[35] Where the dominant tenement is registered land the easement will not become a legal interest until registration; see para.5–04, above. A legal easement may be acquired by prescription in registered land without being registered; see para.5–09, above.

[36] Land Registration Act 1925, s.70(2). There would appear to be a duty on the Registrar notwithstanding the Land Registration Rules 1925, rr.41 and 199, which give him a discretion; see *Dances Way, West Town, Hayling Island, Re* [1962] Ch. 490 at 508, per Diplock L.J.

[37] *Dances Way, West Town, Hayling Island, Re* [1962] Ch. 490 at 507, per Upjohn L.J.

[38] Land Registration Act 1925, s.70(3); Land Registration Rules 1925, r.41.

[39] (2000) 81 P. & C.R. 404.

[40] See *Blacklocks v J. B. Developments (Godalming) Ltd* [1982] Ch. 983 and *Nurdin & Peacock Plc v D. B. Ramsden & Co Ltd* [1999] 1 E.G.L.R. 119.

[41] (2000) 81 P. & C.R. 404 at 423.

Pending actions

5–11   An action in which the existence of an easement over land is directly in issue is
a pending land action as defined in section 17(1) of the Land Charges Act 1972
and registrable under section 5(1)(a) of that Act in the register of pending actions
kept under section 1(1)(b). The registration of such an action is intended to ensure
that anybody taking the land during the pendency of the action shall know of it
and be on notice as to the relief claimed in it. If, therefore, the land is registered,
a caution against dealings with it may be registered pursuant to section 59(1) of
the Land Registration Act 1925.[42] An action by a servient owner for a declaration
that a right has been extinguished by abandonment is also a pending land action
registrable as such, since the land to which it relates (that is the easement) is land
comprised in the title against which the caution is registered.[43]

The registration of such actions may, however, in some circumstances serve little purpose, since any easement will be binding on a purchaser of the servient tenement as an overriding interest.[44] Moreover, the court may order the removal of
a caution where the cautioner can be equally well protected by undertakings
designed to ensure that his claim will be binding on a transferee or where it is
clear that it would be so binding whether or not protected by caution.[45] Where, on
the other hand, there is no dispute as to the existence of the easement, and there
is merely a claim for damages for breach of contract, then the action is not a pending action and the registration of a caution is not appropriate.[46]

3.—The Scheme under the Land Registration Act 2002

5–12   As indicated in para.5–01 above, the 2002 Act came into force on October 13,
2003. The 2002 Act is supplemented by the Land Registration Rules 2003, which
came into force on the same date. The 2002 Act largely gives effect to the recommendations of the Law Commission.[47]

No substantive registration

5–13   In the same way as under the Land Registration Act 1925, it is not possible to
have a separate registered title in relation to an easement. The 2002 Act provides
for some easements to have overriding status, and thus bind the registered proprietor of the servient tenement, and for other easements to require protection by
notice against the title to the servient tenement.[48]

---

[42] *Greenhi Builders Ltd v Allen* [1979] 1 W.L.R. 156 (right of support). Browne-Wilkinson J.
 considered registration to be eminently appropriate because a mandatory injunction was claimed.
[43] *Willies-Williams v National Trust* (1993) 65 P. & C.R. 359.
[44] (1993) 65 P. & C.R. 359, at 363.
[45] (1993) 65 P. & C.R. 359, at 363.
[46] *Regan & Blackburn Ltd v Rogers* [1985] 1 W.L.R. 870 (right of way).
[47] (2001) Law Com. No. 271. The recommendations in relation to easements were at *ibid.*, paras
 4–24–4–26, 5–37–5–38, 8–23–8–25 and 8–65–8–73.
[48] The matters that can be the subject of separate substantive registration are contained in s.2 of the
 2002 Act; although the list now includes a *profit à prendre* in gross (unlike under the 1925 Act) it
 does not include easements.

The effect of first registration of the dominant tenement

Although the provisions differ slightly depending on whether the title is freehold   **5–14**
or leasehold and depending on whether the title is absolute, good leasehold, qualified or possessory, the general position is that the effect of registration is that the
estate in the dominant tenement is vested in the proprietor together with all interests (such as easements) subsisting for the benefit of the estate.[49] The benefit of
an appurtenant right may be entered in the register at the time of the first registration if the Registrar is satisfied that the right subsists as a legal estate and benefits the registered estate; if the Registrar is not so satisfied, he may enter details
of the right claimed with such qualification as he considers appropriate.[50] If it
appears to the Registrar that an agreement prevents the acquisition of rights of
light or air for the benefit of the registered estate, he may make an entry in the
property register of that estate.[51]

The effect of first registration of the servient tenement

Although the provisions differ slightly depending on whether the title is freehold   **5–15**
or leasehold and depending on whether the title is absolute, good leasehold, qualified or possessory, the general position is that the effect of registration is that the
estate in the servient tenement is vested in the proprietor subject only to such
easements as are the subject of an entry in the register in relation to the estate or
unregistered interests which have overriding status under Schedule 1 to the 2002
Act.[52] One category of interests which has overriding status is: "a legal easement
or profit à prendre".[53] Thus the servient tenement is bound by any legal easement
even if the legal easement is unregistered. But in order for the servient tenement
to be bound on first registration by an equitable easement, such easement must be
protected by an entry in the register. Where rules so provide, a person applying for
first registration must provide to the Registrar such information as the rules may
provide about any interest affecting the estate to which the application relates
which falls within Schedule 1 (and, as has been seen, this Schedule includes legal
easements) and is of a description specified by the rules.[54] The relevant rules
provide that the applicant for first registration must provide information to the
Registrar about legal easements which are within his actual knowledge and which
affect the estate to which the application relates; this duty does not apply to an
interest that is apparent from the deeds and documents of title accompanying the
application.[55] Where the applicant provides information about a disclosable overriding interest under this rule, the Registrar may enter a notice in the register in
respect of that interest.[56] Further, on first registration, the Registrar must enter a

[49] Land Registration Act 2002, ss.11, 12.
[50] Land Registration Rules 2003, rule 33.
[51] Land Registration Rules 2003, rule 36.
[52] Land Registration Act 2002, ss.11, 12.
[53] Land Registration Act 2002, Sch.1, para.3.
[54] Land Registration Act 2002, s.71(a).
[55] Land Registration Rules 2003, rule 28.
[56] Land Registration Rules 2003, rule 28(4).

notice in the register of the burden of any interest which appears from his examination of title to affect the registered estate, unless the interest appears to be of a
trivial or obvious character, or the entry of the notice would be likely to cause confusion or inconvenience.[57]

Cautions against first registration of the servient tenement

5–16   A person is entitled to lodge a caution against the registration of title to an unregistered legal estate if he claims to be entitled to an interest (such as an easement)
affecting that estate (and the estate is capable of substantive registration).[58] Where
an application for substantive registration of that estate is made, the Registrar must
give the cautioner notice of the application and of his right to object to it.[59] Apart
from this effect of the registration of a caution, such registration has no effect.[60]
The 2002 Act contains further detailed provisions in relation to such cautions.[61]
The only caution which can be registered under the 2002 Act is a caution against
first registration; it is no longer possible to register a caution against dealings (as
it was under the Land Registration Act 1925).

Notices

5–17   A notice is an entry in the register in respect of the burden of an interest affecting
a registered estate. The fact that an interest is the subject of a notice does not
necessarily mean that the interest is valid but does mean that the priority of the
interest, if valid, is protected for the purposes of considering the effect of a registered disposition.[62] The 2002 Act contains detailed provisions as to notices.[63]
Where the notice is in respect of an order under the Access to Neighbouring Land
Act 1992, the application must be for an agreed notice rather than a unilateral
notice.[64]

Dispositions of registered land

5–18   Subject to an exception which is not material, the registered proprietor of a registered estate has power to make a disposition of any kind permitted by the general law in relation to an interest of that description.[65] A registrable disposition of
a registered estate only has effect if it complies with such requirements as to form
and content as rules may provide.[66] Rules may apply this provision (as to content
and form) to any other kind of disposition which depends for its effect on

---

[57] Land Registration Rules 2003, rule 35.
[58] Land Registration Act 2002, s.15.
[59] Land Registration Act 2002, s.16(1).
[60] Land Registration Act 2002, s.16(2).
[61] Land Registration Act 2002, ss.17–22.
[62] Land Registration Act 2002, s.32.
[63] Land Registration Act 2002, ss.32–39.
[64] Land Registration Rules 2003, rule 80(c).
[65] Land Registration Act 2002, s.23.
[66] Land Registration Act 2002, s.25(1).

registration.[67] There are two different types of disposition which need to be considered in the present context. The first is a transfer of the registered title. While reference will be made to the case of a transfer of the registered title to the dominant tenement, the discussion will focus on the case of a transfer of the registered title to the servient tenement. The second type of disposition is the express grant or reservation of an easement.

The effect of a registered disposition of the dominant tenement

The transfer of the registered title to the dominant tenement, when completed by registration, will vest in the transferee all of the interests (including easements) subsisting for the benefit of the estate.   **5–19**

The effect of a registered disposition of the servient tenement

If there is a registered disposition of the servient tenement for valuable considera-   **5–20**
tion, the disponee has priority over any interest affecting the servient tenement immediately before the disposition unless that interest is protected at the time of registration.[68] In the case of an easement, the available protection will be either a notice of the easement in the register relating to the servient tenement or the easement having overriding status under Schedule 3 to the 2002 Act.[69] To identify those easements which have overriding status, it is necessary to apply three provisions. The first is the general provision contained in Schedule 3, para.3 to the 2002 Act. The second provision is contained in Schedule 12, para.9 to the 2002 Act and this modifies the general provision in the case of an easement which was an overriding interest in relation to a registered estate before October 13, 2003. The third provision is contained in Schedule 12, para.10 of the 2002 Act and this further modifies the general provision but only for the period beginning October 13, 2003 and ending October 12, 2006.

Easements as overriding interests on the disposition of the servient tenement

The general provision as to easements which override the effect of a registered dis-   **5–21**
position of the servient tenement refers to those easements which are legal easements *except for* an easement which at the time of the disposition (i) is not within the actual knowledge of the person to whom the disposition is made, and (ii) would not have been obvious on a reasonably careful inspection of the land over which the easement is exercisable.[70] The words after "except for" identify "the exception". This exception does not apply if the person entitled to the easement or profit proves that it has been exercised in the period of one year ending with the day of disposition.[71] It is

---

[67] Land Registration Act 2002, s.25(2).
[68] Land Registration Act 2002, s.29(1). It is important to note that the statutory provisions as to priority only apply where the disposition is made for "valuable consideration" which phrase is defined in Land Registration Act 2002, s.132(1) as not including marriage consideration or a nominal consideration in money.
[69] Land Registration Act 2002, s.29(2).
[70] Land Registration Act 2002, Sch.3, para.3(1).
[71] Land Registration Act 2002, Sch.3, para.3(2).

clear that this general provision only applies to legal, as distinct from equitable, easements. Thus, under the general scheme created by the Land Registration Act 2002, an equitable easement cannot be an overriding interest. This is a deliberate change from the position under the Land Registration Act 1925.

The first modification of the general provision as to easements is effected by Schedule 12, para.9 to the 2002 Act. This provision applies to an easement which was an overriding interest in relation to a registered estate immediately before October 13, 2003 but which would not fall within the general provision in Schedule 3, para.3 if the right had been created on or after October 13, 2003. An example of such an easement could be an equitable easement which was an overriding interest under the Land Registration Act 1925. Where this first modification applies, the general provision in Schedule 3, para.3 to the 2002 Act has effect as if the easement were not excluded from the general provision in Schedule 3, para.3 to the 2002 Act. Therefore in such a case the general provision is modified so that it applies to a legal easement (which is already within the unmodified Schedule 3, para.3) and also to, e.g. equitable easements which were overriding interests under the Land Registration Act 1925; in each case, the general provision operates subject to the exception referred to above.

The second modification of the general provision as to easements is effected by Schedule 12, para.10 to the 2002 Act. This provision is subject to a time limitation in that it only applies for a period of three years beginning on October 13, 2003. In the period during which the second modification applies, the general provision in Schedule 3, para.3 to the 2002 Act applies with the omission of the exception referred to above.

The first and second modifications can operate in combination in an appropriate case.

The express grant or reservation of an easement

5–22 This is the second type of disposition by a registered proprietor referred to in para.5–18, above. The express grant or reservation of an easement is a disposition which is required to be completed by registration.[72] This reference to an express grant does not include a grant of an easement as a result of the operation of section 62 of the Law of Property Act 1925.[73] It follows from the use of the word "express" that an implied grant or reservation of an easement is not a disposition that requires to be completed by registration. If a disposition of a registered estate requires to be completed by registration, it does not operate at law until the relevant registration requirements are met.[74] The relevant registration requirements in relation to the express grant or reservation of an easement are set out in Schedule 2 to the 2002 Act.[75] These are that a notice in respect of the interest created must be entered in the register and, if the interest is created for the benefit of a

[72] Land Registration Act 2002, s.27(2)(d).
[73] Land Registration Act 2002, s.27(7).
[74] Land Registration Act 2002, s.27(1).
[75] Land Registration Act 2002, s.27(4), Sch.2, para 7.

registered estate, the proprietor of the registered estate must be entered in the register as its proprietor. The practical steps which must be taken to effect registration are explained in the Land Registry Practice Guide 62. It should be noted that an easement granted or reserved by a lease is a registered disposition. The Land Registry Practice Guide 62 explains the steps that should be taken to effect registration where the lease is a registered lease and where the lease is not a registered lease.

The overall effect

It may be helpful to describe the overall effect of the general provision as to easements being overriding interests (but without regard to the two modifications of that general provision) and of the requirements as to the express grant or reservation of an easement.[76] The 2002 Act provides that only a legal easement can be overriding in relation to a registered disposition. Any easement which is expressly granted or reserved out of registered land will be a registrable disposition. It will not take effect at law until it is registered. It follows that it can never be an overriding interest under Schedule 3 to the 2002 Act. As a result: **5–23**

(1) no easements or profits that are expressly created after the 2002 Act comes into force will be able to take effect as overriding interests;

(2) no equitable easements, however created, will be capable of overriding a registered disposition;

(3) the only legal easements and profits that will be capable of being overriding interests are:

    (a) those already in existence at the time when the 2002 Act comes into force, that have not been registered;

    (b) those arising by prescription;

    (c) those arising by implied grant or reservation;

    (d) those arising by the operation of section 62 of the Law of Property Act 1925.

Not all legal easements will have overriding status. The only legal easements which will bind a person who acquires an interest under a registered disposition for valuable consideration will be: **5–24**

(1) easements which the disponee actually knows of;

(2) easements which are patent, that is, which are obvious on a reasonably careful inspection of the land over which the easement is exercisable, so that the seller of the land would be obliged to disclose it[77];

(3) easements exercised within one year before the disposition.

---

[76] The following description in paras 5–23 to 5–25 is based on (2001) Law Com. No. 271 at paras 8.67 to 8.72; the position in relation to the modifications of the general position is described at *ibid.*, para.8.73.

[77] See Megarry & Wade's *The Law of Real Property* (6th ed., 2000), para.12–068.

The third case is intended to cover, in particular, the numerous invisible easements such as rights of drainage or the right to run a water supply pipe over a
neighbour's land. Such rights may have existed for many years but because
they may have been created otherwise than by express grant or reservation, they
may not be recorded on the register. The selection of the period of one year is
necessarily arbitrary.

5–25   The new rules in the 2002 Act are designed to encourage the creation of a
straightforward system of standard inquiries as to easements which will prompt
sellers to disclose what they can be reasonably expected to know. This will tend
to lead to the registration of such rights. In general, the seller should be asked to
disclose any unregistered easements affecting the property to be sold of which the
seller is aware, at least to the extent that they were not obvious on a reasonably
careful inspection of the land and, in particular, any easements which have been
exercised in the year preceding the inquiry. The result of such inquiries should be
that the buyer will have actual knowledge of any unregistered legal easements
long before the transaction is completed.

Duty to disclose unregistered interests

5–26   Where rules so provide, a person applying for first registration must provide to
the Registrar such information as the rules may provide about any interest affecting the estate to which the application relates which falls within Schedule 1 (and
this schedule includes legal easements) and is of a description specified by the
rules.[78] Similarly, where rules so provide, a person applying to register a registrable disposition of a registered estate must provide to the Registrar such information as the rules may provide about any unregistered interest affecting the estate
which falls within Schedule 3 (and this schedule includes legal easements subject
to exceptions) and is of a description specified by the rules.[79] Under the Land
Registration Rules 2003, a person applying to register a registrable disposition of
a registered estate must provide information to the Registrar about any of the
interests that fall within Schedule 3 that are within the actual knowledge of the
applicant and affect the estate to which the application relates.[80] Where the applicant provides information about such an interest under this rule, the Registrar
may enter a notice in the register in respect of that interest.[81]

Miscellaneous matters

5–27   A proprietor of a registered estate who claims the benefit of a legal easement which
has been expressly granted over an unregistered legal estate may apply for it to be
registered as appurtenant to his estate.[82] The application must be accompanied by

---

[78] Land Registration Act 2002, s.71(a); see para.5–15, above.
[79] Land Registration Act 2002, s.71(b). The exception is described in para.5–21, above.
[80] Land Registration Rules 2003, rule 57.
[81] Land Registration Rules 2003, rule 57(5).
[82] Land Registration Rules 2003, rule 73(1). The reference in this rule to an "express" grant does not
    include a grant as a result of the operation of s.62 of the Law of Property Act 1925: see rule 73(3).

the grant and evidence of the grantor's title to the unregistered estate.[83] A proprietor of a registered estate who claims the benefit of a legal easement which has been acquired otherwise than by express grant, may apply for it to be registered as appurtenant to his estate.[84] The application must be accompanied by evidence to satisfy the Registrar that the right subsists as a legal estate appurtenant to the applicant's registered estate.[85] If it appears to the Registrar that an agreement prevents the acquisition of rights of light or air for the benefit of the registered estate, he may make an entry in the property register of that estate.[86]

Equitable easements under the 2002 Act

Although the above discussion has made many references to the treatment of equitable easements, it is desirable to describe in one place the treatment of equitable easements under the 2002 Act. An equitable easement may be created in various ways, e.g. pursuant to a specifically enforceable contract to grant or reserve an easement or pursuant to a purported grant or reservation which is a registrable disposition but which is not completed by registration and therefore takes effect in equity only.   **5–28**

If the easement is clearly equitable, the Land Registry will not enter the benefit of it in the register for the dominant land either on first registration or subsequently. This is because the 2002 Act makes provision only for the registration of *legal* interests.[87] Hence, only the benefit of appurtenant *legal* easements can be entered in the register on first registration[88] and only the benefit of *legal* easements can be entered when the dominant land is already registered.[89] However, on first registration of an estate, that estate vests in the registered proprietor "together with all interests subsisting for the benefit of the estate" and this can extend to equitable easements.[90]

If the servient land is registered, an application should be made to enter an agreed or unilateral notice in respect of the equitable easement. Where an equitable easement is granted in a transfer of registered land, the Land Registry will automatically enter notice of the easement in the register for the servient land providing that the title number is entered in panel 2 of Form AP1. On first registration of the servient land, the Land Registry will enter a notice in the register in respect of an equitable easement.

As to the possibility of an equitable easement being an overriding interest, an equitable easement cannot be an overriding interest on first registration of the servient tenement and will not be an overriding interest on a registered

---

[83] Land Registration Rules 2003, rule 73(2).
[84] Land Registration Rules, 2003, rule 74(1). The reference in this rule to an "express" grant does not include a grant as a result of the operation of s.62 of the Law of Property Act 1925: see rule 74(3).
[85] Land Registration Rules 2003, rule 74(2).
[86] Land Registration Rules 2003, rule 76.
[87] Land Registration Act 2002, s.2.
[88] Land Registration Rules 2003, rule 33(1).
[89] Land Registration Act 2002, Sch.2, para.7 and Land Registration Act 2002, rules 73 and 74.
[90] Land Registration Act 2002, s.11(3).

disposition of the registered servient tenement unless it was an overriding interest before October 13, 2003.

Proprietary estoppel and mere equities

5–29   The 2002 Act declares for the avoidance of doubt that, in relation to registered land, each of the following, an equity by estoppel and a mere equity has effect from the time the equity arises as an interest capable of binding successors in title (subject to the rules about the effect of dispositions on priority).[91] The Law Commission report which led to the 2002 Act stated that it was difficult to define a "mere equity" with clarity but it appeared to have the following characteristics:

(1) it is an equitable proprietary right that is capable of binding successive owners of land;

(2) it is ancillary to or dependent upon an equitable estate or interest in the land;

(3) it appears to be used to denote a claim to discretionary equitable relief in relation to property such as a right to set aside a transfer for fraud or undue influence, a right to rectify an instrument for mistake, or a right to seek relief from forfeiture of a lease after a landlord has peaceably re-entered; and

(4) where title is unregistered, it is capable of being defeated by a bona fide purchaser of either a legal estate or an equitable interest for value without notice.

Pending actions

5–30   References in the 2002 Act to an interest affecting an estate or charge include a pending land action within the meaning of the Land Charges Act 1972.[92] The actions concerning easements which are pending land actions within the Land Charges Act 1972 are discussed at para.5–11, above. As a pending land action is within the class of interests affecting an estate or charge, it may be the subject of a notice in the register.[93]

Extinguishment of easements – removal of register entries

5–31   The subject of extinguishment of easements is dealt with in Chapter 12. When an easement has been extinguished, the servient owner will want to have any entries in respect of the easement removed from the register of title. An application for the removal of the appropriate entries in the register of the dominant and/or

---

[91] Land Registration Act 2002, s.116. This provision is discussed in (2001) Law Com. No. 271 at paras 5–29–5–36.

[92] Land Registration Act 2002, s.87(1)(a).

[93] Land Registration Act 2002, ss.32–34 and Land Registration Rules 2003, rule 172. As to notices, see para.5–17, above.

servient land should be in Form AP1. In all cases, the application must be supported by evidence that the easement has indeed been extinguished. The execution of the deed of release of an easement takes effect in accordance with its terms and does not depend upon the later step of removal of the relevant register entries in respect of the easement as the deed of release is not a registrable disposition and does not need to be registered before it takes effect in law. The other forms of extinguishment of an easement equally take effect in accordance with the general law and do not depend upon the subsequent removal of the relevant register entries in respect of the easement.

PART III

PARTICULAR EASEMENTS AND PARTICULAR NATURAL RIGHTS OF A SIMILAR CHARACTER

CHAPTER 6

RIGHTS IN RESPECT OF WATER

1.—INTRODUCTION

In dealing with the rights of riparian and other owners in respect of the water of **6–01** a natural stream flowing through a defined channel, the first distinction to be borne in mind is the distinction between natural rights and acquired rights. It must, moreover, be remembered that a person who is not himself a riparian owner can acquire rights by grant or prescription in a natural stream. The natural rights of a riparian owner, that is, the owner of land intersected or bounded by a natural stream, may be shortly defined as threefold: first, he has a right of user. He can use the water for certain purposes connected with his riparian land. Secondly, he has a right of flow. He is entitled to have the water come to him and go from him without obstruction.[1] Thirdly, he has a right of purity. He is entitled to have the water come to him unpolluted. These common law principles relating to the abstraction of water must, however, now be considered in the light of the restrictions on abstraction imposed by the Water Resources Act 1991 and the duties and

---

[1] See per Lord Wensleydale in *Chasemore v Richards* (1859) 7 H.L.C. 349 at 382; *Tate & Lyle Industries Ltd v Greater London Council* [1983] 2 A.C. 509 at 534.

powers in this regard of the National Rivers Authority (now the Environment Agency) constituted by the Water Act 1989.[2] In the present chapter a riparian owner's natural rights of user and flow in a natural watercourse will be dealt with in section 2 and the effect of those Acts in section 3. Prescriptive rights of user and flow will be considered in sections 4 and 5, artificial watercourses in section 6, purity and pollution in section 7, the acquisition of water rights in section 8, and miscellaneous rights of riparian owners in section 9. Section 10 deals with easements relating to pipes and drains.

2.—NATURAL RIGHTS IN NATURAL WATERCOURSES

(1) *Surface water: defined natural channel*

Rules as to rights of riparian owners

6–02   In *Wood v Waud*[3] the court held that a riparian owner has no property in the water of a stream flowing through or past his land, but is entitled only to the use of it as it passes along for the enjoyment of his property, citing the law as laid down in 1826 by the American Chancellor Kent, thus[4]:

> "Every proprietor of lands on the banks of a river has naturally an equal right to the use of the water. . . . He has no property in the water itself, but a simple usufruct as it passes along."

Since that case the rules as to the natural rights of riparian owners in water flowing through a natural watercourse having a defined and known channel have been successively stated by a series of great judges.

6–03   In 1851 Parke B. in *Embrey v Owen*[5] laid down the law on this subject as follows:

> "The right to have a stream to flow in its natural state without diminution or alteration is an incident to the property in the land through which it passes; but flowing water is publici juris, not in the sense that it is a bonum vacans, to which the first occupant may acquire an exclusive right, but that it is public and common in this sense only, that all may reasonably use it who have a right of access to it, that none can[6] have any property in the water itself,

---

[2] The rights of riparian owners are further affected by the Land Drainage Act 1991, ss.23 and 24 which control obstructions in ordinary watercourses (i.e. watercourses which do not form part of main rivers); and by the Water Resources Act 1991, s.109 which controls structures in, over or under a watercourse which is part of a main river.
[3] (1849) 3 Exch. 748 at 775.
[4] Kent's *Commentaries on American Law* (12th ed., 1896), Vol. III, p. 439; and see *Embrey v Owen* (1851) 6 Exch. 353.
[5] (1851) 6 Exch. 353 at 369.
[6] Except by statute: *Medway Co v Romney (Earl)* (1861) 9 C.B. (n.s.) 575.

except in the particular portion which he may choose to abstract from the stream and take into his possession, and that during the time of his possession only. But each proprietor of the adjacent land has the right to the usufruct of the stream which flows through it.[7] This right to the benefit and advantage of the water flowing past his land, is not an absolute and exclusive right to the flow of all the water in its natural state . . ., but it is a right only to the flow of water, and the enjoyment of it, subject to the similar rights of all the proprietors of the banks on each side to the reasonable enjoyment of the same gift of Providence. It is only, therefore, for an unreasonable and unauthorised use of this common benefit that an action will lie. For such an use it will, even though there may be no actual damage to the plaintiff."[8]

In *Rawstron v Taylor*[9] Parke B. said: "The right to have a stream running in its natural direction does not depend on a supposed grant, but is jure naturae."   **6–04**

In 1858 Lord Kingsdown said in *Miner v Gilmour*[10]:   **6–05**

"By the general law applicable to running streams, every riparian proprietor has a right to what may be called the ordinary use of the water flowing past his land; for instance, to the reasonable use of the water for his domestic purposes and for his cattle, and this without regard to the effect which such use may have, in case of a deficiency, upon proprietors lower down the stream. But, further, he has a right to the use of it for any purpose, or what may be deemed the extraordinary use of it, provided that he does not thereby interfere with the rights of other proprietors either above or below him. Subject to this condition, he may dam up the stream for the purpose of a mill, or divert the water for the purpose of irrigation. But he has no right to interrupt the regular flow of the stream, if he thereby interferes with the lawful use of the water by other proprietors, and inflicts upon them a sensible injury."[11]

In 1875 Lord Cairns again stated the law in *Swindon Waterworks Co v Wilts and Berks Canal Navigation Co*,[12] where the appellants, being riparian owners on the bank of a stream, claimed the right to collect the water of the stream into a   **6–06**

---

[7] i.e. to the reasonable use of the stream for ordinary purposes, e.g. for his domestic purposes and his cattle (*Miner v Gilmour* (1858) 12 Moo. P.C. 131), but not for purposes foreign to or unconnected with his riparian tenement (*McCartney v Londonderry and Lough Swilly Ry Co* [1904] A.C. 301). See para.6–07, below.

[8] See *Sampson v Hoddinott* (1857) 1 C.B. (n.s.) 611.

[9] (1855) 11 Exch. 369 at 382.

[10] (1858) 12 Moo. P.C. 131 at 156.

[11] Buckley J. pointed out in *Rugby Joint Water Board v Walters* [1967] Ch. 397 at 419 that the final sentence of that passage is a wider statement of the law than that adopted in *Embrey v Owen* (1851) 6 Exch. 353, and could be read as extending to permanent abstraction which caused no sensible injury; but the Privy Council was not concerned with permanent abstraction, and it is clear from the authorities reviewed by Buckley J. that permanent abstraction for extraordinary use is not permitted.

[12] (1875) L.R. 7 H.L. 697 at 704. Lord Cairns' judgment has been said to have almost codified the law: *McCartney v Londonderry and Lough Swilly Ry* [1904] A.C. 301 at 304.

permanent reservoir for the supply of an adjacent town; and it was held that this was not a reasonable use of the water within the meaning of the above rules.

> "Undoubtedly", said Lord Cairns L.C., "the lower riparian owner is entitled to the accustomed flow of the water for the ordinary purposes for which he can use the water, that is quite consistent with the right of the upper owner also to use the water for all ordinary purposes, namely, as has been said ad lavandum et ad potandum, whatever portion of the water may be thereby exhausted and may cease to come down by reason of that use. But further, there are uses no doubt to which the water may be put by the upper owner, namely, uses connected with the tenement of that upper owner. Under certain circumstances, and provided no material injury is done, the water may be used and may be diverted for a time by the upper owner for the purpose of irrigation. That may well be done; the exhaustion of the water which may thereby take place may be so inconsiderable as not to form a subject of complaint by the lower owner, and the water may be restored after the object of irrigation is answered, in a volume substantially equal to that in which it passed before. Again, it may well be that there may be a use of the water by the upper owner for, I will say, manufacturing purposes, so reasonable that no just complaint can be made upon the subject by the lower owner. Whether such a use in any particular case could be made for manufacturing purposes connected with the upper tenement would, I apprehend, depend upon whether the use was a reasonable one. Whether it was a reasonable use would depend, at all events in some degree, on the magnitude of the stream from which the deduction was made for this purpose over and above the ordinary use of the water."

6–07 In 1904, Lord Macnaghten dealt with the law in *McCartney v Londonderry and Lough Swilly Railway Co*,[13] where a railway line belonging to the respondents crossed a natural stream, and at the crossing abutted upon the stream for about eight feet on each side. The respondents inserted a pipe into the stream at the crossing, and by means of this pipe, which was laid along the strip of railway line, diverted water to other land belonging to them, about half a mile from the stream, and there consumed it in working their locomotive engines. The appellant, who was a lower riparian owner upon the stream, stopped the pipe, and thereupon the respondents brought their action for a declaration of their right to take the water through the pipe, and for an injunction. It was held, however, that the appellant was justified in the course taken by him and the action failed. Lord Macnaghten said[14]:

---

[13] [1904] A.C. 301, overruling *Sandwich v G.N. Ry* (1878) 10 Ch. D. 707. *Cf. Orr-Ewing v Colquhoun* (1877) 2 App. Cas. 839 at 856; *Rameshur v Koonj* (1878) 4 App. Cas. 121; *Roberts v Richards* (1881) 50 L.J.Ch. 297; 51 L.J.Ch. 944; *Ormerod v Todmorden Joint Stock Mill Co* (1883) 11 Q.B.D. 155; *Kensit v G.E. Ry* (1884) 27 Ch. D. 122; *Roberts v Gwyrfai D.C.* [1899] 2 Ch. 608; *Attwood v Llay Main Collieries* [1926] Ch. 444.

[14] [1904] A.C. 301 at 306, 307.

"There are, as it seems to me, three ways in which a person whose lands are intersected or bounded by a running stream may use the water to which the situation of his property gives him access. He may use it for ordinary or primary purposes, for domestic purposes, and the wants of his cattle. He may use it also for some other purposes–sometimes called extraordinary or secondary purposes–provided those purposes are connected with or incident to his land, and provided that certain conditions are complied with. Then he may possibly take advantage of his position to use the water for purposes foreign to or unconnected with his riparian tenement. His rights in the first two cases are not quite the same. In the third case he has no right at all.

Now it seems to me that the first question your Lordships have to consider is, under what category does the proposed user of the railway company fall? Certainly it is not the ordinary or primary use of a flowing stream, nor is it, I think, one of those extraordinary uses connected with or incidental to a riparian tenement which are permissible under certain conditions. In the ordinary or primary use of flowing water a person dwelling on the banks of a stream is under no restriction. In the exercise of his ordinary rights he may exhaust the water altogether. No lower proprietor can complain of that. In the exercise of rights extraordinary but permissible, the limit of which has never been accurately defined and probably is incapable of accurate definition, a riparian owner is under considerable restrictions. The use must be reasonable. The purposes for which the water is taken must be connected with his tenement, and he is bound to restore the water which he takes and uses for those purposes substantially undiminished in volume and unaltered in character."

Mutual rights and liabilities

The rules set out in the above judgments relate to the user and flow of overground water in a defined natural stream, to which user and flow every riparian owner has a natural right. These rules were tersely expressed by Erle C.J., in *Gaved v Martyn*[15] as follows:

6–08

"The flow of a natural stream creates mutual rights and liabilities between all the riparian proprietors along the whole of its course. Subject to reasonable use by himself, each proprietor is bound to allow the water to flow on without altering the quantity or quality."

To this may be added that as between himself and lower riparian owners the upper owner is not only bound to allow the water to flow on, but is entitled to insist that it shall flow on. "He has the right to have the natural stream come to him in its natural state, in flow, quantity and quality, and to go from him without obstruction."[16]

---

[15] (1865) 19 C.B. (n.s.) 732 at 759.
[16] *Chasemore v Richards* (1859) 7 H.L.C. 349, 382, per Lord Wensleydale.

Any obstruction by a lower riparian owner of such a character that it might reasonably be expected that injury would be caused to an upper riparian owner is actionable at the suit of the latter.[17]

User ordinary and extraordinary

6–09   The question what is a lawful user of the water by each riparian owner in the exercise of his natural rights depends on the circumstances of each case, and it is impossible to define precisely the limits which sever the permitted use of the water from its wrongful application. Thus, as regards the distinction drawn above by Lord Macnaghten between the ordinary or primary purposes and the extraordinary or secondary purposes to which the riparian owner may apply the water, this distinction may be different in different places and at different times. It has been said that the user which was at one time extraordinary might by changes in the condition of the property become ordinary; and also that a user which might be extraordinary in an agricultural district might not be extraordinary in a manufacturing district.[18]

Extraordinary user

6–10   Among purposes extraordinary but permissible Lord Cairns, in *Swindon Waterworks Co v Wilts and Berks Canal Navigation Co*,[19] mentions manufacturing purposes, which were dealt with in *Dakin v Cornish*,[20] where Alderson B. applied the test whether the same quantity of water continued to run in the river as if none of it had entered the manufacturing premises of the upper riparian owner. In dealing with the same user, Vaughan Williams L.J. in *Baily & Co v Clark, Son & Morland*[21] laid down that the riparian owner must not interfere with the lawful use of the water by owners above or below him or inflict on them a sensible injury. As has been seen, the right of a riparian owner to an extraordinary use does not enable a water company to divert water to supply a town,[22] nor does it enable a railway company which owns a tenement on a stream to divert water to a place outside that tenement and use it to supply locomotives along its line[23]; nor does it enable water to be diverted to supply a lunatic asylum and county jail.[24]

---

[17] *Orr-Ewing v Colquhoun* (1877) 2 App. Cas. 839 at 856; *M'Glone v Smith* (1888) 22 L.R.Ir. 559; *Ambler (Jeremiah) & Son Ltd v Bradford (Mayor)* (1902) 87 L.T. 217; *Tate & Lyle Ltd v Greater London Council* [1983] 2 A.C. 509 at 534.

[18] per Lord Esher in *Ormerod v Todmorden Joint Stock Mill Co Ltd* (1883) 11 Q.B.D. 155 at 168.

[19] (1875) L.R. 7 H.L. 697 at 704; see para.6–06, above.

[20] Referred to by Alderson B. in *Embrey v Owen* (1851) 6 Exch. 353 at 360.

[21] [1902] 1 Ch. 649 at 665. See *Sharp v Wilson* (1905) 93 L.T. 155, where the court held that for manufacturing purposes the defendants had dealt unreasonably with water.

[22] *Swindon Waterworks Co v Wilts and Berks Canal Navigation Co* (1875) L.R. 7 H.L. 697; see para.6–06, above; and see *Owen v Davies* [1874] W.N. 175; *Roberts v Gwyrfai District Council* [1899] 2 Ch. 612.

[23] *McCartney v Londonderry and Lough Swilly Ry* [1904] A.C. 301; see para.6–07, above.

[24] *Medway Co v Earl of Romney* (1861) 9 C.B. (n.s.) 575.

Swindon Waterworks Co v Wilts and Berks Canal Navigation Co[25] and   **6–11**
McCartney v Londonderry and Lough Swilly Railway Co[26] were applied by
Lawrence J. in *Attwood v Llay Main Collieries Ltd*,[27] in which the defendant was
held not to be entitled to draw water from a river in order to turn it into steam for
working the defendant's colliery undertaking. Dealing with the right of a riparian
owner to take water for extraordinary purposes, Lawrence J. said[28]:

> ". . . that he may also take and use the water for extraordinary purposes, if
> such user be reasonable and be connected with the riparian tenement, pro-
> vided that he restores the water so taken and used substantially undiminished
> in volume and unaltered in character."

In *Rugby Joint Water Board v Walters*[29] the plaintiff sought an injunction to   **6–12**
restrain the defendant from abstracting water from the river Avon for the spray
irrigation of his land. On occasion he took as much as 60,000 gallons a day. It was
in evidence that, although the abstraction had no visible or measurable effect on
the river, it amounted to a considerable volume of water, only a very small part
of which was returned to the river. Buckley J., holding that the defendant was not
entitled to take water from the river for spray irrigation and granting an injunction, applied the dictum of Lord Macnaghten in *McCartney v Londonderry &
Lough Swilly Railway Co*[30] and the decision of Lawrence J. in *Attwood v Llay
Main Collieries Ltd*[31] that a riparian owner is not entitled to take water from a
stream for extraordinary purposes without returning it to the stream in substantially unlimited quantity, a decision which Buckley J. found wholly consistent
with the principles laid down in *Wood v Waud*[32] and *Embrey v Owen*.[33] If a riparian owner permanently abstracts water, he deprives other riparian owners of any
use of the water so abstracted and thus infringes their rights. They are then entitled to complain, even without proof of damage.[34] The question whether the effect
of the abstraction is such as to cause them sensible injury is consequently irrelevant.[35] Buckley J. observed[36] that no attempt had been made by judges in the past
to define what uses can be regarded as "ordinary" uses, referred to by Lord Cairns

---

[25] (1875) L.R. 7 H.L. 697.
[26] (1904) A.C. 301.
[27] [1926] Ch. 444.
[28] [1926] Ch. 444 at 458.
[29] [1967] Ch. 397, disapproving *Lord Norbury v Kitchin* (1863) 3 F. & F. 292 (as inconsistent with
McCartney v Londonderry and Lough Swilly Ry [1904] A.C. 301) and *Earl of Sandwich v Great
Northern Ry* (1878) 10 Ch. D. 707 (as not accurately reflecting the law as stated in *Embrey v Owen*
(1851) 6 Exch. 353). The plaintiff had statutory authority to take the whole flow of the river, but it
sued as riparian owner.
[30] [1904] A.C. 301 at 307; see para.6–07, above.
[31] [1926] Ch. 444.
[32] (1849) 3 Exch. 748; see para.6–02, above.
[33] (1851) 6 Exch. 353; see para.6–03, above.
[34] *Attwood v Llay Main Collieries Ltd* [1926] Ch. 444.
[35] *Rugby Joint Water Board v Walters* [1967] Ch. 397 at 423.
[36] [1967] Ch. 397 at 424.

in *Swindon Waterworks Co v Wilts and Berks Canal Navigation Co*[37] as uses *ad lavandum et ad potandum*. That they extended to reasonable domestic uses and to watering cattle was clear. His Lordship said that, without attempting either to draw the line of demarcation between what are ordinary uses for this purpose and what extraordinary, or to suggest how it should be drawn, he felt no doubt that spray irrigation of the kind and upon the scale employed by the defendant could not be regarded as an ordinary use.

6–13   The decision in *Rugby Joint Water Board v Walters*[38] does not, of course, mean that water can never be drawn from a river for irrigation. In *Swindon Waterworks Co v Wilts and Berks Canal Navigation Co*[39] Lord Cairns mentions irrigation among extraordinary purposes. Parke B. in *Embrey v Owen*[40] said that if the irrigation takes place, not continuously, but at intermittent periods when the river is full, and no damage is done thereby to the working of a mill on the stream, and the diminution of the water is not perceptible to the eye, it is not prohibited. In *Chasemore v Richards*[41] Coleridge J. referred to irrigation as a perfectly legitimate mode of exercising the natural rights of an upper riparian owner if he thereby did not abridge the natural rights of a lower riparian owner—a result which would follow if the upper owner by irrigation exhausted the running stream. *Rugby Joint Water Board v Walters*[42] was distinguished in *Cargill v Gotts*,[43] where there was a prescriptive right to take water for irrigation of a farm from a mill pond forming part of a river at a distance of some 500 yards from the dominant tenement. With the introduction of crop-spraying the amount taken had increased tenfold, to as much as 400 gallons a day, between 1927 and 1977. Nevertheless, the Court of Appeal found that the right was a right to take water for farming purposes, that the character of the dominant tenement had not changed, and that the increase in the amount of water taken did not affect the nature or quality of the right asserted during the prescriptive period.

In *Attwood v Bovis Homes Limited*,[44] a prescriptive right of drainage had been acquired in favour of farmland on which the defendant proposed to build houses. The development would not increase the runoff, provided suitable attenuation measures were employed. Neuberger J. held, distinguishing the right of way cases,[45] that in cases of easements of drainage (as with easements of support and eavesdrop), the test is whether there has been a change in the dominant tenement of such a kind as to throw a substantially greater burden on the servient tenement. Since the development would not have that effect, the right was not affected.

---

[37] (1875) L.R. 7 H.L. 697 at 704; see para.6–06, above.
[38] [1967] Ch. 397.
[39] (1875) L.R. 7 H.L. 697 at 704.
[40] (1851) 6 Exch. 353 at 372.
[41] (1857) 2 H. & N. 150. See also *Sampson v Hoddinott* (1857) 1 C.B. (n.s.) 603, per Cresswell J., in which case the question was as to the right to impede the flow by means of channels cut for irrigation.
[42] [1967] Ch. 397.
[43] [1981] 1 W.L.R. 441.
[44] [2001] Ch. 379.
[45] See paras 9–05 to 9–11, below.

Cargill v Gotts and *Attwood v Bovis Homes Ltd* have both been considered, with a large number of other cases concerning other easements (principally rights of way), by the Court of Appeal in *McAdams Homes Ltd v Robinson*.[46] Both of the earlier cases were approved. As a result of that review, the court held that there were two questions to be answered. The first was whether any changes in relation to the dominant land represented a "radical change in the character" or a "change in the identity" of the dominant land as opposed to a mere change or intensification in the use of the dominant land. The second question was whether the changed use of the dominant land would result in a substantial increase or alteration in the burden on the servient land. It was only if there was a radical change in the dominant land and a substantial increase in the burden on the servient land that the dominant owner's right to enjoy the easement would be suspended or lost.

Natural rights are part of the fee simple

In dealing with riparian land it should not be forgotten that the natural rights above referred to are in law parts of the fee simple. Thus it was said by Parker J. in *Portsmouth Borough Waterworks Co v London Brighton and South Coast Railway*[47]:   **6–14**

> "When a riparian owner sells part of his estate, including land on the banks of a natural stream, it is not necessary to make any express provision as to the grant or reservation of the ordinary rights of a riparian proprietor. These rights are not easements to be granted or reserved as appurtenant to what is respectively sold or retained, but are parts of the fee simple and inheritance of the land sold or retained. If it be desired to alter or modify these rights, it can only be done by the grant or reservation of such rights in the nature of easements as the nature of the case may require. If no such rights are granted or reserved the vendor remains, and the purchaser becomes, a riparian owner, and retains or acquires all the ordinary rights of a riparian owner."

Where a riparian owner who had, or may have had, a prescriptive right to pollute the stream granted part of his land without any reservation, he could not as between himself and the grantee continue to pollute.[48]

Who are riparian owners

The question whether a particular piece of land sustains the character of a riparian tenement is a question of fact, and must be determined according to the special circumstances. In *Attwood v Llay Main Collieries* Lawrence J. said[49]:   **6–15**

---

[46] [2004] 3 E.G.L.R. 93.
[47] (1909) 26 T.L.R. 175.
[48] *Crossley & Sons Ltd v Lightowler* (1866) 2 Ch. App. 478.
[49] [1926] Ch. 444 at 459.

"[The] expression ['riparian tenement'] in my opinion connotes, in addition to contact with the river, a reasonable proximity to the river bank. The proposition that every piece of land in the same occupation which includes a portion of the river bank and therefore affords access to the river is, in my opinion, far too wide. In order to test it, let me take an extreme case: nobody in their senses would seriously suggest that the site of Paddington Station and Hotel is a riparian tenement, although it is connected with the river Thames by a strip of land many miles long, nor could it reasonably be suggested that the whole of a large estate of, say, 2,000 acres was a riparian tenement, because a small portion of it was bounded by a stream."

6–16 It is settled that the rights of a riparian owner do not depend on his ownership of the soil of the stream.[50] To give rise to the existence of riparian rights it is necessary that the land in respect of which they are claimed should be in contact with the flow of the stream, but lateral contact is as good *jure naturae* as vertical,[51] that is to say, a man has as much right to water flowing past his land as he has to water flowing over his land. In the case of a tidal river the foreshore of which is left bare at low water, it was said that, although each bank is not always in contact with the flow of the stream, it is in such contact for a great part of every day in the regular course of nature; which fact is an amply sufficient foundation for a natural riparian right.[52] Where a riparian owner grants away a part of his land not abutting on the stream the grantee has no water rights in respect of such part.[53] Again, it has been held that a lessee of mines under land adjoining a stream, who also enjoys a grant from the surface owner of the use of the water for colliery purposes, is not as regards the user of the water a riparian owner.[54] The position of a person holding from a riparian owner a licence to use the water of the stream was dealt with in *Stockport Waterworks Co v Potter*,[55] *Ormerod v Todmorden Joint Stock Mill Co*[56] and *Kensit v G.E. Railway*.[57]

First occupant acquires no right to divert

6–17 Reverting to the earlier cases in which the law as to water rights was stated, it seems that in discussing the question whether the right to receive the water is one of the ordinary incidents of the ownership of the soil, or an additional right claimed as an easement, a misconception formerly took place. The right to the corporeal thing, water itself, was confounded with the incorporeal right to have the stream

---

[50] *Lyon v Fishmongers' Co* (1876) 1 App. Cas. 673. In the case of land bounded by a non-navigable stream the ownership is presumed to extend *ad medium filum* of the soil of the stream (*City of London Commissioners v Central London Ry* [1913] A.C. 379), even where the conveyance appears to exclude the soil (*Mellor v Walmseley* [1905] 2 Ch. 179).

[51] *North Shore Ry Co v Pion* (1889) 14 App. Cas. 621.

[52] (1889) 14 App. Cas. 621.

[53] *Stockport Waterworks Co v Potter* (1864) 3 H. & C. 326; *Ormerod v Todmorden Joint Stock Mill Co* (1883) 11 Q.B.D. 155.

[54] *Insole v James* (1856) 1 H. & N. 243.

[55] (1864) 3 H. & C. 300.

[56] (1883) 11 Q.B.D. 155.

[57] (1884) 27 Ch. D. 122. See paras 6–69 to 6–73, below.

flow in its accustomed manner.[58] Upon this a further error was founded—that the first occupant or appropriator of water had a right to continue to divert the stream to the extent of such appropriation, no matter how injurious such diversion might be to the rights of parties who should afterwards seek to use the stream. The question was debated—what nature of property existed by law, or could exist, in air, light and water. It was attempted to rest the right to the enjoyment of these elements upon the first occupancy of a common right. Thus, Blackstone, in his chapter on "Title by Occupancy", after remarking that a property in goods and chattels might be acquired by occupancy—"the original and only primitive method of acquiring any property at all" laid it down that:

> "the benefit of the elements—light, air, and water—can only be appropriated by occupancy. If I have an ancient window overlooking my neighbour's ground, he may not erect any blind to obstruct the light; but if I build my house close to his wall, which darkens it, I cannot compel him to demolish his wall, for there the first occupancy is rather in him than in me. If my neighbour makes a tanyard, so as to annoy, and render less salubrious the air of my house or gardens, the law will furnish me with a remedy; but if he is first in possession of the air, and I fix my habitation near him, the nuisance is of my own seeking, and may continue. If a stream be unoccupied, I may erect a mill thereon, and detain the water, yet not so as to injure my neighbour's prior mill or his meadow, for he hath by the first occupancy, acquired a property in the current."[59]

The last two illustrations of Blackstone, however, are directly at variance with the later decisions upon this subject.[60] And the question has since been set at rest by the considered judgment of Lord Denman C.J. in *Mason v Hill*,[61] in which he laid it down that there is no authority in English law for the proposition that the first occupant, though he may be proprietor of the land above, has any right by diverting the stream to deprive the owner of the land below of the natural flow of the water. "It has long been established that the first occupant cannot acquire an exclusive right to running water."[62]

No act of appropriation necessary

It was also at one time made a question whether the simple fact of water running in a natural channel through land was sufficient to confer upon the landowner the   **6–18**

---

[58] *Mason v Hill* (1833) 5 B. & Ald. 1.

[59] Bl.Com. 402.

[60] *Mason v Hill* (1833) 5 B. & Ald. 1; *Bliss v Hall* (1838) 4 Bing.N.C. 183; *Sturges v Bridgman* (1879) 11 Ch. D. 852.

[61] (1833) 5 B. & Ald. 1, where the earlier authorities are reviewed at length. See also *Acton v Blundell* (1843) 12 M. & W. 324, para.6–26, below, where Tindall C.J. compared the case of the stream running in its natural course over the surface with the case of an underground spring; *Wright v Howard* (1823) 1 Sim. & St. 190.

[62] per Bowen L.J. in *Ormerod v Todmorden Joint Stock Mill Co Ltd* (1883) 11 Q.B.D. 155 at 171.

right to control his neighbour's interference, or whether there must be some tangible perception or active appropriation by the landowner of the benefit of the water.[63] It is now settled that no act of appropriation is necessary.[64] It has in effect been decided that every proprietor of land along the stream has, without ever having used the water, a right to maintain an action against any person who diverts it, unless the person so diverting it has acquired a legal title to do so, if the diversion diminishes the flow of water to an extent greater than that necessarily incident to the reasonable use of the water by the proprietor above in the exercise of his similar right. For instance, if a person erects a mill, and thereby interferes with the course of the stream to such an extent, he is liable to an action for such diversion at the suit of any proprietor of land lying lower down the stream, although the latter has never applied the water to a beneficial purpose, and brings an action only one day before the time requisite to give the owner of the mill a prescriptive right to a use of the water exceeding the natural right.[65]

(2) Surface water: no defined channel

Right to appropriate

6–19   The natural right to the flow of water applies only to water flowing in some defined natural channel; and therefore the owner of land upon which there is surface water arising out of springy or boggy ground and flowing in no definite channel, or water arising occasionally at one spot but having no defined course, has a right to get rid of such water by draining the land in any way he pleases, although, if not so disposed of, it might ultimately have reached the course of a natural stream.[66] The right of the riparian owner to the natural flow of water cannot extend further than the right to the flow of the stream itself and to the water flowing in some defined[67] natural channel, either subterranean or on the surface, communicating directly with

[63] See *Bealey v Shaw* (1805) 6 East 208; *Saunders v Newman* (1818) 1 B. & Ald. 258; *Williams v Morland* (1824) 2 B. & C. 910, and the considered judgment of Lord Denman in *Mason v Hill* (1833) 5 B. & Ald. 1.

[64] *Orr-Ewing v Colquhoun* (1877) 2 App. Cas. 854.

[65] See the judgments in *Embrey v Owen* (1851) 6 Exch. 368 and *Sampson v Hoddinott* (1857) 1 C.B. (n.s.) 611, where the action was by a reversioner; also *Wood v Waud* (1849) 3 Exch. 772; *Miner v Gilmour* (1858) 12 Moo.P.C. 156; *Crossley & Sons Ltd v Lightowler* (1866) 2 Ch. App. 478; *Roberts v Gwyrfai District Council* [1899] 2 Ch. 608; *McCartney v Londonderry and Lough Swilly Ry* [1904] A.C. 301; *Sharp v Wilson, Rotheray & Co* (1905) 93 L.T. 155; *Attwood v Llay Main Collieries Ltd* [1926] Ch. 444.

[66] *Rawstron v Taylor* (1855) 11 Exch. 369.

[67] "A watercourse consists of bed, banks and water, yet the water need not flow continually, and there are many watercourses which are sometimes dry. There is, however, a distinction to be taken in law between a regular flowing stream of water, which at certain seasons is dried up, and those occasional bursts of water which, in times of freshet or melting of ice and snow, descend from the hills and inundate the country. To maintain the right to a watercourse or brook, it must be made to appear that the water usually flows in a certain direction and by a regular channel, with banks or sides. It need not be shown to flow continually, as stated above, and it may at times be dry; but it must have a well-defined and substantial existence": *Angell on Watercourses*. Compare the explanation stated below of "defined channel". The elements of a watercourse are usefully considered in *Lee v Rural Municipality of Arthur* (1964) 46 D.L.R. (2d) 448, Manitoba Q.B.

the stream itself.[68] *In Broadbent v Ramsbotham*[69] the owner of the soil was held not to be liable to an action for draining a pond the water of which occasionally, when it exceeded a certain depth, escaped and squandered itself over the surface, some of it augmenting a natural stream, but by no defined channel.

The defendant in *Rugby Joint Water Board v Walters*,[70] in addition to drawing **6–20** water for irrigation from the River Avon, drew it from a reservoir which he constructed by enlarging a short length of a natural ditch which ran through his land into the river. The ditch, and hence the reservoir, was fed by piped overflows and drains, by surface water and by percolating water, but not by natural spring water. The water feeding the reservoir was not taken out of the old channel, but at the point at which it would have found its way into the channel. Buckley J. held that the defendant was entitled to impound the water at the point where it entered his reservoir, being the point at which if not intercepted the water would, before the construction of the reservoir, have passed from private ownership into a channel in which riparian rights would have attached to it, and to use it as he thought fit.

So the higher occupier has the right to appropriate surface water flowing over **6–21** his land in no defined channel, even though this deprives the lower landowner of the benefit of that water and even though he may have enjoyed the benefit for many years.[71] The conventional view is that this right is not qualified by any restriction to the effect that it must be exercised in a reasonable manner. The motive of the abstracting party is irrelevant and no action will lie against him even if it can be shown that he acted out of malice.[72] The conventional view is that it follows from the fact that he is not liable for deliberate injury to his neighbour's land, that he cannot be liable for negligence and he owes his neighbour no duty to take care in abstracting water.[73] However, the conventional view may now need to be re-considered in the light of more recent and far-reaching developments in the law of nuisance.[74]

Right to discharge

The occupier of land has no right: (a) to discharge on to his neighbour's land water **6–22** which he has artificially brought on to his land[75] or water that has come naturally

[68] *Rawstron v Taylor* (1855) 11 Exch. 369.
[69] (1856) 11 Exch. 602.
[70] [1967] Ch. 397; see para.6–12, above, applying *Broadbent v Ramsbotham* (1856) 11 Exch. 602 and *Chasemore v Richards* (1859) 7 H.L.C. 349, below.
[71] *Home Brewery Company Limited v William Davis & Co (Leicester) Limited* [1987] Q.B. 339 at 345E–H.
[72] *Bradford Corp v Pickles* [1895] A.C. 587.
[73] *Stephens v Anglian Water Authority* [1987] 1 W.L.R. 1381; *Langbrook Properties Ltd v Surrey County Council* [1970] 1 W.L.R. 161.
[74] See the decisions in *Leakey v National Trust* [1980] Q.B. 485; *Holbeck Hall Hotel Ltd v Scarborough Borough Council* [2000] Q.B. 836; *Bybrook Barn Garden Centre Ltd v Kent County Council* [2001] B.L.R. 55; *Rees v Skerrett* [2001] 1 W.L.R. 1541; *Delaware Mansions Ltd v Westminster City Council* [2002] 1 A.C. 321; *Abbahall Ltd v Smee* [2003] 1 W.L.R. 1472; *Marcic v Thames Water Utilities Ltd* [2004] 2 A.C. 42; *Green v Lord Somerleyton* [2004] 1 P. & C.R. 520 (referred to in para.6–22 below); and *Dobson v Thames Water Utilities Ltd* [2008] 2 All E.R. 362.
[75] *Baird v Williamson* (1863) 15 C.B. (n.s.) 317.

on to his land but which he has artificially, even if unintentionally, accumulated there[76]; or (b) by artificial erection on his land to cause water to flow on to his neighbour's land in a manner in which it would not, but for such erections, have done.[77] He is, however, under no obligation to prevent water that has come naturally on to his land (and has not been artificially concentrated, retained or diverted) from passing naturally on to his neighbour's land.[78] It was stated in *Palmer v Bowman* that the right to allow natural drainage onto lower land is an incident of ownership of the higher land and so its enjoyment cannot give rise to a prescriptive right.[79] *Palmer v Bowman* was distinguished, and explained, in *Green v Lord Somerleyton*[80] as turning on the fact that it concerned the drainage away of rainwater falling onto land, whereas in *Green v Lord Somerleyton* the easement of drainage related to water in dykes on the dominant land being drained through dykes on the servient land. In that case, it was held that in the absence of a relevant easement of drainage, the defendant, an owner and occupier of land, could owe to the owner of neighbouring land a measured duty of care[81] to take such steps as were reasonable in all the circumstances to prevent damage to the neighbouring land from water flooding on it from the defendant's land. On the facts of that case, it was held that there was a relevant easement of drainage acquired by implied reservation or prescription but if there had not been, there would not have been a breach of the duty of care because, first, there was an express provision in a deed exempting the defendant from liability in certain specified events, which had occurred, and, secondly, because in all the circumstances, the defendant had not failed to take reasonable steps to prevent the flooding.

Position of occupier of lower land

6–23   An occupier of land is entitled to protect his land against flood water from the sea or from an overflowing river even if this causes the flood water to flow on to his neighbour's land in greater quantities with greater violence than it otherwise would have done.[82] The neighbour's remedy is to erect his own embankment. Similarly, the owner of lower land is not obliged to receive water running off higher land; he may put up barriers or otherwise pin it back even though this may cause damage to the occupier of the higher land, provided that he does no more

---

[76] *Whalley v Lancashire & Yorkshire Ry* (1884) 13 Q.B.D. 131.

[77] *Hurdman v North Eastern Ry* (1878) 3 C.P.D. 168. The statement of the law in this paragraph is taken from the judgment of Mr Piers Ashworth Q.C. sitting as a deputy High Court judge in *Home Brewery Co Limited v William Davies & Co (Leicester) Limited* [1987] 1 Q.B. 339.

[78] *Smith v Kenrick* (1849) 7 C.B. 515; *Rylands v Fletcher* (1868) L.R. 3 H.L. 330 at 338–339, per Lord Cairns L.C.; *Gartner v Kidman* (1962) 108 C.L.R. 12 at 49, per Windeyer J.

[79] *Palmer v Bowman* [2000] 1 W.L.R. 842 approving this part of the decision in the *Home Brewery* case (above). In *Palmer* the owner of the higher land was seeking to establish the right to drain into defined ditches on the lower land so as to found a claim to the ancillary right to enter the lower land and clean out the ditches.

[80] [2004] 1 P. & C.R. 520.

[81] As described in *Leakey v National Trust* [1980] Q.B. 485.

[82] *R. v Sewers Commissioners for the Levels of Pagham, Sussex* (1828) 8 B. & C. 355 at 360 (sea); *Gerrard v Crowe* [1921] 1 A.C. 395 (river).

than is reasonably necessary to protect his enjoyment of his own land, does not act for the purpose of injury to his neighbour and uses reasonable care and skill.[83] If, however, it is established that the lower occupier's use of his land in taking such preventative steps went beyond what was reasonable and that the resultant damage to his neighbour's land was reasonably foreseeable or if the lower occupier propels water already naturally on his land on to his neighbour's land, he will be liable in nuisance and/or trespass.[84]

(3) *Underground water: channel defined and known*

If a natural stream flows through a defined underground channel, then, as soon as **6–24** the channel is known, the owners of the land above it, and, if it continues on the surface, the riparian owners on each side of the continued channel, have the same rights, and the same rights of action for diversion or obstruction of water higher up in the channel, as they would have had if the stream were wholly above ground.[85]

"Defined" for this purpose means physically or actually defined; in other words a "defined channel" is a channel. A "known" channel is a channel whose course had become actually known, by excavation or otherwise, or can be gathered by reasonable inference from existing and observed facts in the natural or pre-existing condition of the surface of the ground; as, for instance, a stream, such as the River Mole, which disappears into the ground and reappears, presumably as the same stream, lower down.[86]

(4) *Underground water: channel not defined and known*

Right to divert or appropriate

In the case of underground water flowing through undefined and unknown channels the above rules as to the natural rights of riparian owners do not apply. **6–25** For it is settled by *Chasemore v Richards*[87] that every man has the right to divert or appropriate all water of this nature which he can find on his own

---

[83] *Home Brewery Company Limited v William Davies & Co (Leicester) Limited* [1987] 1 Q.B. 339 at 349–352, applying *Gartner v Kidman* (1962) 108 C.L.R. 12 and rejecting the dictum of Lord Dunedin in *Gibbons v Lenfestey* (1915) 84 L.J.P.C. 158 at 160 (a case on the law of Guernsey).

[84] *Home Brewery Company Limited v William Davies & Co (Leicester) Limited* (above).

[85] *Dickinson v Grand Junction Canal Co* (1852) 7 Exch. 282 at 301; *Chasemore v Richards* (1859) 7 H.L.C. 374; *Black v Ballymena Township Commissioners* (1886) 17 L.R.Ir. 459; *Bradford Corp v Ferrand* [1902] 2 Ch. 655, 660; *Bleachers' Association Ltd v Chapel-en-le-Frith R.D.C.* [1933] Ch. 356.

[86] *Black v Ballymena Township Commissioners*, above; *Bradford Corp v Ferrand*, above; *Bleachers' Association Ltd v Chapel-en-le-Frith R.D.C.*, above.

[87] (1859) 7 H.L.C. 376; applied in *Rugby Joint Water Board v Walters* [1967] Ch. 397 at 424, above; see also paras 6–44 to 6–46, below.

land.[88] "Percolating water below the surface of the earth is a common reservoir in which nobody has any property, but of which everybody has (as far as he can) the right of appropriating the whole",[89] and this right the landowner can exercise notwithstanding that the stream which the neighbour owns may be diminished in consequence of the diverted or appropriated water not coming into it.[90] Again, it has been laid down that no action will lie against a man who by digging in his own land drains his neighbour's land, either by intercepting the flow of water percolating through the soil, or by causing water already collected on his neighbour's soil to percolate away.[91] The conventional view is that no action will lie in negligence or nuisance against a man who, by extracting water from his own land, causes the land of his neighbour to collapse.[92] However, the conventional view may now need to be re-considered in the light of more recent and far-reaching developments in the law of nuisance.[93]

6–26   In *Acton v Blundell*,[94] which decided that the owner of Blackacre through which underground water percolates in an undefined channel has no interest in such water which will enable him to maintain an action against a neighbour, who, by mining in the usual manner in his own land, lays dry a well on Blackacre, Tindal C.J. distinguished the case of the stream running in its natural course and the case of an underground spring as follows[95]:

> "The ground and origin of the law which governs streams running in their natural course would seem to be this, that the right enjoyed by the several proprietors of the lands over which they flow is, and always has been, public and notorious: that the enjoyment has been long continued—in ordinary cases, indeed, time out of mind—and uninterrupted; each man knowing what he receives and what has always been received from the higher lands, and what he transmits and what has always been transmitted to the lower. The rule, therefore, either assumes for its foundation the implied assent and agreement of the proprietors of the different lands from all ages, or perhaps

---

[88] *Ballard v Tomlinson* (1885) 29 Ch. D. 115 at 123; *Salt Union v Brunner* [1906] 2 K.B. 822; *English v Metropolitan Water Board* [1907] 1 K.B. 588 at 602. But an express grant of all streams that might be found in certain closes prevented the grantor from working mines under adjoining land so as to divert underground water from wells in the closes: *Whitehead v Parks* (1858) 2 H. & N. 870.

[89] *Ballard v Tomlinson* (1885) 29 Ch. D. 115 at 121, per Lord Brett M.R.

[90] *Bradford Corp v Pickles* [1895] A.C. 587.

[91] *Ballacorkish Mining Co v Harrison* (1873) L.R. 5 P.C. 60, where this rule was held to apply between a surface owner and the mine owner.

[92] *Stephens v Anglian Water Authority* [1987] 1 W.L.R. 1381.

[93] See the decisions in *Leakey v National Trust* [1980] Q.B. 485; *Holbeck Hall Hotel Ltd v Scarborough Borough Council* [2000] Q.B. 836; *Bybrook Barn Garden Centre Ltd v Kent County Council* [2001] B.L.R. 55; *Rees v Skerrett* [2001] 1 W.L.R. 1541; *Delaware Mansions Ltd v Westminster City Council* [2002] 1 A.C. 321; *Abbahall Ltd v Smee* [2003] 1 W.L.R. 1472; *Marcic v Thames Water Utilities Ltd* [2004] 2 A.C. 42; *Green v Lord Somerleyton* [2004] 1 P. & C.R. 520 (referred to in para.6–22, above); and *Dobson v Thames Water Utilities Ltd* [2008] 2 All E.R. 362.

[94] (1843) 12 M. & W. 324. See *New River Co v Johnson* (1860) 2 E. & E. 435 (deciding that there is no distinction for this purpose between water already collected in a well and water which would otherwise have flowed into it); *R. v Metropolitan Board of Works* (1863) 3 B. & S. 710.

[95] (1843) 12 M. & W. 324 at 349–352.

it may be considered as a rule of positive law (which would seem to be the opinion of Fleta and Blackstone), the origin of which is lost by the progress of time; or it may not be unfitly treated as laid down by Mr Justice Story, in his judgment in the case of Tyler v. Wilkinson, in the courts of the United States,[96] as 'an incident to the land; and that whoever seeks to found an exclusive use must establish a rightful appropriation in some manner known and admitted by the law'. But in the case of a well sunk by a proprietor in his own land, the water which feeds it from a neighbouring soil does not flow openly in the sight of the neighbouring proprietor, but through the hidden veins of the earth beneath its surface: no man can tell what changes these underground sources have undergone in the progress of time: it may well be, that it is only yesterday's date, that they first took the course and direction which enabled them to supply the well: again, no proprietor knows what portion of water is taken from beneath his own soil: how much he gives originally, or how much he transmits only, or how much he receives: on the contrary, until the well is sunk, and the water collected by draining into it, there cannot properly be said, with reference to the well, to be any flow of water at all. In the case, therefore, of the well, there can be no ground for implying any mutual consent or agreement, for ages past, between the owners of the several lands beneath which the underground springs may exist, which is one of the foundations on which the law as to running streams is supposed to be built; nor, for the same reason, can any trace of a positive law be inferred from long-continued acquiescence and submission, whilst the very existence of the underground springs or of the well may be unknown to the proprietors of the soil.

But the difference between the two cases with respect to the consequences, if the same law is to be applied to both, is still more apparent. In the case of the running stream, the owner of the soil merely transmits the water over its surface: he receives as much from his higher neighbour as he sends down to his neighbour below: he is neither better nor worse: the level of the water remains the same. But if the man who sinks the well in his own land can acquire by that act an absolute and indefeasible right to the water that collects in it, he has the power of preventing his neighbour from making any use of the spring in his own soil which shall interfere with the enjoyment of the well. He has the power, still further, of debarring the owner of the land in which the spring is first found, or through which it is transmitted, from draining his land for the proper cultivation of the soil: and thus, by an act which is voluntary on his part, and which may be entirely unsuspected by his neighbour, he may impose on such neighbour the necessity of bearing a heavy expense, if the latter has erected machinery for the purposes of mining, and discovers, when too late, that the appropriation of the water has already been made. Further, the advantage on one side, and the detriment to

---

[96] Mason (U.S.) 401.

the other, may bear no proportion. The well may be sunk to supply a cottage, or a drinking-place for cattle; whilst the owner of the adjoining land may be prevented from winning metals and minerals of inestimable value. And, lastly, there is no limit of space within which the claim of right to an underground spring can be confined: in the present case, the nearest coal-pit is at the distance of half a mile from the well: it is obvious the law must equally apply if there is an interval of many miles."

6–27   The principle of *Acton v Blundell*[97] was applied in *Salt Union v Brunner*,[98] although the underground liquid drawn off by the defendants in the course of pumping operations carried on by them on their own land was brine mainly formed by the dissolution of rock-salt in the plaintiffs' salt mines, and although it was found as a fact that the defendants had, by such operations, abstracted a large quantity of salt from the beds of rock-salt belonging to the plaintiffs, and that if the defendants' brine-pumping were continued, more of the plaintiffs' rock would be dissolved, and the salt abstracted therefrom. Notwithstanding these facts it was held that the defendants were guilty of no actionable wrong. It is to be observed that, as pointed out by Sir John Pennycuick V.-C. in *Lotus Ltd v British Soda Co Ltd*,[99] the action was based upon the removal of salt by pumping and not upon any resulting subsidence.

6–28   The decision in *Grand Junction Co v Shugar*,[100] which seems inconsistent with the rule above stated as to percolating underground water, must be explained as relating to a direct tapping of an overground stream flowing in a defined channel, and not to a mere withdrawal of percolating underground water.[101]

6–29   The principles laid down in *Acton v Blundell*[102] also apply where the surface and the mines beneath it belong to different owners, the surface having been granted and the mines retained. The owner of the mine is not responsible if, in working the mines, he drains the water from the surface. In *Ballacorkish Mining Co v Harrison*[103] Lord Penzance, delivering the advice of the Privy Council, said:

"The grant of the surface cannot carry with it more than the absolute ownership of the entire soil would include.

That absolute ownership is held not to include a right to be protected from loss of water by percolation into openings made in the soil of a neighbouring

---

[97] (1843) 12 M. & W. 324.
[98] [1906] 2 K.B. 822. As to the right of support which has been claimed from underground water, see para.10–03, below.
[99] [1972] Ch. 123 at 130, see para.10–08, below.
[100] (1871) 6 Ch. App. 483; see the report in 24 L.T. 402.
[101] *Jordeson v Sutton, Southcoates and Drypool Gas Co* [1899] 2 Ch. 217 at 251; *English v Metropolitan Water Board* [1907] 1 K.B. 588 at 601.
[102] (1843) 12 M. & W. 324.
[103] (1873) L.R. 5 P.C. 49 at 63; see *Littledale v Lonsdale* [1899] 2 Ch. 233n. As to a mine owner's rights in working his mines, see also the Scottish decision in *Scots Mines Co v Leadhills* (1859) 34 L.T. 34.

owner. How, then, can the grant of the surface only be held to include such a protection?

To hold otherwise might not improbably result in rendering the reservation of mines and minerals wholly useless. Percolation of water into mines to some extent is an almost necessary incident of mining. And if the grant of the surface carries with it a right to be protected from any loss of surface water by this percolation, the owner of the surface would hold the owner of the mines at his mercy, for he would be entitled by injunction to inhibit the working of the mines at all.

It is not at variance with this view that the case of Whitehead v Parks[104] was decided, because in that case there was a lease and a distinct grant of the injured springs eo nomine."

If, however, the grant of the surface were made for some express purpose neces-   **6–30** sarily and obviously requiring the continuance of a supply of surface water, the principle laid down in the above passage might come into conflict with the principle that a man may not derogate from his own grant. It is conceived, however, that even in such a case the surface owner could not claim a continuance of the surface water so as to prevent the working of the minerals. The reservation of the minerals would, it is thought, include all the natural and legal incidents consequent upon the working necessary to win them.

Surface springs

As will have been seen above, the rules regulating the right of flow laid down as   **6–31** to water flowing in an undefined channel differ from those which apply to defined channels. In the case of water flowing from surface springs there is often a difficulty in deciding whether they fall under the rules as to defined or undefined channels.[105] Where a natural defined stream issued from a springhead, it was held that the "stream" began at the springhead, and that the owner of the land could only take such water from either as was incident to his right as riparian owner.[106] The same principle applied even where at some remote period the springhead had been built round.[107]

3. — STATUTORY RESTRICTIONS ON RIPARIAN OWNERS' RIGHTS

The Water Act 1973 provided for the establishment of nine regional water author-   **6–32** ities and the Welsh National Water Development Authority, which took over the functions and duties of the former river authorities. The Water Act 1989 provided

---

[104] (1858) 2 H. & N. 870.
[105] See *Ennor v Barwell* (1860) 2 Giff. 423; *Briscoe v Drought* (1860) 11 Ir. C.L.R. 250.
[106] *Dudden v Clutton Union* (1857) 1 H. & N. 627; *Ewart v Belfast Guardians* (1881) 9 L.R.Ir. 172; *Bunting v Hicks* (1894) 70 L.T. 458; *Rugby Joint Water Board v Walters* [1967] Ch. 397 at 424.
[107] *Mostyn v Atherton* [1899] 2 Ch. 360.

for the transfer of the functions of the authorities established in accordance with the 1973 Act to the National Rivers Authority and the companies appointed to be water or sewerage undertakers. The National Rivers Authority was a body corporate established in accordance with the 1989 Act. Its functions and duties were set out in the Water Resources Act 1991. These included: (a) management of water resources,[108] including abstraction licensing; (b) control of water pollution[109]; (c) land drainage and flood protection[110]; and (d) certain fishery and navigation functions. It had a general duty to promote conservation and recreational interests[111] and to have regard to the duties imposed on water and sewerage undertakers which might be affected by the exercise of its powers.[112] With effect from April 1, 1996, the National Rivers Authority was abolished and all its functions and duties transferred to the Environment Agency, a body corporate established under the Environment Act 1995.[113] The position of the riparian owner is particularly affected by Part II, Chapter II of the Water Resources Act 1991, which contains provisions for controlling the abstraction and impounding of water and thus affects the riparian owner's common law rights and duties. These provisions are amended by Part I (ss.1–33) of the Water Act 2003. Part I of the 2003 Act has been brought into force gradually and nearly all of its provisions are now in force.[114] Part I of the 2003 Act is concerned with long-term sustainable use of water resources against the background of climate change. There are new restrictions in the 2003 Act on what were previously exempt uses of water. The new provisions are designed to give to the Environment Agency the ability to manage and rebalance the allocation of water between various classes of abstractor and the environment.

Basic rule

6–33   Section 24(1) of the Water Resources Act 1991 provides that no person shall abstract water or cause or permit any other person so to abstract any water, except in pursuance of a licence under the Act granted by the Authority (now the

---

[108] Water Resources Act 1991, Pt II.
[109] Water Resources Act 1991, Pt III.
[110] Water Resources Act 1991, Pt IV and the Land Drainage Act 1991.
[111] Water Resources Act 1991, s.2(2) and s.16, repealed by Environment Act 1995, s.120 and Sch.24.
[112] Water Resources Act 1991, s.15(1).
[113] Environment Act 1995, ss.2, 6; SI 1996/186. In this connection, it is the duty of the Agency to take all such action as it may from time to time consider, in accordance with the directions (if any) of the Secretary of State, to be necessary or expedient for the purpose of conserving, redistributing or otherwise augmenting water resources in England and Wales and of securing the proper use of water resources in England and Wales: *ibid.*, s.6(2).
[114] The provisions of Part I (ss.1–33) of the Water Act 2003 have been brought into force on different dates pursuant to a number of commencement orders, as follows: April 1, 2004 (SI 2004/641), October 1, 2004 (SI 2004/2528), April 1, 2005 (SI 2004/641 and SI 2005/968), April 1, 2006 (SI 2006/984). The provisions of ss.5, 7, 8(2) and 32 and some of the repeals in Sch.9 Pt I are not in force as of July 26, 2008. The statutory provisions are supplemented by the Water Resources (Abstraction and Impounding) Regulations 2006 (SI 2006/641) and the Water Resources (Abstraction and Impounding) (Amendment) Regulations 2008 (SI 2008/165).

Environment Agency) and in accordance with the provisions of that licence. Although there are exceptions, the general rule is that a licence is required to abstract[115] water from a source of supply. For the purposes of the Act, "source of supply" means any inland waters except any which are "discrete waters", that is, "lakes, ponds or reservoirs which do not discharge to other inland water or underground strata . . . in which water is or may at any time be contained".[116]

In the case of an inland water, a person is entitled to apply for a licence if, as respects the place (or, if more than one, each of the places) at which the proposed abstractions are to be effected he satisfies the Agency that (a) he has, or at the time when the proposed licence is to take effect will have, a right of access to land contiguous to the inland waters at that place (or places) and (b) he will continue to have such a right for the period of at least one year beginning with the date when the proposed licence is to take effect, or until it is to expire (if sooner).[117] In the case of underground strata, a person is entitled to apply for a licence if he satisfies the Agency that (a) he has, or at the time when the proposed licence is to take effect will have, a right of access to land consisting of or comprising those underground strata and (b) he will continue to have such a right for the period of at least one year beginning with the date when the proposed licence is to take effect, or until it is to expire (if sooner).[118] The Agency may, in particular, take evidence of a person's right to occupation of land to be evidence of his right of access to it.[119] Persons who are in the process of obtaining a right of access to the relevant land, either by negotiation or compulsory purchase, may apply for a licence if they can satisfy the Agency that the process that will lead to the acquisition of the necessary rights has started.[120] The Agency will publish notice of the application and give notice of the same to the water undertaker for the relevant area.[121]

---

[115] "Abstract" in the Water Resources Act 1991 means the doing of anything whereby any of that water is removed from a source of supply (either permanently or temporarily) including anything whereby the water is so removed for the purpose of being transferred to another source of supply: *ibid.*, s.221(1). Where, however, there is a single hydrological system with interconnected sources of supply and a single means of abstraction, the abstraction takes place at the immediate source of supply and not at any other, more remote, source and therefore only needs one licence: *British Waterways Board v National Rivers Authority*, [1993] Env. L.R. 239.

[116] Water Resources Act 1991, s.221(1). "Inland water" means inter alia any river, stream or other watercourse, whether natural or artificial and whether tidal or not, and any lake or pond, whether natural or artificial or any reservoir or dock or so much of any channel, creek, bay, estuary or arm of the sea as does not already fall within the definition. "Source of supply", however, does not include a lake or pond which does not discharge to any other inland water, or one of a group of lakes or ponds where none of the groups discharges to any inland water outside the group. "Underground strata" means strata subjacent to the surface of any land. Water contained in any excavation into underground strata, where the level depends on water entering it from those strata, is to be treated as water contained in the underground strata: *ibid.*, s.221(3)(b).

[117] Water Resources Act 1991, s.35(2) as substituted by Water Act 2003, s.11.

[118] Water Resources Act 1991, s.35(3) as substituted by Water Act 2003, s.11.

[119] Water Resources Act 1991 inserted by Water Act 2003, s.11.

[120] Water Resources Act 1991, s.35(4) as amended by Water Act 2003, s.11.

[121] For the publicity and notice requirements, see Water Resources Act 1991, s.37 as substituted by Water Act 2003, s.14; as to the power of the Secretary of State to permit a dispensation in these respects: see Water Resources Act 1991, s.37A, inserted by Water Act 2003, s.14.

Abstraction licences

6–34   Each licence to abstract water must be one of the following three types: (a) a full licence to abstract water from one source of supply over a period of 28 days or more for any purpose ("a full licence"); (b) a licence to abstract water from one source of supply for a period of 28 days or more for the purpose of: (i) transferring water to another source of supply; or (ii) transferring water to the same source of supply, but at another point, in the course of dewatering activities in connection with mining, quarrying, engineering, building or other operations (whether underground or on the surface) and in either case without intervening use ("a transfer licence"); (c) a licence to abstract water from one source of supply over a period of less than 28 days ("a temporary licence"). In the Water Resources Act 1991 as amended by the Water Act 2003, a reference to a licence to abstract water is taken to be a reference to all types of licence unless it is clear that a different meaning is intended.[122]

The Agency has a discretion subject to the provisions of the Act as to whether to grant or refuse a licence, and may grant a licence containing such provisions as it considers appropriate.[123] The Secretary of State has power to call in applications and to cause a local inquiry to be held.[124] There is a right of appeal to the Secretary of State[125] and thence a limited right of appeal to the High Court.[126]

The full licence must, and other licences may, specify inter alia whether it is to remain in force until revoked or is to expire at a specified time, the quantity of water which may be abstracted during a specified period or periods, provision for determining what quantity of water is to be taken to have been abstracted, the means by which the water may be abstracted, the purposes for which the abstracted water is to be used and the dates on which the licence takes effect and on which it expires.[127] The licence must specify the person to whom it is granted and he is the holder of the licence for the purposes of the Act.[128]

---

[122] Water Resources Act 1991, s.24A, inserted by Water Act 2003, s.1.

[123] Water Resources Act 1991, s.38(2). For the factors which the water authority must take into account in dealing with an application: *ibid.*, ss.38, 39A, 39B and 40, as amended by Water Act 2003, ss.14–18.

[124] Water Resources Act 1991, ss.41–42, as amended by Water Act 2003, ss.13, 16.

[125] Water Resources Act 1991, s.43, as amended by Water Act 2003, s.14.

[126] Water Resources Act 1991, s.69.

[127] Water Resources Act 1991, s.46, as amended by Water Act 2003, s.19. If the licence is for a term exceeding 12 years, every full licence must, and every transfer licence may, specify a minimum value for the quantity of water: see Water Resources Act 1991, s.46(2A) inserted by Water Act 2003, s.19. As to the possibility of a limited extension to the validity of the licence, see Water Resources Act 1991, s.46A as inserted by Water Act 2003, s.20.

[128] Water Resources Act 1991, s.47, as amended by Water Act 2003, s.19. As to succession to the licence, see Water Resources Act 1991, ss.59A–59D as amended by Water Act 2003, s.23 and Water Resources Act 1991, s.67. As to modification, variation and revocation of licences, see Water Resources Act 1991, ss.51–55, 61, 61A and 62, as amended by Water Act 2003.

The exceptional cases

There are several exceptional cases where a licence to abstract water is not nec-   **6–35**
essary,[129] of which the following are relevant to the enjoyment of riparian rights
and easements in respect of the supply of water. There were originally, under the
Water Resources Act 1991, further exceptional cases but these have been
removed by the Water Act 2003.

A licence is not required for any abstraction of a quantity of water not exceeding 20 cubic metres in any period of 24 hours if it does not form part of a continuous operation, or a series of operations, whereby in the aggregate more than
20 cubic metres of water are abstracted during that period.[130] What is a series of
operations is a question of fact.[131]

The restrictions on abstraction also do not apply to abstractions in the course
of or resulting from land drainage works or emergency abstractions to prevent
immediate danger of interference with any mining, quarrying, engineering, building or other.[132] The restrictions also do not apply to any transfer of water from one
area of inland water to another by a harbour navigation or conservancy authority
in the exercise of their statutory function[133] or to the use of water for various miscellaneous purposes including fire-fighting.[134]

Effect on common law rights

For the purposes of Chapter II of Part II of the Water Resources Act 1991, a per-   **6–36**
son who is for the time being the holder of a licence under that Chapter to abstract
water is taken to have a right to abstract water to the extent authorised by the
licence and in accordance with its provisions.[135]

Before the coming into force of the Water Act 1973, a person who suffered damage as a result of an abstraction pursuant to a licence might have contemplated
whether he could bring an action against the abstractor in nuisance or negligence or
even for breach of contract. There was (and still is) no statutory impediment to an
action for negligence or for breach of contract, if a claim were otherwise available.

---

[129] The exceptions are contained in Water Resources Act 1991, s.27. In addition, the Secretary of State
may make regulations for further cases (to be referred to as "exemptions") in which the restriction
on abstraction (and, in the case of abstractions from underground strata, the other restrictions in
s.24) shall not apply: Water Resources Act 1991, s.33A, inserted by Water Act 2003, s.9. See the
Water Resources (Abstraction and Impounding) Regulations 2006 (SI 2006/641) and the Water
Resources (Abstraction and Impounding) (Amendment) Regulations 2008 (SI 2008/165); Part 3
of the 2006 Regulations modifies the statutory provisions as apply to abstraction and impounding
by the Agency.

[130] Water Resources Act 1991, s.27(1), as amended by Water Act 2003, s.6. The quantity specified
may be varied by a statutory instrument made under *ibid.*, s.27A.

[131] *Cargill v Gotts* [1981] 1 W.L.R. 441.

[132] Water Resources Act 1991, s.29 as amended by Water Act 2003, s.7.

[133] Water Resources Act 1991, s.26. This is the subject of a prospective amendment by Water Act
2003, s.5 (not yet in force).

[134] Water Resources Act 1991, s.32, as amended by Fire and Rescue Services Act 2004, s.53(1),
Sch.1, para.79.

[135] Water Resources Act 1991, s.48(1).

However, where a person abstracted water in pursuance of a licence he was not liable for common law nuisance to another riparian owner even though he had no defence at common law.[136] Section 48(2) of the Water Resources Act 1991 provided as follows:

> "In any action brought against a person in respect of the abstraction of water from a source of supply, it shall be a defence. . . . for him to prove (a) that the water was abstracted in pursuance of a licence under this Chapter and (b) that the provisions of the licence were complied with."

The grant of a licence, therefore, provided a statutory defence to the holder of the licence[137] in relation to a claim for common law nuisance and, it seems, to any person whom he caused or permitted to abstract water in pursuance of the licence. The terms of the licence must have been complied with; the licence would not provide a partial defence where one of its terms was broken. The position has now been radically altered by the introduction of the statutory duty in section 48A of the Water Resources Act 1991, as amended by the Water Act 2003. Under the new provisions, the defence provided by section 48(2) of the Water Resources Act 1991 is not available in the case of a claim for breach of statutory duty under section 48A of the 1991 Act, introduced by the Water Act 2003. Conversely, where section 48A applies,[138] that section provides that no claim can be made in any civil proceedings by a person in respect of loss and damage caused by the abstraction except where the claim is made in accordance with section 48A.[139] This new section is considered below.

If a person abstracts water without a licence in one of the exceptional cases where no licence is required,[140] his defence to a common law claim by a riparian owner previously depended entirely on the common law. The fact that he fell within one of the exceptions only exempted him from liability to a statutory penalty; it did not provide a defence to an action at common law. In such a case there was nothing to prevent such a person from applying for a licence and thus obtaining a statutory defence, against a common law claim in nuisance, under section 48 of the Water Resources Act 1991.[141] Under the new statutory duty created by section 48A, the possibility of a claim for breach of statutory duty arises, whether the abstractor has a licence or relies on one of the exceptional cases

---

[136] Under Water Resources Act 2003, s.48(2). The licence did not and still does not provide a defence to an action for negligence or breach of contract: *ibid.*, ss.48(4), 48A(6). The statutory defence was not available to persons who abstracted water under a "licence of right" if the action was brought before September 1, 1992: *ibid.*, Sch.7, para.2.

[137] *Scott-Whitehead v National Coal Board* (1985) 33 P. & C.R. 263 at 272.

[138] For a case where loss and damage has been suffered but where s.48A does not apply, see s.48A(7); in such a case the operation of s.48 is not affected by s.48A.

[139] Nothing in s.48A affects a claim for negligence or breach of contract.

[140] Water Resources Act 1991, s.27, as amended by Water Act 2003. See above, para.6–35.

[141] The statutory authority must not derogate from "protected rights" when granting a licence; but these rights do not necessarily correspond with common law rights: see below.

where no licence is required (or indeed has no right to abstract water) but, as described above, where section 48A applies, that section provides that no claim can be made in any civil proceedings by a person in respect of loss and damage caused by the abstraction except where the claim is made in accordance with section 48A.

Statutory duty

The Water Act 2003 has introduced section 48A into the Water Resources Act 1991. Under the new section 48A, subject to certain exceptions, a person who abstracts water from any inland waters or underground strata ("an abstractor") must not by that abstraction cause loss or damage to another person. A person who suffers such loss or damage ("a relevant person") may bring a claim against the abstractor. The claim is treated as a claim in tort for breach of statutory duty. In proceedings in respect of a claim under section 48A, the court may not grant an injunction against the abstractor if that would risk interrupting the supply of water to the public, or would put public health or safety at risk. Except as is provided by section 48A, no claim may be made in civil proceedings by a person, whether or not a relevant person, against an abstractor in respect of loss or damage caused by his abstraction of water. Nothing in section 48A prevents a claim for negligence or for breach of contract. Section 48A does not apply, and no claim may be brought under it, where the loss or damage is caused by an abstractor acting in pursuance of a licence under Chapter II of Part II of the Water Resources Act 1991 and is loss or damage in respect of which a person is entitled to bring a claim under section 60 of the 1991 Act,[142] or would be so entitled if there were a breach of the duty referred to in section 60, or in respect of which a person would have been entitled to bring a claim under section 60, but for an express provision disapplying that duty, or constituting grounds on which a person is entitled to apply to the Secretary of State under section 55 of the 1991 Act (or would be so entitled but for section 55(2)) for the revocation or variation of that licence. Section 48A is subject to section 79 of the 1991 Act, which deals with drought orders.

6–37

Effect of the Water Resources Act 1991 on easements

An easement already acquired at common law is not lost by reason of an illegal abstraction, although the easement cannot lawfully be exercised until a licence has been obtained,[143] and the illegal abstraction gives rise to a statutory penalty.[144] Furthermore, a person entitled at common law to abstract water does not lose his

6–38

---

[142] Water Resources Act 1991, s.60 is considered in para.6–39, below.
[143] *Cargill v Gotts* [1981] 1 W.L.R. 441; one sentence in the judgment of Templeman L.J. in *Cargill v Gotts* at 446, was held to be too widely expressed in *Bakewell Management Ltd v Brandwood* [2004] 2 A.C. 519 at [38] and [59] but this does not affect the above text.
[144] Water Resources Act 1991, s.24(4), (5).

right to sue for damages for interference with that right notwithstanding that that abstraction is prohibited by section 24 of the Water Resources Act 1991.[145]

Liability of water authority

6–39   The Agency has a duty not to grant a licence authorising the abstraction of water so as to derogate from any rights which, at the time the application is determined, are "protected rights" under the Water Resources Act 1991.[146] If, however, the Agency, in breach of such duty, grants a licence, the grant is not invalid and cannot be restrained by prohibition or injunction, but the person having a "protected right" may sue the Agency in damages for breach of statutory duty.[147] A "protected right" is not necessarily the same as the common law right to restrain an abstraction of water, and is comprehensively defined.[148]

As a result of this statutory duty, the holder of a licence to abstract water has a right of action against the Agency if it grants another licence which prevents him from abstracting water to the extent authorised by his licence.[149] Similarly, a person who is in a position to abstract water without a licence by virtue of subsection (1) of section 27 has a right of action against the Agency if he is prevented from exercising his right to the extent specified in that subsection by the granting of a licence to another person.[150]

4.—PRESCRIPTIVE RIGHTS IN NATURAL WATERCOURSES

Defined channel

6–40   In the case of water flowing through a natural watercourse with a defined channel, rights may be acquired by prescription which interfere with what would otherwise be the natural rights of other proprietors above and below.[151] "Easements to take water, whether express or prescriptive, are rarely if ever defined by reference to quantity as well as or instead of by reference to the purposes for which the water may be abstracted".[152] A riparian owner may by user acquire a right to use the water in a manner not justified by his natural rights; but such acquired right has no operation against the natural rights of a landowner higher up or lower down, unless it affects the use such landowner has of the stream, or his power to

---

[145] *Cargill v Gotts* [1981] 1 W.L.R. 441 (Lawton and Brandon L.JJ., Templeman L.J. dissenting). The Court of Appeal considered the effect of the Water Resources Act 1963, s.135(8).

[146] See Water Resources Act 1991, ss.39(1), 39A and 39B, as amended by Water Act 2003, ss.16–18.

[147] Water Resources Act 1991, s.60(1), (2). For defences available to the Agency, *ibid.*, s.60(5) and Sch.7.

[148] Water Resources Act 1991, s.39A, as inserted by Water Act 2003, s.17.

[149] Water Resources Act 1991, ss.39(1), 39A(1)(a) and 48, as amended by Water Act 2003.

[150] Water Resources Act 1991, ss.27(1), 39(1) and 39A(1)(b), as amended by Water Act 2003.

[151] *White (John) & Sons v White* [1906] A.C. 72. What is said in this section of this chapter must be read in the light of the water legislation as to which see section 3 of this chapter, above.

[152] *Cargill v Gotts* [1981] 1 W.L.R. 441 at 448, per Templeman L.J.

use it, so as to raise the presumption of a grant, and so render the tenement above or below a servient tenement.[153]

Before the Prescription Act 1832, 20 years' exclusive enjoyment of water in any particular manner afforded a strong presumption of right in the party so enjoying it derived from grant or Act of Parliament.[154] In *Prescott v Phillips*[155] it was ruled "that nothing short of twenty years' undisturbed possession of water diverted from the natural channel, or raised by a weir, could give a party an adverse right against those whose lands lay lower down the stream and to whom it was injurious". The right of diverting water, which in its natural course would flow over or along the land of a riparian owner, can be created only by grant, or enjoyment from which a grant may be presumed, or by statute. Such an easement exists for the benefit of the dominant owner alone, and the servient owner acquires no right to insist on its continuance.[156] The right, whether of a riparian or a non-riparian owner, to take water from the land of another is a right for all purposes according to the ordinary and reasonable use to which the dominant land might be applied at the time of the supposed grant.[157] In assessing what is ordinary and reasonable use, there are two questions to be answered. The first is whether any changes in relation to the dominant land represent a "radical change in the character" or a "change in the identity" of the dominant land as opposed to a mere change or intensification in the use of the dominant land. The second question is whether the changed use of the dominant land would result in a substantial increase or alteration in the burden on the servient land. It is only if there is a radical change in the dominant land and a substantial increase in the burden on the servient land that the dominant owner's right to enjoy the easement would be suspended or lost.[158]

A riparian owner may acquire a prescriptive right to pen back a stream,[159] or to divert part of a stream by means of a stone,[160] but he can acquire no such right in any navigable river.[161] Similarly, a lower riparian owner can acquire a right to place a hatch on the land of the upper owner to regulate the flow of water[162] or for the latter purpose to go on the land of the upper owner and open lock gates.[163] Similarly the lower riparian owner can acquire a right to go on the land of an

6–41

---

[153] *Sampson v Hoddinott* (1857) 1 C.B. (n.s.) 590.

[154] *Cox v Matthews* (1673) 1 Vent. 237; *Bealey v Shaw* (1805) 6 East 208; see *Dewhirst v Wrigley* (1834) Coop.Pr.Cas. 329.

[155] (1798) unreported, cited in *Bealey v Shaw* (1805) 6 East 208 at 213; *Mason v Hill* (1833) 5 B. & Ad. 23.

[156] per Cockburn C.J. in *Mason v Shrewsbury and Hereford Ry* (1871) L.R. 6 Q.B. 578 at 587. See, however, the opinion of Blackburn J. in the same case.

[157] *Cargill v Gotts* [1981] 1 W.L.R. 441, applying *Williams v James* (1867) L.R. 2 C.P. 577 and *R.C.P. Holdings Ltd v Rogers* [1953] 1 All E.R. 1029.

[158] *McAdams Homes Ltd v Robinson* [2004] 3 E.G.L.R. 93.

[159] *Cooper v Barber* (1810) 3 Taunt. 110.

[160] *Holker v Porritt* (1875) L.R. 10 Ex. 62.

[161] *Vooght v Winch* (1819) 2 B. & Ald. 662.

[162] *Wood v Hewett* (1846) 8 Q.B. 913; *Moody v Steggles* (1879) 12 Ch. D. 266; see *Greenslade v Halliday* (1830) 6 Bing. 379.

[163] See *Simpson v Godmanchester Corp* [1897] A.C. 696. Compare *Beeston v Weate* (1856) 5 E. & B. 986, para.6–47, below.

upper riparian owner and bank up the stream.[164] Again, the right to a fishing weir may be acquired in non-navigable rivers by grant from other riparian owners, or by enjoyment, or by any means by which such rights may be constituted.[165] Even in a navigable river a riparian owner can acquire an interest in its water power as derived from a reservoir artificially formed by a dam across the channel.[166] It should be noted here that section 2 of the Prescription Act refers to a claim to a watercourse, words which have been held to include a claim to have water, which would otherwise flow down to the plaintiff's land, diverted over other land.[167]

No defined channel

6–42   There can be no express grant or reservation of water which percolates in an unidentified channel, because water is not the subject of property; though a landowner, while unable to reserve percolating water out of land conveyed by him, can reserve the right to obtain water from such land, and the reservation of such a right can be made to run against the land conveyed by a covenant on the part of the grantee for himself and his successors not to do anything on the land or any part or parts of it whereby water obtained therefrom would be diminished.[168] In the absence of such a covenant the owner of land containing underground water which percolates in undefined channels and flows to the land of a neighbour is entitled to divert or appropriate the percolating water within his own land so as to deprive his neighbour of it, and whether or not by exercising such right he intends to injure his neighbour is immaterial.[169]

6–43   Because no grant can be made, and therefore inevitably no grant can be presumed, in the case of water which percolates in an undefined course, no right to the uninterrupted flow of such water can be acquired by prescription.[170] Similarly, no claim by prescription can be established to water percolating through the banks of a stream.[171]

6–44   The owner of the land containing the percolating water cannot control its course and therefore cannot prevent its appropriation, and because he cannot indicate his dissent an adjoining landowner cannot prescribe against him. If, therefore, he extracts the percolating water, no matter how long his neighbour has enjoyed it, his neighbour cannot complain. The principle was settled in

---

[164] *Roberts v Fellowes* (1906) 94 L.T. 279.
[165] *Rolle v Whyte* (1868) L.R. 3 Q.B. 286; *Leconfield v Lonsdale* (1870) L.R. 5 C.P. 657; *Barker v Faulkner* [1898] W.N. 69.
[166] *Hamelin v Bannerman* [1895] A.C. 237.
[167] *Mason v Shrewsbury and Hereford Ry* (1871) L.R. 6 Q.B. 578. See *Staffordshire and Worcestershire Canal Co v Birmingham Canal Co* (1866) L.R. 1 H.L. 254.
[168] *Simeon, Re* [1931] Ch. 525.
[169] *Bradford Corp v Pickles* [1895] A.C. 587.
[170] *Chasemore v Richards* (1859) 7 H.L.C. 349 at 370, 385, 386; *Palmer v Bowman* [2000] 1 W.L.R. 842, explained in *Green v Lord Somerleyton* [2004] 1 P. & C.R. 520 as turning on the fact that it concerned the drainage away of rainwater falling onto land whereas in *Green* the easement of drainage related to water in dykes on the dominant land being drained through dykes on the servient land.
[171] *Roberts v Fellows* (1906) 94 L.T. 281.

Chasemore v Richards,[172] where the House of Lords approved and acted on the unanimous opinion of the judges, delivered by Wightman J. The plaintiff occupied an ancient mill on the River Wandle and he and his predecessors had for more than 60 years used and enjoyed the flow of the river for the purpose of working the mill. The river was in part fed by percolating underground water. The defendant, who represented the Local Board of Health of Croydon, pumped up by means of a well large quantities of percolating water which otherwise would have found its way to the river. The plaintiff unsuccessfully brought an action against the defendant for the diversion, detention and interruption of the underground water.

Having referred to *Embrey v Owen*,[173] *Rawstron v Taylor*,[174] *Broadbent v Ramsbotham*[175] and *Acton v Blundell*,[176] and having explained the apparently inconsistent cases of *Balston v Bensted*[177] and *Dickinson v The Grand Junction Canal Co*,[178] Wightman J. said[179]:   **6–45**

"In such a case as the present, is any right derived from the use of the water of the River Wandle for upwards of twenty years for working the plaintiff's mill? Any such right against another, founded upon length of enjoyment, is supposed to have originated in some grant which is presumed from the owner of what is sometimes called the servient tenement. But what grant can be presumed in the case of percolating waters, depending upon the quantity of rain falling or the natural moisture of the soil, and in the absence of any visible means of knowing to what extent, if at all, the enjoyment of the plaintiff's mill would be affected by any water percolating in and out of the defendant's or any other land? The presumption of a grant only arises where the person against whom it is to be raised might have prevented the exercise of the subject of the presumed grant; but how could he prevent or stop the percolation of water?"

Later he said[180]:

"The question then is, whether the plaintiff has such a right as he claims jure naturae to prevent the defendant sinking a well in his own ground at a distance from the mill, and so absorbing the water percolating in and into his own ground beneath the surface, if such absorption has the effect of diminishing the quantity of water which would otherwise find its way into the

[172] (1859) 7 H.L.C. 349.
[173] (1851) 6 Exch. 353; see para.6–03, above.
[174] (1855) 11 Exch. 369; see para.6–04, above.
[175] (1856) 11 Exch. 602; see para.6–19, above.
[176] (1843) 12 M. & W. 324; see para.6–26, above.
[177] (1808) 1 Camp. 463.
[178] (1852) 7 Exch. 282.
[179] (1859) 7 H.L.C. 349 at 370.
[180] (1859) 7 H.L.C. 349 at 370, 371.

River Wandle, and by such diminution affects the working of the plaintiff's mill. It is impossible to reconcile such a right with the natural and ordinary rights of landowners, or to fix any reasonable limits to the exercise of such a right. Such a right as that contended for by the plaintiff would interfere with, if not prevent, the draining of land by the owner."

6–46   In the same case Lord Wensleydale said[181] with reference to the plaintiff's claim, as based on the possession of his mill for 30 or 60 years:

"I do not think that the principle on which prescription rests can be applied; it has not been with the permission of the proprietor of the land that the streams have flowed into the river for twenty years or upwards: 'qui non prohibet quod prohibere potest, assentire videtur.' But how here could he prevent it? He could not bring an action against the adjoining proprietor; he could not be bound to dig a deep trench in his own land to cut off the supplies of water, in order to indicate his dissent. It is going very far to say, that a man must be at the expense of putting up a screen to window lights, to prevent a title being gained by twenty years' enjoyment of light passing through a window. But this case would go very far beyond that. I think that the enjoyment of the right to these natural streams cannot be supported by any length of user if it does not belong of natural right to the plaintiff."

5.—MISCELLANEOUS PRESCRIPTIVE RIGHTS

To take water

6–47   Independently of the prescriptive rights of user and flow which are mainly called in question between riparian owners, other miscellaneous rights may be mentioned. Thus a landowner can acquire by prescription the right to go on to his neighbour's land and draw water there from a spring[182] or from a pump.[183] Similarly, A, a non-riparian owner, was held to have acquired by prescription the right to go onto the land of B, an adjoining riparian owner, to turn the water from a natural stream into an artificial channel which passed from the stream across B's land to A's land, and to repair such channel.[184]

To discharge water: eavesdrop

6–48   As regards discharging water upon adjoining land, it was said by Bowen L.J. in *Chamber Colliery Co v Hopwood*[185] that the mere discharge of water by A, an

---

[181] (1859) 7 H.L.C. 349 at 385, 386.
[182] *Race v Ward* (1855) 4 E. & B. 702.
[183] *Polden v Bastard* (1865) L.R. 1 Q.B. 156.
[184] *Beeston v Weate* (1856) 5 E. & B. 986.
[185] (1886) 32 Ch. D. 549 at 558.

upper proprietor, on to the land of B, a lower proprietor, may easily establish a right on the part of A to go on discharging, because so long as the discharge continues there is submission on the part of B to proceedings which indicate a claim of right on the part of A. It is, however, difficult for B "to establish a right to have the flow continued, just as it would be very difficult to make out that because for twenty years my pump has dripped on to a neighbour's ground, therefore he has a right at the end of twenty years to say that my pump must go on leaking".

In the case of eaves, it has been laid down that though everyone in building is **6–49** bound so to construct his house as not to overhang his neighbour's property, and construct his roof in such a manner as not to throw the rainwater upon the neighbouring land,[186] yet according to our law a man may acquire a right, by user, to project his wall or eaves over the boundary line of his property, or discharge the rain running from the roof of his house upon the adjoining land. The case of projecting buildings over a boundary will be dealt with in a subsequent chapter.[187] The easement of eavesdrop was recognised by the Court of Exchequer in *Thomas v Thomas*.[188] In *Pyer v Carter*[189] there was an easement for the defendant to have the rainwater flow from his eaves on to the plaintiff's roof, and for the plaintiff to have such water, together with the water originally falling on to his own roof, carried away by a drain on the defendant's land.

There are ancient decisions recognising similar easements in the case of a **6–50** discharge of water on to the neighbouring land by means of a gutter or leaden pipe.[190] "If a man hath a sue, that is to say, a spout, above his house, by which the water used to fall from his house, and another levies a house paramount the spout, so that the water cannot fall as it was wont but falls upon the walls of the house, by which the timber of the house perishes, this is a nuisance."[191] Where a man who had not acquired any easement of eavesdrop built his roof with eaves which discharged rainwater by a spout into adjoining premises, whereby the reversion in such premises was damaged, the reversioner could sue.[192] It was not necessary to prove that rain had actually fallen.[193]

The right of eavesdrop will not be lost by raising the house.[194] The occupier of **6–51** a house who has a right to have the rain fall from the eaves of it upon another man's land cannot by spouts discharge it upon such land in a body.[195] For such an

---

[186] Com.Dig. Action on the Case for a Nuisance, A.
[187] See Ch.11, below.
[188] (1835) 2 C.M. & R. 34.
[189] (1857) 1 H. & N. 916.
[190] *Lady Browne's Case* (1572) 3 Dyer 319b, cited in *Sury v Pigott* (1625) Palmer 446; Com.Dig. Action on the Case for a Nuisance, A; *Baten's Case* (1610) 9 Rep. 53b, recognised in *Fay v Prentice* (1845) 1 C.B. 828.
[191] Rolle, Abr. Nusans, G. 5, citing 18 Edw. 3, 22b; Vin.Abr. Nusance, G. 5.
[192] *Tucker v Newman* (1839) 11 A. & E. 40.
[193] *Fay v Prentice* (1845) 1 C.B. 828.
[194] *Harvey v Walters* (1872) L.R. 8 C.P. 162, considered in *McAdams Homes Limited v Robinson* [2004] 3 E.G.L.R. 93 at [32] and [87]. The *McAdams Homes* case considered the effect of an alteration in the dominant tenement on an easement acquired by implied grant or by prescription and is referred to at para.6–13, above.
[195] *Reynolds v Clarke* (1725) 2 Ld.Raym. 1399.

act trespass would not lie, but case.[196] The flow of water for 20 years from the eaves of a house will not give a right to the neighbour to insist that the house shall not be altered so as to diminish the quantity of water flowing from the roof.[197] It may be noted here that a legal origin was presumed for the right of discharging water from a highway through a pipe on to adjoining land.[198]

6.—ARTIFICIAL WATERCOURSES

Basis of rights

6–52   Artificial watercourses occur frequently, especially in parts of the country where mining is carried on. A common instance of an artificial watercourse is where a system of draining is created for a mine whereby the water is pumped up and flows away from the mining property through the lands of several neighbouring landowners to join some river or lake.[199] Another instance is where an artificial watercourse is constructed for diverting water from a natural stream for use at a mill not itself situate on the natural stream.[200] The rights in the water of artificial watercourses have been the subject of numerous judicial decisions.

Sir Montague Smith, in delivering the advice of the Privy Council in *Rameshur v Koonj*,[201] said:

> "There is no doubt that the right to the water of a river flowing in a natural channel through a man's land and the right to water flowing to it through an artificial watercourse constructed on his neighbour's land, do not rest on the same principle. In the former case each successive riparian proprietor is, prima facie, entitled to the unimpeded flow of the water in its natural course, and to its reasonable enjoyment as it passes through his land, as a natural incident to his ownership of it. In the latter, any right to the flow of the water must rest on some grant or arrangement, either proved or presumed, from or with the owners of the lands from which the water is artificially brought, or on some other legal origin."

Again, it was said by Vaughan Williams L.J. in *Baily & Co v Clark, Son & Morland*[202] that in the case of an artificial watercourse any right to the flow of the water must be based on some grant, whether in the nature of an easement or

---

[196] *Reynolds v Clarke*, above.
[197] *Arkwright v Cell* (1839) 5 M. & W. 233; *Wood v Waud* (1849) 3 Exch. 748; *Greatrex v Hayward* (1853) 8 Exch. 291 at 293, 294.
[198] *Att-Gen v Copeland* [1902] 1 K.B. 690.
[199] *Arkwright v Cell* (1839) 5 M. & W. 233; *Wood v Waud* (1849) 3 Exch. 748.
[200] *Burrows v Lang* [1901] 2 Ch. 502.
[201] (1878) 4 App. Cas. 121 at 126; a case in which disapproval was expressed of Lord Denman's ruling, in *Magor v Chadwick* (1840) 11 A. & E. 586, that the law of natural and artificial watercourses was the same.
[202] [1902] 1 Ch. 649 at 664.

otherwise. The basis of every right to the flow of the water must be an agreement, expressed or presumed from the user, with the owners of the land through which the stream runs.

In ascertaining the rights in respect of an artificial watercourse, there must be taken into account, first, the character of the watercourse, whether it is temporary or permanent, secondly, the circumstances under which it was presumably created, and thirdly, the mode in which it has in fact been used and enjoyed.[203]

Permanent artificial watercourses

The court may conclude that the watercourse is a permanent one,[204] because, for example, it is penned up by embankments,[205] and in this case it is settled that prescriptive rights may be acquired.[206] The enjoyment on which the claim to such a prescriptive right is based must be "as of right", that is, not by leave[207] or under a mistake.[208] There must also be a capable grantor of the easement.[209]   **6–53**

In the case of an artificial watercourse the origin of which is unknown the proper conclusion from the user of the water and other circumstances may be that the watercourse was originally constructed upon the condition that all the riparian owners should have the same rights as they would have had if the watercourse had been a natural one.[210] The result of such a conclusion would, it seems, be that not only could prescriptive rights be acquired, but also that the riparian owners would have in the water the ordinary rights known as natural rights.

Temporary artificial watercourses

On the other hand, the court may conclude that the watercourse is a temporary one, constructed for a temporary purpose,[211] as where a watercourse was constructed and maintained for the purposes of a mill,[212] or for draining a mine.   **6–54**

---

[203] per Stirling L.J., *Baily & Co v Clark, Son & Morland* [1902] 1 Ch. 649 at 668; applied in *Bartlett v Tottenham* [1932] 1 Ch. 114. And see *North-Eastern Ry v Elliot* (1860) 1 J. & H. 145 at 154, per Sir William Page Wood V.-C. (a case of a drowned mine).

[204] *Baily & Co v Clark, Son & Morland*, above; *Lewis v Meredith* [1913] 1 Ch. 571 at 580. In *Gaved v Martyn* (1865) 19 C.B. (n.s.) 732, the court held that the "lower launder" (one of the three streams in question in the action) was a good example of a stream artificially made but in its origin supplied by a natural spring, and subject to prescription, i.e. in effect, that this watercourse was a permanent one.

[205] *Wood v Waud* (1849) 3 Exch. 748 at 777, 778, per Pollock C.B.

[206] *Ivimey v Stocker* (1866) 1 Ch. App. 406, 409; *Powell v Butler* (1871) Ir.R. 5 C.L. 309; *Rameshur v Koonj* (1878) 4 App. Cas. 128; *Blackburne v Somers* (1879) 5 L.R.Ir. 1; *Scott-Whitehead v National Coal Board* (1985) 53 P. & C.R. 263.

[207] *Gaved v Martyn* (1865) C.B. (n.s.) 732.

[208] *Chamber Colliery Co v Hopwood* (1886) Ch. D. 549.

[209] *McEvoy v G.N. Ry* [1900] 2 I.R. 325.

[210] *Sutcliffe v Booth* (1863) 32 L.J.Q.B. 136; *Roberts v Richards* (1881) 50 L.J. Ch. 297; *Baily & Co v Clark, Son & Morland* [1902] 1 Ch. 665; *Whitmores (Edenbridge) Ltd v Stanford* [1909] 1 Ch. 427 at 439. In *McCartney v Londonderry & Lough Swilly Ry*, the stream was in fact artificial, but the case was argued on the hypothesis that it was a natural one: see [1904] A.C. 301 at 303.

[211] *Hanna v Pollock* [1900] 2 I.R. 664.

[212] *Burrows v Lang* [1901] 2 Ch. 502.

6–55   The rules applicable to cases of this nature were discussed by Lord Abinger in delivering the judgment of the Court of Exchequer in *Arkwright v Cell*.[213] That case turned upon the right of lower riparian owners, the occupiers of mills situate on a stream which drained a mine, to compel the mine-owners to continue such discharge. The court held that no such right existed. Lord Abinger, delivering the judgment of the court, said[214]:

> "The stream . . . was an artificial watercourse, and the sole object for which it was made, was to get rid of a nuisance to the mines, and to enable their proprietors to get the ores which lay within the mineral field drained by it: and the flow of water through that channel was, from the very nature of the case, of a temporary character, having its continuance only whilst the convenience of the mine-owners required it, and, in the ordinary course it would, most probably, cease when the mineral ore above its level should have been exhausted. . . .
>
> What, then, is the species of right or interest, which the proprietor of the surface, where the stream issued forth, or his grantees, would have in such a watercourse, at common law, and independently of the effect of user under the recent statute, 2 & 3 Will. 4, c. 71? He would only have a right to use it for any purpose to which it was applicable, so long as it continued there. An user for twenty years, or a longer time, would afford no presumption of a grant of the right to the water in perpetuity; for such a grant would, in truth, be neither more nor less than an obligation on the mine-owner not to work his mines by the ordinary mode of getting minerals, below the level drained by that sough, and to keep the mines flooded up to that level, in order to make the flow of water constant, for the benefit of those who had used it for some profitable purpose. How can it be supposed that the mine-owners could have meant to burthen themselves with such a servitude, so destructive to their interests:-and what is there to raise an inference of such an intention? The mine-owner could not bring any action against the person using the stream of water, so that the omission to bring an action could afford no argument in favour of the presumption of a grant; nor could he prevent the enjoyment of that stream of water by any act of his, except by at once making a sough at a lower level, and thus taking away the water entirely;-a course so expensive and inconvenient, that it would be very unreasonable, and a very improper extension of the principle applied to the case of lights, to infer from the abstinence from such an act, an intention to grant the use of the water in perpetuity, as a matter of right . . .
>
> It remains to be considered, whether the statute 2 & 3 Will. 4, c. 71, gives to Mr Arkwright and those who claim under him, any such right; and we are clearly of opinion that it does not. The whole purview of the Act shews that it applies only to such rights as would before the Act have been acquired

---

[213] (1839) 5 M. & W. 203.
[214] (1839) 5 M. & W. 203 at 231–234. See also para.1–116, above.

by the presumption of a grant, from long user. The Act expressly requires enjoyment for different periods, 'without interruption', and therefore necessarily imports such a user as could be interrupted by someone 'capable of resisting the claim'; and it also requires it to be 'of right'. But the use of the water in this case could not be the subject of an action at the suit of the proprietors of the mineral field lying below the level of the Cromford Sough, and was incapable of interruption by them at any time during the whole period, by any reasonable mode; and as against them it was not 'of right'; they had no interest to prevent it; and until it became necessary to drain the lower part of the field, indeed at all times, it was wholly immaterial to them what became of the water, so long as their mines were freed from it."

After *Arkwright v Cell*,[215] where the rights of lower riparian owners when asserted as against the creator of an artificial stream were discussed, there came before the same court *Wood v Waud*,[216] where the question arose as to the same rights when asserted, not as against the creator of a stream, but as against upper riparian owners who diverted it. In the last-mentioned case water from the working of a colliery had for more than 20 years flowed through two artificial channels called the Bowling Sough and Low Moor Sough. The first passed directly through the plaintiffs' land. The second passed into a natural stream, the Bowling Beck, which, so augmented, passed through the plaintiffs' land. The defendants, having works on each channel above the points where they respectively arrived at the plaintiffs' land and at the Bowling Sough, diverted the water of each. The channels were subterranean, but the court determined the question as it would have stood if they had been surface streams. Pollock C.B., delivering the judgment of the court, said[217]:

6–56

"It appears to us to be clear, that, as they have a right to the use of the Bowling Beck, as incident to their property on the banks and bed of it, they would have the right to all the water which actually formed part of that stream, as soon as it had become part,[218] whether such water came by natural means, as from springs, or from the surface of the hills above, or from rains or melted snow, or was added by artificial means, as from the drainage of lands or of colliery works; and if the proprietors of the drained lands or of the colliery augmented the stream by pouring water into it, and so gave it to the stream, it would become part of the current; no distinction could then be made between the original natural stream and such accessions to it.

But the question arises with respect to an artificial stream not yet united to the natural one.

---

[215] (1839) 5 M. & W. 203.
[216] (1849) 3 Exch. 748.
[217] (1849) 3 Exch. 748 at 779, 780.
[218] See *Dudden v Clutton Union* (1857) 1 H. & N. 627.

The proprietor of the land through which the Bowling Sough flows has no right to insist on the colliery owners causing all the waters from their works to flow through their land. These owners merely get rid of a nuisance to their works by discharging the water into the sough, and cannot be considered as giving it to one more than another of the proprietors of the land through which that sough is constructed; each may take and use what passes through his land, and the proprietor of land below has no right to any part of that water until it has reached his own land—he has no right to compel the owners above to permit the water to flow through their lands for his benefit; and, consequently, he has no right of action if they refuse to do so.

If they pollute the water, so as to be injurious to the tenant below, the case would be different.

We think, therefore, that the plaintiffs have no right of action for the diversion of that water. The question as to the Low Moor Sough is less favourable to the plaintiffs, for this sough does not pass through their land at all.

We are of opinion, that, if the plaintiffs would not be entitled to the water of the soughs if above ground, their being below ground in this case would probably make no difference. It does not certainly make a difference in favour of the plaintiffs."[219]

6–57   Of *Wood v Waud*[220] it was said by Blackburn J. in *Mason v Shrewsbury and Hereford Railway*[221] that this was in effect a decision that an active enjoyment in fact for more than the statutory period was not an enjoyment as of right, if during the period it was known that it was only permitted so long as some particular purpose was served. The nature of the sough showed that though the water had in fact flowed for 60 years, yet from the beginning it was only intended to flow so long as the coal owners did not think fit otherwise to drain their mine, and so was precarious.

6–58   In accordance with *Wood v Waud*, it was held in *Greatrex v Hayward*[222] that the flow of water for 20 years from a drain made for agricultural improvements did not give to the person through whose land it flowed a right to the continuance of the flow, so as to preclude the proprietor of the land drained from altering his drains for improvement and so cutting off the supply.

6–59   Again, in *Bartlett v Tottenham*,[223] it was held, in accordance with the two cases last cited, that no right could be acquired by prescription to receive water overflowing from a tank along an artificial watercourse constructed for a temporary purpose.

6–60   It follows from the above authorities that where the enjoyment of an artificial watercourse depends on temporary circumstances, no right to the uninterrupted

---

[219] cf. *Wardle v Brocklehurst* (1859) 1 E. & E. 1058 at 1060; *Staffordshire and Worcestershire Canal Co v Birmingham Canal Co* (1866) L.R. 1 H.L. 254; *Brymbo Water Co v Lester's Lime Co* (1894) 8 R. 329.
[220] (1849) 3 Exch. 748.
[221] (1871) L.R. 6 Q.B. 578 at 584.
[222] (1853) 8 Exch. 291.
[223] [1932] 1 Ch. 114.

flow of water can by prescription be acquired either against the creator of the stream[224] or against upper riparian owners through whose land the stream passes.[225]

Meaning of "temporary purpose"

As regards the question whether a watercourse should be held to have been con- **6–61** structed for a temporary purpose within the principle of the decision of *Arkwright v Cell*,[226] it was said by Farwell J. in *Burrows v Lang*[227] that the meaning of "temporary purpose" is not confined to a purpose that happens to last in fact for a few years only, but includes a purpose which is temporary in the sense that it may in the reasonable contemplation of the parties come to an end.

Watercourse not on neighbour's land

Again, it seems that it is more difficult to presume an agreement as to enjoyment **6–62** when a watercourse is constructed entirely over the land of the creator than in the case of water pumped over the land of a neighbour.[228]

7.—IMPURITY AND POLLUTION

Purity

Every riparian owner on the banks of a natural stream is entitled as a natural right **6–63** to have the stream flow past his land without sensible alteration in its character or quality.[229] He is accordingly entitled to insist that the water shall not be polluted by the refuse of a factory or the sewage of a town[230]; that very soft water shall not be made very hard water[231]; and that the water shall not be raised in temperature.[232] The right arises in respect of the ownership of the bank, independently of the ownership of the bed of the stream.[233] Anyone who fouls the water infringes the riparian owner's right of property, and he can therefore maintain an action to restrain pollution without proving that there has been actual damage.[234] The right is not affected by the use made of the water by the riparian owner or

---

[224] *Arkwright v Cell* (1839) 5 M. & W. 203; *Burrows v Lang* [1901] 2 Ch. 502.
[225] *Wood v Waud* (1849) 3 Exch. 748; *Mason v Shrewsbury and Hereford Ry* (1871) L.R. 6 Q.B. 578.
[226] (1839) 5 M. & W. 203.
[227] [1901] 2 Ch. 508; see *Wright v Macadam* [1949] 2 K.B. 744.
[228] *Burrows v Lang*, above; see *McEvoy v G.N. Ry* [1900] 2 I.R. 333.
[229] *Young (John) & Co v Bankier Distillery Co* [1893] A.C. 698; *Scott-Whitehead v National Coal Board* (1985) 53 P. & C.R. 263.
[230] *Magor v Chadwick* (1840) 11 A. & E. 571; *Crossley & Sons Ltd v Lightowler* (1867) 2 Ch. App. 478; *Jones v Llanrwst U.D.C.* [1911] 1 Ch. 393.
[231] *Young (John) & Co v Bankier Distillery Co* [1893] A.C. 698; see also *Scott-Whitehead v National Coal Board* (above) (high chloride content caused by water discharged from mine workings).
[232] See *Tipping v Eckersley* (1855) 2 K. & J. 264; *Pride of Derby and Derbyshire Angling Association v British Celanese Ltd* [1953] Ch. 149.
[233] *Jones v Llanrwst U.D.C.* [1911] 1 Ch. 393 at 402.
[234] [1911] 1 Ch. 393.

whether, as against lower riparian owners, he is entitled to extract water for that purpose.[235] The natural right to purity extends to underground water.[236] Again, it is settled that prima facie no man has a right to use his land in such a way as to be a nuisance to his neighbour.[237] Accordingly, if a man puts poison or filth on his land, with the result that water percolating underground from his own to his[238] neighbour's land is polluted, the neighbour has a right of action. The right of action is in the tort of nuisance or under the rule in *Rylands v Fletcher* and is governed by the general rule as to remoteness of damage in tort, so that the foreseeability of harm of the relevant type is a prerequisite of liability.[239]

6–64   The fact that the stream has already been polluted by A is not a defence to an action to restrain pollution by B.[240] Again, if the acts of several persons which independently would not produce pollution result in producing pollution when combined, each of them may be restrained.[241] The grantee of a right of fishing can obtain an injunction to restrain pollution without proving actual pecuniary loss, because the pollution is the disturbance of a legal right,[242] and the defendant in such an action is not in a position to set up *jus tertii* against a possessory title.[243] On the other hand, an inhabitant of a town who, in common with other inhabitants, has been accustomed to take water from a river passing the town, cannot maintain an action for pollution; his only remedy is by indictment.[244]

Rights acquired by prescription

6–65   As in the case of the natural rights of user and flow, so in the case of the natural right of purity rights may be acquired by prescription which interfere with the natural right. Section 2 of the Prescription Act refers to claims which may be lawfully made by custom, prescription, or grant to any watercourse or the use of any water. A claim to a watercourse within the section includes a claim to send through another's watercourse either polluted water[245] or sand and rubble,[246] and generally it is clear that a right may be acquired by prescription to pollute a stream,[247] but such a right can only be acquired by the continuance of perceptible

---

[235] *Scott-Whitehead v National Coal Board* (above) at pp. 271–212.

[236] *Hodgkinson v Ennor* (1863) 4 B. & S. 229. As has been seen, para.6–25, above, every man has the right to appropriate all underground water percolating through an undefined channel on his land.

[237] *Ballard v Tomlinson* (1885) 29 Ch. D. 126.

[238] *Turner v Mirfield* (1865) 34 Beav. 390; *Ballard v Tomlinson* (1885) 29 Ch. D. 126.

[239] *Cambridge Water Co v Eastern Leather Plc* [1994] 2 A.C. 264, HL, reversing the Court of Appeal who held that liability under *Ballard v Tomlinson* was strict.

[240] *Crossley & Sons Ltd v Lightowler* (1867) 2 Ch. App. 478.

[241] *Blair v Deakin* (1887) 57 L.T. 522; *Pride of Derby and Derbyshire Angling Association Ltd v British Celanese Ltd* [1953] Ch. 149.

[242] *Fitzgerald v Firbank* [1897] 2 Ch. 96; *Nicholls v Ely Beet Sugar Factory Ltd (No. 2)* [1936] Ch. 343.

[243] *Fitzgerald v Firbank* [1897] 2 Ch. 96; *Nicholls v Ely Beet Sugar Factory Ltd* [1931] 2 Ch. 84.

[244] *R. v Bristol Dock Co* (1810) 12 East 429.

[245] *Wright v Williams* (1836) 1 M. & W. 77.

[246] *Carlyon v Lovering* (1857) 1 H. & N. 784. Compare *Murgatroyd v Robinson* (1857) 7 E. & B. 391.

[247] *Baxendale v McMurray* (1867) 2 Ch. App. 790; *Att-Gen v Dorking Guardians* (1882) 20 Ch. D. 595; *McIntyre v McGavin* [1893] A.C. 268, 274 (refuse from factory); *Brown v Dunstable Corp* [1899] 2 Ch. 378 (sewage).

injury for 20 years.[248] There can be no prescription where the pollution is unknown to and unexpected by the plaintiff. The prescription period does not start to run until actual damage is caused.[249] Householders may obtain a prescriptive right to discharge sewage into a local authority's sewers.[250]

There can, however, be no prescriptive right to justify a public nuisance[251]; and, as title by prescription is founded upon the presumption of a grant, if no grant could lawfully have been made, by reason of statutes passed to prevent pollution, no presumption can arise and a claim to a prescriptive right must fail.[252] The control of pollution of water is now principally regulated by Part III of the Water Resources Act 1991. A person commits an offence if he causes or knowingly permits any poisonous, noxious or polluting matter or any solid waste matter to enter any controlled waters, unless the entry occurs or the discharge is made under and in accordance with a consent under Chapter II of Part III of the Water Resources Act 1991 or certain other authorisations or licences.[253]

6–66

The circumstances in which an offence is committed under section 85 of the Water Resources Act 1991 and, in particular, the meaning of "causes" in that section have been considered by the House of Lords in *Environment Agency v Empress Car Co (Abertillery) Ltd*.[254] A person causes a pollutant to enter controlled waters if he actively did something, with or without the occurrence of other factors, which produced a situation in which the polluting matter could escape, even though what he did was not the immediate cause of the pollution. Where a necessary condition of the actual escape which happened was also the act of a third party or a natural event, the justices should consider whether that act or event should be regarded as a normal fact of life or something extraordinary. If it was an ordinary occurrence, it would not negative the causal effect of the defendant's acts, even if it was not foreseeable that it would happen to that particular defendant, or take that particular form; however, if it could be regarded as something extraordinary, it would be open to the justices to hold that the defendant did not cause the pollution. Whether an act or event was ordinary or extraordinary was one of fact and degree to which the justices should apply their common sense and knowledge of what happened in the area.

---

[248] *Goldsmid v Tunbridge Wells Improvement Commissioners* (1866) 1 Ch. App. 349; *Liverpool Corp v Coghill* [1918] 1 Ch. 307.

[249] *Scott-Whitehead v National Coal Board* (1983) 53 P. & C.R. 263.

[250] *Harrington v Derby Corp* [1905] 1 Ch. 205 at 219, per Buckley J.

[251] *Att-Gen v Barnsley* [1874] W.N. 37; *Butterworth v West Riding Rivers Board* [1909] A.C. 45, 57; and see *George Legge and Son Ltd v Wenlock Corp* [1938] A.C. 204. The *George Legge* case (and *Hulley v Silversprings Bleaching and Dyeing Co* [1922] 2 Ch. 268) were considered in *Bakewell Management Ltd v Brandwood* [2004] 2 A.C. 519, and see the discussion of that decision at para.4–125, above.

[252] *Hulley v Silversprings Bleaching and Dyeing Co* [1922] 2 Ch. 268 at 282, per Eve J.

[253] An injunction may be granted to restrain an anticipated breach of the statute: *Att-Gen v Wellingborough U.D.C.* (1974) 72 L.G.R. 507 (a decision under the Rivers (Prevention of Pollution) Act 1951, s.7 (repealed by the Control of Pollution Act 1974, s.108 and Sch.4).

[254] [1999] 2 A.C. 22. In *Environment Agency v Brock* [1998] J.P.L. 968, the existence of a latent defect in the equipment did not mean that the defendant had not caused the resulting pollution.

In the *Empress Car* case, the defendant had a diesel tank on its premises. An unknown third party opened a tap on the tank. The tap had no lock. The diesel escaped from the tank via the tap and thence into a storm drain and thence to a river. The defendant was held to be responsible as it had maintained the diesel tank on its land and it was open to the justices to hold that it had caused the pollution.

Consent for the discharge of effluent or other matter may be given by the Environment Agency,[255] subject in certain cases to reference to the Secretary of State,[256] and an appeal against refusal of consent lies to him.[257] In so far as effluent may now, by virtue of a consent having been given, be discharged into a stream without contravening any statute, a prescriptive right to discharge may be acquired to the detriment of lower riparian owners who fail to take the necessary steps to protect their interests.

Rights acquired by agreement: rights of licensees

6–67   As regards artificial watercourses, we have seen that in some cases the proper conclusion may be that the watercourse was originally constructed upon the condition that all the riparian owners should have the same rights as they would have had if the watercourse had been a natural one.[258] In these cases it seems that the riparian owners would have the natural right of purity. In other cases the proper conclusion may be that the watercourse was a temporary one constructed for a temporary purpose. It would appear that, apart from prescription, appropriation of the water by a person entitled to appropriate it gives such a person the right to insist that the water shall not be polluted to his injury.[259]

6–68   In *Whaley v Laing*[260] the plaintiff, by permission of a canal company, made a communication from the canal to his own premises, by which water was brought on to them, with which water he fed his boilers. The defendant fouled the water in the canal, whereby the water as it came into the plaintiff's premises was fouled, and by the use of it his boilers were injured. The defendant had no permission from the canal owners to do what he did. The Court of Exchequer gave judgment for the plaintiff, on the ground that, as the defendant was the cause of dirty water flowing on to the plaintiff's premises without any right to do so, the plaintiff was entitled to maintain an action against him. The court expressly abstained from

---

[255] For the various offences of polluting controlled waters, see Water Resources Act 1991, s.85; for defences in respect of authorised discharges, see *ibid.*, s.88. For definition of "controlled water", see *ibid.*, s.104: in brief the expression covers: (i) territorial waters up to three miles from the territorial sea baselines; (ii) coastal waters, i.e. waters to the landward of those baselines up to the limit of the highest tide/freshwater limit; (iii) lakes or ponds which discharge directly or indirectly into a river or watercourse and rivers and watercourses which are neither public sewers or drains for drain into a public sewer; and (iv) groundwaters.

[256] Water Resources Act 1991, s.88(2) and Sch.10. The functions of the National Rivers Authority under those provisions have now been transferred to the Environment Agency by the Environment Act 1995, s.2.

[257] Water Resources Act 1991, Sch.10, para.4.

[258] See para.6–53, above.

[259] See para.6–54, above.

[260] (1857) 2 H. & N. 476; (1858) 3 H. & N. 675.

giving any opinion upon the question whether an action would have been maintainable against the defendant if the defendant had diverted the water, or if the plaintiff had been obliged to go to the canal and fetch the water instead of its flowing into his premises. In the Exchequer Chamber the judgment was reversed, but for reasons involving no dissent from the ground on which judgment in the court below was based. The judgments in the Exchequer Chamber show, however, that it was considered very doubtful whether a person, having a mere permission from a riparian owner to take water out of a stream, can maintain an action against a wrongdoer for diverting or fouling the stream higher up.

The question as to the right of a licensee from a riparian owner to receive pure **6–69**
water arose in the case of a natural stream in *Stockport Waterworks Co v Potter*.[261] The plaintiff sued the defendant for fouling the water of the Mersey, coming to its waterworks through a tunnel which it had made under a grant from a riparian proprietor. The Court of Exchequer held that it was not entitled to sue. The reason of the decision is given in the judgment of Pollock C.B. and Channell B. (in which Wilde B. concurred) as follows[262]:

"It is difficult to perceive any possible legal foundation for a right to have the river kept pure, in a person situate as this company is.

There seems to be no authority for contending that a riparian proprietor can keep the land abutting on the river the possession of which gives him his water rights, and at the same time transfer those rights or any of them, and thus create a right in gross by assigning a portion of his rights appurtenant.

It seems to us clear that the rights which a riparian proprietor has with respect to the water are entirely derived from his possession of land abutting on the river. If he grants away any portion of his land so abutting, then the grantee becomes a riparian proprietor and has similar rights. But if he grants away a portion of his estate not abutting on the river, then clearly the grantee of the land would have no water rights by virtue merely of his occupation. Can he have them by express grant? It seems to us that the true answer to this is that he can have them against the grantor[263] but not so as to sue other persons in his own name for the infringement of them. The case of Hill v. Tupper,[264] recently decided in this Court, is an authority for the proposition that a person cannot create by grant new rights of property so as to give the grantee a right of suing in his own name for an interruption of the right by a third party."

This case was approved in the Court of Appeal in *Ormerod v Todmorden Joint* **6–70**
Stock Mill Co Ltd[265] and treated as expressly deciding that a riparian owner cannot, except as against himself, confer on one who is not a riparian owner any right

---

[261] (1864) 3 H. & C. 300.
[262] (1864) 3 H. & C. 300 at 326, 327.
[263] *Hamelin v Bannerman* [1895] A.C. 237.
[264] (1863) 2 H. & C. 121; para.1–26, above.
[265] (1883) 11 Q.B.D. 155.

to use the water of the stream, and that any user of the stream by a non-riparian proprietor, even under a grant from a riparian proprietor, is wrongful if it sensibly affects the flow of the water by the lands of other riparian proprietors. Bowen L.J. said[266]:

> "The only legitimate user by him [a riparian proprietor] of the water, other than such rights as he may have acquired by prescription, is for purposes connected with his ordinary occupation of the land upon the bank."

6–71   In *McCartney v Londonderry and Lough Swilly Railway Co*[267] the House of Lords held that A, an upper riparian owner on a natural stream, had no right, as between himself and B, a lower riparian owner, to divert the water to a place outside A's tenement and there consume it for purposes unconnected with the tenement, although the damage suffered or likely to be suffered by B was small.

From *McCartney v Londonderry and Lough Swilly Railway Co*[268] it would appear that a lower riparian owner, even though his flow of water was not diminished or injured in quality (provided that the facts were not such as to bring the case within the maxim *de minimis non curat lex*), could prevent an upper riparian owner from permitting a third person to use the stream. Such user would be foreign to or unconnected with the tenement of the upper riparian owner, and the permission given would therefore be in excess of the rights of such owner.

6–72   In *Kensit v G.E. Railway*[269] a person who held a licence from an upper riparian owner on a natural stream took water from the stream, and after using it for purposes unconnected with the riparian owner's tenement returned it to the stream unaltered in quality or quantity. A lower riparian owner having brought an action to restrain this user, the Court of Appeal refused an injunction. The grounds of their decision were thus stated by Cotton L.J.[270]:

> "The plaintiffs say, and they are right, that a riparian owner is in this position, that he can maintain an action for interference with his right, even although he does not shew that at the time he has suffered any actual damage and loss. But then we must consider what the right of a riparian owner is as regards the lower riparian owners. It is this, that he has a right to take and use the water as it runs past him for all reasonable purposes. . . . Then, as against the upper proprietors, he has this right, he is entitled to have the flow of the water in the natural bed of the river coming down to him unaltered in quality and quantity, subject only to the right of the upper proprietors, such as he has against the proprietors below him, to take the water for reasonable purposes. Then he has this right, that where the stream comes

---

[266] (1883) 11 Q.B.D. 155, at 172.
[267] [1904] A.C. 301 at 310, 313; and see para.6–07, above.
[268] [1904] A.C. 301.
[269] (1884) 27 Ch. D. 122.
[270] (1884) 27 Ch. D. 122, at 130.

opposite to or through his land it shall come in its ordinary and accustomed channel.

Now has that been interfered with? I am of opinion it has not. The quantity and quality of the stream when it comes into the plaintiffs' land is the same as it always was."

Lindley L.J. pointed out[271] that, so long as the defendant did only what he was then doing, there was no possibility of injury.

The principles applied by the House of Lords in *McCartney v Londonderry and Lough Swilly Railway Co*[272] and by the Court of Appeal in *Kensit v G.E. Railway*[273] seem at first sight inconsistent. Lord Lindley was a party to both decisions, and they are to be reconciled (if at all) in the manner pointed out by him in his judgment in the House of Lords in *McCartney v Londonderry and Lough Swilly Railway Co*,[274] where he stated that the ratio decidendi in *Kensit v G.E. Railway*[275] was that what was there complained of never could grow into a prescriptive title, inasmuch as all the water taken was returned unaltered in quantity or quality. **6–73**

8.—ACQUISITION OF WATER RIGHTS

Acquisition by express grant

Water rights may be acquired by express grant.[276] As to the construction of an express grant, it has been laid down that the grant of a "watercourse" may mean: (1) the right to the running water; or (2) the drain which contains the water; or (3) the land over which the water flows.[277] In the absence of words showing a contrary intention, a grant of a watercourse will be held to mean the grant of the right to the running water,[278] but the natural meaning of "watercourse" seems to be the channel, whether natural or artificial, through which a stream flows.[279] The reservation of a right to make a watercourse included the right to divert water and to use the water diverted.[280] A "spring of water" means a natural source of water of a definite and well-marked extent.[281] A "stream" is water which runs in a defined course, so as to be capable of diversion.[282] The same word was held not to include **6–74**

---

[271] (1884) 27 Ch. D. 122, at 135.

[272] [1904] A.C. 301.

[273] (1884) 27 Ch. D. 122.

[274] [1904] A.C. 301, at 313.

[275] (1884) 27 Ch. D. 122.

[276] *Mitchell v Potter* [2005] EWCA Civ 88, *The Times*, January 24, 2005 concerned the construction of an express grant: see para.6–89, below.

[277] *Taylor v St Helens Corp* (1877) 6 Ch. D. 264, at 271, where the effect of the grant of an artificial watercourse was considered.

[278] *Taylor v St Helens Corp* (1877) 6 Ch. D. 264.

[279] *Remfry v Natal (Surveyor-General)* [1896] A.C. 558, at 560; *Anderson v Cleland* [1910] 2 I.R. 377; but see *Doe d. Earl of Egremont v Williams* (1848) 11 Q.B.D. 700.

[280] *Remfry v Natal (Surveyor-General)* [1896] A.C. 558.

[281] *Taylor v St Helens Corp* (1877) 6 Ch. D. 264.

[282] *Taylor v St Helens Corp* (1877) 6 Ch. D. 264.

either the spring or water soaking through marshy ground.[283] In *Northam v Hurley*[284] it was held, on the construction of the grant of a watercourse from the land of the grantor to the land of the grantee, that the grantor had acted wrongfully in altering the channel on his own land, although no damage had occurred to the grantee from such alteration. The effect of special words in an express grant or reservation of water was also considered in *Rawstron v Taylor*,[285] *Lee v Stevenson*[286] and *Finlinson v Porter*.[287] A grant (in pursuance of a statute) of the exclusive right of drainage through a watercourse gave the grantee, not merely an easement, but (for the purpose of rating) possession of the watercourse.[288]

6–75   A grant of all streams of water that might be found in land, when at the time of the grant there was one stream and several wells, was held to include the underground water in the land; the grantor could not, nor could anyone claiming under him, do anything the effect of which could be to drain such underground water from the land.[289] On the other hand, a grant of an artificial watercourse as shown in a plan, with the stream and springs flowing into or feeding the same, was held to be a grant of the artificial channel and of the definite springs and streams feeding it, and of such other water as should run into and down the channel as it stood, and not to justify the grantees in enlarging the channel so as to carry off more water.[290]

Acquisition by custom

6–76   Water rights may also be acquired by custom.[291]

9.—MISCELLANEOUS RIGHTS OF RIPARIAN OWNERS

To place erections on bed

6–77   The owner of both banks of a non-tidal river may build on the bed, provided that he does not alter the natural flow of the water above or below his property.[292] Again, the owner of one bank only cannot as against the opposite owner build on his own moiety of the bed in such a manner as to interfere with the natural flow of the stream;

---

[283] *McNab v Robertson* [1897] A.C. 129.
[284] (1853) 1 E. & B. 665.
[285] (1855) 11 Exch. 369.
[286] (1858) 27 L.J.Q.B. 263.
[287] (1875) L.R. 10 Q.B. 188.
[288] *Holywell Union v Halkyn Drainage Co* [1895] A.C. 117.
[289] *Whitehead v Parks* (1858) 2 H. & N. 870.
[290] *Taylor v St Helens Corp* (1877) 6 Ch. D. 264; *McNab v Robertson* [1897] A.C. 129.
[291] *Bastard v Smith* (1837) 2 Mood. & R. 129; *Gaved v Martyn* (1865) 19 C.B. (n.s.) 732 (customary right to divert); *Carlyon v Lovering* (1857) 1 H. & N. 784 (customary right to pollute); *Harrop v Hirst* (1868) L.R. 4 Exch. 43 (customary right to use of water).
[292] *Orr-Ewing v Colquhoun* (1877) 2 App. Cas. 839; see *Greyvensteyn v Hattingh* [1911] A.C. 355; *Radstock Co-operative & Industrial Society Ltd v Norton-Radstock U.D.C.* [1968] Ch. 605, distinguished by O'Connor J. in *Leakey v The National Trust* [1978] Q.B. 849 (whose judgment was approved by the Court of Appeal [1980] 1 Q.B. 485 at 413) and not followed by the Court of Appeal in *Bybrook Barn Centre Ltd v Kent County C.C.* [2001] B.L.R. 55.

and was restrained, although there was no proof that damage had been sustained or was likely to be sustained.[293] This principle has been extended to tidal navigable rivers.[294] As regards the rights of erection possessed by a riparian owner generally, it seems that he may erect a post for a ferry or for mooring a boat, or plant stakes to prevent poaching,[295] or place an erection on his own bank to protect it.[296] A riparian owner cannot, however, complain of a decrease in the depth of water when the only effect of that decrease is to obstruct the public right of navigation.[297]

To divert flood water

A riparian owner has a right to raise the banks upon his own land so as to prevent   **6–78** the water from overflowing his land, with this restriction, that he does not occasion injury to the property of others.[298] If an extraordinary flood is seen to be coming on land, the owner may, at least in the case of an artificial watercourse, protect his land from it without being responsible for the consequences, although his neighbour may be injured.[299] If, on the other hand, the flood has already come, the owner must not, for the purpose of getting rid of the mischief, injure his neighbour.[300]

Navigable rivers

The public have a right to use a navigable river for navigation similar to the right   **6–79** which they have to pass along a public highway through private land,[301] and an artificial navigable river may be dedicated as a public highway,[302] but the analogy between a navigable river and a public highway is not complete.[303] The right of navigation in tidal waters rests on the Crown's ownership of the land beneath those waters.[304] The position is more obscure in the case of non-tidal waters, where the bed of the river belongs to the riparian owners. It seems that a public right of navigation in a non-tidal river depends upon (a) the navigability of the river, and (b) proof of actual use since time immemorial.[305] Reliance cannot be placed on the presumption of dedication which, in the case of rights of way, arises

---

[293] *Bickett v Morris* (1866) L.R. 1 H.L.Sc. & Div 47.

[294] *Att-Gen v Earl of Lonsdale* (1868) L.R. 7 Eq. 377; *Att-Gen v Terry* (1874) 9 Ch. App. 423; see *Exeter Corp v Earl of Devon* (1870) L.R. 10 Eq. 232.

[295] *Withers v Purchase* (1889) 60 L.T. 821; compare *Att-Gen v Wright* [1897] 2 Q.B. 318.

[296] *Ridge v Midland Ry* (1888) 53 J.P. 55; see *Bickett v Morris* (1866) L.R. 1 H.L.Sc. & Div 47.

[297] *Tate & Lyle Food and Distribution Ltd v Greater London Council* [1983] 2 A.C. 509 (distinguishing *Bickett v Morris* (1866) L.R. 1 H.L.Sc. & Div 47).

[298] *Menzies v Breadalbane* (1828) 3 Bligh (n.s.) 414, at 418; *R. v Trafford* (1831) 1 B. & Ald. 874; *Att-Gen v Earl of Lonsdale* (1868) L.R. 7 Eq. 377.

[299] *Nield v L. & N.W. Ry* (1874) L.R. 10 Ex. 4; see *Whalley v Lancashire and Yorkshire Ry* (1884) 13 Q.B.D. 131 at 136, 140; *Maxey v G.N. Ry* (1912) 106 L.T. 429. Compare the similar right on the seashore; *R. v Pagham* (1828) 8 B. & C. 355.

[300] *Whalley v Lancashire and Yorkshire Ry* (1884) 13 Q.B.D. 131.

[301] *Orr-Ewing v Colquhoun* (1877) 2 App. Cas. 839; see *Original Hartlepool Co v Gibb* (1877) 5 Ch. D. 713.

[302] *Att-Gen v Simpson* [1901] 2 Ch. 671 at 716; see *Simpson v Att-Gen* [1904] A.C. 476 at 494.

[303] *Att-Gen v Simpson* [1901] 2 Ch. 671 at 687; [1904] A.C. 476 at 509.

[304] *Gann v Free Fisheries of Whitstable* (1865) 11 H.L. Cas. 192.

[305] *Wills Trustees v Cairngorm Canoeing and Sailing School* 1976 S.L.T. 162.

from 20 years' user by the public under section 31 of the Highways Act 1980, because those provisions do not apply to rivers.[306] In the case of the soil of navigable rivers, there may be also public rights incidental to the right of navigation, such as fixing moorings and anchoring.[307] Otherwise mooring to the bank would amount to a trespass against the land of the riparian owner; a public right of way on foot along a towpath does not confer a right to maintain moorings and gangplanks on the bank.[308]

As regards the right of access, it is settled that in general a riparian owner on a navigable river has, subject to the public right of navigation, the same right of access to the river as such an owner has on a non-navigable river.[309] The public have no right of access without the permission of, as a grant from, the landowner and have no right to land, moor or use the banks as a towpath.

10.—PIPES AND DRAINS

Acquisition of rights

6–80   Pipes and drains are artificial watercourses to which the usual rules as to acquisition of easements apply. Easements in respect of them may be acquired by express grant or reservation, implied grant or reservation, by virtue of the operation of section 62 of the Law of Property Act 1925, or by prescription in the usual way. By reason of the fact that pipes are usually buried in the ground, however, difficulty may arise in connection with the requirement for an implied grant under the rule in *Wheeldon v Burrows* that the right should be "continuous and apparent" and the requirement for the acquisition of an easement by prescription that user must have been as of right and not "*clam*".

6–81   As to implied grant, it has long been held that where the owner of adjoining houses conveys one to a purchaser, such house is entitled to the benefit of the drains from his house and subject to all drains necessarily used for the benefit of the adjoining house without express reservation or grant.[310] A drain is regarded as "apparent" for these purposes not only if there are visible signs of its presence but if the purchaser must have known some such drainage existed.[311] There is no doubt, moreover, that a right to use a pipe supplying or carrying away water is in its nature "continuous".[312]

---

[306] *Att-Gen, ex rel. Yorkshire Trust v Brotherton* [1992] 1 A.C. 425; for the difference between the incidents of a right of way over land and right of navigation, see per Lord Oliver at 434A–G.

[307] *Att-Gen v Wright* [1897] 2 Q.B. 318; *Denaby v Anson* [1911] 1 K.B. 171.

[308] *Sussex Investments Limited v Jackson* [1993] E.G.C.S. 441.

[309] *Lyon v Fishmongers' Co* (1876) 1 App. Cas. 662 (distinguished in *Tate & Lyle Food and Distribution Ltd v Greater London Council* [1983] 2 A.C. 509); *North Shore Ry Co v Pion* (1889) 14 App. Cas. 612; *Hindson v Ashby* [1896] 2 Ch. 1 at 30.

[310] *Pyer v Carter* (1857) 1 H. & N. 916; *Nicholas v Chamberlain* (1606) Crow. Jac. 121; *Watts v Kelson* (1870) L.R. 6 Ch. App. 166.

[311] *Pyer v Carter* (above).

[312] *Watts v Kelson* (above) at 174. There was held to be an implied grant of a right of drainage in *McAdams Homes Limited v Robinson* [2004] 3 E.G.L.R. 93, see at [8].

As to prescription, the test is whether successive owners of the servient land, **6–82** assuming them to have been reasonable persons, diligent in the protection of their interests, either must have known or must be taken to have had a reasonable opportunity of becoming aware of the existence of the pipe or drain in question under or through their property.[313] Where (a) it is obvious that the dominant tenement requires a water supply or drainage, (b) the pipes in question were originally installed with the servient owner's knowledge[314] and (c) the course of a pipe or drain can readily be inferred, given the known source of supply or point of discharge, this requirement is unlikely to defeat a prescriptive claim. Where, however, there was no evidence of the regular presence of the dominant owner on the servient land, the servient owner was not aware of the presence of the pipe and the user, though not surreptitious, was unknown to and unsuspected by the servient owner, it was held that no prescriptive right had been acquired.[315]

Express grant

When considering (whether for the purpose of drafting or construing) express **6–83** grants or reservations in connection with pipes and drains, it is important to bear in mind the distinctions between the following rights:

   (i) the right to lay pipes;
   (ii) the right to use pipes;
   (iii) the right to a supply of water (or, in the case of drains, the right to discharge);
   (iv) the right to maintain or repair a pipe.

Similar principles apply to gas pipes or wires and cables for conducting electricity or transmitting signals.

Right to lay pipes

In *Trailfinders v Razuki*,[316] a lease for 21 years reserved **6–84**

"the free and uninterrupted running and passage of water, soil, gas and electric current from other buildings and lands of the landlords . . . through the channels, sewers, drains, water courses, pipes, wires and other conduits which are now, or may hereafter during the term hereby granted be in, under or over the demised premises".

The plaintiffs wished to pass computer cables over the defendant's property. The judge rejected the arguments that: (1) the reservation was limited to cables existing

---

[313] *Dalton v Angus* (1881) 6 App. Cas. 740; *Union Lighterage Co v London Graving Dock Co* [1902] 2 Ch. 557; *Lloyds Bank v Dalton* [1942] 2 Ch. D. 352.
[314] See *Schwann v Cotton* [1916] 2 Ch. 459.
[315] *Barney v B.P. Truckstops Ltd* [1995] N.P.C. 5; *Liverpool Corp v Coghill* [1918] Ch. 307.
[316] [1988] 2 E.G.L.R. 46.

at the date of grant; (2) "electric current" was limited to mains supply and did not apply to low voltage impulses passing along computer cables; and (3) cables attached to the wall would be "on" rather than "in" the demised premises, but held that the reservation did not enable the plaintiffs to enter the demised premises to lay computer cables, albeit they would be entitled to enter to repair or replace existing cables. Even a reservation of "the passage of gas, water and other pipes and electric wires through the demised premises" does not authorise the laying of a new system of pipes.[317]

6–85   In *Simmons v Midford*[318] by contrast, there was granted a right "to lay and maintain drains, sewers, pipes and cables over under and along" a strip of land which was to be kept as a roadway and "the free and uninterrupted passage and running of water, soil, gas and electricity there through and the right to enter upon and open up the said land for the purposes of laying, maintaining and repairing the said drains". The owner of the servient land sought to connect a drain to the drain under the roadway but it was held that (a) the pipe belonged to the dominant owner; alternatively (b) the dominant owner was entitled to the exclusive use of the pipe.[319] The reference to "maintain", meaning "keep", was regarded as indicating that ownership was to remain with the person who laid the pipe on the basis that, had it been intended that the pipe should belong to the land owner, the grantee could not have removed it without his consent and the grant of a right to keep it there would have been inappropriate.[320] Rejecting the argument that the grant of a right to a flow through the pipe would be unnecessary if the intention was that the pipe should belong to the owner of the dominant land, Buckley J. observed that the ownership of an enclosed drain and the right to a flow through it might well be in different ownership and the grantee of a right to construct such a drain would be well advised to obtain at the same time an explicit grant of a right to a flow through it.[321] Furthermore he held that a grant of a right to lay pipes in the above terms would permit the grantee to remove the pipe and put in a bigger or better one or one following a different line under the servient land.[322]

6–86   In *Coopind (UK) Ltd v Walton Commercial Group Ltd*[323] the question arose whether the grant to a tenant in his lease of "a right to receive a supply of gas" entitled him to instal a bigger gas pipe in a different position from the one existing at the date of grant under the servient land. It was held on the facts and in the

---

[317] *Taylor v British Legal Right Assurance Company Limited* (1925) 94 L.J. Ch. 284 on appeal from [1925] 1 Ch. 395.

[318] [1969] 2 Ch. 415.

[319] Applying *Lee v Stevenson* (1858) E.B. & E. 512.

[320] [1969] 2 Ch. 415, at 422D–G. It seems doubtful whether this was what the draftsman meant by "keep" in that context. However that may be, the House of Lords have now held that *Simmons v Midford* was wrongly decided in so far as it treated the question of ownership of the pipe as being affected by the terms agreed between the parties; it is only such intention as can be presumed from the degree and object of annexation that is material for those purposes: *Melluish v B.M.I. (No. 3) Ltd* [1996] A.C. 454, at 473C–G.

[321] *Simmons v Midford* [1969] 2 Ch. 415, at 424A.

[322] [1969] 2 Ch. 415, at 422B–D.

[323] [1989] 1 E.G.L.R. 241.

light of the specific wording of the lease that it did, but the court recognised that a possible meaning of such an expression might be a right to receive whatever gas could be obtained through the gas main existing at the date of grant. Plainly it is desirable that the draftsman should make explicit what installation rights are intended to be conferred.

In *Martin v Childs*[324] there was conveyed with a house "a right to run water, electricity and other services through any pipes, cables, wires or other channels ('the Conduits') ... and the right to enter onto ... the Retained Land [of the Vendor] for the purpose of installing, repairing, maintaining, cleansing and inspecting the Conduits." The purchasers' successors entered the servient land to instal a new pipe in a different position so as to secure an adequate water supply. The Court of Appeal held that the grant did not extend to a right to instal a conduit over a route different to those existing at the date of grant[325] or confer the right to alter the position or size of existing water pipes; "installing" more appropriately referred to the provision of other services where there was not at the date of the conveyance an existing conduit.[326] Conversely, in *Dixon v Hodgson*[327] it was held that the ordinary and natural meaning of a right to use and connect to service-conducting installations that were in, on or over the servient tenement, for the benefit of the dominant tenement, which was a site on which a bungalow was being built, such bungalow needing to be provided with a drain, was that the dominant owner could do whatever was necessary to connect the drains on the dominant land with drains on the servient land. Such a construction of the express grant made the grant of the right to use and connect reasonably effective.

Care must be taken when granting or reserving rights through pipes etc., which may be laid in the future, to limit such rights to installations laid during the perpetuity period. In *Dunn v Blackdown Properties Limited*,[328] Cross J. held that a grant of a right to use sewers and drains "hereafter to pass" under the servient tenement was perpetuitous and invalid. A right to enter on land to construct, lay down, alter, repair, renew, cleanse or maintain sewers, water courses, cesspools, gutters, drains, water pipes, gas pipes, electric wires or cables or other like works, provided that it is ancillary to a valid right to use such installations, is not within the rule against perpetuities.[329] The grant of a future easement after July 16, 1964 not confined within the perpetuity period will probably now be saved by the "wait and see" rule introduced by the Perpetuities and Accumulations Act 1964.[330]

6–87

Right of flow and right of supply

The distinction between a right of supply and a right of flow was drawn in *Schwann v Cotton*,[331] where a testator devised adjoining properties to different

6–88

[324] [2002] EWCA Civ 283.
[325] [2002] EWCA Civ 283 at [12] per Pill L.J.
[326] [2002] EWCA Civ 283 at [27] per Mummery L.J.
[327] [2007] 1 E.G.L.R. 7.
[328] [1961] Ch. 433.
[329] Law of Property Act 1925, s.162(1)(d)(iv), as explained in *Dunn v Blackdown Properties Ltd* (above).
[330] Perpetuities and Accumulations Act 1964, ss.3 and 15(5).
[331] [1916] 2 Ch. 460.

parties; the plaintiff's property received a supply of water by a pipe through the
defendant's property from the property of a third party; it was argued for the
defendant that the plaintiff had not proved any right to a supply of water and that
therefore the right to a flow through the pipe over his land was precarious and
incapable of existing as an easement, but this argument was rejected as irrelevant
to the question whether there was a right to a flow over the defendant's land.

6–89   In *Beauchamp v Frome Rural District Council*[332] the plaintiffs had been
granted "the right as now enjoyed in common with others having the same right
to a water supply to the hereditaments hereinbefore described through pipes from
a spring". The local authority acquired the pipes and the source and laid additional service pipes, thus decreasing the supply to the plaintiff's farm. It was held
that the right granted was to have the residue of the water after the other persons
entitled had taken what they wanted, but only by way of the installations existing
at the date of the grant; the plaintiffs were entitled to object to the drawing off of
water by further or larger service pipes which decreased the supply coming to
them. In *Mitchell v Potter*,[333] the grant was of:

> "Full right and liberty for purchasers and their successors in title to take
> water from the reservoir situated . . . on the vendors' adjoining land to the
> south of the property in common with the owner thereof, the right to convey
> the same through the pipeline now laid from the said reservoir to the said
> property and to draw from the said reservoir such an amount of water as may
> be reasonably required for domestic and farming purposes."

The grantor's spring fed a small reservoir which in turn fed into a pipe which
crossed the grantor's land, the water within the pipe dropping by gravity and then
leading into a pipe on the grantee's land and to his farm. On the grantor's land there
was a spur which fed water to the grantor's bungalow, which was upstream of the
grantee's farm. The claimant was the grantee and the defendant was the successor
of the grantor. The defendant relied on the words "in common with the owner" and
on the decision in *Beauchamp v Frome Rural District Council*.[334] The Court of
Appeal derived no assistance from authority, saying that there was no identical
grant in the cases cited. The grant had to be construed in the light of the circumstances at the date of grant. The grant was of sufficient water from the reservoir
from the spring. The grantor was only entitled to the residue after the grantee's
rights had been exercised.

6–90   In *Rance v Elvin*[335] the plaintiff was granted a right to a free and uninterrupted
flow of water through pipes situated under the retained land of his vendor. The
supply came from the local water company. Subsequently they installed a meter
on the servient tenement and charged the servient owner for all the water used by

---

[332] [1938] 1 All E.R. 595.
[333] [2005] EWCA Civ 88, *The Times*, January 24, 2005.
[334] [1938] 1 All E.R. 595.
[335] (1985) 50 P. & C.R. 9.

both tenements. It was held at first instance that the plaintiff's right to a water supply was incapable of constituting an easement since it imposed a positive obligation on the servient tenement to pay for the water supply so as to maintain an uninterrupted flow, but the Court of Appeal held that this analysis confused the right to a supply and the right to the uninterrupted passage of such water as might come into the pipes. The plaintiff was only claiming the latter; as long as there was a supply, the defendant was not entitled to interrupt it and there was to be implied an obligation on the part of the plaintiff to reimburse the cost of the water received. If the defendant terminated his own supply, then the plaintiff could make his own arrangements with the water company to supply the pipe; accordingly the plaintiff's right was a valid easement and the defendant was not entitled to interfere with the pipe.

The same analysis was applied to a grant of a right of passage of electricity **6–91** in *Duffy v Lamb*,[336] where it was held that the same principles apply to rights to the passage of water, soil,[337] gas, electricity and telephone communications. Accordingly the servient owner was held liable for having switched off the dominant owner's electricity sub-meter which was situated on the servient land. The obligation of the servient owner is to take no positive step to prevent the entry of water/electricity onto his land as well as its subsequent passage, but he is not obliged to ensure a supply. It appears that he has no obligation to continue to pay for the supply, but the Court of Appeal left open[338] the question whether he can invite the supplier to take steps to discontinue the supply which involve interfering with installations on the servient land (as by removing part of the circuit).

These cases[339] were considered in *Cardwell v Walker*[340] which concerned **6–92** express grants of a right to the passage of electricity through the servient land. At the date of the grants the supply of electricity was controlled by recording meters or by coin operated meters on the dominant land. Later, the servient owner proposed the modification of the meters so that they would be operated by tokens and the tokens would be available for sale by the servient owner. This proposal was accepted and implemented. Later the servient owner sold the servient land. The new owner removed the fuses (apparently) on the servient land and it was accepted that that was an actionable interference with the easement. The new servient owner denied that he was under a positive obligation to sell tokens and relied on the general absence of a positive obligation on a servient owner.[341] It was held that the arrangement to replace the meters with token operated meters was not intended to deprive the grantees of the unrestricted right to the passage of electricity through the servient land. If the original servient owner wished to

---

[336] (1997) 75 P. & C.R. 364, CA.
[337] The reference to soil seems inapposite, since the dominant owner would hardly be asserting a right to a supply.
[338] (1997) 75 P. & C.R. 364 at 372, per Millett L.J.; at 373 per Morritt L.J. and at 374 per Ward L.J.
[339] i.e. *Rance v Elvin* (1985) 50 P. & C.R. 9 and *Duffy v Lamb* (1997) 75 P. & C.R. 364.
[340] [2004] 2 P. & C.R. 122.
[341] Relying on *Jones v Price* [1965] 2 Q.B. 618 at 631; *Duke of Westminster v Guild* [1985] Q.B. 688 at 700D–G; *Rance v Elvin*; and *Duffy v Lamb*.

stop supplying tokens, he would have to revert to the previous arrangements. The new servient owner was in the same position. There was an analogy with the cases about the provision of keys to gates or doors which blocked a right of way[342] and also an analogy with the case[343] where the servient owner did not commit a nuisance by laying speed restricting ramps across a road over which there ran a right of way provided always that the ramps remained in good condition; when the ramps ceased to be in good condition their presence constituted an interference with the right of way.

Right to repair

6–93   As with other easements, the dominant owner is entitled to enter the servient tenement to carry out works to clear or repair water courses, pipes and drains.[344] After the repairs have been effected, the surface of the land must be restored to its previous condition.[345] This right applies irrespective of the ownership of the pipe. If the servient owner builds over the pipe, thus interfering with the dominant owner's access for the purpose of repair, he may be ordered to remove the obstruction.[346] Although the dominant owner has no duty to repair the pipe, if he fails to do so and matter escapes from the pipe, that will amount to a trespass to the servient property and he will be liable for damage consequent on that trespass.[347]

Excessive use

6–94   If the dominant owner makes excessive use of a right of drainage by discharging more matter than the system is designed to cope with, thus causing flooding of the servient land, he will be liable in nuisance. What amounts to excessive use will depend on the terms of the grant construed in the light of the circumstances surrounding its creation, which may include the capacity of an existing system[348] or the size of the buildings on the dominant land at the date of grant.[349] The question of excessive user of a right of drainage acquired by an implied grant or by prescription (in the context of an alteration in the dominant tenement) was considered in detail in *McAdams Homes Limited v Robinson*.[350] The Court of Appeal

---

[342] *Johnstone v Holdway* [1963] 1 Q.B. 601 and *Dawes v Adela Estates Ltd* (1970) 216 E.G. 1406.

[343] *Saint v Jenner* [1973] 1 Ch. 275.

[344] *Jones v Pritchard* [1908] 1 Ch. 630 at 638; *Duke of Westminster v Guild* [1985] 1 Q.B. 688 at 700E; *Beeston v Weate* (1856) 5 E. & B. 986; *Roberts v Fellows* (1906) 94 L.T. 279; *Finlinson v Porter* (1875) L.R. 10 Q.B. 188; *Birkenhead Corp v London & North Western Ry Company* (1885) 15 Q.B.D. 572.

[345] *Thurrock Grays & Tilbury Joint Sewage Board v E.J. & W. Goldsmith* (1914) 79 J.P. 17.

[346] *Goodhart v Hyett* (1884) 25 Ch. D. 182; *Abingdon Corp v James* [1940] Ch. 287; *Rickmansworth Water Co v J.W. Ward & Sons Ltd* [1990] E.G.C.S. 91.

[347] *Jones v Pritchard* (above) at 638; *Simmons v Midford* (above) at 422A–B, where Buckley J. stated that the object of a drainpipe is to protect the dominant owner from liability for the escape of water and soil on to the servient land.

[348] *Gardner v Davis* [1999] E.H.L.R. 13, CA.

[349] *Wood v Saunders* (1875) 10 Ch. App. 582; see para.1–138, above.

[350] [2004] 3 E.G.L.R. 93.

held that the question of excessive user should be determined by asking two questions: first, whether the alteration in the dominant tenement involved a "radical change in character" or a "change in identity" and, secondly, whether the alteration would result in a substantial increase or alteration in the burden on the servient land. The trial judge had held that an alteration in the dominant tenement from a bakery to two houses was a radical change in character. The Court of Appeal held that this was a decision that he was entitled to reach. The trial judge had also held that the alteration would result in a substantial increase in the burden on the servient tenement. The Court of Appeal again held that this was a conclusion the trial judge was entitled to reach although the case was very borderline. In commenting on this second issue, Neuberger L.J. stated that in comparing the user of the easement at the time of its grant with the user following the alteration of the dominant tenement, one was entitled to take into account possible intensifications in user which the grantee of the easement could properly make in relation to the easement. Accordingly, the dominant owner would not automatically be defeated just because the user of the easement after the alteration would be greater than the actual user at the date of creation of the easement. Further, the servient owner would not automatically fail just because it could be shown that that dominant owner could properly intensify the user without any alteration in the dominant tenement to an extent which exceeded the user after the alteration was carried out. The comparison should be between the likely range of levels from the dominant tenement in its condition at the date of creation of the easement and from the dominant tenement after alteration.[351]

---

[351] See [2004] 3 E.G.L.R. 93 at [62]–[66].

CHAPTER 7

RIGHT TO LIGHT

1.—ACQUISITION OF EASEMENT OF LIGHT

Introduction

The right to flowing water in a natural stream, it has already been shown, is an **7–01** ordinary right of property requiring no length of time to fortify it. The right to light seems to depend, however, upon very different grounds. The natural rights of the owner of property in this respect seem to be defined by the legal maxim, *cujus est solum ejus est usque ad coelum et ad inferos*. The strict right of property entitles the owner to so much light only as falls perpendicularly on his land. The passage of light over lands unencumbered by buildings must necessarily have existed from time immemorial: but the use of the light so passing, by means of windows in a house or otherwise, confers no right unless it has been continued for 20 years.

A landowner can acquire the right to the reception of light in a lateral direction without obstruction; such a right is an easement. In the absence of such an easement benefiting a neighbour's land, a landowner may build to the very extremity of his own land, and no action can be maintained against him for disturbing his neighbour's privacy by opening windows which overlook the adjoining property.[1] It is competent to such neighbour to obstruct the windows so opened by building against them on his own land, at any time during 20 years after their construction, and thus to prevent the acquisition of the easement of light[2]; if, however, that period is once suffered to elapse, his long acquiescence becomes evidence of title to such an easement.

---

[1] *Chandler v Thompson* (1811) 3 Camp. 80; *Tapling v Jones* (1865) 11 H.L.C. 290 at 305.

[2] See per Littledale J. in *Moore v Rawson* (1824) 3 B. & C. 340; *Tapling v Jones*, above; and, as showing that a railway company has in this respect the same rights as an individual, see *Bonner v G.W. Ry* (1883) 24 Ch. D. 1; *Foster v London, Chatham & Dover Ry* [1895] 1 Q.B. 711.

In *Penwarden v Ching*,[3] a case decided before the Prescription Act 1832, a claim by the defendant to have light pass through a window which had been made 21 years before action was resisted by the plaintiff on the ground that the window was shown not to be an ancient window. Tindal C.J. said: "The question is, not whether the window is what is strictly called ancient, but whether it is such as the law, in indulgence to rights, has in modern times so called, and to which the defendant has a right."

Presumption of grant

7–02   The right to light can be claimed by prescription at common law or by lost grant as well as under the Prescription Act.[4] Where light is claimed by either of the two first-mentioned methods a grant must be presumed[5] and the enjoyment must be as of right[6]; but where light is claimed under section 3 of the Prescription Act, then, as has been seen,[7] it is not necessary to presume a grant,[8] or that the actual enjoyment should be as of right.[9]

The mode in which an easement, including a right to light, may be acquired, namely, by grant, express or implied, or by prescription, has already been considered[10]; but certain questions, peculiar to the easement of light, will now be examined.

User in respect of vacant land

7–03   It is clear that the right to light cannot be acquired by user in respect of vacant land.

Where the right to light is claimed by prescription at common law or by lost grant, the last-mentioned rule is laid down in the reporter's marginal note to *Roberts v Macord*,[11] which appears to be sound. The note runs as follows:

> "The use of an open space of ground in a particular way requiring light and air for twenty years does not give a right to preclude the adjoining owner from building on his land so as to obstruct the light and air."[12]

Where the right to light is claimed under the Prescription Act 1832, the enjoyment must have been had to and for a "building", in which there must be some aperture.

---

[3] (1829) Moo. & Mal. 400 at 401.
[4] *Aynsley v Glover* (1874) 10 Ch. App. 283, para.4–06, above; *Tisdall v McArthur & Co (Steel and Metal) Ltd* [1951] I.R. 228.
[5] *Gardner v Hodgson's Kingston Brewery Co* [1903] A.C. 229 at 239.
[6] *Colls v Home and Colonial Stores* [1904] A.C. 179 at 206.
[7] See para.4–25, above.
[8] *Tapling v Jones* (1865) 11 H.L.C. 290.
[9] *Colls v Home and Colonial Stores* [1904] A.C. 179 at 205; see para.4–24, above.
[10] Chs 3 and 4.
[11] (1832) 1 Mood. & R. 230.
[12] See, e.g. *Garritt v Sharp* (1835) 3 A. & E. 325; *Potts v Smith* (1868) L.R. 6 Eq. 311 at 318; *Scott v Pape* (1886) 31 Ch. D. 554 at 571; *Harris v De Pinna* (1886) 33 Ch. D. 238.

This aperture may be a skylight,[13] or the glass roof and sides of a greenhouse,[14] but not an ordinary doorway.[15] The aperture defines the area which is to be kept free over the servient tenement.[16] In the case, however, of an alteration of the dominant tenement, the preservation of the right to light depends, not on identity of aperture, but upon identity of light.[17]

In assessing damages for obstruction of the light to a building, regard may be had to the potentialities of the dominant tenement as a building site.[18]

Actual user by building need not be shown

For the purpose of a claim under the Act no actual enjoyment of the light (in the   **7–04** sense of user and occupation of the dominant tenement) need be shown; it is sufficient that the aperture existed, and that the light might have been used at any time[19] but if the aperture was completely boarded up during the prescription period, no easement is acquired.[20] The "internal arrangement rule"[21] relates to the scope of the right acquired and not to the question whether it was acquired at all.[22] The fact that a room has been used for a purpose requiring less than a normal quantity of light does not diminish the amount of light claimable therefor.[23]

2.—EXTENT OF RIGHT ACQUIRED BY USER

The basic principles

The decision of the House of Lords in *Colls v Home and Colonial Stores Ltd*[24]   **7–05** established the basic principle that the measure of the light to which right is acquired, of which it has to be seen whether there is such diminution as to cause

---

[13] *Harris v Kinloch* [1895] W.N. 60; *Boston v Isted* [1903] 1 Ch. 405; *Smith v Evangelization Society (Incorporated) Trust* [1933] Ch. 515.

[14] *Clifford v Holt* [1899] 1 Ch. 698; *Born v Turner* [1900] 2 Ch. 211; *Allen v Greenwood* [1980] Ch. 119.

[15] *Levet v Gas Light & Coke Co* [1919] 1 Ch. 24.

[16] *Scott v Pape* (1886) 31 Ch. D. 554 at 575.

[17] *Andrews v Waite* [1907] 2 Ch. 500.

[18] *Griffith v Richard Clay & Sons Ltd* [1912] 1 Ch. 291; *Wills v May* [1923] 1 Ch. 317; and see *Scott v Goulding Properties Ltd* [1973] I.R. 200.

[19] *Courtauld v Legh* (1869) L.R. 4 Exch. 126 (a case of an unfinished house); *Cooper v Straker* (1888) 40 Ch. D. 21 (window with iron shutters only opened occasionally); *Collis v Laugher* [1894] 3 Ch. 659 (window spaces opened, but no window sashes put in); *Smith v Baxter* [1900] 2 Ch. 138 (windows obscured by shelves).

[20] *Smith v Baxter* (above); *Tamares Ltd v Fairpoint Properties Ltd* [2006] EWHC 3589; [2007] 1 W.L.R 2148 at [12].

[21] See paras 7–23 to 7–25, below.

[22] [2007] 1 W.L.R. 2148 at [14].

[23] *Price v Hilditch* [1930] 1 Ch. 500.

[24] [1904] A.C. 179; *Allen v Greenwood* [1980] Ch. 119 at 130, per Goff L.J.; *Lyme Valley Squash Club Ltd v Newcastle-under-Lyme B.C.* [1985] 2 All E.R. 405 at 411, per Blackett-Ord V.-C. The question as to what is sufficient light is considered in detail in *Charles Semon & Co v Bradford Corp* [1922] 2 Ch. 737. As to nuisance being the test, see in particular [1904] A.C. 179 at 185, per Lord Halsbury L.C.; *ibid.*, 204, per Lord Davey, and *ibid.*, 210, per Lord Lindley. See also *Paul v Robson* (1914) 83 L.J.P.C. 304; *Ough v King* [1967] 1 W.L.R. 1547.

a nuisance, is the light required for the beneficial use of the building for any ordinary purpose for which it is adapted. That decision has further made it clear that the nature and extent of the prescriptive right to light acquired by user was not altered by the Prescription Act 1832, which was only concerned with the conditions or length of user.[25] The nature of the right is in fact the same whether it be claimed by prescription at common law, or under the statute,[26] or by lost grant, or by grant implied on a disposition by the owner of two tenements,[27] or under a grant of "lights" among the general words of a deed.[28]

Before *Colls v Home and Colonial Stores Ltd*[29] considerable doubt existed as to the extent of the right acquired by enjoyment, that is to say, whether the access of light through a window for the necessary period entitled the owner to object to any substantial diminution of the light which had been accustomed to pass through the window; or whether the adjoining owner might build so as substantially to diminish the light, provided that no actual nuisance was created. After a long controversy *Colls v Home and Colonial Stores Ltd*[30] settled the question in the latter sense; but some mention of the previous cases appears to be desirable.

Decisions before Colls v Home and Colonial Stores Ltd

7–06 The necessity of showing that the diminution of light was such as to cause a nuisance is generally found in the earlier authorities, of which the first appears to be *Aldred's Case*,[31] an action on the case for building a pigsty and obstructing lights, in which it was resolved that the action was well maintainable,

> "for in a house four things are desired, habitatio hominis, delectatio inhabitantis, necessitas luminis, et salubritas aeris, and for nuisance done to three of them an action lies, sc. (1) To the habitation of a man, for that is the principal end of a house. (2) For hinderance of the light, for the ancient form of an action on the case was significant, sc., quod messuagium horrida tenebritate obscuratum fuit," etc.

"Horrida tenebritate" certainly suggests an obstruction amounting to a nuisance.

7–07 In *Fishmongers' Co v East India Co*,[32] in refusing an application to restrain building so as to stop up lights, Lord Hardwicke said:

---

[25] [1904] A.C. 179 at 183, per Lord Halsbury L.C.; *ibid.*, 198, 199, per Lord Davey; and see *Price v Hilditch* [1930] 1 Ch. 500; *Masonic Hall Co v Sheffield Corp* [1932] 2 Ch. 17.

[26] [1904] A.C. 179; see *Kelk v Pearson* (1871) 6 Ch. App. 809 at 813.

[27] *Leech v Schweder* (1874) 9 Ch. App. 472 at 474.

[28] (1874) 9 Ch. App. 472. In *Frogmore Developments Ltd v Shirayama Shokusan Co Ltd* [2000] 1 E.G.L.R. 121, a grant of "the right to the free and unobstructed passage of light and air to the premises at all times" conferred a right to a quantity of light to be measured in accordance with the decision in *Colls v Home and Colonial Stores Ltd*; the reference to "unobstructed" was not intended to create a greater right.

[29] [1904] A.C. 179.

[30] [1904] A.C. 179; and see *Charles Semon & Co v Bradford Corp* [1922] 2 Ch. 737.

[31] (1611) 9 Co.Rep. 58a.

[32] (1752) 1 Dick. 163 at 164, 165.

"As to the question whether the plaintiffs' messuage is an ancient building, so as to entitle them to the right of the lights, and whether the plaintiffs' lights will be darkened, I will not determine it here; for if it clearly appeared that what the defendants are doing is what the law considers as a nuisance. I would put it in a way to be tried . . .

But I am of opinion it is not a nuisance contrary to law; for it is not sufficient to say it will alter the plaintiffs' lights, for then no vacant piece of ground could be built on in the city; and here will be seventeen feet distance, and the law says it must be so near as to be a nuisance. It is true the value of the plaintiffs' house may be reduced by rendering the prospect less pleasant, but that is no reason to hinder a man from building on his own ground."

In *Back v Stacey*[33] Best C.J. directed the jury that it was not sufficient to constitute an illegal obstruction that the plaintiff had in fact less light than before, nor that his warehouse, the part of his house principally affected, could not be used for all the purposes for which it might otherwise have been applied. He said that in order to give a right of action and sustain the issue there must be a substantial deprivation of light, sufficient to render the occupation of the house uncomfortable and[34] to prevent the plaintiff from carrying on his accustomed business (that of a grocer) on the premises as beneficially as he had formerly done. His Lordship added that it might be difficult to draw the line, but the jury must distinguish between a partial inconvenience and a real injury to the plaintiff in the enjoyment of the premises.   **7–08**

In *Clarke v Clark*[35] the defendant had erected a building which undoubtedly diminished the amount of lateral light coming to the plaintiff's ancient window, and rendered the plaintiff's room less cheerful, especially during the winter months. But Lord Cranworth refused an injunction, saying that there was not such an obstruction of light as to amount to a nuisance. He said[36]:   **7–09**

"The window in question still receives greatly more light than falls to the lot of inhabitants of towns generally. . . . What the plaintiff was bound to show was, that the buildings of the defendant caused such an obstruction of light as to interfere with the ordinary occupations of life . . .

The real question is not what is, scientifically estimated, the amount of light intercepted, but whether the light is so obstructed as to cause material inconvenience to the occupiers of the house in the ordinary occupations of life."

In *Yates v Jack*[37] the same judge, holding that the defendant's new buildings would materially interfere with the quantity of light necessary or desirable for the   **7–10**

---

[33] (1826) 2 C. & P. 465.
[34] *Quaere* "or"; see *Dent v Auction Mart Co* (1866) L.R. 2 Eq. 238 at 245.
[35] (1865) 1 Ch. App. 16. See also the discussion about this date of the alternative remedies of an injunction or damages in *Jackson v Newcastle* (1864) 3 De G.J. & Sm. 275.
[36] (1865) 1 Ch. App. 16 at 20, 21.
[37] (1866) 1 Ch. App. 295.

plaintiffs in the conduct of their business, restrained the defendant from building so as to darken, injure or obstruct any of the ancient lights of the plaintiffs as the same were enjoyed previously to the taking down by the defendant of his buildings on the opposite side of the street, and also from permitting to remain any buildings already erected which would cause any such obstruction. The judgment in this case indicates no intention on Lord Cranworth's part to depart from the rule laid down by him in *Clarke v Clark*,[38] but the effect of the order (as set out above) was to preserve to the plaintiffs the whole of the light previously enjoyed by them, without any express reference to the question whether it could be diminished without causing a nuisance. The form of the order in *Yates v Jack*,[39] which was in use for many years after that decision, and probably contributed to the uncertainty which existed as to the nature of the dominant owner's rights,[40] was in this respect modified in *Colls'* case.[41]

In *Durell v Pritchard*,[42] *Curriers' Co v Corbett*[43] and *Robson v Whittingham*,[44] Knight-Bruce and Turner L.JJ. followed *Clarke v Clark*,[45] in each case refusing to grant an injunction on the ground that no material damage had been shown.

7–11   In *Kelk v Pearson*,[46] the principle was clearly stated by James L.J., who said:

> "On the part of the plaintiff it was argued before us that this was an absolute right—that now, under the statute 2 & 3 Will. 4, c. 71, he had an absolute and indefeasible right by way of property to the whole amount of light and air which came through the windows into his house . . .
>
> Now I am of opinion that the statute has in no degree whatever altered the pre-existing law as to the nature and extent of this right. The nature and extent of the right before that statute was to have that amount of light through the windows of a house which was sufficient, according to the ordinary notions of mankind, for the comfortable use and enjoyment of that house as a dwelling-house, if it were a dwelling-house, or for the beneficial use and occupation of the house if it were a warehouse, a shop, or other place of business. That was the extent of the easement—a right to prevent your neighbour from building upon his land so as to obstruct the access of sufficient light and air, to such an extent as to render the house substantially less comfortable and enjoyable";

---

[38] (1865) 1 Ch. App. 16.

[39] (1866) 1 Ch. App. 295.

[40] See, e.g. the judgments in *Dent v Auction Mart Co* (1866) L.R. 2 Eq. 238; *Martin v Headon* (1866) L.R. 2 Eq. 425; and *Calcraft v Thompson* (1867) 15 W.R. 367, which cannot now be altogether relied upon as good law.

[41] See per Lord Macnaghten [1904] A.C. 179 at 193.

[42] (1865) 1 Ch. App. 244.

[43] (1865) 4 De G.J. & Sm. 764.

[44] (1866) 1 Ch. App. 442.

[45] See fn.35, above.

[46] (1871) 6 Ch. App. 809 at 811.

and he went on to say that the absolute and indefeasible right given by the statute was not greater. Mellish L.J. laid down the rule in different terms; but it does not appear that he intended to differ from the above observations of James L.J.[47]

In *City of London Brewery Co v Tennant*[48] the same rule was repeated and applied, and an injunction was refused, Lord Selborne being a party to the decision.[49]

The alternative view, that the access of light through a window for the neces-   **7–12**
sary period entitled the owner to object to any substantial diminution of the light which had been accustomed to pass through the window, rested primarily on words which were used by Tindal C.J. in summing up to the jury in *Parker v Smith*[50] and which suggested that no diminishment of light could be tolerated. Parke B. in *Wells v Ody*[51] adopted the law as laid down by Tindal C.J. in *Parker v Smith*[52] and it received further support from the Court of Appeal in *Scott v Pape*[53] and *Warren v Brown*.[54] The last-mentioned case was overruled by the House of Lords in *Colls v Home and Colonial Stores Ltd*[55] and it follows that the line of authority of which *Parker v Smith*[56] is the earliest case can no longer be regarded as good law.

Colls v Home and Colonial Stores Ltd

In *Colls v Home and Colonial Stores Ltd*[57] Lord Davey (with whom Lord   **7–13**
Robertson agreed) expressly approved[58] James L.J.'s statement of the principle in *Kelk v Pearson*.[59] Later in his speech Lord Davey described the measure of the right to light through ancient windows as being that which is required for the ordinary purposes of inhabitancy or business of the tenement according to the ordinary notions of mankind. Lord Lindley approved a similar statement of the doctrine in *City of London Brewery Co v Tennant*,[60] saying[61]:

"That doctrine . . . is that generally speaking an owner of ancient lights is entitled to sufficient light according to the ordinary notions of mankind for

---

[47] See *Colls v Home and Colonial Stores Ltd* [1904] A.C. 179 at 200, per Lord Davey.
[48] (1873) 9 Ch. App. 212.
[49] *Leech v Schweder* (1874) 9 Ch. App. 463 (a case of grant).
[50] (1832) 5 C. & P. 438 at 439, 440; and see *Pringle v Wernham* (1836) 7 C. & P. 377.
[51] (1836) 7 C. & P. 410.
[52] (1832) 5 C. & P. 438.
[53] (1886) 31 Ch. D. 554.
[54] [1902] 1 K.B. 15.
[55] [1904] A.C. 179. In that case Joyce J. had followed the decision of Wright J. in *Warren v Brown* [1900] 2 Q.B. 722, before its reversal by the Court of Appeal [1902] 1 K.B. 15. The Court of Appeal [1902] 1 Ch. 302, reversed the decision of Joyce J., but the House of Lords restored it, incidentally vindicating the decision of Wright J. in *Warren v Brown*.
[56] (1832) 5 C. & P. 438.
[57] [1904] A.C. 179.
[58] [1904] A.C. 198.
[59] (1871) 6 Ch. App. 809 at 811; see para.7–11, above.
[60] (1873) 9 Ch. App. 212 at 216, 217.
[61] [1904] A.C. 179 at 208.

the comfortable use and enjoyment of his house as a dwelling-house, if it is a dwelling-house, or for the beneficial use and occupation of the house if it is a warehouse, a shop, or other place of business. The expressions 'the ordinary notions of mankind', 'comfortable use and enjoyment', and 'beneficial use and occupation' introduce elements of uncertainty; but similar uncertainty has always existed and exists still in all cases of nuisance, and in this country an obstruction of light has commonly been regarded as a nuisance, although the right to light has been regarded as a peculiar kind of easement."

The decisions after Colls v Home and Colonial Stores Ltd

7–14   The effect of the authorities, down to and including *Colls v Home and Colonial Stores*,[62] was stated by Farwell J. in *Higgins v Betts*[63] as follows:

"Apart from express contract or grant, the owner of a house has no right to any access of light to the windows thereof over his neighbour's land until he has acquired it by prescription or under the Act. When he has so acquired it, he has a house with an easement of light attached to it. Any substantial interference with his comfortable use and enjoyment of his house according to the usages of ordinary persons in that locality, is actionable as a nuisance at common law. His neighbour's brick burning or fried fish shop may be a nuisance in respect of smell, his pestle and mortar in respect of noise, and in like manner his neighbour's new building may be a nuisance in respect of interference with light. The difference between the right to light and the right to freedom from smell and noise is that the former has to be acquired as an easement in addition to the right of property before it can be enforced, the two latter are ab initio incident to the right of property. But the wrong done is in both cases the same, namely, the disturbance of the owner in his enjoyment of his house. Inasmuch as the acquisition of the easement was a necessary condition precedent to the right to sue, the courts appear in many cases to have addressed themselves rather to the extent of the easement acquired and the amount of such easement taken away by the defendant, than to the sufficiency for ordinary purposes of the amount of light left, so much so that many expressions can be found that lend support to the argument that the right to light was a right of property for which trespass would lie. The dominant owner was never entitled either by prescription or under the Act to all the light that came through his windows. It was not enough to show that some light had been taken, but the question always was whether so much had been taken as to cause a nuisance. But for many years the tendency of the courts had been to measure the nuisance by the amount taken from the light acquired, and not to consider whether the amount left was sufficient for

---

[62] [1904] A.C. 179.
[63] [1905] 2 Ch. 210 at 214, 215.

the reasonable comfort of the house according to ordinary requirement. If a man had a house with unusually excellent lights, it was treated as a nuisance if he was deprived of a substantial part of it, even although a fair amount for ordinary purposes was left. It is in this respect that Colls' case[64] has, to my mind, readjusted the law. It is still, as it has always been, a question of nuisance or no nuisance, but the test of nuisance is not–How much light has been taken, and is that enough materially to lessen the enjoyment and use of the house that its owner previously had? but–How much is left, and is that enough for the comfortable use and enjoyment of the house according to the ordinary requirements of mankind?"

Shortly after the decision in *Colls v Home and Colonial Stores*[65] the question was again considered in *Kine v Jolly*,[66] which was argued successively in three courts. Kekewich J., in granting to the dominant owner an injunction against an obstruction, said[67]: **7–15**

"The great cause of complaint has been of the obstruction of light to what has been called the morning-room. . . . That there has been a large obstruction of light by the erection of the defendant's house is abundantly clear, and I think it is also clear that there has been a large interference with the cheerfulness of the room. . . . I am convinced that the character of the room is altered, and that though still a well-lighted room, it has lost in the obstruction of light one of its chief charms and advantages. . . . Having given all the circumstances full consideration, I have come to the conclusion that the obstruction of light to the morning-room is a nuisance within the meaning of the authorities on that subject."

This decision was affirmed by a majority of the Court of Appeal; and an appeal to the House of Lords also failed, the House being equally divided in opinion. Difficulty was caused by the learned judge's finding that the room was "still a well-lighted room"; but Lord Loreburn interpreted this as meaning that it was well lighted, not according to the standard to be expected in the actual locality and surroundings, but according to the standard of a crowded city.[68] It seems clear that the decision stood by reason of the express finding that there was a nuisance.

In *Masonic Hall Co v Sheffield Corporation*,[69] Maugham J. held that, when a room in a building receives light through windows which have acquired a right to light under the Prescription Act, and are on different sides of the building, the owner of land on either side can as a general rule build only to such a height as, **7–16**

---

[64] [1904] A.C. 179.
[65] [1904] A.C. 179.
[66] [1905] 1 Ch. 480; [1907] A.C. 1.
[67] [1905] 1 Ch. 480 at 483.
[68] [1907] A.C. 1 at 3.
[69] [1932] 2 Ch. 17.

if a similar building were erected on the other side, would not deprive the room of so much light as to cause a nuisance. The grounds of the decision were that in such a case the nature of the restrictive obligation imposed on the servient owners on each side is that they will not so build as by their joint action to cause a nuisance to the dominant owner. The proposition that the defendant, building on one side, was entitled to build to such an extent as, with the light coming from the other side, would leave sufficient light had to be qualified so as to preserve the right of the owner on the other side to a reasonable utilisation of his land.[70] Maugham J. cannot have been merely adjusting the rights of the servient owners *inter se*; for if the servient owner, building in excess of his quota, had derogated from the rights of the servient owner who was not, it would have been for the latter to complain; but damages were awarded to the plaintiff. It must follow that if the first servient owner exceeds his quota, the second remains entitled to build to the extent of his. A situation of some difficulty would arise if the first owner builds, without appreciable injury to or objection from the dominant owner, and the second owner builds, the combined result being to create a nuisance.

7–17   Referring to the statement of the law made by James L.J. in *Kelk v Pearson*[71] and to the speech of Lord Lindley in *Colls v Home and Colonial Stores Ltd*[72] in which he approved a similar statement in *City of London Brewery Co v Tennant*,[73] Goff L.J., delivering the leading judgment in *Allen v Greenwood*,[74] said: "Those passages do, in my judgment, tie the measure of the light to the nature of the building and the purposes for which it is normally adapted." In that case the building under consideration was a greenhouse and it had been argued, in reliance on a dictum of Bray J. in *Ambler v Gordon*,[75] that the right to light was a right not to have the light diminished below a certain standard, that the standard amount of light was that required for ordinary residence or business in the building in question, that ordinary business meant a business requiring an ordinary amount of light, and that light was not necessarily to be measured by that required for the business in fact being carried on in the building or the business for which the building was adapted.

The Court of Appeal disapproved Bray J.'s dictum. Goff L.J. (with whom Orr L.J. agreed) said[76]:

> "It seems that what is ordinary must depend upon the nature of the building and to what it is ordinarily adapted. If, therefore, the building be, as it is in this case, a greenhouse, the normal use of which requires a high degree of light, then it seems to me that that degree is ordinary light."

---

[70] [1932] 2 Ch. 17 at 22, 23.
[71] (1871) 6 Ch. App. 809 at 811; see para.7–11, above.
[72] [1904] A.C. 179 at 208; see para.7–13, above.
[73] (1873) 9 Ch. App. 212 at 216, 217.
[74] [1980] Ch. 119 at 130.
[75] [1905] 1 K.B. 417 at 424.
[76] [1980] Ch. 119 at 131.

Buckley L.J. said[77]:

> "I think the following formulation of the principle can be distilled [from
> *Colls v Home and Colonial Stores Ltd*[78]]: the amount of light to which a
> dominant owner is entitled under a prescriptive claim is sufficient light,
> according to ordinary notions, for the comfortable or beneficial use of the
> building in question, again according to ordinary notions, for such purposes
> as would constitute normal uses of a building of its particular character. If
> the building be a dwelling-house, the measure must be related to reasonable
> standards of comfort as a dwelling house. If it be a warehouse, a shop or a
> factory, the measure must be related to reasonable standards of comfort or
> beneficial use (for comfort may not be the most appropriate test in the case
> of such a building) as a warehouse, a shop or a factory as the case may be.
> These may very probably differ from the standards which would apply to a
> dwelling-house. If the building be a greenhouse, the measure must, in my
> opinion, be related to its reasonably satisfactory use as a greenhouse."

The test in *Colls v Home and Colonial Stores Ltd* was considered and applied in
Midtown v City of London Real Property Co Ltd.[79] The dominant tenement was an
office building which enjoyed good natural light passing over the servient tenement.
The proposed development on the servient tenement would significantly reduce the
light to that office building. However, the office building had always been lit by electric lighting, at all times of the day and all seasons of the year. All of the proposed
redevelopments of the office building which had been contemplated also proceeded
on the basis that the new office buildings would be lit by electric lighting. The defendant argued that in those circumstances, the reduction in the natural light to the office
building would not be a nuisance as it would not interfere with the beneficial use and
occupation of the dominant tenement. This submission was rejected. The judge was
concerned that a submission of this kind had not been made in an earlier case.
Further, the submission if correct might result in there never being a successful challenge to an interference with a right to light. Further, the judge considered that there
might be benefits in having illumination provided by natural light as compared with
electric lighting. In addition, one had to take account of the potential of other reasonable uses of the dominant tenement which might seek to take advantage of the
natural light. However, the fact that the office building had always been lit by electric lighting was relevant when the court came to consider whether the appropriate
remedy for an infringement was an injunction or damages. In the event, the court
refused to grant an injunction to restrain the infringement of the right to light.

   In *Tamares Ltd v Fairpoint Properties Ltd*[80] the judge found that the effect of
the obstruction would be that the landing of a staircase would be better lit but the

---

[77] [1980] Ch. 119 at 134, 135.
[78] [1904] A.C. 179.
[79] [2005] EWHC 33 (Ch.); [2005] 1 E.G.L.R. 65.
[80] [2007] 1 W.L.R. 2148 at [28] to [32].

treads would be worse lit and that the shift of the light from the treads to the landing had probably made matters worse to a material extent *if the use of electric
light was ignored.* He found, however, that "in the real world situation" in which,
for safety reasons, the stairs should probably be properly lit by electric light at all
times, he would regard the complaint as a trivial one but held that he was
required, on the authority of *Midtown*, to employ an "artificial test" and leave
artificial light out of account. We respectfully question whether this is right. It is
one thing to ignore electric light when the area in question is well lit by natural
light before the obstruction but quite another to do so when the area already
needed electric light at all times to enable it to be used safely. In such a case the
obstruction has made no practical difference — the judge called it "trivial" and
would not have found that it fell on the "real injury" side of the line — and it is
difficult to see why it should be actionable in the tort of nuisance.

Unusually good light

7–18   The dominant owner is entitled to such a degree of light as is indicated in the passages in the judgments of Goff and Buckley L.JJ. in *Allen v Greenwood*[81] quoted
above, irrespective of the knowledge of the servient owner of the use being made
of the dominant tenement. Prior to that case, however, it had been a question of
doubt[82] whether the owner of a tenement who for upwards of 20 years has used
that tenement for a purpose requiring an extraordinary amount of light, and has
in fact enjoyed such light, thereby has a prescriptive right to such extraordinary
enjoyment; though in the case of a lease the court had protected special light
required for the business for which the premises were let, apparently on the
ground that the lessor demised the premises with knowledge that they were to
be used for a purpose requiring an unusually good light and so was bound by an
obligation analogous to that imposed by a restrictive covenant.[83]

In *Allen v Greenwood*[84] the greenhouse in the plaintiffs' garden had been in use
for more than 20 years for the ordinary purposes of a domestic greenhouse when
the defendants, the owners of an adjoining property, so obstructed the light to the
greenhouse that it could no longer be used for the purpose of growing plants,

---

[81] [1980] Ch. 119 at 131, 135.
[82] In addition to *Lanfranchi v Mackenzie* (1867) L.R. 4 Eq. 421 and *Ambler v Gordon* [1905] 1 K.B.
417, the question arose and was discussed in several other cases: see *Dickinson v Harbottle* (1873)
28 L.T. 186; *Cartwright v Last* [1876] W.N. 60; *Theed v Debenham* (1876) 2 Ch. D. 165; *Mackey
v Scottish Widows' Fund Assurance Society* (1877) Ir.R. 11 Eq. 541; *Lazarus v Artistic
Photographic Co* [1897] 2 Ch. 214; *Parker v Stanley* (1902) 50 W.R. 282; *Newham v Lawson*
(1971) 22 P. & C.R. 852. In the last-mentioned case Plowman J. doubted whether church authorities who had a prescriptive right of light through church windows were entitled to claim any greater
degree of protection if the windows were of stained glass than if they were of clear glass; the evidence failed to show that the erection of the defendants' building would prevent the comfortable
use of the church according to the ordinary requirements of people attending church and the plaintiffs accordingly were not entitled to relief.
[83] *Herz v The Union Bank of London* (1854) 2 Giff. 686; and see *Browne v Flower* [1911] 1 Ch. 219
at 226, and para.3–32, above.
[84] [1980] Ch. 119.

though there was still sufficient light for the purpose of working in it. The Court of Appeal found that the defendants and their predecessors as owners of the servient tenement during the period of 20 years were fully aware at all times of the way in which the greenhouse was being used.

Considering the plaintiffs' claim to an extraordinary degree of light, both Goff L.J.[85] and Buckley L.J. referred to and approved a dictum of Malins V.-C. in *Lanfranchi v Mackenzie*[86] where he said:

> "I intend to decide this case on broad general principles, and my view of the law is this, that if there be a particular user, and the quantity of light claimed for that is such as would not belong to the ordinary occupations of life, a person who claims that extraordinary quantity of light cannot establish his right to it unless he can show that he has been in the enjoyment of it for 20 years. If a man cannot establish a right within 20 years to an ordinary quantity of light, how can he establish in a less period the right to an extraordinary? All he can establish is the right to the quantity of light he would be entitled to for ordinary purposes. If he has been in the enjoyment of an extraordinary user for 20 years, that would establish the right against all persons who had reasonable knowledge of it."

At the same time the Court of Appeal disapproved the dictum to the contrary of Bray J. in *Ambler v Gordon*.[87] Lord Davey in *Colls v Home and Colonial Stores Ltd*[88] had thrown some doubt on the dictum of Malins V.-C. in *Lanfranchi v Mackenzie*,[89] but in his speech expressly reserved his opinion on the point, so that the Court of Appeal did not feel itself in any way bound by his words. Goff L.J. said[90]:

> "It is clear that a right to a greater degree of light than such as is normally obtained by prescription could be the subject of a valid grant, and in my judgment, therefore, it is capable of being acquired by prescription. That being so, provided it is enjoyed for the full period of 20 years to the knowledge of the servient owners, I fail to see any ground upon which it should be held not to have been acquired by prescription."

Buckley L.J. said[91]:

> "In the case of an easement of way, the extent of the use to which a claim can be established, whether on foot only or with animals or vehicles,

[85] As stated at para.7–17, above, Orr L.J. agreed with Goff L.J.
[86] (1867) L.R. 4 Eq. 421 at 430.
[87] [1905] 1 K.B. 417 at 424; see para.7–17, above.
[88] [1904] A.C. 179 at 203, 204.
[89] (1867) L.R. 4 Eq. 421 at 430.
[90] [1980] Ch. 119 at 132.
[91] [1980] Ch. 119 at 137, 138.

depends, whether under the doctrine of lost grant or prescription, on the nature of the user which has been enjoyed as of right for a sufficient period. By analogous reasoning it seems to me that the same principle should apply to an easement of light. If in any case it could be shown that a use of the dominant tenement for a period and in circumstances justifying the implication of a lost grant has been such as to make an exceptional amount of light necessary for the particular use to which the tenement has been put, I can see no reason why a lost grant of such an exceptional amount of light should not be presumed. If in any case it can be shown that there has been such a use of the dominant tenement for 20 years or upwards before action brought, I see no reason why a prescriptive right should not be obtained in respect of the dominant tenement to such an exceptional amount of light as may be necessary to the satisfactory enjoyment of that use; but the use, to demonstrate a claim as of right to the exceptional amount of light, must be one which, according to ordinary notions, reasonably requires such an exceptional amount of light and must be known at all material times to the occupier of the servient tenement."

His Lordship left open the question whether the use must be continuous throughout the period in question, a question which did not arise in that case, as there was no dispute that the greenhouse had been used as an ordinary domestic greenhouse throughout the 20-year period.

It was the plaintiffs' case that they were entitled by virtue of their prescriptive right to light to all the benefits of the light, including the rays of the sun, warmth being an inescapable product of daylight, and the judgment of the Court of Appeal was that they were so entitled. Goff L.J. did, however, add[92] a proviso: on other facts, particularly in the case of solar heating, it might be possible and right to separate the heat, or some other property, of the sun from its light, and in such a case a different result might be reached.

7–19   It has been suggested[93] that the case of a commercial, as opposed to a domestic greenhouse would be different, the supposed distinction being supported by reference to *Hill v Tupper*[94] and the principle that an easement must be for the benefit of the dominant tenement and enhance the normal use and enjoyment thereof.[95] The right unsuccessfully claimed in *Hill v Tupper*[96] was in effect a right to prevent commercial competition and clearly there was no benefit to the plaintiff's land as such. It is no objection to the validity of the right claimed that the dominant tenement is used for commercial purposes and the easement is required in connection with the business carried on there.[97] It seems, therefore, that where

---

[92] [1980] Ch. 119 at 134.
[93] In a note by F.R. Crane, Conv. (n.s.) 301.
[94] (1863) 2 H. & C. 121.
[95] *Ellenborough Park, Re* [1956] Ch. 131.
[96] (1863) 2 H. & C. 121.
[97] See *Moody v Steggles* (1879) 12 Ch. D. 261 and the other cases cited at para.1–27, above.

a greenhouse on the dominant land benefits from the access of the light which is claimed it makes no difference whether the greenhouse is being used for domestic or for commercial purposes.

Nuisance

On the question of nuisance or no nuisance there are some further points which are clear. Thus the result of an inquiry whether there is a nuisance may differ according to the locality of the building affected. While in cases of nuisance by obstruction to ancient lights the question of locality is of very much less importance in determining whether such obstruction amounts to an actionable nuisance than in cases relating to other nuisances,[98] and it is probable that no variation in locality can justify the diminution of light below a minimum standard,[99] or afford grounds for reducing the light passing to a room in a manufacturing town to the standard of other inadequately lighted rooms in the neighbourhood, yet the court is entitled to have regard to the locality.[100]   **7–20**

Light from other sources

The court should have regard to light (including light from a skylight),[101] coming from sources other than that which has been obstructed, but only so far as this other light is light which the dominant owner is entitled by grant or prescription to enjoy; light of which such owner may be deprived at any time[102] ought not to be taken into account.[103] In this connection it should be pointed out that, as between the dominant and servient owners, the right to ancient light is a negative easement over the servient tenement considered as a whole; and where the   **7–21**

---

[98] See *Fishenden v Higgs & Hill Ltd* (1935) 153 L.T. 128 at 140, per Romer L.J., and at 142, 143, per Maugham L.J. See also *Colls v Home and Colonial Stores Ltd* [1904] A.C. 179 at 183–185, per Lord Halsbury, and at 210, per Lord Lindley; *Kine v Jolly* [1905] 1 Ch. 480 at 497, per Romer L.J. In the case of nuisance other than obstructions to light, the question varies with locality: *Rushmer v Polsue & Alfieri Ltd* [1906] 1 Ch. 234 at 250; [1907] A.C. 123.

[99] "The standard of lighting required to survive in order to eliminate the existence of a nuisance seems to me of necessity an absolute standard. The human eye requires as much light for comfortable reading or sewing in Darlington Street, Wolverhampton, as in Mayfair. True, no doubt it may be that as a rule buildings are more crowded together in manufacturing districts than in residential neighbourhoods. Lights have been obstructed, and no doubt where they have been ancient compensation has been accepted. True, no doubt it may be that an adequately lighted ground floor back room is a rare find in a manufacturing district. I can see, however, no reason in this for saying that a man whose room in such a locality has been turned into a room no longer adequately lighted for ordinary purposes has not suffered an actionable wrong": *Hortons' Estate Ltd v James Beattie Ltd* [1927] 1 Ch. 75 at 78, per Russell J.

[100] *Ough v King* [1967] 1 W.L.R. 1547.

[101] *Smith v Evangelization Society (Incorporated) Trust* [1933] Ch. 515.

[102] Including, it seems, light reflected back into the plaintiff's window from a wall not belonging to him; see *Price v Hilditch* [1930] 1 Ch. 500 at 505, 506; *Smith v Evangelization Society (Incorporated) Trust* [1933] Ch. 515 at 523; and article in (1934) 20 Conv. 65.

[103] See *Colls v Home and Colonial Stores Ltd* [1904] A.C. 179 at 211, per Lord Lindley; and *Kine v Jolly* [1905] 1 Ch. 480 at 493, per Vaughan Williams L.J., and 497, per Romer L.J.; and [1907] A.C. 7, per Lord Atkinson. Since *Colls v Home and Colonial Stores* it is doubtful whether the words of James V.-C. in *Dyers' Co v King* (1870) L.R. 9 Eq. 442, hold good to their full extent.

servient owner raised part of his tenement and lowered part, so that the net light
was unaltered, it was held that the dominant owner could not complain.[104]

Glazed tiles

7–22   If an actionable nuisance is proved, it is not sufficient for the person who
obstructs the light to offer to patch up the injury by putting glazed tiles in front
of the windows in question. In *Dent v Auction Mart Co*, Page Wood V.-C. said[105]:

> "A person who wishes to preserve his light has no power to compel his
> neighbour to preserve the tiles, or a mirror which might be better, or to keep
> them clean, nor has he covenants for these purposes that will run with the
> land, or affect persons who take without notice; and, therefore, it is quite
> preposterous to say, 'Let us damage you, provided we apply such and such
> a remedy'."

Future use of dominant tenement

7–23   It was laid down by Lord Cockburn C.J. in *Moore v Hall*[106] that the court should
consider not only the actual present use of the premises but also any purpose to
which it may be reasonably expected that in the future may be applicable. This
rule was not altered by the decision in *Colls v Home and Colonial Stores Ltd*.[107]
Lord Davey said that regard might be had not only to the present use but also to
any ordinary uses to which the dominant tenement is adapted, and that a man does
not restrict his right by not using the full measure of light which the law permits,[108] and it was the opinion of Lord Lindley that if the dominant owner
chooses to use a well-lighted room for a lumber-room for which little light is
required, he does not lose his right to use at some future time the same room for
some other purpose for which more light is required.[109] The future use of the
dominant tenement was a relevant factor in the court finding that a development
of the servient tenement would infringe the right to light in *Midtown v City of
London Real Property Co Ltd*.[110]

7–24   In *Price v Hilditch*[111] Maugham J. expressly adopted as the basis of his decision
the observations of Lord Davey and Lord Lindley above referred to. The light
received by a room in a residential house had by reason of the defendant's building operations been diminished to such an extent as no longer to be sufficient for

---

[104] *Davis v Marrable* [1913] 2 Ch. 421.

[105] (1866) L.R. 2 Eq. 238 at 251, 252. See *Black v Scottish Temperance Assurance* [1908] I.R. 541.

[106] (1878) 3 Q.B.D. 178 at 183; and see *Aynsley v Glover* (1874) L.R. 18 Eq. 551 at 554; *Dicker v
Popham, Radford & Co* (1890) 63 L.T. 379.

[107] [1904] A.C. 179.

[108] [1904] A.C. 179 at 202, 203.

[109] [1904] A.C. 179 at 211. The decision in *Martin v Goble* (1808) 1 Camp. 320 has been quoted in
favour of the opposite view. The decision may be supported on a different ground: see [1904] A.C.
179 at 202.

[110] [2005] EWHC 33 (Ch.); [2005] 1 E.G.L.R. 65.

[111] [1930] 1 Ch. 500.

the purposes of an ordinary room, although it was sufficient for the purposes of a scullery, for which the room had long been used. Maugham J. treated as irrelevant the use to which the room had been put, and, in regard to the observations of Lords Davey and Lindley, said[112]:

> "I respectfully adopt those views: and, for myself, I would add that the language of section 3 of the Prescription Act 1832 seems to support them, since the section begins with the words: 'When the access and use of light to and for any dwelling-house, workshop, or other building shall have been actually enjoyed therewith for the full period of twenty years, without interruption, the right thereto shall be deemed absolute and indefeasible.' Nothing is said to indicate that the right is to be measured by the internal arrangements of the building. . . . I think it is reasonably clear that the lost grant which juries were directed to presume before the Act must have been a grant of the access to and use of light over the servient tenement, knowingly permitted by the owners of it, to and for certain windows or lights in the dominant tenement, without any question at all as to the use for which the light had been used (as it is phrased, somewhat incorrectly) in the rooms which were lit from those windows. As was pointed out by Lord Lindley, the fact that a house has been unoccupied for twenty years, or that the shutters have been closed for a month at a time, does not prevent the easement being acquired; and this fact tends to support the view which I have adopted. The statute has created a fresh origin for the easement of light, and enjoyment as of right is not necessary under section 3; but the nature of the easement has not, in my opinion, been altered."

Moore v Hall,[113] *Colls v Home and Colonial Stores Ltd*[114] and *Price v Hilditch*[115]   **7–25** were applied by Millett J. in *Carr-Saunders v Dick McNeil Associates Ltd*[116] where there had been an alteration in the internal arrangements of the second floor of the dominant tenement so that a room on that floor which had the enjoyment of light had been divided into small rooms. The owners of the servient tenement added two storeys to their premises with the result that the second floor of the dominant tenement could no longer, as formerly, conveniently be divided in such a way as to leave the small rooms with an adequate amount of light through the existing windows. According to Millett J.[117] it is necessary to bear three principles in mind:

---

[112] [1930] 1 Ch. 500 at 508.
[113] (1878) 3 Q.B.D. 178.
[114] [1904] A.C. 179.
[115] [1930] 1 Ch. 500.
[116] [1986] 1 W.L.R. 922.
[117] [1986] 1 W.L.R. 922, at 928C–H.

   (i) the right acquired under section 3 of the Act of 1832 is an easement of access of light to a building, not a particular room within it; so the extent of the right is not necessarily to be measured by the internal arrangements of the building;

  (ii) interference with the right constitutes the tort of nuisance; the question is therefore whether there has been such a substantial interference with the enjoyment of the property as to constitute an actionable nuisance, no actionable wrong being committed if the amount of light remaining is sufficient for the comfortable enjoyment of the property, not merely of a particular room;

 (iii) the right of light is not measured by the particular use to which the dominant tenement has been put in the past; the dominant owner is entitled to such access of light as will leave the property adequately lit for all ordinary purposes for which it may reasonably be expected to be used.

What would be an alternative use which might reasonably be expected must, however, be established by evidence and the court will not be satisfied by speculation.[118]

Alterations in windows

7–26 The above discussion concerned alterations in the use of the dominant tenement. There have been many cases which have considered the effect of alterations in the windows themselves. These cases primarily concern the question whether the alteration in the window leads to a loss of, or a suspension of, the pre-existing right to light and are, accordingly, considered in detail at paras 12–29–12–44, below.

Angle of 45 degrees

7–27 Before *Colls v Home and Colonial Stores Ltd*[119] some judges had been inclined, in dealing with the easement of light, to establish a specific test, and referred to the Metropolis Management Amendment Act 1862,[120] which contained the following clause:

> "No building, except a church or chapel, shall be erected, on the side of any new street of a less width than fifty feet, which shall exceed in height the distance from the external wall or front of such building to the opposite side of such street, without the consent in writing of the Metropolitan Board of Works; nor shall the height of any building so erected be at any time subsequently increased so as to exceed such distance without such consent; and in

---

[118] *Tamares Ltd v Fairpoint Properties Ltd* [2007] 1 W.L.R. 2148 at [37].
[119] [1904] A.C. 179.
[120] s.85; repealed by the London Building Act 1894, see now the Building Act 1984 and the Regulations made thereunder. *Cf.* the byelaw of the Metropolitan Board in *Theed v Debenham* (1876) 2 Ch. D. 165 at 168n.

determining the height of such building the measurement shall be taken from the level of the centre of the street immediately opposite the building up to the parapet or eaves of such building."

It would appear, both from the character of the statute and also from the direction to measure the distance in every case, not from the sill of any window, but from the level of the street, that the clause was primarily intended, not to protect the enjoyment of light in private houses, but to ensure the free passage of air and sunlight to the streets themselves. In some cases, however, it was suggested that a rule as to light was there laid down.[121] This question has now been set at rest by *Colls v Home and Colonial Stores Ltd*,[122] where it was laid down that there is no hard and fast rule with regard to the angle of 45 degrees.

> "There is no rule of law", said Lord Lindley,[123] "that if a person has forty-five degrees of unobstructed light through a particular window left to him he cannot maintain an action for a nuisance caused by diminishing the light which formerly came through that window."

A person may be left with much less than 45 degrees of light and yet have suffered no actionable diminution. Thus, where the defendants proposed to erect a building 73ft high with a street 45ft wide separating it from the plaintiffs' building, it was held that, as even the ground-floor windows of the plaintiffs' building would still be unusually well lighted, the plaintiffs could not sustain a *quia timet* action.[124]

> "But experience shows", continues Lord Lindley,[125] "that it is, generally speaking, a fair working rule to consider that no substantial injury is done to him where an angle of forty-five degrees is left to him, especially if there is good light from other directions as well. Lord Justice Cotton pointed this out in Ecclesiastical Commissioners v Kino."[126]

The question as to the angle of 45 degrees had been previously dealt with by Lord Selborne in *City of London Brewery Co v Tennant*,[127] where he also discusses the evidence necessary to sustain an action to restrain lateral obstructions.

---

[121] *Hackett v Baiss* (1875) L.R. 20 Eq. 494. See also *Beadel v Perry* (1866) L.R. 3 Eq. 465; *City of London Brewery Co v Tennant* (1873) 9 Ch. App. 212; *Theed v Debenham* (1876) 2 Ch. D. 165; *Ecclesiastical Commissioners v Kino* (1880) 14 Ch. D. 213.

[122] [1904] A.C. 179.

[123] [1904] A.C. 179 at 210.

[124] *Charles Semon & Co v Bradford Corp* [1922] 2 Ch. 737. Mr Waldram gave evidence.

[125] *Colls v Home and Colonial Stores Ltd* [1904] A.C. 179 at 210.

[126] (1880) 14 Ch. D. 213 at 228. See also *Parker v First Avenue Hotel Co* (1883) 24 Ch. D. 282. The question of the angle of 45 degrees was discussed very fully by Crossman J. in *Fishenden v Higgs and Hill Ltd* (1935) 153 L.T. 128 at 131–133, and his observations were approved by the Court of Appeal. As Maugham L.J. said (*ibid.*, at 143), "No hard-and-fast mathematical standards can be applied".

[127] (1873) 9 Ch. App. 220. See also, as to lateral obstructions, *Clarke v Clark* (1865) 1 Ch. App. 16.

Evidence

7–28   A method employed by expert witnesses to measure the obscuration of light caused by a new building is to estimate the amount of direct sky which will reach a hypothetical table 2ft 9in. high in a particular room. By this method a room is regarded as adequately lit for all ordinary purposes if 50 per cent or more of its area receives not less than one lumen of light at table level. This so-called "50/50 rule", however, is merely a useful guide and not to be applied rigidly without regard to the shape and size of the room or the disposition of the light within it. Its justification is that an owner is unreasonable if he complains that the corners or other parts of the room where good light is not expected are poorly lit, if the room as a whole remains well lit.[128] The proportion of the room which receives the required amount of light is determined by the drawing by a rights of light surveyor of a light contour map known as a "Waldram" diagram after Mr Percy Waldram, who devised the method in the 1920s.

In *Masonic Hall Co v Sheffield Corporation*[129] Maugham J., while conceding the value of such expert evidence, said:

"I think it is safer to rely upon the view expressed in Colls v. Home and Colonial Stores[130] and to consider whether, as a matter of common sense, there is such a deprivation of light as to render the occupation of the house uncomfortable in accordance with the ordinary ideas of mankind."

In *Fishenden v Higgs and Hill*[131] the same judge said, after saying that Mr Waldram's daylight plans were "of great use", that they could not be regarded as in any way conclusive and he added:

"they may, I think, often be exceedingly misleading if the so-called 50–50 rule with regard to the amount of light is applied to a room which has any unusual depth in it, or applied to a room where the windows are in any sense unusual, because the light falling at table height from the window at a particular part of the room depends directly upon the depth of the room and the height of the window."

This emphasises the limitations of the Waldram diagram approach; it is scientific up to a point but the selection of a point half-way back in a room is somewhat

---

[128] Per Millett J. in *Carr-Saunders v Dick McNeil Associates Ltd* [1986] 1 W.L.R. 922 at 927B; see also *Smyth v Dublin Theatre Co Ltd* [1936] I.R. 692; and *Deakins v Hookings* [1994] 1 E.G.L.R. 190, where the 50/50 rule was said to be indicative of the minimum acceptable level of light in modern conditions. The agreed evidence given by the expert witnesses in *Midtown v City of London Real Property Co Ltd* [2005] EWHC 33 (Ch.); [2005] 1 E.G.L.R. 65 was by reference to the 50/50 rule.
[129] [1932] 2 Ch. 17 at 24.
[130] [1904] A.C. 179.
[131] (1935) L.T. 128 at pp. 143 and 144.

arbitrary. It would hardly have been appropriate on the facts of *Colls* where the room affected was 100 feet deep.

In *Ough v King*[132] the so-called "Waldram" method was treated as not being decisive and the Court of Appeal held that it was admissible to have regard to the higher standards expected for comfort as the years go by. Lord Denning M.R. said[133] that he thought that it was very helpful for a judge in light cases to have a view of the premises.

Bad light

Some uncertainty exists as to the right to protect ill-lighted premises.[134] In the course of the argument in *Colls v Home and Colonial Stores Ltd*[135] Lord Robertson said:

7–29

> "Can a man by making one window where there should be five to give proper light, and living twenty years in this cave, prevent his neighbour from building a house which would have done no harm to the light if there had been five windows?"

This dictum suggests that the owner of a badly-lighted building has only himself to blame. In the earlier case of *Dent v Auction Mart Co*,[136] however, Sir William Page Wood V.-C. rejected an argument on the part of the defendant that the plaintiffs might have made their windows larger, saying that it was not for the defendant to tell the plaintiffs how they were to construct their premises and pointing out that if they did alter their windows the alterations would not be protected by any easement. Certainly in Ireland the view seems to have been that it was particularly important to protect premises which were so badly lit that the smallest interference with the existing light would substantially inconvenience the occupier.[137] Probably the Irish cases would be followed in England and Wales.

Whether or not protection will be given appears to depend upon the degree of lighting of the whole or the several parts of the room or premises, and other factors, such as the nature of the light abstracted or left.[138]

---

[132] [1967] 1 W.L.R. 1547. See also *McGrath v The Munster and Leinster Bank Ltd* [1959] I.R. 313; *Gamble v Doyle* (1971) 219 E.G. 310. In *Voyce v Voyce* (1991) 62 P. & C.R. 290, the evidence was too scanty to establish an actionable nuisance.

[133] [1967] 1 W.L.R. 1547 at 1552.

[134] The matter is discussed in Hudson "Light for Inadequate Windows" 48 Conv. (n.s.) 408.

[135] [1904] A.C. 179 at 181.

[136] (1866) L.R. 2 Eq. 238 at 251.

[137] *O'Connor v Walsh* (1908) 42 I.L.T.R. 20 (Lord Meredith M.R. and Court of Appeal in Ireland); *McGrath v Munster and Leinster Bank Ltd* [1959] I.R. 313; see also *Cannon v Hughes* [1937] I.R. 284. But see *Litchfield-Speer v Queen Anne's Gate Syndicate Ltd (No. 2)* [1919] 1 Ch. 407, where P. O. Lawrence J. refused relief in respect of a kitchen which was already poorly lighted.

[138] This proposition is adopted from Bodkin "The Acquisition of Rights to Light for Badly-lighted Premises" 38 Conv. (n.s.) 4.

3.—Custom of London

7–30   By the custom of London,[139] a man might rebuild his messuage or house upon an
ancient foundation to what height he pleased, though thereby the ancient windows or lights of the adjoining house were stopped, if there were no agreement
in writing to the contrary.[140] Although the new building may go to any height, its
foundations may not extend laterally beyond the original foundations.[141] The custom was originally declared in *Plummer v Bentham* in relation to messuages or
houses; it was expressly held that there was no such custom in relation to other
erections or buildings. The decision in *Wynstanley v Lee*[142] was only concerned
with houses. However, in *Perry v Eames*[143] Chitty J. held that the custom applied
to the site of the late Bankruptcy Court in the City of London but the decision in
Plummer v Bentham does not appear to have been cited to the court. In *Bowring
Services Ltd v Scottish Widows Fund & Life Assurance Society*,[144] a deputy High
Court judge held that he should not depart from the decision of Chitty J.
However, since the evidence of custom and the declaration in *Plummer v
Bentham* was to the effect that there was no such custom in relation to buildings
other than houses, and since the matter was not properly explored in *Perry v
Eames* it is suggested that the court should still proceed today on the basis of the
only custom declared to exist in *Plummer v Bentham*.

This custom remains effective where the light is claimed by prescription at
common law or under the doctrine of lost modern grant. But where the right is
claimed under the Prescription Act 1832, the custom is overriden by the words in
section 3: "any local custom or usage notwithstanding".[145]

---

[139] There was a similar custom in York: see the case of *Bland v Mosley* cited in *Hughes v Keymish*
(1490) 1 Bulstrode 115.
[140] Com. Dig. London, N. (5); *Plummer v Bentham* (1757) 1 Burr. 248; *Wynstanley v Lee* (1818) 2
Swan 333.
[141] *Hughes and Keene's Case* (1490) Godbolt 183, reported as *Hughes v Keymish* (1490) 1 Bulstrode
115 and *The Case of the City of London* Calthorp 649.
[142] (1818) 2 Swan 333.
[143] [1891] 1 Ch. 658 at 667.
[144] [1995] 1 E.G.L.R. 158.
[145] *Perry v Eames* [1891] 1 Ch. 667. See *Salters' Co v Jay* (1842) 3 Q.B. 109; *Truscott v Merchant
Tailors' Co* (1856) 11 Exch. 855; *Cooper v Hubbuck* (1862) 12 C.B. (n.s.) 456.

CHAPTER 8

AIR

1.—RIGHT TO AIR

Introduction

It is common conveyancing practice expressly to provide against the acquisition of **8–01** a right of access of light and air, and it was probably as a result of this practice that it was at one time usual in referring to decisions upon the access to light to describe them as cases of light and air, and a formula of this description crept into both pleadings and evidence.[1] This, however, is inaccurate. The grounds upon which the court will restrain the obstruction of light may differ widely from the grounds upon which it will restrain the obstruction of air.[2] Moreover, while, generally speaking, the modes in which a right to the access of light and a right to the access of defined air can be acquired are similar,[3] a right to the access of light is within section 3 of the Prescription Act 1832,[4] while a right to the access of air is within section 2.[5]

No right to the passage of air over an unlimited surface

A general right to the access of air passing over the unlimited surface of neigh- **8–02** bouring land cannot be acquired by prescription.[6] The ground of this rule is that a right cannot be acquired against others by a user which they cannot interrupt.[7] Thus in *Webb v Bird*,[8] the plaintiff's windmill was built in 1829; the defendant,

---

[1] *City of London Brewery Co v Tennant* (1873) 9 Ch. App. 221; *Bryant v Lefever* (1879) 4 C.P.D. 172; see *Dent v Auction Mart Co* (1866) L.R. 2 Eq. 252.

[2] *City of London Brewery Co v Tennant*, above; *Baxter v Bower* (1875) 44 L.J.Ch. 625.

[3] *Cable v Bryant* [1908] 1 Ch. 263.

[4] See para.4–23, above.

[5] See para.4–22, above, and para.8–06, below.

[6] The old authorities to the contrary are mentioned in the 14th ed. of this book, but they can no longer be considered to be good law and are at most of historical interest.

[7] *Harris v De Pinna* (1886) 33 Ch. D. 238 at 262, per Bowen L.J. (a claim to the uninterrupted access of air to a structure for storing timber).

[8] (1861) 10 C.B. (n.s.) 268; (1862) 13 C.B. (n.s.) 841; accepted by Lord Denning M.R. in *Phipps v Pears* [1965] 1 Q.B. 76 at 83 as stating the law.

in 1860, built a schoolhouse within 25 yards of the mill which obstructed the currents of air that would otherwise have passed to the mill; and for the obstruction an action was brought which failed. The Court of Exchequer Chamber held that the plaintiff's claim could not be supported upon the presumption of a grant, which only arose where the person against whom the right was claimed might have prevented the exercise of the subject of the supposed grant; and in the case of the windmill such prevention would be, if not absolutely impossible, yet so difficult that no presumption of a grant could be founded upon non-prevention. Blackburn J. said that he wished to guard against its being supposed that anything in the judgment affected the common law right that might be acquired to the access of air through a window.

8–03   In *Bryant v Lefever*[9] the plaintiff and the defendants were occupiers of adjoining houses, which had remained in the same condition for 30 years. The defendants, in rebuilding, raised their house, thereby causing the plaintiff's chimney to smoke. The plaintiff having brought an action claiming a right to have the free access of air to his chimneys, the Lords Justices held that the action failed. There was no natural right to such access; for the establishment of such a right would prevent every adjoining owner from making a reasonable use of his land. Neither could the right be acquired by prescription, for the claim was vague and uncertain, and the enjoyment incapable of being interrupted by any reasonable means. Cotton L.J. added that it was unnecessary to say whether, if the uninterrupted flow of air through a definite aperture or channel over a neighbour's property had been enjoyed as of right for a sufficient period, a right by way of easement could be acquired.

Air through a defined aperture or channel

8–04   While, as appears from the authorities above referred to, a general right to the access of air passing over the unlimited surface of neighbouring land cannot be acquired by prescription (though it can be the subject of covenant), on the other hand a right to the access of air can be acquired by prescription where such access is enjoyed either through a definite aperture in the dominant tenement or through a definite channel over adjoining property.[10]

8–05   In *Gale v Abbott*[11] and *Dent v Auction Mart Co*[12] injunctions were granted to remove and prevent impediments to ventilation. In the first case the defendant was ordered to remove a skylight which he had placed over his yard, and which

---

[9] (1879) 4 C.P.D. 172; *Hunter v Canary Wharf Ltd* [1997] A.C. 655.

[10] *Bass v Gregory* (1890) 25 Q.B.D. 481, where the plaintiff succeeded in establishing a prescriptive right to ventilate a cellar by a shaft communicating with a disused well. See also *Moseley v Bland*, 2 Roll.Abr. 141, Nusans, G. pl. 16 (cited in *Aldred's Case* (1610) 9 Co Rep. 57b); *Aldin v Latimer Clark, Muirhead & Co* [1894] 2 Ch. 437, 446; *Chastey v Ackland* [1895] 2 Ch. 389 at 402; *Cable v Bryant* [1908] 1 Ch. 264; *Hunter v Canary Wharf Ltd* [1997] A.C. 655. It is not sufficient for the plaintiff to prove only a casual and temporary obstruction depending on the direction of the wind: *Johnson v Wyatt* (1863) 2 De G.J. & S. 17 at 26.

[11] (1862) 8 Jur. (n.s.) 987.

[12] (1866) L.R. 2 Eq. 238.

materially impeded the passage of air to the window of the plaintiff's kitchen. In the second case Sir William Page Wood V.-C. said[13]:

> "There is a staircase lighted in a certain manner by windows which, when opened, admit air. The Defendants are about to shut up these windows, as in a box with the lid off, by a wall about eight or nine feet distant, and some forty-five feet high; and in that circumscribed space they propose to put three water-closets. There are difficulties about the case of air as distinguished from that of light; but the Court has interfered to prevent the total obstruction of all circulation of air; and the introduction of three water-closets into a confined space of this description is, I think, interference with air which this Court will recognise on the ground of nuisance."

In some cases, even a right to air through a defined aperture or channel has been treated as arising only by covenant. Thus in *Hall v Lichfield Brewery Co*,[14] in which the plaintiff, who had for 30 years enjoyed a free access of air to his slaughterhouse through two apertures, brought an action for the obstruction of this air. Fry J. said that the right to have an access of air to an aperture in the building could undoubtedly be acquired at law, and that for this purpose the court would imply a covenant. In the case of a dwelling-house the covenant to be implied would be not to interrupt the free use of salubrious air. In the case of a slaughterhouse the covenant to be implied would be not to interrupt the free access of air suitable for a slaughterhouse. Fry J. said that the right to defined air could not be claimed by grant, and therefore not by prescription; and he referred to the words of Littledale J. in *Moore v Rawson*[15] to the effect that such a right more properly arises by covenant. It would seem, however, that a right to the passage of defined air is a negative easement, or a right *ne facias*. As such it may be the subject of a grant, and it is now clear that it is claimable by prescription,[16] including prescription under section 2 of the Prescription Act 1832. **8–06**

Derogation from grant

On the principle that a grantor may not derogate from his grant, it has been held that where land is expressly granted for carrying on a particular business the grantor cannot interrupt air so as to interfere with that business.[17] Similarly, where there was an express grant of land with a stable on it (which stable was ventilated by defined apertures) the grantor could not subsequently erect anything **8–07**

---

[13] (1866) L.R. 2 Eq. 238 at 252.
[14] (1880) 49 L.J.Ch. 655. See also *Harris v De Pinna* (1886) 33 Ch. D. 255; *Chastey v Ackland* [1895] 2 Ch. 389 at 402.
[15] (1824) 3 B. & C. 332.
[16] See *Dalton v Angus* (1881) 6 App Cas. 740 at 798, per Lord Selborne L.C., at 823, per Lord Blackburn; *Bass v Gregory* (1890) 25 Q.B.D. 481 at 483; *Aldin v Latimer Clark, Muirhead & Co* [1894] 2 Ch. 437; *Simpson v Godmanchester Corp* [1897] A.C. 696 at 709; *Cable v Bryant* [1908] 1 Ch. 259 at 263; and see paras 1–38–1–41, above.
[17] *Aldin v Latimer Clark, Muirhead & Co* [1894] 2 Ch. 437, paras 3–32–3–51, above.

on his adjoining property which by interfering with the air prevented the use of the stable as a stable.[18] A grantee may have an implied easement of necessity to go on to the grantor's land to erect an air-duct without which the grantee's business cannot be carried on legally.[19]

Right to prevent access of impure air not an easement

8–08   It may be observed here that the right to a lateral passage of air, as to a flow of water, superadds a privilege to the ordinary rights of property, and is quite distinct from that right which every owner of a tenement, whether ancient or modern, possesses to prevent his neighbour transmitting to him air or water in impure condition; this latter right is one of the ordinary incidents of property, requiring no easement to support it, and can be countervailed only by the acquisition of an easement for that purpose by the party causing the nuisance.

2.–CUSTOM OF LONDON

8–09   In *Curriers' Co v Corbett*[20] it was argued, from air not being mentioned in section 3 of the Prescription Act, that the custom of London, as to building on an ancient foundation[21] was not affected by it so far as it related to the obstruction of air, and on this ground a formal objection was made to a decree of the Vice-Chancellor for an injunction. Turner L.J. said that he should not be disposed to come to any decision in the absence of evidence that the custom applied to air, as well as to light. In any event, it is now clear that, while not expressly mentioned, air is within section 2.[22]

---

[18] *Cable v Bryant* [1908] 1 Ch. 259; see para.3–34, above.
[19] *Wong v Beaumont Property Trust Ltd* [1965] 1 Q.B. 173; see para.3–124, above.
[20] (1865) 4 De G.J. & Sm. 764.
[21] For the extent of this custom, in relation to light, see para.7–30, above.
[22] See para.8–06, above.

CHAPTER 9

RIGHTS OF WAY

1.—NATURE OF RIGHTS OF WAY

Different kinds of ways

Rights of way are at once the most familiar and the most important of the class **9–01** of affirmative easements, which impose upon the owner of the servient tenement the obligation to submit to something being done within the limits of his own property.

Rights of this nature are susceptible of almost infinite variety: they may be limited as to the intervals at which they may be used—as a right to be exercised during daylight,[1] or (formerly) as a way for a parson to carry away his tithe.[2] Again, they may be limited as to the actual extent of user authorised—as a footway, horseway, carriageway, or driftway. Or they may be limited as to the purposes for which they may be exercised; thus there may be a way for agricultural purposes only,[3] or for the carriage of coals only,[4] or for the carriage of all articles except coals.[5]

---

[1] *Collins v Slade* (1874) 23 W.R. 199.
[2] *James v Dods* (1834) 2 Cr. & M. 266.
[3] *Reignolds v Edwards* (1741) Willes 282.
[4] *Iveson v Moore* (1700) 1 Ld.Raym. 486.
[5] *Stafford v Coyney* (1827) 7 B. & C. 257. See also *Tomlin v Fuller* (1681) 1 Mod. 27; *Jackson v Stacey* (1816) Holt N.P.C. 455; *Bidder v North Staffordshire Ry* (1878) 4 Q.B.D. 412.

There may be both a private right of way and a public highway over the same road.[6] A private right of way is not necessarily destroyed either by the public acquiring a right of way over the same road[7] or by a public highway over the same road being extinguished by an order of a magistrates' court under section 116 of the Highways Act 1980[8] or by a private Act.[9] The existence of a right of way over common land is not inconsistent with the land being "common land" within the meaning of section 22(1) of the Commons Registration Act 1965.[10]

Excessive user

9–02   It is critical to determine the extent of the right which the dominant owner is entitled to enjoy. User which goes beyond the right will amount to a trespass on the servient land. Conversely, one cannot determine whether an act done by the servient owner constitutes actionable interference with the right until the precise scope of the right has been determined. User which goes beyond the right is generally termed "excessive", but confusion often arises because the different reasons for user being "excessive" are not always distinguished. It is suggested that it is helpful to break this topic down by asking a series of questions:

1. What is the physical extent of the way?
2. What mode of use (i.e., on foot, vehicular) is permitted?
3. Is the way being used to gain access to land other than the dominant tenement?
4. Is use limited to any particular purpose?
5. Are there any other limitations on the manner of use, such as frequency, times, size or weight of vehicles?
6. Does the use being made of the way interfere with the legitimate rights of others similarly entitled?

These questions arise both in the case of easements acquired by use and those acquired by grant but the approach to answering them and the applicable rules are very different in each case. The extent of a right acquired by user is measured by the extent and purpose of the user on which the acquisition of the right was based, but the extent of a right acquired by express grant depends on the terms of the grant properly construed in the light of all relevant factors. The extent of a right acquired by implied grant is governed by considerations similar to those governing a right acquired by use.[11]

---

[6] *Brownlow v Tomlinson* (1840) 1 Man. & G. 484; *Att-Gen v Esher Linoleum Co Ltd* [1901] 2 Ch. 647; *Pullin v Deffel* (1891) 64 L.T. 134.

[7] *Duncan v Louch* (1845) 6 Q.B. 904; *R. v Chorley* (1848) 12 Q.B. 515.

[8] *Walsh v Oates* [1953] 1 Q.B. 578 (a case under the Highway Act 1835, s.91 (since repealed)).

[9] *Wells v London, Tilbury and Southend Ry* (1877) 5 Ch. D. 126.

[10] *Land in Weston, Northamptonshire, Re* Ref. No. 26/D/29 (Commons Commissioners) [1972] C.L.Y. 352.

[11] *McAdams Homes Limited v Robinson* [2004] EWCA Civ 214; [2004] 3 E.G.L.R. 93.

2. — EXTENT OF RIGHTS OF WAY ACQUIRED BY USER

The relevant principle

Where a right of way is acquired by user, since user is not continuous and may **9–03** vary, there may be difficulty in determining the scope of the right acquired. The general rule is that, where a right of way is acquired by user, the extent of the right must be measured by the extent of the user.[12] Although *Coke*[13] classified ways into an ascending hierarchy of footway, packway or driftway and cartway, each category including and extending those below, there is no presumption in English law that by establishing a particular right one necessarily becomes entitled to the lesser rights on the principle that the greater includes the lesser. So a right to drive vehicles does not necessarily include the right to drive cattle.[14]

There is not, then, in English law any positive division of rights of way into distinct classes. Applying the general principle that every easement is a restriction of the rights of property of the party over whose lands it is exercised, the real question appears to be, on the peculiar facts of each case, whether proof has been given of a right coextensive with that amount of inconvenience sought to be imposed by the right claimed. It is obvious that, in some cases, a right to drive cattle might be productive of greater inconvenience than a right to drive carts, and vice versa. It will, therefore, be for the court to infer the extent of the supposed grant from the actual amount of injury proved under all circumstances attending it. If it appeared that the way had been used for all the purposes required by the claimant, there would be strong evidence of a general right, while, on the other hand, proof that the party, having occasion for a particular use, had not made that use of the way in question, would be almost conclusive evidence that he had not a right of way for that particular purpose.

This statement of principle is supported by *Cowling v Higginson*[15] where it was **9–04** held that proof of user for farming purposes did not necessarily prove a right of way for the purpose of conveying coal, the produce of a mine lying under the defendant's land. In the course of the argument, Lord Abinger C.B. observed[16]:

> "The extent of the right must depend upon the circumstances. If a road led through a park, the jury might naturally infer the right to be limited; but if it went over a common, they might infer that it was a way for all purposes. Using a road as a footpath would not prove a general right; nor proof that a

---

[12] *Finch v Great Western Ry* (1879) 5 Ex.D. 254 at 258; *Mills v Silver* [1991] Ch. 271.

[13] Co.Litt. 56A. For text of this passage, see 16th ed. of this work at para.9–03.

[14] *Ballard v Dyson* (1808) 1 Taunt. 279. A full account of this case is given in the 16th edition of this work at para.9–04. *Ballard v Dyson* was applied by the Court of Appeal in *British Railways Board v Glass* [1965] Ch. 538, a case where there was an express grant, the court taking the view that the words "with all manner of cattle" enlarged rather than limited the nature of the right granted, a driftway for cattle being a more onerous right than a mere right of way with horses and carts.

[15] (1838) 4 M. & W. 245.

[16] (1838) 4 M. & W. 245 at 252.

party had used a road to go to church only. Some analogy should be shewn between farming and mining purposes."

In his judgment, Lord Abinger C.B. said[17]:

> "I do not give any opinion upon the effect of the evidence; but I should certainly say that it is not a necessary inference of law, that a way for agricultural purposes is a way for all purposes, but that is a question for the jury in each particular case. . . . If a way has been used for several purposes, there may be a ground for inferring that there is a right of way for all purposes; but if the evidence shews a user for one purpose, or for particular purposes only, an inference of a general right would hardly be presumed."[18]

It is settled that proof of user with horses and carts will establish a right of user with mechanically propelled vehicles.[19]

Purposes of user: alteration of dominant tenement

9–05   Where there is an alteration in the dominant tenement the question arises whether the fact of user, over a long period, for the purposes of the dominant tenement as it was during that period establishes a right of user for additional or new purposes of the dominant tenement in its altered state. Speaking generally, and subject to considerations of degree, the answer appears to be in the negative. In *Williams v James*,[20] which was a case of alleged excessive user of a prescriptive way, the decision being that user for the purpose of carting hay grown on land adjoining the dominant tenement was not, in the circumstances, colourable or excessive, Bovill C.J. said[21]:

> "In all cases of this kind which depend upon user the right acquired must be measured by the extent of the enjoyment which is proved. When a right of

---

[17] (1838) 4 M. & W. 245 at 255, 256, the language of Parke B., both in the course of the argument (at 251–254) and in his judgment (at 256, 257), suggests that he thought that evidence of use of a way generally would support a right to use it for all purposes, but in *Wimbledon and Putney Commons Conservators v Dixon* (1875) 1 Ch. D. 362 at 371 (see para.9–06, below), Mellish L.J. expressed the view that Parke B. did not have present to his mind the question of a change in the dominant tenement. Mellish L.J. preferred the language of Lord Abinger, adding that user of a way for purposes connected with the occupation of the land in its existing state might be considered to be a user for Lord Abinger's "particular purposes".

[18] *cf. Dare v Heathcote* (1856) 25 L.J.Ex. 245. Today it is, of course, in the absence of a jury, a question for the judge.

[19] *Lock v Abercester Ltd* [1939] Ch. 861. The grounds of this decision, though not the decision itself, may be respectfully questioned; for it appears to have been decided or assumed that a right to user with horses and carts was sufficiently established, for the purposes of the Prescription Act, s.2, by proof of user for a period ending, not at the commencement of the action, but about eight years before. Contrast *R.P.C. Holdings Ltd v Rogers* [1953] 1 All E.R. 1029 at 1031; and see the Prescription Act 1832, s.4, and para.4–39, above; para.12–101, below. See also *Att-Gen v Hodgson* [1922] 2 Ch. 429.

[20] (1867) L.R. 2 C.P. 577. *Cf. Bradburn v Morris* (1876) 3 Ch. D. 812.

[21] (1867) L.R. 2 C.P. 577 at 580.

way to a piece of land is proved, then that is, unless something appears to the contrary, a right of way for all purposes according to the ordinary and reasonable user to which that land might be applied at the time of the supposed grant. Such a right cannot be increased so as to affect the servient tenement by imposing upon it any additional burthen."

Willes J. said[22]:

"I agree ... that ... where a way has to be proved by user, you cannot extend the purposes for which the way may be used, or for which it might be reasonably inferred that parties would have intended it to be used. ... To be a legitimate user of the right of way, it must be used for the enjoyment of the nine acre field, and not colourably for other closes. I quite agree also with the argument that the right of way can only be used for the field in its ordinary use as a field. The right could not be used for a manufactory built upon the field. The use must be the reasonable use for the purposes of the land in the condition in which it was while the user took place."

In *Wimbledon and Putney Commons Conservators v Dixon*,[23] where the user   **9–06**
proved was a user for farming purposes only—except for two or three slight circumstances, the enlargement of a farmhouse, the replacing of a mud cottage by a brick cottage, and apparently the taking away of gravel—the court declined to presume a grant of a way for all purposes, and restrained the defendant from carting building materials for a new house. The Lords Justices, affirming Lord Jessel M.R., held that the property could not be so changed as substantially to increase or alter the burden upon the servient tenement. James L.J. said[24]:

"I am satisfied that the true principle is ... that you cannot from evidence of user of a privilege connected with the enjoyment of property in its original state, infer a right to use it, into whatsoever form or for whatever purpose that property may be changed, that is to say, if a right of way to a field be proved by evidence of user, however general, for whatever purpose, qua field, the person who is the owner of that field cannot from that say, I have a right to turn that field into a manufactory, or into a town, and then use the way for the purposes of the manufactory or town so built."

Mellish L.J.[25] expressed the opinion that the true rule was that laid down by Bovill C.J. and Willes J. in *Williams v James*,[26] that is to say,

---

[22] (1867) L.R. 2 C.P. 577 at 582.
[23] (1875) 1 Ch. D. 362. *Cf.* the dicta of North J. in *New Windsor (Mayor) v Stovell* (1884) 27 Ch. D. 665 at 672.
[24] (1875) 1 Ch. D. 362 at 368.
[25] (1875) 1 Ch. D. 362 at 370, 371.
[26] (1867) L.R. 2 C.P. 577 at 580, 582, above. See also *Cargill v Gotts* [1981] 1 W.L.R. 441, where the Court of Appeal applied the principle in *Williams v James* and *R.C.P. Holdings Ltd v Rogers* [1953] 1 All E.R. 1035, to a right to take water: see para.6–40, above.

"that when a right of way to a piece of land is proved, then that is, unless something appears to the contrary, a right of way for all purposes according to the ordinary and reasonable use to which that land might be applied at the time of the supposed grant".

Where, however, a right of way to a dwelling-house had been acquired by user, there was no excess of user by opening a small shop.[27]

9–07   The question came again before the court in *R.P.C. Holdings Ltd v Rogers*.[28] There the plaintiff sought to restrain the defendant from trespassing on a track passing over the plaintiff's golf course to the defendant's field. The defendant had recently established on this field, and was about to enlarge, a camping site for caravans. The defendant proved that from about 1880 down to a few years before the commencement of the action the track had been used for the ordinary agricultural purposes of the field, and on this ground[29] he established a right of way by prescription at common law. The question then arose whether this right was a right to use the track for agricultural purposes only, or a right to use it for all purposes, including the purposes of the camping site. Harman J., after considering *Cowling v Higginson*,[30] *Williams v James*[31] and *Wimbledon and Putney Commons Conservators v Dixon*,[32] decided against the defendant. He said[33]:

"It seems to me as a result of these three authorities that the question of the extent of the right is one which I as a juryman have got to determine, but that I am not to conclude from the mere fact that while the property was in one state the way was for all purposes for which it was wanted, therefore, that is a general right exercisable for totally different purposes which only came into existence at a later date. Sitting as a juryman I can feel no doubt that the way here was a way limited to agricultural purposes, and that to extend it to the use proposed would be an unjustifiable increase of the burden of the easement."

9–08   In *British Railways Board v Glass*[34] the Court of Appeal by a majority (Harman and Davies L.JJ., Lord Denning M.R. dissenting) held that the defendant had acquired a prescriptive right to use a level-crossing over the plaintiff's railway for the purposes of a caravan site which was situate in a field on the north side of the railway line. The plaintiff on the pleadings admitted that the whole of the field

---

[27] *Sloan v Holliday* (1874) 30 L.T. 757.
[28] [1953] 1 All E.R. 1029. See also *Ward (Helston) Ltd v Kerrier District Council* [1984] R.V.R. 18 (right of way limited to use in connection with a slaughterhouse).
[29] See para.4–05, above.
[30] (1838) 4 M. & W. 245.
[31] (1867) L.R. 2 C.P. 577.
[32] (1875) 1 Ch. D. 362.
[33] [1953] 1 All E.R. 1035 at 1036. See also *Ironside, Crabb and Crabb v Cook, Cook and Barefoot* (1981) 41 P. & C.R. 326.
[34] [1965] Ch. 538.

constituted the site. Over the years there had been a substantial increase in the number of caravans using the site, but Harman and Davies L.JJ. held, applying *Williams v James*,[35] that, no radical change having occurred in the character of the dominant tenement, the mere increase in the number of caravans using the site and the consequent increase in the user of the crossing did not amount to an excessive user of the prescriptive right, and there had been no such increase in the burden of the easement as would justify the plaintiff in seeking an injunction. Saying that if there were a radical change in the character of the dominant tenement, then the prescriptive right would not extend to it in that condition, Harman L.J.[36] instanced a change of a small dwelling-house to a large hotel.

In *Woodhouse & Co Ltd v Kirkland (Derby) Ltd*[37] Plowman J. found that the   **9–09** plaintiff had established a prescriptive right of way over a passageway owned by the defendant for the plaintiff's reasonable business purposes and that this extended to, inter alia, use by its customers, the identity of the persons using the passage for such business purposes being immaterial. The user by the plaintiff's customers had greatly increased, but Plowman J. held, applying *British Railways Board v Glass*,[38] that there had been no excessive user, since the user had not been of a different kind or for a different purpose. His Lordship found it unnecessary on the facts to consider whether an increase in user, if very great, could ever of itself amount to excessive user.

In *Giles v County Building Constructors (Hertford) Ltd*[39] the defendant   **9–10** intended to demolish two houses on the dominant tenement and to erect thereon a three-storey block of six flats, a bungalow and seven garages which would be served by a vehicular right of way, which had been acquired by prescription. It was held that this development did not involve a radical change in the character of, nor a change of identity of, the dominant tenement and so did not involve excessive user of the right of way.

The same approach was applied, by analogy, in *Mills v Silver*,[40] where it was   **9–11** held that a lost grant of a right of way was to be presumed over a rough track across a hill farm, which track used to be impassable with vehicles in wet weather. The question arose whether the dominant owner was entitled to improve it by putting down several hundred tons of stone. Dillon L.J. said[41]:

"A prescriptive right of way differs from a right of way by express grant in that the extent of a prescriptive right of way is limited by the nature of the user from which it has arisen. . . . If the dominant owner under a prescriptive

---

[35] (1867) L.R. 2 C.P. 577.
[36] [1965] Ch. 562. A further example of a radical change is supplied by *Maiden Farm Ltd v Nicholson* (1956) 3 D.L.R. (2d) 236, a case dealing with an express grant; it was held there was excessive user when the defendant had built a beach resort on the dominant tenement and the private right of way was being used by hundreds of members of the public.
[37] [1970] 1 W.L.R. 1185.
[38] [1965] Ch. 538.
[39] (1971) 22 P. & C.R. 978.
[40] [1991] Ch. 271.
[41] [1991] Ch. 271, at 287B.

grant cannot increase the burden on the servient tenement by building further
buildings—e.g. additional houses—on the dominant tenement, I do not see
why he should be entitled to increase the burden on the servient tenement by
building a made road over the servient tenement, so as to make the way
usable at times of the year and in weather conditions when it was not passable before."

9–12   In *Attwood v Bovis Homes Limited*,[42] the defendants were proposing to build
1,000 houses on what had been farmland, in favour of which an easement of
drainage through ditches over the plaintiff's land had been acquired by prescription. Neuberger J. tentatively suggested[43] that the rule as to rights of way

> ... "may be that, if there is a subsequent radical change in the use of the
> dominant tenement, a right of way acquired by prescription can only con-
> tinue to be used in connection with the dominant tenement if the Court can
> be satisfied that the change cannot result in the use of the way being greater
> in quantum or different in character from that which it was [for the period
> establishing the prescriptive right]. The onus would be on the owner of the
> dominant tenement, and would, I suspect, normally be difficult to satisfy in
> relation to a right of way."

9–13   The purpose to be served by a prescriptive right is determined likewise by the
purpose for which the way was used during the whole period relied on to establish it. A change during the prescription period will not be material. In *Loder v
Gaden*,[44] a right of way for all purposes was claimed over a lane in proceedings
begun in 1996. Until 1977 the dominant land had been used only for agricultural
purposes and it was accepted that there were rights over the lane for those purposes. Subsequently and with growing intensity the land was used as a haulage
depot. Since nothing had happened before 1977 to give any hint to the owner of
the land that a use was being established other than that of agricultural land, it
was held that the right was limited to that purpose.

9–14   The extent of an easement acquired by user was considered in detail by the
Court of Appeal in the important case of *McAdams Homes Limited v Robinson*.[45]
This case concerned a right acquired by an implied grant rather than by prescription but it was said that, at least in the great majority of cases, there should be
little difference in the principles applicable to the two types of case.[46] The case
concerned a right of drainage rather than a right of way but the leading right of
way cases in this area were considered in detail and were relied upon for the
purpose of stating general principles which apply both to rights of way and other
easements.

---

[42] [2001] Ch. 379.
[43] [2001] Ch. 379, at 388D.
[44] (1999) 78 P. & C.R. 223.
[45] [2004] EWCA Civ 214; [2004] 3 E.G.L.R. 93.
[46] [2004] EWCA Civ 214, at [22] and [79].

The first judgment in *McAdams Homes* was given by Neuberger L.J. He held   **9–15**
that the cases established the following propositions:

(1)   where the dominant land is used for a particular purpose at the time an
easement is created, an increase, even if substantial, in the intensity of
that use, resulting in a concomitant increase in the use of the easement,
cannot of itself be objected to by the servient owner[47];

(2)   excessive use of an easement by the dominant land will render the
dominant owner liable in nuisance; in most cases where the extent, and
even the nature, of the grant is in dispute the question of excessive user
will be unhelpful because one can only determine whether the use is
excessive once one has decided the extent of the grant;

(3)   where there is a change in the use of or the erection of new buildings
on the dominant land, without having any effect on the nature or extent
of the use of the easement, the change, however radical, will not affect
the right of the dominant owner to use the easement[48];

(4)   a number of cases bear on the converse question, namely, the effect of a
change in the use of the dominant tenement which results, or may result,
in an alteration in the manner or extent of the use of the easement[49];

(5)   the issue as to the extent of an easement acquired by implied grant or
by prescription should be determined by answering two questions;

(6)   the first question was: whether the development of the dominant land
represented a "radical change in the character" or a "change in the
identity" of the dominant land as opposed to a mere change or intensification in the use of the dominant land;

(7)   the second question was: whether the use of the dominant land as redeveloped would result in a substantial increase or alteration in the burden on the servient land;

(8)   it is only if the redevelopment of the dominant land resulted in a radical change in its character and would lead to a substantial increase in
the burden that the dominant owner's right to enjoy the easement
would be suspended or lost;

(9)   where both requirements are satisfied, the dominant owner's right to
enjoy the easement will be ended, or at least suspended, so long as the
radical change of character and substantial increase in burden are
maintained;

---

[47] See *British Railways Board v Glass* [1965] Ch. 538 and *Cargill v Gotts* [1981] 1 W.L.R. 441.

[48] See *Luttrel's Case* (1601) 4 Co. Rep. 86a; *Watts v Kelson* (1870) 6 Ch. App. 166; *Atwood v Bovis Homes Limited* [2001] Ch. 371, and *Harvey v Walters* (1873) L.R. 8 C.P. 162.

[49] These cases included *Williams v James* (1867) L.R. 2 C.P. 577; *Wood v Saunders* (1875) 10 Ch. App. 582; *Wimbledon and Putney Commons Conservators v Dixon* (1875) 1 Ch. D. 362; *Milner's Safe Company Limited v Great Northern & City Railway Company* [1907] 1 Ch. 208; *R.P.C. Holdings Limited v Rogers* [1953] 1 All E.R. 1029; *British Railways Board v Glass*; [1965] Ch. 538; *Giles v County Building Constructors (Hertford) Limited* (1971) 22 P. & C.R. 978; and *Ray v Fairway Motors (Barnstaple) Limited* (1968) 20 P. & C.R. 261.

(10) although not all the cases were entirely consistent and clear, the above approach was principled, consistent and coherent;

(11) it was a potentially unsatisfactory feature of the principles that both questions might be said to involve an exercise which may have a rather uncertain outcome; the questions had to be expressed in a generalised way and each case would very much turn on its own facts, with regard to the particular easement, the position on the ground at the date of the grant, the surrounding circumstances at the date of grant, and the nature and effect of the redevelopment that has subsequently taken place.[50]

Neuberger L.J. then applied these principles to the facts of the case; as the case concerned a right of drainage rather than a right of way, the application of the principles to the facts is considered at para.6–94, above.

9–16   Nourse L.J. gave the second judgment. He made the following observations about the authorities:

(1) in general, authorities on prescriptive easements apply equally to implied easements and vice versa;

(2) in general, authorities on rights of way apply equally to rights of drainage;

(3) the authorities on rights of way from *Williams v James* onwards establish that the right impliedly granted or prescriptively acquired is a right for all purposes according to the ordinary and reasonable use to which the dominant tenement might be applied at the time of the implied or supposed grant;

(4) the authorities on rights of way subsequent to *Williams v James* fall into two broad categories; first, those where there has been a change in the character of the dominant tenement leading to a substantial increase in the burden of the easement, in which cases use of the right has been restrained; second, those in which there has been no such change but a considerable increase in the use of the right in which cases the use has been allowed to continue;

(5) in the first category of case are *Wimbledon and Putney Commons Conservators v Dixon* and *R.P.C. Holdings Limited v Rogers*; in the second category of case are *British Railways Board v Glass*, *Giles v County Building Constructors (Hertford) Limited* and *Cargill v Gotts*.

9–17   Peter Gibson L.J. gave a short judgment which concentrated on the fact that the right arose pursuant to an implied grant. The grant of the easement was to correspond to the facility which the grantor himself found necessary to use at the time of the implied grant. To determine whether the subsequent user is excessive, comparison must be made with what was the user at the time of the implied grant. The question was one of fact and degree.

---

[50] This comment was made in the context of a case which involved an implied grant and the comment needs adaptation in a case where one is concerned with an easement acquired by prescription.

3.—EXTENT OF RIGHTS OF WAY ACQUIRED BY GRANT

(1) *Construction of the grant and physical extent*

In the case of an express grant the language of the instrument must be referred to. **9–18**
The court will have regard to the conveyance as a whole, including any plan that
forms part of it, even though the plan is not mentioned in the parcels clause or is
said to be for identification purposes only.[51]

Moreover the plan may be referred to to establish the intention of the parties as
to the use to which the land is to be put.[52] Where the dimensions of the way are
defined by reference to a driveway to be constructed pursuant to a covenant in the
conveyance, the extent of the grant may be ascertained from the terms of the
covenant.[53] It is for the court to construe that language in the light of the circumstances.[54] These may include the terms of a planning permission, being a public
document available to a purchaser; a conveyance should be construed on the footing that neither party intends that it should involve the vendor in any infringement
of his planning obligations.[55] It may also be permissible to look at the contract for
sale in a case where the conveyance is not clear, at least in a case where it is
referred to in the recitals to the conveyance.[56]

The circumstances may also include the physical characteristics of the land at **9–19**
the date of the grant which may help determine both the physical extent of the
servient land and the mode of user intended. It has been said that the question of
construction must always be approached by reading the text of the grant in a practical way, looking at the geographical and commercial realities.[57] However, a
right of way expressly granted is not necessarily limited by the physical characteristics of the site of the easement at the time of the grant; the language of the
grant may be such that the topographical circumstances cannot properly be
regarded as restricting the scope of the grant according to the language of it.[58] In
West v Sharp, a grant of a right of way over and along a piece of land marked
"reserved for road" and coloured brown on a plan which showed a 40-foot wide
strip coloured brown was held to confer a right of way over the whole strip, not
limited to the width of the track existing on the strip at the date of grant or the
tarmac surface later added to it.

In the absence of any clear indication of the intention of the parties, the maxim **9–20**
that a grant must be construed most strongly against a grantor must be applied.[59]
But a question of construction is a question of law in respect of which no burden

---

[51] *Scott v Martin* [1987] 1 W.L.R. 841.
[52] *Stafford v Lee* (1992) 65 P. & C.R. 172.
[53] *Soper v Leeman-Hawley* [1992] N.P.C. 95.
[54] *Callard v Beeney* [1930] 1 K.B. 353.
[55] *Scott v Martin* (above) at 849H–850A.
[56] *Peacock v Custins* [2001] 2 All E.R. 827 at [31].
[57] *Hillman v Rogers* [1987] N.P.C. 183, per Robert Walker L.J.
[58] *West v Sharp* (2000) 79 P. & C.R. 327, per Mummery L.J. at 332, applying *Keefe v Amor* [1965] 1
Q.B. 334.
[59] *Williams v James* (1867) L.R. 2 C.P. 577 at 581: *Wood v Saunders* (1875) 10 Ch. App. 584N.

of proof lies on either side.[60] In particular, in construing a grant the court will consider (1) the *locus in quo* over which the way is granted; (2) the nature of the *terminus ad quem*; and (3) the purpose for which the way is to be used.[61]

9–21   *Partridge v Lawrence*[62] concerned the width of a right of way created by an express grant. The deed of grant stated that the width of the way was to be no greater and no less than the width on an annexed plan. The plan was an identified architect's plan but the annexed plan was distorted in photocopying and had no recognisable scale. It was held that the court was entitled to consider the original architect's plan from which it was clear that the width of the way was to be 5.5m. The Court of Appeal commented on the earlier case of *Scarfe v Adams*,[63] where it had been suggested that it was not permissible to admit extrinsic evidence where the terms of the deed appeared to be clear. It was stated in *Partridge v Lawrence* that extrinsic evidence of relevant background was always admissible to assist in the construction of the deed, relying on *Investors Compensation Scheme Ltd v West Bromwich Building Society*.[64] This will not, however, include direct evidence of subjective intention or opinion evidence, both of which are inadmissible on a question of the interpretation of a document.[65]

9–22   In *Thomas v Allan*,[66] a grant in 1992, which was ambiguous as to whether the right of way extended to the verges of a track, was construed against the background of two earlier grants of 1961 and 1983, which earlier grants clearly did not include the verges, with the result that the 1992 grant was also held not to extend to the verges.

9–23   It is also relevant to refer here to *P&S Platt Ltd v Crouch*,[67] although this case concerned an implied grant and/or a grant under section 62 of the Law of Property Act 1925. The Court of Appeal restated that the approach of the court as to the admission of evidence as to background matters was that stated in *Prenn v Simmonds*[68] and that evidence of antecedent negotiations, as distinct from evidence as to the genesis and aim of the transaction, was not to be admitted. There is this further consideration that, where a document grants a proprietory right, it may be relied upon by or against persons who were not parties to the original transaction and know little or nothing of the circumstances surrounding it or the contractual context in which it was made. It is suggested that this consideration would support a relatively conservative application of the *Investors Compensation Scheme* principles.

---

[60] *Scott v Martin* (above) at 846D.

[61] *Cannon v Villars* (1878) 8 Ch. D. 415; *Bulstrode v Lambert* [1953] 1 W.L.R. 1064; *Sketchley v Burger* (1893) 69 L.T. 754. See also *Laurie v Winch* (1952) 4 D.L.R. 449.

[62] [2004] 1 P. & C.R. 14.

[63] [1981] 1 All E.R. 843 at p.851.

[64] [1998] 1 W.L.R. 896 at p.912. A stricter approach seems to be being applied in Australia under the Torrens system; see *Westfield Management v Perpetual Trustee* [2007] HCA 45 at [5] and [37]–[41], applied in *Sertari Pty Ltd v Narimba Developments Pty Ltd* [2007] NSWCA 324 at [13], where it was held that extrinsic material apart from the physical characteristics of the tenements was not relevant to the construction of instruments registered under the Real Property Act 1900.

[65] *Young v Brooks* [2008] EWCA Civ 816 at [12].

[66] [2004] S.C. 393.

[67] [2004]1 P. & C.R. 242.

[68] [1971] 1 W.L.R. 1381.

(2) *Mode of user: the relevance of the locus in quo*

The basic principle

It seems that, subject to any qualifying words in the grant, the authorised mode **9–24**
or quality of user (with or without vehicles, etc.) is as general as the physical
capacity of the *locus in quo* at the time of the grant will admit, unless in any
particular case (which must be rare) some limitation on mode of user can be
gathered from the surrounding circumstances. In *Cannon v Villars*,[69] where the
court was considering the extent of an implied right of way arising under an
agreement to grant a lease of premises for the purpose of a business, Sir George
Jessel M.R. said:

> "As I understand, the grant of a right of way per se and nothing else may be
> a right of footway, or it may be a general right of way, that is a right of way
> not only for people on foot but for people on horseback, for carts, carriages,
> and other vehicles. Which it is, is a question of construction of the grant, and
> that construction will of course depend on the circumstances surrounding, so
> to speak, the execution of the instrument. Now one of those circumstances,
> and a very material circumstance, is the nature of the locus in quo over
> which the right of way is granted. If we find a right of way granted over a
> metalled road with pavement on both sides existing at the time of the grant,
> the presumption would be that it was intended to be used for the purpose for
> which it was constructed, which is obviously the passage not only of foot-
> passengers, but of horsemen and carts. Again, if we find the right of way
> granted along a piece of land capable of being used for the passage of car-
> riages, and the grant is of a right of way to a place which is stated on the face
> of the grant to be intended to be used or to be actually used for a purpose
> which would necessarily or reasonably require the passing of carriages,
> there again it must be assumed that the grant of the right of way was
> intended to be effectual for the purpose for which the place was designed to
> be used, or was actually used.
>
> Where you find a road constructed so as to be fit for carriages and of the
> requisite width, leading up to a dwelling-house, and there is a grant of a right
> of way to that dwelling-house, it would be a grant of a right of way for all
> reasonable purposes required for the dwelling-house, and would include,
> therefore, the right to the user of carriages by the occupant of the dwelling-
> house if he wanted to take the air, or the right to have a waggon drawn up to
> the door when the waggon was to bring coals for the use of the dwelling-
> house. Again, if the road is not to a dwelling-house but to a factory, or a
> place used for business purposes which would require heavy weights to be
> brought to it, or to a wool warehouse which would require bags or packages

---

[69] (1878) 8 Ch. D. 415 at 420, 421. This dictum of Sir George Jessel M.R. was applied in *St Edmundsbury
and Ipswich Diocesan Board of Finance v Clark (No. 2)* [1975] 1 W.L.R. 468 at 476, 477.

of wool to be brought to it, then a grant of a right of way would include a right to use it for reasonable purposes, sufficient for the purposes of the business, which would include the right of bringing up carts and waggons at reasonable times for the purpose of the business.[70] That again would afford an indication in favour of the extent of the grant. If, on the other hand, you find that the road in question over which the grant was made was paved only with flagstones, and that it was only four or five feet wide, over which a waggon or cart or carriage ordinarily constructed could not get, and that it was only a way used to a field or close, or something on which no erection was, there, I take it, you would say that the physical circumstances showed that the right of way was a right for foot-passengers only. It might include a horse under some circumstances, but could not be intended for carts or carriages. Of course where you find restrictive words in the grant, that is to say, where it is only for the use of foot-passengers, stated in express terms, or for foot-passengers and horsemen, and so forth, there is nothing to argue. I take it that is the law. Prima facie the grant of a right of way is the grant of a right of way having regard to the nature of the road over which it is granted and the purpose for which it is intended to be used; and both those circumstances may be legitimately called in aid in determining whether it is a general right of way, or a right of way restricted to foot-passengers, or restricted to foot-passengers and horsemen or cattle, which is generally called a drift-way, or a general right of way for carts, horses, carriages, and everything else."

9–25   *Todrick v Western National Omnibus Co*[71] was a case in which the quality of the user was limited by the physical characteristics of the way. It was held that the grant of a right of way, with or without vehicles, over a road seven feet nine inches wide at its entrance, supported by a retaining wall, and clearly not intended for heavy vehicles, did not authorise user by motorbuses.

9–26   In *Watts v Kelson*[72] and *Robinson v Bailey*[73] it was admitted that a grant in general terms of "a right of way" authorised user with vehicles; and it is submitted that the true principle appears in the passage in the judgment of Jenkins J. in *Kain v Norfolk*,[74] where he says:

"[Counsel] says, and I think he is supported by authority, that a right given to the grantee of property at all times hereafter to go, pass and repass over

---

[70] See *Bulstrode v Lambert* [1953] 1 W.L.R. 1064.

[71] [1934] Ch. 190; reversed on other grounds [1934] Ch. 561; explained on this point in *Robinson v Bailey* [1948] 2 All E.R. 791. See further, para.9–64, below. See also *Cousens v Rose* (1871) L.R. 12 Eq. 366.

[72] (1870) 6 Ch. App. 166 at 170n.

[73] [1948] 2 All E.R. 791 at 793.

[74] [1949] Ch. 163 at 168. The decision in the case, which raised the question whether the grantee in 1919 of a right of way "with or without horses carts and agricultural machines and implements" was entitled to convey sand in lorries from a gravel pit subsequently opened on the dominant tenement, was not founded on the passage quoted, but on the fact that the grant, properly construed, included the right of carting loads, with any kind of "cart", including a motor lorry. See para.9–63, below.

and along a certain way without any reference to horses, carriages, carts or anything else, will, per se, unelaborated as it is, give a right of way for all purposes, that is to say, a right to pass with vehicles as well as on foot, provided that the way to which the grant refers is a way suitable at the date of the grant for use by vehicles. I think that accords with the statement of the law contained in the judgment of Jessel M.R. in Cannon v. Villars."[75]

Other decisions involving the construction of an express grant

In *Bulstrode v Lambert*,[76] a conveyance of a house and a passage or yard running alongside it and leading to a building retained by the vendor and used as an auction mart reserved a right for the vendor, his tenants and workmen and others authorised by him, to pass and repass with or without vehicles over and along the passage or yard for the purpose of obtaining access to the auction mart. Upjohn J. held that the vendor's successor in title had the right to bring vans and pantechnicons over the yard for the purpose of transporting furniture and other chattels to and from the auction mart; also the right (without causing undue inconvenience to the servient owner) to bring these vehicles to a point in the yard beyond which it was physically impossible for them to pass, and to carry the goods thence into the mart by hand; and also the right (as to which there was no previous authority) to halt the vehicles in the yard (which was a cul-de-sac) as often and for so long as might be necessary for the purpose of loading and unloading. This last-mentioned right was necessary for the enjoyment of the right reserved.[77] A right to halt to load and unload will not, however, be implied in the case of the grant of a right of way if the circumstances are such that there is no necessity to be able to do so in order to enjoy the right of access granted, as where for example there is an adequate parking or loading area on the dominant land.[78] Where, however, the grant is of the right to use the road as opposed merely to pass or repass over it, it seems that that will entitle the grantee to stop to load and unload and to use the road for all other purposes by which property adjoining a street would normally be accommodated, provided such user does not interfere unreasonably with the use of the road by its owner or those equally entitled.[79]

In *Keefe v Amor*[80] Russell L.J., delivering the leading judgment of the Court of Appeal, observed[81] that the terms of the grant in *Bulstrode v Lambert*[82] were "very

9–27

9–28

---

[75] (1878) 8 Ch. D. 415; see para.9–24, above.

[76] [1953]1 W.L.R. 1064. See also *V.T. Engineering Co Ltd v Richard Barland and Co Ltd* (1968) 19 P. & C.R. 890.

[77] See para.1–90, above. See also *Graham v Philcox* [1984] Q.B. 747, where a right to park was conceded.

[78] *London & Suburban Land & Building Co (Holdings) Limited v Carey* (1991) 69 P. & C.R. 480.

[79] *Snell & Prideaux Limited v Dutton Mirrors Limited* [1995] 1 E.G.L.R. 259 at 262M–263A and 264G.

[80] [1965] 1 Q.B. 334. The Court of Appeal considered its decision in *Dyer v Mousley* (1962) unreported, Bar Library transcript No. 315.

[81] [1965] 1 Q.B. 346.

[82] [1953] 1 W.L.R. 1064.

particular". In *Keefe v Amor*[83] the particular considerations present in the language in *Bulstrode v Lambert* were absent, but the Court of Appeal nevertheless held that on the construction of the transfer of a dwelling-house "together also with a right of way over" a strip of land some 20 feet wide and coloured brown on the plan annexed to the transfer, the right extended to vehicular traffic of any sort and was not limited by the physical characteristics of the site at the time of the grant. At that time (1930) there was at the frontage to the highway a continuous wall, except for a gap four feet six inches wide between two brick pillars. Inside, a gravelled strip eight feet wide, in appearance like a footpath rather than a roadway, led to a doorway three feet wide to the plaintiff's property and to a gap some seven feet wide leading to the remainder of the defendant's property. In 1962 the defendant had widened the entrance from the highway to about seven feet six inches wide by rehanging the original gate and hanging another, three feet wide, alongside, which she kept locked, claiming to be entitled to do so.

9–29   In *Charles v Beach*[84] a common vendor granted to the owner of the dominant tenement and reserved in the conveyance of the servient tenement the right to use "the path or roadway" lying between the two properties; at the date of the conveyances two-thirds of the "path" had been a flower-bed. The question arose whether the plaintiff was entitled to vehicular access over the whole of the "path". The Court of Appeal held that where at the date of grant there is a physical obstruction to the free enjoyment of access by the dominant owner, it is a matter of construction whether the grant is to be given a restricted meaning so as to deny access at the point of obstruction: the question is one of degree: the more transient or insubstantial the obstacle, the readier the Court will be to infer an intention to override the obstruction: the flower-bed was too transient to override or qualify the words of grant.

9–30   In *McIlraith v Grady*[85] there had been a grant in 1901 "with or without horses carts and carriages to pass and repass through over and along" a yard leading from a main road to the back of shop premises. In 1953 the shopkeeper built a small wall at the back of his premises so that thereafter vehicles stopped in the yard to load and unload. The Court of Appeal held that, just as in *Bulstrode v Lambert*,[86] there was by implication a right to halt and unload, so in the present case there was necessarily imported, in addition to an actual right to pass and repass, a right to stop for a reasonable time for the purpose of loading and unloading.

9–31   It has been held in Ireland that the grant of a right of way on foot over a passage does not authorise the grantee to have carried through the passage burdens not ordinarily carried by foot passengers in the use of a footway.[87] But where tenants of a supermarket had been granted "full and free right of way on foot

[83] [1965] 1 Q.B. 334.
[84] [1993] E.G.C.S. 124, CA.
[85] [1968] 1 Q.B. 468.
[86] [1953] 1 W.L.R. 1064.
[87] *Austin v Scottish Widows' Fund Assurance Society* (1881) 8 L.R.Ir. 385.

only" along pedestrian walkways leading to the car parks which they and their customers were also entitled to use, it was held that in the circumstances of the grant it must have been contemplated that the customers would be supplied with trolleys and that the use of the walkways by customers with trolleys was therefore not a trespass.[88]

An easement of way does not give a right to pass sewage through pipes laid **9–32** along the route of its way.[89] On the other hand, a covenant that the owners of the lands conveyed should have the full use and enjoyment of all roads "in as full, free, complete and absolute manner to all intents and purposes whatsoever as if the same were public roads" entitled them not only to the use of the roads for the purpose of transit, or for the purposes for which public roads could be used at the date of the deed, but also to authorise a gas company to open one of the roads for the purpose of laying a gas main to serve the needs of the occupiers.[90]

A way may be granted to pass either with or without vehicles. "Vehicles" has **9–33** been said to be a word of very wide import which covers all manner of vehicles, whatever their mode of propulsion[91] so the grantee of a right of footway without vehicles was not entitled to instal an inclinator, although he could build steps of a kind which would not unduly interfere with the right of the servient owner.[92] It has also been held that a right on foot includes the right to walk dogs which, provided they do not stray from the way, may be leashed or unleashed and that a vehicular right includes the right to use horse-drawn carriages and carts and horses whether ridden or led and the right to lead, but not to drive, cows and other animals on foot.[93]

(3) *The dominant tenement*

The general rule is that a right of way may only be used for gaining access to the **9–34** land identified as the dominant tenement in the grant. It was expressed thus by Romer L.J. in *Harris v Flower & Sons*[94]:

> "If a right of way be granted for the enjoyment of close A, the grantee, because he owns or acquires close B, cannot use the way in substance for passing over close A to close B."

It was said in the same case that, as every easement is a restriction upon the rights of property of the owner of the servient tenement, no alteration can be made in

---

[88] *Soames-Forsythe Properties Limited v Tesco Stores Limited* [1991] E.G.C.S. 22.
[89] *Penn v Wilkins* [1975] 2 E.G.L.R. 113.
[90] *Selby v Crystal Palace Gas Co* (1862) 4 De G.F. & J. 246.
[91] *Hanny v Lewis* (1998) 9 B.P.R. 97,702; *Kain v Norfolk* [1949] 1 Ch. 163; *Barry v Fenton* [1952] N.Z.L.R. 990; *Robmet Investments Pty Limited v Don Chen Pty Limited* (1997) 8 B.P.R. 15,461.
[92] *Hanny v Lewis* (above).
[93] *White v Richards* (1993) 68 P. & C.R. 105 at 114–115.
[94] (1904) 74 L.J.Ch. 127 at 132.

the mode of enjoyment of the dominant tenement the effect of which will be to increase such restriction beyond its legitimate limit.[95] The question, of course, is what that legitimate limit is.

9–35   *Harris v Flower and Sons* was applied by Graham J. in *Bracewell v Appleby*[96] where the defendant, who owned a house to which there was a right of way "of the fullest description", bought an adjoining plot of land and built another house on it, and was held to have no right as the owner of the dominant tenement to extend the grant of the easement to the adjoining plot.

9–36   The same principle was applied in *Jobson v Record* where a farm and farmhouse had the benefit of the grant of a right of way "for all purposes connected with the use and enjoyment of the property hereby conveyed being used as agricultural land". The grantee sought to use the road to extract timber felled on land adjoining the farm and stored on the farm. It was held that, while forestry was agricultural use, timber storage was not. Either the timber storage was a separate operation or the road was being used for the accommodation of the adjoining plantation; in either case the use being made of the way was not authorised by the grant.[97]

9–37   *Harris v Flower & Sons* was distinguished in *Graham v Philcox*.[98] There a right of way granted to the tenant of a first floor flat in a coach house passed to the purchaser of the whole building under section 62 of the Law of Property Act 1925. It was argued that, as the dominant tenement for the benefit of which the way was now claimed, namely the coach house, was greater than the dominant tenement for the benefit of which the way was originally granted, namely the first floor flat, the plaintiffs could not use the way now that the coach house was one dwelling and the two flats had been combined into one. May L.J. doubted whether excessive user ever extinguishes or suspends an easement, as opposed to entitling the servient owner to have the excessive user restrained. He also rejected the suggestion that "a mere alteration of the dominant tenement" could extinguish or affect entitlement to the use of the easement and held, applying *Wright v McAdam*, that the effect of section 62 was to annex the benefit of the easement to the whole coach house. Purchas L.J. treated the right as in effect a right to gain access to a single dwelling unit.[99] It is submitted that this case is really concerned with the operation of section 62 and does not affect the principle of the rule in *Harris v Flower & Sons*.

9–38   *Harris v Flower and Sons* was again distinguished in *National Trust v White*.[100] The National Trust had the benefit of a right of way to a historic site. It was held that they and their visitors were entitled to use the way for access to a car park on nearby land for the purpose of going on to visit the historic site. The car park was not to be treated as an enlargement of the dominant tenement.

[95]   (1904) 74 L.J.Ch. 127, at 132 per Vaughan Williams L.J.
[96]   [1975] Ch. 408.
[97]   *Jobson v Record* (1997) 75 P. & C.R. 375. See also *White v Chandler* [2001] 1 N.Z.L.R. 28.
[98]   [1984] Q.B. 747.
[99]   [1984] Q.B. 747, at 765A.
[100]   [1987] 1 W.L.R. 907; this case is further discussed at para.9–68, below.

This decision was explained by the Court of Appeal in *Das v Linden Mews Limited*[101] as a case where the use of the car park was ancillary to or part and parcel of the use of the way for the purpose of the original grant, namely getting to the historic site; this was to be distinguished from a case where what is being asserted is a right to use the way to access land that is not part of the dominant tenement. In *Das* the owners of two houses in a London mews, which enjoyed rights of way over the mews, acquired plots at the end of the mews on which they wished to park their cars. The argument that the parking of cars on the plots was ancillary to the use of the dominant tenement and that the lawful exercise of the easement extended to accommodating any use that was ancillary to use of the dominant tenement was rejected.[102] The principle seems to be that access to land which is ancillary to the use of the way for the purpose of the grant is permissible but access to land which is ancillary to the enjoyment of the dominant tenement is not.[103]

9–39

In Alvis v Harrison,[104] the party enjoying a right of access from a driveway into some woodland was entitled to construct a road through the woodland to the main road, which was not to be treated as a contiguous tenement because the dominant owner already had a right of access to the main road over the driveway; the new road would therefore merely provide a substitute means of access without altering the volume of traffic. This decision makes it clear that the reason for restricting the benefit of an easement of way to the dominant tenement alone is that to use it for the benefit of future tenements is likely to generate more traffic and so increase the burden.[105]

9–40

In *Britel v Nightfreight*,[106] a right had been granted for P "and all by its authority at all times and for all purposes in connection with the present and future use of the [grantee's land] to go pass and repass over" a road. The question was whether this extended to passage for the purpose of constructing drainage works on the dominant land intended to benefit the land of a third party. It was held that it did, because the land to which access was sought was the dominant land.

9–41

It does not, of course, follow that the mere fact that the grantee uses the way to enter close A makes close B incapable of access from close A. The question must always be whether the ostensible use of the way for the purposes of the dominant tenement is genuine or colourable: "the true point to be considered . . . should

9–42

---

[101] [2002] EWCA Civ 590 at [20]; [2003] 2 P. & C.R. 58.

[102] The opposite result was reached by the Court of Appeal in *Wall v Collins* [2007] EWCA Civ 444; [2007] 3 W.L.R. 459 at [52] where a garage on adjoining land was held to be ancillary to the ordinary residential use of the dominant tenement, applying *Massey v Boulden* [2003] 1 W.L.R. 1792; *Das v Linden Mews* was not cited. This gives rise to the possibilities that either *Das* was wrongly decided or that this part of the decision in *Wall* was decided *per incuriam*. The present editors' view is that *Das* is irreconcilable with *Massey*, see para.9–44, below.

[103] This appears to have been the ratio of the Ontario Court of Appeal in *Mackenzie v Matthews* (1999) 180 D.L.R. (4th) 674 where it was held, applying *National Trust v White* (above), that use of a right of way to get access to a vehicle turnaround on land adjoining the dominant tenement was proper but use to access a commercial building on adjoining land was not.

[104] (1990) 62 P. & C.R. 10, HL (a Scottish Appeal).

[105] (1990) 62 P. & C.R. 10, at 17.

[106] [1988] 4 All E.R. 432.

seem to be, quo animo the party went to the close; whether really and bona fide to do business there, or merely in his way to some more distant place."[107] If land is granted with a right of way, the fact that the way is expressed to be to a particular point or place on the land does not necessarily or usually prevent the right from being annexed to all the land.[108] Indeed, there is a prima facie presumption that an easement is intended to be appurtenant to the dominant tenement and every part of it.[109]

9–43   Notwithstanding the above qualifications and distinctions, the rule in *Harris v Flower and Sons* has recently been reaffirmed and explained by the Court of Appeal. In *Peacock v Custins*[110] the claimants owned a parcel of land which enjoyed the benefit of a right of way granted "at all times and for all purposes in connection with the use and enjoyment of the property hereby conveyed". They also owned an adjoining parcel. Both parcels were farmed as one unit by their tenant who used the way for the purpose of farming both parcels. The evidence was that the farmer needed to use the way about six times a year and that farming both parcels necessitated one or two more visits than farming one.

The judge at first instance refused to make a declaration that the claimants were not entitled to use the way for gaining access to the second parcel on the ground that it did not involve any significant additional user of the way. The appeal was allowed, Schiemann L.J. explaining the principle as follows:

"The right to use a right of way is determined by the terms of the grant, specifying the dominant tenement for the purposes of which the right is created. Trespass is whatever is not permitted by the grant. The right is not to use the way for the purposes of benefiting any property provided that the total user does not exceed some notional maximum user which the beneficiary might have been entitled to make for the purposes of the dominant tenement. If that were the test, the beneficiary might in some circumstances use the way entirely for purposes other than those of the dominant tenement. The right is to use the way for the purposes of the dominant tenement only. The grant, when made, had a notional value which would be identified by reference to those purposes and their likely impact. Use for other purposes would be likely to carry its own notional commercial value. The Claimants are claiming to use a way granted for the limited purposes of the 15 acres of red land for the extended or additional purpose of accessing and cultivating at the same time the further 10 acres of the blue land. That extended or additional use is of self evident commercial value to the Claimants, but any value attaching to it cannot have been embraced in the notional value attached to

---

[107] *Lawton v Ward* (1697) 1 Ld.Raym. 75, note (a). See also *Skull v Glenister* (1864) 16 C.B. (n.s.) 81 and *Harris v Flower and Sons* (1904) 74 L.J.Ch. 127. *Cf. Gordon and Regan, Re* (1985) 15 D.L.R. (4th) 641.

[108] *Callard v Beeney* [1930] 1 K.B. 353; see para.1–12, above. As to the identification of the dominant tenement, see para.1–10, above.

[109] *Short v Patrial Holdings Pty Ltd* (1994) 6 B.P.R. 97534 per Meagher J.A.

[110] [2001] 2 All E.R. 827.

the actual right of way for the benefit of the red land . . . The authorities . . . confirm that, where a Court is being asked to declare whether the right to use a way comprises a right to use it to facilitate the cultivation of land other than the dominant tenement, the Court is not concerned with any comparison between the amount of use made or to be made of the servient tenement and the amount of use made or that might lawfully be made within the scope of the grant. It is concerned with declaring the scope of the grant, having regard to its purposes and the identity of the dominant tenement. The authorities indicate that the burden on the owner of the servient tenement is not to be increased without his consent. But burden in this context does not refer to the number of journeys or the weight of the vehicles. Any use of the way is, in contemplation of law, a burden and one must ask whether the grantor agreed to the grantee making use of the way for that purpose."

In *Massey v Boulden*[111] the Court of Appeal held that the result of section 34 of the Road Traffic Act 1988 was that no right of way had been acquired by prescription. That decision was disapproved by the House of Lords in *Bakewell Management Ltd v Brandwood*.[112] However, the Court in *Massey v Boulden* went on to consider the further point as to whether, if a right of way had been acquired, it could be used only for the purpose of accessing a specific piece of land. The facts were that, for a prescriptive period exceeding 20 years, the way had been used to access a residential property. For a period just some two months' short of 20 years, the residential property had been occupied together with two rooms upon an adjoining property. If it were necessary to consider the two rooms as a separate dominant tenement, no right had been acquired by prescription for such a dominant tenement as the relevant period of user was just short of 20 years. The Court of Appeal accepted a submission that the critical question was whether the use made of the two rooms was more than merely ancillary to the use made of the original residential property. On the facts, it was held that the use of the two rooms was merely ancillary to the original residential property. **9–44**

The difficult task of reconciling the earlier decisions was attempted by the deputy judge in *Macepark (Whittlebury) Ltd v Sargant*.[113] He summarised the law as follows: **9–45**

    a)   An easement must be used for the benefit of the dominant land.

    b)   It must not "in substance" be used for the benefit of non-dominant land.

    c)   Under the "ancillary" doctrine, use is not "in substance" use for the benefit of the non-dominant land if (1) there is no benefit to the non-dominant land or if (2) the extent of the use for the benefit of the non-dominant land is insubstantial, i.e. it can still be said that in substance the access is used for the benefit of the dominant land and not for the benefit of both the dominant and the non-dominant land.

[111] [2003] 1 W.L.R. 1792.
[112] [2004] 2 A.C. 519.
[113] [2003] 1 W.L.R. 2284.

   d) "Benefit" in this context includes use of an access in such a way that a profit may be made out of the use of the non-dominant land, e.g. as a result of an arrangement with the owner of the dominant land.

   e) The application of these principles can involve potentially difficult questions of fact and degree.

It was also held in *Macepark* that the principles applied in the same way whether or not the non-dominant land was in the same ownership as the dominant land.[114] On the facts in *Macepark*, it was held that the dominant owner could not use the right of way for the benefit of land other than the dominant land.

9–46   In *Westfield Management Ltd v Perpetual Trustee Company Ltd*[115] a right of way had been created over a site in the centre of Sydney known as Glasshouse to an adjoining site called Skygarden. The owners of Skygarden sought declarations that they were entitled to use the way to gain access to two sites which they had acquired and which adjoined Skygarden and which they wished to redevelop together with Skygarden. The grant was of "full and free right of carriageway . . . to go, pass and repass at all times and for all purposes with vehicles to and from the lots benefited [Skygarden] across the lots burdened [Glasshouse]." It was held (unsurprisingly) by the High Court of Australia that "to and from" did not mean "to and from and across" and that "for all purposes" "encompassed all ends sought to be achieved by those utilising the easement in accordance with its terms", i.e. to get to and from Skygarden alone.[116]

9–47   In *Wilkins v Lewis*[117] there was an express grant of a right of way through the grounds of a house "in connection with the use of Morghew Park Estate as an agricultural and forestry estate". At the date of the conveyance the Estate comprised some 1,200 acres but a further 800 acres were subsequently added. Questions arose (inter alia) as to whether the way could be used:

   a) To obtain access to the 800 acres.

   b) To gain access to commercial shoots held on the estate.

   c) To bring produce grown outside the estate for storage on the estate.

   d) To gain access to a farm shop on the estate.

It was held (a) that to use the way for the purpose of farming land other than that comprised in the original estate was outside the purpose of the grant[118]; (b) that although conducting commercial shoots was not an agricultural activity, the grant covered activities that could be regarded as intrinsic to, or part and parcel of the

---

[114] See also *Alvis v Harrison* (1990) 62 P. & C.R. 10 at 15–16.

[115] [2007] HCA 45. The case is of interest because of the Court's robust rejection of extrinsic evidence in a dispute involving a registered title. For the approach in England see para.9–21, above. The evidence in *Westfield* appears to have been evidence of subjective intent, which would not have been admissible in England either.

[116] [2007] HCA 45, at [30].

[117] [2005] EWHC 1710 (Ch.).

[118] [2005] EWHC 1710, at [30].

running of an agricultural estate to the extent that they made use either of the fact that the land was devoted to agriculture or of the agricultural produce of the estate and were conducted on such a scale that the estate did not lose its character as an agricultural estate[119]; (c) that accordingly access for shooting only on the original estate and running a stall selling produce grown exclusively on the original estate were within the grant[120]; but (d) that using the way as an access to buildings used to store produce from off the estate was not.[121]

(4) *Purpose and quantity of user*

Subject always to the principle discussed above, it appears now to be settled that, subject to any restriction to be gathered from the words of the grant or the surrounding circumstances, a right of way may be used, in the manner authorised by the grant,[122] for any purpose and to any extent for the time being required for the enjoyment of the dominant tenement or any part of it, irrespective of the purpose for which the dominant tenement was used at the date of the grant.[123] It would seem, also, that user of an authorised kind, for example with vehicles, may be had, at least if that particular kind of user is expressly authorised, to any increased extent which the physical state of the *locus in quo* will for the time being allow.[124] It is still a question, however, whether a description, in the grant, of the *terminus ad quem* limits the dominant owner to user for the purposes of that *terminus* as it was at the time.   **9–48**

Allan v Gomme,[125] which was an action of trespass, used to be quoted to support the view that the right to use a way is confined to the use of it for the purposes of the dominant tenement in the condition in which such tenement was at the time of the grant. It appeared that the defendant, having by express reservation a right of way over the plaintiff's premises to a stable and loft on his own land, and to a "space or opening under the said loft and then used as a wood-house", converted the loft and the space thereunder into a cottage, and claimed to use the way as appurtenant to the cottage. A verdict having been found for the plaintiff, the defendant obtained a rule *nisi* for a nonsuit, which was discharged by the Exchequer   **9–49**

---

[119] [2005] EWHC 1710, at [42]–[48]; a formulation designed to exclude ballooning, go-karting, gift shop and café.

[120] [2005] EWHC 1710, at [49].

[121] [2005] EWHC 1710, at [49]–[50].

[122] See para.9–24, above.

[123] *White v Grand Hotel, Eastbourne Ltd* (1912) 106 L.T. 785; [1913] 1 Ch. 113; *Robinson v Bailey* [1948] 2 All E.R. 791; *Alvis v Harrison* (1990) 62 P. & C.R. 10, HL; *Jalnarne Ltd v Ridewood* (1989) 61 P. & C.R. 143 at 156–157.

[124] *Bulstrode v Lambert*, para.9–27, above, where the vehicles, the use by which of the yard was expressly authorised, were not confined to such as could originally have passed through a gate, with a bar over it, which was inside the entrance to the yard at the date of the reservation and had been removed before the dispute in the action arose. But this is subject to the limitation that the user would not become so excessive as to become a nuisance: See *Jelbert v Davis* [1968] 1 W.L.R. 589; *Rosling v Pinnegar* (1986) 54 P. & C.R. 124 and *White v Richards* (1993) 68 P. & C.R. 105.

[125] (1840) 11 A. & E. 759. See also *Luttrel's Case* (1601) 4 Co.Rep. 86a; and see para.12–33, below.

Chamber. The judgment of the court was delivered by Lord Denman C.J., who, while conceding that the words "now used as a woodhouse" were to be taken merely as ascertaining the place where the open space of ground was, was of opinion that the defendant was confined to the use of the way "to a place which should be in the same predicament as it was at the time of the making of the deed" and explained that by this the court meant that the defendant could only use the way "for purposes which were compatible with the ground being open".

9–50   It is now clear, however, that there is no such general rule as *Allan v Gomme*[126] appears to lay down and that that decision can be applied, if at all, only where the grant appears to be of a way to some specific building or thing. In the course of the argument in *Henning v Burnet*[127] Parke B. said of *Allan v Gomme* that the law appeared to him to have been laid down too strictly.

> "No doubt", he added, "if a right of way be granted for the purpose of being used as a way to a cottage, and the cottage is changed into a tan-yard, the right of way ceases; but if there is a general grant of all ways to a cottage, the right is not lost by reason of the cottage being altered."

9–51   In *South Metropolitan Cemetery Co v Eden*,[128] Jervis C.J. remarked:

> "If I grant a man a way to a cottage which consists of one room, I know the extent of the liberty I grant; and my grant would not justify the grantee in claiming to use the way to gain access to a town he might build at the extremity of it. Here the grant is general,–to use the road for the purpose of going to or returning from the land conveyed, or any part thereof; it is not defined, as in the case referred to."

9–52   In *Watts v Kelson*[129] the plaintiff was, by express words contained in the conveyance of his premises, entitled to "a right of way" through the defendant's gateway and close "to a wicket-gate to be erected by the plaintiff leading into the hereinbefore described piece or part of garden ground". The plaintiff's premises contained, beside the garden, a cottage, a number of stalls for feeding cattle, a yard and outbuildings, and a few acres of land. The defendant's gate would admit carriages. The plaintiff did not erect a wicket-gate, but erected a cart-shed on the same spot, and brought carts to it. The defendant having obstructed the way, Lord Romilly M.R. granted an injunction. The defendant contended that the way was granted for so long only as the part of the plaintiff's premises nearest to the proposed wicket-gate should continue to be used as a garden, quoting *Allan v Gomme*,[130] but Lord Romilly, without giving reasons, rejected this contention.

---

[126] (1840) 11 A. & E. 759.
[127] (1852) 8 Ex. 187 at 192.
[128] (1855) 16 C.B. 42 at 57, 58.
[129] (1870) 6 Ch. App. 166.
[130] (1840) 11 A. & E. 759.

In *United Land Co v Great Eastern Railway Co*[131] a railway company had been   **9–53**
empowered to make a railway through Crown lands by an Act which required the
company to make such convenient crossings where the railway traversed the
Crown lands as should in the judgment of certain commissioners be "necessary
for the convenient enjoyment and occupation of the lands". In accordance with
this provision, the company agreed with the commissioners to make "four level
crossings" at certain specific points, "with proper approaches thereto from the
lands on the other side", three of the crossings to be 30 feet wide each, and the
remaining one 20 feet wide. The crossings were made substantially in accordance
with this agreement. The land in question was, at the date of the Act, marsh or
pasture land, and was subject to a statute which prevented building. The land was
subsequently sold free from this restriction and advertised for resale in building
lots, and the defendants, successors in title of the original railway company,
objected to the crossings being used for access to the houses. The objection was
overruled by Malins V.-C., who distinguished the case before him from a grant of
a private right of way on the ground that it was a case of compulsory sale, and
that a railway company dividing land into lots was bound to render it as useful
for all purposes as if no severance had been made. He thought that the width of
the crossings showed that they had not been intended to be used merely for agricultural purposes. The nature of the communications agreed upon had no doubt
reduced the amount of compensation paid.

On appeal,[132] the Court of Appeal in Chancery affirmed this decision, chiefly   **9–54**
for the special reasons given by the Vice-Chancellor, but Mellish L.J. added some
words on the general principle.

> "No doubt", he said,[133] "there are authorities that, from the description of the
> lands to which the right of way is annexed, and of the purposes for which it
> is granted, the Court may infer that the way was intended to be limited to
> those purposes. But if there is no limit in the grant, the way may be used for
> all purposes."

James L.J. said[134] that there was nothing in the circumstances of the case, or in
the situation of the parties, or in the situation of the land, to prevent the words in the
Act from having their full operation. Farwell J. evidently had this passage in the
judgment of James L.J. in mind when he said in *Todrick v Western National
Omnibus Co Ltd*[135]:

> "In considering whether a particular use of a right of this kind is a proper use
> or not, I am entitled to take into consideration the circumstances of the case,

---

[131] (1873) L.R. 17 Eq. 158.
[132] (1875) 10 Ch. App. 586.
[133] (1875) 10 Ch. App. 586 at 590, 591.
[134] (1875) 10 Ch. App. 586 at 590.
[135] [1934] Ch. 190 at 206, 207. See para.9–25, above. This part of Farwell J.'s judgment was approved
by the Court of Appeal [1934] Ch. 561.

the situation of the parties and the situation of the land at the time when the grant was made: see United Land Company v. Great Eastern Railway Company, per James L.J.[136]; and in my judgment a grant for all purposes means for all purposes having regard to the consideration which I have already mentioned. It would be ridiculous to suppose that merely because the grant was expressed to be for all purposes it entitled the owner of the dominant tenement to attempt to use it for something for which obviously it could not be used . . . A grant of this kind must be construed as a grant for all purposes within the reasonable contemplation of the parties at the time of the grant."

9–55   *Newcomen v Coulson*[137] was a case of an award under an Inclosure Act. The award directed that each of the allottees,

> "and the owner or owners for the time being of the lands hereby to them respectively allotted, shall for ever hereafter have and enjoy a way-right and liberty of passage for themselves and their respective tenants and farmers of the said lands and grounds, as well on foot as on horseback, and with their carts and carriages, and to lead and drive their horses, oxen and other cattle, as often as occasion shall require",

over a certain property therein specified; and that, if the allottees or any of them, or any of the owners for the time being of their respective allotments, should "street out" the way, it should be made yards broad at the least between the quick-sets. The allotments were merely agricultural land. The owners of one of the allotments having commenced to build upon their land a number of villa residences, and to metal the road for the purpose of being used with the residences, the owner of the soil of the road and of the adjoining property interfered, and insisted that the way could not be used except for access to agricultural property. His action, and the appeal, were dismissed. Malins V.-C. distinguished *Allan v Gomme*,[138] being of opinion that this was not the case of an easement, but of an arrangement between the owners of the land enclosed for the formation and enjoyment of a way, which meant a way for all purposes. The Court of Appeal held that it was a case of an easement, and relied on the fact that the way was granted as appurtenant to "land", which meant the land and all buildings from time to time to be erected upon it or any part of it.

9–56   *Finch v Great Western Railway Co*[139] was also a case of an award under an Inclosure Act; here the way in question (20 feet wide) was to "remain a private carriage-road and drift-way for the use of the respective owners and occupiers for the time being of the allotment over which the same passes, and of several old

---

[136] (1875) 10 Ch. App. 586 at 590.
[137] (1877) 5 Ch. D. 133.
[138] (1840) 11 A. & E. 759.
[139] (1879) 5 Ex.D. 254.

inclosed meadows and woodlands belonging to [A], a meadow called Broadmead, belonging to [B], and the said inclosed meadow, belonging to [C], to which the same passes". A part of the "allotment over which" the road passed, which had been pasture land, was converted by the defendant company into a cattle-pen for storing cattle in transit, the user of the road being much increased; and, an action having been brought, the court held that the new user could be justified. The court thought that *Allan v Gomme*[140] established no general rule, but turned on the construction of the particular deed referred to. Stephen J., delivering the judgment of the Exchequer Division, said that *United Land Company v Great Western Railway Company*[141] and *Newcomen v Coulson*[142] established the principle that where there is an express grant of a right of way to a particular place, to the unrestricted use of which the grantee is entitled, the grant is not to be restricted to access to the land for the purposes for which access would be required at the time of the grant.

Milner's Safe Co Ltd v Great Northern and City Railway[143] was a case of implied grant. The general principles which apply in the case of an implied grant are essentially the same as the principles which apply in the case of an easement acquired by prescription and are different from the principles which apply to the construction of an express grant. The law as to implied grants has been considered in detail in *McAdams Homes Limited v Robinson*.[144] In *Milner's Safe* the question arose as to the extent of a way to be implied over a common passage which ran along the back of certain houses into a side street. The plaintiff was the owner of two of these houses, deriving title under one limitation in the will, made in 1828, of a testator who died in 1832, and the defendant was the owner of the site of two others of the houses, deriving title under another limitation. The will contained no express provision as to any right of way over the passage. The defendant pulled down the houses on its land and constructed a railway station having one of its entrances opening into the passage which it claimed to use as a thoroughfare for its passengers. Kekewich J. held that, as in the case of a way acquired by prescription, the extent of the right ought to be measured by the user at the time of the grant.[145] He inferred, from evidence of subsequent user, that the passage was at the relevant time used for ordinary business purposes only, and concluded that its user by railway passengers was excessive.[146] *Milner's Safe Co Ltd v Great Northern and City Railway*[147] was distinguished in *Graham v Philcox*[148] on the ground that

9–57

---

[140] (1840) 11 A. & E. 759.

[141] (1873) L.R. 17 Eq. 158.

[142] (1877) 5 Ch. D. 133.

[143] [1907] 1 Ch. 208.

[144] [2004] EWCA Civ 214; [2004] 3 E.G.L.R. 93; *Milner's Safe* was considered in *McAdams Homes* at [38]–[39]. *McAdams Homes* is considered in detail at paras 9–14 to 9–17, above.

[145] Whether the relevant date for this purpose was the date of the will or the date of the death was not decided; see [1907] 1 Ch. 208 at 222.

[146] Appeal against this decision was compromised: [1907] 1 Ch. 208 at 229.

[147] [1907] 1 Ch. 208.

[148] [1984] Q.B. 747. Purchas L.J. (at 762) described as perhaps the most important passage in Kekewich J.'s judgment his quotation ([1907] 1 Ch. 208 at 226) from the judgment of James L.J. in *Wimbledon and Putney Commons Conservators v Dixon* (1875) 1 Ch. D. 362 at 368, quoted at para.9–06, above.

it depended upon the change in the user of the dominant tenement rather than the change in the nature, destruction or enlargement of the area of the dominant tenement.

9–58   In *White v Grand Hotel, Eastbourne*,[149] where the dominant tenement had been converted (in effect) from a private dwelling-house into a hotel, and the court had to consider an oral, and apparently general, grant of a right of way, it was decided that user for the purposes of the hotel was justified. Joyce J.[150] accepted the proposition laid down in *Finch v Great Western Railway*[151] that "where there is an express grant of a private right of way to a particular place, to the unrestricted use of which the grantee of the right of way is entitled, the grant is not to be restricted to access to the land for the purposes of which access would be required at the time of the grant". His decision was affirmed by the Court of Appeal, who considered the law to be settled by *United Land Co v Great Eastern Railway*[152] with which Farwell L.J.[153] thought *Allan v Gomme*[154] to be inconsistent. Lord Cozens–Hardy M.R. said[155]:

> "The plaintiffs' main point was . . . that it was only a right of way for what I may call domestic purposes as distinct from trade purposes; and that it was only for such use as could reasonably be expected to be in the contemplation of the parties at the time when the defendants' house, St Vincent Lodge, was a private residence, and ought not to be altered now that St Vincent Lodge is turned into a [hotel-] garage. We heard that point fully argued by counsel for the appellants and we have come to the conclusion that there is no ground for limiting the right of way in the manner suggested. It is not a right of way claimed by prescription. It is a right of way claimed under a grant, and, that being so, the only thing that the Court has to do is to construe the grant; and unless there is some limitation to be found in the grant, in the nature of the width of the road or something of that kind, full effect must be given to the grant, and we cannot consider the subsequent user as in any way sufficient to cut down the generality of the grant."

9–59   In *South Eastern Railway v Cooper*[156] the predecessors in title of the defendant had owned land through part of which the plaintiff company constructed its railway under statutory powers in 1844, so that the remainder of the defendant's land was completely cut off from the highway which had adjoined the land before the construction of the railway. In order to restore access to the highway, the company

---

[149] (1912) 106 L.T. 785; [1913] 1 Ch. 113, CA, varied in HL on another point sub nom. *Grand Hotel, Eastbourne Ltd v White* (1913) 110 L.T. 209.
[150] (1912) 106 L.T. 788.
[151] (1879) 5 Ex.D. 254; see para.9–56, above.
[152] (1873) L.R. 17 Eq. 158; see para.9–53, above.
[153] [1913] 1 Ch. 113 at 115.
[154] (1840) 11 A. & E. 759.
[155] [1913] 1 Ch. 113 at 116.
[156] [1924] Ch. 211.

made a level-crossing from the defendant's land to the highway, and granted a right of way in general terms. For many years after 1844 the owners of the land had used the crossing for agricultural purposes only; but in 1920 the defendant opened a sandpit upon the land and sold out of it large quantities of sand for commercial purposes, so that the burden of the easement was much increased. The plaintiff company having brought an action to restrain the defendant from using the crossing in excess of the extent to which it was used when the easement was granted, the Court of Appeal held that, the grant being a grant of a general right of way for all purposes and not merely a grant of an "accommodation way" under section 68 of the Railway Clauses Consolidation Act 1845,[157] the user was not restricted to that contemplated when the grant was made.

South Eastern Railway v Cooper[158] was applied by the Court of Appeal **9–60** (Harman and Davies L.JJ., Lord Denning M.R. dissenting) in *British Railways Board v Glass*.[159] In that case a conveyance of land to a railway company was expressed to except a right of crossing the railway and the majority of the Court of Appeal construed the conveyance as operating as a grant of a right of way for all purposes, not limited to the user contemplated when the grant was made. Hence the way was not limited to the agricultural purposes in the contemplation of the parties and could be used for access to a caravan site in the defendant's field.

In the case of a way (for example a level crossing or a bridge) maintained as such **9–61** "accommodation works" as are referred to in section 68 of the Railway Clauses Consolidation Act 1845[160] the dominant owner has no general right of user. The user is not, however, confined to that to which the dominant tenement was put at the time when the way came into existence: the user may be changed, but not so as to impose an added burden on the servient land; and the onus of showing that the burden will not be increased rests on the dominant owner.[161] Where a crossing over a railway is made to accommodate an owner whose land has been intersected, and the lands on the two sides of the railway line subsequently pass into separate ownership, the right of way may be abandoned, in which case it will not be revived if the lands again become vested in the same owner.[162]

In *Robinson v Bailey*[163] a limitation on the permitted quantity and purpose of user **9–62** was sought to be established by inference from the surrounding circumstances.

---

[157] As to the limited permissible use of such ways, see *Great Western Ry v Talbot* [1902] 2 Ch. 759; *Taff Vale Ry v Gordon Canning* [1909] 2 Ch. 48; *British Railways Board v Glass* [1965] Ch. 538 at 553, 554, per Lord Denning M.R. and at 558, 559, per Harman L.J.

[158] [1924] 1 Ch. 211.

[159] [1965] Ch. 538; see para.9–08, above.

[160] The expression "accommodation works" is not defined in the Act, but it is a well-known expression in railway terminology: *T.R.H. Sampson Associates Ltd v British Railways Board* [1983] 1 W.L.R. 170 at 174.

[161] *T.R.H. Sampson Associates Ltd v British Railways Board*, above, applying *Great Western Ry v Talbot* [1902] 2 Ch. 759 and *Taff Vale Ry v Gordon Canning* [1909] 2 Ch. 48 (in both of which the change of user involved an unacceptable increase in the burden). See also *Great Northern Ry v M'Alister* [1897] 1 I.R. 587.

[162] *Midland Ry v Gribble* [1895] 2 Ch. 827.

[163] [1948] 2 All E.R. 791.

The Court of Appeal, affirming Harman J. whose judgment is not reported, recognised that surrounding circumstances can affect the construction of a grant, but considered that they had no limiting effect in that case. The defendant, who was a builder, had bought from the plaintiff a plot on a new building estate, together with "a right of way" over an adjacent roadway, about 25 feet wide, leading to the public highway. At the date of the conveyance this roadway was laid out in a rudimentary fashion, and in the conveyance the plaintiff covenanted to make up and maintain it until it should be taken over as a public road by the local authority. The whole estate in the hands of the plaintiff was subject to a restrictive covenant, which was assumed to be enforceable against the defendant, prohibiting the erection of buildings other than private dwelling-houses and the carrying on of any trade or business on any part. Under a local town planning scheme, building was restricted to residential houses. The defendant covenanted with the plaintiff that only one house should be erected on his plot.

The plaintiff sought to establish that the defendant was not entitled, under the grant to him of "a right of way", to use the roadway for the passage of heavy lorries engaged in carrying to and from the plot builders' materials for which the defendant, who was prevented by current conditions from building a house, was using the plot as a store in connection with his business. The plaintiff admitted that user by lorries was in itself an authorised mode of user, but contended that, in the circumstances, the right granted must be confined inferentially to user for the purposes of a house, and that the persistent use of the road by lorries carrying builders' materials was excessive. It was said that, having regard to the restrictions existing at the time of the grant, the parties must have contemplated that the plot, and consequently the roadway, would be used only for the purposes of a residential house; but the court pointed out that, as between the parties, the authorised use of the plot was not confined to residential use; that the restrictions imposed on the plaintiff, and by the town planning scheme, were not necessarily permanent or immutable; and that the effect of the plaintiff's covenant to maintain the road until it should be taken over as a public road was, if anything, to confirm the view that the road was intended to be used as fully as a public road might be; and they concluded that there was nothing in the surrounding circumstances that limited the unqualified terms of the grant.

9–63   In *Kain v Norfolk*[164] where the defendant, grantee of a right of way "with or without horses carts agricultural machines and implements" was held entitled to use the way for lorries carrying sand from a sandpit recently opened on the dominant land, which at the date of the grant was agricultural, it was conceded that the right was not confined to user for agricultural purposes. The contention was that the words quoted were restrictive, and that "carts" did not include motor-lorries.

---

[164] [1949] Ch. 163.

(5) *Other limitations*

Where a right of way was granted "as at present enjoyed", the words quoted were **9–64** held to refer to the quality, and not to the purpose or extent, of the user.[165] Where a right of way was expressed to be appurtenant to the grantee's land "as used and occupied at the date hereof for the purpose it now is" but was also said to be "for all purposes", it was held that the former expression was only intended to identify the dominant tenement and not to qualify the description of the right granted.[166] If a right of way is granted "in connection with the use of [the dominant tenement] as an agricultural and forestry estate", the way cannot be used for storing produce not grown on the dominant tenement or for activities which are not intrinsic to, or part and parcel of, the running of such an estate.[167]

In *White v Richards*,[168] there was an express reservation of a right to pass on **9–65** foot and with or without motor vehicles over a track so far as necessary for the use and enjoyment of the retained land. At the date of the conveyance, the track was 2.7 metres (8 feet, 10 inches) wide and formed of crushed stone embedded in the topsoil intermittently covered with a well-worn bituminous layer. The Court of Appeal held that the reference in the reservation to motor vehicles, read in the light of the physical characteristics of the track, was to be restricted to vehicles of a certain dimension and weight and upheld the trial judge's order limiting vehicles to those with a wheel base width not exceeding eight feet, an overall width not exceeding nine feet and a laden weight not exceeding 10 tons. Use by 14–16 heavy lorries per day in addition to smaller vehicles, so that the surface of the way became damaged, was held to be excessive use.[169]

(6) *User which interferes with the rights of others*

In *Jelbert v Davis*[170] agricultural land had been conveyed together with "the right **9–66** of way at all times and for all purposes over the driveway . . . leading to the main road in common with all other persons having the like right". The Court of Appeal held that although the wide terms of the grant permitted use of the driveway for vehicular traffic of a kind different from that contemplated at the time of the grant, and therefore for caravans, excessive user of the way such as would interfere with the rights of "other persons having the like right" or cause a legal nuisance would be outside the terms of the grant, looked at in the circumstances

---

[165] *Hurt v Bowmer* [1937] 1 All E.R. 797. See also *Nicklin v Pearson* (1971) 220 E.G. 649 ("as hitherto used and enjoyed"). In *Collins v Slade* (1874) 23 W.R. 199, the same words were held to refer to the time of user, i.e. during specified daylight hours only, the servient owner being entitled to block the way at night.

[166] *McKay Securities Limited v Surrey County Council* [1998] E.G.C.S. 180.

[167] *Wilkins v Lewis* [2005] EWHC 1710 (Ch.) at [46]–[48].

[168] (1993) 68 P. & C.R. 105.

[169] (1993), 68 P. & C.R. 105 at 113. See also *Todrick v Western National Omnibus Co* [1934] Ch. 190 and para.9–25, above.

[170] [1968] 1 W.L.R. 589. Followed in *Grinskis v Lahood* [1971] N.Z.L.R. 502.

at the date it was made. On the evidence, the proposed user of the driveway for 200 camping units (consisting of caravans and/or tents) on the dominant land would be excessive. Lord Denning M.R. referred[171] to the passage in the judgment of Farwell J. in *Todrick v Western National Omnibus Co Ltd*[172] quoted above as having stated the law on this subject. *Jelbert v Davis* was relied on in *Owen v Blathwayt*[173] to resolve questions of priority between grantees of non-exclusive rights of grazing.

9-67   The same approach was adopted by the Court of Appeal in *Rosling v Pinnegar*.[174] A Georgian mansion built by the same architect who was responsible for the White House, Washington, had been conveyed with the right in common with all other persons entitled thereto at all times and for all purposes with or without vehicles to use a certain lane. The lane was narrow and winding and was the only access not only to the mansion but to 25 dwellings in the village. The owner of the mansion opened it to the public and the residents of the village sought an injunction preventing him from causing persons to use the way as a result of public or general invitation. It was held that the mere fact that there had been a change of use of the mansion, in that it was now open to the public, was not itself a breach of the terms of the grant, nor were the residents entitled to complain of the loss of their rural peace and quiet but the resultant user was excessive in that it was such as to interfere unreasonably with the use of the lane by the other persons entitled to use it. Accordingly, injunctions limiting the size of vehicles which could use the lane and the days upon which and the times at which the owner could invite the public to use the lane were appropriate.[175]

9-68   In *National Trust v White*,[176] the National Trust had by virtue of grant the benefit of a right of way over a track leading from the A30 to Figsbury Ring "for all purposes". The local authority formed a one-and-a-half acre car park on land at the side of the track to accommodate members of the public wishing to visit the historic site. The owners of the track complained that their enjoyment of their property was adversely affected by the increase in the volume of traffic and attempted to prevent user of the track and to fence it off from the car park. It was held that the use of the track for access to the car park for the purpose of visiting Figsbury Ring was ancillary to the enjoyment of Figsbury Ring and thus within the terms of the grant, although use of the track for gaining access to the car park for the purpose of enjoying the car park itself would not have been.[177] The car park was not to be treated as an enlargement of the dominant tenement. The use of the track by vehicles going to and from the car park was not excessive, because

---

[171] [1968] 1 W.L.R. 595.
[172] [1934] Ch. 190 at 206, 207. See para.9–25, above.
[173] [2003] 1 P. & C.R. 444.
[174] (1986) 54 P. & C.R. 124.
[175] Following the form of order made in *Kennaway v Thompson* [1981] Q.B. 88.
[176] [1987] 1 W.L.R. 907.
[177] [1987] 1 W.L.R. 907, at 913C, applying dicta of Vaughan Williams and Romer L.JJ. in *Harris v Flower* (1904) 74 L.J.Ch. 127 at 132, which draw a distinction between cases where a way is used for the benefit of additional land and where the user is still essentially for the benefit of the original land.

it was not such as to interfere with the use of the track by the owners or their licensees.[178]

In *Alvis v Harrison*,[179] the appellant owned a house on the west side of the driveway and woodland stretching to the main road on the east side of the driveway; he had a right of access over the driveway and verges by express reservation; he built a road from the driveway through the woodland to the main road with a tarmac bellmouth on the verge of the driveway. The House of Lords held that he was entitled to do so; he was entitled to exercise the right not only for the purposes of the use to which the dominant tenement was being put at the time of the grant but also for any other lawful purposes to which it might later be put, provided he did so *civiliter*, that is reasonably and in a manner least burdensome to the servient tenement: he could also reinforce the verge with tarmac for the better enjoyment of his right, so long as this did not prejudice the servient tenement regarded as a whole; it would be wrong to regard the main road as if it were another contiguous tenement,[180] because the appellant already had a right of access to the main road over the driveway and the burden on the driveway would therefore not be increased.

9–69

4.—MISCELLANEOUS INCIDENTS

Who may use the way

When the grant is in general terms, and there are no circumstances subsisting at the date of the grant, and nothing in the grant itself, sufficient to point in an opposite direction, a way may be used, with the authority of the person entitled to possession of the dominant tenement, by anyone whose user is not inconsistent with the quantity and purpose[181] of user envisaged by the grant. In *Hammond v Prentice Brothers Ltd*, Eve J. said[182]: "After all, the grant is appurtenant to the dominant tenement, and in my opinion in the absence of special circumstances ought to be so construed as to secure to the grantee all that is necessary for the reasonable enjoyment of the dominant tenement." Words in a grant mentioning certain persons as entitled to use, such as tenants, visitors, and the like, are generally to be regarded as illustrative, and not as restrictive.[183]

9–70

Eve J. followed *Baxendale v North Lambert Liberal and Radical Club Ltd*[184] where it was held that a grant, contained in a lease, of full right "for the lessee,

---

[178] Distinguishing *Jelbert v Davis* [1968] 1 W.L.R. 589.

[179] (1990) 62 P. & C.R. 10 (a Scottish appeal).

[180] See paras 9–34–9–47, above.

[181] See para.9–48, above.

[182] [1920] 1 Ch. 201 at 216, followed in *Grinskis v Lahood* [1971] N.Z.L.R. 502.

[183] [1920] 1 Ch. 207, *cf.* the argument on an analogous point, which the court was inclined to accept, in *Kain v Norfolk* [1949] Ch. 163 at 168.

[184] [1902] 2 Ch. 427. See also *Mitcalfe v Westaway* (1864) 34 L.J.C.P. 113 ("assigns, officers, servants and workmen" held not restrictive). As to somewhat similar words in a grant of a *profit à prendre*, see *Reynolds v Moore* [1908] 2 I.R. 641, and *cf. Vickers' Lease, Re* [1947] Ch. 420.

his executors, administrators, and assigns, undertenants and servants" at all times
and for all purposes connected with the use and enjoyment of the premises, to use
a way, extended to members and honorary members of, and all other persons
going lawfully to and from, a workmen's club afterwards established on the
premises. Swinfen Eady J. said that it could not be doubted that, in the ordinary
case of a right of way to a house and premises which could only be used as a private dwelling-house, the right would extend not only to the grantee, but to members of his family, servants, visitors, guests and tradespeople, even though none
of those persons was expressly mentioned in the grant; and that the necessary or
reasonable user of the club premises as a club required that there should be
liberty of passing over the way in question for the persons and vehicles shown to
have used it.[185]

9–71   The point has now been confirmed by the House of Lords. In *Moncrieff v
Jamieson*[186] Lord Hope said that a right of access to a house granted only in
favour of the owner of the dominant tenement and her successors in title could
not be construed too strictly and that the right extended to the proprietor's guests,
visitors, employees and others who came there for the purposes to which the land
was being put as long as that use was within the intended scope of the servitude
and did not impose an undue burden on the servient tenement. He then applied
the same principle to an ancillary right to park on the way.

9–72   In *Thornton v Little*[187] where a right of way was granted, so as to be annexed
to premises then used as a school, to the grantee, her administrators and assigns,
and her and their tenants, visitors and servants, to the intent that the right should
be appurtenant to the premises for all purposes connected with the use, occupation and enjoyment of the same, Kekewich J. seemed inclined to regard the enumeration of permitted persons as exhaustive, but he held that, construing the grant
in the light of the circumstances, "visitors" included pupils.

9–73   In *Keith v Twentieth Century Club Ltd*[188] the sites of certain houses then being
built round a London "square" garden had been conveyed to A, with a grant to A,
his heirs, executors, administrators and assigns, and his and their lessees and sub-
lessees or tenants, being occupiers for the time being of the houses then in course
of erection or thereafter to be erected immediately adjoining the garden, and for
his and their families and friends, in his and their company or without, of free use
and right of ingress, egress and regress at all times into, out of and upon the garden, he and they conforming to such rules as should be ordered by the vendor, his
heirs or assigns, or the committee (if any) of residents to whom the management
of the garden should be committed, and also paying an annual subscription for the
maintenance of the garden. Some of the houses having been acquired by the
defendant and converted into a residential club, certain adjoining residents, who
were entitled to the same right, sought to restrain the defendant from allowing its

[185] This paragraph was referred to and applied in *St Martin le Grand, York, Re* [1990] Fam. 63 at 80.
[186] [2007] 1 W.L.R. 2620 at [38].
[187] (1907) 97 L.T. 24.
[188] (1904) 73 L.J.Ch. 545.

members to use the garden. The owner of the garden was not a party. Two preliminary points of law, namely whether resident members of the club were entitled as of right to use the garden, and whether the defendant was entitled to authorise its members, resident or non-resident, to use it, were answered by Buckley J. in the negative, on the ground that members of the defendant's club were not tenants or friends of the defendant. The learned judge evidently felt that the user of the garden was intended to be confined to owners and occupiers of residential houses adjoining it, and their families and friends, and that, as there was nothing to prevent the houses round the square from being used otherwise than as private dwelling-houses, the words of enumeration in the grant ought to be considered as exhaustive.

In *St Martin le Grand, York, Re*, it was recited in a deed that "the company and its servants" had enjoyed and should continue to enjoy a right of way on foot and with trolleys over a churchyard to and from the street and to and from the company's printing works. It was contended that this right did not extend to the company's licensees but it was held on the evidence and in the light of *Baxendale*[189] that it did.[190]   **9–74**

Route of the way

A right of way should, generally speaking, have a *terminus a quo* and a *terminus ad quem*, so as to be bounded and circumscribed to a place certain,[191] but in *Wimbledon and Putney Commons Conservators v Dixon*,[192] the Court of Appeal was of the opinion that the fact that the occupiers of a tenement to which a way by user was claimed had used, not a definite road marked out between the *termini*, but a number of tracks indifferently, did not prevent the right from being acquired. Again, on the taking of a lease of land in Ireland, the court implied a grant by the lessor to the lessee of a right of way across the lessor's other land by such route as the lessor should from time to time point out.[193] A contract to grant "suitable access" over the land being purchased, the route to be at the discretion of the purchaser, is not too uncertain to amount to an enforceable contract to grant an easement.[194]   **9–75**

In *Davis v Whitby*[195] the dominant tenement enjoyed for 15 years a way by a path across the middle of the garden of the adjoining servient tenement. The route was then altered to a path across the bottom of the garden and enjoyed for a further period of 18 years. It was held by the Court of Appeal, affirming the decision of Burgess V.-C. and applying dicta of Patteson J. in *Payne v Shedden*[196] and Lord   **9–76**

---

[189] *Baxendale v North Lambeth Liberal and Radical Club Ltd* [1902] 2 Ch. 427, see para.9-70, above.
[190] [1990] Fam. 63 at 80–81.
[191] *Albon v Dremsall* (1610) 1 Brownl. 216; Yelv. 163; Com.Dig.Chemin, D.2.
[192] (1875) 1 Ch. D. 362; and see *Barba v Gas and Fuel Corp of Victoria* (1975) 51 A.J.L.R. 219, High Ct. of Australia (pipeline easement).
[193] *Donnelly v Adams* [1905] 1 I.R. 154.
[194] *Callander v Midlothian D.C.* (1997) F.L.T. 865.
[195] [1973] 1 W.L.R. 629, affirmed [1974] Ch. 186.
[196] (1834) 1 Mood. & R. 382 at 383.

Herschell in *Phillips v Halliday*[197] that long user as of right should if possible be presumed to be of legal origin, and, both periods of user being as of right, they should be added together, thus giving a full period of 20 years; and accordingly the right of way was established by prescription. The Court of Appeal rejected an argument that the agreement to a change in the route made the user *precario*, but the rejection of the argument appears to have been based on the facts, and in such a case it seems that the question whether there was consent, so as to defeat a claim as of right, will always arise.

9–77   Questions have arisen, on the construction of particular grants, as to whether a right of way over a road mentioned is a right over its whole length, or over a part only.[198]

9–78   If the site of a way over which a right is granted is not physically apparent, it is for the servient owner to indicate where it is to be.[199] Once he has done so, or the way has been defined by usage, it cannot (except by agreement) be altered.[200]

Realignment of way

9–79   The servient owner has no right to alter the route of an easement of way unless such a right is an express or implied term of the grant of the easement or is subsequently conferred on him.[201] In exceptional circumstances the court might, however, refuse injunctive relief, as it did in the *Greenwich NHS Trust*[202] case, where the realignment improved road safety, the dominant owners had failed to object and the realignment was necessary to achieve an object of substantial public and local importance. The court left open the question whether, in these circumstances, the realignment amounted to a substantial interference with the easement such as to be actionable. In the case of a minor realignment of a road in the course of its improvement which did not cause any overall restriction on its use, it being accepted that the party entitled to a right of way would be entitled to free and unrestricted access over the realigned road, the court declined to order either an injunction or damages in lieu, thus rendering the question whether there had been an actionable interference academic.[203]

---

[197] [1891] A.C. 228 at 231. See para.4–16, above.

[198] *Wood v Stourbridge Ry* (1864) 16 C.B. (n.s.) 222; *Knox v Sansom* (1877) 25 W.R. 864; *Randall v Hall* (1851) 4 De G. & Sm. 343. For a case of mutual mistake in describing a staircase, see *Cowen v Truefit Ltd* [1898] 2 Ch. 551; [1899] 2 Ch. 309.

[199] *Bolton v Bolton* (1879) 11 Ch. D. 968 (way of necessity); *Deacon v South Eastern Ry* (1889) 61 L.T. 377 (express grant); *Nickerson v Barraclough* [1981] Ch. 426 at 445, 446, per Eveleigh L.J.

[200] *Deacon v South Eastern Ry*, above; *Wolland v Marshalsea*, unreported, November 10, 1994, CA. See, however, as to the alteration of an easement of necessity, *Wynne v Pope* (1960) 3 S.A. 37, and para.3–118, above. *Deacon v South Eastern Ry* was distinguished in *Coopind UK Ltd v Walton Commercial Group Ltd* [1989] 1 E.G.L.R. 241, where the grant of a "right to receive a supply of gas" in a lease was held to entitle the tenant to lay a larger gas main along a different route to that already existing.

[201] *Greenwich NHS Trust v London & Quadrant Housing* [1998] 1 W.L.R. 1749, applying *Deacon v S.E. Ry* (1889) 61 L.T. 377 and following the decision of the New Brunswick Court of Appeal in *Gormley v Hoyt* (1982) 43 N.B.R. (2d) 75.

[202] *Greenwich NHS Trust v London & Quadrant Housing* [1998] 1 W.L.R. 1749.

[203] *Crane Road Properties LLP v Hundalani* [2006] EWHC 2066 (Ch.) at [106].

Right to deviate

If an obstruction, not easy of removal, is placed across a way by the servient **9–80**
owner or occupier (or *semble*, by any other person)[204] who is entitled to adjoining land, the person entitled to use the way may, so long as the obstruction continues, deviate onto the adjoining land in order to connect the two parts of the way
on each side of the obstacle.[205] If the obstructing party holds the adjoining land
for a particular estate, the right of deviation is limited to the duration of that
estate.[206] There is, it seems, no other right to deviate.[207]

Access from dominant tenement

Swinfen Eady L.J. in *Pettey v Parsons*[208] said that: **9–81**

> "It is a question of construction in a deed granting a right of way whether the
> way that is granted is a way so that the grantee may open gates, or means of
> access to the way, at any point of his frontage, or whether it is merely a way
> between two points, a right to pass over the road, and is limited to the modes
> of access to the road existing at the date of the grant."

Pickford L.J. said[209] that, assuming the right of access from every part of the land
from which access is required to every part of the way, such access should be
given as will give reasonable opportunity for the exercise of the right.

It has been said that no hard and fast rule emerges from the cases but that the
guidance that they do afford is that, whilst the servient owner may not derogate
from the grant, the dominant owner may not make unreasonable demands. What
would, in a particular case, constitute a derogation from the grant and what would
constitute an unreasonable demand depends on the proper construction of the
grant and then on the factual circumstances.[210]

The grant of a right to pass and repass along a road adjoining the boundary of **9–82**
the dominant tenement for all purposes connected with the use of the property as
a private residence prima facie gives the dominant owner an unfettered right to

---

[204] *Stacey v Sherrin* (1913) 29 T.L.R. 555.
[205] *Selby v Nettlefold* (1873) 9 Ch. App. 111; *Wolland v Marshalsea*, unreported November 10, 1994, CA.
[206] *Selby v Nettlefold* (1873) 9 Ch. App. 111 (tenant for life); *Mann v R.C. Eayrs Ltd* (1973) 231 E.G. 843 (compulsory requisition).
[207] *Bullard v Harrison* (1815) 4 M. & S. 387; *Taylor v Whitehead* (1781) 2 Doug. K.B. 745; and see 1 Wms.Saund. (1871 ed.) 565, n.(3), where it is pointed out that the proposition in Com.Dig.Chemin, D.6 that a right to deviate arises if the way becomes impassable through lack of repair is applicable only to highways.
[208] [1914] 2 Ch. 653 at 667; and see *South Metropolitan Cemetery Co v Eden* (1855) 16 C.B. 42; *Cooke v Ingram* (1893) 68 L.T. 671; *Sketchley v Burger* (1893) 69 L.T. 754; and see *Laurie v Winch* (1952) 4 D.L.R. 449.
[209] [1914] 2 Ch. 669. Applied in *Butler v Muddle* (1995) 6 B.P.R. 97,532 where it was held the access at points extending to 13m out of a frontage of 23m was not reasonable; *Carlson v Carpenter* (1998) 8 B.P.R. 97,693.
[210] *National Trust v White* [1987] 1 W.L.R. 907 at 913G, approved and applied by the Court of Appeal in *Lomax v Wood* [2001] EWCA Civ 1099.

enter the roadway at any point on the boundary and he may change his access point at any time if he so wishes.[211] This is, of course, subject to the proviso that the opening of the new access does not unduly interfere with the rights of others entitled to use the way.[212] Moreover, the words of the grant have to be construed in the light of the surrounding circumstances, which include any physical limitations existing at the date of grant. This may result in the grant being construed as subject to limitations on the opening of new access points.[213]

9–83   In *Perlman v Rayden*,[214] Patten J. considered many of the earlier cases which discussed the ability of the dominant owner to open a new point of access onto the access way. In that case there were arguments based on the detailed terms of the grant and on the physical layout of the dominant and servient land at the date of grant but, notwithstanding these arguments, the Judge held that the dominant owner was entitled to open a new point of access (a new front door in his house) from the dominant land onto the access way.

9–84   In *Well Barn Shoot Ltd v Shackleton*,[215] the Court of Appeal appears to have adopted a different approach. It was held that, as a matter of necessary implication, there was a right to take access into a field at a certain point from a passing track. It was held that there was no necessary implication that there should be any other point of access. The single point of access at the present time satisfied the dominant owner's reasonable requirements. This reasoning appears to have led the court to reject the submission that there could be further points of access in accordance with the principles in *Pettey v Parsons*.

9–85   In Australia it has been held, in reliance on *Pettey v Parsons*, that an easement of way created by express grant, which does not indicate an access or conclusion point for the easement, does not confer a right to enter the dominant tenement from any point along the easement. Thus the owner of the servient tenement may fence the land, even though the fence limits the points at which the dominant owner can enter and leave his property from the right of way, provided that the fence does not prevent reasonable access to the property. What is reasonable is determined by reference to the language of the grant construed in the light of the surrounding circumstances.[216]

Ancillary rights

9–86   The dominant owner is entitled to enter the servient land to effect repairs or to alter the surface of the servient land to accommodate the right granted.[217] So a

---

[211] *Carder v Davies* (1998) 76 P. & C.R. D33 (CA).
[212] *Fairview New Homes Plc v Government Row Residents Association Limited* [1998] E.G.C.S. 92; *Jelbert v Davis* [1968] 1 W.L.R. 589; and see paras 9–66 to 9–69, above.
[213] *Mills v Blackwell* (1999) 78 P. & C.R. D43. The distinction between this case and *Carder v Davies*, above, appears to be that here the boundary wall was a party-wall, whereas there the boundary wall belonged to the dominant owner.
[214] [2004] EWHC 2192 (Ch.).
[215] [2003] EWCA Civ 02.
[216] *Boglari v Steiner School* [2007] VSCA 58 at [26].
[217] See para.1–91, above.

dominant owner may be entitled to enter the servient land to instal lighting if that is reasonably necessary to enable the way to be used safely and conveniently.[218] The grant of a right of way does not, however, carry with it an implied right to have visibility splays at the junction with a highway either provided or kept clear and it is not a derogation from such a grant to obstruct the view from or of the way.[219]

The following summary of the law has been described as "settled for centuries" and uncontroversial.[220] Subject to contrary agreement,   **9–87**

(1) The grantee may enter the grantor's land for the purpose of making the grant of the right of way effective viz. to construct a way which is suitable for the right granted to him[221];

(2) Once the way exists, the servient owner is under no obligation to maintain or repair it[222];

(3) Similarly, the dominant owner has no obligation to maintain or repair the way[223];

(4) The servient owner (who owns the land over which the way passes) can maintain and repair the way, if he chooses;

(5) The dominant owner (in whose interest it is that the way be kept in good repair) is entitled to maintain and repair the way and, if he wants the way to be kept in repair, must himself bear the cost[224];

(6) He has a right to enter the servient owner's land for the purpose but only to do necessary work in a reasonable manner.[225]

If the dominant owner agrees to contribute to the cost incurred by the servient owner in repairing a road but the servient owner improves the road by relaying it to a significantly higher specification, the dominant owner can only be charged for those elements of the work actually undertaken which would have been incurred if the road had merely been repaired in accordance with the covenant and not for work which would have had to be done had the road been so repaired but which was avoided by its having been upgraded.[226]   **9–88**

Under a grant of a free and convenient horse and foot-way, and for carts, etc., "to carry stones, timber, coals and other things whatsoever", it was held that the   **9–89**

---

[218] *Owners of Strataplan 58754 v Anderson* (1990) 9 B.P.R. 97,782.
[219] *Hayns v Secretary of State for the Environment* [1978] 1 E.G.L.R. 134; *McKay Securities Limited v Surrey County Council* (1998) E.G.C.S. 180; to the same effect is a dictum of Young J. in *Finlayson v Campbell* (1997) 8 B.P.R. 97,675 at p. 15, 711. *V.T. Engineering Limited v Richard Barland & Co Limited* (1968) 19 P. & C.R. 890.
[220] *Carter v Cole* [2006] EWCA Civ 398 at [8].
[221] See *Newcomen v Coulson* (1887) 5 Ch. D. 133, 143 per Jessel M.R.
[222] See *Pomfret v Ricroft* (1669) 1 Wms. Saunders (1871 ed.) 557 per Twysden J.; *Taylor v Whitehead* (1781) 2 Doug K.B. 745; and *Jones v Pritchard* [1908] 1 Ch. 630, 637, per Parker J.
[223] See *Duncan v Louch* (1845) 6 Q.B. 904.
[224] *Taylor v Whitehead* (1781) 2 Doug K.B., per Lord Mansfield.
[225] See *Liford's Case* (1614) 11 Co. Rep. 46b, 52a (citing a case in the reign of Edward IV) and *Jones v Pritchard* [1908] 1 Ch. 630, 638 per Parker J.
[226] *Crane Road Properties LLP v Hundalani* [2006] EWHC 2066 (Ch.) at [51].

grantee could lay a framed way along the land for carrying coals, but not a transverse way.[227] Where in 1630 land was granted, excepting and reserving out of the grant all mines of coal with sufficient wayleave to the said mines, and with liberty of sinking pits, it was held that the right was not confined to such ways as were in use at the time of the grant, and that it included the right to instal steam engines and other machinery necessary for draining the pits off.[228] Where, however, A granted land, reserving a wagon or cart road of the width of 18 feet, to be at all times thereafter kept in repair at his own cost, it was held that this reservation did not enable A to lay down a railroad for carrying coals from his neighbouring colliery.[229]

9–90   While a right of way does carry a right to what has been called "vertical swing space", that is, to have the way free from obstruction to such a height as is reasonable,[230] it does not carry the right to use the air space above such height as is sufficient to allow vehicles to pass and repass.[231] Moreover, there is no right of "elbow room": the owner of land abutting a way may build right up to the edge of the way and the dominant owner has no cause for complaint if he is restricted to the exact width of the way.[232]

9–91   In *Perlman v Rayden*[233] it was held that the dominant owner who was entitled to open a new point of access from the dominant land onto an access way, in the form of a new front door to his house, had an ancillary right to construct a step in front of the new door as that was reasonably necessary for the safe and convenient use of the new door. In the same way, the dominant owner had an ancillary right to pave over a part of the servient land, which was formerly laid out for planting, to permit convenient access to the new door.

9–92   A right to park is not normally implied as being ancillary to a right of way[234] but may be in unusual circumstances. In *Moncrieff v Jamieson*,[235] a house in Shetland on the sea shore at the foot of a cliff was conveyed with the benefit of a right of access from a public road 150 yards away to the top of the cliff over a way over the transferor's retained land. The way was steeply sloping and vehicles could not get from it onto the dominant tenement. It was found at first instance that the property was not reasonably capable of comfortable enjoyment without a right to park on the servient tenement adjacent to the dominant tenement such number of vehicles as were reasonably necessary for the use of the dominant

---

[227] *Senhouse v Christian* (1787) 1 T.R. 560. In *Butler v Muddle* (1995) 6 B.P.R. 97,532, the right to pave the way was held to be restricted to so much of the way as was needed for reasonable enjoyment of the way.

[228] *Dand v Kingscote* (1840) 6 M. & W. 174; see *Newcomen v Coulson* (1877) 5 Ch. D. 133 at 139.

[229] *Bidder v North Staffordshire Ry* (1878) 4 Q.B.D. 412.

[230] (1878) 4 Q.B.D. 412.

[231] *Robmet Investments Pty Ltd v Don Chen Pty Ltd* (1997) 8 B.P.R. 97,649.

[232] *Minor v Groves* (1997) 80 P. & C.R. 136; *V.T. Engineering Ltd v Richard Barland & Co Ltd* (above).

[233] [2004] EWHC 2192 (Ch.).

[234] See para.9–106, below.

[235] [2007] 1 W.L.R. 2620.

tenement. The House of Lords upheld the decision that in these special circumstances a right to park was a necessary incident of the right of access.[236]

Amount of way to which grantee entitled

There is a distinction between a private and a public right of way, that the former is **9–93** not necessarily, as the latter is, over every part of the land along which the right exists.[237] The grant of a private right of way along "the passage coloured blue" on a plan confers, it has been said,[238] a prima facie right to the reasonable use of every part of the passage, but an action for disturbance will not lie unless there is a real substantial interference with the enjoyment.[239] Accordingly, where there was granted to the plaintiff a right to use a 40-foot road, it was held that he could not maintain an action in respect of a portico which projected two feet into the carriageway but left ample space for the convenient enjoyment by the plaintiff of the way.[240] On the other hand, where there was a right of way over a driveway nine metres wide the servient owner was not entitled to reduce the width to 4.14 metres.[241] Where there was a fairly narrow surface road which was the only vehicular access to a row of houses, the Court of Appeal said that the judge had been right to proceed on the basis that the neighbours' rights of way extended over the whole width of the roadway.[242]

The question is whether practically and substantially the right of way can be exercised as conveniently as before.[243] In *Pettey v Parsons*,[244] the dominant owner was held entitled to place a gate, to be kept open during business hours and never to be locked, at one end of the way, and to fence in a small portion of it at its wider end.

In *Strick (F.C.) & Co Ltd v City Offices Ltd*[245] the defendants granted to the plain- **9–94** tiffs a lease of offices in a block of buildings. No mention was made in the lease of any right of access from the entrance hall, but it was admitted that the plaintiffs had

---

[236] The decision depended very much on its facts and should not be taken to mean that the owner of any house with a right of access over the grantor's land has an ancillary right to park on the access road because he has nowhere else to park or because the available parking is inconveniently distant: see in particular the speeches of Lords Rodger and Neuberger.

[237] *Hutton v Hamboro* (1860) 2 F. & F. 218, 219; *Pettey v Parsons* [1914] 2 Ch. 653. A grant of a right to pass over certain roads "in the same manner and as fully as if the same were public roads" was held to entitle the grantee to the use of the whole of the roads; *Nicol v Beaumont* (1883) 53 L.J.Ch. 853; *cf. Selby v Crystal Palace Gas Co* (1862) 4 de G.F. & J. 246. A grantee is entitled to have vertical "swing-space", that is, to have the way free from obstruction to such a height as is reasonable, but there is no implied right of lateral "swing-space" which would prevent the servient owner from building on either side of the way; *V.T. Engineering Ltd v Richard Barland & Co Ltd* (1968) 19 P. & C.R. 890; *Minor v Groves* (1997) 80 P. & C.R. 136.

[238] *Sketchley v Burger* (1893) 69 L.T. 754.

[239] *Pettey v Parsons*, above. This point was not argued in *Scott v Martin* [1987] 1 W.L.R. 841 where the question of what injunctive relief might be appropriate against the party who had encroached upon the verge of a private road was remitted by the Court of Appeal to the county court.

[240] *Clifford v Hoare* (1874) L.R. 9 C.P. 362; *West v Sharp* (2000) 79 P. & C.R. 327. See also *Miller v T.G. Dobson and Co Ltd* (1971) 220 E.G. 1595.

[241] *Celsteel Ltd v Alton House Holdings Ltd* [1985] 1 W.L.R. 204 (revd. in part, but not on this point, [1986] 1 W.L.R. 512).

[242] *Simpson v Fergus* (2000) 79 P. & C.R. 398.

[243] *Hutton v Hamboro* (1860) 2 F. & F. 218; *Robertson v Abrahams* [1930] W.N. 79.

[244] [1914] 2 Ch. 653. A question as to the right of the servient owner to make a gate into the way arose, on peculiar facts, in *Earl of Guilford v St George's Golf Club Trust* (1916) 85 L.J.Ch. 669.

[245] (1906) 22 T.L.R. 667.

such right. At the date of the lease the hall was of large dimensions, and the defendants subsequently proposed to diminish the size. The plaintiffs claiming a right of way over every part of the hall, it was held that no such right existed, the plaintiffs being entitled only to a reasonable user.

What constitutes actionable interference with a right of way is discussed further in Chapter 13.[246]

Remedy for excessive user

9–95   Where user of a right of way is excessive the dominant owner will be liable in trespass and may be restrained by injunction.[247] The injunction may require him not to permit licensees to use the right without ensuring that they do not exceed the terms of the grant, for example by parking on a right of way when there is no right to do so.[248] Where it is impossible to sever proper user of an easement from excessive user, the servient owner may stop the whole user.[249] It has been held,[250] in the case of a right of way, that if the excessive user cannot be abated without obstructing the whole user, the servient owner may obstruct the whole of that user, but this is probably wrong, because the servient owner may obtain an injunction restraining the dominant owner from use in excess of the grant, leaving it to the dominant owner to devise means to ensure compliance.[251] It may be reasonable to impose a traffic flow system on the users of a right of way.[252]

5.–PARKING AND STOPPING

Whether an easement

9–96   There appears to be no reason in principle why a right to park a car somewhere in a defined area should not be capable of being an easement provided that (a) it is made appurtenant to a dominant tenement,[253] and (b) the right is not so excessive as to exclude the servient owner and leave him without any use of the area in question for parking or anything else. Indeed, counsel have often accepted or assumed[254]

---

[246] See para.13–06, below.

[247] *Milner's Safe Co Ltd v Great Northern and City Ry* [1907] 1 Ch. 208 at 229.

[248] *Jalnarne Ltd v Ridewood* (1989) 61 P. & C.R. 143.

[249] See para.12–108, below.

[250] *Bernard and Bernard v Jennings and Hillaire* (1968) 13 W.I.R. 501, Trinidad and Tobago CA.

[251] *Hamble Parish Council v Haggard* [1992] 1 W.L.R. 122 at 134D.

[252] See *Saint v Jenner* [1973] Ch. 275, applied by analogy in *Cardwell v Walker* [2004] 2 P. & C.R. 122 (see paras 6–90 to 6–91 above); *Celsteel Ltd v Alton House Holdings* [1985] 1 W.L.R. 204 (revd. in part, but not on this point, [1986] 1 W.L.R. 512).

[253] This sentence up to this point was approved by Lord Neuberger in *Moncrieff v Jamieson* [2007] 1 W.L.R. 2620 at [137].

[254] *Graham v Philcox* [1984] Q.B. 747; *Patel v WH Smith (Eziot) Limited* [1987] 1 W.L.R. 853 at 859H; *Papworth v Lindhaven* [1988] E.G.C.S. 54; *Pavledes v Ryesbridge Properties Limited* (1989) 58 P. & C.R. 459; *Penn v Wilkins*, unreported, February 15, 1966, CA (Civil Division) Transcript No. 36 of 1966, referred to at [1992] 1 W.L.R. 128H; *Bye v Marshall* [1993] C.L.Y. 1627; *Saeed v Plustrade Limited* [2001] R.T.R. 30 at [5], but in the Court of Appeal, Sir Christopher Slade said that he would prefer to leave the point open, it not being necessary to the decision: [2002] 2 E.G.L.R. 19 [22].

and the courts have on a number of occasions now decided[255] that a right to park is capable of being an easement. Any residual doubts on this point have now been dispelled by the decision of the House of Lords in *Moncrieff v Jamieson*.[256]

It is, of course, essential that there must be a dominant tenement nearby to which the right is appurtenant. So in *Le Strange v Pettefar*,[257] a facility of parking cars on waste land which had been enjoyed by a tenant of the landowner not as such but as a member of the general public was held not to pass to the tenant under the statutory general words in the conveyance of the reversion to his property. **9-97**

Secondly, if the right in question did amount to a right to use the whole of the area to the complete exclusion of the owner, it could not be an easement.[258] A right to park a car on a forecourt capable of taking two or three other cars is, however, certainly capable of being an easement and falls on the easement side of what has been called the "ill defined line" between rights in the nature of an easement and rights in the nature of an exclusive right to possess or use.[259] While there would thus appear to be no difficulty about a right to park at large anywhere in a defined area forming the subject-matter of the grant of an easement, a question might arise if the right were such as entirely to exclude the landowner from the area in question: for example, if the right were granted in respect of a single car space reserved for the grantee's sole use and protected by a chain or a lockable post. **9-98**

Such a situation might, at least if the right were granted in a lease, result in the space being regarded as part of the demise.[260]

Where an exclusive right to park cars on a strip of land during normal business hours on weekdays was claimed, the Court of Appeal held that the right claimed was not capable of being an easement because the owner would not have had any reasonable use of the land for parking or any other purpose; the curtailment of his right to use the land for intermittent periods would make his ownership **9-99**

---

[255] *Bilkus v Redbridge LBC* (1968) 207 E.G. 803; *Newman v Jones*, unreported, March 22, 1982, cited in *Handel v St Stephens Close* [1994] 1 E.G.L.R. 70 at 71M; *London & Blenheim Estates Limited v Ladbroke Retail Parks Ltd* [1992] 1 W.L.R. 1278; *Leon Asper Amusements Ltd v Northmain Carwash* (1966) 56 D.L.R. (2d) 173; *Queanbeyan Leagues Club Ltd v Poldune Pty Ltd* (1996) 7 B.P.R. 15,078; *Owners of Strataplan 42472 v Menala Pty Limited* (1998) 9 B.P.R. 97,717; *Hair v Gillman* [2000] 3 E.G.L.R. 74.

[256] [2007] 1 W.L.R. 2620; see in particular per Lord Scott at [47], and per Lord Neuberger at [137].

[257] (1939) 161 L.T. 300.

[258] *Copeland v Greenhalf* [1952] Ch. 488, in which, however, *Wright v Macadam* was not referred to; *London & Blenheim Estates Limited v Ladbroke Retail Parks Limited* (above) at 1288C.

[259] *Hair v Gillman* [2000] 3 E.G.L.R. 74 at 75G. In *Pointon York Group Plc v Poulton* [2006] EWCA Civ 1001 a tenant whose lease conferred an exclusive right to park in seven parking spaces was held to be "occupying" those spaces within the meaning of s.23 of the Landlord and Tenant Act 1954.

[260] *Hilton v James Smith & Sons (Norwood) Ltd* [1979] 2 E.G.L.R. 44, where a tenant was given liberty to use a defined part of a private roadway as a parking area, Ormrod L.J. regarded the tenant as being in possession of that area and entitled to sue in trespass and to place posts around the land (at 46G), but *cf. Simpson v Fergus* (2000) 79 P. & C.R. 39, to the opposite effect; and in *Moncrieff v Jamieson* (above) Lord Neuberger said at [145] that the proposition that a right to park a vehicle in a specific space was incapable of being an easement was open to doubt.

"illusory".[261] Likewise, where the claim was to a right to park on a strip of waste-land an unlimited number of vehicles, the only restriction being one of space availability, it was held that the right claimed would render the ownership of the servient owner illusory and the right could not be an easement.[262] These cases may have to be reconsidered in the light of recent dicta in the House of Lords.

9–100   In *Moncrieff v Jamieson*[263] Lord Scott said that he could not see why a landowner could not grant rights of a servitudal character over his land to any extent that he wished; he also pointed out that an owner of land over which he had granted parking rights could still make use of it by building over or under the parking area or by placing advertising hoardings on the walls and perhaps in other ways; he could see no reason why, if an area of land could accommodate nine cars, the owner could not grant an easement to park nine cars on it, but could grant an easement to park seven or eight; he therefore rejected the tests of whether the owner was left with a "reasonable" degree of use or whether his own-ership had been rendered "illusory" and any test of degree which paid regard to the totality of the land owned by the servient owner as opposed to the land over which the right was enjoyed[264]; he suggested that the true test is whether the servient owner retains possession and, subject to the reasonable exercise of the right in question, control of the servient land.

9–101   Lord Neuberger said that he saw considerable force in this view, expressed himself not satisfied that a right is prevented from being an easement simply because the right granted would involve the servient owner being effectively excluded from the property and thought it contrary to common sense that an arrangement be debarred from being an easement simply because the parties had chosen to identify a precise space over which the right was to be exercised which was just big enough to hold the vehicle in question; it was, however, not neces-sary to decide the point and to do so might produce unforeseen consequences.[265]

9–102   *Moncrieff v Jamieson* has not conclusively decided the problem of whether an *exclusive* right to park in a defined area can be an easement. The appeal was from Scotland; the issue for decision was whether an express grant of a right of way included as an ancillary right the right to park on the way and the right claimed was not a right to park on a space just big enough for the number of vehicles in question; the dicta referred to above were, therefore, *obiter*. Nevertheless, the rea-soning of Lords Scott and Neuberger on this point seems so obviously sensible and the result so practical that it is suggested that courts are unlikely in future to

---

[261] *Batchelor v Marlow* [2001] EWCA Civ 1051; (2001) 82 P. & C.R. 459 reversing [2001] 1 E.G.L.R. 119, where the deputy judge had held that the right claimed, being limited in time, did not, as a matter of degree, amount to such exclusion of the owner as to preclude it subsisting as an easement (see at 125M); but doubted by Lords Scott and Neuberger in *Moncrieff v Jamieson* (above) at [60] and [143].

[262] *Central Midlands Estates Ltd v Leicester Dyers Ltd* [2003] 2 P. & C.R. DG1.

[263] [2007] 1 W.L.R. 2620 at [59].

[264] Disapproving dicta of Judge Baker in *London & Blenheim Estates Limited v Ladbroke Retail Parks Limited* [1992] 1 W.L.R. 1278 at page 1288C.

[265] *Moncrieff v Jamieson* (above) at [137]–[145].

allow the "ouster principle" to prevent an exclusive parking right being regarded as an easement, at least where it is clear that the parties intended it to be.[266]

In their recent Consultation Paper, the Law Commission express some doubt as to whether Lord Scott's test of retention of possession and control is "helpful" and propose an alternative.[267] The present editors cannot see why it should not be. The distinction between possession and control on the one hand and use and occupation on the other is fundamental in property law and is of daily application in cases where the question is whether a document creates a tenancy or a licence or whether an owner has been dispossessed within the meaning of the Limitation Act 1980. Moreover their suggested alternative that a right should be capable of being an easement notwithstanding that it confers exclusive possession on the owner of the dominant tenement, provided that the right is clearly defined, limited in scope so as to restrict the use of the servient land and does not create a tenancy, would appear to fall foul of the very problem foreseen by Lord Neuberger of potentially elevating every licence to make use of land for a limited purpose into a proprietory right.					**9–103**

It would not appear, however, to be any objection to the existence of an easement that charges are made, whether for the parking itself or for the upkeep of the parking area.[268]					**9–104**

If, of course, the grant is, on its true construction, only intended to be personal to the parties, it will only amount to a licence,[269] though a licence may ripen into an easement upon a subsequent conveyance under the operation of section 62 of the Law of Property Act 1925.[270]					**9–105**

Express grant

The grant of a right to "pass and repass" does not per se include a right to park[271]; neither does a "right of access".[272] It was, however, held in *Bulstrode v Lambert*[273]					**9–106**

---

[266] Lord Scott is surely right to have said at [59] that if an easement can be acquired by grant, it can be acquired by prescription, but until and unless *Batchelor v Marlow* is overruled, courts inferior to the House of Lords will be bound to follow it, unless it can be distinguished; one ground for doing so may be that it was a claim to a right by prescription: in *Jackson v Mulvaney* [2003] 1 W.L.R. 360 at [23], Latham L.J. said that in the case of a right expressly granted "the court will undoubtedly lean in favour of the creation of an easement if the intention of the parties was clearly to that end", whereas in the case of a right claimed by prescription, "the court has the more difficult task of assessing the evidence as to alleged use in order to determine whether the alleged right has been established"; alternatively, it may be possible to distinguish *Batchelor v Marlow* on the basis that account was not taken of the sort of concurrent uses open to the servient owner mentioned by Lord Scott. For an article critical of the decision of the Court of Appeal in *Batchelor v Marlow* and referred to in their Lordships' speeches in *Moncrieff v Jamieson*, see "Rights of Parking and the Ouster Principle after Batchelor v Marlow" by Alexander Hill-Smith, [2007] 71 Conveyancer 223.

[267] Law Commission Consultation Paper No. 186 at paras 3.34–3.55.

[268] *London & Blenheim Estates Limited v Ladbroke Retail Parks Limited* (above) at 1288B. And see *Montrose Court Holdings Ltd v Shamash* [2007] EWCA Civ 251.

[269] *cf. IDC Group v Clark* [1992] 2 E.G.L.R. 184.

[270] As happened in *Sweet & Maxwell v Michael-Michaels (Advertising)* [1965] C.L.Y. 2192; and in *Hair v Gillman* (above).

[271] per Megarry J. in *Newman v Jones* (above); *Butler v Muddle* (1995) 6 B.P.R. 97,532.

[272] *Moncrieff v Jamieson* (above).

[273] [1953] 1 W.L.R. 1064.

that a right to pass and repass over a cul-de-sac for the purpose of obtaining access to an auction mart implied the further right to halt vehicles in the cul-de-sac for so long as might be necessary for the purpose of loading or unloading, because such a right was necessary for the enjoyment of the right reserved.[274] It has been argued[275] that this principle would entitle the tenants of a block of flats to park overnight on the basis that the tenants could not substantially enjoy their tenancies without the right to park, but that seems unsustainable. A right to stop to load and unload will not be implied where there is no necessity to do so to enjoy the right of access granted, as where, for example, there is an adequate loading or parking area on the dominant land.[276]

9–107   The grant of a right to "use" a way, however, as opposed merely to pass and repass over it, does entitle the grantee to stop to load and unload and to use the way for all other purposes by which property adjoining a street would normally be accommodated, provided that such use does not interfere unreasonably with the use of the way by its owner or those equally entitled.[277] That description would appear to include parking (so long as this does not obstruct use of the way by others) and it would seem to be implicit in the finding of the Court of Appeal in *Snell & Prideaux Limited v Dutton Mirrors Limited* that "parking and washing vehicles and loading and unloading" were activities that showed that the dominant owner had not intended to abandon his rights, that this is correct. In *Papworth v Lindhaven*[278] where the tenants had been granted "full rights . . . to use . . . the forecourts and roadways in the curtilage" of their flats, counsel conceded and the court accepted that this entitled them to park without charge. That a right to "use" a road includes a right to park was accepted by the court in *McClymont v Primecourt Property Management Limited,*[279] citing this paragraph.

Implied grant

9–108   The purchasers of the reversions on blocks of flats have sometimes sought to exploit their purchase by delineating car spaces on the forecourt or drives or private roads surrounding the block and charging the tenants for the right to

---

[274] See also *McIlraith v Grady* [1968] 1 Q.B. 468 and para.9–30, above. These cases were followed in *Robmet Investments Pty Limited v Don Chen Pty Limited* (1997) 8 B.P.R. 97,649, where Windeyer J. said that the right to stop to unload should be regarded as a normal incident of the grant of a right to pass and repass, but this would appear not to be supported by the English authorities. In *Moncrieff v Jamieson* (above), where vehicles could not access the dominant land from the way (because it was at the bottom of a cliff), it was accepted that the right included the right to turn vehicles round and to station such vehicles for the purpose of loading and unloading and for short visits (meter readers, postmen, repair men): see at [123] per Lord Neuberger.

[275] *Handel v St Stephens Close Limited* (above) at 71G.

[276] *London & Suburban Land and Building Co (Holdings) Ltd v Carey* (1991) 62 P. & C.R. 480; *SS & M Ceramics Pty Ltd v Kin* [1996] 2 Qd. R. 540; *B & Q Plc v Liverpool & Lancashire Properties Limited* [2001] 1 E.G.L.R. 92 (where it was held that there was plenty of space on the dominant tenement to accommodate vehicles wishing to load or unload).

[277] *Snell & Prideaux Limited v Dutton Mirrors Limited* [1995] 1 E.G.L.R. 259 at 262M–263D.

[278] [1988] E.G.C.S. 54.

[279] [2000] E.G.C.S. 139.

park.[280] Often the tenants will have been accustomed to park in those areas for many years without payment without, however, having any express right to do so in their leases. The question will thus arise whether all or any of them acquired parking rights at the time of the grant of their leases by virtue of the operation of section 62 of the Law of Property Act 1925 as a right appertaining or reputed to appertain to each of the flats. Of this situation Megarry J. said in *Newman v Jones*[281]:

> "Where there is a block of flats and the tenants in general regularly park their cars within the curtilage of the block, the liberty, privilege, easement, right or advantage of being allowed to do this will rapidly become regarded as being something which appertains or is reputed to appertain to each of the flats in the block and as being reputed to be appurtenant to each of those flats. Accordingly, on the grant of a lease of one of the flats, I think that section 62(2) of the Law of Property Act 1925 will operate to give the lessee an easement of car parking appurtenant to his leasehold. I do not think that it matters whether the previous occupants of the particular flat did or did not park their cars within the curtilage of the block, or, indeed, whether they had any car. In all ordinary cases the reputation will be that of a right of parking which goes with each of the flats, for there will be no reason for one lessee to have greater rights than another in this respect. The question, 'can the tenants park their cars round the block?' would receive a simple yes, and not an answer which distinguished between one flat and another on the basis of whether previous occupants of the flat in question had been accustomed to park their cars round the block."

The judge then observed that no reputed right would arise if the landlord operated some scheme whereby tenants were required to obtain some licence or parking permit from the landlord or pay for a specified space, nor could any rights arise if a contrary intention had been expressed in the lease. The fact that there is not enough space for every flat owner to park simultaneously is not a reason for denying that any rights exist.[282]

In *Handel v St Stephens Close*,[283] the tenants of a block of flats sought an interlocutory injunction to restrain the landlords from carrying out work to the estate roads to provide secure parking space. The plaintiffs' evidence was to the effect that parking had gone on for many years as if the tenants had that right and that both landlord and tenants believed that they would have such a right when the leases were granted. That was regarded as sufficient to raise a serious issue as to whether section 62 applied and an injunction was granted.

9–109

---

[280] *Newman v Jones* (above); *Overcom Properties v Stockleigh Hall Residents* (1989) 58 P. & C.R. 1; *Handel v St Stephens Close* [1994] 1 E.G.L.R. 70; *Papworth v Lindhaven* [1988] E.G.C.S. 54.
[281] Above.
[282] *Newman v Jones* (above).
[283] [1994] 1 E.G.L.R. 70.

Prescription

9–110   There is no reason why parking rights cannot be acquired by prescription or under the doctrine of lost modern grant. In *Bye v Marshall*,[284] such a claim succeeded. In *Pavledes v Ryesbridge Properties Limited*[285] and *Central Midlands Estates Ltd v Leicester Dyers Ltd*,[286] it failed on the facts. In *Patel v WH Smith (Eziot) Limited*,[287] it should have succeeded if the parties claiming a prescriptive right had not admitted in correspondence during the relevant period that they did not have the right which they were claiming and negotiated for the grant of a licence.[288] In *Batchelor v Marlow* such a claim succeeded at first instance but the appeal was allowed on the ground that the rights claimed were too extensive.[289] In Canada a right for cottage owners to park on a beach beside a lake was held to have been acquired by prescription.[290]

Right to vary, regulate or extinguish parking rights

9–111   Parking rights are often conferred in terms which give the grantor power to control, regulate or alter the parking arrangements. In *Saeed v Plustrade Limited*[291] the tenant of a flat was granted a right in common with twelve others to park on such part of the forecourt as might from time to time be specified by the landlord as reserved for parking when space was available and subject to such regulations as the landlord might make from time to time. There were twelve spaces originally and the landlords proposed to reduce them to four and charge for them. It was held that the power to specify spaces only entitled the landlord to change the location of spaces, not to extinguish the right; the power was conferred on him for the purpose of giving effect to that right, not extinguishing or reducing it. There is, however, no reason why a power to extinguish parking rights on notice cannot be reserved but this would have to be done clearly and expressly.[292]

9–112   Likewise in *Liverpool & Lancashire Properties Limited v B&Q Plc*[293] a warehouse on a retail park was demised with a right for the tenant, its customers and staff to park in a communal car park. The landlord purported to make a regulation pursuant to powers in the lease prohibiting the tenant's staff from using the communal car park until spaces within the demise were fully occupied by parked cars. It was held that the purported regulation was ultra vires because: (1) the regulations sought to determine whether and in what circumstances the right for the staff to use the communal car park might be exercised rather than how it might

---

[284] [1993] C.L.Y. 1627.
[285] (1989) 58 P. & C.R. 459.
[286] [2003] 2 P. & C.R. DG 1.
[287] [1987] 1 W.L.R. 853.
[288] See the explanation and criticism of this case in *Mills v Silver* [1991] Ch. 271 at 284.
[289] [2001] 1 E.G.L.R. 119; [2001] 82 P. & C.R. 459, CA.
[290] *Depew v Wilkes* (2000) 193 D.L.R. (4th) 529 (Ontario Supreme Court) upheld by the Court of Appeal at (2002) 216 D.L.R. (4th) 487.
[291] [2001] R.T.R. 30, upheld on appeal at [2002] 25 E.G.L.R. 19.
[292] [2001] R.T.R. 30 at [18] approved by the Court of Appeal at [2002] 25 E.G.L.R. 19 at [32].
[293] Blackburne J., June 28, 2000 (unreported).

be exercised; (2) by making the use of the communal car park conditional, the regulation had the effect, if and so long as the condition was not fulfilled, of depriving the tenant altogether of the right expressly granted to it by the lease; and (3) by requiring the tenant to use up the car parking spaces shown on the lease plan, the regulation was seeking to determine how the tenant used its own premises even though there was no requirement within the lease that the areas so identified be used by the tenant for that purpose.

In *Montrose Court Holdings Ltd v Shamash*[294] the owners of an estate comprising some 100 residences, on which there were at most 114 parking spaces available, made regulations pursuant to a power reserved in leases and transfers seeking to regulate the use of parking spaces on the service road by the issue of permits, which entitled each household, upon payment of a fee, to bring one car onto the estate and park it for up to 72 hours at a time. It was contended by one of the freeholders on the estate who enjoyed a right to park on the service road that such regulations amounted to a derogation from his grant. The Court of Appeal held that the regulations were perfectly proper. The easement conferred a right to compete with others for a parking space. The regulations did not reduce that right but merely regulated it. The purpose of the regulations was to enable those with a right to compete to do so in an orderly way and to have an opportunity to obtain a space. They were intended for the benefit of all those with a right to park.[295] **9–113**

In *Hunte v E. Bottomley & Sons Ltd*[296] a tenant of a café on an industrial estate was granted a right to pass and repass over the estate roads subject to a proviso that he observed "all regulations of the Landlord relating to the parking or unloading of vehicles or the direction of traffic". The landlord built a wall across the main access road, thus compelling the tenant and his customers to use a more obscure, unattractive and circuitous route, and sought to justify this by reference to the power to make regulations as to the direction of traffic. Ward L.J. said [297]: **9–114**

> "If any meaning has to be given to a proviso which allows the Landlord to make regulations for the direction of traffic, then the most it can mean is that he is allowed to direct in which way traffic will circulate along this roadway round the site. In other words, the most he could possibly do, in my judgment, is say: 'All traffic shall pass in a clockwise direction' or 'It must go in an anti-clockwise direction'; but that is not a justification for blocking the road and saying: 'You can only come halfway along the road, then you turn back and go the way you came.' That, in my judgment, is a wholly fanciful construction of the proviso."

In the High Court of Ireland it has been held that the reservation by a landlord of a right to alter and vary rights granted by leases and to make rules and regulations **9–115**

---

[294] [2006] EWCA Civ 251, distinguishing *Saeed v Plustrade Ltd* (above).
[295] [2006] EWCA Civ 251, at [26].
[296] [2007] EWCA Civ 1168.
[297] [2007] EWCA Civ 1168, at [13].

for the efficient and safe operation of a financial services centre did not entitle him to make rules or alter or vary rights the effect of which would in substance be to extinguish the tenants' expressly granted rights.[298]

9–116   It has been held in Australia that the grant of a right to leave a car in a marked space on land indicated imposes a duty on the grantor to make the grant effective by selecting and marking out a space, though this would not necessarily be final as some occasion might arise for changing the location of the space.[299]

Traffic control measures

9–117   Where a tenant or other landowner enjoys rights of parking and rights of way, it is nevertheless open to the landlord or servient owner to impose measures to regulate the speed and flow of traffic as long as these do not represent a substantial interference with the dominant owner's enjoyment of his rights but are rather designed to enable the drives or other ways to be conveniently and safely used by all those entitled to use them.[300] Indeed, it is plain that such a system may enhance the dominant owner's rights by preventing conflict and obstruction rather than derogating from them and such a system may be necessary to avoid a landlord becoming liable in nuisance because of the obstruction of the way by his other tenants.[301] So in *Celsteel Limited v Alton House Holdings*[302] it was held that a landlord of a block of flats was entitled to impose a new one-way traffic flow system with designated exits and entrances and in *Saint v Jenner*,[303] where the servient owner had installed speed bumps, he and his successors were held to be entitled to retain them provided that they repaired any potholes which appeared as a result of the presence of the bumps (because otherwise they would be adopting a nuisance).

Clamping

9–118   If a motorist parks his car without permission on another person's property, knowing that by doing so he runs the risk of it being clamped, he has no right to damage or destroy the clamp. If he does so, he will be guilty of a criminal offence.[304] The owner of a chattel has no right to retake his property from the land of another when its presence there is due to his own wrongful trespass and no right to use force against the property of the landowner (for example to his fences, gates, clamps or other obstacles) in the process.[305]

---

[298] *Redfont Ltd v Custom House Dock Management Ltd* [1998] 1 E.H.C. 206.
[299] *Owners of Strataplan 42472 v Menala Pty Limited* (1998) 9 B.P.R. 97,717.
[300] *Celsteel Limited v Alton House Holdings Limited* [1985] 1 W.L.R. 204 (reversed on another ground at [1986] 1 W.L.R. 512).
[301] *Hilton v James Smith & Sons (Norwood) Limited* [1979] 2 E.G.L.R. 44, a decision which it is not easy to reconcile with the principle that a servient owner is not responsible for the repair or fitness of the right of way.
[302] Above.
[303] [1973] Ch. 275.
[304] *Lloyd v DPP* [1992] 1 All E.R. 982.
[305] *Stear v Scott* [1992] R.T.R. 226.

It is lawful and not tortious to clamp a vehicle unlawfully parked on private **9–119** property by a motorist who has seen a warning notice to the effect that vehicles parked without proper authority would be clamped and only released on payment of a fee, because the motorist has voluntarily consented to the risk of his car being clamped and remaining clamped until payment of the reasonable cost of clamping and declamping.[306]

The clamper may not, however, (a) exact an unreasonable or exorbitant charge, **9–120** (b) do anything which would cause damage to the car, (c) delay in releasing the car after the owner offers to pay, or (d) fail to provide means for the motorist to communicate his offer. The argument that clamping could be justified in the absence of those conditions (including that of warning of the risk of clamping) by application of the doctrine of distress damage feasant, that is, the right of a landowner to impound trespassing livestock or objects until paid compensation for any damage caused by them, has been rejected.[307]

The act of clamping the wheel of another person's car, however, even when **9–121** that car is trespassing, is an act of trespass to that other person's property unless it can be shown that the owner of the car has consented to or willingly assumed the risk of his car being clamped. So where a person parked on land which was not obviously not part of the highway and did not see the warning sign, she was entitled to the return of the payment she was required to make to get the clamp removed.[308] A person who sees but does not read a warning notice, on the other hand, will probably be held to have assumed the risk of being clamped.

---

[306] *Arthur v Anker* [1996] 2 W.L.R. 602.
[307] [1996] 2 W.L.R. 602.
[308] *Vine v Waltham Forest LBC* [2000] 1 W.L.R. 1283.

CHAPTER 10

SUPPORT

1.—THE RIGHT TO SUPPORT

Right to support

The right to support from the adjacent or subjacent soil may be claimed in respect **10–01** of land in its natural state, or in respect of land subjected to an artificial pressure by means of buildings or otherwise. A further right to support may be claimed for one building from adjacent or subjacent buildings.

> "The right to support of land and the right to support of buildings stand upon different footings as to the mode of acquiring them, the former being prima facie a right of property analogous to the flow of a natural river, or of air; Rowbotham v. Wilson[1] though there may be cases in which it would be sustained as matter of grant (see Caledonian Railway Company v. Sprot[2]); whilst the latter must be founded upon prescription or grant, express or implied: but the character of the rights, when acquired, is in each case the same."[3]

---

[1] (1857) 8 E. & B. 123; affirmed (1860) 8 H.L.C. 348.

[2] (1856) 2 Macq. 449.

[3] *Bonomi v Backhouse* (1858) E.B. & E. 622 at 654, 655, per Willes J.; approved by Lord Selborne L.C. in *Dalton v Angus* (1881) 6 App. Cas. 792. Caution was expressed about this general dictum in *Brace v South Eastern Regional Housing Association Ltd* [1984] 1 E.G.L.R. 144 at 146, 147. Thus, as will be seen, there is no natural right for support of land from water, but it may be possible to acquire (by express or implied grant or by prescription) a right to support of land from water. Further, even if there can be no natural support of land from water, it may be possible to acquire a right of support for buildings on land from water under the land.

Support is usually provided vertically or laterally. In *Rees v Skerrett*[4] there were two terraced houses, one owned by the plaintiff and the other owned by the defendant. The defendant demolished his house leaving the common wall exposed. The common wall was unstable and suffered cracking. The cracking was not attributable to the weight of the roof and the upper parts of the structure borne by the wall but to the effect of wind suction caused by the wind blowing along the front of the terrace and along the wall itself. It was held that the defendant had interfered with the easement of support and was responsible for the cracking to the wall. It was not appropriate to distinguish between "weight support" and "wind support".

"The name 'easement of support' is not perhaps the most eloquent and precise description of what, in essence, is merely a right not to have the support removed without replacement."[5] "A negative right not to have the support removed cannot accurately be expressed in terms of a positive right to have the support maintained."[6] This description of the nature of the right as a negative right which does not place a positive duty on the owner of the servient tenement may be accurate as a matter of property law but is now incomplete in view of recent developments in the law of tort which, in some circumstances, places a measured duty of care on the owner of land in relation to the fact of support to other land.[7]

2.—NATURAL SUPPORT TO LAND

Prima facie rule as to support

10–02   If every proprietor of land were at liberty to dig and mine at pleasure on his own soil, without considering what effect such excavations must produce upon the land of his neighbours, it is obvious that the withdrawal of the lateral support would, in many cases, cause the falling in of the land adjoining. As far as the mere support to the soil is concerned, such support must have been afforded as long as the land itself has been in existence; and in all those cases, at least, in which the owner of land has not, by buildings or otherwise, increased the lateral pressure upon the adjoining soil, he has a right to the support of it, not as an easement but as an ordinary right of property, necessarily and naturally attached to the soil. The leaning of the courts appears to have been in favour of this doctrine at least from the seventeenth century: thus, in Rolle's Abridgment,[8] it is laid down: "It seems that a man who has land closely adjoining my land cannot dig his land so near mine that mine would fall into his pit; and an action brought for such an act would lie."

---

[4] [2001] 1 W.L.R. 1541.
[5] *Byard v Co-operative Permanent Building Society Ltd* (1970) 21 P. & C.R. 807 at 820, per Megarry J.
[6] (1970) 21 P. & C.R. 807, at 821.
[7] These developments are considered at paras 10–32–10–38, below.
[8] Rolle's Abr. 565: Trespass, Justification, (I), pl. 1. (The wording in the text is a translation from the original law French.)

Questions as to support have arisen where the title to land A has been severed from the title to land B which is subjacent to land A vertically; or from the title to land C which is adjacent to land A laterally. The prima facie rule in these cases is that (independently of the result of any facts or instruments connected with the severance) the owner of land A is of common right entitled to have it supported vertically by land B[9] and laterally by land C.[10] But the obligation to support land A laterally only binds that portion of the adjacent land C, the existence of which in its natural state is necessary for the support of land A.[11]

Support from water, silt and liquid pitch

The natural right does not extend to the enjoyment of the support of any under- **10–03**
ground water which may be in the soil, so as to prevent the adjoining owner from draining his soil; the presence of the water in the soil being an accidental circumstance, the continuance of which the landowner has no right to count upon. The distinction has been justified on the ground that when the result of digging is to withdraw land-support, whether subjacent or lateral, from the neighbouring land, the probability of a subsidence of the neighbouring land is more or less obvious, and there is a practical limit of space within which a landowner should know that he cannot dig without running the risk of letting down the neighbouring land; but the landowner cannot tell at what distance the digging on his own land may operate to drain the underground springs on land of other landowners and he would not know what underground springs there are, nor where they are.[12] The distinction has also been explained by the rule that it is not possible to own or have an interest in percolating underground water.[13]

The leading case in relation to water is *Popplewell v Hodkinson*.[14] In that case, land was granted for building subject to a chief rent, and cottages were built upon it, and the owner afterwards granted the adjacent land to the builders of a church, whose excavations so far drained the land on which the cottages stood that the soil subsided and they became cracked and damaged. The church builders, however, were held not responsible. Delivering the judgment of the Court of Exchequer Chamber, Cockburn C.J. said[15]:

---

[9] *Humphries v Brogden* (1850) 12 Q.B. 739; *Caledonian Ry v Sprot* (1856) 2 Macq. 449; *N.E. Ry v Elliott* (1860) 1 J. & H. 145; *Backhouse v Bonomi* (1861) 9 H.L.C. 503.

[10] *Hunt v Peake* (1860) John. 705; *Davis v Treharne* (1881) 6 App. Cas. 460 at 446, per Lord Blackburn; *Dalton v Angus* (1881) 6 App. Cas. 740 at 808, 809, per Lord Blackburn.

[11] *Birmingham Corp v Allen* (1877) 6 Ch. D. 284.

[12] See *Jordeson v Sutton, Southcoates and Drypool Gas Co* [1899] 2 Ch. 217 at 249–250 and 255–256. The existence of such a right of support of land from water would inhibit drainage of land: see *ibid.*, at 256.

[13] The rule is laid down in *Chasemore v Richards* (1859) 7 H.L.C. 349 and *Bradford Corp v Pickles* [1895] A.C. 587 and see paras 6–25–6–30, above. This explanation is given in particular in *Langbrook Properties Ltd v Surrey C.C.* [1970] 1 W.L.R. 161 and *Stephens v Anglian Water* [1987] 1 W.L.R. 1381. This reasoning is criticised in (1988) 104 L.Q.R. 183 (J.G. Fleming).

[14] (1869) L.R. 4 Ex. 248.

[15] (1869) L.R. 4 Ex. 248 at 251, 252.

"Although there is no doubt that a man has no right to withdraw from his neighbour the support of adjacent soil, there is nothing at common law to prevent his draining that soil, if, for any reason it becomes necessary or convenient for him to do so. It may be, indeed, that when one grants land to another for some special purposes, for building purposes, for example, then, since according to the old maxim a man cannot derogate from his own grant, the grantor could not do anything whatever with his own land which might have the effect of rendering the land granted less fit for the special purpose in question than it otherwise might have been."

The court held that there was nothing in the grant to the plaintiff to warrant the inference of an implied condition to prevent the defendant from doing with the adjacent land what was incidental to its ordinary use, namely draining it in order to render it more capable of being adapted to building purposes.

10–04   *Popplewell v Hodkinson*[16] was applied by Plowman J. in *Langbrook Properties Ltd v Surrey County Council*.[17] Strictly, the case was not concerned with the easement of support.[18] Instead, the plaintiff company claimed damages for nuisance and negligence against the defendants, alleging that, by pumping out excavations on land in the vicinity of the plaintiff's land, the defendants had abstracted water percolating beneath the plaintiff's land, causing settlement of the buildings on that land. A preliminary issue was ordered to be tried whether, on the facts pleaded in the statement of claim, the plaintiff had any cause of action against the defendants by reason of any withdrawal of water by the pumping of it from beneath the surface of the land in the vicinity of the plaintiff's land, and Plowman J., after an extensive review of the cases on the withdrawal of percolating water, held that they established that a man may abstract the water under his land which percolates in undefined channels to whatever extent he pleases, notwithstanding that this may result in the abstraction of water percolating under the land of his neighbour and, thereby, cause him injury. In such circumstances the principle of *sic utere tuo ut alienum non laedas* did not operate and the damage was *damnum sine injuria*. There was no room for the law of nuisance or the law of negligence to operate. This case is further discussed in relation to the recent developments in tort at para.10–34, below.

10–05   *Langbrook Properties Ltd v Surrey County Council* was approved by the Court of Appeal in *Stephens v Anglia Water Authority*.[19] It was held that because no-one can have a right or interest in underground percolating water, and because a deliberate abstraction of such water, even when intended to cause harm to a neighbouring owner, was not actionable, it was an inevitable logical consequence that the right to abstract water was exercisable regardless of the consequences, whether

[16] (1869) L.R. 4 Ex. 248.
[17] [1970] 1 W.L.R. 161.
[18] See [1970] 1 W.L.R. 161 at 165A. The reasoning is criticised in (1988) 104 L.Q.R. 183 (J.G. Fleming).
[19] [1987] 1 W.L.R. 1381.

physical or pecuniary, to neighbours. This case is further discussed in relation to the recent developments in tort at para.10–34, below.

In this context, the approach to what is meant by "water" has been restrictive. **10–06** Silt or liquid pitch or brine are not considered to be "water" and there may be a natural right of support for land from such substances. Thus, in *Jordeson v Sutton, Southcoates and Drypool Gas Co*[20] the defendants carried out excavation works upon their property, which adjoined the plaintiff's property, and in the course of such excavation cut through a stratum of running silt, with the result that the plaintiff's houses erected upon his adjoining property subsided. The evidence was conflicting as to whether the stratum of silt could truly be considered to be muddy water or wet sand, and in effect the decision turned upon the view taken by a majority of the Court of Appeal as to the conclusion to be drawn from this evidence; Sir Nathaniel Lindley M.R. and Rigby L.J. holding that the plaintiff's land was supported, not by a stratum of water, but by a bed of wet sand, whilst Vaughan Williams L.J. came to the conclusion that the withdrawal of subterranean water support had caused the subsidence. The decision of a majority of the court was therefore based upon the ordinary law with regard to the right to support.

In *Trinidad Asphalt Co v Ambard*[21] the subsidence of the plaintiff's land **10–07** was caused by the oozing and escape of pitch, which formed the main ingredient of the plaintiff's land, consequent upon excavations on the defendant's adjacent lands. The judgment of the Privy Council was in favour of the plaintiff, but the grounds of the decision were based upon the conclusion that the pitch or asphalt which escaped from beneath the plaintiff's land was not water, but a mineral.

In *Lotus Ltd v British Soda Co Ltd*,[22] the defendants engaged in wild brine **10–08** pumping, that is to say, the extraction from beneath their land of saturated brine resulting from the dissolution of rock salt by water. As the defendants extracted the brine, more water flowed under the plaintiff's land and dissolved further salt and the resulting brine was pumped away to be replaced by yet more water. In consequence the plaintiff's land subsided and serious damage was caused to buildings on the land. Sir John Pennycuick V.-C. said that there was no difference in principle between the removal *in specie* of a support such as wet sand and an operation which consisted, first, in causing a solid support to liquefy and then removing the resultant liquid. As the threat of subsidence was a continuing one, the plaintiff was entitled to an injunction which it claimed restraining further pumping.

In *Brace v South East Regional Housing Association Ltd*[23] Eveleigh L.J., while **10–09** evidently, from his reference to the judgment of Vaughan Williams L.J. in

---

[20] [1899] 2 Ch. 217. See the Brine Pumping (Compensation for Subsidence) Act 1891, and *cf. Salt Union v Brunner* [1906] 2 K.B. 822, which is considered at para.6–27, above.
[21] [1899] A.C. 594.
[22] [1972] Ch. 123.
[23] [1984] 1 E.G.L.R. 144.

Jordeson v Sutton, Southcoates and Drypool Gas Co,[24] feeling some doubt in the matter, nevertheless proceeded upon the assumption that there can be no prescriptive right to support from water itself, and further upon the assumption that where a right of support has been acquired against a neighbour's land that neighbour is not liable for a weakening of support which is attributable only to the withdrawal of water. In *Brace v South East Regional Housing Association Ltd*,[25] however, the plaintiff had a prescriptive right to support for her building from an adjoining building, which was demolished. The removal of that building caused the clay upon which it had been built to dry out and shrink, with consequent subsidence causing damage to the plaintiff's building. The Court of Appeal distinguished the cases which allow immunity to an owner who draws off percolating water to which another owner has no proprietary right and found the defendant liable for the damage caused to the plaintiff's building by the interference with the support to which it was entitled.

10–10   Even though a right to support of land from water is not part of the natural right of support of land, the decision in *Brace* left open the possibility that a right to support of land from water could be acquired.[26] Indeed, this appears to have been recognised by dicta which refer to a landowner not being able to derogate from a grant of land which is to be taken to have implicitly restricted the grantor from abstracting water and letting down the surface of the land.[27] It was also suggested in *Brace* that a right to support from water for land with buildings could be acquired.[28] However, it has been suggested that it would not be possible to have an implied grant in relation to an unknowable and changing subject-matter such as underground water.[29]

3.—SUPPORT OF BUILDINGS BY LAND

No natural right

10–11   There is no natural right to the support of a building per se; thus it was said by Lord Selborne L.C. in *Dalton v Angus*[30]: "Support to that which is artificially imposed upon land cannot exist ex jure naturae, because the thing supported does not itself so exist."

If, however, land has been affected by the withdrawal of support, and a building on it has also been affected, and it is shown that the withdrawal of support would have affected the land in its natural state, in other words, that the land has

---

[24] [1899] 2 Ch. 217.
[25] [1984] 1 E.G.L.R. 144.
[26] See [1984] 1 E.G.L.R. 144 at 146F.
[27] See *Popplewell v Hodkinson* (1869) L.R. 4 Ex. 248 at 252–253.
[28] See [1984] 1 E.G.L.R. 144 at 147.
[29] See *Jordeson v Sutton, Southcoates and Drypool Gas Co* [1899] 2 Ch. 217 at 256.
[30] (1881) 6 App. Cas. 740 at 792; see *Ray v Fairway Motors (Barnstaple) Ltd* (1968) 20 P. & C.R. 261.

been deprived of its natural right of support, damages may be recovered for the consequent injury to the building.[31]

The rule negativing any natural right of support as regards buildings appears to have been acted upon in early cases. Thus it was laid down in *Wilde v Minsterley*[32]:

10–12

> "If A is seised in fee of copyhold land closely adjoining the land of B, and A erect a new house upon his copyhold land, and any part of his house is erected on the confines of his land adjoining the land of B, if B afterwards dig his land so near to the foundation of the house of A, but not in the land of A, that by it the foundation of the messuage, and the messuage itself, fall into the pit, still no action lies by A against B, inasmuch as it was the fault of A himself that he built his house so near the land of B, for he cannot by his (own) act prevent B from making the best use of his land that he can."

In *Wyatt v Harrison*[33] the declaration stated that the plaintiff was possessed of a certain dwelling-house; that the defendant in rebuilding his dwelling-house adjoining, dug so negligently, carelessly, and improperly into the soil and foundation of his own dwelling-house, and so near the soil and foundation of the said dwelling-house of the plaintiff, that by reason thereof the plaintiff's wall gave way and was damaged. To so much of this declaration as "related to the defendant's digging into the soil and foundation of the said dwelling-house of him the defendant, so near to the soil and foundation of the said dwelling-house of the plaintiff that by reason thereof", etc., the defendant demurred. Lord Tenterden said[34]:

10–13

> "The question reduces itself to this, Whether, if a person builds to the utmost extremity of his own land, and the owner of the adjoining land digs the ground there, so as to remove some part of the soil which formed the support of the building so erected, an action lies for the injury thereby occasioned? Whatever the law might be, if the damage complained of were in respect of an ancient messuage possessed by the plaintiff at the extremity of his own land, which circumstance of antiquity might imply the consent of the adjoining proprietor, at a former time, to the erection of a building in that situation,

---

[31] *Brown v Robins* (1859) 4 H. & N. 186; *Hunt v Peake* (1860) John. 705; *Hamer v Knowles* (1861) 6 H. & N. 454; *Richards v Jenkins* (1868) 18 L.T. 437; *Att-Gen v Conduit Colliery Co* [1895] 1 Q.B. 301 at 312. *Smith v Thackerah* (1866) L.R. 1 C.P. 564, which appears to throw some doubt on the principle, is commented on in *Att-Gen v Conduit Colliery Co*, above, at 313, and it is noticeable that in that case *Hamer v Knowles* does not appear to have been cited. Damages may also be recovered for letting down a modern house where the person excavating in the adjoining land is not the owner, but a trespasser: *Jeffries v Williams* (1850) 5 Exch. 792; *Bibby v Carter* (1859) 4 H. & N. 153; or a contractor having no proprietary interest therein: *Keegan v Young* [1963] N.Z.L.R. 720.

[32] (1640) 2 Rolle's Abr. 564, 565, Trespass, Justification (1) pl. 1. (The wording in the text is a translation of the original law French.)

[33] (1832) 3 B. & Ald. 871.

[34] (1832) 3 B. & Ald. 871, at 875, 876.

it is enough to say in this case that the building is not alleged to be ancient, but may, as far as appears from the declaration, have been recently erected; and if so, then, according to the authorities, the plaintiff is not entitled to recover. It may be true that if my land adjoins that of another, and I have not by building increased the weight upon my soil, and my neighbour digs in his land so as to occasion mine to fall in, he may be liable to an action. But if I have laid an additional weight upon my land, it does not follow that he is to be deprived of the right of digging his own ground, because mine will then become incapable of supporting the artificial weight which I have laid upon it. And this is consistent with 2 Rolle's Abridgment Trespass (I.) pl. 1. The judgment will therefore be for the defendant."

10–14 In *Ray v Fairway Motors (Barnstaple) Ltd*[35] the defendant company's land was excavated in such a way that a wall on the plaintiff's land collapsed but without there being any interference with the natural right of support. The Court of Appeal held that, in the absence of an easement of support (which in this case there was), an owner of land could do what he liked, even if the result was the collapse of his neighbour's building; and there was no room, at least so far as the Court of Appeal was concerned, for a duty to exercise reasonable care: *Donoghue v Stevenson*[36] has not affected this rule of law. Fenton Atkinson L.J. suggested, however[37] that the position might have been different if the plaintiff could have shown something beyond the mere removal of soil, or omission to take active steps to prevent its effect; for example the adoption of an unnecessarily dangerous method of removal.

10–15   These cases undoubtedly establish that there is no natural right of support for buildings from land and that if a right of support is to be asserted it must be shown it was acquired as an easement. However, in so far as these cases state that in the absence of an easement of support, there is no cause of action against an adjoining land owner who does acts on his land which adversely affect the support in fact enjoyed by his neighbour, they need to be reconsidered in the light of more recent developments in the law of tort.[38]

Acquisition of right to support

10–16 Although the surface owner where he has encumbered the surface by building has no natural right to the additional support which has become necessary, it is settled by the decision of the House of Lords in *Dalton v Angus*[39] that an enjoyment of such additional support for not less than 20 years will be sufficient to confer a right, subject only to the conditions which limit all acquisitions of rights by length

---

[35] (1968) 20 P. & C.R. 261.
[36] [1932] A.C. 562.
[37] (1968) 20 P. & C.R. 275.
[38] See paras 10–32–10–38, below.
[39] *Angus & Co v Dalton and the Commissioners of Her Majesty's Works and Public Buildings* (1877) 3 Q.B.D. 85; (1878) 4 Q.B.D. 162; sub nom. *Dalton v Angus* (1881) 6 App. Cas. 740.

of enjoyment only. The case is of such importance, and evinced such divergency of view amongst the judges who considered it, that it is thought to merit extensive consideration. The law as established by *Dalton v Angus* is summarised at para.10–25, below.

The decision in Dalton v Angus

The action was brought by Angus & Co, the owners in fee of a coach factory at   **10–17**
Newcastle upon Tyne, to recover damages for injuries to their factory caused by the defendant commissioners, and by their contractor, the defendant Dalton, in excavating the soil of the adjoining property, on which the Probate Office was to be built. It appeared that the plaintiffs' building and the adjoining building on the defendants' land were estimated to be upwards of a hundred years old; that up to the year 1849, being about 27 years before the incident, both houses had been occupied as dwelling-houses; that in that year the plaintiffs' predecessor in title had converted his house into a coach factory, in such a manner as to increase the pressure on the borders of his own soil and consequently on the adjoining property; that this had been done without the express assent of the defendants' predecessor, but openly and without any attempt at concealment; that the defendants had pulled down their house and the wall dividing the two properties without injury to the factory; but that, in excavating in their land for the purpose of providing cellarage (which had not previously existed) for the offices to be built, they had dug below the foundations of the plaintiffs' building without leaving sufficient support, and had thus brought the whole building to the ground.

At the trial Lush J. directed a verdict for the plaintiffs for the damages claimed, but left them to move for a judgment in order to have the questions of law determined. On motion for judgment it was argued for the defendants, first, that the plaintiffs' factory was not entitled to the support claimed; and, secondly, that the commissioners were not responsible for the negligence of their contractor. Upon the second point the court considered itself bound by the decision in *Bower v Peate*[40] to find against the defendants; and this ruling was ultimately affirmed by the Court of Appeal and the House of Lords.

On the first point, which raised the whole question of the law of support, the   **10–18**
judges differed.[41] On appeal[42] Brett L.J. agreed with the majority of the court

---

[40] (1876) 1 Q.B.D. 321.

[41] Lush J., adhering in substance to the view which he had taken at the trial, thought that the plaintiffs ought to succeed; and rested his opinion partly on the doctrine of the presumption of a grant after 20 years' uninterrupted enjoyment and partly on an analogy to the Statutes of Limitation. He thought that the decision in *Bonomi v Backhouse* (1859) E.B. & E. 655; (1861) 9 H.L.C. 503, involved the very point in question. But Cockburn C.J. held that, if any presumption of a grant were derived from 20 years' user, it was open to be rebutted, and that, when it was proved or admitted that no grant or assent was in fact made or given, the presumption was at an end; and further that, the enjoyment not being capable of being interrupted by any reasonable means, no presumption in fact arose. Mellor J. agreed with the Lord Chief Justice, and accordingly judgment was given for the defendants. All the judges agreed that the right to support was not an easement within the Prescription Act.

[42] (1878) 4 Q.B.D. 162.

below; but Cotton and Thesiger L.JJ. being of the contrary opinion, the decision was reversed.[43]

Although, upon the main question, the majority of the Court of Appeal decided in favour of the plaintiffs' contention, the Court was unanimously of opinion that, the construction of the plaintiffs' factory being somewhat unusual, the jury should have been asked to determine whether the weight which had been put upon the adjoining soil was such as the owner of the soil could be reasonably expected to be aware of, and, on this ground, directed the defendants to elect within 14 days whether they would take a new trial.[44] The option was not exercised; and, judgment having been entered for the plaintiffs for damages assessed by a special referee, the defendants appealed to the House of Lords.

10–19   The appeal[45] was, in the House of Lords, twice argued, the second time before seven judges of the High Court who had not yet been parties to any decision in the case.[46] The judges, in answering the questions put to them by the House, were unanimous in advising that the judgment of the Court of Appeal was justified by the authorities; and two only of them[47] disapproved of the principle underlying

[43] Thesiger L.J., while admitting that the presumption of a lost grant was a presumption, not "*juris et de jure*", but liable to be rebutted, held that it could not be rebutted by mere proof by the owner of the servient tenement that no grant was in fact made either at the commencement or during the continuance of the enjoyment; in fact, it "is in the nature of an estoppel by conduct, which, while it is not conclusive so far as to prevent denial or explanation of the conduct, presents a bar to any simple denial of the fact, which is merely the legal inference drawn from the conduct": see at 173. The cases of *Barker v Richardson* (1821) 4 B. & Ald. 579; *Webb v Bird* (1863) 13 C.B. (n.s.) 841; and *Chasemore v Richards* (1859) 7 H.L.C. 349, in which a presumption of this nature had been held to be rebutted, "as direct authorities go no further than to shew that a legal incompetence as regards the owner of the servient tenement to grant an easement, or a physical incapacity of being obstructed as regards the easement itself, or an uncertainty and secrecy of enjoyment putting it out of the category of all ordinary known easements, will prevent the presumption of an easement by lost grant; and on the other hand indirectly, they tend to support the view, that as a general rule where no such legal incompetence, physical incapacity, or peculiarity of enjoyment, as was shewn in those cases, exists, uninterrupted and unexplained user will raise the presumption of a grant, upon the principle expressed by the maxim, 'Qui non prohibet quod prohibere potest assentire videtur'." (at 179)

As to the alleged impossibility or extreme difficulty of obstructing the enjoyment of the right of support, he pointed out that this only exists where the servient tenement, being itself covered with buildings, enjoys a reciprocal benefit from the dominant tenement; and in any case he held himself bound by the authorities not to admit the argument as sufficient.

The judgment of Cotton L.J. was to the same effect. None of the Lords Justices adopted the view expressed by Lush J., that the period of 20 years might be limited for the acquisition of a right to support by analogy to the Limitation Acts (see at 170 and 199); and none of them seems to have considered that the right might be an easement within the Prescription Act (see at 170 and 196).

[44] (1878) 4 Q.B.D. 162 at 187, 204.

[45] (1881) 6 App. Cas. 740.

[46] Pollock B. and Field, Lindley, Manisty, Lopes, Fry and Bowen JJ.

[47] Lindley and Fry JJ.

the authorities, but the reasons on which their opinions were based were very diverse.[48]

In the course of his opinion,[49] Lindley J. discussed the important question   **10–20** whether the enjoyment of support is not after all rather affirmative than negative, and so capable of interruption by the short method of an action of trespass, and, in the absence of interruption, ripening into an easement under section 2 of the Prescription Act. He said[50]:

> "Support, even when lateral, involves pressure on and an actual use of the laterally supporting soil. . . . No trace is to be found in our law books of any action at law or suit in equity based upon any wrong done to the owner of the servient tenement; and the general opinion certainly is that in the absence of actual damage to the soil, no such action or suit could be maintained. Upon principle, I confess I do not see why this should be so. If a person builds so near the edge of his own land as to use his neighbour's land to support his house without his neighbour's consent, I do not see why such neighbour should have no cause of action. The enjoyment of light coming across adjoining land and the enjoyment of the use of such land for support are in some respects entirely different; for no use is made of a man's property by opening a window on other property near it; and a right not to be overlooked is not recognised by our law. At the same time in every case in which the right to lateral support is alluded to, it is treated as analogous to the right to light, and the difference to which I have drawn attention has not been dwelt

[48] Pollock B. and Field and Manisty JJ. did not refer the right to support to any presumption of grant or acquiescence, but treated it as a proprietary right, to be acquired by a de facto enjoyment for 20 years; and the first-named expressly approved of the conclusion arrived at by Lush J. at the trial, that the rule might be derived by analogy from the Statutes of Limitation. On the other hand, Lindley J. (with whom Lopes J. agreed) was of opinion that support was an easement which, after 20 years' open and uninterrupted enjoyment, the court would presume to have been granted, even though it should be proved or admitted that no sealed or written grant had in fact been executed; and that the law which required the servient owner to remove his soil in order to preserve his unrestricted right to let down his neighbour's house, though it did not "commend itself to common sense", was completely established by authority. Fry J. felt the same difficulty in approving of the principles of the decisions, holding that "an excavation for the sole purpose of letting down a neighbour's house is of so expensive, so difficult, so churlish a character, that it is not reasonably to be required in order to prevent the acquisition of a right" (at 775); and adding (at 777) that, as the servient owner cannot, "except by a trespass or an impertinence", ascertain the nature of his neighbour's structure, the incidence of its burden on the soil, or the depth and character of its foundations, the enjoyment is so secret that no right ought to be founded upon it; but he also thought the authorities conclusive against this view being adopted in practice. Lastly, Bowen J., reverting to some extent to the opinions of the Lord Chief Justice and Brett L.J., treated the 20 years' rule as a "canon of evidence", and held that 20 years' user, peaceful, open, and as of right, was sufficient ground for inferring a lawful origin of the user, and that the inference could only be met by showing that there was no such lawful origin, either at law (as by grant or covenant), or in equity (as by agreement or acquiescence); he thought the decisions showed that the enjoyment was capable of interruption. As to the question of notice, upon which the defendants had obtained from the Court of Appeal the option to have the case retried, Lindley, Lopes and Bowen JJ. thought that this should have gone to the jury, while the remaining judges considered the question immaterial.

[49] (1881) 6 App. Cas. 740 at 764.

[50] (1881) 6 App. Cas. 740 at 763, 764.

upon or treated as material. Nevertheless, whatever my own opinion would be, looking at the matter theoretically, I am not prepared to say that an action for damages, or an injunction, could be maintained in such a case as I have supposed. The authority against it, although purely negative, would, in my judgment, be considered as too strong to be got over. If, however, your Lordships should be of a different opinion, I apprehend that it would follow that the Prescription Act[51] would apply to and include an easement of lateral support; and the law upon this important subject would then be contained in the provisions of that statute. But all the Judges before whom this case has come concur in holding the Prescription Act not to apply; and, in the absence of authority to the contrary, I am not prepared to differ from them."

On the same subject Fry J. made the following observations in a contrary sense[52]:

"It has been argued at your Lordships' Bar that the doctrine[53] applies in its simplest form to the right in question; for it has been contended that the act of building a house on one piece of land which derives lateral support from the adjoining soil of a different owner is both actionable and preventible, and that, therefore, time constitutes a valid bar. Is such a building actionable? I think not. The lateral pressure of a heavy building on soft ground which causes an ascertainable physical disturbance in a neighbour's soil would no doubt be trespass; but no one ever heard of an action for the mere increment caused by reason of a new building to the pre-existing lateral pressure of soil on soil, producing no ascertainable physical disturbance. If that were the law no one could rightly build on the edge of his land, unless he built upon a rock; and yet the building of walls and other structures on the borders of land is universally recognised as lawful. Nay more, any erection of a house would give a right of action not only to the adjoining neighbours, but to every owner of land within the unascertainable area over which the increase of pressure must, according to the laws of physics, extend. Such an increase of pressure when unattended with unascertainable physical consequences, is, in my opinion, one of those minima of which the law takes no heed. The distinction between the principles applicable to water collected into visible streams and that running in invisible ones through the ground, affords a very good analogy to the distinction which I draw between the pressure of an adjoining house which produces a visible displacement of the soil, and that which produces no visible or ascertainable result, but is only a matter of inference from physical science or subsequent experiment."

Bowen J.'s observations on the same point[54] appear to indicate that he agreed in principle with Lindley J.

---

[51] Prescription Act 1832, s.2.

[52] (1881) 6 App. Cas. 740 at 775.

[53] Sc., *Qui non prohibet quod prohibere potest assentire videtur.*

[54] (1881) 6 App. Cas. 740 at 784.

The House of Lords[55] unanimously dismissed the appeal; and it is of impor-   **10–21**
tance to note the grounds upon which their Lordships' opinions in favour of this
course proceeded.

Lord Selborne L.C., after showing that the right to support to buildings was not
a natural but a conventional or acquired easement, expressed his agreement[56] with
the views of Lindley J. and Bowen J.,

> "that it is both scientifically and practically inaccurate to describe it as one
> of a merely negative kind. What is support? The force of gravity causes the
> superincumbent land, or building, to press downward upon what is below it,
> whether artificial or natural; and it has also a tendency to thrust outwards,
> laterally, any loose or yielding substance, such as earth or clay, until it meets
> with adequate resistance. Using the language of the law of easements, I say
> that, in the case alike of vertical and of lateral support, both to land and to
> buildings, the dominant tenement imposes upon the servient a positive and
> a constant burden, the sustenance of which, by the servient tenement, is nec-
> essary for the safety and stability of the dominant. It is true that the benefit
> to the dominant tenement arises, not from its own pressure upon the servient
> tenement, but from the power of the servient tenement to resist that pressure,
> and from its actual sustenance of the burden so imposed. But the burden and
> its sustenance are reciprocal, and inseparable from each other, and it can
> make no difference whether the dominant tenement is said to impose, or the
> servient to sustain, the weight."

From these considerations it followed that the right to support was to some extent
affirmative, and so properly the subject, not of covenant only,[57] but of grant. It
was also capable of interruption, if not by action, at least by the removal of the
supporting soil; and if in some cases it did not suit the purpose of the supporting
owner to exercise this right of removal, it was the policy of the law that his inac-
tion (whether due to negligence or to his own preponderating interest) should in
time confer a possessory title upon his neighbour. The right of support then, being
an easement, not purely negative, capable of being granted and also capable of
being interrupted, was within section 2 of the Prescription Act; and the question
of grant or no grant was excluded. And, even though the Prescription Act should
not apply, the presumption of a lost grant could not be rebutted by showing that
no grant had in fact been made. As to the question of notice, a landowner who
sees building operations, or alterations of an existing building, in progress upon
the borders of his property, must have imputed to him the knowledge that the
building will require fresh support from the adjoining land; and, if everything is
done honestly and (as far as possible) openly, he must be fixed with knowledge

[55] The Lords present were Lord Selborne L.C. and Lords Coleridge, Penzance, Blackburn and
   Watson.
[56] (1881) 6 App. Cas. 740 at 793.
[57] See per Littledale J. in *Moore v Rawson* (1824) 4 B. & C. 332 at 340; para.1–38, above.

of the amount of support enjoyed. No question need therefore have been submitted to the jury.

10–22   Lord Penzance expressed the opinion that, if the matter were *res integra*, it might properly be held that a building owner acquired, immediately upon erecting a house, the right to have it supported by the adjacent soil; but he agreed with Fry J. in thinking that length of enjoyment could only confer a title through the acquiescence of another, and that an enjoyment which was both secret and incapable of being interrupted without an unreasonable waste of labour and expense was no evidence of acquiescence, and should not on principle be made the basis of any right. However, he considered that the ruling of Lush J. was entirely supported by the authorities, and that the appeal on this ground should be dismissed.

10–23   Lord Blackburn thought that the fiction of a lost grant, however introduced, was not a rule of evidence which a jury might or might not conform to, but an established doctrine of the court; and that to refuse to administer such a rule, when established, was at least as much a usurpation of legislative authority as it was at first to introduce it. He did not consider that acquiescence or laches was the sole, or indeed the chief, principle on which prescriptive rights were founded. Prescription, or *usucapio*, was a matter, not of natural justice, but of positive law, differing in different countries; and the authorities showed that the English law conferred a right after 20 years' enjoyment. The servient owner had notice that some support was required; and this was enough to put him on inquiry.

Lord Blackburn thought it unnecessary to decide the question whether support was within the Prescription Act. But, incidentally, he supplied an answer to the argument drawn by Fry J.[58] from the impossibility of pushing the doctrine of Lindley J. to its extreme limits. Lord Blackburn said[59]:

"The distinction between a right to light and a right of prospect, on the ground that one is a matter of necessity and the other of delight, is to my mind more quaint than satisfactory. A much better reason is given by Lord Hardwicke in Att.-Gen. v. Doughty,[60] where he observes that if that was the case there could be no great towns. I think this decision, that a right of prospect is not acquired by prescription, shews that, whilst on the balance of convenience and inconvenience, it was held expedient that the right to light, which could only impose a burthen upon land very near the house, should be protected when it had been long enjoyed, on the same ground it was held expedient that the right of prospect, which would impose a burthen on a very large and indefinite area, should not be allowed to be created, except by actual agreement. And this seems to me the real ground on which Webb v. Bird[61] and Chasemore v. Richards[62] are to be supported. The rights there claimed were analogous to prospect in this, that they were vague and

---

[58] (1881) 6 App. Cas. 740 at 775; see para.10–20, above.
[59] (1881) 6 App. Cas. 740 at 824.
[60] (1788) 2 Ves.Sen. 453.
[61] (1861) 10 C.B. (n.s.) 268; (1862) 13 C.B. (n.s.) 841.
[62] (1859) 7 H.L.C. 349.

undefined, and very extensive. Whether that is or is not the reason for the distinction the law has always, since Bland v. Moseley,[63] been that there is a distinction; that the right of a window to have light and air is acquired by prescription, and that a right to have a prospect can only be acquired by actual agreement."

Lord Watson agreed with Lord Selborne in holding that the right of support to a **10–24** building, whether lateral or vertical, was a positive easement; being, as he said, probably influenced by the consideration that a decision that the easement was negative would form an unsatisfactory precedent in Scotland, where positive servitudes alone are capable of being acquired by prescription. He thought that no question of fact need have been submitted to the jury. Lord Coleridge did not deliver a detailed opinion, but expressed his concurrence in the judgments of Lords Selborne and Blackburn. He did not say whether he agreed with the former in holding the easement to be a positive one.

The law as established by Dalton v Angus

The decision of the House of Lords in *Dalton v Angus*[64] may be taken as estab-   **10–25** lishing the rule that 20 years' enjoyment of support to a building, whether from the adjacent or from the subjacent land, being peaceable, open and as of right, will (either by a right springing out of the enjoyment at the common law, or under the Prescription Act, or under the doctrine of lost grant) confer the right to have the support continued; that, if the right is based on the presumption of a grant founded on the enjoyment, the presumption is absolute and cannot be rebutted by showing that no grant has in fact been made; and that, in the absence of any wilful fraud or concealment, the outward appearance of the building is sufficient notice to all persons concerned of the amount of support which it requires.[65]

Acquisition of right of support for buildings by grant

Apart from a title resulting from enjoyment, a title to the easement of support for   **10–26** buildings may be made in other ways. Thus, it follows from the judgments in *Dalton v Angus*[66] that where the title to land A, on which a building has been or is about to be erected, is severed from the title to the subjacent or adjacent land, the right to have such building supported by the subjacent or adjacent land may be acquired by grant whether express or implied. When acquired the right is precisely the same as that of support for land.[67]

---

[63] (1587), cited in 9 Co.Rep. 58a.
[64] (1881) 6 App. Cas. 740.
[65] See *Union Lighterage Co v London Graving Dock Co* [1902] 2 Ch. 557; *Lloyds Bank Ltd v Dalton* [1942] Ch. 466.
[66] (1881) 6 App. Cas. 740 at 792, 809. As to implied grants and reservations of the right to support, see also para.3–74, above.
[67] (1881) 6 App. Cas. 740.

Withdrawal of support in working coal

10–27 Under the Coal Mining Subsidence Act 1991, the person who is responsible for the damage[68] is obliged, subject to certain conditions, to make good or pay compensation for damage occurring to land or buildings as the result of the withdrawal of support in working coal.[69]

4.—SUPPORT OF BUILDINGS BY BUILDINGS

10–28 The principles which have just been discussed in relation to a right of support for buildings from adjacent or subjacent land also apply to the question of a right of support for buildings from adjacent or subjacent buildings.[70] There is no natural right to such support[71]; but it may in the case of buildings belonging to different owners be claimed by prescription,[72] in which case the enjoyment must have been as of right,[73] and therefore open[74]; or by implied grant or reservation.[75] Where a right of support for a building by a building exists it will generally relate to the building as it then stands and thus the obligation is not affected by whether the dominant building from time to time, by reason of settlement, decay or any other cause, leans to a greater or lesser extent on the servient building.[76] A right of support does not entitle the dominant owner to freedom from vibration from the servient building; but if the vibration is sufficiently grave, it may give rise to an action for nuisance.[77]

---

[68] See Coal Industry Act 1994, s.43(1), (8), Sch.6.

[69] s.1. For cases on the predecessor of the 1991 Act, see *Knibb v National Coal Board* [1987] Q.B. 906; *McAreavey v Coal Authority* (1999) 80 P. & C.R. 41. The right of operators licensed under the Coal Industry Act 1994 to withdraw support from land is governed by s.38 of that Act. For the creation of easements by statute, see para.3–02, above. For rights in respect of other minerals, see paras 1–127 and 1–128, above.

[70] The subject is discussed in Bodkin, "Rights of Support for Buildings and Flats" in (1962) 26 Conv. (n.s.) 210.

[71] See *Southwark and Vauxhall Water Co v Wandsworth Board of Works* [1898] 2 Ch. 603 at 612. It was said in that case that in the absence of an easement, the pulling-down owner must be careful to interfere as little as possible with the adjoining house, but he is not bound to take active steps for its protection, or to mitigate a mischief which follows inevitably on the reasonable exercise of his own rights (per Collins L.J. at 612, 613). This view of the law may now have to be reconsidered in the light of more recent developments in the law of tort.

[72] *Lemaitre v Davis* (1881) 19 Ch. D. 281; *Waddington v Naylor* (1889) 60 L.T. 480; *Selby v Whitbread & Co* [1917] 1 K.B. 736 at 751.

[73] *Tone v Preston* (1883) 24 Ch. D. 739.

[74] *Solomon v Vintners' Co* (1859) 4 H. & N. 601; *Lemaitre v Davis*, above; *Gately v Martin* [1900] 2 I.R. 269; *Union Lighterage Co v London Graving Dock Co* [1902] 2 Ch. 557; *Lloyds Bank Ltd v Dalton* [1942] Ch. 466.

[75] See para.3–74, above. Where the owner of building A and building B, which is subjacent to A and supports it, demises A, he cannot withdraw the support, but no covenant is implied by him to repair B: *Colebeck v Girdlers' Co* (1876) 1 Q.B.D. 234 at 243.

[76] *Byard v Co-operative Permanent Building Society Ltd* (1970) 21 P. & C.R. 808 at 821. This general comment particularly applies to an easement of support acquired by implied grant or by prescription. In the case of an express grant of an easement of support, the matter will turn on the terms of the grant. Further, if an extra burden is placed on the servient tenement for a period of 20 years, the right to maintain this extra burden may have been acquired by prescription.

[77] (1970) 21 P. & C.R. 808.

5.—THE NATURE OF THE RIGHT TO SUPPORT

A right of support from land, whether natural or acquired, and whether by way of   **10–29**
support for land alone or for land and buildings, possessed by the owner of the
dominant tenement is not a right to have the whole or any part of the adjacent or
subjacent soil left in its natural state, but simply a right not to have the dominant
tenement appreciably affected by anything done, however carefully,[78] in the
adjoining soil adjacent or subjacent.[79] The obligation of the servient owner is negative, namely, to refrain from any act which will diminish support. He is not
obliged to take active steps to maintain the thing that gives support.[80] There is no
actionable interference with the easement of support in the case of subsidence
caused by the operation of nature on adjoining land after this has been used in a
normal manner not itself diminishing support.[81]

The nature of the right of support for buildings by buildings has been   **10–30**
summarised as follows by Sir Wilfrid Greene M.R. in *Bond v Nottingham
Corporation*[82]:

> "The owner of the servient tenement is under no obligation to repair that part
> of his building which provides support for his neighbour. He can let it fall
> into decay. If it does so, and support is removed, the owner of the dominant
> tenement has no cause for complaint. On the other hand, the owner of the
> dominant tenement is not bound to sit by and watch the gradual deteriora-
> tion of the support constituted by his neighbour's building. He is entitled to
> enter and take the necessary steps to ensure that the support continues by
> effecting repairs, and so forth, to the part of the building which gives the
> support. But what the owner of the servient tenement is not entitled to do is,
> by an act of his own, to remove the support without providing an equivalent.
> There is the qualification upon his ownership of his own building that he is
> bound to deal with it, and can only deal with it, subject to the rights in it
> which are vested in his neighbour."

---

[78] *Humphries v Brogden* (1850) 12 Q.B. 739 at 757; *Hunt v Peake* (1860) John. 705 at 710.
[79] *Bonomi v Backhouse* (1858) E.B. & E. 622 at 657; *Dalton v Angus* (1881) 6 App. Cas. 740 at 808;
Att-Gen v Conduit Colliery Co [1895] 1 Q.B. 301 at 313.
[80] *Sack v Jones* [1925] Ch. 235; *Bond v Nottingham Corp* [1940] Ch. 429 at 438; *Macpherson v
London Passenger Transport Board* (1946) 175 L.T. 279.
[81] *Rouse v Gravelworks Ltd* [1940] 1 K.B. 489 (erosion caused by rainwater in a gravel-pit on adjoining land being blown on to the plaintiff's land).
[82] [1940] Ch. 429 at 438, 439, affirming [1939] Ch. 847; see also *Sack v Jones* [1925] Ch. 235. For a
case which concerned the absence of equivalent support, see *Brace v South East Regional Housing
Association* [1984] 1 E.G.L.R. 144. In *Grimley v Minister of Housing and Local Government*
[1971] 2 Q.B. 96 John Stephenson J. held that on the compulsory purchase of the servient tenement
the owner of the dominant tenement, which enjoyed an easement of support, was not entitled to
notice under para.3(1)(b) of Sch.1 to the Acquisition of Land (Authorisation Procedure) Act 1946,
as the dominant owner was not the owner of land comprised in the order within the meaning of
s.8(1) of that Act and s.3(2) of the Liverpool Corporation (General Powers) Act 1966. (The relevant
provisions of the Acquisition of Land (Authorisation Procedure) Act 1946 were repealed by the
Acquisition of Land Act 1981, s.34(3), Sch.6. See now *ibid.*, ss.2(3), 7(1), 12(1), Sch.1.)

In that case a servient building became subject to a clearance order made under section 26 of the Housing Act 1936[83] and so was required to be demolished, but the order did not extend to the dominant building. It was held that the demolishing servient owner or local authority was bound to provide equivalent support for the dominant building.

When the removal of support is actionable

10–31 The removal of support is not actionable if, upon removal of that support, equivalent support is provided.[84] Further, it is established that no cause of action arises until actual injury is caused to the dominant tenement and time does not begin to run under the Statutes of Limitation until then.[85] Where there are successive subsidences, each creates a separate cause of action.[86] Consequently, a claimant cannot recover damages at law for loss of value of his property due to the risk of future subsidence[87] or for the cost of effecting remedial works designed to prevent anticipated future subsidence,[88] though he might in these circumstances be able to obtain a *quia timet* mandatory injunction provided that the likelihood of future damage is sufficiently proved and that the injunction is in terms clear enough to give the other party adequate indication of the work that has to be done.[89] Moreover, provided that the remedial works have not been done (in which case there would be no jurisdiction to grant an injunction) it seems that damages equal to the cost of remedial works could be awarded in equity in lieu of an injunction.[90] An owner or lessee of minerals is not liable for damage caused to neighbouring land by subsidence occasioned by acts of his predecessor in title, although the damage did not occur until after the owner or lessee came into possession.[91]

---

[83] Repealed.
[84] *Rowbotham v Wilson* (1857) 8 E. & B. 123 at 157; *Bower v Peate* (1876) 1 Q.B.D. 321 at 327.
[85] *Backhouse v Bonomi* (1861) 9 H.L.C. 503; *West Leigh Colliery Co v Tunnicliffe & Hampson Ltd* [1908] A.C. 27. See now the Limitation Act 1980, s.2.
[86] *Darley Main Colliery Co v Mitchell* (1886) 11 App. Cas. 127; *Crumbie v Wallsend Local Board* [1891] 1 Q.B. 503; *Hall v Duke of Norfolk* [1900] 2 Ch. 493 at 503; *Redland Bricks Ltd v Morris* [1970] A.C. 652 at 664.
[87] *West Leigh Colliery Co v Tunnicliffe & Hampson Limited* [1908] A.C. 27.
[88] *Midland Bank Plc v Bardgrove Property Services Limited* (1992) 65 P. & C.R. 153 followed in *Yorkshire Water Services Ltd v Sun Alliance & London Insurance Plc* [1998] Env. L.R. 204. Cf. *Co-operative Wholesale Society Ltd v British Railways Board* [1995] N.P.C. 200 where a bulging wall was held to be a nuisance to the neighbouring owner who was accordingly entitled to demolish the wall and recover the cost as damages.
[89] *Midland Bank Plc v Bardgrove Property Services Limited*, above, at 170, per Sir Christopher Slade.
[90] *Hooper v Rogers* [1975] 1 Ch. 43. This case was not cited in *Midland Bank Plc v Bardgrove Property Services Limited* (above) where the court rejected the claim for damages in lieu on the grounds (a) that there was no need for an injunction because the work had been done and (b) that damages could never be a satisfactory alternative to a *quia timet* injunction. The latter reason would not appear to be sustainable.
[91] *Greenwell v Low Beechburn Coal Co* [1897] 2 Q.B. 165; *Hall v Norfolk (Duke)* [1900] 2 Ch. 493; distinguished on the facts in *Manley v Burn* [1916] 2 K.B. 121.

6. — Support and the Law of Tort

The conventional view

The earlier parts of this chapter have considered cases where there has been no   **10–32**
right of support for land or for buildings, as the case may be. This state of affairs
can arise for various reasons. For example, in the case of support for land,
although land has a natural right of support from other land, it does not have a
natural right of support from water.[92] Further, in the absence of an express or
implied grant, and in the first 20 years after construction of a building before a
right of support is acquired by prescription, a building may in fact take support
from adjoining land but without having a right to do so. In these cases, the courts
have over the years held that the neighbouring landowner may do things on his
own land, such as excavation of the land, or demolition of a building or abstraction of water, which result in foreseeable harm to the land or buildings adjoining
but without being liable in nuisance or negligence.[93] A similar approach was
adopted in a case where there was a right of support. The nature of a right of support has been held to be a negative right; the owner of the dominant tenement may
not take positive steps to interfere with the right but was held to be under no obligation, in particular was held to owe no duty of care, to take steps to maintain
support.[94]

Some general principles of the law of nuisance

Before considering recent developments in the law of nuisance, it is useful to set   **10–33**
out some basic general principles. Private nuisance is an act or omission which is
an interference with, disturbance of, or annoyance to a person in the exercise or
enjoyment of his ownership or occupation of land or of some easement, profit, or
other right used or enjoyed in connection with land.[95] A private nuisance may be
and usually is caused by a person doing, on his own land, something which he is
otherwise lawfully entitled to do. His conduct only becomes a nuisance when the
consequences of his act are not confined to his own land but extend to the land of
his neighbour by:

(1) causing an encroachment on his neighbour's land, when it closely
    resembles trespass;
(2) causing physical damage to his neighbour's land or building or works or
    vegetation upon it;
(3) unduly interfering with his neighbour in the comfortable and convenient
    enjoyment of his land.[96]

---

[92] See para.10–03, above.
[93] See paras 10–12 to 10–14, above.
[94] See paras 10–29 to 10–30, above.
[95] Clerk & Lindsell on Torts (18th ed.), para.19–01.
[96] Clerk & Lindsell on Torts (18th ed.), para.19–06.

The application of these principles is illustrated by the decision in *Hunter v Canary Wharf Ltd*.[97] In that case, the defendant erected a tall building on its land. The effect was to interfere with television signals and the resulting television reception in houses on neighbouring land. The House of Lords held that the owner of land is normally entitled to build on his land. He may do so even where the building interferes with a neighbour's view, or a flow of light or air, in the absence of a relevant restrictive covenant or a relevant easement of light or air. If there is a relevant easement, then any substantial interference with that easement is an actionable nuisance. In the absence of a relevant easement, the erection of the building is not a nuisance even though it interferes with the use and enjoyment of the neighbouring houses. This approach was applied to the complaint of interference with television reception. In the absence of an easement, interference with television reception and, in consequence, the enjoyment of occupation of the houses was not a nuisance.

10–34   The approach in the recent case of *Hunter v Canary Wharf Ltd*[98] can be seen to be consistent with the much older cases where a landowner did something on his own land but which, in the absence of an easement of support, was not a nuisance. The cases decided in accordance with the conventional view of the law appeared to establish the following. If one owner erects a building so as to take support, in fact, from a second owner's building or land but where the first owner has no right of support for his building, the second owner is not constrained in his use of his land and can excavate his land or demolish his building without committing any nuisance, even where it is foreseeable that his action will cause the collapse of the first owner's building.[99]

Further, if the first owner's land depends upon the fact of support from percolating underground water, an adjoining owner may abstract the underground water so as to cause the collapse of the first owner's land, with any buildings on it, in the absence of any right of support from the underground water.[100] Again, even where there is a right of support, because the right is a negative one, which imposes no positive duty on the owner of the servient tenement, that owner may neglect his own property as he sees fit even though it is foreseeable that his neglect will cause the collapse of the land or building of the dominant owner.[101]

---

[97] [1997] A.C. 655.

[98] [1997] A.C. 655.

[99] *Wilde v Minsterley* (1640) 2 Rolle's Abr. 564, 565; *Wyatt v Harrison* (1832) 3 B. & Ald. 871; *Dalton v Angus* (1881) 6 App. Cas. 740 at 804 per Lord Penzance; *Southwark and Vauxhall Water Co v Wandsworth Board of Works* [1898] 2 Ch. 603; *Ray v Fairway Motors (Barnstaple) Ltd* (1968) 20 P. & C.R. 261.

[100] *Popplewell v Hodkinson* (1869) L.R. 4 Ex. 248; *Langbrook Properties Ltd v Surrey County Council* [1970] 1 W.L.R. 161; *Dorset Yacht Co Ltd v Home Office* [1970] A.C. 1004 at 1060; *Stephens v Anglian Water Authority* [1987] 1 W.L.R. 1381. The reasoning in *Stephens* was criticised in (1988) 104 L.Q.R. 183 (J.G. Fleming).

[101] See the cases cited in paras 10–29 and 10–30, above, and, in particular, *Bond v Nottingham Corp* [1940] Ch. 429.

Developments in the law of nuisance

In *Goldman v Hargrave*,[102] the Privy Council held that an occupier of land was   **10–35**
under a duty of care to abate a fire which was started by lightning striking a tree on
his land and which spread to his neighbour's land. It was held that the law in this
area is not static. The decision represented an extension of the responsibilities of a
landowner to his neighbour. This decision was applied in England and Wales in
Leakey v National Trust.[103] The National Trust's land included a natural hill. By reason of natural forces, rocks and soil on the hill slipped onto the neighbouring property at the foot of the hill. The court held that the National Trust owed a duty of care
to prevent damage from slips from their land onto the land of the downhill owner.
The scope of the duty is not equivalent to the normal duty of care in negligence,
which is described by reference to the reasonable man in the circumstances of the
case. The duty is instead described as a "measured duty of care", the content of
which is affected by the personal capabilities and circumstances of the particular
defendant. It does not matter whether the duty is expressed as arising in the tort of
nuisance or the tort of negligence; the relevant duty is the same in either case.[104]
These cases have been repeatedly followed and applied.[105] There are two cases in
particular which need to be considered in the context of support to land; these are
Holbeck Hall Hotel Ltd v Scarborough Borough Council[106] and *Rees v Skerrett*.[107]

The Holbeck Hall case[108]

The plaintiffs were the owners of a hotel and grounds situated at the top of a cliff   **10–36**
overlooking the sea. The defendants owned the land forming the undercliff
between the hotel grounds and the sea. That part of the coast was subject to
marine erosion, there had been some minor landslips over the years and the
defendants had investigated the position. In 1993 a massive landslip caused loss
of support to the hotel grounds and part of the hotel, which had to be demolished.
On the plaintiffs' claim to damages, the trial judge held that the defendants knew
that progressive landslips were likely which at some indeterminate future time
would affect the plaintiffs' land and that, although they neither knew nor foresaw
that the hazard was of such a magnitude that it would be likely to involve the
grounds and the hotel itself, they owed a duty of care to the plaintiffs and had

---

[102] [1967] 1 A.C. 645.

[103] [1980] Q.B. 485.

[104] [1980] Q.B. 485 at 514–515; see also *Delaware Mansions Ltd v Westminster C.C.* [2001] UKHL
55; [2001] 4 All E.R. 737 at [31].

[105] See, for example, *Holbeck Hall Hotel Ltd v Scarborough B.C.* [2000] Q.B. 836; *Bybrook Barn
Centre Ltd v Kent C.C.* [2000] EWCA Civ 300; [2001] L.G.R. 239; *Delaware Mansions Ltd v
Westminster C.C.* [2001] UKHL 55; [2002] 1 A.C. 321; *Rees v Skerrett* [2001] EWCA Civ 760;
[2001] 1 W.L.R. 1541; *Wandsworth L.B.C. v Railtrack Plc* [2001] EWCA Civ 1236; [2002] 2
W.L.R. 512; *Marcic v Thames Water Utilities* [2002] 2 A.C. 42.

[106] [2000] Q.B. 836.

[107] [2001] 1 W.L.R. 1541.

[108] [2000] Q.B. 836; the court approved the earlier first instance decision in *Bradburn v Lindsay*
[1983] 2 All E.R. 408 and followed the unreported decision of the Court of Appeal in *Bar-Gur v
Bruton*, July 29, 1993.

been negligent in failing to conduct further investigations which would have made it clear that further remedial works were required to ensure the long-term stability of the slope. On appeal, it was confirmed that an owner or occupier of land did owe a measured duty of care to prevent danger to a neighbour's land from lack of support due to natural causes where the owner or occupier knew, or was presumed to know, of the defect or condition on his land giving rise to the danger, even though he had not created it, and where it was reasonably foreseeable that the defect or condition would, if not remedied, cause damage to the neighbour's land; that the duty arose when the defect was known and the hazard or danger to the neighbour's land was reasonably foreseeable, in the sense that it was a danger which a reasonable man with knowledge of the defect should have foreseen as likely to eventuate in the reasonably near future; that liability arose only where the defect was patent and it was no answer for a reasonable landowner to say that he did not observe it if a responsible servant did so, or if as a reasonable landowner, he or his responsible agent ought to have seen it; but that, where the defect was latent, the landowner or occupier was not to be held liable simply because he would have discovered it upon further investigation.

It was further held that the scope of the duty depended not only upon the defendant's knowledge of the hazard, the ease and expense of abatement and his ability to abate it, but also upon the extent to which the damage which in fact eventuated was foreseen, and whether it was fair, just and reasonable in all the circumstances to impose a duty. In the circumstances of that case, it was held that justice did not require that a defendant should be held liable for damage which, albeit of the same type, was vastly more extensive than that which was foreseen, or could have been foreseen without extensive further geological investigation. This was particularly so where the defect in the land existed just as much on the plaintiffs' land as on the defendant's land. In those circumstances, the scope of the defendant's duty had been confined to an obligation to take care to avoid damage to the plaintiffs' land which they ought to have foreseen without further geological investigation and since it was not aware of the magnitude of the danger which in fact occurred, it was not liable. *Bond v Nottingham Corporation*[109] was stated to no longer represent the law in relation to the existence of a positive duty to maintain support.[110]

Rees v Skerrett[111]

10–37 This case involved two terraced houses, one owned by the plaintiff and one owned by the defendant. The defendant pulled down his house thereby exposing the common wall between the properties. The exposed wall was unstable and it was held that the defendant whose land was subject to an easement of support had withdrawn support without providing an equivalent and this constituted an actionable interference with the easement. However, the plaintiff had suffered further damage to his property due to rain falling on the unprotected exposed wall

[109] [1940] Ch. 429.
[110] [2000] Q.B. 836 at 856D–G.
[111] [2001] 1 W.L.R. 1541.

leading to damp penetration into his property. This damage could not be claimed as part of the loss attributable to the withdrawal of support. It was accepted that there was no easement to protection from the weather.[112] Nonetheless, the court held, following *Leakey v National Trust*[113] and the *Holbeck Hall* case,[114] that the defendant owed to the plaintiff a measured duty of care which required him to take positive steps to prevent damage to the plaintiff's property consequent upon the demolition and that he was in breach of that duty.

Although the courts in the *Holbeck Hall* case[115] and in *Rees v Skerrett*[116] considered the line of authority culminating in *Bond v Nottingham Corporation*,[117] they do not seem to have been referred to the other authorities referred to in para.10–34, nor is there any discussion of the significance of *Hunter v Canary Wharf Ltd*.[118] It remains to be seen therefore, how far the new developments in the law of nuisance will impact on what had appeared to be established principles of property law in this area. If the recent decisions are right, then where there is a relevant easement of support and the dominant owner interferes with that easement, he will be liable irrespective of negligence. However, where there is no cause of action for interference with an easement of support, there may be, in accordance with the recent statement of the law of nuisance, a measured duty of care which is broken if a neighbour does something which would foreseeably cause damage to a neighbouring owner or fails to take action to avoid such damage. It seems to have been envisaged in the *Holbeck Hall* case that the duty of care in tort will apply even in a case where the owner of the land affected by the absence of support has an easement of support. However, that ignores the decision of the Court of Appeal in *Duke of Westminster v Guild*[119] where it was held that the existence of an easement of drainage (with the dominant owner having a right to enter the servient land to repair the drain and without the servient owner being under any obligation under the law of easements to repair the drain) prevented the court holding that the servient owner also owed a duty of care to the dominant owner. However, if it is the case that no duty is owed where support is enjoyed pursuant to an easement, this has the result that the dominant owner is not owed any positive duty under the law of easements but if he did not have an easement, he would be owed a duty of care and this may be more beneficial to him in that it imposes a positive duty upon the neighbouring owner. In New Zealand, where an easement of support may not be acquired by prescription, it has been held that there is a duty of care in respect of the support of adjoining buildings.[120]

10–38

---

[112] Following *Phipps v Pears* [1965] 1 Q.B. 76.
[113] [1980] Q.B. 485.
[114] [2000] Q.B. 836.
[115] [2000] Q.B. 836.
[116] [2001] 1 W.L.R. 1541.
[117] [1940] Ch. 429.
[118] [1997] A.C. 655.
[119] [1985] Q.B. 688 at 701–703.
[120] *Bognuda v Upton & Shearer Ltd* [1972] N.Z.L.R. 741; see also *Stoneman v Lyons* (1975) 133 C.L.R. 550 at 567 per Stephens J.

CHAPTER 11

PARTY-WALLS, BANKS, BOUNDARY TREES AND BUILDINGS AND ACCESS TO NEIGHBOURING LAND

1.—PARTY-WALLS GENERALLY

Meaning of party-wall

Before 1926 the term "party-wall" (in relation to a wall separating two proper- **11–01**
ties) might mean—(1) a wall of which the two adjoining owners were tenants in
common; or (2) a wall divided longitudinally into two portions, one belonging to
each adjoining owner; or (3) a wall belonging entirely to one adjoining owner, but
subject to an easement in the other to have it maintained as a dividing wall; or (4)
a wall divided longitudinally into two portions, each portion being subject to a
cross-easement in favour of the owner of the other.[1]

---

[1] *Watson v Gray* (1880) 14 Ch. D. 192 at 194.

Before 1926 the primary meaning of "party-wall" was a wall of which the two adjoining owners were tenants in common.[2] Such owners were prima facie tenants in common where there had been common user of the wall.[3] The same conclusion might result where it was not known under what circumstances the wall was built.[4] Where, however, the quantity of land which each adjoining owner contributed to the site of the wall is known, the property in the wall follows the property in the land, and each party is the owner of so much of the wall as stands upon his own land.[5]

A wall could (and still can) be a party-wall up to a certain point, namely, so far as it divides two buildings of unequal height, and an external wall above that point[6]; and a pilaster or portico, or a fascia, which appears to form an integral portion of one house, may be parcel of and pass on a conveyance of another house.[7] The raising of a party-wall by one part owner without the consent of the other is a violation of that other's right of ownership and possession of his half, and is not less so because a private Act provides that it shall be lawful for the owner or part owner of any party-wall to raise it, provided that the wall when raised will be of the substance required by any byelaw.[8]

Walls held in common before 1926, or declared after 1925 to be party-walls

11–02   As a result of the Law of Property Act 1925 a legal estate in an undivided share in land or buildings cannot exist,[9] and it was accordingly provided by transitional provisions[10] that where, immediately before 1926, a party-wall or other party structure was held in undivided shares, the ownership thereof should be deemed to be severed vertically as between the respective owners, and the owner of each part should have such rights to support and of user over the rest of the structure as might be requisite for conferring rights corresponding to those subsisting at the commencement of the Act. It is similarly provided[11] that in the case of a disposition or other arrangement made after 1925 which, if a holding in undivided shares had been permissible, would have created a tenancy in common, a wall or other structure is or is expressed to be made a party-wall or structure, that structure shall be and remain severed vertically as between the respective owners, and the

---

[2] *Watson v Gray* (1880) 14 Ch. D. 192 at 194.
[3] *Cubitt v Porter* (1828) 8 B. & C. 257; *Standard Bank of British S. America v Stokes* (1878) 9 Ch. D. 68 at 71; *Dean v Walker* (1996) 73 P. & C.R. 366.
[4] *Wiltshire v Sidford* (1827) 1 Man. & Ry. K.B. 404.
[5] *Matts v Hawkins* (1813) 5 Taunt. 20. See *Murly v M'Dermott* (1838) 8 A. & E. 138; *Irving v Turnbull* [1900] 2 Q.B. 129.
[6] *Weston v Arnold* (1873) 8 Ch. App. 1084; *Drury v Army & Navy Auxiliary Co-operative Society* [1896] 2 Q.B. 271; *Dean v Walker* (1996) 73 P. & C.R. 366.
[7] *Thrupp v Scruton* [1872] W.N. 60; *Fox v Clarke* (1874) L.R. 9 Q.B. 565; *Francis v Hayward* (1882) 22 Ch. D. 177. *Cf. Laybourn v Gridley* [1892] 2 Ch. 53.
[8] *Moss v Smith* (1977) 76 L.G.R. 284 (Bristol Corporation Act 1926, s.93(1)).
[9] s.1(6).
[10] Law of Property Act 1925, s.39, Sch.1, Pt V, para.1.
[11] Law of Property Act 1925, s.38(1).

owner of each part shall have such rights to support and user over the rest of the structure as may be requisite for conferring rights corresponding to those which would have subsisted if a valid tenancy in common had been created. It appears that "vertically" must be given a wide construction so as to apply to the median plan of the structure: that is to say, if the walls are not truly vertical, the line of severance will still be through the middle, and if the division (for example, a ceiling and floor) is in fact horizontal, the line of severance must be taken through the ceiling and floor as if that were itself vertical.[12] The effect of the Law of Property Act 1925 has been, therefore, to transfer walls which before the Act would have been in the first of the four classes mentioned above[13] into the fourth class.

Rights of support and of user

The Law of Property Act 1925[14] refers to rights of "support" and of "user" in regard to party-walls. Rights of support have already been considered.[15] *Upjohn v Seymour Estates Ltd*[16] provides an example of "user". The plaintiff's half of the wall had in it two recesses. The defendants' half of the wall collapsed, so that the recesses formed apertures, through which dirt and debris were admitted, damaging the plaintiff's stock. Goddard J. found[17] that the defendants   **11–03**

> "by allowing their part of the wall to fall . . . not only withdrew such support as it afforded to the plaintiff's part, and to the rest of his premises, but also deprived him of the right of user over the defendants' wall, which protected the apertures and to which uses he was entitled by the effect of the statute."

In the light of this decision, it may be that the ruling in *Phipps v Pears*,[18] in a case which did not involve a party-wall, that there is no easement to be protected from the weather, needs to be modified in the case of the kind of party-wall which is within section 38 of the Law of Property Act 1925. With such a party-wall, it can be said that the owner of one-half of the wall is entitled to use the other half of the wall, not only for support but also for protection from the weather and this right is conferred by the statute. The owner of one-half of a party-wall can in an action against a third party only recover damages in respect of the one-half vested in him.[19]

---

[12] See *Wolstenholme and Cherry's Conveyancing Statutes* (13th ed.), Vol. 1, pp. 100, 371.

[13] See para.11–01, above.

[14] ss.38, 39, Sch.1, Pt V, para.1.

[15] See Chapter 10, above.

[16] [1938] 1 All E.R. 614.

[17] [1938] 1 All E.R. 614 at 617. The defendants' part of the wall fell because they had demolished the remainder of their building.

[18] [1965] 1 Q.B. 76. *Upjohn v Seymour Estates Ltd* [1938] 1 All E.R. 614 was not cited in *Bradburn v Lindsay* [1983] 2 All E.R. 408 nor in *Rees v Skerrett* [2001] 1 W.L.R. 1541 but neither case involved the demolition of the other part of the party structure; the latter case is discussed at paras 10–37–10–38, above.

[19] *Apostal v Simons* [1936] 1 All E.R. 207.

11–04   In *Jones v Pritchard*[20] Parker J. held that where a man grants a divided moiety of an outside wall of his house with intent to make it a party-wall between his house and a house to be built on the adjoining land, the law will imply the grant and reservation, in favour of the grantor and the grantee respectively, of such easements as may be necessary to carry out the common intention of the parties as to the use of the wall, the nature of the easements varying with the particular circumstances of each case. Subject, however, to such easements, the owner of each half may deal with it in such manner as he pleases, and if he uses it only for the purposes contemplated, and does so without negligence or want of reasonable care and precaution, he will not be liable for any nuisance or inconvenience occasioned by such user. The usual right of a dominant owner to repair the servient tenement applies, so that the owner of one-half of a party-wall may repair the other half so far as is reasonably necessary for the enjoyment of any easement granted or reserved.[21]

Other party-walls

11–05   Where a wall was held in severalty before 1926, or its ownership becomes divided after 1925 and it is not declared to be a party-wall (in which case the statutory provisions last mentioned will not apply), there seems no authority for saying that the rights of the respective owners of the portions of the wall differ from those of the proprietors of any other two walls which abut on each other. It was formerly said that unless prevented by some easement having been acquired, either party would be at liberty to pare away or even entirely to remove his portion, notwithstanding the other half might be unable to stand without the support of it.[22] In *Cubitt v Porter* Bayley J. said[23]:

> "If the wall stood partly on one man's land and partly on another's, either party would have a right to pare away the wall on his side, so as to weaken the wall on the other, and to produce a destruction of that which ought to be the common property of the two."

On this basis, the fact of the close union of the walls could only impose a duty of greater caution than might otherwise be required in removing the materials; reasonable care would have to be used in removing any portion of the wall[24]; and trespass would lie if one adjoining owner in rebuilding goes beyond his own boundary.[25]

---

[20] [1908] 1 Ch. D. 630.
[21] *Jones v Pritchard* [1908] 1 Ch. D. 630 at 638. See paras 1–91–1–92, above. See also the rights conferred by the Access to Neighbouring Land Act 1992, discussed at paras 11–41 *et seq.*, below.
[22] *Wigford v Gill* (1592) Cro.Eliz. 269; *Peyton v London Corp* (1829) 9 B. & C. 725; and see *Phipps v Pears* [1965] 1 Q.B. 76.
[23] (1828) 8 B. & C. 257 at 264; and see *Bradbee v Christ's Hospital* (1842) 4 Man. & G. 714 at 761.
[24] *Kempston v Butler* (1861) 12 Ir.C.L.R. 516; *Southwark and Vauxhall Water Co v Wandsworth Board of Works* [1898] 2 Ch. 612. See *Hughes v Percival* (1883) 8 App. Cas. 443.
[25] *Mayfair Property Co v Johnston* [1894] 1 Ch. 508.

However, the law of tort has now developed so that the adjoining owner may owe a measured duty of care in the tort of negligence or in nuisance to prevent damage caused by the removal of that owner's wall.

2.—THE PARTY WALL ETC. ACT 1996

(1) *Introduction and definitions*

Introduction

In London, over a long period, the general law relating to party-walls had been   **11–06** modified by public and private Acts directed to the problems special to an area with a high density of building.[26] The most recent Act which applied to London only was the London Building Acts (Amendment) Act 1939, in particular Part VI thereof.[27] There were also various local Acts which applied to specific areas outside London.[28] The 1939 Act was considered to be a success and its provisions were taken as the model for the Party Wall etc. Act 1996 which came into force on July 1, 1997 and applies throughout England and Wales.[29] Most of the decisions cited in the discussion of the 1996 Act were in relation to the earlier legislation; the wording of the earlier legislation was not always the same as the wording used in the 1996 Act and care should be taken in applying those decisions to the 1996 Act.

The operation of the 1996 Act

The 1996 Act is a code dealing with "party-walls", "party fence walls" and "party   **11–07** structures" as defined. It should be noted that a wall may be a "party-wall" for the purposes of the 1996 Act although it is not a party-wall under the general law. In the case of those walls and structures within the 1996 Act, the Act confers rights which would not otherwise exist. Those rights necessarily involve an interference

---

[26] The principal public Acts were the Fires Prevention (Metropolis) Act 1774, the Metropolitan Building Act 1855, the London Building Act 1894, the London Building Act 1930 and the London Building Acts (Amendment) Act 1939.

[27] As amended by the Building (Inner London) Regulations 1985, SI 1985/1936.

[28] e.g. the Bristol Improvement Act 1847, ss.27–32; the Middlesex County Council Act 1956, s.37; the Greater Manchester Act 1981, s.43; the Leicestershire County Council Act 1985, s.36; the Nottinghamshire County Council Act 1985, s.5; and the West Glamorgan Act 1987, s.27.

[29] The Party Wall etc. Act 1996 was brought into force on July 1, 1997 by the Party Wall etc. Act 1996 (Commencement) Order 1997 (SI 1997/670) subject to the saving provisions in art.4 of the Order to the effect that ss.1, 2 and 6 were not to apply to any work commenced before September 1, 1997 in accordance with any agreement, easement or right, other than a right arising under or by virtue of the 1996 Act; the savings in art.4 were not to apply to land in Greater London where the London Building Acts (Amendment) Act 1939 applied. By the Party Wall etc. Act 1996 (Repeal of Local Enactments) Order 1997 (SI 1997/671), made pursuant to s.21 of the 1996 Act, Pt VI of the 1939 Act and ss.27–32 of the Bristol Improvement Act 1847 were repealed. The 1996 Act does not apply to land situated in Inner London (i.e. Greater London other than the outer London boroughs) in which there is an interest belonging to one of the four Inns of Court: see s.18. The 1996 Act applies to Crown land: see s.19. The Party Wall etc. Act 1996 is reproduced in Appendix A, below.

with the rights of others at common law.[30] Indeed, where the provisions of the Act are operated, the rights which are brought into existence are in lieu of the common law right of support which would otherwise have existed in relation to a party-wall.[31] However, it is expressly provided that nothing in the 1996 Act authorises any interference with any easement of light[32] or other easements in or relating to a party-wall or prejudicially affects the right of any person to preserve or restore any right or other thing in or connected with a party-wall in case of the party-wall being pulled down or rebuilt.[33] Further, the 1996 Act imposes limitations on the exercise of rights which would otherwise exist.[34] Where the 1996 Act applies, it is not open to an owner to carry out building works which fall within the ambit of the Act without complying with the requirements of the Act.[35] The procedural requirements of the 1996 Act will be treated as matters of importance and it was said in relation to the similar procedural requirements of the 1939 Act:

> "Section 46 et seq. of the Act of 1939 give a building owner a statutory right to interfere with the proprietary rights of the adjoining owner without his consent and despite his protests. The position of the adjoining owner whose proprietary rights are being compulsorily affected, is intended to be safeguarded by the surveyors appointed pursuant to the procedure laid down by the Act. Those surveyors are in a quasi-judicial position with statutory powers and responsibilities. It therefore seems to me important that the steps laid down by the Act should be scrupulously followed throughout and short cuts are not desirable."[36]

Definitions of "party-wall", "party fence wall" and "party structure"

11–08   Unless the context otherwise requires, these terms are defined by the 1996 Act. "Party-wall" is defined for the purposes of the 1996 Act as meaning:

---

[30] For an example, where a building owner who had carried out extensive work without complying with the predecessor of the 1996 Act was liable for substantial damages, see *Louis v Sadiq* (1996) 74 P. & C.R. 325.

[31] *Selby v Whitbread & Co* [1917] 1 K.B. 736; *Louis v Sadiq* (1996) 74 P. & C.R. 325.

[32] Thus giving statutory effect to the decision in *Crofts v Haldane* (1867) L.R. 2 Q.B. 194.

[33] The Party Wall etc. Act 1996, s.9. A predecessor of s.9 was s.101 of the London Building Act 1894, the Act considered in *Selby v Whitbread & Co* [1917] 1 K.B. 736, so that it would seem that s.9 is subject to the decision in that case. In *Arena Property Services v Europa 2000* [2003] EWCA Civ 1943 the question arose whether, if there was an easement to have a soil vent pipe on the adjoining property, that right was extinguished by a surveyor's award under the 1996 Act. The Court of Appeal held that the existence of the easement had not been established but that, if it had been, the award would merely have authorised the work and not extinguished any easement. The case raised but did not decide the question whether compensation under s.7(2) can only be determined by a surveyor appointed under s.10, with consequent limitation on the rights of appeal imposed by s.10(16) and (17).

[34] See *Standard Bank of British South America v Stokes* (1878) 9 Ch. D. 68 and *Knight v Pursell* (1879) 11 Ch. D. 412.

[35] *Standard Bank of British South America v Stokes* (1878) 9 Ch. D. 68 at 77; *Louis v Sadiq* (1996) 74 P. & C.R. 325. In *London & Manchester Assurance Co Ltd v O. & H. Construction Ltd* [1989] 2 E.G.L.R. 185, the court ordered the demolition of works which had been carried out without compliance with the 1939 Act.

[36] *Gyle-Thompson v Wall St (Properties) Ltd* [1974] 1 W.L.R. 123 at 130, per Brightman J.

"(a) a wall which forms part of a building and stands on lands of differ-
      ent owners to a greater extent than the projection of any artificially
      formed support on which the wall rests; and

(b) so much of a wall not being a wall referred to in the foregoing para-
      graph (a) as separates buildings belonging to different owners."[37]

Accordingly, by reason of paragraph (b) of the definition, a wall may be a party-wall
for the purposes of the 1996 Act even though it stands entirely on one
person's land, provided that it separates buildings belonging to different owners.
Whereas at common law the question whether a wall is a party-wall is to be determined by reference to the interests in it of adjoining owners, the determining factor
for the 1996 Act is not title but the position and use of the wall.[38] So:

(a) a wall standing over a junction line between two owners is a party-wall,
      even though it is built into on one side only, the adjoining site being
      vacant;

(b) a wall standing and built into on one side of the junction line, with a
      vacant site on the other side, is not a party-wall; but

(c) if a building be then put up on the vacant site and built into the existing
      wall on the adjoining site, that wall will become a party-wall.[39]

For the purposes of the 1996 Act, a party-wall is essentially a wall forming part
of a building, and it must be a vertical structure.[40] It seems from the references in
the definition to "part of a building" and "so much of a wall" that a wall may be
a party-wall for only part of its length and only part of its height.[41]

"Party fence wall" means "a wall (not being part of a building) which stands on   **11–09**
lands of different owners and is used or constructed to be used for separating such
adjoining lands but does not include a wall constructed on the land of one owner
the artificially formed support of which projects into the land of another owner."[42]

"Party structure" means "a party wall and also a floor partition or other structure separating buildings or parts of buildings approached solely by separate staircases or separate entrances from without."[43]

---

[37] Party Wall etc. Act 1996, s.44.
[38] See *Knight v Pursell* (1879) 11 Ch. D. 412 at 414.
[39] *Knight v Pursell* (1879) 11 Ch. D. 412; *Frederick Betts Ltd v Pickfords Ltd* [1906] 2 Ch. 87.
[40] *Reading v Barnard* (1827) 1 Moo. & Malk. 71; *cf.* Law of Property Act 1925, s.38 and para.11–02,
      above. See also the definition of "party structure" in the 1996 Act.
[41] This was clearly established to be the case in relation to earlier legislation where, however, the def-
      inition was not identical: see *Weston v Arnold* (1873) 8 Ch. App. 1084 (Bristol Improvements Acts
      1840 and 1847) and *Drury v Army & Navy Auxiliary Co-operative Society* [1896] 2 Q.B. 271;
      London, Gloucestershire and North Hants Dairy Co v Morley and Lanceley [1911] 2 K.B. 257
      (both concerning the London Building Act 1894). Although the facts are not clearly stated, this
      appears to be the reason for the decision in *Johnston v Mayfair Property Co* [1893] W.N. 73. For
      further proceedings between the same parties, but possibly concerning a different wall, see *Mayfair
      Property Co v Johnston* [1894] Ch. 508.
[42] Party Wall etc. Act 1996, s.20.
[43] Party Wall, etc. Act 1996, at s.20.

Definitions of "owner", "adjoining owner", "adjoining occupier" and "building owner"

11–10   The following definitions apply for the purposes of the 1996 Act unless the context otherwise requires:

"Owner" is defined to include:

> "(a)   a person in receipt of, or entitled to receive, the whole or part of the rents or profits of land;
>
> (b)   a person in possession of land, otherwise than as a mortgagee or as a tenant from year to year or for any lesser term or as a tenant at will;
>
> (c)   a purchaser of an interest in land under a contract for purchase or under an agreement for lease, otherwise than under an agreement for a tenancy from year to year or for a lesser term."[44]

It is possible to have more than one owner, with each owner owning a different interest.[45] In the case of joint owners of an interest, all of the joint owners are together "the owner".[46] A person who collects rents as agent for an owner is not himself an owner.[47] A statutory tenant under the Rent Act 1977 is not an "owner".[48] Under an earlier definition, which made no reference to purchasers or to agreements for lease, a tenant in possession having an equitable interest only under an agreement for lease for a term was held to be an "owner".[49] However, if the agreement for lease provided that the tenant was to be a tenant at will until the granting of the lease, he was not an "owner".[50] The position is now governed by paragraph (c) of the definition in the 1996 Act. A person is not entitled to serve a notice under the 1996 Act on the basis that although he is not currently an "owner" he expects to become one before the notice expires.[51] In relation to an earlier definition which referred to occupation of "any land or tenement" it was held to be sufficient if the person was in occupation of a part of the relevant land or tenement.[52]

"Adjoining owner" and "adjoining occupier" respectively mean "any owner and any occupier of land, buildings, storeys or rooms adjoining those of the building owner."[53]

---

[44] Party Wall, etc. Act 1996, at s.20.

[45] *List v Tharp* [1897] 1 Ch. 260; *Crosby v Alhambra Co Ltd* [1907] 1 Ch. 295.

[46] *Lehmann v Herman* [1993] 1 E.G.L.R. 172. The decision in *Crosby v Alhambra Co Ltd* [1907] 1 Ch. 295 concerned service of notice on an "adjoining owner" and it was stated *obiter* that it may be sufficient to serve such a notice on one of the joint owners of an interest; however, the definition of "adjoining owner" in s.5(32) of the London Building Act 1894 referred to "the owner or one of the owners" and that was relied on to support the conclusion that service on one of joint owners of an interest would suffice.

[47] *Solomons v R. Gertzenstein Ltd* [1954] 2 Q.B. 243.

[48] *Frances Holland School v Wassef* [2001] 2 E.G.L.R. 88.

[49] *Cowen v Phillips* (1863) 33 Beav. 18; *List v Tharp* [1897] 1 Ch. 260.

[50] *Orf v Payton* (1904) 69 J.P. 103.

[51] *Spiers & Son Ltd v Troup* (1915) 84 L.J.K.B. 1986.

[52] *Fillingham v Wood* [1891] 1 Ch. 51, considering *Hunt v Harris* (1865) 19 C.B. (n.s.) 13.

[53] Party Wall etc. Act 1996, s.20.

"Building owner" means "an owner of land who is desirous of exercising rights under this Act."[54]

Under an earlier definition of building owner which referred to "one of the owners" it was held that this did not mean that one of joint owners of an interest could act as building owner on his own behalf and not on behalf of the other joint owners; the reference was instead to one layer of ownership, for example freehold, or head leasehold or sub-leasehold.[55] The same position would seem to apply with the present definition. In relation to the same structure, an owner can be a building owner and his neighbour be an adjoining owner and later the roles may be reversed.[56]

Definitions of "foundation" and "special foundations"

The following definitions apply for the purposes of the 1996 Act unless the context otherwise requires.   **11–11**

"Foundation" in relation to a wall means "the solid ground or artificially formed support resting on solid ground on which the wall rests."[57]

"Special foundations" means "foundations in which an assemblage of steel beams or rods is employed for the purpose of distributing any load."[58]

(2) *Rights of owners of adjoining lands*

Rights of owners of adjoining lands where junction line not built on

The rights of owners of adjoining land vary depending on whether the junction line is built on or not.[59] The more important rights are those which are granted where the junction line is built on.[60] The reference to the junction line not being built on is used in a particular sense in the statute. The rights considered in this paragraph apply where nothing is built at the line of junction or where the only thing which is built at the line of junction is a boundary wall (which is not a party fence wall or the external wall of a building).[61] If a building owner wishes to build on the line of junction a wall placed wholly on his own land, he must serve on the adjoining owner a notice, at least one month before he intends the building work to start, which indicates his desire to build and describes the intended wall.[62] The service of such a notice gives the building owner the right within the period of between one and twelve months[63] from the service of the notice to place   **11–12**

---

[54] Party Wall, etc. Act 1996, at s.20.
[55] *Lehmann v Herman* [1993] 1 E.G.L.R. 172.
[56] See *Leadbetter v Marylebone Corp* [1904] 2 K.B. 893.
[57] Party Wall, etc. Act 1996, at s.20.
[58] Party Wall, etc. Act 1996, at s.20.
[59] See Party Wall, etc. Act 1996, ss.1 and 2.
[60] See Party Wall, etc. Act 1996, s.2.
[61] Party Wall, etc. Act 1996, s.1(1).
[62] Party Wall, etc. Act 1996, s.1(5).
[63] Because the time-limit is a statutory time-limit it is strict.

on the land of the adjoining owner below the level of such land any projecting footings and foundations as are necessary for the construction of the wall.

Where a building owner builds a wall wholly on his own land in accordance with these provisions, he shall do so at his own expense and shall compensate the adjoining owner and the adjoining occupier for any damage to property occasioned thereby.[64] In an earlier provision which referred to "damage", the reference was held to be to structural damage and not to compensation for loss of trade.[65] The current provision expressly refers to "damage to property" which equally would not include compensation for loss of trade. If the parties disagree as to the amount of compensation, the same is to be determined in accordance with the machinery laid down in the 1996 Act.[66] The 1996 Act now confers a general right to compensation for any loss or damage caused to an adjoining owner or adjoining occupier.[67]

With the previous written consent of the adjoining owner, the building owner may go further and build a party-wall or a party fence wall on the line of junction. If the building owner wishes to do this, he must serve on the adjoining owner a notice, at least one month before he intends the building work to start, which indicates his desire to build and describes the intended wall.[68] If the adjoining owner consents in writing, within 14 days from service of the building owner's notice, to the building of a party-wall or a party fence wall, then such wall may be built in such position as may be agreed.[69] The expense of building such wall is to be defrayed from time to time by the two owners in such proportion as has regard to the use made or to be made of the wall by each of them and to the cost of labour and materials prevailing at the time when that use is made by each owner respectively.[70] It follows that if the adjoining owner does not consent in writing to the building of the party-wall or party fence wall, the building owner may only build an external wall or a fence wall, as the case may be, wholly on his own land and at his own expense.[71] Any dispute as to these provisions between the building owner or adjoining owner or occupier is to be determined in accordance with the machinery laid down in the 1996 Act.[72]

---

[64] Party Wall, etc. Act 1996, s.1(7).

[65] *Adams v Marylebone B.C.* [1907] 2 K.B. 822; a distinction was drawn between fixtures which were part of the real property and chattels which were not in *Video London Sound Studios Ltd v Asticus (GMS) Ltd*, Technology and Construction Court, March 6, 2001.

[66] See Party Wall, etc. Act 1996, s.10 and paras 11–22 *et seq.*, below.

[67] See Party Wall, etc. Act 1996, s.7(2) and para.11–20, below.

[68] Party Wall, etc. Act 1996, s.1(2).

[69] Party Wall, etc. Act 1996, s.1(3)(a).

[70] Party Wall, etc. Act 1996, ss.1(3)(b), 11(3). As regards subsequent use by an adjoining owner and the liability to contribute to the expense, see *ibid.*, s.11(11).

[71] Party Wall, etc. Act 1996, s.1(4). "External wall" is not defined for the purposes of the 1996 Act. This phrase was defined for the purposes of the London Building Acts (Amendment) Act 1939 (by adopting the definition in s.5 of the London Building Act 1930) as "an outer wall or vertical enclosure of any building, not being a party wall". In *Pembery v Lamdin* [1940] 2 All E.R. 434 (following *Green v Eales* (1841) 2 Q.B. 225), it was held that a covenant in a lease, which referred to "the external parts of the premises" included a wall that formed part of the enclosure of the premises whether or not it was a wall exposed to the atmosphere or a wall which adjoined another building.

[72] See Party Wall etc. Act 1996, s.10 and paras 11–22 *et seq.*, below.

Rights of owners of adjoining lands where junction line built on

This is the principal set of rights conferred by the 1996 Act. These rights are con-   **11–13**
ferred in a case where the lands of adjoining owners are built on at the line of
junction or where a boundary wall being a party fence wall or the external wall
of a building has been erected at the line of junction.[73] In such cases the building
owner has the rights set out below:

(a) A right to underpin,[74] thicken, or raise a party structure, a party fence
wall, or an external wall which belongs to the building owner and is built
against a party structure or party fence wall.[75] Where work of this kind
is not necessary on account of defect or want of repair of the structure or
wall concerned, the right is exercisable: (a) subject to making good all
damage occasioned by the work to the adjoining premises or to their
internal furnishings and decorations; and (b) where the work is to a party
structure or external wall, subject to carrying any relevant flues and
chimney stacks up to such a height and in such materials as may be
agreed between the building owner and the adjoining owner concerned
or, as is determined under the machinery laid down by the 1996 Act. The
relevant flues and chimney stacks are those which belong to an adjoining owner and either form part of or rest on or against the party structure
or external wall.[76] As to the possibility of apportionment of the expense
of the work, see para.11—25, below.

(b) A right to make good, repair, or demolish and rebuild a party structure
or party fence wall in a case where such work is necessary on account
of defect or want of repair of the structure or wall.[77] As to the possibility of apportionment of the expense of the work, see para.11–25, below.

    In relation to the predecessor of this provision it was held that the
rebuilding had to be in the same form so that the building owner could
not widen apertures[78]; nor could he reduce the height of a party-wall.[79]
Reducing the height of a party-wall is now permitted by section 2(2)(m)
of the 1996 Act. Dampness in a wall will not necessarily be a defect or
want of repair; rather, the question is whether the matter complained
of renders the wall less effective for the purposes for which it is used
or intended to be used. Where there is a defect or want of repair, the
right conferred by the Act is to make good the party structure so that
it becomes effective for the purposes for which it is to be used; in

[73] Party Wall, etc. Act 1996, s.2(1).
[74] For the circumstances in which a building owner may be required to underpin, see Party Wall, etc.
Act 1996, s.6 and para.11–18, below.
[75] Party Wall, etc. Act 1996, s.2(2)(a).
[76] Party Wall, etc. Act 1996, s.2(3).
[77] Party Wall, etc. Act 1996, s.2(2)(b).
[78] *Burlington Property Co Ltd v Odeon Theatres Ltd* [1939] 1 K.B. 633.
[79] *Gyle-Thompson v Wall St (Properties) Ltd* [1974] 1 W.L.R. 123.

determining the proper way of making good the defect due regard is to be had to the convenience of the adjoining owner.[80]

(c) A right to demolish a partition which separates buildings belonging to different owners but does not conform with statutory requirements and to build instead a party-wall which does so conform.[81] A building or structure which was erected before the passing of the 1996 Act (July 18, 1996) is deemed to conform with statutory requirements if it conforms with the statutes regulating buildings or structures on the date on which it was erected.[82]

(d) A right in the case of buildings connected by arches or structures over public ways or over passages belonging to other persons, to demolish the whole or part of such buildings, arches or structures which do not conform with statutory requirements and to rebuild them so that they do so conform.[83] A building or structure which was erected before the passing of the 1996 Act (July 18, 1996) is deemed to conform with statutory requirements if it conforms with the statutes regulating buildings or structures on the date on which it was erected.[84]

(e) A right to demolish a party structure which is of insufficient strength or height for the purposes of any intended building of the building owner and to rebuild[85] it of sufficient strength or height for the said purposes (including rebuilding to a lesser height or thickness where the rebuilt structure is of sufficient strength and height for the purposes of any adjoining owner).[86] This right is exercisable subject to (a) making good all damage occasioned by the work to the adjoining premises or to their internal furnishings and decorations; and (b) carrying any relevant flues and chimney stacks up to such a height and in such materials as may be agreed between the building owner and the adjoining owner concerned, or in the event of dispute, as is determined by the machinery laid down by the 1996 Act. The relevant flues and chimney stacks are those which belong to an adjoining owner and either form part of or rest on or against the party structure.[87]

(f) A right to cut into a party structure for any purpose (which may be or include the purpose of inserting a damp-proof course).[88] This right is

---

[80] *Barry v Minturn* [1913] A.C. 585, where dampness in a garden wall was not a defect or want of repair; the case also contains comments on the extent, if at all, to which the history of the wall is relevant.

[81] Party Wall, etc. Act 1996, s.2(2)(c).

[82] Party Wall, etc. Act 1996, s.2(2), (8).

[83] Party Wall, etc. Act 1996, s.2(2)(d).

[84] See fn.82, above.

[85] In the same form; see fnn.78 and 79, above.

[86] Party Wall, etc. Act 1996, s.2(2)(e). As to the liability of the building owner to make a fair allowance for disturbance and inconvenience where the adjoining premises are laid open in consequence of the exercise of this right, see *ibid.*, s.11(6) and para.11–25, below.

[87] Party Wall, etc. Act 1996, s.2(4).

[88] Party Wall, etc. Act 1996, s.2(2)(f).

exercisable subject to making good all damage occasioned by the work to the adjoining premises or to their internal furnishings and decorations.[89]

(g) A right to cut away from a party-wall, party fence wall, external wall or boundary wall any footing or any projecting chimney breast, jamb or flue or other projection on or over the land of the building owner in order to erect, or underpin any such wall or for any other purpose.[90] This right is exercisable subject to making good all damage occasioned by the work to the adjoining premises or to their internal furnishings and decorations.[91]

(h) A right to cut away or demolish parts of any wall or building of an adjoining owner overhanging the land of the building owner or over-hanging a party-wall, to the extent that is necessary to cut away or demolish the parts to enable a vertical wall to be erected or raised against that wall or building of the adjoining owner.[92] This right is exercisable subject to making good all damage occasioned by the work to the adjoining premises or to their internal furnishings and decorations.[93]

(j) A right to cut into the wall of an adjoining owner's building in order to insert a flashing or other weather-proofing of a wall erected against that wall.[94] This right is exercisable subject to making good all damage occasioned by the work to the wall of the adjoining owner's building.[95]

(k) A right to execute any other necessary works incidental to the connection of a party structure with the premises adjoining it.[96]

(l) A right to raise a party fence wall, or to raise such a wall for use as a party-wall, and to demolish a party fence wall and rebuild it as a party fence wall or as a party-wall.[97]

(m) A right subject to the provisions of section 11(7), to reduce, or to demolish and rebuild, a party-wall or party fence wall to (i) a height of not less than two metres where the wall is not used by an adjoining owner to any greater extent than a boundary wall; or (ii) a height currently enclosed upon by the building of an adjoining owner.[98] This right is exercisable subject to (a) reconstructing any parapet or replacing an existing parapet with another one; or (b) constructing a parapet where one is needed but did not exist before.[99]

(n) A right to expose a party-wall or party structure hitherto enclosed subject to providing adequate weathering.[100]

[89] Party Wall, etc. Act 1996, s.2(5).
[90] Party Wall, etc. Act 1996, s.2(2)(g).
[91] Party Wall, etc. Act 1996, s.2(5).
[92] Party Wall, etc. Act 1996, s.2(2)(h).
[93] Party Wall, etc. Act 1996, s.2(5).
[94] Party Wall, etc. Act 1996, s.2(2)(j).
[95] Party Wall, etc. Act 1996, s.2(5).
[96] Party Wall, etc. Act 1996, s.2(2)(k).
[97] Party Wall, etc. Act 1996, s.2(2)(l).
[98] Party Wall, etc. Act 1996, s.2(2)(m). S.11(7) is considered at para.11–25, below.
[99] Party Wall, etc. Act 1996, s.2(7).
[100] Party Wall, etc. Act 1996, s.2(2)(n).

Where the right is exercisable subject to the building owner making good damage, the statutory provisions make it clear that the reference to "damage" is physical damage to specified buildings or furnishings or decorations rather than a reference to compensation for loss of profits or inconvenience or disruption.[101] However, the 1996 Act now confers on adjoining owners and adjoining occupiers a general right to compensation for any loss or damage which might result to them by reason of any work executed pursuant to the 1996 Act.[102] The 1939 Act lays down requirements for the building owner to serve a "party structure notice" and permits the adjoining owner to serve a "counter-notice".

Party structure notice

11–14   Before exercising any right conferred by section 2 (described in para.11–13, above), a building owner must serve on the adjoining owner a notice in writing stating the name and address of the building owner, the nature and particulars of the proposed work, the time at which it will be begun and, where the proposed work includes the construction of special foundations, the notice must give particulars by providing plans, sections and details of construction of the special foundations with reasonable particulars of the loads to be carried thereby.[103] The notice must be sufficiently clear and intelligible so as to enable the adjoining owner to know what counter-notice he may wish to give under the 1996 Act.[104] Such a notice is referred to in the 1996 Act as a "party structure notice". The requirement as to notice does not apply unless the building owner is seeking to exercise one of the rights conferred by section 2; thus, where the building owner wishes to demolish a building on his own land without cutting into the party-wall, no party structure notice need be served.[105] The notice must be served by or on behalf of the building owner.[106] Where the interest of the building owner is held jointly, the notice must be served on behalf of all of the joint owners.[107]

The notice must be served on the adjoining owner. There may be various layers of interest, the owners of which are separately adjoining owners; all such layers must be served.[108] It was held, *obiter*, in relation to the definition of "adjoining owner" under the London Building Act 1894, that where the relevant

---

[101] Under earlier statutory provisions, a reference to "damage" was construed to mean physical damage and did not include compensation for loss of trade: *Adams v Marylebone B.C.* [1907] 2 K.B. 822; a distinction was also drawn between fixtures which were part of the real property and chattels which were not in *Video London Sound Studios Ltd v Asticus (GMS) Ltd*, Technology and Construction Court, March 6, 2001.

[102] See Party Wall etc. Act 1996, s.7(2) and para.11–20, below.

[103] Party Wall etc. Act 1996, s.3(1). For the possibility of a claim by an adjoining owner in relation to the increased cost to the adjoining owner caused by special foundations, see para.11–25, below.

[104] *Hobbs, Hart & Co v Graver* [1899] 1 Ch. 11. For the general law in relation to the need for reasonable clarity in notices, see *Mannai Investment Co Ltd v Eagle Star Life Assurance Co Ltd* [1997] A.C. 749.

[105] *Major v Park Lane Co* (1866) L.R. 2 Eq. 453.

[106] For the definition of "owner" and "building owner" and cases there cited, see para.11–10, above.

[107] *Lehmann v Herman* [1993] 1 E.G.L.R. 172.

[108] *List v Tharp* [1897] 1 Ch. 260; *Crosby v Alhambra Co Ltd* [1907] 1 Ch. 295.

interest of the adjoining owner was held jointly, it was sufficient to serve one of the joint owners.[109] However, the definition in the 1894 Act referred to "one of the owners", whereas the current definition refers to "any owner" so that the earlier decision cannot safely be relied upon.

A party structure notice must be served at least two months before the date (stated in the notice) as that on which the work is to begin.[110] A party structure notice ceases to be effective if the work to which the notice relates is not begun within 12 months after service of the notice and is not prosecuted with due diligence.[111] Because the time-limit is imposed by statute, the time-limit is a strict one. However, if there is a difference between the building owner and the adjoining owner in relation to the notice and that difference is determined by an award under the 1996 Act, the time for doing the work is to be regulated by the award and this six-month time-limit does not apply.[112] A party structure notice does not need to be served if the building owner obtains the consent in writing of the adjoining owner and the adjoining occupiers that he may exercise any right conferred on him by the section.[113] Further, a party structure notice need not be served before complying with a notice served under any statutory provisions dealing with dangerous or neglected structures.[114] The court may restrain a building owner from proceeding upon an invalid notice if he refuses formally to withdraw it.[115]

The courts are likely to be unsympathetic to a person who commences work to a party-wall without having served the notice required by the Act. An interim injunction will almost certainly be granted[116] and it has been said that the building owner should not be allowed to gain a forensic advantage by his failure and that the court will accordingly take a reasonably robust approach to any issue as to causation of damage.[117]

The adjoining owner's response to the party structure notice

Following the service of a party structure notice, the adjoining owner may choose **11–15** not to do anything, in which event 14 days after service of the party structure notice he is deemed to have dissented from the notice and a difference is deemed to have arisen between the parties.[118] The 1996 Act contains machinery for the determination of that difference.[119] Alternatively, the adjoining owner may, within 14 days after service of the party structure notice, express his written

---

[109] *Crosby v Alhambra Co Ltd* (above).
[110] Party Wall, etc. Act 1996, s.3(2)(a).
[111] Party Wall, etc. Act 1996, s.3(2)(b).
[112] *Leadbetter v Marylebone Corp* [1905] 1 K.B. 661.
[113] Party Wall, etc. Act 1996, s.3(3)(a).
[114] Party Wall, etc. Act 1996, s.3(3)(b).
[115] *Sims v Estates Co* (1866) 14 L.T. 55.
[116] As in *Udal v Dutton* [2007] EWHC 2862.
[117] *Roadrunner Properties Ltd v Dean* [2003] EWCA Civ 1816 at [28]–[29], where the building owner's contractor had used a Kango hammer to cut a chase for heating pipes in a party-wall.
[118] Party Wall, etc. Act 1996, s.5.
[119] Party Wall, etc. Act 1996, s.10, and see paras 11–22 *et seq.*, below.

consent to the party structure notice to prevent a difference being deemed to have arisen.[120] In addition there are two sets of circumstances in which the adjoining owner may wish to serve a counter-notice.[121]

Counter-notice

11–16   A counter-notice may seek to impose three requirements on the building owner. The first possible requirement relates to a party fence wall or party structure; in such a case the adjoining owner may require the building owner to build in or on the party fence wall or party structure, as the case may be, such chimney copings, breasts, jambs or flues, or such piers or recesses or other like works as may reasonably be required for the convenience of the adjoining owner.[122] The second possible requirement relates to special foundations; in such a case, where the adjoining owner consents to the special foundations, he may require them to be placed at a specified greater depth than that proposed by the building owner or to be constructed of sufficient strength to bear the load to be carried by columns of any intended building of the adjoining owner; or he may require both of these.[123] The third possible requirement is not referred to in the section dealing with counter-notices but is mentioned in a later section dealing with the sharing of expenses between the building owner and the adjoining owner. The third possible requirement is that if a building owner serves a notice relying on section 2(2)(m) proposing to reduce the height of a party-wall or a party fence wall, the adjoining owner may serve a counter-notice requiring the building owner to maintain the existing height of the wall. The resulting liability of the adjoining owner to contribute to the additional expense is discussed in para.11–25, below. If a counter-notice is served it must specify the works required to be executed and must be accompanied by plans, sections and particulars thereof.[124] The counter-notice must be served within one month after service of the party structure notice.[125] A building owner on whom a counter-notice is served must comply with the requirements of that counter-notice unless the execution of the works required by the counter-notice would be injurious to him or cause unnecessary inconvenience to him or unnecessary delay in the execution of the works pursuant to the party structure notice.[126]

The building owner's response to a counter-notice

11–17   Following the service of a counter-notice the building owner may choose not to do anything, in which event 14 days after service of the counter-notice, he is deemed to have dissented from the counter-notice and a difference is deemed to

---

[120] Party Wall, etc. Act 1996, s.5.
[121] Party Wall, etc. Act 1996, s.4.
[122] Party Wall, etc. Act 1996, s.4(1)(a).
[123] Party Wall, etc. Act 1996, s.4(1)(b).
[124] Party Wall, etc. Act 1996, s.4(2)(a).
[125] Party Wall, etc. Act 1996, s.4(2)(b).
[126] Party Wall, etc. Act 1996, s.4(3).

have arisen between the parties.[127] The 1996 Act contains machinery for the determination of such a difference.[128] Alternatively, the building owner may, within 14 days after service of the counter-notice, express his written consent to the counter-notice to prevent a difference from being deemed to have arisen.[129]

Adjacent excavation and construction

The 1996 Act imposes certain obligations to underpin (or otherwise strengthen or safeguard the foundations of) the building or structure of the adjoining owner in the following two sets of circumstances. Both sets of circumstances arise where a building owner proposes to excavate, or excavate for and erect a building or structure within a specified distance from any part of a building or structure of an adjoining owner. The first set of circumstances is where a building owner proposes to excavate, or excavate for and erect a building or structure, within a distance of 3m measured horizontally from any part of a building or structure of the adjoining owner and any part of the proposed excavation, building or structure will within those 3m extend to a lower level than the level of the bottom of the foundations of the building or structure of the adjoining owner.[130] The second set of circumstances is where a building owner proposes to excavate, or excavate for and erect a building or structure, within a distance of 6m measured horizontally from any part of a building or structure of an adjoining owner and any part of the proposed excavation, building or structure will within those 6m meet a plane drawn downwards in the direction of the excavation, building or structure of the building owner at an angle of 45 degrees to the horizontal from the line formed by the intersection of the plane of the level of the bottom of the foundations of the building or structure of the adjoining owner with the plane of the external face of the external wall of the building or structure of the adjoining owner.[131] In these two sets of circumstances, the building owner may, and if required by the adjoining owner, he must at the expense of the building owner underpin or otherwise strengthen or safeguard the foundations of the building or structure of the adjoining owner so far as may be necessary.[132] Where the buildings or structures of different owners are within the respective distances of 3m and 6m mentioned above, the owners of those buildings or structures are deemed to be adjoining owners for this purpose.[133]

11–18

In both sets of circumstances, the 1996 Act imposes requirements as to giving of notice and for a response to such notice. In any such case, at least one month before beginning to excavate, or excavate for and erect a building or structure, the building owner must serve on the adjoining owner a notice in writing of his

[127] Party Wall, etc. Act 1996, s.5.
[128] Party Wall, etc. Act 1996, s.10 and see paras 11–22 *et seq.*, below.
[129] Party Wall, etc. Act 1996, s.5.
[130] Party Wall, etc. Act 1996, s.6(1).
[131] Party Wall, etc. Act 1996, s.6(2).
[132] Party Wall, etc. Act 1996, s.6(3).
[133] Party Wall, etc. Act 1996, s.6(4).

proposals.[134] The notice must state whether the building owner proposes to underpin or otherwise strengthen or safeguard the foundations of the building or structure of the adjoining owner.[135] The notice must be accompanied by plans and sections showing the site and depth of any excavation the building owner proposes to make and the site of the building or structure (if any) proposed to be erected by the building owner.[136]

If an owner on whom the building owner's notice is served does not serve a notice indicating his consent to it within 14 days of service, he is deemed to have dissented from the notice and a dispute is deemed to have arisen between the parties.[137] The 1996 Act contains machinery for the determination of such a difference.[138] The building owner's notice ceases to be effective if the work to which the notice relates has not been begun within the period of 12 months after its service and is not prosecuted with due diligence.[139]

In the two sets of circumstances referred to above, the building owner is obliged to compensate the adjoining owner and any adjoining occupier for any loss or damage which may result to any of them by reason of any work executed in these circumstances.[140]

On completion of the work, the building owner must, if he is so requested by the adjoining owner, supply him with particulars, including plans and sections, of the work.[141]

These provisions do not relieve the building owner from any liability to which he would otherwise be subject for injury to the adjoining owner or any adjoining occupier by reason of the work executed by the building owner.[142]

Execution of works

11–19   Nothing in the 1996 Act authorises the building owner to place special foundations on land of an adjoining owner without his previous written consent.[143] A building owner must not exercise any right conferred on him by the 1996 Act in such manner or at such time as to cause unnecessary inconvenience to the adjoining owner or to the adjoining occupier.[144] In particular, where a building owner in exercising any right conferred on him by the 1996 Act lays open any part of the adjoining land or building, he must at his own expense make and maintain so long as may be necessary a proper hoarding, shoring, or fans or temporary construction for the protection of the adjoining land or building and for the

---

[134] Party Wall, etc. Act 1996, s.6(5).
[135] Party Wall, etc. Act 1996, s.6(5).
[136] Party Wall, etc. Act 1996, s.6(6).
[137] Party Wall, etc. Act 1996, s.6(7).
[138] Party Wall, etc. Act 1996, s.10 and paras 11–22 *et seq.*, below.
[139] Party Wall, etc. Act 1996, s.6(8).
[140] Party Wall, etc. Act 1996, s.7(2).
[141] Party Wall, etc. Act 1996, s.6(9).
[142] Party Wall, etc. Act 1996, s.6(10).
[143] Party Wall, etc. Act 1996, s.7(4); "special foundations" are defined in s.20, see para.11–11, above.
[144] Party Wall, etc. Act 1996, s.7(1).

security of the adjoining occupier.[145] Any works executed in pursuance of the 1996 Act must comply with the provisions of statutory requirements and must be executed in accordance with such plans, sections and particulars as may be agreed between the owners or, in the event of a difference between the owners, determined pursuant to the 1996 Act.[146] This means that no deviation may be made from such plans, sections and particulars unless the deviation is agreed between the owners or, in the event of a difference between the owners, is determined to be appropriate pursuant to the 1996 Act.[147]

Compensation

The building owner shall compensate any adjoining owner and any adjoining occupier for any loss or damage which may result to any of them by reason of any work executed in pursuance of the 1996 Act.[148] This general provision is new in the 1996 Act and is in addition to the more specific provisions which require the making good of damage to property.[149] The duty to compensate extends to adjoining occupiers as well as adjoining owners. The reference to work is possibly ambiguous but it seems that it extends to the process of doing the work in question as well as the existence of the completed work.   **11–20**

Power of entry by building owner

A building owner, his servants, agents and workmen, may during usual working hours enter and remain on any premises for the purpose of executing any work pursuant to the 1996 Act and may remove any furniture or fittings or take any other action necessary for that purpose.[150] If the premises are closed, the building owner, his servants, agents and workmen, may, if accompanied by a constable or other police officer, break open any fences or doors in order to enter the premises.[151] Before entering any premises pursuant to these statutory rights, a building owner must give to the owner and occupier of the premises, in the case of an emergency, such notice of his intention to enter as may be reasonably practicable and, in any other case, notice in a period of not less than 14 days ending with the day of the proposed entry.[152] "Emergency" is not defined in the 1996 Act; it has been held in another context to mean "a condition of things causing a reasonable apprehension of the near approach of danger".[153] A surveyor appointed or   **11–21**

---

[145] Party Wall, etc. Act 1996, s.7(3).
[146] Party Wall, etc. Act 1996, s.7(5)(a).
[147] Party Wall, etc. Act 1996, s.7(5)(b). For settlement of differences, see *ibid.*, s.10 and para.11–22, below.
[148] Party Wall, etc. Act 1996, s.7(2).
[149] See Party Wall, etc. Act 1996, ss.1(7), 2(3), (4), (5) and (6).
[150] Party Wall, etc. Act 1996, s.8(1). If an occupier interferes with this right of entry, he may commit a criminal offence, see *ibid.*, s.16 and para.11–31, below.
[151] Party Wall, etc. Act 1996, s.8(2).
[152] Party Wall, etc. Act 1996, s.8(3), (4).
[153] *The Larchbank* [1943] A.C. 299 at 304 per Lord Atkin; the occurrence of that condition need not be sudden: *ibid.* See also, *Higgins v Bernard* [1972] 1 W.L.R. 455.

selected under the disputes determination provisions of the 1996 Act may during usual working hours enter and remain on any land or premises for the purpose of carrying out the object for which he is appointed or selected.[154] No land or premises may be so entered by such a surveyor unless the building owner who is a party to the dispute concerned serves the like notice as is referred to above on the owner and the occupier of the land and premises.[155]

(3) *Settlement of disputes*

Appointment of surveyors

11–22   The 1996 Act refers in a number of places to a dispute arising or being deemed to have arisen between the building owner and the adjoining owner.[156] A dispute may relate to a question of fact, or a question of law, or a question of mixed fact and law.[157] The 1996 Act contains machinery for the determination of such a dispute. The machinery provides for the parties to concur in the appointment of one surveyor (called "the agreed surveyor") or, alternatively, for each party to appoint one surveyor and for the two surveyors to select a third surveyor (all of whom are called "the three surveyors").[158] All appointments and selections must be in writing and may not be rescinded by either party.[159] The 1996 Act contains detailed provisions for the cases where a party refuses or neglects to make an appointment and where an appointed surveyor refuses or neglects to act or dies or becomes incapable of acting.[160] The agreed surveyor or the three surveyors, or any two of the three surveyors, are required to settle by an award any matter which is connected with any work to which the Act applies and which is in dispute between the building owner and the adjoining owner.[161] Either of the parties or either of the surveyors appointed by the parties may call upon the third surveyor who has been duly selected to determine the disputed matters whereupon the third surveyor must make the necessary award.[162] There is provision for one surveyor to proceed to make an award ex parte but this is a drastic power and the preconditions for the exercise of the power must be established; if they are not the award will be a nullity.[163] The determination which the surveyor or surveyors are

---

[154] Party Wall, etc. Act 1996, s.8(5). If an occupier interferes with this right of entry, he may commit a criminal offence, see s.16, *ibid.*, and para.11–31, below.

[155] Party Wall, etc. Act 1996, s.8(6).

[156] See Party Wall, etc. Act 1996, ss.1(8), 2(3)(b), (4)(b), 5, 6(7), 7(5), 11(2), (8), 12(1), (2) and 13(2).

[157] *Selby v Whitbread & Co* [1917] 1 K.B. 732.

[158] Party Wall, etc. Act 1996, s.10(1).

[159] Party Wall, etc. Act 1996, s.10(2). For a case where an informal appointment, not in writing, was invalid, see *Gyle-Thompson v Wall St (Properties) Ltd* [1974] 1 W.L.R. 123.

[160] Party Wall, etc. Act 1996, s.10(3), (4), (5), (6), (7), (8) and (9).

[161] Party Wall, etc. Act 1996, s.10(10).

[162] Party Wall, etc. Act 1996, s.10(11).

[163] Party Wall, etc. Act 1996, s.10(6), (7); and see *Frances Holland School v Wassef* [2001] 2 E.G.L.R. 88.

required to make under the 1996 Act is more in the nature of an expert determination than an arbitration award.[164]

The award

The award may determine the right to execute and the time and manner of executing any work and generally any other matter arising out of or incidental to the dispute, including the costs of making the award. This is subject to the proviso that any period appointed by the award for executing any work must not, unless otherwise agreed by the building owner and the adjoining owner, begin to run until after the expiration of the period prescribed by the 1996 Act for service of the notice in respect of which the dispute arises or is deemed to have arisen.[165] The reasonable costs incurred in making or obtaining an award and the cost of reasonable inspections of work to which the award relates and any other matter arising out of the dispute are to be paid by such of the parties as the surveyor or surveyors making the award determine.[166] Where the surveyors appointed by the parties make an award, they must serve it forthwith on the parties.[167] Where an award is made by the third surveyor, he must, after payment of the costs of the award, serve it forthwith on the parties or their appointed surveyors; if the award is served on the appointed surveyors, they must serve it forthwith on the parties.[168] The importance of prompt service is that the statutory time-limit of 14 days after service for appealing the award runs from service on the party who wishes to appeal.[169]

11–23

The function of the surveyors is to adjust the differences which have arisen between the adjoining owner and the building owner under the 1996 Act. The question for the surveyors is how far the building owner is right in seeking to impose his requirements and how far the adjoining owner is right in making cross-demands. It is beyond the powers of the surveyors to purport to decide future disputes that have not yet arisen or to seek to lay down how the wall is to be dealt with in uncertain future circumstances.[170] It is within the powers of the surveyors to impose on the building owner a continuing obligation as to maintenance, although such an obligation may be undesirable in practice and it may be preferable to secure a similar object by requiring the building owner to carry out works which will produce a similar long-term result.[171] It is not the function of the surveyors to determine which party was at fault in respect of a collapse of a party-wall.[172]

---

[164] *Chartered Society of Physiotherapy v Simmonds Church Smiles* [1995] 1 E.G.L.R. 155, where the jurisdiction was described as *sui generis*.
[165] Party Wall, etc. Act 1996, s.10(12).
[166] Party Wall, etc. Act 1996, s.10(13).
[167] Party Wall, etc. Act 1996, s.10(14).
[168] Party Wall, etc. Act 1996, s.10(15).
[169] Party Wall, etc. Act 1996, s.10(17).
[170] *Leadbetter v Marylebone Corp* [1904] 2 K.B. 893.
[171] *Marchant v Capital & Counties Plc* [1983] 2 E.G.L.R. 156.
[172] *Woodhouse v Consolidated Property Corp Ltd* [1993] 1 E.G.L.R. 174.

A building owner who serves a party structure notice which leads to the making of an award cannot avoid his obligations under the award by transferring his land to a third party after the notice but before the making of the award.[173]

An award which provides that in certain circumstances the adjoining owner may enter on the land of the building owner and carry out remedial works and recover the expense from the building owner did not create an interest in land which could be protected by a caution under the Land Registration Act 1925.[174]

Challenges to the award

11–24   The 1996 Act provides that the award is to be conclusive and is not to be questioned in any court except as expressly provided by the 1996 Act itself.[175] The method of challenge laid down in the 1996 Act is by way of an appeal to the county court. But if the award is outside the powers of the surveyors, it is a nullity and of no effect and need not be appealed.[176] The safer course, however, may be to claim in proceedings brought under CPR Pt 52 that the award is a nullity and, in the alternative, that the award should be varied.[177]

Either of the parties to the difference may within 14 days of the service[178] of the award on that party appeal to the county court against the award. The obligations on the maker of the award to serve the award promptly were described in para.11–23, above. As the time-limit is laid down by statute, it is strict[179]; the court is not given any power to extend this time-limit.

On such an appeal, the county court may rescind the award or modify it in such manner and make such order as to costs as it thinks fit.[180] It was held in relation to the 1939 Act and the former rules of court that the county court might reopen the matter in its entirety and might receive evidence which was not put before the surveyors; the question before the court was what award ought to be made and not whether the award was made by a competent surveyor having regard to the evidence before him[181] but the provisions of the 1939 and 1996 Acts are not identical. After some initial uncertainty, it is now settled that appeals under the 1996 Act are governed by CPR, Pt 52, and the Practice Direction made

---

[173] *Selby v Whitbread & Co* [1917] 1 K.B. 736; in that case unusually, and apparently wrongly, the building owner had done the work before being authorised to do so by the award.

[174] *Observatory Hill Ltd v Camtel Investments SA* [1997] 1 E.G.L.R. 140.

[175] Party Wall, etc. Act 1996, s.10(16).

[176] *Stone and Hastie, Re* [1903] 2 K.B. 463; *Leadbetter v Marylebone Corp* [1904] 2 K.B. 893; *Burlington Property Co Ltd v Odeon Theatres Ltd* [1939] 1 K.B. 633; *Gyle-Thompson v Wall St (Properties) Ltd* [1974] 1 W.L.R. 123; *Marchant v Capital & Counties Plc* [1983] 2 E.G.L.R. 156; *Woodhouse v Consolidated Property Corp Ltd* [1993] 1 E.G.L.R. 174; *Frances Holland School v Wassef* [2001] 2 E.G.L.R. 88.

[177] A course sanctioned by the Court of Appeal in *Zissis v Lukomski* [2006] EWCA Civ 341; [2006] 1 W.L.R. 2778 at [47].

[178] Provisions as to service are contained in Party Wall, etc. Act 1996, s.15.

[179] Conceded in *Riley Gowler Ltd v National Heart Hospital Board of Governors* [1969] 3 All E.R. 1401. The 14-day time-limit is statutory and overrides CPR Pt 52 PD para.17.3 which provides for 28 days: *Zissis v Lukomski* (above) at [40].

[180] Party Wall, etc. Act 1996, s.10(17).

[181] *Chartered Society of Physiotherapy v Simmonds Church Smiles* [1995] 1 E.G.L.R. 155.

under that Part.[182] CPR, Pt 52, r.11 provides that every appeal is limited to a review of the decision of the person from whose decision an appeal is brought unless a practice direction makes different provision for a particular category of appeal or the court considers that in the circumstances of an individual appeal it would be in the interests of justice to hold a re-hearing. Further, unless it orders otherwise the appeal court will not receive (a) oral evidence; or (b) evidence which was not before the lower court. CPR, Pt 52 PD, para.9.1, however, provides for the appeal to be by way of re-hearing where the person from whom the appeal is brought did not hold a hearing to come to his decision or did hold a hearing to come to that decision but the procedure adopted did not provide for the consideration of evidence. Given that an award under the Act is non-speaking and made without a hearing, the Court of Appeal has indicated that any appeal will be by way of a re-hearing and will ordinarily require the court to receive evidence in order to reach its own conclusion on whether the award was wrong.[183]

(4) *Expenses in respect of party structures*

Expense of works

The 1996 Act contains detailed provisions dealing with who should bear the expense of carrying out works in pursuance of the 1996 Act.[184] The general position is that, except as expressly provided to the contrary, the expenses of work under the 1996 Act are to be defrayed by the building owner.[185] Any dispute as to the responsibility for expenses is to be settled pursuant to the machinery laid down by the 1996 Act.[186]   **11–25**

An expense mentioned in section 1(3)(b) is to be defrayed as therein provided.[187]

Where work is carried out in exercise of the right mentioned in section 2(2)(a), and the work is necessary on account of a defect or want or repair of the structure or wall concerned, the expenses are to be defrayed by the building owner and the adjoining owner in such proportion as has regard to the use which the owners respectively make or may make of the structure or wall concerned and responsibility for the defect or want or repair concerned, if more than one owner makes use of the structure or wall concerned.[188]

Where work is carried out in exercise of the right mentioned in section 2(2)(b), the expenses are to be defrayed by the building owner and the adjoining owner in

---

[182] *Zissis v Lukomski* (above) at [41], approving the suggestion made in the previous edition of this work.
[183] *Zissis v Lukomski,* at [41]–[42].
[184] Party Wall etc. Act 1996, s.56.
[185] Party Wall, etc. Act 1996, s.11(1).
[186] Party Wall, etc. Act 1996, s.11(2).
[187] Party Wall, etc. Act 1996, s.11(3).
[188] Party Wall, etc. Act 1996, s.11(4).

such proportion as has regard to the use which the owners respectively make or may make of the structure or wall concerned and responsibility for the defect or want of repair concerned, if more than one owner makes use of the structure or wall concerned.[189]

Where the adjoining premises are laid open in exercise of the right mentioned in section 2(2)(e), a fair allowance in respect of disturbance and inconvenience is to be paid by the building owner to the adjoining owner or occupier.[190]

Where a building owner proposes to reduce the height of a party-wall or party fence wall under section 2(2)(m), the adjoining owner may serve a counter-notice under section 4 requiring the building owner to maintain the existing height of the wall and in such a case, the adjoining owner must pay to the building owner a due proportion of the cost of the wall so far as it exceeds 2m in height or the height currently enclosed upon by the building of the adjoining owner.[191]

Where a building owner is required to make good damage under the 1996 Act, the adjoining owner has a right to require that the expenses of such making good be determined in accordance with the machinery for dispute resolution laid down in the 1996 Act and paid to him in lieu of the carrying out of the work of making good.[192]

Where works are carried out and some of the works are carried out at the request of the adjoining owner or in pursuance of a requirement made by him, the adjoining owner must defray the expenses of carrying out the works requested or required by him.[193]

Where consent in writing has been given to the construction of special foundations on the land of the adjoining owner and the adjoining owner erects any building or structure and its cost is found to be increased by reason of the existence of the said foundations, the owner of the building to which the said foundations belong must, on receiving an account with any necessary invoices and other supporting documents within the period of two months beginning with the day of the completion of the work by the adjoining owner, repay to the adjoining owner so much of the cost as is due to the existence of the said foundations.[194]

Where use is subsequently made by the adjoining owner of work carried out solely at the expense of the building owner, the adjoining owner must pay a due proportion of the expense incurred by the building owner in carrying out that work; and for this purpose, the building owner is taken to have incurred expenses calculated by reference to what the cost of the work would be if it were carried out at the time when that subsequent use is made.[195]

---

[189] Party Wall, etc. Act 1996, s.11(5).

[190] Party Wall, etc. Act 1996, s.11(6).

[191] Party Wall, etc. Act 1996, s.11(7).

[192] Party Wall, etc. Act 1996, s.11(8).

[193] Party Wall, etc. Act 1996, s.11(9).

[194] Party Wall, etc. Act 1996, s.11(10). The reference to "the owner of the building" would appear to be a reference to the person who is the owner of the building at the later time, rather than the building owner who originally constructed the foundations.

[195] Party Wall, etc. Act 1996, s.11(11).Where the original building owner has transferred his property, it would appear that his successor in title is entitled to this contribution from the adjoining owner: *Mason v Fulham Corp* [1910] 1 K.B. 631, considered in *Selby v Whitbread & Co* [1917] 1 K.B. 736.

Security for expenses

An adjoining owner may by written notice require the building owner, before he   **11–26**
begins any work in the exercise of the rights conferred by the 1939 Act, to give
such security as may be agreed between the owners or, in the event of a dispute,
determined pursuant to the machinery laid down by the 1996 Act.[196]

Where an adjoining owner requires a building owner to carry out any work the
expenses of which are to be defrayed in whole or in part by the adjoining owner
or where the adjoining owner serves notice on the building owner requiring security as aforesaid, then the building owner may, before beginning the work to
which the requirement or notice relates, serve written notice on the adjoining
owner requiring him to give such security as may be agreed between the owners
or, in the event of a dispute, determined pursuant to the machinery laid down by
the 1996 Act.[197]

The Act does not specify the financial liabilities in respect of which security
may be required. Presumably, they will include security for the satisfactory completion of the proposed work and for those matters for which the party seeking
security might subsequently be able to claim a contribution or compensation from
the party providing the security.

Somewhat curiously, the 1996 Act does not lay down any express sanction for
the building owner who does not comply with an obligation on him to give security whereas the position of an adjoining owner who does not comply with a
requirement that the adjoining owner provide security is expressly provided for. If
the adjoining owner does not comply with the building owner's notice requiring the
adjoining owner to give security, the requirement or notice by the adjoining owner
which entitled the building owner to call for security ceases to have effect.[198]

Accounts: claims by the building owner

If the building owner is entitled to be reimbursed, or is entitled to a contribution,   **11–27**
in relation to his expenditure, he may within two months of the completion of the
relevant work deliver to the adjoining owner an account in writing showing particulars and expenses of the work and any deductions to which the adjoining
owner or any other person is entitled in respect of old materials or otherwise. In
preparing the account, the work is to be estimated and valued at fair average
rates and prices according to the nature of the work, the locality and the cost
of labour and materials prevailing at the time when the work is executed.[199]
Within one month after delivery of the account, the adjoining owner may give
notice in writing to the building owner stating any objection he may have and
thereupon a dispute is deemed to have arisen between the parties.[200] Conversely,

---

[196] Party Wall, etc. Act 1996, s.12(1).
[197] Party Wall, etc. Act 1996, s.12(2).
[198] Party Wall, etc. Act 1996, s.12(3).
[199] Party Wall, etc. Act 1996, s.13(1).
[200] Party Wall, etc. Act 1996, s.13(2). For the procedure as to the settlement of a dispute, see s.10
ibid., and paras 11–22 *et seq.*, above.

if the adjoining owner does not give such a notice, he is deemed to have no objection to the building owner's account.[201] Delivery of an account is a condition precedent to recovery.[202] As the time-limits are laid down by statute, they are strict.

Accounts: claims by the adjoining owner

11-28   It was pointed out in para.11–25, above, that there can be circumstances in which an adjoining owner is entitled to recover the amount by which the cost to the adjoining owner of carrying out his own building works is increased by reason of the existence of special foundations. The relevant provision refers to the service of an account on the owner of the building to which the special foundations belong.[203] However the 1996 Act does not contain any provisions (similar to those referred to above when dealing with claims by the building owner against the adjoining owner) requiring the recipient of the account to serve notice disputing the account within 14 days. Further, there are no provisions which require the service of an account, or which require there to be a notice of dispute within a specified time, in relation to an adjoining owner's claim for compensation under section 1(7) or section 7(2) of the 1996 Act.

Recovery of expenses

11-29   All expenses to be defrayed by an adjoining owner in accordance with an account delivered by a building owner must be paid by the adjoining owner.[204] Until the adjoining owner pays to the building owner such expenses, the property in any works executed under the 1996 Act to which the expenses relate is vested solely in the building owner.[205] Further, any sum payable pursuant to the 1996 Act (whether by the adjoining owner to the building owner or vice versa) otherwise than by way of fine, is recoverable summarily as a civil debt.[206]

(5) *Miscellaneous*

Service of notices, etc.

11-30   The 1996 Act contains its own provisions as to service of notices or other documents required or authorised under the 1996 Act to be served by any person on any other person.[207]

---

[201] Party Wall, etc. Act 1996, s.13(3).
[202] *Spiers & Sons Ltd v Troup* (1915) 84 L.J.K.B. 1986.
[203] Party Wall, etc. Act 1996, s.11(10).
[204] Party Wall, etc. Act 1996, s.14(1).
[205] Party Wall, etc. Act 1996, s.14(2); or, in the absence of any provision to the contrary in a subsequent conveyance, in his successor in title: see *Mason v Fulham Corp* [1910] 1 K.B. 631.
[206] Party Wall, etc. Act 1996, s.17.
[207] Party Wall, etc. Act 1996, s.15.

Such a document may be served on a person: (a) by delivering it to him in person; or (b) by sending it by post to him at his usual or last-known residence or place of business in the United Kingdom; or (c) in the case of a body corporate, by delivering it to the secretary or clerk of the body corporate at its registered or principal office or sending it by post to the secretary or clerk of that body corporate at that office.[208]

In the case of a notice or other document required or authorised to be served under the 1996 Act on a person as owner[209] of premises, it may be served by: (a) addressing it to "the owner" of the premises (naming them); or (b) delivering it to a person on the premises or, if no person to whom it can be delivered is found there, fixing it to a conspicuous part of the premises.[210]

In addition to the provisions of the 1996 Act, there is also the general provision in the Interpretation Act 1978 to the effect that service is deemed to be effected by properly addressing, prepaying and posting a letter containing the document and, unless the contrary is proved, to have been effected at the time at which the letter would be delivered in the ordinary course of post.[211]

Offences

If an occupier of land or premises refuses to permit a person to do anything which he is entitled to do with regard to the land or premises under section 8(1) (dealing with rights of entry by or on behalf of the building owner) or section 8(5) (dealing with rights of entry by a surveyor appointed or selected for the purposes of resolving a dispute) and the occupier knows or has reasonable cause to believe that the person is so entitled the occupier is guilty of an offence.[212] If a person hinders or obstructs a person in attempting to do anything which he is entitled to do with regard to land or premises under section 8(1) or section 8(5) and the first-mentioned person knows or has reasonable cause to believe that the other person is so entitled, then the first-mentioned person is guilty of an offence.[213] A person guilty of such an offence is liable on summary conviction to a fine of an amount not exceeding level 3 on the standard scale.[214]

11–31

Crown land

Crown land was exempt from the operation of the London Building Acts (Amendment) Act 1939. The position is now reversed under the 1996 Act and it is expressly provided that the Act applies to Crown land.[215]

11–32

---

[208] Party Wall, etc. Act 1996, s.15(1).
[209] For the definition of "owner", see Party Wall, etc. Act 1996, s.20 and para.11–10 above.
[210] Party Wall, etc. Act 1996, s.15(2).
[211] Interpretation Act 1978, s.7.
[212] Party Wall, etc. Act 1996, s.16(1).
[213] Party Wall, etc. Act 1996, s.16(2).
[214] Party Wall, etc. Act 1996, s.16(3).
[215] Party Wall, etc. Act 1996, s.19; this section specifies in detail the land which has been referred to above as "Crown land".

Exemptions

11–33   The 1996 Act does not apply to land which is situated in inner London and in which there is an interest belonging to one of the four Inns of Court.[216]

3.—BANKS, HEDGES AND DITCHES

11–34   In the case of banks or hedges separating fields, the ownership is thus determined: if two fields are separated by an artificial ditch and a bank or hedge, the bank or hedge and the ditch, prima facie and in the absence of proof to the contrary,[217] are presumed to belong to the owner of the field immediately adjoining the bank or hedge,[218] but if there be a bank with ditches at each side of it, then there is no presumption as to the ownership of the bank, and the question must be determined by acts of ownership.[219]

Where parcels on the Ordnance Survey map are bounded by a hedge, it is the invariable practice of the Ordnance Survey Office, of which the court will take judicial notice,[220] to run the boundary through the centre of the hedge. Consequently, if parcels so bounded are conveyed by reference to the Ordnance Survey map, their boundary will be in the centre of the hedge, and any presumption to the contrary will be rebutted.[221]

4.—BOUNDARY TREES AND BUILDINGS

Boundary trees

11–35   As regards boundary trees, there is no authority in English law that an easement can be acquired to compel a man to submit to the invasion of his land by the roots

---

[216] Party Wall, etc. Act 1996, s.18(1); the reference to inner London is to Greater London other than the outer London boroughs: see Local Government Act 1963, s.2(1) and Interpretation Act 1978, s.5, Sch.1.

[217] *Marshall v Taylor* [1895] 1 Ch. 641; *Craven v Pridmore* (1902) 18 T.L.R. 282; *Henniker v Howard* (1904) 90 L.T. 157; *Simcox v Yardley* (1905) 69 J.P. 66; *Falkingham v Parley, The Times*, March 11, 1991.

[218] *Alan Wibberley Building Ltd v Insley* [1989] 1 W.L.R. 894. For earlier cases, see *Noye v Reed* (1827) 1 Man. & Ry. K.B. 63 at 65; *Guy v West* (1808) cited in 2 Selwyn N.P., 13th ed., 1244. See also the explanation given by Lawrence J. in *Vowles v Miller* (1810) 3 Taunt. 137 at 138; and, for a review of the cases, see per Scrutton L.J. in *Collis v Amphlett* [1918] 1 Ch. 232 at 259, 260. The rule seems to have been applied in *Weston v Lawrence Weaver Ltd* [1961] 1 Q.B. 402, in which the defendant's property was separated from a private road by a ditch, bank and hedge.

[219] *Guy v West*, above. So-called "fencing easements" are referred to at paras 1–78–1–85 *et seq.*, above, where rights analogous to easements are considered.

[220] *Davey v Harrow Corp* [1958] 1 Q.B. 60.

[221] *Fisher v Winch* [1939] 1 K.B. 666; *Rouse v Gravelworks Ltd* [1940] 1 K.B. 489; *Davey v Harrow Corp*, above. *Fisher v Winch* was distinguished in *Alan Wibberley Building Ltd v Insley* [1989] 1 W.L.R. 894 on the ground that the ditch in *Fisher v Winch* existed before the boundary was drawn. Where a ditch does not pass by conveyance, because the plan refers to the boundaries as on the Ordnance Survey map, it cannot pass under s.62(1) of the Law of Property Act 1925; Jarvis v Aris (July 14, 1961, unreported: see 232 L.T.Jour. 229).

or branches of a tree planted on his neighbour's soil. The principal objections to the acquisition of such an easement by user consist in the perpetual change in the quantity of inconvenience imposed by it, and, in the case of penetrating roots, the secrecy in the mode of enjoyment. It is now settled that the encroachment of boughs or roots of trees (whether planted or self-growing) over and within the land of the adjoining owner is not a trespass or occupation which by lapse of time can become a right, but is (or may be) a nuisance.[222]

Overhanging branches

The owner or occupier of land which is overhung by the branches of a tree grow-   **11-36** ing on adjoining land is entitled, without notice, if he does not trespass on the adjoining land, to cut the branches, however old they may be, so far as they over-hang[223]; but this right does not carry with it a right to appropriate the severed branches or the fruit growing thereon.[224] That right is not affected by the exis-tence of a tree preservation order.[225] If the overhanging branches are not in fact doing damage it may be that the only right is to cut back the overhanging por-tions[226]; but an action lies where the overhanging branches are actually doing damage, such as through interfering with the growth of fruit trees,[227] or poison-ing cattle.[228] On the other hand, the owner or occupier has no right of action if his cattle eat poisonous leaves on the branches on the adjoining land, not overhang-ing his own land,[229] nor possibly if poisonous leaves from branches which do not overhang fall on to his own land.[230]

In *Cheater v Cater*,[231] where A had let a farm which was overhung by yew trees   **11-37** standing on A's adjoining land, and the tenant's mare died as a result of eating the yew branches, it was held by the Court of Appeal (following the judgment of Mellish L.J. in *Erskine v Adeane*[232]) that, as the tenant had taken the farm with the yew trees overhanging, he must abide the consequences, and had no cause of

---

[222] The law in relation to encroachment by tree roots has now been reviewed by the House of Lords in *Delaware Mansions Ltd v Westminster C.C.* [2002] 1 A.C. 321. For earlier cases, see *Lemmon v Webb* [1894] 3 Ch. 1 at 24; [1895] A.C. 1; *Davey v Harrow Corp* [1958] 1 Q.B. 60; *Morgan v Khyatt* [1964] 1 W.L.R. 475. It seems that the ownership of a tree goes with the land in which the tree was first planted, and that the place where it was planted may be a matter of inference. On this obscure subject, see *Masters v Pollie* (1620) 2 Roll.Rep. 141; *Anon.* (1622) 2 Roll.Rep. 255; *Waterman v Soper* (1697) 1 Ld.Raym. 737; *Holder v Coates* (1827) 1 Moo. & M. 112; *Lemmon v Webb* [1894] 3 Ch. 1 at 20; *Hetherington v Galt* (1905) 7 F. (Ct. of Sess.) 706. As to the liability of a highway authority for trees growing in highways, see *Hurst v Hampshire C.C.* (1997) 96 L.G.R. 27.
[223] *Lemmon v Webb*, above.
[224] *Mills v Brooker* [1919] 1 K.B. 555.
[225] Town and Country Planning Act 1990, s.198(6)(b).
[226] *Smith v Giddy* [1904] 2 K.B. 451; 73 L.J.K.B. 894.
[227] *Smith v Giddy* [1904] 2 K.B. 451; 73 L.J.K.B. 894.
[228] *Crowhurst v Amersham Burial Board* (1878) 4 Ex.D. 5.
[229] *Ponting v Noakes* [1894] 2 Q.B. 281.
[230] *Smith v Giddy* (1904) as reported in 73 L.J.K.B. 894 at 896; *cf. Wilson v Newberry* (1871) L.R. 7 Q.B. 31; *Giles v Walker* (1890) 24 Q.B.D. 656; but see *Davey v Harrow Corp* [1958] 1 Q.B. 60.
[231] [1918] 1 K.B. 247. The principle was recognised in *Shirvell v Hackwood Estates Co* [1938] 2 K.B. 577.
[232] (1873) 8 Ch. App. 756 at 761.

action. What the position of the tenant would have been if the danger had first arisen after the date of the lease was not decided.

11-38   A landowner may also apply to the court under the Access to Neighbouring Land Act 1992 for an access order on the ground that it is reasonably necessary for the preservation of his land to cut back, fell, remove or replace any tree or other growing thing which is or is in danger of becoming damaged, diseased, dangerous, insecurely rooted or dead.[233]

Encroaching roots

11-39   The rights of the owner or occupier of land which is invaded by the roots of a tree growing on adjoining land appear to be exactly the same as his right in respect of overhanging branches.[234] Where damage has occurred, damages have been awarded,[235] and an injunction has been granted restraining the defendant from causing or permitting the roots to encroach so as to cause a nuisance.[236]

Building projecting over boundary

11-40   Speaking generally, the ownership of a building includes the air-space above it.[237] While, however, the grant of a building may well include parts of it which project beyond its apparent boundary,[238] such a grant will not normally include anything above or below the projecting part.[239]

After some conflict of authority, it appears to be settled that the invasion of air-space by projecting buildings, advertising signs, jibs, cranes or the like constitutes a trespass, actionable whether actual damage is caused or not.[240] The right to maintain such a projection may, it seems, be acquired as an easement.[241]

---

[233] Access to Neighbouring Land Act 1992, s.1(4); and see para.11–41, below.

[234] *Lemmon v Webb* [1894] 3 Ch. 1; [1895] A.C. 1; *Butler v Standard Telephones and Cables Ltd* [1940] 1 K.B. 399; *McCombe v Read* [1955] 2 Q.B. 429. See George, "Liability for Damage Caused by Tree Roots" (1963) 27 Conv (n.s.) 179 *et seq.*

[235] The basis for liability has now been restated in *Delaware Mansions Ltd v Westminster C.C.* [2002] 1 A.C. 321. For earlier cases, see *Butler v Standard Telephones and Cables Ltd*, above; *McCombe v Read*, above; *Bunclark v Hertfordshire C.C.* [1977] 2 E.G.L.R. 114.

[236] *McCombe v Read*, above. In this case it was stated in evidence that the roots of a poplar normally extend to one-and-a-half times the height of the tree. See also *King v Taylor* [1976] 1 E.G.L.R. 132 and *Elliott v Islington B.C.* [1991] 1 E.G.L.R. 167.

[237] According to the maxim *cujus est solum ejus est usque ad coelum*, see *Kelsen v Imperial Tobacco Co (of Great Britain and Ireland) Ltd* [1957] 2 Q.B. 334, applied in *Haines v Florensa* (1990) 59 P. & C.R. 200, CA; but only to such height as is necessary for the ordinary use and enjoyment of the land: *Bernstein v Skyviews & General Ltd* [1978] Q.B. 479.

[238] *Francis v Hayward* (1882) 22 Ch. D. 177 (considered in *William Hill (Southern) Ltd v Cabras Ltd* (1987) 54 P. & C.R. 42); *Truckell v Stock* [1957] 1 W.L.R. 161 (projecting footings and eaves); *cf. Laybourn v Gridley* [1892] 2 Ch. 53 (overhanging part of building included in a lease of the building, but also in subsequent conveyance of the property overhung).

[239] *Corbett v Hill* (1870) L.R. 9 Eq. 671 (first floor room projecting over ground floor of adjoining house); *Truckell v Stock*, above. Contrast *Gifford v Dent* [1926] W.N. 336.

[240] *Kelsen v Imperial Tobacco Co (of Great Britain and Ireland) Ltd*, above; *Lemmon v Webb* [1894] 3 Ch. 1 at 18; *Anchor Brewhouse Developments Ltd v Berkeley House (Docklands Developments) Ltd* [1987] 2 E.G.L.R. 173.

[241] *Harris v De Pinna* (1885) 33 Ch. D. 238 at 260; *Lemmon v Webb*, above.

5.—Access to Neighbouring Land

(1) *Introduction and definitions*

Introduction

There are many different easements which authorise the owner of the dominant ten- **11–41**
ement to enter upon the servient tenement for wide or for limited purposes. The
widest of these easements would appear to be a general right of way for all purposes, but there are also recognised easements which permit the owner of the dominant tenement to enter upon the servient tenement for the sole purpose of carrying
out repairs to buildings on the dominant tenement, for example, for the purpose of
repairing overhanging eaves, or undersailing foundations or a flank wall.[242] Further,
where there is a right of way or a right to use conduits of various kinds, there will
generally be, as an incident of that right, a right to enter the servient tenement for
the purpose of repairing the way or the conduit in question. In addition, in relation
to certain structures which are party structures, a building owner may be able to
enter on the land of an adjoining owner under the Party Wall, etc. Act 1996.[243]
Further, some statutes give specific powers of entry on land for specific purposes.[244]

However, there are many other circumstances where one owner of property
wishes to enter his neighbour's land in order to carry out necessary works of
repair which cannot otherwise be carried out or which can only be carried out on
the owner's own land at much greater expense than would be incurred if he could
have access to his neighbour's land for that purpose. In the absence of an easement or specific statutory provision, before 1992, there was nothing that such an
owner could do to compel his neighbour to co-operate with him. The neighbour
was entitled to insist that no such entry should take place, however unreasonable
such an attitude might be. This fact was illustrated by a series of cases involving
"entry" on neighbouring land which took the form of the oversailing into the
air-space above the neighbouring land of the jib of a crane stationed on the
adjoining land on which the owner was carrying out building works. In those
cases the courts generally held that the oversailing jib was a trespass which
could be restrained by an interlocutory injunction regardless of the fact that the
jib might cause the plaintiff no harm and the inability of the defendant to use
such a crane might be very burdensome on him.[245] However, the position is now

---

[242] See, e.g. *Ward v Kirkland* [1967] Ch. 194; *Williams v Usherwood* (1983) 45 P. & C.R. 235. A right
of entry to repair, rebuild or renew will not, however, entitle the party with the benefit of it to carry
out a comprehensive redevelopment involving a completely different structure: *Risegold Ltd v
Escala Ltd* [2008] EWHC 21; [2008] 1 E.G.L.R. 13.

[243] See para.11–21, above.

[244] See the various statutes referred to in *Anchor Brewhouse Developments Ltd v Berkeley House
(Docklands Developments) Ltd* [1987] 2 E.G.L.R. 173 at 178J.

[245] See *Woollerton and Wilson Ltd v Richard Costain Ltd* [1970] 1 W.L.R. 411; *John Trenberth Ltd v
National Westminster Bank Ltd* (1979) 39 P. & C.R. 104; *Anchor Brewhouse Developments Ltd v
Berkley House (Dockland Developments) Ltd* [1987] 2 E.G.L.R. 173; and *London & Manchester
Assurance Co Ltd v O. & H. Construction Ltd* [1989] 2 E.G.L.R. 185.

alleviated by the Access to Neighbouring Land Act 1992 and it is that Act with which the remainder of this chapter is concerned.

The Access to Neighbouring Land Act 1992

11–42   The Access to Neighbouring Land Act 1992 was passed "to enable persons who desire to carry out works to any land which are reasonably necessary for the preservation of that land to obtain access to neighbouring land in order to do so".[246] The rights which are granted by the 1992 Act are in some respects rather limited and those rights can only be enforced by applying to the courts for an "access order".[247] The 1992 Act came into force on January 31, 1993.[248]

Definitions of "land", "dominant land" and "servient land"

11–43   The only definition of "land" in the 1992 Act is to the effect that "land" does not include a highway. Accordingly, in other respects, the definition of "land" provided by the Interpretation Act 1978 applies: this defines "land" as including buildings and other structures, land covered with water, and any estate, interest, easement, servitude or right in or over land.[249] The definition of land includes a party-wall.[250] Because the 1992 Act does not expressly mention the Crown, it will not be binding in relation to Crown lands. The 1992 Act defines, for the purposes of the Act, what is meant by "dominant land" and by "servient land". The "dominant land" is any land to which a person wishes to carry out works.[251] The "servient land" is any land adjoining or adjacent to the dominant land upon which any person desires to enter for the purpose of carrying out works to the dominant land.[252]

Definition of "entry"

11–44   "Enter" and "entry" have a wide statutory meaning in the 1992 Act. Any reference to an "entry" upon any servient land is defined to include a reference to the doing on the servient land of anything necessary for carrying out works to the dominant land which are reasonably necessary for its preservation and "enter" is to be construed accordingly.[253] Further, the Act applies in relation to any obstruction of, or other interference with, a right over, or interest in, any land as it applies in relation to an entry upon that land and "entry" and "enter" are to be construed

---

[246] This quotation is from the long title of the Act. The 1992 Act was preceded by Law Comm. No. 151 which recommended that there be legislation of the kind now embodied in the 1992 Act; it should be noted, however, that the recommendations of the Law Commission were not identical to the provisions as enacted. Part of the report was referred to by the Court of Appeal in *Dean v Walker* (1996) 73 P. & C.R. 366.

[247] An "access order" is an order under s.1 of the 1992 Act.

[248] Access to Neighbouring Land Act 1992 (Commencement) Order 1992, SI 1992/3349.

[249] Interpretation Act 1978, s.5, Sch.1.

[250] *Dean v Walker* (1996) 73 P. & C.R. 366.

[251] Access to Neighbouring Land Act 1992, ss.1(1)(a), 8(3).

[252] Access to Neighbouring Land Act 1992, ss.1(1)(a), 8(3).

[253] Access to Neighbouring Land Act 1992, s.8(1).

accordingly.[254] In the simple case of one landowner going on to his neighbour's land the language of the statute will be easily understood. However, there will be cases where the statutory language will appear somewhat artificial and unnatural. Take the example of adjoining plots, Blackacre and Whiteacre. Whiteacre has the benefit of a right of way over Blackacre. In the ordinary language of easements, Whiteacre is the dominant tenement and Blackacre is the servient tenement. Suppose the owner of Blackacre wishes to carry out preservation work to a building on Blackacre and for that purpose he needs to obstruct the right of way over Blackacre to Whiteacre. In the language of the 1992 Act, the building, or the relevant part of it is "the dominant tenement", the land over which the right of way runs and which is to be obstructed is the "servient tenement" on which the owner of Blackacre will "enter" (even though it is his own land).

(2) *The right to apply for an access order*

The access order

The basic right given by the 1992 Act is to enable certain persons in certain circumstances to apply for an "access order". Any person who, for the purposes of carrying out works to any land (the "dominant land"), desires to enter upon any adjoining or adjacent land (the "servient land") and who needs, but does not have, the consent of some other person to that entry, may make an application to the court for an "access order" against that other person.[255] No qualifications as to ownership or occupation of the dominant land are prescribed for the persons who may apply for an access order. Accordingly, persons other than the owner or occupier of the dominant land may apply for an access order; that this is indeed the position is emphasised by the references to persons "connected with" the applicant in section 2 of the 1992 Act.[256] The statutory provisions appear to apply to a wide range of situations. No doubt, the most common case will be where the owner or occupier of one property applies to be allowed to enter on his neighbour's property for the purpose of carrying out works to the owned or occupied property. But the Act will also apply, for example, to someone who has the benefit of a right of way over a track and who wishes to enter on land adjoining the track in order to do works to the track[257]; the track will be the dominant land and the adjoining land will be the servient land. Further, the Act will apply to a tenant of a block of flats who has the benefit of a right to a supply through a conduit which also runs through other flats; such a tenant will be able to seek an access order permitting entry to those other flats for the purposes of doing works of

11–45

---

[254] Access to Neighbouring Land Act 1992, s.8(2).

[255] Access to Neighbouring Land Act 1992, s.1(1).

[256] See para.11–58, below.

[257] In such a case it would be necessary to consider whether the applicant in fact needs the consent of some other person on account of the ancillary rights of the dominant owner to repair, or sometimes even improve, the servient land: see *Newcomen v Coulson* (1877) 5 Ch. D. 133 and *Nationwide Building Society v James Beauchamp* [2001] 3 E.G.L.R. 6; compare *Mills v Silver* [1991] Ch. 271.

repair to the conduit; the conduit will be the dominant land and the other flats will be the servient land.

The proposed works

11–46   The applicant must satisfy the court that the works are reasonably necessary for the preservation of the whole or any part of the dominant land and that they cannot be carried out, or would be substantially more difficult to carry out, without entry upon the servient land.[258] This requirement is expressed in the Act, in the first instance, in general terms but it is supplemented by a number of specific provisions.

Basic preservation works

11–47   The first such specific provision deals with what are defined as "basic preservation works". In the case of "basic preservation works", if the court is satisfied that it is reasonably necessary to carry out those works then those works are to be taken as being reasonably necessary for the preservation of the land.[259] "Basic preservation works" are defined as any of the following:

(1) the maintenance, repair or renewal of any part of a building or other structure comprised in, or situate on, the dominant land;

(2) the clearance, repair or renewal of any drain, sewer, pipe or cable so comprised or situate;

(3) the treatment, cutting back, felling, removal or replacement of any hedge, tree, shrub or other growing thing which is so comprised and which is, or is in danger of becoming, damaged, diseased, dangerous, insecurely rooted or dead.[260]

The purpose of this list of basic preservation works appears to be to identify those works which are most likely to give rise to the need for an access order, but leaving open the possibility that other works might still satisfy the general test for an access order.

11–48   A second specific provision is that if the court thinks it fair and reasonable in all the circumstances of the case, works may be regarded for the purposes of the 1992 Act as being reasonably necessary for the preservation of any land or as being "basic preservation works" which it is reasonably necessary to carry out to any land, notwithstanding that the works incidentally involve the making of some alteration, adjustment or improvement to the land, or the demolition of the whole or any part of a building or structure comprised in or situate upon the land.[261] This provision emphasises the narrowness of the class of works which can be the

---

[258] Access to Neighbouring Land Act 1992, s.1(2).
[259] Access to Neighbouring Land Act 1992, s.1(4).
[260] Access to Neighbouring Land Act 1992, s.1(4).
[261] Access to Neighbouring Land Act 1992, s.1(5).

subject of an access order. It is not possible to assert that works of improvement are works which are reasonably necessary for the preservation of land; the only works of improvement which can be taken into account are works which are incidental to the works of preservation and, even then, only when the court thinks it is fair and reasonable to allow them to be included.

A third specific provision is that where any works are reasonably necessary for   **11–49**
the preservation of the whole or any part of the dominant land, the doing to the dominant land of anything which is requisite for, incidental to, or consequential on, the carrying out of those works is to be treated for the purposes of the 1992 Act as the carrying out of works which are reasonably necessary for the preservation of that land.[262]

A fourth specific provision is that if it is reasonably necessary for a person to   **11–50**
inspect the dominant land:

(a) for the purpose of ascertaining whether any works may be reasonably necessary for the preservation of the whole or any part of that land;
(b) for the purpose of making any map or plan, or ascertaining the course of any drain, sewer, pipe or cable, in preparation for, or otherwise in connection with, the carrying out of works which are so reasonably necessary; or
(c) otherwise in connection with the carrying out of any such works,

the making of such an inspection is to be taken for the purposes of the 1992 Act to be the carrying out to the dominant land of works which are reasonably necessary for the preservation of that land.[263] If an application is made for an access order to permit inspection on the ground set out in paragraph (a) above and as a result of such an inspection it is found that works are indeed reasonably necessary for the preservation of the land, it would then seem to be necessary to make a further application for an access order to permit entry for the works.

Alternatively, it might be possible to ask the court to make an order permitting the inspection and further providing that in the event of it appearing to the applicant that works are reasonably necessary for the preservation of the land, the applicant is to be permitted to apply in the current proceedings for an access order to permit entry for that work. It would not be possible to dispense with the requirement of a further hearing because the court, and not just the applicant, must be satisfied that the works are reasonably necessary for the preservation of the dominant land.

The statutory test for the making of an access order

The 1992 Act does not give any guidance as to how to approach the question of   **11–51**
whether the works cannot be carried out, or would be substantially more difficult to carry out, without entry on the servient land. The statutory test appears to involve a consideration of the physical practicability of doing the work rather

---

[262] Access to Neighbouring Land Act 1992, s.1(6).
[263] Access to Neighbouring Land Act 1992, s.1(7).

than a consideration of the comparative cost of rival methods of doing the work. No doubt, in many cases where one method of doing the work is simple and another is substantially more difficult, the simple method will be much less expensive than the difficult method and, indeed, the expense will be the reason why the applicant wishes to have an access order. Any saving in the costs of doing the work which results from the making of an access order is relevant in determining the amount of any consideration which is required to be paid (in the case of non-residential land) as a condition of the access order.[264] Where the applicant satisfies the court (with or without the assistance of the specific provisions referred to above) that the works are reasonably necessary for the preservation of the whole or any part of the dominant land and that the works cannot be carried out, or would be substantially more difficult to carry out, without entry upon the servient land then, subject to a specified statutory exception, the court must make an access order.[265]

The statutory exception

11–52   The statutory exception applies where the court is satisfied that, if it were to make an access order:

(a) the respondent to the application or any other person would suffer interference with, or disturbance of, his use or enjoyment of the servient land, or

(b) the respondent to the application or any other person (whether of full age or capacity or not[266]) in occupation of the whole or any part of the servient land would suffer hardship,

to such a degree by reason of the entry (notwithstanding any requirement of the 1992 Act or any term or condition that may be imposed under it[267]) that it would be unreasonable to make the access order.[268] Where the statutory exception is established to the satisfaction of the court, it must not make an access order.[269]

(3) *Terms and conditions of access orders*

Mandatory provisions

11–53   The 1992 Act contains detailed provisions as to what an access order must contain and what it may contain. An access order must specify:

---

[264] See para.11–57, below.
[265] Access to Neighbouring Land Act 1992, s.1(2).
[266] It is not clear why the words "whether of full age or capacity or not" appear in Access to Neighbouring Land Act 1992, s.1(3)(b) but not in s.1(3)(a), nor in s.2(2) nor (4), nor is it clear what is the effect of such omission.
[267] As to the possible imposition of terms and conditions, see para.11–56, below.
[268] Access to Neighbouring Land Act 1992, s.1(3).
[269] Access to Neighbouring Land Act 1992, s.1(3).

(a) the works to the dominant land that may be carried out by entering upon the servient land in pursuance of the order;

(b) the particular area of servient land that may be entered upon by virtue of the order for the purpose of carrying out those works to the dominant land; and

(c) the date on which, or the period during which, the land may be so entered upon.[270]

Where an access order has been made and it is necessary to know what is the servient land for the purposes of the provisions of the 1992 Act, the servient land is the land so specified in the access order.[271] In the ordinary case, the period specified in the access order will be the period which is expected to be needed for the works which are then intended to be done. It has been suggested[272] that the language of the 1992 Act is literally open to the interpretation that it may be possible to apply for an access order which permits entry on the servient land whenever in the future particular works of preservation of the dominant land may become necessary. If this interpretation were to prevail it would enable, for example, the owner of a property with a flank wall which immediately abutted a neighbour's land to apply for an access order in perpetuity to enable the owner of the flank wall to enter on the neighbour's land for the purpose of repointing the flank wall at any time in the future when repointing was needed. It is doubtful, however, whether this interpretation of the 1992 Act is correct. It is a precondition to the making of an access order that the court is satisfied that works are reasonably necessary for the preservation of the dominant land; accordingly, it would not be open to the court to make an order which permitted a person to carry out works which were not reasonably necessary for the preservation of the dominant land at the date of the order and without the court determining at a subsequent date that those works had become reasonably necessary.

The court's discretion as to terms

In addition to the matters which the access order must specify, the court has considerable discretion as to the imposition of other terms and conditions as to the carrying out of the work, as to compensation, as to the payment of a consideration by the applicant to the respondent, as to the respondent's expenses and as to the giving of security for sums payable. **11–54**

Terms and conditions as to the carrying out of the work

An access order may impose upon the applicant or the respondent such terms and conditions as appear to the court to be reasonably necessary for the purpose of avoiding or restricting: **11–55**

---

[270] Access to Neighbouring Land Act 1992, s.2(1).
[271] Access to Neighbouring Land Act 1992, s.2(1).
[272] The *Current Law Statutes* annotations on the 1992 Act at pp. 23–27.

(a) any loss, damage, or injury which might otherwise be caused to the respondent or any other person by reason of the entry authorised by the order; or

(b) any inconvenience or loss of privacy that might otherwise be so caused to the respondent or any other person.[273]

In addition to this general provision, the Act provides, in particular, that the order may impose terms and conditions with respect to:

(1) the manner in which the specified works are to be carried out;

(2) the days on which, and the hours between which, the work involved may be executed;

(3) the persons who may undertake the carrying out of the specified works or enter upon the specified land under or by virtue of the order;

(4) the taking of any such precautions by the applicant as may be specified in the order.[274]

Terms and conditions as to compensation

11–56   An access order may impose terms and conditions:

(a) requiring the applicant to pay, or to secure that such person connected with him[275] as may be specified in the order pays, compensation for:

  (i) any loss, damage or injury, or

  (ii) any substantial loss of privacy or other substantial inconvenience,

  which will, or might, be caused to the respondent or any other person by reason of the entry authorised by the order;

(b) requiring the applicant to secure that he, or such person connected with him[276] as may be specified in the order, is insured against any such risks as may be so specified; or

(c) requiring such a record to be made of the condition of the servient land, or of such part of it as may be so specified, as the court may consider expedient with a view to facilitating the determination of any question that may arise concerning damage to that land.[277]

Terms and conditions as to consideration

11–57   The court has power to include in an access order provision requiring the applicant to pay to the respondent such sum by way of consideration for the privilege of

---

[273] Access to Neighbouring Land Act 1992, s.2(2).
[274] Access to Neighbouring Land Act 1992, s.2(3).
[275] For the meaning of persons "connected with" the applicant, see para.11–58, below.
[276] For the meaning of persons "connected with" the applicant, see para.11–58, below.
[277] Access to Neighbouring Land Act 1992, s.2(4).

entering the servient land pursuant to the access order as appears to the court to be fair and reasonable having regard to all the circumstances of the case, including, in particular:

(1) the likely financial advantage of the order to the applicant and any persons connected with him[278]; and

(2) the degree of inconvenience likely to be caused to the respondent or any other person by the entry.[279]

The reference to "the likely financial advantage of the order" is spelt out in some detail as meaning in all cases a sum of money equal to the greater of the following amounts:

(a) the amount (if any) by which so much of any likely increase in the value of any land:

(i) which consists of or includes the dominant land, and

(ii) which is owned or occupied by the same person as the dominant land,

as may reasonably be regarded as attributable to the carrying out of the specified works exceeds the likely cost of carrying out those works with the benefit of the access order; and

(b) the difference (if it would have been possible to carry out the specified works without entering upon the servient land) between:

(i) the likely cost of carrying out those works without entering upon the servient land; and

(ii) the likely cost of carrying them out with the benefit of the access order.[280]

There is an important limitation on this power in that no payment may be ordered by way of consideration (as distinct from compensation) if and to the extent that the works which the applicant desires to carry out by means of the entry are works to residential land.[281] "Residential land" is defined by the Act to mean so much of any land as consists of:

(a) a dwelling or part of a dwelling;

(b) a garden, yard, private garage or outbuilding which is used and enjoyed wholly or mainly with a dwelling; or

(c) in the case of a building which includes one or more dwellings, any part of the building which is used and enjoyed wholly or mainly with those dwellings or any of them.[282]

---

[278] For the meaning of persons "connected with" the applicant, see para.11–58, below.

[279] Access to Neighbouring Land Act 1992, s.2(5).

[280] Access to Neighbouring Land Act 1992, s.2(6).

[281] Access to Neighbouring Land Act 1992, s.2(5).

[282] Access to Neighbouring Land Act 1992, s.2(7).

Connected persons

11–58   When making provision for terms and conditions as to compensation and consideration, the Act refers to persons "connected with" the applicant. The Act defines the persons who are to be regarded as "connected with" the applicant as:

(1) the owner of any estate or interest in, or right over, the whole or any part of the dominant land;

(2) the occupier of the whole or any part of the dominant land; and

(3) any person whom the applicant may authorise[283] to exercise the power of entry conferred by the access order.[284]

Terms and conditions as to expenses and security

11–59   The court may make provision for the reimbursement by the applicant of any expenses reasonably incurred by the respondent in connection with the application which are not otherwise recoverable as costs.[285] The Act does not otherwise give any directions as to how the court should determine liability for the parties' costs of the application and accordingly the court retains its usual discretion in this respect.

The court may make provision for the giving of security by the applicant for any sum that might become payable to the respondent or any other person, whether by way of compensation, or as consideration or pursuant to an obligation to indemnify the applicant.[286]

Terms varying the usual effect of an access order

11–60   The Act sets out the usual effect of an access order but in some respects authorises the court to vary or exclude the usual effect of such an order. The effect of an access order and the court's powers in this respect are considered below.

(4) *The effect of an access order*

General provisions as to the effect of an access order

11–61   The Act contains a number of general provisions as to the effect of an access order and then goes on to set out a number of detailed consequences of the making of an access order. The court has power to vary or exclude some of the specified detailed consequences.

An access order requires the respondent, so far as he has power to do so, to permit the applicant or any of his associates to do anything which the applicant

---

[283] Under s.3(7) of the 1992 Act.
[284] Access to Neighbouring Land Act 1992, s.2(8).
[285] Access to Neighbouring Land Act 1992, s.2(9)(a).
[286] Pursuant to s.2 or 3 of the 1992 Act: *ibid.*, s.2(9)(b).

or associate is authorised or required to do under or by virtue of the order or section 3 of the Act, which sets out some of the effects of the order.[287] The Act contains further provisions identifying who else, in addition to the respondent, is bound by the order.[288] The applicant's "associates" are such number of persons, whether or not servants or agents of his, whom he may reasonably authorise to exercise the power of entry conferred by the access order as may be reasonably necessary for carrying out the specified works.[289] Where the applicant or any of his associates is authorised or required under or by virtue of an access order or section 3 of the Act to enter, or do any other thing, upon the servient land, he shall not (as respects that access order) be taken to be a trespasser from the beginning on account of his, or any other person's, subsequent conduct.[290] Accordingly, if the applicant or his associates enter on the servient land and at all times operate within the terms of the access order, they will not be trespassers on the servient land. If the applicant or his associates do something which is not permitted by the access order, then that activity may constitute a trespass on the servient land at the time it is carried out, but it will not relate back so as to make the applicant or his associates trespassers from the time when they first entered on the servient land.[291]

Specific provisions as to the effect of an access order

Except as otherwise provided by or under the 1992 Act, an access order authorises the applicant or any of his associates,[292] without the consent of the respondent: **11–62**

(a) to enter upon the servient land for the purposes of carrying out the specified works;

(b) to bring on to that land, leave there during the period permitted by the order and, before the end of that period, remove, such material, plant and equipment as are reasonably necessary for the carrying out of those works; and

(c) to bring on to that land any waste arising from the carrying out of those works, if it is reasonably necessary to do so in the course of removing it from the dominant land.[293]

In making the access order, the court may vary or exclude, in whole or in part, any authorisation which would otherwise be conferred as in (b) or (c) above.[294]

---

[287] Access to Neighbouring Land Act 1992, s.3(1).

[288] Access to Neighbouring Land Act 1992, s.4, and see para.11–67, below.

[289] Access to Neighbouring Land Act 1992, s.3(7).

[290] Access to Neighbouring Land Act 1992, s.3(6).

[291] The effect of Access to Neighbouring Land Act 1992, s.3(6) is to negative any possible application of the rule as to relation back of trespass laid down in the *Six Carpenters' Case* (1610) 8 Co. Rep. 146a; see Hansard, HL, Vol. 535, col. 893 and the Law Comm. No. 151, para.4.111.

[292] For the meaning of "associates" see Access to Neighbouring Land Act 1992, s.3(7) and para.11–61, above.

[293] Access to Neighbouring Land Act 1992, s.3(2).

[294] Access to Neighbouring Land Act 1992, s.3(4).

Nothing in the 1992 Act or in any access order can authorise the applicant or any of his associates to leave anything in, on or over the servient land (otherwise than in discharge of their duty to make good that land) after their entry for the purpose of carrying out works to the dominant land ceases to be authorised under or by virtue of the order.[295] Accordingly, the Act does not extend to permitting the applicant to leave any foundation or footing or prop or conduits of any kind in, on or over the servient land.

Unless the specified statutory effect of the order is expressly varied or excluded, an access order requires the applicant:

(1) to secure that any waste arising from the carrying out of the specified works is removed from the servient land forthwith;

(2) to secure that, before the entry ceases to be authorised under or by virtue of the order, the servient land is, so far as reasonably practicable, made good; and

(3) to indemnify the respondent against any damage which may be caused to the servient land or any goods by the applicant or any of his associates which would not have been so caused had the order not been made.[296]

Any of the requirements set out in (1) to (3) above may be expressly varied or excluded by the court.[297] In particular, if the court is satisfied that it is reasonably necessary for any such waste as may arise from the carrying out of the specified works to be left on the servient land for some period before removal, the access order may, instead of the requirement set out in (1) above, include provision authorising the waste to be left on that land for such period as may be permitted by the order and requiring the applicant to secure that the waste is removed before the end of that period.[298]

(5) Procedure

The court

11–63   Both the High Court and the county court have jurisdiction under the 1992 Act.[299] Where the Act refers to "the court", the reference is to the High Court or a county court.[300] However, it is provided by the High Court and County Courts Jurisdiction Order 1991, as amended by the 1992 Act, that an application under the 1992 Act must be commenced in the county court.[301]

---

[295] Access to Neighbouring Land Act 1992, s.3(2).
[296] Access to Neighbouring Land Act 1992, s.3(3).
[297] Access to Neighbouring Land Act 1992, s.3(4).
[298] Access to Neighbouring Land Act 1992, s.3(5).
[299] Access to Neighbouring Land Act 1992, s.7(1).
[300] Access to Neighbouring Land Act 1992, s.8(3).
[301] 1991 Order, art.6A, introduced by 1992 Act, s.7(2).

The application

An application for an access order must be made in accordance with Part 8 of the   **11–64**
Civil Procedure Rules 1998.[302] The application must set out:

(1) details of the dominant land and the servient land involved and whether the dominant land includes or consists of residential property;
(2) the work required;
(3) why entry to the servient land is required with plans (if applicable);
(4) the names and addresses of the persons who will be carrying out the work;
(5) the proposed date when the work will be carried out; and
(6) what (if any) provision has been made by way of insurance in the event of possible injury to persons or damage to property arising out of the proposed work.[303]

The owner and the occupier of the servient land must be defendants to the application.[304] The 1992 Act provides for Rules of Court to be made to provide a procedure which may be followed where the applicant does not know, and cannot reasonably ascertain, the name of any person whom he desires to make respondent to the application, and to enable such an applicant to make such a person respondent by description instead of by name.[305] The Civil Procedure Rules 1998 contain a general rule as to the circumstances in which a claim form may be issued under Part 8 without naming a defendant.[306]

(6) *Miscellaneous*

No contracting out

Any agreement, whenever made, is void if and to the extent that it purports to prevent a person from applying for an access order or restrict his right to do so.[307]   **11–65**

Registration

An application for an access order is regarded as a pending land action for the   **11–66**
purposes of the Land Charges Act 1972 and the Land Registration Act 2002.[308] In the case of unregistered land, a pending land action will not bind a purchaser without express notice unless it is registered.[309] In the case of registered land, a

---

[302] CPR, Pt 56, r.4, 56PD, para.11.1.
[303] CPR, Pt 56, r.4, 56PD, para.11.2.
[304] CPR, Pt 56, r.4, 56PD, para.11.3.
[305] Access to Neighbouring Land Act 1992, s.4(3).
[306] CPR, Pt 8, r.2A.
[307] Access to Neighbouring Land Act 1992, s.4(4).
[308] Access to Neighbouring Land Act 1992, s.5(6).
[309] Land Charges Act 1972, s.5(7).

pending land action may be protected only by a notice under the Land Registration Act 2002.[310] After the access order is made, it may be registered in the register of writs and orders affecting land under section 6 of the Land Charges Act 1972[311] or protected by notice under the Land Registration Act 2002.[312] The rights conferred on a person by or under an access order are not capable of having overriding status under the Land Registration Act 2002.[313] In any case, where an access order is discharged under the 1992 Act and the order had been protected by an entry registered under the Land Charges Act 1972 or by a notice under the Land Registration Act 2002, the court may by order direct that the relevant registration is cancelled.[314]

Persons bound by access order

11–67   The respondent, or respondents, are of course bound by the access order. In addition, the access order is, subject to the provisions of the Land Charges Act 1972 and the Land Registration Act 1925 (or the Land Registration Act 2002),[315] binding on:

(1) any of his successors in title to the servient land; and

(2) any person who has an estate or interest in, or right over, the whole or any part of the servient land which was created after the making of the order and who derives his title to that estate or interest or right under the respondent.[316]

References in the 1992 Act to the respondent are to be construed so as to extend to persons who are bound by the order.[317] These provisions apply equally to an access order which has been varied under the 1992 Act.[318] The reference to a right over land as distinct from an estate or interest in land would seem to include the rights of a licensee. If the respondent's interest is subdivided, it would seem that the subsequent owners of that interest should be liable only to the extent that the estate or interest they have acquired is directly subject to the order. If a person who was not originally a respondent to the application becomes bound by the access order, he may wish to take advantage of terms and conditions in the order which are beneficial to him. Such a person is entitled to enforce the access order or any of its terms as if he were the respondent, as respects anything falling to be done after the order becomes binding on him, but only if and to the extent that the court thinks it just and equitable to allow him to do so.[319] This provision applies

---

[310] Land Registration Act 2002, ss.32(1), 87(1)(a).
[311] 1992 Act, s.5(1).
[312] See the 1992 Act, s.5(4)(b) as amended by the Land Registration Act 2002, Sch.11.
[313] 1992 Act, s.5(5), as amended by Land Registration Act 2002, Sch.11.
[314] 1992 Act, s.5(4), as amended by the Land Registration Act 2002, Sch.11.
[315] For the provisions as to registration of an access order, see para.11–66, above.
[316] Access to Neighbouring Land Act 1992, s.4(1).
[317] Access to Neighbouring Land Act 1992.
[318] Access to Neighbouring Land Act 1992, s.6(1).
[319] Access to Neighbouring Land Act 1992, s.4(2).

equally to an access order that has been varied under the 1992 Act.[320] It is difficult to see circumstances where it would not be just as against the applicant to allow a person who has become bound by the order to take advantage of the correlative benefits of the order. It may be that the reference to the need for the court to decide whether it is just and equitable to allow the order to be enforced by a third party is to ensure that such a result is just and equitable as regards the original named respondent.

Variation of access orders

Where an access order has been made, the court may, on the application of any party to the proceedings in which the order was made or of any other person on whom the order is binding[321]: **11–68**

    (1) discharge or vary the order or any of its terms or conditions;
    (2) suspend any of its terms or conditions; or
    (3) revive any term or condition suspended pursuant to (2).[322]

A further application can be made in relation to an access order which has been previously varied.[323]

Damages for breach of an access order

If any person contravenes or fails to comply with any requirement, term or condition imposed upon him by or under the 1992 Act, the court may, without prejudice to any other remedy available, make an order for the payment of damages by him to any other person affected by the contravention or failure who makes an application to the court for such damages.[324] The power of the court is discretionary. The Act does not give any guidance as to the nature of the damages which would be recoverable, nor the measure of damage which would be applied. Presumably, the ordinary rules as to foreseeability, proximity and remoteness would apply. The statutory power to award damages recognises that the applicant may have another cause of action, for example, in trespass or in nuisance. The person claiming damages pursuant to the Act must show that he is a "person affected by the contravention or failure"; accordingly, the claimant need not have been a party to the original proceedings. **11–69**

---

[320] Access to Neighbouring Land Act 1992, s.6(1).
[321] See para.11–67, above.
[322] 1992 Act, s.6(1).
[323] Access to Neighbouring Land Act 1992.
[324] 1992 Act, s.6(2).

PART IV

EXTINGUISHMENT OF EASEMENTS

CHAPTER 12

EXTINGUISHMENT OF EASEMENTS

1.—BY OPERATION OF LAW

How an easement may be extinguished by operation of law

An easement may be extinguished by operation of law. Thus, it has been said that **12–01** a way of necessity is limited by the necessity which created it, and when such necessity ceases the right of way is extinguished.[1] Again, where an easement is created by grant for a certain period, when that period has elapsed the easement comes to an end.[2]

So, again, an easement will be extinguished where the purpose for which it was created has come to an end. Thus, where a statute conferred upon a company the right to take water to supply a canal, the right ceased when the canal was abandoned.[3]

It may be that an easement can be extinguished by frustration if circumstances supervening since the grant mean that there is no practical possibility of its ever again benefiting the dominant tenement in the manner contemplated by the grant,[4] but it is unlikely that facts insufficient to support an abandonment will support an

---

[1] *Holmes v Goring* (1824) 2 Bing. 76; 9 Moore 166; it was, however, pointed out in *Huckvale v Aegean Hotels* (1989) 58 P. & C.R. 163 that the proposition stated in the side note in Bingham's Report does not appear to have been necessary to the decision and was doubted in *Proctor v Hodgson* (1855) 10 Exch. 824; see also *B.O.J. Properties Ltd v Allen's Mobile Home Park Ltd* (1979) 108 D.L.R. (3d) 305.

[2] *Beddington v Atlee* (1887) 35 Ch. D. 323. See paras 3–09 and 3–10, above.

[3] *National Guaranteed Manure Co v Donald* (1859) 4 H. & N. 8 explained in *Huckvale v Aegean Hotels* (above) as a case where the dominant tenement had effectively ceased to exist by being converted into something entirely different in kind, viz. a railway.

[4] *Huckvale v Aegean Hotels* (1989) 58 P. & C.R. 163 at 173, per Slade L.J.

extinguishment[5] and the onus of proof on the party alleging extinguishment is just as heavy.[6]

Extinguishment by unity of ownership

12–02   As an easement is a charge imposed upon the servient tenement for the advantage of the dominant tenement, when these are united in the same owner, the easement is extinguished; the special kind of property which the right to the easement conferred, so long as the tenements belonged to different owners, is now merged in the general rights of property.[7]

The doctrine of the extinction of easements by unity of ownership proceeds on the ground that the loss of an easement is a permanent injury to the inheritance. In order, therefore, that the easement should be entirely extinguished, it is essential that the owner of the two tenements should have an estate in fee simple in both of them of an equally perdurable nature.[8]

> "Where the tenant", says Littleton, "hath as great and as high estate in the tenements as the lord hath in the seigniory; in such case, if the lord grant the services to the tenant in fee, this shall enure by way of extinguishment. Causa patet."[9]

Upon which Coke observes[10]:

> "Here Littleton intendeth not onely as great and high an estate, but as perdurable also, as hath beene said, for a disseisor or tenant in fee upon condition hath as high and great an estate, but not so perdurable an estate, as shall make an extinguishment."

In a previous section, speaking of seigniories, rents, *profits à prendre*, etc., he says:

> "They are said to be extinguished when they are gone for ever, et tunc moriuntur, and can never be revived; that is, when one man hath as high and perdurable an estate in the one as in the other."[11]

Unless this be the case, the easement, of whatever species it be, is suspended only so long as the unity of ownership continues, and revives again upon the separation of the tenements.

---

[5] (1989) 58 P. & C.R. 163, at 170, per Nourse L.J.

[6] (1989) 58 P. & C.R. 163, at 171, per Butler-Sloss L.J.

[7] The following cases decide that a man cannot have an easement over his own land: *Roe v Siddons* (1888) 22 Q.B.D. 236; *Metropolitan Ry v Fowler* [1892] 1 Q.B. 165; *Kilgour v Gaddes* [1904] 1 K.B. 461.

[8] Conversely, unity of possession without unity of ownership may not prevent the establishment of a prescriptive right.

[9] s.561.

[10] Co.Litt. 313b.

[11] Co.Litt. 313a.

"Suspence commeth of suspendeo, and in legal understanding is taken when a seigniorie, rent, profit apprender, etc., by reason of unitie of possession of the seigniorie, rent, etc., and of the land out of which they issue, are not in esse for a time, et tunc dormiunt, but may be revived or awaked."[12]

So strictly has this doctrine been construed that no extinguishment was held to have taken place where the king was seised of one tenement "of a pure fee simple indeterminable", *jure coronae*, and of the other of an estate in fee simple, determinable on the birth of a Duke of Cornwall.[13]

Extent of application of doctrine

As regards the extent of application of the doctrine that extinguishment results **12–03** from the union in the same owner of absolute interests in the dominant and servient tenements, it was said by Alderson B. in *Pheysey v Vicary*[14] that no easement of absolute necessity to the dominant tenement is extinguished by unity of ownership. This statement was applied to a right of way in *Margil Pty Ltd v Stegul Pastoral Pty Ltd*.[15] The doctrine, however, appears to be applicable to rights in the nature of easements, such as the right to have a fence repaired.[16] It is also applicable to various sorts of easements. Thus, where the absolute owner of Blackacre, who has a right of way over Whiteacre, purchases an absolute interest in Whiteacre, the right of way is extinguished by the unity of ownership.[17] So as regards prescriptive rights in water, if the same person becomes absolute owner of the land from which a stream of water flows and also of the land into which it flows, the easement which the latter might have claimed is extinguished.[18]

With respect to natural rights in water, the question of the effect of unity of ownership was raised and discussed in the early case of *Sury v Pigot*,[19] which was an action for stopping a natural water-course. According to the report in Popham, of the judgment of Whitlock C.J. where a thing exists by reason of prescription, unity will extinguish it; but where the thing exists *ex jure naturae*, it is not extinguished.[20] The report of this case in Latch[21] refers to rent being extinguished, as well as a way. This is because it does not exist during the unity. It is, however, said to be "otherwise of a thing which exists, notwithstanding the unity". A warren is given as an example.

---

[12] Co.Litt. 313a.
[13] *R. v Hermitage* (1692) Carth. 239, followed in *Cockburn, Re* (1896) 27 O.R. 450 and *Lonegren and Reuben, Re* (1987) 37 D.L.R. (4d) 491, affirmed (1988) 50 D.L.R. (4th) 431. See also *James v Plant* (1836) 4 A. & E. 749 at 766, where it was held that the momentary seisin of a release to uses was insufficient to work a merger by unity of seisin.
[14] (1847) 16 M. & W. 484 at 490.
[15] [1984] 2 N.S.W.L.R. 1 (Needham J.).
[16] See Dyer 295b, pi. 19; *Sury v Pigot* (1625) Palm. 444; *Boyle v Tamlyn* (1827) 6 B. & C. 329.
[17] *Heigate v Williams* (1607) Noy 119; *James v Plant* (1836) 4 A. & E. 749.
[18] *Ivimey v Stacker* (1866) 1 Ch. App. 396 at 407. Consider *Holland v Deakin* (1828) 7 L.J. (o.s.) K.B. 145; and see *Pheysey v Vicary* (1847) 16 M. & W. 484 at 489.
[19] (1625) Pop. 166; Lat. 153; 3 Bulst. 339; Palm. 444.
[20] (1625) Pop. 166 at 170. See *Wood v Waud* (1849) 3 Ex. 748 at 775, where the above was approved by the Court of Exchequer.
[21] (1625) Lat. 153.

The above decisions as to the effect of unity in extinguishing an existing easement should be compared with the decisions referred to above[22] as to the effect of unity during the prescriptive period upon the acquisition of an easement.

Effect of severance

12–04 When two tenements become completely united, and, as it were, fused into one, the owner may modify the previous relative position of the different parts at his pleasure. If he exercises this right so that the part which previously served the other no longer does so—as, for instance, by changing the direction of a spout which emptied the rainwater of one house on the adjoining one—it has never been doubted that on subsequent severance no easement will revive.[23]

It has been contended that if he neglects to do so, and again severs the tenements, all easements having the qualities of being both continuing and apparent, as well as those which existed by necessity, will be revived upon the severance. In the 11th Hen. 7[24] it was decided, "that a customary right in the city of London to have a gutter running in another man's land was not extinguished by unity of possession". It was argued that if the purchaser of both tenements had destroyed the gutter, the right would not have revived; to which Danvers J. replied: "If the matter were so, it might have been pleaded specially: it would be a good issue." It will be found that the classes of easements with respect to which revivor is supposed to take place correspond with those already considered, as being acquired by the implied grant resulting either from the disposition of the owner of the two tenements, or from the easement being of necessity. It is in practice immaterial whether the foundation of the right be a new grant or a revival of the old right; but the former is the more correct view of the title to the right, and it is certainly more in harmony with the general principles of the law of easements.[25]

Vesting in one owner having different estates

12–05 The particular case where the dominant and servient tenements become vested in the same owner for different estates or interests has been dealt with by many judges. Thus, Page Wood V.-C. in *Simper v Foley*[26] expressed the opinion that the effect of such a union of ownership was not to extinguish an easement, but merely to suspend it so long as the union of ownership continued; and that upon the severance of the ownership the easement revived. Again, it was said by Bayley B. in *Canham v Fisk*[27] that a unity of possession merely suspends; there must be a unity of ownership to destroy the prescriptive right. Again, it was said by Alderson B. in *Thomas v Thomas*[28]:

---

[22] See para.4–57, above.
[23] Hen. 7, f. 25; *Lady Browne's Case*, cited in *Sury v Pigot* (1625) Palm. 446.
[24] Fol. 25.
[25] *Holmes v Goring* (1824) 2 Bing. 76.
[26] (1862) 2 J. & H. 555 at 563, 564.
[27] (1831) 2 Cr. & J. 126.
[28] (1835) 2 C.M. & R. 34 at 41. See also the judgment of Eyre C.J. in *Whalley v Tompson* (1799) 1 Bos. & P. 375, and the opinion of the Court of Common Pleas in *Buckby v Coles* (1814) 5 Taunt. 314.

"If I am seised of freehold premises, and possessed of leasehold premises adjoining, and there has formerly been an easement enjoyed by the occupiers of the one as against the occupiers of the other, while the premises are in my hands, the easement is necessarily suspended, but it is not extinguished, because there is no unity of seisin; and if I part with the premises, the right, not being extinguished, will revive."

The application of the above rules to individual cases is not always easy. Three   **12–06**
principles should be borne in mind, namely (1) no one can derogate from his own grant[29]; (2) the law does not allow the coexistence in the same ownership of (a) a right to an easement (such as a right of way) over Whiteacre, and (b) an interest in possession in Whiteacre[30]; (3) if two such rights or interests become vested in the same owner, and he continues to exercise his right of way, the law will attribute this exercise to his interest in possession in Whiteacre, and not to his easement.[31]

Upon this subject there have been the following decisions. Where the owner in   **12–07**
fee of the dominant tenement acquired an outstanding lease in the servient tenement but subsequently parted with the lease, it was held in effect that during the union of ownership the easement of light was not extinguished, and that upon a severance of the ownership the easement revived.[32] Again, where A, the owner in fee of the dominant tenement, granted a lease thereof to X and subsequently sold his reversion in fee to B, who was the owner in fee in possession of the servient tenement, it was held in effect that during X's term the easement of light continued, there being no extinguishment. A could not derogate from his grant so as to interfere with X's right to the easement, nor could B standing in the place of A.[33] In such a case on the falling in of X's lease extinguishment would of course follow.

Merger of interests in dominant tenement

An easement is appurtenant to land, rather than to any particular interest in land.   **12–08**
So if a lessee of the dominant tenement acquires the freehold, he does not thereby lose the benefit of an easement granted by his lease, which enures for the term of the original grant.[34] Indeed, by virtue of section 62 of the Law of Property Act 1925, he will acquire a perpetual right.[35] This will be so even if the servient tenement is itself under lease (as a result of which, in the absence of any reservation of a right to do so, the reversioner would not be capable of granting a right over the servient land having effect during the term of the lease), since the grant effected by section 62 will take effect in reversion on the tenancy and bind the freehold reversion, the dominant owner being entitled to enjoy the easement during the term of the merged lease of his premises in accordance with the original

---

[29] *Browne v Flower* [1911] 1 Ch. 224.
[30] *Ladyman v Grave* (1871) 6 Ch. App. 763 at 768.
[31] *Bolton v Bolton* (1879) 11 Ch. D. 971. See *Bright v Walker* (1834) 1 C.M. & R. 219.
[32] *Simper v Foley* (1862) 2 J. & H. 555.
[33] *Richardson v Graham* [1908] 1 K.B. 39 (see the judgment of Kennedy L.J. at 46).
[34] *Wall v Collins* [2007] 3 W.L.R. 459 at [15]–[19].
[35] [2007] 3 W.L.R. 459 at [20]–[27].

grant.[36] Nor will the acquisition of his freehold by the lessee of the servient tenement affect the burden of the easement, at least for the period of the lease.[37]

2.—BY STATUTE

Expressly or by implication

12–09   An easement may be extinguished by statute. The extinguishment may have resulted from express words, for example from the words of section 8 of the Inclosure (Consolidation) Act 1801[38] or section 68 of the Inclosure Act 1845, providing that "ways shall be for ever stopped up and extinguished"[39]; or from the words of the special Act of a railway company.[40] The extinguishment may also result by necessary implication from a statute. Thus, where the legislature distinctly authorises the doing of a thing which is physically inconsistent with the continuance of an existing right, the right is gone.[41] An Act should not, however be construed so as to interfere with somebody's property rights without compensation unless the court is obliged so to construe it.[42] Accordingly, where a landlord was obliged by Part XI of the Housing Act 1985 to erect a wall for fire precaution purposes which blocked his tenant's access to a rear bin area, it was held that the tenant's right of access was not extinguished and so might revive if circumstances changed, but that the fact that the wall was erected in order to comply with a statutory duty was a complete defence to an action in nuisance.[43] Generally speaking, where a statute which extinguishes a right is repealed, the repeal will not revive the right.[44]

As regards the extinguishment of private rights of way under the Inclosure Acts, it should be mentioned that a proviso in section 8 of the Inclosure (Consolidation) Act 1801[45] required an order of two justices for stopping up an "old or accustomed road". It seems that this proviso only applied to public roads, and not to private ones.[46] Where the road is stopped up under the Inclosure Act 1845, no order of the justices is required.[47]

---

[36] [2007] 3 W.L.R. 459 at [28]–[29].

[37] [2007] 3 W.L.R. 459 at [18].

[38] Repealed by the Commons Act 1899, s.23, Sch.2.

[39] At s.68; *Turner v Crush* (1879) 4 App. Cas. 221.

[40] See *Att-Gen v Great Central Ry* [1912] 2 Ch. 124.

[41] *Yarmouth Corp v Simmons* (1878) 10 Ch. D. 518, where it was shown that the construction of a pier authorised by statute would be physically inconsistent with the existence of a public right of way.

[42] *Jones v Cleanthi* [2006] EWCA Civ 1712; [2007] 1 W.L.R. 1604 at [82]. The common law principle is now reflected by Article 1 of the First Protocol to the European Convention on Human Rights incorporated into British law by the Human Rights Act 1998.

[43] [2006] EWCA Civ 1712; [2007] 1 W.L.R. 1604, distinguishing *Yarmouth Corp v Simmons* (above).

[44] Interpretation Act 1978, s.16(1)(a); *Gwynne v Drewitt* [1894] 2 Ch. 616 (the case of a public right of way).

[45] See fn.1, above.

[46] *White v Reeves* (1818) 2 Moore 23.

[47] See ss.62–68. The "old inclosures" referred to in these sections are discussed and explained in *Hornby v Silvester* (1888) 20 Q.B.D. 797. As to the construction of local Inclosure Acts giving powers to stop up roads, see, further, *Logon v Burton* (1826) 5 B. & C. 513; *R. v Hatfield* (1835) 4 A. & E. 156. As to the effect of an order under the Highways Act 1980, see para.9–01, above.

Lands compulsorily taken

Where lands compulsorily taken under one of the numerous statutes giving **12–10** compulsory powers are subject to an easement which is disturbed in exercise of statutory powers, the person entitled to the easement cannot in general bring an action for disturbance; nor is he entitled to notice to treat. His remedy is by claiming compensation as for lands injuriously affected.[48] However, the easement will not be completely extinguished and will bind the land in the hands of persons other than the acquiring authority.[49] The statutes which expressly confer powers to extinguish easements are referred to in the following paragraphs.

Where a railway company's private Act extinguished, without compensation, "all rights of way in, over, and affecting" certain "footways", the clause affected only public rights, and did not extinguish a private right of way.[50]

The London Building Acts did not affect easements. The provisions which authorise the raising of party-walls confer no authority to raise them to the prejudice of a neighbour's right to light.[51]

The Housing Act 1985[52] enacts that upon the purchase of land by a local **12–11** housing authority pursuant to Part IX of the Act dealing with slum clearance, then, subject to agreement to the contrary and to provisions governing statutory undertakers and telecommunications apparatus, all private rights of way and all rights of laying down, erecting, continuing, or maintaining apparatus on, under or over that land, and all other rights or easements in or relating to that land shall be extinguished, subject to the payment of compensation.

Comparable provisions are contained in the Town and Country Planning Act **12–12** 1990,[53] the Planning (Listed Buildings and Conservation Areas) Act 1990,[54] the Requisitioned Land and War Works Act 1948,[55] the New Towns Act 1981,[56] and the Civil Aviation Act 1982.[57]

Of particular importance is Part IX of the Town and Country Planning Act 1990. **12–13** Under s.226 a local authority has power to acquire compulsorily land in its area (a)

---

[48] See, under the Lands Clauses Consolidation Act 1845, *Eagle v Charing Cross Ry* (1867) L.R. 2 C.P. 638; *Bedford v Dawson* (1875) L.R. 20 Eq. 353; *Wigram v Fryer* (1887) 36 Ch. D. 87; *Kirby v Harrogate School Board* [1896] 1 Ch. 437; *M.S. & L. Ry v Anderson* [1898] 2 Ch. 394; *Long Eaton v Midland Ry* [1902] 2 K.B. 574; and under s.10 of the Compulsory Purchase Act 1965, *Wilson's Brewery Ltd v West Yorkshire M.B.C.* (1977) 34 P. & C.R. 224.

[49] See the cases cited in the last footnote and further, by analogy, cases concerning restrictive covenants: *Marten v Flight Refuelling* [1982] Ch. 115; *Elm Avenue, Re* [1984] 1 W.L.R. 1398; *Brown v Heathlands NHS Trust* [1996] 1 All E.R. 133.

[50] *Wells v London, Tilbury and Southend Ry* (1877) 5 Ch. D. 126.

[51] See, e.g. on 14 Geo. 3, c. 78, *Titterton v Conyers* (1813) 5 Taunt. 465 and *Wells v Ody* (1836) 1 M. & W. 452; on 18 & 19 Vict. c. 122, ss.83, 85, *Crofts v Haldane* (1867) L.R. 2 Q.B. 194; and, on a Bristol Improvement Act, *Weston v Arnold* (1873) 8 Ch. App. 1084. The London Building Acts (Amendment) Act 1939, s.54 contains an express provision to the like effect.

[52] s.295; see also Housing Act 1988, Sch.10, para.4.

[53] ss.236 and 237.

[54] s.51(1).

[55] s.4(2).

[56] s.19 (as amended by the Telecommunications Act 1984, s.109(1), Sch.4, para.79(3)).

[57] s.46(2)(c); and see *London Regional Transport v Imperial Group Pension Trust Ltd* [1987] 2 E.G.L.R. 20, on the London Transport Act 1964, s.14.

if they think the acquisition will facilitate the carrying out of development or rede-velopment or improvement on or in relation to the land or (b) which is required[58] for a purpose which it is necessary to achieve in the interests of the proper planning of an area in which the land is situated. The authority cannot exercise their powers under (a) unless they think that the development is likely to contribute to the pro-motion or improvement of the economic or social or environmental well-being of their area. An acquisition under s.226, or an appropriation for a purpose for which land could have been acquired under s.226, is called an acquisition or appropriation "for planning purposes".[59]

The construction of any building or the carrying out of work on land which has been acquired or appropriated by a local authority for planning purposes (whether done by the authority or by a person deriving title under them) is authorised if done in accordance with planning permission, notwithstanding that it involves interfer-ence with an easement or breach of a restrictive covenant.[60] Compensation is payable for such interference under the compulsory purchase legislation,[61] i.e. on the basis of diminution in the value of the claimant's land, and does not include any ransom or loss of bargaining position element.[62]

12–14   It follows that one way for a developer to overcome either a refusal on the part of a dominant owner to negotiate the release of a right necessary to allow the devel-opment to go ahead or an excessive demand for payment for such a release is to per-suade the local authority to acquire the development site and then transfer it back to the developer, subject to suitable indemnities as to the compensation. It remains to be seen whether a decision of a local authority to participate in such a scheme would be vulnerable to judicial review on the ground that an acquisition whose chief purpose was to save the developer money was ultra vires or on other grounds. The pre-acquisition paper trail probably needs to demonstrate serious intransigence on the part of the dominant owner to justify the exercise of these powers simply for the purpose of defeating an easement. If, however, the dominant owner wishes to mount a challenge to the local authority's decision, he must do so promptly by way

---

[58] "Required" seems to mean less than indispensable but more than desirable: *Chesterfield Properties v Secretary of State for the Environment* [1997] EWHC Admin 709 at [19].

[59] Town and Country Planning Act 1990, s.246(1).

[60] Town and Country Planning Act 1990, s.237.

[61] i.e. under section 63 or 68 of the Lands Clauses Consolidation Act 1845 or under s.7 or 10 of the Compulsory Purchase Act 1965.

[62] *Wrotham Park Settled Estates v Hertsmere Borough Council* [1993] 2 E.G.L.R. 15 (a restrictive covenant case), approving the reasoning and the analysis of the case-law of Judge Marder Q.C. sit-ting in the Lands Tribunal reported at [1991] 1 E.G.L.R. 230. There may, however, be a question as to whether this is consistent with the analysis of Millett L.J. in *Jaggard v Sawyer* [1995] 1 W.L.R. 269 at 291F that the dominant tenement derives part of its value from having appurtenant to it the right to prevent development on the servient tenement. For other cases on compensation for over-riding easements, see *Glover v North Staffordshire Ry* (1850) 16 Q.B. 912; *Ford v Metropolitan and Metropolitan District Rly Cos* (1886) 17 Q.B.D. 12; *Furness Ry v Cumberland Building Society* (1884) 52 L.T. 144; *Bernard v Great Western Rly* (1902) 86 L.T. 798; *Ward v Wychavon D.C.* [1986] 2 E.G.L.R. 205, where the compensation was assessed at nil where an alter-native route had been provided (all rights of way); *Eagle v Charing Cross Rly* (1867) L.R. 2 C.P. 638; *Clark v London School Board* (1874) L.R. 9 Ch. 120; *London, Tilbury and Southend Ry & Gowers Schools, Re* (1889) 24 Q.B.D. 326 (rights of light).

of judicial review proceedings: it will be too late to raise it years later when the development begins to interfere with his easement or covenant.[63]

Section 237 of the Town and Country Planning Act 1990 was considered in *R. v City of London Corporation Ex p. Mystery of the Barbers of London*[64] where it was held that the section applied even after the original purpose for which the land had been acquired had been achieved and even where the statutory authority was seeking to interfere with a right which it had itself granted.   **12–15**

That case was in turn considered in *Midtown v City of London Real Property Co Ltd*,[65] in which a local authority, the Corporation of the City of London, had acquired a small area of land ("the relevant land"), and a large area of other land, for the purpose of redevelopment following war damage. Shortly after its acquisition, the local authority sold the relevant land to a purchaser who carried out a development which was a part of the contemplated redevelopment. A small part of that development was on the relevant land. The local authority retained the other land it had acquired and used it to create a new road. The defendant was a successor in title who proposed to demolish the earlier development and construct a major new development. A small part of its new development was on the relevant land. It claimed to be entitled to rely on s.237 of the Town and Country Planning Act 1990 in relation to the relevant land.   **12–16**

The Judge referred to part of the judgment of Dyson J. in the *Barbers* case where it was said, *obiter*, that if the subsequent development was by a successor in title of the local authority which had originally acquired or appropriated the land for planning purposes, the subsequent development must be related in some way to those planning purposes. That *obiter* view was adopted and applied. It was said that this requirement applied whether the local authority or a successor in title owned the land at the time of the proposed subsequent development. If the local authority still owned the land it could re-appropriate the land for the proposed development. If a successor in title owned the land, the subsequent development had to be related to the original planning purpose. It was held that the development in that case was not so related and the defendant could not rely on s.237.[66]

Statutory title

In the event of an easement already acquired by prescription vesting in the owner of the dominant tenement by statutory authority, the prescriptive title will merge in the statutory title, and if the operation of the statute be limited to a period the easement will be lost on the expiration of the period.[67] In *New Windsor Corporation v Taylor*, Lord Davey said[68]:   **12–17**

---

[63] *Ford-Camber Ltd v Deanminster Ltd* [2007] EWCA Civ 458.

[64] [1996] 2 E.G.L.R. 128. See also *Edmunds v Stockport Metropolitan B.C.* [1990] 1 P.L.R. 1 and *Sutton L.B.C. v Bolton* [1993] 2 E.G.L.R. 181 (concerning restrictive covenants rather than an easement).

[65] [2005] EWHC 33 (Ch.); [2005] 1 E.G.L.R. 65.

[66] In these circumstances, the Judge did not need to deal with an argument based on the Human Rights Act 1998, to the effect that s.237 should be "read down" so as to avoid an infringement of Article 1 of the First Protocol in Part II of Sch.1 to the 1998 Act.

[67] *Manchester Corp v Lyons* (1882) 22 Ch. D. 287; *New Windsor Corp v Taylor* [1899] A.C. 41.

[68] [1899] A.C. 41 at 49.

"I hold it to be an indisputable proposition of law that where an Act of Parliament has according to its true construction, to use the language of Littledate J., 'embraced and confirmed' a right which had previously existed by custom or prescription, that right becomes henceforward a statutory right, and that the lower title by custom or prescription is merged in and extinguished by the higher title derived from the Act of Parliament."

3.—BY RELEASE

(1) *Express release*

Form of release

12–18   An easement may be extinguished by express release. It would appear that, in the case of easements, as of other incorporeal rights, an express release, to be effectual at law, must be under seal.[69] This rule, however, must not be taken to exclude a written instrument not under seal, or even a parol declaration, as evidence to show the character of any act done, or any cessation of enjoyment; and in equity an easement may be lost or modified by agreement.[70]

12–19   The effect of an agreement to release an easement followed by a sale of the dominant land with the benefit of the easement, before completion of the release, was considered in *Allen v Jones*.[71] At the date of the agreement, the dominant land was owned by a Mr Turner. He contracted that he would release a right of way over part of an access to the dominant land. The agreement complied with section 2 of the Law of Property (Miscellaneous Provisions) Act 1989. Before completion of that agreement by execution of a deed of release, Mr Turner sold the dominant land to Mr and Mrs Jones. The benefit of the right of way passed to Mr and Mrs Jones. The benefit of the agreement to release the easement was not contended to be an overriding interest under section 70 of the Land Registration Act 1925. It was held that as the agreement was not under seal it did not operate as an effective express release of the easement. It was also held that it was not possible to spell an implied release out of this agreement to release the easement. Although the agreement was binding in equity on Mr Turner, the Joneses did not have notice of the agreement when they bought and were not bound by such equity. The principles of mutual benefit and burden did not apply, not least because the Joneses were not intending to take the benefit under the agreement.

[69] Co. Litt. 264b; Com. Dig. Release (A. 1), (B. 1). See judgment of Willes J. in *Lovell v Smith* (1857) 3 C.B. (n.s.) 127; but see *Norbury v Meade* (1821) 3 Bli. 241. In *Poulton v Moore* [1915] 1 K.B. 400, a release of a right of way resulted from a deed operating by estoppel.

[70] *Davies v Marshall* (1861) 10 C.B. (n.s.) 710; *Fisher v Moon* (1865) 11 L.T. 623; *Waterlow v Bacon* (1866) L.R. 2 Eq. 514. *Cf. Salaman v Glover* (1875) L.R. 20 Eq. 444, where a lease was held to be controlled by the terms of a prior agreement. On and after September 27, 1989, a contract for the release of an easement must be made in writing so as to comply with s.2 of the Law of Property (Miscellaneous Provisions) Act 1989.

[71] [2004] EWHC 1119 (QB).

The principles of proprietary estoppel did not affect the position of the Joneses as they had themselves not done anything which would cause those principles to apply to them and they did not have notice of the circumstances which might cause those principles to apply to Mr Turner's conduct.

In *Robinson Webster (Holdings) Ltd v Agombar*,[72] a transfer contained a   **12–20**
covenant to erect a wall across an access way "to the effect that the right of way . . . shall be extinguished". The Judge held[73] that in so far as there was a pre-existing right of way over the access in question, the terms of the deed either amounted to an immediate release by deed or constituted an agreement to release the easement. If the latter, it was said to be binding in equity upon successors in title but this point was not further explained.

(2) *Implied release*

Licence given by the owner of the dominant tenement to the owner of the servient tenement

If the owner of the dominant tenement authorises an act of a permanent nature to   **12–21**
be done on the servient tenement, the necessary consequence of which is to prevent his future enjoyment of the easement, it is thereby extinguished.[74] Provided that the authority is exercised, it is immaterial whether it was given by writing or by parol.[75]

Extinguishment by cessation or alteration of user

Unless the easement is granted for a term of years, the rights conferred by an   **12–22**
easement are perpetual and, accordingly, are actually or potentially valuable rights. Therefore it is not lightly to be inferred that the owner of such a right should give it up for no consideration. Thus in *Tehidy Minerals Ltd v Norman*[76] the Court of Appeal held that abandonment of an easement or a *profit à prendre* can only be treated as having taken place where a person entitled to it has demonstrated a fixed intention never at any time thereafter to assert the right himself or to attempt to transmit it to anyone else. In that case the subjection by commoners of their rights of grazing to the control of an association was, as the Court of Appeal found, only a temporary and terminable arrangement, not sufficient to infer abandonment.

---

[72] [2002] 1 P. & C.R. 243.

[73] [2002] 1 P. & C.R. 243 at [72].

[74] *Winter v Brockwell* (1807) 8 East 308; *Liggins v Inge* (1831) 7 Bing. 682; *Davies v Marshall* (1861) 10 C.B. (n.s.) 697; *Johnson v Wyatt* (1863) 9 Jur. (n.s.) 1333; *Armstrong v Sheppard & Short Ltd* [1959] 2 Q.B. 384 at 399–401, per Lord Evershed M.R.; and see *Bosomworth v Faber* (1992) 69 P. & C.R. 288; see also Cullity, "The Executed Licence" (1965) 29 Conv. (n.s.) 19.

[75] *Liggins v Inge* (1831) 7 Bing. 682.

[76] [1971] 2 Q.B. 528 at 553, applied in *Yateley Common, Hampshire, Re* [1977] 1 W.L.R. 840 (rights of common: no abandonment when user prevented by requisitioning). See also *Gotobed v Pridmore* (1970) 115 S.J. 78; *Williams v Usherwood* (1983) 45 P. & C.R. 235; *Benn v Hardinge* (1992) 66 P. & C.R. 246; *Bosomworth v Faber* (1992) 69 P. & C.R. 288; *Snell & Prideaux v Dutton Ltd* [1995] 1 E.G.L.R. 259; and paras 12–84 to 12–89, below.

12–23   Nonetheless it is the policy of the law, favouring the freedom of property, that no restriction should be imposed upon one tenement without a corresponding benefit arising from it to another, and so it is essential to the validity of an easement that it should contribute to the more beneficial enjoyment of the dominant tenement. If, therefore, any alteration be made in the disposition of the dominant tenement, of such a nature as to make it incapable ever again of benefiting from the particular easement, the status of the land as a dominant tenement, to which the easement was attached, and which is an inherent condition of its existence, is determined. Such alteration must, of course, be of a permanent character, evincing an intention of ceasing to take the particular benefit, or otherwise an easement might be lost by the mere pulling down of the tenement for the purposes of necessary repair.[77]

12–24   In this context it is necessary to distinguish between two classes of easements. First, continuous easements, namely those of which the enjoyment is or may be continuous without the necessity of interference by man; such as a right to light. These easements require for their enjoyment a permanent adaptation of the dominant tenement. Secondly, discontinuous easements, namely those of which the enjoyment can only be had by the interference of man; such as a right of way. These easements require no permanent adaptation of the dominant tenement. In the case of both these classes of easements questions arise as to the effect in law of (1) the actual cessation of enjoyment, and (2) an alteration in the mode of user, whether accompanied or not by an alteration of the dominant tenement. Under the last head must be considered those difficult cases where, instead of there being an intention to relinquish the right, an attempt has been made to usurp a greater right than the dominant owner was entitled to, or to enjoy it in a different manner; and here it may be pointed out that in the case of continuous easements it may often be a matter of great difficulty to ascertain the extent of the usurpation or excess, in other words, to sever the increased burden attempted to be imposed on the servient tenement. In the case of discontinuous easements the extent of the acts of usurpation or excess can usually be easily ascertained; in other words, the increased burden can be severed.

12–25   The law as to the abandonment of an easement appears to have developed in its own way. Thus, it is to be contrasted with the rules of the abandonment of the benefit of a contract. It is not possible to have a unilateral abandonment of the benefit of a contract[78] but it seems to be possible to have a unilateral abandonment of the benefit of an easement. Further, although many of the cases of abandonment of easements can be analysed in terms of estoppel by acquiescence, or other estoppels, this analysis is not appropriate for all the decisions. The law as to abandonment of continuous easements appears to have been settled for some time but the law relating to the abandonment of discontinuous easements has been the subject of several important recent decisions.

---

[77] *Luttrel's Case* (1601) 4 Rep. 86; *Staight v Burn* (1869) 5 Ch. App. 163; *Ecclesiastical Commissioners v Kino* (1880) 14 Ch. D. 213. *Cf.* per Fry J. in *National Provincial Co v Prudential Co* (1877) 6 Ch. D. 757 at 764.
[78] *The Hannah Blumenthal* [1983] 1 A.C. 854; *Collin v Duke of Westminster* [1985] Q.B. 581.

(a) *Continuous easements*

Intention to abandon right

The cases in which this question has most frequently been raised have been cases **12–26** relating to the easement of light, where there has been an actual cessation for a longer or shorter period of the old enjoyment. It appears from these cases that the law has fixed no precise time during which this cessation must continue. The material inquiry must always be whether there was an intention to abandon the right.

An example of an intention to abandon

Certain acts will clearly show the intention to abandon; for example the shutting **12–27** up of windows with bricks and mortar for 20 years.[79] Again, in the leading case of *Moore v Rawson*,[80] the plaintiff pulled down his wall, in which there were some ancient windows, and rebuilt it as a blank wall. Fourteen years later the defendant erected a building in front of this blank wall. Three years afterwards the plaintiff opened in the blank wall a window in the place of one of the ancient windows, and sued the defendant for obstruction. The action failed, the court holding that the plaintiff had abandoned his right. In his judgment in that case it was said by Littledale J. that if a man pulls down a house and does not make any use of the land for two or three years, or converts it into tillage, he may be taken to have abandoned all intention of rebuilding the house, and consequently the right to the light has ceased.[81]

An example of no intention to abandon

On the other hand, the mere alteration of a building containing ancient lights does **12–28** not imply abandonment.[82] Nor, again, does the mere pulling down of a building destroy the right.[83] Thus, in *Ecclesiastical Commissioners v Kino*,[84] a church became vested in the commissioners upon trust to pull it down and sell the site. The church having been pulled down, but not yet sold, the defendant commenced to build upon the adjoining land in a way which would have obstructed the light to the ancient church windows had they still been subsisting. In an action brought by the commissioners, the defendant was restrained from obstructing the lights of any building to be erected on the site of the church, so far as such lights occupied the same position as the lights of the church. The Court of Appeal thought that the commissioners were entitled to sell the land with the right to rebuild. James L.J. said[85]:

---

[79] *Lawrence v Obee* (1814) 3 Camp. 514.

[80] (1824) 3 B. & C. 332.

[81] (1824) 3 B. & C. 332, at 341. See also the judgment of Tindal C.J. in *Liggins v Inge* (1831) 7 Bing. 682 at 693.

[82] *Greenwood v Hornsey* (1886) 33 Ch. D. 471. See *Stokoe v Singers* (1857) 8 E. & B. 31.

[83] The Harman Committee (see para.4–38, above) thought that nothing was required, or could usefully be done, to preserve the rights of destroyed or damaged dominant or prospectively dominant buildings.

[84] (1880) 14 Ch. D. 213.

[85] (1880) 14 Ch. D. 213 at 219.

"It appears to me that when a building, in which there are ancient lights, has been taken down, though the actual enjoyment of the light has been suspended, there is nothing to prevent the owner from applying to the Court for an injunction to restrain an erection which would interfere with the easement of the ancient lights, where the Court is satisfied that he is about to restore the building with its ancient lights. That was so decided by Lord Justice Giffard in Staight v. Burn."[86]

Onus of proving intention

12–29   The question turning upon intention, there has been discussion as regards the onus of proving this intention. It seems that where a house is rebuilt shortly after it has been pulled down, and rebuilt in such a way that the new windows will receive a considerable portion of the light which went into the old windows, it is unnecessary to give further evidence of intention to preserve the right.[87]

On the other hand, in *Moore v Rawson*[88] Lord Abbott C.J. said:

"It seems to me that, if a person entitled to ancient lights pulls down his house and erects a blank wall in the place of a wall in which there had been windows, and suffers that blank wall to remain for a considerable period of time, it lies upon him at least to shew, that, at the time when he so erected the blank wall, and thus apparently abandoned the windows which gave light and air to the house, that was not a perpetual, but a temporary abandonment of the enjoyment; and that he intended to resume the enjoyment of those advantages within a reasonable period of time. I think that the burden of shewing that lies on the party who has discontinued the use of the light. By building the blank wall, he may have induced another person to become the purchaser of the adjoining ground for building purposes, and it would be most unjust that he should afterwards prevent such a person from carrying those purposes into effect."

12–30   *Wilson's Brewery Ltd v West Yorkshire M.B.C.*[89] concerned an easement of support. The claimant's building had a right to support from the adjoining building. Notwithstanding this, the adjoining building was pulled down in 1938 and the replacement building arguably did not provide any, or as much, support. The replacement adjoining building was pulled down in 1973 by the respondent and the question arose, in the context of a claim for compensation for injurious affection,[90] whether the claimant still had a right of support in 1973. It was held that for there to be abandonment of an easement, there must be clear and unequivocal evidence of intention on the part of the dominant owners to abandon that easement and such an intention had not been shown.

---

[86] (1869) 5 Ch. App. 163.
[87] *Scott v Pape* (1886) 31 Ch. D. 554 at 567; *Smith v Baxter* [1900] 2 Ch. 138 at 142.
[88] (1824) 3 B. & C. 332 at 336.
[89] (1977) 34 P. & C.R. 224.
[90] Pursuant to s.10 of the Compulsory Purchase Act 1965.

Necessity for act by owner of servient tenement

From the language of the judges in cases before *Stokoe v Singers*,[91] it does not **12–31**
appear to be necessary, where a building containing ancient lights has been
altered, that after the alteration the servient owner should have done any act on
the faith that the easement had been extinguished. In *Stokoe v Singers*,[92] on the
other hand, there are dicta to the effect that in order to make out an extinguishment of the easement such an act is essential; but these dicta have never been
followed. While there appears to be no sufficient authority in our law for requiring any such act as the condition of the extinguishment of an easement, yet such
an act, unopposed by the owner of the dominant tenement, as in the case of *Moore
v Rawson*,[93] would be almost conclusive evidence that there was no intention to
preserve the easement.

Alteration in mode of user: general rule

In cases where there has been no actual cessation of user of the continuous **12–32**
easement, but there is an alteration in the mode of user, whether accompanied or
not by an alteration of the dominant tenement, the rule seems to be that where the
alteration does not impose any additional burden on the servient tenement, there
is no extinguishment of the easement, but that an alteration which imposes an
additional restriction or burden may destroy the easement altogether.[94] Where the
amount of excess user can be ascertained or separated,[95] the excess alone will be
bad and the original right will remain; but where the original and the excessive
uses are so blended together that it is impossible, or even difficult, to separate
them, it seems that the right to enjoy the easement will be altogether lost.

The decision in Luttrel's Case

An early decision on the effect of alteration of the dominant tenement is *Luttrel's* **12–33**
Case,[96] an action brought for the diversion of water, which has ever since been
treated as a leading authority. The plaintiff owned two old fulling mills, in a
ruinous condition, which enjoyed a supply of water from a watercourse. The plaintiff pulled down the fulling mills and erected in their place two grist mills, for the
purpose of which he diverted the supply of water. It was argued that the alteration
from fulling mills to grist mills might be injurious to the owner of the watercourse,
because he might have corn mills himself, and be injured by the proximity of

---

[91] (1857) 8 E. & B. 31.
[92] (1857) 8 E. & B. 31.
[93] (1824) 3 B. & C. 332.
[94] For the first branch of the rule, see the cases quoted, paras 12–34 to 12–38, below; for the second
branch, see paras 12–40 *et seq.*, below; and compare the cases as to discontinuous easements,
paras 12–66 *et seq.*, below.
[95] An example by reference to a profit is given in *Luttrel's Case* (1601) 4 Rep. 86a: if a house enjoying a right of estovers is enlarged, the right will not enure for the benefit of the addition but is not
lost as regards the original grant.
[96] (1601) 4 Rep. 86a, recognised and applied in modern cases—e.g. *Colls v Home and Colonial
Stores* [1904] A.C. 179 at 202; *Att-Gen v Reynolds* [1911] 2 K.B. 888 at 896.

others; and it was further contended that a man may not preserve an easement by rebuilding on the same spot, and in the same manner, unless the previous destruction has been caused by some act of God, as by tempest or lightning. The Court of Exchequer Chamber held, however, that the alteration from fulling mill to grist mill was not one of substance, but only of quality, and was not prejudicial to the owner of the watercourse, so that the prescription remained. In *Luttrel's Case*[97] a further case[98] is mentioned, of a grant to a corporation, the members of which were afterwards incorporated under another name; it was held that they retained all their franchises and privileges, because no person would be prejudiced by the change.

Illustrations of the rule

12–34   In *Saunders v Newman*,[99] where the claim in the declaration was for a mill generally, the right to the discharge of water was held not to be lost by an alteration in the dimensions of the mill-wheel. Abbott J. said[100]:

> "The owner [of a mill] is not bound to use the water in the same precise manner, or to apply it to the same mill; if he were, that would stop all improvements in machinery. If, indeed, the alterations made from time to time prejudice the right of the lower mill, the case would be different."

12–35   In *Hall v Swift*[101] the plaintiff had a right to water flowing from the defendant's land across a lane to his own land. Previously, the stream had meandered down the lane before it flowed into the plaintiff's land. But the plaintiff varied the course by making a straight cut to his own premises. This, it was contended, negatived the right. Lord Tindal C.J. said[102]:

> "I think that these objections to the verdict ought not to prevail . . . If so, any alteration, however slight, would destroy the right, however long established. No authority has been cited in support of such a proposition; and I think it cannot be maintained."

12–36   In *Hale v Oldroyd*[103] the plaintiff had a right to a flow of surplus water to an ancient pond. Instead of using the water to supply that pond, he had during 30 years past used it to supply three more recent ponds. It was held he had not abandoned or lost his right to the flow of water by such user. Parke B. said[104]:

---

[97] (1601) 4 Rep. 86a.
[98] Hen. 6 at 12.
[99] (1818) 1 Barn. & Ald. 258.
[100] (1818) 1 Barn. & Ald. 258 at 261.
[101] (1838) 4 Bing.N.C. 381 (a case of an alteration in the enjoyment of a natural right).
[102] (1838) 4 Bing.N.C. 383.
[103] (1845) 14 M. & W. 789. *Cf. Davis v Morgan* (1825) 4 B. & C. 8.
[104] (1845) 14 M. & W. 789 at 793.

"The use of the old pond was discontinued only because the plaintiff obtained the same or a greater advantage from the use of the three new ones. He did not thereby abandon his right, he only exercised it in a different spot; and a substitution of this nature is not an abandonment."

Rolfe B. said[105]:

"If the plaintiff had even filled up the [old] pond, that would not in itself amount to an abandonment, although, no doubt, it would be evidence of it."

In *Watts v Kelson*[106] the right to a watercourse which had been used to supply cattle-sheds was held not to be lost by the erection of cottages in their place. **12–37**

In *McAdams Homes Limited v Robinson*[107] the dominant tenement benefited **12–38** from a right of drainage acquired pursuant to an implied grant. The dominant tenement was altered from a bakery to two houses. It was held that this was a radical change in the character of the dominant tenement which would involve a substantial increase in the burden on the servient tenement and that, at least, the easement was in suspense while that state of affairs continued. The Court of Appeal considered the possibility (without deciding the point) that the alteration of the dominant tenement involved in demolition of the bakery building without any intention of erecting a new bakery building might have resulted in the loss of the easement.

The easement of eavesdrop might be extinguished by an alteration of the **12–39** projection of the roof from which it could be inferred that the dominant owner meant to direct the rainwater into a different channel. Where, however, a greater burden is not thrown on the servient tenement, such an easement will not be lost either by increasing the projection[108] or by raising the house.[109]

Additional burden imposed on servient tenement

Of the rule referred to above,[110] the second branch (which states that an alteration **12–40** of the dominant tenement which imposes an additional burden on the servient tenement may destroy the continuous easement altogether) is illustrated by *Angus v Dalton*,[111] where it was pointed out that any easement of lateral support which might have attached to the plaintiffs' premises as they originally were had been lost by the taking down of the old house and substituting a building of an entirely different construction,[112] but the cases in which the suggestion has been most

---

[105] (1845) 14 M. & W. 789 at 793.
[106] (1870) 6 Ch. App. 166.
[107] [2004] EWCA Civ 21; [2004] 3 E.G.L.R. 93. For further discussion of this case, see paras 9-03 to 9-13, above.
[108] *Thomas v Thomas* (1835) 2 C.M. & R. 34.
[109] *Harvey v Walters* (1872) L.R. 8 C.P. 162.
[110] See para.12–32, above.
[111] (1877) 3 Q.B.D. 85 at 102 (see paras 10–17 *et seq.*, above); *cf. Ray v Fairway Motors (Barnstaple) Ltd* (1968) 20 P. & C.R. 261.
[112] Contrast *Lloyds Bank Ltd v Dalton* [1942] Ch. 466 at 471 *et seq.*

frequently made that the continuous easement has been destroyed are cases relating to the easement of light.[113] These decisions are numerous, and for a long time there was much doubt about the doctrine. In view of the importance of the questions raised, some of the decisions must now be considered.

12–41   One of the most important of the early decisions was *Martin v Goble*,[114] where a building having been used for upwards of 20 years as a malt-house was converted into a dwelling-house. In an action for obstruction of light, the question for the jury was held to be whether, if the building had remained in the condition of a malt-house, a proper degree of light for making malt was prevented entering the windows by the obstruction. Macdonald C.B. said that the converting of the building from a malt-house to a dwelling-house could not affect the rights of the owner of the adjoining ground, for "no man could by any act of his, suddenly impose a new restriction upon his neighbour".[115] This decision has been much criticised,[116] but may be supported on the ground that (to use the language of *Luttrel's Case*) "the alteration affected the substance and not only the quality of the tenement".[117]

Alterations in windows

12–42   In several subsequent decisions including *Renshaw v Bean*[118] and *Hutchinson v Copestake*[119] it was laid down that where an owner of the dominant tenement altered his ancient lights, or opened additional lights, he had not necessarily lost or suspended his admitted right; but that the alterations or the opening of the additional lights justified the owner of the servient tenement in obstructing the ancient lights, if in fact the doing so was unavoidable in the exercise of his right to obstruct the new lights. Accordingly it was held in equity that in such a case an injunction would not be granted to restrain the obstruction, except upon the terms of the plaintiff blocking up the new lights and restoring the ancient lights to their previous position.[120]

---

[113] See Lord Davey's words in *Colls v Home and Colonial Stores* [1904] A.C. 202: "It would be contrary to the principles of the law relating to easements that the burden on the servient tenement should be increased or varied from time to time at the will of the owner of the dominant tenement. . . . I do not propose to discuss at length the question how far a variation in a tenement will destroy an easement appurtenant to it. The law on that subject is as old as Luttrel's Case" (1601) 4 Rep. 86a.

[114] (1808) 1 Camp. 320. See also *Cherrington v Abney* (1709) 2 Vern. 646; *East India Co v Vincent* (1740) 2 Atk. 83.

[115] (1808) 1 Camp. 320 at 323.

[116] See *Moore v Hall* (1878) 3 Q.B.D. 178; *Dent v Auction Mart Co* (1866) L.R. 2 Eq. 238 at 250.

[117] (1601) 4 Rep. 86a. See *Colls v Home and Colonial Stores* [1904] A.C. 202; see also *Cotterell v Griffiths* (1801) 4 Esp. 69, per Lord Kenyon; *Chandler v Thompson* (1811) 3 Camp. 80, in which the judgment of Le Blanc J. appears to be in accordance with the view afterwards adopted in the House of Lords; *Garritt v Sharp* (1835) 3 A. & E. 325, per Lord Denman; *Graham v Philcox* [1984] Q.B. 747. It is doubtful how far *Blanchard v Bridges* (1835) 4 A. & E. 176 can now be relied on: see *Scott v Pape* (1886) 31 Ch. D. 554, per North J. at 561, and per Bowen L.J. at 573.

[118] (1852) 18 Q.B. 112.

[119] (1861) 9 C.B. (n.s.) 863. See also *Wilson v Townend* (1860) 1 Dr. & Sm. 324; *Turner v Spooner* (1861) 1 Dr. & Sm. 467; *Binckes v Posh* (1861) 11 C.B. (n.s.) 324; *Davies v Marshall* (1861) 1 Dr. & Sm. 557; *Curriers' Co v Corbett* (1865) 2 Dr. & Sm. 355.

[120] *Cooper v Hubbuck* (1860) 30 Beav. 160; *Weatherley v Ross* (1862) 1 H. & M. 349.

The decision in Tapling v Jones

The whole subject was reviewed in *Tapling v Jones*,[121] a case which was carried **12–43**
to the House of Lords. This was an action for obstructing the lights of the house
of the plaintiff, who had altered the size and position of his lower windows, which
were ancient, so that the new windows occupied parts only of the old apertures.
He had also added upper windows in such a position that it was impossible for
the adjoining owner to obstruct them without also obstructing the ancient portion
of the new lower windows. The defendant, who was tenant of the adjoining property, built thereon a wall which obstructed the whole of the plaintiff's windows.
Subsequently the plaintiff restored his lower windows to their original size and
position, blocked up his new upper windows, and called on the defendant to pull
down his wall, but the defendant refused. At the trial a verdict was found for the
plaintiff subject to a special case which was argued before the Court of Common
Pleas. There was much difference of opinion, but in the result judgment was
entered for the plaintiff.[122] This was affirmed in the Exchequer Chamber, where
there was also much difference of opinion.[123] The House of Lords affirmed
the Exchequer Chamber. The question in dispute turned on the nature of the right
to light acquired under the Prescription Act; and the theory of this right was
discussed by the judges in the House of Lords.[124]

Lord Westbury, after citing section 3 of the Act,[125] observed that the right to **12–44**
light now depended upon positive enactment, and did not require, and therefore
ought not to be rested on, any presumption of grant, or fiction of a licence having
been obtained from the adjoining proprietor. He said[126]:

"The right is declared by the statute to be absolute and indefeasible, and it
would seem therefore that it cannot be lost or defeated by a subsequent temporary intermission of enjoyment, not amounting to abandonment. Moreover
this absolute and indefeasible right, which is the creation of the statute, is not
subjected to any condition or qualification; nor is it made liable to be affected
or prejudiced by any attempt to extend the access or use of light beyond that
which, having been enjoyed uninterruptedly during the required period, is
declared to be not liable to be defeated."

He could not accept the reasoning on which the decisions in *Renshaw v Bean*[127]
and *Hutchinson v Copestake*[128] were founded. He said[129]:

[121] (1861) 11 C.B. (n.s.) 283; affirmed (1862) 12 C.B. (n.s.) 826; affirmed (1865) 20 C.B. (n.s.) 166;
11 H.L.C. 290.
[122] (1861) 11 C.B. (n.s.) 283.
[123] (1862) 12 C.B. (n.s.) 826.
[124] *Tapling v Jones* (1865) 11 H.L.C. 290.
[125] See para.4–23, above.
[126] (1865) 11 H.L.C. 290 at 304, 305.
[127] (1852) 18 Q.B. 112.
[128] (1861) 9 C.B. (n.s.) 863.
[129] (1865) 11 H.L.C. 290 at 307.

"Upon examining the judgments [in those cases] it will be seen that the opening of the new windows is treated as a wrongful act done by the owner of the ancient lights, which occasions the loss of the old right he possessed; and the Court asks whether he can complain of the natural consequence of his own act. I think two erroneous assumptions are involved in or underlie this reasoning; first, that the act of opening the new windows was a wrongful one; and secondly, that such wrongful act is sufficient in law to deprive the party of his right under the statute."

His Lordship's opinion was that the defendant's wall, so far as it obstructed the access of light to the plaintiff's ancient unaltered windows, was an illegal act from the beginning.

12–45   Lord Cranworth gave similar reasons for his judgment, and expressed his dissent from the reasoning in *Renshaw v Bean*.[130] Lord Chelmsford said that he did not see that the defendant's case would be benefited if it were established, contrary to the express words of the statute, that the right to the enjoyment of light rested on the footing of a grant. He stated the law to be that the right acquired by user must necessarily be confined to the exact dimensions of the opening through which the access of light and air had been permitted. As to anything beyond, the parties possessed exactly the same relative rights which they had before. The owner of the privileged window did nothing unlawful if he enlarged it, or made a new window in a different situation. The adjoining owner was at liberty to build upon his own ground so as to obstruct the addition to the old window, or shut out the new one; but he did not acquire his former right of obstructing the old window, which he had lost by acquiescence; nor did the owner of the old window lose his absolute and indefeasible right to it, which he had gained by length of user. The right continued uninterruptedly until some unequivocal act of intentional abandonment was done by the person who had acquired it, which would remit the adjoining owner to the unrestricted use of his own premises. Lord Chelmsford said[131]:

"It will, of course, be a question in each case, whether the circumstances satisfactorily establish an intention to abandon altogether the future enjoyment and exercise of the right. If such an intention is clearly manifested, the adjoining owner may build as he pleases upon his own land; and should the owner of the previously existing window restore the former state of things, he could not compel the removal of any building which had been placed upon the ground during the interval; for a right once abandoned is abandoned for ever."

On the other hand a person, by endeavouring to extend a right, could not manifest an intention to abandon it; he evinced his determination to retain it, and acquire something more; and the enlarging of an ancient window would be no cause

---

[130] (1852) 18 Q.B. 112.
[131] (1865) 11 H.L.C. 290 at 319.

of forfeiture, because the act was not unlawful. Lord Chelmsford also thought that *Renshaw v Bean*[132] could not be supported.

Decisions following Tapling v Jones

The decision of the House of Lords in *Tapling v Jones*[133] has been uniformly **12–46** followed since it was given.[134] With respect, however, to its bearing on earlier decisions, it has been pointed out by Sir A. Hobhouse, when delivering the judgment of the Privy Council in *Frechette v La Compagnie Manufacturiere de St Hyacinthe*,[135] that the plaintiff in *Tapling v Jones*[136] succeeded in getting protection for nothing but his old lights; and that it may be inferred from the judgments that, if the plaintiff had so mixed up his old lights with his new ones that they could not be distinguished, he would have failed. He said[137]:

> "It is true that in that case the protection given to the ancient light carried with it incidentally protection to the new lights. But the only reason why it did so was that the new lights could not be obstructed without obstruction to the ancient light. New lights are no encroachment, nor did the plaintiff's decree aggravate the defendant's servitude, for he was only prevented from building so as to obstruct the ancient lights."

The authorities analysed

It is convenient to analyse the authorities as follows: **12–47**

(1) cases of an increase in the size of the window;
(2) cases of a decrease in the size of the window;
(3) cases of an alteration in the plane of the window.

Increase in size of window

It has been seen that in *Colls v Home and Colonial Stores*[138] it was laid down that **12–48** an obstruction, to be actionable, must amount to a nuisance. Since that decision it seems that an increase in the size of an ancient window will not increase the

---

[132] (1852) 18 Q.B. 112.
[133] (1865) 11 H.L.C. 290.
[134] See *Martin v Headon* (1866) L.R. 2 Eq. 425, 433; *Staight v Burn* (1869) 5 Ch. App. 163; *Newson v Pender* (1884) 27 Ch. D. 43; *Scott v Pape* (1886) 31 Ch. D. 554; *Smith v Baxter* [1900] 2 Ch. 138. It may be observed, however, that the question of nuisance or no nuisance was not considered in *Tapling v Jones* (1865) 11 H.L.C. 290, and that the tacit assumption that when the building was altered a right to light had been actually acquired under s.3 of the Prescription Act appears (having regard to s.4) to have been incorrect. See *Colls v Home and Colonial Stores* [1904] A.C. 179 at 189.
[135] (1883) 9 App. Cas. 170. The judgment of Farwell J. in *News of the World v Allen Fairhead & Sons* [1931] 2 Ch. 402 at 405, 406, is to the same effect; see para.12–52, below.
[136] (1865) 11 H.L.C. 290.
[137] (1883) 9 App. Cas. 186.
[138] [1904] A.C. 179; see para.7–05, above.

burden of the servient tenement, seeing that any obstruction which would be a nuisance to the enlarged window would a fortiori have been a nuisance to the original window.

Decrease in size of window

12–49   It would seem clear that, after an alteration in an ancient window whereby its size was decreased, the dominant proprietor would not be entitled to prevent the erection of buildings which, though obstructing the altered window, would not, before the alteration, have caused an illegal obstruction within the rule laid down in *Colls*.[139] This principle was applied in *Ankerson v Connelly*.[140] There an easement of light had been acquired in respect of ancient windows, but the dominant tenement was amply lighted by means of light other than that which came through the ancient windows. The defendant, who was the dominant owner, rebuilt his tenement so as practically to exclude all light other than that coming through the ancient windows. The plaintiff, who was the servient owner, erected an obstruction which prevented any access of light to the ancient windows, which obstruction the defendant pulled down. The plaintiff thereupon applied for a declaration that the defendant was not entitled to any easement of light over the plaintiff's land. The evidence showed that, after the rebuilding, the plaintiff's obstruction would materially interfere with the access of light to the defendant's ancient windows, whereas before the rebuilding it would not have caused such an interference as, since *Colls*,[141] would have justified an injunction. In the result the plaintiff succeeded. The Court of Appeal laid down that in the case of alteration there must be substantial identity between the altered premises and the old ones before the protection of ancient lights can be obtained, and held that as a matter of fact the reconstruction had destroyed this identity. They also held that what the servient owner had done would not have been the subject of an injunction prior to the alterations made by the dominant owner.

12–50   After *Ankerson v Connelly*[142] the question was further considered in *Bailey (W.H.) & Son Ltd v Holborn and Frascati Ltd*.[143] That was a case, not of the dominant owner decreasing the size of his window, but of his consenting to an obstruction of light coming over one of several servient tenements, by which obstruction his light had been diminished. From the judgment of Sargant J.[144] it seems that in his opinion a decrease by the dominant owner in the size of his window would not entirely negative his right to an easement of light, though it would not give him any further right so as to prevent the erection of a building which he could not have prevented had the size of the window not been decreased.

---

[139] [1904] A.C. 179; see para.7–05, above.
[140] [1906] 2 Ch. 554; [1907] 1 Ch. 678. The foregoing part of this paragraph was inserted in the 8th edition of this work by Mr (afterwards Judge) Roope Reeve; and his words were cited with approval by Sargant J. in *Bailey (W.H.) & Son Ltd v Holborn and Frascati Ltd* [1914] 1 Ch. 598 at 602, 603.
[141] [1904] A.C. 179.
[142] [1906] 2 Ch. 554; [1907] 1 Ch. 678.
[143] [1914] 1 Ch. 598.
[144] [1914] 1 Ch. 602 at 603.

The difficulty in these cases arises in defining and applying under the altered **12–51** circumstances the rights of the owner of the old easement. It has been pointed out that in many cases where lights have been altered it may, since *Colls v Home and Colonial Stores*,[145] be a matter of extreme difficulty to show that an interference with light is capable of legal remedy, having regard to the great difficulty of showing whether what is existing under the present conditions would have been a nuisance under the conditions formerly existing.[146]

The dominant owner is strictly speaking entitled to his old easement, but to nothing more; and if in any particular case the evidence enables the court to distinguish between the interference which, having regard to his old easement, the dominant owner can prevent, and that which he cannot prevent, the old easement can be protected accordingly. If, however, the evidence does not enable the court to make this distinction—in other words, if it be impossible to sever any increased burden—then the question will arise whether the old easement has or has not been lost. In *Ankerson v Connelly*,[147] Warrington J. decided that in such a case the old easement had been lost; but the Court of Appeal refused to deal with the question.

News of the World Ltd v Allen Fairhead & Sons Ltd[148] was a case where the **12–52** evidence did not enable the court to make this distinction. The plaintiff company was the lessee of certain buildings in the City of London which were entitled to receive light over the defendant's property. In 1925 the plaintiff's buildings were pulled down, and a new building was erected with numerous windows fronting the defendant's buildings (the servient tenement). At the trial no proper survey plan was produced showing the partial coincidence between the old and the new windows, and it was clear that the plaintiff's architect had never considered the question of preserving ancient lights. Such partial coincidences as did exist were not the result of any intention on the part of the plaintiff or its architect to preserve ancient lights, but were purely fortuitous. After the plaintiff's new buildings had been completed, the defendant pulled down its existing buildings and began to erect in their place new buildings of much greater height. In 1931 the plaintiff, fearing that its light would be obstructed, sued for an injunction and damages.

Farwell J. dismissed the action. He held that the mere lack of evidence of any **12–53** intention to preserve the ancient lights was not by itself sufficient to prove an intention to abandon them, even though the amount of coincidence between the old and new windows was comparatively very small. On the ground floor, moreover, there were undoubtedly substantial coincidences between new apertures and the old windows, and the plaintiff still had a right to ancient lights in regard to these particular apertures. In these circumstances Farwell J. had to consider whether the defendant's new building would obstruct the plaintiff's ancient lights to a sufficient extent to cause a nuisance.

---

[145] [1904] A.C. 179.
[146] *Andrews v Waite* [1907] 2 Ch. 510, where the evidence enabled the court to surmount this difficulty.
[147] [1906] 2 Ch. 549; [1907] 1 Ch. 682.
[148] [1931] 2 Ch. 402.

The learned judge began his judgment by referring to the well-known observations of Farwell J. in *Higgins v Betts*,[149] pointing out that the test of nuisance is: How much light is left, and is that enough for the comfortable use and enjoyment according to the ordinary requirements of mankind? The learned judge then dealt with the question how, in applying that test, he was to ascertain whether there was a nuisance or not. The plaintiff had contended that the right way to apply this test was to treat the windows as only consisting of the portion through which the ancient light passed, and to treat the remaining portion as blocked up. The court should then, according to the plaintiff's argument, have ascertained whether the obstruction to the window so treated was such as to cause a nuisance. Dealing with this argument of the plaintiff, Farwell J. said[150]:

> "They rely on Colls v. Home and Colonial Stores,[151] where Lord Lindley said:
>
> > 'As regards light from other quarters, such light cannot be disregarded; for, as pointed out by James V.-C. in the Dyers' Co. v. King,[152] the light from other quarters, and the light the obstruction of which is complained of, may be so much in excess of what is protected by law as to render the interference complained of non-actionable. I apprehend, however, that light to which a right has not been acquired by grant or prescription, and of which the plaintiff may be deprived at any time, ought not to be taken into account.'
>
> The plaintiffs say that in applying that principle, in order to see whether there is a nuisance, I must exclude all light except that passing through those portions of the new apertures which correspond with the old. They say that Tapling v. Jones[153] is to the same effect.
>
> If that is so, I am bound to give effect to those decisions, but I cannot accept the view either that Tapling v. Jones[154] decided anything of the kind, or that Lord Lindley ever intended to suggest that it did."

12–54   The learned judge, after pointing out that the question in *Tapling v Jones* was whether the alteration and reinstatement of the plaintiff's building had amounted to abandonment, and explaining that Lord Lindley was clearly speaking of light to which a right had not been acquired and of which the plaintiff could be deprived at any time, said[155]:

> "I can well understand that if a man has a room lighted, both by ancient lights and by non-ancient lights, obstructible by outsiders, then, if an obstruction is threatened to the ancient lights, the Court cannot say to the plaintiff, 'you are

---

[149] [1905] 2 Ch. 210 at 215. The judge in *Higgins v Betts* was Sir George Farwell; the judge in *News of the World Ltd v Allen Fairhead & Sons* (above) was Sir Christopher Farwell.
[150] [1931] 2 Ch. 402 at 405.
[151] [1904] A.C. 179 at 210.
[152] (1870) L.R. 9 Eq. 438.
[153] (1865) 11 H.L.C. 290.
[154] (1865) 11 H.L.C. 290.
[155] [1931] 2 Ch. 402 at 406, 407.

at present getting enough light from the other windows to prevent this obstruction being a nuisance, and therefore you cannot complain' since the result might be that if the obstructive windows were subsequently blocked the plaintiff might be left with a room wholly unsuitable for ordinary occupation.

But on the other hand it cannot be right that anything the plaintiff himself does should increase the burden on the servient tenement, and I cannot believe that the learned Lords in Tapling v. Jones or Lord Lindley in the Colls case[156] ever contemplated that a plaintiff could pull down his old building and put up a new building totally different in every respect, except for some slight coincidences in the old and new window spaces, and then say to the Court, 'Treat all my present light facilities as blocked out, leaving me nothing but a comparatively small peephole of ancient light, and then give me relief because that very inadequate amount of ancient light space will be made more inadequate by the defendants' proposed acts'. If that were the law, the plaintiff by his own acts would have greatly increased the burden on the servient tenement.

The true view is this. If the plaintiff pulls down the building with ancient light windows and erects a new building totally different in every respect, but having windows to some extent in the same position as the old windows, he cannot require the servient owners to do more than see that the ancient lights, if any, to which he is still entitled are not obstructed to the point of nuisance. He cannot require them not to obstruct non-ancient light merely because a portion of the window through which that non-ancient light enters his premises, also admits a pencil of ancient light. If the obstruction of the pencil itself causes a nuisance the plaintiff is entitled to relief, but if taking the building as it stands, the pencil obstruction causes no nuisance at all, the plaintiff is not entitled to relief."

After referring to observations of Warrington J. in *Ankerson v Connelly*,[157] Farwell J. said that in the case before him it was also impossible to determine the exact result of the threatened obstruction.

Farwell J.'s decision appears to establish clearly that the principle that a dominant **12–55** owner is not entitled to increase the burden on the servient tenement by altering the size and position of ancient buildings is paramount to the consideration that obstructive light is not to be taken into account in estimating whether the servient owner's obstruction amounts to an actionable nuisance.

Alteration of plane of window

Alterations may be made, not only in the size or area of a window, but in its plane **12–56** and inclination; and the question whether an alteration of this latter kind would suffice to extinguish an easement of light has been much discussed. It is now settled that alterations of this kind stand on the same footing as alterations of size, and do not, unless they are of such a character as substantially to change the nature of the easement,[158] amount to abandonment.

---

[156] [1904] A.C. 179.
[157] [1906] 2 Ch. 544 at 548, 549.
[158] See para.12–64, below.

12–57   Thus, in *National Provincial Plate Glass Insurance Co v Prudential Assurance Co*,[159] a building containing ancient lights had been pulled down and rebuilt; and the old dormer window of three faces, which lighted the ground floor, had been converted into a skylight partially coextensive with the old window, but of a different shape. The defendants having obstructed the light to this skylight, the plaintiffs brought their action. On the motion for an injunction Lord Jessel M.R., while refusing the interlocutory injunction on the ground that the obstruction was complete before the action was brought, expressed his opinion that the easement formerly belonging to the ground floor window had not been lost; for, although the plane or direction of the glass had been altered the aperture remained substantially the same.[160] At the trial, Fry J. awarded damages for the obstruction of the ground floor window. He said[161]:

> "It is said that the access of light to the dwelling-house must be identical, and that the right claimed and the enjoyment which has existed must be of access of light through identical apertures. Now in its breadth that proposition is not true, because the case of Tapling v. Jones[162] has shewn that you may destroy the identical aperture by taking away the surrounding lines of that aperture and yet leave your right to light intact. Furthermore, I find nothing whatever in the statute which refers expressly to a window or aperture. I find in the statute a reference to the access of light, and in my view the access of light might be described as being the freedom with which light may pass through a certain space over the servient tenement; and it appears to me that, wherever for the statutory period a given space over the servient tenement has been used by the dominant tenement for the purpose of light passing through that space, a right arises to have that space left free so long as the light passing through it is used for or by the dominant tenement.[163] I come to that conclusion for this reason—that you do not want a statute to give you a right of access in your own premises to light through your own aperture. The statute is wanted to assure your right in the space over the servient tenement.
>
> But then it is said that the cases have to a large extent proceeded upon the form and size of the aperture or window; and that is perfectly true, because, of course, the opening in the dominant tenement is the limit which defines the boundaries of the space over the servient tenement. It is for that reason that in all the cases the Court has had regard to the aperture in the dominant tenement by means of which the space over the servient tenement has been useful to the dominant tenement."

[159] (1877) 6 Ch. D. 757.

[160] His Lordship also thought that the windows in the upper floors, which had been set back about 5ft 8in., were no longer the same windows so as to retain their right to light; but it appeared on the hearing that these windows were not affected by the defendant's building, and the case cannot therefore be regarded as a decision on this point. See and consider the cases next quoted.

[161] (1877) 6 Ch. D. 757, 764.

[162] (1865) 11 H.L.C. 290.

[163] Since *Colls v Home and Colonial Stores* [1904] A.C. 179, expressions to this effect must not be taken literally, but must be taken to refer to the right as defined by that decision.

To the same effect is *Barnes v Loach*,[164] where a wall containing ancient windows had been set back, and windows had been made in the new wall of the same size and in the same relative positions as those in the old wall, but in a different plane; and it was held that the right to light remained. It was also held in the same case that the dominant owner had not, by erecting a wall and a window in it, outside and at an angle with an ancient window, lost the easement of light attached to the ancient window.

12–58

Again, in *Bullers v Dickinson*,[165] the plaintiff's premises stood on the site of an old toll-house which had projected obliquely into the street, and had enjoyed an easement of light for the windows on the ground floor; the toll-house had recently been pulled down, the site of the projecting part being sold for widening the street, and the plaintiff's premises being forthwith erected on the remainder. The plaintiff's ground floor window, for which he claimed protection, was substantially on the same level as the old window; but it stood further back, and, of course, at a different angle to the street. On an action being brought to restrain an interference with the new window, the defendant objected that the plaintiff had lost or abandoned his right; but Kay J. overruled the objection.

12–59

Alterations in windows generally: the decision in Scott v Pape

In *Scott v Pape*[166] the whole question as to the effect of an alteration in a building was fully considered. The plaintiff, who was the owner of buildings having ancient lights looking into a lane, had pulled down his buildings within 20 years before action was brought, and erected larger buildings on the site. The new buildings contained windows on all the floors. Parts of six windows on the first floor of the new building occupied a large portion of the area formerly covered by three ancient lights; and for this portion of such area the plaintiff claimed protection. It was a material element in the case that the plaintiff, in rebuilding, had slightly advanced his wall into the lane, the gain varying from a foot to three feet, five inches. Upon these facts North J., who heard the action, declined to infer abandonment, and granted an injunction to[167]:

12–60

"Restrain the defendant from permitting to remain erected any wall, etc., so as to darken, injure, or obstruct any of the ancient lights of the Plaintiff's premises, as the same were enjoyed by means of those portions of the windows on the first floor of the Plaintiff's old buildings, which have not been blocked up in the rebuilding of the Plaintiff's premises."

This was affirmed by the Court of Appeal. Cotton L.J., after referring to section 3 of the Prescription Act, continued[168]:

12–61

---

[164] (1879) 4 Q.B.D. 494.
[165] (1885) 29 Ch. D. 155.
[166] (1886) 31 Ch. D. 554.
[167] (1886) 31 Ch. D. 554 at 563.
[168] (1886) 31 Ch. D. 554 at 569, 570.

"What alteration, then, will deprive the Plaintiff of his right, this right which can be claimed only in respect of a dwelling-house, workshop, or other building? Will the alteration of the purpose or object for which the building is to be used, as the conversion of a workshop into a house, or of a house into a workshop, have this effect? It will not: that is definitely settled by the case of Ecclesiastical Commissioners v. Kino.[169] The old building there was a church, and that which was to be built on the site of the church was a warehouse, an entire alteration of the purposes and of the character of the building. Then will moving back the plane of the wall deprive the Plaintiff of his right? In my opinion, no. It is difficult to see how the mere fact of moving back can do so, and in fact there is authority against such a proposition. Then if moving it back will not, will simply moving it forward have this effect? In my opinion both the moving back and the moving forward may destroy the right, because the new building when constructed may, either by being substantially advanced or substantially set back, be so placed that the light which formerly went into the old windows will not go into the new. If a building is set back, say 100 feet, it will not enjoy the same cone of light that was enjoyed before, but will have an entirely different cone, and it may be moved so far forward that it will not enjoy the same light as that enjoyed by the old building. In my opinion the question to be considered is this, whether the alteration is of such a nature as to preclude the Plaintiff from alleging that he is using through the new apertures in the new wall the same cone of light, or a substantial part of that cone of light, which went to the old building. If that is established, although the light must be claimed in respect of a building, it may be claimed in respect of any building which is substantially enjoying a part, or the whole, of the light which went through the old aperture."

12–62   Bowen L.J., developing the same principle, said[170]:

"The measure of the enjoyment and the measure of the right acquired are not the windows and apertures themselves, which would involve a continuing structural identity of the windows, but the size and position of the windows, which necessarily limit and define the amount of light which arrives ultimately for the house's use."

Fry L.J. added his opinion that the "access of light" referred to in the Prescription Act was not access through the aperture or window, but access or freedom of passage over the servient tenement; and that the "right thereto", which is by the statute rendered "absolute and indefeasible", is a right to the same access and use of light to and for any dwelling-house, workshop, or other building. The Act, he said, was silent as to identity of aperture, as it was silent as to identity of building.

12–63   The above judgments are misleading in so far as they suggest that the right acquired under the Prescription Act is a right to the whole of "that particular light

[169] (1880) 14 Ch. D. 213; see para.12–28, above.
[170] (1886) 31 Ch. D. 554 at 572.

which has come to" a building.[171] As has been already seen, since the decision in *Colls v Home and Colonial Stores*[172] it is established that the right acquired is a right only to freedom from nuisance by obstruction. With this qualification the decision in *Scott v Pape*[173] has put the law as to the effect upon an easement of light of an alteration in the dominant tenement on a clear and definite footing; and it must now be taken that, if and so long as the dominant tenement continues to enjoy the same or some part of the same light formerly enjoyed, no abandonment will be inferred.[174] In *Andrews v Waite* Neville J. said[175]:

> "It seems to me that the question which has to be determined is, whether proof is necessary of identity of the window or aperture through which the light claimed has been admitted to the dominant building, or whether the true matter for investigation is the identity of the light which has been so admitted. . . . I think the real test is, as I said before, identity of light and not identity of aperture, or entrance for the light."

Present rule as to inferring abandonment

Where the alteration is such that none of the existing windows can be said **12–64** substantially to correspond with an ancient window, even though part of the space occupied by each may be identical, no difficulty arises; and, as it cannot be proved that any window in respect of which a right had been acquired has been in fact obstructed, abandonment may be inferred.[176] *Hutchinson v Copestake*[177] may be referred to this principle, and, so interpreted, may stand even without *Renshaw v Bean*.[178] To the same effect are *Health v Bucknall*,[179] where the new windows did not cover more than one-fourth of the former area, and the opinions of the judges in *Newson v Pender*,[180] where the whole question was discussed.

In any case, it is essential to the preservation of the right that the dominant owner, when effecting the alteration, should preserve clear and definite evidence of the size and position of the former windows.[181]

---

[171] See *Colls v Home and Colonial Stores* [1904] A.C. 179 at 189, per Lord Macnaghten.

[172] [1904] A.C. 179; para.7–05, above.

[173] (1886) 31 Ch. D. 554.

[174] *Greenwood v Hornsey* (1886) 33 Ch. D. 471; *Smith v Baxter* [1900] 2 Ch. 138; *Andrews v Waite* [1907] 2 Ch. 500; *cf. Raper v Fortescue* [1886] W.N. 78; *London and Tilbury Ry, Re* (1889) 24 Q.B.D. 326.

[175] [1907] 2 Ch. 500 at 509, 510.

[176] *Pendarves v Monro* [1892] 2 Ch. 611; *cf. Ankerson v Connelly* [1906] 2 Ch. 544; [1907] 1 Ch. 678; *News of the World v Allen Fairhead & Sons* [1931] 2 Ch. 402.

[177] (1861) 9 C.B. (n.s.) 863; para.12–42, above.

[178] (1852) 18 Q.B. 112.

[179] (1869) L.R. 8 Eq. 1.

[180] (1884) 27 Ch. D. 43.

[181] *Fowlers v Walker* (1881) 51 L.J.Ch. 443; *Scott v Pape* (1886) 31 Ch. D. 554; *Pendarves v Monro* [1892] 2 Ch. 611. In *Arcedeckne v Kelk* (1858) 2 Giff. 683; *Staight v Burn* (1869) 5 Ch. App. 163; *Dyer's Co v King* (1870) L.R. 9 Eq. 438; and *Bourke v Alexandra Hotel Co* [1877] W.N. 30 it was held that a plaintiff who obscured the light of his house, but left a substantial part unaffected, was not thereby disentitled to an injunction.

Restoration after alteration

12–65   Upon the question whether a party who has lost his rights by altering his tenement is still at liberty to restore his tenement to its former condition and recur to his former enjoyment, it would seem that on principle he would have no such right, as he would have clearly evinced an intention to relinquish his former mode of enjoyment.[182] In addition to the actual encroachment, the uncertainty caused by the attempted extension of the right would of itself impose a heavier burden upon the owner of the servient tenement, if such return to the original right were permitted.

(b) *Discontinuous easements*

Cessation of user: the general rule

12–66   Although it was stated in earlier editions of this book that

> "there seems to be no doubt that discontinuous easements may be lost by mere non-user, provided such cessation to enjoy be accompanied by the intention to relinquish the right,"

that statement could be misleading. The true rule would appear to be that mere non-user without more, however long, cannot amount to abandonment.[183] Such non-user is evidence from which abandonment may be inferred but must be regarded in the context of the circumstances as a whole.[184] The non-user may be explained by the fact that the dominant owner had no need to use the easement, in which case it will not be enough to establish abandonment.[185] A presumption of abandonment will arise where there are circumstances adverse to the user and sufficient to explain the non-user, combined with a substantial length of time during which the dominant owner has acquiesced in that state of affairs[186] or where the dominant owner does some act clearly indicating the firm intention that neither he nor any successor in title of his should thereafter make use of the

---

[182] See the judgment of Pollock C.B. in *Jones v Tapling* (1862) 12 C.B. (n.s.) 864 and the judgment of Lord Chelmsford in *Tapling v Jones* (1865) 11 H.L.C. 319. See also *Moore v Rawson* (1824) 3 B. & C. 332; *Garritt v Sharp* (1835) 3 A. & E. 325; *South Metropolitan Cemetery Co v Eden* (1855) 16 C.B. 42.

[183] *Benn v Hardinge* (1992) 66 P. & C.R. 246; *Ward v Ward* (1852) 7 Ex. 838 at 839. See also *Guth v Robinson* (1972) 1 B.P.R. 9,209; *Riley v Pentilla* [1974] V.R. 547; *Treweeke v 36 Wolseley Rd Pty Ltd* (1973) 128 C.L.R. 274; *Kileel & Kingswood Realty Ltd, Re* 108 D.L.R. (3d) 362; *Grill v Hockey* (1994) 5 B.P.R. 97,365; *Cavacourt Pty Ltd v Durian Holdings Pty Ltd* (1998) 9 B.P.R. 97,761, applying this sentence in the 16th ed.

[184] *Swan v Sinclair* [1924] 1 Ch. 254 at 274, per Sargant L.J. citing *Goddard on Easements* (8th ed.) at 521.

[185] *Benn v Hardinge* (above) at 257. As in *Williams v Sandy Lane (Chester) Ltd* [2006] EWCA Civ 1738 at [52]–[59], where the non-use of a route since 1976 was to be accounted for by reason of the fact that a more convenient route was available.

[186] *Swan v Sinclair* (above) at 268; *McIntyre v Porter* [1983] 2 V.L.R. 439.

easement.[187] It has been said that abandonment is not to be lightly inferred: owners of property do not normally wish to divest themselves of it unless it is to their advantage to do so, notwithstanding that they may have no present use for it.[188] Further, if the dominant owner does not have any present need to exercise his right and does not object to conduct of the servient owner which temporarily renders the exercise of those rights difficult or impossible, it would be undesirable if such general and good neighbourly conduct could not be indulged in for fear of losing those rights for all time.[189]

Precisely because enjoyment is by its nature discontinuous and because cessation of enjoyment may take place without any alteration in the dominant tenement (by contrast with a right of light case), it would be difficult to determine when a cessation of use alone would amount to abandonment, but as Lord Denman said in *R. v Chorley*:   **12–67**

> "It is not so much the duration of the cesser as the nature of the act done by the grantee of the easement or of the adverse act acquiesced in by him and the intention in him that either the one or the other indicates, which are material for consideration by the jury."[190]

The position may be different if the servient owner is induced by reliance on the apparent abandonment by the dominant owner to incur substantial expense. Such a situation might result in the dominant owner becoming estopped from denying that the easement had been released or abandoned, but in such a case it would seem that the facts supporting the estoppel need to be expressly pleaded and proved.[191]

Any minimum period of non-user?

Accepting that non-user is not enough on its own, the question nevertheless arises whether any minimum period of cessation of use is fixed by law without which there cannot be abandonment.   **12–68**

Coke appears to have been of opinion that, when a title by prescription was once acquired, it could only be lost by non-user during a period equal to that required for its acquisition. "It is to be knowne that the title, being once gained by prescription or custom, cannot be lost by interruption of the possession for ten or twenty yeares."[192] At this time the analogy to the Limitation Act 1623[193] had not been introduced into the law.

---

[187] *Williams v Usherwood* (1983) 54 P. & C.R. 235 at 256, citing *Gotobed v Pridmore* (1971) E.G. 759; *Tehidy Minerals Limited v Norman* [1971] 2 Q.B. 528.
[188] per Buckley L.J. in *Gotobed v Pridmore* (above).
[189] per Stuart Smith L.J. in *Snell & Prideaux Limited v Dutton Mirrors Limited* [1995] 1 E.G.L.R. 259 at 262D.
[190] *R. v Chorley* (1858) 12 Q.B. 515 at 519.
[191] per Hoffmann L.J. in *Snell & Prideaux Limited v Dutton Mirrors Limited* (above) at 264J–K; and see the passage from the judgment of Page Wood V.-C. in *Crossley & Sons Limited v Lightowler* (1866) L.R. 3 Eq. 272, cited at 377, below. For a case where estoppel was alleged but the plea failed on the facts, see *Costagliola v Bunting* [1958] 1 W.L.R. 580.
[192] Co.Litt. 114b.
[193] See para.4–05, above.

12–69 In *Doe d. Putland v Hilder*,[194] Lord Abbott C.J., in delivering the judgment of the court, said:

> "One of the general grounds of a presumption is, the existence of a state of things, which may most reasonably be accounted for, by supposing the matter presumed. Thus the long enjoyment of a right of way by A. to his house or close, over the land of B., which is a prejudice to the land, may most reasonably be accounted for, by supposing a grant of such right by the owner of the land: and if such a right appear to have existed in ancient times, a long forbearance to exercise it, which must be inconvenient and prejudicial to the owner of the house or close, may most reasonably be accounted for, by supposing a release of the right. In the first class of cases, therefore, a grant of the right, and in the latter, a release of it, is presumed."

12–70 Littledale J., in the case of *Moore v Rawson*,[195] though he did not cite the above authority, expressed an opinion in accordance with it, that discontinuous easements could only be lost by cessation of enjoyment during 20 years; the learned judge distinguished between these easements and a right to light and air, principally on the ground that the former, as far as their acquisition by prescription was concerned, could only be acquired by enjoyment accompanied with the consent of the owner of the land, while the enjoyment of the latter required no such consent, and could only be interfered with by some obstruction. He said[196]:

> "According to the present rule of law a man may acquire a right of way, or a right of common, (except, indeed, common appendant) upon the land of another, by enjoyment. After twenty years' adverse enjoyment the law presumes a grant made before the user commenced, by some person who had power to grant. But if the party who has acquired the right by grant ceases for a long period of time to make use of the privilege so granted to him, it may then be presumed that he has released the right. It is said, however, that as he can only acquire the right by twenty years' enjoyment, it ought not to be lost without disuse for the same period; and that as enjoyment for such a length of time is necessary to found a presumption of a grant, there must be a similar non-user, to raise a presumption of a release. And this reasoning, perhaps, may apply to a right of common or of way."[197]

12–71 It is tolerably clear from the judgment of Lord Denman C.J. in *R. v Chorley*, however, that there is no minimum period. While in a case of mere acquiescence the

---

[194] (1819) 2 B. & Ald. 782 at 791.
[195] (1824) 3 B. & C. 332 at 339 *et seq.*
[196] (1824) 3 B. & C. 332 at 339.
[197] A covenant the benefit of which runs with an easement may be enforceable even though not relied on for 40 years: *Holmes v Buckley* (1691) 1 Eq.Cas.Abr. 27. There are some observations on this case, as bearing on the law of covenants running with the land, in *Austerberry v Corp of Oldham* (1885) 29 Ch. D. 750 at 777, 782; see para.1–97, above.

court should not rely on a period of less than 20 years, a lesser period of non-use coupled with any act clearly indicative of an intention to abandon the right would have the same effect as an express release "without any reference to time".[198]

In *Bower v Hill*,[199] Lord Tindal C.J. said that an obstruction to a way of a **12–72** permanent character, if acquiesced in for 20 years, would be evidence of a renunciation and abandonment of the right, but it is plain on the authorities that there is no particular period of non-use which is enough on its own. In the earlier case of *Seaman v Vawdrey*,[200] where a right of access to mines had been reserved by a conveyance of 1704, but had never been exercised, it had been held that the right had not been released by this non-user. In *Dogherty v Beasley*,[201] where the plaintiff brought an action against the defendant for obstructing the plaintiff's right of way over the defendant's close, and the defendant pleaded in effect that the plaintiff had not used the way for 20 years, Joy C.B. said that the question really came to this: Was the plaintiff obliged to use the way, and if he did not make use of it for twenty years, was he to be excluded by a plea such as the defendant's? He said[202]: "We think not. The question is not whether the non-user may not be evidence . . . but whether it is per se an absolute bar. We think that we must allow the demurrer." In *Cook v Bath*,[203] Lord Malins V.-C. held that 30 years' non-user without more was insufficient to extinguish a right of way.

In *Benn v Hardinge*,[204] the Court of Appeal held that non-use for 175 years of a **12–73** right implied from the laying out of a way pursuant to the directions in an enclosure award did not raise any presumption of abandonment in circumstances where nobody had any occasion to use the way, there being an alternative means of access.

Cessation of user: no indication of intention to abandon

The following cases illustrate the doctrine that a mere intermittence of the user, or **12–74** a slight alteration in the mode of enjoyment, when unaccompanied by any intention to renounce the right, does not amount to an abandonment.

In *Payne v Shedden*[205] issue was taken upon a plea of right of way; and it **12–75** appeared that, by agreement of the parties, the line and direction of the way used had been varied, and at certain periods wholly suspended. Patteson J. was of the opinion[206] that the occasional substitution of another track might be considered as substantially the exercise of the old right and "evidence of the continued enjoyment of it", and that the suspension by agreement was not inconsistent with the

---

[198] *R. v Chorley* (1848) 12 Q.B. 515 at 519; see passage cited at para.12–76, below.
[199] (1835) 1 Bing.N.C. 555. *Cf. Drewett v Sheard* (1836) 7 C. & P. 465.
[200] (1810) 16 Ves. 390.
[201] (1835) 1 Jones Exch.Rep.(Ir.) 123.
[202] (1835) 1 Jones Exch.Rep.(Ir.) 123 at 129.
[203] (1868) L.R. 6 Eq. 177.
[204] (1992) 66 P. & C.R. 246, CA.
[205] (1834) 1 Mood. & R. 382. The defendant failed to establish any right of way. See also *Can v Foster* (1842) 3 Q.B. 581; *Hale v Oldroyd* (1845) 14 M. & W. 789.
[206] (1834) 1 Mood. & R. 382 at 383.

right. Patteson J.'s dictum was applied by the Court of Appeal in *Davis v Whitby*,[207] in which the route of a passageway had been altered by agreement.

12–76   In *R. v Chorley*[208] the defendants were indicted for obstructing a public footway over a lane by driving carts. The lane was so narrow that carts could not pass without damage to persons on foot. The defence was that the defendants had a private right of way with carts, etc., to a malthouse, etc., situated in the lane, and that the public right of footway had been acquired subsequently to the private right, and was qualified by or subject to it[209]; and the question was, whether the privilege was extinguished by the acquiescence of the dominant owners in the user of the way by the public—a user which was inconsistent with its use as a cartway by the defendants. The learned judge at the trial told the jury that nothing short of 20 years' user by the public, in a way inconsistent with the private user, would destroy the right. Lord Denman C.J., on making a rule absolute for a new trial for misdirection, after saying[210] that if

> "the learned judge had done no more than remark that, if a mere ceasing to use the private way, or a mere acquiescence in the interruption by the public were relied on, it would be prudent in them not to rely on such mere cesser or acquiescence unless shewn for twenty years, we think such a remark . . . would have been no misdirection,"

proceeded as follows[211]:

> "As an express release of the easement would destroy it at any moment, so the cesser of use coupled with any act clearly indicative of an intention to abandon the right would have the same effect without any reference to time. For example, this being a right of way to the defendant's malthouse, and the mode of user by driving carts and waggons to an entrance from the lane into the malthouse yard, if the defendant had removed his malthouse, turned the premises to some other use, and walled up the entrance, and then for any considerable period of time acquiesced in the unrestrained use by the public, we conceive the easement would have been clearly gone. It is not so much the duration of the cesser as the nature of the act done by the grantee of the easement, or of the adverse act acquiesced in by him, and the intention in him which either the one or the other indicates, which are material for the consideration of the jury."[212]

---

[207] [1974] Ch. 186 at 191.

[208] (1848) 12 Q.B. 515.

[209] See *Brownlow v Tomlinson* (1840) 1 Man. & G. 484; *Elwood v Bullock* (1844) 6 Q.B. 383; *Morant v Chamberlin* (1861) 6 H. & N. 541.

[210] (1848) 12 Q.B. 515 at 518.

[211] (1848) 12 Q.B. 515 at 519.

[212] The court, it will be seen, expressed no distinct opinion on the point left open in *Stokoe v Singers* (1857) 8 E. & B. 31, para.12–31, above, whether or not, to make out an abandonment, the servient owner should have done some act on the faith that the easement had been abandoned, but in the latter case Lord Campbell said of *R. v Chorley* (1848) 12 Q.B. 515: "It is an authority that an abandonment is effectual if communicated and acted upon. It goes no further."

In *Ward v Ward*[213] a right of way was held not to have been lost by mere non-user   **12–77**
for a period much longer than 20 years, it being shown that the way was not used
because the owner had a more convenient mode of access through his own land.
Alderson B. said[214]:

> "The presumption of abandonment cannot be made from the mere fact of
> non-user. There must be other circumstances in the case to raise that pre-
> sumption. The right is acquired by adverse enjoyment. The non-user, there-
> fore, must be the consequence of something which is adverse to the user."

In *Lovell v Smith*[215] the owner of a right of way had, about 30 years before the   **12–78**
action, agreed with the servient owner to use, in lieu of part of the old way, a new
way over the servient owner's land, and therefore he discontinued to use the old
way, and used the new. The court held that the mere non-user of the old way and
the user of the new one for more than 20 years, under such circumstances, fur-
nished no evidence of an intention to abandon the old right.

In *Cook v Mayor and Corporation of Bath*[216] there had formerly been a right   **12–79**
of way through a back door, which had been closed for 30 years, and then opened
and used for four years before the obstruction. Malins V.-C. held that there had
been no abandonment. He said[217]:

> "It is always a question of fact, to be ascertained by a jury, or by the Court,
> from the surrounding circumstances, whether the act amounts to an aban-
> donment, or was intended as such. If in this case the Defendants had com-
> menced building before this backdoor had been re-opened, I should have
> been of opinion that the Plaintiff had, by allowing it so to remain closed, led
> them into incurring expense, and therefore could not prevent them acting on
> the impression that he intended to abandon his right."

In *James v Stevenson*[218] it was held that mere non-user of some of the roads over   **12–80**
which a right of way existed, where no occasion for user had arisen, coupled with
the use by the servient owner of those parts of the roads for farm purposes, did
not constitute abandonment; and to the same effect is *Cooke v Ingram*.[219]

In *Midland Railway v Gribble*,[220] on the other hand, where, on the intersection   **12–81**
of land by a railway, a crossing had been provided for the purpose of communication between the severed parts, it was held that, on the alienation by the owner
of the part on one side of the railway without reserving any right of way over it,
the right to use the crossing was finally abandoned.

[213] (1852) 7 Exch. 838.
[214] (1852) 7 Exch. 838 at 839.
[215] (1857) 3 C.B. (n.s.) 120. See *Hulbert v Dale* [1909] 2 Ch. 570.
[216] (1868) L.R. 6 Eq. 177.
[217] (1868) L.R. 6 Eq. 177 at 179.
[218] [1893] A.C. 162.
[219] (1893) 68 L.T. 671.
[220] [1895] 2 Ch. 827.

12–82   In *Young v Star Omnibus Co*,[221] the plaintiffs claimed, and were held entitled to, a right of way over a strip of land 10 feet wide in the occupation of the defendants. Some years prior to the commencement of the action the plaintiffs erected on their land a summer-house which projected over a strip of land to the extent of two feet four inches. The defendants having obstructed the way, this action was brought, and the defendants pleaded extinguishment or abandonment on the part of the plaintiffs. It was held that the erection of the summer-house was at best only a partial abandonment, and constituted no defence to the action.

12–83   In *Hall v Swift*,[222] where it appeared that it was about 40 years since a stream of water from natural causes ceased to flow in its accustomed course, and the stream did not return to that course until 19 years before the action was brought, the court held that the right to the flow of water was not lost. Tindal C.J. said[223]:

> "It is further objected that the right claimed has been lost by desuetude, the water having many years since discontinued to flow in its accustomed channel, and having only recommenced flowing nineteen years ago. That interruption, however, may have been occasioned by the excessive dryness of seasons or from some other cause over which the plaintiff had no control. But it would be too much to hold that his right is therefore gone; otherwise, I am at a loss to see why the intervention of a single dry season might not deprive a party of a right of this description, however long the course of enjoyment might be."[224]

Non-user over a long period due to some legal impediment cannot amount to abandonment. So in *Yateley Common, Hampshire, Re*[225] rights of common over land which had been requisitioned for use as an aerodrome were held by Foster J. not to have been abandoned.

12–84   In *Williams v Usherwood*,[226] in which a right of way was found to have been abandoned, Cumming-Bruce L.J., delivering the judgment of the Court of Appeal, said:

> "The relevant case law is conveniently given in concise form in the judgment of Buckley L.J. in Gotobed v. Pridmore.[227] We quote:

---

[221] (1902) 86 L.T. 41.
[222] (1838) 6 Scott 167; 4 Bing.N.C. 381. See observations on this case by Patteson J. in *Can v Foster* (1842) 3 Q.B. 586. *Hall v Swift* is a case of a natural right, not an easement, but the same principle applies in both types of case.
[223] (1838) 6 Scott 167 at 170.
[224] *cf. Hale v Oldroyd* (1845) 14 M. & W. 789.
[225] [1977] 1 W.L.R. 840. See also *Mann v R. C. Eayrs Ltd* (1974) 231 E.G. 843.
[226] (1983) 45 P. & C.R. 235 at 256.
[227] (1970) 115 S.J. 78; (1971) E.G. 759. The case is not otherwise reported. Cumming-Bruce L.J. was quoting from Court of Appeal (Civil Division) Transcript No. 498A of 1970, pp. 12D–14D (December 16, 1970). Buckley L.J.'s judgment was the judgment of the Court. See also *Costagliola v English* (1969) 210 E.G. 1425. The *Gotobed* test was recently applied by the Court of Appeal in *CDC2020 Plc v Ferreira* [2005] EWCA Civ 611; [2005] 3 E.G.L.R. 15, where a right of way granted expressly for purposes connected with the use of 3 garages was held not to have been abandoned although the 3 garages had been demolished and their site occupied by other structures and used unlawfully for over 30 years.

'To establish abandonment of an easement the conduct of the dominant owner must, in our judgment, have been such as to make it clear that he had at the relevant time a firm intention that neither he nor any successor in title of his should thereafter make use of the easement . . . Abandonment is not, we think, to be lightly inferred. Owners of property do not normally wish to divest themselves of it unless it is to their advantage to do so, notwithstanding that they may have no present use for it.'

We quote also from a passage cited by Buckley L.J. from the judgment of Sir Ernest Pollock MR. in Swan v. Sinclair[228]:

'Non-user is not by itself conclusive evidence that a private right of easement is abandoned. The non-user must be considered with, and may be explained by, the surrounding circumstances. If those circumstances clearly indicate an intention of not resuming the user then a presumption of a release of the easement will, in general, be implied and the easement will be lost.' "

In *Benn v Hardinge*,[229] the Court of Appeal held that non-use for 175 years of a right implied from the laying out of a way pursuant to the directions in an enclosure award did not raise any presumption of abandonment in circumstances where nobody had any occasion to use the way, there being an alternative means of access. The principle to be applied was said to have been authoritatively laid down by the Court of Appeal in *Gotobed v Pridmore*.   **12–85**

In *Charles v Beach*[230] the failure of the dominant owner to create a formed access between the dominant tenement and the rear two-thirds of the driveway over which the right was granted during a period of 60 years was not evidence of abandonment. In *Carder v Davies*[231] it was contended that by building a wall the owner of the dominant tenement had abandoned the right of access onto a way at any point adjoining his land. Peter Gibson L.J. said: **12–86**

"Where the easement owner is in no way limited by the words of an easement to access at any particular point, it matters not that he builds a wall, erects a fence or grows a hedge, which by its nature would not allow convenient access through onto the easement. He is able, if he wishes, to change the access point at any time."

In *Snell & Prideaux Limited v Dutton Mirrors Limited*,[232] the following conduct on the part of the dominant owner was held insufficient to evidence an intention to abandon the right to vehicular use of the passage over which there was an express grant of a 12-foot right of way: **12–87**

[228] [1924] 1 Ch. 254 at 266.
[229] (1992) 66 P. & C.R. 246, CA.
[230] [1993] E.G.C.S. 124.
[231] (1998) 76 P. & C.R. D33, CA, but *cf. Mills v Blackwell* (1999) 78 P. & C.R. D43.
[232] [1995] 1 E.G.L.R. 259.

    (i) the bricking up of a gateway on the dominant owner's land giving access to the street, which rendered a passage useless for the purpose of passing and repassing but which did not stop it being used occasionally for parking, washing and loading and unloading vehicles;

    (ii) the replacement of the buildings on the dominant owner's land with a new factory intended for a different purpose;

    (iii) the provision of direct access to the new factory from the street and of a loading bay opening directly on to the street;

    (iv) the construction of a door on to the passage not wide enough to give vehicular access to the yard at the rear of the new premises;

    (v) acquiescence by the dominant owner in the erection of a pillar in the middle of the passage precluding vehicular access to the factory, to the erection of a fence enclosing a substantial area of the passage, to the use of part of the passage as a storage area and parking space and to the erection of gates across the mouth of the passage (the gates being left open during the working week and the dominant owner being provided with a key).

As to the first four points relating to the reconfiguration of the dominant owner's factory, the court held that these could not amount to a clear intention to abandon rights when those rights had, albeit only to some extent and occasionally, actually continued to be exercised. As to the acquiescence relied upon, the obstructions in question were all easily removable, or the servient owner had failed to discharge the burden of proving that they were not.

12–88   In *CDC2020 Plc v Ferreira*[233] a conveyance granted a right of way over land "for all purposes connected with the use and enjoyment of the three garages erected on" the dominant tenement. The garages had been demolished and their site occupied by other structures and the way used unlawfully for gaining access to other land for over 30 years. The dominant owner then redeveloped his land and constructed three garages on it. It was held that the easement had not been abandoned.

12–89   A mistaken belief that a right has been lost will not constitute abandonment. So in *Obadia v Morris*[234] Plowman J. held that a mistaken impression that the merger of a lease in the freehold reversion had destroyed a right of way was inconsistent with an intention to abandon.

Indication of intention to abandon

12–90   In *Crossley & Sons Ltd v Lightowler*[235] the plaintiffs were carpet manufacturers, and had carried on business on the banks of the River Hebble from 1840 to 1864. A supply of pure water was necessary for their business. The defendants claimed a right to foul the stream with the refuse of dye-works, which had been carried on

[233] [2005] EWCA Civ 611; [2005] 3 E.G.L.R. 15.
[234] (1974) 232 E.G. 333.
[235] (1866) L.R. 3 Eq. 279; (1867) 2 Ch. App. 478.

before 1839, but had then been shut up and abandoned, and reopened by the defendants in 1864. Page Wood V.-C. said[236]:

> "The question of abandonment, I quite concede to the counsel for the Defendants, is a very nice one. On that a great number of authorities have been cited, which appear to me to come to this, that the mere non-user of a privilege or easement of this description, is not, in itself, an abandonment that in any way concludes the claimant; but the non-user is evidence with reference to abandonment. The question of abandonment is a question of fact that must be determined upon the whole of the circumstances of the case. . . . It has always been held to be of considerable importance, that a person in possession of a certain right, and leaving the right wholly unused for a long period of time, and having given so far an encouragement to others to lay out their money, on the assumption of that right not being used, should not be allowed at any period of time to resume his former right, to the damage and injury of those who themselves have acquired a right of user, which the recurrence to this long disused easement will interfere with."

On appeal Lord Chelmsford L.C. said[237]:   **12–91**

> "The authorities upon the subject of abandonment have decided that a mere suspension of the exercise of a right is not sufficient to prove an intention to abandon it. But a long continued suspension may render it necessary for the person claiming the right to shew that some indication was given during the period that he ceased to use the right of his intention to preserve it. The question of abandonment of a right is one of intention, to be decided upon the facts of each particular case. Previous decisions are only so far useful as they furnish principles applicable to all cases of the kind. The case of R. v. Chorley,[238] shews that time is not a necessary element in a question of abandonment as it is in the case of the acquisition of a right."

His Lordship, on the facts, held that, the ancient dye-works having been dismantled without any intention of erecting others, the right had been abandoned.

In *Swan v Sinclair*[239] the Court of Appeal (Warrington and Sargant L.JJ., Lord   **12–92** Pollock M.R. dissenting) held that abandonment might be inferred where there was non-formation or non-user of the way and continuous obstruction of the way for more than 50 years. All the judges accepted the dictum of Alderson B. in *Ward v Ward*,[240] but the two Lords Justices held, while the Master of the Rolls was

---

[236] (1866) L.R. 3 Eq. 279 at 292, 293.
[237] (1867) 2 Ch. App. 478 at 482. Applied in *McIntyre v Porter* [1983] 2 V.R. 439, Supreme Court of Victoria, where *Ward v Ward* (1852) 7 Exch. 838 and *Gotobed v Pridmore* (1970) 115 S.J. 78; (1971) E.G. 759 were distinguished.
[238] (1848) 12 Q.B. 515.
[239] [1924] 1 Ch. 254.
[240] (1852) 7 Exch. 838; para.12–77, above.

unable to hold, that in the present case, as distinguished from that one there were facts, other than the mere non-user, which raised the presumption of abandonment. This decision was affirmed on other grounds by the House of Lords,[241] Viscount Cave L.C. remarking,[242] however, that even if the right of way had been effectively granted, the non-user of the way, coupled with acquiescence in the continuance of walls running across it, and (since 1883) in the additional obstruction caused by the filling up of the strip of land comprising one of the lots, would, according to the decisions of *Moore v Rawson*,[243] *Bower v Hill*[244] and *R. v Chorley*,[245] have afforded good ground for inferring a release or abandonment of the easement. The effect of the transactions was, however, at most to create a contractual relationship under which the several purchasers might have been called upon to clear the land and form the road; until that had been done there would be no effectual creation of the easement of passage. In fact no right of way ever came into existence. Viscount Finlay said[246]:

> "The scheme contemplated that it should come into existence when the road at the back of the premises had been made and the other provisions of the conditions had been complied with. As this never took place, the right of way remained a mere possibility of the future."

Lord Shaw of Dunfermline said[247]:

> "All the arguments as to non-use of a subject which is res mere facultatis can find no place in the present case. For there was no res, no right, and the physical basis of the right, including the very construction of the road over which the right of way was to run, has never yet been in existence."

12–93 *Swan v Sinclair* was distinguished in *Charles v Beach*,[248] where there was a complete, as opposed to conditional, grant of a right of way; in those circumstances the Court of Appeal held that the failure of the dominant owner to create a formed access between the dominant tenement and the rear two-thirds of the driveway over which the right was granted during a period of 60 years was not evidence of abandonment.

12–94   Where a cessation to enjoy has been accompanied by indications of an intention to abandon the right, as by a disclaimer, there is authority for saying that a shorter period than that of the non-user in *Swan v Sinclair*[249] will be sufficient to extinguish the right. Such direct evidence of intention appears to have been

---

[241] [1925] A.C. 227.
[242] [1925] A.C. 227 at 237.
[243] (1824) 3 B. & C. 339; para.12–70, above.
[244] (1835) 1 Bing.N.C. 555; para.12–72, above.
[245] (1848) 12 Q.B. 515; para.12–71, above.
[246] [1925] A.C. 227 at 240.
[247] [1925] A.C. 227 at 243.
[248] [1993] E.G.C.S. 124, CA.
[249] [1924] 1 Ch. 254; [1925] A.C. 227.

treated in the same manner as the similar indications afforded by a change in the status of the dominant tenement. Such non-user, accompanied by confessions that the party had no right, would at all events be strong evidence, and in effect almost conclusive evidence, that he never had any such right.

In *Norbury v Meade*[250] Lord Eldon L.C. said: **12–95**

> "In the case of a right of way over the lands of other persons, being an easement belonging to lands, if the owner chooses to say, I have no right of way over those lands, that is disclaiming that right of way; and though the previous title might be shown, a subsequent release of the right might be presumed."

In *Howton v Hawkins*[251] lessees, to whom had been granted rights of way over   **12–96** land retained by the lessor by mutual agreement, enclosed within the gardens of their respective properties parts of the retained land so that the whole was enclosed. The lessor, who had not objected to the enclosure for 40 years, was held to have no right to do so, even if he did not know of it. Therefore when the reversion was sold the lessor was obliged to accept that the retained land had been added to the gardens of the properties concerned.[252]

In *Williams v Usherwood*[253] two houses were built with a shared driveway   **12–97** between them. The ownership of the driveway was split approximately down the middle. The original owners of the houses (A and B) were granted rights of way over the parts of the driveway that each did not own. However, the layout was such that A did not in fact benefit from the driveway and a fence was erected separating the driveway from A's house. It was held that B had acquired title by adverse possession of the half width of the driveway originally owned by A and A had abandoned his right of way over the other width of the driveway owned by B.

In *Bosomworth v Faber*,[254] a party entitled to a prescriptive right to a supply of   **12–98** water from a tank at a particular point entered into a licence entitling him to construct a new tank at a different point and take his supply from that. The licence was determinable on notice and was subsequently determined. The Court of Appeal held that the previous prescriptive right was impliedly abandoned when the licence was accepted and the new tank system installed and the old tank demolished.

Similarly in *Robinson Webster (Holdings) Ltd v Agombar*[255] there was held to be abandonment of any pre-existing right of way when the dominant owner accepted a licence to use the way, such licence being terminable by one week's notice and at a nominal fee.

---

[250] (1821) 3 Bligh 211, 241, 242.
[251] (1966) 110 S.J. 547.
[252] Where a right of way had ceased to be used because an access had been made elsewhere, an injunction to restrain its obstruction by a padlocked gate was refused: *Waveney D.C. v Wholgemouth*, *The Times*, July 11, 1985.
[253] (1983) 45 P. & C.R. 235.
[254] (1992) 69 P. & C.R. 288.
[255] [2002] 1 P. & C.R. 243 at [72].

Summary

12–99   In *Odey v Barber*[256] Silber J. said that the approach of the courts to a claim that a right of way has been abandoned could be summarised by the following principles set out in this work and the cases cited above:

(a) whether a person intends an abandonment is not a subjective question; it is always a question of fact to be ascertained from the surrounding circumstances whether the act amounts to an abandonment or was intended as such;

(b) abandonment depends on the intention of the person alleged to be abandoning the right of way as perceived by the reasonable owner of the servient tenement; to establish abandonment of an easement the conduct of the dominant owner must have been such as to make it *clear* that he had at the relevant time *a firm intention* that neither he nor any successor in title of his should thereafter make use of the easement; (the judge's emphasis)

(c) abandonment is not to be lightly inferred; owners of property do not normally wish to divest themselves of it unless it is to their advantage to do so, notwithstanding that they may have no present use for it;

(d) non-user is not by itself conclusive evidence that a private right is abandoned; the non-user must be considered with and may be explained by the surrounding circumstances.

Partial user

12–100   Where the extent of the right is known, and does not (as in the case of a right claimed by prescription) have to be gathered from user, user to something less than the full extent does not prejudice the full right,[257] although it has been said that there is no logical or legal reason why there cannot be a partial abandonment of the full extent of an easement.[258]

Effect of Prescription Act 1832

12–101   A question upon this point under the Prescription Act 1832 was suggested in the first edition of this work,

"Whether, in all cases where an easement is claimed by prescription, the user must possess all the qualities requisite to confer a title down to the very commencement of the suit; and therefore, although the right may have clearly existed at an earlier period, it is destroyed by a subsequent user not possessing those essential qualities."[259]

---

[256] [2006] EWHC 3109 (Ch.); [2008] 2 W.L.R. 618 at [103].

[257] *Keewatin Power Co Ltd v Lake of the Woods Milling Co Ltd* [1930] A.C. 640 at 657; *Bulstrode v Lambert* [1953] 1 W.L.R. 1064 at 1068.

[258] per Stuart Smith L.J. in *Snell & Prideaux Limited v Dutton Mirrors Limited* [1995] 1 E.G.L.R. 259 at 261J citing *Drewett v Sheard* (1836) 7 Car. & P. 465.

[259] See, e.g. *Hyman v Van den Bergh* [1907] 2 Ch. 516; affirmed [1908] 1 Ch. 167 (a case of light).

It has already been seen that, by the statute, the period of user to acquire an easement must be that immediately preceding the commencement of an action,[260] and, if the statute had been held to be obligatory in all cases upon parties to proceed under it, many ancient rights would have been lost on grounds which at the common law would have been insufficient to produce that result, and which the legislature, in framing the statute, did not appear to contemplate. For example, where, within the period requisite to confer an easement, there has been a unity of possession of the dominant and servient tenements, no right under the statute can be acquired,[261] and supposing the right to be ancient, the incidental operation of the statute would have been, in such a case, to destroy it. So of any other failure of the requisite qualities of the user.

Another anomaly would also have arisen as to the mode of losing an easement, which would be different in the case of an easement claimed by express grant and by prescription. Thus, a right of way by express grant would not be determined by unity of possession, as it would have been if claimed by prescription.

This inconvenience has been obviated by considering the Prescription Act 1832 **12–102** as an affirmation statute, which does not take away the common law.[262] In *Onley v Gardiner*[263] where the defendant failed in proving a sufficient title under the statute in consequence of a unity of possession, the court allowed the defendants to amend by pleading a right by prescription generally. In *Richards v Fry*,[264] where it was suggested in argument that if "a party had a right three years ago, which he released, and then that an action was brought against him for a trespass committed before the release, if he pleads according to the letter of the statute, i.e. a user for thirty years before the commencement of the suit, he would be defeated, although the act in question was perfectly justifiable at the time", Patteson J. observed[265]: "He might not be able to avail himself of the statute, but he would have a defence at common law."

In accordance with this view, statements occur in several later cases to the effect that the Prescription Act has not taken away any of the methods of claiming easements which existed before that Act was passed. The rule has been so laid down by Mellish L.J. in *Aynsley v Glover*,[266] by Lord Blackburn in *Dalton v Angus*,[267] by Stirling J. in *Smith v Baxter*,[268] and by Lord Lindley in *Gardner v Hodgson's Kingston Brewery Co.*[269] Again, as regards *profits à prendre*, Lord Hatherley in 1871[270] held that rights of common could be established by prescription at common law independently of the statute.

[260] s.4; see para.4–43, above.
[261] See para.4–57, above, and the cases there cited.
[262] Bacon Ab., Stat.G.
[263] (1838) 4 M. & W. 496.
[264] (1838) 3 Nev. & P.K.B. 67.
[265] (1838) 3 Nev. & P.K.B. 67 at 72.
[266] (1875) 10 Ch. App. 283 at 285.
[267] (1881) 6 App. Cas. 740 at 814.
[268] [1900] 2 Ch. 138.
[269] [1903] A.C. 229 at 238.
[270] *Warrick v Queen's College, Oxford* (1871) 6 Ch. App. 716.

It should be remembered, however, that by the combined effect of section 1, section 2 or section 3 and section 4 of the Prescription Act 1832 a right under the Act is not established by user for the prescribed period in gross, but remains inchoate until it is brought into question by action[271] and consequently, in many of the cases referred to in this chapter, where a tenement had been altered after enjoying a right for the prescribed period, the question would seem to have been not whether the right, supposed to have been acquired under the Act, had been abandoned, but whether, having regard to the alteration, a right had been acquired at all. In *Andrews v Waite*,[272] a light case where a building had enjoyed light since 1879 but had been altered in 1888 and 1895, Neville J. expressed the opinion that no distinction can be drawn between what, in the way of alteration, involves the loss of the right to light when once indefeasibly acquired, and what is sufficient to prevent the acquisition of the right during the 20 years.

Effect of excessive user

12–103   In the case of discontinuous easements the previously existing right will not be affected by acts of excessive user or usurpation, if (as is usually the case) the extent of the excess can be ascertained. Thus, if a party having a right of footway were to use it as a carriageway, though he might thereby become liable to an action for such trespass, he might nevertheless sustain an action for any disturbance of his footway. The right thus sought to be usurped would, in the mode of its enjoyment, be altogether distinct from the previous easement.

12–104   In *Graham v Philcox*[273] in the Court of Appeal, May L.J. (with whom Purchas L.J. agreed) said:

> "I doubt whether any excessive user, at least of a discontinuous easement, in whatever respect the use may be excessive, will ever of itself bring to an end or indeed suspend such an easement . . .[274] The owner of the servient tenement upon which, ex hypothesi, the excessive burden is placed is entitled to have that excessive user restrained. The fact that a court may grant an appropriate injunction or make a declaration to this end does not in my judgment either extinguish or suspend the easement. Provided that the owner of the dominant tenement subsequently reverts to lawful use of the easement, his prior excessive use of it is then irrelevant."

May L.J. went on to say[275] that the statement of Romer L.J. in *Harris v Flower and Sons*[276] that "If a right of way be granted for the enjoyment of close A, the grantee, because he owns or acquires close B, cannot use the way in substance for passing over close A to close B", must be considered in the context of the facts

---

[271] See para.4–44, above.
[272] [1907] 2 Ch. 500 at 509.
[273] [1984] Q.B. 747 at 756. For the facts of this case, see para.3–140, above.
[274] May L.J. at this point referred to pp. 346, 347 of the 14th ed. of this book.
[275] [1984] Q.B. 747 at 756, 757.
[276] (1905) 74 L.J.Ch. 127 at 132.

of that particular case, and pointed out that in none of the cases[277] on which counsel for the servient owners had relied was "there suggestion that a mere alteration
of a dominant tenement to which a right of way may be appurtenant is sufficient
to extinguish it, or indeed to affect the entitlement to its use unless as the result
of that alteration the extent of the user is thereby increased."

In *Harris v Flower & Sons*[278] the excessive user by which it was attempted to   **12–105**
impose an additional burden on the servient tenement consisted in the use of a
right of way for obtaining access to buildings erected partly on the land to which
the right of way was appurtenant and partly on other land. A claim was put forward on behalf of the plaintiffs that the right of way had been abandoned, on the
ground that, as it was practically impossible to separate the lawful from the excessive user, the right of way could not be used at all. This contention failed, however, the court holding that there had been no abandonment, but that the user of
the way for access to the buildings so far as they were situate upon land to which
the right of way was not appurtenant was in excess of the rights of the defendants,
and a declaration was made accordingly, with liberty to apply.[279]

In *Milner's Safe Co Ltd v G. N. & City Railway Co*[280] a house which enjoyed   **12–106**
a right of way had been pulled down and a railway station erected on the site, and
a claim by the dominant owner to use the way for access to the station failed. It
was further argued for the servient owner that the dominant tenement had been so
altered that the dominant owner could not help exceeding the right if it used it at
all, and, the good user not being severable from excess of user, the right was suspended. Kekewich J. gave effect to the argument, saying[281]: "It may be correct to
say that the right is suspended, for I suppose it is presumably capable of being
revived, but what I hold is that it is not under present circumstances exercisable
at all." On appeal,[282] however, the case was compromised on the basis that the
railway company should be restrained from using the right of way by licensing or
inviting any person using their railway station as travellers to pass along it, but
that the restraint should not extend to the company using the way for the purposes
of access by its officers, clerks or servants or by any person not being a traveller
or intending traveller reasonably visiting the company's premises, so that this
case may be considered to be in line with the principle that excessive user will
not ever lead to suspension of a discontinuous easement.

[277] *Allan v Gomme* (1840) 11 A. & E. 759; *Harris v Flower and Sons* (1905) 74 L.J.Ch. 127; *Ankerson v Connelly* [1906] 2 Ch. 644; *Milner's Safe Co Ltd v Great Northern and City Ry* [1907] 1 Ch. 208.
[278] (1905) 74 L.J.Ch. 127. Where a way is used to reach land the use of which is ancillary to the use of the dominant tenement, the user is not excessive: *National Trust for Places of Historic Interest or Natural Beauty v White* [1987] 1 W.L.R. 907.
[279] This analysis of *Harris v Flower* was adopted by the High Court of Australia in *Westfield Management Ltd v Perpetual Trustee Company Ltd* [2007] H.C.A. 45 at [27].
[280] [1907] 1 Ch. 208, see para.9–57, above. See also, as to the extinguishment of a right of way by alteration of the dominant tenement, *Allan v Gomme* (1840) 11 A. & E. 772; *Henning v Burnet* (1852) 8 Ex. 191; para.9–49, above. For another example of an injunction restraining the dominant owner from licensing others to use the way except on terms, see *Jalnarne Limited v Ridewood* (1989) 61 P. & C.R. 143.
[281] [1907] 1 Ch. 208 at 227.
[282] [1907] 1 Ch. 208 at 229, 230.

12–107   In *Hamble Parish Council v Haggard*,[283] Millett J. said that the compromise of the *Milner's Safe* case suggests that, where it is possible, however difficult, to make lawful use of a right of way or other discontinuous easement, the servient owner is entitled to an injunction to restrain excessive user and throw the burden of disentangling the two users and stopping the excessive user upon the dominant owner, but not to obstruct the user altogether. In that case an express grant entitled the parish council to use a way so as to get access to a field intended eventually to be used for burials, but not to the existing churchyard or church. The judge suggested that one way that the dominant owner might seek to prevent excessive user might be to erect a fence with a locked gate between the two parcels.[284]

12–108   Nevertheless, it appears that if the owner of the servient tenement cannot otherwise abate the excessive user of the easement he may obstruct the whole use of it. So where a person who has a right to send down clean water through a drain sends down foul water, so that is it impossible to sever the good user from the excessive user, the servient owner may stop the whole discharge[285] and where the dominant tenement was altered from a bakery to two houses leading to a substantial increase in the burden on the drains, it was held that the right of drainage was at least suspended while that state of affairs continued.[286] Where, however, a right had been acquired to pollute water by a certain manufacture, it was said that the right would not be destroyed by altering the materials used.[287]

---

[283] [1992] 1 W.L.R. 122 at 134D.
[284] [1992] 1 W.L.R. 122 at 136E.
[285] *Cawkwell v Russell* (1856) 26 L.J.Ex. 34; *Hill v Cock* (1872) 26 L.T. 185; *Charles v Finchley Local Board* (1883) 23 Ch. D. 767 at 775. See also *Bernard and Bernard v Jennings and Hillaire* (1968) 13 W.I.R. 501, Trinidad and Tobago CA, where a dominant owner having a right of footway claimed an unlimited right of way, and it was held that if the excessive user of an easement cannot be abated without obstructing the whole user, the owner of the servient tenement may obstruct the whole of that user, and the servient owner was therefore entitled to block the way and erect a fence in order to prevent the dominant owner from exercising an unlimited right of way.
[286] *McAdams Homes Ltd v Robinson* [2004] EWCA Civ 214; [2004] 3 E.G.L.R. 93.
[287] *Baxendale v MacMurray* (1867) 2 Ch. App. 790 at 794.

PART V

DISTURBANCE OF EASEMENTS

CHAPTER 13

WHAT AMOUNTS TO A DISTURBANCE

1.—THE NATURE OF THE CAUSE OF ACTION

Nuisance and disturbance compared

Because the owner of an easement is not in any sense in possession of the servient **13–01** tenement, his action for interference with his easement cannot be in trespass, since that is a cause of action which can only be maintained by a person in possession. His only remedies are abatement or an action for nuisance.[1] There is a distinction as to the foundation of the right of action for a private nuisance, properly so called, and an action for the disturbance of an easement. No proof of any right in addition to the ordinary right of property is required in the case of the former; for example, where an action is brought for polluting the air, or establishing an offensive trade.

On the other hand, to maintain an action for a disturbance of an easement to receive air by a window, proof of the accessorial right must be given.[2] Yet the incidents of the two classes of rights, as far as concerns the remedies for any infringement of them, are similar, and in many cases an action may be founded on both; thus, in *Aldred's Case*[3] the plaintiff complained of the stoppage of his windows, and that the defendant had erected a wooden building and kept hogs in it, by means of which his easement of light was obstructed, and his enjoyment of his property diminished by the smell of the hogs. Both injuries are called nuisances, and the same principles as to the nature of the remedies for them apply indiscriminately to both.[4]

---

[1] *Paine & Co Limited v St Neots Gas & Coke Co* [1939] 3 All E.R. 812 at 823–824, per Luxmoore L.J., citing *Aldred's Case* (1610) 9 Co.Rep. 57b and *Higgins v Betts* [1905] 2 Ch. 210.

[2] *Paine & Co Ltd v St Neots Gas and Coke Co Ltd* [1938] 4 All E.R. 492; [1939] 3 All E.R. 812.

[3] (1611) 9 Co.Rep. 57b.

[4] This statement of principle in the 14th edition of this book was approved by Stamp L.J. delivering the judgment of the Court of Appeal in *Saint v Jenner* [1973] Ch. 275, 280.

Need for sensible diminution of enjoyment

13–02 It is not every interference with the full enjoyment of an easement that amounts in law to a disturbance; there must be some sensible abridgment of the enjoyment of the tenement to which it is attached, although it is not necessary that there should be a total destruction of the easement. The injury complained of must be of a substantial nature, in the ordinary apprehension of mankind, and not one arising merely from the caprice or peculiar physical constitution of the party aggrieved.[5]

13–03 To establish his cause of action, therefore, the claimant has to prove:

(1) his title to the easement by express or implied grant or reservation or prescription;
(2) the scope of the easement, which in the case of an express easement will depend on the construction of the grant, in the case of an implied easement, on the circumstances giving rise to the implication and, in the case of prescription on the nature of the use made of the servient land at the beginning of and throughout the period relied upon;
(3) that there has been a substantial interference with the right to which he is entitled.

2.—DISTURBANCE OF VARIOUS EASEMENTS

Watercourses

Interference with the watercourse of another

13–04 The following acts have been held to be actionable interferences with a right to a watercourse:

(1) polluting the water in the watercourse,[6]
(2) diverting the water so that there is no longer sufficient water for a mill,[7] even if the stream is already choked and obstructed,[8]
(3) attaching a small pipe to a larger one so as to take water from it,[9]

---

[5] In *Leon Asper Amusements Ltd v Northmain Carwash* (1966) 56 D.L.R. (2d) 173, the plaintiff, who owned a theatre, had an easement which permitted theatre patrons to park after 6 p.m. on the servient tenement; the owners of the servient tenement attempted to direct patrons as to where they should park; it was held that this was an interference with the easement. In *Jackson v Mulvaney* [2003] 1 W.L.R. 360, the dominant owner had a right to use the servient land as a communal garden for recreational and amenity purposes. The servient owner removed a flower bed in the garden without notice and without giving the dominant owner an opportunity to recreate or relocate it or its contents elsewhere. This was held to be an interference with the right.
[6] *Aldred's Case* (1611) 9 Co.Rep. 57b, 59a.
[7] 2 Rolle, pl. 8, 9.
[8] *Bower v Hill* (1835) 1 Bing.N.C. 549.
[9] *Moore v Browne* (1572) Dyer 319b, pl. 17.

(4) opening a drain into a sewer on the servient land,[10]

(5) any act which prevents the dominant owner drawing water from a spring.[11]

Interference with land of another by alterations to watercourse

If an owner of land for his own convenience diverts or interferes with the course of a stream, he must take care that the new course provided for it is sufficient to prevent mischief from an overflow to his neighbour's land.[12] He will be liable if such an overflow takes place.[13] Liability will be strict if the possibility of flooding was foreseeable. It is not a defence to say that something was not a nuisance when constructed. If a person constructs a culvert to carry a natural stream, he is under a high obligation to see that the stream continued to flow and must enlarge the culvert if it later proves inadequate, albeit due to factors which are not of his making.[14] This may be so even if it is necessary to acquire extra land in order to abate the nuisance.[15]

13–05

Private rights of way

As regards the disturbance of private rights of way, it has been laid down that whereas in a public highway any obstruction is a wrong if appreciable, in the case of a private right of way the obstruction is not actionable unless it is substantial.[16] Again, it has been said that for the obstruction of a private way the dominant owner cannot complain unless he can prove injury; unlike the case of trespass, which gives a right of action though no damage be proved.[17] In *Hutton v Hamboro*,[18] where the obstruction of a private way was alleged, Cockburn C.J. laid down that the question was whether practically and substantially the right of way could be exercised as conveniently as before.

In *Keefe v Amor*[19] Russell L.J. said that the grantee of a right of way could only object to such activities of the owner of the land, including retention of obstructions, as substantially interfered with the use of the land in such exercise of the defined right as for the time being was reasonably required. It must not be forgotten that the grant of a private way ordinarily speaking confers only a right to a reasonable use of the way by the grantee in common with others[20]; and the question as to what is a reasonable use has been said to be a question for the jury.[21]

13–06

---

[10] *Lee v Stevenson* (1858) E.B. & E. 512.

[11] "If one does something to prevent another from going to a spring, etc., or from drawing from a spring, such persons may fall to the assize." Bracton Lib. 4, f. 233.

[12] *Sedleigh Denfield v O'Callaghan* [1940] A.C. 880 at 888 per Viscount Maugham.

[13] *Greenock Corp v Caledonian Ry* [1917] A.C. 556.

[14] *Bybrook Barns Centre Limited v Kent C.C.* [2001] B.L.R. 55.

[15] *Marcic v Thames Water Utilities Limited* [2002] 2 All E.R. 55 at [91], reversed on appeal at [2004] 2 A.C. 42.

[16] *Pettey v Parsons* [1914] 2 Ch. 662. See *Pullin v Deffel* (1891) 64 L.T. 134; also *Celsteel Ltd v Alton House Holdings Ltd* [1985] 1 W.L.R. 204 (reversed, but not on this point, [1986] 1 W.L.R. 374).

[17] *Thorpe v Brumfitt* (1873) 8 Ch. App. 650 at 656.

[18] (1860) 2 F. & F. 218.

[19] [1965] 1 Q.B. 334 at 347.

[20] *Clifford v Hoare* (1874) L.R. 9 C.P. 362 at 371. See *Harding v Wilson* (1823) 2 B. & C. 96; *Strick v City Offices* (1906) 22 T.L.R. 667; *Robertson v Abrahams* [1930] W.N. 79.

[21] *Hawkins v Carbines* (1857) 27 L.J.Ex. 46.

13–07   In *B. & Q. Plc v Liverpool & Lancashire Properties Limited*,[22] the owners of a
retail park had granted B. & Q. a lease of a retail warehouse with a right to pass
and repass over a service yard at the rear of one of the other units. The landlords
proposed to construct an extension which would reduce the area of the yard and
the turning circle available to B. & Q.'s vehicles, albeit that turning facilities were
available to B. & Q. within their own demise. Blackburn J. adopted the following
propositions of law[23]:

> (1) the test of an actionable interference is not whether what the grantee is
>   left with is reasonable, but whether his insistence upon being able to
>   continue the use of the whole of what he contracted for is reasonable;
> (2) it is not open to the grantor to deprive the grantee of his preferred *modus
>   operandi* and then argue that someone else would prefer to do things
>   differently, unless the grantee's preference is unreasonable or perverse;
> (3) if the grantee has contracted for the "relative luxury" of an ample right,
>   he is not to be deprived of that right, in the absence of an express reser-
>   vation of a right to build upon it, merely because it is a relative luxury
>   and the reduced, non-ample right would be all that was reasonably
>   required[24];
> (4) the test is one of convenience and not of necessity or reasonable necessity;
>   providing that which the grantee is insisting upon is not unreasonable, the
>   question is "Can the right of way be substantially and practically exercised
>   as conveniently as before?"[25];
> (5) the fact that an interference with an easement is infrequent and, when it
>   occurs, is relatively fleeting, does not mean that the interference cannot
>   be actionable.

Applying those tests, the judge held that the right granted could not be used so
conveniently as before and granted an injunction.

13–08   The fifth proposition above was based on *C.P. Holdings Limited v Dugdale*,[26]
where British Rail had granted a right at all times to pass and repass across the
bed of a disused railway line. The way granted formed part of the access road to
a business park. A successor to British Rail wished to reopen the line and run a
small number of trains each day, building a level crossing at the point where the
access road crossed the line. Park J. held that, though the access road with a level
crossing would still provide reasonable facilities for entering and leaving the

---

[22] [2001] 1 E.G.L.R. 92.
[23] [2001] 1 E.G.L.R. 92, at 96G, 96L and 99D.
[24] See also *West v Sharp* (2000) 79 P. & C.R. 327 at 332, per Mummery L.J but see the reservations
of Patten J. concerning the precise formulation of this proposition in *Perlman v Rayden* [2004]
EWHC 2192 (Ch.), where the issue was as to the width of a way needed for access to repair the
property on the dominant land.
[25] This test was applied in *Hitchman v Wilbraham* [2007] L.T.L. 17/03/08, where it was held that the
narrowing of a lane with some rocks had not caused any substantial interference but the parking of
cars opposite the claimant's entrance had.
[26] [1998] N.P.C. 97.

park, the temporary obstruction of the way would amount to actionable interference with the easement; the correct test was whether insistence by the park owner on users of the park being able to continue to use the access road without the possibility of being held up by a level crossing was reasonable; it was, particularly since the evidence showed it was what the owner bargained and paid for.

In *Greenwich NHS Trust v London & Quadrant Housing*,[27] the court left open **13–09** the question whether the realignment of a right of way would constitute an actionable interference if the realigned route was equally convenient, describing this as a difficult and far-reaching question, but granted a declaration that the dominant owners were not entitled to an injunction to prevent the realignment.[28]

In deciding what is a substantial interference with the dominant owner's reason- **13–10** able user of the way, all the circumstances must be considered; for example, the reciprocal rights of the persons entitled to use the way[29]; also the case of persons carrying burdens along the way.[30] Certain acts by the servient owner have been held to be obstruction, such as building on the way[31]; or ploughing up the way, which makes it not so easy as it was before[32]; or erecting a building so as to leave a tunnel only 10 feet high[33]; or constructing ramps which, though not a disturbance when first erected, become such due to deterioration of the road surface.[34] There is, however, no principle of law which precludes the owner of land building right up to the boundary of his land. If this land abuts on a right of way, building right up to the edge of the way does not interfere with the right of way. The dominant owner has no cause for complaint if he is restricted in his user of the way to the exact width of the way.[35]

The owner of a right of way cannot recover damages for physical damage to **13–11** the servient tenement. The right to damages lies in the unlawful interference with the right to use the way, and if there is no substantial interference there is no cause of action.[36] So failure to clear rutted snow is not an unlawful interference with the right to use the way and will not found a cause of action.[37]

---

[27] [1998] 1 W.L.R. 1749.

[28] The circumstances in which it would be appropriate to make a negative declaration of the kind made in the *Greenwich NHS Trust* case were considered in *Well Barn Shoot Ltd v Shackleton* [2003] EWCA Civ 02 where a similar negative declaration was made to the effect that certain activities would not amount to an actionable interference with the right in question, which was a profit of shooting.

[29] *Shoesmith v Byerley* (1873) 28 L.T. 553. And see especially the remarks of Lord Jessel M.R. as to reasonable user in *Original Hartlepool Co v Gibb* (1877) 5 Ch. D. 713 (access to a wharf on a navigable river, which is a public highway).

[30] *Austin v Scottish Widows Fund Assurance Society* (1881) 8 L.R.Ir. 385.

[31] *Lane v Capsey* [1891] 3 Ch. 411. See *Phillips v Treeby* (1862) 3 Giff. 632.

[32] Rolle, Ab., Nusans, G. 1. See *Nicol v Beaumont* (1883) 50 L.T. 112.

[33] *V. T. Engineering Ltd v Richard Barland & Co Ltd* (1968) 19 P. & C.R. 890.

[34] *Saint v Jenner* [1973] Ch. 275 (applying *Sedleigh-Denfield v O'Callaghan* [1940] A.C. 880); see para.1–95, above. As to liability for the acts of strangers, see para.14–35, below.

[35] *Minor v Groves* (1997) 80 P. & C.R. 136; *V.T. Engineering Ltd v Richard Barland & Co Ltd* (1968) 19 P. & C.R. 890; *Drumonde v Moniz* (1997) 105 O.A.C. 295; *Fallowfield v Bourgault* (2003) 235 D.L.R. (4th) 263.

[36] *Weston v Lawrence Weaver* [1961] 1 Q.B. 402.

[37] *Clutterham v Anglian Water Authority*, *The Times*, August 14, 1986, CA, but for the common duty of care now owed by occupiers of servient land, see Occupiers' Liability Act 1984, paras 1–99 *et seq.*, above.

Gates and doors

13–12 With respect to the particular disturbance of a private right of way caused by the servient owner erecting a gate across the way, the following dictum by Jones J. occurs in his report of *James v Hayward*.[38]

> "If a private man has a way across the land of J.S. by prescription or grant, J.S. cannot make a gate across the way; and if on a private way a gate cannot be made, a multo fortiori it cannot be made on a highway which would be prejudicial to many."

In *Andrews v Paradise*[39] the plaintiff recovered judgment against the defendant for breach of covenant for quiet enjoyment, the breach consisting of the erection of a gate across a way. The case was argued on demurrer, which admitted the plaintiff's allegation that the defendant had erected a gate across the way, *per quod* the plaintiff's tenant was obstructed. In *Kidgill v Moor*[40] a declaration by the plaintiff (owner in reversion of the dominant tenement) against the defendant for fastening a gate made across a private way was held good after verdict.

13–13 Modern cases have placed the law on a clearer footing. It has been held in the Court of Appeal in England that a gate is not necessarily an interference with a private right of way. To be actionable the interference must be substantial.[41] And it has been held in Ireland that whether a gate is or is not an interference with the right is a matter of fact.[42] In both the last-mentioned cases the erection of a gate across a private way was held to be no interference with the right, proper facilities being given to the dominant owner,[43] who, on his part, is under an obligation to shut after him a gate which has been left unlocked for his convenience.[44]

13–14 In Australia the effect of *Pettey v Parsons*[45] has been said to leave it open to the owner of land to make any use of his land open to an owner, including the erection of gates and fences, so long as there is no real substantial interference with the enjoyment of the right of way. There is a natural presumption that the servient owner should be entitled to fence his land; the servient owner is

---

[38] (1631) Sir W. Jones 222; Cro.Car. 184. The words of Jones J. do not occur in Croke's report.
[39] (1724) 8 Mod. 318.
[40] (1850) 9 C.B. 364.
[41] *Pettey v Parsons* [1914] 2 Ch. 662 at 666; applied in *Siggery v Bell* [2007] All E.R. (D) 40; see also *Lister v Rickard* (1969) 113 S.J. 981.
[42] *Ffynn v Harte* [1913] 2 I.R. 327.
[43] See also *Deacon v S.E. Ry* (1889) 61 L.T. 377, where the erection of gates across a private right of way was held justifiable. And gates may even be placed across public highways. "You may, as a matter of law, have a gate upon a public highway", said Scrutton J. in *Att-Gen v Meyrick & Jones* (1915) 79 J.P. 515; but it must not be locked: *Guest Estates Ltd v Milner's Safes Ltd* (1911) 28 T.L.R. 59.
[44] See also *Baypeak Pty Ltd v Lim* [2005] V.S.C. 77 at [30] where it was held in the Supreme Court of Victoria that any person who is entitled to open a gate in the exercise of a right of way acts unreasonably if, having opened the gate, he leaves it open when he knows or ought to know that it is, or may be, necessary to keep in the stock depastured on the land and the Court granted an injunction to restrain the defendants from leaving the gate open unless the circumstances afforded some reason or excuse for doing so.
[45] [1914] 2 Ch. 662.

entitled to fence the common boundary and the dominant owner is entitled to access to the right of way by means of gates at such points as reasonably meet his requirements, subject, of course, to any express or implied terms of the grant.[46]

It has been held further that the erection of four internal gates of "Queensland style" construction on a right of way 1 km long did amount to substantial interference with the right,[47] but the presence of a single unlocked boom gate did not[48]; that the erection of four gates in the space of 50 metres was a substantial interference, as would be two gates, unless a section of fence were removed so that the dominant owner could get access to his land by only having to go through one gate[49]; and that the erection of two bolted but unlocked gates across a road leading from a factory, which resulted in traffic congestion, was a substantial interference.[50] The installation of an unmanned code-operated barrier across a private road over which three schools and the residents of the estate had a statutory right of way, the object being to defeat "rat-running", has been held to be a recipe for chaos and to constitute a very substantial interference.[51]

Whether the erection of gates is an actionable nuisance may depend on the motive of the party erecting them. If his behaviour is "unneighbourly" and motivated by malice or the desire to be awkward so as to further some ulterior motive, his conduct is likely to be held to be tortious.[52]

Locks

In *Dawes v Adela Estates Ltd*,[53] Sir John Pennycuick V.-C. held that the locking of   **13–15** an outer door to a house divided into flats was not a substantial interference if the tenants of the flats were provided with keys to the door. On the other hand the fact that the postman could not obtain access to the building with the tenants' mail amounted to an interference and the owner of the house had to make arrangements for his admittance.[54] If a gate across a private way is locked, it is not necessarily an answer to a complaint of the obstruction to say that keys will be supplied.[55] The maintenance of locked gates and insistence on the making of a prior appointment for access and identification of persons exercising the right is substantial interference with a right of way expressed to be at all times for the purposes of forestry, even

---

[46] per Bryson J. in *Owners of Strataplan 42472 v Menala Pty Limited* (1998) 9 B.P.R. 97,717, citing *Powell v Landon* (1944) 45 S.R. (NSW) 136 at 139 and *Dunell v Phillips* (1982) 2 B.P.R. 9,517 at 9,522.

[47] *Sinclair v Jutt* (1996) 9 B.P.R. 97,705.

[48] *Carlson v Carpenter* (1998) 8 B.P.R. 97,693.

[49] *Siggery v Bell* [2007] EWHC 2167 (Ch.).

[50] *Dresdner v Scida* [2003] NSWSC 957.

[51] *The Sisters of the Sacred Heart of Mary Ltd v Kingston Borough Council* [2008] All E.R. (D) 209.

[52] *Owers v Bailey* [2006] 39 L.S. Gaz. 34.

[53] (1970) 216 E.G. 1405.

[54] *Geoghegan v Henry* [1922] 2 I.R. 1; the same conclusion was reached in *Gohl v Hendon* [1930] S.A.S.R. 158. In *Lister v Rickard* (1969) 113 S.J. 981 it was held that the servient owner was not bound to close the gates, for it was not reasonably necessary for the enjoyment of the dominant owner's land that the gates should be kept closed.

[55] *Guest Estates Ltd v Milner's Safes Ltd* (1911) 28 T.L.R. 59; *Rafique v Trustees of the Walton Estate* (1992) 65 P. & C.R. 356, *cf. Johnstone v Holdway* [1963] 1 Q.B. 601.

though the access in question was to land which had been the largest explosives depot in Europe and was still hazardous and there was such a regime in place at the date of grant of the lease containing the easement.[56]

Light

13–16   To maintain an action for obstructing light it is not sufficient to show that the light is less than before. The plaintiff must show that the obstruction complained of is a nuisance.[57] The measure of the right to light laid down by the House of Lords and the matters to which the court should have regard in deciding the question of nuisance or no nuisance have already been stated and discussed.[58] In particular, it has been pointed out that the court should have regard to light coming from sources other than that which has been obstructed, but only so far as this other light is light which the dominant owner is entitled by grant or prescription to enjoy.[59]

13–17   Assuming, for example, a room having windows in walls facing both east and west, the windows in either wall being amply sufficient to light the room without the assistance of the light coming through the windows in the other wall; assuming, also the windows in the eastern wall to have enjoyed the access of light for more than 20 years, and those in the western wall to have been open for less than the statutory period. In such a case, in an action for obstruction to the ancient windows in the eastern wall, could regard be had to the light enjoyed through the windows in the western wall, of which the owner of the building would be liable to be deprived at any moment? The answer to this question should, in accordance with the words of the judges referred to above,[60] be in the negative.

It should be pointed out, however, that in practice it may be difficult to limit the light coming from other sources to light to which the dominant owner has acquired a right, for such a qualification might and probably would involve questions of the rights of third persons. Moreover, as regards a claim to light under the Prescription Act, it is now settled that even after 20 years' enjoyment the right remains inchoate until some action is commenced in which the right is called in question.[61]

It is no answer to an action for disturbance of light that the plaintiff has himself slightly diminished the light.[62] It is otherwise if the result of the plaintiff's act is to render the burden on the servient tenement more onerous; as, for example, if the plaintiff, by altering his premises, diminishes the light coming to them by means other than through the ancient windows, with the result that an obstruction,

---

[56] *Forestry Commission v Omega Pacific Limited*, unreported, January 13, 2000.

[57] *Colls v Home and Colonial Stores* [1904] A.C. 179.

[58] See paras 7–05 *et seq.*, above. For a useful summary of some of the "key points of legal principle" that have to be borne in mind, see *Tamares Ltd v Fairpoint Properties Ltd* [2007] 1 W.L.R. 2148 at [19].

[59] See para.7–21, above.

[60] See para.7–21, above.

[61] *Hyman v Van den Bergh* [1908] 1 Ch. 167.

[62] See *Arcedeckne v Kelk* (1858) 2 Giff. 683; *Staight v Burn* (1869) 5 Ch. App. 163; *Barnes v Loach* (1879) 4 Q.B.D. 494.

which before the alteration would have been immaterial, effects a substantial diminution in his light.[63]

Disturbance of secondary easements

An action lies as well for a disturbance of the secondary easements, without which the primary one cannot be enjoyed, as for a disturbance of the primary easement itself.[64] So acts will be restrained which would interfere with the right of the dominant owner to go onto the servient land to repair the subject-matter of the easement.[65]   **13–18**

3.—CLAUSES PERMITTING DEVELOPMENT

Effect of clauses permitting development

It is quite common, particularly in leases, to find the grant of an easement quali-   **13–19**
fied by a reservation of a right to develop or alter the servient tenement in such manner as the servient owner shall think fit, notwithstanding that the access of light or air to the dominant tenement and (sometimes) any other easement appurtenant to the dominant tenement may be obstructed or interfered with.[66] The effect of such a provision is a matter of construction in each case but the court will lean against a construction which would entitle the servient owner to deprive the dominant tenement of all access of light and air or the whole benefit of any other easement such as a right of access.

Such a provision may, however, permit acts which would otherwise amount to an   **13–20**
unjustified obstruction to or interference with an easement and would otherwise be an actionable nuisance but not acts which would for practical purposes destroy the easement. In that case the servient owner can obstruct or interfere with a dominant owner's rights, provided the dominant owner is left with reasonable enjoyment of them, though not necessarily in so convenient a manner or to such an extent as at the date of grant. So, where leases of flats contained a grant of rights of access over the forecourt but also such a provision as is under discussion, and the landlord wished to delineate parking spaces on the forecourt with lockable posts and grant exclusive licences of the spaces, it was held that he was entitled to do so, despite the fact that the scheme proposed would substantially interfere with the rights of access granted by the leases and otherwise amount to an actionable nuisance.[67]

---

[63] *Ankerson v Connelly* [1906] 2 Ch. 544; [1907] 1 Ch. 678; *News of the World v Allen, Fairhead & Sons* [1931] 2 Ch. 402. See *Bailey (W.H.) & Son Ltd v Holborn and Frascati Ltd* [1914] 1 Ch. 602.

[64] "If one is prohibited from going to a spring he has the action quare quis obstruxit, because he to whom a right to draw water is granted, is also granted a right of way to the spring and access to it": Bracton. Lib 4, f. 233; *Race v Ward* (1857) 7 E. & B. 384. And see *Peter v Daniel* (1848) 5 C.B. 568.

[65] See para.1–91 above.

[66] For the effect of such a clause in cases involving the acquisition of a right to light, see paras 4–26 to 4–28, above.

[67] *Overcom Properties v Stockleigh Hall Residents Management Ltd* (1988) 58 P. & C.R. 1.

13–21   In *Paragon Finance Plc v City of London Real Property Company Limited*[68] a lease granted rights of light but contained a provision that nothing in it should operate to prevent or restrict the development of any land not comprised in the lease, without prejudice to the covenant for quiet enjoyment. The judge accepted that those words were to be construed in the same way as in *Overcom*[69] as permitting acts which would otherwise amount to an unlawful interference with the easement but not acts which would destroy it.

  The judge went on to hold, however, that such clauses are to be construed restrictively and against the grantor on the principle that the court will not construe a general provision in a lease, particularly an exception couched in general terms, so as to take away with one hand that which has already been granted by the other in the dispositive provisions of the lease.[70] He therefore held that the clause only applied to land of the landlord owned by the landlord at the date of the lease.[71]

13–22   In *Petra Investments Limited v Jeffrey Rogers Limited*[72] a lease of a unit in a shopping centre reserved to the landlord the right to rebuild or alter the buildings and any other premises then or during a specified period belonging to the landlord in any manner whatsoever and to use or let them for any purpose notwithstanding that the access of light or air might be diminished, obstructed or interfered with or that any other right appertaining to or enjoyed by the premises or the tenant might be diminished or prejudicially affected. Counsel accepted that this clause did not oust entirely the doctrine of derogation from grant but submitted that it indicated various types of activity by the landlord (alteration, letting for any purpose) that were contemplated as not necessarily being inconsistent with the irreducible minimum implicit in the grant. The judge accepted that but observed that he did not find it helpful in identifying what that "irreducible minimum" was or what obligations (positive or negative) were thereby owed by the landlord; the most that the clause showed was that not every alteration to the centre, either physical or in terms of use, was contemplated as being incompatible with the tenant's rights; he was "inclined to think" that the circumstances of the grant imposed an obligation not so to alter the common parts of the centre as to cause it to lose its character as a retail shopping mall.[73]

13–23   In *Saeed v Plustrade Limited*,[74] a tenant of a flat had along with twelve others been granted the right to park on part of the forecourt; the lease reserved to the landlord the right to alter the building or adjoining buildings and to build on adjoining property to such height as he should think fit and so that the access of light and air should, until interrupted, be deemed to be enjoyed by consent and so that the enjoyment thereof should not prevent such redevelopment. The landlords

---

[68] [2002] 1 E.G.L.R. 97; [2002] L. & T.R. 139.
[69] *Overcom Properties v Stockleigh Hall Residents Management Ltd* (1988) 58 P. & C.R. 1.
[70] See *William Hill (Southern) Ltd v Cabras* (1986) 54 P. & C.R. 42.
[71] [2002] 1 E.G.L.R. 97, where both judgments are reported.
[72] [2000] 3 E.G.L.R. 120.
[73] [2000] 3 E.G.L.R. 120, at 126J–M.
[74] [2001] R.T.R. 30, upheld on appeal at [2002] 2 E.G.L.R. 19.

took the parking spaces out of commission for over three years while they refurbished flats in the block and then proposed to reduce them from 12 or 13 to 4, relying (inter alia) on that reservation. It was held that the reservation only protected the landlord in respect of infringements of rights to light and air and not to any other easement.[75] Both the interruption of the right to park and the proposed reduction were substantial interference with the rights granted and damages were awarded for past breach and declaratory and injunctive relief granted.[76]

In *Green v Ashco Horticulturalist Ltd*[77] the lease of Mr Green's shop reserved   **13–24** apparently unlimited power to the landlord to deal with adjoining land and premises, including power to build without regard to the diminution in light and air enjoyed by the lessee. It was held that, read as a whole, the operation of the clause was confined to easements of light and air and did not permit the erection of gates across a passageway.[78]

In *Platt v London Underground Limited*[79] the claimant took a lease for five   **13–25** years of a kiosk situated within the exit from Goodge Street underground station. The judge found on the facts that at the date of the lease it had been contemplated by the parties that the exit would be part of the station operation while the station was open but in fact the exit was only operational during the morning rush hour. This affected the claimant's trade and he claimed damages for derogation from grant. The landlord relied (inter alia) on a term in the lease which stated that the tenant should not be entitled to raise any objection in respect of the construction, working, or carrying on by the company of its present or any future undertaking or works. The judge held that those words did not give the company carte blanche to carry on or manage its undertaking in any way it liked, irrespective of the damage it might do to the business carried on at the kiosk. Such a construction, carried to its logical conclusion, would mean that the company could close the access to the exit altogether, which cannot have been envisaged by the parties and would be repugnant to the whole grant; provisions such as this have to be interpreted relatively strictly and in such a way as to be consistent with the rights granted to the tenant under the lease; a relatively strict approach is appropriate because the purpose of such a clause is to cut down a right granted.

The lesson for the draftsman wishing to preserve his client's right to develop or   **13–26** participate in the development of adjoining land is that he must spell out fully and expressly the rights which he wishes to reserve or the clause will be construed restrictively. If he wishes to be able to develop land not owned by the grantor or after-acquired land, he must say so. If he wishes to be able to do things notwithstanding that they interfere substantially with the use of the property for the very purpose for which it was demised or sold, he must make that clear. Such frankness in drafting, of course, may well attract the red pen of the other party's solicitor but the alternative is to run the risk that the clause proves not to meet the grantor's aspirations.

---

[75] See [2001] R.T.R. 30 at [19] and on appeal [2002] 2 E.G.L.R. 19 at [27].
[76] For form of order see [2001] R.T.R. 30, at [20] and [50].
[77] [1966] 1 W.L.R. 989.
[78] per Cross J. at pp. 895H to 896B.
[79] [2001] 2 E.G.L.R. 121.

13–27   The point is not academic. It is not unusual for shopping centres or office complexes to require after a time substantial refurbishment and redesign of the common parts and areas to refresh their "offer" and give them an up-to-date image. Such works may be disruptive to trade, intrusive, involve permanent interference with existing easements and result in a permanent change of trading emphasis that, while it may be welcome to some occupiers, may be judged adverse by others.

Reserving rights to light

13–28   While the existence of any easement which a land owner is either granted or acquires by user may inhibit the development of adjoining land, the problem is particularly acute in the case of light. This is because the acquisition of an easement of light under the Prescription Act 1832 depends only on the light having been actually enjoyed for the necessary period; it does not have to have been enjoyed "as of right". One consequence of this is that a tenant can acquire a right to light over adjoining land of his landlord[80]—which is an exception to the general rule that prescription operates only for and on behalf of and against the freehold.

13–29   It will be instructive, therefore, to identify the problems which should be anticipated by a would-be lessor:

> (1) if the building to be let has already acquired rights to light, those rights will pass to the tenant under section 62 of the Law of Property Act 1925, unless the parties to the lease agree otherwise;
>
> (2) as we have seen, the tenant can in due course acquire rights to light over adjoining land of his landlord, unless he is allowed to enjoy the light with his landlord's written consent;
>
> (3) the tenant can acquire rights by prescription over neighbouring land, which the landlord might subsequently acquire and wish to develop;
>
> (4) if the tenant acquires rights to light either at the grant of the lease or subsequently, this may not only prevent the landlord developing his own adjoining land but may prevent him being in a position to negotiate an advantageous deal with a neighbouring developer and/or enable the tenant to demand his share of any deal that is going.

13–30   Accordingly leases (and transfers) often contain a variety of mechanisms with a view to preventing these various consequences, in the form of reservations or declarations or provisos or covenants. The precise wording has to be scrutinised to see whether:

> a) the clause only defuses s.62, so that rights do not pass at the moment of grant but can be acquired later[81];

---

[80] *Morgan v Fear* [1907] A.C. 425.
[81] As in *Mitchell v Cantrill* (1887) 37 Ch. D. 36.

b) the clause operates as a written consent under s.3 of the Prescription Act to enjoy light until the grantor is ready to develop adjoining land— which will prevent prescription over the grantor's land but not over that of a third party; or

c) the clause reserves to the grantor (i) the right to release or dispose of rights which the tenant may have or may acquire for the benefit of the building over adjoining land of third parties or (ii) the right to authorise a third party to interfere with the building's light.[82]

In *RHJ Ltd v FT Patten (Holdings) Ltd*[83] the Court of Appeal reviewed the author-   **13–31** ities on this area of the law and held that a reservation of a right to build on adjoining land was a sufficient agreement for the purpose of s.3 so as to prevent the acquisition of rights to light by prescription, notwithstanding that it did not refer to light and was not expressed permissively.

---

[82] As (arguably) in *Haynes v King* [1893] Ch. 439. For a discussion of all the cases bearing on this topic in the context of easements of light, see paras 4–26 to 4–28, above.
[83] [2008] EWCA Civ 151; [2008] 18 E.G. 128.

REMEDIES FOR DISTURBANCE

Kinds of remedy

The remedies for any disturbance of an easement are of two kinds: (1) by act of   **14–01**
the party aggrieved; and (2) by act of law.

1.—REMEDIES BY ACT OF THE PARTY

Abatement

It is a general rule of law that a person who suffers a nuisance is entitled to abate   **14–02**
it. So a person may enter on to his neighbour's land in order to put an end to the
nuisance.[1] Thus, if there is interference with an easement, for example obstruction of a right of way,[2] the owner of the dominant tenement may exercise this
right of abatement. A land owner may also take steps to abate excessive use of an
easement.[3] Some of the older cases went so far as to say that, in the case of
obstruction of a right to light or of a way, the dominant owner could enter on the
servient land and demolish his neighbour's house,[4] even if it was inhabited,[5] but

---

[1] *Baten's Case* (1610) 9 Rep. 54b; *Perry v Fitzhowe* (1845) 8 Q.B. 757 at 775; *Raikes v Townsend*
(1804) 2 Smith 9; and see examples in 2 Rolle, Ab., Nusans S.W.
[2] As in *Chamberlain v Lindon* [1998] 1 W.L.R. 1252.
[3] *Greenslade v Halliday* (1830) 6 Bing. 379; *Hill v Cock* (1872) 26 L.T. 185.
[4] *R. v Rosewell* (1699) 2 Salk. 459; *Thompson v Eastwood* (1852) 8 Ex. 69.
[5] *Lane v Capsey* [1891] 3 Ch. 411.

it is inconceivable that such an extreme step would now be permitted. The circumstances in which there will be a right to abate were described in very restricted terms in *Burton v Winters*,[6] confining the right to simple cases which would not justify the expense of legal proceedings and urgent cases which required an immediate remedy. Moreover the right is subject to a number of limitations. It must be exercised with extreme caution and restraint. The onus is on the person exercising the right to prove that he has not exceeded his entitlement[7] and, if he has, he risks having committed a criminal offence.[8]

Who may abate

14–03   The owner in fee of a dominant tenement can abate even if the tenement be in the occupation of a tenant.[9] The party in possession may abate although the nuisance existed before his entry.[10]

Limitations on the right to abate

14–04   The cases show that the right to abate is subject to the following limitations, which will be discussed in more detail below:

(1) abatement is only appropriate in simple cases which would not justify the expense of legal proceedings or in urgent cases where an immediate remedy is required; it will not be appropriate in cases which raise difficult questions of fact or law or where there is a question as to the proportionality of the remedy;

(2) abatement is not permissible if the court has already refused to grant a mandatory injunction;

(3) where there is a choice of methods, abatement must be effected by the least mischievous, as long as that does not cause damage to innocent parties;

(4) the person abating the nuisance must not cause any unnecessary damage;

(5) notice to remedy the nuisance must generally be given to the wrongdoer except (a) in an emergency or (b) when no entry on the other's land is involved;

(6) the right will be lost if it is not exercised promptly.

---

[6] [1993] 1 W.L.R. 1077.

[7] *Lagan Navigation Co v Lambeg Bleaching, Dyeing and Finishing Co* [1927] A.C. 226 at 246,where cutting away banks to allow flood water to escape was held to be unjustifiable even upon the supposition that the works which had caused the floods constituted a nuisance, for the abator had failed to prove that he had not done any unnecessary damage and that there was no alternative method.

[8] Under the Criminal Damage Act 1971, s.5, but it is a defence to prove that he destroyed the property in question in order to protect an interest in property vested in himself and that he believed that the interest was in immediate need of protection and that the means of protection adopted were reasonable in all the circumstances: see *Chamberlain v Lindon* [1998] 1 W.L.R. 1252.

[9] *Proud v Hollis* (1822) 1 B. & C. 8.

[10] *Brent v Haddon* (1620) Cro.Jac. 555.

Simple cases

In *Burton v Winters*[11] Lloyd L.J. said: **14–05**

> "Ever since the assize of nuisance became available, the courts have
> confined the remedy by way of self-redress to simple cases, such as an over-
> hanging branch or an encroaching root, which would not justify the expense
> of legal proceedings, and urgent cases which require an immediate remedy."

He went on to cite the following passage from Blackstone:

> "And the reason the law allows this private and summary method of doing
> oneself justice is because injuries of this kind, which obstruct or annoy such
> things as are of daily convenience and use, require an immediate remedy;
> and cannot wait for the slow progress of the ordinary forms of justice."[12]

Refusal of injunction

In *Lane v Capsey*[13] Chitty J. left open the question as to whether the dominant   **14–06**
owner retained a right to abate a nuisance when he had applied for an injunction
requiring the demolition of five houses which obstructed his right of way but such
an injunction had been withheld. This question has now been answered by *Burton
v Winters*.[14] In that case the defendant had constructed a garage so that half in
width of one of the walls of the garage was on the plaintiff's land. The court dismissed the plaintiff's claim for an injunction requiring the removal of the relevant
part of the wall and adjourned the claim for damages so that valuation evidence
could be given. The plaintiff nonetheless asserted a right to abate the trespass.
The Court of Appeal treated the law as to the abatement of a trespass as the same
as the law as to the abatement of a nuisance and said[15]:

> "Self redress is a summary remedy, which is justified only in clear and
> simple cases, or in an emergency. Where a plaintiff has applied for a manda-
> tory injunction and failed, the sole justification for a summary remedy has
> gone. The court has decided the very point in issue. This is so whether the
> complaint lies in trespass or in nuisance. In the present case, the court has
> decided that the plaintiff is not entitled to have the wall on her side of the
> boundary removed. It follows that she has no right to remove it herself."

Least mischievous remedy

A party entitled to a watercourse may enter the land of a person who has occasioned   **14–07**
a nuisance to a watercourse to abate it; but he can only interfere so far as his

---

[11] [1993] 1 W.L.R. 1077.
[12] Blackstone, *Commentaries*, Book III, Chapter 1.
[13] [1891] 3 Ch. 411.
[14] [1993] 1 W.L.R. 1077.
[15] [1993] 1 W.L.R. 1077 at 1082.

interference is positively necessary,[16] and if there are two methods of abating he must choose the least mischievous,[17] for he is bound to abate the nuisance in the most reasonable manner.[18] In several cases abatements have been held reasonable.[19]

No unnecessary damage

14-08   In abating a private nuisance a party is bound to use reasonable care that no more damage be done than is necessary for effecting his purpose[20] without injury to third parties,[21] and it appears that in abating a public nuisance the same degree of caution is required.[22]

In *Rea v Sheward*,[23] where goods were wrongfully placed by the plaintiff on the defendant's land, it was held that they might lawfully be removed to and deposited on the plaintiff's own land; and an action of trespass brought by the plaintiff was dismissed.

Previous request to abate

14-09   It is not entirely settled when the dominant owner must give notice of his intention to abate before actually entering on to the servient land. It is clear that notice is necessary where abatement involves pulling down an inhabited house.[24] Again, notice is necessary where the land on which the nuisance arose has since passed into the possession of a person not responsible for the nuisance,[25] except in a case of emergency, when notice is not necessary before entry is made.[26] In *Delaware Mansions v Westminster City Council*[27] it was held that the owner of a tree was entitled to notice before the party whose property had been damaged by the tree's

---

[16] *Roberts v Rose* (1865) L.R. 1 Exch. 82; *Greenslade v Halliday* (1830) 6 Bing. 379.

[17] *Roberts v Rose* (1865) L.R. 1 Exch. 82.

[18] *Hill v Cock* (1872) 26 L.T. 186.

[19] e.g. *Roberts v Rose*, above; *McCartney v Londonderry and Lough Swilly Ry* [1904] A.C. 301.

[20] Com.Dig Action on the Case for a Nuisance, D. 4; *Greenslade v Halliday* (1830) 6 Bing. 379; *Perry v Fitzhowe* (1846) 8 Q.B. 757; *Davies v Williams* (1851) 16 Q.B. 546; and see *Hill v Prideaux* (1595) Cro.Eliz. 384.

[21] *Roberts v Rose* (1865) L.R. 1 Exch. 82.

[22] In *Colchester Corp v Brooke* (1845) 7 Q.B. 339, the court put the cases of private and public nuisances on the same footing with regard to the care to be used in removing them. According to the latter case, and *Dimes v Petley* (1850) 15 Q.B. 276 at 283, an individual is not justified in abating a public nuisance, unless it does him a special injury; and in the case of a nuisance in a public highway "he can only interfere with it as far as is necessary to exercise his right of passing along the highway and . . . cannot justify doing any damage to the property of the person who has improperly placed the nuisance in the highway, if, avoiding it, he might have passed on with reasonable convenience". In *Bateman v Bluck* (1852) 18 Q.B. 870 at 876, Lord Campbell C.J. goes so far as to say that he cannot justify unless "there was no way in which he could exercise [his right] without the removal".

[23] (1837) 2 M. & W. 424.

[24] *Perry v Fitzhowe* (1846) 8 Q.B. 757; *Davies v Williams* (1851) 16 Q.B. 546; *Jones v Jones* (1862) 1 H. & C. 1; *Lane v Capsey* [1891] 3 Ch. 411.

[25] *Penruddock's Case* (1598) 5 Rep. 100b; *Jones v Williams* (1843) 11 M. & W. 176.

[26] In both *Penruddock's Case*, above, and *Jones v Williams*, above, an exception is made in cases of immediate danger; and see *Lemmon v Webb* [1894] 3 Ch. 1 at 13.

[27] [2001] UKHL 55; [2001] 1 A.C. 321.

encroaching roots incurred the cost of underpinning, so as to give the tree owner an opportunity of avoiding further damage by the removal of the tree. It is thought that considerations of neighbourliness will nowadays result in the courts insisting on notice whenever it is practically feasible for notice to be given.

There are dicta to the effect that except in the case of emergency, notice is always necessary before entering on to the servient tenement,[28] at least if it involves a trespass thereon; but these may not have affected earlier authorities where it was said that notice is not necessary if the person in occupation created the nuisance.[29]

It is certainly the law that (except in the case of emergency) notice is necessary when the occupier of the servient tenement is not responsible for the creation or continuance of the nuisance,[30] and possibly in all cases where he has not created it.[31]

When a request is necessary it may be made to the lessor who created the nuisance or to the lessee, for the continuance is a nuisance by the lessee.[32]

In the case of nuisance caused by overhanging branches no entry on to another's land is necessary in order to abate and therefore notice is not required.[33]

No delay

In Prosser & Keeton, *The Law of Torts* (4th ed., 1971), p. 641, it was said: **14–10**

> "Consequently the privilege [of abatement] must be exercised within a reasonable time after knowledge of the nuisance is acquired or should have been acquired by the person entitled to abate; if there has been sufficient delay to allow resort to legal process, the reason for the privilege fails, and the privilege with it."

The textbook cited *Moffett v Brewer*,[34] where it was said:

> "This summary method of redressing a grievance, by the act of an injured party, should be regarded with great jealousy, and authorised only in cases of particular emergency, requiring a more speedy remedy than can be had by the ordinary proceedings at law."

These passages were approved in *Burton v Winters*[35] where it was held that the plaintiff lost any right to abate which she may have had because not only did she

---

[28] *Lemmon v Webb* [1895] A.C. 1, per Lord Herschell at 5, per Lord Davey at 8. In the case of a right of way, entry on to the servient tenement would not be a trespass.

[29] *Jones v Williams* (1843) 11 M. & W. 176, per Parke B. at 181, cited by the Court of Appeal with apparent approval in *Lemmon v Webb* [1894] 3 Ch. 1; see also *Earl of Lonsdale v Nelson* (1823) 2 B. & C. 302, per Best J. at 312; and *Job Edwards v Birmingham Navigations* [1924] 1 K.B. 341, per Scrutton L.J. at 355.

[30] *Jones v Williams* (1843) 11 M. & W. 176.

[31] *Earl of Lonsdale v Nelson* (1823) 2 B. & C. 302, per Best J. at 311.

[32] *Brent v Haddon* (1620) Cro.Jac. 555.

[33] *Lemmon v Webb* [1895] A.C. 1.

[34] (1848) Iowa 1 Greene 348 at 350, per Greene J.

[35] [1993] 1 W.L.R. 1077; followed in *Co-operative Wholesale Society Ltd v British Railways Board* [1995] N.P.C. 200.

have time to bring proceedings for an injunction, she actually did bring such proceedings. The outcome of those proceedings was that her application for an injunction was refused and she was held entitled to an award of damages in lieu of an injunction. The refusal of an injunction and an award of damages in lieu thereof was an additional reason why the plaintiff was not entitled to assert a right to abate a trespass or nuisance.[36]

Effect of abatement

14–11 The ability of the person suffering a nuisance to enter another's land to abate it does not relieve that other from liability.[37] If the injured party prefers not to abate the nuisance, he will not lose his right to damages or prejudice his chances of getting an injunction. If, on the other hand, he does abate the nuisance, he is still entitled to damages for losses arising before the abatement and to the reasonable expenditure he has incurred in abating the nuisance.[38]

Apprehended injury

14–12 The occupier of land cannot abate an apprehended nuisance. In 1617 it was said by Croke J.:

> "If the boughs of your tree grow over my land, I may cut them off; but I cannot justify cutting them before they grow over my land, for fear they should grow over."[39]

Again it was said by Coke C.J.:

> "Whether the Defendant may pull down the nusans before the house be made, and so come to be a nusans; I do much doubt of this; here it is only said Conatus fuit to edifice this house, and rear up the timber, the Defendant hath no hurt by this, for he may afterwards leave off again; the Defendant is not to pull this down . . . for his intent only."[40]

Generally, some injury must have been sustained before redress can be had. Thus, if a party intending to build a house, which will obstruct ancient lights, erects fences of timber for the purpose of building, there is no right to pull them down. However, a nuisance may exist although no actual damage has accrued: "If a house be built the eaves of which project over my land, I need not wait till any water actually falls from them, but may pull them down at once."[41]

---

[36] See paras 14–86 *et seq.*, below.
[37] *Bradburn v Lindsay* [1983] 2 All E.R. 408 (applying *Leakey v National Trust for Places of Historic Interest or Natural Beauty* [1980] Q.B. 483).
[38] *Delaware Mansions Ltd v Westminster City Council* [2001] UKHL 55; [2001] 1 A.C. 321 at [38]; *Abbahall Ltd v Smee* [2002] EWCA Civ 1831; [2003] 1 W.L.R. 1472 at [28].
[39] *Morris v Baker* (1617) 1 Rolle 393 at 394.
[40] *Morrice v Baker* (1616) 3 Bolst. 196 at 197. See *Penruddock's Case* (1598) 5 Co.Rep. 101.
[41] 2 Rolle, Ab., 145, Nusans U; *Fay v Prentice* (1845) 1 C.B. 828.

2.—REMEDIES BY ACT OF LAW

Action in High Court

The remedy by act of law for the disturbance of an easement is by an action for **14–13** nuisance.[42] An action in which an easement over land is directly in issue is a "pending land action"[43] registrable[44] in the register of pending actions.[45] The court may grant an injunction "in all cases in which it appears to the court to be just and convenient so to do".[46] The Court of Appeal and the High Court also have jurisdiction to award damages in addition to, or in substitution for, an injunction.[47]

Action in county court

By the County Courts Act 1984, amended by the Courts and Legal Services Act **14–14** 1990 and supplemented by the High Court and County Courts Jurisdiction Order 1991 (as amended), the county court now has a very wide jurisdiction to deal with various causes of action which arise and the various remedies which are sought in disputes involving easements.[48]

(1) *Parties to actions*

Who may sue

It has already been stated that a right to sue for the disturbance of an easement is **14–15** a right in nuisance and that the difference between such a right and an ordinary right to sue in nuisance is that the existence of the easement must be established.[49] In relation to the right to sue in nuisance generally, the traditional view that the claimant has to have a proprietary or possessory right in relation to the land affected by the nuisance[50] has now been reaffirmed by the House of Lords.[51]

---

[42] *Paine & Co v St Neots Gas & Coke Co* [1939] 3 All E.R. 812 at 823.

[43] Land Charges Act 1972, s.17(1).

[44] Land Charges Act 1972, s.5(1)(a).

[45] Land Charges Act 1972, s.1(1); *Greenhi Builders v Allen* [1979] 1 W.L.R. 156; *Willies Williams v National Trust* (1993) 65 P. & C.R. 359.

[46] Supreme Court Act 1981, s.37(1).

[47] Supreme Court Act, 1981, s.50. The ultimate derivation of this section is the Chancery Amendment Act 1858 (Lord Cairns' Act), s.2. All courts administer law and equity concurrently: Supreme Court Act 1981, s.49.

[48] See County Courts Act 1984 (as amended by the Courts and Legal Services Act 1990), s.15 (actions of contract and tort), s.21 (actions for the recovery of land and where title is in question), s.23 (equity jurisdiction), s.38 (remedies) and the High Court and County Courts Jurisdiction Order 1991, art.6A (Access to Neighbouring Land Act 1992).

[49] See para.13–01, above.

[50] *Malone v Laskey* [1907] 2 K.B. 141; *Foster v Warblington U.D.C.* [1906] 1 K.B. 648; and *Newcastle-under-Lyme Corp v Wolstanton Ltd* [1947] Ch. 92 (Evershed J.), reversed on appeal on another ground: [1947] Ch. 427.

[51] *Hunter v Canary Wharf Ltd* [1997] A.C. 655 overruling *Khorasandjian v Bush* [1993] Q.B. 727.

In the case of an easement which has been proven to exist,[52] it would seem sufficient if the claimant has a proprietary or possessory right to the dominant tenement and, pursuant to that right, a right to the benefit of the easement. Furthermore, it will be sufficient in some cases, for example in the case of the claimant's home, for the claimant to be an occupier of the dominant tenement, and to have, pursuant to his rights of occupancy, a right to the benefit of the easement. If the claimant has a sufficient proprietary or possessory right in the dominant tenement but he is not entitled as against the owner of the dominant tenement to the benefit of the easement, for example, because it has been expressly excluded from the rights conferred upon him, then it would seem that he does not have a cause of action for disturbance of the easement.

Tenants

14–16   An injunction to restrain an obstruction to light has been granted at the suit of a yearly tenant[53] and of a tenant whose lease had expired after the obstruction, but who had agreed to renew,[54] and in *Jones v Chappell*[55] Lord Jessel M.R. said that so far as he was aware, it had never been decided that a weekly tenant could not have an injunction, and if a weekly tenant and his landlord were to join in a suit to restrain a nuisance he would not find the slightest difficulty in granting an injunction. In *Jacomb v Knight*,[56] where a yearly tenant filed a bill against adjoining tenants holding under the same landlord to restrain a slight obstruction to light, and the landlord after the filing of the bill gave the plaintiff notice to quit, so that at the time of the hearing less than eight months of the tenancy remained unexpired, Lord Romilly M.R. granted a mandatory injunction; but the Court of Appeal, taking into consideration the extent of the plaintiff's interest, and the balance of convenience and inconvenience, dismissed the bill without costs, and without prejudice to an action for damages. The owner of a house, who has no intention of residing there, may have an injunction against an obstruction to the windows simply on the ground of the effect of such an obstruction on the value of the property.[57] The court may, however, grant damages in lieu of an injunction on the ground that the claimant has only a limited interest.[58]

It seems, accordingly, that in any case (and not only in the case of light) an injunction to restrain a nuisance may be obtained by a tenant who holds by the year[59] or by the week,[60] but in such a case the injunction may be limited to the duration of the claimant's tenancy,[61] or may be refused without prejudice to a

---

[52] For the need to prove title to the easement, see paras 14–43 to 14–45, below.
[53] *Inchbald v Robinson* (1869) 4 Ch. App. 388.
[54] *Gale v Abbott* (1862) 8 Jur. (n.s.) 987.
[55] (1875) L.R. 20 Eq. 539.
[56] (1863) 32 L.J. Ch. 601.
[57] *Wilson v Townend* (1860) 1 Dr. & Sm. 324.
[58] *McGrath v The Munster and Leinster Bank Ltd* [1959] I.R. 32. See paras 14–88 *et seq.*, below.
[59] *Inchbald v Robinson* (1869) 4 Ch. App. 388.
[60] *Jones v Chappell* (1875) L.R. 20 Eq. 539.
[61] *Simper v Foley* (1862) 2 J. & H. 555.

claim for damages.[62] Tenants have been added as co-plaintiffs by amendment at the trial.[63] The respective owners or occupiers of adjoining buildings will not, as a general rule, be allowed to join in one action for relief in respect of the obstruction of light.[64]

Reversioner

A reversioner can sue for injury to the reversion, but not otherwise. It follows that **14–17** the injury must have some effect on the reversion.[65] In many cases, the injury will not have any effect on the reversion until the reversion comes into possession at a future date and in those cases the injury will not affect the reversion, unless it is an injury of an enduring kind. But there will be cases where the disturbance of the easement will have an immediate effect on the reversion and so will be actionable at the suit of the reversioner. An example of the latter case is where the dominant tenement is let on the terms of a lease which permit a reduction in the rent payable in the event of the right of way to the dominant tenement being obstructed. In that event, on the obstruction of the right of way, the reversioner loses rent and therefore suffers damage for which he has a cause of action against the person responsible for disturbing the easement.[66]

The action by a landlord for an injury to land in the possession of his tenant **14–18** may be traced to very early times. There are several cases in the Year Books where such actions have been maintained, not only for a permanent damage or destruction of the land,[67] but also for transient acts commencing and ending during the tenancy, but which occasioned loss to the landlord. Such acts are: ousting a tenant,[68] menacing tenants at will, whereby they determined their tenancies,[69] improperly setting up a court, and, by frequent distresses on the tenants for not attending the court, impoverishing them so that they were unable to pay their

---

[62] *Jacomb v Knight* (1863) 32 L.J. Ch. 601.

[63] *House Property and Investment Co v H. P. Horse Nail Co* (1885) 29 Ch. D. 190.

[64] *Bendir v Anson* [1936] 3 All E.R. 326.

[65] The rule laid down in Com.Dig., Action on the Case for a Nuisance, B., on the authority of *Bedingfield v Onslow* (1685) 3 Lev. 209 and *Jesser v Gifford* (1767) 4 Burr. 2141, is: "If the nuisance is to the damage of the inheritance, he in the reversion shall have an action for it." The authorities relied on by the court in *Bedingfield v Onslow* were 19 Hen. 6, 45; 12 Hen. 6, 4; 2 Rolle, Ab. 551; and the following note of *Love v Pigott* (1587) Cro.Eliz. 56: "It was said that there are divers precedents, that if a lessee for years be sued in Court-Christian for tythes, he in the reversion may have a prohibition." And see *Jackson v Pesked* (1813) 1 M. & S. 234; 14 R.R. 417; *Alston v Scales* (1832) 9 Bing. 3; *Hopwood v Schofield* (1837) 2 Mood. & R. 34; *Tucker v Newman* (1839) 11 A. & E. 40; *Fay v Prentice* (1845) 1 C.B. 828; *Kidgill v Moor* (1850) 9 C.B. 364; *Metropolitan Association v Petch* (1858) 5 C.B. (n.s.) 504.

[66] This example is based on the facts of *Ehlmer v Hall* [1993] 1 E.G.L.R. 137, which did not itself concern the disturbance of an easement.

[67] As in 19 Hen. 6, 45, where land in the possession of a tenant at will was subverted by a stranger, and it was held that the tenant at will should have an action of trespass, because he could not have the profit of the land, and the landlord another action of trespass for the destruction of land: Bro.Ab. Trespas. pi. 131; 2 Rolle, Ab., 551, Trespas. N. pl. 3.

[68] 12 Hen. 6, 4.

[69] 9 Hen. 7, 7; 1 Rolle, Ab., 108, pl. 21; Com.Dig. Action on the Case of Misfeasance, A. 6; cited by Holt C.J., *Keeble v Hickeringill* (1809) 11 East 576; *Bell v Midland Ry* (1861) 10 C.B. (n.s.) 307.

rent,[70] fouling water with the refuse of a lime-pit, in which the defendant steeped calves' skins and sheep-skins, which caused the plaintiff's tenants to leave his houses[71]; or, taking toll of a tenant who was exempt from toll.[72]

14–19　　According to the modern authorities, an interference will be injurious to the reversion if it be something which will in the future continue to the time when the reversion falls into possession, or it be something which in the present operates as a denial of the right of the reversioner, or if it causes a present actual loss to the reversioner.

14–20　　As regards the first head of injury, it was laid down by Cotton L.J. in *Rust v Victoria Graving Dock Co*[73] that as a general rule a reversioner cannot get any damages for a wrongful act unless the damage is such as will endure and be continuing when the reversion becomes an estate in possession. The rule has been more recently stated by Parker J. in *Jones v Llanrwst U.D.C.*[74] as follows:

> "It is reasonably certain that a reversioner cannot maintain actions in the nature of trespass, including, I think, actions for infringement of natural rights arising out of his ownership of land, without alleging and proving injury to the reversion. If the thing complained of is of such a permanent nature that the reversion may be injured, the question of whether the reversion is or is not injured is a question for the jury: Simpson v. Savage.[75] I take 'permanent', in this connection, to mean such as will continue indefinitely unless something is done to remove it. Thus, a building which infringes ancient lights is permanent within the rule, for, though it can be removed before the reversion falls into possession, still it will continue until it be removed. On the other hand, a noisy trade, and the exercise of an alleged right of way, are not in their nature permanent within the rule, for they cease of themselves, unless there be some one to continue them. In my opinion, what is complained of in the present case is of a permanent nature within the rule. The sewage of Llanrwst will continue to be turned into the Conway unless and until something is done to divert it elsewhere. It is not a case only of the present intention of the defendants, but of the necessary consequences of the physical conditions, if nothing is done to alter them."

14–21　　Under the second of the above heads of injury to the reversion there fall the following decisions. Where a reversioner sued on the ground that the defendant had erected a roof to the obstruction of an ancient light, Lord Tenterden held that the reversioner had a good cause of action, because it was an injury to the right; and

---

[70] *Earl of Suffolk's Case*, 13 Hen. 4, 11; 1 Rolle, Ab., 107, pl. 7; Com.Dig. Action on the Case for a Disturbance, A. 6; cited by Willes J. in *Bell v Midland Ry*, above.

[71] *Prior of Southwark's Case*, 13 Hen. 7, 26; cited by Wray C.J. in *Aldred's Case* (1611) 9 Rep. 59a.

[72] 43 Edw. 3, 29; 2 Rolle, Ab. 107, pl. 8.

[73] (1887) 36 Ch. D. 132.

[74] [1911] 1 Ch. 393 at 404, followed by Sargant J. in *White v London General Omnibus Co* [1914] W.N. 78. As to the meaning of "permanent", see *Shelfer v City of London Electric Lighting Co* [1895] 1 Ch. 287 at 299–317.

[75] (1856) 1 C.B. (n.s.) 47.

the effect of letting the obstruction stand might be that from the death of witnesses the evidence of its erection might be lost, and so the injury become permanent.[76] In the case of the same obstruction a second action was brought for its continuance, and the court held that if the erection were in the first instance an injury to the reversion, the continuance must be so likewise. Such continuance would render the proof of the title more difficult at a future time. Lord Tenterden said in the first action that the injury might "become permanent", not that it was so; and the recovery of damages in the second action shows that judgment in the first was given for the past obstruction, not for its permanence.[77] So, again, a reversioner could sue for obstruction to an ancient light caused by a hoarding which might have been put up "in denial of the plaintiffs right".[78] In such cases, said Sir George Jessel M.R., there was an injury to the right which might be lost if the reversioner were not able to institute proceedings.[79]

Again, it was said that such an obstruction, if acquiesced in for a sufficient time, would be evidence of the abandonment of the right.[80] With this should be compared the case where a stranger entered on demised land in exercise of an alleged right of way, and it was said that such acts would be no evidence of right against the reversioner, who accordingly could not sue.[81]

The third head of injury is where the disturbance of the easement causes a **14–22** present actual loss to the reversioner. An example of such a case is suggested by *Ehlmer v Hall*,[82] which did not concern the disturbance of an easement. In that case, the defendant negligently damaged the plaintiff's premises which were let to a tenant. The terms of the tenancy provided that the rent payable thereunder was suspended during a period when there was damage from insured risks. The damage in question was such damage and so for the period until the damage was repaired the reversioner was not entitled to receive rent from the tenant. The plaintiff sued the defendant for the lost rent. The defendant, relying on *Rust v Victoria Graving Dock Co*,[83] contended that the damages were not recoverable. The Court of Appeal held that "the general rule" referred to in the *Rust* case[84] was not of universal application and held that the reversioner had suffered damage for which he was entitled to recover. A similar result would apply where the disturbance of an easement resulted in a present financial disadvantage to the reversioner. In *Rust v Victoria Graving Dock Co*[85] the plaintiff had claimed damages for the diminution in the value of his reversion as a result of temporary damage to his premises, but this claim was disallowed. This part of the decision was

---

[76] *Shadwell v Hutchinson* (1829) 3 C. & P. 615.
[77] *Shadwell v Hutchinson* (1831) 4 C. & P. 334.
[78] *Metropolitan Association v Petch* (1858) 5 C.B. (n.s.) 504.
[79] *Mott v Shoolbred* (1875) L.R. 20 Eq. 22 at 24.
[80] *Bower v Hill* (1835) 1 Bing.N.C. 549 at 555.
[81] *Baxter v Taylor* (1832) 4 B. & Ald. 72.
[82] [1993] 1 E.G.L.R. 137.
[83] (1887) 36 Ch. D. 113.
[84] See at para.14–20, above.
[85] (1887) 36 Ch. D. 113.

explained in *Ehlmer v Hall*[86] on the basis that the plaintiff in the *Rust* case had not sold his reversion during the period that the premises were damaged and did not intend to do so and, when the reversion fell into possession, the fact that the premises had been damaged earlier would not affect the value at that time.

14–23   Having regard to the above rules, the right of a reversioner to sue is considered in the case of actions for the disturbance of easements; in the case of actions for the disturbance of natural rights; and in the case of actions for trespass, which are relevant in considering the law of easements because a trespass which is allowed to continue may ripen into an easement.

Reversioner's action for disturbance of easements

14–24   The reports contain several instances of a reversioner's action for the disturbance of easements where ancient lights had been obstructed by the erection of a permanent structure,[87] where rights in respect of a watercourse had been disturbed[88]; and where a private way had been permanently obstructed.[89]

Reversioner's action for disturbance of natural rights

14–25   Of a reversioner's action for the disturbance of natural rights there are also some examples. Where the water of a natural stream had been polluted (the right of purity being infringed), and the pollution would not cease unless and until something was done to divert it, a reversioner had a good cause of action.[90] In the case of nuisances arising from noise and smoke, a reversioner was held to have no right of action, on the ground that the nuisances might cease at any moment[91]; but where a house was structurally injured by vibration caused by the adjoining owner, the reversioner could sue.[92]

It is to be observed that in *Baxter v Taylor*[93] Taunton and Parke JJ. held that entry in exercise of an alleged right of way on to land in the possession of a tenant would

---

[86] [1993] 1 E.G.L.R. 113.

[87] *Jesser v Gifford* (1767) 4 Burr. 2141; *Shadwell v Hutchinson* (1829) 3 C. & P. 615; (1831) 4 C. & P. 334; *Metropolitan Association v Petch* (1858) 5 C.B. (n.s.) 504; *Wilson v Townend* (1860) 1 Dr. & Sm. 324. See also the words of Lord Jessel M.R. in *Mott v Shoolbred*, above, and of Parker J. in *Jones v Llanrwst U.D.C.* [1911] 1 Ch. 404, quoted at para.14–20, above.

[88] *Bedingfield v Onslow* (1685) 3 Lev. 209; *Peter v Daniel* (1848) 5 C.B. 568. See *Egremont v Pulman* (1829) Mood. & M. 404; *Bell v Twentyman* (1841) 1 Q.B. 766.

[89] *Bower v Hill* (1835) 1 Bing.N.C. 549; *Bell v Midland Ry* (1861) 10 C.B. (n.s.) 287. See *Hopwood v Schofield* (1837) 2 Mood. & R. 34; *Kidgill v Moor* (1850) 9 C.B. 364. As to a reversioner suing in respect of rights connected with a public highway, see *Dobson v Blackmore* (1847) 9 Q.B. 1004; *Mott v Shoolbred* (1875) L.R. 20 Eq. 22.

[90] *Jones v Llanrwst U.D.C.* [1911] 1 Ch. 393.

[91] *Mumford v Oxford, etc. Ry* (1856) 1 H. & N. 34; *Simpson v Savage* (1856) 1 C.B. (n.s.) 347; *Jones v Chappell* (1875) L.R. 20 Eq. 539; *Cooper v Crabtree* (1882) 20 Ch. D. 589; *House Property and Investment Co v H. P. Horse Nail Co* (1885) 29 Ch. D. 190; *White v London General Omnibus Co* [1914] W.N. 78.

[92] *Shelfer v City of London Electric Lighting Co* [1895] 1 Ch. 287; *Colwell v St Pancras B.C.* [1904] 1 Ch. 707. See *Kirby v Chessum* (1914) 30 T.L.R. 660, where the reversioner's wall was in danger from adjoining excavation.

[93] (1832) 4 B. & Ald. 72.

not be evidence of right against the reversioner; and that neither the noise complained of in *Mumford v Oxford, etc., Railway*,[94] nor the smoke and noise complained of in *Simpson v Savage*,[95] was a disturbance of an easement (the onus of establishing which, if disputed, would be on the plaintiff), but an injury, not of a permanent kind, to a natural right. A natural right would prima facie subsist after the determination of the term; and unless the reversioner suffered the injurious acts to continue after the end of the term,[96] they would not be likely to afford an obstacle, by way of evidence, to the maintenance of the right; for the evidence afforded by them might be rebutted by proof of the subsistence of the tenancy during the continuance of them; whereas in the case of the disturbance of an easement the proof of its existence is equally affected by acts of interference with the enjoyment of it, whether the dominant tenement has been under lease or not.[97]

Reversioner's action for trespass

Where an adjoining owner had committed a trespass of a permanent nature by building a wall on the demised land the reversioner could sue.[98] So it was where the defendant had built a wall on the demised land and placed timber thereon overhanging a yard,[99] and again, where the adjoining owner had erected a roof with eaves projecting over the demised land and discharging rainwater on to it.[100] In the case, however, of a simple trespass (as where a stranger entered in exercise of an alleged right of way) the reversioner had no right of action.[101]   **14–26**

Earlier decisions on reversioner's right to sue

The following discussion of earlier decisions on the right of a reversioner to sue was contained in some of the former editions of this book, and is retained here as it is believed that it is still relevant. To enable a reversioner to maintain the action, said Parke J. in *Baxter v Taylor*,[102]   **14–27**

> "it was necessary for him to allege and prove that the act complained of was injurious to his reversionary interest, or that it should appear to be of such a permanent nature as to be necessarily injurious. A simple trespass, even accompanied with a claim of right, is not necessarily injurious to the reversionary estate."

---

[94] (1856) 1 H. & N. 34; see para.14–28, below.
[95] (1856) 1 C.B. (n.s.) 347; see para.14–28, below.
[96] As to the effect of which, see *Palk v Shinner* (1852) 18 Q.B. 575.
[97] See *Johnstone v Hall* (1856) 2 K. & J. 414; *Crump v Lambert* (1867) L.R. 3 Eq. 409; *Mott v Shoolbred* (1875) L.R. 20 Eq. 22; *Jones v Chappell* (1875) L.R. 20 Eq. 539. *Cooper v Crabtree* (1881) 19 Ch. D. 193, where the reversioner failed, was a simple case of trespass.
[98] *Mayfair Property Co v Johnston* [1894] 1 Ch. 508.
[99] *Jackson v Pesked* (1813) 1 M. & S. 234. See *Alston v Scales* (1832) 9 Bing. 3; *Raine v Alderson* (1838) 4 Bing.N.C. 702.
[100] *Tucker v Newman* (1839) 11 A. & E. 40.
[101] *Baxter v Taylor* (1832) 4 B. & Ald. 72.
[102] (1832) 4 B. & Ald. 76. See *Damper v Bassett* [1901] 2 Ch. 350.

14–28   *Baxter v Taylor*[103] was acted upon in *Simpson v Savage*[104] in which the court held that no action lies by a reversioner for a smoke nuisance caused by lighting fires in a factory and causing smoke to issue so as to be a nuisance to the reversioner's tenants and make them give notice to quit; and a very similar point was decided in *Mumford v Oxford, etc., Railway*,[105] where the complaint was for causing loud noises, and the court held that the action would not lie.[106] In both cases the court relied upon the fact that the injury complained of was not of a permanent character, although unquestionably the repetition of such acts would furnish evidence against the reversioner, whether he might be able to rebut it or not. In *Kidgill v Moor*,[107] Maule J., referring to the dictum of Parke J. in *Baxter v Taylor*,[108] said: "My brother Parke does not say that it would not be evidence, if the party claimed a right of way, and meant to assert it": and in *Tickle v Brown*[109] Patteson J. said: "Before the statute, the acts of tenants might be evidence against the reversioners, yet their naked declarations were not so."

14–29   In *Palk v Shinner*,[110] there being a user of 20 years, during the first 15 years of which the premises were under lease, Erle J. said:

> "If this case had arisen before the statute, there would have been good evidence to go to the jury . . . notwithstanding the existence of the tenancy. And the question is still to be left to the jury in the same way."[111]

It seems unjust to deprive the reversioner of an immediate remedy in respect of acts which may at a future time furnish evidence against him, and which, though he may possibly in many cases be able then to rebut, must in all cases involve him in trouble and expense, by affecting the evidence of his right. The point is akin to that which is raised in an action by a reversioner for obstructions by others to the enjoyment of easements by his tenants, the ground of which action is that the evidence of the right of the reversioner to the easement is affected, as his acquiescence in the obstruction would furnish evidence against him of a renunciation and abandonment of it.[112]

14–30   In *Kidgill v Moor*[113] the plaintiff sued for the locking of a gate across a way to which the tenants of the plaintiff were entitled in respect of the tenement of which he was the reversioner and it was objected, on motion in arrest of judgment, that

---

[103] (1832) 4 B. & Ald. 76.
[104] (1856) 1 C.B. (n.s.) 352.
[105] (1856) 1 H. & N. 34.
[106] *cf.* the old authorities referred to in *Bell v Midland Ry* (1861) 10 C.B. (n.s.) 287, as to the right of action for causing tenants to leave their tenements.
[107] (1850) 9 C.B. 364 at 372.
[108] (1832) 4 B. & Ald. 76.
[109] (1836) 4 A. & E. 369 at 378.
[110] (1852) 18 Q.B. 568 at 575.
[111] And see the judgments in *Daniel v North* (1809) 11 East 372; *Lineham v Deeble* (1859) 9 Ir.C.L.R. 309; *Cooper v Crabtree* (1882) 20 Ch. D. 589; *Hanna v Pollock* [1900] 2 Ir.R. 664.
[112] See per Tindal C.J. in *Bower v Hill* (1835) 1 Bing.N.C. 549.
[113] (1850) 9 C.B. 364.

the act complained of was not of a permanent character; but the court held that the declaration was good, as such an act might amount to as permanent an injury to the reversionary interest as the building of a wall, and that the question whether the plaintiff was injured in his reversionary estate was one of fact for the jury.

In *Metropolitan Association v Petch*[114] a declaration in an action by a rever-   **14–31**
sioner for obstructing ancient lights by the erection of a hoarding was sustained, the court holding that such an erection might be an injury to the reversion, and that it was for the jury to determine. In that case also the judges laid down that the way in which the act might injure the reversioner would be by affording evidence in denial of the right. According to the last class of cases, the jury might find for the plaintiff if the act complained of would furnish any evidence in denial of the right. It is difficult to discover any principle upon which the reversioner should be without remedy by action in respect of a series of separate acts of obstruction furnishing evidence in denial of the right, while he has such action in the case of the wooden hoarding intervening, or why a series of trespasses in the assertion of a right of way should not give a right of action to a reversioner.

Continuing disturbance

If the disturbance be continued, a fresh action may be maintained from time to   **14–32**
time by the persons then entitled to sue,[115] but nowadays a claimant should ask for an injunction if there is reason to think that the interference will be repeated or he may find himself estopped from suing again on the principle that a litigant has a duty to bring forward his whole case.

Parties liable to be sued

The party creating the disturbance is liable to an action, whether he be the owner   **14–33**
of the servient tenement or not.[116] He remains liable for all consequential damage even though he is no longer in possession and is unable to prevent the damage continuing.[117] Thus, if the person in possession has leased the premises he remains liable,[118] and if a contractor erects a building on another's land he remains liable if it is a nuisance.[119]

For the continuance of a disturbance each successive owner in occupation of the servient tenement is liable, though it may have been begun before his estate commenced.[120]

---

[114] (1858) 5 C.B. (n.s.) 504.
[115] *Penruddock's Case* (1598) 5 Rep. 101; *Wilson v Peto* (1821) 6 Moore 47; *Shadwell v Hutchinson* (1831) 2 B. & Ald. 97; *Battishill v Reed* (1856) 18 C.B. 696; *Darley Co v Mitchell* (1886) 11 App. Cas. 127; *Crumbie v Wallsend Local Board* [1891] 1 Q.B. 503.
[116] Com.Dig. Action on the Case for a Nuisance, B.; *Thompson v Gibson* (1841) 7 M. & W. 456; *Wettor v Dunk* (1864) 4 F. & F. 298. See *Corby v Hill* (1858) 4 C.B. (n.s.) 556; *Wilson v Peto* (1821) 6 Moore (C.P.) 47.
[117] *Rosewell v Prior* (1701) 12 Mod. 635 at 639.
[118] (1701) Mod. 635.
[119] *Thompson v Gibson* (1841) 7 M. & W. 456.
[120] *White v Jameson* (1874) L.R. 18 Eq. 303; *Broder v Saillard* (1876) 2 Ch. D. 692; see also *Manley v Burn* [1916] 2 K.B. 121.

Where, however, the party was not the original creator of the disturbance, a request must be made to remove it before any action is brought; but it is sufficient if such request is made to the party in possession, though he be only lessee.[121]

The acts of two or more persons may, taken together, constitute such a nuisance that the court in separate actions will restrain each of them from doing the acts constituting the nuisance, although the act of one taken alone would not amount to a nuisance.[122]

Landlord and tenant

14–34   If the owner of land on which a nuisance exists lets the land, an action for the continuance will lie, at the option of the party injured,[123] either against the tenant[124] or (subject to the following qualifications) against the landlord.[125]

No action for the continuance of a nuisance lies against the landlord for an act of his tenant done during the tenancy[126] unless it be done by the landlord's authority.[127] An injunction will not be granted against a landlord who has no power to further the interference by his tenant with the rights of the injured party.[128]

Generally speaking, a landlord is liable for a nuisance on premises occupied by his tenant—(1) where he takes from the tenant a covenant to do things which result in the nuisance[129]; (2) where he lets the premises for a purpose likely to result in and resulting in the nuisance[130]; (3) where he relets the premises after a nuisance upon them has been created,[131] if he knew or ought to have known of the nuisance before the letting, and whether or not he takes a covenant from the

---

[121] *Penruddock's Case* (1598) 5 Rep. 101; *Brent v Haddon* (1620) Cro.Jac. 555. A request to a former occupier while in possession will suffice: *Salmon v Bensley* (1825) Ry. & M. 189. There appears to be no recent authority in favour of the proposition in the text.

[122] *Lambton v Mellish* [1894] 3 Ch. 163, where there were several actions; *cf. Blair v Deakin* (1887) 57 L.T. 522, where there was one action against one such person. And see *Nixon v Tynemouth* (1888) 52 J.P. 504.

[123] i.e. if he be a stranger, and not a tenant or his licensee: *Robbins v Jones* (1863) 15 C.B. (n.s.) 240.

[124] *Broder v Saillard* (1876) 2 Ch. D. 692. Unless, *semble*, the tenant neither knew nor ought to have known of the nuisance; *Wilkins v Leighton* [1932] 2 Ch. 106; *Sedleigh-Denfield v O'Callaghan* [1940] A.C. 880.

[125] *Christian Smith's Case* (1633) Sir W. Jones 272; *Rosewell v Prior* (1701) 12 Mod.Rep. 635; *R. v Pedly* (1834) 1 A. & E. 822; *Todd v Flight* (1860) 9 C.B. (n.s.) 377, in which the previous authorities are reviewed; *Att-Gen v Bradford Canal Proprietors* (1866) L.R. 2 Eq. 71; *Mason v Shrewsbury Ry* (1871) L.R. 6 Q.B. 585.

[126] *Cheetham v Hampson* (1791) 4 T.R. 318; *Rich v Basterfield* (1847) 4 C.B. 783; *R. v Pedly* (1834) 1 A. & E. 827, per Littledale J.; *Preston v Norfolk Ry* (1858) 2 H. & N. 735; *Bishop v Bedford Charity* (1859) 1 E. & E. 697; *Bartlett v Baker* (1864) 3 H. & C. 153. As to a tenancy from year to year, see *Gandy v Jubber* (1864) 5 B. & S. 485; 9 B. & S. 15; *Bowen v Anderson* [1894] 1 Q.B. 164; *cf. Kieffer v Le Seminaire de Quebec* [1903] A.C. 85, where it was held that under Canadian law the landlord was not liable.

[127] *Harris v James* (1876) 45 L.J.Q.B. 545; *Phillips v Thomas* (1890) 62 L.T. 793.

[128] *Celsteel Ltd v Alton House Holdings Ltd* [1986] 1 W.L.R. 512 (reversing on this point [1985] 1 W.L.R. 204). See para.14–70, below.

[129] *Burt v Victoria Graving Dock Co* (1882) 47 L.T. 378.

[130] *Winter v Baker* (1887) 3 T.L.R. 569; *Jenkins v Jackson* (1888) 40 Ch. D. 77; *Tetley v Chitty* [1986] 1 All E.R. 663.

[131] *Sandford v Clarke* (1888) 21 Q.B.D. 398; *Bowen v Anderson* [1894] 1 Q.B. 164.

tenant to remedy or stop the nuisance[132]; (4) if he lets the premises and has either undertaken the duty to repair or reserved the right to enter and do repairs. It would seem that the defendant's knowledge, or means of knowledge, has no relevance to the question of his liability in this last type of case.[133]

It seems to have been held that a tenant for years, occupying a house which was an obstruction to light, erected before his tenancy, was not liable to be sued for damages for its continuance; for he had no authority to abate it.[134]

Where the landlord was not made a party the court has refused to grant against a lessee a mandatory injunction to pull down buildings which infringed a right of light.[135]

Liability for act of stranger

In all cases the defendant must be shown to be in some sense responsible for the continuance of the act complained of. The occupier of land on which is something, not done or placed there by himself, which causes a nuisance to other land is liable if he continues the nuisance, that is, if with knowledge or presumed knowledge of its existence he fails to take reasonable means to bring it to an end when he has ample time to do so; or if he adopts the nuisance by making any use of the erection or artificial structure which constitutes it.[136] So, where a landlord granted a right of way to a tenant and the way was obstructed by other tenants of the landlord parking their cars, he had a duty to take steps for the removal of the obstruction.[137]

14–35

Liability for acts of contractor

The further question, how far an owner who employs a contractor to perform work for him is liable for the consequences of the contractor's negligent or wrongful acts, has been much discussed.

14–36

Where the work contracted to be done is itself unlawful, or necessarily involves the doing of some unlawful act, the employer is clearly liable.[138]

Where the act contracted to be done is in itself lawful, and involves no special risk or duty which the employer has neglected, it is equally clear that the employer is not liable.[139]

Where, on the other hand, the work contracted to be done is hazardous to third persons, or is otherwise of such a nature as to cast a duty upon the person

14–37

---

[132] *Brew Bros Ltd v Snax (Ross) Ltd* [1970] 1 Q.B. 612.

[133] See *Gwinnell v Earner*, above; *Nelson v Liverpool Co* (1877) 2 C.P.D. 311; *Wilchick v Marks and Silverstone* [1934] 2 K.B. 56 at 66; *Wringe v Cohen* [1940] 1 K.B. 229; *Heap v Ind Coope and Allsopp Ltd* [1940] 2 K.B. 476; *Mint v Good* [1951] 1 K.B. 517.

[134] *Ryppon v Bowles* (1615) Cro.Jac. 373.

[135] *Barnes v Allen* [1927] W.N. 217.

[136] *Sedleigh-Denfield v O'Callaghan* [1940] A.C. 880.

[137] *Hilton v James Smith & Sons (Norwood) Ltd* [1979] 2 E.G.L.R. 44 (applying *Sedleigh-Denfield v O'Callaghan*, above).

[138] *Ellis v Sheffield Co* (1853) 2 E. & B. 767.

[139] *Quarman v Burnett* (1840) 6 M. & W. 499; *Reedie v L. & N.W. Ry* (1849) 4 Ex. 244; *Knight v Fox* (1850) 5 Ex. 721; *Gayford v Nicholls* (1854) 9 Ex. 702; *Kiddle v Lovett* (1885) 16 Q.B.D. 605.

undertaking it, the employer is bound to see that proper and reasonable precautions are taken, and is liable for any omission in this respect. Nor is it sufficient that, by the contract between employer and contractor, it is stipulated that the precautions shall be taken by the contractor; the employer must also take care that the stipulation is carried out.[140] Delivering the judgment of the court in *Pickard v Smith*,[141] in which the plaintiff was injured by falling into a cellar opening, Williams J. said:

> "Unquestionably, no one can be made liable for an act or breach of duty, unless it be traceable to himself or his servant or servants in the course of his or their employment. Consequently, if an independent contractor is employed to do a lawful act, and in the course of the work he or his servants commit some casual act of wrong or negligence, the employer is not answerable. To this effect are many authorities which were referred to in the argument. That rule is, however, inapplicable to cases in which the act which occasions the injury is one which the contractor was employed to do; nor, by a parity of reasoning, to cases in which the contractor is intrusted with the performance of a duty incumbent upon his employer, and neglects its fulfilment, whereby an injury is occasioned. Now, in the present case, the defendant employed the coal-merchant to open the trap in order to put in the coals; and he trusted him to guard it whilst open, and to close it when the coals were all put in. The act of opening it was the act of the employer, though done through the agency of the coal merchant; and the defendant, having thereby caused danger, was bound to take reasonable means to prevent mischief. The performance of this duty he omitted; and the fact of his having intrusted it to a person who also neglected it, furnishes no excuse, either in good sense or law."

14–38   In *Bower v Peate*,[142] where the defendant was held liable for the act of his contractor in letting down a house entitled to support, the rule was put even more strongly by Cockburn C.J., thus:

> "A man who orders a work to be executed, from which, in the natural course of things, injurious consequences to his neighbour must be expected to arise, unless means are adopted by which such consequences may be prevented, is bound to see to the doing of that which is necessary to prevent the mischief, and cannot relieve himself of his responsibility by employing someone else—whether it be the contractor employed to do the work from which the danger arises or some independent person—to do what is necessary to prevent the act he has ordered to be done from becoming wrongful. There is an

---

[140] *Hole v Sittingbourne Ry* (1861) 6 H. & N. 488; *Pickard v Smith* (1861) 10 C.B. (n.s.) 470; *Gray v Pullen* (1864) 5 B. & S. 970; *Holliday v National Telephone Co* [1899] 2 Q.B. 392; *The Snark* [1900] P. 105.

[141] (1861) 10 C.B. (n.s.) 470 at 480.

[142] (1876) 1 Q.B.D. 321 at 326, 327. The decision was approved by the House of Lords in *Dalton v Angus* (1881) 6 App. Cas. 740 at 791, 829.

obvious difference between committing work to a contractor to be executed from which, if properly done, no injurious consequences can arise, and handing over to him work to be done from which mischievous consequences will arise unless preventive measures are adopted. While it may be just to hold the party authorizing the work in the former case exempt from liability for injury, resulting from negligence which he had no reason to anticipate, there is, on the other hand, good ground for holding him liable for injury caused by an act certain to be attended with injurious consequences if such consequences are not in fact prevented, no matter through whose default the omission to take the necessary measures for such prevention may arise."

The first part of the passage above quoted was, in *Hughes v Percival*,[143] objected to by Lord Blackburn as being so broadly stated as to appear to conflict with *Quarman v Burnett*,[144] but the substance of the law is quite clear, and was in fact applied in *Hughes v Percival*[145] itself. There the defendant, having authorised a contractor to perform some building operations which involved a use of the party-wall between his premises and the plaintiff's, and a risk to the plaintiff's premises themselves, was held liable for damage caused to the plaintiff's premises in the course of the operations by workmen employed by the contractor. Lord Fitzgerald said[146]:   **14–39**

"The law has been verging somewhat in the direction of treating parties engaged in such an operation as the defendant's as insurers of their neighbours, or warranting them against injury. It has not, however, reached quite to that point. It does declare that under such a state of circumstances it was the duty of the defendant to have used every reasonable precaution that care and skill might suggest in the execution of his works, so as to protect his neighbours from injury, and that he cannot get rid of the responsibility thus cast on him by transferring that duty to another. He is not in the actual position of being responsible for injury, no matter how occasioned, but he must be vigilant and careful, for he is liable for injuries to his neighbour caused by any want of prudence or precaution, even though it may be culpa levissima."[147]

(2) *Title to the easement*

Easements

Where a landowner is enjoying the de facto benefit of an easement, for instance, of support for his buildings, but has no title to an easement, he cannot of course   **14–40**

---

[143] (1883) 8 App. Cas. 443 at 447.
[144] (1840) 6 M. & W. 499 (a case concerned with vicarious liability: see para.14–36, above).
[145] (1883) 8 App. Cas. 443.
[146] (1883) 8 App. Cas. 443 at 455.
[147] *cf.* as to the liabilities of local authorities for the default of their contractors, *Smith v West Derby Board* (1878) 3 C.P.D. 423; *Hardaker v Idle Council* [1896] 1 Q.B. 335; *Penny v Wimbledon Council* [1898] 2 Q.B. 212; [1899] 2 Q.B. 72; *Hill v Tottenham Council* (1899) 79 L.T. 495.

sue the lawful owner of the land providing the de facto benefit for its disturbance. Where, however, something is done on property A, to the detriment of property B, by X, a stranger to A, there is authority for the proposition that the owner or occupier of B can sue X without alleging or proving any easement, even though, vis-à-vis the owners and occupiers of A, B has no natural right of immunity against the consequences of the thing done by X.[148] This proposition, however, cannot be regarded with certainty as a general statement of the law. Each of the authorities which supports it concerns action against a stranger (that is not the owner or occupier of the quasi-servient tenement) for the disturbance of de facto support enjoyed by buildings on the quasi-dominant tenement. There is one authority which suggests that even against a stranger title to the easement must be shown.[149]

Profits

14–41   On the other hand, it is quite clear that the person in actual enjoyment of a *profit à prendre* can maintain an action of trespass against any person who disturbs his enjoyment,[150] save the owner of the servient tenement and persons holding under him; as against the latter a good title to the *profit à prendre* must be shown. The reason given for the distinction from easements in this respect is that a profit à prendre is an interest capable of existing in gross and is protected by an action in trespass; possession, therefore, is all that need be proved.[151] On the other hand, an easement is protected by an action in nuisance and it depends for its existence upon being attached to a dominant tenement; its mode of origin must therefore be proved.[152]

Equitable easements

14–42   Where a landowner has a right in the nature of an easement arising from an application of equitable principles,[153] he may sue the owner of the servient tenement

---

[148] *Jeffries v Williams* (1850) 5 Exch. 792; *Bibby v Carter* (1859) 4 H. & N. 153; *Richards v Jenkins* (1868) 18 L.T. 437 at 443, 444; *Keegan v Young* [1963] N.Z.L.R. 720.

[149] *Paine & Co v St Neots Gas & Coke Co* [1938] 4 All E.R. 592; [1939] 3 All E.R. 812, per Goddard L.J. at first instance, and, on appeal, per Luxmoore L.J.; Scott and Finlay L.JJ. expressing no opinion. In *Keegan v Young* [1963] N.Z.L.R. 720, however, the decision was distinguished. In *Salmond on Torts* (6th ed.), p. 302, Sir John Salmond suggested that as against a stranger de facto possession of an easement was sufficient if the disturbance produced harmful effects to the dominant tenement, but where the act complained of produced no such harmful effects a legal right had to be proved even against a stranger. Thus, a landowner could sue a stranger for interfering with de facto support to buildings, for blocking up his windows, or for interfering with his water supply, but not for interfering with his use of a right of way across another's land. This distinction, however, may not be valid since *Paine & Co v St Neots Gas & Coke Co*, above, where an interference with a de facto water supply was held not actionable.

[150] *Fitzgerald v Firbank* [1897] 2 Ch. 96.

[151] *Paine & Co v St Neots Gas & Coke Co* [1938] 4 All E.R. 592 at 597; [1939] 3 All E.R. 812 at 823.

[152] [1938] 4 All E.R. 598; [1939] 3 All E.R. 823 at 824.

[153] See, e.g. *Ward v Kirkland* [1967] Ch. 194; *E. R. Ives Investments Ltd v High* [1967] 2 Q.B. 379.

for a disturbance of this right and obtain an injunction.[154] The right is capable of binding a successor in title to the servient tenement,[155] and a stranger to the servient tenement may be sued for a disturbance of the right.

(3) *Pleadings*

Allegation of title

Whenever a party claims more than he is entitled to of common right, he must allege in his pleading that he ought to have that which he demands.[156]   **14–43**

In early authorities a distinction is taken as to the mode of alleging title in actions against strangers and in actions against the terre-tenant of the servient tenement: in the former case it was admitted that a general allegation, "that he had and ought to have the right claimed", was sufficient; whilst in the latter case it was said that a title by grant or prescription must be shown, it being an attempt to "put a charge upon" the defendant.[157] By subsequent decisions it appears to have been held that in all actions for disturbance of an easement, whether the action be brought against the servient owner or a stranger, a general allegation of right was sufficient.[158] Where, however, the defendant justified his act by virtue of an easement he was obliged to set out the particular title upon which he relied, whether by grant or prescription.[159]

Pleadings after the Prescription Act 1832

In the case of actions brought after the Prescription Act 1832 modifications in pleading were introduced by section 5 of the Act.[160] Under this section it is necessary for the claimant to allege enjoyment "as of right" in claiming a prescriptive right of way,[161] but not in claiming a prescriptive right to light[162]; enjoyment   **14–44**

---

[154] *Ward v Kirkland* [1967] Ch. 194; *Celsteel v Alton House Holdings Ltd* [1985] 1 W.L.R. 204 (not affected on this point by the decision of the Court of Appeal at [1986] 1 W.L.R. 512), followed in *Thatcher v Douglas* [1996] New L.J. 282.

[155] *E. R. Ives Investments Ltd v High* [1967] 2 Q.B. 379. For the circumstances where an equitable easement is binding on a successor in title to the servient tenement and the relevance of the Land Charges Act 1972 and the Land Registration Act 1925, see para.2–36, above.

[156] *Wyatt v Harrison* (1832) 3 B. & Ald. 871; *Tebbutt v Selby* (1837) 6 A. & E. 786; *Laing v Whaley* (1858) 3 H. & N. 675 at 901.

[157] *St John v Moody* (1687) 3 Keb. 528 at 531; *Winford v Wollaston* (1689) 3 Lev. 266; *Blockley v Slater* (1693) 1 Lut. fol. 119. *Cf. Bullard v Harrison* (1815) 4 M. & S. 387.

[158] *Sands v Trefuses* (1640) Cro.Car. 575; *Villers v Ball* (1689) 1 Show. 7; *Tenant v Goldwin* (1705) 1 Salk. 360; S.C. 2 Ld.Raym. 1089; *Rider v Smith* (1790) 3 T.R. 766; 2 Wms.Saund. 113a, note; 2 Notes to Saund. 361; Com.Dig. Pleader (C. 39); see also *Trower v Chadwick* (1836) 3 Scott 699; 3 Bing.N.C. 334; *Paine & Co v St Neots Gas & Coke Co* [1939] 3 All E.R. 812 at 823; [1938] 4 All E.R. 592 at 598.

[159] See Com.Dig. Chimin, D. 2; 1 Wms.Saund. 624; *Bird v Dickinson* (1701) 2 Lut. 1526; *Grimstead v Marlowe* (1792) 4 T.R. 717; *Bailey v Appleyard* (1838) 8 A. & E. 167.

[160] See para.4–48, above.

[161] *Holford v Hankinson* (1844) 5 Q.B. 584. For a modern example, see *Copeland v Greenhalf* [1952] Ch. 488 at 490.

[162] See *Colls v Home and Colonial Stores* [1904] A.C. 179 at 205.

as of right meaning an enjoyment *nec vi, nec clam, nec precario.*[163] If the other party intends to rely on any proviso, exception, incapacity, disability, contract, agreement or other matter mentioned in the Act, or on any cause or matter of fact or of law not inconsistent with the simple fact of enjoyment, he must specially allege it.

14–45   "The simple fact of enjoyment" was explained in the judgments quoted below to mean a continuous enjoyment as of right, and as an easement. Having regard to these words, the courts held that it was necessary to allege specially things consistent with such enjoyment, for example a tenancy for life,[164] or a licence extending over the whole period,[165] or such facts as that during the first part of the period of enjoyment the user was in exercise of a statutory right; and the statutory right having ceased, the enjoyment was continued for the rest of the period,[166] but that it was not necessary to allege specially things inconsistent with such enjoyment—for example unity of ownership, or stealth, or leave given during the period,[167] all of which could be given in evidence under a general traverse.

14–46   In *Tickle v Brown*[168] it was held that where a defendant justifies under an enjoyment of 20 or 40 years, if the plaintiff relies upon a licence covering the whole of that period he must plead such licence specially, but a licence granted and acted upon during the period may be given in evidence under the general traverse of the enjoyment "as showing that there was not, at the time when the agreement was made, an enjoyment as of right; and so the continuity is broken, which is inconsistent with the simple fact of enjoyment during the forty or twenty years".

14–47   In *Beasley v Clarke*[169] Tindal C.J. said:

> "Under a plea denying that the Defendant had used the way for forty years, as of right and without interruption, the Plaintiff is at liberty to shew the character and description of the user and enjoyment of the way during any part of the time; as that it was used by stealth, or in the absence of the occupier of the close and without his knowledge, or that it was merely a precarious enjoyment by leave or licence, or any other circumstances which negative that it is an user or enjoyment under a claim of right; the words of the fifth section, 'not inconsistent with the simple fact of enjoyment,' being referable, as we understand the statute, to the fact of enjoyment as before stated in the Act, viz. an enjoyment claimed and exercised 'as of right'."

---

[163] See *Gardner v Hodgson's Kingston Brewery* [1903] A.C. 229 at 238.
[164] *Pye v Mumford* (1848) 11 Q.B. 666; *Warburton v Parke* (1857) 2 H. & N. 64. See s.7 of the Act, para.4–50, above.
[165] *Tickle v Brown* (1836) 4 A. & E. 369 at 382.
[166] *Kinloch v Nevile* (1840) 6 M. & W. 795.
[167] *Monmouth Canal Co v Harford* (1834) 1 C.M. & R. 614; *Beasley v Clarke* (1836) 2 Bing.N.C. 705; *Onley v Gardiner* (1838) 4 M. & W. 496; *R.P.C. Holdings Ltd v Rogers* [1953] 1 All E.R. 1029 at 1036A–B; *Mills v Silver* [1991] Ch. 271 at 277G–H.
[168] (1836) 4 A. & E. 369.
[169] (1836) 2 Bing.N.C. 705 at 709.

In *Onley v Gardiner*[170] the Court of Exchequer decided that unity of actual pos- **14–48** session was inconsistent with the simple fact of enjoyment as of right, and, therefore, need not be specially pleaded. The simple fact of enjoyment, referred to in section 5, is an enjoyment as of right; and proof that there was an occasional unity of actual possession is as much in denial of that allegation as the occasionally asking permission would be; because the enjoyment during the unity of possession could not be an enjoyment as of an easement.

The disabilities and exceptions mentioned in sections 7 and 8 must be alleged **14–49** in answer to a pleading claiming an easement under the Act[171]; so must the fact that the enjoyment was under a statutory right which ceased before the expiration of the required period of enjoyment[172]; or that the servient owner and his agents were absent from the neighbourhood and ignorant of the enjoyment during the whole period; or, in short, any other facts which would rebut the inference of a right by prescription or grant. Sections 7 and 8 only apply to the easements included in section 2, so that those sections cannot be set up in answer to a claim to an easement of light by virtue of 20 years' enjoyment.

Pleading prescriptive rights under the Civil Procedure Rules

The above requirements must now be read in connection with the rules of plead- **14–50** ing established under the Civil Procedure Rules.[173] CPR Pt 16.4 provides that particulars of claim must include a concise statement of the facts on which the claimant relies. The claimant should state all the facts necessary for the purpose of formulating a complete cause of action. Where a claim is made for an injunction or declaration in respect of or relating to any land, the particulars of claim must state whether or not the injunction or declaration relates to residential premises and identify the land.[174]

Where a claim is based upon a written agreement, a copy of the contract or documents constituting the agreement should be attached to or served with the particulars of claim and the original should be available at the hearing.[175] In his defence, the defendant must state (a) which of the allegations in the particulars of claim he denies; (b) which allegations he is unable to admit or deny, but which he requires the claimant to prove; and (c) which allegations he admits.[176] Where the defendant denies an allegation, he must state his reasons for doing so and, if he intends to put forward a different version of events from that given by the claimant, he must state his own version.[177] A party may: (1) refer in his statement

---

[170] (1838) 4 M. & W. 498.
[171] *Pye v Mumford* (1848) 11 Q.B. 666. As to pleading where a tenancy for life is alleged, see *ibid.*; also *Clayton v Corby* (1842) 2 Q.B. 813.
[172] *Kinloch v Nevile* (1840) 6 M. & W. 795.
[173] Made under the Civil Procedure Act 1997.
[174] CPR 16PD.7.1.
[175] CPR 16PD.7.3.
[176] CPR Pt 16.5(1).
[177] CPR Pt 16.5(2).

of case to any point of law on which his claim or defence is based; (2) give in his statement of case the name of any witness he proposes to call; and (3) attach to or serve with his statement of case a copy of any document which he considers is necessary to his claim or defence (including an expert's report).[178] All pleadings must be verified by a statement of truth in the form required by the rules. Further guidelines on the contents of statements of case may be found in Appendix 2 to the Chancery Guide.[179] In particular, it is provided that any matter which, if not stated might take another party by surprise, should be stated.

14–51   The general allegations and denials which were sufficient within section 5 of the Prescription Act 1832 are now insufficient. Accordingly, in an action to restrain the obstruction of an alleged private right of way, the plaintiff was held bound in pleading to state the title by which he claimed, and whether by grant or by prescriptive user.[180] Where in trespass the defendants pleaded that the *locus in quo* was a highway, they were ordered to show the mode in which they claimed that it had become a highway, and to give particulars of dedication.[181]

14–52   Whether the action be brought against the servient owner or a stranger, a party cannot safely allege his right to an easement generally, but should state specifically the manner in which he claims title to the easement, whether by grant (actual or lost), prescription at common law, or under the Prescription Act[182]; and in many cases it is advisable to plead, alternatively, a title by all three methods.[183] As the right to an easement exists in respect of the dominant tenement, the pleading usually states the possession of the tenement by the party, and that by reason thereof he was entitled to the right in question.

14–53   A pleading under the Prescription Act was required to state the enjoyment to have been without interruption.[184] Under a plea of 40 years' user, according to the statute, evidence of what took place before that period was admissible as showing the state of things at the commencement of the 40 years' enjoyment.[185] The necessity of giving particulars of a claim to an easement by prescription is less strict in the county court.[186]

---

[178] CPR 16PD.13.3.

[179] Civil Procedure, (2008 ed.) Vol. 2, 1A–208.

[180] *Harris v Jenkins* (1882) 22 Ch. D. 481; *Farrell v Coogan* (1890) 12 L.R.Ir. 14. See *Pledge v Pomfret* [1905] W.N. 56.

[181] *Spedding v Fitzpatrick* (1888) 38 Ch. D. 410.

[182] *Harris v Jenkins* (1882) 22 Ch. D. 481; and see *Smith v Baxter* [1900] 2 Ch. 138 at 146; *Hyman v Van den Bergh* [1907] 2 Ch. 516 at 524; [1908] 1 Ch. 167 at 169, 176; *cf. Spedding v Fitzpatrick* (1888) 38 Ch. D. 410; *Pledge v Pomfret* [1905] W.N. 56.

[183] In *Tehidy Minerals v Norman* [1971] 2 Q.B. 528 at 543, the Court of Appeal expressed the view that the coexistence of three separate methods of prescribing was anomalous and undesirable, for it resulted in much unnecessary complication and confusion. The court expressed the hope that it might "be possible for the Legislature to effect a long-overdue simplification in this branch of the law". It has not yet done so.

[184] per Patteson J. in *Richards v Fry* (1838) 7 A. & E. 698 at 701.

[185] *Lawson v Langley* (1836) 4 A. & E. 890.

[186] See *Pugh v Savage* [1970] 2 Q.B. 373.

Pleading grant

According to modern practice, a lost grant, if relied upon, should be pleaded[187]; but **14–54** claims based on lost grant have been added by amendment at the trial.[188] Formerly, the names of the parties to, and the date of, the supposed grant had to be stated[189]; but on averment that the deed had been lost profert was excused.[190] The statement of date and parties is no longer necessary.[191] Today it is accepted that, inasmuch as the grant is fictional, particulars will not be ordered of the persons by whom it was made and to whom and exactly when.[192] On the other hand, a party is entitled to know whether or not it is alleged that a lost grant was notionally made before or after certain dates, for example, before or after a private Act,[193] and may be ordered to plead accordingly, in which case he has the right to elect either alternative grants so as to cover the entire period of years or one specific period only, but, if he pleads in the alternative, he is at risk as to costs.[194]

There appears to be no precedent of a pleading of an easement arising from the disposition of the owner of two tenements; but it seems that, as in the case of easements of necessity, the right must be pleaded as arising by implied grant from the joint owner at the time of severance. The pleading might allege the joint ownership and subsequent conveyance, and aver the apparent and continuous nature of the easement, and its existence at the period of severance.

A pleading of an easement of necessity must, in like manner, allege the joint ownership at the time of the conveyance, and that the easement is essential to the full enjoyment of the principal thing conveyed or reserved.[195]

The party should describe in his pleading the nature of the right in question. Thus, in an action for the disturbance of a way, he should state the *terminus a quo* and *ad quem*, and the kind of way he claims, as a footway, etc.[196] A precise local description, as by alleging the land to be in any particular place, is not, however, requisite; and it is not necessary, although it is convenient, to give the intervening closes.[197]

Pleading damage

As regards the allegation and proof of damage, the rule should be borne in mind **14–55** that actual perceptible damage is not indispensable as the foundation of an action.

---

[187] *Smith v Baxter* [1900] 2 Ch. 147.
[188] *Brown v Dunstable Corp* [1899] 2 Ch. 380 at 387; *Gardner v Hodgson's Kingston Brewery Co* [1900] 1 Ch. 601.
[189] *Hendy v Stephenson* (1808) 10 East 55. See *Doe d. Fenwick v Reed* (1821) 5 B. & Ald. 232; *Liven v Wilson* (1825) 3 Bing. 115.
[190] *Read v Brookman* (1789) 3 T.R. 151.
[191] See the pleadings in *Duke of Norfolk v Arbuthnot* (1879) 4 C.P.D. 293; *Brown v Dunstable Corp* [1899] 2 Ch. 380.
[192] *Tremayne v English Clays Layering Pochin & Co Ltd* [1972] 1 W.L.R. 657; and see *Gabriel Wade & English Ltd v Dixon & Cardus Ltd* [1937] 3 All E.R. 900.
[193] *Palmer v Guadagni* [1906] 2 Ch. 494.
[194] *Palmer v Guadagni* [1906] 2 Ch. 494; *Tremayne v English Clays Levering Pochin & Co Ltd* [1972] 1 W.L.R. 657.
[195] *Proctor v Hodgson* (1855) 10 Ex. 824; *Bullard v Harrison* (1815) 4 M. & S. 387.
[196] See Com.Dig. Action on the Case for a Disturbance, B. (1); Chimin, D. (2); *Harris v Jenkins* (1882) 22 Ch. D. 481.
[197] *Simpson v Lewthwaite* (1832) 3 B. & Ald. 226; *Harris v Jenkins* (1882) 22 Ch. D. 481.

It is sufficient to show the violation of a right, in which case the law will presume damage.[198] Again, wherever any act injures another's rights and would be evidence in future in favour of the wrongdoer, an action may be maintained for the invasion of the right without proof of specific injury.[199] These rules have been applied in the case of actions of trespass to land[200]; in the case of actions for diversion of water (where it has been pointed out that the defendant might by the diversion acquire a right injurious to the plaintiff[201]); in the case of actions for pollution of water[202]; and in the case of actions for the disturbance of rights of way.[203]

In applying these rules, however, it is necessary to bear in mind the distinction between various "rights". Thus, where water was taken from a river by the licensee of an upper riparian owner, a lower riparian owner was refused an injunction on the ground that the water taken was returned undiminished in quantity and undeteriorated in quality, so that the acts of the licensee could never grow into a prescriptive title, and the right of the lower riparian proprietor was not in fact interfered with.[204] Again, as regards support, a landowner has the right to insist that his land shall not be let down by his neighbour's excavation; but supposing the neighbour were to excavate, the landowner has no right of action at law unless and until subsidence follows.[205]

In the case of an action for diversion of water, the principle that to sustain the action actual damage need not be alleged or proved applies not only in the case of natural rights, but also where rights in respect of water have been acquired by grant or user,[206] or arise under a statute.[207]

Allegation of disturbance

14–56   In *Mersey & Irwell v Douglas*,[208] an action on the case for a disturbance, it was held sufficient to allege a disturbance generally, without showing the particular manner of the disturbance.[209]

---

[198] per Parke B. in *Embrey v Owen* (1851) 6 Ex. 353 at 368; per Littledale J. in *Williams v Morland* (1824) 2 B. & C. 910 at 916.
[199] 1 Wms.Saund. 626.
[200] See the judgment of Lord Holt C.J. in *Ashby v White*, 1 Sm.L.C. (13th ed.), p. 253; (1703) 2 Ld.Raym. 938.
[201] *Wilts & Berks Canal Navigation Co v Swindon Waterworks Co* (1874) 9 Ch. App. 457 at 458; *Roberts v Gwyrfai D.C.* [1899] 2 Ch. 610. See *Embrey v Owen*, above; *Bickett v Morris* (1866) L.R. 1 H.L.Sc. 60; *Harrop v Hirst* (1868) L.R. 4 Ex. 47; *McCartney v Londonderry and Lough Swilly Ry* [1904] A.C. 313.
[202] *Jones v Llanrwst U.D.C.* [1911] 1 Ch. 402.
[203] *Bower v Hill* (1835) 1 Bing.N.C. 555; *Clifford v Hoare* (1874) L.R. 9 C.P. 372.
[204] *Kensit v G.E. Ry* (1884) 27 Ch. D. 130. See *McCartney v Londonderry and Lough Swilly Ry*, above, cf. *Ormerod v Todmorden Joint Stock Mill Co* (1883) 11 Q.B.D. 155; and see paras 6–70 to 6–73, above.
[205] *Backhouse v Bonomi* (1861) 9 H.L.C. 503; *Midland Bank Plc v Bardgrove Property Services Ltd* (1992) 65 P. & C.R. 153.
[206] *Northam v Hurley* (1853) 1 E. & B. 665; *Rawstron v Taylor* (1855) 11 Ex. 369; *Harrop v Hirst* (1868) L.R. 4 Ex. 47.
[207] *Rochdale Co v King* (1849) 14 Q.B. 122.
[208] (1802) 2 East 497.
[209] Com.Dig Action on the Case for a Disturbance, B. (1); Anon. (1566) 3 Leon. 13; *Dawney v Dee* (1620) Cro.Jac. 605.

In *Tebbutt v Selby*,[210] however, Patteson J. appears to have doubted whether such a general allegation of obstruction would be sufficient, and nowadays particulars would undoubtedly be ordered.

In a pleading by the reversioner he must show that he sues in that capacity, and allege that the disturbance is to the injury of his reversionary estate.[211]

(4) *Remedy by injunction*

Powers of court

The remedy which was afforded at common law for the continuous disturbance of 　**14–57** easements or other nuisances, by an indefinite series of actions for damage, was obviously, in many cases, quite inadequate; and the Court of Chancery always exercised the power of interfering, by injunction, to stop the whole mischief complained of.[212]

The foundation of the plaintiff's right in such cases being a right at common law, the Court of Chancery, before finally granting equitable relief, at one time required that the legal right of the person seeking relief should be established in a proceeding at law.[213] Since the Judicature Act 1873, the jurisdiction both of the Court of Chancery and of the common law courts has been vested in the High Court of Justice, and today all courts have power to entertain legal and equitable claims and defences alike.[214]

Perpetual injunctions

Before a perpetual injunction can be granted to restrain a private nuisance or the 　**14–58** disturbance of an easement, the court as a general rule requires the party to establish his legal right and the fact of its violation. But when these things have been established, then, unless there be something special in the case, the party is entitled as of course to an injunction to prevent the recurrence of that violation.[215] An easement is a legal right. The remedy by injunction is in aid of that legal right. The owner of the right is entitled to a prohibitory (or negative), as opposed to a mandatory,[216] injunction, not in the discretion of the court, but of course; unless

---

[210] (1837) 6 A. & E. 793.

[211] *Jackson v Pesked* (1813) 1 M. & S. 234.

[212] *Robinson v Byron* (1785) 1 Bro.C.C. 588 (watercourse); *Thorpe v Brumfitt* (1873) 8 Ch. App. 650 (way); *Arcedeckne v Kelk* (1858) 2 Giff. 683; *Herz v Union Bank of London* (1854) 2 Giff. 686; and *Wilson v Townend* (1860) 1 Dr. & Sm. 324 (light); *Hunt v Peake* (1860) John. 705 (natural right of support); *N.E. Ry v Elliott* (1863) 10 H.L.C. 333 (easement of support).

[213] See *Imperial Gas Light & Coke Co v Broadbent* (1859) 7 H.L.C. 600; *Cardiff Corp v Cardiff Waterworks Co* (1859) 4 De G. & J. 596; *Eaden v Firth* (1863) 1 H. & M. 573; *Roskell v Whitworth* (1870) 5 Ch. App. 459. It never was a ground of demurrer that the legal right had not yet been tried, though it was a ground for not granting interlocutory injunctions.

[214] Supreme Court Act 1981, s.49.

[215] *Imperial Gas Co v Broadbent* (1859) 7 H.L.C. 612; *Fullwood v Fullwood* (1878) 9 Ch. D. 176; *Martin v Price* [1894] 1 Ch. 285; *Regan v Paul Properties Ltd* [2006] EWCA Civ 1391; [2007] Ch. 135.

[216] See para.14–65, below.

there is something special in the case, for instance laches, or the fact that the disturbance is only trivial or occasional.[217] The cost to the defendant of complying with a negative injunction is not a factor to be taken into account.[218] The grounds on which the court acts in granting an injunction were thus stated by Page Wood L.J. in *Att-Gen v Cambridge Consumers Gas Co*[219]:

"Where the Court interferes by way of injunction to prevent an injury in respect of which there is a legal remedy, it does so upon two grounds, which are of a totally distinct character; one is that the injury is irreparable, as in the case of cutting down trees; the other that the injury is continuous, and so continuous that the Court acts upon the same principle as it used in older times with reference to bills of peace, and restrains the repeated acts which could only result in incessant actions, the continuous character of the wrong making it grievous and intolerable. As an illustration of this class of case, I may refer to *Soltau v De Held*,[220] where the annoyance from the ringing of the bell was in itself slight, but it was so continuous that the Court thought fit to arrest the nuisance brevi manu, and save the complainant all further annoyance."

"Irreparable injury" has been referred to as meaning injury which cannot be compensated in damages.[221]

14–59   To obtain an injunction, proof of actual damage is not necessary where a right of property has been infringed[222]; or where the parties to a contract for valuable consideration with their eyes open have contracted that a particular thing shall not be done.[223] Again, where the wrong is of a recurring nature an injunction may be obtained even though the actual damage is slight.[224] The court, however, will not interfere by injunction where the violation of a legal right is trivial,[225] nor will it interfere by injunction to restrain actionable wrongs for which damages are the proper remedy.[226]

---

[217] *Cowper v Laidler* [1903] 2 Ch. 339 at 341.
[218] *Redland Bricks Ltd v Morris* [1970] A.C. 652 at 664.
[219] (1868) 4 Ch. App. 71 at 80, 81.
[220] (1852) 2 Sim. (n.s.) 133.
[221] *Att-Gen v Hallett* (1847) 16 M. & W. 581; *Mogul Steamship Co v M'Gregor* (1885) 15 Q.B.D. 486.
[222] *Jones v Llanrwst U.D.C.* [1911] 1 Ch. 393 at 402 (where Parker J. refers to other authorities); *Thorpe v Brumfitt* (1873) 8 Ch. App. 656; *Pennington v Brinsop Hall Coal Co* (1877) 5 Ch. D. 772.
[223] *Doherty v Allmann* (1873) 3 A.C. 709 at 719.
[224] *Clowes v Staffordshire Waterworks Co* (1872) 8 Ch. App. 142.
[225] *Coulson v White* (1743) 3 Atk. 21; *Att-Gen v Sheffield Gas Consumers' Co* (1853) 3 De G.M. & G. 304; *Swaine v G.N. Ry* (1864) 10 Jur. (n.s.) 191; *Durrell v Pritchard* (1865) 1 Ch. App. 244; *Cooke v Forbes* (1867) L.R. 5 Eq. 166; *Att-Gen v Cambridge Consumers' Gas Co* (1868) 4 Ch. App. 71; *Llandudno Urban Council v Woods* [1899] 2 Ch. 705; *Behrens v Richards* [1905] 2 Ch. 614; *Armstrong v Sheppard & Short Ltd* [1959] 2 Q.B. 384; *Tamares Ltd v Fairpoint Properties Ltd* [2006] EWHC 3589 (Ch.); [2007] 1 W.L.R. 2148.
[226] *Wood v Sutcliffe* (1851) 2 Sim. (n.s.) 165; *London and Blackwall Ry v Cross* (1886) 31 Ch. D. 369.

Can a final injunction be varied?

Does the court have jurisdiction to vary or discharge a final injunction restrain- **14–60**
ing interference with an easement if circumstances change? The question arose in
Rosling v Pinnegar (No.2).[227] The facts of the original case are set out in
para.9–67, above. The case resulted in a detailed order limiting the size of vehicles which could use the lane at the days and times when the owner of
Hammerwood House could open it to the public. Subsequently the owner
acquired ownership of a substantial part of the lane (subject to the rights of way
of the villagers), obtained planning permission to fell certain trees and proposed
to widen the lane so as to create three passing places with a view to addressing
the congestion which had been a major ground for the grant of the injunction.

The judge at first instance held that he had no jurisdiction to vary or discharge
a final injunction but considered the facts *de bene esse* and found that the
improvements proposed would increase the traffic and thus the interference with
the villagers' rights; he would therefore not have varied the order even if he had
jurisdiction to do so.

The Court of Appeal were prepared to assume (1) that an express "liberty to
apply" gives the court power to review the terms of a final order in relation to the
working out or carrying out of it; (2) that in very exceptional cases, such as where
there has been a fundamental and unforeseen change of circumstances, the court
has a residual power to review the exercise of its discretion granting a final
injunction; and (3) that RSC Ord. 45, r.11 (which gives the court power to stay
execution of an order or grant "other relief" on the ground of matters which have
occurred since the date of the order) was applicable. Nevertheless, in the light of
the judge's findings of fact, they held that the matters relied on were not such serious, relevant and unforeseen changes of circumstances as could possibly justify
the Court in varying the injunction.

On the point of principle it is submitted, first, that "liberty to apply", unless **14–61**
expressly extended to include the power to apply for the subsequent variation of
the order, only applies to its "working out" and so confers no jurisdiction to vary
a final order. Secondly, it is very doubtful whether there is any residual jurisdiction to vary a final order. In *Co-operative Insurance Society Limited v Argyll
Stores (Holdings) Limited*[228] Lord Hoffmann said that there was no case in this
jurisdiction in which a final order of the Court had been varied or discharged
except when the activity enjoined had been legalised by statute and suggested that,
even if there were such a jurisdiction if circumstances changed radically, circumstances which were predictable when the order was made would not suffice.[229] In

---

[227] [1998] EWCA Civ 1510.
[228] [1998] A.C. 1 at 18A.
[229] In making these remarks Lord Hoffmann probably had in mind the Australian case of *CSIRO v
Perry* (1988) 92 F.L.R. 182 at 185, in which it was said that the researches of counsel had not discovered any case in Australia or England in which a permanent injunction had been dissolved in
a subsequent action but the court dissolved an injunction on the ground that the prohibited act had
subsequently been authorised by statute.

argument in *Att-Gen v Colchester Corporation*[230] Lord Goddard C.J. rejected the suggestion that an order once made could be dissolved.[231]

14–62   In *Midtown Limited v City of London Real Property Company Limited*,[232] the claimant was seeking an injunction to prevent the defendant building in a way which would interfere with the claimants' right of light. The evidence showed that the claimants had proposals for redeveloping their own building. The Judge observed that, if an injunction were granted, it would be unfortunate if the property was subsequently redeveloped and the windows and the rights enjoyed by those windows were no longer used. The claimants' counsel submitted that the defendant could in those circumstances apply to the Court for a discharge of any perpetual injunction but the Judge doubted this in view of Lord Hoffmann's dicta in *Co-operative Insurance Society Limited v Argyll Stores (Holdings) Limited*.[233] Counsel then suggested that the situation could be dealt with by an undertaking on the part of the claimants to agree to have any perpetual injunction discharged in the event that they no longer wished to use the easements of light protected by the injunction but the Judge (Peter Smith J.) was unconvinced that this was a satisfactory solution.

14–63   It is now provided by CPR Pt 3.1(7) that the power of the court to make an order under the CPR includes a power to vary or revoke the order. In *Lloyds Investment (Scandinavia) Ltd v Christen Ager-Hanssen*,[234] Patten J. stated his understanding of the effect of that provision in the following passage:

> "This is not confined to purely procedural orders and there is no real guidance in the White Book as to the possible limits of the jurisdiction. Although this is not intended to be an exhaustive definition of the circumstances in which the power under CPR Part 3.1(7) is exercisable, it seems to me that, for the High Court to revisit one of its earlier orders, the Applicant must either show some material change of circumstances or that the judge who made the earlier order was misled in some way, whether innocently or otherwise, as to the correct factual position before him. The latter type of case would include, for example, a case of material non-disclosure on an application for an injunction. If all that is sought is a reconsideration of the order on the basis of the same material, then that can only be done, in my judgment, in the context of an appeal. Similarly it is not, I think, open to a party to the earlier application to seek in effect to re-argue that application by relying on submissions and evidence which were available to him at the

---

[230] [1955] 2 Q.B. 207.
[231] See also *St Nazaire Co, Re* (1879) 12 Ch. D. 88; *Jordan v Norfolk C.C.* [1994] 1 W.L.R. 1353 (on analysis, a case of the "working out" of the previous order); *Phonographic Performance Limited v Maitra* [1998] 1 W.L.R. 870 at 879F–G (where the Court of Appeal envisaged application being made for the discharge of an injunction awarded in default of defence—but setting aside or varying such a judgment was expressly provided for in the rules: RSC, Ord. 19, r.9).
[232] [2005] EWHC 33; [2005] 1 E.G.L.R. 65.
[233] [1998] A.C. 1 at 18.
[234] [2003] EWHC 1740 (Ch.).

time of the earlier hearing, but which, for whatever reason, he or his legal representatives chose not to employ."

In *Advent Capital Plc v GN Ellinas Imports-Exports Ltd*[235] Colman J. said that he **14–64** agreed with that analysis and added:

"if a permanent prohibitory injunction is granted on the assumption that the private rights of the party to be protected will continue to exist into the future and to require such protection but yet as matters turn out, those rights do at some future time cease to exist or to be enforceable either by statute or operation of law, that would normally be a situation where the jurisdiction of a judge of first instance could be engaged upon an application to revoke the original order and it would not be necessary or appropriate to appeal the original order out of time. Thus in this case, if by a change in the law which occurred after the making of the order of Morison J. the rights which it was the purpose of that order to protect ceased to exist, the underlying assumption of that order would have gone and it would be open to this court to decide whether in consequence the order should be revoked."

Mandatory injunction

The jurisdiction to grant a mandatory injunction, even on interlocutory motion, **14–65** has often been asserted.[236] A distinction was taken in some early cases between those injunctions which merely prevent the doing of an act and those the consequence of which, either directly or indirectly, will be to compel a party to do some act, as to fill up a ditch,[237] or pull down a wall[238]; the former being granted on motion, the latter only at the trial. This distinction, however, though recognised, does not appear to have been strictly adhered to: indeed, in one case,[239] Lord Eldon, though he refused the order, as prayed, specifically to repair the banks of a canal and stop-gates and other works, purposely made an order in such a form as to have the same effect, by making it difficult for the defendant to avoid completely repairing his works. And in commenting on this case, in *Blakemore v Glamorganshire Canal Navigation*,[240] Lord Brougham L.C. said:

". . . if the Court has this jurisdiction, it would be better to exercise it directly and at once; and I will further take leave to add, that the having recourse to

---

[235] [2005] EWHC 1242 (Comm) at [74].
[236] *Mexborough v Bower* (1843) 7 Beav 127; *Hervey v Smith* (1855) 1 K. & J. 389; *Beadel v Perry* (1866) L.R. 3 Eq. 465; *Westminster Brymbo, etc., Co v Clayton* (1867) 36 L.J.Ch. 476; *Shephard Homes v Sandham* [1971] Ch. 340; but see *Locabail International Finance Ltd v Agroexport* [1986] 1 W.L.R. 657 at 663, 664.
[237] *Robinson v Byron* (1785) 1 Bro.C.C. 588.
[238] *Ryder v Bentham* (1750) 1 Ves.Sen. 543.
[239] *Lane v Newdigate* (1804) 10 Ves. 192.
[240] (1832) 1 My. & K. 154 at 184; *cf.* the observations of Lord Jessel M.R. in *Smith v Smith* (1875) L.R. 20 Eq. 500 at 504; and *Bidwell v Holden* (1890) 63 L.T. 104.

a roundabout mode of obtaining the object, seems to cast a doubt upon the jurisdiction."

The court has now departed from the "roundabout mode", and where an injunction is granted, the effect of which is to require the performance of a certain act, such as the pulling down and removal of buildings, the order is made in a direct mandatory form, and not in the indirect form formerly in use.[241]

14-66   Such an injunction may order the pulling down of work done or erected after the commencement of an action, or after notice given to the defendant that his erecting it will be objected to[242] even where the work or erection was completed before the writ was issued.[243] On the question of granting such an injunction it is important to see if the defendant knew that he was doing wrong.[244] Further, an injunction may not be granted if the injury to the claimant can be estimated and sufficiently compensated by an award of damages,[245] and is restricted to cases where extreme or very serious damage would ensue from not granting it[246]; although these are now factors which may justify an award of damages in lieu of an injunction rather than a refusal of an injunction *ab initio*.[247]

14-67   Unlike a prohibitory injunction, a mandatory injunction is entirely discretionary and can never be granted "as of course", every case depending upon its own particular circumstances,[248] but it may be granted *quia timet*.[249] So in *Snell & Prideaux Limited v Dutton Mirrors Limited*,[250] where the Court of Appeal held that a right to use a passage for vehicles had not been abandoned and had been obstructed by a new building, an injunction requiring the building to be demolished was refused and damages awarded equal to the diminution in value of the plaintiffs' property caused by the restriction of the access in circumstances where:

(a) the defendants had not ridden roughshod over clear and long exercised rights but rather had acted on the bona fide but (as it turned out) mistaken advice of their solicitors and had an arguable case;

(b) the defendants had invited the plaintiffs to apply for an interlocutory injunction before they started building but the plaintiffs had not done so because they did not wish to give an undertaking in damages; and

---

[241] *Jackson v Normanby Brick Co* [1899] 1 Ch. 438; *Seton's Judgments and Orders* (7th ed.), pp. 369, 539.

[242] *Kelk v Pearson* (1871) 6 Ch. App. 809; *Smith v Day* (1880) 13 Ch. D. 651; *Clifford v Holt* [1899] 1 Ch. 698.

[243] *Lawrence v Horton* (1890) 62 L.T. 749; *Mortimer v Bailey* [2004] EWCA Civ 1514; [2005] 1 E.G.L.R. 75.

[244] *Smith v Smith* (1875) L.R. 20 Eq. 500 at 503; *Lawrence v Horton* (1890) 62 L.T. 749; *Pugh v Howells* (1984) 48 P. & C.R. 298.

[245] *Isenberg v East India House Estate Co Ltd* (1863) 3 De G.J. & S. 263.

[246] *Durell v Pritchard* (1865) 1 Ch. App. 244.

[247] See para.14-86, below.

[248] *Smith v Smith* (1875) L.R. 20 Eq. 500 at 503; *Gaskin v Balls* (1879) 13 Ch. D. 324; *Shiel v Godfrey* [1893] W.N. 115; *Tollemache & Cobbold Breweries Ltd v Reynolds* [1983] 2 E.G.L.R. 158.

[249] See below.

[250] [1995] 1 E.G.L.R. 259, distinguishing *Krehl v Burrell* (1879) 11 Ch. D. 146.

(c) the plaintiffs had made no use of the access for many years and had an alternative access to the premises.

There must be no delay or acquiescence on the part of the plaintiff if he is to be granted a mandatory injunction,[251] unless this can be adequately explained.[252] Indeed, in circumstances where there had been both delay and acquiescence and where the plaintiff deliberately refrained from applying for an interlocutory injunction so as to avoid having to give an undertaking in damages, the claim for a mandatory injunction was struck out as vexatious and an abuse of the process of the court.[253]   **14–68**

Quia timet injunction

There may arise a situation where it is apprehended that there may be injury to an easement or natural right, although the injury has not so far occurred. In such a case an injunction may be obtained in a *quia timet* action. Such an action is broadly applicable in two types of case.[254] First, in a case where the defendant has as yet done no hurt to the claimant but is threatening to do works which will render irreparable harm to him or his property if carried to completion. Cases of this kind are normally, though not always, concerned with negative injunctions. The second type of case arises where the claimant has been fully recompensed in law and in equity for the damage he has suffered (for example by an award of damages and an injunction restraining the defendant from further activity) but where he alleges that the earlier actions of the defendant may lead to future causes of action, for example, where the defendant has constituted a menace to the claimant's land by withdrawing support from it or depositing on it soil from his mining operations.[255] Here the court has jurisdiction to grant a mandatory injunction ordering the defendant to carry out positive works. These two types of case will now be considered in turn.   **14–69**

In the first type of case the defendant may be carrying on an activity which, when completed, may infringe the rights of the claimant, for example, by erecting a building which threatens to obstruct a right of light[256] or way,[257] or by so mining his land as to threaten to interfere with the support of the land of the claimant.[258] If an injunction to restrain the activity is to be granted there must be a strong probability that the activity will cause injury to the claimant.[259] Although   **14–70**

[251] See, e.g. *Baxter v Bower* (1875) 23 W.R. 805.
[252] *Redland Bricks Ltd v Morris* [1970] A.C. 652 at 665.
[253] *Blue Town Investments Limited v Higgs & Hill Plc* [1991] 1 W.L.R. 696; but *cf. Oxy Electric Limited v Zainuddin* [1991] 1 W.L.R. 115.
[254] *Redland Bricks Ltd v Morris* [1970] A.C. 652 at 665.
[255] *Kennard v Cory Bros & Co Ltd* [1922] 1 Ch. 265; *Redland Bricks Ltd v Morris* [1970] A.C. 652.
[256] *Litchfield-Speer v Queen Anne's Gate Syndicate* [1919] 1 Ch. 407, where it was said that the decision in *Colls v Home and Colonial Stores* [1904] A.C. 179 had not abrogated the right to relief in a *quia timet* action.
[257] *Celsteel Ltd v Alton House Holdings Ltd* [1985] 1 W.L.R. 204; [1986] 1 W.L.R. 512.
[258] *Siddons v Short and Harley & Co* (1877) 2 C.P.D. 572.
[259] *Pattisson v Gilford* (1874) L.R. 18 Eq. 259; *Fletcher v Bealey* (1884) 28 Ch. D. 688 at 698; *Att-Gen v Manchester Corp* [1893] 2 Ch. 87 at 92; *Litchfield-Speer v Queen Anne's Gate Syndicate* [1919] 1 Ch. 407 at 411.

it has sometimes been said that the apprehended injury must be irreparable,[260] this is probably not so, it being necessary to show only that an actionable injury be apprehended.[261]

14–71   The alleged intention of the defendant to interfere with the rights of the claimant must normally be accompanied and evidenced by some activity,[262] for example laying the foundations of a house which when built would interfere with a right to light. This is, however, unnecessary if the avowed intentions of the defendant are to commence the activity, provided that there is a real probability that he will carry out such intentions.[263] If the servient tenement is held under a long lease and the threat of interference with the rights of the dominant owner comes from the lessee it is not appropriate to grant an injunction against a lessor who has no power to do anything further towards the interference.[264]

14–72   Instead of granting an injunction the court may make a declaration that the defendant cannot carry on his activity to its fulfilment and may give liberty to apply for an injunction.[265]

14–73   In the second type of case the conditions for the grant of a *quia timet* injunction, when a mandatory order is sought, are far more stringent. In *Redland Bricks Ltd v Morris*[266] the principles upon which the court's discretion should be exercised were considered. The respondents owned and farmed some eight acres of land which was valued at £12,000 or thereabouts. The appellants used adjoining land to excavate clay for their brick-making business. Due to this activity support to the respondents' land was withdrawn and it started to slip into the appellants' land. Despite remedial works carried out by the appellants the slipping continued. The respondents began proceedings in the county court and the judge found that there was a strong possibility of further slips with serious loss to the respondents. It was agreed that works to prevent further slipping would cost the appellants up to £35,000. The judge, in addition to awarding damages to the respondents for damage already suffered and granting an injunction restraining further excavations, ordered the appellants to "take all necessary steps to restore the support" to the respondents' land.

14–74   The appellants appealed to the Court of Appeal who upheld the decision of the county court judge, but a further appeal to the House of Lords was allowed. Lord Upjohn, delivering a judgment with which the remainder of the House agreed, set out[267] the principles applicable to the grant of mandatory injunctions *quia timet* which may be summarised as follows:

[260] See, e.g. *Fletcher v Bealey* (1884) 28 Ch. D. 688, per Pearson J. 698; *Litchfield-Speer v Queen Anne's Gate Syndicate* [1919] 1 Ch. 407, 411, per P. O. Lawrence J.

[261] *Siddons v Short and Harley & Co* (1877) 2 C.P.D. 572.

[262] See, e.g. *Phillips v Thomas* (1890) 62 L.T. 793.

[263] *cf. Lord Cowley v Byas* (1877) 5 Ch. D. 944, where the Court of Appeal, reversing Sir James Bacon V.-C., found no such intentions.

[264] *Celsteel Ltd v Alton House Holdings Ltd* [1986] 1 W.L.R. 512 (reversing on this point [1985] 1 W.L.R. 204). In subsequent proceedings (*Celsteel Ltd v Alton House Holdings Ltd (No. 2)* [1986] 1 W.L.R. 666) the lessee failed in a claim against the lessor that the injunction granted against the lessee represented a breach of the covenant for quiet enjoyment contained in the lease.

[265] *Litchfield-Speer v Queen Anne's Gate Syndicate* [1919] 1 Ch. 407.

[266] [1970] A.C. 652.

[267] [1970] A.C. 652 at 665–667.

(1) the plaintiff must show a very strong probability that grave damages will accrue to him in the future;

(2) damages will not be a sufficient or adequate remedy if such damage does happen;

(3) the cost to the defendant to do works to prevent or lessen the likelihood of a future apprehended wrong is an element to be taken into account. Where the defendant has acted without regard to his neighbour's rights, or has tried to steal a march on him or has tried to evade the jurisdiction of the court or, to sum it up, has acted wantonly and quite unreasonably in relation to his neighbour, he may be ordered to repair his acts by doing positive work to restore the *status quo* even if the expense to him is out of all proportion to the advantage thereby accruing to the plaintiff.[268] Where, however, the defendant has acted reasonably, the cost of remedying by positive action his earlier activities is important for two reasons: first, because no legal wrong has yet occurred (for which the plaintiff has not been recompensed in law and in equity) and may never occur again, or at least only on a smaller scale than anticipated; secondly, because if damage does occur he has his action in law and remedies in equity. Considering these factors, the court must balance the amount to be expended under a mandatory order by the defendant against the anticipated possible damage to the plaintiff in deciding whether it is unreasonable to inflict such expenditure on a potential wrongdoer. The court can order works to be done which will merely lessen the likelihood of further injury[269];

(4) if a mandatory injunction is granted, the defendant must know exactly what he has to do as a matter of fact.[270]

On the facts of the case the House of Lords held that the decision of the county court judge could not stand. Although the respondents had satisfied conditions (1) and (2) above, they had failed under (3) and (4). The appellants had not behaved unreasonably but only wrongly. Moreover, the terms of the order imposed upon the appellants an unqualified obligation to restore support without giving them any indication of what was to be done. It would have cost at least £30,000 to prevent further damage and this offended condition (3).   **14–75**

Interim injunctions

It is in the nature of disputes concerning easements that there will be a need to apply for interim injunctions either to restrain an alleged disturbance of an easement or to restrain conduct pursuant to an alleged entitlement to an easement. The modern principles on which applications for interim injunctions are considered   **14–76**

---

[268] *Woodhouse v Newry Navigation Co* [1898] 1 I.R. 161.

[269] *Kennard v Cory Bros & Co Ltd* [1922] 1 Ch. 265 at 274; affirmed [1922] 2 Ch. 1.

[270] *Att-Gen v Staffordshire County Council* [1905] 1 Ch. 336 at 342; *Fishenden v Higgs & Hill Ltd* (1935) 153 L.T. 128 at 142.

effectively date from the decision of the House of Lords in *American Cyanamid Co Ltd v Ethicon Ltd*,[271] which changed the pre-existing rule as to the strength of the case that a party seeking an interim injunction had to show. Accordingly, the decisions of the courts before 1975 in cases concerning easements must now be reconsidered and are no longer authoritative. Accordingly, those decisions which were referred to in previous editions of this work are not repeated here. Instead, brief reference will be made to the modern principles.[272]

Strength of the claimant's case

14–77   Before the decision in *American Cyanamid*, a claimant had to show a prima facie case of entitlement to an injunction. The decision in *American Cyanamid* swept away this requirement and replaced it with the lesser requirement that in the case of a negative or prohibitory injunction,[273] the claimant need only establish a serious issue to be tried. If the claimant does so, then the court goes on to consider whether damages would be an adequate remedy to either party and, if damages would not be, the court will then decide the outcome of the application by reference to the balance of convenience.

In the case of an application for a mandatory interim injunction, the court requires a very high degree of assurance that at the trial it will appear that the injunction was rightly granted.[274] In cases where a right of light is being infringed, the court has compelled the defendant to pull down the infringing building where he had endeavoured to steal a march on the plaintiff by hurrying on with the building works after being served with notice of the proceedings,[275] or had evaded service of the writ,[276] and continued the building after due warning from the plaintiff.

Adequacy of damages

14–78   If the claimant would be adequately compensated by an award of damages if he succeeds at the trial, and the defendant would be able to pay them, no injunction should be granted, however strong the claimant's case. However, this will usually not be the position in cases involving disputes as to easements. If damages are not an adequate remedy for the claimant the court will go on to consider whether, if an interim injunction is granted to the claimant but the defendant succeeds at trial, the defendant would be adequately compensated in damages which would then have to be paid by the claimant, and whether the claimant would be able to pay those damages. If damages would be an adequate remedy for the defendant in

---

[271] [1975] A.C. 396; but see *Series 5 Software Ltd v Clarke* [1996] 1 All E.R. 853.
[272] A fuller treatment of the relevant principles and case law is contained in *Snell's Equity* (29th ed.), at pp. 660 *et seq.*
[273] *Locabail International Finance Ltd v Agroexport* [1986] 1 W.L.R. 657 at 664.
[274] *Locabail International Finance Ltd v Agroexport* [1986] 1 W.L.R. 657; *Films Rover International Ltd v Cannon Film Sales Ltd* [1987] 1 W.L.R. 670.
[275] *Daniel v Ferguson* [1891] 2 Ch. 27; *Mathias v Davies* [1970] E.G.D. 370.
[276] *Von Joel v Hornsey* [1895] 2 Ch. 774.

those circumstances, then the defendant's prospects of success at the trial should not prevent the grant of an interim injunction to the claimant. In many cases concerning easements, it will not be clear that damages are an adequate remedy for the defendant in those circumstances.

Balance of convenience

If there is doubt as to the adequacy of damages, the court must then consider where the balance of convenience, or the balance of justice,[277] lies. The question for the court is whether the injustice that would be caused to the defendant if the claimant was granted an injunction and later failed at the trial outweighed the injustice that would be caused to the claimant if the injunction was refused and he succeeded at the trial.[278] This question will involve the consideration of a wide range of factors. "Where other factors appear to be evenly balanced it is a counsel of prudence to take such measures as are calculated to preserve the status quo."[279] Thus a new venture on the part of the defendant may be restrained where an established business would not be. The *status quo* refers to the period immediately preceding the issue of the writ (or the notice of motion if substantially later) and not to the period before the conduct complained of.[280] The court should not embark on anything resembling a trial of the action on conflicting affidavits but sometimes on undisputed facts the strength of one party's case is disproportionate to that of the other party and this may be taken into account in tipping the balance in an otherwise balanced case.

14–79

The limits of the above guidelines

The approach in *American Cyanamid* was to lay down guidelines as to the exercise of what remains essentially a discretionary matter where the object is to do what is "just and convenient".[281] Thus in a case where it is plain that the claimant is in the right, the balance of convenience will play no part, for example where the claimant's title is clear and the defendant's trespass is indisputable.[282]

14–80

Conduct of the parties

As part of the balancing exercise called for in the exercise of the discretion as to the grant of an interim injunction, the court will have regard to relevant conduct by both parties. Thus the conduct of the claimant in delaying the application for the interim injunction will be material. A lesser degree of acquiescence or laches suffices to debar a claimant from interim relief than from obtaining a permanent injunction.[283]

14–81

---

[277] The expression preferred by Sir John Donaldson M.R. in *Francome v Mirror Group Newspapers Ltd* [1984] 1 W.L.R. 892 at 898.

[278] *Films Rover International Ltd v Cannon Film Sales Ltd* [1987] 1 W.L.R. 670.

[279] *American Cyanamid Ltd v Ethicon Ltd* [1975] A.C. 396 at 408, per Lord Diplock.

[280] *Garden Cottage Foods Ltd v Milk Marketing Board* [1984] A.C. 130 at 140.

[281] Supreme Court Act 1981, s.37(1).

[282] *Patel v W.H. Smith (Eziot) Ltd* [1987] 1 W.L.R. 853.

[283] See para.14–68, above, and para.14–85, below.

REMEDIES FOR DISTURBANCE

Illustrations

14–82 The *American Cyanamid* guidelines have been applied in recent cases involving easements, including *Huckvale v Aegean Hotels Ltd*[284] and *Handel v St Stephens Close Ltd*.[285]

Undertaking as to damages

14–83 Where the claimant obtains an interim injunction, an undertaking by him to the court to pay any damages which the respondent sustains which the court considers the applicant should pay must be inserted in the order unless the court orders otherwise[286]; and where an interim injunction has been granted on such an undertaking, and afterwards at the trial the claimant does not obtain an injunction, an inquiry as to damages will be directed unless the circumstances are exceptional,[287] even though the claimant obtained the order without misrepresentation, concealment, or default.[288]

Undertaking to pull down

14–84 In some cases the court has ordered a motion for an interim injunction to stand over until the trial, on the defendant undertaking to abide by any order which may be made at the trial as to pulling down the additional buildings to be erected,[289] but no such undertaking is required in order to found the jurisdiction of the court over buildings erected after the commencement of the action.[290]

Delay

14–85 As regards delay, it has been held that, even though there has been no such acquiescence as to amount to the constructive grant of a right, a party may be barred by delay from obtaining an injunction.[291] There may be a difference between the acquiescence which will justify the refusal of an interim and of a perpetual injunction.[292]

---

[284] (1989) 58 P. & C.R. 163.

[285] [1994] 1 E.G.L.R. 70.

[286] CPR 25PD.5.1.

[287] *Lunn Poly Ltd v Liverpool & Lancashire Properties Ltd* [2006] EWCA Civ 430; [2006] 2 E.G.L.R. 29 at [42]–[44].

[288] *Griffith v Blake* (1884) 27 Ch. D. 474, where the Lords Justice dissented from an opinion to the contrary expressed by Lord Jessel M.R. in *Smith v Day* (1882) 21 Ch. D. 421.

[289] *Wilson v Townend* (1860) 1 Dr. & Sm. 324.

[290] *Smith v Day* (1880) 13 Ch. D. 651. *Cf. Aynsley v Glover* (1874) L.R. 18 Eq. 544 at 553, per Lord Jessel M.R.; *Mackey v Scottish Widows' Fund Assurance Society* (1876) Ir.R. 10 Eq. 113; *Greenwood v Hornsey* (1886) 33 Ch. D. 471.

[291] *Wicks v Hunt* (1859) John. 372; *Cooper v Hubbuck* (1860) 30 Beav. 160; *Gaskin v Balls* (1879) 13 Ch. D. 324; *Young v Star Omnibus Co* (1902) 86 L.T. 41; *Bracewell v Appleby* [1975] Ch. 408. See *Hogg v Scott* (1874) L.R. 18 Eq. 444; *Smith v Smith* (1875) L.R. 20 Eq. 503; *Gooden v Ketley* (1997) 73 P. & C.R. 305.

[292] *Johnson v Wyatt* (1863) 2 De G.J. & S. 18; *Turner v Mirfield* (1865) 34 Beav. 390.

(5) *Award of damages in lieu*

Power to award damages

The question whether for any particular disturbance of an easement a party could   **14–86**
obtain damages, or an injunction, or both, depended for a long time on the different jurisdictions of the courts of common law and equity. In some cases a party
came into a court of equity for an injunction and was sent to a court of law to
recover damages, being thus bandied about from one court to another.[293] Even
after the Chancery Amendment Act 1858 (commonly known as Lord Cairns'
Act)[294] had conferred a power to award damages either in addition to or in substitution for an injunction, doubt remained as to whether damages could be
awarded in a case in which the injunction was asked for to restrain a threatened
injury, and was not resolved until the decision in the affirmative of the House of
Lords in *Leeds Industrial Co-operative Society v Slack*.[295]

The decision of the House of Lords has, of course, determined once and for all   **14–87**
the question that the jurisdiction exists, but the question as to the circumstances
in which the jurisdiction should be exercised is quite another matter. In *Krehl v
Burrell*,[296] in which the plaintiff claimed a mandatory injunction to restrain building on a passage over which he had a right of way, and the defendant contended
that only damages should be given, Sir George Jessel M.R. said:

> "If I acceded to this view, ... I should add one more to the number of
> instances which we have from the days in which the Bible was written until
> the present moment, in which the man of large possessions has endeavoured
> to deprive his neighbour, the man with small possessions, of his property,
> with or without adequate compensation."

Those words should be borne in mind, and so also should the words of Lindley
L.J. in *Shelfer v City of London Electric Lighting Co*,[297] where he said:

> "Ever since Lord Cairns' Act was passed the Court of Chancery has repudi-
> ated the notion that the Legislature intended to turn that Court into a tribunal
> for legalizing wrongful acts; or in other words, the Court has always protested
> against the notion that it ought to allow a wrong to continue simply because
> the wrongdoer is able and willing to pay for the injury he may inflict;"

and so again should the words of Buckley J. in *Cowper v Laidler*[298]:

---

[293] See *Ferguson v Wilson* (1866) 2 Ch. App. 77.
[294] s.2, repealed by the Supreme Court Act 1981, s.152(4), Sch.7; see now *ibid.*, s.50.
[295] [1924] A.C. 851, disapproving *Dreyfus v Peruvian Guano Co* (1889) 43 Ch. D. 316. The problem
  had been left unresolved in *Martin v Price* [1894] 1 Ch. 276 and *Litchfield-Speer v Queen Anne's
  Gate Syndicate* [1919] 1 Ch. 407.
[296] (1878) 7 Ch. D. 551 at 555; affirmed (1879) 11 Ch. D. 146; but distinguished in *Snell & Prideaux
  Ltd v Dutton Mirrors Ltd* [1995] 1 E.G.L.R. 259.
[297] [1895] 1 Ch. 287 at 315, 316.
[298] [1903] 2 Ch. 337 at 341.

"The Court has affirmed over and over again that the jurisdiction to give damages where it exists is not so to be used as in fact to enable the defendant [in an action for disturbance of an easement] to purchase from the plaintiff against his will his legal right to the easement."

Having referred to the words of Lindley L.J. in *Shelfer v City of London Electric Lighting Co*,[299] quoted above, Buckley J. continued:

"To refuse to aid the legal right by injunction and to give damages instead is in fact to compel the plaintiff to part with his easement for money."

As Lord Finlay said in *Leeds Industrial Co-operative Society v Slack*,[300] referring to the words of Lindley L.J. and the first of the two passages in Buckley J.'s judgment quoted above:

"These passages bring out very clearly the scope of the Act and the care taken to prevent abuse of its powers."

Disregard of them and of other such dicta would lead up to a practice under which the court would, as Lord Sumner said in the same case,[301]

"fix the price at which an intending tortfeasor should be judicially licensed to violate the rights of another", and would "allow the big man . . . to have his way, and to solace the little man for his darkened and stuffy little house by giving him a cheque that he does not ask for."

Should the remedy be injunction or damages?

14–88   The appropriateness of the comparative remedies of an injunction or damages was discussed in a long line of cases (chiefly relating to the easement of light), and the effect of many of these cases was thus stated in the eighth (1908) edition of this work[302]:

"Where the defendant has erected or substantially erected his building, either after action brought, or otherwise with notice of the plaintiff's right and in defiance of his protests, the judges have absolutely refused to allow him to compensate the plaintiff with damages, but have forced him to pull down his buildings.[303] Except, however, for such cases of wilful breach of

---

[299] [1895] 1 Ch. 217 at 315, 316.
[300] [1924] A.C. 851 at 861.
[301] [1924] A.C. 851 at 871, 872.
[302] By Mr Raymond Roope Reeve (1908).
[303] *Smith v Smith* (1875) L.R. 20 Eq. 500; *Gaskin v Balls* (1879) 13 Ch. D. 324; *Parker v Stanley* (1902) 50 W.R. 282; see now also *Pugh v Howells* (1984) 48 P. & C.R. 298 and *Deakins v Hookings* [1994] 1 E.G.L.R. 190.

duty, the courts have declined to fetter their discretion by laying down any absolute rule, and have considered each case upon its own circumstances. The tendency of the earlier decisions[304] was to award damages in preference to a mandatory injunction whenever the injury to the plaintiff could be reasonably estimated in money—whenever, in fact, the injury was not irreparable except by the restoration of the status quo ante. At a later period, however, the inclination of the judges was to exercise the discretion only in cases where the damage to the plaintiff, although not so trifling as to exclude the jurisdiction altogether, was yet small in amount and capable of being amply compensated by a money payment, or when there were special circumstances which would make it oppressive to grant an injunction.[305] It seems also that damages might be awarded even for injury done after the issue of the writ,[306] and possibly for injury which may be expected to accrue after judgement."[307]

The cases before *Colls v Home and Colonial Stores*[308] laid down the following principles to guide the court in the exercise of its discretion whether to grant an injunction or to award damages: where a legal right has been established, the plaintiff is prima facie entitled to an injunction,[309] and in cases of continuing actionable nuisance the jurisdiction to award damages ought only to be exercised in very exceptional circumstances.   **14–89**

In *Shelfer v City of London Electric Lighting Co*[310] an injunction was granted to restrain a continuing nuisance by noise and vibration. It was a case where damages would have been an entirely inadequate remedy.[311] In the course of his judgment, Lindley L.J. said[312]:   **14–90**

"Without denying the jurisdiction to award damages instead of an injunction, even in cases of continuing actionable nuisances, such jurisdiction ought not to be exercised in such cases except under very exceptional circumstances. I

---

[304] *Johnson v Wyatt* (1863) 2 De G.J. & S. 18; *Isenberg v East India House Estate Co* (1863) 3 De G.J. & S. 263; *Bowes v Law* (1870) L.R. 9 Eq. 636; *Ball v Derby* (1874) referred to by Sir George Jessel M.R. in *Aynsley v Glover* (1874) L.R. 18 Eq. 544 at 555, and by Kekewich J. in *Dicker v Popham, Radford & Co* (1890) 63 L.T. 379 at 381; *Lady Stanley of Alderley v Earl of Shrewsbury* (1875) L.R. 19 Eq. 616; *National Co v Prudential Co* (1877) 6 Ch. D. 757; *Holland v Worley* (1884) 26 Ch. D. 578.

[305] *Senior v Pawson* (1866) L.R. 3 Eq. 330; *Aynsley v Glover* (1874) L.R. 18 Eq. 544; *Smith v Smith* (1875) L.R. 20 Eq. 500; *Allen v Ayres* [1884] W.N. 242; *Dicker v Popham* (1890) 63 L.T. 379; *Young v Star Omnibus Co* (1902) 86 L.T. 41.

[306] *Davenport v Rylands* (1865) L.R. 1 Eq. 302; *Fritz v Hobson* (1880) 14 Ch. D. 542; *Chapman v Auckland Union Guardians* (1889) 23 Q.B.D. 298.

[307] See *Dicker v Popham* (1890) 63 L.T. 379.

[308] [1904] A.C. 179.

[309] *Martin v Price* [1894] 1 Ch. 285; *Shelfer v City of London Electric Lighting Co* [1895] 1 Ch. 287; *Jordeson v Sutton, Southcoates and Drypool Gas Co* [1899] 2 Ch. 217; see *Cowper v Laidler* [1903] 2 Ch. 337 at 341.

[310] [1895] 1 Ch. 287.

[311] See *Fishenden v Higgs and Hill Ltd* (1935) 153 L.T. 128 at 144, per Maugham L.J.

[312] [1895] 1 Ch. 287 at 316, 317. *Cf. Colls v Home and Colonial Stores* [1904] A.C. 179 at 212.

will not attempt to specify them, or to lay down rules for the exercise of judicial discretion. It is sufficient to refer, by way of example, to trivial and occasional nuisances: cases in which the plaintiff has shewn that he only wants money; vexatious and oppressive cases; and cases where the plaintiff has so conducted himself as to render it unjust to grant him more than pecuniary relief. In all such cases as these, and in all others where an action for damages is really an adequate remedy—as where the acts complained of are already finished—an injunction can be properly refused."

14–91 In the same case, however, A.L. Smith L.J., in the course of his judgment, indicated the principles which, in his opinion, should guide the court in the exercise of its discretion. His observations, which were obiter dicta,[313] were as follows[314]:

"Many judges have stated, and I emphatically agree with them, that a person by committing a wrongful act . . . is not thereby entitled to ask the Court to sanction his doing so by purchasing his neighbour's rights, by assessing damages in that behalf, leaving his neighbour with the nuisance, or his lights dimmed, as the case may be. In such cases the well-known rule is not to accede to the application, but to grant the injunction sought, for the plaintiffs legal right has been invaded, and he is prima facie entitled to an injunction."

The Lord Justice, after pointing out that there were cases in which this rule might be relaxed, and in which damages might be awarded in substitution for an injunction, and mentioning that a plaintiff might by his acts or laches disentitle himself, continued as follows:

"In my opinion, it may be stated as a good working rule that—

(1) If the injury to the plaintiff's legal rights is small,
(2) And is one which is capable of being estimated in money,
(3) And is one which can be adequately compensated by a small money payment,
(4) And the case is one in which it would be oppressive to the defendant to grant an injunction:—

then damages in substitution for an injunction may be given.

There may also be cases in which, though the four above-mentioned requirements exist, the defendant by his conduct, as, for instance, hurrying up his building so as if possible to avoid an injunction, or otherwise acting with a reckless disregard to the plaintiffs rights, has disentitled himself from asking that damages may be assessed in substitution for an injunction.

It is impossible to lay down any rule as to what, under the differing circumstances of each case, constitutes either a small injury, or one that can be

---

[313] See *Fishenden v Higgs and Hill Ltd* (1935) 153 L.T. 128 at 144.
[314] [1895] 1 Ch. 287 at 322, 323.

estimated in money, or what is a small money payment, or an adequate compensation, or what would be oppressive to the defendant."[315]

It would seem that, when this frequently quoted "good working rule" is read in its proper context, A.L. Smith L.J. did not really differ from Lindley L.J. and that, although he went further than Lindley L.J. in formulating principles to guide the court in subsequent cases, he was anxious so to express himself as not to fetter the court in the exercise of its discretion.

Rights of light cases

In *Colls v Home and Colonial Stores*,[316] Lord Macnaghten considered the **14–92** approach to be followed by the court in granting damages or an injunction to prevent obstruction of an easement of light; in earlier editions of this work this was described as "the rule to be followed", but the Court of Appeal has recently pointed out[317] that Lord Macnaghten himself described these remarks merely as "practical suggestions" and said that he "did not put them forward as carrying any authority":

> "In some cases, of course, an injunction is necessary–if, for instance, the injury cannot fairly be compensated by money–if the defendant has acted in a high-handed manner–if he has endeavoured to steal a march upon the plaintiff or to evade the jurisdiction of the Court. . . . But if there is really a question as to whether the obstruction is legal or not, and if the defendant has acted fairly and not in an unneighbourly spirit, I am disposed to think that the Court ought to incline to damages rather than an injunction. It is quite true that a man ought not to be compelled to part with his property against his will, or to have the value of his property diminished, without an Act of Parliament. On the other hand, the Court ought to be very careful not to allow an action for the protection of ancient lights to be used as a means of extorting money."

In *Kine v Jolly*[318] Cozens-Hardy L.J. said that the tendency of the speeches in **14–93** *Colls v Home and Colonial Stores*[319] was to go a little further than was done in *Shelfer v City of London Electric Lighting Co*[320] and to indicate that, as a general rule, the court ought to be "less free in granting mandatory injunctions than it was in years gone by" but it has now been pointed out by the Court of Appeal[321] that that "tendency" was only evident in the speech of Lord MacNaghten, who had

---

[315] [1895] 1 Ch. 287 at 322–323.
[316] [1904] A.C. 179 at 193.
[317] In *Regan v Paul Properties Ltd* [2006] EWCA Civ 1319; [2007] Ch. 135 at [39]–[45].
[318] [1905] 1 Ch. 480 at 496, 504.
[319] [1904] A.C. 179.
[320] [1895] 1 Ch. 287.
[321] In *Regan v Paul Properties Ltd* [2007] Ch. 135.

made it clear that what he was saying was not intended to be authoritative. Nevertheless, in *Slack v Leeds Industrial Co-operative Society*[322] the "good working rule" was affirmed and applied by the Court of Appeal.

14–94   In *Price v Hilditch*,[323] Maugham J. declined to grant a mandatory injunction and ordered an inquiry as to damages. In *Fishenden v Higgs and Hill Ltd*[324] the scope of the "good working rule" was fully considered by Crossman J. and the Court of Appeal (Lord Hanworth M.R., Romer and Maugham L.JJ.). Crossman J. found as a fact, and the Court of Appeal agreed with him, that a building which was being erected by the defendants would, when completed, cause a nuisance by interference with the plaintiffs' ancient lights. Crossman J., after reviewing the authorities, came to the conclusion that the "good working rule" obliged him to grant an injunction unless all the conditions mentioned by A.L. Smith L.J. existed. He treated the "good working rule" as a rule which had to be applied in its entirety in every case and decided that in the case before him, the "good working rule" had not been complied with because (a) he was not satisfied that the injury to the plaintiffs' rights was small within the meaning of the rule; (b) he could not say that it was capable of being estimated in money; (c) he did not think it was capable of being compensated by a small money payment; and (d) he did not think the case was one where it would be oppressive to the defendants to grant an injunction.

14–95   The Court of Appeal refused to treat the *Shelfer* case[325] as laying down any inflexible rule which might hamper the court in the exercise of its discretion. Lord Hanworth M.R.,[326] after referring to a number of authorities, including the speeches of Lords Macnaghten and Lindley in *Colls v Home and Colonial Stores*[327] and the judgments of Vaughan Williams and Cozens-Hardy L.JJ. in *Kine v Jolly*,[328] said:

> "It seems to me, therefore, that these rules in the *Shelfer case* must now be taken with the concomitant passages to which I have referred in later cases, in *Colls*[329] and in *Kine v. Jolly*,[330] and that we ought to incline against an injunction if possible."

Romer L.J. said[331]:

---

[322] [1924] 2 Ch. 475. The case had been remitted to the Court of Appeal by the House of Lords, who had decided by a majority that the court had jurisdiction to award damages in lieu of an injunction in a *quia timet* action. See para.14–86, above.
[323] [1930] 1 Ch. 500.
[324] (1935) 153 L.T. 128.
[325] [1895] 1 Ch. 287.
[326] (1935) 153 L.T. 128 at 139.
[327] [1904] A.C. 179.
[328] [1905] 1 Ch. 480.
[329] [1904] A.C. 179.
[330] [1905] 1 Ch. 480.
[331] (1935) 153 L.T. 128 at 141.

"Where the four conditions enunciated by A.L. Smith L.J. are fulfilled, I do not doubt that a court will grant damages in lieu of an injunction. But it by no means follows that A.L. Smith L.J. intended to say or did say or in fact could say that in all cases in which these four conditions do not prevail, the injunction must be granted; he could not have intended to have fettered the discretion imposed upon the court by Lord Cairns' Act. The fact that he did not do that is apparent, I think, from the judgment of Lindley L.J. in the same case."

The Lord Justice then read the passage from the judgment of Lindley L.J. already quoted[332] and part of the above-quoted observations of Lord Macnaghten in *Colls v Home and Colonial Stores*.[333]

Maugham L.J.[334] expressed the opinion that the "good working rule" was not a universal or even a sound rule in all cases of injury to light and said that he agreed with the rule as propounded by Lindley L.J.[335]

Romer L.J. said[336] that in his opinion the case was one where the interference was small and could be compensated in damages and that it would be oppressive to grant an injunction. In other words, even if the "good working rule" was applicable, the plaintiff ought not to obtain an injunction.

The Court of Appeal refused an injunction and the case was sent back to the **14–96** trial judge for damages to be assessed by him. In previous editions of this work the view was expressed that, in light of those observations of the Court of Appeal, it seemed doubtful whether the "good working rule" was to be applied to any case where an alleged injury to lights was in question; that the court had a discretion which should be exercised on the broad principles laid down by Lindley L.J. in the *Shelfer* case[337] and by Lord Macnaghten in *Colls v Home and Colonial Stores*[338] and that perhaps the nearest approach to a working rule was the explanation of the observations of A.L. Smith L.J., given by Romer L.J. in *Fishenden v Higgs and Hill Ltd*.[339]

While accepting that *Fishenden* is "relevant to determining ... the proper approach to the 'good working rule' and to the four conditions laid down in

---

[332] [1895] 1 Ch. 287 at 316, 317; see para.14–90, above.
[333] [1904] A.C. 179 at 193; see para.14–92, above.
[334] (1935) 153 L.T. 128 at 144.
[335] [1895] 1 Ch. 287 at 316, 317; see para.14–90, above.
[336] (1935) 153 L.T. 128 at 142.
[337] [1895] 1 Ch. 287 at 316, 317; see para.14–90, above.
[338] [1904] A.C. 179.
[339] (1935) 153 L.T. 128 at 141, see para.14–94, above. In *McGrath v The Munster and Leinster Bank Ltd* [1959] I.R. 32, the dictum of Lord Macnaghten was applied in granting damages in lieu of an injunction to the plaintiff, a lessee, who sued for an interference with light. In *Mathias v Davies* (1970) 114 S.J. 268 the same dictum was applied by the Court of Appeal when granting an injunction to restrain an interference with light where the defendant had built in the face of protests from the plaintiff; Russell L.J. said that there was no arguable case to oppose the injunction because of the "high-handed manner of the defendant". In *Prow v Chaplin* (1964) 108 S.J. 463 the interference with the plaintiffs' light would have been estimable in money, but Widgery J. granted an injunction because the plaintiffs had protested and it would be unfair to force them to move from their house.

Shelfer", the Court of Appeal has recently, in *Regan v Paul Properties Ltd*,[340] stated that *Fishenden* was decided on the ground "that the amount of damages was not itself determinative of whether an injunction should be granted" and re-affirmed and applied the "good working rule"; they went on to hold that the trial judge had been wrong to hold that the onus was on the claimant to show why an injunction should not be granted; rather the court's discretion to award damages in lieu of an injunction should not be exercised so as to deprive a claimant of his prima facie right except under very exceptional circumstances.

14–97   While no-one could dispute the decision in *Regan* as to the onus borne by the claimant, *Fishenden* and *Regan* are difficult to reconcile on their facts. Both were cases of residential premises, where there would be appreciable interference with the light to the main living room of a flat. In *Fishenden* the Court of Appeal envis-aged that the damages would be substantial and that one of the conditions of the "good working rule" would therefore not be complied with but felt able to inter-fere with the discretion of the trial judge because he had approached the matter on the basis that all four conditions had to be met, which was not correct. Moreover the Court undoubtedly took the view (a) that the good working rule had not been necessary to the decision in *Shelfer* and (b) that it applied with less force to a light case. Perhaps both cases should simply be regarded as cases where the appellate court disagreed with the exercise of the trial judge's discretion (in *Fishenden* largely on grounds of the claimant's delay in objecting) and felt enti-tled to interfere because they were able to identify an error of principle in the trial judge's approach.

The modern approach

14–98   The "working rule" of A.L. Smith L.J. in *Shelfer v City of London Electric Lighting Co*[341] was applied in *Jaggard v Sawyer*,[342] where the authorities were reviewed and damages awarded in lieu of injunction. In that case the defendants were the owners of a house in a cul-de-sac which had the benefit of a private right of way over the cul-de-sac. The defendants acquired a further plot of land con-tiguous to the house and built a second house on it. The only means of access to the second house was over the cul-de-sac and then over a driveway formed across the garden of the first house. The construction of the driveway was a breach of a restrictive covenant binding the defendants and of which the plaintiff had the ben-efit. Further, the defendants' right of way over the cul-de-sac was not available for giving access to the new plot and the use of the road for such purpose was a trespass on the part of the road owned by the plaintiff. The plaintiff did not seek an interlocutory injunction to restrain the breach of the restrictive covenant nor the trespass on his part of the road.

---

[340] [2006] EWCA Civ 1391; [2007] Ch. 135.
[341] [1895] 1 Ch. 287.
[342] [1995] 1 W.L.R. 269. See also *Bracewell v Appleby* [1975] Ch. 408, which was a very similar case. *Jaggard v Sawyer* was considered by the Court of Appeal in *Gooden v Ketley* (1997) 73 P. & C.R. 305.

At trial the judge found that the defendants' user of the second house would **14–99** involve a continuing trespass and breach of the restrictive covenant; that the defendants had not acted in blatant and calculated disregard of the plaintiff's rights; that the defendant had known of but had failed to appreciate the effect of the covenant; and that the plaintiff had not sought interlocutory relief. He further held that the injury to the plaintiff's rights was small; that the value of the injury was capable of being estimated in money; that the injury was one which could be adequately compensated by a small money payment and that in all the circumstances it would be oppressive to the defendant to grant injunctions to restrain the trespass and the breach of covenant.[343]

His decision was upheld by the Court of Appeal. Sir Thomas Bingham M.R. **14–100** said[344]:

> "It is important to bear in mind that the test is one of oppression, and the court should not slide into an application of a general balance of convenience test. But oppression must be judged as at the date the court is asked to grant an injunction, and . . . the court cannot ignore the reality with which it is then confronted. It is relevant that the plaintiff could at an early stage have sought interlocutory relief, which she would seem very likely to have obtained; but it is also relevant that the defendants could have sought a declaration of right. These considerations are not decisive. It would weigh against a finding of oppression if the defendants had acted in blatant and calculated disregard of the plaintiffs rights, of which they were aware, but the judge held that this was not so, and the plaintiffs solicitors may be thought to have indicated that damages would be an acceptable remedy."

Millett L.J. added:

> "AL Smith L.J.'s check list has stood the test of time; but it needs to be remembered that it is only a working rule and does not purport to be an exhaustive statement of the circumstances in which damages may be awarded instead of an injunction."

The trial judge had awarded the plaintiff damages by reference to the sum that the defendants might reasonably have paid for a right of way and the release of the covenant. He held that the defendants should have been prepared to pay not less than £6,250 which, split among the plaintiff and other residents in a similar position, yielded £694.44 per resident and this sum was awarded to the plaintiff.[345]

---

[343] So if an alternative access is made available it may be appropriate to refuse an injunction and award damages as in *Doe v Cogente Pty Ltd* (1997) 94 L.G.E.R.A. 305; B.P.R. Case Notes 3, 102,202.

[344] [1995] 1 W.L.R. 269 at 283.

[345] See [1993] 1 E.G.L.R. 197 at 202F and 203D.

14–101 In *Greenwich NHS Trust v London Quadrant Housing*,[346] planning permission had been granted for the construction of a new hospital subject to a condition requiring the realignment of the road over which there were rights of way in favour of several premises. The court made a declaration that, although the servient owner had no right to alter the route of the easement, the dominant owners were not entitled to an injunction[347] to restrain the re-alignment because:

(1) the realignment was an improvement, in particular in the matter of road safety,

(2) the dominant owners had been given the opportunity to object and had not done so, and

(3) the re-alignment was necessary to achieve an object of substantial public importance.[348]

14–102 In a case where the claimant had evinced a willingness to settle the dispute on payment of a cash sum, that can properly be reflected in an award of damages.[349] It is no objection in such a case that the award may be large. In such a case the first and third conditions of the "good working rule" do not apply. The essential prerequisite of an award of damages is that it should be oppressive to the defendant to grant an injunction.[350] So it seemed, prior to the recent decision of the Court of Appeal in *Regan v Paul Properties*,[351] that the courts were moving away from the "good working rule" in favour of approaching the exercise of the discretion more broadly, in the light of the factors identified by Sir Thomas Bingham in *Jaggard v Sawyer* and Lindley L.J. in *Shelfer*.

14–103 In *Das v Linden Mews Limited*[352] the Court of Appeal, having agreed with the judge that the owners of houses in a mews were not entitled to an easement of access to their gardens for parking purposes, remitted the case to him to consider whether damages should be awarded in lieu of injunction and what the measure of any damages should be. The Court identified the following factors as relevant to whether damages were the more appropriate remedy:

(1) the fact that the finding of trespass was based on a claim to extend the dominant tenement rather than on excessively burdensome use of the way;

---

[346] [1998] 1 W.L.R. 1749.

[347] The declaration was also to the effect that the dominant owners were not entitled to damages but this appears to have been in respect of that part of the claim based on breach of a restrictive covenant and the case advanced and accepted as to the easement was that the defendant should be satisfied by an award of damages in respect of the easement: see [1998] 1 W.L.R. 1749, at 1755E–G.

[348] The circumstances in which it will be right for the court to grant a negative declaration of this kind were considered by the Court of Appeal in *Well Barn Shoot v Shackleton* [2002] EWCA Civ 2; see para.14–147, below.

[349] This is entirely consistent with what Lindley L.J. said in *Shelfer*: see para.14–90, above.

[350] *Gafford v Graham* [1999] 3 E.G.L.R. 75, CA.

[351] [2006] EWCA Civ 1391; [2007] Ch. 135; see below.

[352] [2002] EWCA Civ 590; [2002] 2 E.G.L.R. 76.

(2) the fact that use of the way would unlock an asset, namely a parking space, without placing any practical burden on the servient owner;

(3) the fact that the servient owner's amenity and convenience were not affected;

(4) delay in bringing proceedings, albeit that it fell short of that which would make it unconscionable to enforce the servient owner's rights.

In *Mortimer v Bailey*[353] a house extension had been built in breach of a restric-   **14–104**
tive covenant not to build without the claimants' consent. The defendant took the view that refusal of consent had been unreasonable in view of the grant of planning permission and built the extension in spite of the claimant's protests. Proceedings were not commenced or an interim injunction sought for about two months, during which time the extension was almost completed. The judge held that the refusal of consent had been reasonable and that the extension adversely affected the value and enjoyment of the claimants' property. He assessed the diminution in the value of the claimants' property at £20,000 and decided that a reasonable sum for the claimants to have required to permit the development would have been £40,000, but held that damages were not an adequate remedy and that the proper approach was to grant a mandatory injunction requiring the defendant to demolish the extension.

The Court of Appeal held that, although failure to seek an interim injunction is a factor which may be taken into account, there is no general rule that debars a person who has made clear at the outset his objection to the breach and his intention to bring proceedings for it from obtaining a final injunction to have the offending building pulled down. *Gafford v Graham*[354] was distinguished principally on the ground that there the claimant had made clear that his principal objective was money, and the good working rule in *Shelfer*[355] applied.

In *Midtown Limited v City of London Real Property Company Limited*[356] the   **14–105**
owners and tenants of a building in Fetter Lane, London sought an injunction to prevent the erection of buildings which would interfere with their rights of light. The judge held that the infringement of the claimants' light would amount to an actionable nuisance but refused an injunction. In the case of the freeholders, he did so because:

(1) their only interest was in money;

(2) the diminution in the value of their property was capable of calculation;

(3) they would suffer no present loss because of the existence of continuing leases;

(4) their redevelopment proposals would make the injunction academic;

(5) they had unreasonably rebuffed the defendant's attempts to negotiate;

---

[353] [2004] EWCA Civ 1514; [2005] 1 E.G.L.R. 75.
[354] [1999] 3 E.G.L.R. 75.
[355] [1895] 1 Ch. 287.
[356] [2005] EWHC 33; [2005] 1 E.G.L.R. 65.

(6) an injunction would be oppressive in that it would prevent the defendant pursuing a worthwhile development;

(7) it was accepted by the defendant that damages could include a compensatory payment by reference to a reasonable price for the release of the easement in addition to compensation for the diminution in value of the property.

The tenant's claim for an injunction was refused because:

(1) they had failed to respond to the defendant's approaches;

(2) they had no capital interest which would be diminished in value by the infringement;

(3) neither their existing use nor their proposed future use would in practical terms be affected;

(4) their evidence as to the importance of having natural light (as opposed to a view or airiness) for the purposes of their business had not been convincing.

The judge observed that the damages to which the tenants would be entitled were probably limited to the right to participate in the extraction of compensation for release of the rights of light. He directed an enquiry as to the damages to be divided between the landlord and the tenant.

14–106   In *Regan v Paul Properties Ltd*,[357] however, the trial judge held that a development in the course of construction would result in an actionable interference to the light enjoyed by the living room of the claimant's maisonette but awarded damages in lieu of injunction on the basis that, in the case of an infringement of light, refusing an injunction and leaving the claimant with an award of damages was not an exceptional course; indeed the onus was on the claimant to persuade the court that he should not be left to a remedy in damages.

The Court of Appeal held that that was wrong and that *Shelfer* was authority for the following propositions:

(1) A claimant is prima facie entitled to an injunction against a person committing a wrongful act, such as a continuing nuisance, which invades the claimant's legal right.

(2) The wrongdoer is not entitled to ask the court to sanction his wrongdoing by purchasing the claimant's rights on payment of damages assessed by the court.

(3) The court has jurisdiction to award damages instead of an injunction, even in cases of a continuing nuisance; but the jurisdiction does not mean that the court is "a tribunal for legalising wrongful acts" by a defendant, who is able and willing to pay damages.

---

[357] [2006] EWCA Civ 1391; [2007] Ch. 135.

(4) The judicial discretion to award damages in lieu should pay attention to well settled principles and should not be exercised to deprive a claimant of his prima facie right "except under very exceptional circumstances".

(5) Although it is not possible to specify all the circumstances relevant to the exercise of the discretion or to lay down rules for its exercise, the judgments indicated that it was relevant to consider the following factors: whether the injury to the claimant's legal rights was small; whether the injury could be estimated in money; whether it could be adequately compensated by a small money payment; whether it would be oppressive to the defendant to grant an injunction; whether the claimant had shown that he only wanted money; whether the conduct of the claimant rendered it unjust to give him more than pecuniary relief; and whether there were any other circumstances which justified the refusal of an injunction.[358]

The Court then considered how its discretion should be exercised in the circumstances. They held: (a) that the reduction of light in the affected room was from 67 per cent to 42–45 per cent of its area and that this was not a "small injury"; (b) that the diminution in value of the flat was about £5,500 and that this was not a "small money payment"; (c) that it was not correct to compare that with the cost to the defendant of having to comply with the court's order; (d) that the sum of equitable compensation when linked to a proportion of the net development profit would not be small; (e) that the defendants' losses resulting from the order were not determinative of the issue of oppressiveness; and (f) that the defendants had proceeded with the development despite Mr Regan's protests in reliance on advice which turned out to be wrong at their own risk. In the circumstances it was not oppressive to grant an injunction to protect Mr Regan's right to light rather than to force him "to accept compensation for losing the light in respect of his home".[359] **14–107**

The decision in *Regan* suggests that the principles applicable to the choice of remedy for infringement of rights to light are no different to those applicable to the infringement of any other easement or indeed any other property right. Nonetheless, it is suggested that Lord Macnaghten's "practical suggestions" had much to be said for them and have certainly been so regarded by the courts over the years. There will be many cases where either the interference in question is of no very great concern to the claimant (except as a bargaining chip), where the claimant's interest is purely financial or where there are considerations arising out of the claimant's conduct which make it inequitable to grant an injunction.[360] The courts will, however, be very likely to grant an injunction in a case where the claimant's enjoyment of the habitable rooms of his home is materially affected. **14–108**

---

[358] [2006] EWCA Civ 1391; [2007] Ch. 135, at [36].
[359] [2006] EWCA Civ 1391; [2007] Ch. 135, at [70]–[75].
[360] As in *Midtown* and in *Fishenden* (above).

14–109   In *Tamares Ltd v Fairpoint Properties Ltd*[361] the judge found that the light to
two basement windows would be affected to an actionable extent (if one ignored
the use of artificial light) but that, given that artificial light would have been
required anyway for safety reasons, the infringement was trivial and did not merit
an injunction. He considered that all the conditions in *Shelfer* were met.[362] He
awarded damages in lieu of £50,000.[363] In the course of his judgment he extracted
the following useful propositions from the judgment of Millett L.J. in *Jaggard v
Sawyer*[364]:

> (i) damages in substitution for an injunction relate to the future, not the
> past. They inevitably extend beyond the damages to which the
> claimant may be entitled at law;
>
> (ii) the nature of the cause of action is immaterial. "The jurisdiction to
> award damages in substitution for injunction has most commonly
> been exercised in cases where the Defendant's building has infringed
> the Plaintiff's right to light . . .";
>
> (iii) the question of whether to grant an injunction or award damages
> instead is decided "by reference to the circumstances as they exist at
> the date of the hearing";
>
> (iv) "It has always been recognised that the practical consequence of with-
> holding injunctive relief is to authorise the continuance of an unlawful
> state of affairs, If, for example, the Defendant threatens to build in such
> a way that the Plaintiff's light will be obstructed and he is not
> restrained, then the Plaintiff will inevitably be deprived of his legal
> right." This results not from the award of damages, but from the refusal
> of the injunction;
>
> (v) a claimant who has established both a legal right and a threat to
> infringe it is prima facie entitled to an injunction to protect it; "special
> circumstances" are needed to justify withholding the injunction;
>
> (vi) nevertheless, the grant of an injunction, like all equitable remedies, is
> discretionary. Many proprietary rights cannot be protected at all by the
> common law and the owner must submit to unlawful interference with
> his rights and be content with damages. "If he wants to be protected,
> he must seek equitable relief, and he has no absolute right to that. In
> many cases, it is true, an injunction will be granted almost as of
> course; but this is not always the case, and it will never be granted if
> this would cause injustice to the Defendant.";
>
> (vii) the danger of misappropriating the claimant's property rights needs to
> be balanced by the danger that a mandatory injunction would "deliver
> over the Defendants to the Plaintiffs bound hand and foot, in order to be

---

[361] [2006] EWHC 3589 (Ch.); [2007] 1 W.L.R. 2148.
[362] [2006] EWHC 3589 (Ch.); [2007] 1 W.L.R. 2148, at [57].
[363] See his second decision at [2007] 1 W.L.R. 2167.
[364] [1995] 1 W.L.R. 269 at 284–289.

made subject to any extortionate demand that he may, by possibility, make . . ."[365];

(viii) A.L. Smith L.J.'s "good working rule" is a "check-list" that "has stood the test of time; but it needs to be remembered that it is only a working rule and does not purport to be an exhausting statement of the circumstances in which damages may be awarded instead of an injunction.";

(ix) "Reported cases are merely illustrations of circumstances in which particular judges have exercised their discretion, in some cases by granting an injunction, and in others by awarding damages instead. Since they are all cases on the exercise of discretion, none of them is a binding authority on how the discretion should be exercised. The most that any of them can demonstrate is that in similar circumstances it would not be wrong to exercise a discretion in the same way. It does not follow that it would be wrong to exercise it differently.";

(x) "The outcome of any particular case usually turns on the question: would it in all the circumstances be oppressive to the Defendant to grant the injunction to which the Plaintiff is prima facie entitled? Most of the cases in which the injunction has been refused are cases where the Plaintiff has sought a mandatory injunction to pull down a building which infringes his right to light or which has been built in breach for a restrictive covenant. In such cases the court is faced with a fait accompli. The jurisdiction to grant a mandatory injunction in those circumstances cannot be doubted, but to grant it would subject the Defendant to a loss out of all proportion to that which would be suffered by the Plaintiff if it were refused and would indeed deliver him to the Plaintiff bound hand and foot to be subjected to any extortionate demands the Plaintiff might make.";

(xi) "In considering whether the grant of an injunction would be oppressive to the Defendant, all the circumstances of the case have to be considered. At one extreme, the Defendant may have acted openly and in good faith and in ignorance of the Plaintiff's right and thereby inadvertently placed himself in the position where the grant of an injunction would either force him to yield to the Plaintiff's extortionate demands or expose him to substantial loss. At the other extreme, the Defendant may have acted with his eyes open and in full knowledge that he was invading the Plaintiff's rights, and carried on his work in the hope that by presenting the court with a fait accompli, he would compel the Plaintiff to accept monetary compensation. Most cases . . . fall somewhere in between."

In *Jacklin v Chief Constable of West Yorkshire*[366] the judge granted an injunction   **14–110**
requiring the removal of works which obstructed a vehicular right of way belong-

---

[365] The "bound hand and foot" expression is taken by Millett L.J. from Lord Westbury L.C. in *Isenberg v East India House Estate Co Ltd* (1863) 3 De G.J. & S. 263 at 273.
[366] [2007] EWCA Civ 181.

ing to the claimant. He found that the first three conditions set out in *Shelfer* had been satisfied but that the defendant had failed to show that the grant of an injunction would be oppressive. The Court of Appeal held that the four conditions were cumulative[367] and that the fourth condition had to be met if an injunction was to be withheld, and declined to interfere with the judge's exercise of his discretion.

14–111   The non-joinder of a necessary party may make damages the only remedy which can be given.[368]

(6) *Measure of damages*

Heads of damage

14–112   Where user of an easement is excessive, the servient owner will have an action in trespass.[369] Where the exercise of the easement is obstructed or interfered with, the dominant owner will have an action in nuisance. In the following paragraphs, we will call the former "trespasses" and the latter "obstructions" and where we want to refer to both kinds of case indiscriminately, we will call them "infringements". In either kind of case, damages may be recovered:

(a) at common law for past trespasses or obstructions; and
(b) in a case where an injunction is refused and damages are awarded in lieu, for trespasses or obstructions which will continue into the future.

Damages may be awarded under any of the following heads:

(i) damages to compensate for actual financial loss resulting from the infringement;
(ii) damages representing the diminution in the value of the injured party's property resulting from the infringement;
(iii) loss of amenity (temporary or permanent), resulting from the infringement;
(iv) damages on the "wayleave" or "user" basis for past infringements;
(v) damages representing the loss of the injured party's bargaining position, i.e. a sum which the dominant owner could reasonably have been expected to have been able to negotiate for the release, or the servient owner could reasonably have been expected to have had to pay for the grant, of the right in question in respect of both past and, where damages are awarded in lieu of injunction, future infringements;
(vi) aggravated damages.

---

[367] [2007] EWCA Civ 181, at [48]. This might be thought to contradict the ratio of *Fishenden v Higgs and Hill Ltd* (1935) 153 L.T. 128, which was that an injunction could be refused even though one of the *Shelfer* conditions was not met. Nevertheless, it is clear that oppressiveness is a vital consideration.

[368] *Barnes v Allen* [1927] W.N. 217.

[369] e.g. *Bracewell v Appleby* [1975] Ch. 408; *Jaggard v Sawyer* [1995] 1 W.L.R. 269.

Damages under each of these heads will be considered in turn.

The general rules

The general rule is that a successful plaintiff in an action in tort can recover dam-   **14–113**
ages equivalent to the loss which he has suffered. If he has suffered no loss, the
most that he can recover is nominal damages. A second general rule is that, where
the plaintiff has suffered loss to his property or some proprietary right, he can
recover damages equivalent to the diminution in value of the property or the
right.[370]

Financial loss

The obstruction of an easement may be the direct cause of financial loss to the   **14–114**
dominant owner. An obvious example is where a right of way to business prem-
ises is obstructed and this results in a loss of profits by the business carried on
upon the dominant land.[371] Financial loss of this kind is perhaps less likely to be
caused in a trespass case but could be, where use outside the proper scope of the
easement had interfered with the use to which the servient owner was able to put
his own land. If the injured party exercises his right to abate a nuisance or trespass, he can recover the reasonable cost of so doing.[372]

Diminution in value

In many cases, however, the claimant will have suffered no financial loss as a   **14–115**
result of the trespass or obstruction. He may nevertheless be able to recover damages equivalent to the diminution in value of his property or his right during the
period of the infringement under the second general rule stated above. This head
of damage is more likely to be applicable where the diminution in value is permanent because the court has decided to award damages in lieu of injunction,[373]
but could also apply to cases where a temporary infringement has diminished the
value of the land affected during the period of, or on account of, any dispute.[374]

Obstruction of light

A special example of this kind of damages is provided by the way in which rights   **14–116**
of light surveyors have conventionally put a value upon the obstruction of rights
to light. This is done by preparing Waldram diagrams showing the 0.2 per cent

---

[370] *Stoke on Trent Council v W&J Wass Ltd* [1988] 1 W.L.R. 1406 at 1410G–H.
[371] e.g. *Rose v Groves* (1843) 5 M. & G. 613 (loss of custom to Thames-side public house in
Bermondsey caused by obstruction of river access); *Hunte v E Bottomley & Sons Ltd* [2007]
EWCA Civ 1168 (obstruction of estate road leading to a café); *Yankwood Ltd v Havering LBC*
[1998] E.G.C.S. 75 (interference with bridleways used by equestrian centre).
[372] See para.14–11, above.
[373] As in *Snell & Prideaux v Dutton Mirrors* [1995] 1 E.G.L.R. 259, where a right of way was nar-
rowed by the defendant's building but the court did not order its removal.
[374] As in *Owers v Bailey* [2006] 39 L.S. Gaz. 34. And see *Wildtree Hotels Ltd v Harrow LBC* [2001]
2 A.C. 1 (compensation awarded for temporary interference).

sky factor contours on a before and after obstruction basis, from which the area of light lost to the rooms lit by the apertures in question can be calculated. For the purpose of calculating compensation the affected rooms are divided into four equal zones known respectively as the front zone, the first zone, the second zone and the makeweight area. Loss of light in the front zone is regarded as very serious and that area of loss is given a weighting of 1.5. Loss of light in the second zone is given a weighting of 0.5 and loss of light in the makeweight area is taken at 0.25. By the application of these factors the loss is thus given a value equivalent to first zone loss, known as "EFZ".[375] The EFZ figures are then aggregated and multiplied by a rate per square foot per annum of between £3 and £5, depending on location. That gives an annual value which is then capitalised by the application of a suitable years purchase figure. The valuation formula can thus be expressed as follows: EFZ × [£3–£5] × YP. It can be seen that this approach is in essence a way of calculating the diminution in capital value of the areas affected by loss of light and thus of the dominant tenement. Very many rights of light disputes have been resolved on this basis.

Parasitic damages

14–117   Damages on the diminution in value basis are not restricted to the loss suffered by the apertures which enjoy rights to light but may be recovered in respect of loss caused as a result of the obstruction of other apertures and for the depreciation in value of other buildings or land affected by the obstruction. Such damages in respect of an interest other than that which the tort was designed to protect are sometimes called "parasitic", although the use of this expression has been roundly condemned by Lord Denning M.R.[376] So in *London Tilbury & Southend Railway Company v Gowers Walk School Trustees*[377] the owners of buildings which had acquired rights to light pulled them down and erected a new building on the site, certain parts of the windows of which coincided with the old windows, while others did not. The defendant erected a warehouse which obstructed the windows in the new building. It was held that the claimants were entitled to compensation[378] in respect of the whole of the windows so obstructed, including those which did not coincide with those in the old building and which therefore enjoyed no right to light. Lord Esher M.R. said[379]:

> "Supposing the company had been in the ordinary position of owners of land and not affected by any statute and had then done what they have done, the Trustees would have been entitled to sue them in a common law action for interference with ancient lights; could the Plaintiffs in such an action have recovered damages in respect of injury to all the lights affected, the new as

[375] The process is not unlike the measurement of retail premises in terms of zone A ("ITZA") for valuation purposes.
[376] In *Spartan Steel Alloys v Martin & Co* [1973] Q.B. 27 at 35F.
[377] (1889) 24 Q.B.D. 326.
[378] The claim was for compensation under the Railway Clauses Act 1845.
[379] At p.329.

well as the old? On this point the rule seems to me to be that where a Plaintiff has a cause of action for a wrongful act of the Defendant the Plaintiff is entitled to recover for all the damage caused which was the direct consequence of the wrongful act and so probable a consequence that, if the Defendant had considered the matter, he must have foreseen the whole damage would result from that act. If that be so, and a person puts up buildings, the inevitable consequence of their erection being to obstruct ancient and modern lights, should he not be taken to have foreseen that in obstructing the one he would obstruct the other? If that were proved in a common law action, the Plaintiff would be entitled to damages for the whole of the consequences of the wrongful act of obstructing ancient lights, which would include damage to the new as much as to the old lights."

That decision was applied by a subsequent Court of Appeal in *Griffith v Richard* **14–118** *Clay & Sons*.[380] There the plaintiff owned two old and dilapidated houses, the front windows of which had acquired rights to light. He also owned a piece of land at the rear of the houses. The defendant erected a building on the opposite side of the street which obstructed the plaintiff's windows. It was found that the houses were ripe for redevelopment and that the whole site would be suitable for a warehouse or factory. It was held that the damages recoverable were not limited to the diminution in the value of the houses but extended to the diminution in value of the whole of the plaintiff's property considered as one building site. The reason was that an injunction, had one been sought in time and obtained, "*would have enured for the benefit of the whole site*".[381]

Similarly, in *Wills v May*[382] the plaintiff owned two houses which he had **14–119** bought with a view to redeveloping the site of both for commercial purposes. The defendant obstructed the light to one of the houses. It was held that the Court was entitled to take into account not only the immediate damage to the house whose light had been obstructed but also the diminution in value of the site of both houses treated as a development site, albeit that the site of one house would not become available for development for 14 years because it was under lease. Lawrence J. awarded £50 for the immediate damage to the affected house plus £100 for the permanent damage to the whole site.

Loss of amenity

When the infringement affects the amenity of the affected premises, damages **14–120** reflecting that loss of amenity may also be recovered. These may include damages for inconvenience and, in a rights of light case, for such factors as loss of sky visibility and loss of sunlight.[383] There is no distinction in this regard between

---

[380] [1912] 2 Ch. 291.

[381] See per Cozens-Hardy M.R. at pp. 296–297 and per Buckley L.J. at p. 301.

[382] [1923] 1 Ch. 317.

[383] *Carr-Saunders v Dick McNeill Associates Ltd* [1986] 1 W.L.R. 922. In *Wandsworth LBC v Railtrack Plc* [2001] 1 W.L.R. 368, affirmed on appeal at [2002] Q.B. 756, damages were awarded for public nuisance caused by pigeon droppings from a railway bridge fouling the footpath below.

nuisance causing physical damage to property and nuisance causing inconvenience and interfering with comfort.[384] There is little guidance as to how such damages should be assessed. In *Bone v Seal*[385] the Court of Appeal suggested that in nuisance cases courts should have regard to the level of damages awarded in analogous personal injury cases, but this criterion is likely to be of limited application in a property law context. A better yardstick may be awards of damages for loss of amenity in landlord and tenant cases where landlords have failed to repair residential premises or have been guilty of acts amounting to derogation from grant.[386] Damages under this head will tend to be modest and the courts will be careful not to allow double recovery for the same item where damages for diminution in value and/or aggravated damages are also being awarded.[387]

The wayleave or user basis

14–121   The two general rules set out in para.14–113 above are subject to exceptions. One well established exception arises in cases of trespass to land. The exception originated in wayleave cases, where the defendant had trespassed by carrying coals along an underground way through the plaintiff's mine. Although the value of his land had not been diminished by the trespass, the plaintiff recovered damages equivalent to what he would have received if he had been paid for a wayleave.[388] In those cases the measure of damage was the going rate in the locality for such a wayleave.

The principle of those cases was then applied to cases of wrongful trespass on the surface of land and wrongful retention of the possession of land in circumstances where the claimant would not otherwise have made use of the land, the measure of damage being, not the diminution in the value of the land to the claimant, but the value to the defendant of the use he had made of the claimant's land.[389]

In *Whitwham* Rigby L.J. put the matter thus, at 543:

> "There is nothing special in the nature of a wayleave, and there is nothing special for this purposes in an underground way. The principle is that a trespasser shall not be allowed to make use of another person's land without in some way compensating that other person for that user. Where the trespass consists in using a way over the Plaintiff's land, a convenient way of assessing damages may be by an inquiry as to wayleave, which, when there is a customary rate of charge for wayleave in the locality, may furnish a convenient

---

[384] At 384D.

[385] [1975] 1 All E.R. 787.

[386] See Woodfall, *Landlord and Tenant*, Vol. 1, para. 13.089.2 and cases there cited.

[387] *Owers v Bailey* [2006] 39 L.S. Gaz. 34.

[388] *Martin v Porter* (1839) 5 M. & W. 351; *Jegon v Vivian* (1871) L.R. 6 Ch. App. 742, and *Phillips v Homfray* (1871) L.R. 6 Ch. App. 770.

[389] *Whitwham v Westminster Brymbo Coal & Coke Co* [1896] 2 Ch. 538 (land used for tipping colliery waste); *Penarth Dock Engineering Co Ltd v Pounds* [1963] 1 Lloyds Rep. 359 (use of a dock); *Swordheath Properties Ltd v Tabet* [1979] 1 W.L.R. 285 (use of a flat); see *Att-Gen v Blake* [2001] 1 A.C. 268 at 278D–279E per Lord Nicholls.

measure of damages; but the principle is that in some way or other, if you can do nothing better then by rule of thumb, the trespasser must be charged for the use of the land."

As Patten J. said in *Perlman v Rayden*,[390] "The wayleave principle assumes a willing and reasonable claimant and not one who would seek an exorbitant fee for the use of his land in order to deter consent being sought". He awarded £10,000 as damages on the user principle for unlawful use of a roadway to facilitate the carrying out of building works.[391]

In *Experience Hendrix v PPX Enterprises*[392] the Court of Appeal considered how damages are to be quantified under this principle. The defendant had, in breach of an agreement, licensed masters of recordings which it was not entitled to licence. There was no proof that this had caused the claimant any loss. The claimant applied for an account of the profits, alternatively damages on the "user" basis. The Court of Appeal held that the proper remedy would be a reasonable sum for the defendant's use of the material in breach of contract assessed by reference to the fees that might have been agreed between willing parties; the cases in which the appropriate remedy is an account of profits[393] will be exceptional. Mance L.J. held that damages on the user basis may be recovered at common law for a past infringement, even if an injunction is awarded for the future. In other words, this measure of damages is not confined to cases where damages are awarded in lieu of injunction. This is so even if the claimant can prove no financial loss and even if the claimant would not have granted a licence permitting the infringement. **14–122**

It has been suggested that where damages are assessed on this basis, interest should not be awarded, since "it would spell double recovery" and "would amount to awarding interest upon interest".[394] In *Whitwham*, Chitty J. said that to award interest "would be to treat the Plaintiffs as having invested their damages at interest in the hands of the Defendants".[395] We are quite unable to follow this reasoning. Interest is routinely awarded on awards of mesne profits, damages for trespass and arrears of rent, taking account, of course, of the fact that the liability accrued over a period and not at a single date, and there is no reason for not adopting the same approach in a case involving use of land which goes beyond that authorised by an easement. **14–123**

Damages in lieu—the "negotiating basis"

At common law damages can only be recovered for past loss but it is possible to recover damages for a trespass or other wrong expected to continue into the **14–124**

---

[390] [2004] EWHC 2192 at [102].
[391] In *Sinclair v Gavaghan* [2007] EWHC 2256 (Ch.), the same judge awarded £5,000 for unlawful use of a small area of land to facilitate construction works in circumstances where the use of the land had been merely convenient, but not essential.
[392] [2003] 1 All E.R. (Comm) 830, CA.
[393] Such as *Att-Gen v Blake* [2001] 1 A.C. 268 (book royalties as a result of spying).
[394] *McGregor on Damages*, 17th ed., para.15–043.
[395] [1896] 1 Ch. 894 at 899 (upheld on appeal at [1896] 2 Ch. 538).

future where the Court has jurisdiction to award an injunction and instead awards damages in lieu under section 50 of the Supreme Court Act. In such a case damages are assessed by reference to such sum as reasonable and willing negotiating parties would have prospectively agreed as the price for the consent or grant necessary to legitimate the wrongful conduct.[396] In principle this is no different to the "wayleave" basis, except that the former compensates for the loss of the ability to enforce the right for the future, usually in perpetuity, while the latter compensates for the usurpation of the right in the past.[397]

Not a "ransom price"

14–125   The assessment of damages on this basis assumes a hypothetical negotiation on the footing that each party is willing to agree a proper but not a "ransom price which a very reluctant plaintiff might put on it".[398] That the actual parties or one of them was in fact most unwilling to negotiate is irrelevant.[399] The proper price will have regard to the amount of profit which the defendant would expect from its development of the site.[400]

Sir Thomas Bingham's dictum that the price is not a "ransom price" is, at first sight, puzzling because, of course, it is the power to hold the other party to ransom by the threat of an injunction which creates the claimant's bargaining position. It is thought that what Sir Thomas meant to emphasise is that the price is moderated by:

(a) the artificial assumption that both parties are to be taken to be willing to do a deal;

(b) ignoring any personal agenda of either party;

(c) the assumption that they are taken to be negotiating before either is irrevocably committed;

(d) the awareness of the seller that he may not get another chance to realise a capital sum for releasing or granting the required right;

(e) the availability of possible alternatives, e.g. acquiring an alternative access[401] or cutting back the proposed development to a point where the light obstruction caused is not actionable.

---

[396] *Wrotham Park v Parkside Homes* [1974] 1 W.L.R. 798; *Jaggard v Sawyer* [1995] 1 W.L.R. 269 and *Att-Gen v Blake* [2001] 1 A.C. 268.

[397] This is illustrated by the facts of *Whitwham v Westminster Brymbo Coal & Coke Co* [1896] 1 Ch. 894; on appeal [1896] 2 Ch. 538: the claim for unauthorised tipping on rather under half of the plaintiff's land was for £1,104; further tipping was restrained by injunction leaving what the judge called "a residual tipping value"; after this was pointed out, counsel agreed a figure of £550.

[398] per Sir Thomas Bingham M.R. in *Jaggard v Sawyer* [1995] 1 W.L.R. 269 at 282H.

[399] per Peter Gibson L.J. in *Experience Hendrix v PPX Enterprises Inc* [2003] 1 All E.R. (Comm) 83 at [57] citing Brightman J. in *Wrotham Park v Parkside Homes* (above) at 815C.

[400] per Millett J. in *Carr Saunders v Dick McNeill Associates Ltd* [1986] 1 W.L.R. 2167.

[401] In *Sinclair v Gavaghan* [2007] EWHC 2256 (Ch.) the claimant sought £125,000 damages for trespass in the course of the execution of building works but the judge awarded £5,000 because access could have been obtained without trespassing, albeit less conveniently.

In *Carr-Saunders v Dick McNeill Associates Ltd* Millett J. awarded damages of **14–126** £8,000, although he had assessed the diminution in value of the dominant tenement on the evidence of rights of light surveyors at only £3,000, in order to take into account both loss of amenity and loss of bargaining position. He did so unassisted by any evidence as to the value of these two factors. Following that decision, the practice grew up among rights of light surveyors of applying a multiplier of about 3 to the EFZ calculation described in para.14–116 above. The use of that particular factor would appear to have no proper valuation or legal basis, albeit that other cases have produced not dissimilar results.[402]

Damages are compensatory

This approach is not to be regarded as a departure from the principle that dam- **14–127** ages are awarded so as to compensate the victim for his loss; in these circumstances, where damages are awarded in lieu of injunction, the dominant owner is being compensated for the loss of the bargaining position represented by the right to obtain an injunction to prevent infringement of his easement.[403] In *Midtown Limited v City of London Real Property Company Limited*,[404] it was accepted by counsel for the defendant in a case involving infringement of rights of light that damages could include a compensatory payment by reference to a reasonable price for the release of the right, in addition to a sum representing diminution in the value of the property, and an enquiry as to damages was ordered in lieu of an injunction.

Date of assessment

The correct date for assessing damages on this basis is normally the date before **14–128** the infringement started[405] but it has been said that the position might be different in a case where one party concealed its acts from the other so as to steal a march and postpone the date at which the other realised that his rights were being

---

[402] In *Deakins v Hookings* [1994] 1 E.G.L.R. 190 the judge would (if he had not granted an injunction) have awarded damages of £4,500, being 15 per cent of the value of the development, although he put the diminution in value of the dominant tenement at only £1,500. In *Marine & General Mutual Life Assurance Society v St James Real Estate Co Ltd* [1991] 2 E.G.L.R. 178 the deputy judge awarded damages of £18,000 (by reference to a comparable transaction), though the plaintiff's valuation evidence put the diminution in value at £6,375 and the defendant's evidence put it at nil. In *Mortimer v Bailey* [2004] EWCA Civ 1514; [2005] 1 E.G.L.R. 75, the judge assessed the diminution in value of the claimants' house at £20,000 but put the sum reasonably required to permit the development at £40,000: see at [20]–[21]. In *Horsford v Bird* [2006] UKPC 3, the Privy Council doubled an award based on the diminution in value of the land encroached upon to take into account the value of that land to the trespasser.

[403] *Jaggard v Sawyer* [1995] 1 W.L.R. 269, explaining *Surrey County Council v Bredero Homes* [1993] 1 W.L.R. 1361. This analysis in terms of compensation for loss of bargaining position was approved as correct by the House of Lords in *Att-Gen v Blake* [2001] 1 A.C. 268 at 281G per Lord Nicholls, where it is also said that it comes to the same thing as the price payable for the compulsory acquisition of a right. See also *WWF-World Wide Fund for Nature v World Wrestling Federation* [2007] EWCA Civ 286; [2008] 1 W.L.R. 445.

[404] [2005] EWHC 33; [2005] 1 E.G.L.R. 65.

[405] *Lunn Poly Ltd v Liverpool and Lancashire Properties Ltd* [2006] 2 E.G.L.R. 29.

infringed, in which case it might be appropriate to shift the imaginary negotiations forward in time.[406]

The use of hindsight

14–129 This raises the question to what extent the court may make use of hindsight in assessing loss on this basis. Obviously in a real negotiation taking place before the infringement the negotiators would have to estimate the likely profit and make assumptions (about which there might be considerable scope for disagreement) about a number of factors.[407] By the time of trial, however, a number of those unknowns will have become known and a more accurate assessment of the profit can be made.

In *Amec Developments Ltd v Jury's Hotel Management (UK) Ltd*,[408] the judge, Mr Anthony Mann Q.C., said[409]:

> "The negotiation analysis is not pursued rigorously to its logical end. I do not have to imagine a negotiation in which the parties have to guess at something that events have in fact made certain. In carrying out my exercise, I can take into account the actual events that have happened, and the actual benefits accrued, as at the date of trial."

As authority for this proposition, the judge cited the approach of Brightman J. in *Wrotham Park* and dicta of Lord Nicholls in *Att-Gen v Blake* that "the defendant must make a reasonable payment in respect of the benefit he has gained". The judge then went on to assess the damages on the basis of what the evidence showed about the actual level of gain to the defendant. Later in his judgment, he said that the fact that one was allowed to take into account what had actually happened in terms of assessing the actual gain did not shift the date of the hypothetical negotiation but merely made sure that it had "at least one foot in the realms of reality and limits the possibility of over- or under-compensation".[410]

14–130   In *Lunn Poly Ltd v Liverpool & Lancashire Properties Ltd*[411] however, Neuberger L.J. (with whom Scott Baker and Auld L.JJ. agreed) said[412]:

> "Although I see the force of what Mr. Mann said in his judgment, it should not, in my opinion, be treated as being generally applicable to events after the date of breach where the Court decided to award damages in lieu on a negotiating basis as at the date of breach. After all, once the Court has

---

[406] *Amec Developments Ltd v Jurys Hotel Management (UK) Ltd* [2001] 1 E.G.L.R. 81 at 86L–87A.
[407] Similar language was used by Mance L.J. in *Experience Hendrix* (above) at [35] where he spoke of "a reasonable sum having regard to the financial benefit obtained" from holding an unlawful pop concert.
[408] [2001] 1 E.G.L.R. 81.
[409] At 84A–C.
[410] *Amec Developments Ltd* at 86M.
[411] [2006] 2 E.G.L.R. 29.
[412] At [28] and [29].

decided on a particular valuation date for assessing negotiating damages, consistency, fairness, and principle can be said to suggest that a judge should be careful before agreeing that factors that existed at that date should be ignored, or that a factor that occurred after that date should be taken into account, as affecting the negotiating stance of the parties when deciding the figure at which they would arrive.

In my view the proper analysis is as follows. Given that negotiating damages under the Act are meant to be compensatory, and are normally to be assessed or valued at the date of breach, principle and consistency indicate that post valuation events are normally irrelevant. However, given the quasi equitable nature of such damages, the judge may, where there are good reasons, direct a departure from the norm, either by selecting a different valuation date or by directing that a specific post-valuation-date event can be taken into account."

The question in that case was whether the judge was right to hold that the hypothetical negotiators (of the price for the right to block up a fire door) should not be supposed to take into account that the tenant's negotiating position would have been weakened because his lease was liable to forfeiture on an unrelated ground. It was not concerned with the assessment of the likely profit. Moreover, Neuberger L.J. stressed that the way in which damages in lieu are to be assessed is very flexible, that there are no absolute rules and said that he could see no reason why the court should not be able to order the defendant simply to pay over to the claimant a proportion of a capital sum which it made as a result of selling its interest with the benefit of the breach of the claimant's rights.[413]

The law would appear to be that it will often be appropriate to take evidence of actual costs and/or profit (where that is known) into account for the purpose of arriving at a fair figure to compensate the claimant for the wrong which has been done to him[414]; the imaginary negotiation is a useful tool but it is not a straitjacket. The situation is different from one where a market value assessment on a particular date is required by contract or statute.   **14–131**

The division of the profit

The amount of profit is only one relevant factor in the assessment of what the claimant might have obtained as the price for his consent.[415] It remains, of course, to decide how much of that profit the claimant could reasonably have expected to receive and the defendant to have to pay. That will be a matter for evidence and   **14–132**

---

[413] At [24].
[414] See the judgment of Chadwick L.J. in *WWF-World Wide Fund for Nature & World Wrestling Federation Entertainment Inc* [2007] EWCA Civ 286; [2008] 1 W.L.R. 445 at [29] where he explains that Brightman J.'s award of damages in *Wrotham Park* was based on the actual profit of the development and at [59] where he speaks of the court's "flexible response to the need to compensate the claimant for the wrong which has been done to him".
[415] per Millett L.J. in *Jaggard v Sawyer* [1995] 1 W.L.R. 269 at 291D.

judgment in every case; the decided cases show a wide range, which only empha-sises that it all depends on the facts. In *Wrotham Park*, the judge awarded 5 per cent of the actual profit—but there were special reasons for a low award. In *Bracewell v Appleby* the award was £2,000 out of an estimated profit of £5,000—so 40 per cent. In *Jaggard v Sawyer* the trial judge took a figure which he described as between a quarter and a third of the hypothetical profit.[416] In *Deakins v Hookings*[417] the judge would (if he had not granted an injunction) have awarded damages equal to 15 per cent of the value of the benefit of the development to the defendant. In *Tamares Ltd v Fairpoint Properties*, the judge took one-third of the average of the surveyor's loss of profit estimates and rounded it down "on account of the relatively modest nature of the infringement"; the result was about 28.5 per cent of the estimated profit.[418] In *Wynn-Jones v Bickley*,[419] the judge awarded 50 per cent of the estimated profit facilitated by the trespass. In *Small v Oliver and Saunders (Developments) Ltd*,[420] the judge based his award on 35 per cent of the development profit.

There is no decided case in which an account of the development profits—i.e. 100 per cent—has been awarded as damages for nuisance. Although there are circumstances in which an account can be an appropriate remedy for breach of contract or fiduciary duty,[421] it is almost certainly never an available remedy for nuisance by obstruction of an easement.[422]

14–133   Moreover, where several parties enjoy rights over the same land, all of which would require to be bought off to make the conduct in question lawful, any indi-vidual claimant will only be entitled to a share of the "pot" which the developer could reasonably be expected to be prepared to make available. The courts have so far only had to deal with the relatively simple case of a known number of per-sons entitled to precisely the same right,[423] but more complicated situations can arise, particularly in relation to obstruction of light, where the effect on the claimants and other potential claimants differs markedly but the overall pot is likely to be limited. Another complication in such a case, which may impact on what any individual might reasonably expect to be paid, is the risk borne by the developer that not everybody will come to terms and that he may need to take account of the likely cost of dealing with the more intransigent, if necessary by litigation.

---

[416] See [1993] 1 E.G.L.R. 197 at 203D.

[417] [1994] 1 E.G.L.R. 190.

[418] [2007] 1 W.L.R. 2167 at [37].

[419] [2006] EWHC 1991.

[420] [2006] EWHC 1293 (Ch.) at [96].

[421] See *Att-Gen v Blake* [2001] 1 A.C. 268.

[422] *Forsyth-Grant v Allen* [2008] EWCA Civ 505; [2008] 26 E.G. 118.

[423] In *Bracewell v Appleby* [1975] Ch. 408, where the pot was divided equally between five owners of the servient land and in *Jaggard v Sawyer* [1995] 1 W.L.R. 269, where the pot was divided between nine owners. In *Small v Oliver and Saunders (Developments) Ltd* [2006] EWHC 1293 (Ch.); [2006] 3 E.G.L.R. 152, a breach of restrictive covenant case, the claimant's damages of £3,720 were calculated by taking 35 per cent of the development profit and dividing it by the 48 persons entitled to enforce the covenant.

Other considerations

In *Tamares (Vincent Square) Limited v Fairpoint Properties (Vincent Square)*   **14–134**
Limited (No.2)[424] the deputy judge synthesised the principles concerning damages in lieu to be derived from the previous cases as follows:

(1) the overall principle is that the court must attempt to find what would be
    a "fair" result of a hypothetical negotiation between the parties;
(2) the context, including the nature and seriousness of the breach, must be
    kept in mind;
(3) the right to prevent a development gives the owner of the right a signif-
    icant bargaining position;
(4) the owner of the right with such a bargaining position will normally be
    expected to receive some part of the likely profit from the development;
(5) if there is no evidence of the likely size of the profit, the court can do its
    best by awarding a suitable multiple of the damages for loss of
    amenity[425];
(6) if there is evidence of the likely size of the profit, the court should nor-
    mally award a sum which takes into account a fair percentage of the
    profit;
(7) the size of the award should not in any event be so large that the devel-
    opment would not have taken place had such a sum been payable;
(8) after arriving at a figure which takes into consideration all the above and
    any other relevant factors, the court needs to consider whether the "*deal
    feels right*".

In that case the judge assessed the profit from the relevant part of the development at £174,500 and awarded £50,000 as damages guided to some extent by the
decision of the Lands Tribunal in *Stokes v Cambridge Corporation*.[426]

Use of comparables

It is not, however, thought that the derivation of a reasonable price from an esti-   **14–135**
mate or account of the profit to be made will always be appropriate. There will be
many cases where what would be a reasonable price can be demonstrated by reference to comparables—i.e. what others have agreed in relation to the same development or in similar situations. The use of comparables is generally regarded by
valuers as a more accurate valuation approach than the use of a residual valuation
method, which necessarily involves a number of variables. In *Marine & General
Mutual Life Assurance Society v St James Real Estate Co Ltd*,[427] the judge
awarded damages of £18,000 by reference to a comparable transaction, although

---

[424] [2007] EWHC 212; [2007] 1 W.L.R. 2167.
[425] As in *Carr Saunders v Dick McNeill Associates Ltd* [1986] 1 W.L.R. 922.
[426] (1961) 13 P. & C.R. 77.
[427] [1991] 2 E.G.L.R. 178.

the plaintiff's valuer had put the diminution in value at £6,375 and the defendant had put it at nil. In *Harris v Williams-Wynne*,[428] the judge awarded £8,000 as the price that would have been agreed for the release of a covenant, rejecting an approach based on a residual valuation method, relying on evidence of actual agreements made by one of the parties and observing that any deal would have been a "horse-trade" and not the result of a sophisticated calculation.

Statutory rights of access

14–136 A factor which would obviously affect the parties' negotiating position would be the existence of any statutory right to obtain the grant of the right in question and the measure of compensation payable pursuant to statute. It is likely, however, that the developer will be prepared to pay more, perhaps significantly more, for a negotiated grant in order to avoid the delay, cost and uncertainty of having to operate the statutory procedure.

In *Severn Trent Water Limited v Barnes*[429] a water undertaker had laid 20 metres of main on the claimant's land without serving notice of entry and was sued for trespass. The Court of Appeal approved an award of damages consisting of a sum equal to the statutory compensation (£100) plus a further sum representing loss of bargaining opportunity (£500) but overruled that part of the decision of the trial judge in which he had awarded a third sum by way of compensation for the use of the pipe pending judgment.

14–137 In *Horsford v Bird*,[430] however, the Privy Council awarded damages for trespass in lieu of injunction as at the date of action brought and mesne profits for 6 years prior to that date and for a further 2 years to the date on which an injunction was refused, at 7.5 per cent per annum of the capital value awarded. As Mr Hodge Q.C., sitting as a deputy judge, pointed out in *Wynn-Jones v Bickley*,[431] it would have been more in line with earlier authority to award a capital sum assessed as at the date of the infringement and added interest until the date of judgment, but it may be that the Privy Council were not in a position to do that because the value of the land had been agreed at first instance as at the later date. It may not, of course, make much difference whether the court awards a capital sum assessed at the earlier date plus interest or a capital sum assessed as at the later date with mesne profits from the earlier date, unless property values have altered significantly between the two dates. It is suggested that the court can adopt whichever approach produces the fairest result in all the circumstances.

Aggravated damages

14–138 The basic conditions for an award of aggravated damages are first, exceptional or contumelious conduct or motives on the part of the defendant in committing the wrong, and secondly, mental distress, injury to feelings, indignity, insult, humili-

---

[428] [2005] EWHC 151 (Ch.) at [57]–[59], upheld on appeal on other points at [2006] EWCA Civ 104.
[429] [2004] 2 E.G.L.R. 95.
[430] [2006] UKPC 3; [2006] 1 E.G.L.R. 75.
[431] [2006] EWHC 1991.

ation and a heightened sense of injury or grievance sustained by the claimant.[432] So, in a case where the defendant had deliberately and maliciously blocked access to the claimant's house, used intimidatory and insulting language to the female claimant, had done so in order to force the claimants to give him a right of access to which he was not entitled and succeeded in forcing the claimants to sell up and move house, the court awarded a total of £4,500 aggravated damages in addition to damages for loss of amenity and for diminution in value of the claimants' property.[433]

In *Perlman v Rayden*,[434] Patten J. awarded aggravated damages to compensate the claimant for mental distress caused by the defendant exceeding his rights. He held that aggravated damages may be awarded for mental distress increased by the defendant's conduct during or after the tortious act and that it was relevant to take into account: **14–139**

  (i) the defendant's motives for committing the tort and resisting any claim for compensation;
  (ii) any deliberate misleading of the claimant or concealment of what was being or had been done; and
  (iii) the fact that any wrongdoing had been denied.

By contrast, in *Cardwell v Walker*[435] Neuberger J. on appeal overturned an award of aggravated damages where a servient owner had withheld tokens necessary to operate electricity meters for five days, although the judge described that conduct as a "mean and unpleasant act".

(7) *Practice*

Plans and photographs

In cases involving disputes about easements an understanding of the topography is all-important for determining the meaning or scope of the grant, express or implied, for deciding whether the right in question has been substantially interfered with or exceeded and for determining what relief is appropriate. Practitioners would do well to heed the following advice of Lady Justice Arden concerning plans and photographs given in the context of an appeal but scarcely less apposite in the context of preparation for a hearing at first instance: **14–140**

"The problem is this: there are a significant number of cases which involve this court using plans, maps, diagrams and photographs, and more importantly, understanding them. These cases usually concern land. Many cases of this

---

[432] *Appleton v Garrett* [1997] 8 Med. L.R. 75 at 77–78, per Dyson J.
[433] *Owers v Bailey* LTL 27/9/2006.
[434] [2004] EWHC 2192.
[435] [2003] EWHC 3117.

kind, however, ... are prepared in a way which makes it very difficult for members of this court, when reading the papers in preparation for the appeal hearing, to read the plan, map, diagram or photograph correctly, or to follow fully the submissions of the parties about those documents or the property which is the subject of the dispute. In these circumstances, the court cannot be certain about what the plan, diagram, map or photograph shows until the appeal is opened and they are fully explained. Those who prepare bundles or skeleton arguments would do well to remember that a plan, map, diagram or photograph which is clear to people who are fully familiar with the case may well not be wholly clear to a judge coming to the case for the first time. The problem is often exacerbated when the case comes to this court, and the parties very properly put into the appeal bundle some only of the maps, plans, diagrams or photographs. When that happens, this court does not have all the information which the court below had. In my judgment, it is absolutely essential in any case of this kind, where the court is going to have to grapple with plans, maps, diagrams or photographs, that there is at least one plan, photograph or map which leaves the court in no real doubt about the location of all the relevant features. The skeleton arguments should also identify that photograph, map, plan or diagram at an early point, so this court is left in no doubt when it is pre-reading its papers for the hearing. Very often, in my experience, this court is (for example) either given some only of the plans, or photocopies which do not have the colouring referred to in the original documents or by the judge in his judgment, or copies with parts cut off, or without compass points, or where appropriate, a statement of the scale. Those who prepare skeleton arguments for cases in this court or appeal bundles should please bear in mind that the court has properly and easily to understand any map, plan, diagram or photograph which is material in the appeal."[436]

Form of injunction

14–141 Most of the cases on the disturbance of easements in which the form of the injunction to be granted has been considered have been concerned with rights of light.[437] In *Dent v Auction Mart Co*[438] Page Wood V.-C. referred to earlier authorities and adopted the form of injunction settled by Lord Cranworth in 1866 in *Yates v Jack*.[439] This order (the form of which was followed until 1904) restrained the defendant

---

[436] *Hunte v E. Bottomley & Sons Ltd* [2007] EWCA Civ 1168 at [30]; the case concerned obstruction of a right of way.

[437] In *Seton* (7th ed.) will be found forms of injunction against interference with the right of support (p. 565), rights of way (p. 574), rights in respect of the flow or user of water (p. 582), and the right to purity of water (p. 605).

[438] (1866) L.R. 2 Eq. 238.

[439] (1866) 1 Ch. App. 295 at 298; para.7–10, above.

"from erecting any building so as to darken, injure, or obstruct any of the ancient lights of the Plaintiffs as the same were enjoyed previously to the taking down by the Defendant of his buildings on the opposite side of the street, and also from permitting to remain any buildings already erected which will cause any such obstruction."

Lord Cranworth, in the same case, following *Stokes v City Offices Co*,[440] added a proviso enabling the parties to come before the chief clerk in order to have it ascertained whether any proposed addition to the building would or would not be a violation of the injunction; but this proviso was not inserted as a matter of course in subsequent orders.

Since it was definitively laid down in *Colls v Home and Colonial Stores*[441] that **14–142** the easement of light confers only the "right to be protected against a particular form of nuisance", and not the right to the whole of the light as it was previously enjoyed, the form of the order in *Yates v Jack*[442] was not appropriate as it stood. It was disapproved as a common form order in *Colls*,[443] and suggestions for an alteration in the form of order were made by Lord Macnaghten[444]:

"The common form of injunction which has been in use since the case of *Yates v Jack*[445] is not, I think, altogether free from objection. I think it would be better that the order, when expressed in general terms, should restrain the defendant from erecting any building so as to cause a nuisance or illegal obstruction to the plaintiffs ancient windows, as the same existed previously to the taking down of the house which formerly stood on the site of the defendant's new buildings. If the action is brought to a hearing before the defendant's new buildings are completed, and there seems to be good ground for the plaintiffs apprehensions, an order, I think, might be conveniently made in that form with costs up to the hearing, and liberty to the plaintiff within a fixed time after completion to apply for further relief by way of mandatory injunction or damages, as he may be advised."

In *Anderson v Francis*,[446] Swinfen Eady J. followed the above suggestions of Lord Macnaghten, and the form so suggested has now been adopted as the common form order.[447]

It is as a general rule improper to couple an injunction to restrain interference **14–143** with rights of air with an injunction to restrain interference with rights of light.

---

[440] (1865) 2 H. & M. 650.
[441] [1904] A.C. 179 at 212, per Lord Lindley.
[442] (1866) 1 Ch. App. 295.
[443] [1904] A.C. 179 at 193, per Lord Macnaghten; per Lord Davey at 201; per Lord Lindley at 207.
[444] [1904] A.C. 179 at 194.
[445] (1866) 1 Ch. App. 295.
[446] [1906] W.N. 160.
[447] See the orders made in *Higgins v Betts* [1905] 1 Ch. 217; *Andrews v Waite* [1907] 2 Ch. 500 at 510; and *Vere v Minter* [1914] W.N. 89. Other forms of injunctions dealing with the obstruction of ancient lights are given in *Seton* (7th ed.), pp. 553 *et seq.*

For an injunction to protect air is not granted unless a separate case be made for it.[448] Where, however, a separate case is made in respect of air, injunctions have been granted by the courts.[449]

Reference to a surveyor

14-144 There are cases[450] where the court, after deciding that there is an obstruction to be restrained, has, by consent of the parties, referred it to a surveyor to say what alteration will be sufficient to remedy the obstruction. Thus, in *Abbott v Holloway*,[451] an order was by consent made to refer it to an independent surveyor to determine whether the erection of the defendants' buildings, having regard to the increased height thereof, would depreciate to any and what extent the value of the plaintiffs' premises; the defendants to pay to the plaintiffs the sum (if any) so determined; the surveyor to be agreed upon by the parties, or in default to be appointed by the judge, and his fees to be borne by the parties equally; the defendants to pay the plaintiffs' taxed costs of the action; the surveyor not to be attended by anyone on behalf of the parties, or to take evidence.

The court now has power[452] to appoint an assessor to assist the court in dealing with a matter in which he has skill and experience. Provision for the appointment of such a person is made in the Civil Procedure Rules and Practice Directions.[453]

14-145 In *Colls v Home and Colonial Stores*,[454] Lord Macnaghten made the following observations[455]:

"It will be observed that in *Back v. Stacey*[456] the learned judge told the jury who had viewed the premises that they were to judge rather from their own ocular observation than from the testimony of any witnesses, however respectable, of the degree of diminution which the plaintiff's ancient light had undergone. Now a judge who exercises the functions of both judge and jury cannot be expected to view the premises himself, even if he considers himself an expert in such matters. But I have often wondered why the Court does not more frequently avail itself of the power of calling in a competent adviser to report to the Court upon the question. There are plenty of experienced surveyors accustomed to deal with large properties in London who might be trusted to make a perfectly fair and impartial report, subject, of

---

[448] See para.8–01, above.

[449] *Dent v Auction Mart Co* (1866) L.R. 2 Eq. 238 at 255; *Chastey v Ackland* [1895] 2 Ch. 389 at 391, 392; *Cable v Bryant* [1908] 1 Ch. 260.

[450] *Jessel v Chaplin* (1856) 2 Jur. (n.s.) 931; *Att-Gen v Merthyr Tydfil Local Board of Health* [1870] W.N. 148; but see *Att-Gen v Colney Hatch Lunatic Asylum* (1868) 4 Ch. App. 146.

[451] [1904] W.N. 124.

[452] Under the Supreme Court Act 1981, s.70 and the County Courts Act 1984, s.63.

[453] CPR Pt 35, r.15 and 35 PD 7.

[454] [1904] A.C. 179.

[455] [1904] A.C. 179 at 192. See also *Fishenden v Higgs & Hill* (1935) 153 L.T. 128 at 144, per Maugham L.J. The court's attitude to the appointment of a court expert was discussed in *Abbey National Mortgages Plc v Key Surveyors Nationwide Ltd* [1996] 3 All E.R. 184.

[456] (1826) 2 C. & P. 465.

course, to examination in Court if required. I am not in the least surprised
that the plaintiffs in the present case objected to a report from a disinterested
surveyor, but in my opinion the Court ought to have obtained such a report
for its own guidance."

Although it has been doubted whether a judge should himself visit the premises **14–146**
in question and use his own senses to ascertain whether an injury has been committed, for he may be mistaken, and it is his duty to decide on sworn evidence,[457]
he may, however, inspect the premises.[458] In *Ough v King*,[459] Lord Denning M.R.
said that it was helpful for the judge to have a view in light cases.

Declaratory relief

The court may be faced by difficult questions of fact and degree when consider- **14–147**
ing what conduct would amount to an infringement of an easement or to excessive user infringing the rights of others. In such a case it may be sufficient to
determine the rights of the parties in the form of a declaration coupled with
liberty to apply for an injunction if necessary,[460] or it may be appropriate to make
a detailed order prohibiting specified conduct or prescribing the times at and
manner in which certain activities may take place,[461] or prescribing the dimensions of vehicles which may use a right of way.[462]

   In *Well Barn Shoot v Shackleton*,[463] the owners of a shooting estate of
1,500 acres had shooting rights over a farm which consisted of a farmhouse, two
barns, some outbuildings in a farmyard and an area of garden and grazing land of
about 13 acres. The owner of the farm obtained planning permission to convert
the redundant farm buildings to housing. He sought a declaration that no element
of the proposed development would necessarily cause (a) any unreasonable interference with the ordinary exercise of the sporting rights or (b) any other breach
or derogation from the sporting rights.

   The judge granted that negative declaration upon the farmer's undertaking to
enter into covenants limiting the height of fences and walls and prohibiting construction work during the shooting season, subject to a proviso that the development be carried out in accordance with the planning consent and section 106
agreement and that the farm comply with the undertakings and covenants.

   The Court of Appeal held that there is jurisdiction to grant such a negative declaration; that it is a matter of discretion for the trial judge whether to do so and
that the critical question is the practicality and utility of making such an order.
Sedley L.J. warned:

---

[457] *Jackson v Duke of Newcastle* (1864) 3 De G.J. & S. 275; *Leech v Schweder* (1874) 22 W.R. 292.
[458] See *Kine v Jolly* [1905] 1 Ch. 480 at 499; *Buckingham v Daily News Ltd* [1956] 2 Q.B. 534.
[459] [1967] 1 W.L.R. 1547 at 1552.
[460] See *Jelbert v Davis* [1968] 1 W.L.R. 589.
[461] As in *Rosling v Pinnegar* (1986) 54 P. & C.R. 124, followed in *Butler v Muddle* (1995) 6 B.P.R.
97,532 (whether number of openings on to way was unreasonable).
[462] As in *White v Richards* (1993) 68 P. & C.R. 105.
[463] [2002] EWCA Civ 2.

"In the ordinary case a Judge should not readily set out to anticipate trouble. The risk is that such an enterprise, rather than head off trouble, will provoke or aggravate it. To make declarations predicated upon undertakings which are proleptic in form and proactive in effect, but are made in necessary ignorance of the situations in which they will be invoked, is more often than not to court trouble. Such cases stand in contrast to those where some identifiable step can be forbidden because it either has violated or inevitably will violate one party's rights, or can be declared lawful because it can have no such effect."

(8) *Costs*

Calderbank offers

14–148   Since disputes about easements usually concern the entitlement of one or the other party to do something and since the primary relief sought is usually either a declaration or injunction, there is little scope for the defendant to protect himself by a payment into court. In these circumstances either party may seek to protect himself on costs by making a "Calderbank" offer, that is an offer expressed to be "without prejudice save as to costs". Such an offer will not be admissible on the substantive issues but will be admissible when costs come to be considered. If the offer is more advantageous to the offeree than the outcome of the action, then the offeror will have a strong claim to have an order for costs made in his favour.[464] Such an offer needs to state the offeror's proposals as to the costs of the proceedings to date. Even if it does not, however, it should still be taken into account, especially if made at an early stage and in a case where the costs are proportionately high compared to the value of the matter in issue. If the recipient of such an offer regards it as insufficient, he ought to state what would be sufficient. If the offer is unclear to him he ought to seek clarification. If he does not, he is at risk on costs.[465]

Part 36 offers

14–149   Alternatively, provisions are now made by the Civil Procedure Rules for either party to protect himself on costs by making an offer in a form and having the contents prescribed.[466] An offer made in accordance with these requirements is called a Part 36 offer. It must be in writing and must (a) state that it is intended to have the consequences set out in Part 36; (b) specify a period of not less than 21 days within which the defendant will be liable for the claimant's costs if the offer is accepted; (c) state whether it relates to the whole of the claim or part of it or to

---

[464] *Cutts v Head* [1984] Ch. 290, the leading case on Calderbank offers, which concerned a dispute over the right of access to a fishery.
[465] *Phillis Trading Limited v 86 Lordship Road Ltd* [2001] 2 E.G.L.R. 85; [2001] EWCA Civ 350. Clarification may also be sought in the case of Part 36 offers: CPR Pt 36, r.8.
[466] CPR Pt 36.

an issue and, if so, to what part or issue; and (d) state whether it takes into account any counterclaim.[467] A Part 36 offer to pay or accept a sum of money is treated as inclusive of all interest until (generally) 21 days after the date of the offer.[468] It is therefore critical to take interest into account when deciding what offer to make. The fact that a Part 36 offer had been made must not be communicated to the trial judge until the case has been decided.[469]

The costs consequences of acceptance of a defendant's or a claimant's Part 36 offer are prescribed by the rules.[470] If the claimant fails to better a Part 36 offer, he will generally be ordered to pay the defendant's costs from the latest date upon which the offer could have been accepted without court order.[471] If the claimant does better than his own Part 36 offer, the court may award him an enhanced rate of interest and indemnity costs.[472] **14–150**

---

[467] CPR Pt 36, r.2(2).
[468] CPR Pt 36, r.3(3).
[469] CPR Pt 36, r.13(2).
[470] CPR Pt 36, r.10.
[471] CPR Pt 36, r.14(2).
[472] CPR Pt 36, r.14(3).

APPENDICES

STATUTES, RULES AND ORDERS

Appendix A—Statutes

Appendix B—Regulations

APPENDIX A

Prescription Act 1832

(2 & 3 WILL. 4, C. 71)

An Act for shortening the time of prescription in certain cases.

[1ST AUGUST 1832]

Whereas the expression "time immemorial, or time whereof the memory of man runneth not to the contrary," is now by the Law of England in many cases considered to include and denote the whole period of time from the Reign of King Richard the First, whereby the title to matters that have been long enjoyed is sometimes defeated by shewing the commencement of such enjoyment, which is in many cases productive of inconvenience and injustice;

Claims to right of common and other profits à prendre, not to be defeated after thirty years enjoyment by merely showing the commencement; after sixty years enjoyment the right to be absolute, unless had by consent or agreement

1. No claim which may be lawfully made at the common law, by custom, prescription, or grant, to any right of common or other profit or benefit to be taken and enjoyed from or upon any land of our sovereign lord the King, or any land being parcel of the duchy of Lancaster or of the duchy of Cornwall, or of any ecclesiastical or lay person, or body corporate, except such matters and things as are herein specially provided for, and except tithes, rent, and services, shall, where such right, profit, or benefit shall have been actually taken and enjoyed by any person claiming right thereto without interruption for the full period of thirty years, be defeated or destroyed by showing only that such right, profit, or benefit was first taken or enjoyed at any time prior to such period of thirty years, but nevertheless such claim may be defeated in any other way by which the same is now liable to be defeated; and when such right, profit, or benefit shall have been so taken and enjoyed as aforesaid for the full period of sixty years, the right thereto shall be deemed absolute and indefeasible, unless it shall appear that the same was taken and enjoyed by some consent or agreement expressly made or given for that purpose by deed or writing.

A1–001

In claims of right of way or other easement the periods to be twenty years and forty years

A1–002   **2.** No claim which may be lawfully made at the common law, by custom, prescription, or grant, to any way or other easement, or to any watercourse, or the use of any water, to be enjoyed or derived upon, over, or from any land or water of our said lord the King, or being parcel of the duchy of Lancaster or of the duchy of Cornwall, or being the property of any ecclesiastical or lay person, or body corporate, when such way or other matter as herein last before mentioned shall have been actually enjoyed by any person claiming right thereto without interruption for the full period of twenty years, shall be defeated or destroyed by showing only that such way or other matter was first enjoyed at any time prior to such period of twenty years, but nevertheless such claim may be defeated in any other way by which the same is now liable to be defeated; and where such way or other matter as herein last before mentioned shall have been so enjoyed as aforesaid for the full period of forty years, the right thereto shall be deemed absolute and indefeasible, unless it shall appear that the same was enjoyed by some consent or agreement expressly given or made for that purpose by deed or writing.

Claim to the use of light enjoyed for 20 years

A1–003   **3.** When the access and use of light to and for any dwelling house, workshop, or other building shall have been actually enjoyed therewith for the full period of twenty years without interruption, the right thereto shall be deemed absolute and indefeasible, any local usage or custom to the contrary notwithstanding, unless it shall appear that the same was enjoyed by some consent or agreement expressly made or given for that purpose by deed or writing.

Before mentioned periods to be deemed those next before suits

A1–004   **4.** Each of the respective periods of years herein-before mentioned shall be deemed and taken to be the period next before some suit or action wherein the claim or matter to which such period may relate shall have been or shall be brought into question and that no act or other matter shall be deemed to be an interruption, within the meaning of this statute, unless the same shall have been or shall be submitted to or acquiesced in for one year after the party interrupted shall have had or shall have notice thereof, and of the person making or authorizing the same to be made.

In actions on the case, the claimant may allege his right generally, as at present. In pleas to trespass and certain other pleadings, the period mentioned in this Act may be alleged. Exceptions, etc. to be replied to specially

A1–005   **5.** In all actions upon the case and other pleadings, wherein the party claiming may now by law allege his right generally, without averring the existence of such right from time immemorial, such general allegation shall still be deemed sufficient, and if the same shall be denied, all and every the matters in this Act mentioned and provided, which shall be applicable to the case, shall be admissible in evidence to sustain or rebut such allegation; and that in all pleadings to actions of trespass, and in all other pleadings wherein before the passing of this Act it would have been necessary to allege the right to have existed from time immemorial, it shall be sufficient to allege the enjoyment thereof as of right by the occupiers of the tenement in respect whereof the same is claimed for and during such of the periods mentioned in this Act as may be applicable to the case, and without claiming in the name or right of the owner of the fee, as is now usually done; and if the other party shall intend to rely on any proviso, exception, incapacity, disability, contract, agreement, or other matter herein-before mentioned, or on any cause or matter of fact or of law not inconsistent with the simple fact of enjoyment, the same shall be specially alleged and set forth in answer to the allegation of the party claiming, and shall not be received in evidence on any general traverse or denial of such allegation.

Presumption to be allowed in claims herein provided for

6. In the several cases mentioned in and provided for by this Act, no presumption shall be allowed or made in favour or support of any claim, upon proof of the exercise or enjoyment of the right or matter claimed for any less period of time or number of years than for such period or number mentioned in this Act as may be applicable to the case and to the nature of the claim.   **A1–006**

Proviso for infants, etc

7. Provided also, that the time during which any person otherwise capable of resisting any claim to any of the matters before mentioned shall have been or shall be an infant, idiot, non compos mentis, feme covert, or tenant for life, or during which any action or suit shall have been pending, and which shall have been diligently prosecuted, until abated by the death of any party or parties thereto, shall be excluded in the computation of the periods herein-before mentioned, except only in cases where the right or claim is hereby declared to be absolute and indefeasible.   **A1–007**

What time to be excluded in computing the term of forty years appointed by this Act

8. Provided always, that when any land or water upon, over, or from which any such way or other convenient watercourse or use of water shall have been or shall be enjoyed or derived hath been or shall be held under or by virtue of any term of life, or any term of years exceeding three years from the granting thereof, the time of the enjoyment of any such way or other matter as herein last before mentioned, during the continuance of such term, shall be excluded in the computation of the said period of forty years, in case the claim shall within three years next after the end or sooner determination of such term be resisted by any person entitled to any reversion expectant on the determination thereof.   **A1–008**

Limitation

9. This Act shall not extend to Scotland [. . .][1]   **A1–009**
10. [. . .][2]   **A1–010**
11. [. . .][3]   **A1–011**

[1] Words repealed by Statute Law Revision Act 1874 (c. 35).
[2] Repealed by Statute Law Revision Act 1874 (c. 35).
[3] Repealed by Statute Law Revision Act 1874 (c. 35).

Law of Property Act 1925

(15 GEO, C. 20)

An Act to consolidate the enactments relating to conveyancing and the law of property in England and Wales.

[9TH APRIL 1925]

PART I

GENERAL PRINCIPLES AS TO LEGAL ESTATES, EQUITABLE INTERESTS AND POWERS

Legal estates and equitable interests

A2–001   **1.**—(1) The only estates in land which are capable of subsisting or of being conveyed or created at law are—

(a) An estate in fee simple absolute in possession;
(b) A term of years absolute.

(2) The only interests or charges in or over land which are capable of subsisting or of being conveyed or created at law are—

(a) An easement, right, or privilege in or over land for an interest equivalent to an estate in fee simple absolute in possession or a term of years absolute;
(b) A rentcharge in possession issuing out of or charged on land being either perpetual or for a term of years absolute;
(c) A charge by way of legal mortgage;
(d) [. . .]¹ and any other similar charge on land which is not created by an instrument;
(e) Rights of entry exercisable over or in respect of a legal term of years absolute, or annexed, for any purpose, to a legal rentcharge.

Limitation and Prescription Acts

A2–002   **12.** Nothing in this Part of this Act affects the operation of any statute, or of the general law for the limitation of actions or proceedings relating to land or with reference to the acquisition of easements or rights over or in respect of land.

Party structures

A2–003   **38.**—(1) Where under a disposition or other arrangement which, if a holding in undivided shares had been permissible, would have created a tenancy in common,

---

¹ Words repealed by Tithe Act 1936 (c. 43), Sch.9 and Finance Act 1963 (c. 25), Sch.14 Pt.VI.

a wall or other structure is or is expressed to be made a party wall or structure, that structure shall be and remain severed vertically as between the respective owners, and the owner of each part shall have such rights to support and user over the rest of the structure as may be requisite for conferring rights corresponding to those which would have subsisted if a valid tenancy in common had been created.

(2) Any person interested may, in case of dispute, apply to the court for an order declaring the rights and interests under this section of the persons interested in any such party structure, and the court may make such order as it thinks fit.

Conveyances to be by deed

52.—(1) All conveyances of land or of any interest therein are void for the purpose of conveying or creating a legal estate unless made by deed.   **A2–004**

General words implied in conveyances

62.—(1) A conveyance of land shall be deemed to include and shall by virtue of   **A2–005**
this Act operate to convey, with the land, all buildings, erections, fixtures, commons, hedges, ditches, fences, ways, waters, water-courses, liberties, privileges, easements, rights, and advantages whatsoever, appertaining or reputed to appertain to the land, or any part thereof, or, at the time of conveyance, demised, occupied, or enjoyed with, or reputed or known as part or parcel of or appurtenant to the land or any part thereof.

(2) A conveyance of land, having houses or other buildings thereon, shall be deemed to include and shall by virtue of this Act operate to convey, with the land, houses, or other buildings, all outhouses, erections, fixtures, cellars, areas, courts, courtyards, cisterns, sewers, gutters, drains, ways, passages, lights, watercourses, liberties, privileges, easements, rights, and advantages whatsoever, appertaining or reputed to appertain to the land, houses, or other buildings conveyed, or any of them, or any part thereof, or, at the time of conveyance, demised, occupied, or enjoyed with, or reputed or known as part or parcel of or appurtenant to, the land, houses, or other buildings conveyed, or any of them, or any part thereof.

(3) A conveyance of a manor shall be deemed to include and shall by virtue of this Act operate to convey, with the manor, all pastures, feedings, wastes, warrens, commons, mines, minerals, quarries, furzes, trees, woods, underwoods, coppices, and the ground and soil thereof, fishings, fisheries, fowlings, courts leet, courts baron, and other courts, view of frankpledge and all that to view of frankpledge doth belong, mills, mulctures, customs, tolls, duties, reliefs, heriots, fines, sums of money, amerciaments, waifs, estrays, chief-rents, quitrents, rentscharge, rents seck, rents of assize, fee farm rents, services, royalties jurisdictions, franchises, liberties, privileges, easements, profits, advantages, rights, emoluments, and hereditaments whatsoever, to the manor appertaining or reputed to appertain, or, at the time of conveyance, demised, occupied, or enjoyed with the same, or reputed or known as part, parcel, or member thereof.

For the purposes of this subsection the right to compensation for manorial incidents on the extinguishment thereof shall be deemed to be a right appertaining to the manor.

(4) This section applies only if and as far as a contrary intention is not expressed in the conveyance, and has effect subject to the terms of the conveyance and to the provisions therein contained.

(5) This section shall not be construed as giving to any person a better title to any property, right, or thing in this section mentioned than the title which the conveyance gives to him to the land or manor expressed to be conveyed, or as conveying to him any property, right, or thing in this section mentioned, further or otherwise than as the same could have been conveyed to him by the conveying parties.

(6) This section applies to conveyances made after the thirty-first day of December, eighteen hundred and eighty-one.

Restrictions on the perpetuity rule

A2–006   **162.**—(1) For removing doubts, it is hereby declared that the rule of law relating to perpetuities does not apply and shall be deemed never to have applied—

(a) To any power to distrain on or to take possession of land or the income thereof given by way of indemnity against a rent, whether charged upon or payable in respect of any part of that land or not; or

(b) To any rentcharge created only as an indemnity against another rentcharge, although the indemnity rentcharge may only arise or become payable on breach of a condition or stipulation; or

(c) To any power, whether exercisable on breach of a condition or stipulation or not, to retain or withhold payment of any instalment of a rentcharge as an indemnity against another rentcharge; or

(d) To any grant, exception, or reservation of any right of entry on, or user of, the surface of land or of any easements, rights, or privileges over or under land for the purpose of—

  (i) winning, working, inspecting, measuring, converting, manufacturing, carrying away, and disposing of mines and minerals;

 (ii) inspecting, grubbing up, felling and carrying away timber and other trees, and the tops and lops thereof;

(iii) executing repairs, alterations, or additions to any adjoining land, or the buildings and erections thereon;

(iv) constructing, laying down, altering, repairing, renewing, cleansing, and maintaining sewers, watercourses, cesspools, gutters, drains, water-pipes, gas-pipes, electric wires or cables or other like works.

(2) This section applies to instruments coming into operation before or after the commencement of this Act.

Legal easements

A2–007   **187.**—(1) Where an easement, right or privilege for a legal estate is created, it shall enure for the benefit of the land to which it is intended to be annexed.

(2) Nothing in this Act affects the right of a person to acquire, hold or exercise an easement, right or privilege over or in relation to land for a legal estate in common with any other person, or the power of creating or conveying such an easement right or privilege.

Rights of the public over commons and waste lands

A2–008   **193.**—(1) Members of the public shall, subject as hereinafter provided, have rights of access for air and exercise to any land which is a metropolitan common within the meaning of the Metropolitan Commons Acts, 1866 to 1898, or manorial waste, or a common, which is wholly or partly situated within [an area which immediately before 1st April 1974 was]² a borough or urban district, and to any land which at the commencement of this Act is subject to rights of common and to which this section may from time to time be applied in manner hereinafter provided:

Provided that—

(a) such rights of access shall be subject to any Act, scheme, or provisional order for the regulation of the land, and to any byelaw, regulation or order made thereunder or under any other statutory authority; and

(b) the Minister shall, on the application of any person entitled as lord of the manor or otherwise to the soil of the land, or entitled to any common-able rights affecting the land, impose such limitations on and conditions as to the exercise of the rights of access or as to the extent of the land to be affected as, in the opinion of the Minister, are necessary or desirable for preventing any estate, right or interest of a profitable or beneficial nature in, over, or affecting the land from being injuriously affected, [for conserving flora, fauna or geological or physiographical features of the land,]³ or for protecting any object of historical interest and, where any such limitations or conditions are so imposed, the rights of access shall be subject thereto; and

(c) such rights of access shall not include any right to draw or drive upon the land a carriage, cart, caravan, truck, or other vehicle, or to camp or light any fire thereon; and

(d) the rights of access shall cease to apply—
   (i) to any land over which the commonable rights are extinguished under any statutory provision;
   (ii) to any land over which the commonable rights are otherwise extinguished if the council of the county [[, county borough]⁴ or metropolitan district]⁵ [. . .]⁶ in which the land is situated by resolution assent to its exclusion from the operation of this section, and the resolution is approved by the Minister.

(2) The lord of the manor or other person entitled to the soil of any land subject to rights of common may by deed, revocable or irrevocable, declare that this section shall apply to the land, and upon such deed being deposited with the Minister the land shall, so long as the deed remains operative, be land to which this section applies.

(3) Where limitations or conditions are imposed by the Minister under this section, they shall be published by such person and in such manner as the Minister may direct.

---

² Words inserted by Local Government Act 1972 (c. 70), s.189(4).
³ Words inserted by Countryside and Rights of Way Act 2000 (c. 37), Sch.4, para.1.
⁴ Words inserted by Local Government (Wales) Act 1994 (c. 19), Sch.16, para.7(1).
⁵ Words inserted by Local Government Act 1985 (c. 51), s.16, Sch.8, para.10(5).
⁶ Words repealed by Local Government Act 1972 (c. 70), s.273(1), (3), Sch.30.

(4) Any person who, without lawful authority, draws or drives upon any land to which this section applies any carriage, cart, caravan, truck, or other vehicle, or camps or lights any fire thereon, or who fails to observe any limitation or condition imposed by the Minister under this section in respect of any such land, shall be liable on summary conviction to a fine not exceeding [£20][7] for each offence.

(5) Nothing in this section shall prejudice or affect the right of any person to get and remove mines or minerals or to let down the surface of the manorial waste or common.

(6) This section does not apply to any common or manorial waste which is for the time being held for Naval, Military or Air Force purposes and in respect of which rights of common have been extinguished or cannot be exercised.

General definitions

A2–009   **205.**—(1) In this Act unless the context otherwise requires, the following expressions have the meanings hereby assigned to them respectively, that is to say—

> (ii) "Conveyance" includes a mortgage, charge, lease, assent, vesting declaration, vesting instrument, disclaimer, release and every other assurance of property or of an interest therein by any instrument, except a will; "convey" has a corresponding meaning; and "disposition" includes a conveyance and also a devise, bequest, or an appointment of property contained in a will; and "dispose of" has a corresponding meaning;
>
> (ix) "Land" includes land of any tenure, and mines and minerals, whether or not held apart from the surface, buildings or parts of buildings (whether the division is horizontal, vertical or made in any other way) and other corporeal hereditaments; also a manor, an advowson, and a rent and other incorporeal hereditaments, and an easement, right, privilege, or benefit in, over, or derived from land; [. . .][8] and "mines and minerals" include any strata or seam of minerals or substances in or under any land, and powers of working and getting the same [. . .][9] and "manor" includes a lordship, and reputed manor or lordship; and "hereditaments" means any real property which on an intestate occurring before the commencement of this Act might have devolved upon an heir;
>
> (x) "Legal estates" mean the estates, interests and charges, in or over land (subsisting or created at law) which are by this Act authorised to subsist or to be created as legal estates; "equitable interests" mean all the other interests and charges in or over land [. . .][10] an equitable interest "capable of subsisting as a legal estate" means such as could validly subsist or be created as a legal estate under this Act;

---

[7] Figure substituted by Criminal Justice Act 1967 (c. 80), Sch.3, Pt I.

[8] Words repealed by Trusts of Land and Appointment of Trustees Act 1996 (c. 47), Sch.4, para.1.

[9] Words repealed by Trusts of Land and Appointment of Trustees Act 1996 (c. 47), Sch.4 para.1.

[10] Words repealed by Trusts of Land and Appointment of Trustees Act 1996 (c. 47), Sch.4, para.1.

Rights of Light Act 1959

(C. 56)

An Act to amend the law relating to rights of light, and for purposes connected therewith.

[16TH JULY 1959]

1.—[. . .]¹   **A3–001**

Registration of notice in lieu of obstruction of access of light

2.—(1) For the purpose of preventing the access and use of light from being taken   **A3–002**
to be enjoyed without interruption, any person who is an owner of land (in this
and the next following section referred to as "the servient land") over which light
passes to a dwelling-house, workshop or other building (in this and the next following section referred to as "the dominant building") may apply to the local
authority in whose area the dominant building is situated for the registration of a
notice under this section.

(2) An application for the registration of a notice under this section shall be in
the prescribed form and shall—

  (a) identify the servient land and the dominant building in the prescribed
      manner, and
  (b) state that the registration of a notice in pursuance of the application is
      intended to be equivalent to the obstruction of the access of light to the
      dominant building across the servient land which would be caused by
      the erection, in such position on the servient land as may be specified
      in the application, of an opaque structure of such dimensions (including,
      if the application so states, unlimited height) as may be so specified.

(3) Any such application shall be accompanied by one or other of the following certificates issued by the Lands Tribunal, that is to say,—

  (a) a certificate certifying that adequate notice of the proposed application
      has been given to all persons who, in the circumstances existing at the
      time when the certificate is issued, appear to the Lands Tribunal to be
      persons likely to be affected by the registration of a notice in pursuance
      of the application;
  (b) a certificate certifying that, in the opinion of the Lands Tribunal, the case
      is one of exceptional urgency, and that accordingly a notice should be
      registered forthwith as a temporary notice for such period as may be
      specified in the certificate.

(4) Where application is duly made to a local authority for the registration of a
notice under this section, it shall be the duty of [that authority to register the
notice in the appropriate local land charges register, and—

¹ Repealed by Statute Law (Repeals) Act 1974 (c. 22), s.1, Sch. Pt IV.

(a) any notice so registered under this section shall be a local land charge; but
(b) section 5(1) and (2) and section 10 of the Local Land Charges Act 1975 shall not apply in relation thereto][2].

(5) Provision shall be made by rules under section three of the Lands Tribunal Act, 1949, for regulating proceedings before the Lands Tribunal with respect to the issue of certificates for the purposes of this section, and, subject to the approval of the Treasury, the fees chargeable in respect of those proceedings; and, without prejudice to the generality of subsection (6) of that section, any such rules made for the purposes of this section shall include provision—

(a) for requiring applicants for certificates under paragraph (a) of subsection (3) of this section to give such notices, whether by way of advertisement or otherwise, and to produce such documents and provide such information, as may be determined by or under the rules;
(b) for determining the period to be specified in a certificate issued under paragraph (b) of subsection (3) of this section; and
(c) in connection with any certificate issued under the said paragraph (b), for enabling a further certificate to be issued in accordance (subject to the necessary modifications) with paragraph (a) of subsection (3) of this section.

Effect of registered notice and proceedings relating thereto

A3–003   **3.**—(1) Where, in pursuance of an application made in accordance with the last preceding section, a notice is registered thereunder, then, for the purpose of determining whether any person is entitled (by virtue of the Prescription Act, 1832, or otherwise) to a right to the access of light to the dominant building across the servient land, the access of light to that building across that land shall be treated as obstructed to the same extent, and with the like consequences, as if an opaque structure, of the dimensions specified in the application,—

(a) had, on the date of registration of the notice, been erected in the position on the servient land specified in the application, and had been so erected by the person who made the application, and
(b) had remained in that position during the period for which the notice has effect and had been removed at the end of that period.

(2) For the purposes of this section a notice registered under the last preceding section shall be taken to have effect until either—

(a) the registration is cancelled, or
(b) the period of one year beginning with the date of registration of the notice expires, or
(c) in the case of a notice registered in pursuance of an application accompanied by a certificate issued under paragraph (b) of subsection (3) of the last preceding section, the period specified in the certificate expires

---

[2] Words substituted (with savings) by Local Land Charges Act 1975 (c. 76), ss.17(2), 19(2)–(4), Sch.1.

without such a further certificate as is mentioned in paragraph (c) of subsection (5) of that section having before the end of that period been lodged with the local authority,

and shall cease to have effect on the occurrence of any one of those events.

(3) Subject to the following provisions of this section, any person who, if such a structure as is mentioned in subsection (1) of this section had been erected as therein mentioned, would have had a right of action in any court in respect of that structure, on the grounds that he was entitled to a right to the access of light to the dominant building across the servient land, and that the said right was infringed by that structure, shall have the like right of action in that court in respect of the registration of a notice under the last preceding section:

Provided that an action shall not be begun by virtue of this subsection after the notice in question has ceased to have effect.

(4) Where, at any time during the period for which a notice registered under the last preceding section has effect, the circumstances are such that, if the access of light to the dominant building had been enjoyed continuously from a date one year earlier than the date on which the enjoyment thereof in fact began, a person would have had a right of action in any court by virtue of the last preceding subsection in respect of the registration of the notice, that person shall have the like right of action in that court by virtue of this subsection in respect of the registration of the notice.

(5) The remedies available to the plaintiff in an action brought by virtue of subsection (3) or subsection (4) of this section (apart from any order as to costs) shall be such declaration as the court may consider appropriate in the circumstances, and an order directing the registration of the notice to be cancelled or varied, as the court may determine.

(6) For the purposes of section four of the Prescription Act, 1832 (under which a period of enjoyment of any of the rights to which that Act applies is not to be treated as interrupted except by a matter submitted to or acquiesced in for one year after notice thereof)—

(a) as from the date of registration of a notice under the last preceding section, all persons interested in the dominant building or any part thereof shall be deemed to have notice of the registration thereof and of the person on whose application it was registered;

(b) until such time as an action is brought by virtue of subsection (3) or subsection (4) of this section in respect of the registration of a notice under the last preceding section, all persons interested in the dominant building or any part thereof shall be deemed to acquiesce in the obstruction which, in accordance with subsection (1) of this section, is to be treated as resulting from the registration of the notice;

(c) as from the date on which such an action is brought, no person shall be treated as submitting to or acquiescing in that obstruction:

Provided that if, in any such action, the court decides against the claim of the plaintiff, the court may direct that the preceding provisions of this subsection shall apply in relation to the notice as if that action had not been brought.

Application to Crown land

A3–004   **4.**—(1) Subject to the next following subsection, this Act shall apply in relation to land in which there is a Crown or Duchy interest as it applies in relation to land in which there is no such interest.

(2) Section three of the Prescription Act, 1832, as modified by the preceding provisions of this Act, shall not by virtue of this section be construed as applying to any land to which (by reason that there is a Crown or Duchy interest therein) that section would not apply apart from this Act.

(3) In this section "Crown or Duchy interest" means an interest belonging to Her Majesty in right of the Crown or of the Duchy of Lancaster, or belonging to the Duchy of Cornwall, or belonging to a government department, or held in trust for Her Majesty for the purposes of a government department.

Power to make rules

A3–005   **5.**—(1) [. . .][3]

(2) Any rules made [under section 14 of the Local Land Charges Act 1975 for the purposes of section 2 of this Act][4] shall (without prejudice to the inclusion therein of other provisions as to cancelling or varying the registration of notices or agreements) include provision for giving effect to any order of the court under subsection (5) of section three of this Act.

A3–006   **6.** [. . .][5]

Interpretation

A3–007   **7.**—(1) In this Act, except in so far as the context otherwise requires, the following expressions have the meaning hereby assigned to them respectively, that is to say—

"action" includes a counterclaim, and any reference to the plaintiff in an action shall be construed accordingly;

["local authority", in relation to land in a district or a London borough, means the council of the district or borough, and, in relation to land in the City of London, means the Common Council of the City;][6]

"owner", in relation to any land, means a person who is the estate owner in respect of the fee simple thereof, or is entitled to a tenancy thereof (within the meaning of the Landlord and Tenant Act, 1954) for a term of years certain of which, at the time in question, not less than seven years remain unexpired, or is a mortgagee in possession (within the meaning of the Law of Property Act, 1925) where the interest mortgaged is either the fee simple of the land or such a tenancy thereof;

"prescribed" means prescribed by rules made by virtue of subsection (6) of section fifteen of the Land Charges Act, 1925, as applied by section five of this Act.

---

[3] Repealed (with savings) by Local Land Charges Act 1975 (c. 76), ss.17(2), 19, Schs 1, 2.
[4] Words substituted by Local Land Charges Act 1975 (c. 76), ss.17(2), 19(2)–(4), Sch.1.
[5] Repealed by Northern Ireland Constitution Act 1973 (c. 36), s.41(1), Sch.6, Pt I.
[6] Definition substituted (with savings) by Local Land Charges Act 1975 (c. 76), ss.17(2), 19(2)–(4), Sch.1.

(2) References in this Act to any enactment shall, except where the context otherwise requires, be construed as references to that enactment as amended by or under any other enactment.

Short title, commencement and extent

8.—(1) This Act may be cited as the Rights of Light Act, 1959.

A3–008

(2) This Act, except sections one and six thereof, shall come into operation at the end of the period of three months beginning with the day on which it is passed.

(3) This Act shall not extend to Scotland.

(4) This Act, [. . .]⁷, shall not extend to Northern Ireland.

Town and Country Planning Act 1990

(C. 8)

An Act to consolidate certain enactments relating to town and country planning (excluding special controls in respect of buildings and areas of special architectural or historic interest and in respect of hazardous substances) with amendments to give effect to recommendations of the Law Commission.

[24TH MAY 1990]

BE IT ENACTED by the Queen's most Excellent Majesty, by and with the advice and consent of the Lords Spiritual and Temporal, and Commons, in this present Parliament assembled, and by the authority of the same, as follows:—

Compulsory acquisition of land for development and other planning purposes

226.—(1) A local authority to whom this section applies shall, on being authorised to do so by the Secretary of State, have power to acquire compulsorily any land in their area which—

A4–001

(a) is suitable for and required in order to secure the carrying out of development, redevelopment or improvement; or

(b) is required for a purpose which it is necessary to achieve in the interests of the proper planning of an area in which the land is situated.

(2) A local authority and the Secretary of State in considering for the purposes of subsection (1)(a) whether land is suitable for development, re-development or improvement shall have regard—

(a) to the provisions of the development plan, so far as material;

---

⁷ Words repealed by Northern Ireland Constitution Act 1973 (c. 36), s.41(1), Sch.6 Pt I.

(b) to whether planning permission for any development on the land is in force; and

(c) to any other considerations which would be material for the purpose of determining an application for planning permission for development on the land.

(3) Where a local authority exercise their power under subsection (1) in relation to any land, they shall, on being authorised to do so by the Secretary of State, have power to acquire compulsorily—

(a) any land adjoining that land which is required for the purpose of executing works for facilitating its development or use; or

(b) where that land forms part of a common or open space or fuel or field garden allotment, any land which is required for the purpose of being given in exchange for the land which is being acquired.

(4) It is immaterial by whom the local authority propose that any activity or purpose mentioned in subsection (1) or (3)(a) should be undertaken or achieved (and in particular the local authority need not propose to undertake an activity or to achieve that purpose themselves).

(5) Where under subsection (1) the Secretary of State has power to authorise a local authority to whom this section applies to acquire any land compulsorily he may, after the requisite consultation, authorise the land to be so acquired by another authority, being a local authority within the meaning of this Act.

(6) Before giving an authorisation under subsection (5), the Secretary of State shall—

(a) if the land is in a non-metropolitan county, consult with the councils of the county and the district;

(b) if the land is in a metropolitan district, consult with the council of the district; and

(c) if the land is in a London borough, consult with the council of the borough.

(7) The [1981 c. 67.] Acquisition of Land Act 1981 shall apply to the compulsory acquisition of land under this section.

(8) The local authorities to whom this section applies are the councils of counties, districts and London boroughs.

Power to override easements and other rights

A4–002   237.—(1) Subject to subsection (3), the erection, construction or carrying out or maintenance of any building or work on land which has been acquired or appropriated by a local authority for planning purposes (whether done by the local authority or by a person deriving title under them) is authorised by virtue of this section if it is done in accordance with planning permission, notwithstanding that it involves—

(a) interference with an interest or right to which this section applies, or

(b) a breach of a restriction as to the user of land arising by virtue of a contract.

(2) Subject to subsection (3), the interests and rights to which this section applies are any easement, liberty, privilege, right or advantage annexed to land and adversely affecting other land, including any natural right to support.

(3) Nothing in this section shall authorise interference with any right of way or right of laying down, erecting, continuing or maintaining apparatus on, under or over land which is—

(a) a right vested in or belonging to statutory undertakers for the purpose of the carrying on of their undertaking, or
(b) a right conferred by or in accordance with the telecommunications code on the operator of a telecommunications code system.

(4) In respect of any interference or breach in pursuance of subsection (1), compensation—

(a) shall be payable under section 63 or 68 of the [1845 c. 18.] Lands Clauses Consolidation Act 1845 or under section 7 or 10 of the [1965 c. 56.] Compulsory Purchase Act 1965, and
(b) shall be assessed in the same manner and subject to the same rules as in the case of other compensation under those sections in respect of injurious affection where—
  (i) the compensation is to be estimated in connection with a purchase under those Acts, or
  (ii) the injury arises from the execution of works on land acquired under those Acts.

(5) Where a person deriving title under the local authority by whom the land in question was acquired or appropriated—

(a) is liable to pay compensation by virtue of subsection (4), and
(b) fails to discharge that liability,

the liability shall be enforceable against the local authority.

(6) Nothing in subsection (5) shall be construed as affecting any agreement between the local authority and any other person for indemnifying the local authority against any liability under that subsection.

(7) Nothing in this section shall be construed as authorising any act or omission on the part of any person which is actionable at the suit of any person on any grounds other than such an interference or breach as is mentioned in subsection (1).

Interpretation of Part IX

246.—(1) In this Part—

A4–003

(a) any reference to the acquisition of land for planning purposes is a reference to the acquisition of it under section 226 or 227 of this Act or section 52 of the [1990 c. 9.] Planning (Listed Buildings and Conservation Areas) Act 1990 (or, as the case may be, under section 112 or 119 of the 1971 Act or section 68 or 71 of the 1962 Act); and

(b) any reference to the appropriation of land for planning purposes is a reference to the appropriation of it for purposes for which land can be (or, as the case may be, could have been) acquired under those sections.

Access to Neighbouring Land Act 1992

(C. 23)

An Act to enable persons who desire to carry out works to any land which are reasonably necessary for the preservation of that land to obtain access to neighbouring land in order to do so; and for purposes connected therewith.

[16TH MARCH 1992]

BE IT ENACTED by the Queen's most Excellent Majesty, by and with the advice and consent of the Lords Spiritual and Temporal, and Commons, in this present Parliament assembled, and by the authority of the same, as follows—

Access orders

A5–001 **1.**—(1) A person—

(a) who, for the purpose of carrying out works to any land (the "dominant land"), desires to enter upon any adjoining or adjacent land (the "servient land"), and

(b) who needs, but does not have, the consent of some other person to that entry,

may make an application to the court for an order under this section ("an access order") against that other person.

(2) On an application under this section, the court shall make an access order if, and only if, it is satisfied—

(a) that the works are reasonably necessary for the preservation of the whole or any part of the dominant land; and

(b) that they cannot be carried out, or would be substantially more difficult to carry out, without entry upon the servient land;

but this subsection is subject to subsection (3) below.

(3) The court shall not make an access order in any case where it is satisfied that, were it to make such an order—

(a) the respondent or any other person would suffer interference with, or disturbance of, his use or enjoyment of the servient land, or

(b) the respondent, or any other person (whether of full age or capacity or not) in occupation of the whole or any part of the servient land, would suffer hardship,

to such a degree by reason of the entry (notwithstanding any requirement of this Act or any term or condition that may be imposed under it) that it would be unreasonable to make the order.

(4) Where the court is satisfied on an application under this section that it is reasonably necessary to carry out any basic preservation works to the dominant land, those works shall be taken for the purposes of this Act to be reasonably necessary for the preservation of the land; and in this subsection "basic preservation works" means any of the following, that is to say—

(a) the maintenance, repair or renewal of any part of a building or other structure comprised in, or situate on, the dominant land;

(b) the clearance, repair or renewal of any drain, sewer, pipe or cable so comprised or situate;

(c) the treatment, cutting back, felling, removal or replacement of any hedge, tree, shrub or other growing thing which is so comprised and which is, or is in danger of becoming, damaged, diseased, dangerous, insecurely rooted or dead;

(d) the filling in, or clearance, of any ditch so comprised;

but this subsection is without prejudice to the generality of the works which may, apart from it, be regarded by the court as reasonably necessary for the preservation of any land.

(5) If the court considers it fair and reasonable in all the circumstances of the case, works may be regarded for the purposes of this Act as being reasonably necessary for the preservation of any land (or, for the purposes of subsection (4) above, as being basic preservation works which it is reasonably necessary to carry out to any land) notwithstanding that the works incidentally involve—

(a) the making of some alteration, adjustment or improvement to the land, or

(b) the demolition of the whole or any part of a building or structure comprised in or situate upon the land.

(6) Where any works are reasonably necessary for the preservation of the whole or any part of the dominant land, the doing to the dominant land of anything which is requisite for, incidental to, or consequential on, the carrying out of those works shall be treated for the purposes of this Act as the carrying out of works which are reasonably necessary for the preservation of that land; and references in this Act to works, or to the carrying out of works, shall be construed accordingly.

(7) Without prejudice to the generality of subsection (6) above, if it is reasonably necessary for a person to inspect the dominant land—

(a) for the purpose of ascertaining whether any works may be reasonably necessary for the preservation of the whole or any part of that land,

(b) for the purpose of making any map or plan, or ascertaining the course of any drain, sewer, pipe or cable, in preparation for, or otherwise in connection with, the carrying out of works which are so reasonably necessary, or

(c) otherwise in connection with the carrying out of any such works,

the making of such an inspection shall be taken for the purposes of this Act to be the carrying out to the dominant land of works which are reasonably necessary for the preservation of that land; and references in this Act to works, or to the carrying out of works, shall be construed accordingly.

Terms and conditions of access orders

A5–002   **2.**—(1) An access order shall specify—

(a) the works to the dominant land that may be carried out by entering upon the servient land in pursuance of the order;

(b) the particular area of servient land that may be entered upon by virtue of the order for the purpose of carrying out those works to the dominant land; and

(c) the date on which, or the period during which, the land may be so entered upon;

and in the following provisions of this Act any reference to the servient land is a reference to the area specified in the order in pursuance of paragraph (b) above.

(2) An access order may impose upon the applicant or the respondent such terms and conditions as appear to the court to be reasonably necessary for the purpose of avoiding or restricting—

(a) any loss, damage, or injury which might otherwise be caused to the respondent or any other person by reason of the entry authorised by the order; or

(b) any inconvenience or loss of privacy that might otherwise be so caused to the respondent or any other person.

(3) Without prejudice to the generality of subsection (2) above, the terms and conditions which may be imposed under that subsection include provisions with respect to—

(a) the manner in which the specified works are to be carried out;

(b) the days on which, and the hours between which, the work involved may be executed;

(c) the persons who may undertake the carrying out of the specified works or enter upon the servient land under or by virtue of the order;

(d) the taking of any such precautions by the applicant as may be specified in the order.

(4) An access order may also impose terms and conditions—

    (a) requiring the applicant to pay, or to secure that such person connected with him as may be specified in the order pays, compensation for—
        (i) any loss, damage or injury, or
        (ii) any substantial loss of privacy or other substantial inconvenience,

    which will, or might, be caused to the respondent or any other person by reason of the entry authorised by the order;

    (b) requiring the applicant to secure that he, or such person connected with him as may be specified in the order, is insured against any such risks as may be so specified; or

    (c) requiring such a record to be made of the condition of the servient land, or of such part of it as may be so specified, as the court may consider expedient with a view to facilitating the determination of any question that may arise concerning damage to that land.

(5) An access order may include provision requiring the applicant to pay the respondent such sum by way of consideration for the privilege of entering the servient land in pursuance of the order as appears to the court to be fair and reasonable having regard to all the circumstances of the case, including, in particular—

    (a) the likely financial advantage of the order to the applicant and any persons connected with him; and

    (b) the degree of inconvenience likely to be caused to the respondent or any other person by the entry;

but no payment shall be ordered under this subsection if and to the extent that the works which the applicant desires to carry out by means of the entry are works to residential land.

(6) For the purposes of subsection (5)(a) above, the likely financial advantage of an access order to the applicant and any persons connected with him shall in all cases be taken to be a sum of money equal to the greater of the following amounts, that is to say—

    (a) the amount (if any) by which so much of any likely increase in the value of any land—
        (i) which consists of or includes the dominant land, and
        (ii) which is owned or occupied by the same person as the dominant land,

    as may reasonably be regarded as attributable to the carrying out of the specified works exceeds the likely cost of carrying out those works with the benefit of the access order; and

    (b) the difference (if it would have been possible to carry out the specified works without entering upon the servient land) between—
        (i) the likely cost of carrying out those works without entering upon the servient land; and
        (ii) the likely cost of carrying them out with the benefit of the access order.

(7) For the purposes of subsection (5) above, "residential land" means so much of any land as consists of—

(a) a dwelling or part of a dwelling;
(b) a garden, yard, private garage or outbuilding which is used and enjoyed wholly or mainly with a dwelling; or
(c) in the case of a building which includes one or more dwellings, any part of the building which is used and enjoyed wholly or mainly with those dwellings or any of them.

(8) The persons who are to be regarded for the purposes of this section as "connected with" the applicant are—

(a) the owner of any estate or interest in, or right over, the whole or any part of the dominant land;
(b) the occupier of the whole or any part of the dominant land; and
(c) any person whom the applicant may authorise under section 3(7) below to exercise the power of entry conferred by the access order.

(9) The court may make provision—

(a) for the reimbursement by the applicant of any expenses reasonably incurred by the respondent in connection with the application which are not otherwise recoverable as costs;
(b) for the giving of security by the applicant for any sum that might become payable to the respondent or any other person by virtue of this section or section 3 below.

Effect of access order

A5–003   **3.**—(1) An access order requires the respondent, so far as he has power to do so, to permit the applicant or any of his associates to do anything which the applicant or associate is authorised or required to do under or by virtue of the order or this section.

(2) Except as otherwise provided by or under this Act, an access order authorises the applicant or any of his associates, without the consent of the respondent,—

(a) to enter upon the servient land for the purpose of carrying out the specified works;
(b) to bring on to that land, leave there during the period permitted by the order and, before the end of that period, remove, such materials, plant and equipment as are reasonably necessary for the carrying out of those works; and
(c) to bring on to that land any waste arising from the carrying out of those works, if it is reasonably necessary to do so in the course of removing it from the dominant land;

but nothing in this Act or in any access order shall authorise the applicant or any of his associates to leave anything in, on or over the servient land (otherwise than in discharge of their duty to make good that land) after their entry for the purpose of carrying out works to the dominant land ceases to be authorised under or by virtue of the order.

(3) An access order requires the applicant—

(a) to secure that any waste arising from the carrying out of the specified works is removed from the servient land forthwith;

(b) to secure that, before the entry ceases to be authorised under or by virtue of the order, the servient land is, so far as reasonably practicable, made good; and

(c) to indemnify the respondent against any damage which may be caused to the servient land or any goods by the applicant or any of his associates which would not have been so caused had the order not been made;

but this subsection is subject to subsections (4) and (5) below.

(4) In making an access order, the court may vary or exclude, in whole or in part,—

(a) any authorisation that would otherwise be conferred by subsection (2)(b) or (c) above; or

(b) any requirement that would otherwise be imposed by subsection (3) above.

(5) Without prejudice to the generality of subsection (4) above, if the court is satisfied that it is reasonably necessary for any such waste as may arise from the carrying out of the specified works to be left on the servient land for some period before removal, the access order may, in place of subsection (3)(a) above, include provision—

(a) authorising the waste to be left on that land for such period as may be permitted by the order; and

(b) requiring the applicant to secure that the waste is removed before the end of that period.

(6) Where the applicant or any of his associates is authorised or required under or by virtue of an access order or this section to enter, or do any other thing, upon the servient land, he shall not (as respects that access order) be taken to be a trespasser from the beginning on account of his, or any other person's, subsequent conduct.

(7) For the purposes of this section, the applicant's "associates" are such number of persons (whether or not servants or agents of his) whom he may reasonably authorise under this subsection to exercise the power of entry conferred by the access order as may be reasonably necessary for carrying out the specified works.

Persons bound by access order, unidentified persons and bar on contracting out

4.—(1) In addition to the respondent, an access order shall, subject to the provisions of the Land Charges Act 1972 and the Land Registration Act 2002, be binding on—   **A5–004**

(a) any of his successors in title to the servient land; and

(b) any person who has an estate or interest in, or right over, the whole or any part of the servient land which was created after the making of the order and who derives his title to that estate, interest or right under the respondent;

and references to the respondent shall be construed accordingly.

(2) If and to the extent that the court considers it just and equitable to allow him to do so, a person on whom an access order becomes binding by virtue of subsection (1)(a) or (b) above shall be entitled, as respects anything falling to be done after the order becomes binding on him, to enforce the order or any of its terms or conditions as if he were the respondent, and references to the respondent shall be construed accordingly.

(3) Rules of court may—

(a) provide a procedure which may be followed where the applicant does not know, and cannot reasonably ascertain, the name of any person whom he desires to make respondent to the application; and

(b) make provision enabling such an applicant to make such a person respondent by description instead of by name;

and in this subsection "applicant" includes a person who proposes to make an application for an access order.

(4) Any agreement, whenever made, shall be void if and to the extent that it would, apart from this subsection, prevent a person from applying for an access order or restrict his right to do so.

Registration of access orders and of applications for such orders

A5–005 **5.**—(1) In section 6(1) of the Land Charges Act 1972 (which specifies the writs and orders affecting land that may be entered in the register) after paragraph (c) there shall be added—

"(d) any access order under the Access to Neighbouring Land Act 1992."

(2) [*Repealed by Land Registration Act 2002, Sch.11*].

(3) [*Repealed by Land Registration Act 2002, Sch.11*].

(4) In any case where—

(a) an access order is discharged under section 6(1)(a) below, and

(b) the order has been protected by an entry registered under the Land Charges Act 1972 or by a notice under the Land Registration Act 2002,

the court may by order direct that the entry, notice or caution shall be cancelled.

(5) The rights conferred on a person by or under an access order [shall not be capable of falling within paragraph 2 of Schedule 1 or 3 to the Land Registration Act 2002 (overriding status of person in actual occupation)][1].

(6) An application for an access order shall be regarded as a pending land action for the purposes of the Land Charges Act 1972 and the Land Registration Act 2002.

---

[1] Words substituted by Land Registration Act 2002, Schedule 11.

Variation of orders and damages for breach

6.—(1) Where an access order or an order under this subsection has been made, the court may, on the application of any party to the proceedings in which the order was made or of any other person on whom the order is binding—   A5–006

(a) discharge or vary the order or any of its terms or conditions;

(b) suspend any of its terms or conditions; or

(c) revive any term or condition suspended under paragraph (b) above;

and in the application of subsections (1) and (2) of section 4 above in relation to an access order, any order under this subsection which relates to the access order shall be treated for the purposes of those subsections as included in the access order.

(2) If any person contravenes or fails to comply with any requirement, term or condition imposed upon him by or under this Act, the court may, without prejudice to any other remedy available, make an order for the payment of damages by him to any other person affected by the contravention or failure who makes an application for relief under this subsection.

Jurisdiction over, and allocation of, proceedings

7.—(1) The High Court and the county courts shall both have jurisdiction under this Act.   A5–007

(2) In article 4 of the High Court and County Courts Jurisdiction Order 1991 (which provides that proceedings in which the county courts and the High Court both have jurisdiction may, subject to articles 5 and 6, be commenced either in a county court or in the High Court) for the words "and 6" there shall be substituted the words ", 6 and 6A"; and after article 6 of that Order there shall be inserted—

"6A. Applications under section 1 of the Access to Neighbouring Land Act 1992 shall be commenced in a county court."

(3) The amendment by subsection (2) above of provisions contained in an order shall not be taken to have prejudiced any power to make further orders revoking or amending those provisions.

Interpretation and application

8.—(1) Any reference in this Act to an "entry" upon any servient land includes a reference to the doing on that land of anything necessary for carrying out the works to the dominant land which are reasonably necessary for its preservation; and "enter" shall be construed accordingly.   A5–008

(2) This Act applies in relation to any obstruction of, or other interference with, a right over, or interest in, any land as it applies in relation to an entry upon that land; and "enter" and "entry" shall be construed accordingly.

(3) In this Act—

"access order" has the meaning given by section 1(1) above;

"applicant" means a person making an application for an access order and, subject to section 4 above, "the respondent" means the respondent, or any of the respondents, to such an application;

"the court" means the High Court or a county court;

"the dominant land" and "the servient land" respectively have the meanings given by section 1(1) above, but subject, in the case of servient land, to section 2(1) above;

"land" does not include a highway;

"the specified works" means the works specified in the access order in pursuance of section 2(1)(a) above.

Short title, commencement and extent

A5–009   **9.**—(1) This Act may be cited as the Access to Neighbouring Land Act 1992.

(2) This Act shall come into force on such day as the Lord Chancellor may by order made by statutory instrument appoint.

(3) This Act extends to England and Wales only.

Party Wall, etc. Act 1996

(C. 40)

An Act to make provision in respect of party walls, and excavation and construction in proximity to certain buildings or structures, and for connected purposes.
[18TH JULY 1996]

BE IT ENACTED by the Queen's most Excellent Majesty, by and with the advice and consent of the Lords Spiritual and Temporal, and Commons, in this present Parliament assembled, and by the authority of the same, as follows—

Construction and repair of walls on line of junction

New building on line of junction

A6–001   **1.**—(1) This section shall have effect where lands of different owners adjoin and—

(a) are not built on at the line of junction; or

(b) are built on at the line of junction only to the extent of a boundary wall (not being a party fence wall or the external wall of a building),

and either owner is about to build on any part of the line of junction.

(2) If a building owner desires to build a party wall or party fence wall on the line of junction he shall, at least one month before he intends the building work to start, serve on any adjoining owner a notice which indicates his desire to build and describes the intended wall.

(3) If, having been served with notice described in subsection (2), an adjoining owner serves on the building owner a notice indicating his consent to the building of a party wall or party fence wall—

(a) the wall shall be built half on the land of each of the two owners or in such other position as may be agreed between the two owners: and

(b) the expense of building the wall shall be from time to time defrayed by the two owners in such proportion as has regard to the use made or to be made of the wall by each of them and to the cost of labour and materials prevailing at the time when that use is made by each owners respectively.

(4) If, having been served with notice described in subsection (2), an adjoining owner does not consent under this subsection to the building of a party wall or party fence wall, the building owners may only build the wall—

(a) at his own expense; and

(b) as an external wall or a fence wall, as the case may be, placed wholly on his own land,

and consent under this subsection is consent by a notice served within the period of fourteen days beginning with the day on which the notice described in subsection (2) is served.

(5) If the building owner desires to build on the line of junction a wall placed wholly on his own land he shall, at least one month before he intends the building work to start, serve on any adjoining owner a notice which indicates his desire to build and describes the intended wall.

(6) Where the building owner builds a wall wholly on his own land in accordance with subsection (4) or (5) he shall have the right, at any time in the period which—

(a) begins one month after the day on which the notice mentioned in the subsection concerned was served, and

(b) ends twelve months after that day,

to place below the level of the land of the adjoining owner such projecting footings and foundations as are necessary for the construction of the wall.

(7) Where the building owner builds a wall wholly on his own land in accordance with subsection (4) or (5) he shall do so at his own expense and shall compensate any adjoining owner and any adjoining occupier for any damage to his property occasioned by—

(a) the building of the wall;

(b) the placing of any footings or foundations placed in accordance with subsection (6).

(8) Where any dispute arises under this section between the building owner and any adjoining owner or occupier it is to be determined in accordance with section 10.

Repairs, etc., of party wall: rights of owner

2.—(1) This section applies where lands of different owners adjoin and at the line of junction the said lands are built on or a boundary wall, being a party fence wall or the external wall of a building, has been erected.   **A6–002**

(2) A building owner shall have the following rights—

(a) to underpin, thicken or raise a party structure, a party fence wall, or an external wall which belongs to the building owner and is built against a party structure or party fence wall;

(b) to make good, repair, or demolish and rebuild, a party structure or party fence wall in a case where such work is necessary on account of defect or want of repair of the structure or wall;

(c) to demolish a partition which separates buildings belonging to different owners but does not conform with statutory requirements and to build instead a party wall which does so conform;

(d) in the case of buildings connected by arches or structures over public ways or over passages belonging to other persons, to demolish the whole or part of such buildings, arches or structures which do not conform with statutory requirements and to rebuild them so that they do so conform;

(e) to demolish a party structure which is of insufficient strength or height for the purposes of any intended building of the building owner and to rebuild it of sufficient strength or height for the said purposes (including rebuilding to a lesser height or thickness where the rebuilt structure is of sufficient strength and height for the purposes of any adjoining owner);

(f) to cut into a party structure for any purpose (which may be or include the purpose of inserting a damp proof course);

(g) to cut away from a party wall, party fence wall, external wall or boundary wall any footing or any projecting chimney breast, jamb or flue, or other projection on or over the land of the building owner in order to erect, or underpin any such wall or for any other purpose;

(h) to cut away or demolish parts of any wall or building of an adjoining owner overhanging the land of the building owner or overhanging a party wall, to the extent that it is necessary to cut away or demolish the parts to enable a vertical wall to be erected or raised against the wall or building of the adjoining owner;

(j) to cut into the wall of an adjoining owner's building in order to insert a flashing or other weather-proofing of a wall erected against that wall;

(k) to execute any other necessary works incidental to the connection of a party structure with the premises adjoining it;

(l) to raise a party fence wall, or to raise such a wall for use as a party wall, and to demolish a party fence wall and rebuild it as a party fence wall or as a party wall;

(m) subject to the provisions of section 11(7), to reduce, or to demolish and rebuild, a party wall or party fence wall to—
   (i) a height of not less than two metres where the wall is not used by an adjoining owner to any greater extent than a boundary wall; or
   (ii) a height currently enclosed upon by the building of an adjoining owner;

(n) to expose a party wall or party structure hitherto enclosed subject to providing adequate weathering.

(3) Where work mentioned in paragraph (a) of subsection (2) is not necessary on account of defect or want of repair of the structure or wall concerned, the right falling within that paragraph is exercisable—

(a) subject to making good all damage occasioned by the work to the adjoining premises or to their internal furnishings and decorations; and

(b) where the work is to a party structure or external wall, subject to carrying any relevant flues and chimney stacks up to such a height and in such materials as may be agreed between the building owner and the adjoining owner concerned or, in the event of dispute, determined in accordance with section 10;

and relevant flues and chimney stacks are those which belong to an adjoining owner and either form part of or rest on or against the party structure or external wall.

(4) The right falling within subsection (2)(e) is exercisable subject to—

(a) making good all damage occasioned by the work to the adjoining premises or to their internal furnishings and decorations; and

(b) carrying any relevant flues and chimney stacks up to such a height and in such materials as may be agreed between the building owner and the adjoining owner concerned or, in the event of dispute, determined in accordance with section 10;

and relevant flues and chimney stacks are those which belong to an adjoining owner and either form part of or rest on or against the party structure.

(5) Any right falling within subsection (2)(f), (g) or (h) is exercisable subject to making good all damage occasioned by the work to the adjoining premises or to their internal furnishings and decorations.

(6) The right falling within subsection (2)(j) is exercisable subject to making good all damage occasioned by the work to the wall of the adjoining owner's building.

(7) The right falling within subsection (2)(m) is exercisable subject to—

(a) reconstructing any parapet or replacing an existing parapet with another one, or

(b) constructing a parapet where one is needed but did not exist before.

(8) For the purposes of this section a building or structure which was erected before the day on which this Act was passed shall be deemed to conform with statutory requirements if it conforms with the statutes regulating buildings or structures on the date on which it was erected.

Party structure notices

3.—(1) Before exercising any right conferred on him by section 2 a building owner shall serve on any adjoining owner a notice (in this Act referred to as a "party structure notice") stating—   **A6–003**

(a) the name and address of the building owner;

(b) the nature and particulars of the proposed work including, in cases where the building owner proposes to construct special foundations, plans, sections and details of construction of the special foundations together with reasonable particulars of the loads to be carried thereby; and

(c) the date on which the proposed work will begin.

(2) A party structure notice shall—

(a) be served at least two months before the date on which the proposed work will begin;
(b) cease to have effect if the work to which it relates—
    (i) has not begun within the period of twelve months beginning with the day on which the notice is served; and
    (ii) is not prosecuted with due diligence.

(3) Nothing in this section shall—

(a) prevent a building owner from exercising with the consent in writing of the adjoining owners and of the adjoining occupiers any right conferred on him by section 2, or
(b) require a building owner to serve any party structure notice before complying with any notice served under any statutory provisions relating to dangerous or neglected structures.

Counter notices

A6–004 **4.**—(1) An adjoining owner may, having been served with a party structure notice serve on the building owner a notice (in this Act referred to as a "counter notice") setting out—

(a) in respect of a party fence wall or party structure, a requirement that the building owner build in or on the wall or structure to which the notice relates such chimney copings, breasts, jambs or flues, or such piers or recesses or other like works, as may reasonably be required for the convenience of the adjoining owner;
(b) In respect of special foundations to which the adjoining owner consents under section 7(4) below, a requirement that the special foundations—
    (i) be placed at a specified greater depth than that proposed by the building owner; or
    (ii) be constructed of sufficient strength to bear the load to be carried by columns of any intended building of the adjoining owner,
or both.

(2) A counter notice shall—

(a) specify the works required by the notice to be executed and shall be accompanied by plans, sections and particulars of such works, and
(b) be served within the period of one month beginning with the day on which the party structure notice is served.

(3) A building owner on whom a counter notice has been served shall comply with the requirements of the counter notice unless the execution of the works required by the counter notice would—

(a) be injurious to him;
(b) cause unnecessary inconvenience to him; or

(c) cause unnecessary delay in the execution of the works pursuant to the party structure notice.

Disputes arising under sections 3 and 4

5. If an owner on whom a party structure notice or a counter notice has been served does not serve a notice indicating his consent to it within the period of fourteen days beginning with the day on which the party structure notice or counter notice was served, he shall be deeemed to have dissented from the notice and a dispute shall be deemed to have arisen between the parties.

A6–005

Adjacent excavation and construction

Adjacent excavation and construction

6.—(1) This section applies where—

A6–006

(a) a building owner proposes to excavate, or excavate for and erect a building or structure, within a distance of three metres measured horizontally from any part of a building or structure of an adjoining owner; and

(b) any part of the proposed excavation, building or structure will within those three metres extend to a lower level than the level of the bottom of the foundations of the building or structure of the adjoining owner.

(2) This section also applies where—

(a) a building owner proposes to excavate, or excavate for and erect a building or structure, within a distance of six metres measured horizontally from any part of a building or structure of an adjoining owner; and

(b) any part of the proposed excavation, building or structure will within those six metres meet a plane drawn downwards in the direction of the excavation, building or structure of the building owner at an angle of forty-five degrees to the horizontal from the line formed by the intersection of the plane of the level of the bottom of the foundations of the building or structure of the adjoining owner with the plane of the external face of the external wall of the building or structure of the adjoining owner.

(3) The building owner may, and if required by the adjoining owner shall, at his own expense underpin or otherwise strengthen or safeguard the foundations of the building or structure of the adjoining owner so far as may be necessary.

(4) Where the buildings or structures of different owners are within the respective distances mentioned in subsections (1) and (2) the owners of those buildings or structures shall be deemed to be adjoining owners for the purposes of this section.

(5) In any case where this section applies the building owner shall, at least one month before beginning to excavate, or excavate for and erect a building or

structure, serve on the adjoining owner a notice indicating his proposals and stating whether he proposes to underpin or otherwise strengthen or safeguard the foundations of the building or structure of the adjoining owner.

(6) The notice referred to in subsection (5) shall be accompanied by plans and sections showing—

(a) the site and depth of any excavation the building owner proposes to make;
(b) if he proposes to erect a building or structure, its site.

(7) If an owner on whom a notice referred to in subsection (5) has been served does not serve a notice indicating his consent to it within the period of fourteen days beginning with the day on which the notice referred to in subsection (5) was served, he shall be deemed to have dissented from the notice and a dispute shall be deemed to have arisen between the parties.

(8) The notice referred to in subsection (5) shall cease to have effect if the work to which the notice relates—

(a) has not begun within the period of twelve months beginning with the day on which the notice was served; and
(b) is not prosecuted with due diligence.

(9) On completion of any work executed in pursuance of this section the building owner shall if so requested by the adjoining owner supply him with particulars including plans and sections of the work.

(10) Nothing in this section shall relieve the building owner from any liability to which he would otherwise be subject for injury to any adjoining owner or any adjoining occupier by reason of work executed by him.

Rights, etc.

Compensation, etc.

A6–007   7.—(1) A building owner shall not exercise any right conferred on him by this Act in such a manner or at such time as to cause unnecessary inconvenience to any adjoining owner or to any adjoining occupier.

(2) The building owner shall compensate any adjoining owner and any adjoining occupier for any loss or damge which may result to any of them by reason of any work executed in pursuance of this Act.

(3) Where a building owner in exercising any right conferred on him by this Act lays open any part of the adjoining land or building he shall at his own expense make and maintain so long as may be necessary a proper hoarding, shoring or fans or temporary construction for the protection of the adjoining land or building and the security of any adjoining occupier.

(4) Nothing in this Act shall authorise the building owner to place special foundations on land of an adjoining owner without his previous consent in writing.

(5) Any works executed in pursuance of this Act shall—

(a) comply with the provisions of statutory requirements; and

(b) be executed in accordance with such plans, sections and particulars as may be agreed between the owners or in the event of dispute determined in accordance with section 10;

and no deviation shall be made from those plans, sections and particulars except such as may be agreed between the owners (or surveyors acting on their behalf) or in the event of dispute determined in accordance with section 10.

Rights of entry

8. —(1) A building owner, his servants, agents and workmen may during usual working hours enter and remain on any land or premises for the purpose of executing any work in pursuance of this Act and may remove any furniture or fittings or take any other action necessary for that purpose.

A6–008

(2) If the premises are closed, the building owner, his agents and workmen may, if accompanied by a constable or other police officer, break open any fences or doors in order to enter the premises.

(3) No land or premises may be entered by any person under subsection (1) unless the building owner serves on the owner and the occupier of the land or premises—

(a) in case of emergency, such notice of the intention to enter as may be reasonably practicable;

(b) in any other case, such notice of the intention to enter as complies with subsection (4).

(4) Notice complies with this subsection if it is served in a period of not less than fourteen days ending with the day of the proposed entry.

(5) A surveyor appointed or selected under section 10 may during usual working hours enter and remain on any land or premises for the purpose of carrying out the object for which he is appointed or selected.

(6) No land or premises may be entered by a surveyor under subsection (5) unless the building owner who is a party to the dispute concerned serves on the owner and the occupier of the land or premises—

(a) in case of emergency, such notice of the intention to enter as may be reasonably practicable;

(b) in any other case, such notice of the intention to enter as complies with subsection (4).

Easements

9. Nothing in this Act shall—

A6–009

(a) authorise any interference with an easement of light or other easements in or relating to a party wall; or

(b) prejudicially affect any right of any person to preserve or restore any right or other thing in or connected with a party wall in case of the party wall being pulled down or rebuilt.

Resolution of disputes

Resolution of disputes

A6–010   **10.**—(1) Where a dispute arises or is deemed to have arisen between a building owner and an adjoining owner in respect of any matter connected with any work to which this Act relates either—

> (a) both parties shall concur in the appointment of one surveyor (in this section referred to as an "agreed surveyor"); or
> (b) each party shall appoint a surveyor and the two surveyors so appointed shall forthwith select a third surveyor (all of whom are in this section referred to as "the three surveyors").

(2) All appointments and selections made under this section shall be in writing and shall not be rescinded by either party.

(3) If an agreed surveyor—

> (a) refuses to act;
> (b) neglects to act for a period of ten days beginning with the day on which either party serves a request on him;
> (c) dies before the dispute is settled; or
> (d) becomes or deems himself incapable of acting,

the proceedings for settling such dispute shall begin de novo.

(4) If either party to the dispute—

> (a) refuses to appoint a surveyor under subsection (1)(b), or
> (b) neglects to appoint a surveyor under subsection (1)(b) for a period of ten days beginning with the day on which the other party serves a request on him,

the other party may make the appointment on his behalf.

(5) If, before the dispute is settled, a surveyor appointed under paragraph (b) of subsection (1) by a party to the dispute dies, or becomes or deems himself incapable of acting, the party who appointed him may appoint another surveyor in his place with the same power and authority.

(6) If a surveyor—

> (a) appointed under paragraph (b) of subsection (1) by a party to the dispute; or
> (b) appointed under subsection (4) or (5),

refuses to act effectively, the surveyor of the other party may proceed to act ex parte and anything so done by him shall be as effectual as if he had been an agreed surveyor.

(7) If a surveyor—

   (a) appointed under paragraph (b) of subsection (1) by a party to the
      dispute; or
   (b) appointed under subsection (4) or (5),

neglects to act effectively for a period of ten days beginning with the day on
which either party or the surveyor of the other party serves a request on him, the
surveyor of the other party may proceed to act ex parte in respect of the subject
matter of the request and anything so done by him shall be as effectual as if he
had been an agreed surveyor.

   (8) If either surveyor appointed under subsection (1)(b) by a party to the dispute refuses to select a third surveyor under subsection (1) or (9), or neglects to
do so for a period of ten days beginning with the day on which the other surveyor
serves a request on him—

   (a) the appointing officer; or
   (b) in cases where the relevant appointing officer or his employer is a party
      to the dispute, the Secretary of State,

may on the application of either surveyor select a third surveyor who shall have
the same power and authority as if he had been selected under subsection (1) or
subsection (9).

   (9) If a third surveyor selected under subsection (1)(b)—

   (a) refuses to act;
   (b) neglects to act for a period of ten days beginning with the day on which
      either party or the surveyor appointed by either party serves a request on
      him; or
   (c) dies, or becomes or deems himself incapable of acting, before the dis-
      pute is settled,

the other two of the three surveyors shall forthwith select another surveyor in his
place with the same power and authority.

   (10) The agreed surveyor or as the case may be the three surveyors or any two
of them shall settle by award any matter—

   (a) which is connected with any work to which this Act relates, and
   (b) which is in dispute between the building owner and the adjoining owner.

   (11) Either of the parties or either of the surveyors appointed by the parties may
call upon the third surveyor selected in pursuance of this section to determine the
disputed matters and he shall make the necessary award.

   (12) An award may determine—

   (a) the right to execute any work;
   (b) the time and manner of executing any work; and
   (c) any other matter arising out of or incidental to the dispute including the
      costs of making the award;

but any period appointed by the award for executing any work shall not unless
otherwise agreed between the building owner and the adjoining owner begin to

run until after the expiration of the period prescribed by this Act for service of the notice in respect of which the dispute arises or is deemed to have arisen.

(13) The reasonable costs incurred in—

(a) making or obtaining an award under this section;
(b) reasonable inspections of work to which the award relates; and
(c) any other matter arising out of the dispute,

shall be paid by such of the parties as the surveyor or surveyors making the award determine.

(14) Where the surveyors appointed by the parties make an award the surveyors shall serve it forthwith on the parties.

(15) Where an award is made by the third surveyor—

(a) he shall, after payment of the costs of the award, serve it forthwith on the parties or their appointed surveyors; and
(b) if it is served on their appointed surveyors, they shall serve it forthwith on the parties.

(16) The award shall be conclusive and shall not except as provided by this section be questioned in any court.

(17) Either of the parties to the dispute may, within the period of fourteen days beginning with the day on which an award made under this section is served on him, appeal to the county court against the award and the county court may—

(a) rescind the award or modify it in such manner as the court thinks fit; and
(b) make such order as to costs as the court thinks fit.

Expenses

Expenses

A6–011 **11.**—(1) Except as provided under this section expenses of work under this Act shall be defrayed by the building owner.

(2) Any dispute as to responsibility for expenses shall be settled as provided in section 10.

(3) An expense mentioned in section 1(3)(b) shall be defrayed as there mentioned.

(4) Where work is carried out in exercise of the right mentioned in section 2(2)(a), and the work is necessary on account of defect or want of repair of the structure or wall concerned, the expenses shall be defrayed by the building owner and the adjoining owner in such proportion as has regard to—

(a) the use which the owners respectively make or may make of the structure or walls concerned; and
(b) responsibility for the defect or want of repair concerned, if more than one owner makes use of the structure or wall concerned.

(5) Where work is carried out in exercise of the right mentioned in section 2(2)(b) the expenses shall be defrayed by the building owner and the adjoining owner in such proportion as has regard to—

    (a) the use which the owners respectively make or may make of the structure or wall concerned; and
    (b) responsibility for the defect or want of repair concerned, if more than one owner makes use of the structure or wall concerned.

(6) Where the adjoining premises are laid open in exercise of the right mentioned in section 2(2)(e) a fair allowance in respect of disturbance and inconvenience shall be paid by the building owner to the adjoining owner or occupier.

(7) Where a building owner proposes to reduce the height of a party wall or party fence wall under section 2(2)(m) the adjoining owner may serve a counter notice under section 4 requiring the building owner to maintain the existing height of the wall, and in such case the adjoining owner shall pay to the building owner a due proportion of the cost of the wall so far as it exceeds—

    (a) two metres in height; or
    (b) the height currently enclosed upon by the building of the adjoining owner.

(8) Where the building owner is required to make good damage under this Act the adjoining owner has a right to require that the expenses of such making good be determined in accordance with section 10 and paid to him in lieu of the carrying out of work to make the damage good.

(9) Where—

    (a) works are carried out, and
    (b) some of the works are carried out at the request of the adjoining owner or in pursuance of a requirement made by him,

he shall defray the expenses of carrying out the works requested or required by him.

(10) Where—

    (a) consent in writing has been given to the construction of special foundations on land of an adjoining owner; and
    (b) the adjoining owner erects any building or structure and its cost is found to be increased by reason of the existence of the said foundations,

the owner of the building to which the said foundations belong shall, on receiving an account with any necessary invoices and other supporting documents within the period of two months beginning with the day of the completion of the work by the adjoining owner, repay to the adjoining owner so much of the cost as is due to the existence of the said foundations.

(11) Where use is subsequently made by the adjoining owner of work carried out solely at the expense of the building owner the adjoining owner shall pay a due proportion of the expenses incurred by the building owner in carrying out that

work; and for this purpose he shall be taken to have incurred expenses calculated by reference to what the cost of the work would be if it were carried out at the time when that subsequent use is made.

Security for expenses

A6–012 **12.**—(1) An adjoining owner may serve a notice requiring the building owner before he begins any work in the exercise of the rights conferred by this Act to give such security as may be agreed between the owners or in the event of dispute determined in accordance with section 10.

(2) Where—

(a) in the exercise of the rights conferred by this Act an adjoining owner requires the building owner to carry out any work the expenses of which are to be defrayed in whole or in part by the adjoining owner, or

(b) an adjoining owner serves a notice on the building owner under subsection (1),

the building owner may before beginning the work to which the requirement or notice relates serve a notice on the adjoining owner requiring him to give such security as may be agreed between the owners or in the event of dispute determined in accordance with section 10.

(3) If within the period of one month beginning with—

(a) the day on which a notice is served under subsection (2); or

(b) in the event of dispute, the date of the determination by the surveyor or surveyors,

the adjoining owner does not comply with the notice or the determination, the requirement or notice by him to which the building owner's notice under that subsection relates shall cease to have effect.

Account for work carried out

A6–013 **13.**—(1) Within the period of two months beginning with the day of the completion of any work executed by a building owner of which the expenses are to be wholly or partially defrayed by an adjoining owner in accordance with section 11 the building owner shall serve on the adjoining owner an account in writing showing—

(a) particulars and expenses of the work; and

(b) any deductions to which the adjoining owner or any other person is entitled in respect of old materials or otherwise;

and in preparing the account the work shall be estimated and valued at fair average rates and prices according to the nature of the work, the locality and the cost of labour and materials prevailing at the time when the work is executed.

(2) Within the period of one month beginning with the day of service of the said account the adjoining owner may serve on the building owner a notice stating any objection he may have thereto and thereupon a dispute shall be deemed to have arisen between the parties.

(3) If within that period of one month the adjoining owner does not serve notice under subsection (2) he shall be deemed to have no objection to the account.

Settlement of account

14.—(1) All expenses to be defrayed by an adjoining owner in accordance with an account served under section 13 shall be paid by the adjoining owner. **A6–014**

(2) Until an adjoining owner pays to the building owner such expenses as aforesaid the property in any works executed under this Act to which the expenses relate shall be vested solely in the building owner.

Miscellaneous

Service of notices, etc.

15.—(1) A notice or other document required or authorised to be served under this Act may be served on a person— **A6–015**

(a) by delivering it to him in person;

(b) by sending it by post to him at his usual or last-known residence or place of business in the United Kingdom; or

(c) in the case of a body corporate, by delivering it to the secretary or clerk of the body corporate at its registered or principal office or sending it by post to the secretary or clerk of that body corporate at that office.

(2) In the case of a notice or other document required or authorised to be served under this Act on a person as owner of premises, it may alternatively be served by—

(a) addressing it "the owner" of the premises (naming them), and

(b) delivering it to a person on the premises or, if no person to whom it can be delivered is found there, fixing it to a conspicuous part of the premises.

Offences

16.—(1) If— **A6–016**

(a) an occupier of land or premises refuses to permit a person to do anything which he is entitled to do with regard to the land or premises under section 8(1) or (5); and

(b) the occupier knows or has reasonable cause to believe that the person is so entitled,

the occupier is guilty of an offence.

(2) If—

    (a) a person hinders or obstructs a person in attempting to do anything which he is entitled to do with regard to land or premises under section 8(1) or (5); and

    (b) the first-mentioned person knows or has reasonable cause to believe that the other person is so entitled,

the first-mentioned person is guilty of an offence.

(3) A person guilty of an offence under subsection (1) or (2) is liable on summary conviction to a fine of an amount not exceeding level 3 on the standard scale.

Recovery of sums

A6–017   **17.** Any sum payable in pursuance of this Act (otherwise than by way of fine) shall be recoverable summarily as a civil debt.

Exception in case of Temples, etc.

A6–018   **18.**—(1) This Act shall not apply to land which is situated in inner London and in which there is an interest belonging to—

    (a) the Honourable Society of the Inner Temple,

    (b) the Honourable Society of the Middle Temple,

    (c) the Honourable Society of Lincoln's Inn, or

    (d) the Honourable Society of Gray's Inn.

(2) The reference in subsection (1) to inner London is to Greater London other than the outer London boroughs.

The Crown

A6–019   **19.**—(1) This Act shall apply to land in which there is—

    (a) an interest belonging to Her Majesty in right of the Crown,

    (b) an interest belonging to a government department, or

    (c) an interest held in trust for Her Majesty for the purposes of any such department.

(2) This Act shall apply to—

    (a) land which is vested in, but not occupied by, Her Majesty in right of the Duchy of Lancaster;

    (b) land which is vested in, but not occupied by, the possessor for the time being of the Duchy of Cornwall.

Interpretation

A6–020   **20.**—(1) In this act, unless the context otherwise requires, the following expressions have the meanings hereby respectively assigned to them—

"adjoining owner" and "adjoining occupier" respectively mean any owner and any occupier of land, buildings, storeys or rooms adjoining those of the building owner and for the purposes only of section 6 within the distances specified in that section;

"appointing officer" means the person appointed under this Act by the local authority to make such appointments as are required under section 10(8);

"building owner" means an owner of land who is desirous of exercising rights under this Act;

"foundation", in relation to a wall, means the solid ground or artificially formed support resting on solid ground on which the wall rests;

"owner" includes—

(a) a person in receipt of, or entitled to receive, the whole or part of the rents or profits of land;

(b) a person in possession of land, otherwise than as a mortgagee or as a tenant from year to year or for a lesser term or as a tenant at will;

(c) a purchaser of an interest in land under a contract for purchase or under an agreement for a lease, otherwise than under an agreement for a tenancy from year to year or for a lesser term;

"party fence wall" means a wall (not being part of a building) which stands on lands of different owners and is used or constructed to be used for separating such adjoining lands, but does not include a wall constructed on the land of one owner the artificially formed support of which projects into the land of another owner;

"party structure" means a party wall and also a floor partition or other structure separating buildings or parts of buildings approached solely by separate staircases or separate entrances;

"party wall" means—

(a) a wall which forms part of a building and stands on lands of different owners to a greater extent than the projection of any artificially formed support on which the wall rests; and

(b) so much of a wall not being a wall referred to in paragraph (a) above as separates buildings belonging to different owners;

"special foundations" means foundations in which an assemblage of beams or rods is employed for the purpose of distributing any load; and

"surveyor" means any person not being a party to the matter appointed or selected under section 10 to determine disputes in accordance with the procedures set out in this Act.

Other statutory provisions

A6–021

21.—(1) The Secretary of State may by order amend or repeal any provision of a private or local Act passed before or in the same session as this Act, if it appears to him necessary or expedient to do so in consequence of this Act.

(2) An order under subsection (1) may—

(a) contain such savings or transitional provisions as the Secretary of State thinks fit;

(b) make different provision for different purposes.

(3) The power to make an order under subsection (1) shall be exercisable by statutory instrument subject to annulment in pursuance of a resolution of either House of Parliament.

General

Short title, commencement and extent

A6–022   **22.**—(1) This Act may be cited as the Party Wall, etc. Act 1996.

(2) This Act shall come into force in accordance with provision made by the Secretary of State by order made by statutory instrument.

(3) An order under subsection (2) may—

(a) contain such savings or transitional provisions as the Secretary of State thinks fit;
(b) make different provision for different purposes.

(4) This Act extends to England and Wales only.

Countryside and Rights of Way Act 2000

(C. 37)

An Act to make new provision for public access to the countryside; to amend the law relating to public rights of way; to enable traffic regulation orders to be made for the purpose of conserving an area's natural beauty; to make provision with respect to the driving of mechanically propelled vehicles elsewhere than on roads; to amend the law relating to nature conservation and the protection of wildlife; to make further provision with respect to areas of outstanding natural beauty; and for connected purposes.

[30TH NOVEMBER 2000]

BE IT ENACTED by the Queen's most Excellent Majesty, by and with the advice and consent of the Lords Spiritual and Temporal, and Commons, in this present Parliament assembled, and by the authority of the same, as follows—

Vehicular access across common land, etc.

A7–001   **68.**—(1) This section applies to a way which the owner or occupier (from time to time) of any premises has used as a means of access for vehicles to the premises, if that use of the way—

(a) was an offence under an enactment applying to the land crossed by the way, but

(b) would otherwise have been sufficient to create on or after the prescribed date, and to keep in existence, an easement giving a right of way for vehicles.

(2) Regulations may provide, as respects a way to which this section applies, for the creation in accordance with the regulations, on the application of the owner of the premises concerned and on compliance by him with prescribed requirements, of an easement subsisting at law for the benefit of the premises and giving a right of way for vehicles over that way.

(3) An easement created in accordance with the regulations is subject to any enactment or rule of law which would apply to such an easement granted by the owner of the land.

(4) The regulations may in particular—

(a) require that, where an application is made after the relevant use of the way has ceased, it is to be made within a specified time,

(b) specify grounds on which objections may be made and the procedure to apply to the making of objections,

(c) require any matter to be referred to and determined by the Lands Tribunal, and make provision as to procedure and costs,

(d) make provision as to the payment of any amount by the owner of the premises concerned to any person or into court and as to the time when any payment is to be made,

(e) provide for the determination of any such amount,

(f) make provision as to the date on which any easement is created,

(g) specify any limitation to which the easement is subject,

(h) provide for the easement to include any specified right incidental to the right of way,

(i) make different provision for different circumstances.

(5) In this section—

"enactment" includes an enactment in a local or private Act and a byelaw, regulation or other provision having effect under an enactment;

"owner", in relation to any premises, means—

(a) a person, other than a mortgagee not in possession, who is for the time being entitled to dispose of the fee simple of the premises, whether in possession or in reversion, or

(b) a tenant under a long lease, within the meaning of the Landlord and Tenant Act 1987;

"prescribed" means prescribed by regulations;

"regulations" means regulations made, as respects England, by the Secretary of State and, as respects Wales, by the National Assembly for Wales.

(6) Regulations under this section shall be made by statutory instrument, and no such regulations shall be made by the Secretary of State unless a draft has been laid before, and approved by a resolution of, each House of Parliament.

Land Registration Act 2002

(C. 9)

An Act to make provision about land registration; and for connected purposes.
[26TH FEBRUARY 2002]

BE IT ENACTED by the Queen's most Excellent Majesty, by and with the advice and consent of the Lords Spiritual and Temporal, and Commons, in this present Parliament assembled, and by the authority of the same, as follows:—

Freehold estates

A8–001   **11.**—(1) This section is concerned with the registration of a person under this Chapter as the proprietor of a freehold estate.

(2) Registration with absolute title has the effect described in subsections (3) to (5).

(3) The estate is vested in the proprietor together with all interests subsisting for the benefit of the estate.

(4) The estate is vested in the proprietor subject only to the following interests affecting the estate at the time of registration—

   (a) interests which are the subject of an entry in the register in relation to the estate,
   (b) unregistered interests which fall within any of the paragraphs of Schedule 1, and
   (c) interests acquired under the Limitation Act 1980 (c. 58) of which the proprietor has notice.

(5) If the proprietor is not entitled to the estate for his own benefit, or not entitled solely for his own benefit, then, as between himself and the persons beneficially entitled to the estate, the estate is vested in him subject to such of their interests as he has notice of.

(6) Registration with qualified title has the same effect as registration with absolute title, except that it does not affect the enforcement of any estate, right or interest which appears from the register to be excepted from the effect of registration.

(7) Registration with possessory title has the same effect as registration with absolute title, except that it does not affect the enforcement of any estate, right or interest adverse to, or in derogation of, the proprietor's title subsisting at the time of registration or then capable of arising.

Leasehold estates

A8–002   **12.**—(1) This section is concerned with the registration of a person under this Chapter as the proprietor of a leasehold estate.

(2) Registration with absolute title has the effect described in subsections (3) to (5).

(3) The estate is vested in the proprietor together with all interests subsisting for the benefit of the estate.

(4) The estate is vested subject only to the following interests affecting the estate at the time of registration—

(a) implied and express covenants, obligations and liabilities incident to the estate,
(b) interests which are the subject of an entry in the register in relation to the estate,
(c) unregistered interests which fall within any of the paragraphs of Schedule 1, and
(d) interests acquired under the Limitation Act 1980 (c. 58) of which the proprietor has notice.

(5) If the proprietor is not entitled to the estate for his own benefit, or not entitled solely for his own benefit, then, as between himself and the persons beneficially entitled to the estate, the estate is vested in him subject to such of their interests as he has notice of.

(6) Registration with good leasehold title has the same effect as registration with absolute title, except that it does not affect the enforcement of any estate, right or interest affecting, or in derogation of, the title of the lessor to grant the lease.

(7) Registration with qualified title has the same effect as registration with absolute title except that it does not affect the enforcement of any estate, right or interest which appears from the register to be excepted from the effect of registration.

(8) Registration with possessory title has the same effect as registration with absolute title, except that it does not affect the enforcement of any estate, right or interest adverse to, or in derogation of, the proprietor's title subsisting at the time of registration or then capable of arising.

Dispositions required to be registered

27.—(1) If a disposition of a registered estate or registered charge is required to be completed by registration, it does not operate at law until the relevant registration requirements are met.   **A8–003**

(2) In the case of a registered estate, the following are the dispositions which are required to be completed by registration—

(a) a transfer,
(b) where the registered estate is an estate in land, the grant of a term of years absolute—
    (i) for a term of more than seven years from the date of the grant,
    (ii) to take effect in possession after the end of the period of three months beginning with the date of the grant,
    (iii) under which the right to possession is discontinuous,
    (iv) in pursuance of Part 5 of the Housing Act 1985 (c. 68) (the right to buy), or
    (v) in circumstances where section 171A of that Act applies (disposal by landlord which leads to a person no longer being a secure tenant),
(c) where the registered estate is a franchise or manor, the grant of a lease,
(d) the express grant or reservation of an interest of a kind falling within section 1(2)(a) of the Law of Property Act 1925 (c. 20), other than one

which is capable of being registered under the Commons Registration Act 1965 (c. 64),

(e) the express grant or reservation of an interest of a kind falling within section 1(2)(b) or (e) of the Law of Property Act 1925, and

(f) the grant of a legal charge.

(3) In the case of a registered charge, the following are the dispositions which are required to be completed by registration—

(a) a transfer, and

(b) the grant of a sub-charge.

(4) Schedule 2 to this Act (which deals with the relevant registration requirements) has effect.

(5) This section applies to dispositions by operation of law as it applies to other dispositions, but with the exception of the following—

(a) a transfer on the death or bankruptcy of an individual proprietor,

(b) a transfer on the dissolution of a corporate proprietor, and

(c) the creation of a legal charge which is a local land charge.

(6) Rules may make provision about applications to the registrar for the purpose of meeting registration requirements under this section.

(7) In subsection (2)(d), the reference to express grant does not include grant as a result of the operation of section 62 of the Law of Property Act 1925 (c. 20).

Effect of registered dispositions: estates

A8–004   **29.**—(1) If a registrable disposition of a registered estate is made for valuable consideration, completion of the disposition by registration has the effect of postponing to the interest under the disposition any interest affecting the estate immediately before the disposition whose priority is not protected at the time of registration.

(2) For the purposes of subsection (1), the priority of an interest is protected—

(a) in any case, if the interest—
  (i) is a registered charge or the subject of a notice in the register,
  (ii) falls within any of the paragraphs of Schedule 3, or
  (iii) appears from the register to be excepted from the effect of registration, and

(b) in the case of a disposition of a leasehold estate, if the burden of the interest is incident to the estate.

(3) Subsection (2)(a)(ii) does not apply to an interest which has been the subject of a notice in the register at any time since the coming into force of this section.

(4) Where the grant of a leasehold estate in land out of a registered estate does not involve a registrable disposition, this section has effect as if—

(a) the grant involved such a disposition, and

(b) the disposition were registered at the time of the grant.

Nature and effect

32.—(1) A notice is an entry in the register in respect of the burden of an interest **A8–005** affecting a registered estate or charge.

(2) The entry of a notice is to be made in relation to the registered estate or charge affected by the interest concerned.

(3) The fact that an interest is the subject of a notice does not necessarily mean that the interest is valid, but does mean that the priority of the interest, if valid, is protected for the purposes of sections 29 and 30.

Entry on application

34.—(1) A person who claims to be entitled to the benefit of an interest affecting **A8–006** a registered estate or charge may, if the interest is not excluded by section 33, apply to the registrar for the entry in the register of a notice in respect of the interest.

(2) Subject to rules, an application under this section may be for—

(a) an agreed notice, or
(b) a unilateral notice.

(3) The registrar may only approve an application for an agreed notice if—

(a) the applicant is the relevant registered proprietor, or a person entitled to be registered as such proprietor,
(b) the relevant registered proprietor, or a person entitled to be registered as such proprietor, consents to the entry of the notice, or
(c) the registrar is satisfied as to the validity of the applicant's claim.

(4) In subsection (3), references to the relevant registered proprietor are to the proprietor of the registered estate or charge affected by the interest to which the application relates.

Unregistered interests

37.—(1) If it appears to the registrar that a registered estate is subject to an **A8–007** unregistered interest which—

(a) falls within any of the paragraphs of Schedule 1, and
(b) is not excluded by section 33,

he may enter a notice in the register in respect of the interest.

(2) The registrar must give notice of an entry under this section to such persons as rules may provide.

Registrable dispositions

38. Where a person is entered in the register as the proprietor of an interest under **A8–008** a disposition falling within section 27(2)(b) to (e), the registrar must also enter a notice in the register in respect of that interest.

Duty to disclose unregistered interests

A8–009 **71.** Where rules so provide—

    (a) a person applying for registration under Chapter 1 of Part 2 must provide to the registrar such information as the rules may provide about any interest affecting the estate to which the application relates which—
      (i) falls within any of the paragraphs of Schedule 1, and
      (ii) is of a description specified by the rules;
    (b) a person applying to register a registrable disposition of a registered estate must provide to the registrar such information as the rules may provide about any unregistered interest affecting the estate which—
      (i) falls within any of the paragraphs of Schedule 3, and
      (ii) is of description specified by the rules.

Proprietary estoppel and mere equities

A8–010 **116.** It is hereby declared for the avoidance of doubt that, in relation to registered land, each of the following—

    (a) an equity by estoppel, and
    (b) a mere equity,

has effect from the time the equity arises as an interest capable of binding successors in title (subject to the rules about the effect of dispositions on priority).

SCHEDULE 1

UNREGISTERED INTERESTS WHICH OVERRIDE FIRST REGISTRATION EASEMENTS AND PROFITS A PRENDRE

A8–011 **3.** A legal easement or profit a prendre.

SCHEDULE 2

REGISTRABLE DISPOSITIONS: REGISTRATION REQUIREMENTS

SCHEDULE PART 1 REGISTERED ESTATES

Creation of Other Legal Interest

A8–012 **7.**—(1) This paragraph applies to a disposition which—

    (a) consists of the creation of an interest of a kind falling within section 1(2)(a), (b) or (e) of the Law of Property Act 1925, and
    (b) is not a disposition to which paragraph 4, 5 or 6 applies.

(2) In the case of a disposition to which this paragraph applies—

(a) a notice in respect of the interest created must be entered in the register, and
(b) if the interest is created for the benefit of a registered estate, the proprietor of the registered estate must be entered in the register as its proprietor.

(3) Rules may provide for sub-paragraph (2) to have effect with modifications in relation to a right of entry over or in respect of a term of years absolute.

SCHEDULE 3

UNREGISTERED INTERESTS WHICH OVERRIDE REGISTERED DISPOSITIONS
EASEMENTS AND PROFITS A PRENDRE

3.—(1) A legal easement or profit a prendre, except for an easement, or a profit a   **A8–013**
prendre which is not registered under the Commons Registration Act 1965 (c. 64), which at the time of the disposition—

(a) is not within the actual knowledge of the person to whom the disposition is made, and
(b) would not have been obvious on a reasonably careful inspection of the land over which the easement or profit is exercisable.

(2) The exception in sub-paragraph (1) does not apply if the person entitled to the easement or profit proves that it has been exercised in the period of one year ending with the day of the disposition.

APPENDIX B

The Local Land Charges Rules 1977

(SI 1977/985)

Made . . . 3 June 1977

Laid before Parliament . . . 20 June 1977

Coming into Operation . . . 1 August 1977

Title and commencement

1.—These Rules may be cited as the Local Land Charges Rules 1977 and shall come into operation on 1st August 1977.

B1–001

Interpretation

2.—(1) The Interpretation Act 1889 shall apply to the interpretation of these Rules as it applies to the interpretation of an Act of Parliament.

B1–002

(2) In these Rules, unless the context otherwise requires—

"the Act" means the Local Land Charges Act 1975;
"charge" means a local land charge or a matter which is registrable in a local land charges register;
"description" in relation to a charge means a description which is sufficient to indicate—
    (a) the nature of any agreement, certificate, notice, order, resolution, scheme or other instrument or document (not being a statute or an instrument embodying statutory provisions) which comprises the charge or in connection with which the charge came into existence;
    (b) where apparent from the instrument or document, the date on which the charge came into existence;
    (c) any statutory provision (other than section 1(1)(e) of the Act or a provision specified in the part of Schedule 2 appropriate for the charge) under or by virtue of which the charge is a local land charge or registrable, or which comprises the charge;

. . . . .

"register" means local land charges register;

. . . . .

(3) In these Rules, unless the context otherwise requires, a rule or schedule referred to by number means the rule or schedule so numbered in these Rules and a form designated by letter means the form so designated in Schedule 1.

(4) In these Rules, unless the context otherwise requires, any reference to an enactment is a reference to that enactment as amended, extended or applied by or under any other enactment.

Parts of the register

B1–003   **3.**—The register shall continue to be divided into parts, for the registration of different types of charge, as follows:—

. . . . .

Part 11, for charges falling within section 2(4) of the Rights of Light Act 1959 ("light obstruction notices");

. . . . .

Application for registration

B1–004   **4.**—(1) Without prejudice to rule 10(1) below, an application to a registering authority for registration of a charge shall be in writing and shall contain a description of the charge and any other particulars necessary to enable the registering authority to register the charge in accordance with these Rules.

(2) An application for registration may be sent by post to, or left at the office of, the registering authority.

Delivery of applications

B1–005   **5.**—(1) For the purposes of section 10(5) of the Act, it shall be regarded as practicable for a registering authority to register a charge on the day on which the application for registration is delivered or treated in accordance with paragraph (2) below as having been delivered.

(2) An application for registration delivered between the time when the office of the registering authority closes and the time when it next opens shall be treated as having been delivered immediately after that interval.

Registration

B1–006   **6.**—(1) Every charge shall be registered by reference to the land in the area of the registering authority affected by the charge, in such a manner as to show the situation and extent of that land.

(2) Subject to rule 7, the registration of a charge shall be effected by entering in the part of the register appropriate for that charge the particulars specified in Schedule 2 in relation to that part.

Use of existing registers

B1–007   **7.**—Where the particulars of a planning charge or other charge which are required by these Rules to be entered in the register have been entered in another record maintained and kept open for public inspection in pursuance of a statutory obligation, it shall be a sufficient compliance with that requirement to enter in the register a reference whereby the particulars in that other record can readily be traced.

Amendment and cancellation of registrations

8.—(1) Without prejudice to any other provisions of these Rules . . .   **B1–008**

    (a) where a registered charge has been varied or modified or any registration is incorrect, the registering authority shall amend the registration accordingly;

    (b) where a registered charge has been discharged, ceased to have effect or ceased to be a charge, the registering authority shall cancel the registration.

. . . . .

Light obstruction notices

10.—(1) An application under section 2(2) of the Rights of Light Act 1959 for   **B1–009** registration of a light obstruction notice shall be in Form A and shall be accompanied by the certificate of the Lands Tribunal relating to the notice.

(2) On receiving the application and the certificate the registering authority shall file them and register the notice in accordance with rule 6.

(3) Where, after a temporary certificate has been filed and before the period for which it operates has expired a definitive certificate is lodged with the registering authority, they shall file the definitive certificate with the application and amend the registration accordingly.

(4) On receiving an office copy of a judgment or order directing the registration of a light obstruction notice to be varied or cancelled, the registering authority shall file the office copy with the application for that registration and shall amend or cancel the registration accordingly.

(5) The person on whose application the notice was registered, or any owner of the servient land or part of it who is a successor in title to that person, may within a year from the date of registration apply in Form B for—

    (a) amendment of the registered particulars of the position or dimensions of the structure to which registration is intended to be equivalent, so as to reduce its height or length or to increase its distance from the dominant building; or

    (b) cancellation of the registration;

and on receiving any such application the registering authority shall file it and amend or cancel the registration accordingly.

(6) Without prejudice to the preceding paragraphs of this rule, the registering authority shall cancel the registration of a notice—

    (a) where in relation to the notice a temporary certificate has been filed and no definitive certificate has been filed, on the expiration of the period of operation specified in the temporary certificate;

    (b) in any other case, on the expiration of 21 years from the date of registration;

and thereupon any document relating to the notice and filed pursuant to these Rules shall be taken off the file.

(7) In this rule "definitive certificate" means a certificate issued by the Lands Tribunal under section 2(3)(a) of the Rights of Light Act 1959 and "temporary

certificate" means a certificate so issued under section 2(3)(b) of that Act; "dominant building" and "servient land" have the meanings assigned to them by section 2(1) of that Act; and "owner" has the meaning assigned to it by section 7(1) of that Act.

Searches

B1–010   **11.**—(1) [Subject to rule 16 (Requisition and issue of official search certificates by electronic means)][1] [a][2] person who wishes to make a personal search shall, if so requested by the registering authority, state his name and address and indicate the parcel of land in respect of which he wishes to search.

(2) A requisition for an official search of the register and the official search certificate shall be in Form C.

(3) A separate personal search or (as the case may be) a separate requisition for an official search shall be made in respect of each parcel of land against which a search is required, except where for the purpose of a single transaction the search is required in respect of two or more parcels of land which have a common boundary or are separated only by a road, railway, river, stream or canal.

(4) [Subject to rule 16 (Requisition and issue of official search certificates by electronic means)][3] [a][4] n official search certificate shall, where there are subsisting registrations, be accompanied by a schedule substantially in accordance with Schedule 2 (or such numbered parts of it as may be appropriate) showing the particulars of the registrations.

Office copies

B1–011   **12.**—On the written request of any person, and on payment of the prescribed fee, the registering authority shall supply an office copy of any registration or any document, map or plan deposited with or filed by that authority in connection with a registration.

Use of forms

B1–012   **13.**—[Subject to rule 16 (Requisition and issue of official search certificates by electronic means)][5] [e][6] xcept for the purposes of schedules accompanying official search certificates in accordance with rule 11(4) above, no forms other than those supplied by Her Majesty's Stationery Office [or, until the Lord Chancellor otherwise directs, clear and legible facsimiles of such forms][7] may be used for the purposes of these Rules.

Fees

B1–013   **14.**—The fees specified in Schedule 3 shall be payable under the Act and every fee shall be paid in advance.

[1] Words inserted by SI 1995/260, r.2.
[2] Words inserted by SI 1995/260, r.2.
[3] Words inserted by SI 1995/260, r.2.
[4] Words inserted by SI 1995/260, r.2.
[5] Words inserted by SI 1995/260, r.2.
[6] Words inserted by SI 1995/260, r.2
[7] Words inserted by SI 1978/1638, r.3.

Transitional provisions

15.—(1) Any application or requisition which— **B1–014**

    (a) was sent to the registering authority before 1st August 1977;

    (b) was not dealt with by the registering authority before that date;

    (c) could have been made under these Rules if they had been in force;

shall be treated as an application or requisition under these Rules and shall be dealt with by the registering authority accordingly.

(2) As respects registrations subsisting on 31st July 1977, registering authorities shall not be bound to register or to disclose by an official certificate of search or otherwise any particulars the registration or disclosure of which could not be required by or under the Rules applicable on that date to such registrations.

(3) Notwithstanding the provisions of these Rules, the forms prescribed by the rules applicable on 31st July 1977 to charges may, until the Lord Chancellor otherwise directs, be used, with such adaptations as may be appropriate, for the purposes of these Rules.

Requisition and issue of official search certificates by electronic means

[**16.**—(1) A requisition for an official search of the register may be made by elec- **B1–015**
tronic means, notwithstanding section 231(1) of the Local Government Act 1972[8]
(service of documents on local authorities), where the local authority to whom it
is made consents to the use of those means.

(2) An official search certificate may be issued by electronic means where the person requiring the search consents to the use of those means.

(3) Where a requisition is made under paragraph (1), or a certificate issued under paragraph (2), all the information that would otherwise be required by these Rules to be set out in Form C shall be transmitted electronically together with—

    (a) in the case of a requisition, the name of the person making the requisition or his solicitor; or

    (b) in the case of a certificate, the name and office of the person certifying the search and the name of the registering authority.

(4) The signatures otherwise required by these Rules shall not be transmitted.][9]

---

[8] 1972, c.70.
[9] Added by SI 1995/260, r.3.

SCHEDULE 1

FORMS

Form A

APPLICATION FOR REGISTRATION OF A LIGHT OBSTRUCTION NOTICE

B1–016 I, ... of . . . ., being the
freehold owner *or* the tenant of a term of years of which over 7 years remain unex-
pired *or* the mortgage in possession[1] of . . . .

. . . .

. . . .

. . . .[2],

which is shown on the plan attached hereto, hereby apply to the . . . .
Council for registration of this notice under section 2 of the Rights of Light Act
1959 against the building known as . . . .

. . . .

. . . .

. . . .[3]

Registration of this notice is intended to be equivalent to the obstruction of the
access of light to the said building across my land which would be caused by the
erection of an opaque structure on all the boundaries of my land *or* in the position
on my land marked on the attached plan[4] and of unlimited height
or . . . .

. . . .

. . . .

. . . .

. . . .[5]

Signed . . . .

Date . . . .

[1] Delete inapplicable words.

[2] Insert description of servient land.

[3] Insert description of dominant building (wherever practicable, a map or plan of the building should be attached).

[4] Delete inappropriate words.

[5] Delete "of unlimited height" if inappropriate and insert description of height and other dimensions.

Form B

APPLICATION TO AMEND OR CANCEL A LIGHT OBSTRUCTION NOTICE WITH STATUTORY DECLARATION

Application

I, ... of . . . ., being the   **B1–017**
owner of the interest described below in the land known
as . . . .

. . . .

. . . .

[1] Delete inapplicable words.

[2] Delete and insert as appropriate.

[3] If an amendment is required, give particulars; if a cancellation, delete sentence.

[4] Give names and addresses of persons indicated; if there are no such persons, delete sentence.

hereby apply for the amendment *or* the cancellation[1] of the light obstruction notice registered on my application *or* on the application of . . . . of . . . .[2]
The amendment which I require is . . . .

. . . .

. . . .[3]

The consent to this application by the following persons, being persons who would be entitled to apply for the registration of a light obstruction notice, is attached: . . . .

. . . .

. . . .[4]

Signed . . . .

Date . . . .

Statutory Declaration

I, ... of, ... solemnly
and sincerely declare that: —

   (a) I am the freehold owner *or* the tenant for a term of years of which over
        7 years remain unexpired *or* the mortgage in possession[1] of . . . .   [1] Delete inapplicable words.

        . . . .

        . . . .[2];   [2] Insert description of servient land.

   (b) the light obstruction notice referred to above was registered on my   [3] Delete and
        application *or* on the application of . . . .   insert as
        of . . . .[3];   appropriate.

   (c) there are no other persons who would be entitled to apply for the registra-
        tion of a light obstruction notice . . . .[4]   [4] Insert if appropriate "apart from the persons named above."

And I make this solemn declaration, conscientiously believing the same to be true,
by virtue of the Statutory Declarations Act 1835.

Declared by the said . . . .
at . . . . this . . . day of
. . . . before me . . . .

                                   A Commissioner for Oaths *or*
                                   a practising solicitor.

Form C

REQUISITION FOR SEARCH AND OFFICIAL CERTIFICATE OF SEARCH

Requisition for Search

¹ Delete if
inappropriate.

² Delete if
inappropriate.

B1–018

Official number ....
Name of registering authority ....
An official search is required in [Part........................of]¹ the register of local land charges kept by the above-named registering authority for subsisting registration against the land [defined in the attached plan and]² described below:

....

....

....

....

Signature of applicant ....

or his solicitor ....

Date ....

Official Certificate of Search

³ Delete
inapplicable
words.

It is hereby certified that the search requested above reveals no subsisting registration *or* the registrations described in the Schedule hereto³ up to and including the date of this certificate.

⁴ Insert name of
registrating
authority.

Signed ....

On behalf of .... ⁴

Date ....

SCHEDULE 2

PARTICULARS OF REGISTRATIONS

B1–019

Part 11: light obstruction notices
Rights of Light Act 1959, section 2(4)

Description of charge	Description of dominant building	Name and address of applicant and short description of his interest in servient land	Position and dimension of structure to which registration equivalent	Date of temporary Lands Tribunal certificate (if any) and of its expiration	Date of definitive Lands Tribunal certificate	List of documents filed	Date of registration
1	2	3	4	5	6	7	8

Part 12: drainage scheme charges
Land Drainage Act 1976, section 31(4)

Description of charge	Originating authority	Place where relevant documents may be inspected	Date of registration
1	2	3	4

SCHEDULE 3

FEES

[Item	Fee	**B1–020**
	£	
1. Registration of a charge in Part 11 of the register	[60.00]	
2. Filing a definitive certificate of the Lands Tribunal under rule 10(3)	[2.10]	
3. Filing a judgment, order or application for the variation or cancellation of an entry in Part 11 of the register	[6.30]	
4. Inspection of documents filed under rule 10 in respect of each parcel of land	[2.10]	
5. Personal search in the whole or in part of the register	[10.00]	
and in addition, in respect of each parcel of land above one, where under rule 11(3) the search extends to more than one parcel, subject to a maximum of £13.00	[1.00]	
6. Official search (including issue of official certificate of search)—		
(a) in any one part of the register	[1.90]	
(b) in the whole of the register	[5.00]	
and in addition, in respect of each parcel of land above one, where under rule 11(3) more than one parcel is included in the same requisition (whether the requisition is for a search in the whole or in any part of the register), subject to a maximum of £13.00	[0.80]	
7. Office copy of any entry in the register (not including a copy or extract of any plan or document filed pursuant to these Rules)	[1.40][10]	
8. Office copy of any plan or other document filed pursuant to these Rules	such reasonable fee as may be fixed by the registering authority according to the time and work involved][11]	

[10] Fees 1–7, substituted by SI 1998/1190, Local Land Charges (Amendment) Rules, Sch.1.
[11] Substituted by SI 1992/194, Local Land Charges (Amendment) Rules, r.2.

The Lands Tribunal Rules 1996

(SI 1996/1022)

Made ... 27 March 1996

Coming into force ... 1 May 1996

PART VI

APPLICATIONS UNDER SECTION 2 OF THE RIGHTS OF LIGHT ACT 1959

Form of application

B2–001 **21.**—(1) An application for a certificate of the Lands Tribunal under section 2 of the Rights of Light Act 1959 shall be in Form 1.

(2) An application under paragraph (1) shall be accompanied by two copies of the application which the applicant proposes to make to the local authority in whose area the dominant building is situated.

Publicity

B2–002 **22.**—(1) Upon receipt of an application the registrar shall determine what notices are to be given, whether by advertisement or otherwise, to persons who appear to have an interest in the dominant building referred to in rule 21(2).

(2) For the purpose of paragraph (1), the registrar shall require the applicant to provide any documents or information which it is within his power to provide.

(3) The notices that the registrar determines shall be given under this rule shall be given by the applicant who shall notify the registrar in writing once this has been done setting out full particulars of the steps he has taken.

Issue of temporary certificate

B2–003 **23.**—(1) Where the Tribunal is satisfied that exceptional urgency requires the immediate registration of a temporary notice in the register of local land charges, it shall issue a temporary certificate in Form 2.

(2) A temporary certificate shall not last longer than six months.

Issue of definitive certificates

B2–004 **24.** The Tribunal shall issue a certificate in Form 3 or, where a temporary certificate has been issued under rule 23, in Form 4, once it is satisfied that the notices which the registrar has determined shall be given under rule 22 have been duly given.

Rule 2.   SCHEDULE 1   **B2–005**

Rule 21.   FORM 1

Application for Certificate under section 2 of the Rights of Light Act 1959

To:—The Registrar, Lands Tribunal
Strike out words not applicable   **B2–006**
I/We. . . ..

of. . .. .

being [owner(s)] [tenant(s)] for a term of years certain expiring in 19   ]

[mortgagee(s) in possession] of (*here describe the servient land*) . . .. apply to the Lands
Tribunal for the issue of a certificate that adequate publicity has been given to my/our proposed application for the registration in the register of local land charges of the . . .. Council of a notice
under section 2 of the Rights of Light Act 1959.

I/We attach two copies of the proposed application.
Application for temporary certificate. Strike out if not applicable.
[I/We also apply for the issue of a certificate authorising the registration forthwith of the proposed
notice as a temporary notice. The case is one of exceptional urgency because (*here insert reasons*)
. . ..].

To the best of my/our knowledge persons likely to be affected by the registration of the notice are
(*here insert names and addresses of all persons in occupation of the dominant building or having a
proprietary interest in it*) . . ..

All communications regarding this application should be addressed to me/us at the address shown
above (*or* to my/our solicitor/agent . . .. of . . ..].
Dated . . ..
Signed . . ..

Rule 23.   FORM 2

Temporary Certificate for Registration of a Notice under section 2 of the Rights of Light Act 1959

I hereby certify that for reasons of exceptional urgency a temporary notice may be registered by (*name*   **B2–007**
of applicant) . . .. forthwith against the building specified in the attached Form of Application
for the registration of a notice under section 2 of the Rights of Light Act 1959.

A notice registered under the said application shall not have effect after the effluxion of . . ..
months from the date of registration unless before the expiration of that period a further certificate of
this Tribunal has been lodged with the registering authority stating that due publicity has been given
to the proposed registration.
Dated . . ..
Signed . . ..

Registrar
Lands Tribunal

Rule 24.   FORM 3

Certificate for Registration of a Notice under section 2 of the Rights of Light Act 1959

B2–008   I certify that adequate notice of the proposed application by (*name of applicant*) . . . . a copy
of which is attached to this certificate, to register a notice under section 2 of the Rights of Light Act
1959 against the (*description of dominant building as specified in the application*) . . . . has
been given to all persons who, in the circumstances existing at the present time, appear to the Lands
Tribunal to be persons likely to be affected by the registration of such a notice.
Dated . . . .
Signed . . . .

Registrar
Lands Tribunal

Rule 24.   FORM 4

*Certificate for Registration of a Notice under section 2 of the Rights of Light Act 1959 following
Registration of a Temporary Notice*

B2–009   I certify that adequate notice of the application by (*name of applicant*) . . . . to register a notice
under section 2 of the Rights of Light Act 1959 against (*description of dominant building as specified
in the application*) . . . . has been given to all persons who, in the circumstances existing at the
present time, appear to the Lands Tribunal to be persons likely to be affected by the registration of
such a notice.

A temporary certificate authorising the registration of a temporary notice was issued by the Lands
Tribunal on . . . . 19 . . . .
Dated . . . .
Signed . . . .

Registrar
Lands Tribunal

Fees
B2–010   The following fees are prescribed by the Lands Tribunal (Amendment) Rules 1996 (SI 1996/1021).

On lodging an application:

(1) for a definitive certificate . . . £250
(2) for a temporary and a definitive certificate . . . £300

Vehicular Access Across Common and Other Land (England) Regulations 2002

(SI 2002/1711)

Made . . . 2002

Coming into force in accordance with regulation 1(1) . . . July 4, 2002

The Secretary of State for Environment, Food and Rural Affairs, in exercise of
the powers conferred on her by section 68 of the Countryside and Rights of Way
Act 2000,[1] hereby makes the following Regulations a draft of which has been laid
before and approved by resolution of each House of Parliament:

[1] 2000, c. 27.

Title, commencement and extent

1.—(1) These Regulations may be cited as the Vehicular Access Across Common and Other Land (England) Regulations 2002 and shall come into force on the day after the date on which they are made.

(2) These Regulations shall apply to land in England only.

(3) For the purposes of paragraph (2), "land" means any land which is crossed by a way used as a means of access for vehicles to premises.

B3–001

Interpretation

2.—(1) In these Regulations—

"the Act" means the Countryside and Rights of Way Act 2000;

"the applicant", "the land" and "the land owner" have the meanings given in regulation 3(2);

"compensation sum" means the amount of compensation payable by the applicant;

"easement" means an easement subsisting at law for the benefit of the premises and giving a right of way for vehicles;

"the parties" means the applicant and the land owner and "party" shall be construed accordingly;

"the premises" means the premises served by the way in respect of which an application for an easement is made;

"the value of the premises" has the meaning given in regulation 11(4).

(2) Any reference in these Regulations to a numbered regulation shall be construed as a reference to the regulation so numbered in these Regulations.

B3–002

Entitlement to make an application

3.—(1) An owner of any premises may, as respects a way to which section 68 of the Act applies, apply for the creation of an easement in accordance with these Regulations.

(2) For the purposes of these Regulations, the owner who makes an application shall be referred to as "the applicant", the land crossed by the way shall be referred to as "the land" and the person who, for the time being, has the freehold title to the land, shall be referred to as "the land owner".

B3–003

Prescribed date

4. The prescribed date for the purpose of section 68(1)(b) of the Act is 5th May 1993.

B3–004

Nature of easement

5. An easement created in accordance with these Regulations shall—

(a) be subject to any limitation agreed by the parties or determined by the Lands Tribunal;

(b) include any right incidental to the right of way agreed by the parties or determined by the Lands Tribunal; and

B3–005

(c) be subject to any rule of law which would apply to the easement had it been acquired by prescription.

Procedure for making an application

B3–006   **6.**—(1) An application for the easement shall be made by the applicant serving a notice on the land owner.

(2) The application must be served within 12 months of the date on which these Regulations come into force or, if later, the date on which the relevant use of the way has ceased.

(3) The application shall contain the information specified in paragraph 1, and be accompanied by the information specified in paragraph 2, of the Schedule to these Regulations.

Unopposed applications

B3–007   **7.**—(1) Where the land owner does not object to the application he shall, within three months of receipt of the application, serve a notice on the applicant, agreeing to the application.

(2) The notice shall contain the following information—

(a) the name and address of the land owner and a description of his interest in the land; and
(b) a statement confirming that upon payment of the compensation sum he will provide a written receipt.

(3) The notice shall be accompanied by evidence of the land owner's title to the land.

Opposed applications

B3–008   **8.**—(1) Where the land owner has objections to the application, he shall, within three months of receipt of the application, serve a notice (a "counter notice") on the applicant, objecting to the application.

(2) Objections to the application may be made on the following grounds—

(a) the applicant has served the application after the expiry of the period for service;
(b) the applicant has not provided the information required by regulation 6(3);
(c) information provided by the applicant is not correct;
(d) the easement should be subject to limitations other than those (if any) described in the application;
(e) any rights incidental to the right of way which are described in the application as being rights which should be included in the easement, are not agreed;
(f) the value of the premises is not agreed.

(3) The counter notice shall contain the following information—

(a) the name and address of the land owner and a description of his interest in the land;

(b) the objections to the application; and

(c) any alternative proposals.

(4) The counter notice shall be accompanied by—

(a) any evidence relevant to the objections and alternative proposals; and

(b) evidence of the land owner's title to the land.

Amended application and amended counter notice

9.—(1) Within two months of receipt of a counter notice, the applicant may serve on the land owner an amended application addressing the objections and any alternative proposals set out in the counter notice.   **B3–009**

(2) An amended application shall contain the information specified in paragraph 1 of the Schedule to these Regulations and shall be accompanied by any evidence relevant to the applicant's response to the objections and any alternative proposals set out in the counter notice.

(3) Where the applicant has served an amended application on the land owner, the land owner shall, within two months of receipt of the amended application—

(a) serve a notice on the applicant agreeing to the amended application and confirming that upon payment of the compensation sum he will provide a written receipt, or

(b) serve an amended counter notice on the applicant objecting to the amended application.

(4) An amended counter notice shall comply with regulation 8(2), (3) and (4)(a) and, for this purpose,—

(a) references in regulation 8(2) and (3) to the application, except for the reference in sub-paragraph (a) of regulation 8(2), shall be treated as references to the amended application; and

(b) an objection may also be made on the ground that the applicant has served the amended application after the expiry of the period for service or has not provided the information required by paragraph (2) of this regulation.

(5) Where the land owner has served an amended counter notice on the applicant, the applicant may, within two months of receipt of the amended counter notice, serve a notice on the land owner agreeing to the amended counter notice.

Lands Tribunal

10.—(1) Where a counter notice has been served, either party may, where there is a dispute relating to any matter other than the value of the premises, request the Lands Tribunal to determine the matter in dispute by sending a notice of reference to the Lands Tribunal in accordance with the Lands Tribunal Rules 1996.[2]   **B3–010**

(2) The notice of reference shall have annexed to it—

---

[2] SI 1996/1022, amended by SI 1997/1965 and SI 1998/22.

(a) the application;

(b) the counter notice; and

(c) if applicable, the amended application and amended counter notice.

Calculation of the compensation sum

B3–011　**11.**—(1) Subject to paragraph (2), the compensation sum shall be 2 per cent of the value of the premises.

(2) Where the premises were in existence on—

(a) 31st December 1905; or

(b) 30th November 1930,

the compensation sum shall be 0.25 per cent or 0.5 per cent of the value of the premises respectively.

(3) Where the premises are in residential use and replaced other premises on the same site which were also in residential use ("the former premises"), the compensation sum shall be calculated in accordance with paragraph (2) by reference to the date on which the former premises were in existence.

(4) For the purposes of these Regulations, the value of the premises shall be calculated as at the valuation date on the basis of the open market value of the premises with the benefit of the easement.

(5) In paragraph (4), the "valuation date" means the date as at which the premises are valued for the purposes of the application, being a date no more than 3 months before the date on which the application is served.

Determination of the compensation sum in default of agreement

B3–012　**12.**—(1) Where no agreement can be reached on the value of the premises, either party may serve on the other a notice (the "valuation notice") requiring the amount to be determined by a chartered surveyor.

(2) Where a valuation notice has been served, the appointment of a chartered surveyor shall be agreed by the parties within one month of the service of the valuation notice and, where agreement on such appointment cannot be reached, either party may request the President of the Royal Institution of Chartered Surveyors to appoint a chartered surveyor.

(3) Where a chartered surveyor has been appointed in accordance with paragraph (2), the following provisions shall apply as appropriate—

(a) where the appointment has been made by the President of the Royal Institution of Chartered Surveyors, the parties shall be equally liable for the costs of that appointment;

(b) unless the parties agree that the chartered surveyor shall act as an independent expert, he shall act as an arbitrator and the provisions of the Arbitration Act 1996[3] shall apply; and

(c) where the chartered surveyor acts as an independent expert, the parties shall—

---

[3]　1996, c. 23.

     (i) be bound by his final decision; and

    (ii) each party shall bear their own costs and shall be equally liable for the fees and costs of the chartered surveyor.

Payment of the compensation sum

13.—(1) Where—   **B3–013**

    (a) the land owner has notified the applicant in accordance with regulation 7 or 9(3)(a);

    (b) the applicant has notified the land owner in accordance with regulation 9(5); or

    (c) any matters in dispute have been determined in accordance with regulation 10 or 12,

the applicant shall pay the compensation sum to the land owner.

   (2) The compensation sum shall be paid within two months of—

    (a) the date of notification under regulation 7 or paragraph (3)(a) or (5) of regulation 9, as the case may be; or

    (b) where a determination is made under regulation 10 or 12, the date of the determination, or if more than one such determination is made, the date of the last determination.

   (3) The land owner shall, within one month from the date of receipt of the compensation sum, provide the applicant with a written receipt for that sum.

Payment into court

14. Where—   **B3–014**

    (a) the land owner does not serve a notice in accordance with either regulation 7 or 8; or

    (b) the applicant has served an amended application on the land owner and the land owner fails to act in accordance with regulation 9(3),

the applicant may, within two months of the expiry of the period for service of a notice under regulation 7, 8 or 9(3), as the case may be, pay the compensation sum into a county court in accordance with the Court Funds Rules 1987.[4]

Creation of the easement

15. Upon payment of the compensation sum either—   **B3–015**

    (a) to the land owner in accordance with regulation 13; or

    (b) into court in accordance with regulation 14,

the easement shall be created.

---

[4] SI 1987/821, amended by SI 1988/817, SI 1990/518, SI 1991/1227, SI 1997/177, SI 1999/1021, SI 2000/2918 and SI 2001/703.

Notices

B3–016 **16.**—(1) A notice under these Regulations shall be in writing and may be served by sending it by post.

(2) Where any notice is required by these Regulations to be served within a specified period, the parties may, except in the case of an application, agree in writing to extend or further extend that period.

Abandonment, etc. by applicant

B3–017 **17.**—Where the applicant withdraws or otherwise fails to continue with the application at any stage, he shall be liable for the reasonable costs incurred by the land owner.

SCHEDULE

Regulation 6(3)

INFORMATION TO BE PROVIDED BY THE APPLICANT

B3–018 1. The application shall contain the following information—
  (a) the name and address of the applicant;
  (b) a description of the premises;
  (c) a description of the applicant's interest in the premises;
  (d) details of the current use of the premises and the use during the period giving rise to the entitlement to apply for the easement;
  (e) where the relevant use of the way has ceased, the date of the cessation;
  (f) where the premises, or, where regulation 11(3) applies, the former premises, were in existence on 31st December 1905 or 30th November 1930, a statement confirming those facts;
  (g) the nature of the use of the access, including any limitation or incidental right to which the easement should be subject or which should be included in the easement;
  (h) the dimensions of the width of the way; and
  (i) the proposed compensation sum to be paid to the land owner in respect of the easement, together with the basis on which it is calculated.

2. The application shall be accompanied by—
  (a) a map of an appropriate scale (1:1250 or 1:2500) showing the premises (marked in blue), the way (marked in red) and sufficient other land to establish the exact location of the premises and the way in relation to the surrounding area;
  (b) evidence (which may include a statutory declaration) that—

    (i) the way is a way to which section 68 of the Act applies; and
    (ii) where the application is served after 12 months of the date on which these Regulations come into force, either that the relevant use of the way has not ceased or that such use ceased no more than 12 months before the date on which the application is served; and

  (c) an estimate prepared by a chartered surveyor of the value of the premises as at the valuation date, and "valuation date" has the same meaning for this purpose as in regulation 11(4).

Land Registration Rules 2003

(SI 2003/1417)

PART 4

FIRST REGISTRATION

Duty to disclose unregistered interests that override first registration

28.—(1) Subject to paragraph (2), a person applying for first registration must provide information to the registrar about any of the interests that fall within Schedule 1 to the Act that—   **B4–001**

(a) are within the actual knowledge of the applicant, and
(b) affect the estate to which the application relates, in Form DI.

. . .

(3) In this rule and in Form FR1, a "disclosable overriding interest" is an interest that the applicant must provide information about under paragraph (1).

(4) Where the applicant provides information about a disclosable overriding interest under this rule, the registrar may enter a notice in the register in respect of that interest.

First registration—entry of beneficial rights

33.—(1) The benefit of an appurtenant right may be entered in the register at the time of first registration if—   **B4–002**

(a) on examination of the title, or
(b) on receipt of a written application providing details of the right and evidence of its existence, the registrar is satisfied that the right subsists as a legal estate and benefits the registered estate.

(2) If the registrar is not satisfied that the right subsists as a legal interest benefiting the registered estate, he may enter details of the right claimed in the property register with such qualification as he considers appropriate.

First registration—entry of burdens

35.—(1) On first registration the registrar must enter a notice in the register of the burden of any interest which appears from his examination of the title to affect the registered estate.   **B4–003**

(2) This rule does not apply to—

(a) an interest that under section 33 or 90(4) of the Act cannot be protected by notice,

(b) a public right,

(c) a local land charge,

(d) an interest which appears to the registrar to be of a trivial or obvious character, or the entry of a notice in respect of which would be likely to cause confusion or inconvenience.

First registration—note as to rights of light and air

B4–004   **36.** On first registration, if it appears to the registrar that an agreement prevents the acquisition of rights of light or air for the benefit of the registered estate, he may make an entry in the property register of that estate.

PART 6

REGISTERED LAND: APPLICATIONS, DISPOSITIONS AND MISCELLANEOUS ENTRIES

Applications

Duty to disclose unregistered interests that override registered dispositions

B4–005   **57.**—(1) Subject to paragraph (2), a person applying to register a registrable disposition of a registered estate must provide information to the registrar about any of the interests that fall within Schedule 3 to the Act that—

(a) are within the actual knowledge of the applicant, and

(b) affect the estate to which the application relates, in Form DI.

. . .

(3) In this rule and in Form AP1, a "disclosable overriding interest" is an interest that the applicant must provide information about under paragraph (1).

(4) The applicant must produce to the registrar any documentary evidence of the existence of a disclosable overriding interest that is under his control.

(5) Where the applicant provides information about a disclosable overriding interest under this rule, the registrar may enter a notice in the register in respect of that interest.

Miscellaneous Entries

Application for register entries for express appurtenant rights over unregistered land

B4–006   **73.**—(1) A proprietor of a registered estate who claims the benefit of a legal easement or profit a prendre which has been expressly granted over an unregistered legal estate may apply for it to be registered as appurtenant to his estate.

(2) The application must be accompanied by the grant and evidence of the grantor's title to the unregistered estate.

(3) In paragraph (1) the reference to express grant does not include a grant as a result of the operation of section 62 of the Law of Property Act 1925.

Application for register entries for implied or prescriptive appurtenant rights

74.—(1) A proprietor of a registered estate who claims the benefit of a legal easement or profit a prendre, which has been acquired otherwise than by express grant, may apply for it to be registered as appurtenant to his estate. **B4–007**

(2) The application must be accompanied by evidence to satisfy the registrar that the right subsists as a legal estate appurtenant to the applicant's registered estate.

(3) In paragraph (1) the reference to an acquisition otherwise than by express grant includes acquired as a result of the operation of section 62 of the Law of Property Act 1925.

Qualified register entries for appurtenant rights

75.—(1) This rule applies where a proprietor of a registered estate makes an application under rule 73 or rule 74 and the registrar is not satisfied that the right claimed subsists as a legal estate appurtenant to the applicant's registered estate. **B4–008**

(2) The registrar may enter details of the right claimed in the property register with such qualification as he considers appropriate.

Note as to rights of light or air

76. If it appears to the registrar that an agreement prevents the acquisition of rights of light or air for the benefit of the registered estate, he may make an entry in the property register of that estate. **B4–009**

INDEX